Collector
Subscription Offer

25-Page Price Guide to Collectibles & Antiques

Name _____

Address _____

City _____

State/Zip _____

Phone _____

❑ Check here for advertising information on **Collector Magazine & Price Guide**

CREDIT CARD ORDERS CALL 1-800-334-7165

4 WEEKS FREE
to
Antique Trader Weekly

Name _____

Address _____

City _____

State/Zip _____

Phone

❑ Check here for advertising information

Antique Trader Publications

NO POSTAGE NECESSARY IF MAILED IN THE UNITED STATES

BUSINESS REPLY MAIL

FIRST CLASS MAIL PERMIT NO.50 DUBUQUE, IA

POSTAGE WILL BE PAID BY ADDRESSEE

Antique Trader Publications
PO BOX 1050
DUBUQUE IA 52004-9969

Antique Trader Publications

NO POSTAGE NECESSARY IF MAILED IN THE UNITED STATES

BUSINESS REPLY MAIL

FIRST CLASS MAIL PERMIT NO.50 DUBUQUE, IA

POSTAGE WILL BE PAID BY ADDRESSEE

Antique Trader Publications
PO BOX 1050
DUBUQUE IA 52004-9969

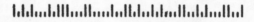

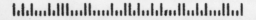

Twelfth Edition
Antique Trader Books
ANTIQUES & COLLECTIBLES
PRICE GUIDE

1996 ANNUAL EDITION

ANTIQUE TRADER BOOKS
Antiques & Collectibles Price Guide

Edited by
Kyle Husfloen

An illustrated comprehensive price guide to the entire field of
antiques and collectibles for the 1996 market

Antique Trader Books
P.O. Box 1050
Dubuque, IA 52004

STAFF

Assistant Editor . . . . Elizabeth Stephan

Editorial Assistant . . . . Ruth Willis

Production Coordinator . . . . Aaron J. Roeth

Production Assistant . . . . Karen Sodt

Production Assistant . . . . Lynn Bradshaw

Cover Design . . . . Jaro Sebek

Customer Service/Order Fulfillment . . . . Bonnie Rojemann

ISBN: 0-930625-11-0
ISSN: 1083-8430

**Other books and magazines published by
Antique Trader Publications:**

American Pressed Glass & Bottles Price Guide
American & European Decorative & Art Glass Price Guide
American & European Art Pottery Price Guide
American & European Furniture Price Guide
American Military Collectibles Price Guide
German Military Collectibles Price Guide
Japanese & Other Foreign Military Collectibles Price Guide

Ceramics Price Guide	The Antique Trader Weekly
Toy Trader	Collector Magazine & Price Guide
DISCoveries	The Big Reel
Postcard Collector	Baby Boomer Collectibles
Maloney's Resource Directory	Military Trader
Rockin' Records	Comics Values Annual
Metalwares Price Guide	Garage Sale Manual & Price Guide

**To order additional copies of this book or
other publications listed above, contact:**

Antique Trader Publications
P.O. Box 1050
Dubuque, Iowa 52004
1-800-334-7165

A WORD TO THE READER

The Antique Trader has been publishing a comprehensive annual price guide to all types of antiques and collectibles since 1984. The material for this reference, which covers hundreds of categories of antiques and collectibles, is compiled by our staff with contributions from outside experts.

Over the years, we continue to strive to adjust the emphasis of our price guide so it accurately reflects the changing marketplace. Years ago, glassware, ceramics and furniture were the most popular, sought-after categories; Barbie lunch boxes garnered little or no attention. Clearly, interests change. And likewise, the emphasis of our price guide adjusts.

We work to expand our coverage every year and add new categories to our compilations as the collecting markets evolve. In this edition we are pleased to introduce a number of new categories which reflect important trends in the collectibles market. These major new categories include: Barbie Dolls & Collectibles; Lunch Boxes; PEZ Dispensers; Pop Culture Collectibles; Radio & Television Memorabilia; Records & Record Jackets; Space Age Collectibles; Sporting Collectibles; Tobacciana; and Western Character Collectibles. With the addition of these categories to our comprehensive coverage of the more traditional areas, we are able to offer you the broadest possible coverage of all aspects of the collecting marketplace. In our 12th edition (1996) we have also made it a point to expand our listings of more market sensitive "collectibles" which are being bought and sold with even higher demand and which appeal to an even broader market. Character Collectibles, Advertising Items, Toys and Disneyana are fields we have particularly focused in on as well as modern, collectible types of glass and ceramics.

The Antique Trader Price Guide continues to pride itself on presenting the most accurate and detailed descriptions possible for each item. Too many price guides include only a short, often vague, description of a piece in their listings. These one-line computer-generated listings have limited value since price alone doesn't put the piece in a proper market perspective. Factors like color, condition and general rarity all influence the price a particular piece will realize.

We always include a good variety of black and white photographs to illustrate our listings. Readers give great value to photographs in a price guide because they help to illustrate important details which determine the value of a piece, whether it be furniture, glass, china or a toy or doll.

A great many of our categories are introduced by a brief paragraph that explains the history of the item and helps establish its place in the collecting field. Throughout this guide, categories are cross-referenced to other related listings.

The currency and care with which our staff develops and prepares our material certainly makes it one of the most authoritative and in-depth guides available. We make it a point to educate as well as inform.

As with all pricing guides, keep in mind that this book should be used only as a *guide* to prices. It is not intended to set prices. There are sometimes regional variations from one area of the country to another and, in general, prices may be somewhat higher in large metropolitan areas where collector competition is keenest. We pride ourselves in compiling a price guide that reflects the broadest average prices for every major category of antique and collectible, but specific sale prices may be included which reflect a specific sale of a rare and unique item and our careful descriptions are meant to explain this to readers. Though prices have been double-checked and every effort has been made to assure accuracy, neither the compilers, editor nor publisher can assume responsibility for any losses that might be incurred as a result of consulting this guide, or of errors, typographical or otherwise.

Our *Antiques & Collectibles Price Guide* follows an alphabetical format with all categories listed alphabetically. We, however, organize the various categories of Ceramics, Furniture and Glassware into their own sections with individual categories arranged alphabetically within that section. Therefore all types of glass, including the major types such as Carnival, Custard, Depression and Pattern, are located within the Glass section. A complete and expanded Index and cross-references in the text have been provided for your convenience.

Any number of collectors, dealers and experts have aided us in compiling our latest volume; however, special thanks must go to the following authorities who helped in selecting material to be used in this guide: Sandra Andacht, Little Neck, New York; Marilyn Dipboye, Warren, Michigan; Cecil Munsey, Poway, California; and Ruth Eaves, Marmora, New Jersey.

Photographers who have contributed to this issue include: E.A. Babka, East

Dubuque, Illinois; Al Bagdade, Northbrook, Illinois; Stanley L. Baker, Minneapolis, Minnesota; Dorothy Beckwith, Platteville, Wisconsin; Donna Bruun, Galena, Illinois; Herman C. Carter, Tulsa, Oklahoma; J.D. Dalessandro, Cincinnati, Ohio; Bill Freeman, Smyrna, Georgia; Jeff Grunewald, Chicago, Illinois; Jim Martin, Monmouth, Illinois; Louise Paradis, Galena, Illinois; Joyce Roerig, Waltersboro, South Carolina; Ruth Eaves, Marmora, New Jersey; Molly Schroeder, Danville, Illinois; and Tom Wallace, Chicago, Illinois.

For other photographs, artwork, data or permission to photograph in their shops, we sincerely express appreciation to the following auctioneers, galleries, museums, individuals and shops: Americana Shop, Chicago, Illinois; Bell Tower Antique Mall, Covington, Kentucky; Bertoia/Brady Auctions, Vineland, New Jersey; Block's Box, Trumbull, Connecticut; Burmese Cruet, Montgomeryville, Pennsylvania; Busby Land & Auction Company, Ridge Farm, Illinois; Butterfield & Butterfield, San Francisco, California; Fred & Jan Carlson, Hillsboro, Oregon; The Cedars - Antiques, Aurelia, Iowa; Norm & Diana Charles, Hagerstown, Indiana; Christie's, New York, New York; Collector's Auction Services, Oil City, Pennsylvania; Collector's Sales & Services, Middletown, Rhode Island; D. & L. Antiques, North Berwick, Maine; Davis Auction House, Phelps, New York; DeFina Auctions, Austenburg, Ohio; Gail DePasquale, Leavenworth, Kansas; Marilyn Dipboye, Sterling Heights, Michigan; William Doyle Galleries, New York, New York; DuMouchelle's, Detroit, Michigan; Dunnings Auction Service, Elgin, Illinois; Robert Edwards Auctions, Hoboken, New Jersey; T. Ermert, Cincinnati, Ohio; The Galena Shoppe, Galena, Illinois; Garth's Auctions, Inc., Delaware, Ohio; Glass-Works Auctions, East Greenville, Pennsylvania; Glick's Antiques, Galena, Illinois; Morton M. Goldberg Auction Galleries, New Orleans, Louisiana; Robert Gordon, San Antonio, Texas; and Grunewald Antiques, Hillsborough, North Carolina.

Also to Harmer Rooke Galleries, New York, New York; Vicki Harmon, San Marcos, California; the Gene Harris Antique Auction Center, Marshalltown, Iowa; the late William Heacock, Marietta, Ohio; The House in the Woods Auction Gallery, Eagle, Wisconsin; International Carnival Glass Assoc., Mentone, Indiana; Jackson's Auctions, Cedar Falls, Iowa; Doris Johnson, Rockford, Illinois; Jewel Johnson, Tulsa, Oklahoma; James Julia, Fairfield, Maine; Just Kids Nostalgia, Huntington, New York; Maryann Kennedy, Marshall, Minnesota; Agnes Koehn Antiques, Cedar Rapids, Iowa; Peter Kroll, Sun Prairie, Wisconsin; Lang's Sporting Collectables,

Raymond, Maine; Jim Ludescher, Dubuque, Iowa; Joy Luke Gallery, Bloomington, Illinois; Manion's International Auction House, Kansas City, Kansas; J. Martin, Mt. Orab, Ohio; Robert T. Matthews, West Friendship, Maryland; Randall McKee, Kenosha, Wisconsin; McMasters Doll Auctions, Cambridge, Ohio; Dr. James Measell, Berkley, Michigan; William Miller, Rockford, Illinois; Nauck's Vintage Records, Spring, Texas; Neal Auction Company, New Orleans, Louisiana; Nostalgia Galleries, Elmont, New York; Nostalgia Publications, Inc., Hackensack, New Jersey; O'Gallerie, Inc., Portland, Oregon; Pettigrew Auction Gallery, Colorado Springs, Colorado; Dave Rago Arts & Crafts, Lambertville, New Jersey; R.A.M. Quality Auctions, Joliet, Illinois; Raven & Dove, Wilmette, Illinois; Jane Rosenow, Galva, Illinois; Robert W. Skinner, Inc., Bolton, Massachusetts; Sotheby's, New York, New York; Stanton's Auctioneers & Realtors, Vermontville, Michigan; Michael Strawser, Wolcottville, Indiana; Rose Mary Taylor, Pecatonica, Illinois; Temples Antiques, Minneapolis, Minnesota; Theriault's, Annapolis, Maryland; Town Crier Auction Service, Burlington, Wisconsin; Treadway Gallery, Cincinnati, Ohio; Lee Vines, Hewlett, New York; Vintage Cameras and Imagery, Hardwick, Vermont; Doris Virtue, Galena, Illinois; Bruce & Vicki Waasdorp, Clarence, New York; Chris Walker Auctions, Potosi, Wisconsin; Richard Wolfers Auctions, Inc., San Francisco, California; Wolf's Auctioneers and Appraisers, Cleveland, Ohio; Woody Auctions, Douglass, Kansas; and Yesterday's Treasures, Galena, Illinois.

Today's antiques and collectibles market is certainly booming. And our Antiques & Collectibles Price Guide is positioned to support this huge and diverse market by offering the best, most well-rounded price guide available.

The staff of The Antique Trader Antiques & Collectibles Price Guide welcomes all letters from readers, especially those of constructive critique, and we make every effort to respond personally.

Kyle Husfloen, Editor

ON THE COVERS:

Front cover: top left - early rare Maytag washing machine sign; bottom, left to right - a fine walnut Victorian Renaissance Revival substyle cylinder-front secretary-bookcase; a Moorcroft pottery vase; a No. 1 Barbie doll.

Back cover: left - a grouping of collectible copper wares; right - pieces in Franciscan's Apple pattern.

1996 Antiques Market Report

Now that we've arrived in the last half of the 1990s and are quickly moving towards a new millennium it's interesting to take a moment to reflect on collecting trends, past and present.

The hobby of collecting, as a serious pastime, is really only about 100 years old; it was during the 1890s that a handful of pioneer collectors began beating the backroads of New England in search of early American artifacts like Historical Staffordshire China and Pilgrim Century furniture. At first they were considered somewhat eccentric but by the early 20th century these few had inspired dozens more happy hunters.

It was during the 1920s that the antiques market really boomed as the interest in early American furniture, glass and ceramics entered the mainstream of public consciousness. Chippendale and Duncan Phyfe furniture, early American pattern glass and lacy Sandwich glass became familiar to thousands of readers of the day's popular magazines. Decorating with antiques became a major trend and many furniture and glassware manufacturers introduced reproductions or adaptations of pieces featured in antiques shops and shows.

The 1920s also saw the birth of specialized collecting periodicals, such as The Magazine Antiques. Many more reference books were being published and the hobby of collecting became a frequent topic of interest. Of course, in these early years, only "true" antiques were considered worthy of acquiring. Most items produced after 1830 were not deemed worthy of consideration. How times have changed!

The major trend in collecting during the past 25 years has been the astounding expansion of the market. No longer are only real antiques of interest to the collecting public. In fact, "antiques" in the legal sense (100 years old) are today only a fraction of the whole collecting realm.

Beginning in the 1960s there was a surge of interest in newer collectibles and areas of collecting never before explored. Depression glass, insulators, fruit jars and brand new mass-produced, mass-marketed 'collectibles' such as Avon bottles and Jim Beam whiskey decanters made a splash in collecting circles. The trend for 'new' collectibles continued unabated in the early 1970s especially the field of limited edition collector plates and Hummel figurines. The hard economic times of the 1970s and early 1980s hit these collecting markets quite hard, but today most of them have regained some stability and interest continues.

The economic problems of the 1970s and 1980s also affected the field of "real" antiques. But these more stable markets weather the hard times more easily. By the late 1980s, the world of fine arts and antiques was booming again.

Between the realm of mass-marketed modern collectibles and high-ticket early antiques lies the major segment of today's collecting market. This is the realm of collecting which you'll find covered in the majority of the categories listed in this price guide. Most listings in this reference are priced in the $10 to $10,000 range which is considered the 'low to mid-market' area. Of all areas of collecting during the past quarter-century, this is undoubtedly the range that has seen the strongest market growth.

Today we are seeing a major broadening of collecting interests, especially in artifacts less than 50 years old. With millions of post-World War II 'baby boomers' now reaching middle age and eager to collect materials from their childhood and youth, it's easy to see what drives this collecting trend.

Even the major New York auction houses like Christie's and Sotheby's have bowed to this reality. In the past year, they have featured major specialty sales of pop memorabilia and guitars, Hollywood entertainment memorabilia and movie posters and more. Christie's East even offered a unique auction of G.I. Joe action figures from the 1960s, which celebrated their 30th Anniversary in 1994.

Although the big city auction houses across the country still offer the major sales of the very finest early art and high-priced antiques, it is clear they have realized there's a tremendous interest and big money to be made by catering to the low and middle priced collecting market.

Specialized sales have been offered on such 'hot' collectibles as lunch boxes and comic character drinking glasses. Especially popular are materials relating to TV Westerns and science fiction and space-related shows of the 1950s and 1960s. Bonanza, one of the longest-running TV Westerns, gave us lunch boxes and toy figures which are in great demand today. And Maverick, another Western classic, has fewer collectibles but the recent major motion picture based on that show certainly increased demand for them. In the realm of space and science fiction, there is almost a cult following today for shows such as Outer Limits, Lost in Space, and of course, Star Trek. Early toys, games and promotional materials from these and other such shows always bring good prices. For instance, the Star Trek "Super Phaser II Target Game" from 1976 was listed in 1990 at $45.00 but this past year had reached $55.00. An early Star Trek board game from 1967, when the show was still in production, can bring over $100.00 today. Similar trends occur with all the most popular TV shows of the past.

From coast to coast, shows, auctions and dealers are aware of the public's interest in a vast array of collectibles. Mass-market publications, a wide range of specialty collecting publications and even popular TV shows help hype this market. Remember, it wasn't that long ago that leading talk-show host Oprah Winfrey featured a segment on collectible cookie jars!

One of the most active areas of collecting today is toys and one of the major segments of this market is Barbie dolls and accessories. Today new Barbies are snapped up as quickly by adult collectors as by little girls. Special 'limited edition' Barbies escalate dramatically in value in just a short time. Meanwhile, the classic No. 1 Barbie, which we listed in our 1986 Annual Price Guide for $725.00 is listed in this current edition at over $2,000.00. So desirable are all things Barbie that Hallmark, the famous greeting card and Christmas ornament maker, now offers special Barbie tree ornaments each year.

Along with the wide and continually growing range of collecting specialties there has also been noteworthy growth in collecting clubs. It is these groups of well organized collectors which help to stabilize and maintain the wide range of collectibles. As most people today are aware, there's a collector for nearly everything imaginable. And, most of these collectors belong to one or more collecting clubs. These organized clubs often publish informative newsletters which help expand the interest and understanding of their field. And, most hold an annual convention where collectors gather to share, learn, buy and sell. By following the pricing trends established by members of these clubs, we can learn a great deal about a wide range of popular collectibles.

Another major trend influencing the expansion of the collecting market is the huge growth in the number of available books and price guides that cover all facets of the market. Antique Trader Books has become a major contributor to this expansion of information for collectors. We have introduced a number of specialized price guides including ones covering all types of glass, general ceramics, Art Pottery, comic books, rock and roll records, military collectibles, and furniture. By the end of 1995, other new volumes on metalwares, 20th American ceramics and White Ironstone China will also be added. Whatever your collecting interest may be, there is probably a reference which will benefit you.

How strong were sale prices last year? Overall in the hundreds of categories we covered, values remained steady with no dramatic short-term rises or drops. In every case, the rarest pieces and those in top condition lead the way, with items in average condition just holding their own. The old adage about buying what you like but buying the best you can afford still holds true!

What does the future hold for collectors? That is a difficult question to answer, but I see no reason to doubt that collecting, as a popular pastime, will continue to grow and expand well into the 21st century. Many collectors will continue to search out toys and artifacts of their youth while others will gather early items which represent a specific era or event. Special commemorations, such as the 50th Anniversary of the end of World War II, spur interest in material from that era, and other wars, world's fairs and political campaigns of the past still draw attention from dedicated collectors. The Desert Storm operation of a few years ago inspired a short spat of collectibles such as trading cards but only time will tell if these and other ephemeral items of today will become tomorrow's collectibles. After all, no one could have foreseen that a set of Superman Gum cards, ca. 1940, would be listed in this year's price guide for nearly $3,000.00!

Today's collectors must nurture and support the next generation of young collectors, their children and grandchildren. Not everyone may be interested in 'antique' artifacts, but today's collecting world offers hundreds of other new collectibles which can offer beginning collectors a chance to participate in the joy and excitement of gathering reminders of our cultural and social history.

—Kyle Husfloen, Editor

ABC PLATES

These children's plates were popular in the late 19th and early 20th centuries. An alphabet border was incorporated with nursery rhymes, maxims, scenes or figures in an apparent attempt to "spoon feed" a bit of knowledge at mealtime. They were made of ceramics, glass and metal. A boon to collectors is the fine book, A Collector's Guide to ABC Plates, Mugs and Things *by Mildred L. and Joseph P. Chalala (Pridemark Press, Lancaster, Pennsylvania, 1980).*

CERAMIC

Alphabet Plate with U.S. Capitol

5¾" d., center scene of "The Blind Girl," polychrome decoration (tiny stain spot) **$110.00**

6⅛" d., biblical scenes, brown transfer-printed center scene of three people in a prison setting titled "Scared History of Joseph and his brethren - Joseph interpreting the dreams of the chief butler and baker," decorated w/green, yellow & pink enamel, raised alphabet border **66.00**

6¼" d., children's activities, brown transfer-printed center scene of three Dutch-type children, embossed deaf alphabet border, marked "Hansley & Co. Longton" **247.50**

6¼" d., green transfer-printed center scene of wooden dolls, embossed alphabet border, red rim stripe.........**181.50**

7" d., colored transfer-printed center scene of boy in period attire carrying a basket, printed alphabet border, Meakin **110.00**

8½" d., brown transfer-printed view of "Independence Hall, Philadelphia," embossed alphabet border, trimmed in pink, green & blue, minute rim flake **55.00**

8½" d., hunting scene, green, red &

brown transfer-printed center scene of hunter, hounds, fox & horse, embossed alphabet border **150.00**

8½" d., scene of the U.S. Capitol building transfer-printed in brown, titled "At Washington," trimmed in pink, green & blue, embossed alphabet border (ILLUS.) **60.50**

TIN

"Mary Had A Little Lamb" Tin Plate

3½" d., Girl on Swing lithographed center scene, printed alphabet border **65.00**

5⅝" d., "Hey, Diddle Diddle," cat playing a fiddle, dog, dish & spoon & cow jumping over the moon lithographed center scene, printed alphabet border..................................**75.00**

6" d., embossed bust profile of George Washington w/stars around head & "Washington" below, embossed alphabet border (minor dents, light rust) **170.50**

6¼" d., "Jumbo," embossed standing elephant in center, embossed alphabet border (dents, some rust) **115.50**

8" d., enamelware, central black transfer of a clock face w/Arabic & Roman numerals on white, printed alphabet border (edge chips) **99.00**

8" d., "Mary Had A Little Lamb" verse above scene of Mary & the lamb, embossed alphabet border (ILLUS.)...............**110.00 to 135.00**

8" d., "Who Killed Cock Robin?," Cock Robin bird & verse embossed center scene, embossed alphabet border **150.00**

8¼" d., "Hey Diddle Diddle," center scene of a cat w/fiddle, dog sitting up & a cow jumping over the moon, alphabet border on curved rim.........**203.50**

ADVERTISING ITEMS

Thousands of objects made in various materials, some intended as gifts with purchases, others used for display or given away for publicity, are now being collected. Also see *AUTOMOTIVE COLLEC-TIBLES, BANKS, BASEBALL MEMO-RABILIA, BIG LITTLE BOOKS, BLACK AMERICANA, BOTTLE OPENERS, BOTTLES & FLASKS, BREWERIANA, BUSTER BROWN COLLECTIBLES, CALENDAR PLATES, CANS & CONTAINERS, CARNIVAL GLASS, CHARACTER COLLECTIBLES, COCA-COLA ITEMS, COOKBOOKS, DISNEY COLLECTIBLES, FANS, KITCHEN-WARES, JEWEL TEA AUTUMN LEAF WARES, MATCH SAFES, MUCHA (Alphonse) ARTWORK, OLD SLEEPY EYE POTTERY, PAPERWEIGHTS, PARRISH (Maxfield) ARTWORK, PENNSBURY POTTERY, RADIO & TELEVISION MEMORABILIA, SALES-MAN'S SAMPLES, SCOUTING ITEMS, SHEET MUSIC, SPACE AGE COL-LECTIBLES, STICKPINS, TOBAC-CIANA, TOYS, TRADE CARDS, TRADE CATALOGS, TRAYS, SERVING & CHANGE, WATCH FOBS, WATT POT-TERY, WESTERN CHARACTER COL-LECTIBLES, and WORLD'S FAIR COLLECTIBLES.*

Alarm clock, "Red Goose Shoes," by Gilbert **$275.00**

Alarm clock, "Standard Brand Shoes," by Gilbert **75.00**

Star Kist Alarm Clock

Alarm clock, "Star Kist Tuna," pale blue metal case w/handle & bells at the top & short legs at the base, dial w/dark blue Arabic numerals & a picture of Charlie Tuna & a sign on a hook reading "Sorry Charlie," ca. 1969, scratches, 4" d. (ILLUS.) **71.50**

Ashtray, "B.F. Goodrich - 100th Anniversary," rubber tire shape w/clear glass insert, 1970 ....**22.00**

Ashtray, "Lowell Hand Cream," cobalt blue glass, hat-shaped......................**25.00**

Ashtray, "Penn Reels, Philadelphia," Bakelite, embossed w/sailfish............**24.50**

Ashtray, "Pepsi-Cola," black glass, rectangular, center depicts a bottle cap beside "say Pepsi please," calender border, 1963, 4 x 5"..........**125.00**

Ashtray, "Royal Crown Cola," glass, ca. 1940 ....**18.00**

Wyandotte Products Ashtray

Ashtray, "Wyandotte Products," brass, cast in the form of an arrowhead, the oval indented center w/raised wording "Wyandotte Products," American Indian figures at the sides & a campfire scene at the top, tarnished, 3½ x 5" (ILLUS.) **71.50**

Backbar bottle, "Pointer" arched above & "Maryland Rye" arched below an oval frame w/"Pointer The Gottschald Co. - Baltimore, MD" around the edge & model of a Pointer dog in the center, clear glass w/white, gold & blue label-under-the-glass, tooled mouth, smooth base, 11¼" h...**1,750.00**

Bank, "Pioneer Life Insurance Co., Rockford, Illinois," truck-shaped **30.00**

Bank, "Red Goose Shoes," cast iron, model of a goose, painted red, 4¼" h...**150.00**

Bank, "Mrs. Sanitary Diaper Service," plastic, model of a truck **30.00**

Bank, "Sinclair H-C Gasoline," litho-graphed tin, pump-shaped, green & white **50.00**

Blotter, "Bond Bread," illustration of a portable television w/a baseball scene on the screen **15.00**

Blotter, "Buster Brown Shoes," pictures Buster & Tige, ca. 1910, unused **25.00**

Blotter, "Carter's Ink," pictures Inky Racer **30.00**

Blotter, "Carter's Ink," pictures people of the world **24.00**

Blotter, "Fleers 1¢ Double Bubble Gum" **18.00**

Blotter, "Kellogg's Cereal," pictures boy in a wagon, ca. 1916...................**18.00**

Blotter, "Malt Extract, Long Island

Bottling Co., Brooklyn," 1910,
unused **18.00**
Blotter, "Philadelphia Transit Safety,"
includes illustrations of children
playing & a 1920 calendar **20.00**
Blotter, "Planters Peanuts," peanut-
shaped **45.00**
Blotter, "Reid's Ice Cream,"
ca. 1910 ....**22.00**
Blotter, "Royal Portable Typewriter,"
die-cut, ca. 1920, unused **32.00**

Texaco Motor Oil Blotter

Blotter, "Texaco Motor Oil," a colorful
scene of a man standing looking
under the hood of an early auto w/a
lady seated at the wheel, a billboard
in the background reads "The Easy
Pour Two Quart Can - You don't
need oil until you need two quarts -
Texaco Motor Oil," ca. 1920s, 3 x 6"
(ILLUS.) **121.00**
Blotter, "Texaco Motor Oil," colorful
scene of a pit crew working on an
early race car, text at left side reads
"Under the rack and strain of racing
wise drivers used Texaco Motor Oil -
Protect your car the same way, "
3 x 6" **231.00**
Blotter, "Texaco Roofing," colorful
scene of a kneeling workman
holding a roll of the roofing, printed
w/"Texaco Roofing - Ready to Lay -
Prepared to Stay" & additional
advertising copy, 3½ x 6" (corner
tips slightly bent) **88.00**
Blotter, "Zilatone - Reestablishes
normal liver bile & bowel function,"
red & yellow **5.00**
Book, "Evans Fur Company," history
of furs, 1914 ....**20.00**
Book, "Kellogg's," entitled "Book of
Games," includes "Sambo," 1931 ......**65.00**
Book, "Kellogg's," entitled "Kellogg's
Funny Jungleland Moving-Pictures,"
in color, 1909 ....**30.00 to 40.00**
Book, "Kellogg's," entitled "Kellogg's
Funny Jungleland Moving Pictures,"
1932 ....**25.00**
Book ends, "Hartford Fire Insurance
Co.," bronze, dated 1935, pr. **75.00**
Booklet, "Aunt Jemima," die-cut,
includes recipes, ca. 1906 ....**175.00**
Booklet, "Chase & Sanborn," entitled

"After Dinner Tricks & Puzzles,"
1896 ....**40.00**
Booklet, "Gold Dust," entitled "Brite
Spots" twins pictured throughout,
1937 ....**45.00**
Booklet, "Jell-O," entitled "The
Jell-O Girl Entertains," eight
color illustrations signed by Rose
O'Neill ....**25.00 to 35.00**
Booklet, "Merchants Gargling Oil,"
ca. 1890 ....**12.00**
Booklet, "Metropolitan Life Insurance
Co.," entitled "First Aid in the Home,"
1914, 64 pp. **9.00**
Booklet, "Monarch Stoves," entitled
"Dora's Diary," includes cartoons by
Louis Fisher, recipes & advertising **9.00**
Booklet, "Planters Peanuts," entitled
"Our Fighting Forces," illustrations
include U.S. & enemy uniforms,
insignias, etc., 1943 ....**25.00**
Booklet, "Warner's Log Cabin Reme-
dies," products & testimonials **15.00**
Bottles, miniature, "Pepsi-Cola," six-
pack w/holder **75.00**
Bottle carrier, "Pepsi-Cola," cloth,
white w/red trim, 1940s **35.00**
Bottle carrier, "Pepsi-Cola," wooden,
six-pack size, ca. 1930s, 8 x 9" **95.00**
Business card, "Planters Peanuts,"
peanut-shaped **60.00**
Cake pan, "Swans Down Cake Flour,"
tin, six-sided, small ....**20.00 to 30.00**
Calendar, 1889, "Aetna Insurance
Co.," lithographed cardboard, color
scene at the top of an early steam
fire wagon pulled by two racing
horses w/a burning building in the
background, agent name across
the bottom, all months intact,
6¼ x 9½" **385.00**
Calendar, 1890, "Aultman Miller,"
colorful, two months to each
sheet **100.00**

1892 Hood's Calendar

Calendar, 1892, "Hood's Sarsaparilla," round w/a circle of children's

faces, w/pad, minor soiling (ILLUS. bottom previous page) **93.50**

Calendar, 1892, "Metropolitan Life Insurance Company," lithographed cardboard, diamond-shaped, w/a rectangular center reserve featuring a pretty young girl in a long pink dress w/light blue ribbon tied around her neck, small calendar sheets at the sides, agent name at the bottom, 13½" sq. (minor soiling) **55.00**

Calendar, 1893, "The Prudential Insurance Company," round cardboard, bust portrait of a young girl w/short curly blonde hair framed by calendar sheets, advertising on the bottom sheet, 9" d. (minor soiling) **82.50**

Hood's 1894 Calendar

Calendar, 1894, "Hood's Sarsaparilla," die-cut cardboard, colorful oval portrait of a lovely young lady wearing a large flowered hat, advertising & calendar pages from March through December below, very minor soiling, 5½" w., 8¾" h. (ILLUS.) **55.00**

Calendar, 1902, "John Hancock Mutual Life Insurance Co.," lithographed cardboard, nearly square w/large top scene of a young girl asleep snuggled next to a large St. Bernard dog, month sheets across the bottom, print titled "The Protector of the Home," 9½ x 10½" (minor water stain, rounded corners) **203.50**

Calendar, 1905, "James Lally Jr. - Dealer in Flour, Grain and Hay," die-cut cardboard, the top w/a cut-out circle w/large edge roses framing a winter scene of a young child feeding chickens, 7" w., 12" h. (minor soiling on paper, creases on cardboard) **22.00**

Calendar, 1906, "Youth's Companion," tri-fold cardboard, self-framed three-part color scene of marching

Colonial Minute Men, month blocks across the bottom, magazine premium, published by the Perry Mason Company, Boston, Massachusetts, 24¾" l. 11½" h. (minor edge wear & fold marks) **60.50**

Marble City Garage Calendar

Calendar, 1913, "Marble City Garage," lithographed paper, large colorful scene of a pretty lady carrying a large armful of flowers & climbing into an early automobile w/a man at the wheel, printed advertising in the upper right corner & a small calendar pad at the center bottom, piece missing at the top center, tears at sides, framed, 18½" w., 23½" h. (ILLUS.) **550.00**

Calendar, 1914, "Whitehead Hoag" celluloid, ruler & letter opener combination **20.00**

Calendar, 1916, "Belle Plaine Candy Kitchen," embossed & die-cut cardboard, a horizontal garden scene w/gazebo w/a boy & girl kissing, pastel coloring, complete calendar pad (very minor soiling) **121.00**

Calendar, 1925, "Western Ammo," hunting scene **250.00**

Calendar, 1935, "Wrigley's Spearmint Gum," colorful three-quarter length portraits of two early female radio stars, very minor soiling, 9 x 15½" (ILLUS. top next page)....................**154.00**

Calendar, 1936, "Hercules Powder Co.," long color print shows a boy standing & holding a rifle, his hunting dog seated by his side, both gazing up at distant flying ducks, titled "Day's End" & signed "Frederic Stanley," grouping of the months below, in bright colors of orange, red & green, 13" w., 30" h. (very minor soiling) **77.00**

Calendar, 1937, "DeLaval Cream Separators," store advertising............**25.00**

Wrigley's Gum Calendar

Calendar, 1937, "Mobilgas," shows "Along The Magnolia Trail," 11½ x 13" **150.00**

Calendar, 1942, "Royster Field Tested Fertilizer," w/print by Charlotte Becker of baby & blue Teddy bear, 4¾ x 8" **22.00**

Calendar, 1943, "Texaco Gasoline," six different colorful seasonal scenes above a two-month calendar listing w/a memo section & advertising along the bottom of the page (minor soiling, edge wear) **55.00**

Calendar, 1950, "Royal Crown Cola," pictures Wanda Hendrix **35.00**

Calendar, 1954, "American Airlines," 12 pp. **20.00**

Charm, "Planters Peanuts," plastic, figure of Mr. Peanut **25.00**

Checkerboard, "Hires Root Beer," cardboard, folding, the back printed w/a color picture of the smiling Hires baby holding a piece of bread, a package of the product & a glass of root beer beside him, printed advertising copy above & below, ca. 1892, 12" sq. open (water stains, tear on back) **203.50**

Cigarette lighter, "Camel," brass, w/embossed suede pouch **45.00**

Clicker, "PEZ," lithographed tin, illustration of girl wearing a PEZ hat **35.00**

Clicker, "Poll Parrot Shoes," tin, 1⅞" l. **22.00**

Clicker, "Red Goose Shoes," tin **25.00**

Clock, "AC Spark Plugs," electric wall-type, round plastic, sunburst-molded outer ring in orange printed in black w/"AC Fire Ring Spark Plugs," center dial in cream & yellow w/Arabic numerals & "Change Now," 16" d. (scratches, soiling) **165.00**

Clock, "American Express Money Orders," electric wall-type, square metal w/a bowed glass front, light-up

American Express Clock

style, beige ground w/red & blue lettering & highlights, reads "American Express Money Orders Sold Here," sweep seconds hand, minor rust spotting, 13" sq. (ILLUS.) **82.50**

Calumet Baking Powder Clock

Clock, "Calumet Baking Powder," wall regulator, wood case w/glass door over white dial w/Roman numerals, lower door in black w/gold lettering reading "Time To Buy Calumet Baking Powder - 'Best by Test'," early 20th c., soiling at winding hole, some spotting at top on wood, 18" w., 38" h. (ILLUS.) **385.00**

Clock, "Crosley," neon wall-type, octagonal w/neon around the edges framing the glass door opening to the white dial framed w/another band of neon, the dial w/Arabic numerals & "Time For Crosley," blue & white, w/sweep seconds hand, 21½" w. (soiling, paint loss to edges of glass door) **467.50**

Clock, "Ever-Ready Safety Razor," wall-type, embossed painted metal, rectangular w/rounded corners, round white dial w/Arabic numerals, a bald smiling man shaving in the

Ever-Ready Safety Razor Clock

center, "Ever-Ready" above the dial & "Safety Razor" below, gold & black lettering, instructions painted on back, staining along edge of dial, minor paint chipping & scratches, overall paint cracking & dented edges & rust pitting, 12½ x 18" (ILLUS.) **935.00**

Clock, "Hamm's Beer," electric wall-type, illuminated, revolving water fall & campsite scene, overall 19 x 60" **600.00**

Clock, "It's Time For Ice Cream," wall-type, copper, a cartouche-shaped waffle patterned copper sheet w/double round lobes at top & base mounted w/pink, blue & green jewels, a large figural copper ice cream cone at the top, the dial w/Arabic numerals at the center, w/key, gold-colored lettering, 14½" w., 27" h. (very minor scratches) **605.00**

Clock, "Kelly-Springfield Tires," table model, vinyl & metal, the arched vinyl case w/in-curved sides & flat front & back, round metal bezel & glass-fronted dial w/Arabic numerals, printed in gold above the dial "Kelly-Springfield Tires," printed at bottom front "When It's Time To Buy Tires - Call - Danielski & Co. - Hanover 88...," 5" w., 4¾" h. (minor wear) **110.00**

Clock, "Oilzum Motor Oil," electric wall-type, round dial printed in the center in orange, black & white w/the Oilzum man's head logo & "Oilzum Motor Oil," Arabic numerals around the edges, sweep seconds hand, glass front, 14½" d. **1,650.00**

Clock, "Quaker State Motor Oil," electric wall-type, square plastic printed w/Arabic numerals around

"Ask For Quaker State Motor Oil," sweep seconds hand, printed in green & black, 16" sq. **66.00**

Clock, "Pepsi-Cola," electric wall-type, rectangular plastic face, light-up type, base of frame reads "Pepsi," ca. 1970, 14 x 18" **150.00**

Clock, "Pepsi-Cola," electric wall-type, square glass front in wooden frame, face lettered "Time for Cloverdale Mineral Water - Pepsi-Cola," ca. 1930s, 15" sq. **500.00**

Clock, "Reading Beer," electric wall-type, round w/white dial & black Arabic numerals, black & red lettering reading "Reach for Reading - The Friendly Beer for Modern People," 14½" d. (very minor scratches) **165.00**

Wetherill's Paints Neon Clock

Clock, "Wetherill's Atlas Paints," neon wall-type, octagonal case w/glass cover, a black ribbon band on the cover over a band of neon framing the round black, white & yellow dial w/Arabic numerals, printed in the center "Wetherill's - Estab. 1807 - Atlas Paints," plastic cover behind glass cracked & repaired, 18" w., 18" h. (ILLUS.) **412.50**

Coloring book, "Peter Pan Peanut Butter," unused **15.00**

Comic book, "B.F. Goodrich," entitled "P.F. Magic Shoe Adventure" & featuring the Rocket Kids, 1962.........**22.00**

Comic book, "Kellogg's - Corn Flakes," dated 1912, 7 x 10".............**35.00**

Comic book, "Post Sugar Crisps Cereal," entitled "Baseball Facts & Fun," 1955, 52 pp. **30.00**

Comic book, electric company, "Reddy Kilowatt," entitled "The Mighty Atom," 1973.........................**35.00**

Comic book, "Remington Arms," entitled "Let's Go Shooting" **15.00**

Compact, "Lydia Pinkham," adver-tising on both sides **75.00**

Costume, "Planters Peanuts," molded plastic full-sized body costume in beige w/a black hat that buckles on, gold-embossed lettering around the hat, 18" d., 47" h. (minor fading to lettering) **550.00**

Counter display, "Carrara's Ice Cream" mechanical, a large papier-maché ice cream cone w/a man w/moving eyes arising out of the top, red lettering, early 20th c., 40½" h. (soiling, chipping & cracking) **1,900.00**

Gillette Counter Display

Counter display, "Gillette Safety Razor," die-cut cardboard, a large figure of Santa Claus at the top of a world globe w/a winter landscape across the bottom, in red, white & blues, printed at the top "At old Saint Nicholas' request - We offer you the Yuletide's Best," w/"Gillette Safety Razor" & red diamond logo across the center of the globe (ILLUS.).......**505.00**

Counter display, "Lyons Polar Maid Ice Cream," composition model of a large ice cream cone in brown w/a cream-colored top, mounted in a cast-iron framework w/conical base, 48" h. (paint chipping & scratches) ..**660.00**

Counter display, "Red Goose Shoes," die-cut lithographed, easel-back cardboard, pictures young girl & logo, ca. 1905 ....**545.00**

Counter display, "Winchester," die-cut cardboard, illustrates an Indian, promotes shot gun barrels, 5' h. **158.00**

Counter display bottle, oversized, "Stag Beer," teal blue glass w/paper label, ca. 1930s, 27" h. **200.00**

Counter display box, "Brownie Brand Peanuts," wooden w/image & advertising stenciled in green on inside of lid & front panel **135.00**

Counter display box, "George's Corn & Bunion Shields," oak, dovetailed construction w/inside glass cover,

brand name embossed on outside front, full label inside lid, mint.............**90.00**

Counter display box, "West Beach & Motor Hair Net," deep square wooden box w/printed advertising on the front & a colorful lithograph inside the lid picturing a bathing beauty standing on the running board of an early car at the beach, ca. 1918, 6½" w., 5½" h. (minor wear)..**275.00**

Ingersoll Watches Case

Counter display case, "Ingersoll Watches," brown wood-grained metal in a checkered design, tall upright rectangular case w/slanting form & narrow chamfered base rim, interior fitted w/slotted cardboard w/velvet lining, "Ingersoll" printed at the top front, cream label w/black lettering on the back, very minor scratches & wear, 6 x 9½", 14¼" h. (ILLUS.) **110.00**

Counter display case, "Panco Soles and Heels," metal & wood, upright shallow rectangular box w/interior shelving, a wide arched crestrail printed w/pictures of a shoe sole & heel & "Panco Soles and Heels - Guaranteed to Outwear Best Leather 2 to 1," further advertising on the sides & back, printed in yellow, black & red, 15" w., 35" h. (scratches, soiling) **176.00**

Counter display case, "Tooke Kum-Seald Handkerchief," rectangular wooden case w/molded top & flaring platform base & glass front, the interior divided into five slots, gold lettering at the bottom front reads "Tooke Kum-Seald Handkerchief - Tooke," back opens to fill, 8 x 22", 12" h. (very minor scratches & wear)..**154.00**

Counter display figure, "Dutch Boy Paints," molded composition figure of the Dutch boy kneeling & holding a paint brush in one hand, original paint, 12" h. **300.00**

Counter display figure, electric company, "Reddy Kilowatt," plastic, a flattened figure of Reddy in red w/a cream-colored head, hands & feet on a rectangular black base, 5¼" h. **130.50**

Counter display figure, "Esso Gasoline," large composition model of a friendly looking recumbent German Shepherd dog, wearing a narrow black collar w/an oval "Esso" tag, natural coloring, 44" l., 22" h. (age cracks, minor chipping) **1,320.00**

Counter display figure, "Poll Parrot Shoes," china model of a parrot on stand, 1930s, 8" h. **85.00**

Counter display figure, "RCA," model of Nipper the dog, papier-maché painted white & brown, 11" h. (crack to front leg, chipping, soiling) **247.50**

Counter display figure, "Red Goose Shoes," chalkware, model of a goose, 8" h. **65.00**

Counter display figure, "Spalding," terra cotta, the figure of a barefoot black boy, the Spalding mascot, wearing a yellow vest, flowered shirt, green britches & a baseball cap, proferring a baseball in his right hand, the figure mounted on a pedestal base inscribed "Spalding's Li'l Ball Boy Mascot," America, ca. 1912, 43½" h. (restorations).........**9,200.00**

La Palina Display Jar

Counter display jar, "La Palina Cigars," clear glass, paneled cylindrical sides w/a metal rim band & glass lid, embossed on the front "La Palina - The Quality Cigar - Since 1896," on a separate wood base w/"La Palina" across the front, lettering on base faded, minor rust spotting on metal band, 6½" w., 8" h. (ILLUS.) **132.00**

Planters Peanuts Barrel Jar

Counter display jar, cov., "Planters Peanuts," clear glass barrel-shaped jar embossed w/figures of Mr. Peanut, glass lid w/peanut finial, original "Planters Salted Peanuts" red & gold paper label, figures w/worn silver paint, 8" d., 10½" h. (ILLUS.) **302.50**

Counter display jar, cov., "Planters Peanuts," clear glass "clipper" jar & metal lid **125.00**

Counter display jar, cov., "Planters Peanuts," clear glass jar w/peanuts at corners & original glass lid w/peanut finial ....**225.00 to 250.00**

Counter display jar, cov., "Planters Peanuts," clear glass, octagonal, peanut finial on lid, embossed "PENNANT SALTED PEANUTS 5 CENTS" on front & back panels, Mr. Peanut figure raised on four panels, 12½" h. **135.00**

Counter display jar, cov., "Pyramid Salted Nuts," clear glass, octagonal, w/original paper label **150.00**

Creamer, "Kellogg's," clear glass, reads "Correct Cereal" **17.50**

Heinz Baked Beans Crock

Crock, "Heinz Baked Beans," electric,

brown Albany-glazed pottery, embossed "Heinz" logo on the front w/raised wording "Heinz Oven Baked Beans 57," mismatched lid, early 20th c., 11" h. (ILLUS.)..............**55.00**

Dispenser, counter-type, "Heinz Vinegar," clear glass, barrel-shaped, 10" h..**185.00**

Doll, "Arbuckle Coffee," Jill, lithographed stuffed cloth **62.00**

Doll, "Arbuckle Coffee," Mary & lamb, lithographed stuffed cloth...................**65.00**

Doll, "Cream of Wheat," stuffed cloth, figure of Rastus, the black chef holding a bowl of the cereal, black & white striped pants, red & cream bowl, early 20th c., 20" h. (overall soiling) **88.00**

Doll, "Ceresota Flour boy," uncut cloth **200.00**

Doll, "Kellogg's," Chiquita Banana girl, uncut cloth, ca. 1944...................**45.00**

Doll, "Kellogg's Rice Krispies," Crackle, lithographed uncut cloth, Arnold Printworks, 1948.....................**45.00**

Doll, "Kellogg's," Papa Bear, stuffed cloth, 1926 ....**120.00**

Dolls, "Kellogg's," Goldilocks & Three Bears (Mama, Papa & Baby), ca. 1920, mint condition, the set....................................**325.00 to 350.00**

Uneeda Bisquits Boy Doll

Doll, "Uneeda Bisquits," composition body w/painted blue eyes, closed mouth & molded & painted hair, cloth body w/composition lower arms & legs, wearing original pink & white striped romper & yellow rain slicker & hat, composition feet molded as black boots, original tag on clothes, original Uneeda Bisquit box, two pinback buttons on his coat, one reading "I Signed Up," the other commemorating Nabisco's 50th Anniversary (1898-1948),

minor touch-up & crazing, 15" h. (ILLUS. below left) **425.00**

Door push plate, "Nesbitt's," porcelain, black & yellow ground w/white, black & orange lettering reading "Nesbitt's - the finest orange...Take Home A Carton," an orange, black & white bottle cap to the right, 32½" l., 3½" h. (very minor scratches & edge chipping) **165.00**

Peg Top Door Push Plate

Door push plate, "Peg Top Cigars," porcelain, cream ground w/brown lettering & a brown cigar, reads "The Old Reliable - Peg Top - 5¢," minor edge chipping & rust, 4 x 12½" (ILLUS.) **148.50**

Door push plate, "Salada Tea," porcelain, black lettering on a yellow ground reading "Delicious - 'Salada' Tea - Flavour," 32" l., 3" h. (minor scratches, edge chipping & rust) **137.50**

Door push plate, "7-Up," porcelain, reads "Fresh Up with 7-Up" **50.00**

Egg separator, "Jewel Stoves," metal, embossed **18.00**

Fan, hand-type, "Chambers Undertakers," woven wicker, flat rounded form printed in black "Chambers - One of the Largest Undertakers in the World," early 20th c., 12 x 13½" (minor soiling) **16.50**

Feather duster, "Chicago Carriage," long turned wood handle, patent-dated "Dec. 22, 1902," 19½" l. (minor wear) **49.50**

Folder, "Moore's Fountain Pens," six-sided, fold-out type......................**35.00**

Game, "Dr. Daniels Veterinarian Dice Game," also reads "Don't gamble - Use Dr. Daniels remedies," dice enclosed in glass dome, dated 1903..**385.00**

Game, "En-Ar-Co Glass National Refining Co.," entitled "Auto Road Game," 1919, in original envelope.....**35.00**

Game, "Lord Calvert Whiskey,"

dominoes, ca. 1939, the set..............**65.00**

Hosiery box, "Buster Brown," 1920s ...**50.00**

Humidor, cov., "Blue Boar Tobacco," yellow stoneware w/brown transfer scene **100.00**

Jigsaw puzzle, "White Sewing Machine Co.," lithographed cardboard, rectangular, one side w/a large colored advertisement for the White Sewing Machine w/a classically-garbed lady standing beside the sewing machine above two men & vignette scenes, the reverse w/a puzzle map of the Unites States, late 19th c., framed, 14½ x 20" (minor soiling) **137.50**

Jug, miniature, "Compliments of Hirsch Bro. & Co., Mfg's of Cider & Vinegar, Louisville, KY," stoneware **75.00**

Kite, electric company, pictures Reddy Kilowatt **72.50**

Atlas Equipment Pocket Knife

Knife, pocket-type, "Atlas Equipment Corp.," white celluloid handles w/inlaid metal logo & "Atlas Equipment Corp. - Pittsburgh, Pa.," two blades, scissors & nail file, made in Germany, minor scratches & soiling (ILLUS.) **27.50**

Lamp, "Sunkist Tuna," table model, composition & chalkware, figural Charlie Tuna, 1960s **125.00**

Marbles, "Weather-Bird Shoes - Best For Boys, Best For Girls," glass, five cat's-eye type, 1950s, in original giveaway box **75.00**

Grand Orient Wall Mirror

Mirror, wall-type, "Grand Orient," black diamond-shaped wooden frame w/ornate floral & geometric decoration incised at the top & bottom, & yellow & black lettering reads "Smoke Grand Orient" across the top, patent-dated "July 24, 1883," scratches on mirror, very minor paint loss, 16" w., 17" h. (ILLUS. bottom previous column) **440.00**

Mirror, wall-type, "Kist Beverages," reads "Get Kist Here," 12" d..............**95.00**

Socony Pocket Mirror

Mirror, pocket-type, "Socony Motor Gasoline," round, printed w/"So - N - Y" & logo reading "Socony Motor Gasoline - Standard Oil Co. of New York," early 20th c., minor soiling, 3¼" d. (ILLUS.) **82.50**

Mirror w/thermometer, "Royal Crown Cola," metal frame **150.00**

Mug, cov., "Good Cheer Cigar," lithographed tin, cylindrical w/strap handle **80.00**

Mug, "Sprudel Water & Salt from West Baden, Indiana," china, pictures building & gnome **125.00**

Salada Tea Paper Dispenser

Paper roll dispenser, counter-type, "Salada Tea," cast-iron framework on a rectangular wooden base, black & yellow porcelain sign at top bar reads " 'Salada Tea' - Always Delicious," w/a roll of paper, minor rust on cast iron & minor edge chipping on sign, 29" l., 16" h. (ILLUS.) **258.50**

Paperweight, "Northway Motor Mfg.,"

Detroit," bronze, detailed aerial view of plant & two hand-cranked motors **350.00**

Paperweight, "Parched Rolled Oats Brand - Nebraska City Cereal Mills," clear glass top w/milk white glass base **130.00**

Paperweight, "Planters Peanuts," glass w/paper insert illustrating Mr. Peanut & a tennis player, dated 1938 ....**75.00**

Peanut butter maker, "Planters Peanuts," figural Mr. Peanut w/grinder between ears, w/box, 12" h. ....**35.00 to 45.00**

Pen, fountain-type, "Bell Telephone Co.," Esterbrook, mint condition **45.00**

Pen, fountain-type, "Pepsi-Cola," the clip in shape of soda bottle **100.00**

Pen & pencil set, "Red Goose Shoes," in tin box w/ruler markings on the cover & dealer imprint, the set **160.00**

Pencil, mechanical, "Planters Peanuts," figural Mr. Peanut at top **20.00**

Pencil, mechanical, "Planters Peanuts," plastic, floating Mr. Peanut figure in top section, 6" l. (very minor wear) **22.00**

Pencil, mechanical, "Shell Oil," little figural "Shell" on clip **35.00**

Pencil, mechanical, "Tea Table Mills" ...**7.00**

Pencil clip, "7-Up," celluloid.................**30.00**

Pencil holder, "Oxydol Soap," celluloid, reads "Sho Makes Clothes White!" & pictures a black Mammy **69.00**

Sleepy Eye Pillow Top Cover

Pillow top cover, "Sleepy Eye Milling Co.," cloth, colorful scene depicting Chief Sleepy Eye greeting President Monroe, framed (ILLUS.) **750.00**

Pinback button, "Philip Morris," gold-plated metal, pictures Johnny **22.00**

Pinback button, "Sweet Caporal Cigarettes," celluloid, 1930s **20.00**

Pinback button, "The Tubular Cream Separator, Different from Others," celluloid, depicts child & woman w/device, 1⅛" l. **65.00**

Plate, bread & butter, "Mobil Oil," china, w/Pegasus logo **45.00**

Playing cards, "Chevron," die-cut, illustrates an oil can, the deck.............**18.00**

Playing cards, "Fleetwing Gasoline," double-deck set **35.00**

Playing cards, "Winchester," 1929, the deck **325.00**

Pot holder, electric company, pictures Reddy Kilowatt, in original package **40.00**

Punchboard, "Planters Peanuts," for chances to win a tin of "Planters Cocktail Peanuts - 2 cents a try," colorful, unused in original tissue wrapping paper, 1940s **85.00**

Puppet, hand-type, "Dutch Boy Paints," Dutch Boy figure, 1956, in original package, 12" h..................**65.00**

Columbus Flour Rolling Pin

Rolling pin, "Columbus Flour," milk white glass w/turned wooden handles, printed light brown flour bag & wording "Use Columbus Flour...," minor soiling & fading to graphics, late 19th c., 18" l. (ILLUS.) **962.50**

Ruler, "Ramson Mfg.," wooden, pictures carriages **25.00**

Salt & pepper shakers, "RCA Victor," Lenox China, model of Nipper, "His Master's Voice," pr. **50.00**

Salt & pepper shakers, "Tappan Range Mfg.," ceramic, figural chef, 4" h., pr. **18.00**

Sewing kit, "Lydia Pinkham," metal, tube-shaped **25.00**

Magnolia Condensed Milk Crate

Shipping Crate, "Magnolia Brand Condensed Milk," wooden, each end decorated w/debossed black-painted wording in upper right

"Magnolia Brand" & in lower left "Condensed Milk ," slanted banner through the center reads "4 Doz. Cans Premium Coupon 14 oz. each Net," also in small letters at the bottom "Borden's Condensed Milk Co., N.Y.," bottom cracked, wear, small pieces gone, 13 x 19", 7" h. (ILLUS. bottom previous page) **27.50**

Shipping Crate, "Mobiloil," wooden, rectangular w/stenciled black lettering & red gargoyle logo on end, three-board sides & single-board ends, 10½ x 21", 16" h. (overall soiling) **93.50**

Shinola Shoe Horn

Shoe horn, "Shinola," metal, colorful printed advertising w/two brushes & a can of the product w/"Shinola - The Wonderful Shoe Polish" at the tip, minor edge paint chipping, 4" l. (ILLUS.) **99.00**

Store window decals, "Muriel Cigar," picture of Edie Adams on both sides, 6 x 8", pr. **36.00**

String holder, "Red Goose Shoes," cast iron figural goose.....................**950.00**

Tablespoon, "Banner Buggies," silver plate, picture of buggy in bowl **25.00**

Tape measure, "Lewis Lye," white celluloid, pictures lye can w/Quaker logo in blue, dated 1918, 1½" d...................................**50.00 to 75.00**

Teaspoon, "Baker (Walter) Cocoa," silver plate, La Belle Chocolatiere figural handle **50.00**

Teaspoon, "Doe-Wah-Jack (Dowagiac, Michigan) Round Oak Stoves," silver plate, figural Indian handle, stove in bowl **75.00**

Thermometer, "American Fence & Posts," porcelain, 6" w., 19" l. **135.00**

Thermometer, "Dr. Pepper," tin, ca. 1960s, 20" h.................................**90.00**

Thermometer, "Grapette," metal, bottle cap-shaped, 11" d. **95.00**

Thermometer, "Mail Pouch Tobacco," porcelain, white lettering on a dark blue ground, rounded ends, printed at the top "Treat Yourself to The Best," printed at the bottom "Chew Mail Pouch Tobacco," 8" w., 38¾" h. (edge chipping, mounting holes)........**93.50**

Thermometer, "Mentholatum - Pure Drugs - Prescriptions," blue & white porcelain, 7 x 27" **62.00**

Thermometer, "Nesbitt's," tin, illustrates a professor saying "Don't Say Orange Say Nesbitt's," 7 x 27"...........**75.00**

Thermometer, "Pepsi-Cola," tin, illustrates a large bottle beside the thermometer, reads "Bigger" at the top & "Better" at the bottom, 1940s, 6 x 16"..**150.00**

Thermometer, "Pepsi-Cola," tin, printed at top "Buy Pepsi-Cola - Big, Big Bottle," 1940s, 7 x 27".....................**150.00**

Pepsi-Cola Thermometer

Thermometer, "Pepsi-Cola," tin, oblong, large embossed bottle cap at the top, reads "The Light refreshment" at the bottom, late 1950s, scratches & minor paint chipping, 7 x 27" (ILLUS.) **88.00**

Thermometer, "Prestone Anti-Freeze," enameled metal, grey, blue & red, reads "Safe & You Know It," 36" l. ....**75.00 to 100.00**

Thermometer, "Red Devil's Lighter Fluid," porcelain, narrow rectangular form, a colored picture of the product at the top above the scale, printed at the bottom w/" 'The Fluid With A Thousand Lights'," & "Full 4 Oz.," red, white & orange, 3 x 11½" (minor scratches & soiling) **198.00**

Thermometer, "Tums," metal, tall narrow form w/cream & yellow lettering on a dark blue ground, the thermometer down the center, reads "Tums - for the Tummy - Tums -

Quick Relief for Acid Indigestion - Heartburn," 4" w., 9" h. (very minor scratches & soiling).............................**55.00**

Victor Traps Thermometer

Thermometer, "Victor Guaranteed Traps," painted wood, narrow rectangular shape w/a rounded top, printed at the top w/a small skunk above "When The Mercury Is Low - Furs Are High," at the bottom w/"Victor Guaranteed Traps For All Fur Bearing Animals and Destructive Rodents - You Can Buy Them Here," black on cream, minor paint cracking, soiling & touch-up, 4 x 15" (ILLUS.) **165.00**

Tool caddy, "Stanley," wood, long rectangular open box w/pointed end panels joined at the top by a bar handle, printed in black on sides & ends "Stanley - Helps You Do Things Right," ca. 1940s, 36" l., 20" h. (one side piece missing).........**44.00**

Toy, automobile, "Roi Tan Cigars," lithographed tin w/two-sided sign on the roof, ca. 1939, mint in box **195.00**

Rosemary Foods Coaster Wagon

Toy coaster wagon, "Rosemary Foods," steel, w/rubber-rimmed metal tires, green w/yellow lettering along the sides reading "Rosemary Foods - The Highest Standard of

Purity and Excellence," rust & overall paint loss, 15 x 34", 14" h. (ILLUS. bottom previous column) **44.00**

Toy periscope, "Cracker Jack" prize ...**35.00**

Star Brand Shoes Racer

Toy race car, "Star Brand Shoes," lithographed tin, red w/white lettering & wheels, die-cut driver wearing blue, printed on the side "Star Brand Shoes Are Better," & printed on tail "The Winner," minor scratches, ca. 1917, 8½" l., 3" h. (ILLUS.) **1,980.00**

Toy whistle, "Buster Brown," tin, 1930s **45.00**

Tumbler, "Moxie," glass, flared rim, embossed **25.00**

Pepsi-Cola Commemorative Tumbler

Tumbler, "Pepsi-Cola," clear glass printed w/"Buffalo Rock - Pepsi-Cola - Birmingham, Alabama - 2nd Grand Opening - October 1971" (ILLUS.).....**44.00**

Tumblers, "Fisk Tires," clear glass, ca. 1940, set of 4 ....**25.00**

Umbrella, miniature, "Travelers Insurance Company," enameled metal, mint on card **15.00**

Yard long print w/calendar, "Pabst Brewing Co.," long narrow colorful lithograph w/various American Indian scenes & artifacts & a large bust portrait of an Indian Chief in feathered headdress, small calendar pages printed along the top & edges, printed at the bottom "Pabst Extract Indian Calendar," copyright

Pabst Yard Long Print-Calendar

by C.W. Henning, 1906
(ILLUS.) **1,300.00**

(End of Advertising Section)

ALMANACS

Almanacs have been published for decades. Commonplace ones are available at $4 to $12; those representing early printings or scarce ones are higher.

Ayer's Almanac, 1875..........................**$7.00**
Ayer's American Almanac, 1890 ....**7.00**
Farmer's Almanac, 1827 ....**57.50**
Hostetter's Almanac, 1907...................**6.00**
Shaker Almanac, 1886.......................**40.00**
Swamp Root Almanac, Indian
   designs on cover, 1913.....................**18.00**

ARCHITECTURAL ITEMS

Giltwood Putto Ornament

In recent years the growing interest in and support for historic preservation has spawned a greater appreciation of the fine architectural elements which were an integral part of early buildings, both public and private. Where, in decades past, fine structures might be razed and doors, fireplace mantels, windows, etc., hauled to the dump, today all interior and exterior details from unrestorable buildings are salvaged to be offered to home restorers, museums and even builders who want to include a bit of history in a new construction project.

Baseboard fragment, copper-plated
   cast iron, geometric incised design
   of double stars w/a raised ring of
   dots in the center, egg-and-dart
   lower border band, designed by
   Adler and Sullivan, Chicago, for The
   Chicago Stock Exchange Building,
   ca. 1893, 17$\frac{1}{16}$" x 24"....................**$632.50**
Building ornaments, winged putti,
   each in carved giltwood & shown
   wearing a blindfold & holding a
   flute, the legs emanating from a
   carved scroll acanthus, American-
   made, 19th c., 14$\frac{1}{2}$" l., pr. (ILLUS.
   of one)..**2,185.00**
Column capital, carved & painted
   wood, of the Corinthian order,
   19th c., 28$\frac{1}{2}$" h. **1,092.50**
Columns w/composite capitals,
   carved & painted wood, labeled, late
   19th c., 4' 10" h., pr. (losses) **374.00**

Decorated Window Cornices

Cornices, carved, painted & stenciled
   wood, each w/a shaped & cut-out
   cresting centering a basket filled
   w/fruits & stenciled flowers, the
   corners w/fruit-filled compotes
   flanking a broad horizontal band of
   stenciled leafage & flowers framed
   by gilt painted moldings, all on a
   dark green ground, probably New
   England, ca. 1835, 42" l., 15" h., pr.
   (ILLUS.) **2,300.00**
Door, painted pine, two long panels
   above two short panels, good old

blue paint, cast-iron fittings, 19th c.,
29" w., 6' 6" h. **302.50**
Fan carving, carved & painted wood,
vestiges of paint, 19th c., 72" l.,
20½" h. **632.50**
Fireplace mantel, painted soft wood,
Federal style, the long rectangular
shelf w/a molded edge above two
plain rectangular panels separated
by three almond-shaped sunbursts,
reeded pilasters down the sides, old
paint, early 19th c., overall 61¾" w.,
5' 1½" h. **1,650.00**
Fireplace mantel, painted & gessoed
pine, Federal style, the molded
platform above a fluted & stellate-
carved frieze, two panels below
decorated w/baskets of fruit &
festoons of grapes & leaves tied
w/bow-knots, centering a rectangular raised panel depicting a
chariot pulled by lions, a winged
trumpeting putto in the foreground,
raised panels flanking depicting
Diana the Huntress, reeded pilasters
flanking the fireplace opening, painted off-white, attributed to Robert
Welford, Philadelphia, Pennsylvania,
ca. 1805, 88½" w., 5' 3" h. **3,450.00**

Art Nouveau Fireplace Surround

Fireplace surround, cast iron, Art
Nouveau style, wide flat top section
flaring down to pierced & cast stylized scrolling, the wide canted sides
w/scroll-cast bases, dark patina,
Hector Guimard, France, ca. 1900,
33½" w., 36" h. (ILLUS.) **3,737.00**
Fireplace surround, marble, the
foliate-carved white marble surround
inlaid w/green & liver white striated
panels, carved w/leaves & w/a
beaded border, George II period,
England, mid-18th c., 83½" l.,
4' 5" h. **20,700.00**
Gates, painted wood, the curved top
bar above a lattice design w/a cen-

Early Wooden Gates

tral six-spoke wheel w/the spokes
radiating out to the sides of the
framework, worn paint, American-
made, mid-19th c., each half 37" w.,
4' 5" h., pr. (ILLUS.) **1,380.00**
Gates, wrought iron, Art Deco style,
tall rectangular sections w/a narrow
barred side panel beside a wide
panel w/stepped bar rectangles
above a pair of large scrolls at the
bottom, Raymond Subes, ca. 1925,
98½" l., 6' 7¾" h., pr.....................**7,475.00**
Newel post, cast iron, Modern style,
the rectangular slender post w/a
spherical foot & oval terminal cast
w/an elliptical design, the terminal
w/flamboyant scrolled foliage,
designed by Adler & Sullivan for the
Chicago Stock Exchange Building,
ca. 1893, on a black metal mount,
5' 5" h. **3,450.00**
Paneled room wall section, painted
pine, in three sections, comprising
a fireplace surround & two closet
doors w/surrounds, each section
w/molded cornice above a fluted
frieze w/raised rectangular panels
below, the doors retaining their "HL"
hinges, the fireplace surround w/a
molded & serpentine shelf above,
painted off-white, Philadelphia,
ca. 1775, sections 96" w., 44½" w.
& 50⅞" w., overall 8" h., the
group...**10,350.00**

ART DECO

*Interest in Art Deco, a name given an
art movement stemming from the Paris
International Exhibition of 1925, is at an
all-time high and continues to grow. This
style flowered in the 1930s and actually
continued into the 1940s. A mood of
flippancy is found in its varied
characteristics—zigzag lines resembling
the lightning bolt, sometimes steps, often*

the use of sharply contrasting colors such as black and white and others. Look for Art Deco prices to continue to rise. Also see JEWELRY (MODERN).

Bowl, silver plate, the circular deep body raised on a flaring round foot & flanked by two wide arches w/round rosewood rim tab handles, stamped "DESNY PARIS MADE IN FRANCE DEPOSE," w/logo, 1930s, 4⅜" h...**$3,450.00**

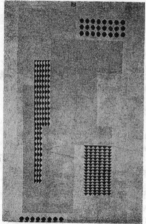

Art Deco Carpet

Carpet, room-size, the beige field set w/overlapping rectangles in shades of orange & taupe & set w/patterns of triangles & dots, woven signature "da Silva Bruhns" w/weaver's monogram (?), ca. 1925, 8 x 13' (ILLUS.) **17,250.00**

Carpet, room-size, central section w/a grid of nine circles in green, brown & beige, within a beige border, by Paul Follot, woven monogram in the reverse resembling a stylized hand in brown, ca. 1938, 11' 2" w., 11' 4" l................**10,350.00**

Art Deco Mantel Clock

Clock, mantel-type, onyx & ormolu, the arched onyx case centered by a small round dial w/Arabic numerals

framed by a fan-form panel of cast ormolu morning glory vines & flowers, angled lower sides & flat rectangular base, Europe, ca. 1930, minor chips, 18½" l., 11½" h. (ILLUS. bottom previous column) **747.50**

Clock, table model, model of a sky-scraper, Bakelite, by Hammond, w/calendar **75.00**

Skyscraper Table Lamp

Lamp, table model, cast iron, cast as a model of stepped skyscraper on a cross-form base, applied bronze patina, ca. 1925, unsigned, some patina loss, 30⅞" h. (ILLUS.) **977.50**

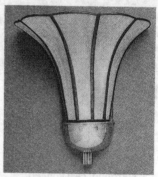

Art Deco Wall Sconce

Wall sconces, leaded glass & brass, the half-round brass mount supporting a five-paneled petal-form shade w/mottled amber glass panels, 13" h., pr. (ILLUS. of one) **690.00**

ART NOUVEAU

Art Nouveau's primary thrust was between 1890 and 1905 but commercial Art Nouveau productions continued until

about World War I. This style was a
rebellion against historic tradition in art.
Using natural forms as inspiration, it is
primarily characterized by undulating or
wave-like lines. Many objects were made in
materials ranging from glass to metals.
Interest in Art Nouveau still remains high,
especially for jewelry in the Nouveau taste.
Also see JEWELRY (Antique) and MUCHA
(Alphonse) ARTWORK.

Art Nouveau Jardiniere

Jardiniere, bronze & ceramic, figural,
the bronze mount cast w/the masks
of maidens on either side amid
poppy blossoms, buds & foliage,
conjoined by whiplash devices,
enclosing a deep cobalt blue glazed
ceramic liner w/an additionai tinned
liner, bronze w/dark brown patina,
France, ca. 1900, 25⅜" l.
(ILLUS.) **$2,875.00**

Jardiniere & pedestal, earthenware,
the bulbous footed bowl molded in
high-relief w/a series of full-length
Art Nouveau maidens twisting
around the sides & clothed in
revealing drapery, the pedestal
molded in high-relief around the top
w/three busts of young women
w/flowing hair, their drapery swirling
down the sides to the flaring foot,
the upper sides & ladies glazed in
white, the draperies glazed in
turquoise blue, attributed to Delphin
Massier, France, ca. 1900, 5' 11" h.,
pr. (restorations, minor chips &
losses) **21,850.00**

Figural Art Nouveau Vases

Lamp, table model, alabaster,
partially draped female figure supporting a globe overhead, 32¾" h.....**977.50**

Vases, parcel-gilt bronze, figural, tall
slender & slightly waisted cylindrical
body w/a flaring ruffled mouth, a
flaring lily pad-cast foot, one cast in
relief w/a gilt female fairy against a
ground of tall leaves, the other cast
w/a male fairy against a wave-cast
ground, brown patina, by Charles
Louchet, impressed "LOUCHET,"
France, ca. 1900, 10" h., pr. (ILLUS.
bottom previous column) **2,013.00**

Vase, gilt bronze & ceramic, figural,
the vessel glazed in mottled blue-
green & turquoise shading to deep
olive green & cast w/side handles at
base, fitting into a mount cast
w/swirling waves from which a nude
maiden arises, w/a cluster of seaweed applied at one upper corner,
impressed mark on bottom, bronze,
unsigned, ca. 1900, 17¼" h. **4,313.00**

Ornate Art Nouveau Vase

Vase, silvered-metal, figural, the tall
slender complexly shaped two-
handled body cast w/openwork
leafage & set near the base
w/figures of a maiden in a flowing
gown & a young girl holding a
basket of rose blossoms, unsigned,
probably by Wurttembergische
Metallwarenfabrik(WMF), Germany,
ca. 1900, 27¾" h. (ILLUS.) **1,380.00**

AUDUBON PRINTS

*John James Audubon, American
ornithologist and artist, is considered the*

finest nature artist in history. About 1820 he conceived the idea of having a full color book published portraying every known species of American bird in its natural habitat. He spent years in the wilderness capturing the beauty in vivid color only to have great difficulty finding a publisher. In 1826 he visited England, received immediate acclaim, and selected Robert Havell as his engraver. "Birds of America," when completed, consisted of four volumes of 435 individual plates, double-elephant folio size, which are a combination of aquatint, etching and line engraving. W.H. Lizars of Edinburgh engraved the first ten plates of this four volume series. These were later retouched by Havell who produced the complete set between 1827 and early 1839. In the early 1840s, another definitive work, "Viviparous Quadrupeds of North America," containing 150 plates, was published in America. Prices for Audubon's original double-elephant folio size prints are very high and beyond the means of the average collector. Subsequent editions of "Birds of America," especially the chromolithographs done by Julius Bien in New York (1859-60) and the smaller octavo (7 x 10½") edition of prints done by J.T. Bowen of Philadelphia in the 1840s, are those that are most frequently offered for sale.

Boat-Tailed Grackle - Plate CLXXXVII, hand-colored engraving by Robert Havell, Jr., London, 1827-38, framed, 23½ x 32" (laid-down, subtle fading, minor foxing) **$826.50**

Canada Lynx (Male) - Plate XVI, hand-colored lithograph by J.T. Bowen, Philadelphia, ca. 1845, framed 21¼ x 27¼" (pale mat stain, trace of soiling, tiny edge tears on disbound edge) **4,313.00**

Common American Deer

Common American Deer - Plate LXXXI, hand-colored lithograph by J.T. Bowen, Philadelphia, ca. 1845, some tiny spots of foxing, minor soiling at sheet edges, stitch

holes on disbound edge, framed, 21⅝ x 27" (ILLUS.bottom previous column) **4,025.00**

Little Screech Owl - Plate XCVII, hand-colored engraving by Robert Havell, Jr., London, 1827-38, framed, 24½ x 32" (laid-down, scattered foxing & staining) **1,380.00**

Painted Finch - Plate LIII, hand-colored engraving by Robert Havell, Jr., London, 1827-38, framed, 26⅛" x 39½" (small stain, small repaired tears, tiny losses, slight edge discoloration) **3,105.00**

Pileated Woodpecker - Plate CXI, hand-colored engraving by Robert Havell, Jr., London, 1827-38, 25⅛ x 38⅛" (light foxing & soiling, mainly in margins, repaired circular tear, backed w/tape on verso in the tree, small paper loss in the top sheet edge, soiling in extreme sheet edges verso) **12,075.00**

Pinnated Grous - Plate CLXXXVI, hand-colored engraving by Robert Havell, Jr., London, 1827-38, 25¾ x 39⅛" (mat stain, bit of light discoloration in the sky, 25mm tear in top sheet edge, edges of paper hinged to back mat w/linen tape) ..**7,475.00**

Purple Heron - Plate CCLVI, hand-colored engraving by Robert Havell, Jr., London, 1827-38, framed, 26 x 38½" (foxing at top, pale staining, some surface soiling & tears in margins, old binding holes) **6,900.00**

Rice Bunting - Plate 54, hand-colored engraving by Robert Havell, Jr., London, 1827-38, 25⅝ x 38½" (a few very slight handling creases & minor soiling in the margins, a few fox marks visible only on the verso) **1,265.00**

Ruff-necked Humming-bird - Plate CCCLXXIX, hand-colored engraving by Robert Havell, Jr., London, 1827-38, 26 x 39¼" (few traces of ink & a bit of soiling near lower right platemark, soiling in sheet edges) **4,313.00**

Rusty Grackle - Plate CLVII, hand-colored engraving by Robert Havell, Jr., London, 1827-38, unframed, 26 x 39⅛" (traces of foxing & soiling along edges, a few stitch holes along disbound edge, offprint on verso) **1,840.00**

Tell-Tale Godwit or Snipe - Plate CCCVIII, hand-colored engraving by Robert Havell, Jr., London, 1827-38, framed, 25⅝ x 38⅛" (very light soiling, small losses & minor traces of glue along disbound edge) **2,530.00**

White-Crowned Pigeon - Plate

CLXXVII, hand-colored engraving by
Robert Havell, Jr., London, 1827-38,
framed, 24¾ x 38⅛" (faint light stain,
few specks of foxing & small abra-
sion, small loss to edge) **5,175.00**
White-fronted Goose - Plate
CCLXXXVI, hand-colored engraving by Robert Havell, Jr., London,
1827-38, framed, 24⅞ x 37⅝"
(horizontal crease, repaired tear
in margin, slight soiling & small
tears in edge) **6,440.00**
Winter Wren, Rock Wren - Plate
CCCLX, hand-colored engraving
by Robert Havell, Jr., London,
1827-38, unframed, (few tiny
specks of foxing, some soiling on
edges, stitch holes along disbound
edge)...**1,495.00**
Yellow Shank - Plate CCLXXXVII,
hand-colored engraving by Robert
Havell, Jr., London, 1827-38,
unframed, 14⅝ x 20⅝" (some faint
soiling & foxing in margins, tiny tears
in edges) **4,830.00**

Zenaida Dove

Zenaida Dove - Plate CLXII, hand-
colored engraving by Robert Havell,
Jr., London, 1827-38, fine tiny fox
marks, soiling & soft creases at
edges, framed, overall 26⅜ x 39⅜"
(ILLUS.) **3,220.00**

AUTOGRAPHS

*Value of autographs and autograph letters
depend on such factors as content, scarcity
and the fame of the writer. Values of good
autograph material continue to rise. A.L.S.
stands for "autographed letter signed," L.S.
for "letter signed," D.S. for "document signed"
and S.P. for "signed photograph." Also see*

*POP CULTURE COLLECTIBLES and
RECORDS & RECORD JACKETS.*

Armstrong, Louis (1901-71),
American jazz musician, signed
recording contract, spelling out
terms, signed in lower right by
Armstrong & his manager Joseph
Glaser, dated "October 3rd,
1935".......................................**$1,035.00**
Astaire, Fred (1899-1987), American
dancer & actor, SP, black & white
bust portrait of a smiling Mr. Astaire,
signed in the upper right in black ink
"Fred Astaire," ca. 1950s, 8 x 10 .....**863.00**
Autry, Gene (1907-) American
cowboy movie & radio star, S.P.,
8 x 10"..**45.00**
Bankhead, Tallulah (1903-68),
American actress, S.P., sepia tone
photo of the actress sitting wearing
a period gown, inscribed in black ink
"To West From Tallulah," ca. 1920s,
matted & framed, 8½ x 11" **345.00**

Irving Berlin-Signed Music

Berlin, Irving (1888-1989), American
composer, autographed sheet music
cover for "White Christmas," inscribed in blue ink in the center left side
"All Good Wishes - Irving Berlin,"
framed, 9 x 12" (ILLUS.) **920.00**
Cagney, James (1899-1986),
American actor, S.P., black & white
bust portrait of the smiling actor,
signed in lower right in black ink
"Regards to Wilbur Powell -
James Cagney," framed, 11 x 14" ...**460.00**
Colbert, Claudette (1903-),
American actress, S.P., black &
white half-length portrait of the
actress, inscribed in the lower right
in blue ink "To Sydney with my
sincere good wishes Claudette
Colbert," ca. 1940s, 11 x 14" **460.00**
Cooper, Gary (1901-61), American
actor, S.P., black & white head
portrait of the actor, signed in the

lower right corner in black ink "To Bob - with deep regard, and appreciation for starting me off in the movies -- Sincerely, Gary Cooper," ca. 1940s, unframed, 11 x 13½" **633.00**

Flynn, Errol, (1909-59), American actor, S.P., black & white photograph of Flynn as Sir Robin of Locksley in "The Adventures of Robin Hood," inscribed in black ink on lower right corner "To The Boys Club All my good wishes Errol Flynn," unframed, 10 x 13" **1,380.00**

Gable, Clark (1901-60), American actor, S.P., black & white bust portrait of a clean-shaven Mr. Gable, inscribed in lower right hand corner in blue ink "To Beulah The Gal on Duty Clark," the raised letters 'Clarence Sinclair Bull' underneath the inscription, ca. late 1920s - early 1930s, unframed, 10 x 13" **1,725.00**

Signed Judy Garland Photo

Garland, Judy (1923-69), American actress, S.P., black & white three-quarters portrait of Judy wearing a tramp outfit & holding a large bouquet of roses, torn from a magazine, inscribed "Joan dear - with all my love, Judy," mounted on cardboard, 9½ x 12½" (ILLUS.) **2,185.00**

Hepburn, Katharine, (1909-), American actress, A.L.S. to Sydney Guilaroff on Spencer Tracy's stationery responding to sympathy wishes on Tracy's death, in black ink, dated July 17, 1967, w/original envelope **3,220.00**

Holly, Buddy (1936-59), Rock & Roll musician, A.L.S., a handwritten letter w/details concerning his early career, dated August, 1957, matted & framed w/a black & white photograph, 16 x 32"..............................**8,050.00**

Presley, Elvis (1935-77), American singer & actor, signed menu from the Las Vegas Hilton, signed on the

Menu Signed by Elvis

front in blue ink "Best Wishes - Elvis Presley," ca. 1974, 8½ x 11" (ILLUS.) **1,150.00**

Presley, Elvis (1935-77), American singer & actor, blue ball point pen autograph & inscription reading "Best Wishes - Elvis Presley," matted & framed w/a color photograph & small plaque, 21 x 33".....................................**977.00**

Signed Roy Rogers Cowboy Hat

Rogers, Roy (1911-), movie & TV cowboy actor, signed cowboy hat, tan felt worn by Rogers, inside rim tag reading "CUSTOM MADE FOR ROY ROGERS - KING OF THE COWBOYS," inscribed on the brim in black ink "To Frank - Roy Rogers" (ILLUS.) **368.00**

Roosevelt, Theodore (1858-1919), 26th President of the United States, letter to Commander Peary on White House stationery, thanks Peary for a photograph of his son & offered a dose of spirited praise & encouragement, dated March 13, 1908.........**6,600.00**

AUTOMOBILE LITERATURE

Book, "The Gasoline Automobile," 1915, McGraw Hill, hard cover, 259 pp..**$20.00**

Book, "Practical Treatise on Automobiles," 1910, illustrated, 419 pp.....**45.00**

Buick brochure, 1965, 44 pp. **25.00**
Chevrolet owner's manual, 1936.......**45.00**
Chrysler booklet, 1938, shows
   fifteen cars in color, 8½ x 11".............**50.00**
Edsel owner's manual, 1957.............**60.00**
Ford sales booklet, 1951 ....**30.00**
**Hupmobile Eight promotional
   booklet,** 1930, 9 x 12", 16 pp. **40.00**
Lincoln "Zephyr" sales booklet,
   1937 ....**35.00**
Mack Truck maintenance manual,
   "Series E. Mack Truck," 1930,
   136 pp. **18.00**
Magazine, Buick, 1939, January..........**10.00**
Magazine, Chicago Show Number,
   1914, illustrates all types of cars........**55.00**
Magazine, Motor Age, 1902, May........**20.00**
Magazine, Motor Age, 1906,
   December 27, articles include
   coverage of the "New" Oldsmobile **22.00**
Oakland owner's manual, 1926 ....**65.00**
Oldsmobile dealer color folder, featuring the "Holiday Sedans" (four-
   door hard tops), 1955 ....**25.00**
Pierce Arrow showroom brochure,
   1931, full-color paintings of various
   models, all colored pictures border-
   ed in silver, 36 pp., 10 x 14½"..........**385.00**
Tucker showroom folder, w/14"
   picture of a car, 1946, 17 x 22" **38.00**

AUTOMOBILES

1931 Ford Model A Coupe

Buick, 1948 Roadmaster station
   wagon **$18,000.00**
Cadillac, 1934 Model 355D, Series
   10 town sedan **20,000.00**
Chevrolet, 1928 cabriolet conver-
   tible **18,000.00**
Chevrolet, 1940 deluxe four-door
   sedan...**3,000.00**
Chevrolet, 1957 Bel Air conver-
   tible **27,000.00**
Chevrolet, 1964 Impala SS, two-door
   hard top...**3,600.00**
Chrysler, 1927 Model H 60 road-
   ster...**17,000.00**
Chrysler, 1947 Windsor town &
   country **31,000.00**

Chrysler, 1968 Imperial, red & black,
   hard top, four-door, all original,
   odometer reading 43,550............**12,500.00**
Duesenberg, 1927 Model A, four-
   window sports sedan **45,000.00**
Ford, 1929 Model A roadster **8,000.00**
Ford, 1930 Model A pickup truck,
   restored..**6,900.00**
Ford, 1931 Model A Deluxe coupe,
   five-window model, fully restored
   (ILLUS.) **10,000.00**
Ford, 1932 Model B roadster **25,000.00**
Ford, 1934 Model 40 cabriolet **27,000.00**
Ford, 1948 "woodie" station
   wagon **35,000.00**
Ford, 1951 F-1 pick-up truck...........**8,000.00**
Ford, 1951 "woodie" station wagon,
   fully restored **6,600.00**
Ford, 1955 Thunderbird convert-
   ible **25,000.00**
Ford, 1962 Fairlane 500, four-
   door..**2,250.00**
Ford, 1965 Mustang two-door hard
   top..**4,250.00**
Ford, 1966 Mustang coupe **4,800.00**
Franklin, 1931 Model 153 sedan ..**21,000.00**
Hupmobile, 1932 Model B-216
   Century 6, four door.....................**4,750.00**
Lincoln, 1937 Zephyr coupe.........**40,000.00**
Mercedes Benz, 1958 Model 190 SL
   roadster..**21,000.00**
Packard, 1955 Patrician sedan.......**7,000.00**
Pontiac, 1932 two-door sedan......**12,750.00**
Pontiac, 1967 G.T.O. post
   coupe **11,000.00**
Rolls Royce, 1934 Model 20/25 two-
   door coupe...................................**38,000.00**
Sears, 1908 Model H runabout **10,000.00**
Willys-Knight, 1923 touring car....**12,000.00**

AUTOMOTIVE COLLECTIBLES

Also see CANS & CONTAINERS.

Michelin Air Compressor

Air Compressor, "Michelin," painted metal, a figure of the Michelin man w/a hose coming from his mouth, seated astride a bullet-shaped metal compressor w/top loop handle, ca. 1920-30, paint wear, 11" h. (ILLUS. bottom previous page) **$962.50**

Air pump meter, "The Arno Air Meter," cast iron painted red & silver, the arched compartment w/"The Arno Air Meter" above a small window on one side & "AIR" in large letters on the other side, on flaring wedge feet, Model 30 C, 6" w., 14" h.....................................**209.00**

Atlas Antifreeze Tester

Antifreeze tester, metal, glass & rubber, a large rubber bulb atop a metal-framed glass tube above round metal base printed "Atlas Colder Antifreeze...," a hose issuing from the base, minor scratches, 18" h. (ILLUS.) **66.00**

Bumper sign, tin, "State Farm Insurance," 1938, mint in package.............**18.00**

Chauffeur's badge, 1919, Michigan....**65.00**

Chauffeur's badge, 1925, New York ..**28.50**

Chauffeur's badge, 1928, Iowa **12.00**

Chauffeur's badge, 1928, New York ..**10.00**

Chauffeur's badge, 1937, Ohio **18.00**

Chauffeur's badge, 1940, Indiana **18.00**

Chauffeur's badge, 1944, Colorado ...**12.50**

Chauffeur's badge, 1949, Ohio **18.00**

Chauffeur's license, 1919, Michigan..**65.00**

Clothes brush, "Pontiac," oval green plastic back printed in yellow w/Pontiac Indian head logo & advertising for a Chicago, Illinois dealership, ca. 1950s, 6¾" l..............**22.00**

Counter display figure, "Michelin Tires," standing reinforced plaster figure of the Michelin man w/a banner across his chest reading "Michelin Tires," all-original, 32" h. (overall wear) **1,237.50**

Driving mitts, horsehide, marked "Osborn Motor Hardware," pr..........**165.00**

Gasoline pump globe, "American Gas," milk white lenses in a metal frame, lenses w/a wide dark ring w/white lettering, 15" d. (scratches, minor edge chipping & fading) **302.50**

Gasoline pump globe, "Amoco," Gill glass body, white lettering on a dark ground, 13½" d.............................**302.50**

Gasoline pump globe, "Atlantic," milk white glass Gill body, Atlantic logo printed in red, white & blue, 13½" d. (soiling at base) **242.00**

Gasoline pump globe, "Duro Gasoline," three-piece milk white glass, wide green ring printed in white "Duro Gasoline," white center circle w/a large "D" in red & green, 13½" d.....................................**308.00**

Gasoline pump globe, "Elreco," milk white glass w/a red circle in the center crossed by a white bar w/red lettering "Elreco," outer white circle w/"Buy miles - Not gallons - Premium," 13½" d. **330.00**

Gasoline pump globe, "Esso," Gill body, milk white glass lenses w/red lettering, metal base, 13½" d. (soiling, water stains on inside).......**302.50**

Gasoline pump globe, "Falcon," plastic, large yellow & brown flying falcon behind a green center band printed in white lettering "Falcon," 13½" d. **467.50**

Gasoline pump globe, "General Motor Fuel," three-piece white metal frame w/milk white glass lenses, black diagonal band printed in yellow "General," a shield w/helmeted head behind band in yellow w/red lettering "Motor Fuel," 15" d. (very minor wear)..................**660.00**

Gasoline pump globe, "Golden 97 Ethyl," Hull glass body, milk white w/colored printing & company logo, 12½" d. (very minor scratches) **385.00**

Indian Gas Pump Globe

Gasoline pump globe, "Indian Gas," milk white glass one-piece style w/a large red dot in the center framed by "Indian Gas" in blue letters, "Havo-line" down the side, chips on the flange base, 15½" d. (ILLUS. bottom previous page) **1,045.00**

Gasoline pump globe, "Lubrite Sky-Hy," glass lenses in a metal frame, 15" d. lens (soiling & paint loss to frame, lens very good) **770.00**

Magnolia Gas Pump Globe

Gasoline pump globe, "Magnolia Gasoline," red metal frame w/milk white glass lenses decorated w/a large white magnolia blossom framed by green leaves & surrounded by red lettering outlined in blue reading "Magnolia Gasoline," scratches on the inside of the lenses, 16" d. (ILLUS.) **1,650.00**

Gasoline pump globe, "Metro," red metal body w/white lenses printed in red & green, 15" d. (very minor scratches) **330.00**

Musgo Gas Pump Globe

Gasoline pump globe, "Musgo," milk white glass printed in colors w/a bust portrait of an Indian chief wearing a feathered headdress framed by a wide ring printed "Musgo - Michigans Mile Maker," dated "Sept. 1928," 13½" d. (ILLUS.) **5,225.00**

Gasoline pump globe, "Penreco," glass lenses & metal frame, the lenses printed w/a statue of William Penn on a tall square pedestal base

behind the logo "Penreco," ca. 1920s-30s, 15" d. lens (paint flaking) **770.00**

Gasoline pump globe, "Purgo Radiator Service," green metal body, yellow & green background w/black lettering outlined in white reading "Purgo Radiator Service - Cleans - Flushes - Leakproofs!," white starburst in background, 16½" d..**605.00**

Gasoline pump globe, "Red Crown Gas," milk white glass, molded in the form of a crown w/"Red Crown Gas" molded in a band around the base, factory prototype, undecorated, 16" h. (very minor soiling) **660.00**

Richfield Ethyl Pump Globe

Gasoline pump globe, "Richfield Ethyl," metal frame w/milk white glass lenses, printed w/a large blue shield bordered in yellow, a small blue & white eagle above yellow lettering reading "Richfield Ethyl" & a small circle w/"Ethyl - Property of Richfield Oil Co. Copyright 1928 R.O. Co. of Calif.," overall soiling & scratches, 15" d. (ILLUS.) **660.00**

Gasoline pump globe, "Royal Gas," red metal frame w/milk white glass lenses printed "Royal Gas" framing a map of the state of Maine, 15" d. (paint chipping on frame) **825.00**

Gasoline pump globe, "Shell," milk white glass in a molded shell shape, red letters, 18" w., 18" h. (letters repainted, minor soiling) **385.00**

Gasoline pump globe, "Texaco," milk white glass, three-piece globe on metal base, printed w/a large red star w/a green "T" & "Texaco" in black, 13½" d. (soiling, fading) **357.50**

Gasoline pump globe, "Texaco Sky Chief," Gill body, milk white glass w/white banner reading "Sky Chief" over a long wing w/the Texaco logo, grey paint on the frame, 13½" d......**495.00**

Gasoline pump globe, "Tydol," black metal body w/milk white glass lenses printed in orange & black, 14½" d.

(minor soiling, reverse side scratched & faded)............................**385.00**

Gasoline pump globe, "White Eagle," figural hollow milk white glass eagle w/pointed beak, 20¾" h. (very minor soiling) **1,870.00**

Gas station attendant's hat, "Esso," dark cloth w/plastic band & oval red, blue & white logo patch on front, size 6⅞" (minor soiling & wear) **88.00**

Gas tank gauge, "Tank-o-Scope," slender metal & clear plastic cylindrical gauge, w/cylindrical wooden case marked "Tank-o-Scope Automotive Service Co., Milldale, Conn." gauge 16" l. (case soiled, scratches & w/minor nicks, minor wear on gauge) **22.00**

Glare shield, "Face-A-Lite," metal mount w/L-form green visor, w/original illustrated black & white box w/red lettering reading "Face-A-Lite," ca. 1930s, 7¾" l., 5¾" h. (one side of box gone, tears & soiling on box)..**60.50**

Head lamps, brass & glass, pedestal base below wide round clear lens & a small red lens at the back, a long swing handle at the top, patent-dated "Feb. 15, 1927," 11" h., pr. (polished) **170.50**

Head lamps, "Neverout," brass & glass, ringed pedestal base below a wide round clear lens w/a smaller red lens at the back, ringed vent top flanked by a fixed brass loop handle, marked by the Rose Mfg. Co., Philadelphia, early 20th c., 9" h., pr. (repolished, minor wear) **198.00**

Headlight lenses, "Ford," for Model A, 1930-31, pr. **20.00**

Hood ornament, "Dodge," chrome, Art Deco style, standing winged lady w/upstretched arms, base marked "Dodge Bros." **85.00**

Winged Female Hood Ornament

Hood ornament, chrome, figure of a winged female w/streaming hair & holding a small wheel out ahead, the long flat wing of clear hard plastic etched w/four lines, minor wear (ILLUS.) **88.00**

Hood ornament, chromed brass, model of a leaping greyhound, made for Lincoln, 8¾" l. (some chrome

wear, bottom of cap & tip of tail missing) **110.00**

Hood ornament, German silver, a figure of a standing Abraham Lincoln posed w/one arm behind his back, marked on base "Copyright 1927 LT Bargick Byron III," offered by the Ford Motor Company between 1927 & 1929, 6½" h. (some soiling) **275.00**

Horn, "Mercedes," brass w/original black paint, 1930s............................**40.00**

Inkwell, silver-plated, molded as two race car drivers in a vintage car, the hood & trunk opening to reveal two inkwells, by Wurttembergische Mettalwaren Fabrik, stamped w/firm's marks, 14" l.....................**2,300.00**

Key chain, "Chrysler," 1942, pictorial ..**30.00**

Key chain, "General Motors Power-ama," 1955................................**10.00**

License plates, 1905, New Hamp-shire, porcelain, pr. **85.00**

License plates, dealer-type, 1910, Massachusetts, porcelain, pr. **65.00**

License plates, 1911, Connecticut, porcelain, pr. **85.00**

License plates, 1911, Vermont, porcelain, pr. **75.00**

License plates, 1912, New Jersey, porcelain, pr. **85.00**

License plates, 1913, Maine, porcelain, pr. **60.00**

License plates, 1913, Pennsylvania, porcelain, pr. **75.00**

License plates, 1914, Massa-chusetts, porcelain, pr.......................**75.00**

License plates, 1915, Connecticut, porcelain, pr. **85.00**

License plates, 1931, Texas, pr.........**60.00**

License plates, 1931, Virginia, pr........**85.00**

License plates, 1935, Nevada, mint in package, pr. **50.00**

License plates, 1936, Texas Centennial, pr. **100.00**

License plates, 1937, New York, pr. **50.00**

Mirror, wall-type, long rectangle w/a printed green border w/pine sprigs & a colored landscape vignette at the top w/deer, advertising printed at the bottom "Courtesy Chevrolet Co. - Chevrolet - Cadillac - Sales and Service - Phone 2241 - Choteau, Montana," 12 x 22" (chipping to edges & corners of glass) **137.50**

Moto meter, "Boyce," cast iron & glass, universal model, a metal frame holding a glass thermometer, flaring metal wings at the base above the scalloped cap, paint chipping inside thermometer (ILLUS. top next page)....................**148.50**

Motor oil bottle, "Mobil Gargoyle,"

Boyce Moto Meter

clear glass, flat sides, spill-proof top,
1 qt. **95.00**
Motor oil bottle, "Shell," clear glass
w/raised logo & embossed rib
design, 1 qt., 14" h. **85.00**
Motor oil rack, rectangular wire rack
w/high center wire carrying handle
above eight compartments holding
clear glass bottles w/metal pointed
pouring caps, bottles w/embossed
"Standard Oil" circular logos,
9 x 17", 15" h. (one cap missing,
soiling, minor rust) **467.50**
Postcard, "Ford Model T," illustrates
the touring car...................................**20.00**

Ford Fordor Sedan Poster

Poster, Ford "De Luxe Fordor Touring
Sedan," cardboard, a black car on a
green & grey ground w/red, white &
black lettering, 1930s, bent corners,
minor soiling, 21½ x 36"
(ILLUS.) **247.50**
Puzzle, jigsaw-type, "Firestone Motor
Tire Service," illustrates a map of
the world, 1930s, complete in
original box **50.00**
Radiator cap, for Model A Ford...........**12.00**
Radiator cooling water bag, canvas,
printed w/an apple logo & adver-
tising reading "Hirsch-Weis Original
Auto Motor Self-Cooling Water Bag
... Manufactured by Hirsch-Weis
Canvas Products Co. - Portland,
Oregon," 11½ x 19" (soiling) **33.00**
Radiator flag holder set, 1940s, mint
in original box....................................**18.00**
Salesman award from Chevrolet,
silver plated pot metal, figural, a
striding man wearing a business suit

& carrying a folder under his arm, on
a book-shaped base, marked "Go-
Getter - It Shall Be Done - The Go
Get It and Keep It Campaign -
Presented in Appreciation," ca.
1940s (minor tarnish) **137.50**
Spark plug cap setter, "Chevrolet,"
key-shaped metal, embossed w/the
Chevrolet logo & "The Key to
Chevrolet Performance," w/nine
fold-out setters (minor wear) **60.50**
Spark plug cleaner & regapper,
"AC," cylindrical metal body
w/flanged base painted green, blue,
orange & cream, printed "AC - Spark
Plug Cleaning and Re-Gapping
Service - Dirty or Worn Spark Plugs
Waste 1 Gallon of Gas in 10," 11" d.,
22" h. (minor rust, scratches & paint
chipping) **110.00**
Taxi cab roof light, metal & glass, a
glass tube in black w/clear lettering
"TAXI," mounted between chrome
cylinders w/pointed yellow bulb ends
& raised on short chrome bell-
shaped supports, 13" l. (minor
soiling) **143.00**

Shell Test Tube Holder

Test tube holder, "Shell," cast iron, a
large shell embossed "Shell" above
a platform base w/two indentations
for test tubes, embossed red
lettering, white paint spotting &
scratches, 8¾" h. (ILLUS.) **275.00**

AVIATION COLLECTIBLES

*Recently much interest has been shown
in collecting items associated with the
early days of the "flying machine." In
addition to relics, flying adjuncts and
literature relating to the early days of
flight, collectors also seek out items that*

picture the more renowned early pilots, some of whom became folk-heroes in their own lifetimes, as well as the early planes themselves.

Banquet menu, in honor of Col. Charles Lindbergh, by the City of Wilmington, Delaware, 1920s **$65.00**

Book, "Charles Lindbergh - His life," by Dan Van Every, first edition, 1927..**40.00**

Book, "Lindbergh, The Lone Eagle, His Life & Epoch Making Flight," by Burt, 1928 ....**28.00**

Book, "The Story of Lindbergh - The Lone Eagle," by Richard J. Beamish, first edition, 1927 ....**40.00**

Card game, "Lindy," Parker Bros., 1927..**35.00**

Gasoline pump globe, "Aero Mobilgas," milk glass lenses w/a new metal frame, the flying red Pegasus logo above "Aero Mobilgas" 15" d...**2,420.00**

Gasoline pump globe, "Pittman Streamlined Gasoline," blue Gill rippled glass body, milk white lenses printed in the center w/a flying plane w/"Pittman" arched above & "Streamlined - Gasoline" on two lines below, 13½" d. (minor surface scratches on one lens)................**7,700.00**

Sinclair Aircraft Gas Globe

Gasoline pump globe, "Sinclair Aircraft," one-piece milk glass globe w/fired-on background w/white lettering & a single-wing plane at the center, minor discoloration, ca. 1925-28, 16" w., 16" h. (ILLUS.) ...**4,400.00**

Lapel pin, metal, figural plane, "Spirit of St. Louis" on cowling, portrait of Lindbergh & name on rudder **45.00**

Mug, porcelain, barrel-shaped w/squared handle, h.p. blue & brown background w/a black outlined Spirit of St. Louis plane, base inscribed "To Thomas - From Your Aunt Elsie - Dec. 25, 1930," scratch on the back, 3½" h. (ILLUS. top next column) **110.00**

Spirit of St. Louis Mug

Pin, "Air America," sterling silver, wing-shaped **125.00**

Pin, model of the Spirit of St. Louis plane, celluloid, on original card **110.00**

Plate, portrait of Colonel Charles Lindbergh, commemorating his flight, dated 1927, 8½" sq. **60.00**

Print, lithograph of first Beaumont Race, Bleriot, France, 1911, framed...**775.00**

Program, "All American Air Maneuvers," 1949.............................**30.00**

Sheet music, "Ameilia Earhart's Last Flight"...**25.00**

Sheet music, "Oh Charlie Is My Darling," cover photo of Charles Lindbergh..**25.00**

Straight razor, black handles w/inlaid brass biplanes at each end & "Spirit of St. Louis" inlaid in center of handle, mint in original box **375.00**

Tapestry, machine-woven half-length portrait of Charles Lindbergh in front of The Spirit of St. Louis, France, ca. 1927, framed 22½ x 23½"..................**82.50**

Toy, model of the "Spirit of America," windup lithographed tin, orange & yellow w/blue lettering, ca. 1930, 6" l.,6⅝" w. (motor not working) **201.00**

Watch, pocket-type, Charles Lindbergh, The Statue of Liberty & The Eiffel Tower on the case **300.00**

BABY MEMENTOES

Everyone dotes on the new baby and through many generations some exquisite and unique gifts have been carefully selected with a special infant in mind. Collectors now seek items from a varied assortment of baby mementoes, once tokens of affection to the newborn babe. Also see CHILDREN'S BOOKS and CHILDREN'S MUGS.

Baby caddy, pink plastic sailboat

holds four glass jars, sail embossed w/a lamb & "S.S. Lullaby," ca. 1950s, 17¼" l. **$30.00**

Ornate Wicker Baby Carriage

Carriage, woven wicker, the deep sides w/large tightly woven scrolls, a deep S-scroll front, on a metal framework continuing to form back arms joined by a turned wooden grip, four wire-spoked wheels, bearing a metal tag stamped "Block," early 20th c., 18½ x 44", 26" h. (ILLUS.) **1,495.00**

Feeding dish, china, ABC border, w/cats & turtle decoration, ca. 1920-30...**65.00**

Feeding dish, china, lustre glaze decorated w/an elf & flowers, marked "Germany".............................**55.00**

Feeding dish, china, depicts children dressed in cute hats & winter coats in center, ABC's in gold, Germany.....**80.00**

Feeding dish, china, depicts two girls dancing w/butterflies, marked "Nippon" **105.00**

Feeding dish, china set in a stainless steel warmer base, decorated w/the Three Bears scene, Excello...............**55.00**

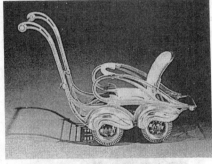

Rare Aluminum Perambulator

Perambulator, cast aluminum, unusual streamlined Art Deco design w/swirled loop open arms flanking the back-facing upholstered seat, wing-form wheel cap & metal

wheels, long slender scroll handles joined by a bar, stamped "NOVA," probably Italian, ca. 1930, 14 x 50", 35½" h. (ILLUS.) **6,600.00**

Push cart, wicker & wood, a low-sided rectangular natural wicker basket atop a wooden framework w/front bars flanking a carved wood dapple grey-painted rocking horse raised on a small steel-spoked & rimmed wheel, two large steel wheels at the back, high curved iron handle supports at the back, worn original varnish w/black & gold striping, horse w/worn harness & saddle, 19th c., 65" l. (horse mane missing, tail needs reattachment, wear, some damage & age cracks) **2,805.00**

BANKS

Acrobat Bank

Original early mechanical and cast-iron still banks are in great demand with collectors and their scarcity has caused numerous reproductions of both types and the novice collector is urged to exercise caution. The early mechanical banks are especially scarce and some versions are seldom offered for sale but, rather, are traded with fellow collectors attempting to upgrade an existing collection. Numbers before mechanical banks refer to those in John Meyer's Handbook of Old Mechanical Banks. However, a recently published book, Penny Lane - A History of Antique Mechanical Toy Banks, by Al Davidson, provides updated information and the number from this new volume is indicated in parenthesis at the end of each mechanical bank listing.

In past years, our standard reference for cast-iron still banks was Hubert B. Whiting's book Old Iron Still Banks, but because this work is out of print and a *beautiful new book, The Penny Bank Book - Collecting Still Banks by Andy and Susan Moore pictures and describes numerous additional banks, we will use the Moore numbers as a reference preceding each listing and indicate the Whiting reference in parenthesis at the end. The still banks listed are old and in good original condition with good paint and no repair unless otherwise noted. An asterisk (*) indicates this bank has been reproduced at some time.*

MECHANICAL

1	**Acrobat,** PL 1 (ILLUS.)	**$5,520.00**
2	**Afghanistan** (PL 3)	**3,220.00**
4	**Always Did 'Spise a Mule,** on bench (PL 250)	**1,725.00**
7	**Artillery -** eight-sided Block House, no soldier	**2,400.00**
6	**Artillery -** Square Block House (PL 11)	**3,220.00**
8	**Atlas -** "Money Moves the World" (PL 13)	**5,175.00**
9	**Bad Accident** (PL 20)	**3,220.00**
12	**Bear -** Paws Around Tree Stump (PL 30)	**700.00 to 800.00**
15	**Bill E. Grin,** bust, turns eyes, sticks out tongue (PL 33)	**2,645.00**
16	**Bird on Roof** (PL 36)	**1,650.00 to 1,700.00**
23	**Boy on Trapeze** (PL 50)	**3,450.00**
22	**Boys -** Stealing Watermelons (PL 53)	**1,955.00**
26	**Buffalo -** Butting Buffalo (PL 90), replaced trap	**5,175.00**
33	**Cabin** (PL 90), replaced trap	**1,610.00**

Calamity Bank

34	**Calamity -** Football, PL 94, (ILLUS.)	**19,550.00**
	Called Out Bank, soldier standing on top of a pyramid, J. & E. Stevens Co., Connecticut, ca. 1900 (PL 95)	**12,650.00**

42	**Chief Big Moon** (PL 108)	**2,000.00 to 2,200.00**

Circus Bank

47	**Circus** (PL 114), replaced crank (ILLUS.)	**14,950.00**
49	**Clown on Globe** (PL 127), slight fading	**5,175.00**
52	**Cow -** Milking or Kicking (PL 327)	**4,600.00**
54	**Creedmore -** New (Tyrolese Bank), PL 358	**690.00**
53	**Creedmore -** Soldier aims Rifle at Target in Tree Trunk (PL 137)	**805.00**
56	**Darktown Battery** (PL 146)	**3,400.00**
57	**Dentist** (PL 152)	**16,100.00**
72	**Dog -** Trick, modern w/one piece base (PL 482)	**1,495.00**
76	**Education & Economy** (Bank of) Patented April 30, 1895 (PL 23)	**750.00**
	Elephant, w/Howdah, w/tusks, pull tail (PL 175)	**450.00 to 550.00**
91	**Ferris Wheel** (PL 188)	**6,900.00**
95	**Fortune Teller Safe** (PL 195)	**575.00**
101	**Frog on Rock** (PL 203), w/original box	**3,105.00**
99	**Frogs -** Two (PL 200)	**1,495.00**

Girl Skipping Rope Bank

109	**Girl Skipping Rope,** PL 217, yellow dress (ILLUS. bottom previous column)	**48,300.00**
110	**Globe on Stand**	**225.00**
113	**Goat** - Little Billy (PL 34)	**1,725.00**
116	**Goat** - Butting (PL 91)	**748.00**
	Greedy Nigger Boy, aluminum version of "Jolly Nigger," attributed to Urlwin, New Zealand (PL 222)	**805.00**
146	**Hall's Liliput Bank with Tray** (PL 230)	**1,017.50**
123	**Hold the Fort** (PL 240)	**7,475.00**
	Horse Race, w/straight base (PL 246)	**6,325.00**
128	**Independence Hall Tower** (PL 255)	**805.00**
129	**Indian Shooting Bear** (PL 257)	**2,100.00 to 2,500.00**
	Jolly Nigger with High Hat, moves ears, Starkie Patent, aluminum (PL 272)	**950.00**
143	**Leap Frog** (PL 292)	**2,990.00**

Lion & Monkeys Bank

147	**Lion and Monkeys,** PL 300 (ILLUS.)	**3,220.00**
148	**Lion Hunter** (PL 301), coin trap relaced	**4,600.00**
	Little Joe Bank, Small Hat (PL 305)	**1,610.00**
154	**Magician** (PL 315)	**3,500.00 to 4,000.00**

Mule Entering Barn Bank

159	**Mikado** (PL 326)	**63,000.00**
165	**Monkey & Parrot** (PL 333)	**805.00**
162	**Monkey,** Coin in Stomach (PL 330)	**3,220.00**
169	**Mule Entering Barn,** PL 342 (ILLUS. bottom previous column)	**900.00 to 1,250.00**
178	**Organ Bank** - with Boy & Girl (PL 368), minor paint wear	**1,925.00**
177	**Organ Bank** - with Monkey, Cat and Dog (PL 369)	**1,350.00**
187	**Patronize the Blind Man and His Dog** (PL 379)	**12,650.00**
189	**Pelican** (PL 381)	**4,025.00**

Trick Pony Bank

196	**Pony** - Trick, PL 484 (ILLUS.)	**1,380.00**
203	**Punch & Judy** (PL 404)	**2,750.00 to 3,450.00**
214	**Santa Claus at Chimney** (PL 428)	**1,380.00**

Tammany Bank

224	**Tammany,** PL 455 (ILLUS.)	**500.00**
226	**Teddy and the Bear in Tree** (PL 459)	**1,800.00 to 2,100.00**
231	**Uncle Sam with Satchel & Umbrella** (PL 493)	**3,200.00 to 3,900.00**

William Tell Bank

237 **William Tell,** PL 565 (ILLUS.)................................**850.00**

245 **Zoo** (PL 576) **1,725.00**

STILL

1487 **Automobile** - Auto (4 passengers), large wheels, cast iron, A.C. Williams Co., 1912-31, 6¾" l. , 3½" h. ....**375.00 to 400.00**

1482 **Automobile** - Limousine, w/ driver, cast iron w/steel wheels, Arcade Mfg. Co., Illinois, (No. 05 model), ca. 1921, 8$\frac{1}{16}$" l., 3½" h...........**3,500.00**

Baseball Player Bank

18 **Baseball Player,** cast iron, A.C. Williams Co., 1909-34, 5¾" h., W. 10 (ILLUS.) ....**375.00 to 400.00**

1450 **Battleship** - "Oregon" (small), cast iron, J. & E. Stevens Co., Connecticut, 1891-1906, 4⅞" l., 3⅞" h. (W. 144) **275.00**

717 **Bear** - Bear with Honey Pot, cast iron, Hubley Mfg. Co., ca. 1936, 6½" h. (W. 327)*....**120.00**

715 **Bear** - Begging Bear, cast iron, A.C. Williams, ca. 1910 & Arcade Mfg. Co., Illinois, 1910-25, 5⅜" h. (W. 330) ....**100.00 to 125.00**

705 **Bear** - Seated Panda, white metal, "Vanio, 1938," American-made, 4$\frac{5}{16}$" h. **110.00**

694 **Bear** - Teddy Bear (no embossing), cast iron, Arcade, 1905-25, 4" l. (W. 331 variant)* **99.00**

84 **Black Boy** - Two-Faced Black Boy (Negro Toy Bank) cast iron, A.C. Williams, 1901-19, 3⅛" h. (W. 44).......**125.00 to 150.00**

Aunt Jemima Bank

168 **Black Woman** - Aunt Jemima (Mammy with Spoon), cast iron, A.C. Williams Co., 1905-30s, 5⅞" h., W. 17* (ILLUS.)...............................**150.00**

169 **Black Woman** - Aunt Jemima (Mammy with Spoon), cast iron, slot between legs, American-made, 5⅞" h. **148.50**

176 **Black Woman** - Mammy with Hands on Hips, cast iron, Hubley Mfg. Co., Pennsylvania, 1914-46, 5¼" h. (W. 20) *..............................**125.00**

557 **Buffalo** - Buffalo (large), American-made, 1970, 8" l., 5" h...........................**110.00**

560 **Buffalo** - Buffalo (small), cast iron, Arcade, 1920 - 25 & A. C. Williams, 1920-34, 4½" l., 3⅛" h. (W. 208)*......................**71.50**

1213 **Building (House)** - House with Bay Window, cast iron, American-made, 1874, 2$\frac{5}{16}$ x 3 x 4 ⅞" **467.50**

1202 **Building** - Independence Hall Tower, cast iron, Enterprise Mfg., ca. 1876, 3⅞ x 3⅞", 9½" h. **577.50**

1122 **Building** - Roof "Bank," cast iron, J. & E. Stevens, 1887, 3¼ x 3¾", 5¼" h. (W. 366) **225.00**

1124 **Building** - Roof Bank, cast iron, Grey Iron, 1903-28, 3¼ x 3¾", 5¼" h....**200.00 to 225.00**

1080 **Building** - State Bank, cast iron, Kenton, ca. 1900s, 3½ x 4⅝", 5⅞" h. (W. 445) ...**198.00**

"Tower" Bank

1198 **Building** - "Tower Bank," cast iron, "1890" on the door w/a combination lock, Kyser & Rex, ca. 1890, 6⅞" w., 6⅞" h., W. 437 (ILLUS.) ....**875.00 to 900.00**

1008 **Building** - Two-Story, (Six-Sided), cast iron, American-made, 2⅜" x 2⁷⁄₁₆", 3⅜" h. (W. 358) **325.00**

241 **Buster Brown & Tige,** cast iron, A.C. Williams, 1910-32, 5½" h. (W. 2)*.......................**192.50**

768 **Camel** - Camel, Small, cast iron, Hubley Mfg. Co. & A.C. Williams, 1920-30s, 4¾" h.................................**102.00**

925 **Cash Register** - Cash Register with mesh, cast iron, Arcade, 1910-25, 3¾" h. (W. 241) **71.50**

353 **Cat** - Cat with ball, cast iron, American-made, 5⅝" l., 2½" h....................................**165.00**

1539 **Clock** - World Time Bank - printed cards inside visible windows indicated times at 24 world capitols, cast iron & paper, Arcade, 1910-20, 4⅛" h. (W. 172) **275.00**

Clown Bank

211 **Clown,** standing figure w/ pointed hat, cast iron, A.C. Williams, ca. 1908, 6³⁄₁₆" h., W. 29* (ILLUS.) ......**80.00 to 100.00**

1317 **Coronation Crown** (Elizabeth II) cast iron, England, 1953, 3" d., 3³⁄₁₆" h....................................**75.00**

553 **Cow** - Cow, standing animal, cast iron, A.C. Williams, ca. 1920, 5¼" l., 3⅜" h. (W. 200)*..............................**150.00**

413 **Dog** - Boston Bull, Seated, cast iron, Hubley, 1930-40, 5⅝" l., 4⅜" h. (W. 114) **110.00**

359 **Dog** - Dog on Tub, cast iron, A.C. Williams, 1920-34, 4¹⁄₁₆" h. (W. 54) **104.50**

443 **Dog** - Fido on Pillow, cast iron, Hubley, 1920s, 7⅜" w/base, 5¾" h. (W. 336) **185.00**

440 **Dog** - Newfoundland, standing animal, cast iron, Arcade, 1910-mid-30s, 5⅜" l, 3⅝" h. (W. 107) **75.00**

405 **Dog** - Pugdog, Seated, cast iron, Kyser & Rex, 1889, 3½" h. (W. 111) **60.50**

439 **Dog** - St. Bernard with Pack (small), cast iron, A.C. Williams, 1905-30, 5½" l., 3¾" h. (W. 106)*.......................**60.00**

419 **Dog** - Scottie, Seated, cast iron, Hubley, 1930-40, 4⅞" h. (W. 110) **150.00**

418 **Dog** - Spaniel with Trap, cast iron, Hubley Mfg. Co., 1930s, 6" l., 3¾" h. (W. 109) **150.00**

615 **Duck** Bank, cast iron, A.C. Williams, 1909-35, 4⅞" h. (W. 211)...............**150.00 to 175.00**

616 **Duck on Tub** ("Save for a Rainy Day"), cast iron, Hubley, 1930-36, 5⅜" h. (W. 323)..............**100.00 to 125.00**

619 **Duck** - Round Duck, cast iron, original paint, large Kenton-type trap, Kenton Hardware Mfg. Co. 1936-40, 4⅞" d., 4" h. (W. 325) **225.50**

462 **Elephant** - Circus Elephant, seated animal wearing child's straw sailor hat w/ribbon, cast iron, Hubley Mfg. Co., 1930-40, 3⅞" h.....................**195.00**

483 **Elephant** - Elephant on Tub, no blanket, cast iron, A.C. Williams, 1920s, 5⅜" h. (W. 59) ....**125.00 to 150.00**

Elephant with Howdah Bank

474 **Elephant** - Elephant with
     Howdah (large), cast iron,
     A.C. Williams, 1910-30s,
     6⅜" l., 4⅞" h., W.63*
     (ILLUS.)................................**110.00**
459 **Elephant** - Elephant with
     Howdah (small), cast iron,
     A.C. Williams, 1912-34, 4" l.,
     3" h. (W. 68)*..........................**71.50**
1666 **Elephant** - Elephant with
     Raised Trunk, silvered lead,
     trick lock, Germany, 1920s,
     6⅛" l., 3¹⁵⁄₁₆" h..........................**75.00**
472 **Elephant** - Elephant with
     Tucked Trunk, cast iron,
     Arcade, 1910-32, 4⅝" l.,
     2¾" h. (W. 67)...........**50.00 to 75.00**
461 **Elephant** - Seated Elephant,
     Trumpeting, raised trunk
     touching forehead, white
     metal, key locked trap, Vanio,
     ca. 1936, 5" h. **85.00**

English Throne Bank

1325 **English Throne** (Elizabeth II),
     aluminum, Reuben Wine-
     berg, England, 1953, 3⅜" h.
     (ILLUS.)...................................**40.00**
785 **Globe** - Globe on Wire Arc,
     cast iron, Arcade, 1900-13,
     4⅝" h. (worn paint) **137.50**
512 **Horse** - Horse on Wheels, cast
     iron, A.C. Williams, ca. 1920,
     4¼" l., 5" h., W. 87 (ILLUS. top
     next column) **148.50**

Horse on Wheels Bank

518 **Horse** - Prancing Horse, Cana-
     dian, cast iron, American-
     made, 4⅛ x 4⅞" **45.00**
519 **Horse** - White Horse on Base,
     cast iron, George C. Knerr,
     1973, 10" l, 9½" h...................**71.50**
524 **Horseshoe** - Horseshoe with
     Wire Mesh, wire cylinder
     supported on horseshoe ends
     centered w/horse heads, cast
     iron, 1910-25, 3" w., 3¼" h.
     (W. 239) **125.00**
1371 **Ice Cream Freezer** (North Pole
     Bank) - "Save Your Money
     and Freeze It," nickeled cast
     iron, Grey Iron Casting Co.,
     1922-28, 2⅝" d., 4¼" h.
     (W. 156)* ....**125.00 to 175.00**
239 **Indian** - Indian Seated on Log,
     cast iron, A. Ouve, artist,
     American, ca. 1970, 3⅝" h......**75.00**
784 **Liberty Bell** - Washington Bell,
     cast iron, Grey Iron Casting
     Co., 1900-05, 3⅞" d.,
     3¾" h.....................................**325.00**
742 **Lion** - Lion, small, cast iron,
     A.C. Williams, 1934, 3⅝" l.,
     2½" h. (W. 94) **80.00**

Lion on Tub Bank

747 **Lion -** Lion on Tub, small, cast
iron, A.C. Williams, 4⅛" h.
(W. 61) **125.00**

747 **Lion -** Lion on Tub, plain, cast
iron, A.C. Williams, 1920s,
7⅜" h. (W. 58).........**75.00 to 100.00**

746 **Lion -** Lion on Tub, Decorated
with cord in mouth, cast iron,
A.C. Williams, 1920-34, 5½" h.,
W. 57* (ILLUS. bottom
previous page) **125.00**

759 **Lion -** Lion, Tail Right, cast
iron, A.C. Williams, 1920s,
4¹⁵⁄₁₆" l., 3½" h. (W. 91)* **159.50**

758 **Lion -** Quilted Lion, cast iron,
American-made, 4¾" l.,
3¾" h.....................................**395.00**

36 **"Middy Bank"** (has clapper),
English Admiralty character,
cast iron, American-made,
ca. 1887, 5¼" h.
(W. 26)* ....**125.00 to 150.00**

178 **Mulligan** (Policeman), slot
between legs, American-
made, 5¾" h. (W. 606) **300.00**

8 **Officer** (Cadet), cast iron,
Hubley Mfg. Co., 1905-15,
5¾" h. (W. 7)*.........................**425.00**

186 **Oriental Boy on Pillow**
(conversion), cast iron,
Hubley Mfg. Co., 1920s,
5¼ x 6¼", 5½" h. **250.00**

"The Wise Pig" Bank

609 **Pig -** "The Wise Pig," seated
on haunches w/plaque w/writing
across stomach, painted cast
iron, Hubley Mfg. Co., ca.
1930-36, 6⅝" h. W. 175*
(ILLUS.)................................**100.00**

566 **Rabbit -** Begging Rabbit, cast
iron, A.C. Williams Co.,
1908-20s, 5⅛" h. (W. 98)*.....**203.50**

570 **Rabbit -** Large Seated, Rabbit,
cast iron, Wing pre-1906,
Hubley 1906-20, 4⅜" l., 4⅝"
h. (W. 100)*...........................**295.00**

Small Reindeer Bank

736 **Reindeer -** Small Reindeer
(Elk), cast iron, standing
animal w/antlers, A.C. Williams Co., 1910-35 & Arcade,
1913-32, 4⅞" l., 6¼" h.,
W. 195 (ILLUS.) ....**50.00 to 75.00**

721 **Rhino,** cast iron, Arcade,
1910-25, 5" l., 2⅝" h.
(W. 252) **425.00**

547 **Rooster,** yellow body paint &
red comb, cast iron, Arcade,
1910-25, 4⅝" h. (W. 187)* **159.50**

75 **Rumpelstiltskin,** "Do You
Know Me" on feet & base,
cast iron, American-made,
ca. 1910, 2⁵⁄₁₆" w., 6" h.
(W. 49) ....**275.00 to 300.00**

Safe - Burglar Proof House
Safe, cast iron w/nickel
plating, round design
w/florette on door, scalloped
apron, J.& E. Stevens Co.,
Connecticut, patent 1897,
5⅞" h.......................................**66.00**

887 **Safe -** National "Safe," cast
iron w/nickel plating, openwork sides, J.& E. Stevens

Santa with Tree Bank

Co., 1896-1928, 2¼ x 2½",
3⅜" h. **65.00**

891 **Safe -** "Security Safe Deposit,"
cast iron, Kyser & Rex (?),
ca. 1881, 2⅜ x 2¹³⁄₁₆", 3⅞" h. **75.00**

61 **Santa Claus -** Santa with Tree,
cast iron, old polychrome
paint, Hubley, 1914-30,
5⅞" h. W. 32* (ILLUS.
bottom previous page) **295.00**

660 **Squirrel with Nut,** cast iron,
American-made, 3" w., 4⅛" h.
(W. 250) **522.50**

World War I Tank Bank

1435 **Tank -** "Tank Bank U.S.A.
1918," model of a World
War I tank, cast iron, A.C.
Williams, 1920s, 3¹¹⁄₁₆" l.,
3" h. (ILLUS.) ....**100.00 to 125.00**

857 **Telephone -** Pay Phone Bank,
cast iron, J. & E. Stevens,
1926, 3 x 3¹¹⁄₁₆ x 7⅞⁄₁₆"............**368.50**

1428 **Zeppelin -** "Graf Zeppelin,"
cast iron, A.C. Williams,
1920-34, 6⅝" l.,
1¾" h. (W.171)......**150.00 to 200.00**

POTTERY

Rare Pottery Dog Bank

Apple, redware w/old red
finish, 3½" d.........................**192.50**

Dog, seated Spaniel facing
viewer, buff clay w/heavy
coleslaw mane, worn amber
glaze w/green & brown,
attributed to Shenandoah
Valley region, very minor
coleslaw damage, 6½" h.
(ILLUS.)............................**1,100.00**

Dog's head, modeled as a
Spaniel-type head w/long
ears, yellowware w/runny

green & brown glaze, 4" h.
(repaired chip on back
edge) **126.50**

Ovoid body, redware, tapering
to a tiny molded mouth, overall runny brown glaze, 4¼" h.
(minor chips) **275.00**

Pig, standing, yellowware
w/overall brown & blue
sponging, 6" l. (chips on feet
& coin slot) **132.00**

Ram's head, modeled w/long
curled horns, facial details &
fur, mottled brown Rocking-
ham glaze, 3" h. (chips) **71.50**

TIN

Unusual Tin House Bank

Barrel, "Happy Days," J.
Chein & Co.............................**38.00**

Clown head, lever-operated
semi-mechanical multi-
colored, J. Chein & Co.,
5" h. (PL 118) **65.00**

House, plain rectangular sides
w/a steeply pitched roof w/a
large center chimney, smoke-
decorated, 19th c., 7½" l.,
7½" h. (ILLUS.).....................**431.00**

Monkey Tips Hat Bank

Monkey tips hat, semi-mechanical, J. Chein & Co., ca. 1940, PL 336 (ILLUS. bottom previous page) ....**50.00 to 60.00**

WOODEN

Wooden House Bank

House, carved & painted pine, a two-story house w/a cupola centering the low-pitched hinged roof, arched painted windows & door, raised on a rectangular foundation w/steps at each side above a stepped platform base, painted brown & blue w/white trim, late 19th c., 11" l., 10½" h. (ILLUS.) **1,610.00**

Unusual Tower Bank

Tower, carved & painted wood, a square three-tier tower building w/double rows of incised windows at each graduated tier, a stepped peak w/a flat scroll-cut finial, on a finely molded base, early 19th c., small losses to

base molding, 19½" h. (ILLUS.)...............................**1,035.00**

(End of Banks Section)

BARBERIANA

A wide variety of antiques related to the tonsorial arts have been highly collectible for many years, especially 19th and early 20th century shaving mugs and barber bottles and, more recently, razors. We are now combining these closely related categories under one heading here for easier reference. A selection of other varied pieces relating to barbering will also be found below.

BARBER BOTTLES

Amber Hobnail Barber Bottle

Amber, Hobnail patt., Hobbs, Brockunier & Co. (ILLUS.) **$299.00**
Amber, bulbous base below a tall

Art Nouveau Barber Bottle

stick neck, orange & white
enameled dot & floral design,
sheared lip, rough pontil, 8" h. **55.00**

Amethyst, squatty bulbous base
below a tall lady's leg neck, gilded &
enameled w/stylized Art Nouveau
florals, rolled lip w/stopper, rough
pontil, 8" h. (ILLUS. bottom
previous page) **209.00**

Blue opalescent, Swirl patt., bulbous
body below a tall lady's leg neck,
rolled lip, smooth base, 7½" h. **93.50**

Cobalt blue, enameled w/white &
gold daisies **200.00**

Cranberry, Inverted Thumbprint
patt. **269.00**

Cranberry opalescent, Hobnail patt.,
Hobbs, Brockunier & Co. **369.00**

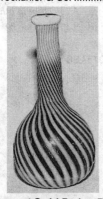

Opalescent Swirl Barber Bottle

Cranberry opalescent, Swirl patt.,
bulbous base below a tall cylindrical
neck, rolled lip, smooth base, 7½" h.
(ILLUS.) **104.50**

Cranberry opalescent, Swirl patt.,
ovoid body tapering to a short stick
neck w/sheared lip, smooth squared
base, w/stopper, 8¼" h **110.00**

Lime green, spherical body below a
tall stick neck, white & brown
enameled dot & daisy design, rough
pontil, 8" h. (enamel wear) **66.00**

Spatter, tall tapering waisted cylindrical body, cobalt blue & white opal
spatter in ribbed band molded design, rolled lip, smooth base, 12" h.,
pr. (small chip on base of one) **209.00**

White opalescent, polka dot patt. **199.00**

RAZORS

OHO Duetsch Razor

Safety razor, "Gillette Safety Razor,"
goldtone metal, double edge, in
original leather box w/blades in
original blue box w/NRA
emblem, 1930s, the set **62.50**

Straight razor, "Keen Kutter - Hollow
Ground," K746, back of razor
marked "Simmons Hdwe. Co. Mfgs.
& Distributors," celluloid handle,
w/original box (wear to box) **11.00**

Straight razor, "OHO Deutsch," black
celluloid handle w/German silver
inlaid end scrolls & the name in
inlaid script, handle of blade
engraved "OHO Deutsch - Hans,"
Germany, early 20th c., w/original
box, minor box wear (ILLUS.) **22.00**

SHAVING MUGS
(Porcelain unless otherwise noted)

Fraternal

**Ancient Order of Foresters of
America,** decorated w/emblem of
flags in a shield, a deer, eagle &
name in gold, base marked "Phila.
Supply House" **135.00**

Odd Fellows, w/"Acme Lodge 469"
& dated "1923" on front....................**150.00**

Occupational

Butcher, depicts butcher & a lady in
butcher shop, two marks on
bottom...**325.00**

Railroad engineer, decorated w/a
steam locomotive marked "ES & C,"
ca, 1870s (chip on the base) **275.00**

Railroad engineer, scene includes
engineer & fireman on a steam
engine & coal car, name in gold,
base marked C.F. Haviland &
"Boston China Decorating Works -
L. Cooley, Charles St. Boston" **395.00**

Tailor, decorated w/a scene of a tailor
cutting cloth, name in gold **145.00**

General

China, decorated w/berry vines
trimmed w/gold & a gold name,
Barber Supply logo on the base,
excellent condition **95.00**

China, decorated w/flowers & name
in gold **65.00**

China, patriotic design decorated
w/an eagle, flags, a shield & world
globe, name in gold, base marked
"T. & V. Limoges"............................**110.00**

GENERAL ITEMS

Barber chair, walnut w/carved lions'
heads, 1880s, restored **1,100.00**

Barber pole, porcelain & stained glass, "Koken," 48" h....................**1,200.00**

Early Barber Pole

Barber pole, turned & painted wood, a large spherical knob above a turned ring over the long slender pole painted w/narrow red & wide white stripes & dark blue trim, soiling, paint chips, minor wood cracking, 40½" h. (ILLUS.)...............**495.00**

Barber pole, turned & painted wood, a large knob top above a ring-turned knop above the long slightly flaring shaft w/knob base, very worn & weathered red & white repaint, made to be side-mounted, 72" l. (age cracks, damage) **935.00**

Barber pole, turned & painted wood, the tall pole w/a large knob top in white above a squatty urn-form turning above two long cylindrical sections w/red & white stripes separated by a ring-turned center section, ring-turned base on block foot, weathered red, white & blue repaint, 73" h. plus added stand (age cracks, puttied repair, base edge damage)................................**385.00**

Barber Shop Shaving Stand

Barber shop shaving stand, light-up type, nickel-plated chrome, a stepped round foot supporting a tall slender pole fitted w/arms, one for soap mug, one a shaving brush & one a razor strop, the pole topped by an arched adjustable lighted mirror, minor wear to strop & crack in razor, 5' 2" h. (ILLUS. bottom previous column) **198.00**

Mustache grooming kit, traveling-type, celluloid handles, beveled mirror & leather case, the set............**35.00**

Razor blade bank, china, figural donkey, advertising Listerine Shaving Cream **34.00**

Razor hone, "Shapleigh Hardware Diamond King," w/original litho-graphed box......................................**45.00**

Shaver, electric, "Norelco Sportsman," Bakelite cover, w/all accessories, leather case & instructions, mint in box **250.00**

Federal Shaving Mirror

Shaving mirror, table model, Federal style, inlaid mahogany, a rectan-gular line-inlaid frame around the mirror swiveling between two block- and baluster-turned uprights w/acorn finials, on a bow-front case w/a pair of drawers w/small brass knobs, on small ogee bracket feet, New England, 1790-1810, 7¼ x 19", 20" h. (ILLUS.) **460.00**

Shaving mirror, table model, George III style, mahogany, the arched rectangular mirror plate flanked by reeded uprights w/ivory vase finials, the bowfronted platform w/tulipwood banding & three drawers on turned ivory feet, England, late 18th c., 9 x 21", 23½" h..............................**1,265.00**

Storage jar, cov., "Barbicide," tall clear glass cylinder w/domed metal cover suspending a metal bar & cup, white printed label on the front, marked "King Research Inc. #4764 -

Glass - Made in Canada," 4" d.,
9¾" h. (scratches) **27.50**

BARBIE DOLLS & COLLECTIBLES

At the time of her introduction in 1959 no one could have guessed that this statuesque doll would become a national phenomenon and, eventually, the most famous girl's plaything ever produced.

Over the years Barbie and her growing range of family and friends have evolved with the times, serving as an excellent mirror on the fashion and social changes taking place in American society. Today, after more than 30 years of continual production, Barbie's popularity continues unabated, both among young girls and older collectors. Early and rare Barbies can sell for remarkable prices and everyone hopes to find mint condition "#1 Barbie."

Also see LUNCH BOXES

DOLLS

Allan, Ken's Friend

Allan, ca. 1963, painted red hair, pink lips, straight leg, wearing original jacket, blue swim trunks, one cork sandal w/blue strap, loose wrist tag, in box, small hair rub, jacket discolored, waistband stretched, box discolored & stained, no box insert (ILLUS.) **$65.00**

Barbie, "#1 Barbie," brunette hair w/original ponytail, blue eyeliner, red lips, finger paint, toe paint, straight leg, wearing gold loop earrings & black & white one-piece swimsuit, white-rimmed eyeglasses w/blue lenses, in box w/neck insert, near mint (slight wear & touch-up, smoke 'tanned') **2,200.00**

Complete #2 Ponytail Barbie

Barbie. "#2 Ponytail Barbie," brunette hair in original set, faded red lips, finger & toe paint, hoop earrings, black & white striped one-piece swimsuit, black #1 open-toed shoes & white-rimmed glasses w/blue lenses, in box w/cardboard neck insert, pedestal stand & pink cover booklet, near mint (ILLUS.) **5,100.00**

#3 Ponytail Barbie & Box

Barbie, "#3 Ponytail Barbie," light blonde hair, full red lips, brown eyeliner, nostril paint, finger & toe paint, straight leg, wearing black & white striped one-piece swimsuit, pearl earrings, black #1 open-toed shoes w/holes, in box w/pedestal & pink cover booklet, near mint, hair rubber bands missing, box discolored (ILLUS.) **1,400.00**

Barbie, "#5 Ponytail Barbie," titian hair, red lips, straight leg, finger & toe paint, black & white striped one-piece swimsuit, near mint (faint fading to upper lip, eyebrows faded, left leg slightly shorter) **450.00**

Barbie, "#5 Ponytail Barbie," 1961,

yellow blonde hair, coral lips, finger
paint, toe paint, straight leg, nude
(rubbing, hair loosely retied) **150.00**

American Girl Barbie

Barbie, "American Girl Barbie," 1965,
blonde, beige lips, finger paint, bent
leg, original one-piece swimsuit,
eyebrows slightly faded, left leg
won't bend, ends of toes missing,
swimsuit worn & damaged
(ILLUS.) **320.00**
Barbie, "American Girl Barbie," 1966,
brunette, high-color face paint w/full
dark pink lips, nostril paint, faint
cheek blush, bent-leg, finger & toe
paint, original one-piece swimsuit,
near mint......................................**1,000.00**
Barbie, "Barbie with Growin' Pretty
Hair," ca. 1970, wearing pink satin
dress w/hair accessories, never
removed from box (box slightly
discolored & worn) **300.00**
Barbie, "Bubblecut Barbie," 1964,
bubblecut blonde hair, white lips
w/pink tint, finger paint, toe paint,
straight leg, nude **60.00**

Bubblecut Barbie & Box

Barbie, "Bubblecut Barbie," 1964,
bubblecut light golden blonde hair,
faded white lips, finger paint, toe
paint, straight leg, nude (finger & toe
paint rubs) **70.00**
Barbie, "Bubblecut Barbie," titian hair,
full pink lips, finger, toe & nostril
paint, straight leg, wearing red nylon
one-piece swimsuit, pearl earrings &
wrist tag, in box w/neck insert, black
wire stand & blue cover booklet,
near mint (ILLUS. bottom
previous column) **175.00**
Barbie, "German Barbie,"
International Series, ca. 1986, never
removed from box (box discolored &
slightly worn) **95.00**
Barbie, "India Barbie," International
Series, ca. 1981, never removed
from box (box slightly discolored &
worn at corners) **130.00**
Barbie, "Living Barbie," 1970, titian
hair, pink lips, cheek blush, twist 'n
turn, rooted eyelashes, bendable
arms, legs & ankles, wearing
original one-piece silver & gold
swimsuit w/orange net jacket (lip
rubs, face pale, worn color on
swimsuit) **55.00**

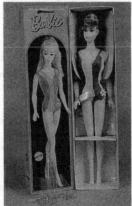

Standard Barbie & Box

Barbie, "Standard Barbie," ca. 1969,
light brown hair, blue eyes, red lips,
cheek rouge, original one-piece
bright green & pink swimsuit, never
removed from box, w/insert, clear
plastic stand, wrist tag & booklet in
cellophane bag, box front faded &
'real eyelashes' marked out
(ILLUS.) **550.00**
Barbie, "Swirl Ponytail Barbie," 1964,
light blonde hair, white lips w/pink
tint, finger paint, toe paint, straight
leg, wearing one-piece red nylon
swimsuit (played-with, some wear &
repaint)..**180.00**

Swirl Ponytail Barbie

Barbie, "Swirl Ponytail Barbie," titian hair, pink lips, finger & toe paint, straight leg, pearl earrings, wearing No. 822 'Barbie in Switzerland' outfit including dress, felt belt, hat, flower bouquet, white open-toed shoes, 'Barbie in Switzerland' poster & cellophane bag, w/box, ears slightly faded, one belt stringhole torn, box discolored & slightly damaged (ILLUS.) **425.00**

Barbie, "Talking Barbie," 1971, brunette, pink lips, rooted eyelashes, faint cheek blush, wearing white two-piece swimsuit w/gold cover-up, wrist tag, in box w/plastic stand, never removed from box (non-working, box very worn)....**220.00**

Barbie, "Talking Barbie," titian hair, wearing a two-piece white swimsuit w/gold cover-up, ca. 1969, near mint in box (box worn, booklets missing, non-working) **260.00**

Twist 'N Turn Barbie

Barbie, "Twist 'n Turn Barbie," ca. 1969, brunette, wearing pink & white one-piece swimsuit, never removed from box, light colored spot above left eyebrow, light brown mark on left hand (ILLUS.)............................**230.00**

Barbie & Ken Gift Set

Barbie & Ken, "Barbie & Ken Gift Set," original boxed set w/blonde Barbie & Ken dolls & various outfits, ca. 1962, complete in sealed package, light box staining, the set (ILLUS.)............................**1,050.00**

Christie, "Twist 'n Turn Christie," ca. 1969, short dark hair, wearing one-piece yellow & print swimsuit, never removed from box, tint of red in the hair..**190.00**

Boxed Francie Dolls

Francie, "Black Francie," ca. 1965, Twist 'n Turn, black hair, wearing original two-piece swimsuit, never removed from box, box slightly discolored (ILLUS. right) **1,500.00**

Francie, "No Bangs Francie," ca. 1969, Twist 'n Turn, brunette, wearing original short red & white dress, never removed from box, face light colored (ILLUS. left) **1,250.00**

Ken, ca. 1961, blond flocked hair, beige lips, straight leg, wearing original jacket, red swim trunks w/white stripe, yellow towel & cork sandals w/red straps, in box w/neck insert, black wire stand, blue cover booklet, near mint (ILLUS. top next page) **160.00**

Early Ken & Box

Ken, "Malibu Ken Surf's Up" gift set, Malibu Ken w/yellow & red & blue coat, yellow beach shoes, blue swim fins, towel, face mask, snorkel & goggles, booklet, skim board, never removed from box, plastic torn, skim board loose, cover discolored (ILLUS.) **300.00**

Malibu Ken Set

Midge, 1964, blonde, pink lips, straight leg, finger & toe paint, wearing blue nylon two-piece swimsuit, near mint (slight rubs, swimsuit slightly worn) **40.00**

Midge, 1964, brunette hair, pink lips, finger paint, toe paint, straight leg, nude (two pin holes in upper torso)..**40.00**

Midge, 1964, titian, pink lips, finger & toe paint, straight leg, wearing two-piece nylon orange & chartreuse swimsuit, in box w/insert, near mint (ILLUS. top next column) **70.00**

Scott, ca. 1979, never removed from box (box slightly discolored & worn)..**60.00**

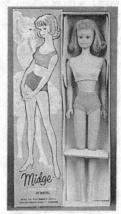

Early Midge & Box

Skipper, pale blonde hair, pink lips, straight leg, wearing headband w/plastic covering on head, wearing one-piece swimsuit & wrist tag, gold wire stand, box insert, shoes, comb & brush in cellophane sleeves, ca. 1963, near mint in box (headband discolored, booklet missing, some box & insert wear) **135.00**

Skooter, blonde hair, pink lips, straight leg, wearing original two-piece swimsuit, wrist tag w/gold wire stand, box insert, booklet, shoes, comb & brush in cellophane sleeve, ca. 1964, mint in box (box slightly age discolored w/worn edges) **140.00**

Skooter in Box

Skooter, ca. 1964, titian, light beige lips, one painted nostril, straight leg, wearing original two-piece swimsuit, red shoes, wrist tag, in box w/insert & gold wire stand, near mint (ILLUS.) **175.00**

Stacey, "Twist 'n Turn Stacey," short red hair, wearing flower print one-piece swimsuit, ca. 1969, never removed from box (front cellophane torn, taped top & bottom) **280.00**

Stacey, "Twist 'n Turn Stacey," 1967, titian hair, wearing one-piece red nylon swimsuit w/button accents, never removed from box..................**345.00**

Tutti in Box

Tutti, bendable & poseable, blonde hair w/pink ribbon, pink lips, cheek blush, wearing pink, yellow & green dress, in box w/accessories, never removed from box, top of face light colored, box slightly discolored (ILLUS.) **95.00**

CLOTHING & ACCESSORIES

Barbie Sportscar in Box

Automobile, "Barbie's Own Sportscar," an orange Austin Healy w/aqua interior, ca. 1962, by Irwin, near mint in box, car slightly faded, few cracks in white on tires, box slightly discolored & damaged (ILLUS.) **185.00**

Bicycle, "Barbie Ten Speeder," ca. 1973, yellow plastic w/white handles, light, seat & attached tote basket, colored decals, in box (some decals loose, box age-discolored) **17.50**

Carrying case, Barbie & Francie, red vinyl w/red handle, pictures Barbie on the front, made in France, some discoloring, two small tears on both sides of bottom inside lid seam, w/four pink hangers **70.00**

Clothing set, Barbie, "Barbie-Q," No. 962, includes rose dress, white apron, chef hat, white open-toe shoes, rolling pin, metal knife, spoon & spatula w/red handles, checkered pot holder, unboxed, mint, the set **50.00**

Clothing set, Barbie, "Debutante Ball," No. 1666, includes aqua gown w/rose accent, stole, clear open-toe shoes w/glitter, gold clutch purse, white long gloves, unboxed, the set (gown faded & soiled, stole ties worn & lining soiled, purse closure worn) **70.00**

Clothing set, Barbie, "Friday Night Date," No. 979, includes white underdress, corduroy jumper w/felt appliqués, black tray w/logo, two "orange" glasses w/cotton & one straw, black open-toe shoes, unboxed, near mint, the set (slight wear on jumper) **45.00**

Clothing set, Barbie, "Fringe Benefits," No. 3401, ca. 1969, includes dress, suede boots, hanger, booklet, label on box, never removed from box (box slightly discolored, wear on corners & several small tears)...........................**55.00**

Clothing set, Barbie, "Happy Go Pink," No. 1868, pink & white dress, pink shoes w/bow, pink nylon stockings on cardboard forms, The World of Barbie booklet, pink hanger attached to green cardboard backing, never removed from box (box slightly discolored, one corner loose & torn) **190.00**

Clothing set, Barbie, "Lunch on the Terrace," No. 1649, includes dress

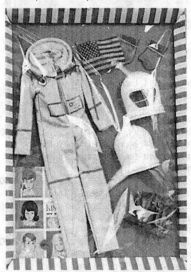

Rare "Miss Astronaut" Set

& matching hat, unboxed, near mint, the set (arm holes slightly worn) **85.00**

Clothing set, Barbie, "Miss Astronaut," No. 1641, space suit & accessories, never removed from package (ILLUS. bottom previous page) **700.00**

Clothing set, Barbie, "Pink Moonbeams," No. 1694, ca. 1964, includes nightgown, robe, pink open-toe shoes, hanger, booklet, label on box, never removed from box (box slightly discolored) **310.00**

Clothing set, Barbie, "Registered Nurse," No. 991, includes white nurse dress w/attached metal pin, matching hat, cape, white open-toe shoes, black-rimmed glasses w/clear lenses, water bottle, medicine bottle, metal spoon, diploma, loose, near mint, the set (diploma creased & slightly soiled, water bottle spout w/small dent) **55.00**

Clothing set, Barbie, "Barbie Round the Clock Gift Set," ca. 1963, includes brunette 'bubblecut' Barbie w/pink lips & three complete outfits, near mint in box (small amount of green on each ear, left side of box opened w/tape closure, box slightly discolored) **4,300.00**

Clothing set, Barbie, "Ruffles 'n Swirls," No. 1783, ca. 1969, includes dress w/belt, blue high-tongue shoes, hanger, booklet, label on box, never removed from box (box slightly discolored) **40.00**

Barbie "Silver Polish" Set

Clothing set, Barbie, "Silver Polish," No. 1492, silver gown & yellow long

jacket, never removed from package (ILLUS.) **120.00**

"Solo in the Spotlight" Set

Clothing set, Barbie, "Solo in the Spotlight," No. 982, black gown w/ruffled bottom, w/accessories, never removed from package (ILLUS.) **275.00**

Clothing set, Barbie, "White Magic," No. 1607, ca. 1964, includes white satin coat w/matching hat, silver clutch purse, white short nylon gloves, booklet, label on box, never removed from box (box slightly discolored & faded, corners worn) **170.00**

Barbie "Winter Wedding" Set

Clothing set, Barbie, "Winter

Wedding," No. 1880, white fur-trimmed wedding gown, veil & accessories, never removed from package (ILLUS.) **180.00**

Clothing set, Barbie, "Yellow Mello," No. 1484, yellow velour dress w/braid trim, yellow stockings, yellow pilgrims, near mint, unboxed, the set **85.00**

Clothing set, Francie, "Get-Ups 'N Go," No. 7711, red & white cheerleader dress w/"M," red nylon tights, red hat, "Go Team" banner, megaphone w/"M," red pompons, white knee-high boots w/molded laces, ca. 1973, never removed from package (cardboard backing slightly discolored & worn) **55.00**

Clothing set, Francie, "Midi Duet," No. 3451, ca. 1970, includes gown, long vest, pink square toe shoes, hanger, booklet, label on box, never removed from box (box discolored & slightly worn) **80.00**

Clothing set, Francie, "Style Setters," No. 1268, ca. 1966, includes a dress, coat, stockings, blue soft shoes, hanger & booklet, never removed from box (label missing, box slightly discolored) **225.00**

Clothing set, Francie, "Sugar Shears," No. 1229, ca. 1965, includes dress, slip, pink fishnet stockings on cardboard form, purse, record player, one record, hanger, booklet, label on box, never removed from box (box slightly discolored, wear on corners) **200.00**

Clothing set, Ken, "Army and Air Force," No. 797, includes shirt, pants, tan & blue hats, blue necktie, black & tan cotton socks, blue & brown shoes, metal 'wings,' cardboard poster, unboxed, near mint, the set (necktie rubber band broken)...**50.00**

Clothing set, Ken, "Drum Major," No. 775, includes jacket w/braid trim & shoulder attachments, pants, hat w/gold trim, baton, unboxed, the set (red faded on jacket trim, hat flat, gold baton discolored) **25.00**

Clothing set, Ken, "Ken in Switzerland," No . 776, grey fleece shorts w/attached ribbon suspenders & eight silver button accents, white short sleeve shirt & button accents, white ribbed knee-high socks, black ankle boots, black felt hat w/white braided band & attached feather, painted ceramic stein w/metal lid, plastic pipe, travel pamphlet & booklet w/blue cover, attached to yellow cardboard backing, paper label, never removed from box..**160.00**

Clothing set, Ken, "The Prince," No. 772, green & gold brocade jacket, white collar, green & gold tights, cape, hat w/'jewel' & feather, slippers, pillow w/attached clear shoe, paper program & Exclusive Fashions booklet, never removed from card, in cellophane bag (box missing, bottom of bag open) **230.00**

Clothing set, Skipper, "Flower Showers," No. 1939, ca. 1964, includes raincoat, hat, pink boots, hanger, booklet, label on box, never removed from box (box slightly discolored) **45.00**

Clothing set, Skipper, "Get-ups 'N Go," No. 7847, yellow & white dotted long dress w/ribbon belt & white sleeves, white nylon overskirt, yellow tulle headband w/ribbon & flowers, flower bouquet, white flat shoes, ca. 1973, never removed from package (shoes loose in package, backing slightly discolored & worn) **25.00**

Clothing set, Skipper, "Masquerade Party," No. 1903, ca. 1963, includes tutu, panties, hat, mask, black shoes w/yellow pompons, invitation, booklet, label on box, store sticker, never removed from box (box slightly discolored & worn)...**90.00**

Barbie Cookbook

Cookbook, "Barbie's Easy-As-Pie Cookbook," ca. 1964, Random House, hard cover, pages discolored w/some stains, writing on inside first page (ILLUS.) **80.00**

Display box, "Barbie & Midge," dated 1963, cardboard w/cardboard insert w/notched tops, corners slightly worn& discolored (ILLUS. top next page) **250.00**

Barbie & Midge Display Box

Game, board-type, Barbie "Queen of the Prom," 1963, complete in original box **60.00**

Midnight, Barbie's horse, ca. 1981, near mint in box (box slightly discolored) **17.50**

Pen holder, Barbie, dated 1961, black plastic w/photos of a typewriter, paper & pencil & Barbie sitting on a chair w/paper & pencil, zipper on top (few scuffs on pictures, small gold spot on back, ends of cloth on zipper frayed) **70.00**

Plate, "The 1959 Barbie Bride-To-Be," by Susie Morton, from the collection entitled 'High Fashion Barbie' (blonde Ponytail), limited edition, Danbury Mint, No. C4893, w/box & certificate **20.00**

Plate, "The 1960 Solo in the Spotlight," by Susie Morton, from the collection entitled 'High Fashion Barbie' (blonde Ponytail), limited edition, Danbury Mint, No. C4893, w/box & certificate............................**30.00**

Shelves, "Portable Home Display," ca. 1963, includes cardboard & metal 'stage' w/metal bar to hang clothing, near mint in box (cardboard corners slightly worn, one creased) **240.00**

Stand for #1 Barbie, round black plastic base w/two metal prongs, near mint......................................**1,700.00**

Table cover, "Barbie - Party Maid," white crepe paper w/Barbie outline design, blonde hair & wearing a pink striped dress & sitting on a bench holding a gift, Barbie logo above her head, purple & pink design above the logo, gold paper label w/price removed, American Greetings, ca. 1964, never removed from box, in plastic bag w/cardboard backing, cloth 54 x 104" (cover discolored, gold label worn & w/a small side tear) **160.00**

Tea set, "Barbie 25th Anniversary," 1984, 14 piece set in 'velvet' lined box, near mint in box in white cardboard sleeve (missing certificate, upper box clasp slightly rusted, sleeve age discolored w/faded pink stains) **55.00**

Trading cards, Barbie Deluxe First Edition set, ca. 1990, never removed from box, the set **22.50**

Trading cards, "Barbie & Ken Jumbo Trading Cards," includes 35 cards numbering from 176-210, complete in box, ca. 1962 (box discolored, worn & damaged) **360.00**

Barbie Wrist Watch Set

Wrist watch set, "Barbie," dated 1971, includes a watch w/gold trim & blonde-haired Barbie w/a blue dress, her arms form the 'hands' of the watch, includes three plastic interchangeable wristbands in pink, 'denim' & white, a red plastic case w/yellow insert, cardboard label & paper label on the side, some wear (ILLUS.) **65.00**

(End of Barbie Dolls Section)

BASEBALL MEMORABILIA

Roger Maris-Signed Ball

Baseball was named by Abner Doubleday as he laid out a diamond-shaped field with four bases at Cooperstown, New York. A popular game from its inception, by 1869 it was able to support its first all-professional team, the Cincinnati Red Stockings. The National

League was organized in 1876 and though the American League was first formed in 1900, it was not officially recognized until 1903. Today, the "national pastime" has millions of fans and collecting baseball memorabilia has become a major hobby with enthusiastic collectors seeking out items associated with players such as Babe Ruth, Lou Gehrig, and others who became legends in their own lifetimes. Though baseball cards, issued as advertising premiums for bubble gum and other products, seem to dominate the field there are numerous other items available. Also see: SPORTS MEMORABILIA.

Baseball, autographed by Roger Maris, unofficial game-used ball, inscribed in ink "To Johnny - Best of Luck - Roger Maris," dated June 7, 1962 (ILLUS.) **$633.00**

Baseball, autographed by Jackie Robinson, official National League "Ford Frick" ball, signed on the sweet spot.....................................**2,760.00**

Baseball, autographed by Babe Ruth, official American League "Barnard" ball signed on the sweet spot **5,175.00**

Baseball, 1930 St. Louis Cardinals team-signed ball, official National League ball signed by 28 team members including Jesse Haines, Gus Mancuso & Jim Bottomly.........**978.00**

Baseball, 1938 New York Yankees team-signed ball, official Joe DiMaggio League Ball, signed by 21 members of the team, Lou Gehrig's signature on the sweet spot..........**1,035.00**

Baseball, 1939 Boston Red Sox team-signed ball, official American League ball signed by 25 members of the team including rookie Ted Williams as well as Doerr, Pennock, Craemer & Foxx.............................**748.00**

Baseball, 1955 Brooklyn Dodgers team-signed ball, official National

Early Frank Baker Card

League ball signed by 23 team members including Walter Alston, Gil Hodges, Duke Snider, Pee Wee Reese & Jackie Robinson as well as Frank Kellert & Karl Spooner........**1,150.00**

Baseball card, Frank Baker T-231 Fans series card, front shows a sepia portrait of Baker in New York Yankees uniform, reverse contains his batting average through 1921 & the wording "I select Frank Baker leading batter of all 3d basemen, packed with FANS cigarettes," rounded corners, slight crease in upper left (ILLUS. bottom previous column) **1,380.00**

Baseball card, 1933, Goudey Gum Co. - Big League Chewing Gum, Babe Ruth, half-length color picture of Ruth in batting stance, No. 149, advertising & overview of Ruth career on reverse.........................**4,180.00**

Baseball card, 1952, Topps Gum, Dom DiMaggio, No. 22 ....**80.00**

Baseball card, 1953, Topps Gum, Satchell Paige, No. 220 ....**345.00**

Baseball card, 1954, Topps Gum, Don Mueller, No. 42...........................**12.00**

Baseball card, 1954, Topps Gum, Duane Pillette, No. 107.......................**8.50**

Baseball card, 1954, Topps Gum, Hank Aaron rookie card, No. 128 ....**978.00**

Baseball card, 1955, Topps Gum, Ted Williams, No. 2..........................**225.00**

Baseball card, 1957, Topps Gum, Bob Clemente, No. 76 ....**130.00**

Baseball card, 1957, Topps Gum, Mickey Mantle, No. 407 ....**260.00**

Baseball card, 1958, Topps Gum, Willie Mays, No. 5 ....**145.00**

Yastrzemski Rookie Card

Baseball card, 1960, Topps Gum, Carl Yastrzemski rookie card, No. 148 (ILLUS.).............................**196.00**

Baseball card, 1961, Topps Gum, Roy Campanella, No. 480 ....**30.00**

Baseball card, 1962, Topps Gum, Mickey Mantle..................................**368.00**

Baseball card, 1965, Topps Gum, Bob Uecker, No. 519 ....**30.00**

Baseball card, 1969, Topps Gum, Bob Gibson, No. 200 ....**15.00**

Baseball card, 1969, Topps Gum, Willie Stargell, No. 545 ....**10.00**

Baseball card, 1974, Topps Gum, Dave Parker, No. 252 ....**17.00**

Baseball card, 1976, Topps Gum, George Brett, No. 19.........................**42.00**

Baseball card, 1979, Topps Gum, Mike Schmidt, No. 610........................**8.00**

Bat, miniature, wooden, souvenir of 1942 World's Series...........................**50.00**

Bat, Ernie Banks game-used Hillerich & Bradsby professional model, markings indicate season, Banks' uniform number "14" written in marker on the knob.......................**4,025.00**

Early Baseball Book

Book, "Beadle's Dime Baseball Player - A Compendium of the Game," by Henry Chadwick, 1860, first edition in a plain buckram binding, the flyleaf inscribed "President of the Excelsior Base Ball Club Brooklyn," cover detached (ILLUS.) **2,530.00**

Book, "How I Would Pitch to Babe Ruth," by Tom Seaver, hard cover, w/dust jacket **15.00**

Book, "I Managed Good But Boy Did They Play Bad," by Jim Bouton, w/dust jacket, 1973 ....**12.00**

Book, "It's Good To Be Alive," by Roy Campanella, Boston, 1959, first edition, illustrated..............................**15.00**

Book, "Red Sox Fever," by Ellery Clark, first edition, w/dust jacket **20.00**

Book, "Spaulding Official Baseball Rules - National & American League," 1923...................................**30.00**

Book, "Yogi," by Yogi Berra, Doubleday, 1961, first edition, autobiography **23.00**

Calendar, 1943, advertising "Old Judge Irradiated Coffee," a large picture at the top of two cardinals

St. Louis Cardinals Calendar

framed by a band w/black & white photographs of members of the 1942 World Champion St. Louis Cardinals team, advertising in yellow & calendar pads in white on a red ground, some creases (ILLUS.) **460.00**

Calendar proof, 1951, a sample proof w/a full-color image of Lou Gehrig in the sky behind a young blond boy playing baseball, marked "Brown & Bigelow - Remembrance Advertising - Saint Paul 4, Minnesota," 16 x 31" (folded)..........**403.00**

Babe Ruth Christmas Card

Christmas card, signed by Babe Ruth, printed w/line-drawn Christmas designs in red, green & gold (ILLUS.) **2,185.00**

Contract, Babe Ruth's 1930-31 contract w/the New York Yankees, a two-year agreement for the then-record salary of $80,000.00 per season, dated March 10, 1930 ...**29,900.00**

Figures, china, a pitcher standing on a rocky mound wearing a blue & white striped cap & shirt, white pants & black & blue socks w/brown shoes, the batter standing on a

Victorian Baseball Figures

similar mound wearing a red & white
striped cap & shirt, white pants &
black & red socks w/brown shoes,
blond hair & natural coloring,
Heubach, Germany, ca. 1890s,
wooden bat not original, 15" h., pr.
(ILLUS.) **7,986.00**

Game, pinball-type, "Five In One
Game," wooden frame w/glass top,
1930s, excellent condition **125.00**

Glove, leather, embossed w/"Willy
Mays" facsimile signature,
MacGregor, No. 300 ....**55.00**

Jersey, 1965 Don Drysdale Los
Angeles Dodgers home flannel
jersey, "Dodgers" name & "53,"
produced by Tim McAuliffe Inc., size
46, signed by Drysdale on the front,
front tags & Drysdale's name........**5,750.00**

Jersey, Reggie Jackson 1985 Los
Angeles Angels home white jersey,
all correct labels & tags, autograph-
ed by Jackson on the front............**1,150.00**

Magazine, "Baseball Magazine," May,
1940...**35.00**

Magazine, "Saturday Evening Post,"
1963, Leo Durocher cover & feature
story...**28.00**

Newspaper, "New York Daily
Graphic," July 5, 1873, cover of
Philadelphia Athletic ball club &
featuring Cap Anson.........................**300.00**

Pen & pencil set, bat-shaped, "Pee
Wee Reese" & "Brooklyn Dodgers,"
mint in box, the set..........................**165.00**

Photograph, black & white shot of
Earle Combs in his 1939 uniform,
signed by Combs, 8 x 10" **345.00**

Photograph, autographed photo of
Lou Gehrig, an original Burke
portrait signed to Jake Powell, "To
Jake, with kindest personal regards,
Lou "Sis" Gehrig" **7,820.00**

Photograph, a Burke photo of Leon

"Goose" Goslin, signed by Goslin,
4 x 6"...**184.00**

Photograph, original team photo of
the 1905 New York Highlanders,
featuring Jack Chesbo, Clark Griffith
& Willie Keeler, long & narrow view
(side edges ragged) **805.00**

1913 Cleveland Indians Photo

Photograph, original sepia team
photo of the 1913 Cleveland
Indians, including Joe Jackson &
Napoleon Lajoie, players' names
written on the bottom in ink, border
tears at edges, creases at corners,
8 x 13" (ILLUS.) **1,840.00**

Photograph, New York Yankees
1949 team photo, 21 x 32" (few
small areas adhered to the
glass) **483.00**

Photograph, panoramic view of the
1905 World Series, by the Pictorial
News Company, shot at the Polo
Grounds during the second game of
the series, caption reads "Athletics
in the Field, Bender Pitching," on
coated stock board, 8 x 36" **920.00**

Photograph, 1910 Philadelphia
Athletics sepia tone premium photo,
published by the Baseball Magazine
Co., the team pictured in uniform,
includes Connie Mack, Harry Davis,
Frank Baker, Eddie Plank, Eddie
Collins & Chief Bender, 14 x 24".....**368.00**

Postcard, signed by Joe Tinker, w/a
lengthy handwritten inscription, sent
from Orlando, Florida, pasted to an
album page **863.00**

Postcards, photo-type, a set of 10
real photo cards of Babe Ruth
swinging a bat, each signed in bold
ink by Ruth, near mint condition, the
set..**10,350.00**

Premium 'blankets,' uncut sheet of
felt B-1 Blankets containing 18
complete blankets including Joe
Jackson, Chapman & Huggins, as
well as several partials, printed in
monotone apparently as a proof,
early 20th c. **1,725.00**

Press pin, 1913 Philadelphia
Athletics World Series pin w/ribbon
& metal medallion, produced by J.

E. Caldwell, the pin bears the Baseball Writers logo, medallion features the team logo, faded green & gold ribbon printed "PRESS" **2,530.00**

Press pin, 1927 New York Yankee World Series model, enameled gilt-metal, shield-shaped w/a red band at the top above a white band & a blue band near the base, reads "Press - World Series - American League - 1927," near mint **2,530.00**

1938 Cincinnati Press Pin

Press pin, 1938 Cincinnati All-Star Game pinback button, celluloid w/a white ground, team logo in red & blue w/red lettering reading "Press - All Star Game - Crosley Field - Cincinnati - 1938," original back paper intact (ILLUS.) **7,590.00**

Program, 1889 World Series between the New York Giants & the Brooklyn Baseball Club, a score card - program for the second game of the series, dated "October 15, 1889" in pencil (some staining, chipping on cover) **1,265.00**

Program, 1938 World Series between the New York Yankees & the Chicago Cubs **275.00**

Program, 1944 World Series, Cincinnati Browns vs St. Louis Cardinals.................................**120.00**

Program, 1963 New York Yankees 'Old Timers Day' program autographed by 32 Old Timers including Joe McCarthy, Sam Rice, Joe DiMaggio, Jackie Robinson, Jimmie Foxx, Carl Hubbell, Dizzy Dean & others, the occasion was to honor Sam Ric, elected to the Hall of Fame that year............................**920.00**

Record book, 1954 World Series, Gillette premium.................................**10.00**

Restaurant jersey, grey flannel baseball jersey from DiMaggio's restaurant team in San Francisco, made by Stroh's of San Francisco, sewn on number "3," signed by Joe DiMaggio on the front **1,150.00**

Scorecard, 1871 game between the Philadelphia Athletics & the New York Mutuals, first year of the National Association, scored, a Peck & Snyder advertisement on the back **1,150.00**

Season pass, 1925 National League Philadelphia Base Ball Club pass issued to Thomas Shibe, owner of the team, an embossed image of a Quaker standing on a dome in a pitching pose, border in blue enamel **863.00**

Season pass, 1930 New York Giants 14k gold pass issued to first Commissioner of Baseball, Kenesaw Mountain Landis, rectangular w/arched top, the same design as the Charles Dana Gibson 1930 silver pass, inscribed "Hon. K.M. Landis & Party" **3,220.00**

Sheet Music, "Husky Hans," dedicated to Honus Wagner & w/his black & white photograph in uniform on the cover, written by Wm. J. Hartz, early 20th c., 10¾ x 14"........**550.00**

Uniform, child's, Babe Ruth jersey & pants, Wilson, size 30, the set **300.00**

Uniform, Gary Gentry 1971 Mets flannel road uniform, game-worn, consisting of a jersey & pants, excellent condition, 2 pcs.............**2,300.00**

Yearbook, 1954 New York Giants **100.00**

Yearbook, 1961 San Francisco Giants **35.00**

Yearbook, 1961 Chicago White Sox....**10.00**

BASKETS

Miniature "Buttocks" Baskets

The American Indians were the first basket weavers on this continent and, of necessity, the early Colonial settlers and their descendants pursued this artistic handicraft to provide essential containers for berries, eggs and endless other items to be carried or stored. Rye straw, split willow and reeds are but a few of the wide variety of materials used. The Nantucket baskets, plainly and sturdily constructed, along with those made by other specialized groups, would seem to draw the greatest attention in this area of collecting. Also see INDIAN ARTIFACTS & JEWELRY and SHAKER ITEMS.

"Buttocks" basket, miniature, 10-rib construction, woven splint, 3 x 3⅝", 2" h. plus bentwood handle............**$115.50**

"Buttocks" basket, miniature, 16-rib construction, woven splint, minor damage, 5¼ x 5½", 3" h. plus bentwood handle (ILLUS. left) **192.50**

"Buttocks" basket, miniature, 16-rib construction, woven natural & blue-green splint, 5 x 5½", 3¼" h. plus bentwood handle **241.50**

"Buttocks" basket, miniature, 20-rib construction, woven splint, 4½ x 5¼", 2¾" h. plus bentwood handle **170.50**

"Buttocks" basket, miniature, 24-rib construction, woven splint w/traces of gold paint, 5½ x 6", 3½" h. plus bentwood handle **176.00**

"Buttocks" basket, miniature, 26-rib construction, woven splint, well shaped, 7¼ x 8½", 4" h. plus bentwood handle (ILLUS. right) **203.50**

"Buttocks" basket, 20-rib construction, woven splint, natural patina, well shaped, 10 x 10", 6" h. plus bentwood handle (minor damage)..**82.50**

"Buttocks" basket, 20-rib construction, woven splint, bentwood handle w/'eye of God' design, old worn patina, 14 x 16", 9" h. plus bentwood handle **225.50**

"Buttocks" basket, 22-rib construction, woven splint, old worn patina, 11" l., 7" h. plus bentwood handle **159.50**

"Buttocks" basket, 22-rib construction, woven splint, dark patina, w/faint two-tone design, 14 x 17", 9" h. plus bentwood handle **165.00**

"Buttocks" basket, 24-rib construction, woven splint, well made, natural patina, 11 x 12", 6" h. plus bentwood handle (minor damage)..**148.50**

Large "Buttocks" Basket

"Buttocks" basket, 30-rib construction, woven splint, finely woven w/good detail, natural patina, 9" d., 6" h. plus bentwood handle **385.00**

"Buttocks" basket, 34-rib construction, woven splint, gold old worn natural patina, 16 x 17", 9½" h. plus bentwood handle (ILLUS. bottom previous column) **104.50**

Field (or gathering) basket, woven splint, squared bottom & sides w/a rounded wrapped rim, small bentwood rim handles, old patina, 22" d., 9" h. **181.50**

Flower gathering basket, woven splint, flat oval slightly curved up on two sides, old worn varnish, 12 x 15½", 5" h. plus bentwood handle **71.50**

Goose feather basket, woven splint, large barrel-shaped container w/bentwood rim handles, 21½" h. (minor repair) **225.50**

Loom basket, hanging-type, woven splint, natural dark patina w/black & faded red, 11½" w., 8½" h. (crest has some missing pieces & repair, one handle missing)...........................**71.50**

Market basket, woven splint, low round sides, wrapped rim, old patina, 7" d., 4" h. plus bentwood handle (minor damage)....................**137.50**

Market basket, woven splint, round w/wrapped rim, weathered two-tone weaving w/faded red stripe, 11½" d., 5½" h. plus bentwood handle **170.50**

Market Basket from Ohio

Market basket, woven splint, rectangular bottom, w/low sides & wrapped oblong rim, pair of swivel bentwood rim handles, old finish, old pencil inscription on base "Leesville, Ohio," 12 x 18½", 7" h. plus handles (ILLUS.) **110.00**

Market basket, woven splint, square base w/rounded sides & round wrapped rim, weathered greyish finish, 11½ x 12", 7½" h. plus bentwood handle **104.50**

"Melon" basket, miniature, 10-rib construction, oval, woven splint w/diamond design at handles, wrapped handle, 4¼" l. **148.50**

Nantucket basket, finely woven splint, round w/wrapped rim, wooden swing handle, Nantucket

Island, Massachusetts, early
20th c., 8¾" d., 10¼" h.....................**330.00**

Nantucket basket, finely woven splint
& cane, wrapped rim above deep
sides & a wooden base, bentwood
swing handle, early 20th c., 10" d.,
12" h. plus handle **431.00**

Nantucket basket, finely woven splint
& cane, wrapped rim above deep
sides & a wooden base, bentwood
swing handle, branded "C.W.
Chapin" on handle & twice on base,
late 19th c., 13" d. **1,495.00**

Nantucket baskets, finely woven
splint, wrapped rim, oval wooden
base, wooden swing handle, labeled
"by Davis Hall, Nantucket, Mass.,"
nested set of six, 6¾" to 13" l.,
the set **7,150.00**

Storage basket, woven splint,
rectangular bottom w/oval sides &
rim, natural tan & dark brown
w/printed designs in rectangles,
11½" l., 3½" h.....................................**93.50**

Large Storage Basket

Storage basket, woven splint, deep
rounded sides w/a heavy wrapped
rim, angular bentwood handle, old
dark patina, wear, minor damage &
soiling, 15½" d., 9½" h. plus handle
(ILLUS.) **93.50**

Storage basket, woven splint, deep
rectangular sides w/wrapped rim, &
bentwood end handles, old dark
paint, 18½ x 29", 14" h. plus handles
(some damage)................................**385.00**

Utility basket, woven splint, rectangular w/low flat sides, natural & red
stain, 9 x 12", 4" h. **49.50**

Decorated Utility Basket

Utility basket, woven splint, rectangular, natural w/printed double-leaf
designs in faded red & green, small
end rim handles, some damage,

9½ x 13", 4¾" h. plus handles
(ILLUS.) **148.50**

Utility basket, woven splint, rectangular base below deep flat sides to
an oval wrapped rim, small loop end
bentwood rim handles, 8¾ x 9½",
5½" h. plus handles (stains, minor
rim damage).......................................**49.50**

Utility basket, woven splint, rectangular bottom w/slightly flaring sides
to a wrapped oblong rim, center
bentwood handle, weathered grey
finish, 10¼ x 16½", 7" h. plus
handle (minor damage).....................**82.50**

Utility basket, woven splint, rectangular w/wrapped rim, light natural
patina, 9½ x 11½", 7¼" h. plus
bentwood handle **126.50**

Utility basket, woven splint, round
deep sides w/a wrapped rim &
bentwood handle, good old patina,
17 x 18", 9" h. plus handle **159.50**

Utility basket, woven splint, round
w/deep sides, wrapped rim
w/bentwood end handles, 20" d.,
10½" h..**137.50**

BELLS

Figural Lady Bell

Figural bell, brass, full-skirted lady in
18th c. costume wearing a small hat
& holding a fan, 2½" d., 5⅝" h.
(ILLUS.) **$75.00**

Figural bell, brass, a standing warrior
wearing a helmet & holding a club
above his head, scenes of warriors
around the sides & an inscription
around the flanged base, Hemony-
type, 3" d., 6½" h. (ILLUS. top
next page) **125.00**

Figural bell, china w/scene of two
black cats & "Bon Soir," one cat has
blue bow & one has red bow,
2⅝" d., 3¼" h. **65.00**

Figural Warrior Bell

Fire bell, brass, on a square wood
base, 14" d., 17" h............................**220.00**
Shop bell, cast brass bell on steel
spring, mid-19th c., 2½ x 3" bell.......**140.00**

BIG LITTLE BOOKS

Buck Rogers - 25th Century A.D.

*The original "Big Little Books" and
"Better Little Books" small format series
were originated in the mid-30s by
Whitman Publishing Co., Racine,
Wisconsin, and covered a variety of
subjects from adventure stories to tales
based on comic strip characters and movie
and radio stars. The publisher originally
assigned each book a serial number. Most
prices are now in the $25.00 - $50.00 range
with scarce ones bringing more.*

**Buck Rogers in the War with the
Planet Venus,** No. 1437, 1938........**$60.00**
Buck Rogers, 25th Century A.D.,
No. 742, 1933 (ILLUS.) ....**50.00 to 75.00**
Buffalo Bill and the Pony Express,
No. 713, 1934 ....**30.00**
Bugs Bunny and Klondike Gold,
No. 1455, 1947 ....**28.00**

Bugs Bunny, Accidental Adventure,
No. 5758, 1973 (reissue of
No. 2929) **25.00**
**Captain Frank Hawks Air Ace and
the League of Twelve,** No. 1444,
1938..**20.00**
**Captain Midnight & the Secret
Squadron vs The Terror of the
Orient,** No. 1488, 1942....................**55.00**
**Captain Midnight and Sheik Jomak
Khan,** No. 1402, 1946 ....**20.00**
**Charlie Chan, Inspector of the
Honolulu Police,** No. 1478, 1939.....**35.00**
**Charlie Chan Solves a New
Mystery,** No. 1459, 1940...................**45.00**
**Chester Gump at Silver Creek
Ranch,** No. 734, 1933.......................**35.00**
**Dick Tracy and the Boris Arson
Gang,** No. 1163, 1935 ....**30.00**
**Dick Tracy and the Racketeer
Gang,** No. 1112, 1936 ....**50.00**
Dick Tracy and the Spider Gang,
No. 1446, 1937..................................**60.00**
Dick Tracy and Yogee Yamma,
No. 1412, 1946..................................**30.00**
Dick Tracy in Chains of Crime,
No. 1185, 1936 ....**45.00**
Dick Tracy vs Crooks in Disguise,
No. 1479, 1939 ....**50.00**
**Flash Gordon and the Perils of
Mongo,** No. 1423, 1940 ....**50.00**
**Flash Gordon and the Witch Queen
of Mongo,** No. 1190, 1936 ....**50.00**
Gang Busters Step In, No. 1433,
1939..**20.00**
**Gene Autry and the Land Grab
Mystery,** No. 1439, 1945...................**20.00**
Gene Autry in Law of the Range,
No. 1483, 1939 ....**35.00**
George O'Brien in Gun Law, RKO
movie edition, No. 1418, 1935 ....**40.00**
G-Man vs the Red X, No. 1147,
1936...**22.00**
Houdini's Big Little Book of Magic,
No. 715, 1933 ....**35.00**
Invisible Scarlet O'Neil, No. 1403,
1942...**25.00**
**Jack Armstrong and the Ivory
Treasure,** No. 1435, 1937 ....**25.00**
Little Miss Muffet, No. 1120, 1936......**30.00**
**Lone Star Martin of the Texas
Rangers,** No. 1405, 1939.................**22.00**
Mickey Rooney, Himself, No. 1427,
1939..**25.00**
Mickey Mouse, The Mail Pilot,
No. 731, 1933 ....**45.00**
Popeye and Queen Olive Oyl,
No. 1458, 1949 ....**20.00**
Popeye the Sailor Man, No. 1422,
1947...**20.00**
Punch Davis of the Aircraft Carrier,
No. 1440, 1945 ....**35.00**
Tailspin Tommy and the Lost

Transport, No. 1413,
1939 ....**25.00 to 30.00**
Tarzan of the Screen, No. 778,
1934...**40.00**
Tarzan Escapes, No. 1182,
1936 ....**30.00 to 40.00**
Tex Thorne Comes Out of the West,
No. 1440, 1937 ....**45.00**
Tim McCoy in the Westerner,
No. 1193, 1936 ....**42.00**
Tiny Tim (The Adventures of),
No. 767, 1935 ....**30.00**
Treasure Island, movie edition
w/Jackie Cooper, No. 1141(0),
1934...**18.00**

RELATED BOOKS
The Adventures of Dick Tracy,
Detective, Big Big Books,
No. 4055, 1934 ....**160.00**
Buck Jones and the Night Riders,
Big Big Books, No. 4069, 1937
(¼" piece missing from spine)..........**100.00**
Daktari, Night of Terror, Ivan Tors',
A Big Little Book, No. 2018, 1968......**10.00**
Little Orphan Annie (The Story of),
Big Big Books, No. 4054,
1934 ....**100.00 to 125.00**

BIRDCAGES

Mahogany & Wire Birdcage

Although probably not too many people specialize in just collecting birdcages, many who keep birds as pets enjoy keeping them in old or antique cages. The shiny brass birdcages widely produced earlier in this century by firms such as Hendryx are also popular decorative accent pieces in the homes of antiques lovers who may use them to hold a fern or potted plant rather than a live bird. Note that the very large and elaborate cages produced in the 19th

century are the ones which today bring the highest prices on the collecting market.

Mahogany & wire, a high domed center section flanked by vaulted side sections, large turned wood cap w/pointed finial, fitted w/thin sliding trays in the wooden base, England, 19th c., 14¼ x 32½", 38½" h. (ILLUS.) **$3,738.00**

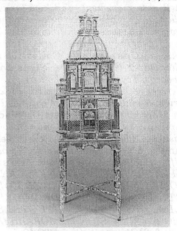

Tall Wirework Birdcage

Wirework, green-painted & parcel-gilt, a high domed top w/a cupola above a two-tier cage w/small round turrets at the corners of the top tier, one working & seven false doors, on a conforming wooden stand w/ring-turned legs joined by a cross-stretcher, England, late 19th c., later paint, alterations (ILLUS.) **9,775.00**

BLACK AMERICANA

Figural Andirons

Over the past decade or so this field of

collecting has rapidly grown and today almost anything that relates to Black culture or illustrates Black Americans is considered a desirable collectible. Although many representations of Blacks, especially on 19th and early 20th century advertising pieces and housewares, were cruel stereotypes, even these are collected as poignant reminders of how far American society has come since the dawning of the Civil Rights movement, and how far we still have to go. Other pieces related to this category will be found from time to time in such categories as Advertising Items, Banks, Character Collectibles, Kitchenwares, Cookie Jars, Signs and Signboards, Toys, and several others.

Reference books dealing with Black Americana include Black Collectibles *by Lynn Morrow (1983);* Collecting Black Americana *by Dawn E. Reno (Crown Publishers, 1986); and* Black Collectibles, Mammy and her friends *by Jackie Young (Schiffer Publishing Ltd., 1988). Also see ADVERTISING ITEMS, BANKS, CANS & CONTAINERS, CHARACTER COL-LECTIBLES, CHILDREN'S BOOKS, DOLLS, DOORSTOPS, POSTERS, RADIO & TELEVISION MEMORABILIA, SIGNS & SIGNBOARDS and TOYS.*

Andirons, cast iron, figural, modeled as a black man & black woman, dressed in early 19th c. attire, found in Georgia, overall deep pitting, ca. 1825-45, 16½" h., pr. (ILLUS.) **$825.00**

Ashtray, floor model, cast iron, full-figure black butler wearing a frock coat, vest & bow tie, standing & holding a wide shallow tray w/'fins' at each side to hold boxes of matches, very tall slender legs on a square foot, decorated in red, black & white, ca. 1930s, 35" h. (overall paint crazing) **770.00**

Auto cloth, "Cadie," black character on package front **30.00**

Book, "Little Black Sambo Story Book" by Helen Bannerman & Frank Ver Beck, Henry Altemus Co., Philadelphia, 1930 (slight wear on cover) **145.00**

Book, "Watermelon Pete & Other Stories," small format w/illustrated cover & color illustrations by Elizabeth Gordon, hard cover, 68 pp. **27.00**

Can, Luzianne Coffee, 3 lb. **110.00**

Candy box, cov., the cover w/a label featuring a scene of a black boy & girl on a teeter-totter made from a peppermint stick, excellent condition, large **200.00**

Card game, "Old Maid," cards w/six

black characters, 1940s, the deck **45.00**

Clothes brush, simple shaped wooden handle painted as a black Mammy, 6" l. (some paint chipping) **40.00**

Decanter with "Cake Walk" Scene

Decanter w/original clear facet-cut mushroom-shaped stopper, tapering cylindrical body on a cushion foot, the angled shoulder to a slender tall cylindrical neck w/flaring rim, sapphire blue enameled w/a scene of a black man in striped pants, long-tailed jacket, cane & top hat doing a high-stepped dance, enameled "Cake Walk," 3" d., 11¼" h. (ILLUS.) **195.00**

Doll, Chase (Martha) cloth black woman, stockinette face & body, face thickly painted, brown eyes & strong features, black short wig,

Martha Chase Black Woman

applied ears, painted lower arms &
legs, wearing original brightly printed
red cotton long skirt & blouse, white
neck scarf & apron, red bandanna,
underclothes & black socks, missing
shoes, late 19th c., 26" h.
(ILLUS. bottom previous page) **8,050.00**

Doll, cloth black baby, embroidered
stockinette, nicely shaped face
w/eyes of simulated ivory w/black
button pupils, embroidered lips,
applied ears, looped wool hair,
fabric body, wearing a white cotton
skirt & blouse, old black-coated cloth
shoes, early 20th c., 20½" h. **4,312.00**

Doll, cloth black child, embroidered
eyes, eyebrows & small mouth,
applied nose & ears, sock hair,
fabric body w/mitten hands, wearing
a long faded yellow cotton dress,
early 20th c., repairs to the body,
21½"..**805.00**

Doll, cloth black "Mammy" doll, life-
sized, black woman wearing a
flowered cotton dress, white
organdy apron & cap w/a white
cotton kerchief around her neck &
red shoes, painted eyes & mouth,
now mounted on a black metal
base, 20th c. **575.00**

Doll, cloth black woman, stockinette,
black button eyes over white kid
eyes, hide eyebrows & hair,
stockinette body w/mitten hands,
leather shoes, wearing a black
cotton dress w/white apron, black
coat w/black fur trim, velvet hat,
early 20th c., 20" h. **1,495.00**

Doll, lithographed cloth, uncut, "Uncle
Mose," Aunt Jemima premium,
1924...**120.00**

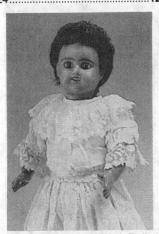

Denamur Bisque Black Doll

Doll, Denamur bisque head black girl
doll, marked "E 6 D," fixed brown

glass eyes, open mouth w/teeth,
pierced ears, black skin wig, straight
limb composition walker body,
redressed in a white cotton gown &
underwear, paint surfaced on arms
& hands frail, France, ca. 1890,
16" h. (ILLUS.) **1,150.00**

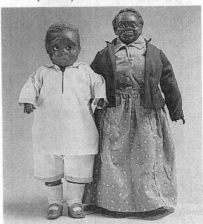

Black Character Dolls

Doll, Head (Magge) plaster shoulder-
head black woman, well-detailed
face, painted eyes, smiling closed
mouth, pierced ears, hair molded as
a thick braid over the crown of her
head, fabric body w/composition
lower arms, wearing a bright green
printed cotton dress & dark green
jacket, pen-inscribed on sole of
shoes "This doll belongs to Jeanne
Head, Magnolia, unmarked, one of
the very first by Magge Head 1952,"
19½" h. (ILLUS. right) **747.00**

Boxed "Julia" Doll

Doll, "Julia," from the TV series, Twist
n' Turn model, wearing one-piece
nurse's outfit, never removed from
the box, ca. 1968 (ILLUS.) **165.00**

Kammer & Reinhardt Black Girl Doll

Doll, Kammer & Reinhardt bisque
head character girl, marked "101- 0,"
painted brown eyes, closed mouth,
black mohair wig, straight limb
composition body, wearing a red &
white gingham dress & white apron,
no socks or shoes, Germany, ca.
1909, 11" h. (ILLUS.) **3,162.00**

Doll, Moss (Leo) so-called
composition head black boy,
character face w/fixed brown glass
eyes, down-turned mouth, knitted
brows, tears falling from eyes, fabric
body w/composition lower arms,
wearing a white cotton shirt w/sailor
collar, matching pants, socks & blue
oilcloth shoes, "LM" scratched on
back of head, 18" h.
(ILLUS. left, previous page) **1,840.00**

Black 'Stockinette' Doll

Doll, 'stockinette' cloth black child,
pleasingly shaped face w/eyes of
simulated ivory w/black button
pupils, embroidered lips, applied
ears, looped wool hair, fabric body,

wearing a white cotton skirt &
blouse, old black coated cloth
shoes, early 20th c., 20½" h.
(ILLUS.) **4,312.00**

Doll clothing, Julia "Brrr-Furrr" set,
includes dress, matching coat
w/attached belt, fur hat, blue hinge-
tongue shoes, booklet, label on box,
store sticker, ca. 1969, never
removed from box (box discolored &
worn corners) **140.00**

Doorstop, cast iron, figural black man
carrying a satchel & looking back
over his shoulder, Hubley, 5⅛" w.,
7½" h...**950.00**

Figure, bisque, black man standing &
holding a chicken, fine coloring,
7½" h...**250.00**

"Emperor Jones" Movie Poster

"The Green Eyed Monster" Movie Poster

Figure, bisque, black boy seated on chamber pot eating a slice of watermelon, Germany **145.00**

Game, board-type, "Little Black Sambo" **135.00**

Movie film, "Little Black Sambo," 16mm, Castle Films, mint **70.00**

Movie poster, "Emperor Jones," starring Paul Robeson, color bust portrait of the star, tempera and/or gouache on board, United Artists, 1933, 24½ x 32" (ILLUS. previous page) **3,162.00**

Movie poster, "The Green Eyed Monster," The Norman Film Mfg.

"Paradise in Harlem" Poster

"Up Jumped The Devil" Poster

Co., 1921, colored lithograph showing a seated black couple, one-sheet, linen backed, 27 x 41" (ILLUS. bottom previous page) **4,312.00**

Movie poster, "Paradise in Harlem," starring Frank Wilson & Mamie Smith, colored lithograph w/sketched vignettes, black, yellow & red lettering on a red background, Jubilee, 1939, one-sheet, linen backed, 27 x 41" (ILLUS. previous column) **517.00**

Movie poster, "Up Jumped The Devil," starring Mantan Moreland & Shelton Brooks, black, white & red serigraph, Toddy, 1940, one-sheet, 28 x 42" (ILLUS. bottom previous column) **575.00**

Mug, china, transfer-printed scene of a black man playing a banjo, Warwick China, IOGA mark, early 20th c. **150.00**

Painting of the "Dancers"

Painting, water-color on paper, pictures a black couple in bright costume dancing, titled "Dancers," American school, ca. 1830, 5½ x 9" (ILLUS.) **2,990.00**

Pinback button, "NAACP," blue w/white lettering, 1951, ⅞" d. **40.00**

Pipe, carved wood, an alligator carved on the stem, a black man behind the bowl w/a stick in his hand & down the alligator's throat, 12" l. **850.00**

Pitcher, tankard, earthenware, transfer-printed scenes titled "The Wren's Nest - The home of Uncle Remus, Atlanta, Ga.," & "A Georgia Cotton Field," also marked "Seventh Annual Convention Railway Mail Association, Atlanta, Ga., June 1909," Ridgways, England, 12½" h. **310.00**

Plate, china, advertising "Coon Chicken Inn," Syracuse China Co., 9½" d. **250.00**

Platter, china, advertising "Coon Chicken Inn," Syracuse China Co., 8 x 11½" **375.00**

Poster, lithographed paper, "George

Comic Minstrel Poster

Thatcher's Minstrels - The Darktown
Brotherhood vs. The Blackville
League," a colorful comic baseball
scene w/black players in action, in
walnut shadowbox frame, late
19th c., 29 x 39½" (ILLUS.)...........**4,950.00**
Salt & pepper shakers, ceramic,
figural Mammy & chef, Pearl China,
3" h., pr. **60.00**
Salt & pepper shakers, china, figural
boy & watermelon, Japan, pr. **75.00**
Salt & pepper shakers, plastic,
figural Aunt Jemima & Uncle Mose,
F. & F. Mold & Die Works,
3½" h., pr. **50.00**
Salt & pepper shakers, plastic,
figural Aunt Jemima & Uncle Mose,
F. & F. Mold & Die Works,
5¼" h., pr. **65.00**

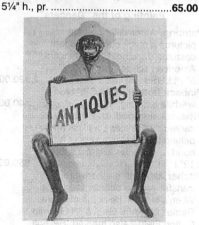

Figural "Antiques" Sign

Sign, "Antiques," figural, a relief-
molded figure of a black man
holding a rectangular metal sign
reading "ANTIQUES," colorful old
repaint, ca. 1940, several small old
repairs, 4' 5½" h. (ILLUS.)...............**467.50**
Sign, "O'Baby Chocolate Dairy Drink,"
lithographed cardboard, caricature
of a black boy holding a bottle of the
product, reads "O'Baby - Chocolate

"O'Baby" Chocolate Drink Sign

Dairy Drink - Pure - Wholesome -
Tasty - "Ain't dat sumptin" - It's
pasteurized - No Preservatives,"
printed in brown, green, orange,
white & black, paint loss quarter of
the way up at bottom, edge wear,
14¼ x 22½" (ILLUS.) **71.50**

Figural Barber Sign

Sign, "Elijah Cook - Barber," figural,
carved & painted wood, finely
carved figure of a black man holding
a bunch of cigars in one hand & a
striped bat in the other, standing
atop a tall platform base painted
w/ "Elijah Cook - Barber - Cigars
5¢," wearing green pants & tan shirt,
lettering in red & blue on a light
green ground, minor fading,
scratches & paint chips, ca. 1940-
50s, 15½ x 20½", 5' 1" h.
(ILLUS.) **1,430.00**
Slave document, states that "Mr.
Capps buys a Negro of Joseph
Bates for $679.00, Dec. 14, 1846,"

written in blue & brown ink, found near Mobile, Alabama, 7½ x 12¼" (fold lines & a few pinpoint holes) **247.50**

Soap dish, cast iron, figural Mammy **195.00**

Spoon, sterling silver, figural black boy's head on handle, enameled watermelon in bowl, small...............**260.00**

Statue of a Young Black Man

Statue, copper over plaster, depicting a young black man sitting on a tree stump, wearing a jacket, pants, scarf & suspenders, in a contemplative mood, "Virginia Blend" written on the base, early 20th c., 9" h. (ILLUS.) **220.00**

Syrup pitcher, plastic, figural Aunt Jemima, F. & F. Mold & Die Works, ca. 1949 ....**65.00**

Rare Tobacco Jar

Tobacco jar, cov., bisque porcelain, triangular form molded in relief on one side w/a black man playing cards, the legs molded as a grouping of tobacco pipes, the cover realistically molded as a deck of cards w/a die finial, hand-painted in color, Austria, ca. 1890-1910 (ILLUS.) **577.50**

Toy, battery-operated tin, "Strutting Sam," black man does a jig on a pedestal base, mint in box, 10½" h..**550.00**

Toy, windup tin, "Be Bop Jigger," black man dancing on a lithographed pedestal base, Louis Marx & Co., New York, New York **450.00**

Toy, windup tin, "Louis Armstrong," figural, playing the trumpet **425.00**

Windup 'Talking Head' Toy

Toy, windup tin 'talking head,' depicting a dandified black man w/top hat, his articulated neck & jaw

Early Mechanical Toy

moving w/clockwork mechanism & cam driven to give him the appearance of guffawing, early 20th c., 7" h. (ILLUS. previous page)..**517.00**

Toy, mechanical, "Old Mammy Washing Clothes," a colorfully dressed white-haired black woman stands on a platform & bends over an open wood tub to scrub a sheet, turning her head & bending at her waist when wound, Ives Corp., Bridgeport, Connecticut, ca. 1890, 11" h. (ILLUS. bottom previous page)...**13,800.00**

Trade card, "Fairbanks Soaps," color lithograph showing two black boys standing beside a large wooden tub of steaming water, advertising on back, 3½ x 5" **28.00**

Rare Union Porcelain Works Vase

Vase, china, cylindrical tapering at the bottom to a flared foot, h.p. decoration of a black banjo player wearing a straw hat, high-collared jacket & striped pants, geometric bands at the top & bottom edges, Union Porcelain Works, black ink mark "UPW," 3½" d., 7" h. (ILLUS.) **2,750.00**

(End of Black Americana Section)

BOOK ENDS

Brass, bust of Theodore Roosevelt, overall tarnishing, 4½" w., 6½" h., pr. (ILLUS. top next column) **$11.00**

Brass, model of Wirehaired Fox Terriers, ca. 1929, pr. **85.00**

Theodore Roosevelt Book Ends

Brass & Bakelite, model of an elephant w/a Bakelite head & arched brass body, Chase, 3½" w., 4¾" h., pr...**299.00**

Bronze, figural, depicting a kneeling nude child on a self base, rich brown patina, from a model by Barretto Parsons, one signed "E. Barretto Parsons Copy 1913" & stamped "Gorham Co. Founders QSC," the other inscribed "E.B. Parsons © 1913" & stamped "Gorham Co. Founders QSC," 6¼" h., pr. **1,035.00**

Bronze, figural, a seated female nude w/a book in her lap, inscribed "M. LeVerrier," on marble base, green patina, France, early 20th c., 7¼" h., pr...**345.00**

Bronze finish, model of an eagle, Frankart, pr. **35.00**

Cast iron, Art Deco style, circle w/figure of a nude female in the center, gold paint, 7" h., pr...............**185.00**

Cast iron, figural hooded monk crouched reading w/wall of books behind him, signed "B&H," Bradley & Hubbard, pr. **135.00**

Cast iron, figural Indian Chief, copper finish, pr. **70.00**

Cast iron, kissing Dutch children, No. 332, Hubley, pr. **165.00**

Cast iron, figural "The Thinker," copper finish, 4½" w., 6" h., pr. **45.00**

Cast iron, model of a fighting cock, life-like, late 19th c., 7 x 9 x 10", pr...**295.00**

Cast iron, model of a dog, seated Setter, head up, gilt finish, pr. **24.00**

Cast iron, model of a spread-winged eagle w/head turned to side, on a low base, 7" h., pr. **302.50**

Cast iron, relief-molded bust of an Indian w/single feather in hair, against a textured ground, original polychrome paint, 6¼" h., pr. **187.00**

Ceramic, figural Cubist-style, modeled as a stylized standing cowboy w/hat pulled down over his face & leaning against a wall, white crackle glaze, J. Fabre, inscribed "Fabre - Edition Kaza - France," w/a Galleries Lafayette, Paris retail label, ca. 1922, 4¼ x 5⅜", 10½" h., pr...**431.00**

Copper, hand-wrought, Arts & Crafts style, hammered & stitched border, original rich dark brown patina, die-stamped "open box" mark of Dirk Van Erp, San Francisco, California, early 20th c., 3½ x 4½", pr. **330.00**

BOOKS

(Also see CHILDREN'S BOOKS, BIG LITTLE BOOKS, CHARACTER COL-LECTIBLES, DISNEY COLLECTIBLES, RADIO & TELEVISION MEMORABILIA, SPACE AGE COLLECTIBLES and WESTERN CHARACTER COLLECT-IBLES.)

ANTIQUES RELATED

Archer, Margaret & Douglas, "Glass Candlesticks," 1975, Collector Books, illustrated color plates, 112 pp...**$30.00**

Bain, David, & Bruce Harris, editors, "Mickey Mouse - Fifty Happy Years," 1977, Harmony Books, illustrated, stiff covers, 255 pp.........................**50.00**

Barbour, Raymond E., "Sandwich, Town That Glass Built, Sandwich Glass History," 1948, 318 pp. **25.00**

Barret, Richard Carter, "Bennington Pottery and Porcelain," 1958, black & white photos, hard cover w/dust jacket.....................................**55.00**

Belknap, E. McCamly, "Milk Glass," 1949, Crown Publishers, w/dust jacket **60.00**

Blake, Sylvia Dugger, "Flow Blue China," 1971, Wallace-Homestead, illustrated, color plates, 48 pp. **25.00**

Bolton, Ethel Standwood & Coe, Eva Johnston, "American Samplers," 1973, Pyne Press reprint, 416 pp.................................**77.00**

Camehl, Ada Walker, "The Blue-China Book," 1916, black & white photos, hard cover **38.50**

Clinton County Historical Association, "Reflections - The Story of Redford Glass," 1979, black & white & color photographs, soft cover **93.50**

Downs, Joseph, "American Furniture," 1952, 9½ x 12¼" **115.50**

Fales, Dean & Bishop, Robert & Nelson, Cyril I., "American Painted Furniture, 1660-1880" 1972, E.P. Dutton, first edition, illustrated, 298 pp. **225.50**

Flayderman, Norman, "Scrimshaw & Scrimshanders - Whales and Whalemen," 1972, limited edition, author-signed, 293 pp. **275.00**

Greaser, Arlene & Paul, "Homespun Ceramics," 1964, black & white & one color photo, soft cover, 59 pp. **88.00**

Grimmer, Elsa, "Wave Crest Ware," 1979, Wallace-Homestead, 26 color plates, stiff covers, 96 pp. **35.00**

Grover, Ray & Lee, "Art Glass Nouveau," 1968, Charles E. Tuttle Co., color illustrations, 231 pp. **45.00**

Hartung, Marion T., "Carnival Glass in Color," 1967, illustrated, color plates **40.00**

Hartung, Marion T., "Northwood Pattern Glass," 1967, illustrated, 100 pp...**33.00**

Hollister, Paul M., "The Encyclopedia of Glass Paperweights," 1969, C.N. Potter, illustrated, 312 pp. **25.00**

Jacobs, Celia, "Pocket Book of American Pewter," 1960, auto-graphed, 85 pp., 4⅛ x 5½" **44.00**

Kerfoot, J.B., "American Pewter," 1924, Houghton Mifflin, first edition, illustrated, 239 pp., 8¾" x 11¼" **55.00**

Koch, Robert, "Louis C. Tiffany: Rebel in Glass," 1963, Crown, illustrated, 246 pp. **125.00**

Lagerberg, Ted & Vi, "Collectible Glass - #1," 1966, 207 color plates **28.00**

Lagerberg, Ted & Viola, "Collectible Glass - #3 - Emil J. Larson and Durand Glass," 1967, 234 color plates **39.00**

Larsen, Ellouise Baker, "American Historical Views on Staffordshire China," 1974 Dover reprint, black & white photos, soft cover, 345 pp. (cover slightly worn) **93.50**

Lee, Ruth Webb, "Antique Fakes and Reproductions," 1950, black & white photographs, hard cover, 317 pp.......**60.50**

Lee, Ruth Webb, & Rose, James, "American Glass Cup Plates," 1948, black & white photos, hard cover, 445 pp. **55.00**

Lichten, Frances, "Folk Art of Rural Pennsylvania," 1964, Charles Scribner, 276 pp. **104.50**

Little, Nina F., "Little by Little," original box **181.50**

Lockwood, Luke Vincent, "Colonial Furniture in America ," 1901, Scribner's first edition, 641 pp. (binding worn) **225.00**

McClinton, Katharine M., "Collecting

American 19th Century Silver," 1968, Scribner, illustrated, 280 pp. **27.00**

McClinton, Katharine M., "Collecting American Glass," 1950, Gramercy Press, illustrated, hard covers, 64 pp. **16.50**

McKearin, George and Helen "American Glass," 1942, third printing, black & white photographs, autographed by authors, w/dust jacket, hard cover, 634 pp. **143.00**

Miller, Robert W., "The Art Glass Basket," 1972, Wallace-Homestead, illustrated w/color plates, softbound, 32 pp. **30.00**

Montgomery, Charles, "American Furniture: The Federal period in the Henry Francis du Pont Winterthur Museum," 1966, Viking, illustrated, 497 pp. **159.50**

Munsey, Cecil, "The Illustrated Guide to the Collectibles of Coca-Cola," 1972, Hawthorn Books, illustrated, 333 pp. **50.00**

Nutting, Wallace, "Furniture Treasury," 1950, Macmillan, three volumes **82.50**

Pearson, J. Michael & Dorothy T., "American Cut Glass for the Discriminating Collector," 1965, Vantage Press, 2 volumes, 204 pp. **80.00**

Revi, Albert C., "American Art Nouveau Glass," 1968, Thomas Nelson, illustrated in black & white & color, 476 pp. **34.00**

Revi, Albert C., "American Pressed Glass and Figure Bottles," 1964, Thomas Nelson, illustrated, 446 pp. ...**55.00**

Rice, Alvin H. & Stoudt, John Baer, "The Shenandoah Pottery," 1929, Shenandoah Publishing, illustrated, 277 pp (minor cover wear) **192.50**

Robacker, Earl & Ada, "Spatterware and Sponge," 1978, 8¾ x 11¼" **165.00**

Savage, George, "18th Century English Porcelain," 1964, Spring Books, illustrated, hard cover w/dust jacket, 435 pp. **99.00**

Smith, Alan, "The Illustrated Guide to Liverpool Herculaneum Pottery, 1796-1840," 1970, Barrie & Jenkins, black & white & color illustrations, hard cover w/dust jacket, 142 pp. **93.50**

Time-Life Books, "Encyclopedia of Collectibles," illustrated, 16 volumes, the set **240.00**

Traub, Jules S., "The Glass of Desire Christian, Ghost for Gallé," 1978, The Art Glass Exchange, full-page color plates, 143 pp. **130.00**

CIVIL WAR RELATED

More books have been written about the Civil War era (1861-65) than any other period in the history of our country. The following listing includes books by and about those directly involved in the fighting, overall history of the conflict and the years following.

"Boy Spy of the Civil War," by Kerby **17.50**

"Corporal Si Klegg," 1888, by Hinman **47.50**

"Dan McCook's Regiment - 52nd O.V.I.," by Rev. Nixon Stewart, 1900, cloth covers (minor edge wear) **93.50**

"Photographic History of the Civil War," 1911, 50th Anniversary edition, blue bindings, 10 vols. **650.00**

"Spy of Rebellion," by Pinkerton, 688 pp. **57.50**

"Story of an American Sailor," 1888, by Brooks, 336 pp. (fair condition) **35.00**

PRESIDENTS & HISTORICAL FIGURES

The following listing includes a wide cross-section of books by and about former Presidents of the United States and other persons of note.

"Abraham Lincoln - The Prairie Years & The War Years," by Carl Sandburg, 1926, six volume set in binder (edge wear on binder) **82.50**

"The Life & Heroic Deeds of Admiral Dewey," by Louis S. Young, 1899 ....**110.00**

"Personal Memoirs of U.S. Grant," by U.S. Grant, 1885, first edition, 2 vols. **75.00**

"The Marvelous Career of Theodore Roosevelt & The Story of His African Trip," by John C. Winston Co., 1910, depicts Teddy in black & white oval photo on front cover, hard cover **95.00**

"The Strange Death of President Harding, Diaries of Gaston Mann," first edition **45.00**

STATE & LOCAL

CONNECTICUT

"History of Warebury & Naugatuck Valley, Connecticut," Volume II, 1918 ....**40.00**

ILLINOIS

"Mitchell's Illinois in 1837-38," Philadelphia, 1837, second printing, fold-out color map, rebound **250.00**

INDIANA

"History of Marshall County, Indiana," 1890................................**60.00**

IOWA

"Atlas of O'Brien County, Iowa," 1924 (inner hinges weak)...............**45.00**

MARYLAND

"Old Homes & History of Montgomery County," by Farquhar, autographed by author ...**35.00**

MASSACHUSETTS

"Guide to Historic Plymouth, Tercentenary Committee," 1921, 96 pp. **12.00**

"The Maritime History of Massachusetts 1783-1860," by Samuel Morison, 47 plate maps including Boston Harbour................**55.00**

NEW YORK

"Views of Albany," 1912, all photographs, including horse & buggy scenes, 24 pp..................................**22.00**

WASHINGTON

"Tacoma, Washington Land Co.," 1888, promotional book, illustrated, w/ads, hard cover, 72 pp.................................**65.00 to 75.00**

BOOTJACKS

Painted Wood Bootjack

Cast iron, figural "Naughty Nellie," 4½ x 9½"...**$88.00**
Cast iron, model of a Boxer dog........**825.00**
Cast iron, model of a cricket, scrolling detail, late 19th c., 11½" l.................**175.00**

Wooden, painted, a long narrow board painted black & decorated in red, yellow & green & inscribed "GUD," hanging hole at the end, Pennsylvania, 19th c., 20" l. (ILLUS.) **690.00**

BOTTLE OPENERS

Corkscrews were actually the first bottle openers and these may date back to the mid-18th century, but bottle openers as we know them today, are strictly a 20th century item and came into use only after Michael J. Owens invented the automatic bottle machine in 1903. Avid collectors have spurred this relatively new area of collector interest that requires only a modest investment. Our listing, by type of metal, encompasses the four basic types sought by collectors: advertising openers; full figure openers which stand alone or hang on the wall; flat figural openers such as the lady's leg shape; and openers with embossed, engraved or chased handles.

The numbers following figural openers are taken from Mike Jordan's book Figural Bottle Openers *(1981).*

Cast iron, full figure alligator w/head up & jaws open, polychrome paint, John Wright Co., 5" l. (J-125)...........**$80.00**
Cast iron, full figure drunk at lamp post, leg down, polychrome paint, Wilton Products, 4⅛" h. (J-3) **20.00**
Cast iron, full figure drunk at palm tree, bald-headed man leaning against tree, worn original polychrome paint, Wilton Products, 4" h. (J-16) **25.00**
Cast iron, full figure drunk at point sign post, leg out, polychrome paint, John Wright Co., 4⅜" h. (J-2) ....**50.00 to 60.00**
Cast iron, full figure drunk at sign post, worn polychrome paint, sign marked "1000 Islands," Wilton Products, 4" h. (J-5) **20.00**
Cast iron, full figure elephant, seated w/trunk curled back touching forehead, head tilted back, Wilton Products, polychrome paint, some wear, 3⅝" h. (J-88) **32.50**
Cast iron, full figure parrot (large), large notched crest & long tail on perch, John Wright Co., 3" h. (J-61) ....**50.00 to 70.00**
Cast iron, wall-mounted, bear's head, polychrome paint, John Wright Co. (J-165) ....**125.00 to 150.00**
Cast iron, wall-mounted, full figure

drunk (Hanging Drunk), poly-
chrome paint, Wilton Products
(J-156) ....**75.00 to 125.00**
Cast iron, wall-mounted, head of a
clown, polychrome paint w/polka dot
bow tie, John Wright Co. 4⅜" h.
(J-158) ....**100.00 to 150.00**
White metal, full figure swordfish,
good paint, John Wright Co.
(J-128) **35.00**

BOTTLES & FLASKS

BITTERS

*(Numbers with some listings below
refer to those used in Carlyn Ring's For
Bitters Only.)*

Begg's Dandelion Bitters

African Stomach Bitters, Spruance,
Stanley & Co., round, amber,
9⅝" h...**$60.00**
Allen's (William) Congress Bitters,
rectangular, emerald green, ¾ qt.,
10" h...**1,375.00**
Appetine Bitters (under) Geo. Benz
& Sons - St. Paul, Minn., w/"Pat.
Nov. 23, 1897" on base, square,
scrolls along sides of label panel,
reddish amber, 8¼" h.....................**522.50**
Atwood Quinine Tonic Bitters, rectangular, aqua, 8⁷⁄₁₆" h. **86.50**
Baker's Orange Grove - Bitters,
square w/roped corners, applied
mouth, smooth base, medium
amber, 9½" h. **165.00**
Baker's Orange Grove - Bitters,
square w/roped corners, applied
mouth, smooth base, golden yellow
amber, ca. 1865-70, 9½" h. **330.00**
Baker's Orange Grove - Bitters,
square w/roped corners, applied
mouth, smooth base, medium

gasoline puce, ca. 1865-70,
9½" h..**1,320.00**
Baker's Orange Grove - Bitters,
square w/roped corners, applied
mouth, smooth base, medium to
dark puce, 9½" h. **750.00**
Baker's Orange Grove - Bitters,
square w/roped corners, yellow
amber, ¾ qt...................................**302.50**
Baker's (E.) Premium Bitters, Rich-
mond, Va., oval, aqua, 6¾" h..........**187.00**
**Ball's (Dr.) Vegetable Stomachic
Bitters,** Northboro, Mass., rec-
tangular, aqua, 6⅞" h......................**220.00**
Barto's Great Gun Bitters, Reading,
Pa., cannon shape, golden
yellow amber 3½" d., 11" h. **6,380.00**
Bavarian, Hoffheimer Brothers, St.
Louis & Cincinnati, square, amber,
9¼" h...**275.00**
Beggs' Dandelion Bitters,
rectangular, lettering reads base to
shoulder, amber, 7¾" h.................**1,045.00**
Beggs' Dandelion Bitters,
rectangular, lettering reads base to
shoulder, medium amber, 7¾" h.
(ILLUS.) **330.00**
Bell's Cocktail, Jas. M. Bell & Co.,
New York, lady's leg shape, applied
mouth w/ring, amber, pt...**400.00 to 450.00**
Berliner Magen Bitters Co., square,
medium amber, 9" h..........................**49.50**
Bishop's (Dr.) - Wa-Hoo Bitters -
Wahoo Bitter Co. - New Haven
Conn, rectangular, smooth base,
applied mouth, medium yellowish
amber, 10½" h.................................**522.50**

Bismarck Bitters

Bismarck Bitters, W.H. Muller, New
York, U.S.A., rectangular, base
embossed "W.T. & Co., 2, U.S.A.,"
smooth base, tooled lip, medium
amber, 6⅛" h. (ILLUS.) **93.50**
Bourbon Whiskey Bitters, barrel-
shaped, deep strawberry puce,
9¼" h. ....**440.00 to 467.50**

Bourbon Whiskey Bitters, barrel-
shaped, ten-rib, puce, 9¼" h. 302.50
Bourbon Whiskey Bitters, barrel-
shaped, red puce, 9¼" h. 412.50
Brown's Celebrated Indian Herb
Bitters, Patented Feb. 11, 1868,
figural Indian Queen, amber,
12¼" h. 412.50
Brown's Celebrated Indian Herb
Bitters - Patented 1867, figural
Indian Queen, chocolate amber,
12¼" h. 605.00

Brown's Celebrated Herb Bitters

Brown's Celebrated Indian Herb
Bitters - Patented 1867, figural
Indian Queen, deep chocolate,
12¼" h.(ILLUS.) 1,072.00
Brown's Celebrated Indian Herb
Bitters - Patented 1867, figural
Indian Queen, yellow shading to
amber, 12¼" h. 880.00
Brown's Celebrated Indian Herb
Bitters - Patented Feb. 11, 1868,
figural Indian Queen, rolled lip,
smooth base, deep amber, ca.
1870-80, 12½" h. 687.50
Brown's Celebrated Indian Herb
Bitters, Patented 1868, figural
Indian Queen, lime green,
13½" h. 7,810.00
Bryant's Stomach Bitters, 8-sided
lady's leg shape, emerald green,
pontil, 12⅝" h. 5,170.00
Byrne (Professor Geo. J.) New York
- The Great Universal Compound
Stomach Bitters Patented 1870,
square, yellow w/green tone,
10½" h. 6,160.00
Caldwells Herb Bitters (below) The
Great Tonic, triangular, golden
yellow amber,12⅜" h. 330.00
California Fig Bitters, square,
amber, 2½" sq., 9¾" h. 50.00
California Wine Bitters, M. Keller,

Los Angeles, w/monogram "MK" in
shield, round, light to medium apple
green, 12¼" h. 12,870.00
Canton (star) Bitters, round w/lady's
leg neck, medium yellowish amber,
12½" h..203.50
Cassin,s - Grape Brandy - Bitters,
viola-shaped, applied mouth, brilliant
yellowish green, 10" h. 20,200.00
Clarke's Sherry Wine Bitters,
Rockland, ME, rectangular, aqua,
2½ x 3½", 9⅝" h. 125.00

Mrs. E. Emma Cobb's Bitters

Cobb's (Mrs. E. Emma) - Dr. Cobb's
Compound - Herbal Bitters,
square, smooth base, tooled lip,
amber, 8¼" h. (ILLUS.) 302.50
Coleman's (Dr. A.W.) Anti
Dyspeptic and Tonic Bitters,
rectangular, applied mouth, iron
pontil, deep yellowish green,
9¼" h..3,080.00
Congress Bitters (on two sides),
rectangular, applied mouth, smooth
base, aqua, 10¼" h..........................302.50
Constitution Bitters - A.M.S.2 1864
(on two sides) - Seward & Bentley,
Buffalo, NY., rectangular, medium
amber, 9½" h. 467.50
Constitution Bitters - A.M.S.2 1864
(on two sides) - Seward & Bentley,
Buffalo, NY., rectangular, amber,
9½" h...1,210.00
Doyle's - Hop - Bitters - 1872 (on
shoulders), square, yellowish olive,
9⅝" h..632.50
Drakes Plantation Bitters - Patented
1862, cabin-shaped, six-log,
arabesque variant, amber, 10" h.
(D-102)...225.00
Drakes Plantation Bitters - Patented
1862, cabin-shaped, six-log,
arabesque variant, olive yellow,
10" h. (D-102) 797.00
Drakes Plantation Bitters - Patented

1862, cabin-shaped, five-log, golden amber, 10" h. (D-109) **253.00**

Drakes Plantation Bitters - Patented 1862, cabin-shaped, five-log, root beer amber, 10" h. (D-109) **198.00**

Drake's (S T) 1860 Plantation Bitters - Patented 1862, no "X," cabin-shaped, four-log, yellowish amber, 10¼" h. (D-110) **88.00**

Drake's (S T) 1860 Plantation Bitters - Patented 1862, no "X," cabin-shaped, four-log, yellow w/olive green tones, 10¼" h. (D-110)......................................**3,630.00**

Drake's (S T) 1860 X Plantation Bitters - Patented 1862, cabin-shaped, four-log, yellowish amber, 10¼" h. (D-110) **150.00**

Drake's (S T) 1860 Plantation Bitters - Patented 1862, no "X," cabin-shaped, six-log, medium copper puce, 10" h. (D-103)............**302.50**

Drake's (S T) 1860 Plantation X Bitters - Patented 1862, cabin-shaped, six-log, amber, 10" h. (D-105)...**60.00**

Drake's (S T) 1860 Plantation X Bitters - Patented 1862, cabin-shaped, six-log, deep burgundy puce,10" h. (D-105).......................**577.50**

Drake's (S T) 1860 Plantation X Bitters - Patented 1862, cabin-shaped, six-log, deep reddish puce, 10" h. (D-105) ....**150.00 to 170.00**

Drake's (S T) 1860 Plantation X Bitters - Patented 1862, cabin-shaped, six-log, deep yellowish olive, 10" h. (D-105) **1,100.00**

Drake's (S T) 1860 Plantation X Bitters - Patented 1862, cabin-shaped, six-log, light to medium golden yellow, 10" h. (D-105)...........**346.50**

Drake's (S T) 1860 Plantation X Bitters - Patented 1862, cabin-

Drake's Plantation Bitters

shaped, six-log, medium emerald green, 10" h. (D-105) **7,370.00**

Drake's (S T) 1860 Plantation X Bitters - Patented 1862, cabin-shaped, six-log, medium yellowish topaz, 10" h. (D-105)......................**577.50**

Drake's (S T) 1860 Plantation X Bitters - Patented 1862, cabin-shaped, six-log, reddish puce, 10" h., D-105 (ILLUS. bottom previous column) **148.50**

Drake's (S T) 1860 Plantation X Bitters - Patented 1862, cabin-shaped, six-log, topaz puce, 10" h. (D-105) **440.00**

Drake's (S T) 1860 Plantation X Bitters - Patented 1862, cabin-shaped, six-log, yellowish amber, 10" h. (D-105) **198.00**

Drake's (S T) 1860 Plantation X Bitters - Patented 1862, cabin-shaped, six-log, dense amber, 10" h. (D-108) **220.00**

Drake's (S T) 1860 Plantation X Bitters - Patented 1862, cabin-shaped, six-log, light to medium pinkish puce, 10" h. (D-108) **2,860.00**

Drake's (S T) 1860 Plantation X Bitters - Patented 1862, cabin-shaped, six-log, olive yellow, 10" h. (D-108) **935.00**

Drake's (S T) 1860 Plantation X Bitters - Patented 1862, square, cabin-shaped, six-log, greyish moss green, 10" h. (D-106) **11,000.00**

Drake's (S T) 1860 Plantation X Bitters - Patented 1862, square, cabin-shaped, six-log, light to medium yellowish lime green, 10" h. (D-106) **6,710.00**

Drake's (S T) 1860 Plantation X Bitters - Patented 1862, square, cabin-shaped, six-log, medium green w/yellow tone, 10" h. (D-106)......................................**6,600.00**

Drake's (S T) 1860 Plantation X Bitters - Patented 1862, square, cabin-shaped, six-log, strawberry puce, 10" h. (D-106)......................**137.70**

Eastman's (Dr. E.P.) Yellow Dock, Lynn, Mass., rectangular w/wide beveled corners, aqua, pt. **770.00**

Excelsior Herb Bitters, Washington, N.J., H.V. Mattison, rectangular, medium amber, 10⅛" h.................**715.00**

Fischs (Doctor) Bitters - W.H. Ware, Patent 1866, figural fish, light yellow amber, 11¾" h. **440.00**

Fish (The) Bitters - W.H. Ware, Patented 1866, figural fish, reddish amber, 11½" h. **165.00**

Fish (The) Bitters - W.H. Ware, Patented 1866, figural fish, lime green, 11⅜" h. **4,440.00**

Fish (The) Bitters - W.H. Ware, Patented 1866, figural fish, yellowish olive green, 11⅜" h. **2,200.00**

Fleschhut's (Dr.) Celebrated Stomach, La Porte, Pa., square, aqua, ¾ qt. **330.00**

Frank's (Sol) - Panacea Bitters - Frank Hayman & Rhine - Sole Proprietors - New York, lighthouse shape, medium amber, 10¼" h. **1,485.00**

Garnett's Compound Vegetable Bitters, Richmond, VA., oval, amber, 6½" h. **467.50**

Gates (C.) & Cos. - Life of Man - Bitters, "C. Gates Son & Company, MIddleton, Annapolis County, Nova Scotia" on paper labels, rectangular, aqua, 8" h...**65.00**

German Hop Bitters

German Hop - Bitters - Dr. C.D. Warner - Reading, Mich., (also on base) Warner - 1880 - Warner - 1880, square, medium amber, 10" h. (ILLUS.) **253.00**

Gilbert's - Sarsaparilla - Bitters - N.A. Gilbert & Co. - Enosburgh Falls, VT., octagonal, medium yellowish amber, 8¾" h. **495.00**

Globe Bitters

Globe Bitters, Manufactured only by - Byrne Bros & Co., New York (also on shoulder) Globe Bitters - Byrne Bros. & Co., New York, round, amber, ground wear, overall stain & small flake on lip, 11" h. (ILLUS. bottom previous column) **315.50**

Goodins (Dr.) Comp Gentian Bitters, square w/three vertical ribs on each side, applied smooth base, aqua, 9⅝" h. **2,750.00**

Golden Bitters, Geo. C. Hubbel & Co., rectangular w/roofed shoulders, aqua, 10⅜" h...................................**440.00**

Greeley's Bourbon Bitters, barrel-shaped, ten rings above & below center band, copper, 9⅜" h...............**198.00**

Greeley's Bourbon Bitters, barrel-shaped, ten rings above & below center band, medium greyish olive green, 9⅜" h. **1,100.00**

Greeley's Bourbon Bitters, barrel-shaped, ten rings above & below center band, medium plum puce, 9⅜" h..**440.00**

Greeley's Bourbon Bitters, barrel-shaped, ten rings above & below center band, smoky topaz w/olive tone, 9⅛" h................................**632.50**

Hall's Bitters - E.E. Hall New Haven, Established 1842, barrel-shaped, ten-rib, medium yellowish amber, 9⅛" h..**385.00**

Hall's Bitters - E.E. Hall, New Haven, Established 1842, barrel-shaped, ten-rib, olive yellow, 9⅛" h. **357.50**

Hardy (Dr. Manly) Genuine Jaundice Bitters, Bangor, Me., rectangular, aqua, 7" h....................**198.00**

Harter's (Dr.) Wild Cherry Bitters, St. Louis - Design Patented, rectangular, amber, 4½" h. **30.00**

Hart's Star Bitters

Hart's Star Bitters - (circle enclosing) O.B.L.P.C. & a five-pointed star (enclosing) 1868 - Philadelphia - Pa., oval, aqua, 9¼" h. (ILLUS.) **275.00**

**Henley's (Dr.) Wild Grape Root IXL
Bitters,** celery green, 12½" h. **1,017.00**
**Henley's (Dr.) Wild Grape Root IXL
Bitters,** yellowish olive green,
12½" h. **1,760.00**
Herb (H.P.) Wild Cherry Bitters,
Reading, Pa., cabin-shaped, square
w/cherry tree motif & roped corners,
amber, 8⅞" h. **242.00**
Herb (H.P.) Wild Cherry Bitters,
Reading, Pa., square, cabin-shaped
w/cherry tree motif & roped corners,
emerald green, 10" h. **3,410.00**
Herb (H.P.) Wild Cherry Bitters,
Reading, Pa., square, cabin-shaped
w/cherry tree motif & roped corners,
yellowish amber, 10" h. **797.50**
Hi-Hi Bitters, Hi-Hi Bitters Co., Rock
Island, Ill., triangular, yellowish
green, 9⅜" h. **253.00**
Hoffeld's (A.) - Liver Bitters -
Louisville Chemical - Manufacturing
Co. - Louisville KY, square, medium
amber, 9¾" h. **632.50**
Holtzermann's Stomach Bitters,
cabin-shaped w/four roofs, sample
size, w/paper label, amber,
4" h...**1,150.00**

Holtzermann's Bitters

**Holtzermann's - Patent Stomach
Bitters,** cabin-shaped, stylized logs,
medium amber, 9¼" h. (ILLUS.) ...**1,430.00**
**Holtzermans Patent Stomach
Bitters** (on shoulders), cabin-
shaped w/four roofs, w/paper label,
amber, 9⅝" h. (ILLUS. top next
column) **357.50**
**Holtzermans Patent Stomach
Bitters** (on shoulders), cabin-
shaped w/four roofs, w/paper label,
reddish amber, 9⅝" h. **209.00**
Hoofland's (Dr.) German Bitters -
Liver Complaint - C.M. Jackson,
Philadelphia - Dyspepsia & C.,

Holtzermans with Paper Label

rectangular, aqua, w/paper label,
8" h. **70.00**
**Horse Shoe Bitters - Horse Shoe
Medicine Co.** (embossed motif of
running horse) - Collinsville, Ills.,
horseshoe-shape, amber,
8⅝" h. **2,750.00**
**Hostetter's (Dr. J.) Stomach Bitters
- 18 Fluid Oz.,** square, amber,
8¾" h. (H-197) **15.00**
Hostetter's (Dr. J.) Stomach Bitters,
square, w/paper label reading
"Hostetter's Celebrated Stomach
Bitters," amber, 9" h.(H-195)..............**40.00**

Hostetter's Stomach Bitters

Hostetter's (Dr. J.) Stomach Bitters,
square, deep olive green, 9" h.,
H-195 (ILLUS.)................................**121.00**
Hostetter's (Dr. J.) Stomach Bitters,
square, dark olive amber, 9½" h.
(H-194)...**143.00**
Hostetter's (Dr. J.) Stomach Bitters,
square, dark olive green, 8¾" h.
(H-199)...**121.00**
Hostetter's (Dr. J.) Stomach Bitters,
square, yellow w/olive tone, 8¾" h.
(H-199)...**121.00**

Hostetter's (Dr. J.) Stomachic Bitters, square, amber, 8¾" h. (H-198)..**495.00**
Indian Vegetable & Sarsaparilla - Bitters - Geo. C. Goodwin - Boston, rectangular, pontil, aqua, 8⅜" h. **231.00**
Jackson's (Dr. H.A.) Bitters, rectangular, aqua, ca. 1845-55, 7½" h. **412.50**
Johnson's Calisaya Bitters - Burlington, Vt., square, collared mouth w/ring, deep reddish copper puce, ca. 1870-80, 10" h. **385.00**
Johnson's Indian Dyspeptic Bitters, rectangular, aqua, ca. 1845-55, 6⅝" h...**385.00**

Kelly's Old Cabin Bitters

Kelly's Old Cabin Bitters - Patented 1863, cabin-shaped, medium amber, 9⅝" h. (ILLUS.) ....**1,650.00 to 1,850.00**
Keystone Bitters, barrel-shaped, amber, ¾ qt., 9¾" h. **577.00**
Kimball's Jaundice - Bitters - Troy, N.H., rectangular, yellowish olive amber, ca. 1850-60, 7" h. **412.50**

Lediard's Stomach Bitters

Lediard's Celebrated Stomach Bitters, square, medium to deep

emerald green, ca. 1855-65, 9½" h. (ILLUS.) **2,090.00**
Litthauer Stomach Bitters (paper label), Hartwig Kantorowicz, Posen, Ham - burg, Paris, square case gin-shape, milk white, miniature, 3¾" h...**121.00**
Litthauer Stomach Bitters - Hartwig Kantorowicz - Posen Wronkerstr No. 6 - embossed fish inside Star of David, square case gin shape, deep amber, ca. 1870-90, 10" h. **99.00**
Loew's (Dr.) Celebrated Stomach Bitters & Nerve Tonic - The Loew & Sons Co., Cleveland, O., square, light to medium yellowish or apple green, ca. 1890-1910, 9¼" h. **220.00**
Loftus Peach Bitters, cylindrical w/lady's leg shaped neck, green w/yellow tone, ca. 1880-1900, 11½" h..**176.00**
Loveridges - Wahoo - Bitters - Buffalo, NY, flask-shaped, medium yellowish olive, ca. 1860-70, 7" h.....**330.00**
Lowell's Invigorating Bitters - Boston, Mass., square, ca. 1870-80, 8⅛" h...............................**77.00**
Lowerre & Lyon's (Drs.) - Restorative Bitters, rectangular, ca. 1845-55, aqua, 8¾" h.................**797.00**
Lyford's (Dr.) Bitters, C.P. Herrick, Tilton, N.H., oval, aqua, 8½" h. **110.00**

Moffat Phoenix Bitters

Moffat (Jno.) - Price $1 - Phoenix Bitters - New York, rectangular w/wide beveled corners, pontil scarred base, applied mouth, yellowish olive green, 5½" h. (ILLUS.) **495.00**
Morning (Star) Inceptum 5869 Bitters - Patented 5869, triangular, amber, 12⅞" h. (ILLUS. top next page)..**220.00**
National Bitters - Patent 1867, figural ear of corn, medium amber, 12⅝" h..**330.00**

Morning (Star) Bitters

National Bitters - Patent 1867, figural
ear of corn, medium pinkish
strawberry puce, 12⅝" h. **1,540.00**
**Niagara Star Bitters (John W.
Steele's),** John W. Steele's Niagara
Bitters, square w/roofed shoulders,
three stars on roof & 1864, collared
mouth w/ring, amber, 10" h. **632.50**

Old Continental Bitters

Old Continental - Bitters, rectangular w/roofed shoulders, light to
medium yellowish amber, 9⅞" h.
(ILLUS.) **253.00**
Old Homestead Wild Cherry Bitters
- Patent (on shoulders), cabin-
shaped w/shingles, medium
strawberry puce, 9⅞" h. **1,045.00**
**Old Sachem Bitters and Wigwam
Tonic,** barrel-shaped, ten-rib,
medium amber, ca. 1860-70,
9½" h..**357.50**
Oswego Bitters, (star) 25¢ (star),
oval, medium amber, 7" h. **82.50**
Owen's (Dr.) European Life Bitters,
Detroit, aqua, 7" h. **165.00**

**Petzold's (Dr.) Genuine German
Bitters,** Incpt. 1862, embossed
"Pat'd 1884" on shoulder, oval,
figural beehive, 17 ribs, yellowish
amber, 7⅞" h. **275.00**
(Pineapple), Patd October 1st 1870
by A.L. Lacraix, pineapple-shaped,
aqua, 8⅞" h..................................**1,870.00**
(Pineapple), C. & Co., N.Y., pineapple-shaped, medium yellowish
amber, 8⅞" h. **121.00**
Reed's Bitters, cylindrical, lady's leg
neck, smooth base, applied mouth,
amber, 12½" h. **275.00**
**Roback's (Dr. C.W.) Stomach
Bitters,** Cincinnati, O, barrel-
shaped, golden yellow w/olive tone
barrel, 9⅜" h. **231.00**
**Roback's (Dr. C.W.) Stomach
Bitters,** Cincinnati, O, barrel-
shaped, medium amber, 9⅜" h. **159.50**
**Roback's (Dr. C.W.) Stomach
Bitters,** Cincinnati, O, barrel-
shaped, yellowish amber, 9⅜" h. **198.00**
**Roback's (Dr. C.W.) Stomach
Bitters,** Cincinnati, O, barrel-
shaped, amber, 10" h.....................**187.00**
**Roback's (Dr. C.W.) Stomach
Bitters,** Cincinnati, O, barrel-
shaped, medium olive green,
10" h...**5,720.00**
**Roback's (Dr. C.W.) Stomach
Bitters,** Cincinnati, O, barrel-
shaped, medium yellowish amber,
10" h...**495.00**
Rocky Mountain - Tonic Bitters -
1840 Try Me 1870, square,
yellowish amber, 9⅞" h. **165.00**
Romaines' - Crimean - Bitters -
Patend (sic) 1863 - W. Chilton &
Co., square, applied mouth, smooth
base, medium yellowish amber,
ca. 1860-70, 9⅜" h. **357.50**
Schroeder's Bitters Louisville and
Cincinnati - Established 1845, lady's

Dr. Soule Hop Bitters

leg neck, tooled lip, smooth base,
amber, 5³⁄₁₆" h. **330.00**
**Skinner's (Dr.) Celebrated 25 Cent
Bitters,** So. Reading, Mass.,
rectangular, 8½" h............................**121.00**
Soule (Dr.) - Hop - Bitters - 1872
(embossed on shoulders), hop
flowers & leaf motif one side (same
side has "1872" on shoulder),
square, dark amber, 9¾" h.
(ILLUS. bottom previous page) **82.50**
Soule (Dr.) - Hop - Bitters - 1872
(embossed on shoulders), hop
flowers & leaf motif one side (same
side has "1872" on shoulder),
square, light golden amber,
7¾" h. **148.50**
Soule (Dr.) - Hop - Bitters - 1872
(embossed on shoulders), hop
flowers & leaf motif one side (same
side has "1872" on shoulder),
square, deep root beer amber,
9¾" h. **99.00**
Steinfield's French Cognac Bitters,
First Prize, Paris Exhibition, square,
applied mouth, smooth base, yellow
w/olive tone, 9⅞" h......................**3,410.00**

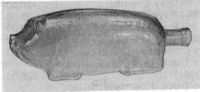

Suffolk Bitters

Suffolk Bitters - Philbrook & Tucker,
Boston, model of a pig, whittled,
yellowish amber, 10⅛" l. (ILLUS.)....**715.00**

Sunny Castle Stomach Bitters

Sunny Castle Stomach Bitters, Jos.
Dudenhoefer, Milwaukee, square,
amber, w/label, some spotting
outside on two panels, 9" h.
(ILLUS.) **71.50**

Swain's (C.H.) Bourbon Bitters,
square, medium yellowish olive,
2⅝" w., 9" h.......................................**275.00**
Tyree's (W.R.) Chamomile Bitters -
1 - 0 - 8 - 8, square w/semi-cabin
shaped shoulder, medium amber,
9½" h...**577.50**
Wahoo & Calisaya Bitters - Jacob
Pinkerton - Jacob Pinkerton, square,
puce w/amber tints, 9⅝" h. **467.50**
Wahoo & Calisaya Bitters - Jacob
Pinkerton - Jacob Pinkerton, square,
yellowish amber, 9⅝" h....................**495.00**
Walker's Tonic Bitters, round, lady's
leg neck, medium yellowish amber,
11½" h..**467.50**
Warner's Safe Bitters, embossed
safe & Trade Mark, Rochester N.Y.,
oval, smooth base, applied mouth,
amber, 7½" h. **522.50**
Whitwell's Temperance Bitters,
Boston, rectangular, pontil, aqua,
7¾" h...**143.00**
Wilder's (Edw.) Stomach Bitters -
five story house design - Edw.
Wilder & Co., Wholesale Druggists,
Louisville, KY, building shape
w/hobnailed corners, clear,
10½" h..**187.00**
**Wood's (Dr.) Sarsaparilla & Wild
Cherry Bitters,** rectangular, pontil
aqua, 9" h..**264.00**

CONTEMPORARY

Ezra Brooks

Kachina Doll

American Legion Salute....................**50.00**
Badger Boxer **9.00**
Big Bertha **9.00**
Buffalo Hunt **9.00**
Canadian Loon..................................**27.50**
Clown, Shriner **9.50**
Dakota Cowboy.................................**43.50**
Fire Engine OMB, 1974......................**40.00**
F.O.E. Eagle, 1979.............................**17.50**

Gold Miner..9.00
Indianapolis 500 Pace Car
  1980 Pace Car (Pontiac) 33.00
Jack of Diamonds...............................9.00
Kachina Doll No. 1, 1972 (ILLUS.)......95.00
Kachina Doll No. 3 (1974)..................68.50
Kachina Doll No. 8 ....55.00
Moose...34.00
Old Ez, Scops Owl, No. 4 (1980)........16.00
Phoenix Bird 27.00
Shrine Fez (1976) 9.00
South Carolina Fighting
  Game Cock 10.00
Tennis Player 9.00
V.F.W.Decanter, No. 185, cobalt
  blue, red, white & gold 75.00
Washington Salmon 27.00
Whopping Crane 17.50
Zimmerman Old Hat 9.00

Jim Beam

Ambulance, 1931 Ford......................45.00

Antique Trader

Antique Trader, 1968 (ILLUS.)............21.00
Bobby Unser Racing Car, Olsonite
  Eagle (1975) 39.00
Boys' Town (1973) 11.50

Female Cardinal

Cardinal, female, 1973 (ILLUS.
  bottom previous column) 18.50
Cathedral Radio (1979)......................22.50
Churchill Downs Kentucky Derby
  1969 95th Pink Roses.......................35.00
Circus Wagon (1979) 24.00
Conventions
  1971 No. 1 Denver...........................14.50
  1974 No. 4 Lancaster 89.00
  1981 No. 11 Las Vegas 26.50
  1982 No. 12 New Orleans 42.50
Corvette (1984)
  red 59.00
  black...82.00
Dining Car (1982) 69.00
Donkey & Elephant Politicals
  1956 Ashtrays, pr. 29.00
  1964 Boxers, pr. 61.00
Ducks Unlimited
  1979 Canvasback Drake (No. 5).....35.00
  1985 Pintail (No. 11) 35.00
  1990 Swan 50.00
Duesenberg Model J., light blue
  (1981) 95.00
Emmett Kelly (1973) 45.00
Executives
  1955 Royal Porcelain.....................287.50
  1958 Grey Cherub 169.00
  1964 Royal Gold Diamond 39.00
  1967 Prestige..................................20.00
Figaro (1977) 109.00
Fire Chief's Car (1981)......................66.00
Fire Truck, 1917 Mack Pumper
  (1982) 125.00
Fire Truck, 1930 Model "A" Ford
  (1983) 129.00
Harolds Club
  1957 Man in Barrel No. 1 ....385.00
  1965 Pinwheel 55.00
  1973 VIP 20.00
Hula Bowl (1975)...............................11.00
Idaho (1963).....................................40.00
King Kamehameha (1972)..................45.00
King Kong (1976) 15.00
Locomotive
  Grant (1979) 62.00
Magpies (1977) 11.50
Model A Ford, 1903, red & black
  (1978) 30.00
Model A Ford, 1928, Pheaton
  (1980) 45.00
Model T Ford, green & black (1974)....29.00
National Fresh Water Fishing Hall
of Fame
  1974 Bluegill 45.00
  1975 Rainbow Trout.........................45.00
  1981 Catfish....................................20.00
New Zealand Kiwi Bird (1974)............45.00
Oldsmobile, 1904, (1972)...................45.00
Police Car, 1929 Model A Ford
  Pheaton (1982) 75.00
Preakness Pimlico.............................22.00
Sigma Nu Fraternity, Kentucky
  (1977) 12.00

Stingray, red or silver (Corvette) **59.00**
Stone Mountain (1974) **15.00**
Stutz Bearcat (1977) **35.00**
Tank Car (1983) (J.B. Turner RR) **29.00**
Telephone Pioneers
   1975 1907 Wall Telephone
   (No. 1) **125.00**

Tombstone Arizona

Tombstone, Arizona, 1970 (ILLUS.).....**7.00**
Turtle (1975) **45.00**
Volkswagen (1973), red or blue,
   each **52.00**
West Virginia (1963) **72.00**
Woodie 1929 Station Wagon (1983) ..**49.00**
Zimmerman
   1965 Two-Handled Jug...................**62.00**

FIGURALS

Bust of three people, two men & one
   woman, atop of waisted paneled
   column, probably Europe, ca. 1880-
   1910, milk white cased in clear,
   13½" h..**200.00**
Monument, applied collared mouth,
   clear w/amethyst tint, 11¾" h.........**110.00**
Negro waiter, frosted, clear glass
   body & frosted black, smooth base,
   ground lip, 14¼" h........................**1,430.00**
Pistol, ground lip w/metal screw on
   cap, smooth base, medium sapphire
   blue, 7½" l **412.50**

FLASKS

   Flasks are listed according to the
numbers provided in American Bottles &
Flasks and Their Ancestry *by Helen*
McKearin and Kenneth M. Wilson.

GI-1 - Washington bust below
   "General Washington" - American
   Eagle below nine stars & standing
   on oval frame w/inner band of 18
   pearls, horizontal beading w/vertical
   medial rib, plain lip, pontil, aqua,
   pt..**302.50**

GI-2 - Washington bust below
   "General Washington" - American
   Eagle w/shield w/seven bars on
   breast, head turned to right, edges
   w/horizontal beading w/vertical
   medial rib, plain lip, pontil, light
   green, pt. ....**200.00 to 225.00**
GI-3 - Washington bust below
   "General Washington," no epaulets
   on uniform - American Eagle
   w/shield w/seven bars on breast,
   head turned to right, resting on oval
   frame w/olive branches on either
   side, edges w/horizontal beading
   w/vertical medial rib, plain lip,
   pontil, aqua, pt. (minor interior
   stains) **330.00**
GI-6a - Washington bust below
   "General Washington" - American
   Eagle w/shield w/seven bars on
   breast, head turned to right, resting
   on oval frame w/ "J.R.," & olive
   branches on either side of oval,
   horizontal beading w/vertical medial
   rib, plain lip, pontil, clear, pt. **1,100.00**
GI-18 - "Washington" above bust -
   "Baltimore Glass Works." in
   semicircle around Battle Monument,
   Baltimore, three vertically ribbed
   edges w/heavy medial rib, plain lip,
   pontil, aqua, pt. **110.00**
GI-20 - Washington bust (facing right)
   below "Fells," "Point" below bust -
   Baltimore Monument w/ "Balto"
   below, plain lip, vertical medial rib,
   pontil, aqua, pt. **143.00**
GI-20 - Washington bust (facing right)
   below "Fells," "Point" below bust -
   Baltimore Monument w/"Balto"
   below, plain lip, vertical medial rib,
   pontil, light puce, pt. **1,045.00**
GI-21 - Washington bust (facing right)
   below "Fells," "Point" below bust -
   Baltimore Monument w/"Balto"
   below, plain lip, vertical medial rib,
   pontil, aqua, qt. **275.00**
GI-31 - "Washington" above bust -
   "Jackson" above bust, plain lip, open
   pontil, amber, pt., 7" h.....................**132.00**
GI-32 - "Washington" above bust,
   uniform without bars on lapel -
   "Jackson" above bust, plain lip,
   pontil, medium yellow olive, pt. **154.00**
GI-34 - "Washington" above bust
   (facing right) - "Jackson" above bust,
   plain lip, vertically ribbed edges
   w/heavy medial rib, pontil, olive
   green, ½ pt.......................................**165.00**
GI-35 - "Washington" bust (facing
   right), not in oval panel - Large tree
   in foliage w/nine buds, plain lip,
   aqua, qt. **71.50**
GI-37 - Washington bust below "The

Father of His Country" - Taylor bust, "Gen. Taylor Never Surrenders, Dyottville Glass Works, Philad.a," plain lip, smooth edges, pontil, medium brownish amber, qt., 8⅛" h. **907.50**

GI-37 - Washington bust below "The Father of His Country" - Taylor bust, "Gen. Taylor Never Surrenders, Dyottville Glass Works, Philad.a," plain lip, smooth edges, pontil, medium pinkish amethyst, qt., 8⅛" h. **2,970.00**

GI-38 - Washington bust below "The Father of His Country" - Taylor bust, "Gen. Taylor Never Surrenders, Dyottville Glass Works, Philad.a," plain lip, smooth edges, pontil, aqua, pt. **346.50**

GI-39 - Washington bust below "The Father of His Country" - Taylor bust, "Gen. Taylor Never Surrenders," plain lip, smooth edges, pontil, deep amethyst, pink, qt. **1,210.00**

GI-40a - Washington bust below "The Father of His Country" - Taylor bust, "Gen Taylor Never Surrenders," smooth edges, sheared lip, pontil, cobalt blue, pt. (small chip & bruise on base, flake on mouth) **1,980.00**

GI-40a - Washington bust below "The Father of His Country" - Taylor bust, "Gen Taylor Never Surrenders," smooth edges, sheared lip, pontil mark, deep yellowish olive, pt. **412.50**

GI-40c - Washington bust below "The Father of His Country" - Taylor bust, "Gen Taylor Never Surrenders" & arc of 28 tiny beads below bust, smooth edges, sheared lip, pontil, medium emerald green, pt. (light inside stain) **302.50**

GI-41 - Washington bust below "The Father of His Country" - Taylor bust "Gen. Taylor Never Surrenders," plain lip, smooth edges, pontil, deep olive green, ½ pt. **4,290.00**

GI-42 - Washington bust below "The Father of His Country" - Taylor bust, "A Little More Grape Captain Bragg, Dyottville Glass Works, Philad.a," smooth edges, plain lip, pontil, aqua, qt. **98.00**

GI-42 - Washington bust below "The Father of His Country" - Taylor bust, "A Little More Grape Captain Bragg, Dyottville Glass Works, Philad.a," smooth edges, plain lip, pontil, medium emerald green, qt. **260.00**

GI-43 - Washington bust below "The Father of His Country" - Taylor bust below "I Have Endeavour'd To Do My Duty," plain lip, smooth edges,

pontil, dark green, qt. (lip w/tiny flakes) **1,210.00**

GI -54 - Washington bust without queue - Taylor bust in uniform, open pontil, bluish green, qt., 8¾" h. **286.50**

GI -54 - Washington bust without queue - Taylor bust in uniform, open pontil, deep aqua, qt., 8¾" h. **192.50**

GI -54 - Washington bust without queue - Taylor bust in uniform, open pontil, dark reddish puce, qt., 8¾" h. **1,760.00**

GI -54 - Washington bust without queue - Taylor bust in uniform, open pontil, light green, qt., 8¾" h. **250.00**

GI -54 - Washington bust without queue - Taylor bust in uniform, open pontil, yellow w/olive tone, qt., 8¾" h. **495.00**

GI-65 - "General Jackson" surrounding bust - American Eagle w/shield on oval frame, "J.T. & Co." below oval frame, thirteen small five-pointed stars above eagle, horizontal beading w/vertical medial rib, plain lip, pontil mark, pale green, pt. ..**71.50**

GI-67 - "General Jackson" surrounding bust - American Eagle w/shield on oval frame, "J.T. & Co." below oval frame, eight six-pointed stars & one five-pointed star above eagle, horizontal beading w/vertical medial rib, plain lip, pontil mark, brilliant aqua, pt. **2,805.00**

GI-71 - Taylor bust, facing left, w/ "Rough and Ready" below - Ringgold bust, facing left w/"Major" in semicircle above bust & "Ringgold" in semicircle beneath bust, heavy vertical ribbing, plain lip, pontil mark, aqua, pt. **132.00**

GI-71 - Taylor bust, facing left, w/ "Rough and Ready" below - Ringgold bust, facing left w/"Major" in semicircle above bust & "Ringgold" in semicircle beneath bust, heavy vertical ribbing, plain lip, pontil mark, pale amethyst, pt. **907.50**

GI-73 - Taylor bust, facing left, w/ "Genl Taylor" above - Washington Monument without statue "Fells Point" in semicircle above & "Balto" below, vertically ribbed edges w/heavy medial rib, plain lip, pontil, aqua, pt. **132.00**

GI-73 - Taylor bust, facing left, w/ "Genl Taylor" above - Washington Monument without statue "Fells Point" in semicircle above & "Balto" below, vertically ribbed edges w/heavy medial rib, plain lip, pontil, light greyish green, pt. **715.00**

GI-74 - Taylor bust, facing right, w/ "Zachary Taylor" above & "Rough & Ready" below - "Corn For The World" above cornstalk, plain lip, vertically ribbed w/heavy medial rib, pontil mark, aqua, pt. **330.00**

GI-75 - Taylor bust, facing right, w/ "Zachary Taylor" above & "Rough & Ready" below - "Corn For The World" above cornstalk, plain lip, smooth edges, pontil mark, olive green, pt. **5,115.00**

GI-77 - Taylor bust below "Rough & Ready" - American Eagle w/shield w/eight vertical & three horizontal bars on breast, head turned left, "Masterson" above 15 five-pointed stars above eagle, horizontally corrugated w/vertical medial rib, plain lip, open pontil, aqua, qt. **990.00**

GI-81 - "Lafayette" above bust & "S & C" below - "DeWitt Clinton" above bust & "C-T" below, plain lip, pontil mark, brilliant yellowish olive green, ½ pt. **632.50**

GI-84 - "Lafayette" above bust & "T.S." & bar below - Masonic arch, pillar & pavement w/Masonic emblem inside the arch, horizontal corrugated edges, horizontal rib at base, plain lip, pontil mark, olive, green ½ pt. **1,870.00**

Lafayette Flask

GI-85 - "Lafayette" above bust & "Covetry (sic) - C-T" below - French liberty cap on pole & semicircle of eleven five-pointed stars above, "S & S" below, fine vertical ribbing, two horizontal ribs at base, plain lip, pontil mark, deep yellowish amber, pt. (ILLUS.) **330.00**

GI-86 - "Lafayette" above bust & "Coventry - C-T" below - French liberty cap on pole & semicircle of eleven five-pointed stars above,

"S & S" below, fine vertical ribbing, two horizontal ribs at base, plain lip, pontil mark, olive amber, ½ pt. ....**550.00 to 575.00**

GI-87 - "Lafayette" above bust & "Coventry - C-T" below - French liberty cap on pole above "S & S" below, three vertical ribs close together, plain lip, pontil mark, olive green, ½ pt....................................**4,400.00**

GI-89 - "Lafayette" above bust - Masonic emblem, smooth edges w/a narrow vertical rib, plain lip, pontil mark, deep yellowish olive, ½ pt. **1,485.00**

GI-94 - Franklin bust below "Benjamin Franklin" - Dyott bust below "T.W. Dyott, M.D.," edges embossed "Where Liberty Dwells There Is My Country" & "Kensington Glass Works Philadelphia," plain lip, pontil, pale aqua, pt. **253.00**

GI-97 - Franklin bust obverse & reverse, vertical ribbing, plain lip, pontil mark, deep aqua, qt. **1,705.00**

GI-97 - Franklin bust obverse & reverse, vertical ribbing, plain lip, pontil mark, emerald green, qt. **2,630.00**

GI-99 - "Jenny Lind" above bust - View of Glasshouse w/"Glass Works" above & "Huffsey" below, calabash, smooth sides, broad sloping collar, pontil, bright yellow w/hint of olive tones, qt. **770.00**

GI-103 - "Jeny (sic) Lind" above bust - View of Glasshouse, calabash, heavy vertical ribbing pontil mark, aqua, qt. **93.50**

GI-104 - "Jeny (sic) Lind" above bust - View of Glasshouse, calabash, vertically ribbed edges, rounded collar, pontil, sapphire blue, qt. **4,840.00**

'Jeny' Lind Flask

GI-104 - "Jeny (sic) Lind" above bust -

View of Glasshouse, calabash, vertically ribbed edges, rounded collar, pontil, yellowish root beer amber, qt. (ILLUS.) **12,430.00**

GI-108 - Jenny Lind bust, obverse & reverse, wearing broad plain bertha, large lyre below, scroll-type shape, edges paneled vertically & forming flaring ten-sided scalloped base or foot, plain lip, pontil, aqua, pt. **550.00**

GI-111 - Kossuth bust profile between "Bridgeton, New Jersey" - Sloop sailing & flying a pennant, vertically ribbed edges, plain lip, aqua, pt. **198.00**

GI-112a - Kossuth bust in full uniform w/feathered hat below "Louis Kossuth" - Frigate sailing to left above "U.S. Steam Frigate Mississippi," "S. Huffsey" not in inscription, "Ph. Doflein Mould Maker Nth 5t 84" on base, calabash, fluted edges, aqua, qt. **275.00**

GI-113 - "Kossuth" above bust - tall tree in foliage, calabash, smooth edges, iron pontil, light green, qt. ....**125.00 to 175.00**

GI-113 - "Kossuth" above bust - tall tree in foliage, calabash, smooth edges, iron pontil, olive yellow, qt. **467.50**

GI-114 - Draped bust facing right - Draped bust facing left, both in classical mode, vertically ribbed edges, plain lip, pontil, yellowish amber, ½ pt......................................**275.00**

Columbia Bust Flask

GI-117 - Columbia bust w/ "Kensington" below - American Eagle w/head turned to right & w/ "Union. Co." below, aqua, pt. (ILLUS.) ....**650.00 to 675.00**

GI-122 - Columbia bust - American Eagle, vertically ribbed edges, plain lip, pontil, clear, pt. **3,850.00**

GII-1 - American Eagle on oval, head

turned to right obverse & reverse, horizontally beaded edges w/narrow vertical medial rib, plain sheared lip, open pontil, whittled, many seed bubbles, aqua, pt. **275.00**

GII-4a - American Eagle on oval w/13 large pearls on inner band & 10 stars in semicircle above eagle, horizon-tally beaded w/narrow vertical medial rib, plain lip, aqua, pt. **165.00**

GII-7 - American Eagle w/head turned left on small oval - circular 32 ray sunburst, large circular beading w/heavy vertical medial rib, plain lip, pontil mark, clear, pt. **2,035.00**

GII-7 - American Eagle w/head turned left on small oval - circular 32 ray sunburst, large circular beading w/heavy vertical medial rib, plain lip, pontil mark, clear w/vaseline tint, pt. **2,420.00**

GII-10 - American Eagle w/"W. Ihmsen's" above & "Glass" below - Sheaf of Rye w/ "Agriculture" above & farm implements below, vertically ribbed edges, plain lip, open pontil, aqua, pt. **1,045.00**

GII-11 - American Eagle on oval w/head turned to left & 11 tiny stars in semicircle above eagle - inverted Cornucopia with Produce, horizon-tally beaded w/vertical medial rib, plain lip, brilliant aqua, ½ pt. **264.00**

GII-12 - American Eagle on oval w/head turned to left "W.C." in oval frame below eagle - inverted Cornucopia with Produce, horizon-tally beaded w/vertical medial rib, plain lip, aqua, ½ pt. **657.50**

GII-14 - American Eagle on oval, head turned to left & eleven tiny stars in semicircle above eagle - inverted Cornucopia with Produce, smooth edges, smooth lip, light green, ½ pt. **2,310.00**

GII-19 - American Eagle facing left w/wings raised over & parallel w/body & standing on two furled flags - Morning glory & vining & gadrooning at base of neck on each side, heavy vertical medial rib, plain lip, pontil, aqua, pt. ....**330.00 to 350.00**

GII-24 - American Eagle above oval obverse & reverse, ribbon & two semicircular rows of stars above & elongated eight-point star in oval below, edges corrugated horizontally w/vertical medial rib, plain lip, pontil, aqua, pt. **137.50**

GII-24 - American Eagle above oval obverse & reverse, ribbon & two semicircular rows of stars above & elongated eight-point star in oval below, edges corrugated horizontally w/vertical medial rib, plain lip, pontil, medium yellowish amber, pt. **2,310.00**

GII-30 - American Eagle in large oval medallion obverse & reverse, overall heavy vertical ribbing except for medallions, plain lip, pontil mark, pale bluish green, ½ pt. **715.00**

GII-31 - American Eagle in large oval medallion obverse & reverse, overall heavy vertical ribbing except for medallions, pontil, medium green, qt. **4,730.00**

GII-33 - American Eagle in oval medallion - "Louisville Glass Works Ky.," in oval medallion, entire flask except medallions covered w/heavy vertical ribbing, aqua, ½ pt. **154.00**

GII-38 - American Eagle facing right, poised on a rock formation which supports an American shield, "E Pluribus Unum" inscribed on ribbon held in eagle's mouth - "Dyottville Glass Work's" in semicircle & "Philada." below in slightly curved line, smooth edges, plain lip, aqua, pt. **121.00**

GII-40 - American Eagle on oval obverse & reverse, vertically ribbed edges, short sheared neck, pontil, aqua, pt. **352.50**

GII-41 - American Eagle on oval - large tree in foliage, vertically ribbed edges, plain lip, pontil, aqua, pt. **143.00**

GII-43 - "E Pluribus Unum - One of Many" in arch above American Eagle - "Kennisgton Glass Works Philadelphia" in arch above a cornucopia filled with produce, vertically ribbed edges, plain lip, pontil, aqua, ½ pt. **302.50**

GII-43 - "E Pluribus Unum - One of Many" in arch above American Eagle - "Kennisgton Glass Works Philadelphia" in arch above a cornucopia filled with produce, vertically ribbed edges, plain lip, pontil, clear, ½ pt. **880.00**

GII-45 - American Eagle on oval - Cornucopia with Produce, vertically ribbed edges, plain lip, pontil, aqua, ½ pt. **165.00**

GII-52 - American Eagle w/shield & olive branches below - "For Our Country" below U.S. flag w/20 stars, vertically ribbed edges, plain lip, open pontil, deep olive amber, pt. **2,530.00**

GII-55 - American Eagle w/shield & 13 stars - Bunch of Grapes, vertically ribbed edges, plain lip, pontil, aqua, qt. **145.00**

GII-55 - American Eagle w/shield &

13 stars - Bunch of Grapes, vertically ribbed edges, plain lip, pontil, deep olive green, qt. **3,520.00**

GII-60 - American Eagle in oval beaded medallion - "Liberty" in scroll above beaded medallion around leafy tree, plain lip, smooth edges, olive green, ½ pt. **247.50**

GII-61 - American Eagle below "Liberty" - inscribed in four lines, "Willington - Glass, Co - West Willington - Conn," smooth edges, yellowish olive, ca. 1860-72, qt. **198.00**

American Eagle Flask

GII-62 - American Eagle below "Liberty" - "Willington Glass, Co West, Willington Conn," smooth edges, plain lip, deep olive amber, pt. (ILLUS.) **165.00**

GII-63 - American Eagle below "Liberty" - inscription in five lines, "Willington - Glass - Co - West Willington - Conn.," smooth edges, plain lip, yellowish olive, ca. 1860-72, ½ pt. **198.00**

GII-64 - American Eagle below "Liberty" - inscription in four lines, "Willington - Glass, Co - West Willington - Conn," smooth edges, plain lip, pontil, green, pt. **308.00**

GII-64 - American Eagle below "Liberty" - inscription in four lines, "Willington - Glass, Co - West Willington - Conn," smooth edges, plain lip, pontil, olive amber, ca. 1860-72, pt. **132.00**

GII-64 - American Eagle below "Liberty" - inscription in four lines, "Willington - Glass, Co - West Willington - Conn," smooth edges, plain lip, pontil, yellowish olive, pt. ...**165.00**

GII-68 - American Eagle in flight below seven five-pointed stars - large anchor w/"New London" in a banner above & "Glass Works" in a

banner below, smooth edges, plain
lip, pontil, yellow w/small amber
streak on obverse, ca. 1860-66,
pt. **550.00**

GII-69 - American Eagle w/head
turned left w/thunderbolt in left talon
& olive branch in right - Inverted
Cornucopia with Produce, horizontally beaded w/vertical medial rib,
plain lip, pontil mark, deep aqua,
½ pt. **385.00**

GII-72 - American Eagle w/head
turned to right & standing on rocks -
Cornucopia with Produce, vertically
ribbed edges, plain lip, pontil, olive
amber, pt., 7" h. **165.00**

GII-72a - American Eagle w/head
turned to right & standing on rocks -
Cornucopia with Produce & "X" on
left, vertically ribbed edges, plain lip,
pontil, olive amber, pt. **88.00**

GII-73 - American Eagle w/head
turned to the right & standing on
rocks - Cornucopia with Produce &
"X" on left, vertically ribbed edges,
plain lip, pontil, olive green,
pt., 7" h. **132.00**

GII-76 - Eagle surrounded by
concentric rings obverse & reverse,
vertically ribbed edges, plain lip,
medium green,
pt. **4,730.00**

GII-78 - American Eagle above oval
rings obverse & reverse, edges
w/single vertical rib, plain lip, pontil,
amber, qt. **93.50**

GII-82 - American Eagle above oval
obverse & reverse, w/"Stoddard,
N.H." in oval on reverse, narrow
vertical rib edges, plain lip, pontil,
olive amber, pt. **148.50**

GII-88 - American Eagle above oval -
the diameter of the eagle's head is
⅛" larger, vertically ribbed edges,
plain lip, pontil, olive amber, ½ pt.....**165.00**

GII-103 - American Eagle above oval
obverse & reverse, w/"Pittsburgh,
Pa." in oval on obverse, narrow
vertical rib on edges, collared rim,
dark green, qt..................................**220.00**

GII-106 - American Eagle above oval
obverse & reverse, w/"Pittsburgh,
PA" in oval on obverse, narrow
vertical rib on edges, deep olive
green, pt...**220.00**

GII-106 - American Eagle above oval
obverse & reverse, w/"Pittsburgh,
PA." in oval on obverse, narrow
vertical rib on edges, medium
brilliant green, pt. **1,402.50**

GII-112 - American Eagle above oval
obverse & reverse, w/"Cunningham"
(upper) & "Pittsburgh" (lower) in oval
on obverse & "Glass" (upper) &

"Manufacturers" (lower) in oval on
reverse, narrow vertical ribbing on
edges, light green, pt. **148.50**

GII-126 - Small American Eagle
above a large laurel wreath w/stems
crossed below large ribbon obverse
& reverse, smooth edges, rounded
collar, aqua, ½ pt. **77.00**

GII-138 - American Eagle w/head
turned right & taking off from uneven
ground, plain reverse, smooth
edges, bright golden amber, ½ pt. ...**286.00**

GII-141 - Eagle flying to right w/oval
eye & small hooked beak, right wing
raised parallel to body, left wing
above head, above two pennants
from beak, panel below in the style
of an architectural monument
w/semicircular pediment w/simple
scroll ornament flanking oval -
reverse w/Indian wearing tunic &
crown, facing left & shooting arrow
at small bird in flight, small dog
behind Indian, large rectangular
frame below, aqua, qt., 9⅛" h. **460.00**

GII-142 - American Eagle w/plain
shield in talons & pennant in beak
above monument w/sailing ship at
left, central column & sheaves of
grain at right in pediment above
gallery above rifle & American flag
above frame w/"Continental" - Indian
shooting arrow at bird perched on
tree w/dog at heels, frame below w/
"Cunningham's & Co., Pittsburgh,
Pa.," smooth edges, yellowish
olive, qt. **495.00**

GIII-4 - Cornucopia with Produce -
Urn with Produce, vertically ribbed
edges, plain lip, pontil, olive green,
pt. **222.00**

Cornucopia with Produce Flask

GIII-6 - Cornucopia with Produce -
Urn with Produce, vertically ribbed
edges, plain lip, pontil, medium
emerald green, pt. (ILLUS.) **258.50**

GIII-7 - Cornucopia with Produce -
Urn with Produce, vertically ribbed
edges, sheared lip, pontil, light to
medium emerald green, ½ pt. **203.50**

GIII-12 - Cornucopia with Produce &
curled right - Urn with Produce, plain
lip, vertically ribbed edges,
pontil, olive green, ½ pt. **99.00**

GIII-17 - Cornucopia with Produce &
curled right - Urn with Produce, plain
lip, double rounded collar, iron
pontil, medium to deep bluish green,
pt. **495.00**

GIV-1 - Masonic Emblems - American
Eagle w/ribbon reading "E Pluribus
Unum" above & "IP" (old-fashioned
J) below in oval frame, tooled
mouth, five vertical ribs, deep aqua
w/hint of green, pt. **110.00**

GIV-2 - Masonic Emblems - American
Eagle w/ribbon reading "E Pluribus
Unum" above & "HS" below in oval
frame, tooled mouth, five vertical
ribs, bright pale green, ca. 1815-30,
pt. (light interior stain ring near
shoulder, small sand grain bruise on
mouth) **363.00**

Masonic Arch - Eagle Flask

GIV-18 - Masonic Arch, pillars &
pavement w/Masonic emblems -
American Eagle without shield on
breast, plain oval frame below w/
"KCCNC" inside, smooth edges
w/single vertical rib, plain lip, pontil,
medium yellow olive green, pt.
(ILLUS.) **154.00**

GIV-28A - Masonic Arch, pillars &
pavement w/Masonic emblems
obverse & reverse, arch & pillars
without fluting, plain lip, pontil,
peacock green, ½ pt. **605.00**

GIV-43 - Masonic six-point star w/eye
of God in center all above "A D" -
six-point star w/arm in center all
above "GRJA," sheared mouth,

pontil, bright medium amber,
ca. 1860-70, pt. **121.00**

GV-1 - "Success to the Railroad"
around embossed locomotive -
similar reverse, sheared tooled lip,
straight line base, aqua, ca.
1849-60, pt. **242.00**

GV-1 - "Success to the Railroad"
around embossed locomotive -
similar reverse, sheared tooled lip,
straight line base, cornflower blue,
pt. (weak lettering) **1,045.00**

GV-3 - "Success to the Railroad"
around embossed horse pulling cart
- similar reverse, sheared lip, pontil,
medium olive green, pt. **176.00**

GV-3 - "Success to the Railroad"
around embossed horse pulling cart
- similar reverse, sheared lip, pontil,
olive amber, pt. **220.00**

Railroad Flask

GV-5 - "Success to the Railroad"
around embossed horse pulling cart
- similar reverse, plain lip, pontil,
vertically ribbed edges, olive green,
pt. (ILLUS.) **143.00**

GV-6 - "Success to the Railroad"
around embossed horse pulling cart
obverse & reverse, w/"Success"
above scene, plain lip, pontil,
vertically ribbed edges, clear
w/amethyst tint, pt. **962.50**

GV-7 - Embossed horse pulling cart
obverse & reverse, plain lip, round
collar, pontil mark, deep olive green,
pt. **440.00**

GVI-1 - Baltimore Monument -
embossed vine & grape form a
semicircular frame containing the
inscription "A little more grape Capt
Brag (sic)," smooth sides, plain lip,
pontil mark, strawberry puce,
½ pt. **6,820.00**

GVIII-5a - Sunburst w/twenty-four
rounded rays obverse & reverse,
two dotted concentric rings

enclosing medium-size dot in middle, plain lip, pontil, golden amber, pt.................................880.00

Sunburst Flask

GVIII-10 - Sunburst w/twenty-nine triangular sectioned rays, center raised oval w/"KEEN" reading from top to bottom on obverse & reverse, sheared lip, pontil, yellowish olive amber, ½ pt. (ILLUS.) 522.50

GVIII-14 - Sunburst w/twenty-one triangular sectioned rays obverse & reverse, sunburst centered by ring w/a dot in the middle, pontil, light emerald green, ½ pt. 742.50

Twenty-one Ray Sunburst Flask

GVIII-16 - Sunburst w/twenty-one triangular sectioned rays obverse & reverse, plain lip, open pontil, medium olive green, shallow sliver chip on base corner, ½ pt. (ILLUS.) 231.00

GVIII-18 - Sunburst w/twenty-four rounded rays obverse & reverse, horizontal corrugated edges, plain lip, pontil mark, yellowish amber, ½ pt. 412.50

GVIII-21 - Sunburst w/thirty-six slender rays forming a scalloped ellipse w/five small oval ornaments in center - similar but variations in size of center oval ornaments, open pontil, copper amber, pt. 176.00

GVIII-23 - Sunburst w/thirty-six slender rays forming oval w/five small oval ornaments in center obverse & reverse, plain lip, smooth edges, deep bluish aqua, pt.............495.00

GVIII-25 - Sunburst w/twenty-four slender rays tapering to rounded ends obverse & reverse, five oval-shaped ornaments forming five-petaled flower in middle of sunburst, plain lip, pontil, medium pinkish puce, ½ pt. 2,640.00

GIX-1 - Scroll w/two six-point stars, both large, obverse & reverse, plain, tall neck, moonstone, qt., ...550.00

Louisville Scroll Flask

GIX-8 - Scroll w/heart shaped frame & eight-point star & "Louisville" below medial scroll - reverse the same except for "Glass Works" below medial scroll, vertical medial rib on edge, plain lip, yellowish olive, overall haze & spider crack in upper embossed star, pt. (ILLUS.) 231.00

GIX-34 - Scroll w/large eight-point star above a large pearl over a large fleur-de-lis obverse & reverse, vertical medial rib on edge, tooled broad rounded collar w/lower bevel, iron pontil, deep reddish puce, ½ pt..440.00

GX-19 - Summer Tree - Winter Tree, plain lip, smooth edges, pontil, aqua, qt..120.00

GXI-37 - "For Pike's Peak" above prospector w/tools & cane standing on oblong frame - American Eagle w/pennant above oval frame, collared lip, light yellowish green, pt. 275.00

GXI-46 - "For Pike's Peak" above prospector w/tools & cane - Hunter shooting at stag, molded collar, plain edges, root beer amber, pt. **2,200.00**

GXII-21 - Clasped hands above oval, all inside shield, w/"Union" above - American Eagle above oval frame, amber, qt. **110.00**

GXII-39 - Clasped hands above oval frame inscribed w/"Wm Frank & Sons Pitts," all inside shield w/"Union" above - cannon & American flag, smooth base, collared lip, aqua, pt..........................**82.50**

GXIII-8 - Sailor dancing a hornpipe on an eight-board hatch cover, above a long rectangular bar - banjo player sitting on a long bench, smooth edges, plain lip, pontil mark, yellowish olive green, ½ pt. **632.50**

GXIII-16 - U.S. Army officer in full-dress uniform & mounted on a high stepping steed - large hound walking right, smooth edges, plain lip w/angular collar, pontil scarred base, yellow w/olive tone, pt. **3,080.00**

Flora Temple Flask

GXIII-23 - Flora Temple obverse, plain reverse, smooth edges w/beads at lower neck & shoulder, deep bluish aqua, overall light milky interior haze, pt. (ILLUS.) **495.00**

GXIII-23 - Flora Temple obverse, plain reverse, smooth edges w/beads at lower neck & shoulder, bluish green, pt. **357.50**

GXIII-37 - Sheaf of Grain w/rake & pitchfork crossed behind sheaf - "Westford Glass Co., Westford Conn," smooth sides, dark olive green, ca. 1860-73, ½ pt. **121.00**

GXIII-38 - Sheaf of Grain above crossed rake & pitchfork - large five-pointed star, smooth edges, medium bluish green, qt. **275.00**

GXIII-48 - Anchor w/fork-ended pennants inscribed "Baltimore" & "Glass Works" - Sheaf of Grain w/rake & pitchfork crossed behind sheaf, smooth edges, golden amber, qt. **330.00**

GXIII-83 - five-pointed star - "Ravenna" in arc above "Glass - Works," smooth edges, pontil, deep aqua, pt. **242.00**

GXIV-6 - "Traveler's Companion" arched above & below & framing a large stylized duck - "Lockport" in shallow arch & below "Glass" & above "Works" in straight lines, plain lip, pontil, bright yellow green, pt. **1,650.00**

Chestnut, ribbed pattern swirled to right, cobalt blue, sheared lip, 3½" h..**264.00**

Chestnut, 14 swirled ribs to the left, pontil mark, sheared & tooled lip, bright yellow green, 4" h. **880.00**

Chestnut, 16 vertical ribs, wide sheared mouth, rough pontil, green w/deep brown coloration in the neck, 6" h...**192.50**

Chestnut, 24 ribs swirled to the right, golden yellowish amber, rolled lip, pontil, Zanesville, Ohio, 7⅝" h. **550.00**

Chestnut, 24 ribs swirled to the right, medium amber, rolled lip, pontil, Zanesville, Ohio, 8½" h. **467.50**

Chestnut, 36 broken ribs, yellowish olive amber, sheared lip, pontil, 6½" h..**302.50**

Pitkin, 24 swirled ribs, pontil mark, sheared lip, olive green, 5" h. **275.00**

INKS

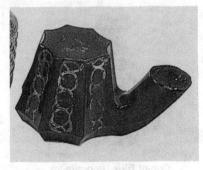

Rare Teakettle Ink

Cylindrical, master size, olive green glass, embossed "Clark's Superior Record Ink - Boston," flared lip, pontil scarred base, olive green, 5⅞" h..**1,650.00**

Cylindrical, master size, sapphire blue glass, embossed "Dr. Sheet's

Ink," smooth base, applied mouth
w/pour spout, 9¾" h. **632.50**

Domed, six-sided w/offset neck,
yellow w/olive tone glass, "J. &
I.E.M.," smooth base, tooled lip, ca.
1875-85, 2" h. **1,595.00**

House-shaped, medium blue green
glass, smooth base, tooled lip,
2½" h. **2,090.00**

Teakettle-type fountain inkwell
w/neck extending up at angle from
base of the tapering hexagonal
body, greyish clambroth opaque
glass, smooth base, ground lip, ca.
1875-85, 2¼" h. **440.00**

Teakettle-type fountain inkwell
w/neck extending up at angle from
base of the tapering hexagonal
body, medium olive green glass, gilt
trim, smooth base, ground lip, small
stress crack in base, ca. 1825-30,
1¾" h. (ILLUS.) **385.00**

Teakettle-type fountain inkwell
w/neck extending up at angle from
base of the tapering hexagonal
body, mint green opaque glass,
smooth base, ground & polished lip,
ca. 1875-85, 2½" h. **715.00**

Umbrella-type (8-panel cone shape),
aqua glass, embossed "Davis &
Miller - D M," pontil scar, rolled lip,
ca. 1845-60, 2⅜" h. **475.00**

Umbrella-type (8-panel cone shape),
aqua glass, "Potter - Champlin -
Westerly - R.I.," open pontil, rolled
lip, ca. 1850-60, 2⅞" h. **1,155.00**

Umbrella-type (8-panel cone shape),
bright yellow w/olive tone glass,
smooth base, tooled lip, ca.
1870-80, 2½" h. **880.00**

Cobalt Blue Umbrella Ink

Umbrella-type (8-panel cone shape),
cobalt blue glass, smooth base,
2⅝" h. (ILLUS.) **577.50**

MEDICINES

Ashbaugh's (Dr. J.) - Wonder of the
World - Pittsburgh, PA., rectangular,
clear, 6" h. **45.00**

**Birmingham's (Dr.) Anti Billious
Blood Purifier,** paneled cylinder,
applied mouth, smooth base, yellow
green, 8½" h. **770.00**

**Brant's Indian - Pulmonary Balsam
-** M.T. Wallace Proprietor, eight-
sided, aqua, 7" h. **65.00**

Craig's Kidney & Liver Cure, oval-
shaped, golden amber,
9½" h. ....**125.00 to 150.00**

Foley's Kidney & Bladder Cure,
Chicago, U.S.A., rectangular,
amber, 4¼" h. **20.00**

**Gladstone's Celery and Pepsin
Compound,** Mastico Medicine Co.,
Danville, Ill., amber, 2¼ x 4⅛",
7⅜" **10.00**

**The Great South American Nervine
Tonic** Trade (monogram) Mark and
Stomach & Liver Cure, oval, clear,
9½" h. ....**70.00 to 90.00**

Hansburns (Allen) Castor Oil,
rectangular, cobalt blue, 3½" h. **35.00**

**Howards - Vegetable Cancer and
Canker Syrup,** flask-shaped
w/applied mouth, smooth base,
deep yellowish amber, 7¼" h. **935.00**

**Jayne's (Dr. D.) Carminative
Balsam,** Philada., aqua,
1⅛ x 4¾" **28.00**

**Jayne's (Dr. D.) Carminative
Balsam,** round, aqua, 5¼" h. **35.00**

**KA:TON:KA - The Great Indian
Remedy,** rectangular, clear, 8¾" h.
(some light stain) **25.00**

Lake's Indian Specific

Lake's (H.) Indian Specific,
rectangular w/deeply beveled
corners & raised frame around
embossing, ring on neck, aqua,
8¼" h. (ILLUS.) **467.50**

**Larookah's (Dr.) - Indian Vegetable
-** Pulmonic Syrup, rectangular, deep
aqua, w/complete label, 8½" h. **55.00**

Merchang (G.W.), Lockport, N.Y.,
rectangular w/beveled corners,
yellowish green, 5" h. **440.00**

Mexican Mustang Liniment, round,
pontil, aqua, 1⁷⁄₁₆ x 3⅞"......................**14.00**
Miles (Dr.) Medical Company, aqua,
8¼" h...**10.00**
Perrines Apple Ginger, cabin-
shaped, amber.................................**245.00**
Rowand & Waltons Panacea,
Philad, rectangular, applied mouth,
open pontil, aqua, 6⅛" h. **880.00**
Sallade & Co. Magic Mosquito Bite
Cure & Insect Destroyer, N.Y.,
oval, aqua, 7¾" h. **25.00**
Schenck's - Seaweek - Tonic,
square, iron pontil, aqua, 9" h. **55.00**
Swaim's - Panacea - Philada.,
cylindrical paneled, green, 3½" d.,
8" h...**60.00**
Swaim's Panacea - Genuine -
Philadelphia, rectangular, open
pontil, aqua, 8" h. **412.50**
U.S.A. Hosp. Dept., cylindrical,
double collar top, crude, whittled,
light yellow amber, qt., 9¼" h. **330.00**
U.S.A. Hosp. Dept., blob top, star on
base, yellow olive, qt.......................**412.50**
Warner's Safe Kidney & Liver Cure,
flattened oval, peened-out version
w/embossed safe on side, amber,
9⅜" h...**30.00**
Warner's Safe Rheumatic Cure
Rochester, NY., U.S.A., w/safe,
oval, amber, w/original paper label,
9¼" h. **75.00**
Warner's Safe Remedies Co. 6 FL.
Oz. Rochester, N.Y., oval, single
collar mouth, clear, 7⅛" h. **40.00**
Wheaton's Sick Head Ache
Remedy, Prepared by Dr. Wm.
Price, rectangular, applied mouth,
iron pontil, deep aqua, 6¼" h. **522.50**
Wishart's (L.Q.C.) - Pine Tree Tar
Cordial Phila. - (embossed pine
tree) Patent 1858, square
w/beveled corners, bright yellowish
olive, 9¾" h. **357.50**
Wyeth (John) & Bro., Philadelphia,
w/dose cap, "Pat. May 16, 1899" on
base & "Take Next Dose At" on
neck, cobalt blue, 6½" h. **35.00**

MILK
Clear, embossed "Climax, Patent
11/15/98," square shape w/original
tin top, ½ pt. **125.00**
Clear, "Dairylea," double baby face......**52.00**
Clear, embossed "Wm. E. Hemming,
Whitesboro, NY," w/original tin top,
pt. **45.00**
Clear, embossed "Patent 1898,"
w/original tin lid & handle, pt. **150.00**
Clear, embossed "Isaac W. Rush-
more, 100 Atlantic Ave, Brooklyn,
NY," w/grey graniteware lid, qt.........**225.00**
Milk white, embossed "Thatcher -

Absolutely Pure Milk" & w/a man
milking a cow, qt. **300.00**

MINERAL WATERS
Alum Water (on shoulder) Bath Alum
Springs, Virginia, applied mouth,
smooth base, yellowish amber,
9⅛" h..**715.00**
Avon Spring Water, cylindrical,
smooth base, applied mouth, deep
green, 9½" h. **797.50**
Boardman (J.) - New York - Mineral
Waters - (embossed star) This
Bottle Is Never Sold, applied mouth,
iron pontil, sapphire blue, 7½" h. **325.00**
Conway (P.) Bottler- Philada - No 8
Hunger St. - & 108 Filbert St.,
applied mouth, iron pontil, cobalt
blue, 7" h..**110.00**
Cox, A.R. - Norristown PA., applied
mouth, iron pontil, medium emerald
green, 7¼" h. **140.00**
Dearborn (J & A) - New York -
Mineral Water, eight-sided, iron
pontil, applied mouth, deep sapphire
blue, 7" h. ....**170.00 to 200.00**
Hamilton, Gray & Co., Proprietors,
Maysville, KY, Blue Lick Water &
embossed stag, applied mouth,
smooth base, black amber, qt.,
9⅜" h...**1,045.00**
Jone's Mineral-Water, Phila. - J.,
applied mouth, iron pontil, light to
medium emerald green, 7¼" h...........**55.00**
Keys - Burlington, N.J., applied
mouth, iron pontil, medium bluish
green, 7" h. **375.00**
Lynch & Clarke, New York,
Saratoga-type, short neck variant,
pontil, crude, yellowish olive amber,
pt., 7½" h. **253.00**
Middletown Mineral Spring Co.,
Natures Remedy, Middletown, VT.,
cylindrical, smooth base, applied
mouth, emerald green, 9⅜" h. **275.00**
Napa - Soda Natural - Mineral
Water, w/original metal closure,
applied mouth, smooth base, deep
sapphire blue, 7¼" h.........................**300.00**
Reid & Cecil - Mineral Water -
Philada. - R. & C., applied mouth,
iron pontil, medium emerald green,
7½" h. **100.00**
Riddle's Philada Mineral Water,
eight-sided, applied mouth, iron
pontil, emerald green, 7¼" h. **350.00**
Robinson, Wilson & Legallse - 102
Sudsbury St - Boston, cylindrical,
iron pontil, applied mouth, deep
green, 6⅞" h. **165.00**
Rockbridge Alum Water, Rockbridge
County, Va., blue green, ½ gal. **286.00**
Roussell (E.) Mineral Water -
Philada. - Patent, cylindrical, open

pontil, applied mouth, medium
emerald green, 6⅞" h. **522.50**
Superior Mineral Water, eight-sided,
iron pontil, cobalt blue......................**220.00**
Twitchell Superior Mineral Water
Philada., applied mouth, iron
pontil, cobalt blue, 7¼" h. **275.00**
Utica Bottling - A.L. EDIC -
Establishment - Superior Mineral
Waters, applied mouth, iron pontil,
light green, 6⅞" h. **70.00**

PEPPERSAUCES
Cathedral-type, Gothic arch
windows, "Cleveland," smooth base,
applied mouth, aqua, 8½" h. **302.50**
Cathedral-type, Gothic arch
windows, "H.E. & Co. - Cin'ti,"
applied mouth, pontil, deep aqua,
8⅜" h. **330.00**

PICKLE BOTTLES & JARS

Superior Pickles Bottle

Aqua, four-sided, cathedral-type
Gothic arch windows, smooth base,
rolled lip, 13⅛" h. **308.00**
Clear, four-sided, cathedral-type
Gothic arch windows, 13" h. **250.00**
Pale green, four-sided, round-topped
paneled sides, cylindrical ringed
neck, cream & grey paper label
reading "Superior Pickles," partial
label torn, ca. 1860s, 13¾" h.
(ILLUS.) **66.00**

POISONS
Cobalt blue, figural skull, embossed
"Pat. June 26th, 1894" on smooth
base, tooled lip, 2¾" h. **1,870.00**
Cobalt blue, flask-shaped, base
embossed "C.L.G. Co. - Patent
Applied For," w/original paper label
reading "Poison Lead & Opium
Wash F.H. Ridgway Pharmacy

Connecticut & Florida Avenues,
N.W. Washington, D.C. CAUTION
Not To Be Taken," smooth base,
tooled lip, 7½" h. **143.00**
Medium amber, coffin-shaped,
embossed "Poison - F.A. Thompson
& Co. - Detroit - Poison," smooth
base, tooled lip, 3" h. **1,210.00**
Medium amber, coffin-shaped,
embossed "Norwich" on smooth
base, tooled lip, 4⅞" h. **550.00**

Rare Poison Bottle

Yellowish amber, cylindrical,
embossed "Poison" flanking a five-
pointed star above a skull &
crossbones, overall diamond-lattice
design around the sides, marked
"S&D" on the smooth base, tooled
lip, ca. 1890-1910, 4⅝" h.
(ILLUS.) **550.00**

SNUFF BOTTLES
Amber, free-blown, square w/cork
closure, original tax stamp & paper
label showing an Indian & reading
"Lorillard 'Maccoboy' Snuff" **60.00**
Deep yellowish olive green, free-
blown, rectangular w/beveled
corners, crude applied wide ring
mouth, pontil scar, 5⅞" h. **143.00**
Medium yellowish olive green, free-
blown, sheared flared mouth, pontil
scar, Netherlands,
7⅞" h..**253.00**
Yellowish olive amber, mold-blown,
"Schabbehard & Compagne: In
Bremen Fiener Rappe" on applied
seal, square body w/flared mouth &
rolled lip, Germany, 8⅝" h. **825.00**

SODAS & SARSAPARILLAS
Backus & Pratt - Binghampton,
N.Y., applied mouth, iron pontil,
clear, 7⅝" h. **95.00**
Baldwin. Tuthill & Co. - 112 Warren
St., N.Y., applied mouth, iron pontil,
medium emerald green, 7" h..............**65.00**

Billings (E.L.), Sac. City, Cal.,
Geyser Soda, blob top, aqua, 7" h.....**45.00**
Brown (H.L. & J.W.) - Hartford, CT.,
applied mouth, iron pontil, dark olive
amber, 6⅜" h. **230.00**
Brown (J.T.) Chemist - Boston -
Double Soda Water, torpedo-form,
collared mouth, deep cobalt blue,
8¾" h. **850.00**
**Buffum Sarsaparilla & Lemon
Mineral Water,** Pittsburgh, ten-
sided, iron pontil, applied mouth,
deep aqua, ca. 1840-50, 7⅞" h.
(two tiny corner base flakes) **231.00**
**Buffum Sarsaparilla & Lemon
Mineral Water,** Pittsburgh, ten-
sided, iron pontil, applied mouth,
deep cobalt, ca. 1845-55, 10½" h.
(polished) **330.00**
B.W. & Co. New York Soda Water,
squat cylindrical form w/heavy
collared mouth, iron pontil mark,
cobalt blue, ½ pt. **308.00**
Craven - Union Glass Works -
Phila., applied mouth, pontil scarred
base, peacock blue, 7⅜" h. **100.00**
Dillon Beverages, soda, painted
label w/cowboy on bucking horse,
1940..**24.00**
**Eagle (W.) - Vestry Varick & Canel
Sts -** Prem'm Soda Water - Union
Glass Works - Phila, applied mouth,
iron pontil, emerald green, 7⅜" h. **50.00**
Espisito (J.), 812 & 814, trademark
"K" inside, Koca Nola, Washington
Ave., Philada., "JE" monogram on
smooth base, Hutchinson stopper,
tooled lip, yellow w/green tint,
7⅝" h. **4,200.00**
Gardner & Co. - Hackettstown, N.J.,
ten-sided, applied mouth, smooth
base, sapphire blue, 6¾" h. **400.00**
Haddock & Sons, torpedo-shaped,
rolled lip, pontil scarred base,
yellowish olive green, 6⅞" h. **850.00**

J.W. Harris Soda Bottle

Hale (C.B.) & Co. - Camden, N.J.,
applied mouth, iron pontil, emerald
green, 6¾" h. **200.00**
Harris (J.W.) - Soda Water - New
Haven - Conn., eight-sided, iron
pontil, applied mouth, light ice to
sapphire blue, chip at shoulder,
ca. 1845-55, 7⅜" h. (ILLUS.
bottom previous column) **412.50**
Harvy (Ira) - Prov. R.I., soda, cylindrical sloping collared mouth, iron
pontil, deep sapphire blue, ½ pt.......**220.00**
**Kane (J.O.) - Dyottville Glass
Works,** Philada, applied mouth, iron
pontil, deep green, 7" h.....................**60.00**

Knicker - Bocker Soda Bottle

Knicker - Bocker - Soda - Water -
18S.S52, ten-sided, applied mouth,
iron pontil, deep sapphire blue,
7⅝" h. (ILLUS.) **190.00**
Lake (J.), Schenectady, N.Y.,
applied mouth, iron pontil, deep
sapphire blue, 7½" h. **525.00**
Owen Casey - Eagle Soda - Works -
Sac City, applied mouth, smooth
base, deep sapphire blue, 7¼" h. **65.00**
Phoenix Glass Works - Brooklyn,
applied mouth, iron pontil, pale
green, 7⅛" h. **400.00**
Premium - Newton, New York,
applied mouth, iron pontil, emerald
green, 7" h. **70.00**
Rahn (D.S.) Perkiomenville, applied
mouth, smooth base, medium bluish
green, 6⅞" h. **400.00**
**Ryer (W.) - Union Glass Works - R -
Philada,** applied mouth, iron pontil,
brilliant deep cobalt blue, 7⅛" h. **425.00**
Seedorf (John), Charleston, SC -
Soda Water, applied mouth, iron
pontil, cobalt blue, 7½" h. **275.00**
Seitz & Bro., Easton, Pa., Premium
Soda Waters, eight-sided, iron
pontil, applied mouth, cobalt blue,
ca. 1840-55, 7⅛" h. **170.00**

Smith (L.C.), applied mouth, iron
  pontil, deep cobalt blue, 7¼" h. **170.00**
Smith (S.) - Auburn, N.Y. - 1856 -
  KR. S - Water, twelve-sided, iron
  pontil, applied mouth, cobalt blue,
  ca. 1856-60, 7¼" h. **350.00**
Smith (S.) - Auburn, N.Y. - 1856 -
  KR. S - Water, ten-sided, applied
  mouth, iron pontil, light to medium
  sapphire blue, 7¾" h. **240.00**
Smith (S.) - Auburn, N.Y. - 1857, ten-
  sided, applied mouth, iron pontil,
  medium cobalt blue, 7¾" h. **140.00**
**Southwich (Adna H.) & Tupper
  (G.O.) -** New York, ten-sided, iron
  pontil, applied mouth, cobalt blue,
  7½" h. **385.00**
Townsend's (Dr.) - Sarsaparilla -
  Albany, N.Y., square, iron pontil,
  bluish green **231.00**
Townsend's (Dr.) - Sarsaparilla -
  Albany, N.Y., square w/beveled
  corners, emerald green, 9¼" h. **236.50**
Townsend's (Dr.) - Sarsaparilla -
  Albany, N.Y., square w/beveled
  corners, iron pontil, applied mouth,
  green w/yellowish tint, ca. 1840-50,
  9½" h. **198.00**
Townsend's (Dr.) - Sarsaparilla -
  Albany, N.Y., square w/beveled
  corners, pontil, olive amber.............**165.00**
Townsend's (Dr.) - Sarsaparilla -
  Albany, N.Y., square w/beveled
  corners, iron pontil, applied mouth,
  yellowish olive amber, 9¾" h. **220.00**
Townsend's (Dr.) - Sarsaparilla -
  Albany, N.Y., square w/beveled
  corners, iron pontil, applied mouth,
  yellowish olive green, 9¾" h. **154.00**
**Tweddle, Jr. (J.) Celebrated Soda
  or Mineral Water -** Barclay Street -
  41 - New York, applied mouth,
  iron pontil, medium bluish green,
  7½" h. **120.00**
**Valentine & Vreeland - Newark, N.J.
  - Supr Soda Water -** Union Glass
  works, - Phila, applied mouth, iron
  pontil, cobalt blue, 7⅜" h. (lightly
  cleaned) **150.00**
**Wynkoop's Katharismic
  Sarsaparilla,** New York,
  rectangular, applied mouth, metallic
  pontil, sapphire blue, 10" h. **5,720.00**

WHISKEY & OTHER SPIRITS

Beer, "Schlitz," royal ruby, 12 oz. **28.00**
Bourbon, "Bininger's Old Kentucky
  Bourbon - 1849 Reserve Distilled in
  1848 - A.M. Bininger & Co., No. 19
  Broad St., N.Y.," square, smooth
  base, applied mouth, yellowish olive,
  ca. 1865-75, 9¾" h. **187.00**
Case gin, "Wistar's Club House,"
  square tapered-form, mushroom

mouth, iron pontil, deep red puce,
  qt. **495.00**
Case gin, dip-molded, square w/deep
  shoulder & rolled lip, pontil mark,
  yellowish olive amber, 15½" h. **475.00**

A.M. Bininger Gin Bottle

Gin, "A.M. Bininger & Co., No. 19
  Broad St., N.Y. - Old London Dock -
  Gin," square w/beveled corners,
  smooth base, applied mouth, yellow
  w/an olive green tone, ca. 1860-70,
  10" h. (ILLUS.) **154.00**
Schnapps, "Udolpho Wolfe's
  Schiedam - Aromatic - Schnapps,"
  rectangular w/cut corners, iron
  pontil, applied mouth, medium root
  beer amber, 7¾" h. **165.00**

Udolpho Wolfe's Schnapps Bottle

Schnapps, "Udolpho Wolfe's
  Schiedam - Aromatic - Schnapps,"
  rectangular w/cut corners, smooth
  base, applied mouth, medium
  pinkish amethyst, ca. 1865-75,
  8¼" h. (ILLUS.) **385.00**
Spirits, mold-blown, globular, 18
  swirled ribs, sheared lip, scarred
  base, yellow w/olive tone,

Pittsburgh-Monongahela area,
6⅜" h. **302.50**

Early Ohio Spirits Bottle

Spirits, mold-blown, globular, 24 ribs
swirled to the right, medium amber,
Zanesville, Ohio, ca. 1830-40,
8½" h. (ILLUS.) **467.50**
Spirits, mold-blown, globular, 24 ribs
swirled, yellowish olive, Zanesville,
Ohio, 8⅜" h. **2,420.00**
Whiskey, "Bennett & Carrol, 120
Wood Street, Pittsburg," barrel-
shaped, applied mouth, smooth
base, amber, 9⅜" h. **522.50**
Whiskey, "E.B. Bevan, I.X.L. Valley
Whiskey, Pittston, Pa." & embossed
w/five-pointed stars on seven of
eight panels, rectangular w/beveled
corners, applied mouth, pontil scar,
reddish amber, 7" h. **1,100.00**
Whiskey, "A.M. Bininger & Co., No.
375 Broadway N.Y.," square,
smooth base, applied mouth,
medium pinkish puce, 9⅞" h. **302.50**
Whiskey, "A.M. Bininger & Co., No.
19 Broad St., New York," cylindrical,
applied mouth & handle, smooth
base, olive green, 7¾" h. **1,155.00**

Early Booz's Whiskey Bottle

Whiskey, "E.G. Booz's Old Cabin
Whiskey - 120 Walnut St. -
Philadelphia - 1840 - E.G. Booz's
Old Cabin Whiskey," cabin-shaped,
smooth base, applied mouth,
yellowish amber, 7¾" h. (ILLUS.
bottom previous column) **1,155.00**
Whiskey, "From the Casper Co.,
Winston Salem, N.C. - New York -
Chicago, St. Louis," cylindrical,
smooth base, tooled lip, cobalt blue,
ca. 1880-1900, 11¾" h. **550.00**
Whiskey, "Duffy Crescent (moon)
Saloon," pig-shaped, sheared
mouth, aqua, 7⅝" l. **880.00**

(End of Bottles Section)

BOXES

Early Hanging Box

Band box, wallpaper-covered, oval,
covered w/a blue paper w/large
orange & yellow fan-shaped
blossoms w/feathery leaf sprigs
separated by small squiggly almond-
shaped devices in yellow,
Pennsylvania, 19th c., 8¼ x 11¾",
6" h. **$4,025.00**
Band box, wallpaper-covered, oval,
the whole decorated w/large green
& cream-painted peacocks on a
grey ground, American-made,
19th c., 10¾ x 14½", 10¼" h. **748.00**
Bride's box, oval bentwood w/laced
seams, painted & decorated pine,
blue ground, the top decorated w/a
scene of a hound chasing deer &
hare w/a German inscription, the
sides w/two bands of polychrome
blossoms, Europe, 19th c., 19" l.
(wear, edge damage, laced seams
damaged on cover) **770.00**
Candle box, cov., hanging-type,

walnut w/some curl, low arched crest w/hanging hole above a slanted rectangular lift-lid above a dovetailed case, one dovetailed drawer below, 14" l. (age cracks, refinished, minor separation at joints) **495.00**

Candle box, hanging-type, pine, triangular back pierced for hanging, above an open rectangular container, worn old dark finish, 12½" l. **137.50**

Decanter box, shagreen w/brass mounts, the domed canted lid w/lifting handle enclosing a velvet-lined interior w/two glass bottles w/silver plate lids engraved w/a crest, on brass paw feet & locking device, George III period, England, late 18th c., 6½" h. **920.00**

Document box, painted & decorated wood, rectangular w/hinged lid, black-painted panels outlined in green, yellow & red, enclosing pierced hearts & swans, the lid inscribed "Amor Et Love," late l9th c., 5⅞ x 11⅛", 5½" h. (damage to corner of lid) **345.00**

Gilt-brass & *pietra dura* **box,** shaped rectangular form, the cover & sides set w/oval stone floral inserts, on agate feet, Europe, 19th c., 4½ x 9½", 5¼" h. **1,150.00**

Glass box, round, metal-hinged glass cover, cobalt blue, cover decorated w/an enameled bird & yellow & gold flowers, base decorated w/yellow & gold flowers & six applied clear wishbone-shaped feet, 5½" d., 4¾" h..**295.00**

Glass box, round, metal-hinged glass cover, golden amber Inverted Thumbprint patt., cover decorated w/applied sapphire blue serpent & enameled green leaves, base decorated w/enameled blue flowers & green leaves, brass ormolu claw feet, 4½" d., 5" h. **275.00**

Hanging box, carved wood, narrow rectangular form w/a tapering rounded end tab pierced w/a hole for hanging, a low-domed sliding cover, carved on one side "A.B. 1799," cover opens to a double-welled compartment, probably Mid-Atlantic States, 2¼ x 13¼" , 1¾" h. (ILLUS.) **748.00**

Inlaid box, pine, dovetail construction, slant top lift lid opening to two interior lidded compartments, inlaid diamond in lid, red stain, 13¾" l...**220.00**

Oak box, Art & Crafts style, oak, cylindrical w/a chamfered edge on

the base & flat cover, the cover carved & painted in color w/a village landscape, unmarked, early 20th c., 5" d., 3" h. **99.00**

Hanging Pipe Box

Pipe box, hanging-type, painted wood, the upright rectangular form w/a pierced arched tab handle above the deep compartment over a small drawer at the base, on a molded base, probably Mid-Atlantic States, early 19th c., 3½ x 5", 17½" h. (ILLUS.) **3,450.00**

Salt box, hanging-type, painted & decorated wood, the crest w/slender scrolls flanking a shaped flat bracket w/round top pierced for hanging above a rectangular hinged lid above a compartment w/two short drawers below, the surface in yellowish white & outlined in dark blue, green & orange, the lid & case w/a floral bouquet flanked by two birds, the case w/a central flower flanked by two birds over the two red-painted drawers w/black & yellow banding & green floral decorations, attributed to S.S. Plank, Berks County, Pennsylvania, ca. 1885, 7½ x 13", 16" h.................**23,000.00**

Silver box, rectangular w/chased scrolls, engraved w/Prince of Wales Plume, Europe, probably France, early l9th c.. 3½" l. **230.00**

Storage box, painted & decorated pine, rectangular w/paneled sliding lid, painted red & decorated w/a potted tulip on the lid, the case sides decorated w/potted tulips within arched panels, the front decorated w/a compass star, Berks County, Pennsylvania, late 18th c., 7⅞ x 13", 5¼" h...........................**10,350.00**

Storage box, painted & decorated

Decorated Bentwood Box

oval bentwood, painted red, the fitted lid decorated w/white & blue stylized flowers & w/single tulips on the sides, Berks County, Pennsylvania, late 18th c., 9¼ x 14", 6" h. (ILLUS.) **1,725.00**

Storage box, painted & decorated wood, rectangular w/three reeded edges enclosing a yellow, ochre & brown-painted sliding lid opening to a single compartment fitted w/a lidded till, the case w/blue, yellow & ochre painted sides, on a molded base, Pennsylvania, 19th c., 4¾ x 12", 6¼" h.............................**8,625.00**

Storage box, painted & decorated oval bentwood, black ground decorated w/large stylized red, yellow, green & white tulip-like flowers around the base & the fitted lid, Berks or Lancaster County, Pennsylvania, late 18th - early l9th c., 11⅛ x 16½", 8" h..**27,600.00**

Storage box, bentwood w/tack construction, yellow paint w/a dark brown band around the rim below the fitted cover, cover w/stenciled floral sprig in red & dark brown, 9¾" d.(worn paint)............................**176.00**

Tobacco box, silver, rectangular, the cover & base engraved w/windmills, the sides engraved w/foliage, the interior of the cover w/two hinged panels engraved w/windmills & opening to reveal similar engraved

Early William & Mary Box

scenes w/fabric backing, Holland, late l9th c., 5" l.. ....**460.00**

Trinket box, heart-shaped maple & pine bentwood, w/a fitted lid & on three bun feet, oxidized patina, New England, probably Connecticut, ca.1825, 5¼ x 6", 3" h...................**1,035.00**

William & Mary box, inlaid walnut, rectangular lid w/a molded edge hinged w/cotter pins & opening to a well, dovetailed case, the front inlaid w/ "TH 1743," molded base, on turned ball feet, Pennsylvania, front left foot replaced, 12½" l., 6" h. (ILLUS.) **5,750.00**

BREWERIANA

Enameled Beer Glasses

Beer is still popular in this country but the number of breweries has greatly diminished. More than 1,900 breweries were in operation in the 1870s but we find fewer than 40 supplying the demands of the country a century later. The small local brewery has either been absorbed by a larger company or forced to close, unable to meet the competition. Advertising items used to promote the various breweries, especially those issued prior to Prohibition, now attract an ever growing number of collectors. The breweriana items listed are a sampling of the many items available. Also see BOTTLES, SIGNS & SIGN-BOARDS and TRAYS.

Beer glass, "Breunig's Lager," blue enameled lettering (ILLUS. left) **$40.00**

Beer glass, "Calumet Beer," red enameled lettering (ILLUS. right) **74.00**

Beer glass, "Klausmann Brewing Co., S. St. Louis, Mo.," embossed pilsner **25.00**

Beer glass, "Dubuque Star,"

Dubuque Star & Imperial Glasses

enameled w/a six-point star & "D"
surrounded by "Dubuque Star
Brewing Co." & a wreath, Dubuque,
Iowa (ILLUS. left) **90.00**
Beer glass, "Imperial Premium,"
enameled royal coat-of-arms w/
"Ajax Select Extra Pale" above
"Imperial Premium," Indianapolis,
Indiana (ILLUS. right).........................**65.00**

Acid-Etched Beer Glasses

Beer glass, "Pacific Beer," acid-
etched, the round logo for the
"Pacific Brewing & Malting Co. -
Tacoma" above "Pacific Beer - Best
East or West," Tacoma,Washington
(ILLUS. left)..**30.00**
Beer glass, "Savoy Style Special
Brew," acid-etched, a leaf cluster &
emblem above "Savoy Style Special
Brew Export Beer - United States
Brewing Co. - Chicago" (ILLUS.
right)...**91.00**
Clock, electric wall model, "Duquesne
Pilsener," round plastic, white dial
w/black Arabic numerals &
advertising "'The Finest Beer in
Town' - Duquesne Pilsener," domed
plastic dial cover printed w/a bust

portrait of a man serving a glass of
beer, red, white & blue lettering,
15" d. (face cover cracked &
scratched) **44.00**
Corkscrew, advertising, "Anheuser
Busch Malt Nutrine," metal **85.00**

Schmidt's Counter Display

Counter display, bronze, "Schmidt's,"
a figure of a bartender carrying two
mugs of beer in front of a half-barrel,
on a chamfered platform base
w/advertising on the front side,
minor wear, 7¾" h. (ILLUS.) **165.00**
Foam scraper, celluloid, "Caparine,
DeKalb, Illinois".................................**25.00**
Foam scraper, celluloid, "Meyer's
Munchener Lowenbrau".....................**25.00**
Foam scraper, celluloid, "Pittsburgh
Brewing Co." **22.50**
Foam scraper, celluloid, "Smoke
Union Made Cigars"...........................**25.00**

Two Modern Pottery Mugs

Mug, pottery, "Americana" pattern,
Ceramarte of Brazil, No. CS17
(ILLUS. left)......................................**550.00**
Mug, pottery, Anheuser-Busch "A" &
flying eagle logo design, Ceramarte
of Brazil, No. CS24 (ILLUS. right) **633.00**
Mug, pottery, tapering cylindrical
form, printed w/logo & "Export Lager

Older Beer Mugs

- Keeley Brewing Co. Chicago, Ill."
(ILLUS. left).....................................**275.00**
Mug, pottery, cylindrical body tapering
at the rim, printed w/a bust of a man
drinking beer above "'Old Times' -
Lager - Henn & Gabler Brewery,
Chicago, U.S.A." (ILLUS.
right)...**303.00**
Mug, pottery, printed w/a castle scene
& "Wurzburger - Light Beer,"
Ceramarte of Brazil for Budweiser,
No. CS-39 (ILLUS. left below) **277.00**

Trommer's Beer Counter Sign

Sign, counter-type, a flat half-round
glass plate inset in a metal frame
w/a molded & textured metal base,
printed in red & black letters on a
clear & white ground "Trommer's
Malt Beers" w/logo (ILLUS.).............**275.00**

Modern Beer Mug & Stein

Stein, clear glass, horn-shaped w/flat
hinged metal lid, printed in color
w/the Budweiser Clydesdales pulling

a beer wagon & titled "Budweiser,
Champion Clydesdales" (ILLUS.
right)...**115.00**

Fauerbach & Koehler's Tap Knobs

Tap knob, "Fauerbach Beer -
Madison, Wis.," chromed metal knob
w/black & orange round disc (ILLUS.
left) **88.00**
Tap knob, "Koehler's Beer," black
plastic w/a red, orange & silver
round disc printed "The Erie Brewing
Co. - Koehler's Beer - Erie, Pa."
(ILLUS. right) **35.00**

Old Style & Point Beer Knobs

Tap knob, "Old Style Lager," black
plastic w/round disc printed
"Heileman's Old Style Lager, G.
Heileman Brewing Co., La Crosse,
Wis." in brown, white, gold & black
(ILLUS. left)......................................**55.00**
Tap knob, "Point Beer," chromed
metal knob w/a blue, white & gold
disc w/"Stevens Point Beverage Co.
- Point Beer" (ILLUS. right) **53.00**
Tap spigot, "Acme," brass, No. 6 ....**85.00**

BROWNIE COLLECTIBLES

*The Brownies were creatures of fantasy
created by Palmer Cox, artist-author, in
1887. Early in this century numerous
articles with depictions of or in the shape
of Brownies appeared.*

Early Brownie Dolls

Crate label, decorated w/Palmer Cox
Brownies, 1930s, 10 x 12" **$14.00**
Cup & saucer, china, colored transfer
of Brownies playing tug-o-war **95.00**
Doll, papier-maché, a Brownie
gentleman wearing a cylindrical cap,
jacket, vest & cravat, molded &
painted facial features, jointed at
shoulders & hips, light wear & paint
flakes, right ankle cracked, right
thumb missing, 9" h. (ILLUS. left) **450.00**
Doll, papier-maché, Brownie
Chinaman, molded & painted facial
features, tiny cap on head attaches
queue, molded & maroon-painted
long coat, white stockings & orange
shoes w/pointed toes, jointed
shoulders & hips, fine crack in right
side seam & legs, both thumbs off,
dent in side of chest, 8½" h. (ILLUS.
right)...**425.00**
Flatware set, child's: knife, fork &
spoon; silver plate, Brownies on
handles, mint in box, the set **65.00**

Brownies "Nine-Pins" Game

Game, "Nine-Pins," ten lithographed
paper-on-cardboard die-cut figures
of Brownies, w/original box

w/colorful cover picture, McLoughlin
Bros., ca. 1893, box in poor
condition (ILLUS.) **1,495.00**
Game, "Ring Toss," by M.H. Miller,
ca. 1920, w/original colorful litho-
graphed box **150.00**
Mug, silver plate, decorated
w/Brownies, authorized by Palmer
Cox **185.00**
Plate, child's, porcelain, decorated
w/Brownies, 7" d. **95.00**

BUCKLES

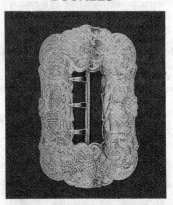

Civil War-Era Gold Buckle

Belt buckle, Bakelite, pinkish ivory
rays w/center-carved floral **$50.00**
Belt buckle, citrine & silver, designed
as a pair of addorsed birds,
centered by an oval citrine mounted
in silver gilt, American hallmark **172.50**
Belt buckle, gold, shaped oblong
form w/scalloped border, each end
chased w/panels of foliate scrolls on
a matted ground enclosing, at the
top, the American eagle w/a
"UNION" banner, w/figures of Liberty
& Justice on the sides, & below, a
Union shield & military trophies,
unmarked, American-made,
ca. 1860, 2½" l. (ILLUS.)..............**1,495.00**

Chinese Jade Buckle

Belt buckle, jade, each section carved w/a bat soaring amid a leafy vine, one side w/a loop to receive the dragon-head terminal, China, late 18th - early l9th c., white, 4⅜" l. (ILLUS. bottom previous page).....**1,150.00**

Belt buckle, sterling silver, chased & pierced florals, Birmingham, England hallmarks, late l9th - early 20th c., 2 x 3½", 2 pcs. **125.00**

Early Shoe Buckles

Shoe buckles, faceted clear glass, copper & silvered metal, curved oval bands set w/faceted clear glass stones w/a copper interior band, in a shagreen case w/blue silk lining, probably English, late 18th c., pr. (ILLUS.) **345.00**

BUSTER BROWN
COLLECTIBLES

Buster Brown Coaster Wagon

Buster Brown was a comic strip created by Richard Outcault in the New York

Herald *in 1902. It was subsequently syndicated and numerous objects depicting Buster (and often his dog, Tige) were produced.*

Bandanna, orange, green & white, illustrated w/all the TV gang including Smilin' Ed & Froggy **$90.00**

Coaster wagon, low-sided rectangular wooden platform stenciled on the sides "Buster Brown," on metal-rimmed wooden wheels, early 20th c., minor wear, 30" l., 13" h. (ILLUS.) **973.50**

Coloring book, ca. 1940, unused........**50.00**

Cup & saucer, china, illustration of Buster pouring tea for Tige **120.00**

Game, "Pin The Tie on Buster," illustrated by Outcault, early 20th c. **125.00**

Kite, advertising, "Buster Brown Shoes," paper, 1940s **38.00**

Pinback button, reads "Buster Brown Shoes," & illustrates Buster & Tige **35.00**

Buster Brown & Tige Plate

Plate, china, round w/scroll-molded rim w/pink trim, a colorful transfer in the center of Buster w/Tige balancing a teakettle on his nose, minor scratches, 7"d. (ILLUS.)...........**82.50**

Rocking horse, painted wood, a flat stylized model of a horse suspended from springs in a wooden framework, airbrushed details in red & a colorful logo on the sides w/the head of Buster Brown & Tige & "Buster Brown" in script, point of purchase item, ca. 1950s, 17¾ x 32", 30" h...............................**440.00**

Shoe tree, single, plastic, figural bust of Buster & Tige forming the handle, 9" l., 4½" h. (minor soiling) **22.00**

BUTTER MOLDS & STAMPS

Early Butter Stamps

While they are sometimes found made of other materials, it is primarily the two-piece wooden butter mold and one-piece butter stamp that attract collectors. The molds are found in two basic styles, rounded cup form and rectangular box form. Butter stamps are usually round with a protruding knob handle on the back. Many were factory made items with the print design made by forcing a metal die into the wood under great pressure, while others had the design chiseled out by hand. For listing of other types of molds see MOLDS - CANDY, FOOD & MISC. category.

Cow stamp, round, carved wood, carved border, dark patina, turned threaded handle, 3⅝" d..................**$220.00**

Eagle stamp, round, carved wood, a well-carved long necked eagle below a small star, a carved serrated border, old patina, turned handle, 3¾"d. (ILLUS. bottom right)....................................**385.00**

Eagle - starflower "lollipop" stamp, carved pine, a crudely carved stylized eagle w/shield on one side, a starflower on the other, old patina, 9" l. (ILLUS. upper left) **990.00**

Flower stamp, round, the carved blossomhead w/a bulbous center flanked by four pairs of long curved petals on a slender stem flanked by fat feathered leaves, zipper-notched border band, turned one-piece handle, scrubbed finish, 4⅝" d...........**93.50**

Flower stamp, round, carved wood, a large pair of angled leaves flanking a small teardrop blossom above three leaves & a crosshatched ground, turned handle, 5⅛"d. (ILLUS. top center) **137.50**

Four-leaf stamp, round, carved wood w/four large oblong leaves on a curved branch, wide zipper-band

border, turned inserted handle, 3¾"d.......................................**93.50**

Hearts stamp, round, carved w/a large heart topped by a small heart flanked by the initials "H" & "R," inserted turned handle, good patina, 4" d.....................................**269.50**

Pineapple stamp, round, carved wood, central design of fruit w/feather foliage surrounding, chip-carved border, one-piece turned handle, old scrubbed grey patina, 4½" d.....................................**110.00**

Pineapple stamp, round, carved w/a round fruit w/a long, fanned top crest, on a slender stem flanked by long feathered leaves, one-piece turned handle, scrubbed finish, 4½" d. (minor age cracks).................**66.00**

Pineapple stamp, half-round carved wood, the fruit in center flanked by pairs of long feathery leaves, turned inserted handle, scrubbed, 7" w.......**214.50**

Pinwheel "lollipop" stamp, carved wood w/four long, curved teardrop-form arms, each separated by a serrated leaf-like device, long tapering handle, 9¾" l. (age cracks) **357.50**

Pinwheel - star "lollipop" stamp, carved wood, one side carved w/a seven-arm pinwheel, the other w/a star, bulbous carved handle, age cracks, edge damage, 7" l. (ILLUS. upper right) **302.50**

Sheaf of wheat stamp, round, deeply carved w/a sheaf of wheat w/a widely fanned top & leaf sprigs below, notch-carved border, one-piece turned handle, good patina, 4⅝" d...**247.50**

Sheaf of wheat stamp, round, carved wood, sheaf flanked by stalks of grain, w/one-piece turned handle, old soft patina, 4¾" d. (age crack in sheaf) **60.50**

Cased Sheaves of Wheat Mold

Sheaves of wheat cased mold, rectangular block divided into two squares each w/a sheaf of wheat flanked by small leaf sprigs, heavy box case, plunger handle, 5 x 7¾" (ILLUS.) **148.50**

Starflower stamp, round, carved wood, rope-carved border, one-piece turned handle, dark brown patina, 2⅞" d. **165.00**

Starflower stamp, round, carved wood, a six-petal starflower w/a small six-point star between each petal, turned handle, old patina, 5" d. (ILLUS. bottom left) **165.00**

Stars cased mold, rectangular block divided into two squares w/serrated edges, each square w/a six-point star, plunger handle, 4½ x 5¼" **148.50**

Strawberry & leaf stamp, round, carved wood, single berry & cluster of three leaves, plain edge, w/inserted turned handle, old soft patina, 3½" d. **165.00**

Sunburst stamp, round, carved wood, dished form w/well carved details, dark patina, 4¾" d. **192.50**

Swan stamp, round, a stylized bird in center framed by a wide carved outer ring, turned screw-in handle, worn patina, 2⅞" d. **82.50**

Tulip stamp, round, carved w/a slender stylized tulip blossom flanked by almond-form devices, one-piece w/whittled handle, worn patina, 3½" d. **220.00**

Tulip stamp, round, large stylized blossom w/U-form centered by a long almond-shaped petal, zipper-band border, w/turned handle, 4½" d. **302.50**

Tulip one side, reverse w/flower stamp, round, carved wood, no handle, scrubbed grey finish, 3½" d...**77.00**

Tulip one side, reverse w/star stamp, round, carved wood, no handle, scrubbed grey finish, 4¼" d...**192.50**

CALENDAR PLATES

Plate with "Gibson-type" Girl

Calendar plates have been produced in

this country since the turn of the century, primarily of porcelain and earthenwares but also of glass and tin. They were made earlier in England. The majority were issued after 1909, largely intended as advertising items.

1909, "Gibson-type" girl bust portrait center (ILLUS.) **$38.00**

1910, Howe Building, Leroy, Illinois center..**18.00**

1910, New York City center scene **36.00**

1910, poppies center, New York advertising **36.00**

1910, sailboats on water center............**35.00**

1923, fish in center **45.00**

CANDLESTICKS & CANDLEHOLDERS

Tiffany Candelabrum

Also see METALS, ROYCROFT ITEMS and SANDWICH under Glass.

Candelabra, bronze & Favrile glass, a scroll-cast domed base set w/green glass "jewels," a central stem issuing four slender curved arms each w/a bulbous candle socket set w/green glass "jewels," rich dark patina, bobeche intact, each base impressed "Tiffany Studios New York - 22324," w/early "T G & D Co." mark, 11¼" h., pr. (ILLUS. of one) **$5,175.00**

Candelabra, sterling silver, four-light, flared circular base, four fluted curved arms rising from fluted pointed center, circular drip pans & fluted sconces, Naylor Brothers, London, England, 1961, retailed by Collingwood, 14" h., pr..................**3,738.00**

Candelabra, sterling silver, five-light, on a flaring base chased w/rocaille scrolls & foliage, rising to a baluster stem similarly chased w/rocaille & trailing leaves, w/a central baluster socket supporting four removable scroll branches w/baluster sockets & shaped circular drip pans, w/removable circular nozzles, Gorham Mfg. Co., Providence, Rhode Island, 1919, 21" h., pr. **7,475.00**

Figural Porcelain Candleholder

Candleholder, porcelain, figural, a black cat w/an arched back, the tail forming the loop handle, on an orange base, Germany, early 20th c., 2 x 4", 5" h. (ILLUS.) **110.00**

Tiffany Candle Lamp

Candle lamp, bronze & glass, the bronze holder w/two animal legs w/animal head terminals flanking the ring holder, the round base w/four animal paws, the ring supporting a teardrop-form opal Favrile glass shade w/iridescent greenish gold pulled feather designs, a beaded bronze candle cup inside, base impressed "Tiffany Studios - New York TGC Co.," 6½" h. (ILLUS.) ...**2,070.00**

Candlestand, wrought iron, curved

tripod base supporting a twisted stem & adjustable arm w/two brass sockets, early 20th c., 5' 3" h. **330.00**

Candlestick, brass, stepped octagonal base w/screw-in ring-turned standard, straight candle socket, 19th c., 5½" h. **275.00**

Candlestick, hand-hammered copper, Arts & Crafts style, a round foot below the cylindrical shaft supporting a wide dished bobeche & a wide-rimmed candle socket, long slender angled strap handles down the sides, early 20th c., 4¾" d., 9" h..................**88.00**

Candlesticks, brass, a circular bobeche above a ring- and trumpet-turned stem on a square domed base w/cusped corners, probably England,18th c., 7¼" h., pr. **1,150.00**

Early Brass Candlesticks

Candlesticks, brass, a scalloped bobeche above a ring-turned cylindrical candlecup over a trumpet-turned stem above a domed petal base, America or England, mid-18th c., 8½" h., pr.(ILLUS.) **1,610.00**

Candlesticks, brass, circular base, tapering paneled standard, bulbous candlecup w/flared rim, w/pushup, 19th c., 9" h., pr...............................**143.00**

Candlesticks, brass, Arts & Crafts style, a flat disc foot centered by a slender rod shaft supporting an ovoid socket, original patina, inscribed "JARVIE," early 20th c., 4½" d., 11" h., pr. **577.50**

Candlesticks, brass, Arts & Crafts style, a bulbous ovoid socket w/a flaring ring raised on a tall slender shaft w/a knobbed base atop a flat disc foot, aged brass finish, Chicago School, early 20th c., unmarked, 5" d., 11" h., pr. **770.00**

Candlesticks, brass, beehive & diamond quilted detail, w/pushup,

English registry mark, 19th c.,
11⅞" h., pr. **165.00**
Candlesticks, bronze, Art Nouveau
style, spherical socket cast as a
lotus blossom bud raised on a
slender twisted organic stem above
the flaring foot composed of
overlapping lily pads w/human
faces, original patina, by Charles H.
Barr, incised "C H BARR 1902,"
Providence, Rhode Island, 1902,
w/bound volume of International
Studio Vol. 6, 1898-99, sticks
11⅜" h., pr. **977.50**
Candlesticks, copper w/silver &
brass wash, cylindrical socket above
a scalloped dished drip pan on
slender legs to the cylindrical
pedestal w/flaring base on tiny bun
feet, the pedestal engraved w/a line
& scroll design, impressed mark of
the Pairpoint Mfg. Co., 11" h., pr.
(finish wear) **201.00**
Candlesticks, pressed flint glass, a
paneled flaring socket above a
double-knop paneled stem attached
w/a glass wafer to a loop pattern
foot, emerald green, probably
Boston & Sandwich Glass Co., ca.
1850, 6⅞" h., pr. (one w/a socket
crack) **2,200.00**
Candlesticks, pressed flint glass,
Acanthus patt. base w/a paneled
baluster-form standard on a domed
paneled foot in opaque white,
w/opaque starch blue tulip-form
sockets, attributed to the Boston &
Sandwich Glass Co., ca. 1850,
11" h., pr. (tiny chip on corner of
one, other w/heat crack in socket
& long crack in the stem) **660.00**
Candlesticks, pressed glass, a
flaring tulip-form socket above a
tapering ringed & ribbed standard on
a ringed & ribbed domed round foot,
opaque starch blue, probably
France, ca. 1840-60, 7¾" h., pr. **148.50**
Candlesticks, sterling silver, plain
baluster-form, the foot rim w/an
applied scrolling design,
monogrammed, Towle, early 20th c.,
10½" h., pr. **460.00**
Candlesticks, silver, square base
w/baluster-form standard, chased
w/leaves, monogrammed,
Russian hallmarks, 14½" h., pr. **632.50**
Chamberstick, hand-hammered
copper, Arts & Crafts style, wide
dished base centering a heavy
cylindrical shaft w/a riveted strap
handle near the top, flattened rim at
socket, bronze patina, impressed
Gustav Stickley mark, Model No. 74,
early 20th c., 9" h. **345.00**

Rush light holder, wrought iron &
wood, w/candle socket
counterweight, wooden base
w/twisted detail & old
worn patina, 8" h. **302.50**
Wall sconces, brass, cast in five
parts w/pierced hanging tab above
scrolled lozenge plate, the oval
domed center w/applied squared
bracket & socket pierced to receive
double scrolled candlearms,
w/separate dished bobeche &
reeded urn-shaped candlecup,
possibly American-made, 18th c.,
8" deep, 7" h., pr. **575.00**

CANDY CONTAINERS

Early Auto Candy Container

*Indicates the container might not have
held candy originally. +Indicates this
container might also be found as a
reproduction. ‡Indicates this container was
also made as a bank. All containers are
clear glass unless otherwise indicated. Any
candy container that retains the original
paint is very desirable and readers should
follow descriptions carefully realizing that
an identical candy container that lacks the
original paint will be less valuable. Also
see HOLIDAY COLLECTIBLES.*

Airplane - w/left side rear door, metal
screw cap & tin propeller, painted
wing & wheels, probably 1930s,
4⅝" l. **$388.00**
Airplane - "Spirit of Goodwill,"
w/screw cap & propeller, Victory
Glass Co., ca. 1930,
4⅝" l. ....**150.00 to 175.00**
Airplane, "Spirit of St. Louis" printed
on tin wings, tin propeller closure,
glass fuselage embossed "W.Glass
Co., Grapeville, Pa.," metal frame &
wheels, late 1920s, 4¾" l., 6 3/16" w.
(slight rust, dent on nose) **345.00**
Amos & Andy in Open Air Taxi -
painted figures, marked "Victory
Glass Co., etc.," w/tin closure,
1928-30, 4½" l. **600.00**
Automobile - coupe w/long hood,

marked "U.S.A.," w/tin closure on
bottom, ca. 1918, 5¼" l. (ILLUS.).....**110.00**
Automobile - V.G. Co. sedan, 4-door,
marked "Avor ¾ oz" & "V.G. Co."
under doors, w/original tin wheels,
5" l..**100.00**
Barney Google & Ball - painted,
marked "Barney Google" across
base under figure, reverse marked
"copyright 1927 - King Features
Syndicate Inc.," 3¾" h......................**350.00**
‡**Barney Google beside bank,**
painted figure, "BARNEY GOOGLE"
in raised letters on bank container,
marked on base under figure
"copyright 1923 - King Features
Syndicate, inc.," 3¹/₁₆"......................**750.00**
Bell - Liberty Bell w/hanger, green,
w/old closure, 3⅜" h..........................**65.00**
*****Boat** - "Remember the Maine," two-
piece dish container, 7¼" l..............**95.00**
Charlie Chaplin beside barrel - figure
beside barrel marked "Geo .
Borgfeldt & Co." on base w/tin
closure on barrel slotted for use as
bank, ca. 1915, figure w/paint,
3⅞" h..**188.00**
Chicken on Oblong Basket - painted
w/closure, 3" h....................................**95.00**
"Chicken on the Nest" - marked on
cardboard closure, J.H. Millstein,
4⅝" h...**40.00**
Chicken - crowing rooster,
original paint, 2⅛" d., 5" h...............**145.00**
"Felix" beside Barrel, painted
character, marked on base
"Copyright 1922-24 - by Pat
Sullivan...," w/tin closure on top of
barrel slotted for use as bank,
3⅜" h. figure....................................**750.00**
Fire Engine - Little Boiler No. 1,
4¾" l., 3" h..**75.00**
+**Fire Engine** - miniature w/solid glass
boiler & hose roll on back, 5" l. **45.00**
*****Gun** - small revolver No. 1, 4¾" l........**45.00**
Horn - trumpet-shaped but no valves,
milk white glass w/gilt trim &
souvenir lettering, color decal of
either bears or Dutch children decor,
ca. 1908, 5½" l. **150.00**
Lamp - candlestick base, clear
pressed glass w/opaque oiled
lithographed paper shade, T.H.
Stough Co., Jeannette, Pa., 2¼" d.,
3⅝" h. base, 1¾" h. shade, 1½" d. at
top & 2" d. at bottom, complete
w/candy..**250.00**
Locomotive - "Mapother's 1892,"
Mogul-type locomotive, all-glass,
metal screw-on closure, 6¼" l.,
3¾" h...**150.00**
Locomotive - "Brainard's 1923," all-
glass, "N.Y.C." on cab doors, tin

closure shows interior of cab
w/figures, 4⅞" l., 2¹³/₁₆" h................**225.00**
Locomotive - curved line No. 888 all-
glass, tin snap-on strip closure,
4⅞" l., 2⅛" h.....................................**50.00**
+**Locomotive** - double window in
engine cab marked "888" below,
American-type locomotive, glass
wheels, 4⅞" l......................................**50.00**
+**Mule Pulling Two-Wheeled Barrel
with Driver** - painted, some marked
"Victory Glass Co.," w/tin cap
closure on back of barrel,
ca. 1936, 4½" l.................**100.00 to 125.00**
Pumpkin Head Policeman, goggles,
cap, hands & legs painted black,
pumpkin orange head w/red mouth
& white teeth, blue coat, metal
screw-on closure, ca. 1920s, 2" d.
base, 4¾" h. **975.00**
Rabbit - pushing chick in shell cart,
original paint & closure, Victory
Glass Co., 4" l., 3⅞" h.....................**350.00**
Rabbit - sitting w/forepaws next to
body, gilt paint, marked on back
"1 oz. AVOR. U.S.A.," metal screw
cap base closure, 5" h **110.00**
Rabbit Mother with Daughter,
standing wearing dress & apron,
marked on back "V/G" & "½ oz. -
AVOR. U.S.A.," 5⅛" h......................**650.00**
Radio - old-time model w/speaker
horn on top of cabinet, marked
"Tune In" on cabinet & marked
"V.G.,...," no paint, no closure,
ca. 1925 ....**170.00**
Santa Claus - with double cuffs.
painted, metal screw-on base
closure, Victory Glass Co., ca. 1927,
4⅜" h. **150.00**

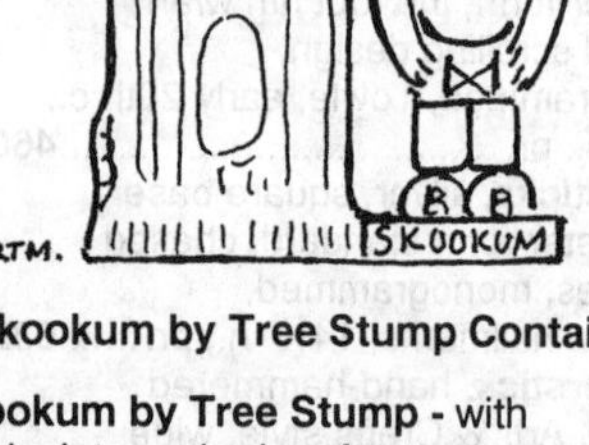

Skookum by Tree Stump Container

‡**Skookum by Tree Stump** - with
bank slot, marked on front
"SKOOKUM," & on back "U.S. DES.
PAT." stump base marked "GEO
BORGFELDT & CO. SOLE
LICENSEE - J.S. SEARS
1916," 3⅝" h. (ILLUS.)....................**350.00**

Tank - World War I, all-glass, some paint w/closure, 4⁵⁄₁₆" **75.00**

Taxi, Checker Cab, w/lithographed tin slide cover marked "Black & White Taxi," & pierced tin wheels, 4½" l..**170.00**

Telephone - candlestick-type, tall musical toy, w/wooden receiver, ca. 1950, 4¼" h. ....**50.00 to 75.00**

Early Telephone Container

Telephone - "Victory Glass Co., Dial Type," wire hanger & wooden receiver, ca. 1944, 4⅞" h. (ILLUS.) ....**40.00 to 47.50**

Telephone - candlestick-type, "Tall," w/wooden receiver, marked "V.G.Co." on base, 7½" h.................**150.00**

Wheelbarrow - w/tin closure over top, 6" l., 2¼" h. **32.50**

CANES & WALKING STICKS

Ornately Carved Walking Stick

Cherry walking stick, the handle

fashioned as a stylized figure of a mermaid relief-carved w/flowing hair & scaled body twisting around a vine relief-carved shaft, initialed "A.V." on the shaft, New England, probably Nantucket, Massachusetts, third quarter 19th c., now mounted on a black metal base, 35¼" l............**$3,737.00**

Mahogany walking stick, turned & flattened ball handle above a slender turned & tapering shaft, New England, early 19th c., 54½" l. **977.00**

Pine walking stick, the tapering shaft carved w/the figures of 26 animals & birds in relief, including a horse, dog, wolf, goat, pig, seal, camel, chickens & other birds, America, late 19th c., now mounted on a black metal base, 36" l. **2,588.00**

Whalebone walking stick, the knop carved in the form of a clenched fist, 19th c., 31½" l. (some age cracks) ..**495.00**

Whalebone walking stick, carved whalebone shaft w/whale's tooth handle carved in the form of a sperm whale, 19th c.. 32" l..............**440.00**

Whalebone, ivory & ebony walking stick, the ivory handle carved as a fist clutching a serpent's head, the serpent's body continuing to a rope-twist tapering ebony shaft ending in a whalebone tip, now mounted on a black metal base, American-made, 19th c., 33¾" l. **2,990.00**

Wooden walking stick, the handle carved in the form of a stylized dog's head w/collar, the tapering shaft intricately carved w/various animals including dogs, rabbits, birds, a fox, fish & two entwined snakes, late 19th c., 35½" l. (ILLUS.)..................**805.00**

CANS & CONTAINERS

Flotex Snowman Antifreeze

The collecting of tin containers has become quite popular within the past several years. Air-tight tins were first produced by hand to keep foods fresh and, after the invention of the tin-printing machine in the 1870s, containers were manufactured in a wide variety of shapes and sizes with colorful designs. Also see: TOBACCIANA.

Almond Paste, Heide's tin, shows workers in improved factory.............**$70.00**

Antifreeze, Flotex Snowman Anti-Freeze 1 qt. can, stylized white snowman against a green ground w/green trim, dark green, white & red lettering, ca. 1935, minor scratches (ILLUS.) **231.00**

Antifreeze, Polar 1 gal. can, dark blue w/a large white polar bear in the lower half, white, red & blue lettering, 6¾" w., 9½" h. (minor rust & scratches) **93.50**

Shell Anti-Freeze

Antifreeze, Shell 1 qt. can, minor scratches, w/contents (ILLUS.) **82.50**

Antifreeze, Snowman 2 gal. can, printed in colors w/a large angular stylized snowman & a band of small black cars, printed w/"Snowman - Completely Denatured Alcohol - The Non-Rusting Antifreeze," 8½" w., 11" h. (minor denting & scratches)...**242.00**

Antifreeze, Thermo 1 gal. can, comic design of a running snowman carrying a can of the product in one hand & a large thermometer across his other shoulder, 1945 copyright, 6½" d., 8" h. (minor denting, scratches & rust) **55.00**

Aspirin, Hobbson's tin, flat...................**12.00**

Axle grease, Eldred 1 lb. can, block lettering reading "Eldred No. 3 Cup Grease," soiling & scratches (ILLUS. top next column) **49.50**

Axle grease, Mica 5 lb. can, cylindrical, 6½" d. (overall rust & soiling) **33.00**

Axle grease, White Rose 1 lb. can, a single white rose on a light background above "White Rose,"

Eldred Axle Grease Can

printed on a narrow base band "Canadian Oil Companies Limited - Branches Throughout Canada," 3½" d., 4½" h. (overall scratches, minor rust)..**66.00**

Baking powder, Calumet 6 oz. can, Indian logo **10.00**

Baking powder, Chef tin, great picture of chef **35.00**

Baking powder, Miss Princine tin, one-cup measuring cup size, unopened..**75.00**

Rough Rider Baking Powder

Baking powder, Rough Rider can, Teddy Roosevelt on horseback, 1901, some damage to paper label, minor rust, 2" d., 3¾" h. (ILLUS.) **66.00**

Biscuit, Crawford & Sons tin, model of a double-decker bus, lithographed passengers in deck, top opens for biscuits, movable wheels, advertising on the sides, England, ca. 1920, 10½" l. **5,060.00**

Biscuit, Crawford & Sons tin, model of a passenger biplane, gold w/black lettering, trim & wheels, movable propeller, British flags on top wing, sides printed "Crawford's Air Service" & "A-One," ca. 1928, w/original box, 16" l. (ILLUS. top next page) **3,450.00**

Crawford's Biplane Biscuit Tin

Biscuit, Huntley & Palmer tin, lithographed scene of Russian peasant & sleigh, 1890s **55.00**

Loose-Wiles "Hiawatha" Box

Biscuit, Loose-Wiles "Hiawatha's Wedding Journey" 2 lb. 8 oz. box w/bail handle, Hiawatha & Indian maiden by waterfall, w/poem (ILLUS.) **175.00**

Biscuit, Saltina 10½ oz. round tin, sailor decoration **45.00**

Brake fluid, Indian Head can...............**22.50**

Candy, English Toffee tin, oblong, pictures Little Red Riding Hood, 1950s, 4 x 6" **55.00**

Candy, Standard Licorice Lozenges 5 lb. store bin, square upright form w/arched glass front panel, reddish orange ground w/black & grey lettering & trim, lithograph of a pretty girl on the lid, 5 x 5", 7½" h. **198.00**

Candy, Walter's Palm Toffee tin, super graphics, 5½ x 11" **100.00**

Candy, Whitman's Prestige Chocolates tin, dome shaped **18.00**

Candy, Whitman's "Salmagundi" 2 lb. box **35.00**

Cigarettes, Camel can, cylindrical w/camel logo on a white paneled ground, ca. 1950s, minor soiling, 3½" d., 3½" h. (ILLUS. top next column) **33.00**

Cigarettes, Half & Half flat fifties tin.......**6.00**

Camel Cigarettes Can

Cigarettes, Kools flat fifties tin **70.00**

Cigarettes, Lucky Strike flat fifties tin, Christmas decoration **45.00**

Cigarettes, Lucky Strike flat fifties, green, red, gold................................**25.00**

Cigarettes, Old Gold flat fifties tin........**50.00**

Cigarettes, Player's Navy cut flat fifties tin, sailor shown.......................**15.00**

Cigarettes, Player's Navy Cut tin, long rectangle w/rounded corners, color scene against blue ground, 3¼ x 5½", 1¼" h.................................**32.00**

Cigars, Armas Del Mundo tin **40.00**

Cigars, Blue Jay vertical tin, square, 3 x 3", 5½" h.....................................**190.00**

Cigars, Cornelius tin, bust portrait of Roman man, 3" d., 6" h...............**165.00**

Cigars, La Corona tin, oval **95.00**

Cigars, La Diligencia Premier tin **45.00**

Cigars, La Fendrich tin, rectangular, bust portrait of man w/a goatee in oval reserve, 3 x 4", 1" h. **30.00**

Cigars, Marshall Field tin, rectangular, bust portrait of white-haired man in a square panel, 3 x 4", 1" h. ....**15.00 to 25.00**

Cigars, Oxford Gems tin, rectangular, small round portrait of an Oxford don within a laurel wreath, 3 x 4", 4" h..**125.00**

Cigars, Red Dot square tin, rectangular, small round center portrait of a pretty lady's head, 2 x 4", 1" h......................................**55.00**

Cigars, Stogie Panetelas vertical tin, square, 4 x 4", 7" h............................**70.00**

Cigars, Webster pocket tin, bust portrait of Daniel Webster **25.00**

Cleanser, Evans Reddy Waterless Cleanser pail, tapering cylinder, a band of small comic bellhops around the bottom & bellhop on cover, wire bail handle, red, yellow & black, w/some contents (scratches, soiling, rust on bottom)................................**66.00**

Cleanser, Lighthouse canister pictures lighthouse, 1950s **12.00**

Cocoa, Droste ¼ oz. sample tin...........**95.00**
Cocoa, Index 5 lb. tin, Montgomery
Ward & Co., pictures girl...................**55.00**
Cocoa, Monarch sample size, lion's
head shown........................**50.00 to 75.00**
Coffee, Admiration 1 lb. can, black
woman serving white couple.............**65.00**
Coffee, American Ace 1 lb can, bust
portrait of flying Ace **22.50**
Coffee, Astor House 1 lb. can,
pictures the hotel **70.00**
Coffee, Berma 1 lb. can, brown &
gold **35.00**
Coffee, Budget Blend 1 lb. can **75.00**
Coffee, Bursley's 1 lb. can **55.00**
Coffee, Cafe' London House 1 lb.
can **50.00**
Coffee, Campbell 4 lb. container,
camel pictured, yellow & red,
8" d., 8" h. **50.00**
Coffee, Comrade 6 lb. pail w/handle,
pictures dog's head.........................**130.00**
Coffee, Continental 1 lb. can...............**50.00**
Coffee, Defiance 1 lb. can.....................**60.00**
Coffee, Delicious 1 lb. can, McTighe
Grocery Co., Binghamton, New
York **35.00**
Coffee, Del Monte 1 lb. can, green,
red & white.....................................**18.00**
Coffee, Franklin's Famous Java ½ lb.
square upright canister w/beveled
corners...**25.00**
Coffee, Golden Rule Blend 1 lb. can,
moss green & gold ....**40.00 to 50.00**
Coffee, Hersh's Best 1 lb. can **80.00**
Coffee, Ideal 1 lb. can, "W" logo on
front..**40.00**
Coffee, Kleeko 1 lb. can, coffee cup &
saucer on front, red & yellow **80.00**
Coffee, Lipton's Yellow Brand 1 lb.
can **50.00**
Coffee, Luzianne Coffee & Chicory
3 lb. pail, red background **65.00**
Coffee, Luzianne Coffee & Chicory
3 lb. pail, white background **75.00**
Coffee, Manhattan 1 lb. can, skyline
scene, key-wind lid **55.00**
Coffee, May-Day 1 lb. can, blue
paper label.....................................**55.00**
Coffee, Old Judge 1 lb. can, small
picture of an owl on front **30.00**
Coffee, Old Southern tall 1 lb. can,
lady in chair w/cup of coffee
decoration, screw-on lid ....**80.00 to 100.00**
Coffee, Omar 1 lb. can..........................**45.00**
Coffee, Ostrander, Loomis & Co. 2 lb.
pail, cylindrical w/red & gold, wire
bail handle **30.00**
Coffee, Peak 1 lb. can, mountain
range in background **30.00**
Coffee, Red Owl sample display can,
red, white & blue **80.00**
Coffee, Regent 1 lb. can **50.00**

Coffee, Royal Dutch 1 lb. can, red
& cream **35.00**
Coffee, Savarin 1 lb. can......................**40.00**
Coffee, Stewart's 1 lb. can, cream &
brown **40.00**
Coffee, Turkey 1 lb. can, turkey on
the front..**15.00**
Coffee, Veteran Brand 1 lb. can,
portrait of Civil War vet,
4¼ x 5¾".......................................**65.00**
Coffee, Vertical 1 lb. can,
striped background **40.00**
Coffee, Yuban 1 lb. can **30.00**
Crackers, Educator tin, hinged lid........**65.00**

Aunt Sue's Dry Cleaner Can

Dry cleaner, Aunt Sue's 1 gal. can,
lady holding fabric over a bowl
within an oval reserve, reads "Aunt
Sue's French Dry Cleaner," printed
in red, black & white, paint drip at
top, soiling, scratches & rust,
6½" w., 10½" h. (ILLUS.) **55.00**
Foot powder, Zanol Military tin,
flattened oval shape, standing
soldier & sailor shaking hands on
front (excellent condition)...................**75.00**
Gum, Colgan's Taffy Tolu tin.............**295.00**
Gun powder, Dead Shot - DuPont
1 lb. tin **300.00**
Gun powder, DuPont Superfine FFF
drum..**45.00**
Hair product, Sweet Georgia Brown
Pomade tin, black person pictured **50.00**

Manhattan Delight Cones Can

Ice cream cones, Manhattan Delight
Sugar Cones can, cylindrical w/blue
& greyish brown ground & lettering,
early 20th c., overall denting &
scratches, 12" d., 14¼" h. (ILLUS.
bottom previous page) **99.00**

Ice cream cones, Quality Sugar
Cones tin, pictures a young girl w/a
cone...**55.00**

Ink erasers, Carter's Rytoff tin.............**20.00**

Lard, Armour's 4 lb. pail.......................**15.00**

Lard, Home Rendered Lard 50 lb.
can, gold ground decorated w/a
pig in center of a red oval, 13" d.,
15" h..**54.00**

Paracide Kills Moths Can

Moth crystals, Paracide Kills Moths
can, a green & black background
w/a large white airplane & black &
white moths, black lettering outlined
in white, very minor scratches &
denting, 3¼" d., 5½" h. (ILLUS.) **27.50**

Motor oil, Capitan Parlube 1 gal. can,
printed in red, white & blue w/a
scene of a large car racing up a
mountain road, 8½" w., 11" h. (minor
denting & scratches) **132.00**

Motor oil, Indy Hi Speed Racing 1 qt.
can, printed in gold, red, white &
black w/a stylized racing car &
checkered flags, 4" d., 5½" h. (very
minor scratches & denting at top) **286.00**

Motor oil, Lucky Penn 1 qt. can,
yellow & red back ground &
lettering, "100% Pure Pennsylvania
Lucky Penn - Motor Oil," 4" d.,
5½" h. (very minor denting &
scratches) **38.50**

Motor oil, Red Hat 1 gal. can,
rectangular upright form w/top
handle, a large Uncle Sam hat
within a black ring, reads "Approved
- Red Hat - Motor oil," cream
background printed in black & red,
scratches, 8" w., 11" h. (ILLUS.
top next column) **990.00**

Motor oil, Speedway 2 gal. can,
printed in yellow, black & white w/a

Red Hat Motor Oil Can

large checkered flag & a small
racing car, 8" w., 11½" h (scratches,
minor rust)......................................**209.00**

Motor oil, Streamline Hi-Speed 2 gal.
can, printed in orange, yellow, blue
& brown, a curved center banner w/
"Streamline - Hi-Speed" & a sleek
stylized auto above "2000 Miles of
Modern Motor Lubrication - Motor
Oil," 8½" w., 11" h. (denting, rust,
scratches) **165.00**

Motor oil, Texaco Marine 1 qt. can, a
printed scene of motor boats around
the bottom, 4" d., 5½" h. (minor rust,
scratches & denting) **165.00**

Motor oil, Tiolene 1 gal. can, dark
blue w/white lettering & a bull's-eye
& arrow in the center, w/contents,
7½" w., 10½" h. (minor scratches) **60.50**

Tydol Motor Oil Can

Motor oil, Tydol 1 qt. can, cylindrical,
green background w/a cream center
circle printed w/black lettering & a
red "flying A" w/cream wings, minor
scratches & denting, 4" d., 5½" h.
(ILLUS.) **49.50**

Mustard plaster, Mother's tin,
illustration of an elderly lady on lid.....**45.00**

Oysters, Captain Jack 1 gal can..........**40.00**

Oysters, Woodfield's 1 gal. pail,
cylindrical w/wire bail handle, yellow

Woodfield's Oysters Pail

A&P Tea Store Bin

ground w/red & green lettering &
trim, a scroll-bordered panel
enclosing wording & a sailing ship
scene, soiling & scratches, 6½" d.,
7½" h. (ILLUS.) **132.00**
Peanut butter, Mosemann's pail,
yellow ground w/animals on the
side **175.00**
Peanut butter, Shedd's 5 lb. pail,
elves & animals shown **50.00**
Peanut butter, Squirrel lb. pail **200.00**
Peanut butter, Uzar 2 lb. pail,
pictures young girl (some fading).....**350.00**
Peanuts, Planters Pennant Salted
Peanuts 10 lb. canister, blue & red
lettering on black background,
pennant w/Mr. Peanut across
center, w/original lid, 8½" d.,
10" h. ....**100.00 to 125.00**
Popcorn, Monarch "Teenie Weenie"
1 lb. pail ....**250.00 to 275.00**
Radiator cement, Indian Head tin,
Indian Chief pictured, bright colors,
unopened **10.00**
Spice, Zanzibar pepper 10 lb. tin,
depicts African woman & monkeys
on paper label, ca. 1924 ....**275.00**
Talcum powder, Dream Girl tin **55.00**
Talcum powder, Palmer's Alomeal,
illustration of a pretty woman **45.00**
Tea, A & P store bin, wooden,
rectangular w/a three-sided paneled
front below a wide slant lid, original
red paint w/gold & black logos,
metal interior, overall soiling,
30" h. (ILLUS. top next column).......**231.00**
Tea, Golden Rule 5 lb. square upright
canister, shield on front, red &
gold **60.00**
Tea, Ridgway's 5 O'clock tin, lady
portraits **250.00**
Tea bags, Tetley rectangular box,
"Tetley Tea Bags" on top & sides,
blue & gold ground w/red & gold
lettering, 3½ x 5", 2" h. (very minor
denting & scratches) **16.50**

Tennis balls, Wilson's can, World
War II issue, contains no rubber,
unopened.......................................**100.00**
Tobacco, Between the Acts flat
pocket tin, full ....**15.00 to 20.00**
Tobacco, Bond Street pocket tin **20.00**
Tobacco, Bon Voyage pocket tin
w/paper label **20.00**
Tobacco, Bootjack Plug pocket tin **185.00**
Tobacco, Buckingham Cut Plug
pocket tin **70.00**
Tobacco, Buckingham trial size tin **300.00**
Tobacco, Bugler pocket tin,
telescopic-type **18.00**
Tobacco, Burley Boy (Bagley's)
pocket tin, little boxer boy, "The
White Man's Hope" ....**650.00 to 750.00**
Tobacco, Central Union Cut Plug
lunch box **65.00**
Tobacco, City Club upright pocket tin,
short ....**325.00 to 375.00**
Tobacco, Clubb's Perique Mixture
pocket tin **20.00**
Tobacco, Constellation (Mayo's) Cut
Plug rectangular square-corner tin **80.00**
Tobacco, Continental Cubes upright
pocket-tin ....**250.00 to 300.00**
Tobacco, Crescent Club Turkish
Mixture rectangular square-corner
tin **50.00**
Tobacco, Culture pocket
tin....................................**100.00 to 125.00**
Tobacco, Devoes Sweet Smoke
upright pocket tin **350.00**
Tobacco, Diamond F Mixture
rectangular square-corner tin.............**80.00**
Tobacco, Dial pocket tin ....**35.00 to 45.00**
Tobacco, Dill's Best horizontal box,
large, 3 x 3 x 6" **20.00**
Tobacco, Dill's Best pocket tin
(short) ....**30.00 to 50.00**
Tobacco, Dill's Best pocket tin (tall).....**40.00**
Tobacco, Dill's (J.G.) Natural Leaf
Bright Cut rectangular square-
corner tin...**35.00**

Tobacco, Dixie Kid Cut Plug lunch pail, black baby boy ....**375.00 to 425.00**

Tobacco, Dixie Kid Cut Plug lunch pail, white baby boy **195.00**

Tobacco, Dixie Queen canister, wide mouth, 6½" h. ....**250.00 to 275.00**

Tobacco, Edgeworth Junior vertical pocket tin ....**50.00 to 75.00**

Tobacco, Edgeworth trial size pocket tin...**60.00**

Tobacco, Edgeworth pocket tin, concave **20.00**

Tobacco, Edgeworth pocket tin, flat **15.00**

Tobacco, Eight Brothers Long Cut lunch pail...**70.00**

Tobacco, Epicure rectangular canister **35.00**

Tobacco, Fairmount pocket tin, 10¢ on scroll ....**225.00 to 250.00**

Tobacco, Forest & Stream pocket tin, two men in canoe ....**400.00 to 450.00**

Tobacco, Four Roses pocket tin, four roses without oval reserve, flat lid....**110.00**

Tobacco, Friends canister, man w/dog **20.00**

George Washington Lunch Box

Tobacco, George Washington Cut Plug lunch box (ILLUS.)....................**65.00**

Tobacco, Gold Dust pocket tin, three miners panning for gold on front ...**2,400.00**

Tobacco, Golden Lustre Long Cut Virginian rectangular square-corner tin **375.00**

Tobacco, Grain Cut Plug pocket tin.................................**100.00 to 125.00**

Tobacco, Granger Rough Cut canister, knobbed lid.........................**38.00**

Tobacco, Granulated 54 tall pocket tin....................................**100.00 to 150.00**

Tobacco, Guide pocket tin.................**250.00**

Tobacco, Half & Half pocket tin, telescopic-type..................................**25.00**

Tobacco, Hand Made Flake Cut canister **50.00**

Tobacco, Hiawatha Long Cut can, depicts three Indians w/bows & arrows, Scotten & Co., Detroit, Michigan, 4 oz.......................................**95.00**

Tobacco, Hickory pocket tin..**50.00 to 60.00**

Tobacco, Hindoo pocket tin................................**900.00 to 1,000.00**

Tobacco, Hi-Plane pocket tin, twin-engine plane...................**125.00 to 150.00**

Tobacco, Hudson Bay Co. Cut Plug pocket tin **10.00**

Tobacco, Jewel of Virginia rectangular square-corner tin............**80.00**

Tobacco, Just Suits canister, small top...**65.00**

Tobacco, Just Suits Cut Plug lunch box **65.00**

Tobacco, Kentucky Club pocket tin..**25.00 to 35.00**

Tobacco, King Edward pocket tin....................................**475.00 to 550.00**

Tobacco, Little San canister **40.00**

Tobacco, Lucky Strike Roll-Cut pocket tin **55.00**

Tobacco, Maryland Club pocket tin, curved flap lid ....**250.00 to 275.00**

Mayo's Cut Plug Lunch Box

Tobacco, Mayo's Cut Plug lunch box, 3¾ x 8", 4¾" h. (ILLUS.) **55.00**

Tobacco, Mayo's Roly Poly Mammy tin......................................**400.00 to 500.00**

Tobacco, Model sample pocket tin......**65.00**

Tobacco, Monopol London Club rectangular square-corner can.........**225.00**

Tobacco, Old Chum tin.......................**30.00**

Tobacco, Old Colony (Bagley's) canister, ashtray lid.............................**50.00**

Tobacco, Old English pocket tin, curved, 3½ x 4" **22.00**

Tobacco, Old Statesman rectangular square-corner tin, bust portrait of older gentleman on lid **300.00**

Tobacco, Paragon pocket tin....................................**300.00 to 325.00**

Tobacco, Pat Hand pocket tin **175.00**

Tobacco, Patterson's Seal lunch box, basketweave design ....**35.00 to 45.00**

Tobacco, Patterson's Tuxedo rectangular canister w/oval top, green..**325.00**

Tobacco, Pedro lunch box.................................**100. 00 to 125.00**

Penn's Tobacco Tin

Tobacco, Penn's Spells Quality tin, square w/hinged lid, red ground w/gold & black pen knib & black & cream lettering, scratches & minor rust, 6½" sq., 2½" h. (ILLUS.) **33.00**

Three Tobacco Tins

Tobacco, Piccadilly Smoking Mixture tin, rectangular w/square corners, light blue & black webbed background w/stylized white flowers & black & white lettering, light wear (ILLUS. center) **12.50**

Tobacco, Pierce's Specialty Virginia rectangular square-corner tin.............**35.00**

Tobacco, Pipe Major pocket tin.....................................**275.00 to 300.00**

Tobacco, Plow Boy can, cylindrical w/colorful paper label w/man sitting on a plow & smoking, speckling on gold paint & water stains & pieces missing on label, 5" d., 6" h. (ILLUS. top next column) **55.00**

Tobacco, Q-Boid pocket tin, pictures cabin **225.00**

Tobacco, Queen Virginia Perique Mixture rectangular square-corner tin...**55.00**

Plow Boy Tobacco Can

Tobacco, Raleigh Plug Cut rectangular square-corner tin..........**200.00**

Tobacco, Red Jacket pocket tin **50.00**

Tobacco, Revelation pocket tin, telescopic-type ....**15.00 to 20.00**

Tobacco, Rex pocket tin, bust portrait of Roman & laurel wreath flanked by torches............................**150.00 to 175.00**

Tobacco, Richmond Club Mixture rectangular square-corner tin.............**30.00**

Tobacco, Rod and Reel Cut Plug rectangular square-corner tin..........**220.00**

Score Card Tobacco Can

Tobacco, Score Card can, cylindrical w/paper label, one side w/crossed baseball bats w/gloves & a mask-type logo, the other side w/an early baseball score card background, one section w/bowling ball & pins, black & white lettering, overall scratches, 3½" d., 5¼" h. (ILLUS.) **357.50**

Tobacco, Shakespeare rectangular square-corner tin..............................**90.00**

Tobacco, Speedboat (Rothman's) Mixture tin, rectangular w/rounded corners, red background w/white & black lettering & oval reserve of a speedboat in one corner, minor

Speedboat Mixture Tin

wear, ca. 1930s, 5¾" l., 3½" h.
(ILLUS.) **253.00**
Tobacco, Stanwix pocket tin,
blue..................................**300.00 to 325.00**
Tobacco, Target pocket tin....**25.00 to 30.00**
Tobacco, Three Feathers pocket
tin....................................**200.00 to 250.00**
Tobacco, Three States Mixture tin,
some wear, 3 x 4", 2" h. (ILLUS.
top, previous page) **30.00**
Tobacco, Turkish Mixture (Allen &
Ginter) rectangular square-corner
tin **180.00**
Tobacco, Tuxedo pocket tin, man
wearing hat **20.00**
Tobacco, Tuxedo pocket tin, man not
wearing hat **25.00**

Twin Oaks Casket Tin

Tobacco, Twin Oaks casket,
rectangular lid above bombé sides
embossed w/large bare oak leaves
& a pair of acorns framing "Twin
Oaks," on small tab feet, red & black
trim, overall scratches, 8½" l., 4" h.
(ILLUS.) **66.00**
Tobacco, Union Leader lunch box,
basketweave w/eagle deco-
ration ....**30.00 to 45.00**
Tobacco, Union Leader pocket tin,
w/eagle **14.00**
Tobacco, Velvet octagonal canister,
shows pipes **45.00**
Tobacco, Velvet pocket tin, w/pipe's
smoke spelling "Velvet" ....**20.00 to 30.00**
Tobacco, Virginia Creeper Curly Cut
rectangular square-corner tin.............**45.00**
Tobacco, Virginia Dare Cut Plug

4 oz. rectangular square-corner
tin **150.00**
Tobacco, Yale Mixture tin,
rectangular w/square corners, light
wear, 3 x 4", 2" h. (ILLUS.
bottom, previous page) **15.00**

Yankee Boy Pocket Tin

Tobacco, Yankee Boy upright pocket
tin, scene of little boy in baseball
uniform holding bat on both sides,
excellent condition
(ILLUS.) ....**550.00 to 575.00**
Typewriter ribbon, Panama round
box, plane flying over canal zone,
2½" d..**20.00**
Typewriter ribbon, Old Town tin,
depicts secretary & typewriter,
unopened, key-wind lid, ca.
1930s **15.00**

CARD CASES

Cloisonne Card Case

*In a more leisurely and sociable era,
ladies made a ritual of "calling" on new
neighbors and friends. Calling card cases
held the small cards engraved or lettered
with the owner's name and sometimes
additionally decorated. The cases were
turned out in a wide variety of styles and
materials which included gold, silver,
ivory, tortoiseshell and leather. A sampling*

of collectible calling card cases is listed below.

Cloisonne & silver gilt, flat rectangular form, a circle of fine scrolls above delicate leafy scrolls within a shaped border, multicolored enamel w/a demantoid garnet, tourmaline & green onyx closure, Russian hallmarks, made for Tiffany & Company, New York, ca. 1890 (ILLUS.) **$2,645.00**

Coin silver, rectangular w/lightly scalloped sides, lightly engraved bands & central quatrefoil w/engraved presentation, small chain handle, 3½" l. **38.50**

Gold (14k), lady's, one side w/the signature in diamonds of Queen Marie of Romania, the other side w/her portrait miniature, 20th c., 3¼" l. **1,840.00**

Mother-of-pearl, rectangular, overall harlequin diamond inlay design w/engraving & a relief-carved bird & flowers at the center, 4" l. (minor edge damage).....................................**71.50**

Silver, rectangular w/flaring rounded top, engraved scrolls around a central cartouche, figural cast cherubs at sides where chain handle attaches, 4" l. **99.00**

Silver-gilt & translucent enamel, enameled translucent pale blue over a *guilloché* ground, the borders chased w/leaftips, diamond-set thumbpiece, marked initials of workmaster Feodor Afanassiev, Fabregé, St. Petersburg, Russia, ca. 1910, 3¼" l. **8,050.00**

Sterling silver, rectangular w/rounded corners, overall delicate floral engraving w/plain round center reserve, jade button clasp, fine chain handle, marked "Sterling," 4" l. **95.50**

Tortoiseshell, rectangular, engraved ivory inlay of two tulip blossoms on long leafy stems on the sides & a small floral sprig on the cover, 4" l. (minor damage, hinge loose) **82.50**

Tortoiseshell, rectangular, the front w/a round ring centered by a finely detailed embossed basket of flowers, 4" l **82.50**

Tortoiseshell, rectangular, the sides centered by a rectangular mother-of-pearl panel framed by bands of abalone, engraved details, 4" l. (minor damage) **121.00**

CARPET BALLS

Early Carpet Balls

Glazed china spheres, about 3½" in diameter, are commonly called "carpet balls" by collectors who seek them out. Originally made for a popular 19th century game called "bowls," these balls were rolled at a smaller ball called a "jack." Because the game could be played indoors on the carpet or taken out to the lawn, the ceramic balls were fired two or more times after the design was applied to ensure their durability.

Black & white cut-sponge overall stylized blossomheads, 3" d. **$225.00**

Black & white criss-crossing wide bands composed of thin lines, 3⅛" d. **165.00**

Black & white small cut-sponge overall blossomheads, 3¼" d. **165.00**

Black & white overall plaid design, 3½" d..**110.00**

Blue cut-sponge overall small blossoms design, 3⅛" d. (ILLUS. far left)..**187.00**

Green cut-sponge spatter overall large blossoms designs, 3⅛" d. (ILLUS. far right) **192.50**

Red & white alternating wide & thin stripes, flakes, pitting, 3⅜" d. (ILLUS. 2nd from right) **192.50**

Red & white overall plaid design w/alternating wide & narrow stripes, 3⅜" d. (ILLUS. 2nd from left) **165.00**

Yellow & white overall plaid design, 3½" d. (wear & chips)........................**71.50**

White & purple overall plaid design, 3½" d. **185.00**

CASH REGISTERS

James Ritty of Dayton, Ohio, is credited with inventing the first cash register. In 1882, he sold the business to a Cincinnati salesman, Jacob H. Eckert, who subsequently invited others into the business by selling stock. One of the purchasers of an early cash register, John J. Patterson, was so impressed with the savings his model brought to his company, he bought 25 shares of stock and became a director of the company in 1884, eventually buying a controlling interest in the National Manufacturing Company. Patterson thoroughly organized the company, conducted sales classes, prepared sales manuals and established salesman's territories. The success of the National Cash Register Company is due as much to these well organized origins as to the efficiency of its machines. Early "National" cash registers, as well as other models, are deemed highly collectible today.

Brass, "National," Model 7, w/original
   top sign **$550.00**
Brass, "National," Model 250 ....**600.00**
Brass, "National," Model 311 ....**650.00**
Brass, "National," Model
   312 ....**425.00 to 450.00**

National Model 313

Brass, "National," Model 313
   (ILLUS.) **750.00**
Brass, "National," Model 317 ....**450.00**
Brass, "National," Model 327 ....**750.00**
Brass, "National," Model
   442XX..............................**600.00 to 650.00**

CASTORS & CASTOR SETS

Castor bottles were made to hold condiments for table use. Some were produced in sets of several bottles housed in silver plated frames. The word also is sometimes spelled "Caster."

Castor set, 4-bottle, clear glass
   bottles cut w/honeycomb & panels &
   etched w/florals, ornate silver plate
   frame decorated w/florals & models
   of an open fan at each corner,
   marked "Derby" **$235.00**

Pickle castor, Amberina mold-blown
   glass Rib patt. insert, ornate silver
   plate frame & tongs..........................**385.00**
Pickle castor, blue opalescent Daisy
   & Fern patt. insert, ornate
   silver plate frame **469.00**

Castor with Clear Stippled Insert

Pickle castor, clear pressed glass
   stippled design insert, ornate silver
   plate frame w/arched & pierced
   handle top, footed base w/flaring
   skirt & tongs, marked "Meriden,"
   5¼" d., 11" h. (ILLUS.) **145.00**

Castor with Paneled Cane Insert

Pickle castor, clear pressed glass
   Paneled Cane patt. insert, ornate
   silver plate frame w/figural fan &
   flowers at the top of the handle,
   marked "Oneida," w/tongs, 4"d.,
   12" h. (ILLUS.) **145.00**
Pickle castor, clear pressed glass S-
   scroll design insert, ornate silver
   plate frame w/arched pierced scroll-
   cast handle, flaring base, marked
   "CMS," w/tongs, 4" d., 11½" h.
   (ILLUS. top next page)....................**145.00**
Pickle castor, cobalt blue blown
   bulbous glass insert w/gold scrolling
   decoration, ornate silver plate frame
   & tongs...**350.00**

Castor with S-Scroll Insert

Pickle castor, cobalt blue spherical blown glass insert decorated overall w/gold & yellow leafy scrolls & vines, ornate silver plate frame w/scrolls at

Ornate Cobalt Blue Castor

top of handle & w/a wide flaring base on small paw feet, marked "Benedict Mfg. Co.," w/tongs, 5⅜" d. 10½" h. (ILLUS.) **395.00**

Pickle castor, cranberry glass corset-shaped insert, ornate silver plate frame w/cover & tongs **295.00**

Pickle castor, cranberry Inverted Thumbprint patt. cylindrical insert, ornate silver plate frame w/angular pierced handle, w/tongs, frame resilvered, 4⅜" d., 10½" h. (ILLUS. top next column) **265.00**

Pickle castor, cranberry glass Inverted Thumbprint patt. insert w/gold enameling on front, silver plate frame & tongs, marked "Barbour Silver Co." **495.00**

Pickle castor, deep cobalt blue insert w/ornate heavy gold enameled flowers & leaves on front & back, ornate silver plate frame w/pleated base & arched handle w/ornate

Cranberry Pickle Castor

sides & top 'knot,' marked "Homan Silver Co.," resilvered **350.00**

Pickle castor, green pressed glass Daisy & Button patt. insert, ornate silver plate frame **349.00**

Pickle castor, honey amber pressed glass Diamond Point patt. insert, ornate footed silver plate frame & tongs, marked "Forbes" **210.00**

Pickle castor, pink & white spatter glass mold-blown Ribbed Pillar patt. insert, ornate silver plate frame **245.00**

Pickle castor, pink glass w/opalescent stripes & enameled floral decoration insert, original silver plate frame w/tongs, rare small size..................................**345.00**

Pickle castor, Pomona glass w/cornflower decoration insert, ornate silver plate frame & tongs, New England Glass Co...................**395.00**

Sapphire Blue Pickle Castor

Pickle castor, sapphire blue Inverted Thumbprint patt. corset-shaped insert decorated w/white enameled lily of the valley, green leaves & gilt trim, in ornate silver plate frame w/scrolls at the top of the handle & a wide flaring base w/small paw feet, marked "Benedict Mfg. Co.," w/tongs, 5½" d., 11¾" h. (ILLUS.)....**475.00**

Pickle castor, sapphire blue glass Inverted Thumbprint patt. insert decorated overall w/colorful lily of the valley, roses, hollyhocks & foliage, ornate silver plate frame & tongs **335.00**

Pickle castor, vaseline pressed glass Diamond Point Disc patt. insert, ornate silver plate frame **135.00**

CAT COLLECTIBLES

GENERAL

Automaton, walking & meowing cat, fur-covered cardboard & papier-maché, key-wind, by Roullet & Decamps, 10" h. **$1,200.00**

Automaton, Puss in Boots cat, clockwork nodder, furry cat wears thigh-high boots, green cap & red cape, 24" h..................................**2,400.00**

Book ends, Art Deco style cats, white metal painted green, 8" h., pr.............**75.00**

Book ends, stretching Siamese cats, aluminum w/antique brass finish, 7" h., pr. **85.00**

Bottle, "Felix the Cat" bubblebath by Colgate-Palmolive, ca. 1960s **20.00**

Bottle, "Sylvester the Cat" bubblebath, never opened, 1988 ....**15.00**

Box, candy tin, "Droste Haarlem Holland," four tabby kittens pictured on lid, near mint, 6¾" l. **24.00**

Box, candy tin, "Langues de Chats Droste Haarlem Holland," artist-signed C. Reichert, long haired cats pictured on lid, near mint, 4 x 7" **22.00**

Cane head, carved ivory cat head, glass eyes, head measures 3½" l., silver collar, rosewood shaft, horn ferrule, English, ca. 1890 ....**1,980.00**

Chinese Cat Lantern

Cigarette holder, ivory cat with ball **125.00**

Cigarettes, Black Cat Cigarettes, soft pack, unopened, wax seal **22.00**

Cookie jar, pink basketweave, white & black cat head lid, McCoy, 10" h...**60.00**

Lantern, porcelain, model of a crouching cat w/tail upcurled around the body, painted in blue w/stylized fur & incorporating cloud swirls, China, Kangxi Period, hairline crack, 6½" l. (ILLUS. bottom previous column) **8,050.00**

Pillow cover, featuring a smoking, banjo-playing cat & "Don't forget the Kitty," lithographed cotton cover, framed..**176.00**

Pin, 18k yellow gold & amethyst, set w/an amethyst head & body w/gold textured accents & turquoise eyes & tail...**460.00**

Plate, milk white glass, Three Kittens, gold paint in good condition, some chips on back rim...........................**19.00**

Plate, frosted clear glass, Three Kittens, marked "Pan American Expo Buffalo 1901," painted lighthouse & shore scene **65.00**

Plate, A-B-C plate, "Come into my Garden, Maud," three cats, bird & florals, blue & white, Allerton's, ca. 1891, 7⁹⁄₁₆" d............................**140.00**

Print, "Yard of Cats," by Guy Bedford, Chicago, framed **235.00**

Rug, hooked rug, dog & cat in field of hearts, 20th c., 20¾ x 37" **2,530.00**

Rug, hooked rug, black & white cat, early 20th c., 21½ x 40½" (some fiber loss, rebacked) **1,495.00**

Salt shaker, Napoli art glass, Palmer Cox Brownies on front of shaker, a cat & a pig on the opposite side, metal top removed, Mt. Washington, 2⁹⁄₁₆" h. **2,400.00**

Salt & pepper shakers, lusterware cats, off-white w/green bows, facial expression "Mmmm good," marked "Made in Japan," 4" h., pr. **15.00**

Stein, pottery, yowling cat on a book, half-liter **2,310.00**

MODELS OF CATS

Shafford Cat Figure

Ceramic, "Blue Ribbon Tortoise
Shell," cream, rust, & brown,
Shafford, Japan, 14½" l.
(ILLUS. bottom previous page)..........**50.00**
Elfinware porcelain, 'moss-ware'
type, a grey cat decorated w/florals
& moss trim, marked
"Germany," early 20th c., 2½" h.........**50.00**
Ironstone china, seated upright w/an
overall design printed in green,
England, late 19th c., 12" h...........**2,990.00**
Jackfield pottery, black-glazed,
England, 7" h., pr. **1,100.00**

Oriental Cat Figures

Porcelain, Oriental sleeping kitten,
white w/gold patches, red & blue
bow, marked "Made in Japan,"
ca. 1930s, 4" l. (ILLUS. right).............**65.00**
Porcelain, Oriental sleeping cat,
white w/gold patches, red bow,
Japan, ca. 1930s, 5½" l. (ILLUS.
left)...**75.00**
Porcelain, kittens in different poses,
Royal Doulton, HN 2579-2584,
retired in 1986, six different, each......**75.00**

Lady & Kitten Figure

Porcelain, lady in 18th c. attire w/lace
trim feeding her kitten, Meissen,
Germany, bows on her back
missing, ca. 1860-80, 4¾" h.
(ILLUS.) **1,950.00**
Porcelain, "Two Love Cats," one
brown & one black cat, Royal
Doulton, HN 259, England,
ca. 1925, 5" h. (ILLUS. top next
column) **1,600.00**
Porcelain, grey Persian mother &

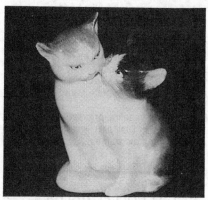

"Two Love Cats" Figure

kitten, 1976 Mother's Day issue,
Goebel, Germany, 5" h. **99.00**
Stoneware pottery, decorated w/a
dark mustard yellow glaze,
attributed to Mcgadore (large
chip in base) **2,350.00**

LOUIS WAIN ITEMS
"Puss in Boots" (The Stump Books),
London, Anthony Treherne & Co.,
Ltd., 1904, 1st Edition, 1⅝ x 6".........**850.00**
Santa postcards feature a cat
dressed in Santa robe with hood,
various humorous winter scenes,
each................................**200.00 to 400.00**
Louis Wain cut-out sets, complete,
each..........................**1,880.00 to 2,500.00**

CELLULOID

Early Auto Dresser Box

*Celluloid was our first commercial
plastic and early examples are now
"antique" in their own right, having been
produced as early as 1868 after the
perfection of celluloid by John Wesley
Hyatt. Earlier in this century other related
"plastics" were also introduced and some
examples of these items are also included.*

Box, cov., lid features an Art
Nouveau-style woman, 8 x 9" **$85.00**

Dresser box, model of an early sedan car, green mother-of-pearl style celluloid w/black fenders & headlights, drawers in the back for face powder, etc., fender & top drawer front reglued, ca. 1930s, 7¾" l., 4" h. (ILLUS.) 495.00

Celluloid Dresser Set

Dresser set: hand mirror, comb, hairbrush, shoe horn, cov. amber glass jar, cov. amber glass hair receiver; sea green mother-of-pearl celluloid, early 20th c., the set (ILLUS.) 66.00

Pin, model of a Scottie dog wearing a beret, Czechoslovakia 35.00

Tape measure, figure of a girl holding flowers..................................115.00

Tape measure, model of a coffee grinder...95.00

Tape measure, model of a kangaroo...65.00

Tape measure, model of a walking bear...85.00

CERAMICS

For additional listings, see Antique Trader Books CERAMICS - POTTERY & PORCELAIN PRICE GUIDE and AMERICAN & EUROPEAN ART POTTERY PRICE GUIDE.

ABINGDON

From about 1934 until 1950, Abingdon Pottery Company, Abingdon, Illinois manufactured decorative pottery, mainly cookie jars, flowerpots and vases. Dec-orated with various glazes, these items are becoming popular with collectors who are especially attracted to Abingdon's novelty cookie jars.

Book ends, model of a horse head, white glaze, pr...................................**$70.00**

Cookie jar, "Choo Choo," engine............................150.00 to 200.00

Cookie jar, "Cutie Pie," blue **185.00**

Cookie jar, "Hippo," decorated **450.00**

Cookie jar, "Hippo," white glaze **150.00**

Cookie jar, "Little Old Lady," green glaze.................................225.00 to 275.00

Cookie jar, "Wigwam"........750.00 to 800.00

Figurine, kneeling nude holding bouquet of flowers, pink w/gold trim, 10" h..**175.00**

Wall pocket, Butterfly patt. ....50.00 to 75.00

ADAMS

TUNSTALL
ENGLAND

Members of the Adams family have been potters in England since 1650. Three William Adamses made pottery, all of it collectible. Most Adams pottery easily accessible today was made in the 19th century and is impressed or marked variously ADAMS, W. ADAMS, ADAMS TUNSTALL, W. ADAMS & SONS, or W. ADAMS & CO. with the word "England" or the phrase "Made in England" added after 1891. Wm. Adams & Son, Ltd. continues in operation today. Also see HISTORICAL & COMMEMORATIVE WARES and STAFFORDSHIRE TRANS-FER WARES.

Bowl, 9" l., rectangular, Calyx Ware, h.p. floral decoration **$45.00**

Pitcher, 6⅝" h., souvenir-type, blue transfer-printed scene, "Mt. Park Hotel, N. Woodstock, N.H."..............**120.00**

Plate, 7¾" d., souvenir-type, blue transfer-printed scene, "Faneuil Hall, Cradle of Liberty, 1742" **45.00**

Plate, 8¾" d., Cows & Sheep patt., dark blue, impressed mark (overall stain & wear to foot) **154.00**

Plate, 9⅜" d., Adam's Rose patt., red,
green & black, impressed "Adams"
(pinpoint edge flakes) **93.50**
Platter, 13½" l., octagonal, Isola Belle
patt., light blue printed mark **126.50**

AUSTRIAN

Ornate Austrian Cake Plate

*Numerous potteries in Austria
produced good-quality ceramic wares over
many years. Some factories were
established by American entrepreneurs,
particularly in the Carlsbad area, and
other factories made china under special
brand names for American importers.
Marks on various pieces are indicated in
many listings. Also see ROYAL VIENNA.*

Bone dishes, scrolled blank,
decorated w/pale yellow roses,
green leaves & brown stems, gold
trim, 6½" l., set of 6 (Carlsbad
Austria) **$95.00**
Bowl, footed, h.p. portrait of four
lovely maidens in elaborate dress in
lovely garden setting w/peacock,
gold trimmed border (Imperial -
Austria Crown China) ......**250.00 to 275.00**
Cake plate w/open handles, the
border decorated in a starburst
design in deep maroon, dark green
& gold w/triangular fan shapes in
gold & moss green at the rim, four-

arm star in center, marked
"Alhambra," 11½" d. (ILLUS.) **110.00**
Chocolate pot, cov., decorated
w/violets on a blue & white ground
w/gold trim (Victoria Austria)............**125.00**

Austrian Compotes & Plate

Compotes, open, 8"d., wide shallow
reticulated bowl raised on a
knobbed pedestal & domed foot,
cobalt blue ground w/gilt trim, the
interior w/a h.p. panel of classical
female subjects, late 19th c., pr.
(ILLUS. right) **977.50**
Condensed milk jar, cov., decorated
w/lavender flowers (Victoria
Carlsbad) **115.00**
Ewer, four-footed, rococo gold scroll
handle, molded scrolls overall,
decorated w/h.p. pink & yellow wild
roses outlined in gold on front &
back, gold rim & feet, 6" d.,
11¾" h. (circle & torch mark
w/"International") **155.00**
Ewer, pillow-form, reticulated handle,
h.p. iris decoration, giant molded
scrolls & lavish gold trim, 8 x 16"
(Victoria - Carlsbad) **360.00**
Ewer, waisted cylindrical footed body
w/small slender neck, ornate handle,
decorated w/colored florals,14" h.....**165.00**
Finger bowls w/underplates, h.p.
decoration of pink roses, gold trim,
set of 6 ....**250.00**

Small Austrian Pitcher with Roses

Pitcher, 4¼" h., 4¼" d., bulbous ovoid body decorated w/h.p. red & yellow roses w/gold trim on pastel background, artist-signed Vienna, Austria (ILLUS. bottom previous page)...**45.00**

Ornate Tankard Pitcher

Pitcher, tankard, 11" h., tall cylindrical body w/a flaring base, C-scroll gilt handle, deep red ground decorated w/heavy leafy scroll gilt borders around rectangular panel h.p. w/a monk drinking wine, gilt borders at rim & base, ca. 1900, beehive mark (ILLUS.) **747.50**
Plate, 8⅞" d., decorated w/large h.p. pink roses & green leaves on an eggshell ground, gold filigree border & rim (O & EG Royal Austria) **18.00**
Plate, 9½" d., wide cobalt blue border band decorated w/silver overlay scrolls, the center h.p. w/a scene of Christopher Columbus, late 19th c., beehive mark (ILLUS. left) **489.00**
Plate, 10" d., pierced for hanging, center decoration of lady & angels on white ground, green & gold decorated border (Victoria Austria) **55.00**
Plates, 7" d., center panels decorated w/large cluster of green & purple grapes, scalloped edge w/dark blue border w/band of gilt tracery encircling center panels, ca. 1884 1909, set of 6 (M.Z. Austria) **342.00**
Vase, 13½" h., 5" w. at base, four-footed, narrow neck w/flared scalloped mouth, high slender double shoulder handles, decorated w/h.p. red, yellow & white carnations, gold outlining on shaded beige-ivory ground, stylized relief-molded leaves at rim & neck, vertical ribs at base, gold trim (crown & seal "RH" Austria) **210.00**

Vase, 14½" h., tall ovoid body tapering to slender cylindrical neck flanked by high loop handles from rim to shoulders, decorated w/heavy enamel fuchsias in realistic colors, cobalt trim on handles extends down sides & around base **360.00**

BAUER POTTERY

The Bauer Pottery was moved to Los Angeles, California from Paducah, Kentucky, in 1909, in the hope that the climate would prove beneficial to the principal organizer, John Andrew Bauer, who suffered from severe asthma. Flowerpots, made of California adobe clay; were the first production at the new location, but soon they were able to resume production of stoneware crocks and jugs, the mainstay of the Kentucky operation. In the early 1930s, Bauer's colorfully glazed earthen dinnerwares, especially the popular Ring-Ware pattern, became an immediate success. Sometimes confused with its imitator, Fiesta Ware (first registered by Homer Laughlin in 1937), Bauer pottery is collectible in its own right and is especially popular with West Coast collectors. Bauer Pottery ceased operation in 1962.

Ashtray, La Linda patt., cobalt blue, 4" sq...**$25.00**
Batter bowl, Ring-Ware patt., yellow...**35.00**
Bowl, 10" d., Ring-Ware patt., green ...**50.00**
Bowl, Ring-Ware patt., light brown, No. 18 ....**40.00**
Butter dish, cov., Monterey patt., ivory **65.00**
Butter dish, cov., Monterey patt., red...**85.00**
Butter dish, cov., Ring-Ware patt., delph (light blue) **135.00**
Butter dish, cov., Ring-Ware patt., green..**130.00**
Butter dish, cov., round, Ring-Ware patt., red ....**150.00 to 175.00**
Candleholder, Ring-Ware patt., yellow..**20.00**

Canister w/wooden lid, oval, Ring-Ware patt., "Coffee," orange **45.00**
Carafe w/copper fittings, Ring-Ware patt., orange.......................................**80.00**
Casserole, cov., Gloss Pastel Kitchenware line, 1½ pt. **35.00**
Casserole, cov., Gloss Pastel Kitchenware line, 1 qt. **45.00**
Casserole, cov., individual, Ring-Ware patt., green **55.00**
Casserole, cov., individual, Ring-Ware patt., red, in wooden frame...**60.00**
Coffee server, cov., Ring-Ware patt., w/copper handle, red **85.00**
Creamer, Ring-Ware patt., black **35.00**
Creamer, Ring-Ware patt., cobalt blue...**16.50**
Creamer, Ring-Ware patt., delph (light blue) **35.00**
Creamer, Ring-Ware patt., red.............**35.00**
Mixing bowl, Atlanta line, cobalt blue, No. 24 ....**65.00**
Mixing bowl, Ring-Ware patt., yellow, No. 36, 5" d. **15.00**
Mixing bowl, Ring-Ware patt., blue, No. 24, 7" d. **20.00**
Mixing bowl, Ring-Ware patt., yellow, No. 18, 8" d. **25.00**
Mixing bowl, Ring-Ware patt., turquoise, No. 12, 9" d. **40.00**
Mixing bowl, Ring-Ware patt., black, No. 9, 10" d. **250.00**
Model of a cowboy hat, yellow **125.00**
Plate, dinner, 9" d., Ring-Ware patt., red..**20.00**
Plate, dinner, 9" d., Ring-Ware patt., yellow...**15.00**
Plate, dinner, 10½" d., Ring-Ware patt., black or white, each **75.00**
Plate, dinner, 10½" d., Ring-Ware patt., red..**50.00**
Plate, chop, 12" d., Ring-Ware patt., red..**75.00**
Plate, chop, 14" d., Ring-Ware patt., green or red, each **75.00**
Plate, chop, 17" d., Ring-Ware patt., red ....**225.00 to 250.00**
Plates, salad, 7½" d., Ring-Ware patt., each a different color, set of 6 ....**105.00**
Salt & pepper shakers, Ring-Ware patt., black, short, pr. **95.00**
Sherbet, footed, Ring-Ware patt., yellow..**35.00**
Teapot, cov., Monterey patt., yellow...**145.00**
Teapot, cov., Ring-Ware patt., cobalt blue **135.00**
Teapot, cov., Ring-Ware patt., red ....**150.00 to 175.00**
Teapot, cov., Ring-Ware patt., Hi-Fire line, rust **125.00**

Tumbler, w/wooden handle, Ring-Ware patt., black, 6 oz. **60.00**
Tumblers, La Linda patt., chartreuse, set of 6...**95.00**
Vase, 9" h., Artware line, w/gold trim... **45.00**
Vase, 12" h., Cal-Art line, No. 508, white **65.00**
Water set: red carafe & six tumbers w/wooden handles; Ring-Ware patt., three tumblers in yellow, three in red, 7 pcs. **250.00**

BAVARIAN

Bavarian Cider Pitcher

Ceramics have been produced by various poteries in Bavaria, Germany, for many years. Those appearing for sale in greatest frtequency today were produced in the 19th and early 20th centuries. Various company marks are indicated with some listings here.

Bowl, 8½" w. octagon, reticulated rim, center w/polychrome scene of youth and maiden in a garden setting, blue & gilt trim, marked "Bavaria" **$22.00**
Bowl, 10" d., 2¼" h., deeply scalloped & scrolled rim w/brushed gold trim, decorated w/large pink roses & buds, green leaves, castle mark w/"RC, Monbijou" **35.00**
Bowl, 11" d., 3" h., deeply scalloped scrolled sides, decorated w/large red roses & green daisies, lavish gold trim, marked "JSPV" (Joyhann Seltmann) **75.00**
Chocolate set: cov. chocolate pot & six cups & saucers; decorated w/roses & floral bouquets, gold trim, 13 pcs. **225.00**
Coffee set: 9¼" h. cov. coffeepot, creamer & cov. sugar bowl; lavish multicolored floral decoration,

scrolled & melon-ribbed blank, gold
rim & trim, crown mark w/"Bavaria -
Creidlitz - Germany," the set............**125.00**
Dish, figural oak leaf, decorated
w/white & pink blossoms w/gold
stems, marked "Old Nuremberg -
Bavaria - Germany," 4½ x 11" **20.00**
Dish, two-part w/center scrolled
handle, fluted & scalloped rim,
decorated w/medallions of Venus &
Mars or Venus & Neptune surrounded by blue, gold tracery & trim,
crown mark w/ "Royal Bavarian -
Germany," 7¾ x 11¼".....................**75.00**
Dresser set: hand mirror & brush;
decorated w/h.p. portrait of beautiful
lady w/long flowing hair, entwined
w/gold streamers & flowers, ornate
handles, R. C. Bavaria, 2 pcs. **155.00**
Fish set: large oval platter & 10
plates; a different fish in underwater
setting on each, marked "Mignon -
Bavaria," the set..........................**1,800.00**
Pitcher, cider, 6½" h., wide tapering
cylindrical body w/angled handle,
h.p. yellow goldenrod flowers &
green leaves on cream background,
dull Roman gold on handle, artist-
signed (ILLUS.)..............................**175.00**
Plate, 6½" d., reticulated rim,
decorated w/red poppies & h.p.
raised gold beading & trim, shades
of pastel blue & pink in ground, gold
leaves on rim, gold edge band,
marked "Schumann - Arzberg
Germany - Bavaria" **15.00**
Plate, 7¾" d., Arbutus patt., pink &
green draped flowers border
decoration w/gold trim.......................**12.00**
Plate, 8½" d., decorated w/scene
of a cat & roses................................**35.00**
Plate, 10½" d., center portrait of
Edwardian woman, crown mark
w/"Bayreuth" **100.00**
Plate, serving, 12⅜" d., gold lattice &
scroll decorated rim, decorated
w/giant pink & white roses on pastel
ground, shield mark w/"Empire -
ZS&Co. - Bavaria - Royal Munich".....**85.00**
Plate, 10" d., pierced to hang,
decorated w/h.p. pink & red roses,
artist-signed **50.00**
Plates, dinner, 10¾" d., white center
w/wide gold-encrusted rim band w/a
delicate floral design, marked
"Bavaria," set of 12 ....**429.00**
Table set: creamer, cov. sugar bowl,
salt & pepper shakers & toothpick
holder; decorated w/h.p. pink roses
& gold trim, artist-signed, marked
"J&C," 5 pcs. **150.00**
Table set: creamer, cov. sugar bowl,
toothpick holder, salt & pepper
shakers; decorated w/h.p. pink

roses, gold trim, artist-signed,
5 pcs. (J&C) **145.00**
Vase, 10" h., figural swan handles,
grape & leaf decoration, artist-
signed, marked "H.A.C. Bavaria".......**65.00**

BELLEEK

Belleek china has been made in Ireland's
County Fermanagh for many years. It is
exceedingly thin porcelain. Several marks
were used, including a hound and harp
(1865-1880), and a hound, harp and castle
(1863-1891). A printed hound, harp and
castle with the words "Co. Fermanagh
Ireland" constitutes the mark from 1891.
Belleek-type china also was made in the
United States last century by several firms,
including Ceramic Art Company,
Columbian Art Pottery, Lenox Inc., Ott &
Brewer and Willets Manufacturing Co.

AMERICAN

Ott & Brewer Potpourri Vase

Bowl, 6" d., 4" h., pedestal base,
everted lobed rim, the exterior
decorated w/pink flowers & green
leaves on a white ground, lustred
interior (Ceramic Art Company) **$95.00**
Bowl, 10¼" d., 4¼" h., pedestal base,
the interior decorated w/daisies &
wild roses on a white ground w/gold
trim (Ceramic Art Company) **135.00**
Condiment jar, cov., white w/gold
trim, in an R. Wallace & Sons
sterling silver holder, 2½" h.,
5" h...**120.00**
Creamer & cov. sugar bowl,
pedestal bases, floral decoration

w/gold trim, 6" h., pr. (Ceramic
Art Company).................................**175.00**
Cup & saucer, demitasse, cream
ground, figural dragon handle, ca.
1895 (Willets) **395.00**
Cup & saucer, decorated w/floral
reserves, cobalt bands (Morgan
Belleek) **145.00**
Humidor, cov., Art Deco design in
gold & salmon lustre on white,
5½" d., 5" h. (wear to finial, slight
rough spots on lid) **220.00**
Mug, decorated w/grapes & leaves,
5" h. (Ceramic Art Company)...........**225.00**
Mug, green base, gold top half w/six-
figure drinking scene decoration,
artist-signed, 5⅝" h. (Willets) **95.00**
Pitcher, miniature, green w/silver
overlay (Ceramic Art Company) **55.00**
Pitcher, tankard, 6¾" h., Vassar
College 1861 emblem on both sides,
24K gold-plated handle, rim, &
emblems, 1911, (Willets) **165.00**
Pitcher, 8⁷⁄₁₆" h., the slightly flaring
cylindrical body molded w/a wide
border of gilt-heightened 'bark'
issuing gilt-tipped twig stumps & at
the front & reverse forked twig
handles, the larger attached to the
ruffled rim & issuing a gilt branch
bearing shaded pink blossoms &
green & tan leaves all delineated in
raised gilding, a smaller branch on
the reverse, the integral compressed
spherical base w/a gilt-banded tan
ground pierced w/a border of white
prunus blossoms & gilt scrolling
foliage, crown & sword mark
between "BELLEEK" & "O & B"
printed in russett, Ott & Brewer,
1883-90 (small chip on spout &
base foliage) **1,035.00**
Pitcher, tankard, 15" h., decorated
w/a scene of a maiden on steps
looking into fish pool, blue
underglaze finish............................**500.00**
Plate, 5½" d., decorated w/h.p. pink
flowers around a gold filigree
center design (Willets) **45.00**
Potpourri vase, cov., purple-ground
ovoid body decorated front &
reverse in raised stippled gilding w/a
large "T" surrounded by gilt-edged
green, iron-red & blue scrolling
foliage above a green-ground
circular foot shaped on the front &
reverse & decorated w/orange,
maroon & gilt teardrops above a
scalloped blue band between gilt
borders repeated around the neck,
the upper body & cover decorated
w/gilt-delin-eated shaded pink
scalework pierced on either side of
the mushroom knop w/two blue &

green foliate-patterned ovals &
interrupted on the sides of the body
w/an arched handle intricately
pierced around colorful floral &
foliate devices heightened in gilding,
crown & sword mark between
"BELLEEK" & "O & B" printed in red,
Ott & Brewer, ca. 1889, minor chip
beneath foot, 13½" d. (ILLUS.) ...**25,300.00**
Salt dip, three-footed, decorated
w/h.p. green & tan leaves & gold
trim, 2" d., 1⅛" h. (Ceramic Art
Company) **64.00**
Stamp box, cov., lid decorated
w/embossed scrolling & a bouquet
of tiny florals on soft green lustre
ground, interior sectioned for
stamps, 1⅝ x 2½", 1½" h.
(Willets) **160.00**
Teapot, cov., white w/silver overlay,
7" d., 3½" h., Ceramic Art Com-pany
(wear to silver on spout &
finial) **135.00**
Vase, 8" h., black matte ground
w/dragonflies & cattails, ca. 1905
(Willets) **285.00**
Vase, 17½" h., cylindrical, deco-rated
w/white feathered birds on brown,
tan & white ground (Willets) **495.00**

IRISH

Figure of a Leprechaun

Bread plate, Limpet patt., 3rd black
mark **185.00**
Butter dish, cov., Harp patt., 3rd
green mark...**78.00**
Butter plate, 5½" d., Shamrock-
Basketweave patt., 3rd black
mark **72.00**
Cake plate, open-handled,
Shamrock-Basketweave patt.,
twig handles, 2nd black mark **200.00**
Coffeepot, cov., Harp-Shamrock
patt., 3rd green mark **160.00**
Coffeepot, cov., Shamrock-Basket-
weave patt., 3rd green mark **185.00**

Cracker jar, cov., Diamond patt.,
2nd green mark.................................**300.00**
Creamer, Undine patt., girl
decoration, 2nd green mark..............**95.00**
Creamer, No. 397, double shell...........**45.00**
Creamer, Mask patt., 4" h., 3rd
black mark **95.00**
Creamer & open sugar bowl,
Lotus patt., 3rd black mark, pr. **125.00**
Creamer & cov. sugar bowl,
Shamrock-Basketweave patt., 2nd
green mark, pr. **85.00**
Cup & saucer, demitasse, Limpet
patt., 3rd black mark **85.00**
Cup & saucer, Artichoke patt., 1st
black mark **195.00**
Cup & saucer, Harp-Shamrock
patt., 2nd black mark **190.00**
Cup & saucer, Harp-Shamrock
patt., 3rd black mark **120.00**
Cup & saucer, Limpet patt., 1st green
mark..**45.00**
Cup & saucer, Mask patt., 3rd
black mark **155.00**
Cup & saucer, Shamrock-
Basketweave patt., tall shape, 3rd
black mark **110.00**
Cup & saucer, Thistle patt., pink
tint, 1st black mark **200.00**
Ewer, jug-form, Typha patt., slender
ovoid body tapering to a slender
neck, decorated w/shamrocks,
7" h., 2nd green mark **95.00**
Figure of a Leprechaun, seated w/a
pot of gold at his feet, yellow lustre
trim, 3" w., 5" h., 2nd black
mark (ILLUS.) **445.00**
Flowerpot, crinkled, 2nd green
mark..**45.00**

Shamrock-Basketweave Honey Pot

Honey pot on stand, Shamrock-
Basketweave patt., beehive-
shaped, 3rd black mark (ILLUS.) **525.00**
Marmalade jar, cov., Shamrock-
Basketweave patt., 2nd green
mark..**85.00**
Model of a greyhound, female,
No. 631, 6¼" h., 2nd green
mark..**425.00**

Irish Belleek Pig

Model of a pig, seated, all-white,
4" l., 3" h., 2nd black mark
(ILLUS.) **375.00**
Mug, Shamrock-Basketweave patt.,
3rd black mark **100.00**
Pitcher, tankard, jug-type, 5½" h
Vine patt., 3rd green mark **140.00**
Plate, 6¼" d., Limpet patt., 3rd
black mark **40.00**
Plate, 6¾" d., Thistle patt., pink tint
trim, 2nd black mark **80.00**
Plate, 8" d., Limpet patt., 3rd black
mark..**50.00**
Salt dip, master size, Limpet patt.,
2nd black mark **65.00**
Salt dip, Shamrock-Basketweave
patt., 3rd black mark **30.00**
Spill vase, Rock patt., 3½" h., 3rd
black mark **100.00**
Sugar bowl, open, No. 447, 4th
green mark..**45.00**
Tea kettle, cov., Shamrock-
Basketweave patt., 2nd green
mark..**225.00**
Tea kettle, cov., Tridacna patt., 1st
black mark **600.00**

Limpet Pattern Teapot

Teapot, cov., Limpet patt., 2nd
green mark (ILLUS.) **260.00**
Tea set: cov. teapot, creamer & open
sugar bowl; Limpet patt., 3rd
black mark, 3 pcs. **585.00**
Tea set: cov. teapot, creamer, open
sugar bowl & six cups & saucers;
Shamrock-Basketweave patt.,
3rd black mark, 15 pcs....................**595.00**

Tray, Neptune patt., 14½ x 17", 2nd
black mark **1,400.00**

Belleek Seahorse Vase

Vase, 3¾" h., 5" l., Seahorse patt.,
cornucopia-form, on a wave-molded
rectangular base, beaded rim vase,
all-white, 1st black mark
(ILLUS.) **325.00**
Vase, 5½" h., Shamrock-Basket-
weave patt., 2nd green mark **95.00**
Vase, 6" h., figural tree stump,
Shamrock patt., 2nd black mark **145.00**
Vase, 6" h., Aberdeen patt.,
decorated w/applied flowers, 3rd
black mark **305.00**
Vase, 7½" h., Aberdeen patt., 2nd
black mark **375.00**

BENNINGTON

Bennington Book Flasks & Poodle

*Bennington wares, which ranged from
stoneware to parian and porcelain, were
made in Bennington, Vermont, primarily
in two potteries, one in which Captain
John Norton and his descendants were
principals, and the other in which
Christopher Webber Fenton (also once
associated with the Nortons) was a
principal. Various marks are found on the
wares made in the two major potteries,
including J. & E. Norton, E. & L.P.
Norton, L. Norton & Co., Norton & Fenton,
Edward Norton, Lyman Fenton & Co.,
Fenton's Works, United States Pottery Co.,*

U.S.P. and others.

*The popular pottery with the mottled
brown on yellowware glaze was also
produced in Bennington, but such wares
should be referred to as "Rockingham" or
"Bennington-type" unless they can be
specifically attributed to a Bennington,
Vermont factory.*

Book flask, binding impressed
"Departed Spirits G," mottled Flint
Enamel glaze, minor edge wear
& small flakes, 5½" h. (ILLUS.
left) **$412.00**
Book flask, binding impressed
"Kossuth," mottled Flint Enamel
glaze, 7¾" h. **1,100.00**
Book flask, "Scroddleware," applied
star & applied molded label reading
"Fenton's Works, Bennington,
Vermont," blue & white "scroddled"
clay, two corners chipped, hairline
along spine, 5⅝" h. (ILLUS.
right)..**2,585.00**
Bottle, figural coachman, mottled Flint
Enamel glaze, impressed "1849"
mark, 10½" h. (professional repair
to hat)..**1,100.00**
Bowl, pudding, 11½" d., mottled
brown Rockingham glaze **85.00**
Churn, stoneware, ovoid body
w/short cylindrical neck w/flared
mouth, eared handles, slip-quilled
cobalt blue stylized floral spray,
impressed mark "E. & L.P. Norton -
Bennington, VT - 3," ca. 1870, repair
to tight line in back, glaze spider on
side, 5 gal., 18" h. (ILLUS. top
next page) **385.00**
Creamer, parian, Pond Lily patt.,
4" h...**110.00**
Figure, parian, a young boy standing
balancing a basket of applied eggs
on one shoulder, his other hand on
his hip, wearing a short jacket, shirt,

E. & L.P. Norton Churn

cravat & kneebreeches, on a round
plinth base, 9¾" h **80.00**

Figure group, parian, a large thick
cross behind two female figures on
a rockwork base, 11¼" h. **82.50**

Jug, stoneware, semi-ovoid, slip-
quilled cobalt blue bird on branch
decoration, impressed mark "J. & E.
Norton, Bennington, Vt. 2," 14½" h.
(minor flakes) **495.00**

Decorated Stoneware Jug

Jug, stoneware, semi-ovoid, slip-
quilled cobalt blue large dotted
peacock perched on a forked tree
stump looking back over its
shoulder, J. & E. Norton, Bennington
mark, minor rim chips & glaze
spiders in back base, ca. 1855,
3 gal., 15½" h. (ILLUS.) **3,410.00**

Jug, stoneware, semi-ovoid, slip-
quilled cobalt blue large three-petal
stylized flower trimmed w/small
leaves & curling stems, impressed
mark "J. & E. Norton - Bennnington,
VT - 4," ca. 1855, 4 gal., 17" h. **632.50**

Jug, stoneware, semi-ovoid, slip-
quilled cobalt blue pair of birds, one
in front of the other & facing
opposite directions, on branches,

impressed mark "J. Norton & Co. -
Bennington, VT - 4," ca. 1860,
stack mark below tail of one bird,
4 gal.,17" h. **1,155.00**

Bennington Flint Enamel Lion

Model of a lion, standing animal
w/tail over his back & one forepaw
resting on a sphere, applied
"coleslaw" mane, tongue up, mottled
Flint Enamel glaze, tail repaired,
10" l. (ILLUS.) **1,265.00**

Model of a Poodle, the standing dog
facing the viewer & holding a basket
in its mouth, "coleslaw" fur trim,
mottled brown Rockingham glaze,
minor coleslaw damage, tail reglued,
9½" l. (ILLUS. center) **1,760.00**

Pitcher, 10" h., parian, Wild Rose
patt., unmarked..............................**195.00**

Pitcher, 11¾" h., tall tapering footed
octagonal body w/wide arched
spout, applied long angled handle,
mottled Flint Enamel glaze,
impressed "1849" mark (chips on
foot from kiln adhesion) **577.50**

Bennington Toby Jar

Toby jar, cov., figural, model of a
man's head w/tricorner hat forming
the cover, molded hair & facial
details, mottled Flint Enamel glaze,
mid-19th c., 6" w., 7" h. (ILLUS.)...**1,265.00**

Vase, 4⅜" h., parian, figural, a cat

seated beside & looking into an ovoid vase, on a rectangular platform base (chip on vase rim) **258.50**

Vase, 8⅞" h., parian, figural, a large eagle w/raised wing looking over its back & perched before a tall leaf-molded flaring vase on a paneled foot.................**247.50**

Washbowl, miniature, footed w/deep curved flaring sides, mottled brown Rockingham glaze, 1⅝" h. **65.00**

Washbowl, molded petal-form interior, mottled Flint Enamel glaze, impressed "1849" mark, 13⅞" d. (chip on foot from kiln adhesion, minor edge flakes, interior wear) **522.50**

Water cooler, stoneware, barrel-shaped, a wide center band w/a large oblong slip-quilled cobalt blue floral bouquet, incised bands highlighted in blue above & below center band, bung hole at base trimmed w/blue dots, impressed mark at top "J. & E. Norton Bennington, VT - 5," 5 gal., 15" h. (small tight hairline in front, minor stone pings & age spider in back).........................**2,090.00**

BERLIN (KPM)

Ornate Berlin Charger

The mark, KPM, was used at Meissen from 1723 to 1725, and was later adopted by the Royal Factory, Konigliche Porzellan Manufaktur, in Berlin. At various periods it has been incorporated with the Brandenburg sceptre, the Prussian eagle or the crowned globe. The same letters were also adopted by other factories in Germany in the late 19th and early 20th centuries. With the end of the German monarchy in 1918, the name of the firm was changed to Staatliche Porzellan Manufaktur and though production was halted during

World War II, the factory was rebuilt and is still in business. The exquisite paintings on porcelain were produced at the close of the 19th century and are eagerly sought by collectors today.

Basket, octagonal w/slot handles & reticulated sides, center decoration of floral bouquet, blue sceptre mark, 7½" w., 4" h................................**$395.00**

Charger, the wide dished form decorated in the center w/a long oval reserve w/two young women wearing diaphanous gowns w/one holding aloft a floral garland, a wide lustre border band ornately decorated w/gilt scrolls, leaves, medallions & diaper designs, artist-signed, blue sceptre mark w/"Germany" & titled "Lebenreigen," late 19th c., 15½" d., (ILLUS.) **6,325.00**

Dinner service: pr. of cov. circular footed bowls, pr. of oval platters, charger, circular serving dish, oval dish, pr. of sauceboats w/attached stands, cov. oval soup tureen, 24 dinner plates, 12 soup plates, 11 dessert plates, square bowl; *Alt-Ozier* borders around h.p. flowers, modern, 58 pcs. **3,163.00**

Jar, cov., decorated w/two portrait scenes of a young couple, cobalt blue & gold on a white background, 7" h.................................**395.00**

Plaque, rectangular, h.p. scene of girl holding a chamberstick, artist-signed, titled "Gute Nacht," framed, 5" w., 7½" h................................**1,500.00**

Plaque, rectangular, a bust portrait of Gitana, a lovely maiden w/flowing dark hair & a red cap, wearing a low-cut draped gown, impressed marks, late 19th c., in ornate gilt plaster shadowbox frame, 6 x 9"...**4,887.00**

Plaque with Child & Cats

Plaque, rectangular, depicting a

young child wearing an off-the-shoulder robe & holding two kittens & a basket of flowers over one arm, impressed KPM mark, 6½ x 9½" (ILLUS.) **3,737.00**

Plaque, rectangular, painted w/a scene of a young woman reclining, wrapped from the shoulder down, her head propped on one raised hand & reading a book, impressed marks, late 19th c., 7⅜ x 9¾" **2,070.00**

Plaque with Christopher Columbus

Plaque, rectangular, decorated w/a scene of Christopher Columbus in prison, chains at his wrists, shown reclining & wrapped in blankets, artist-signed, late 19th c., impressed "KPM" & scepter marks, 8⅞ x 11" (ILLUS.) **4,025.00**

Plaque, oval, depicting a mother w/long wavy blonde hair & wearing a crown holding a young nude child, impressed "K.P.M." & sceptre marks, 11" h.................................**2,300.00**

Plaque, rectangular, painted w/a scene of green fields, white mountains & blue skies, artist-initialed & marked "DIE WAND," 8⅝ x 11⅛" **633.00**

Plaque, oval, depicting a young woman w/long wavy dark hair turned to dexter, artist-signed, impressed "K.P.M." & sceptre marks, late 19th c., 13¼" h...........................**16,100.00**

Plaque, oval, depicting a beautiful young woman w/long wavy dark hair w/a bow to one side, artist-signed, impressed "K.P.M." & "6," late 19th c., 13¼" h............................**8,050.00**

Plaque, rectangular, depicting a young woman in a landscape scene, impressed "K.P.M." & sceptre marks, late 19th c., 10 x 16" **8,625.00**

Plates, dinner, 10⅛" d., underglaze-blue decoration w/gilt leaf & scalework borders, printed "KPM"

marks, early 20th c., set of 21 (chips) **977.50**

BISQUE

Comic Ashtray - Match Holder

Bisque is biscuit china, fired a single time but not glazed. Some bisque is decorated with colors. Most abundant from the Victorian era are figures and groups, but other pieces from busts to vases were made by numerous potteries in the U.S. and abroad. Reproductions have been produced for many years so care must be taken when seeking antique originals.

Ashtray - match holder, figural novelty-type, a comic bust of a grinning man, large winking eyes, wearing a brown cap, red neckerchief & blue shirt, his gaping mouth forming the ashtray & holes in the top of his head for matches, 2⅜" d., 4½" h. (ILLUS.) **$125.00**

Figure of boy in Colonial attire, impressed mold mark No. 5473, artist mark on base, 9½" h. **125.00**

Figure of baby crawling wearing a blue gown w/pink sash & pink slippers, brown real hair, 6" l., 3½" h..**195.00**

Figure of boy playing professor, Heubach mark, 6½" h. **355.00**

Figure of girl w/chicks, Heubach mark, 12" h....................................**325.00**

Figure of lady holding a child, delicate pastel blues, gold highlights, partially glazed, impressed "Heubach" mark, 12½" h.................**265.00**

Figure of North American Indian princess, standing wearing a multicolored feather skirt, feather headdress, pink robe over shoulder, circular white base w/gold decoration, ca. 1850, 3" d., 11" h.....**495.00**

Figure of a young blonde girl dancing,

wearing a green pleated skirt w/white lace collar, pink sanded bow on shoulder & pink sash, marked "Heubach," 3½" d., 6½" h.................**110.00**

Figure of a young blonde girl dancing, wearIng cream & green pleated dress w/white lace collar, marked "Heubach," 4½" d., 8¼" h.................**165.00**

Figure of a young girl holding a bouquet of flowers, marked "Heubach," 7½" h............................**175.00**

Figures of a boy & a girl, colorfully attired, both wearing hats, he playing a mandolin, she striking a tambourine, triangular bases, 11¾" h., pr. **420.00**

Figures of a boy & girl, each wearing flower-decorated peasant-style clothing & carrying a basket, scroll-molded base, Germany, ca. 1890, 14½" h., facing pair................**425.00**

Figures of a man & woman, both wearing peasant costumes, he standing w/an axe in one hand & wiping his brow w/the other, she standing w/a baby in one arm & holding a pitcher in the other hand, pastel coloring, impressed Heubach mark, late 19th c., 12½" h., pr. **725.00**

Figure group, Dutch boy & girl kissing, signed "Heubach," 7" h. **425.00**

Figure group, three Dutch girls holding hands aloft, white bonnets & aprons over green, blue or red dresses, 2½" d. **135.00**

Model of a puppy w/a muzzle, impressed Heubach mark, 5" l. **125.00**

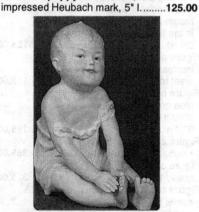

Heubach Piano Baby

Piano baby, seated wearing an off-the-shoulder night shirt, molded & painted hair, blue intaglio eyes, smiling mouth, unjointed body w/hands touching one foot, firing line at side of one leg, unpainted repair on right thumb, tip of little finger &

left wrist, 'sunburst' Heubach mark, 6" h. (ILLUS.) **80.00**

Piano baby, seated wearing a sailor-type outfit & hat w/wide brim, holding a basket of colorful objects between his legs, one arm held aloft, unmarked, 6" h. (two fingers on right hand chipped) **105.00**

Piano baby, crawling on tummy, Heubach mark, 7" l. **250.00**

Piano baby, lying on back, Heubach mark, 7" l. **295.00**

Planter, figure of a girl w/large basket decorated w/birds & flowers, pastel colors w/gold trim, Germany, 2¾ x 7", 7" h..**75.00**

Plaques, oval, pierced for hanging, relief-molded figures of a young man & lady & grape arbor on each one, pink flowers & cream ground, 5½ x 7", pr..**235.00**

Snow baby on red sleigh..................**195.00**

Snow baby sitting **145.00**

Snow baby, stiff neck, painted blue eyes, closed mouth, all-bisque body w/molded & flocked snowsuit, jointed shoulders & hips, 4" l...........**350.00**

Toothpick holder, figural bearded man in elf costume kneeling in front of basketweave holder, pale blue dotted decoration w/gold trim, 4" h. ...**45.00**

Vase, 6¼" h., 3½" d., figural Indian Chief head, w/braids & feather headdress, ca. 1900, blue "crown" & "N" mark **145.00**

Vase, 8" h., figural, a young blond-haired boy wearing a large hat, jacket, waistcoat, striped ribbon belt & kneebritches, holding a badminton racquet & standing in front of a large tree trunk vase, Germany, late 19th - early 20th c. **95.00**

BLUE & WHITE POTTERY

Peacock Salt Box

The category of blue and white or blue and grey pottery includes a wide variety of pottery, earthenware and stoneware items widely produced in this country in the late 19th century right through the 1930s. Originally marketed as inexpensive wares, most pieces featured a white or grey body molded with a fruit, flower or geometric design and then trimmed with bands or splashes of blue to highlight the molded pattern. Pitchers, butter crocks and salt boxes are among the numerous items produced but other kitchenwares and chamber sets are also found. Values vary depending on the rarity of the embossed pattern and the depth of color of the blue trim; the darker the blue, the better. The pattern names used with our listings are taken from two references, Blue & White Stoneware, Pottery, Crockery by Edith Harbin (Collector Books, 1977) and Blue & White Stoneware by Kathryn McNerney (Collector Books, 1981).

Bowl, 5" d., embossed Cosmos patt. **$58.00**
Bowl, 6" d., embossed Wedding Ring patt. **95.00**
Bowl, embossed Apricot & Honeycomb patt. **135.00**
Bowl, small, printed Wildflower patt. **100.00**
Butter crock, cov., embossed Basketweave patt , 7" d. **200.00**
Butter crock, cov., embossed Apricot & Honeycomb patt., w/bail handle................................**150.00 to 200.00**
Butter crock, cover & bail handle, embosssed Butterfly patt. ....**125.00 to 150.00**
Butter crock, cov., embossed Good Luck (Swastika) patt., w/bail handle...**175.00**
Canister, cov., embossed Basketweave patt., "Sugar" **185.00**
Custard cup, sponged Rose patt. **100.00**
Milk crock, embossed Daisy & Lattice patt., 9½" d., 4" h.................**115.00**
Mug, embossed Flying Bird patt. **195.00**
Pitcher, 5" h., side-pour spout, diffused blue **150.00**
Pitcher, 7" h., colorful roses decal decoration **97.00**
Pitcher, 7" h., embossed Dutch Boy & Girl Kissing patt. **200.00**
Pitcher, 7" h., embossed Dutch Children Kissing & Windmill patt. w/embossed tulip petals band above incised lines **175.00**
Pitcher, 7" h., printed Dutch Farm patt. **189.00**
Pitcher, 7½" h., embossed Cherry Cluster patt. ....**150.00 to 200.00**

Pitcher, 8½" h., embossed Cherry Band patt. ....**175.00 to 200.00**
Pitcher, 8½" h., embossed Eagle w/Shield patt. **575.00**
Pitcher, 8½" h., embossed Swan patt. (handle line but sound) **185.00**
Pitcher, 8½" h., embossed Tulip patt. **185.00**
Pitcher, 9" h., embossed Basketweave & Flower (Morning Glory) patt. ....**125.00 to 150.00**
Pitcher, 9" h., embossed Castle & Fishscale patt.................................**225.00**
Pitcher, 10" h., embossed American Beauty Rose patt. **265.00**
Pitcher, wash, 12½" h., embossed Fishscale & Wild Roses patt. **195.00**
Pitcher, embossed Apricot patt. ....**150.00 to 200.00**
Pitcher, embossed doe & fawn decoration **200.00**
Pitcher, water, small, embossed Fishscale & Wild Roses patt. **85.00**
Salt box, cov., hanging-type, embossed Apricot patt. **145.00**
Salt box, wooden lid, hanging-type, embossed Peacock patt. (ILLUS.) **185.00**
Toothbrush holder, embossed Fishscale & Wild Roses patt. **129.00**

BLUE RIDGE DINNERWARES

Summertime Celery Tray

The small town of Erwin, Tennessee was the home of the Southern Potteries, Inc., originally founded by E.J. Owen in 1917 and first called the Clinchfield Pottery.

In the early 1920s Charles W. Foreman purchased the plant and he revolutionized the company's output, developing the popular line of hand-painted wares sold as "Blue Ridge" dinnerwares. Free-hand painted by women from the surrounding hills, these colorful dishes in many patterns, continued in production until the plant's closing in 1957.

Bonbon, Easter Parade patt. **$65.00**
Bonbon, flat shell-shape, Nove Rose
   patt. **55.00**
Bowl, cereal, 6" d., Big Apple patt. **5.00**
Bowl, cereal, 6" d., Dutch Bouquet
   patt., Colonial shape **11.00**
Bowl, cereal, 6" d., Orlinda patt.,
   Colonial shape **10.00**
Bowl, fruit, 5" d., Poinsettia patt. **4.00**
Bowl, fruit, 5" d., Strawberry Patch
   patt. **3.00**
Box, cov., Seaside patt., 3½ x 4½ **96.50**
Cake plate, maple leaf-shaped,
   vitreous china, loop handle, molded
   grape cluster, Chintz patt., 10" l. **50.00**
Cake plate, maple leaf-shaped,
   vitreous china, loop handle, molded
   grape cluster, Fruit Fantasy patt.,
   10" l. **48.00**
Candy box, cov., Calico patt. **128.50**
Candy box, cov., French Peasant
   patt. **159.00**
Celery tray, leaf-shaped, Summer-
   time patt. (ILLUS.) **42.00**
Child's feeding dish, Duck in Hat
   patt. **55.00**
Chocolate set: cov. chocolate pot,
   creamer & open sugar bowl & tray;
   Elegance patt., 4 pcs. **600.00**
Coffeepot, cov., demitasse, Petit
   Point patt. **145.00**
Creamer, Dahlia patt. **12.00**
Creamer, Poinsettia patt. **8.00**
Creamer, Strawberry Patch patt. **6.00**
Creamer & sugar bowl, Carnival
   patt., pr. **25.00**
Creamer & open sugar bowl,
   pedestal-foot, Easter Parade patt.,
   pr. **85.00**
Cup & saucer, demitasse, French
   Peasant patt. **50.00**
Cup & saucer, demitasse, Roseanna
   patt., teal blue **30.00**
Cup & saucer, Dutch Bouquet patt.,
   Colonial shape **12.00**
Cup & saucer, Orlinda patt., Colonial
   shape **12.00**
Cup & saucer, Strawberry Patch patt. .**10.00**
Dinner service for four w/platter &
   oval vegetable bowl, Rutledge patt.,
   Candlewick shape, 22 pcs. **230.00**
Dinner service: eight plates & eight
   cups & saucers; Christmas Tree
   patt., 24 pcs. **850.00**
Gravy boat, Bluebell Bouquet patt. **25.00**
Mixing bowl, Carnival patt., 9½" d. **20.00**
Pie baker, Spindrift patt. **28.00**
Pie server, Sculptured Fruit patt. **32.00**
Pitcher, 6" h., vitreous china, figural
   Chick shape, all-white **75.00**
Pitcher, 6" h., vitreous china, figural
   Chick, floral decoration **95.00**
Pitcher, 7" h., Pansy Trio patt., Spiral
   shape **62.00**

Pitcher, 7" h., Wild Irish Rose patt.,
   Spiral shape **85.00**
Pitcher, 7" h., Sculptured Fruit patt.,
   40 oz. ....**75.00 to 100.00**
Plate, 6" d., Crab Orchard patt. **2.50**
Plate, 6" sq., decorated w/scene of
   rooster on weathervane, signed
   "PV" in circle **40.00**
Plate, bread & butter, 6" d., Dutch
   Bouquet patt., Colonial shape **9.00**
Plate, 6" d., Poinsettia patt. **3.00**
Plate, bread & butter, 6" d.,
   Strawberry Patch patt. **2.00**
Plate, 8" d., Strawberry Patch patt., ...**5.00**
Plate, 8½" d., Flower Bowl patt. **25.00**
Plate, 8½" d., Poinsettia patt.,
   Colonial shape **4.50**
Plate, dinner, 9" d., Bluebell Bouquet
   patt. **7.50**
Plate, dinner, 9⅜" d., Dutch Bouquet
   patt., Colonial shape **16.00**
Plate, dinner, 9½" d., Stanhome Ivy
   patt., Skyline shape **6.00**
Plate, dinner, 10" d., Strawberry
   Patch patt. **7.00**
Plate, dinner, 10¼" d., Thanksgiving
   Turkey patt. **65.00**
Plate, dinner, 10½" d., Fruit Punch
   patt., Colonial shape **16.00**
Plate, 11½" d., Vintage patt., Colonial
   shape **28.00**
Platter, 11" l., oval, Cherry Bounce
   patt. **18.00**
Platter, 11" l., oval, Crab Apple patt. **25.00**
Platter, 13" l., oval, Carnival patt. **18.00**
Platter, 13" l., oval, Cumberland patt. ...**25.00**
Platter, Cocky Locky decoration **95.00**
Platter, oval, Turkey with Acorns patt.,
   Skyline-Clinchfield shape **135.00**
Relish dish, round, Easter Parade
   patt. **75.00**
Salt & pepper shakers, figural
   chickens, model of a hen & rooster,
   hen 4" h., rooster, 4¾" h., pr. (toe
   flake) **85.00**
Server, center-handled, French
   Peasant patt. **95.00**
Snack plates w/cups, Rustic Plaid
   patt., set of six, 12 pcs. **30.00**
Soup plate w/flanged rim,
   Strawberry Patch patt. **9.00**
Soup plate, flat, Sunflower
   patt., Colonial shape, 8" d. **15.00**
Sugar bowl, cov., Strawberry Patch
   patt. **10.00**
Teapot, cov., Champagne Pinks
   patt. **95.00**
Teapot, cov., child's, Duck in Hat
   patt. **125.00**
Teapot, cov., Appleyard patt. **95.00**
Teapot, cov., Spring Hill Tulip patt. ...**110.00**
Vase, 8" h., vitreous china, Mood
   Indigo patt. **85.00**

Vegetable bowl, cov., King's
    Ransom patt. 85.00
Vegetable bowl, open, oval, Carol's
    Roses patt..12.00
Vegetable bowl, open, round, Cherry
    Bounce patt.......................................20.00
Vegetable bowl, open, round,
    Strawberry Sundae patt. 25.00

BOCH FRERES

Boch Freres Vase

The Belgian firm, founded in 1841 and still in production, first produced stoneware art pottery of mediocre quality, attempting to upgrade their wares through the years. In 1907, Charles Catteau became the art director of the pottery and slowly the influence of his work was absorbed by the artisans surrounding him. All through the 1920s wares were decorated in distinctive Art Deco designs and are now eagerly sought along with the hand-thrown gourd-form vessels coated with earthtone glazes that were produced during the same time. Almost all Boch Freres pottery is marked, but the finest wares also carry the signature of Charles Catteau in addition to the pottery mark.

Vase, 12" h., ovoid body tapering to a
    short flaring neck, Art Deco style,
    decorated w/stylized geometric

flowers & triangles in pale turquoise, yellow & brown on a matte black ground, designed by Charles Catteau, printed marks "Ch.Catteau D1110/D" & factory mark, ca. 1925 (ILLUS.) **$690.00**
Vase, 13½" h., ovoid body tapering to a flat molded mouth, decorated w/a central band of stylized florals in mustard yellow & shades of brown highlighted in blue & green on a yellow-dotted white ground w/a black shoulder & base & mustard yellow rim & foot & a blue stripe at the shoulder, matt glaze. ca. 1920, blue stamp mark & inscribed "D. 1854 - V.B.," impressed "914 - K"..**690.00**

BOEHM PORCELAINS

Although not antique, Boehm porcelain sculptures have attracted much interest as Edward Marshall Boehm excelled in hard porcelain sculptures. His finest creations, inspired by the beauties of nature, are in the forms of birds and flowers. Since his death in 1969, his work has been carried on by his wife at the Boehm Studios in Trenton, New Jersey. In 1971, an additional studio was opened in Malvern, England, where bone porcelain sculptures are produced. We list both limited and non-limited editions of Boehm.

ANIMALS
Bobcats, Malvern Studio bone china,
    No. 4001, 1971-74, 8 x 15" **$1,450.00**
Foxes, Malvern Studio bone china,
    No. 4003, 1971-74, 12 x 14" **1,450.00**
Raccoons, Malvern Studio bone
    china, No. 4002, 1971-74,
    11 x 11".......................................**1,450.00**
Red Squirrels, Malvern Studio bone
    china, No. 4004, 1972-74,
    13 x 13½"....................................**2,000.00**

BIRDS
Baby Chickadee, No. 461, 1962-72,
    3" h. ....**150.00 to 175.00**
Barn Owl, Malvern Studio bone
    china, No. 1005, 1972-76,
    21 x 27".......................................**3,500.00**
Black Grouse, Malvern Studio bone
    china, No. 1006, 1972-75,
    13 x 15½"....................................**2,100.00**
Brown Pelican, No. 400-22, 1972-76,
    18 x 25".......................................**9,500.00**
Cygnet (Baby Bird of Peace) on Lily
    Pad, No. 400-13, introduced in
    1971, 3 x 6" ....**350.00 to 375.00**

Everglades Kites, No. 400-24,
1973-76, 14½ x 20½".....................**7,000.00**
Fledgling Red Poll, No. 1084,
introduced in 1968, 4" h. **150.00**

Fledgling Western Bluebirds

Fledgling Western Bluebirds, two
birds, No. 494, 1968-73, 5½" h.
(ILLUS.) **450.00**
Treecreepers, Malvern Studio bone
china, No. 1007, 1972-76,
9 x 17"..**2,800.00**
Varied Thrush w/Parrot Tulips,
No. 400-29, 1974-76, 10" w.,
18" h..**2,600.00**

BRAYTON LAGUNA POTTERY

*Durlin E. Brayton began his operation
in Laguna Beach, California in 1927. After
his marriage a short time later to Ellen
Webster Grieve, who also became his
business partner, the venture became a
successful endeavor. One of the most
popular lines was the* Childrens' *series
which featured a rubber stamp-like mark
with the first name of the child followed
underneath with a line which separates the*

*words "Brayton Pottery." Both white clay
and pink clay were used during Brayton's
production. More than 150 people,
including approximately twenty designers,
were employed by Brayton. Sometimes on
items too small for a full mark, designers
would incise their initials. It was not until
after World War II and the mass
importation of pottery products into the
United States that Brayton's business
declined. Operations ceased in 1968.*

Cookie jar, cov., figural black
Mammy, red dress **$850.00**
Cookie jar, cov., figural Gingham
Dog, red & blue..............................**300.00**
Figure, children's series, "Sally,"
7" h..**95.00**
Figure, South Sea island girl wearing
a sarong...**85.00**
Figures, Abstract man & woman
w/cats, 21" h., pr............................**750.00**
Model of baby elephant, purple..........**70.00**
Model of a calf, purple.......................**35.00**
Model of a fox, No. H57 ....**65.00**
Model of a penquin, 7" h...................**70.00**
Model of a pheasant, turquoise
glaze, 9" h.......................................**80.00**
Planter, figural Mexican woman..........**30.00**
Planter, figural Wolfhound Girl, pink
dress, w/two dogs, 10⅝" h.................**60.00**
Vase, 6½" h., 7¼" d., Art Deco style,
flared mouth, light green glaze **78.00**
Vase, 15½" h., lupine decoration on
seafoam blue ground **150.00**

BUFFALO POTTERY

*Buffalo Pottery was established in 1902
in Buffalo, New York, to supply pottery for
the Larkin Company. Most desirable today
is Deldare Ware, introduced in 1908 in two
patterns, "The Fallowfield Hunt" and "Ye
Olden Days," which featured central
English scenes and a continuous border.
Emerald Deldare, introduced in 1911, was
banded with stylized flowers and geometric
designs and had varied central scenes, the
most popular being from "The Tours of Dr.*

Syntax." Reorganized in 1940, the company now specializes in hotel china.

DELDARE

Candlesticks, artist-signed, ca. 1909,
9½" h., pr. **$875.00**
Card tray, Ye Lion Inn, artist-signed,
7¾" d. **225.00**
Creamer & cov. sugar bowl,
hexagonal, Scenes of Village Life in
Ye Olden Days, pr. **400.00**
Mug, Breakfast at the Three Pigeons,
4½" h. ....**200.00 to 225.00**
Teapot, cov., Scenes of Village
Life in Ye Olden Days,
3¾" h. ....**250.00 to 300.00**
Tea tile, Traveling in Ye Olden Days,
6" d. ....**275.00 to 325.00**

EMERALD DELDARE

Emerald Deldare Kingfisher Vase

Creamer, Dr. Syntax with the Dairy
Maid, 3" h. **450.00**
Mug, Dr. Syntax again filled up his
glass..., 4¼" h. **695.00**
Pitcher, 8¾" h., octagonal, Dr. Syntax
Setting Out to the Lakes **650.00**
Vase, 8"h., 6½" d., bulbous ovoid
body tapering to a short flaring neck,
decorated in shades of green &
white w/a wide central band
featuring kingfishers & water iris,
geometric neck bands & a band of
water lilies around the base, 1911
(ILLUS.) **2,645.00**

MISCELLANEOUS

Cake plate, Vienna patt., blue, ca.
1915..**185.00**
Christmas plate, 1952.........................**50.00**
Christmas plate, 1959.........................**35.00**
Cup & saucer, Blue Willow patt,
regular size **35.00**
Cup & saucer, Blue Willow patt...........**50.00**
Cup & saucer, oversized, Blue
Willow patt. w/Scottish poem **150.00**

Game plate, American Herring Gull
scene, 1907, 9½" d. **60.00**
Game plate, American Woodcock,
9½" d., 1907.....................................**60.00**
Game plate, grouse decoration **70.00**
Game set: 11 x 14" oval platter & four
plates; deer decoration, by R.K.
Beck, 5 pcs. **250.00**

Buffalo "Cinderella" Pitcher

Pitcher, jug-type, 6" h., Cinderella
decoration (ILLUS.) **450.00**
Pitcher, jug-type, 6" h., George
Washington decoration **400.00**
Pitcher, jug-type, Roger Williams
decoration **435.00**
Pitcher, jug-type, 6" h., Landing of
Roger Williams scene **495.00**
Plate, 6" d., Blue Willow patt. **18.00**
Plate, 8¼" d., Vienna patt....................**20.00**
Plate, 10½" d., commemoratve, New
Bedford, Massachusetts, border of
whaling & sea scenes, blue on
white, 1908 ....**135.00**
Tray, Abino ware, sailboat
decoration, 1912, 9¼ x 12" **1,650.00**

CANTON PORCELAIN

Canton Shrimp Dish

This ware has been decorated for nearly two centuries in factories near Canton, China. Intended for export sale, much of it was originally inexpensive blue-and-white hand decorated ware. Late 18th and early 19th century pieces are superior to later ones and fetch higher prices.

Basket & underplate, oval basket w/flanged rim & reticulated sides, conforming underplate, 19th c., 9¾" l., 2 pcs. **$747.50**

Bowl, 9½" d., deep rounded sides w/four-lobe scalloped rim, 19th c. **1,265.00**

Bowl, 10" d., petal-form rim, 19th c. **517.50**

Brush box, rectangular w/divided interior, 19th c., 3⅝ x 7⁵⁄₁₆", 3" h. (glaze imperfections) **632.50**

Butter dish, cover & strainer, flaring plate w/high domed cover w/pointed knob finial, 19th c., 7½" d. (chips) **546.00**

Candlesticks, tall slender cylindrical shafts flaring at the base, the rim w/a broad flattened edge, decorated w/large Oriental buildings in blue on white, late 19th c., 10½" h., pr. **1,610.00**

Cup & saucers, in original crate marked "China," set of 12 ....**1,265.00**

Dish, cov., two-handled, oval, 7" l. **451.00**

Dish, leaf-shaped, 7" w. **220.00**

Dish, octagonal w/deep sides, 19th c., 11¼" w. **316.00**

Pitcher, water, 7½" h., wide ovoid shouldered body tapering to a gently flaring neck w/high arched spout, strap handle, 19th c. (imperfections) **977.50**

Plates, 7½" d., set of 6 ....**231.00**

Plates, luncheon, 8¾" d., 19th c., set of 24 (chips) **1,495.00**

Platter, 13½" d., oval, 19th c. **259.00**

Platter, 14⅞" d., footed, shaped oval edge, 19th c. **1,150.00**

Platter, 17" l., oblong octagonal form, 19th c. (rim chips) **374.00**

Platter, 19" l., chamfered rectangular form, scallop-and-dot, scalework & herringbone border, mid-19th c. (minor rim fritting & underside chip) **920.00**

Sauce tureen, cover & undertray, chamfered rectangular deep body on flaring footring, rabbit's-head end handles, domed cover w/a scroll knop, scenic design w/a trellis diaper border on tureen & cell diaper border on stand, mid-19th c., tureen 7⅛" l., undertray 7¾" l. (chip on cover rim) **805.00**

Serving dishes, rectangular w/canted corners, 19th c., 9¼" l., pr. **546.00**

Shrimp dish, oblong w/one side pulled into a gentle point w/a ribbed & scalloped flanged rim, landscape

scene in the center, 19th c., 9¼" l. (ILLUS.) **632.50**

Soup tureen, cov., oval, 19th c., 9¼ x 11⅝", 7½" h. (imperfections, crack in handle) **747.50**

Soup tureen, cov., boar head handles, stem finial 19th c., 9½ x 12½, 7⅝" h. **862.50**

Vegetable dish, open, rectangular, 8¾" l. **330.00**

CAPO DI MONTE

Capo di Monte Box

Production of porcelain and faience began in 1736 at the Capo-di-Monte factory in Naples. In 1743 King Charles of Naples established a factory there that made wares with relief decoration. In 1759 the factory was moved to Buen Retiro near Madrid, operating until 1808. Another Naples pottery was opened in 1771 and operated until 1806 when its molds were acquired by the Doccia factory of Florence, which has since made reproductions of original Capo-di-Monte pieces with the "N" mark beneath a crown. Some very early pieces are valued in the thousands of dollars but the subsequent productions are considerably lower.

Box w/hinged cover, oval, the sides & top molded in relief w/classical figural scenes decorated in colored enamels, brass fittings, late 19th c., 9⅝" l., 4¼" h. (ILLUS.) **$460.00**

Box w/hinged cover, rectangular, decorated w/h.p. Bacchanalian scenes, late 19th c., blue crown "N" mark, 5" l., 3¼" h. **340.00**

Box w/hinged cover, rectangular each side decorated w/h.p. relief-molded panels of classical figures, blue crown "N" mark, late 19th c., 8" l., 5½" h. **535.00**

Jardiniere & pedestal, the slightly tapering cylindrical jardiniere molded in relief w/classical figures decorated w/colored enamels, the

Capo di Monte Jardiniere & Pedestal

ribbed pedestal w/a flaring top &
stepped base, decorated around the
lower base w/a band of classical
figures, early 20th c., 2 pcs.
(ILLUS.) **990.00**
Lamps, table model, figural, the base
w/the figures of a gentleman & lady
in 18th century attire on an oval
platform, w/a new paneled silk
shantung shade, eletrified, overall
22" h., pr. **575.00**

Capo di Monte Vase

Vases, 8¼" h., cylindrical w/flaring
rim, molded in full-relief w/a
continuous band of classical figures
decorated in colored enamels, late
19th c., slight imperfections, pr.
(ILLUS. one of two) **575.00**

CARLTON WARE

*The Staffordshire firm of Wiltshaw &
Robinson, Stoke-on-Trent, operated the*

*Carlton Works from about 1890 until 1958,
producing both earthenwares and
porcelain. Specializing in decorative items
like vases and teapots, they became well
known for their lustre-finished wares, often
decorated in the Oriental taste. The
trademark Carlton Ware was incorporated
into their printed mark. Since 1958, a new
company, Carlton Ware Ltd., has operated
the Carlton Works at Stoke.*

Ashtrays, Art Deco style, card suit-
shaped, set of 4 ....**$125.00**
Coffeepot, cov., Rouge Royale,
decorated w/a scene of a pagoda,
7¾" h..**375.00**
Dish, leaf-shaped, yellow foxglove
decoration, small................................**39.00**
Sauce boat, yellow buttercup
decoration, small................................**85.00**
Tray, figural maple leaf, 10" l.............**195.00**
Vase, 7" h., ovoid body tapering to
ringed cylindrical base, rim pulled
into four wide points, decorated
w/gold & enamel birds & flowers on
maroon lustre ground, pearlized
interior, original paper label **240.00**
Vase, 10" h., Art Deco style,
decorated w/blue & orange birds,
flowers & intricate gold tracery.........**245.00**

CATALINA ISLAND POTTERY

CATALINA
MADE IN
U. S. A.
POTTERY

*The Clay Products Division of the
Santa Catalina Island Co. produced a
variety of wares during their brief ten-year
operation. The brainchild of chewing-gum
magnate, William Wrigley, Jr., owner of
Catalina Island at the time, and his
business associate D. M. Retton, the plant
was established at Pebbly Beach, near
Avalon in 1927. Its two-fold goal was to
provide year-round work for the island's
residents and building material for
Wrigley's ongoing development of a major
tourist attraction at Avalon. Early
production consisted of bricks and roof and
patio tiles. Later, art pottery, including
vases, flower bowls, lamps and home
accessories were made from a local brown-
based clay and, about 1930, tablewares
were introduced. These early wares carried*

vivid glazes but had a tendency to chip readily and a white-bodied, more chip-resistant clay, imported from the mainland, was used after 1932. The costs associated with importing clay eventually caused the Catalina pottery to be sold to a California mainland competitor in 1937. These wares were molded and are not hand-thrown but some pieces have hand-painted decoration.

Bowl, turquoise glaze, No. 709 ....**$85.00**
Charger, 14" d., oxblood glaze 65.00
Cruet w/original stem stopper,
  Descanso cactus decoration,
  green glaze **225.00**
Model of a sea shell, No. C354 ....75.00
Mug, coffee, red glaze..........................50.00
Tumblers, blue glaze, set of 4 ....**75.00**
Vase, 5" h., oxblood glaze...................75.00
Vase, 5½" h., handled, matte
  cream glaze, No. 812.......................85.00
Vases, 7" h., flared rims, white
  exterior, turquoise interior, pr. 35.00
Vases, 7 x 9", figural conch shell,
  white exterior, pink interior, pr.........**195.00**

CERAMIC ARTS STUDIO OF MADISON

Founded in Madison, Wisconsin in 1941 by two young men, Lawrence Rabbitt and Reuben Sand, this company began as a "studio" pottery. In early 1942 they met an amateur clay sculptor, Betty Harrington and, recognizing her talent for modeling in clay, they eventually hired her as their chief designer. Over the next few years Betty designed over 460 different pieces for their production. Charming figurines of children and animals were a main focus of their output in addition to models of adults in varied costumes and poses, wall plaques, vases and figural salt and pepper shakers.

Business boomed during the years of World War II when foreign imports were cut off and, at its peak, the company employed some 100 people to produce the

carefully hand-decorated pieces.

After World War II many poor-quality copies of Ceramic Arts Studio figurines appeared and when, in the early 1950s, foreign imported figurines began flooding the market, the company found they could no longer compete. They finally closed their doors in 1955.

Since not all Ceramic Arts Studio pieces are marked, it takes careful study to determine which items are from their production.

Candleholder, figural, "Speak No.
  Evil," blonde angel on cloud base,
  5" h...**$58.00**
Console set: candleholder & pr. of
  vases; two-light candleholder, figural
  Triad woman kneeling w/figural
  standing Triad woman vases, one
  facing left & the other facing right,
  3 pcs...95.00
Figurine, Alice in Wonderland **95.00**
Figurine, Bali-Hai, light green w/gold
  accents, 8" h. 59.00
Figurine, Bass Viol Boy, 4¾" h...........60.00
Figurine, Chinese Girl, kneeling,
  Su-Lin, 4" h 18.00
Figurine, Dance Moderne man,
  9⅞" h...39.00
Figurine, Gay 90 Man, first version,
  6¾" h...45.00
Figurine, Gypsy man w/violin, 6⅝" h ...65.00
Figurine, Hunter w/gun, Al the
  Hunter, 7¼" h.................................49.00
Figurine, Lillibeth, Gay Ninety lady,
  6⅜" h...30.00
Figurine, Mexican Girl, Pepita,
  4½" h...25.00
Figurine, Miss Lucindy, Southern
  lady, teal blue & blue, 6⅞" h 30.00
Figurine, Polish Girl 35.00
Figurine, Russian Girl, Petrushka,
  5¼" h...30.00
Figurine, Spanish Man, rhumba
  dancer, blue, 7½" h..........................85.00
Figurine, Wendy, on base w/tall leafy
  plant, 5½" h...................................75.00
Figurine, shelf sitter, Cowboy,
  4½" h...65.00
Figurine, shelf-sitter, Cowgirl, 4½" h....65.00
Figurines, shelf-sitters, Grace &
  Greg, ballet dancers, 6¼" & 7" h.,
  pr...95.00
Figurines, shelf-sitters, Michelle &
  Maurice, 7⅛" & 8¼" h.,
  pr. ....75.00 to 100.00
Figurines, shelf-sitters, Pierrot &
  Pierrette, 6¾" h., pr..........................135.00
Figurines, shelf-sitters, Sun-li & Su-
  Lin, yellow, 6¾" h. & 5½" h., pr. 48.00
Figurines, Dutch Love Boy & Girl,
  4⅞" h., pr. 65.00
Figurines, King's Jester Flutist &

King's Jester Lutist w/metal stands,
11½" h., pr. **185.00**
Figurines, Fire Man & Fire Woman,
11¼" & 11½" h., pr. **450.00**
Figurines, Water Man & Water
Woman, 11¼" & 11½" h., pr. **350.00**
Model of camel, Young Camel,
5⅝" h..**89.00**
Model of a cat w/green bow, Small
Cat or Bright Eyes, 2⅞" h. **15.00**
Model of a dog, Cocker Spaniel,
sitting, 2¾" h. **25.00**
Model of a dog, Collie, shelf-sitter,
5⅛" h..**50.00**
Model of Elsie Elephant, 4¾" h. **40.00**
Model of a turtle w/a cane **32.00**
Model of Mary's lamb, 3⅝" h.............**19.50**
Models of mouse & cheese, cheese
1½" h., mouse 2" h., pr. **25.00**
Models of Mother Bear & Baby Bear
(nesters), brown.................................**95.00**
Models of Mother Bear & Baby Bear
(nesters), white **125.00**
Models of parakeets, shelf-sitters,
"Pudgie" & "Budgie," w/original
metal birdcage, 6" h., pr. **95.00**
Salt & pepper shakers, figural bear,
white, pr...**46.50**
Salt & pepper shakers, figural
Siamese Cats, Thai & Thai-Thai,
large & small, pr.................................**60.00**
Salt & pepper shakers, figural Wee
Dutch Boy & Girl, pr. **20.00**
Toby Jug, seated man in tricorn
hat, 3¼" h...**30.00**
Wall plaque, pierced to hang, figural
Attitude, ballering, 9" h........................**42.50**
Wall plaque, pierced to hang,
Chinese Lantern Man, 8" h. **55.00**
Wall plaque, pierced to hang, figural
Columbine, 8½" h. **75.00**
Wall plaque, pierced to hang, figural
Harlequin, 8⅞" h................**80.00 to 100.00**
Wall plaque, pierced to hang, figural
Zor **48.00**
Wall plaques, pierced to hang, figural
ballet dancers, Grace & Greg, pr. **85.00**
Wall plaques, pierced to hang, model
of a Cockatoo, 7⅞" & 8¼" h.,
pr. ....**60.00 to 80.00**

CHINESE EXPORT

*Large quantities of porcelain have been
made in China for export to America from
the 1780s, much of it shipped from the
ports of Canton and Nanking. A major
source of this porcelain was Ching-te-Chen
in the Kiangsi province but the wares were
also made elsewhere. The largest
quantities were blue and white. Prices*

*fluctuate considerably depending on age,
condition, decoration, etc.*
*CANTON and ROSE MEDALLION
export wares are listed separately.*

Basin, blue "Fitzhugh" patt.,
decorated w/four clusters of large
chrysanthemum heads & symbols
around a central medallion, the rim
molded w/a lip to hold a cover & w/a
pouring spout, ca. 1810, 14½" d.
(cover missing, spout fritted).......**$1,265.00**
Basket & underplate, green
"Fitzhugh" patt., oval basket
w/flattened flaring rim above
reticulated sides trimmed w/yellow,
blue & green enamel, on a
comforming underplate, 10¾" l.,
2 pcs. (minor glaze abrasions)......**1,265.00**
Bowl, 10¼" d., each side decorated
w/a scene of a Chinese family in a
lakeside garden, small figural
cartouches in between, all edged in
grisaille & on a gilt vine ground, the
interior w/a central floral sprig & a
gilt berried vine border, ca. 1780 (gilt
& some enamel rubbed) **863.00**
Bowl, 13" d., *famille rose* palette,
decorated w/two colorful panels of
Chinese families in lakeside garden
settings, smaller panels of birds at
the sides, all bordered in blue &
white flowering scrollwork w/a blue
cell border on the interior above a
central flower cluster, ca. 1780
(restored break at one side).............**748.00**
Charger, gilt & *en grisaille* floral
decoration, late 18th c., 13" d. **316.00**
Coffeepot, cov., lighthouse-style, a
tall tapering cylindrical body
decorated on each side w/a shield
containing the monogram "AMC" in
gilt script below a lovebird crest &
within ermine mantling, all encircled
by gilt stars, mouth & cover
w/narrow borders of blue enamel,
iron-red & gilt, ca. 1790, 9¾" h.
(small kiln flaw to border)................**920.00**
Models of pug dogs, bisque, each
pup reclining w/head raised, his tail
curled around his haunches, the
coat incised w/fur lines & spotted in
brown enamel, the claws & teeth
glazed white, ca. 1800, 6¾" l.,
pr..**1,265.00**
Mug, cylindrical, decorated in shades
of rose, purple, iron-red, yellow,
brown, blue & green w/a spray &
scattered sprigs of flowers beneath
a worn gilt spearhead border around
the rim, the loop handles w/a gilt
heart-shaped thumbpiece, ca.
1770-80, 4⅝" h. (rim chips).............**920.00**
Plate, 9" d., armorial, the center w/the

arms of Pryce impaling More (?), the two crests alternating in four gilt & iron-red cartouches along the rim, gilt spearhead bordering the well, ca. 1740 (some wear, long crack) **230.00**

Plates, 9" d., armorial, each center painted in colored enamels w/a double coat-of-arms beneath a coronet, the rims w/a formal arrangement of strapwork & latticework in grisaille & gilt, ca. 1745, pr. (tiny chips) **690.00**

Platter, 12¾" oval, Auspicious Figures patt., decorated in iron-red, sepia & gold w/four legendary & historic characters alternating w/four still lifes of 'precious objects' around a central floral medallion, the rim w/a wide neoclassical border, first half 19th c. (scattered wear to gilt & enamels) **633.00**

Platter, 14⅞" oval, for the American market, decorated in the center w/a large American flag crossed & ribbon-tied w/a Chinese flag, the rim w/a Rose Medallion-type border of flowers, fruit & butterflies on a gilt ground, ca. 1912-28 (slight gilt & enamel rubbing) **1,840.00**

Platter, 15" oval, blue "Nanking" patt., 19th c. **805.00**

Platter, 18½" oval, the center w/an English griffin crest in gold & shades of brown enamel, a blue enamel & gilt vine along the well & the rim w/a Worcester porcelain-style border containing Chinese bird & flower vignettes in the Canton *famille rose* palette, ca. 1820 (slight wear, strainer missing) **920.00**

Platter, 19⅛" l., oval, blue "Fitzhugh" patt., 19th c. **920.00**

Blue & White Chinese Export Platter

Platters, 15¼" l., rectangular w/chamfered corners, blue on white h.p. decorated of two figures seated

beside a lake w/a standing figure in a small boat on the lake, 18th c., pr. (ILLUS. of one) **2,415.00**

Chinese Export Punch Bowl

Punch bowl, *famille rose* palette, deep rounded sides on a wide foot ring, the exterior in cobalt blue w/traces of a continuous gilt landscape, the white interior decorated w/five large carps & a border of fruiting & flowering vines, exterior gilt very worn, ca. 1750, 15½" d. (ILLUS.) **2,185.00**

Sauce tureens, cov., blue "Nanking" patt., bulbous oval body raised on a low pedestal base, entwined strap end handles & low domed cover w/pine cone finial, decorated w/the Two Birds patt., ca. 1820, 7⅝" l., pr. (one w/a chip & crack, one fritted)..**1,610.00**

Soup plate, armorial, the center w/a coat-of-arms flanked by a savage & a mermaid supporter & above the motto "PER MARE PER TERRAS," all surmounted by a coronet & a badger crest, a border of gilt bamboo intertwined w/flowers around the rim, ca. 1780, 8⅞" d....**1,495.00**

Soup tureen, cover & undertray, blue "Nanking" patt., bulbous oval body raised on a low pedestal w/entwined strap end handles, the stepped domed cover w/pine cone finial, decorated w/the Inclined Pines patt. w/a figure holding a parasol & crossing a bridge in a river landscape, tureen w/a cell diaper band around foot & gilt-trimmed handles, cover w/trellis diaper border edged in spearheads & dumbbells, the cavetto of undertray w/a cell diaper border, ca. 1820, tureen 14⅛" l., undertray 14⅝" l., the set **2,875.00**

Teapot, cov., cylindrical oval body w/angled shoulder to the fitted cover w/acorn finial, entwined strap handle & straight spout, painted front & back w/various Masonic symbols in green, sepia & iron-red enamel &

gilt, one side beneath the sun, the
other the moon, borders in green,
sepia & iron-red, ca. 1790 (spout tip
restored, lines in the body) **863.00**
Tea set: cov. cylindrical teapot
w/undertray, handled cov. sugar
bowl, helmet-shaped creamer, a
saucer dish, cake plate, a berry
dish, ten tea cups, three coffee cups
w/handles & seven saucers; each
piece painted in iron-red
monochrome trimmed w/worn
gilding w/a central grape cluster &
leaves within a husk band & a
fruiting grapevine border around the
gilt-edged rim, ca. 1828, teapot
4" h., 28 pcs. (various
damages) **1,840.00**
Tureen undertray, chamfered
rectangular form, *famille rose*
palette, the center w/a cluster of
roses, the rim bordering in a garland
of pink & orange daisies on a blue
ribbon, ca. 1780, 14⅜" l. (enamel
wear, some glaze flaking) **345.00**
Vase, cov., 10⅞" h., baluster-form
w/a cylindrical neck supporting a
domed cover w/knob finial & flanged
rim, decorated in iron-red w/two
crane & two fruiting boughs of
peaches between deep lappet
borders filled w/chrysanthemum &
pomegranates, early 18th c. (cover
rim chip, tiny foot chip, some glaze
crackling, misfired area)...................**920.00**
Vegetable dish, cov., *famille rose*
palette, chamfered rectangular form,
the cover & interior each painted w/a
Chinese figural scene in rich enamel
colors, all contained within 'rose
medallion' type borders & below a
gilt acorn knop, ca. 1825,
9¾" l...**1,035.00**
Vegetable dish, cov., brown
"Fitzhugh" patt., rectangular
w/notched corners, pine cone finial
on the stepped, domed cover, a
monogram in the center of the
design, 19th c., 9½" l. (glaze wear)..**977.50**

CLARICE CLIFF DESIGNS

*Clarice Cliff was a designer for A.J.
Wilkinson, Ltd., Royal Staffordshire
Pottery, Burslem, England when they
acquired the adjoining Newport Pottery
Company whose warehouses were filled
with undecorated bowls and vases. About
1925 her flair with the Art Deco style was
incorporated into designs appropriately
named "Bizarre" and "Fantasque" and the*

*warehouse stockpile was decorated in vivid
colors. These hand-painted earthenwares,
all bearing the printed signature of designer
Clarice Cliff, were produced until World
War II and are now finding enormous favor
with collectors.*

*Note: Reproductions of the Clarice Cliff
"Bizarre" marking have been appearing on
the market recently.*

Bone dish, Tonquin patt., black........**$20.00**
Bowl, 7" d., ribbed, Peony patt.,
No. 632 S/S **275.00**
Cup & saucer, "Bizarre" ware,
Autumn Crocus patt. **165.00**
Gravy boat & underplate, Tonquin
patt..**43.00**
Plate, 6" d., Tonquin patt.....................**12.00**
Plate, 8" d., Tonquin patt., red.............**20.00**
Platter, 14" l., Tonquin patt., blue.........**75.00**
Teapot, cov., Tonquin patt., purple **125.00**
Toast holder, Tonquin patt., pink **85.00**

COALPORT

BONE COALPORT CHINA
MADE IN ENGLAND
EST. 1750

*Coalport Porcelain Works operated at
Coalport, Shropshire, England, from about
1795 to 1926 and has operated at Stoke-on-
Trent as Coalport China, Ltd., making
bone china since then.*

Cup, demitasse, overall decoration of
small shamrocks, wine & gold
trim **$85.00**
Dish w/pierced handles, Indian Tree
patt., 7½" d..**27.50**
Figure, lady in emerald green flowing
dress holding a fan, artist-signed,
7⅜" h...**85.00**
Plate, 8" d., scalloped rim, floral
decoration, ca. 1890 ....**38.00**
Soup plates, each w/gilt floral &

geometric decoration, 10" d., set
of 10..**575.00**

COPELAND & SPODE

Copeland Luncheon Plates

*W.T. Copeland & Sons, Ltd., have
operated the Spode Works at Stoke,
England, from 1847 to the present. The
name Spode was used on some of its
productions. Its predecessor, Spode, was
founded by Josiah Spode about 1784 and
became Copeland & Garrett in 1843,
continuing under that name until 1847.
Listings dated prior to 1843 should be
attributed to Spode.*

Creamer, decorated w/horse & rider
scenes, "Leaping the Brook," &
"Taking the Leap," Copeland-Spode,
4" h..**$55.00**
Cup & saucer, Chinese Pheasant
patt., embossed floral spray on
blank, Copeland-Spode **35.00**
Cup & saucer, demitasse, Louvain
patt., Copeland-Spode.......................**18.00**
Figure, parian, girl standing w/jug
holding a dog, dated 1876,
signed "L. A. Malepre," 14" h. **550.00**
Pitcher, jug-type, 6 x 6¼", large white
relief male figures in ale house
scene, different scene on opposite
sides w/a third relief figural beneath
the spout representing a seated
toby-like figure drinking ale, rich blue
ground, handle fashioned to
represent a stem of hops w/a cluster
of hops & vine leaves in white relief
extending around the bowl, marked
"Copeland Spode - England" **198.00**

Plate, 10½" d., scenes of Constitution
Hall & Memorial Continental Hall,
light blue transfer, made for J.E.
Caldwell, Copeland-Spode **50.00**
Plates, luncheon, 9" d., scalloped
edge w/molded & gilt-trimmed
scrolls, center color scene of exotic
birds w/three scroll-bordered edge
reserves w/further birds, all against
a light blue ground, Copeland,
19th c., set of 13 (ILLUS. of
part) **2,350.00**

Spode Blue & White Platter

Platter, 20⅝" l., oval w/lightly
scalloped rim, blue & white transfer-
printed decoration w/a large center
landscape scene of Rebecca at the
well, floral sprigs around border,
well-and-tree in center, Spode, mid-
19th c. (ILLUS.)...............................**431.00**
Serving dish, oval w/ruffled edge,
decorated w/green flowers in basket
on white ground, Copeland-Spode,
11" l...**75.00**

CORDEY

*Founded by Boleslaw Cybis in Trenton,
New Jersey, the Cordey China Company
was the forerunner of the Cybis Studio,
renowned for its fine porcelain sculptures.
A native of Poland, Boleslaw Cybis was
commissioned by his government to paint
"al fresco" murals for the 1939 New York
World's Fair. Already a renowned sculptor
and painter, he elected to remain and
become a citizen of this country. In 1942,
under his guidance, Cordey China
Company began producing appealing busts
and figurines, some decorated by applying
real lace dipped in liquid clay prior to
firing in the kiln. Cordey figures were
assigned numbers that were printed or
pressed on the base. The Cordey line was
eventually phased out of production during*

the 1950s as the porcelain sculptures of the Cybis Studios became widely acclaimed.

Box, cov., round w/a scalloped, lightly ribbed & flaring base, domed cover w/molded edge scallops & a grouping of relief-cast colorful flowers & a small bird in the center, No. 7060, 7" d. **$145.00**

Bust of a lady, her hair hanging in long blonde curls & wearing a cap, her V-neck gown w/a flat lace collar, molded blossoms & scrolls at the front base, No. 5014, 5¾" h. **65.00**

Bust of a lady, her head w/a large blossom wreath, a long torso to the scroll-molded base, No. 5003, 5¾" h..**49.00**

Bust of Sir Walter Raleigh, wearing a lace-trimmed shirt & large plumed hat, No. 5034, 8" h. **150.00**

Figure of a boy standing, wearing knee britches, shirt & vest, holding a basket of flowers on his right shoulder, scroll-molded base w/ applied flowers, No. 5048, 10¼" h. **85.00**

Figure of a lady, "Dame Colonial," standing & wearing a dress trimmed w/floral design on skirt, ruffled sleeves & neckline, hair piled high on head, scroll-molded base. No. 5088A, 11" h...............................**85.00**

Figure of a lady, half-length, shown w/her hair pulled back & tied w/ribbons & flowers, wearing a long dress w/puffed sleeves & a square collar w/lace trim, her arms crossed in front holding a large bouquet of flowers, No. 5054, 10" h.....................**95.00**

Figure of a man, standing wearing a large hat w/four pink leaves & white lace trimmed w/gold in bows & streamers, a long pink lace cape w/drapes & folds & white lace top ruffle & shoulder drape, a creamy figured blouse w/many gathers & turned back cuffs & gold-trimmed pink lace streamer down the front, skin-tight pink britches flared & w/bows just below the knees, scrolled uprights on the round base trimmed w/flowers & leaves, No. 4153, 14" h. **115.00**

Plaque, pierced for hanging, face of a lady w/eyes closed, long ringlets & a large hat covered w/flowers, No. 902, 10¾" l. (minor nicks)..........**250.00**

COWAN

R. Guy Cowan first opened a studio pottery in 1913 in Cleveland, Ohio. The

pottery continued to operate almost continuously, at various locations in the Cleveland area, until it was forced to close in 1931 due to financial problems. This fine art pottery, which was gradually expanded into a full line of commercial productions, is now sought out by collectors.

Ashtray, Oriental-style w/gazelle decoration, red & black **$75.00**

Candlesticks, short w/oblong lobed flaring base molded w/small blossoms & scrolls, orange glaze, Mark 6, 3¼" h., pr. **50.00**

Strawberry pot & saucer, pink & green glaze, 6½" h..........................**160.00**

Vase, 9" h., beehive-shaped, apricot & peach glaze **275.00**

CUP PLATES
(EARTHENWARE)

Staffordshire Cup Plate

Like their glass counterparts, these small plates were designed to hold a cup while the tea or coffee was allowed to cool in a saucer before it was sipped from the saucer, a practice that would now be considered in poor taste. The forerunner of the glass cup plates, those listed below are produced in various Staffordshire potteries in England. Their popularity waned after the introduction of the glass cup plate in the 1820s.

Ridgway, India Temple patt., blue, embossed white border, 3⅞" d. **$49.50**

Staffordshire, American Eagle with Shield patt., paneled sides, medium blue, 3¾" w. **385.00**

Staffordshire, Asian landscape scene, light blue, impressed "Opaque Granite China - W. R. & Co.," 4" d. (light stain) **16.50**

Staffordshire, Basket of Flowers patt., dark blue transfer, impressed "Adams" on back, 4" d., ...**154.00**

Staffordshire, Blind Boy patt., scene of boy & mother seated on bench, floral border, medium blue transfer, ca. 1830, Ridgway, 4¼" d. **77.00**

Staffordshire, Bosphorous patt., light blue, T. Mayer, ca. 1840, 4" d. **44.00**

Staffordshire, center reserve w/large clusters of fruit w/a bird, wide flowers & scrolls border, dark blue, ca. 1830, 4¼" d. **121.00**

Staffordshire, center scene of a large grape cluster & vine, flowers border, dark blue, 3½" d. (short hairline on back rim) **77.00**

Staffordshire, cottage in the woods center scene, spearhead & trefoil border, Clews, 3⅝" d. **121.00**

Staffordshire, Lady of the Lake patt., medium blue transfer, Carey, ca. 1830, 3⅞" d. (ILLUS.) **137.50**

Staffordshire, medium blue transfer-printed scene entitled "Italian Scenery, Santa Croce," 4⅝" d. (small flakes) **66.00**

Staffordshire, Parisian Chateau patt., black, R. Hall & Son, ca. 1840, 3¾" d...**44.00**

Staffordshire, recumbent sheep in center, floral border, dark blue, Wild Rose series by Stevenson, ca. 1830, 3¾" d...............................**154.00**

Staffordshire, Shells patt., dark blue, Stubbs, ca. 1830, 4" d............**247.50**

numbered series and thus there can be a wide range available to the collector.

American Bullfrog, "Enchanted Prince," No. 654, 1971-72, 6½" h. ....**$150.00 to 200.00**

Apache "Chato," No. 711, 13" h......**1,500.00**

Burro, "Fitzgerald," No. 632, 1964-83, 7" l...**180.50**

Duckling, "Baby Brother," No. 361, 1962-79, 4½" h. **106.00**

Eleanor of Aquitaine, 1971, 13½" h..**950.00**

First Flight, No. 410, 1966-73, 4½" h...**195.00**

Heidi, No. 432, 1966-73, 7½" h.........**235.00**

Jane Eyre, No. 4047, 1981-84, 12" h...**1,040.00**

Jeanie With The Light Brown Hair, No. 4012, 1979-81, 9½" h. **477.50**

Lady MacBeth, No. 483, 1975-84, 13" h...**2,150.00**

Little Bo Peep, No. 498, 1977-82, 10½" h...**307.00**

Madonna, "Mystical Rose," No. 2092, 17" h., 1950s....................................**575.00**

Oceania, Sea King's Steed, Fantasia collection, No. 694, 1977 ....**2,450.00**

Pegasus, Free Spirit, 1980, 9" h. **110.00**

Peter Pan, No. 430, 1958-70, 7½" h...**534.00**

Rapunzel (pink), No. 468P, 1972-74, 8" h...**519.00**

Rebecca, No. 443, 1964-72, 6½" h...**286.00**

Richard the Lion-Heart, introduced in 1986, 15" h..............................**2,500.00**

Shoshone "Sacajawea," No. 705, 12½" h...**1,500.00**

Sleeping Beauty, No. 4060, 1982, 7½" h...**1,100.00**

Star is Born (A), 9⅞" h. **105.00**

Wendy, No. 433, 1957-82, 6½" h.......**240.00**

Wood Wren & Dogwood, No. 336, 1963-64, 5½" h. **334.00**

CYBIS

Though not antique, fine Cybis porcelain figures are included here because of the great collector interest. They are produced in both limited edition and non-

DELFT

In the early 17th century Italian potters settled in Holland and began producing tin-glazed earthenwares, often decorated with pseudo-Oriental designs based on Chinese porcelain wares. The city of Delft became the center of this pottery production and several firms produced the wares throughout the 17th and early 18th century. A majority of the pieces featured blue on white designs, but polychrome wares were also made. The Dutch Delftwares were also shipped to England and eventually the English copied them at potteries in such cities as Bristol, Lambeth and Liverpool. Although still produced today, Delft peaked in popularity by the mid-18th century.

Garniture set: two baluster-form vases & beaker-shaped vase, painted blue on white, each on the octagonal section & molded on the front w/a rococo scroll-edged cartouche w/a striped & stippled ground reserved w/a panel painted w/a crested bird perched on a flowering tree above a peony, the reverse w/a floral sprig, the necks of the pair w/double-V & cricket motifs, marked "IVDuign" in blue, Holland, 1775-85, De Porceleyne Scotel, 9⅛" & 9¼" h., the set (covers missing, small chips & footrims beveled) **$2,300.00**

Mantel garniture: three baluster-form vases w/covers & pair of beaker vases; painted blue on white, each piece of octagonal section & molded on the front w/a scroll, blossom & petal-edge cartouche decorated w/scalework ground reserved w/an oval painted w/a floral banquet, the reverse w/a foliate branch between bands of scroll devices repeated on the front of the rim, the covers molded on the front w/a blossom above a scalework panel, marked "P:C:" in blue, Holland, ca. 1800, De Porceleyne Fles, 13¾" & 9½" h., the set (various chips & abrasions) **3,132.00**

Delft Charger

Chargers, painted blue & white, decorated w/exotic birds perched on flowering plants, surrounded by alternating birds & flowers on a wide band, marked "GK," Holland, 17th c., 15½" d., pr. (ILLUS. one of two) **1,725.00**

Delft Monteith

Monteith, scalloped rim, painted blue on white, the exterior painted on the front w/two Chinamen seated in a garden, one holding a basket of fruit & foliage, on the reverse a third man seated beneath the moon below the lightly barbed & deeply scalloped rim edge, the interior painted in the center w/a large bunch of grapes, tendrils & leaves within a double-line roundel, England, ca. 1700, 8⁹⁄₁₆" d., glaze pits, glaze chips & abrasions, chip on footrim (ILLUS.) **11,500.00**

Portrait Plaque of Dutch Woman

Plaque, bust portrait of Dutch woman wearing 17th century attire, decorated in blue & white on a dark blue ground, Holland, 16¼" d. (ILLUS.) ...**395.00**

Plaque, half-length portrait of early minstrel playing lute, h.p. brown enamel, signed & impressed marks, late 19th c., mounted in mahogony frame, 17½" d. (ILLUS. top next page) **489.00**

Plate, 12¹³⁄₁₆" d., painted blue on white, decorated w/two Chinamen carrying a pole & standing in a fenced garden beneath a flitting insect, the powder-blue rim reserved w/five floral sprigs & the underside

Hand-painted Framed Delft Plaque

w/four branches & a central leaf spring, England, ca. 1750 (chip & edge abraded) **517.00**

English Delftware Large Plate

Plate, 13¼" d., painted blue on white, fashionable couple conversing between sponged trees in a landscape, the gentleman pointing toward a group of Italianate buildings at the foot of two hills in the distance, England, 1750-60, the cavetto w/chip & rim chips & abrasions (ILLUS.) **805.00**

Plate, 13⅜" d., painted blue on white, decorated w/two ladies conversing between sponged trees & a small house before a distant Italianate building at the foot of small hills, England, 1750-60, (six restored chips & other various chips & edge abrasions) **805.00**

Posset pot, cov., cylindrical body tapering to a short neck & flaring rim w/loop handles, painted blue on white on the front w/insects & birds amid flowering plants flanking the dot- and scroll-decorated tubular spout on reverse & cover w/a

Delft Posset Pot

peacock perched on a rock near a songbird perched on a flowering & fruiting vine beneath an S-scroll border around the neck, the loop handles at the sides similarly decorated to the spout, cover w/a dentil border around the rim & concentric bands around the mushroom knop, marked "S" in blue, a dash & dot in blue, Holland, various restored chips, 9⅛" h., (ILLUS.) **575.00**

Tobacco jars, cov., each painted on the front w/an elaborate cartouche formed by patterned panels & foliate scrolls surmounted by a vase of flowers & inscribed in the scalloped-edge center "HAVANA" or "POMPADOER," three bell marks in blue, Holland, late 18th c., De Drye Clocken, 12⅝" & 12½" h., pr. (one w/neck repair, glaze bruise & glaze crack, damaged knop resoldered).....................................**5,175.00**

Delft Tobacco Jar

Tobacco jars, cov., ovoid bodies w/stepped circular brass covers, each painted on the front w/an elaborate cartouche formed by patterned panels & foliate scrolls surmounted by a vase of flowers & inscribed in the scalloped-edge center "RAPPE D'HOLLANDE" or "SPAANSCHE," the second w/a glaze of light blue tone, three bell marks or Ipkan mark in blue, late 18th c., De Drye Clocken & De Porcelyne Lampetkan, one w/rim notch & shoulder abrasions, both w/rim abrasions, 13¾" h., pr. (ILLUS. one of two) **3,737.00**

Vases, cov., 11⅛" h., baluster-shaped body w/short brass covers, each painted on the front w/a two-chimney house beyond a fountain in a formal garden between allées of trees within a scalloped oval panel surrounded by large peony blossoms & flowering branches, the reverse w/a peony & foliate sprig & the neck w/squiggles & decorative star devices, Holland, 1760-80, pr. (various chips & glaze abrasion)...**2,875.00**

Vases, 11⅜" h., baluster-shaped body sitting on tall cylindrical foot tapering to a tall cylindrical neck w/bulbous top & flaring rim, each painted blue on white w/two pine trees & two rock gardens within roundels alternating w/floral roundels beneath foliate-scroll & *ruyi*-head borders & above a border of patterned *ruyi*-head & icicles, rim decorated w/icicle border flanking the blossom- and leaf- decorated top, marked "2" in blue, early 18th c., Holland, pr. (rim & footrim chips) **1,150.00**

Vase, 14¹⁵⁄₁₆" h., baluster-shaped body sitting on tall cylindrical foot tapering to a tall cylindrical neck w/bulbous top & flaring rim, painted in blue & white on the front & reverse w/two or three Oriental figures in a garden & on either side w/a stag & doe in a roundel surrounded by leafage, all below a flowering vine border & above four blossoms & leaf clusters on spherical knop, Holland, early 18th c. (rim restored, minor glaze abrasions & some crackling)............**575.00**

DOULTON & ROYAL DOULTON

Doulton & Co., Ltd., was founded in Lambeth, London, about 1858. It was operated there till 1956 and often

incorporated the words "Doulton" and "Lambeth" in its marks. Pinder Bourne & Co., Burslem was purchased by the Doultons in 1878 and in 1882 became Doulton & Co., Ltd. It added porcelain to its earthenware production in 1884. The "Royal Doulton" mark has been used since 1902 by this factory, which is still in production. Character jugs and figurines are commanding great attention from collectors at the present time.

ANIMALS & BIRDS

Bear, brown, HN 2659......................**$285.00**

Cat, character, kitten licking hind paw, brown & white, HN 2580, 1941-85, 2¼" h., ...**85.00**

Cat, character, kitten, sleeping, brown & white, HN 2581, 1941-85, 1½" h.,...**85.00**

Cat, character, kitten, sitting licking front paw, tan, HN 2583....................**75.00**

Cat, character, kitten looking up, tan & white, HN 2584, 1941-85, 2" h. **85.00**

Cat, "Lucky," K12, 1932-75, 2¾" h.,....**102.50**

Cat, Persian, white, HN 2539.............**300.00**

Cat, sitting, Flambé, large **95.00**

Dog, Airedale Terrier, "Cotsford Topsail," HN 1024, 1931-68, 4" h. ...**265.00**

Dog, Alsatian, "Benign of Picardy," dark brown coat w/light brown underbody, black highlights, HN 1116, 1937-85, 6" h. **165.00**

Dog, Boxer, "Warlord of Mazelaine," HN 2643, 6½" h. **157.50**

Dog, Bulldog, brindle, HN 1044, small **242.50**

Dog, Bulldog, brindle, HN 1046, 1931-68, 4¾" h. **362.50**

Dog, Bulldog, brown & white, HN 1047, small.................**200.00 to 250.00**

Dog, Bulldog, "Union Jack," British flag over back, HN 6407, 2 x 4", 2½" h.......................................**157.00**

Dog, Bulldog, white, HN 1074, 3" h...**152.00**

Dog, Bulldog Puppy, tan w/dark brown patches over eye & back, K2, 1931-77, 2" h. **100.00**

Dog, Cairn Terrier, "Charming Eyes," HN 1034, medium **375.00**

Dog, Cairn Terrier, "Charming Eyes,"
HN 1035, 3¼" h. **99.50**

Dog, Cairn Terrier, begging,
HN 2589, 4" h. **67.00**

Dog, Cairn Terrier, seated, grey
w/black highlights, K11, 1931-77,
2½" h., ...**65.00**

Dog, character dog, yawning,
HN 1099, 4¼" h. **75.00**

Dog, character dog, w/brown ball,
HN 1103, 2½" h. **67.00**

Dog, character dog, w/plate,
HN 1158, 3" h. **110.00**

Dog, character dog, w/bone in
mouth, HN 1159, 3¾" h. **75.00**

Dog, character dog, "Goworth Victor"
Dalmatian, HN 1113, medium
size **225.00**

Dog, character dog, w/slipper, white
w/black & brown patches, grey
slipper, HN 2654, 1959-85, 3" h.,......**42.00**

Dog, Cocker Spaniel, K 9 ....**57.50**

Dog, Cocker Spaniel, seated w/paw
up, golden brown w/black highlights
K9A, 1931-77 ....**90.00**

Dog, Cocker Spaniel, liver & white,
HN 1002, 1931-60, 6½" h. **350.00**

Dog, Cocker Spaniel, "Lucky Star
of Ware," black w/grey highlights,
HN 1020, 5" h. **110.00**

Dog, Cocker Spaniel, "Lucky Star
of Ware," HN 1021, 3½" h. **132.50**

Dog, Cocker Spaniel, black & white,
HN 1078, 3½" h. **138.00**

Dog, Cocker Spaniel, black & white,
HN 1109, 5" h. **135.00**

Dog, Cocker Spaniel, lying in basket,
white w/brown & black markings,
light brown basket, HN 2585, 1941-
85, 2" h..............................**90.00**

Dog, Cocker Spaniel puppy in basket,
chewing handle, HN 2586, 2½" h. **90.00**

Dog, Cocker Spaniel & Pheasant,
deep brown spots & ears, HN 1001,
8⅜" l., 6¼" h.......................**400.00**

Dog, Cocker Spaniel w/pheasant,
white coat w/dark brown markings,
red brown & green pheasant, HN
1028, 1931-68, 5¼" h., ...**200.00**

Dog, Cocker Spaniel w/pheasant,
white coat w/dark brown markings,
red brown & green pheasant, HN
1029, 1931-68, 3½" h. **175.00**

Dog, Cocker Spaniel, liver & white,
HN 1036, 1¾ x 7", 5¼" h. **165.00**

Dog, Cocker Spaniel & Pheasant,
black & white, HN 1062, small **157.00**

Dog, Collie, "Ashstead Applause,"
HN 1057, 7½" h. **495.00**

Dog, Collie, "Ashstead Applause,"
dark & light brown coat, white chest,
shoulders & feet, HN 1059, 1931-68,
3½" h................................**275.00**

Dog, Dachshund, "Shrewd Saint",

Dog, Dachshund, "Shrewd Saint"
dark brown, light brown feet & nose,
HN 1128, 1937-86, 4" h. **157.50**

Dog, Dachshund, "Shrewd Saint"
HN 1129, 3" h. **150.00**

Dog, Dachshund, red, HN 1140,
medium..............................**245.00**

Dog, Dachshund, brown, HN 1141,
1937-86, 2¾" h. **165.00**

Dog, Doberman Pinscher, "Rancho
Dobe's Storm," HN 2645, 6¼" h. **160.00**

Dog, Dog of Fo, Rouge Flambé glaze,
4¾" h...............................**175.00**

Dog, English Setter, "Maesydd
Mustard," off white coat w/black
high-lights, HN 1049, 1931-60,
7½" h...............................**625.00**

Dog, English Setter, "Maesydd
Mustard," HN 1050, 5¼" h. **155.00**

Dog, English Setter & Pheasant,
HN 2529..............................**275.00**

Dog, English Foxhound, "Tring
Rattler," white, black & brown, HN
1026, 1931-60, 5" h. **425.00**

Dog, Foxhound, seated, white w/dark
brown & black patches over ears,
eyes & back, K7, 1931-77................**90.00**

Dog, Fox Terrier, standing, HN 942,
1927-36, 6" h. **550.00**

Dog, Fox Terrier, HN 943, 5¼" h........**495.00**

Dog, Fox Terrier, white w/black-brown
patches, HN 945, 1927-40, 5½" h....**495.00**

Dog, French Poodle, HN 2631,
medium **200.00**

Dog, Irish Setter, "Pat O'Moy,"
reddish brown, HN 1054, 1931-60,
7½" h...............................**625.00**

Dog, Irish Setter, HN 1055, 5¼" h. ...**170.00**

Dog, Irish Setter, "Pat O'Moy,"
reddish brown, HN 1056, 1931-68,
4" h................................**165.00**

Dog, Labrador, "Bumblikite of
Mansergh," black, HN 2667, 1967-
85, 5¼" h............................**170.00**

Dog, Pekinese, "Biddee of Ifield,"
standing, golden brown w/black
highlights, HN 1012, 1931-85,
3" h................................**125.00**

Dog, Pekinese, seated, golden brown
w/black markings on face & ears,
K6, 1931-77.........................**90.00**

Dog, Pekinese, "Biddee of Ifield,"
seated, butterscotch coat w/black
highlight, HN 1040, 1931-by 1946,
3" h................................**375.00**

Dog, Puppy in basket, lying,
HN 2585, 2" h. **150.00**

Dog, Rough-haired Terrier, "Crackley
Startler," white w/black & brown
markings, HN 1013, 1931-60,
5½" h...............................**375.00**

Dog, Rough-haired Terrier, "Crackley
Startler," white w/black & brown
markings, HN 1014, 1931-85,
3¾" h................................**205.00**

Dog, St. Bernard, lying down, K 19,
miniature, 1¾" h. **67.00**
Dog, Scottish Terrier, Ch. "Albourne
Arthur," HN 1016, small **130.00**
Dog, Sealyham, sleeping, K 4,
miniature **175.00**
Dog, Sealyham, "Scotia Stylist," white
w/light brown patches over eyes &
ears, HN 1031, 1931-55, 4" h. **375.00**
Dog, Sealyham, "Scotia Stylist,"
HN 1032, small **280.00**
Dog, Sealyham, standing - style two,
white w/light brown patches over
eyes & ears, HN 2509, 1938-59,
2½" h. **225.00**
Dog, Springer Spaniel, HN 2516........**272.50**
Dog, Springer Spaniel, HN 2517........**145.00**
Dog, Staffordshire Bull Terrier, white,
HN 1121, 1937-60, 6½" h. **600.00**
Dog, Welsh Corgi, "Spring Robin,"
golden brown w/white & brown
underbody, HN 2558, 1941-68,
5" h. **275.00**
Dogs, Cocker Spaniels sleeping,
white dog w/brown markings &
golden brown dog, HN 2590,
1941-69, 1¾" h. **90.00**
Duck, Mallard Drake, HN 806 ....**150.00**
Duck, Mallard Drake on Rocks (flower
holder), HN 853, 1924-36 ....**275.00**
Fox, stalking, brown & light brown
w/black highlights, HN 147A-1,
1918-by 1946, 1 x 5¼" h. **225.00**
Hare, seated, ears up, light brown &
white, K 39,1940-77, 2¼" h. **100.00**
Horse, "The Gude Grey Mare" w/foal,
HN 2532, 5" h. **300.00**
Penguin, grey & white w/black tips,
K 22, 1940-68, 1¾" h. **245.00**
Penguin, w/chick under wing, black &
white, K 20, 1940-68, 2¼" h. **225.00**

CHARACTER JUGS

Auld Mac Mug

Anne of Cleves, Ears Up, 1980-81,
large, 6" h. **200.00**
'Ard of 'Earing, miniature,
2½" h. **842.00**
'Arriet, tiny, 1¼" h. **170.00**

'Arriet, small, 3½" h. **59.50**
'Arriet, large, 6½" h. **159.00**
'Arry, tiny, 1¼" h. **192.00**
'Arry, small, 3½" h. **79.00**
'Arry, large, 6" h. **159.50**
Athos, miniature, 2¼" h. **45.00**
Auctioneer, large, limited
edition,1988 ....**96.00**
Auld Mac, "A" mark, small, 3½" h. **50.00**
Auld Mac, "A" mark, large, 6¾" h.
(ILLUS.) **92.00**
Bacchus, miniature, 2¼" h...................**39.00**
Bacchus, small, 3½" h. **45.00**
Bacchus, large, 6" h. **65.00**
Beefeater, miniature, 2¼" h. **72.00**
Beefeater, "A" mark, small, w/GR on
handle, 3½" h. **50.00**
Beefeater, large, w/GR on handle **105.00**
Betsy Trotwood, tiny, 1¼" h................**35.00**
Blacksmith, miniature, 2¼" h. **44.00**
Bootmaker, miniature, 2¼" h...............**35.00**
(Sergeant) Buz Fuz, large, 5½" h........**95.00**
Capt. Ahab, small, 3½" h. **55.00**
Capt. Ahab, large, 7" h. **135.00**
Captain Henry Morgan, miniature,
2¼" h...**37.50**
Captain Henry Morgan, small,
3½" h..**49.50**
Captain Henry Morgan, large,
6¾" h..**95.00**
Captain Hook, miniature, 2¼" h. **285.00**
Captain Hook, small, 3½" h. **347.50**
Captain Hook, large, 7¼" h. **500.00**
Cardinal, miniature, 2¼" h. **37.00**
Cavalier, small, 3½" h. **50.00**
Cavalier, "A" mark, large, 7" h...........**150.00**
Chief Sitting Bull & George
Armstrong Custer, Chief sitting
Bull on forward side of jug & Custer
on the reverse, 1984 -
limited edition **147.50**
Cliff Cornell, blue, large **276.00**
Clown w/red hair, large, 6" h..........**2,850.00**
David Copperfield, tiny, 1¼" h. **35.00**
Dick Turpin, mask on hat, gun
handle, miniature, 2¼" h. **37.50**
Dick Turpin, mask on hat, gun
handle, small, 3½" h. **45.00**
Dick Turpin, mask on hat, gun
handle, large, 6" h. **122.00**
Drake, "A" mark, large, 5¾" h.
(ILLUS. top next page) ....**125.00 to 150.00**
Fat Boy, miniature, 2¼" h. **52.00**
Fortune Teller, large, 6¾" h. **450.00**
Friar Tuck, large, 7" h. **375.00**
Gardener, miniature, 2¼" h..................**52.00**
Gardener, small, 3½" h. **70.00**
George Washington, miniature,
2¼" h...**45.00**
George Washington, large, 7½" h. **97.00**
Gladiator, large, 7¾" h.......................**557.00**
Golfer, small, 3½" h. **39.00**
Golfer, large, 7" h...............................**69.00**

Large Drake Mug

Gondolier, miniature, 2¼" h...............383.00
Gondolier, small, 3½" h..................350.00
Gondolier, large, 8" h. 562.50
Gone Away, miniature, 2¼" h. 40.00
Gone Away, small, 3½" h. 53.00
Groucho Marx, large, 7" h. 122.50
Guardsman, miniature, 2¼" h. 45.00
Guardsman, large, 8" h. 69.00
Gulliver, small, 3½" h........................375.00
Gulliver, large, 7½" h. 595.00
Hamlet, large, 7¼" h. 75.00
Izaak Walton, spelled "Izaac" on
   base, large, 7" h..............................79.00
Jarge, small, 3½" h. 147.50
Jarge, large, 6½" h...........................275.00
Jockey, large, 7¾" h. 252.00
John Barleycorn, "A" mark,
   miniature, 2¼" h..............................45.00
John Barleycorn, small, 3½" h............50.00
John Barleycorn, large, 6½" h. 139.00
Johnny Appleseed, large, 6" h. 292.00
John Peel, large, 6½" h. 135.00
Lawyer, miniature, 2¼" h. 45.00
Little Nell, tiny, 1¼" h........................35.00
Lord Nelson, large, 7" h. 350.00
Lumberjack, small, 3½" h...................45.00
Lumberjack, large, 7¼" h. 108.00
Mad Hatter, large, 7¼" h. 125.00
Mae West, large, 7" h..........................95.00
March Hare, large, 6" h......................131.00
Mark Twain, small, 3½" h. 47.50
Mephistopheles, small, 3½" h...........750.00
Mephistopheles, "A" mark, large,
   7" h..550.00
Merlin, miniature, 2¼" h......................41.00
Mikado, small, 3½" h.........................272.50
Mine Host, miniature, 2½" h. 30.00
Mine Host, small, 3½" h......................60.00
Mine Host, large, 7" h. 135.00
Mr. Micawber, tiny, 1¼" h. 95.00
Mr. Micawber, miniature, 2¼" h...........57.50
Mr. Pickwick, tiny, 1¼" h. 135.00
Mr. Pickwick, small, 3½" h. 55.00
Mr. Pickwick, "A" mark, large,
   5¾" h..116.00
Monty, large, 7" h.................................59.50
Old Charley, tiny, 1¼" h.....................115.00
Old Charley, miniature, 2¼" h. 36.00

Old Charley, small, 3½" h....................30.00
Old Charley, large, 5½" h. 103.00
Old King Cole, small, 3½" h. 107.00
Old King Cole, large, 5¾" h..............189.00
Oliver Twist, tiny, 1¼" h. 35.00
Paddy, tiny, 1¼" h................................85.00
Parson Brown, small, 3½" h................51.00
Parson Brown, large, 6½" h. 121.00
Pied Piper, miniature, 2¼" h. 52.50
Pied Piper, small, 3¾" h. 70.00
Pied Piper, large, 7" h..........................98.00
Porthos, small, 3½" h. 55.00
Punch & Judy Man, miniature,
   2¼" h..322.00
Punch & Judy Man, large, 7" h. 562.50
Red Queen, large, 7¼" h. 86.00
Regency Beau, miniature, 2¼" h.......650.00
Regency Beau, small, 3½" h. 525.00
Regency Beau, large, 7¼" h..............948.00
Rip Van Winkle, miniature, 2½" h........36.00
Robin Hood, miniature, 2¼" h. 45.00
Robin Hood, small, 3½" h....................43.00
Robin Hood, large, 7½" h....................90.00
Robinson Crusoe, miniature, 2¼" h....45.00
Robinson Crusoe, large, 7½" h. 85.00
Ronald Reagon, large, 1984, limited
   edition, 7¾" h. 447.50
Sairey Gamp, miniature, 2¼" h. 47.00
Sairey Gamp, small, 3½" h. 51.00
Sairey Gamp, "A" mark, large,
   6¼" h..125.00
Sairey Gamp, large, 6¼" h..................84.00
Sam Johnson, small, 3½" h. 202.00
Sam Johnson, large, 6¼" h 204.00
Sam Weller, tiny, 1¼" h. 90.00
Sam Weller, mid, 4½" h. 150.00
Sam Weller, large, 6½" h....................95.00
Sancho Panza, large, 6½" h..............119.00
Santa Claus, w/doll handle, large,
   1981, 7½" h.....................................122.50
Santa Claus, reindeer handle, large,
   1982, 7¼" h. 150.00
Santa Claus, wreath handle, large,
   7" h..325.00
Scaramouche, small, 3¼" h. 395.00
Scaramouche, large, 7" h.................625.00

Simon the Cellarer Mug

Simon the Cellarer, large, 6½" h.
   (ILLUS.) 135.00
Sir Henry Doulton, small, 1984,
   4½" h..70.00

Sir Thomas Moore, large, 6¾" h. **90.00**
Smuggler, small, 3½" h. **57.50**
Smuggler, large, 7¼" h....................**135.00**
Smuts, large, 6½" h. **1,399.50**
Tam O'Shanter, miniature, 2½" h. **30.00**
Tam O'Shanter, small, 3¼" h. **45.00**
Toby Philpots, small, 3½" h. **45.00**
Toby Philpots, large, 6¼" h..............**142.50**
Tony Weller, miniature, 2¼" h. **45.00**
Tony Weller, small, 3½" h...................**39.00**
Tony Weller, "A" mark, small, 3½" h....**65.00**
Tony Weller, "A" mark, large,
   6½" h..**150.00**
Touchstone, large, 7" h. **220.00**
Town Crier, miniature, 2¼" h............**115.00**
Trapper (The), small, 3½" h...............**50.00**
Trapper (The), large, 7¼" h. **79.00**
Ugly Duchess, small, 3½" h. **234.00**
Ugly Duchess, large, 6¾" h..............**512.50**
Uncle Tom Cobbleigh,
   large, 7" h.................**350.00 to 375.00**
Veteran Motorist, small, 3½" h...........**45.00**
Vicar of Bray, large, 6¾" h. **172.50**
Viking, large, 7½" h...........................**100.00**
Yachtsman, large, w/ life jacket, 8" h...**95.00**

DICKENSWARE
Figurine, Buz Fuz, 1st series, black &
   brown, HN 538, 1922-32, 3¾" h. **80.00**
Figurine, Fat Boy (The), 1st series,
   blue & white, HN 530, 1922-32,
   3½" h..**80.00**
Figurine, Mr. Pickwick, 1st series,
   black & tan, HN 529, 1922-32,
   3¾" h..**80.00**
Figurine, Mr. Pickwick, 2nd series,
   yellow & black, M 41, 1322-83,
   4" h...**70.00**
Figurine, River Boy, blue & green,
   HN 2128, 1962-75 ....**215.00**
Figurine, Sam Weller, 1st series,
   yellow & brown, HN 531, 1922-32,
   4" h...**80.00**
Pitcher, 5½" h., square jug-type, Old
   Curiosity Shop, Nell & Grandfather..**159.00**
Plate, 10¼" d., Micawber **148.00**
Plate, Sam Weller **60.00**

FIGURINES
Adornment, HN 3015, pink &
   lavender striped dress, Gentle Art
   series, limited edition of
   750, 1989......................................**750.00**
Afternoon Tea, HN 1747,
   pink & blue, 1935-82, ...**375.00 to 400.00**
A La Mode, HN 2544, 1974-79..........**159.00**
Alexandra, HN 2398, patterned green
   dress, yellow cape, 1970-76 ....**120.00**
Alice, HN 2158, 1960-80...................**167.50**
Antoinette, HN 2326, white dress,
   1967-79...**120.00**
Autumn Breezes, HN 1911, green &
   black hat, green bodice, pink &
   lavender skirt & muff, 1939-76........**198.00**

Autumn Breezes

Autumn Breezes, HN 1913, green
   skirt, blue bodice & hat, muff,
   1939-71 (ILLUS.) ....**190.00 to 225.00**
Autumn Breezes, HN 2147, white
   dress, black jacket, 1955-71 ....**300.00**
Autumn Glory, HN 2766, bluish grey,
   tan grape basket, limited edition,
   1988...**120.00**
Babie, HN 2121, pink, 1983-92............**55.00**
Bachelor (The), HN 2319, 1964-75 ...**227.50**
Ballerina, HN 2116, lavender dress,
   1953-73 ....**235.00 to 275.00**
Beachcomber, HN 2487, 1973-76 ....**200.00**
Belle o' the Ball, HN 1997, red &
   white, 1947-79 ....**335.00**
Blacksmith (The), HN 2782, brown,
   white & grey, 1987-91 ....**125.00**
Blithe Morning, HN 2021, mauve &
   pink, 1949-71 ....**202.50**
Blithe Morning, HN 2065, red, 1950-
   73 ....**150.00 to 175.00**
Boatman (The), HN 2417, 1971-87 ...**152.50**
Boy Evacuee (The), HN 3202, green
   & blue, 1989 limited edition.............**250.00**
Bride (The), HN 2166, pink,
   1956-76, ...**145.00 to 185.00**
Bridesmaid, M 12, yellow &
   lavender **347.00**
Bridesmaid (The), HN 2196, pale
   blue, 1960-76...................................**110.00**
Bridesmaid (The), HN 2874, white
   w/gold trim, 1980-89 ....**85.00**
Broken Lance (The), HN 2041, blue,
   red & yellow, 1949-75 ....**495.00**
Calumet, HN 2068, 1950-53 ....**608.00**
Camellia, HN 2222, pink dress,
   1960-71..**275.00**
Captain (The), HN 2260, 1965-82 .....**195.00**
Carolyn, HN 2112, 1953-59...............**252.00**
Carpet Seller (The), HN 1464A,
   green & orange, hand closed
   version, 1931-69........**335.00 to 350.00**
Cavalier, HN 2716, 1976-82 ....**195.00**
Centurion (The), HN 2726, 1982-84 ..**163.00**
Charlotte, HN 2423, pale blue & pink,
   1986-92..**129.00**

Chic, HN 2997, pale blue, 1987 ....**170.00**

China Repairman (The), HN 2943,
blue, white & tan, 1983-88 ....**165.00**

Chloe, HN 1479, pink-blue dress,
1931-49...**250.00**

Chloe, HN 1765, white-blue dress,
1936-50...**225.50**

Christine, HN 3172, pink, limited
edition, 1988 ....**225.00**

Christmas Parcels, HN 2851,
1978-82...**194.00**

Clare, HN 2793, 1980-84 ....**190.00**

Clarissa, HN 2345, 1968-81 ....**115.00**

Clockmaker (The), HN 2279,
1961-75...**233.00**

Clown (The), HN 2890, 1979-88........**203.00**

Coachmann (The), HN 2282,
1963-71...**457.50**

Columbine, HN 2185, pale pink
dress, 1957-69..................................**225.00**

Cookie, HN 2218, pink & white,
1958-75...**125.00**

Country Lass, HN 1991, 1975-81 .....**126.00**

Cup of Tea (The), HN 2322,
1964-83...**148.00**

Daisy, HN 1961, pink, 1941-49.........**360.00**

Darby, HN 1427, mottled pink coat,
1930-49...**275.00**

Debut, HN 3046, pale blue, white &
green, 1987-89 ....**170.00**

Debutante, HN 2210, 1963-67...........**269.00**

Delight, HN 1773, green dress,
1936-49 ....**750.00 to 775.00**

Detective (The), HN 2359, brown
coat, 1977-83.....................................**175.00**

Diana, HN 1986, red dress, purple hat
ties, 1946-75...**97.50**

Diana, HN 3266, pink, blue &
white, 1990 ....**100.00**

Drummer Boy, HN 2679, 1976-81 ....**330.00**

Ellen, HN 3020, blue & yellow,
1984-87...**450.00**

Embroidering, HN 2855, 1980-90.....**142.50**

Enchantment, HN 2178, blue dress
w/yellow sleeves, 1957-82 ....**169.00**

Entranced, HN 3186, green, white &
tan, 1988-89......................................**160.00**

Fagin, M 49, brown, 1932-83 ....**60.00**

Francine, HN 2422, 1972-80 ....**85.00**

French Peasant, HN 2075,
1951-55...**475.00**

Friar Tuck, HN 2143, 1954-65...........**425.00**

Gaffer (The), HN 2053, green &
brown, 1950-59.................................**345.00**

Gillian, HN 3042, green dress
w/shoulder straps, 1984-? **119.00**

Girl Evacuee (The), HN 3203, red,
blue & brown, 1989 limited edition...**250.00**

Giselle, HN 2139, blue dress,
1954-69...**361.00**

Giselle, The Forest Glade, HN 2140,
white & blue, 1954-65 ....**300.00**

Good Morning, HN 2671, blue, pink
& brown matte, 1974-76 ....**195.00**

Gossips, HN 2025, 1949-67 ....**285.00**

Grand Manner, HN 2723, lavender &
yellow, 1975-81.................................**225.00**

Granny's Heritage, HN 2031, green
skirt, light multicolored shawl,
1949-69...**362.50**

Granny's Shawl, HN 1642, cream
dress, red shawl, 1934-49 ....**587.00**

Harmony, HN 2824, grey, 1978-84....**235.00**

Harvestime, HN 3084, blue & blue-
grey, 1988-90....................................**195.00**

He Loves Me, HN 2046, flowered
pink dress, 1949-62 ....**247.50**

Her Ladyship, HN 1977, 1945-59 .....**369.50**

Hilary, HN 2335, 1967-80 ....**145.00**

Honey, HN 1909, pink dress,
1939-49...**377.00**

Ibrahim, HN 2095, brown &
yellow, 1952-55.................................**450.00**

Jacqueline, HN 2001, rose dress,
1947-51...**325.00**

Janet, HN 1916, blue bodice, pink
skirt, 1939-49 ....**190.00**

Janice, HN 2022, green &
cream dress, 1949-55 ....**425.00**

January, HN 2697, white w/green
dress, snowdrop flowers, 1987 ....**175.00**

Jean, HN 2032, green dress, red
cloak, 1949-59 ....**220.00**

Jennifer, HN 2392, blue, 1982-92 ....**177.50**

Jovial Monk (The), HN 2144,
1954-76...**172.00**

Juliet, HN 2968, blue & white,
1983-84...**275.00**

Karen, HN 1994, red dress,
1947-55...**395.00**

Kate, HN 2789, white dress w/floral
decoration, 1978-87 ....**155.00**

Kimberley, HN 2969, yellow & white,
1983-84...**275.00**

Lady April, HN 1958, red & purple,
1940-59...**292.00**

Lady Charmian, HN 1948, green
dress w/red shawl,
1940-73 ....**200.00 to 225.00**

Lady Charmian, HN 1949, red dress
w/green shawl, 1940-75...................**182.00**

Lambing Time, HN 1890, brown,
1938-81...**162.50**

Leisure Hour (The), HN 2055, green,
yellow & brown, 1950-65 ....**475.00**

Lily, HN 1798, pink, 1936-71 ....**100.00**

Linda, HN 2106, 1953-76...................**127.00**

Lisa, HN 2310, blue & white matte,
1969-82...**150.00**

Loretta, HN 2337, purple dress,
yellow shawl, 1966-80 ....**145.00**

Lorna, HN 2311, green dress, yellow
shawl, 1965-85 ....**125.00**

Love Letter, HN 2149, pink & blue,
1958-76...**282.50**

Lunchtime, HN 2485, brown,
1973-81...**165.00**

Madonna of the Square, HN 2034, pale green, 1949-51 ....**575.00 to 595.00**
Magic Dragon, HN 2977, cream, 1983-86..**110.00**
Mandy, HN 2476, white, 1982-92 ....**54.50**
Margaret, HN 1989, red & green dress, 1947-59.................................**395.00**
Margaret of Anjou, HN 2012, 1948-53..**800.00**
Marguerite, HN 1928, pink dress, 1940-59..**312.00**
Matilda, HN 2011, 1948-53..............**600.00**
Maureen, HN 1770, pink, 1936-59.....**280.00**

Melanie

Melanie, HN 2271, deep blue dress, gold collar & underskirt, carries bouquet of yellow roses, 1965-81 (ILLUS.) **145.00**
Memories, HN 2030, pink & green, 1949-59 ....**290.00**
Midsummer Noon, HN 2033, pink, 1949-55..**509.00**
Minuet, HN 2019, patterned white dress, 1949-71 ....**225.00**

Miss Demure

Miss Demure, HN 1402, pale pink dress, 1930-75 (ILLUS.) **178.00**
Miss Muffet, HN 1936, red dress, 1940-67..**193.50**
My Pet, HN 2238, 1962-75..................**154.00**

Nicola, HN 2804, red & lilac, 1987....**195.00**
October, HN 2693, white w/blue dress, cosmos flowers, 1987 ....**175.00**
Olga, HN 2463, 1972-75 ....**175.00**
Oliver Twist, M 89, black & tan, 1949-83..**65.00**
Omar Khayyam, HN 2247, brown, 1965-83..**135.00**
Paisley Shawl, M 4, purple & green, 1932-45..**370.00**
Paisley Shawl, HN 1392, red shawl, cream dress, 1930-49.....................**275.00**
Paisley Shawl, HN 1988, red & pink, 1946-75..**170.00**
Penelope, HN 1901, red dress, 1939-75..**258.50**
Peggy, HN 2038, red & white, 1949-79..**93.50**
Phillippa of Hainault, HN 2008, 1948-53..**750.00**
Pied Piper NH 2102, black, red & yellow, 1953-76..............................**250.00**
Polka (The), HN 2156, pink, 1955-69..**213.00**
Queen of the Ice, HN 2435, cream, 1963-86..**195.00**
R.C.M.P., 1873, HN 2555, red, limited edition, 1973 ....**800.00**
R.C.M.P., 1973, HN 2547, red, limited edition, 1973 ....**800.00**
Reverie, HN 2306, peach, 1964-81 ...**225.00**
Robin, M 38, pink & lavender, 1933-45...**800.00**

Roseanna

Roseanna, HN 1926, red dress, 1940-59 (ILLUS.) **287.00**
Royal Governor's Cook, HN 2233, dark blue, white & brown, 1960-84 ..**485.00**
Ruby, HN 1724, red dress, 1935-49..**622.50**
Ruby, HN 1725, blue dress, 1935-49..**672.50**
St. George, No. 2051, green & white, 1950-85..**464.00**
Sally, HN 2741, red & lavender, 1987-91..**132.00**
Sandra, HN 2401, green, 1983-92.....**155.00**

Silversmith of Williamsburg, HN 2208, blue, white & brown, 1960-83.................................**185.00**

Skater (The), HN 2117, white & brown, 1953-71...............................**295.00**

Sleepyhead, HN 2114, orange, blue & white, 1953-55........................**1,500.00**

Soiree, HN 2312, green & cream, 1967-84..**129.00**

Sophistication, HN 3059, pale blue & white, 1987-90.................................**90.00**

Spring Flower, HN 1807, green & blue, 1937-59.....................................**300.00**

Springtime, HN 3033, yellow, cream & green, 1983................................**250.00**

Stephanie, HN 2807, gold, 1977-82...**150.00**

Stitch in Time (A), HN 2352, purple, brown, turquoise, 1966-81...............**150.00**

Summer's Day, HN 2181, white, 1957-62...**256.00**

Suzette, HN 2026, flowered pink dress, 1949-59..................................**295.00**

Sweet & Twenty, HN 1649, green & cream dress, brown sofa, 1934-49...**995.00**

Sweet Anne, M 5, lavender & green, 1932-45...**340.00**

Sweet Anne

Sweet Anne, HN 1496, lavender & rose jacket, cream & lavender skirt, lavender bonnet, 1932-67 (ILLUS.)..**235.00**

Sweeting, HN 1935, pink, 1940-73....**120.00**

Thanksgiving, HN 2446, blue, pink & grey, matte finish, 1972-76..............**225.00**

Top O' the Hill, HN 1833, green & blue, 1937-71.....................................**180.00**

Veronica, HN 1517, red & white dress, 1932-51 (ILLUS. top next column)...**239.00**

Victorian Lady (A), HN 728, pink & purple, 1925-52.................................**325.00**

Votes For Women, HN 2816, gold & grey, 1978-81.....................................**225.00**

Winsome, HN 2220, red, 1960-85.....**145.00**

Winter, HN 2088, lavender, green & red, 1952-59.....................................**350.00**

Veronica

MISCELLANEOUS

Large Royal Doulton Fruit Bowl

Ashtray, figural bust, Dick Turpin........**98.00**

Ashtray, figural bust, Old Charley........**60.00**

Bowl, 3½ x 7", pedestal base, Gallant Fishers series, Jedo border, artist-signed..**185.00**

Bowl, 7"d., Monks series.....................**90.00**

Bowl, small, Sir Roger de Coverly series...**45.00**

Calling card holder, two-handled, Babes in Woods series, 5" d., 3" h...**150.00**

Centerpiece, "tapestry," relief-molded large gold & silver flowers, Doulton - Burslem mark, 9¼" h......................**295.00**

Cigarette lighter, table model, Rip Van Winkle, 1958............................**480.00**

Creamer, & cov. sugar bowl, Bayeux Tapertry series, creamer 3" h., sugar bowl 4½" h., pr..............**150.00**

Cup & saucer, Anne Page..................**60.00**

Cup & saucer, The Gleaners..............**95.00**

Cuspidor, green & gold decoration on cream ground, 7" d. **235.00**

Decanter, "Old Crow Bourbon," crow wears top hat & tuxedo, limited edition 1954-55, 14" h......................**175.00**

Dish, Art Deco style bird among foliage & hearts, cobalt trim, green mottled background, 13" d. **145.00**

Fruit bowl, body flaring to wide rim, sitting on a flared foot, loop handles, decorated inside & out w/large blue flowers on white ground w/green edging, marked, 9½" d., 5¼" h. (ILLUS.) **110.00**

Lamp, kerosene, table model, stoneware, inverted saucer base bolted through metal stem to font, design in yellow, blue & aqua w/milk glass umbrella shade (new?), Lambeth, 12¼" to top of shade **600.00**

Loving cup, handled, Bayeux Tapertry series, 6" h......................**250.00**

Mug, Robin Hood series (Under the Greenwood Tree), scene of Robin Hood, 4¾" h. **210.00**

Pitcher, 4" h., Coaching Days series ...**55.00**

Pitcher, 4¾" h., Jock of The Bushveld **220.00**

Pitcher, 5" h., Coaching Days series ...**65.00**

Pitcher, 6" h., Pipes of Pan.................**215.00**

Pitcher, 6" h., Shakespeare Characters series, "Juliet" **215.00**

Pitcher, 7⅞" h., "Figaro," Doulton - Burslem mark....................................**75.00**

Pitcher, 9" h., Kingsware, 16th century pilgrim golfers scene, ca. 1925 ..**645.00**

Pitcher, 10½" h., decorated w/cobalt blue irises front & back, w/gold flowers scrolling & outlining on white ground, Doulton - Burslem mark **415.00**

Plaque, pierced to hang, Old English Inns series, 13½" d. **100.00**

Plate, 8" d., Coaching Days series......**38.00**

Plate, 8½" d., Geneva patt., blue **88.00**

Royal Doulton Fish Plate

Plate, 9" d., center design of two h.p. "grayling" fish in grey, white & pink w/gold flowers & feathery designs around rim & gold border, artist-signed (ILLUS.)...............................**165.00**

Plate, 9½" d., Gleaners, Old English Scenes series **125.00**

Plate, 10" d., flow blue, floral underglaze, orange tracery over-glaze, Doulton - Burslem **70.00**

Plate, 10" d., rack-type, "The Mayor" ...**65.00**

Plate, 10" d., rack-type, "Roger Salem El Cobler"...**125.00**

Plate, 10¼" d., English Setter, full-body dog **150.00**

Plate, 10¼" d., Pointers, two full-body dogs **150.00**

Plates, 10¼" d., African series, Lion & Lioness, pr. **175.00**

Plate, 10½" d., Bayeux Tapestry series, "Landing at Pevensey" **60.00**

"Willow Pattern Story" Plate

Plate, 10½" d., The Willow Pattern Story series, center scene of man gardening & lady in robes sitting & watching, willow birds in sky, pink border w/rose flowers, verse from Willow story printed on back of plate, dated December 1916 (ILLUS.) **135.00**

Plate, 13½" d., African series, Elephant...**150.00**

Teapot, cov., Bayeux Tapestry series, 5½" h. **225.00**

Tobacco jar w/wooden lid, Issac Walton, Gallant Fishers series, 4¼" h...**150.00**

Tray, decorated w/cottage scene, flambé glaze, 9¼" l. **225.00**

Tray, Robin Hood series "Under the Greenwood Tree," small **30.00**

Umbrella stand, wide cylindrical form, a very wide white band w/oversized dark blue flowers above narrow blue bands around the bottom, marked, 24" h......................**495.00**

Vase, 4" h., flow blue, Babes in the Woods series **525.00**

Vase, 4" h., flower & bird decoration, green & brown, high gloss finish, incised "1881," Doulton - Lambeth marks...**65.00**

Vase, 5" h., 5" d., Bayeux Tapestry series **150.00**

Vase, 5½" h., 2½" d., stoneware, slender waisted cylindrical body w/flared rim, incised scene of twin

Doulton "Twins" Pottery Vase

boys in orange, blue & black, titled
"The Twins" on the reverse, tan
ground w/brown trim (ILLUS.) **175.00**
Vase, 6" h., bulbous body tapering to
a tall, narrow neck, Flambé glaze **200.00**
Vase, 6¾" h., 5" d., globular base &
short wide neck, decorated w/a
band of stylized grapes in purple &
& lavender on a periwinkle ground,
glossy glaze, impressed "ROYAL
DOULTON - ENGLAND - 8683 - AT
- MB" **302.50**

(End of Doulton Section)

DRESDEN

Dresden Oval Bowl

*Dresden-type porcelain evolved from
wares made at the nearby Meissen
Porcelain Works early in the 18th century.
"Dresden" and "Meissen" are often used
interchangeably for later wares. "Dresden"*

*has become a generic name for the kind of
porcelains produced in Dresden and
certain other areas of Germany but
perhaps should be confined to the wares
made in the city of Dresden.*

Bonbon, handled, divided, decorated
w/multicolored flowers on white
ground, ca. 1886, 6½" d. **$85.00**
Bowl, 7¼ x 9¼" oval, w/openwork
edge, decorated w/multicolored
flowers in center & interior, lavish
gold trim, marked "Schumann
Dresden" (ILLUS.) **75.00**
Box, cov., decorated w/raised blue
forget-me-nots & roses, bronze
doré decorative base, 3 x 6" **225.00**
Box, cov., decorated w/h.p. flowers
on white ground, ca. 1886, 3¾" d.
(some wear on gold) **45.00**
Clock, mantel-type, figural, the dial
within a floral encrusted case
flanked by Father Time, putti & a
nursing mother, surmounted by an
allegorical figure, ending in scrolled
feet, raised on a shaped bracket
base on scrolled feet, third quarter
19th c., 32" h. **16,100.00**

Dresden Compote

Compote, open, 5⅝" h., 6¼" w.,
w/openwork edge & foot, bulbous
squared bowl w/slightly tapering rim,
decorated w/multicolored flowers,
green leaves & lavish gold trim,
interior & exterior, marked
"Schumann Dresden" (ILLUS.) **195.00**
Demitasse cups & saucers,
polychrome enamel floral decoration
w/gilt trim, late 19th c., in fitted case,
saucer 4¼" d., 6 sets **546.00**
Figure of a ballerina wearing an
ornate tiered lacy dress, shown
standing w/one leg forward & one

hand holding her skirt as she bows, her other arm extended back, raised on an oval plinth base, ca. 1900, 8 x 11" (tiny piece of lace missing in back) **425.00**

Figure of a lady w/lacy skirt, late 19th c., 7" h. (some lace loss)..........**175.00**

Figure group, three small girls playing Ring Around the Rosie, trimmed w/lace.................................**250.00**

Juice reamer, h.p. decoration, artist-signed, ca. 1890 ....**350.00**

Lamp base, enamel-decorated florals framed w/applied fruits & flowers, Thieme factory marks, late 19th c., 28¼" h...**201.00**

Mint basket, applied rose & blue forget-me-nots, h.p. floral interior decoration, ca. 1920, 2½" h. **250.00**

Plate, 10½" d., round w/heavy gold rim band, the center w/a portrait titled "Konigin Louise," artist-signed **1,295.00**

Plate, 12¾" d., h.p. pastel scene of two deer by stream, artist-signed **55.00**

Serving dish, scalloped, decorated w/h.p. flowers interior & exterior, gold accents, ca. 1881, 5 x 13"..........**95.00**

Vase on stand, 11" h., flaring cylindrical form, the sides painted w/flowers & gilt decoration, late 19th c. **460.00**

Dresden Figural Vase

Vase, cover & stand, 34" h., bulbous baluster-shaped body w/figural cherub handles on shoulder, decorated w/colorful Bacchanalian scene, sitting on pedestal decorated w/applied flowers resting on scrolled base decorated w/like scene, topped w/bulbous cover w/applied flowers, crown & cherubs, late 19th c., damage (ILLUS.) **1,265.00**

FIESTA

Fiesta dinnerware was made by the Homer Laughlin China Company of Newell, West Virginia, from the 1930s until the early 1970s. The brilliant colors of this inexpensive pottery have attracted numerous collectors. On February 28, 1986, Laughlin reintroduced the popular Fiesta line with minor changes in the shapes of a few pieces and a contemporary color range. The effect of this new production on the Fiesta collecting market is yet to be determined.

Ashtray

grey	$72.00
ivory	40.00
light green	42.00
medium green	179.00
rose	63.00

Bowl, individual fruit, 4¾" d.

chartreuse	23.00
light green	20.00
medium green	442.00
red	23.00
turquoise	19.00

Bowl, individual fruit, 5½" d.

cobalt blue	25.00
grey	27.00
ivory	22.00
rose	27.00

Bowl, dessert, 6" d.

light green	27.00
medium green	225.00
turquoise	27.00
yellow	27.00

Bowl, individual salad, 7½" d.

medium green	104.00
red	52.00

Bowl, nappy, 8½" d.

chartreuse	41.00
ivory	29.00
rose	43.00
turquoise	29.50

Bowl, nappy, 9½" d.

forest green	40.00
red	61.00
turquoise	51.50

Bowl, salad, 9½" d.

cobalt blue	50.00
light green	31.50
yellow	28.00

Bowl, fruit, 11¾" d.

light green	175.00
yellow	135.00

Bowl, cream soup

chartreuse	55.00

ivory...41.00
light green...................................35.00
turquoise.....................................34.00
Bowl, salad, large, footed
cobalt blue 260.00
light green..................................253.50
turquoise....................................260.00
Cake plate, 10" d.
cobalt blue 525.00
yellow 491.00
Candleholders, bulb-type, pr.
cobalt blue 96.00
ivory...81.00
turquoise.....................................76.00
yellow 56.00
Candleholders, tripod-type, pr.
red 417.50
turquoise....................................313.00
Carafe, cov.
ivory..190.00
light green..................................172.00
Casserole, cov., two-handled, 10" d.
cobalt blue 182.00
grey 244.00
ivory..141.00
rose 236.00
yellow 117.00
Coffeepot, cov., demitasse, stick handle
turquoise....................................335.00
yellow 265.00
Coffeepot, cov.
chartreuse 358.00
light green..................................130.50
red 200.00
rose 350.00

Fiesta Coffeepot

turquoise (ILLUS.) 128.00
Compote, 12" d., low, footed
ivory..122.50
light green..................................100.00
yellow 107.50
Compote, sweetmeat, high stand
cobalt blue 55.00
ivory...43.00
turquoise.....................................63.00
Creamer, individual size
cobalt blue 18.00
ivory...12.00

light green....................................40.00
yellow 52.00
Creamer, stick handle
cobalt blue 38.00
light green....................................29.00
medium green 20.00
red 36.00
Creamer
chartreuse 22.00
medium green 59.00
red 21.00
yellow 17.50
Creamer & cov. sugar bowl,
individual size, yellow on
cobalt blue tray, 3 pcs. 180.00
Cup & saucer, demitasse, stick handle
chartreuse 272.00
forest green 234.00
red 60.00
rose 330.00
Cup & saucer, ring handle
cobalt blue 29.00
grey 32.00
ivory...24.00
light green....................................23.00
turquoise.....................................25.00
Egg cup
chartreuse 128.00
forest green 117.00
red 57.50
turquoise.....................................53.00
Fork (Kitchen Kraft)
cobalt blue 116.00
yellow (ILLUS. w/bowl) 117.00
Gravy boat
light green....................................29.00
rose 49.00
yellow 29.00
Lid for mixing bowl, size No. 1
red 678.00
Marmalade jar, cov.
light green..................................173.00
yellow 175.00
Mixing bowl, nest-type, size No. 1, 5" d.
light green..................................173.00
red 128.00
Mixing bowl, nest-type, size No. 2, 6" d.
light green....................................67.50
turquoise.....................................61.00
Mixing bowl, nest-type, size No. 3, 7" d.
ivory...48.00
yellow 73.00
Mixing bowl, nest-type, size No. 4, 8" d.
red 82.00
yellow (ILLUS. top next column) ..83.00
Mixing bowl, nest-type, size No. 5, 9" d.
cobalt blue 78.00
turquoise.....................................50.00
Mixing bowl, nest-type, size No. 6, 10" d.
light green..................................103.00
turquoise....................................108.00
Mixing bowl, nest-type, size No. 7, 11½" d.
ivory..234.00
yellow 122.00

Bowl with Spoon & Fork

Mug
forest green	56.00
red	66.00
rose	54.00

Mug, Tom & Jerry style
chartreuse	56.50
cobalt blue	52.50
medium green	71.00
rose	59.00

Mustard jar, cov.
ivory	153.00
red	169.00
turquoise	143.50

Onion soup bowl, cov.
medium green	475.00
yellow	247.50

Pie server (Kitchen Kraft)
cobalt blue	104.50
yellow	57.50

Fiesta Jug Pitcher

Pitcher, jug-type, 2 pt.
cobalt blue	67.50
forest green (ILLUS.)	76.50
light green	57.00
rose	97.00

Pitcher, juice, disc-type, 30 oz.
cobalt blue	92.50
rose	85.00
turquoise	80.00

Pitcher, water, disc-type
chartreuse	216.00
forest green	185.00
light green	112.50
turquoise	79.00

Pitcher, w/ice lip, globular, 2 qt.
cobalt blue	137.00

red	131.00
turquoise	97.00

Plate, 6" d.
forest green	7.00
ivory	4.00
turquoise	3.00

Plate, 7" d.
cobalt blue	7.00
grey	9.00
turquoise	6.00
yellow	6.50

Plate, 9" d.
cobalt blue	14.00
grey	16.00
red	13.00

Plate, 10" d.
cobalt blue	26.00
forest green	28.00
red	26.00
rose	25.50
turquoise	20.00

Plate, grill, 10½" d.
chartreuse	52.00
forest green	43.00
grey	33.00
ivory	27.50
yellow	24.00

Plate, grill, 11½" d.
ivory	42.50
red	44.00
yellow	52.00

Plate, chop, 13" d.
cobalt blue	32.00
forest green	56.00
light green	22.00
medium green	209.00
rose	58.50

Plate, chop, 15" d.
cobalt blue	43.00
grey	125.00
rose	89.00
turquoise	37.00

Platter, 12" oval
forest green	30.50
ivory	22.00
medium green	100.00
rose	37.50
turquoise	23.00

Relish tray w/five inserts
cobalt blue	216.00
light green	113.00
red	212.00

Salt & pepper shakers, pr.
chartreuse	35.00
cobalt blue	15.50
ivory	16.00
red	40.00
rose	29.00

Soup plate w/flanged rim, 8" d.
chartreuse	40.00
grey	43.00
ivory	33.00
rose	42.00
turquoise	27.00

Spoon (Kitchen Kraft)
  cobalt blue (ILLUS. w/bowl)..........**90.00**
Sugar bowl, cov.
  ivory...**28.00**
  medium green **107.00**
  turquoise...................................**25.50**
Syrup pitcher w/original lid
  ivory.......................................**208.00**
  yellow.....................................**176.00**
Teapot, cov., medium size (6 cup)
  cobalt blue **119.00**
  forest green **267.00**
  grey **220.50**
  medium green **378.00**
  yellow **140.00**
Teapot, cov., large size (8 cup)
  cobalt blue **150.00**
  ivory..**116.50**
  light green................................**128.00**
  medium green **585.00**
Tray, Figure 8
  cobalt blue **38.00**
Tumbler, juice, 5 oz.
  ivory..**30.00**
  red **36.00**
  rose **44.50**
Tumbler, water, 10 oz.
  grey **100.00**
  red **52.00**
Utility tray
  cobalt blue **29.00**
Vase, bud, 6½" h.
  cobalt blue **70.00**
  red **65.00**
  turquoise....................................**38.00**
Vase, 8" h.
  red **412.00**
Vase, 10" h.
  ivory..**559.00**
  turquoise..................................**331.00**
  yellow **391.00**
Vase, 12" h.
  ivory..**521.00**
  light green................................**328.00**
  turquoise..................................**567.50**
  yellow **425.00**

FLOW BLUE

Flowing Bue wares, usually shortened to Flow Blue, were made at numerous potteries in Staffordshire, England and elsewhere. They are decorated with a blue that smudged lightly or ran in the firing. The same type of color flow is also found in certain wares decorated with green, purple and sepia. Patterns were given specific names, which accompany the listings here.

ABBEY (George Jones & Sons, ca. 1900)

Coffeepot, cov., 6¼" h....................**$175.00**
Cup & saucer, handleless **85.00**
Relish dish, 5¾ x 11¼" **95.00**
Teapot, cov. **280.00**

ABBEY (Petrus Regout, date unknown)
Bowl **139.00**
Creamer **90.00**
Cup & saucer **38.00**
Plate, grill, 11¼" d. **75.00**

AMOY (Davenport, dated 1844)

Amoy Plate

Cup plate **97.50**
Honey dish **65.00**
Plate, 7" d. **90.00**
Plate, 9" d. (ILLUS.) **120.00**
Plate, 10¼" d. **165.00**
Platter, 16" l. **547.50**
Relish dish, Cameo, large
  (professional restoration) **225.00**
Sauce dish **85.00**
Sugar bowl, cov. **550.00**
Teapot, full panel Gothic, 10" h. **945.00**
Vegetable bowl, open, 9½" d.
  (hairline)......................................**295.00**
Waste bowl, large (edge flakes) **350.00**

ARABESQUE (T.J. and J. Mayer, ca. 1845)
Cup plate **75.00**
Platter, 20¼" l. **1,100.00**
Sugar bowl, cov................................**500.00**

ARGYLE (W.H. Grindley, ca. 1896)

Argyle Platter

Bowl, berry....................................**40.00**
Butter pat......................................**35.00**
Gravy boat **100.00**

Plate, 7" d...35.00
Plate, dinner......................................110.00
Platter, 12 x 17" (ILLUS.)..................250.00
Soup plate w/flanged rim....................65.00

ASHBURTON (W.H. Grindley, ca. 1891)
Bowl, dessert, 5¾" d...........................38.00
Creamer...75.00
Plate, 8" d..45.00
Plate, 9" d..45.00
Plate, 10" d...55.00
Sauce ladle..190.00
Soup tureen, cov. (finial repaired).....325.00
Sugar bowl, cov..................................150.00

BENTICK (Cauldon, ca. 1905)

Bentick Plate

Plate, 6" d..40.00
Plate, 10" d. (ILLUS.)...........................70.00
Turkey platter, 23¾" l.........................950.00

CANDIA (Cauldon Ltd., ca. 1910)
Butter pat...45.00
Gravy boat..165.00
Plate, 6" d..50.00
Plate, 8½" d..75.00
Plate, 10" d...100.00
Platter, small......................................200.00
Platter, large.......................................265.00
Sauce dish..60.00
Soup plate w/flanged rim....................100.00
Vegetable bowl, cov...........................375.00
Vegetable bowl, open.........................125.00

CASHMERE (Ridgway & Morley, G.L. Ashworth, et al., 1840s on)
Bowl, soup, 7" d..................................175.00
Plate, 6" d...150.00
Plate, 9¼" d., back chip (ILLUS. top next column)..............................115.00
Platter, 17½" l...................................1,295.00

CHAPOO (John Wedge Wood, ca. 1850)
Creamer..700.00
Plate, 10½" d.......................................165.00
Sugar bowl, cov..................................595.00
Teapot, cov. (minor professional restoration)......................................895.00

Cashmere Plate

CHATSWORTH (Keeling & Co., ca. 1886)
Plate, 7½" d..40.00
Plate, 9½" d..60.00
Plate, 10" d...80.00
Platter, 11½" l.....................................125.00
Platter, 16" l.......................................195.00
Platter, 18" l.......................................225.00
Sauce tureen, cov., ladle & undertray, 3 pcs. 425.00
Vegetable bowl, cov...........................295.00

CHINESE (Thomas Dimmock, ca. 1845)
Cup & saucer..80.00
Plate..64.00
Sugar bowl, cov..................................375.00
Teapot, cov. 695.00

CLAYTON (Johnson Bros., ca. 1902)

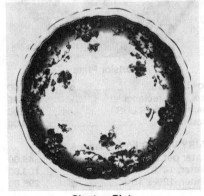

Clayton Plate

Pitcher..200.00
Plate, 6¼" d. (ILLUS.)...........................48.00
Vegetable bowl, open, 7¼ x 9½"........75.00

COBURG (John Edwards, ca. 1860)
Gravy boat..325.00
Plate, 10" d...110.00

CONWAY (New Wharf Pottery, ca. 1891)
Bowl, 9" d...120.00

Plate, 9" d...75.00
Plate, 10" d...90.00
Platter, 8 x 10½"...............................107.00
Soup plate w/flanged rim, 9" d............72.50
Vegetable bowl, open, 9" d. 107.50

DEVON (Alfred Meakin, ca. 1907)
Butter dish, cov. 325.00
Gravy boat...90.00
Sauce ladle...79.00

DUCHESS (W.H. Grindley, ca. 1891)
Bone dish 30.00
Plate, 8" d..35.00
Plate, 10" d..40.00
Platter, 12" l. 135.00
Platter, 15" l. 165.00
Soup plate w/flanged rim....................35.00

DUDLEY (Ford & Sons, ca. 1890)
Platter, 8 x 11"....................................185.00
Platter, 11 x 15"..................................195.00
Platter, 12¼ x 16½"............................195.00

EXCELSIOR (Thomas Fell, ca. 1850)

Excelsior Plate

Bowl, soup 125.00
Box, cov., rectangular 300.00
Plate, 9½" d. (ILLUS.) 35.00
Platter, 11" l. 250.00

FAIRY VILLAS I (W. Adams & Sons)
Butter pat..45.00
Platter, 10" l. 100.00
Platter, 12¾ x 15½" 295.00

FLORAL (Thomas Hughes & Sons, ca. 1895)
Cake stand 450.00
Cheese dish, cov................................435.00
Syrup pitcher w/pewter lid, 6" h. 350.00
Tea tile, 7" d..150.00

FORMOSA (Thos., John & Joseph Mayer, ca. 1850)
Plate, 8⅝" d...75.00
Potato bowl, 12" d. 995.00

Vegetable bowl, 11" d. 465.00

HONG KONG William Ridgway, Son & Co., ca. 1842)
Chamber pot, cov. (chip).................600.00
Sugar bowl, cov...................................750.00
Vegetable bowl, cov..........................850.00
Waste bowl...450.00

INDIAN (possibly F. & R. Pratt, ca. 1840)
Creamer 395.00
Teapot, cov. 195.00
Waste bowl...300.00

IRIS (Arthur Wilkinson - Royal Staffordshire Potteries, ca. 1907)
Pitchers, decorated w/large ivy
  sprays front & back, scrolled handle,
  gold trim, 7" d., 7½"d., 8" d., set of
  3 (barely visible small hairlines on
  rim of 7" pitcher)............................475.00
Plate, 6" d..25.00
Plate, 9" d..75.00
Plate, 10" d..60.00
Sugar bowl, cov...................................195.00

KYBER (John Meir & Son, ca. 1870; Adams & Co., ca. 1891)

Kyber Plate

Creamer 119.50
Honey dish 65.00
Pitcher, 7" h., 1 qt. 475.00
Plate, 8" d. (ILLUS.) 75.00
Plate, 9" d..73.00
Wash pitcher & bowl, 2 pcs. (tiny
  nick on under edge of bowl)..........1,650.00

LA BELLE (W.H. Grindley, ca. 1893)
Bowl, fruit, fluted. 225.00
Butter pat..45.00
Charger, 14" d. 220.00
Cup & saucer (slight crazing) 75.00
Jardiniere, 6 x 7½" 495.00
Pitcher, 8¼" h., 2 qt. (hairline inside
  rim)..550.00
Plate, chop, 11" d. (ILLUS. top next
  page)..175.00

La Belle Chop Plate

LORNE (W.H. Grindley, ca. 1900)
Gravy boat...102.50
Plate, 10" d...65.00
Platter, 12¼" l. ....125.00 to 145.00
Platter, 14" l. 235.00

MADRAS (Doulton & Co., ca. 1900)
Bowl, cereal, 6" d. 32.50
Pitcher, milk 450.00
Plate, 7½" d..55.00
Platter, 14 x 18" 350.00
Platter, 15½" l. 250.00
Vegetable bowl, cov., oval 200.00

MANILLA (Podmore, Walker & Co., ca. 1845)
Creamer..500.00
Gravy boat...345.00
Plate, 9¾" d..92.50
Platter, 12¼ x 15¾"...........595.00 to 695.00
Platter, 13¾ x 17⅝" 795.00
Platter, 17¾" l. 695.00
Teapot, cov. 1,150.00
Vegetable bowl, open, 6¾" x 9.......375.00

MELROSE (Doulton, ca. 1891)
Plate...70.00
Vegetable bowl, cov., 10¾" l. oval 65.00
Vegetable bowl, cov., 11" d..............195.00
Vegetable bowl, cov., handled,
   11" d...225.00

MORNING GLORY (Thos. Hughes & Sons, ca. 1895)
Platter, 10¼ x 15" 250.00
Soup plate w/flanged rim, 9" d.............55.00
Sugar bowl, cov..................................395.00

NANKIN (F. & R. PRATT, ca. 1840)
Cup & saucer, handled......................100.00
Cup & saucer, handled, large............110.00
Plate, 9¼" d...75.00

NON PAREIL (Burgess & Leigh, ca. 1891)
Bowl, 5" d., 3" h. 55.00
Bowl, 6" d., flared rim...........................40.00
Bowl, oval, small 60.00
Butter dish, cov. 237.50

Butter pat...40.00
Cake plate, 10" d. 275.00
Charger, 11½" d.................................395.00
Gravy boat, double spout 325.00
Ladle holder 195.00
Plate, 8½" d...50.00
Platter, 13" l.......................................275.00
Soup plate w/flanged rim, 8¾" d. 80.00
Soup tureen, cov. 750.00
Teapot, cov., (professional finial
   repair) 750.00
Vegetable bowl, cov., 8" d...............365.00

RENOWN (Arthur Wilkinson, ca. 1907)
Plate...89.00
Platter, 15" l. 195.00
Sauce ladle...195.00

ROSEVILLE (John Maddock & Sons, ca. 1891)
Butter pat...35.00
Compote 150.00
Platter, 12 x 17¼" 225.00

SCINDE (J. & G. Alcock, ca. 1840 and Thomas Walker, ca. 1847)

Scinde Plate

Bowl, 3¾" d., 2¾" h...............................95.00
Cup & saucer (round, non-paneled)..195.00
Cup, handleless 120.00
Cup plate 195.00
Gravy boat..415.00
Honey dish 65.00
Pitcher, 8" h..55.00
Plate, 7¼" d..120.00
Plate, 8½" d..135.00
Plate, 9¼" d. (ILLUS.) 110.00
Plate, 10½" d......................................217.50
Platter, 11" l. 385.00
Platter, 10 x 13½" (one chip) 225.00
Platter, 15½" l. 548.00
Platter, 16" l. 800.00
Platter, 16⅛" l., scalloped edge 572.00
Platter, 17¾" l. 900.00
Relish dish, mitten-shaped,
   professional repair (ILLUS. top
   next page)..185.00

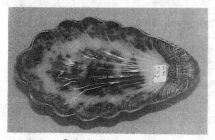

Scinde Relish tray

Soup plate w/flanged rim..................**100.00**
Sugar bowl, cov. ....**450.00 to 495.00**
Tea set: cov. teapot, creamer &
cov. sugar bowl; 3 pcs. **2,285.00**
Toothbrush holder, cov. (pro-
fessional restoration) **750.00**
Vegetable bowl, open, scalloped,
9½" d...**595.00**
Vegetable bowl, open, 8½ x 11¼"
oval **1,075.00**
Waste bowls, pr...............................**300.00**

SHANGHAE (J. Furnival, ca. 1860)
Plate, 7" d..**75.00**
Plate, 9" d..**95.00**
Wash bowl.......................................**795.00**

SOBRAON (probably English, ca. 1850)
Sauce Tureen, cov. **637.50**
Sugar bowl, cov...............................**450. 00**
Vegetable bowl, cov., 10 x 13"..........**545.00**

TEMPLE (Podomore Walker, ca. 1850)
Creamer...**250.00**
Cup & saucer **150.00**
Egg basket **250.00**
Plate, 7" d..**85.00**
Plate, 10" d......................................**120.00**

TONQUIN (W. Adams & Son., ca. 1845)
Plate, 7½" d..**75.00**
Sugar bowl, open **100.00**
Syrup, cover & undertray..................**350.00**

**TOURAINE (Henry Alcock, ca. 1898 and
Stanley Pottery, ca. 1898)**

Touraine Plate

Butter pat...**45.00**
Creamer **279.00**
Cup & saucer **92.50**
Gravy boat.......................................**166.00**
Pitcher, 6½ x 7½" **350.00**
Plate, 7¾" d..**43.00**
Plate, 8" d..**95.00**
Plate, 8½" d..**65.00**
Plate, 8¾" d..**60.00**
Plate, 10" d. (ILLUS.) **95.00**
Platter, 13" l......................................**170.00**
Platter, 10½ x 15" **235.00**
Platter, 15" l. oval.............................**211.00**
Sauce dish..**40.00**
Sugar bowl, cov...............................**325.00**
Vegetable bowl, cov.........................**370.00**
Vegetable bowl, open, 9¾" oval........**125.00**
Waste bowl......................................**125.00**

VERMONT (Burgess & Leigh, ca. 1895)
Bone dish **65.00**
Jardiniere, small.................................**40.00**
Plate, dinner **75.00**
Platter, 10 x 14" **195.00**
Soup plate w/flanged rim...................**60.00**
Tea set: cov. teapot, creamer & cov.
sugar bowl; 3 pcs. **950.00**
Vegetable bowl, cov.........................**275.00**

WALDORF (New Wharf Pottery, ca. 1892)

Waldorf Plate

Bowl, 9" d...**90.00**
Egg platter, 8 x 10¾" (tiny back
flake) **65.00**
Plate, 9" d..**69.00**
Plate, 9¾" d..**70.00**
Plate, dinner, 10" d. (ILLUS.) **78.00**
Soup plate w/flanged rim....................**49.00**

WATTEAU (Doulton & Co., ca. 1900)
Bowl, soup, 8¼" d. **85.00**
Cup & saucer **85.00**
Pitcher, 7½" h **30.00**
Plate, 5½" d..**30.00**
Plate, 6½" d..**38.00**
Platter, 15½" l. **275.00**

Soup plate w/flanged rim, 9¾" d.........**69.00**
Soup plate w/flanged rim, 10¼" d........**95.00**
Soup tureen, cover & undertray,
    3 pcs. **650.00**
Vegetable bowl, open, 10" d. **100.00**

WAVERLY (W.H. Grindley, ca. 1891)
Plate, 8" d....................................**52.00**
Platter, 17" l. (tiny back flakes) **340.00**
Soup plate w/flanged rim....................**55.00**
Vegetable bowl, cov., oval **250.00**

(End of Flow Blue Section)

FRANCISCAN WARE

Apple Pattern Plate & Cup

*A product of Gladding, McBean &
Company of Glendale and Los Angeles,
California, Franciscan Ware was one of a
number of lines produced by that firm over
its long history. Introduced in 1934 as a
pottery dinnerware, Franciscan Ware was
produced in many patterns including
"Desert Rose," introduced in 1941 and
reportedly the most popular dinnerware
pattern ever made in this country.
Beginning in 1942 some vitrified china
patterns were produced under the
Franciscan name also.*

*After a merger in 1963 the company
name was changed to Interpace
Corporation and in 1979 Josiah
Wedgwood & Sons purchased the
Gladding, McBean & Co. plant from
Interpace. American production ceased in
1984.*

Ashtray, Desert Rose patt., 4¾" sq. ...**$75.00**
Ashtray, Desert Rose patt., 4¾ x 9"
    oval **58.00**
Ashtray, individual, leaf-shaped, Ivy
    patt., light green, 4½" w., 4½" l. **30.00**
Ashtray, individual, apple-shaped,
    Apple patt., 4 x 4½"......................**18.00**
Baking dish, Desert Rose patt., 1 qt.,
    8¾" w., 9½" l., 2" h......................**200.00**
Baking dish, Desert Rose patt.,
    1½ qt., 9" w., 14" l., 2½" h...............**250.00**
Baking dish, Forget-Me-Not patt.,
    1½ qt., 14" l., 9" w., 2¼" h...............**125.00**
Baking dish, Meadow Rose patt.,
    1½ qt., 9 x 14" l., 2¼" h..................**225.00**
Bank, model of a pig, Cafe Royal
    patt..**160.00**
Bank, model of a pig, Desert Rose
    patt..**325.00**
Bell, Desert Rose patt., ca. 1941 ....**92.00**
Bowl, fruit, 4½" d., California Poppy
    patt..**15.00**
Bowl, individual fruit, 5" d., Desert
    Rose patt., ca. 1941.......................**6.00**
Bowl, 5½" d., Apple patt., ca. 1940........**6.00**
Bowl, chili, 5½" d., Desert Rose patt.,
    ca. 1941 ....**12.00**
Bowl, cereal, 6" d., Ivy patt., ca.
    1948...**25.00**
Bowl, cereal, 6" d., Meadow Rose
    patt..**12.00**
Bowl, cereal, 6" d., Strawberry Fair
    patt..**14.00**
Bowl, coupe soup, Magnolia patt.,
    1952...**22.00**
Bowl, cream soup, 6" d., Arcadia
    Gold patt., Masterpiece line, ca.
    1941...**20.00**
Bowl, cream soup, Mesa patt.,
    Masterpiece line, ca. 1950 ....**20.00**
Bowl, 7¼" d., Apple patt., ca. 1940......**26.00**
Bowl, salad, 10" d., 3¼" h., Apple
    patt..**91.00**
Bowl, salad, Coronado patt.,
    turquoise gloss.............................**40.00**
Bowl, salad, 11" d., Starburst patt......**100.00**
Bowl, salad, large, Ivy patt., ca.
    1948...**110.00**
Box, cov., heart-shaped, Cafe Royal
    patt., 5 x 5", 2¼" h........................**89.00**
Box, cov., heart-shaped, Desert Rose
    patt., 2½ x 4½".............................**172.00**
Box, cov., Cafe Royal patt., 4¾" d.,
    1¼" h..**85.00**
Butter dish, cov., Starburst patt.,
    ¼ lb., ca. 1954 ....**39.00**
Butter dish, cov., Wheat patt., ca.
    1953...**20.00**
Candleholders, Apple patt., pr. **40.00**
Casserole, cov., Apple patt., 8½" d. **78.00**
Casserole, cov., Desert Rose
    patt..**78.00**
Celery tray, Apple patt.......................**26.50**

Celery tray, Desert Rose patt.,
ca. 1941, 10½" l. **39.50**

Chocolate mug, Apple patt., 3" d.,
4¼" h., 10 oz.................................**95.00**

Cigarette box, cov., Apple patt......**167.00**

Cigarette box, cov., Desert Rose
patt., 3½ x 4½", 2" h.....................**110.00**

Coffeepot, cov., demitasse, Desert
Rose patt. **195.00**

Coffeepot, cov., Ivy patt., ca. 1948....**140.00**

Coffeepot, cov., Sunburst patt..........**103.00**

Coffee server, cov., Ivy
patt. ....**200.00 to 225.00**

Coffee set, demitasse: cov. coffeepot
& two demitasse cups & saucers,
Coronado patt., ivory satin, 5 pcs. **77.50**

Coffee set, demitasse: cov. coffeepot
& six demitasse cups & saucers,
Coronado patt., burgundy
glaze, 13 pcs................................**195.00**

Compote, open, Desert Rose patt.,
tall **78.00**

Compote, open, Apple patt., ca.
1940..**78.00**

Compote, open, Ivy patt., ca.
1948..**112.00**

Creamer, individual, Desert Rose
patt., 3½" h.....................................**35.00**

Creamer, Coronado patt.,
ca. 1936 ....**10.00**

Creamer, large, Desert Rose patt.,
4¼" h..**13.00**

Creamer, Fresh Fruit patt., 4¼" h. **19.00**

Creamer, Magnolia patt., ca. 1952......**42.00**

Creamer, Strawberry Fair patt.,
4¼" h..**32.00**

Creamer & cov. sugar bowl, Apple
patt., ca. 1940, pr............................**30.00**

Creamer & cov. sugar bowl, Desert
Rose patt., ca. 1941, pr. **52.50**

Creamer & cov. sugar bowl, Forget-
Me-Not patt., pr................................**54.00**

Creamer & cov. sugar bowl, Fresh
Fruit patt., pr. **51.50**

Creamer & cov. sugar bowl,
Starburst patt., pr.............................**38.00**

Cup & saucer, demitasse, Apple
patt...**51.00**

Cup & saucer, Apple patt., ca. 1940
(ILLUS. right) **20.00**

Cup & saucer, Apple patt., ca. 1940,
extra large **49.00**

Cup & saucer, Bountiful patt. **35.00**

Cup & saucer, California Poppy patt.,
ca. 1950 ....**26.00**

Cup & saucer, Daisy patt. **15.00**

Cup & saucer, Fresh Fruit patt. **16.00**

Cup & saucer, Ivy patt........................**15.00**

Cup & saucer, Mesa patt.,
Masterpiece line, ca. 1950................**15.00**

Cup & saucer, Moonglow patt.,
Masterpiece line, ca. 1966.................**12.00**

Cup & saucer, Regency patt.,
ca. 1953 ....**29.00**

Cup & saucer, Starburst patt................**6.50**

Cup & saucer, Strawberry Time patt. ...**35.00**

Cup & saucer, Twilight Rose patt.........**35.00**

Dinner service for eight, Apple patt.,
ca. 1940, 48 pcs. **450.00**

Dish, heart-shaped, Cafe Royal
patt...**45.00**

Dish, heart-shaped, Desert Rose
patt., 5¾" l., 5½" w. **122.50**

Goblet, Apple patt..............................**25.00**

Goblet, Desert Rose patt. **250.00**

Goblet, Meadow Rose patt., 6½" h.,
1977..**245.00**

Gravy boat w/attached undertray,
Apple patt..**29.00**

Gravy boat, Coronado patt., coral **12.00**

Gravy boat, Desert Rose patt..............**32.50**

Gravy boat, Ivy patt., ca. 1948 ....**28.00**

Gravy boat, Mesa patt., Masterpiece
line, ca. 1950 ....**35.00**

Gravy boat w/attached undertray,
Strawberry Fair patt., gravy boat
4" h., attached underplate, 8¼" d.......**75.00**

Gravy boat w/attached undertray &
ladle, Starburst patt., ca. 1954,
2 pcs. **40.00**

Marmalade jar, cov., Apple patt., ca.
1940..**95.00**

Mixing bowl set, Apple patt., 3 pcs....**319.00**

Mixing bowl set, Desert Rose patt.,
3 pcs. **337.50**

Mug, Apple patt., ca. 1940, 7 oz. **19.00**

Mug, Autumn patt., ca. 1954 ....**15.00**

Mug, Desert Rose patt., ca. 1941,
7 oz...**20.00**

Mug, coffee, Desert Rose patt.,
10 oz...**30.00**

Mug, Starburst patt., large, ca. 1954....**43.00**

Napkin ring, Apple patt.......................**50.00**

Napkin rings, Desert Rose patt., set
of four in original box **150.00**

Napkin rings, Forget-Me-Not patt.,
set of four in original box.................**165.00**

Napkin rings, October patt., set
of 4 ....**110.00**

Pickle dish, Desert Rose patt.,
11" l..**30.00**

Pie server, Apple patt **32.00**

Pitcher, milk, 6½" h., Apple patt., ca.
1940, 1 qt..**80.00**

Pitcher, milk, 6½" h., Desert Rose
patt., ca. 1941 ....**47.00**

Pitcher, water, 6¾" h., October patt.,
1¾ qt...**110.00**

Pitcher, 8¾" h., w/ice lip,
Apple patt., 92 oz...........................**120.00**

Pitcher, milk, Twilight Rose patt.,
1983..**135.00**

Pitcher, water, Apple patt.,
2 qt. ....**100.00 to 125.00**

Pitcher, water, Coronado patt.,
maroon gloss, ca. 1936 ....**35.00**

Pitcher, water, Meadow Rose patt.....**150.00**

Plate, 6" d., Apple patt., ca. 1940..........**8.00**

Plate, bread & butter, 6" d.,
Strawberry Time patt. **8.00**
Plate, 6¼" d., California Poppy patt. **15.00**
Plate, 6½" d., Coronado patt.,
green gloss glaze..............................**6.00**
Plate, 6½" d., Coronado patt.,
ivory satin glaze **6.00**
Plate, 6½" d., Coronado patt.,
rose gloss glaze **6.00**
Plate, 6½" d., Desert Rose patt.............**7.00**
Plate, bread & butter, 6½" d., Ivy
patt..**7.00**
Plate, 6⅜" d., Apple patt. (ILLUS.
left, with cup and saucer) **5.00**
Plate, bread & butter, Mesa patt.,
Masterpiece line, ca. 1950................**5.00**
Plate, bread & butter, Regency patt.,
ca. 1953 ....**12.00**
Plate, child's, divided, 7¼ x 9",
Apple patt...................................**110.00**
Plate, child's, divided, 7¼ x 9",
Autumn patt. **35.00**
Plate, child's, divided, 7¼ x 9",
Desert Rose patt. **125.00**
Plate, 7½" d., coupe dessert, Desert
Rose patt. **45.00**
Plate, side salad, 4½" w., 8" l.,
crescent-shaped, Apple patt. **35.00**
Plate, side salad, 4½" w., 8" l.,
crescent-shaped, Desert Rose
patt..**30.00**
Plate, side salad, 4½" w., 8" l.,
crescent-shaped, Ivy patt..................**42.50**
Plate, salad, 8" d., California Poppy
patt..**30.00**
Plate, 8" d., Coronado patt., green
gloss glaze...................................**10.00**
Plate, salad, 8½" d., Desert Rose
patt..**13.00**
Plate, salad, 8½" d., Ivy patt.................**10.00**
Plate, salad, 8½" d., Magnolia patt.,
ca. 1952 ....**18.00**
Plate, 9¼" d., Coronado patt., green
gloss glaze...................................**12.00**
Plate, luncheon, 9½" d., Fruit patt. **60.00**
Plate, luncheon, 9½" d., Starburst
patt..**30.00**
Plate, luncheon, 9½" d., Twilight Rose
patt., 1983.....................................**30.00**
Plate, 10" d., California Poppy patt.,
ca. 1950 ....**26.00**
Plate, dinner, 10" d., Bountiful patt.......**30.00**
Plate, dinner, 10" d., Daisy patt............**15.00**
Plate, dinner, 10" d., Fresh Fruit
patt..**17.00**
Plate, dinner, 10" d., Magnolia patt.,
1952...**24.00**
Plate, dinner, 10" d., Poppy patt. **29.50**
Plate, dinner, 10" d., Strawberry Time
patt..**30.00**
Plate, 10½" d., coupe, party w/cup
well, Desert Rose patt.......................**95.00**
Plate, dinner, 10½" d., Autumn patt. **6.00**

Plate, 10½" d., Coronado patt., coral
satin glaze.....................................**25.00**
Plate, dinner, 10½" d., Ivy patt. **20.00**
Plate, dinner, 10½" d., Mesa patt.,
Masterpiece line, ca. 1950................**10.00**
Plate, dinner, 10½" d., Montecito
patt..**12.00**
Plate, dinner, 10½" d., Starburst patt. **9.00**
Plate, dinner, 10½" d., Twilight Rose
patt..**30.00**
Plate, grill/buffet, 11" d., Desert Rose
patt..**85.00**
Plate, 11" l., steak serving-type.,
Desert Rose patt., oval **125.00**
Plate, chop, 12" d., Coronado patt.,
light yellow gloss, ca. 1936 ....**14.00**
Plate, chop, 12" d., Coronado patt.,
maroon gloss, ca. 1936 ....**14.00**
Plate, chop, 12" d., Desert Rose
patt..**82.50**
Plate, 13" d., Ivy patt. **50.00**
Plate, chop, 14" d., Desert Rose
patt...**102.00**
Plate, 8¼" w., 14" l., T.V., w/cup well,
Apple patt....................................**150.00**
Plate, 8¼" w., 14" l., T.V., w/cup well,
Desert Rose patt............................**115.00**
Plate, salad, Mesa patt., Masterpiece
line, ca. 1950 ....**8.00**
Plate, salad, Starburst patt....................**7.00**
Platter, 14" l., Desert Rose patt. **32.50**
Platter, 14" l., Fresh Fruit patt..............**48.00**
Platter, 14" l., Strawberry Fair patt.......**50.00**
Platter, 14" l., Wildflower patt.............**235.00**
Platter, 15" oval, Starburst patt. **55.00**
Platter, 18" oval, Apple patt. **120.00**
Platter, 19" l., Desert Rose patt. **247.50**
Platter, 19" l., Ivy patt........................**250.00**
Platter, 19" l., Meadow Rose
patt. ....**150.00 to 250.00**
Platter, small, Mesa patt.,
Masterpiece line, ca. 1950................**25.00**
Platter, large, Mesa patt.,
Masterpiece line, ca. 1950................**50.00**
Relish dish, Apple patt., 10" l.,
4½" w., 1½" h..................................**30.00**
Relish dish, oval, three-part,
Starburst patt., 12" l **27.00**
Salt & pepper shakers, Apple patt.,
ca. 1940, 2¼" h., pr..........................**25.00**
Salt & pepper shakers, Coronado
patt., coral, pr.................................**12.00**
Salt & pepper shakers, Coronado
patt., light yellow gloss, ca.
1936, pr..**10.00**
Salt & pepper shakers, Desert Rose
patt., ca. 1941, small rosebud
shaped, 2½" h., pr............................**24.50**
Salt & pepper shakers, Forget-Me-
Not patt., pr...................................**48.00**
Salt & pepper shakers, Fresh Fruit
patt., 3" h., pr. **48.00**
Salt & pepper shakers, Magnolia
patt., ca. 1952, pr............................**22.00**

Salt & pepper shakers, Strawberry
Fair, patt., 3" h., pr. **40.00**
Salt shaker & pepper mill, Apple
patt., 6" h., pr. **188.50**
Salt shaker & pepper mill, Meadow
Rose patt., 6" h., pr. **250.00**
Sherbet, footed, Apple patt.,
ca. 1940 ....**20.00**
Sherbet, Ivy patt., ca. 1948................**37.00**
Snack plate, Cafe Royal patt., 8" sq....**75.00**
Snack plate, Meadow Rose
patt. ....**75.00 to 100.00**
Snack set, Starburst., T.V.-type tray
w/cup well, 14" l., 8¼" w., ca. 1954....**85.00**
Soup tureen, cov., flat bottom, Apple
patt., 5 x 8"....................................**425.00**
Soup tureen, cov., flat bottom, Desert
Rose patt., 8" h. **598.00**
Soup tureen, cov., pedestal base,
Apple patt.,10¼" h. **410.00**
Sugar bowl, cov., Coronado patt.,
coral **13.00**
Sugar bowl, cov., large, Desert Rose
patt. **21.50**
Sugar bowl, cov., Fresh Fruit patt.,
3¼" h. **29.00**
Sugar bowl, cov., Ivy patt., 3" h..........**35.00**
Sugar bowl, cov., Strawberry Fair
patt., 3¼" h. **38.00**
Syrup pitcher, Apple patt., ca. 1940,
6¼" h., 1 pt..**72.00**
Syrup pitcher, Desert Rose
patt., 6¼" h., 1 pt..............................**69.00**
Tea bag holder, Apple patt.................**10.00**
Tea canister, cov., Desert Rose
patt. **140.00**
Teapot, cov., Ivy patt., ca. 1948........**168.50**
Teapot, cov., Shasta patt., ...**99.00**
Teapot, cov., Wildflower patt.............**850.00**
Thimble, Apple patt............................**125.00**
Thimble, Desert Rose patt., in
original box **66.50**
Thimble, Forget-Me-Not patt. **55.00**
Tidbit tray, three-tier, Apple patt.........**96.00**
Tile, Apple patt., 6" sq. **31.00**
Tile, Forget-Me-Not patt., 6" sq. **32.00**
Tile, framed, Desert Rose patt.,
7" sq...**65.00**
Toaster cover, Desert Rose patt.,
5½" d., 3" h. **115.00**
Trivet, fluted, Desert Rose patt.,
6" sq...**125.00**
Tumbler, juice, Apple patt...................**26.50**
Tumblers, water, Desert Rose patt.,
5¼" h., set of 7 ....**140.00**
Vase, 5½" h., Coronado patt., white,
ca. 1936 ....**50.00**
Vase, 6" h., Desert Rose patt. **117.50**
Vase, bud, Meadow Rose patt. **100.00**
Vase, 10" h., Coronado patt.,
turquoise, ca. 1936 ....**100.00**
Vegetable bowl, cov., Desert Rose
patt..**100.00**

Vegetable bowl, divided, Apple patt.,
ca. 1940 ....**37.00**
Vegetable bowl, open, Ivy patt.,
7¼" d...**25.00**
Vegetable bowl, open, Apple patt.,
8¼" d...**36.00**
Vegetable bowl, open, Ivy patt.,
8¼" d...**35.00**
Vegetable bowl, open, Forget-Me-
Not patt., 8¾" d. **48.00**
Vegetable bowl, open, oval,
Coronado patt., coral **15.00**
Vegetable bowl, open, round,
Coronado patt., coral **12.00**
Vegetable bowl, open, Fresh
Fruit patt., 9" d. **48.00**
Vegetable bowl, open, round, Ivy
patt...**20.00**
Vegetable dish, divided, Apple
patt., 10" oval....................................**70.00**
Vegetable dish, divided, Desert Rose
patt., 10¾" oval **36.00**
Vegetable dish, open, divided,
Starburst patt., ca. 1954 ....**37.50**
Water set: pitcher & six large
tumblers; Apple patt., 7 pcs. **200.00**

(End of Franciscan Section

FRANKOMA

Frankoma Easter Plate

*John Frank began producing and
selling pottery on a part-time basis during
the summer of 1933 while he was still
teaching art and pottery classes at the
University of Oklahoma. In 1934,
Frankoma Pottery became an incorporated
business that was successful enough to
allow him to leave his teaching position in
1936 to devote full time to its growth. The
pottery was moved to Sapulpa, Oklahoma
in 1938 and a full range of art pottery and
dinnerwares were eventually offered. In
1953 Frankoma switched from Ada clay to
clay found in Sapulpa. Since John Frank's
death in 1973, the pottery has been*

directed by his daughter, Joniece. In early 1991 Richard Bernstein became owner and president of Frankoma Pottery which was renamed Frankoma Industries. Joniece Frank serves as vice president and general manager. The early wares and limited editions are becoming increasingly popular with collectors today.

Bank, walking elephant,
   turquoise **$22.50**
Book end, Dreamer Girl, Onyx Black
   glaze, Ada clay **125.00**
Book end, model of boots w/horse-
   shoes, pr. **45.00**
Christmas card, 1966 ....**20.00**
Christmas card, 1975, Grace Lee &
   Milton Smith **80.00**
Christmas card, 1985 ....**15.50**
Christmas card, 1986 ....**15.50**
Christmas card, 1987 ....**15.50**
Decanter w/stopper, plume design,
   Prairie Green, Ada clay,
   7" rectangular..................................**150.00**
Flower holder, model of a duck, Ada
   clay **150.00**
Model of a puma, No. 114..................**45.00**
Model of Western boot, mottled
   green glaze, 7½" h., 7½" l., pr..........**175.00**
Mug, 1990, (Democratic) donkey **15.50**
Pitcher, 7" h., Wagon Wheel patt,.
   Prairie Green glaze...........................**35.00**
Pitcher w/ice lip, 8" h., Prairie Green
   glaze, Ada clay, No. 5D **140.00**
Planter, model of a swan, jade green
   glaze, Ada clay, No. 222...................**35.00**
Plate, 8½" d., Christmas, 1967, "Gifts
   for the Christ child," depicts the
   three Wise Men...............................**100.00**
Plate, Easter, 1972, "JESUS IS NOT
   HERE...HE IS RISEN," scene of
   Jesus' tomb (ILLUS.) **13.00**
Salt & pepper shakers, model of a
   buffalo, Ada clay, pr. **80.00**
Vase, 3½" h. Prairie Green
   glaze, Ada clay, No. 502...................**60.00**
Vase, 4" h., Wagon Wheel patt,.
   green...**22.00**
Vase, 7" h. Prairie Green glaze, Ada
   clay, No. 63.....................................**55.00**
Vase, 7½" h. Prairie Green glaze, Ada
   clay, No. 79.....................................**150.00**

GAUDY DUTCH

Gaudy Dutch Urn Pattern Plate

This name is applied to English earthenware with designs copied from Oriental patterns. Production began in the 18th century. These copies flooded into this country in the early 19th century. The incorporation of the word "Dutch" derives from the fact that it was the Dutch who first brought the Oriental wares into Europe. The ware was not, as often erroneously reported, made specifically for the Pennsylvania Dutch.

Bowl, 10" d., Single Rose patt.,
   double border band, (several
   enamel flakes) **$440.00**
Cup & saucer, handleless, Single
   Rose patt. **475.00**
Plate, 5⅝" d., Urn patt. (tiny enamel
   flakes) **385.00**
Plate, 8⅛" d., Urn patt. (ILLUS.).........**550.00**

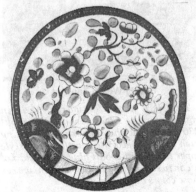

Gaudy Dutch Single Rose Plate

Plate, 9¾" d., Single Rose patt., some
   flaking (ILLUS.) **605.00**
Sugar bowl, cov., boat-shaped,
   Grape patt., enamel flakes, 6" h.
   (ILLUS. top next page)....................**478.50**

Gaudy Dutch Grape Pattern Sugar Bowl

Single Rose Waste Bowl

Waste bowl, Single Rose patt., light overall stain, two hairlines at rim, tiny flakes at foot rim, several enamel flakes 3" h. (ILLUS.) **247.50**

GAUDY WELSH

Gaudy Welsh Tea Set

This is a name for wares made in England for the American market about 1830 to 1860, with some examples dating much later. Decorated with Imari-style copper lustre and cobalt blue, it should not be confused with Gaudy Dutch wares whose colors differ somewhat.

Creamer, four-footed, Tulip patt., small **$125.00**
Creamer, footed, Oyster patt **170.00**
Creamer, Oyster patt., small **85.00**
Cup & saucer, Flower Basket patt.......**75.00**
Cup & saucer, Hexagon patt. **475.00**
Cup & saucer, Tulip patt.......................**75.00**

Cup & saucer, Wagon Wheel patt., small **72.00**
Dessert set: six 6" d. plates, six cups & saucers & 6¾" h. cov. sugar bowl; Tulip patt., 19 pcs. (some damage to cups & saucers) **495.00**
Mug, child's, Oyster patt.......................**95.00**
Mug, Oyster patt., 3" h. **170.00**
Pitcher, jug-type, 4½" h., Oyster patt., Allerton, England **195.00**
Pitcher, 4¾" h., bulbous body, Oyster patt., 1 pt. **205.00**
Pitcher, 6¼" h., figural snake handle, Forget-Me-Not patt.............**295.00**
Plate, 7" d., Columbine patt..................**45.00**
Tea set: cov. teapot, 5" h., cov. sugar creamer, six 5½" plates, five cups & saucers, plus one extra mismatched cup; Oyster patt., cylindrical bodies, stains & minor damage, the set (ILLUS.) **742.50**

HALL

Rose White Salt Shaker

Founded in 1903 in East Liverpool, Ohio, this still-operating company at first produced mostly utilitarian wares. It was in 1911 that Robert T. Hall, son of the company founder, developed a special single-fire, lead-free glaze which proved to be strong, hard and non-porous. In the 1920s the firm became well known for their extensive line of teapots (still a major product) and in 1932 they introduced kitchenwares followed by dinnerwares in 1936 and refrigerator wares in 1938.

The imaginative designs and wide range of glaze colors and decal decorations have led to the growing appeal of Hall wares with collectors, especially people who like Art Deco and Art Moderne design. One of the firm's most famous patterns was the "Autumn Leaf" line, produced as premiums for the Jewel Tea Company.

Helpful books on Hall include, The Collector's Guide to Hall China *by Margaret & Kenn Whitmyer, and* Superior Quality Hall China - A Guide for Collectors *by Harvey Duke (An ELO Book, 1977).*

HALL CHINA

MADE IN U.S.A.

Baker, Orange Poppy patt., French flute shape $25.00
Bowl, salad, 9" d., Orange Poppy patt...20.00
Bowl, salad, 9" d., Red Poppy patt. 25.00
Cake plate, Red Poppy patt., 10⅛" d...22.00
Casserole, cov., Crocus patt., Radiance shape...............................55.00
Casserole, cov., oval, Orange Poppy patt., 8" l. 55.00
Casserole, cov., tab-handled, Pert shape, Cadet blue w/white................35.00
Casserole, cov., Radiance shape, Serenade patt. 44.00
Casserole, cov., Sundial shape, Fantasy patt. 79.00
Casserole, cov., Sundial shape, Chinese Red......................................47.00
Coffeepot, cov., Orange Poppy patt. 40.00
Creamer & cov. sugar bowl, Orange Poppy patt., pr. 60.00
Creamer & cov. sugar bowl, Pert shape, Rose White patt., pr..............34.00
Cup & saucer, Heather Rose patt. 6.00
Custard cup, Orange Poppy patt. 8.00
Drip jar, open, Red Poppy patt., No. 1188 ....28.00
Leftover dish, cov., General Electric refrigerator ware, Delphinium blue.....29.00
Pitcher, Radiance shape, Orange Poppy patt., No. 5 ....30.00
Plate, 9" d., Red Poppy patt. 12.00
Salt shaker, Rose White patt., Pert shape (ILLUS.)....................................8.50
Salt & pepper shakers, handled, Crocus patt., pr. 40.00
Teapot, cov., Baltimore shape, maroon w/gold 35.00
Teapot, cov., Cube shape, green.........50.00
Teapot, cov., Doughnut shape, Chinese Red.....................................400.00

Hollywood Shape Teapot

Teapot, cov., Hollywood shape, maroon (ILLUS.) 30.00
Teapot, cov., Moderne shape, cobalt blue 175.00

Red Poppy Teapot

Teapot, cov., Red Poppy patt., New York shape (ILLUS.) 85.00
Teapot, cov., Streamline shape, Chinese Red, 6-cup size.................100.00
Water server, cov., Adonis line, General Electric 45.00

HAVILAND

Haviland Shrimp Bowl & Plates

Haviland porcelain was originated by Americans in Limoges, France, shortly before the mid-19th century and continues in production. Some Haviland was made by Theodore Haviland in the United States during the last World War. Numerous other factories also made china in Limoges. Also see LIMOGES.

H&C°

Haviland & Co.

Limoges

Bone dish, Blank No. 266.................**$20.00**
Bone dish, Ranson blank **12.50**
Bouillon cup & saucer, Blank
   No. 270 ....**40.00**
Bowl, 5" d., Apple Blossom patt............**15.00**
Bowl, 5" d., berry, Blue Garland patt......**8.00**
Bowl, 5" d., berry, Liberty Blue patt........**8.00**
Bowl, fruit, Ranson blank, gold edge ...**10.00**
Bowl, 6" d., cereal, Liberty Blue patt. **15.00**
Bowl, 8½" d., berry, Blue Garland
   patt. **35.00**
Bowl, 9" oval., serving-type, Liberty
   Blue patt...**45.00**
Cake plate, Clover patt.,
   Blank No. 96 ....**55.00**
Candleholders, Blue Garland patt.,
   pr...**45.00**
Casserole, cov., handled, delicate
   floral decoration interior & exterior
   w/lavish gold trim **195.00**
Chocolate pot, cov., Baltimore Rose
   patt...**250.00**
Chocolate set: cov. chocolate pot &
   two cups & saucers; decorated
   w/dainty sprays of flowers, shades
   of pink, ruffled top, gold tirm,
   5 pcs. **185.00**
Chocolate set: 10" h. cov. chocolate
   pot & four matching cups & saucers;
   decorated w/sprays of small pink
   roses, ribbon handle & finial,
   9 pcs. **425.00**
Coaster, Blue Garland patt., 3½" d. **12.00**
Coffeepot, cov., Apple Blossom patt.,
   pink flowers, green leaves & gold
   trim, red mark "Theodore
   Haviland".......................................**295.00**
Coffeepot, cov., Blue Garland patt. **95.00**
Creamer, Liberty Blue patt. **16.00**
Creamer, Ranson blank, gold edge **40.00**
Creamer & cov. sugar bowl, Apple
   Blossom patt., tall, pr....................**135.00**
Creamer & cov. sugar bowl, Blue
   Garland patt., pr.............................**45.00**
Cup & saucer, demitasse, cobalt blue
   & gilt decoration **45.00**
Cup & saucer, demitasse, decorated
   w/pink roses & green leaf garlands,
   h.p. scrolls on interior & exterior,
   lavish brushed gold scalloped rim,
   marked "Theodore Haviland -
   Limoges - France".............................**24.00**
Cup & saucer, Apple Blossom patt. **25.00**

Cup & saucer, Blank No. 390.............**35.00**
Cup & saucer, Blue Garland patt. **15.00**
Cup & saucer, Clover Leaf patt.,
   Blank No. 98 ....**35.00**
Cup & saucer, Liberty Blue patt. **12.00**
Cup & saucer, Moss Rose patt. **35.00**
Cup & saucer, Ranson blank, gold
   edge..**25.00**
Cup & saucer, St. Lawrence patt.,
   decorated w/pink roses, green
   leaves & blue scrolling, gold trim,
   Wanamaker mark, small **50.00**
Dinner service for eight w/five
   serving pieces, Miramar patt.,
   the set **1,300.00**
Game set: oval platter & twelve
   matching plates; platter w/ornate
   gold handles & wide scalloped rim &
   matching plates, all decorated
   w/wild boars, deer, etc., all artist-
   signed, 13 pcs............................**2,200.00**
Gravy boat, Ranson blank, gold
   edge..**75.00**
Ice cream set: 11 x 16" shallow
   master bowl & six 8" serving bowls;
   overall decoration of h.p. pastel
   multicolored full-grown roses
   w/foliage, heavy gold scalloped
   edge, ca. 1890s, 9 pcs...................**875.00**
Mustard jar, cov., figural white rabbit
   w/gold trim on ears & tail, artist-
   signed, 2" h., 3" l. (chips on cover
   rim)..**300.00**
Oyster plate, four-well, decorated
   w/small yellow roses & brown
   leaves **80.00**
Oyster plate, decorated w/wheat &
   blue flowers.....................................**75.00**
Oyster plate, h.p. decoration of fish
   in gold on cobalt blue ground............**85.00**
Oyster plates, decorated w/green &
   beige florals, gold trim, white
   ground, set of 6 (small flake on
   back of one) **375.00**
Plate, bread & butter, 5" d., Clover
   patt., Blank No. 96 ....**12.00**
Plate, 6" d., Liberty Blue patt.................**5.00**
Plate, 6¼" d., Blue Garland patt.............**7.00**
Plate, 6½" d., Apple Blossom patt.......**12.00**
Plate, salad, 7½" d., Apple Blossom
   patt...**12.00**
Plate, 7½" d., Blue Garland patt...........**13.00**
Plate, 7½" d., Ranson blank, gold
   edge..**10.00**
Plate, 8" d., Apple Blossom patt...........**20.00**
Plate, luncheon, 8½" d., Clover patt.,
   Blank No. 96 ....**18.00**
Plate, luncheon, 8½" d., Liberty Blue
   patt...**22.00**
Plate, 8½" d., Ranson blank, gold
   edge..**14.00**
Plate, dinner, 9½" d., Apple Blossom
   patt...**16.00**

Plate, 9½" d., open-handled, decorated w/h.p. thistles, butterfly & bird, elaborate delicate gold trim, marked "Haviland & Co. - Limoges - France" **48.00**

Plate, dinner, 9¾" d., Liberty Blue patt. **14.00**

Plate, 9¾" d., Ranson blank.................**18.00**

Plate, 10" d., Blue Garland patt............**14.00**

Plates, dessert, 7½" d., scalloped, each decorated w/a different h.p. shore scene in pastels w/browns & golds, ca. 1876, set of 12.................**395.00**

Platter, 12" oval, Apple Blossom patt...**55.00**

Platter, 13" oval, Blue Garland patt......**45.00**

Platter, 13½" l., Ranson blank, gold edge...**75.00**

Platter, 13¾" l., Clover patt., Blank No. 96 ....**48.00**

Platter, 14" l., Blank No. 118, decorated w/small magenta flowers, pale green foliage, brown stems, gold trim, "Theodore Haviland, Limoges, France" **28.00**

Ramekins & underplates, pink roses & green leaves, gold trim, Theodore Haviland - Limoges, set of 4 ....**75.00**

Salt & pepper shakers, Blue Garland patt., 4" h., pr.......................**45.00**

Shrimp set: 10" d., 3½" h. bowl & six 8" salad plates; h.p. decoration of multicolored pastel seashells on peach background w/blue water, gold scalloped borders, bowl decorated on interior & exterior & artist-signed on base, each plate w/different decoration, 7 pcs. (ILLUS.) **375.00**

Soup plate w/flanged rim, Liberty Blue patt., 8½" d. **8.00**

Soup plate w/flanged rim, Ranson blank, gold edge **20.00**

Soup plates w/flanged rims, decorated w/small pale pink & white roses, deep green leaves & scrolling, lacy grey foliage, Blank No. 300, set of 4 ....**100.00**

Sugar bowl, cov., Liberty Blue patt......**24.00**

Sugar bowl, cov., decorated w/h.p. flowers, gold line & trim **12.00**

Sugar bowl, cov., Ranson blank, gold edge...**65.00**

Tea set: cov., teapot, creamer & cov. sugar bowl; rust & yellow floral spray decoration, partly h.p. front & back, scrolled strap handles & finials w/fine gold lattice, gold tirm, teapot, 7¼" sq., creamer & cov. sugar bowl, 6" sq., marked "CFH - FDM," Limoges, France, 3 pcs. **400.00**

Tray, Apple Blossom patt., 9¾" sq. **115.00**

Tray, center-handle, Paradise patt., 7½" l. **30.00**

Tray, scalloped, decorated w/large peonies & gold trim, 13½" l. **125.00**

Vegetable bowl, cov., Blue Garland patt. **75.00**

Vegetable bowl, cov., decorated w/small blue & white floral sprays w/leaves, beading & jeweling, gilt scrolled strap handles, 7½" d., 5" h...**70.00**

Vegetable bowl, cov., oval, Blank No. 205 ....**45.00**

Vegetable bowl, cov., oval, floral decoration w/gold trim.......................**95.00**

Vegetable bowl, cov., oval, Ranson blank, gold edge **110.00**

Vegetable bowl, cov., round, Blank No. 330 ....**75.00**

Vegetable bowl, open, oval, Apple Blossom patt. **25.00**

HISTORICAL & COMMEMORATIVE WARES

Boston State House Pitcher

Numerous potteries, especially in England and the United States, made various porcelain and earthenware pieces to commemorate people, places and events. Scarce English historical wares with American views command highest prices. Objects are listed here alphabetically by title of view.

Most pieces listed here will date between about 1820 and 1850. The maker's name is noted in parenthesis at the end of each entry.

Almshouse, New York platter, flowers w/in medallions border, dark blue, 16½" l. (Ridgway).................**$690.00**

American Villa pitcher, fruit & foliage border, dark blue, 7¼" h. (few pinpoint flakes)................................**715.00**

American Villa plate, fruit & foliage border, dark blue, marked on back "American Villa BB & B," 8½" d........**170.50**

Anti-Slavery (Lovejoy/Tyrant's Foe) cup plate, central inscription, border reserves w/further inscriptions, light blue, 4" d. (light stain) **275.00**

Baker Falls, Hudson River plate, birds, flowers & scrolls border, black 9" d. (Clews) **105.00**

Bald eagle coffeepot, cov., scroll-bordered vignette w/eagle, leafy scroll lappet borders, dark blue, 11" h. (unseen chip on flange of cover, minute flakes on tip of spout, faint hairline in base).....................**4,950.00**

Bank of the United States, Philadelphia plate, spread eagle amid flowers & scrolls border, dark blue, 10" d., Stubbs, (small footrim chips) **345.00**

Battle of Bunker Hill platter, entwined vine border, dark blue, 11⅜" l., Stevenson (scratches, pits on face touched-up & reglazed)....**3,300.00**

Beehive - Washington & Lafayette Portrait Medallion pitcher, large scrolls & florals borders, dark blue, 7¼" h., Stevenson & Williams (restoration to spout & base, portions of body reglazed) **9,900.00**

B & O Railroad (so-called) teapot & cover, floral border, dark blue, 6½" h. (crack at rim & spout, professional handle restoration) **880.00**

Boston Harbor waste bowl, American eagle w/shield super-imposed on cityscape, flowers, foliage & scrolls border, dark blue, Rogers, 3" h. (restored chip, hairline in rim, base stained, foot hairline)....**357.50**

Boston Mails cup plate, light blue transfer of "Gentlemen's Cabin," 3¾" d. (J. & T. Edwards) **132.00**

Boston Mails plate, black transfer of "Gentleman's Cabin," 8¼" d. (J. & T. Edwards) **85.00**

Boston State House dish, leaf-shaped, floral border, dark blue, 5¾" w., Ridgway (restored area in rim) **412.50**

Boston State House pitcher, reverse w/City Hall, New York, rose border, dark blue, 5½" h., Joseph Stubbs (tiny chip on spout) **518.00**

Boston State House pitcher, floral border around the exterior of the neck & prow spout, 8¼" h., spout damaged & reglued, Rogers (ILLUS.) **575.00**

Boston State House plate, floral border, medium blue, 6½" d. (Enoch Wood) **137.50**

Boston State House platter, eagle & floral border, dark blue, 14⅝" l., J. Stubbs (cracked, some scratching & slight discoloration).......................**805.00**

Boston State House sauce tureen, cov., flowers & leaves border, dark blue, 5⅜" h., Rogers (professional restoration to underside of rim, two unrestored hairlines on lid) **440.00**

Boston State House soup tureen, cover & ladle, flowers & leaves border, medium dark blue, tureen 14⅝" l., John Rogers & Son (tureen discolored, hairlines, two footrim chips & ladle notch w/chip & crack, cover finial reglued, slight rim abrasion on ladle) **4,313.00**

Cambridge (England) pepper pot, footed cylindrical body w/mushroom top, dark blue, 3½" h., Ridgway (two tiny foot chips, tiny flakes on top).....**495.00**

Cape Coast Castle on the Gold Coast, Africa platter, shell border w/irregular opening, dark blue, 16" l. (Wood) **1,760.00**

The Capitol, Washington plate, shell border, round center, dark blue, 7½" d., E. Wood (minor glaze wear)...**374.00**

Capitol, Washington soup plate, flowers within medallions border, 10½" d. (Ridgway) **145.00**

Castle Garden, Battery, New York cup plate, shell border, circular center trailing vine around outer edge of center, dark blue, 4⅝" d., Wood (small chip on foot rim) **176.00**

Chillicothe, Men on a Raft platter, floral border, dark blue, 10¾" l., Davenport (short knife mark on face, faint hairline & rim chip on reverse)..**9,900.00**

Christ Church, Oxford (England) plate, figural medallion border, dark blue, 9¾" d., Ridgway (faint star crack on back) **187.00**

Church in the City of New York plate, spred eagle border, dark blue, 6⅛" d., Stubbs (short hairline off the back rim) **302.50**

City Hall, New York sugar bowl, cov., roses border, dark blue, 4¾" h., Stubbs (small chip on lid rim & inner rim of base, some stain) **220.00**

City of Canterbury (England) vege-table dish, squared w/grapevine border, dark blue, 9¾" w., 2¼" h., Wood (stain on foot rim) **357.50**

Columbia College, New York plate, acorns & oak leaves border, dark blue, 7½" d. (Stevenson) **275.00**

Conway, New Hampshire toddy plate, wide flowers & scrolls border, purple, 5" d. (Jackson) **77.00**

Crystal Palace (London, England) sauceboat, small grapevine border, light blue, ca. 1850, 4¾" h. (light staining) **132.00**

Deaf and Dumb Asylum, Hartford, Connecticut chamber pot, Almshouse, New York on reverse & the Capitol, Washington on interior, vining leaf border, dark blue, 10⅞" d., R. Stevenson (rim chip, small hairline beside footrim) **2,875.00**

Deaf & Dumb Asylum Tureen Stand

Deaf and Dumb Asylum, Hartford, Con, (sic) tureen stand, floral & leaf-panel border on the scalloped & barbed rim, 14⅝" l., slight discoloration & large footrim chips, Ridgway (ILLUS.) **1,035.00**

Doctor Syntax Drawing After Nature cup plate, unbordered w/portion of another view at the base, dark blue, 3⅞" d. (Clews) **187.00**

Dreghorn House, Scotland plate, floral border, dark blue, 6½" d. (Hall) **99.00**

Eagle over Landscape Panel cup & saucer, handleless, floral border, dark blue (two tiny rim flakes) **275.00**

The Errand Boy cup plate, unbordered, double transfer, dark blue, Wilkie series, 3½" d. (Clews) **143.00**

Erie Canal Inscription ... DeWitt Clinton Eulogy plate, views of canalboats & locks border, dark blue, 5¾" d **302.50**

Esplanade & Castle Garden, New York pitcher, Boston Almshouse on reverse, vine border, dark blue, 9⁵⁄₁₆" h., R. Stevenson (minor chip issuing hairline around lower handle end) **805.00**

Exchange, Charleston (South Carolina) sauce tureen, cover & undertray, Bank, Savannah on reverse, the cover w/Insane Hospital, Boston, floral & leaf-panel border, dark blue, tureen 8⅜" l., undertray 8⅜" l. (John & William Ridgway) **2,588.00**

Fair Mount Near Philadelphia soup tureen & cover, spread eagles

Fair Mount Soup Tureen
amid flowers & scrolls border, dark blue, 16" l., 12½" h., invisible restoration to base, small chip under lid & foot, short hairline in cover, Stubbs (ILLUS.) **5,060.00**

Famous Naval Heroes pitcher, flowers border, dark blue, unknown maker, 6" h.....................................**690.00**

Fort Gansevoort, New York soup ladle, foliate border, dark blue, 11⅛" l., R. Stevenson (bowl w/two restored rim chips) **1,840.00**

Fort Miller, U.S. plate, grey, 9" d. **110.00**

Franklin's Tomb cup plate, dark blue, 3½" d., Wood (short hairline at rim)..**275.00**

Fulton Market, New York sauce tureen, cover & undertray, cover w/Masonic Hall, Philadelphia & undertray w/Columbia College, New York, foliate-molded handles & feet, dark blue, tureen 8⅜" l., undertray 8⅞" l., the set (R. Stevenson) **2,990.00**

General Jackson, Hero of New Orleans cup plate, black, E. Wood, 3¾"d. (few flakes on extreme edge)...**935.00**

Girard's Bank, Philadelphia cup plate, small flowers & scrolls border, purple, 4" d. (Jackson) **330.00**

Hadley's Falls U. S. plate, sepia, 6⅝" d..**85.00**

Harewood House (England) soup tureen undertray, oval w/end handles, oak leaves & acorn border, dark blue, 14¼" l. (Stevenson) **440.00**

Harvard Hall, Massachusetts plate, floral sprig border purple, 7" d. (Jackson) **99.00**

Highlands, Hudson River undertray, oval w/reticulated rim, shell border, dark blue, 10" l. (Wood) **1,870.00**

Hoboken in New Jersey plate, spread eagles amid flowers & scrolls border, dark blue, 7¾" d. (Stubbs) **176.00**

Hudson, Hudson River platter, birds, flowers & scrolls border, brown, 13½" l. (Clews) **330.00**

Lafayette at Franklin's Tomb sugar bowl, cov., floral border, dark blue, 6⅝" h., E. Wood (minor pinpoints, chip on inner lid flange, hairline in body) **632.50**

Lafayette Portrait Medallion sugar bowl, cov., large floral border, dark blue, 5⅛" h., Stevenson (professional restoration to cover & base, finial & one handle replaced) **3,575.00**

Lake George, State of New York platter, shell border, circular center w/trailing vine around outer edge of center, dark blue, 16½" l., Wood (some scratching, overall slight discoloration) **1,495.00**

Lake George, U.S. vegetable dish, flowers, shells & scrolls border, pink, 11½" l. (Adams)....................**201.00**

Lakes of Kilarney (Ireland) plate, floral border, dark blue, 6½" d. (light overall stain) **55.00**

Landing of General Lafayette at Castle Garden, New York, 16 August, 1824 caster, floral & vine border, dark blue, 4½" h., Clews (minor wear at top) **862.50**

Landing of General Lafayette at Castle Garden, New York, 16 August 1824 mug, floral & vine border, dark blue, Clews, 4¾" h. (cracks) **862.50**

Landing of Gen. Lafayette Platter

Landing of General Lafayette at Castle Garden New York, 16 August 1824 plate, enclosed by primrose & dogwood border, dark blue, 17" l., Clews (ILLUS.)..............**920.00**

Landing of the Fathers at Plymouth, Dec. 22, 1620 plate, pairs of birds & scrolls & four medallions w/ships & inscriptions border, medium blue, 6½" d., Wood (slight rim glaze rub) **181.00**

Louisville, Kentucky platter, groups of flowers & scrolls border, dark

blue, 12½" l., Clews, (slight discoloration) **2,415.00**

Luscombe, Devon (England) plate, grapevine border, dark blue, 6½" d. (Wood) **110.00**

Mendenhall Ferry cup plate, partial spread eagle border, dark blue, 4⅝" d., Stubbs (hairline at rim) **1,980.00**

Military School, West Point, N.Y., U.S. platter, floral & scroll border, pink, 17⅝" l. (Adams)......................**440.00**

Mitchell & Freeman's China and Glass Warehouse, Chatham Street, Boston plate, foliage border, dark blue, 9" d. (Adams)......**440.00**

Mount Vernon Near Washington Vegetable Dish

Mount Vernon Near Washington vegetable dish & cover, floral & leaf-panel borter repeated around the exterior of the dish, 11³⁄₁₆" l., Ridgeway (ILLUS. dish only) **1,955.00**

New York City Hall pitcher, Hospital, New York & Insane Asylum, New York on reverse, foliate border, scroll handle, dark blue, 7³⁄₁₆" h., R. Stevenson (two glaze chips, chip on spout) **1,380.00**

New York from Weehawken sauce tureen, cover & ladle, View from Mount Ida on reverse & Capitol at Washington on interior, floral borders, light blue, 5¾" h. (Charles Meigh)..**495.00**

Passaic Falls, State of New Jersey sauce tureen, cover, undertray & ladle, shells border, Pass in the Catskill Mountains on cover, dark blue, Enoch Wood & Sons, tureen 7¹³⁄₁₆" l., undertray 8¹⁄₁₆" l., the set (tureen footrim chip, cover slightly large & w/riveted repair, chip on handle, slight discoloration on undertray) **805.00**

Peace & Plenty sauce tureen undertray, oval w/end loop handles, wide band of fruit & flowers border,

dark blue, Clews, 8¼" l. (rim glaze
rubs, small chip on back) **330.00**
Pittsburgh - Steamboat
Pennsylvania plate, birds, flowers
& scrolls border, deep maroon,
10½" d. (Clews) **259.00**
Quebec cup plate, floral border, dark
blue, 3⅞" d. (Davenport)..............**1,320.00**
St. Catherine's Hill Near Guilford
(England) cup plate, unbordered,
dark blue, 3½" d., Clews (minute
flake on inner rim) **49.50**
A Ship of the Line in the Downs
(England) bowl, ship flying the
American flag w/a castle in the
background, square form w/shell
border, dark blue, 9" w. (E. Wood &
Sons) **1,610.00**
States series cup plate, three-story
building, two wings & center section,
names of states in festoons
separated by five-point stars border,
dark blue, 3⅞" d. (Clews)................**880.00**
States series cup plate, three-story
mansion, small extension to left,
names of states in festoons
separated by five-point stars border,
dark blue, 4" d., Clews (two tiny
footrim chips, glaze wear on rim) **308.00**
States series mug, mansion
w/winding drive, border w/names of
fifteen states in festoon separated
by five-point stars, dark blue, 3⅛" h.
(Clews)..**1,650.00**
States series soup plate, building,
fishermen w/net, border w/names of
fifteen states in festoons separated
by five- or eight point stars, dark
blue, 10⅜" d. (Clews)......................**357.50**
Staughton's Church, Philadelphia
cup plate, acorns & oak leaves
border, dark blue, mislabeled on
back, 4¼" d., Stevenson (small chip
on back rim) **770.00**
Steamboat soup plate, florals
border, dark blue, 10⅛" d. (light
mellowing on back) **522.50**
Texian Campaigne - Battle of
Buena Vista plate, symbols of war
& "goddess-type" seated border,
light blue, 8¼" d., Anthony Shaw
(chip on foot rim) **137.50**
Troy from Mt. Ida platter, floral &
scroll border, dark blue, 10³⁄₁₆" l., A.
Stevenson, small rim chip
(ILLUS. top next column) **2,300.00**
United States Hotel, Philad(elphi)a
bowl, molded foliate & cable border,
leafy trees frame vignette of three
figures in foreground, hotel in
distance, dark blue, 10¾" d., Tams,
Anderson & Tams Pottery (serious
rim crack & center star crack) **460.00**

Troy from Mt. Ida Platter

View from Ruggle's House,
Newburgh, Hudson River plate,
narrow band of lace w/three small
flowers bunched together & spaced
around border, light blue, 10¾" d.,
(Ridgway)..**55.00**
View Near Fishkill, U.S. plate, black,
10½" d..**120.00**

View of New York Bay Plate

View of New York Bay plate, scrolls
& flowers border, dark blue, 8⅝" d.,
J. Stubbs (ILLUS.) **1,955.00**
View of New York From
Weehawken sauce dish,
medallions w/state seals border,
light blue, 5½" d. (Mellor,
Venables & Co.)................................**49.50**
Virginia Church sugar bowl &
cover, flowers & scrolls border, dark
blue, 7" h. (overall stain in base, few
small inner rim chips)......................**412.50**
Wadsworth Tower waste bowl,
shells border, irregular center, dark
blue, 6½" d., 3¼" h. (Wood).............**330.00**
Washington, His Country's Father -
Fayette, The Nation's Guest
portrait medallion pitcher,
inscriptions on rim, black transfer,
6¾" h., R. Hall & Sons (professional
restoration)....................................**1,540.00**

Washington's Tomb tray, hexagonal w/scroll-embossed rim handles, floral border, dark blue, 7⅞" w. (Wood) **2,750.00**

Welcome Lafayette the Nation's Guest and Our Country's Glory plate, flowers & scrolls border, blue, 8¾" d. (Clews) **1,980.00**

Welcome Lafayette the Nation's Guest and Our Country's Glory plate, embossed scrolls border w/blue trim, dark blue, 10" d., Clews (overall stain, "Y" crack strengthened w/staples)..................**660.00**

West Point Military Academy basket, oval w/reticulated flaring sides & loop end handles, shell border, dark blue, 10¾" l. (Wood) **2,475.00**

Winter View of Pittsfield, Mass. (A) cup plate, double transfer w/the church & hotel, scalloped rim, dark blue, 3⅞" d., Clews (few tiny rim flakes) **181.50**

Winter View of Pittsfield, Mass. (A) platter, floral border w/medallions of center view border, dark blue, 14⅞" l., Clews (small spot of old deteriorating rim repair) **715.00**

Winter View of Pittsfield, Mass. (A) soup plate, floral w/medallions of center view border, dark blue, 8¾" d., Clews (small flakes on back) **412.50**

Worcester Cathedral (England) cup plate, irregular reserve, floral border, dark blue, 3⅞" d (Hall) **93.50**

(End of Historical Section)

HULL

Parchment & Pine Cornucopia-Vase

This pottery was made by the Hull Pottery Company, Crooksville, Ohio, beginning in 1905. Art Pottery was made

until 1950 when the company was converted to utilitarian wares. All production ceased in 1986.

Reference books for collectors include Roberts' Ultimate Encyclopedia of Hull Pottery *by Brenda Roberts (Walsworth Publishing Company, 1992), and* Collector's Guide to Hull Pottery - The Dinnerware Lines *by Barbara Loveless Gick-Burke (Collector Books, 1993).*

Ashtray, figural mermaid to one side, Ebb Tide patt., No. E-8 ....**$98.00**

Bank, figural Corky Pig, Mirror Brown & blue ....**25.00 to 35.00**

Bank, figural pig, embossed floral decoration over glaze, 10" l. **55.00**

Basket, Blossom Flite patt., No. T4-8½", 8½" h. **75.00**

Basket, Blossom Flite patt., pink, 10" h..**80.00**

Basket, Continental patt., No. 55 ....**70.00**

Basket, Ebb Tide patt., pink ground, 8" h..**65.00**

Basket, Imperial patt., two sides pulled up to form handle, supporting a ball, green over dark brown, No. B9, 7½" h......................................**25.00**

Basket, flower, oval, Imperial patt., dark blue & green, No. F24, 6¼ x 7", 6" h..**20.00**

Basket, Imperial patt., No. B-36-9", 9" h..**45.00**

Basket, Orchid patt., No. 305-7", 7" h..**379.00**

Basket, hanging-type, Royal Woodland patt., matte finish, No. W12, 12" h...............................**400.00**

Basket, Sunglow patt., yellow, No. 84, 6½" h.......................................**37.50**

Basket, Tokay patt., 6" h.....................**45.00**

Basket, Tokay patt., round "moon" form, pink, No. 11-10½",10½" h.........**50.00**

Basket, Tokay patt., round "moon" form, green & white, No. 11-10½", 10½" h..**74.00**

Basket, Tokay patt., white ground, No. 15-12", 12" h.............................**160.00**

Basket, Tuscany patt., No. 6-8", 8" h...**50.00**

Basket, Wild Flower patt., No. W16-10½", 10½" h............................**250.00**

Basket, Woodland patt., W-9-8¾", 8¾" h..**117.50**

Basket, Woodland Matte patt., green to cream, No. W22-10½", 10½" h. ...**625.00**

Bottle, figural pink elephant, "Leeds," 7¾" h..**65.00**

Bowl, 7" d., Open Rose patt., pink &
blue, No. 113-7" **75.00**
Bowls, nesting-type, Sunglow patt.,
pink, No. 50, 5½", 7½", 9½", set
of 3..**70.00**
Candleholder, Blossom Flite patt.,
No. T11-3", 3" h. **35.00**
Candleholder, Ebb Tide patt.,
No. E-13, 2¾" h. **18.00**
Candleholder, Magnolia Matte patt.,
No. 27-4", 4" h. **18.00**
Candleholder, Parchment & Pine
patt...**25.00**
Candleholders, Butterfly patt.,
pr...**47.50**
Candleholders, Continental patt., pr. ..**50.00**
Candleholders, Magnolia Gloss patt.,
No. H-24, pr. **60.00**
Candleholders, Woodland patt., No.
W30-3½", 3½" h., pr.......................**67.00**
Candy dish, cov., Continental patt.,
evergreen, No. C62C, 8½" h............**50.00**
Canister, cov., "Cereal," Little Red
Riding Hood patt. **950.00**
Canister, cov., "Coffee," Little Red
Riding Hood patt. **639.00**
Canister, cov., "Salt," Little Red
Riding Hood patt. **850.00**
Canister, cov., "Sugar," Little Red
Riding Hood patt. **629.00**
Casserole, cov., figural hen on nest,
House n' Garden line, Mirror Brown
w/incised rooster decoration inside
base, 14⅜" l., 11" h.........................**95.00**
Casserole, cov., French handle-type,
& warmer, House n' Garden line,
No. 979, Tangerine glaze, 3 pt.,
3 pcs. **80.00**
Casserole, cov., Serenade patt.,
No. 520, blue, 9" d. **100.00**
Coffeepot, cov., House n' Garden
line, Avocado glaze..........................**20.00**
Console bowl, Butterfly patt., white
pebble finish....................................**88.00**
Console bowl, shell-shaped, Ebb
Tide patt., No. E-12, 15¾" l...............**97.50**
Console bowl, Magnolia Matte, pink,
No. 26-12", 12" l............................**105.00**
Console bowl, Parchment & Pine
patt., green, No. S-9, 16" l. **100.00**
Console bowl, Tokay patt., white,
No. 14, 15¾" l................................**110.00**
Console bowl, Wildflower patt.,
yellow/brown matte glaze,
No. W21-12", 12" l. **114.00**
Console bowl, Woodland patt.,
chartreuse & pink, No. W29-14",
14" l. **85.00**
Console set: console bowl & pair of
candleholders; Butterfly patt., bowl
No. B21, candleholders No. B22,
3 pcs. **125.00**
Console set: bowl & pair of candle-
holders; Open Rose patt., 3 pcs. **595.00**

Console set: console bowl & pair of
3½" h. candleholders; Woodland
patt., glossy glaze, heavy gold tirm,
bowl No. W29, candleholders
No. W30, 3 pcs. **120.00**
Cookie jar, cov., Big Apple patt. **20.00**
Cookie jar, cov., Floral patt., No. 48,
8¾" h...**40.00**
Cookie jar, cov., Gingerbread Boy,
brown...**188.00**
Cookie jar, cov., Little Red Riding
Hood patt., No. 967.......................**237.00**
Cookie jar, cov., Little Red Riding
Hood patt., closed basket **282.00**
Cookie jar, cov., Little Red Riding
Hood, closed green basket,
poinsettia decorated **682.50**
Cookie jar, cov., Little Red Riding
Hood patt., red shoes & lavish gold
trim, w/original sticker **645.00**
Cookie jar, cov., Little Red Riding
Hood patt., open basket, painted
underglaze, gold trim & decals,
marked "967 Hull Ware Little Red
Riding Hood Pat. Applied For, USA,"
pre-1943 ....**286.00**
Cookie jar, cov., Little Red Riding
Hood patt., open basket, star
decoration on apron........................**330.00**
Cornucopia-vase, Blossom Flite
patt., No. T-6, 10½" l.......................**73.00**
Cornucopia-vase, Ebb Tide patt.,
No. E3, 7½" h..................................**67.50**
Cornucopia-vase, Ebb Tide patt.,
maroon, No. E-9, 11¾" h. **62.00**
Cornucopia-vase, Imperial patt.,
stylized conch shell, white, No. A53,
4½ x 8"..**18.00**
Cornucopia-vase, Magnolia Matte
patt., No. 19-8½", 8½" h....................**75.00**
Cornucopia-vase, double, Magnolia
Gloss patt., blue, No. H-15-12",
12" h..**70.00**
Cornucopia-vase, Open Rose patt.,
No. 141-8½", 8½" h.........................**110.00**
Cornucopia-vases, Parchment &
Pine patt., Nos. S-2-L&R, 7¾" h.,
pr...**95.00**
Cornucopia-vase, Parchment & Pine
patt., No. S-6, 12" h. (ILLUS.) **60.00**
Cornucopia-vase, Serenade patt.,
yellow, No. 510, 11" h. **60.00**
Cornucopia-vases, Wildflower patt.,
decorated w/pink flowers, green &
yellow trim, No. W5-6½", 6½" h.,
pr...**125.00**
Cornucopia-vase, Wildflower patt.,
No. W7, 7½".....................................**43.00**
Cornucopia-vase, Woodland Gloss
patt., No. W2-5½", 5½" h. **45.00**
Cornucopia-vase, Woodland Gloss
patt., No. W10-11", 11" h. **45.00**
Creamer, Cinderella Blossom patt.,
pink flowers, No. 28-4½", 4½" h.........**18.00**

Creamer, Little Red Riding Hood patt. **105.00**

Creamer, tab-handled, Little Red Riding Hood patt. **272.00**

Creamer, top-pour, Little Red Riding Hood patt. **367.00**

Creamer, Water Lily patt., pink **55.00**

Creamer & open sugar bowl, Little Red Riding Hood patt., pr. **212.00**

Creamer & open sugar bowl, Parchment & Pine patt., Nos. S-12 & S-13, pr. **75.00**

Dish garden, Imperial patt., curved fluted base, white, No. 1406 Scroll, 9" l **8.00**

Dresser jar, cov., Little Red Riding Hood patt. **622.50**

Ewer, Bow-Knot patt., No. B-1, 5½" h. **110.00**

Ewer, Bow-Knot patt., pink, No. B-15-13½", 13½" h. ....**1,200.00 to 1,250.00**

Ewer, Ebb Tide patt., No. E-10, 14" h...**135.00**

Ewer, Magnolia Matte patt., turquoise & pink, No. 14-4¾", 4¾" h..................**44.00**

Ewer, Magnolia Matte, yellow & peach, No. 14-4¾", 4¾" h. **45.00**

Ewer, Magnolia Matte patt., No. 18-13½", 13½" h. **230.00**

Ewer, Open Rose, No. 128-4¾", 4¾" h. **40.00**

Ewer, Orchid patt., pink & blue, No. 311-13", 13" h...........................**650.00**

Rosella Pattern Ewer

Ewer, Rosella patt., No. R-9-6½", 6½" h. (ILLUS.) **43.00**

Ewer, Serenade patt., pink, No. S13, 13¼" h..**194.00**

Ewer, Sueno Tulip patt., No. 109-33-13", 13" h. **312.50**

Ewer, Wildflower patt., pink & blue, No. W2-5½", 5½" h. **32.00**

Ewer, Wildflower patt., W-6-7½", 7½" h...**40.00**

Ewer, Woodland Matte patt., No. W3-5½", 5½" h. **48.00**

Ewer, Woodland Matte patt., No. W24-13½", 13½" h. **200.00**

Figure of The Madonna, white, No. F-40..**25.00**

Flower dish, Continental patt., orange & gold, No. C51, 15⅜" l. **38.00**

Flowerpot, Woodland patt., pink, No. W11-5¾", 5¾" h. **125.00**

Flowerpot w/attached saucer, Sueno Tulip patt., No. 116-33-4¼", 4¼" h.....**78.00**

Fruit bowl, footed, turned-up sides, Serenade patt., No. S15, yellow **45.00**

Jardiniere, Bow-Knot patt., No. B-19-9⅜", 9⅜" h. **650.00**

Jardiniere, Orchid patt., No. 310-6", 6" h...**130.00**

Jardiniere, Sueno Tulip patt., No. 115-33-7", 7" h. **195.00**

Jardiniere, Woodland Matte patt., No. W7-5½", 5½" h. **112.50**

Jardiniere, Woodland Matte patt., No. W-7", 7" h.................................**65.00**

Lamp base, bulbous base tapering to cylindrical neck, brass footed, decorated w/yellow flower & green leaves on white ground, mid-1940s, 7¾" h. **75.00**

Model of a dachshund, black, Novelty line, No. 119-15", 6 x 14" **75.00**

Mug, Serenade patt., No. S22, 8 oz....**50.00**

Mustard jar, cov., Little Red Riding Hood patt. **287.00**

Pitcher, 5½" h., Bow-Knot patt., blue & pink matte glaze, No. B-1-5½".......**160.00**

Pitcher w/ice lip, 6½" h., House n' Garden line, Tangerine glaze **30.00**

Pitcher, 8¼" h., Ebb Tide patt., No. E-4, 8¼", pink.............................**45.00**

Pitcher, 8½" h., Blossom Flite patt., No. T-3..**49.00**

Pitcher, 12" h., Capri patt., No. 87, coral...**85.00**

Planter, baby w/pillow, pink w/gold trim, No. 92, 1951 5½" h. **25.00**

Planter, bust of the Madonna, yellow, No. 24, 7" h. **10.00**

Planter, figure of a boy on a fence, Novelty line, No. 87..............................**20.00**

Planter, Imperial patt., footed, bell-form bowl, No. F34, 5" h. **10.00**

Planter, Imperial patt., fruit decoration, ivory, No. F473, 5 x 8¾"...**8.00**

Planter, model of Bandanna Duck, Novelty line, No. 75, 5 x 7"................**29.50**

Planter, model of Bandanna Duck, No. 76, 3½ x 3½" **40.00**

Planter, model of a Dachshund dog, 14" l., 6" h..**25.00**

Planter, model of two ducks, No. 94, 10" h...**25.00**

Planter, model of a kitten, No. 61, pink **40.00**

Planter, model of lovebirds,
turquoise, Novelty line, No. 93, 6" h...**30.00**
Planter, model of a parrot pulling a
flower blossom-form cart, Novelty
line, No. 60, 9½" l., 6" h. **28.00**
Planter, model of a pheasant, No. 61,
6 x 8"..**25.00**
Planter, model of a pig, leaning on
fence, No. 86, 6¾ x 8" **25.00**
Planter, model of a poodle head,
gold-trimmed, Novelty line, No. 38,
6¼" h..**37.50**
Planter, model of a pink poodle
standing on hind legs w/green
foliage to the back, Novelty line,
No. 114, 8" h. **45.00**
Planter, model of a swan, No. 80........**36.00**

Swan Planter

Planter, model of a swan, yellow
glossy glaze, Imperial line, No. 69,
8½ x 10½", 8½" h. (ILLUS.) **23.00**
Planter, model of a telephone, No.
50, 9" h...**40.00**
Planter, model of twin geese, Novelty
line, No. 95, 7¼" h. **27.50**
Planter, model of a wishing well,
6½" h...**40.00**
Planter, Woodland Matte patt.,
No. W19-10½", 10½" l. **65.00**
Salt & pepper shakers, House n'
Garden line, Avocado glaze, pr. **8.00**
Salt & pepper shakers, figural mush-
room, House & Garden line, pr. **20.00**
Salt & pepper shakers, Little Red
Riding Hood patt., small, 3¼" h.,
pr..**50.00**
Skillet tray, handled, Cook n' Serve
Ware, Continental patt., No. 27,
9¼ x 15½"..**12.00**
Spice jar, cov., Little Red Riding
Hood patt. **625.00**
Stein, Early Utility, Elks BPOE,
No. 496, 6½" h. **42.00**
Sugar bowl, cov., Blossom Flite
Glossy patt., No. T-16.......................**21.50**
Sugar bowl, cov., Little Red Riding
Hood patt. **316.00**

Sugar bowl, open, scroll handles,
Wildflower patt., No. 74, 4¾" h. **50.00**

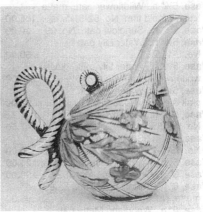

Blossom Flite Teapot

Teapot, cov., Blossom Flite patt.,
No. T14, 8¼" h. (ILLUS.) **60.00**
Teapot, cov., Magnolia Gloss patt.,
blue, No. H-20-6½", 6½" h. **63.00**
Teapot, cov., Parchment & Pine patt.,
green, No. S-11, 6" h. **110.00**
Teapot, cov., Wildflower patt.,
No. 72-8", 8" h..................................**950.00**
Tea set: cov. teapot, creamer & cov.
sugar bowl; Bow-Knot patt., 3 pcs. ..**575.00**
Tea set: cov. teapot, creamer & cov.
sugar bowl; Parchment & Pine patt.,
3 pcs. **170.00**
Tea set: cov. teapot, creamer & cov.
sugar bowl; Woodland Gloss patt.,
green & pink, Nos. W26, W27 &
W28, 3 pcs.......................................**140.00**
Urn, Tokay patt., No. 5, 5½" h.............**50.00**
Vase, 4¾" h., Magnolia Matte patt.,
No. 13-4¾"...**45.00**
Vase, 4¾" h., Orchid patt., No. 303-
4¾"..**55.00**

Bow-Knot Pattern Vase

Vase, 5" h., Bow-Knot patt.,
No. B-2-5" (ILLUS.)...........................**105.00**

Vase, 5" h., Iris patt., peach
No. 411-5"......................................**45.00**
Vase, 5¼" h., Wildflower patt., matte
finish w/gold tirm, No. 52-5¼".........**105.00**
Vase, 5½" h., Sunglow patt., No. 99 ....**30.00**
Vase, 5½" h., Water Lily patt.,
No. L-1- 5½"....................................**50.00**
Vase, 5½" h., Water Lily patt., glossy
white w/gold trim, No. L-2-5½".........**38.00**
Vase, 5½" h., Water Lily patt.,
pink & green, No. L-2-5½" **38.00**
Vase, 5½" h., Wildflower patt.,
No. W3-5½" **47.50**
Vase, 5¾" h., Sunglow patt.,
No. 88-5¾", yellow...........................**20.00**
Vase, 6" h., Mardi Gras patt., pink........**20.00**
Vase, 6" h., Orchid patt., No. 302-6" **90.00**
Vase, 6" h., Sueno Tulip patt., blue
matte, No. 106-33-6".........................**95.00**
Vase, 6" h., Woodland Matte patt.,
No. W-6" **75.00**
Vase, 6¼" h., Magnolia Matte patt.,
pink to blue, No. 11-6¼" **55.00**
Vase, 6¼" h., Magnolia Matte patt.,
No. 15-6¼"...**31.00**
Vase, 6¼" h., Open Rose patt.,
No. 135-6¼".......................................**75.00**
Vase, 6½" h., Bow-Knot patt.,
No. B-5-6½" **60.00**
Vase, 6½" h., two-handled, Dogwood
patt., blue & pink, No. 502-6½" **110.00**
Vase, 6½" h., Magnolia Matte patt.,
brown ground.....................................**40.00**
Vase, 6½" h., Parchment & Pine
patt., No. S-1.....................................**30.00**
Vase, 6½" h., Thistle patt.,
No. 51-6½"...**110.00**
Vase, 7" h., Iris patt., No. 405-7" **60.00**
Vase, 7¼" h., 5¼" d., Puritan-style,
Serenade patt., pink, No. S-4 ....**50.00**
Vase, 7½" h., figural Madonna &
Christ Child head **25.00**
Vase, 8" h., Crab Apple Stoneware....**125.00**
Vase, 8" h., Sueno Tulip patt.,
No. 107-33-8"....................................**110.00**
Vase, 8½" h., Bow-Knot patt.,
No. B-7-8½" **160.00**
Vase, 8½" h., Iris patt.,
No. 402-8½".......................................**105.00**
Vase, 8½" h., Magnolia Matte patt.,
pink & yellow glaze, No. 1-8½" **71.00**
Vase, 8½" h., Magnolia Matte patt.,
No. 2-8½"...**73.00**
Vase, 8½" h., Magnolia Matte patt.,
pink & blue, No. 7-8½" **72.50**
Vase, 8½" h., fan-shaped, Magnolia
Gloss patt., gold side handles,
No. 8-8½" **60.00**
Vase, 8½" h., Orchid patt., pink to
cream, No. 301-8½"...........................**155.00**
Vase, 8½" h., Orchid patt.,
No. 304-8½".......................................**130.00**
Vase, 8½" h., Sunglow patt., figural
flamingo, pink, No. 85-8½"................**25.00**

Vase, 8½" h., Sunglow patt., figural
flamingo, yellow, No. 85-8½" **25.00**
Vase, 8½" h., Wildflower patt., pink,
No. W-9-8½" **150.00**
Vase, 8½" h., Wildflower patt., W-40....**65.00**
Vase, 8½" h., Wildflower,
No. 51-8½"...**245.00**
Vase, 8½" h., Wildflower patt.,
No. 75-8½"...**200.00**
Vase, 8½" h., fan-shaped, Wildflower
patt., No. 78-8½"...............................**350.00**

Woodland Double Bud Vase

Vase, 8½" h., double-bud, Woodland
Glossy patt., No. W-15-8½"
(ILLUS.) **46.00**
Vase, 9" h., Crab Apple Stoneware....**145.00**
Vase, 9" h., Sueno Tulip patt., cream
& blue, No. 101-33-9" **187.50**
Vase, 9¼" h., angel fish form, Ebb
Tide patt., No. E-6.............................**125.00**
Vase, 9½" h., Water Lily patt.,
No. L-11-9½"......................................**145.00**
Vase, 10" h., Imperial patt., embossed
eagle, wheat & stars decoration,
No. F481 ....**20.00**
Vase, 10" h., Parchment & Pine patt.,
No. S-4-10".......................................**45.00**
Vase, 10" h., Sueno Tulip patt.,
No. 101-33-10"..................................**220.00**
Vase, 10" h., Tuscany patt.,
No. 8-10"...**60.00**
Vase, 10½" h., Iris patt., No. 404-
10½", peach & pink...........................**225.00**
Vase, 10½" h., rectangular,
Serenade patt., blue, No. S11 ....**80.00**
Vase, 10½" h., Water Lily patt., peach
& brown, No. L-12-10½" **110.00**
Vase, 10½" h., Wildflower patt., pink
& blue, No. W-14-10½" **175.00**
Vase, 10½" h., Wildflower patt.,
No. W-15-10½" **100.00**
Vase, 10½" h., Wildflower patt., pink
& blue, No. 59-10½"..........................**200.00**

Vase, 10½" h., Woodland Gloss patt.,
   No. W-18-10½" **245.00**
Vase, 11" h., Ebb Tide patt., maroon,
   No. E-7...**100.00**
Vase, 11" h., Ebb Tide patt., salmon,
   No. E-7...**110.00**
Vase, 12½" h., Magnolia Gloss patt.,
   No. H-17-12½" **145.00**
Vase, 12½" h., Magnolia Matte patt.,
   No. 22-12½"......................................**225.00**
Vase, 12½" h., Wildflower patt.,
   No. W-17-12½" **205.00**
Vase, 15" h., Continental patt.,
   persimmon, No. 57 ....**70.00**
Wall plaque, round, Bow-Knot patt.,
   pink, No. B28-10"..........................**1,000.00**
Wall pocket, Bow-Knot patt., model
   of a cup & saucer, pink & blue,
   No. B-24-6", 6" h. **145.00**
Wall pocket, Bow-Knot patt., model
   of a pitcher, No. B-26-6", blue matte
   finish, 6" h. **210.00**
Wall pocket, Little Red Riding Hood
   patt..**437.00**
Wall pocket, shell-form, Royal
   Woodland patt., W13-7½", 7½" h.......**31.50**
Wall pocket, Sunglow patt., model of
   a sad iron, No. 83, pink, 6" h.............**50.00**
Wall pocket, Sunglow patt., model of
   a sad iron, No. 83, yellow, 6" h. **42.00**
Wall pocket, Sunglow patt., model of
   a whisk broom, No. 82, 8¼" h............**26.00**
Wall pocket, shell-form, Woodland
   Gloss patt., No. W13", 7½" h. **85.00**
Wall pockets, heart-shaped, Rosella
   patt., No. R-10-6½", 6½" h., pr...........**65.00**
Window bowl, Scroll patt., Novelty line,
   No. 71, 12½" l. **35.00**
Window box, Serenade patt., blue,
   No. S9-12½", 12½" l. **85.00**
Window box, Serenade patt., pink,
   No. 59-12½" l. **70.00**

(End of Hull Section)

HUMMEL FIGURINES & COLLECTIBLES

The Goebel Company of Oeslau, Germany, first produced these porcelain figurines in 1934 having obtained the rights to adapt the beautiful pastel sketches of children by Sister Maria Innocentia (Berta) Hummel. Every design by the Goebel artisans was approved by the nun until her death in 1946. Though not antique, these figurines with the "M.I. Hummel" signature, especially those bearing the Goebel Company factory mark used from 1934 and into the early 1940s, are being sought by collectors though interest may have peaked some years ago.

Crown Mark
Full Bee Mark
Last Bee Mark

Accordion Boy, crown mark,
   1934-49, 5" h. ....**$350.00 to 400.00**
Adoration, stylized bee mark,
   1956-68, 6¼" h. **225.00**

Adventure Bound

Adventure Bound, last bee mark,
   1972-79, 7½" h. (ILLUS.) **1,750.00**
A Fair Measure, 1972-79,
   5½" h. ....**125.00 to 150.00**
Angel at Prayer fonts, 1956-68,
   2 x 4¾", pr...**60.00**
Angel Duet, three line mark, 1963-71,
   5" h...**130.00**
Angelic Sleep, 1940-57,
   3½ x 5" ....**175.00 to 200.00**
Angel Lights candleholder,
   1972-79...**120.00**
Angel Serenade, 1940-57, 5½" h......**355.00**
Angel with Accordion, 1972-79,
   2¼" h...**45.00**
Apple Tree Boy, 1972-79,
   10" h. ....**500.00 to 600.00**
Apple Tree Girl, 1940-57,
   4" h. ....**150.00 to 200.00**
Apple Tree Girl, 1956-68, 4" h. **106.00**
Apple Tree Girl, 1972-79, 4" h. **80.00**
Apple Tree Girl, 1972-79, 6" h. **123.00**

Apple Tree Girl table lamp,
1972-79, 7½" h. **395.00**
Apple Tree Boy & Girl, 1956-68,
6" h., pr. **180.00**
Apple Tree Boy & Girl, 1972-79,
10½" h., pr. ....**1,000.00 to 1,200.00**
Auf Wiedersehen, 1972-79, 5" h. **125.00**
Autumn Harvest, 1972-79, 4¾" h. **117.00**
Baker, 1940-57, 4¾" h. **168.00**
Band Leader, 1940-57, 5" h. **185.00**
Band Leader, 1956-68,
5" h. ....**150.00 to 175.00**
Band Leader, 1972-79, 5" h. **100.00**
Barnyard Hero, 1963-71, 4" h. **90.00**
Barnyard Hero, 1972-79, 4" h. **87.00**
Barnyard Hero, 1934-49, 5½" h **550.00**
Barnyard Hero, 1940-57,
5½" h ....**375.00 to 400.00**
Barnyard Hero, 1972-79,
5½" h. **165.00**
Bashful, 1972-79, 4¾" h....**100.00 to 125.00**
Begging His Share, 1934-49,
5½" h. ....**550.00 to 600.00**
Be Patient, 1963-71,
6¼" h. ....**125.00 to 150.00**
Be Patient, 1972-79, 6¼" h...............**144.00**
Bird Duet, 1940-57, 4" h....**100.00 to 150.00**
Birthday Serenade, reverse mold,
1956-68, 4¼" h. ....**300.00 to 350.00**
Birthday Serenade, reverse mold,
1956-68, 5¼" h. **400.00**
Birthday Serenade, 1956-68,
4¼" h. **146.00**
Blessed Event, 1956-68, 5½" h........**275.00**
Book Worm, 1940-57,
4" h. ....**220.00 to 260.00**
Book Worm, 1940-57,
5½" h. ....**325.00 to 425.00**
Book Worm, 1972-1979, 5½" h. **143.00**
Book Worm, 1972-79,
9" h. ....**750.00 to 775.00**
Boots, 1972-79, 5½" h. **85.00**
Boots, 1956-68, 6½" h.......**175.00 to 225.00**
Boy with Bird ashtray, 1972-79,
6½" h...**95.00**
Boy with Toothache, 1940-57,
5½" h...**225.00**
Boy with Toothache, 1956-68,
5½" h...**175.00**
Boy with Toothache, 1972-79,
5½" h...**125.00**
Builder, 1963-71, 5½" h.....................**155.00**
Busy Student, 1963-71, 4¼" h. **100.00**
Candlelight, long candle, 1940-57,
6¾" h. ....**550.00 to 575.00**
Candlelight, 1963-71, 6¾" h.............**120.00**
Chef, Hello, 1972-79, 7" h. **150.00**
Chicken-Licken, 1972-79, 4¾" h........**150.00**
Chick Girl, 1940-57, 3½" h **150.00**
Chick Girl, 1956-68, 3½" h **125.00**
Chick Girl, 1972-79, 3½" h..**75.00 to 100.00**
Chick Girl, 1934-49, 4¼" h. **450.00**
Chick Girl, 1956-68,
4¼" h. ....**150.00 to 175.00**

Chick Girl, 1972-79, 4¼" h. **138.00**
Chimney Sweep, 1940-57, 4" h........**138.00**
Chimney Sweep, 1972-79, 4" h..........**65.00**
Chimney Sweep, 1940-57,
5½" h. ....**200.00 to 225.00**
Chimney Sweep, 1972-79, 5½" h......**100.00**
Christ Child, from Nativity set,
1972-79, 1½ x 3¾"............................**35.00**
Confidentially, 1972-79, 5½" h. **162.00**
Congratulations (no socks),
1934-49, 6" h. **390.00**
Coquettes, 1972-79, 5" h...................**144.00**
Culprits, 1940-57, 6¼" h....................**245.00**
Dealer display plaque, 1972-79,
4 x 5½" ....**70.00 to 90.00**
Doctor, 1934-49, 4¾" h. **252.00**
Doll Mother, 1934-49, 4¾" h. **600.00**
Doll Mother, 1956-68, 4¾" h. **148.00**
Duet, 1934-49, 5" h............**350.00 to 400.00**
Duet, 1956-68, 5" h. **175.00**
Easter Greetings, 1972-79, 5½" h. ...**115.00**
Easter Time, 1972-79, 4" h. **125.00**
Farewell, 1940-57,
4¾" h. ....**200.00 to 250.00**
Farm Boy, 1940-57,
5" h. ....**200.00 to 225.00**
Farm Boy, 1956-68, 5" h...................**150.00**
Farm Boy, 1972-79, 5" h...................**130.00**
Favorite Pet, 1963-71, 4½" h.............**160.00**
Favorite Pet, 1972-79, 4½" h.............**140.00**
Feeding Time, 1940-57,
4¼" h. ....**250.00 to 300.00**
Feeding Time, 1940-57, 5½" h.........**275.00**
Feeding Time, 1963-71, 5½" h.........**165.00**
Feeding Time, 1972-79, 5½" h.........**138.00**
Festival Harmony, w/mandolin,
1940-57, 10¾" h. **795.00**
Festival Harmony, w/mandolin,
1972-79, 10¼" h. **240.00**
Flower Madonna, w/color, 1956-68,
8¼" h. ....**200.00 to 250.00**
Flower Madonna, white, 1940-57,
9½" h. **225.00**
Flower Madonna, white, 1956-68,
13" h. **240.00**
Flower Vendor, 1972-79, 5¼" h. **125.00**
Follow the Leader, 1972-79,
7" h. ....**550.00 to 600.00**
For Father, 1940-57, 5½" h. **245.00**
For Mother, 1972-79, 5" h. **102.00**
Friends, 1940-57, 5" h.......**250.00 to 300.00**
Friends, 1956-68, 5" h. **135.00**
Friends, 1972-79, 5" h. **114.00**
Friends, 1956-68, 10¾" h. **975.00**
Friends, 1972-79,
10¾" h. ....**600.00 to 650.00**
Gay Adventure, 1972-79, 5" h...........**102.00**
Girl with Fir Tree candlestick,
1940-57, 3½" h................................**60.00**
Girl with Fir Tree candlestick,
1972-79, 3½" h. **33.00**
Girl with Nosegay, 1940-57, 3½" h....**70.00**
Girl with Trumpet, 1972-79, 2¼" h. **45.00**

Globe Trotter, 1956-68, 5" h. **150.00**
Going to Grandma's, 1972-79,
oval base, 6" h. ....**200.00 to 250.00**
Good Friends, 1940-57, 4" h. **195.00**
Good Friends, 1956-68,
4" h. ....**125.00 to 150.00**
Good Hunting, 1972-79, 5" h. **120.00**
Good Shepherd, 1934-49, 6¼" h. **300.00**
Good Shepherd, 1956-68, 6¼" h. **180.00**
Good Shepherd font, 1956-68,
2¼ x 4¾". **30.00**
Goose Girl, 1934-49,
4" h. ....**275.00 to 300.00**
Goose Girl, 1940-57, 4" h. **175.00**
Goose Girl, 1956-68, 4" h. **115.00**
Goose Girl, 1972-79, 4" h. **80.00**
Goose Girl, 1934-49,
4¾" h. ....**375.00 to 400.00**
Goose Girl, 1940-57,
4¾" h. ....**200.00 to 225.00**
Happiness, 1940-57, 4¾" h. **150.00**
Happy Days, 1956-68, 4¼" h............**120.00**
Happy Days, 1940-57,
5¼" h. ....**300.00 to 325.00**
Happy Pastime,1934-49, 3½" h. **275.00**
Happy Pastime, 1940-57, 3½" h. **240.00**
Happy Pastime, 1956-68, 3½" h. **123.00**
Happy Pastime, 1972-79, 3½" h. **80.00**
Happy Pastime ashtray, 1940-57,
3½ x 6¼" ....**150.00 to 175.00**
Happy Pastime ashtray, 1956-68,
3½ x 6¼" **125.00**
Happy Pastime ashtray, 1972-79,
3½ x 6¼" **70.00**
Happy Traveler, 1940-57, 5" h. **135.00**
Happy Traveler, 1956-68, 5" h. **96.00**
Happy Traveler, 1940-57, 8" h. **500.00**
Happy Traveler, 1972-79, 8" h. **210.00**
Hear Ye, Hear Ye, 1956-68,
5" h..**145.00**
Hear Ye, Hear Ye, 1956-68,
6" h. ....**165.00 to 175.00**

Hear Ye, Hear Ye

Hear Ye, Hear Ye, 1972-79,
6" h. (ILLUS.) **120.00**

Hear Ye, Hear Ye, 1972-79,
7½" h...**250.00**
Heavenly Angel, 1934-49,
4¼" h. ....**175.00 to 200.00**
Heavenly Angel, 1956-68, 4¼" h. **93.00**
Heavenly Angel, 1972-79, 4¼" h. **63.00**
Heavenly Angel, 1956-68,
6" h. ....**125.00 to 150.00**
Heavenly Angel, 1972-79,
6" h. ....**100.00 to 150.00**
Heavenly Protection, 1956-68,
6¾" h..**270.00**
Heavenly Protection, 1934-49,
9¼" h. **750.00**
Heavenly Protection, 1956-68,
9¼" h. ....**600.00 to 650.00**
Heavenly Protection, 1963-71,
9¼" h. **500.00**
Herald Angels candleholder,
1956-68, 2¼ x 4"...............................**144.00**
Home From Market, 1940-57,
4¾" h. ....**150.00 to 175.00**
Home From Market, 1956-68,
4¾" h. ....**80.00 to 100.00**
Home From Market, 1963-71,
4¾" h. ....**80.00 to 90.00**
Home From Market, 1972-79,
4¾" h..**75.00**
Homeward Bound, w/post, 1963-71,
5¼" h..**450.00**
Homeward Bound, 1972-79,
5¼" h..**195.00**
Joyful, 1956-68, 4" h............................**78.00**
Joyful ashtray, 1972-79, 3½ x 6".......**84.00**
Joyful candy box, 1956-68, 6¼" h....**120.00**
Joyous News, Angel w/horn
candleholder, 1956-68, 2" h..............**40.00**
Joyous News, Angel w/lute
candleholder, 1956-68, 2" h..............**37.00**

Joyous News

Joyous News, Angel w/horn
candleholder, 1940-57, 2¾" h.
(ILLUS.) **120.00**
Just Resting, 1940-57,
4" h. ....**150.00 to 175.00**
Just Resting, 1956-68, 3¾" h...........**110.00**
Just Resting, 1972-79, 3¾" h.............**78.00**

Just Resting, 1972-79, 5" h..............**138.00**
Latest News, 1934-49,
  5¼" h. ....**650.00 to 750.00**
Latest News, inscribed "Munchener
  Presse", 1940-57, 5¼" h. **275.00**
Let's Sing, 1934-49,
  3¼" h...........................**200.00 to 250.00**
Let's Sing, 1972-79, 3¼" h. **66.00**
Let's Sing, 1940-57, 3⅞" h. **150.00**
Let's Sing ashtray, 1972-79,
  3½ x 6¾"...**84.00**
Letter to Santa Claus, 1972-79,
  7" h..**175.00**
Little Cellist, 1972-79, 8" h..............**240.00**
Little Drummer, 1940-57, 4¼" h....**169.00**
Little Fiddler, 1940-57, 4¾" h...........**187.00**
Little Fiddler, 1956-68, 6" h..............**175.00**
Little Fiddler, 1972-79,
  10¾" h. ....**550.00 to 600.00**
Little Fiddler plaque, 1934-49,
  5 x 5½"..**240.00**
Little Gardener, 1940-57,
  4" h. ....**125.00 to 150.00**
Little Gardener, 1956-68, 4" h...........**88.00**
Little Goat Herder, 1972-79,
  4¾" h..**85.00**
Little Helper, 1940-57, 4¼" h. **109.00**
Little Helper, 1956-68, 4¼" h. **83.00**
Little Hiker, 1956-68, 4¼" h...............**92.00**
Little Hiker, 1972-79, 4¼" h...............**60.00**
Little Hiker, 1940-57, 5½" h..............**186.00**
Little Hiker, 1956-68, 5½" h..............**168.00**
Little Hiker, 1972-79, 5½" h..............**114.00**
Little Scholar, 1972-79, 5½" h. **108.00**
Little Shopper, 1940-57, 4¾" h...........**142.00**
Little Sweeper, 1940-57, 4½" h...........**150.00**
Little Sweeper, 1956-68, 4½" h...........**87.50**
Little Tailor, 1972-79, 5½" h..............**162.00**
Little Thrifty, 1940-57, 5" h. **200.00**
Little Thrifty, 1972-79, 5" h. **78.00**
Little Tooter, 1940-57, 3¾" h. **85.00**
Little Tooter, 1963-71, 3¾" h. **75.00**
Lost Sheep, 1972-79, 5½" h...........**75.00**
Lost Stocking, 1972-79, 4¼" h. **76.00**
Lullaby candleholder, 1940-57,
  3½ x 5" **180.00**
Lullaby candleholder, 1972-79,
  3½ x 5" **96.00**
Madonna, praying, standing, no halo,
  w/color, 1940-57, 10¼" h............**100.00**
The Mail is Here, 1940-57, 4¼ x 6" ...**595.00**
March Winds, 1934-49,
  5" h. (ILLUS. top next
  column)............................**350.00 to 375.00**
Meditation, 1963-71, 4¼" h. **90.00**
Meditation, 1934-49,
  5¼" h. ....**350.00 to 375.00**
Meditation, 1972-79, 7" h. **200.00**
Merry Wanderer, 1940-57, 4¼" h......**128.00**
Merry Wanderer, seven button
  version, 1956-68, 4¼" h..................**124.00**
Merry Wanderer, 1972-79,
  4¼" h. ....**75.00 to 100.00**

March Winds

Merry Wanderer, 1934-49,
  4¾" h. ....**325.00 to 350.00**
Merry Wanderer, 1940-57, 4¾" h......**176.00**
Merry Wanderer, 1972-79, 4¾" h......**81.00**
Merry Wanderer, 1934-49, 6¼" h......**400.00**
Merry Wanderer, 1972-79, 6¼" h......**138.00**
Merry Wanderer, 1934-49, 7" h........**672.50**
Merry Wanderer, 1956-68,
  7" h. ....**250.00 to 300.00**
Merry Wanderer, 1972-79, 9½" h......**700.00**
Merry Wanderer, 1956-68,
  11¼" h...**1,105.00**
Mother's Darling, 1934-49, 5½" h....**400.00**
Mother's Darling, 1940-57, 5½" h....**238.00**
Mother's Darling, 1972-79, 5½" h.....**125.00**
Mother's Helper, 1972-79, 5" h........**100.00**
Not For You, 1956-68,
  6" h. ....**450.00 to 475.00**
Not For You, 1972-79, 6" h..............**126.00**
Playmates, 1972-79, 4" h. **90.00**
Playmates, 1940-57, 4½" h. **200.00**
Playmates candy box, 1940-57,
  5¼" h...**346.00**
Postman, 1940-57, 5" h. **250.00**
Postman, 1956-68, 5" h. **150.00**
Puppy Love, 1972-79, 5" h...............**135.00**
Quartet plaque, 1956-68, 6 x 6" **175.00**
Retreat to Safety, 1940-57, 4" h........**170.00**
Retreat to Safety, 1972-79, 5½" h....**155.00**
Run-a-way (The), 1972-79, 5¼" h. **130.00**
St. George, 1956-68, 6¾" h...............**295.00**
School Boy, 1940-57, 5½" h. **180.00**
School Boys, 1972-79,
  10¼" h. ....**1,000.00 to 1,100.00**
School Girl, 1940-57, 5¼" h. **205.00**
School Girls, 1956-68, 9½" h........**1,250.00**
Serenade, 1940-57, 4¾" h. **120.00**
Serenade, 1956-68, 4¾" h. **90.00**
Shepherd's Boy, 1972-79, 5½" h......**122.00**
Signs of Spring, 1940-57, 4" h.........**185.00**
Signs of Spring, 1963-71, 4" h.........**130.00**
Singing Lesson ashtray, 1972-79,
  3½ x 6¼"..**170.00**
Sister, 1972-79, 4¾" h. **78.00**

Skier, 1940-57, 5" h. **185.00**
Skier, 1972-79, 5" h. **117.00**
Smart Little Sister, 1956-68, 4¾" d. .**120.00**
Smart Little Sister, 1972-79, 4¾" d. .**125.00**
Soldier Boy, 1963-71, 6" h. **135.00**
Soldier Boy, 1972-79, 6" h. **110.00**

Spring Dance

Spring Dance, 1972-79,
 6½" h. (ILLUS.)................**350.00 to 400.00**
Star Gazer, 1956-68, 4¾" h. **144.00**
Surprise, 1972-79, 4¼" h.............**70.00**
Sweet Music, 1940-57, 5¼" h............**195.00**
Umbrella Boy, 1940-57,
 4¾" h ....**1,675.00 to 1,725.00**
Umbrella Boy, 1956-68,
 8" h. ....**800.00 to 900.00**
Umbrella Boy, 1963-71, 8" h. **840.00**
Umbrella Girl, 1940-57, 4¾" h........**1,735.00**
Umbrella Girl, 1972-79, 8" h. **735.00**
Village Boy, 1940-57, 4" h...............**105.00**
Volunteers, 1972-79, 5½" h...............**156.00**
Watchful Angel, 1972-79, 6¾" h. **168.00**
Wayside Harmony, 1940-57, 4" h. **193.00**
We Congratulate, 1956-68, 4" h........**120.00**
White Angel font, 1934-49,
 1¾ x 3½" **125.00**
Worship, 1940-57, 5" h....................**325.00**
Worship, 1956-68, 12¾" h................**975.00**

(End of Hummel Section)

HUTSCHENREUTHER

The Hutschenreuther family name is associated with fine German porcelains. Carl Magnus Hutschenreuther established a factory at Hohenberg, Bavaria and was succeeded in this business by his widow and sons, Christian and Lorenz. Lorenz later established a factory in Selb, Bavaria (1857) which was managed by Christian and his son, Albert. The family later purchased factories near Carlsbad (1909), Altwasser, Silesia (1918) and Arzberg,

Bavaria and between 1917 and 1927, acquired at least two additonal factories. The firm, noted for the fine quality wares produced, united all these branches in 1969 and continues in production today

Bowl, 2½" d., figural butterfly on rim ..**$48.00**
Cup & saucer, Blue Onion patt............**26.00**
Figure of a ballerina, green, 9" h........**385.00**
Figure of girl w/borzoi, 8½" h. **400.00**
Figure of nude w/deer 9" h.................**450.00**
Figure, "Flame Dancer," 11½" h. **475.00**
Figure group, model of two kissing
 parakeets, yellow & green, artist-
 signed, 13" d., 8½" h.......................**295.00**
Figure group, nude little girls
 dancing, all-white, artist-signed,
 4" h..**250.00**
Figure group, three cherubs holding
 hands & dancing, artist-signed,
 6¾" h..**300.00**
Figure group, three girls playing Ring
 Around the Rosie **4,540.00**
Figures, porcelain, modeled as an
 exotic female dancer & male
 swordsman partially clad in
 costume, headdress & jewels,
 polychrome glazes accented
 w/gilding, w/the firm's printed marks
 & inscribed "C WERNER," female
 figure painted "F," male figure
 painted "M," tallest 12½" h., pr.
 (restoration to one finger) **552.00**
Model of a Siamese cat, cream
 w/brown & blue eyes, 7½" h. **295.00**
Plate, bread & butter, Blue Onion
 patt...**15.50**
Plate, dinner, 10½" d., Blue Onion
 patt...**24.00**
Plate, salad, Blue Onion patt...............**16.50**
Platter, 10½ x 17", h.p. flowers on blue
 ground..**40.00**

IMARI

This is a multicolor ware that originated in Japan, was copied by the Chinese, and imitated by the English and European potteries. It was decorated in overglaze enamel and underglaze-blue. Made in Hizen Province and Arita, much of it was exported through the port of Imari in Japan. Imari often has brocade patterns.

Bowl, 15" d., deep floriform, the
 interior & exterior decorated
 w/naturalistic floral designs
 separated by scrolling floral panels,
 all in underglaze-blue, iron-red,
 green & gold, late l9th c. **$920.00**

Charger, fish scene in center surrounded by floral border decoration, ca. 1870, 15¾" d. **425.00**

Dish, modeled in the form of a stylized fish, decorated in underglaze-blue, enamels & gilt w/a ho-o bird & carp amid plants painted on the backs of two conforming fish, late 19th c., 10" l. **575.00**

Platter, 23" d., fish-form, late l9th c. (small edge chips)............................**460.00**

IRONSTONE

The first successful ironstone was patented in 1813 by C.J. Mason in England. The body contains iron slag incorporated with the clay. Other potters imitated Mason's ware and today much hard, thick ware is lumped under the term ironstone. Earlier it was called by various names, including graniteware. Both plain white and decorated wares were made throughout the 19th century. Tea Leaf Lustre ironstone was made by several firms.

GENERAL

Ironstone Model of a Cat

Coffeepot, cov., low foot on paneled body w/globular base & slender upper portion, gooseneck spout, black floral transfer-printed decoration w/red & green enamel & orange lustre, 10½" h.....................**$198.00**

Coffeepot, cov., Summertime patt, brown on white transfer-printed design, T. & R. Boote **89.00**

Coffeepot, cov., Wheat patt., all-white, Wilkinson, England................**125.00**

Creamer, serpent handle, "gaudy" floral design, marked "Davenport Stone China," 4" h...........................**115.00**

Cup, handleless, Laurel patt., all-white, J. Wedgwood...........................**25.00**

Cup & saucer, miniature, "gaudy," Urn & Flower patt. (cup stained) **242.00**

Cup & saucer, Summertime patt., brown on white, transfer-printed design, T. & R. Boote.....................**25.00**

Dish, square, low sides, "gaudy" floral design, marked "Mason's England," 8¼" sq..**121.00**

Model of a cat, seated animal w/tail curled around the body, decorated overall w/a paisley-like design in green w/bright enamels & heavy gilt, late 19th c., 12" h. (ILLUS.)...........**2,990.00**

Pitcher, miniature, 3⅛" h., paneled sides w/a bulbous base & wide gently flaring neck, transfer-printed Imari-style patt. in blue & red, Mason, ca. 1860 ....**170.50**

Pitcher, 8¼" h., paneled body, Indian patt., green transfer-printed floral design (stains & short hairlines at top of handle) **159.50**

Pitcher, 9" h., polychrome Chusan patt., Wedgwood & Co. **175.00**

Plate, 6½" d., Pearl patt., all-white, Turner & Tomkinson **40.00**

Plate, 8" d., Summertime patt., brown on white, transfer-printed design, T. & R. Boote **20.00**

Plate, 8½" d., "gaudy," Urn & Flowers patt. (stains & minor wear) **165.00**

Plate, 8½" d., Pearl patt., all-white, Turner & Tomkinson **40.00**

Plate, 9" d., "gaudy" floral design w/gilt trim, marked "Ironstone Warrented" w/crown (minor wear)....**132.00**

Plate, 9½" d., Lily of the Valley patt., all-white, Fenton **59.00**

Plate, 9½" d., Pearl patt., all-white, Turner & Tomkinson **49.00**

Platter, 12¼" l., octagonal, "gaudy" vintage design in underglaze-blue w/black, yellow, ochre & two shades of green enameling (stains) **275.00**

Platter, 13½" l., Pearl patt., all-white, Turner & Tomkinson **59.00**

Platter, 15¾" l., "gaudy" floral decoration w/strawberries (minor wear & stains, scratch in one strawberry) **715.00**

Platter, 17¾" l., rectangular w/cut corners, the center w/a stylized Oriental landscape w/figure & temple, scroll band border, blue & white, marked "Oregon Chinese Porcelaine," mid-19th c. (ILLUS. top next page)............................**478.50**

Serving bowl, all-white, Alcock, 9½" sq...**50.00**

Platter with Oriental Scene

Soap dish, Johnson Brothers, England...**9.00**

Soup tureen, cov., President shape, all-white, J. Edwards....................... **275.00**

Soup tureen, cover & undertray, squatty bulbous oval body raised on a pedestal base, the top w/a flaring rim supporting a domed cover w/loop handle, loop end handles, conforming undertray w/tab end handles, India Flowers patt., blue florals w/gilt trim, 12" h., the set (stains, minor hairlines)....................**770.00**

Sugar bowl, cov., Pearl patt., all-white, Turner & Tomkinson................**75.00**

Sugar bowl, cov., Summertime patt., brown on white transfer-printed design, T. & R. Boote.........................**65.00**

Teapot, cov., Hebe patt., all-white **165.00**

Teapot, cov., Poppy patt., all-white....**195.00**

Teapot, cov., Stafford patt., all-white..**195.00**

Teapot, cov., Sydenham patt., all-white **250.00**

Toothbrush holder w/drain, Moss Rose patt., Meakin.......................**75.00**

Tureen, cov., squatty oval body raised on an oval foot, leaf-molded end loop handles, low domed cover w/leaf-molded loop handle, brown transfer-printed design of small exotic birds & exotic flowers on sides & cover, the base interior w/a scene of a parrot on a flowering branch w/a pagoda in the distance, ca. 1800, 7 x 12", 5½" h. (yellowing & overall light crazing) **33.00**

Tureen, cov., wide & waisted octagonal body raised on a flaring foot, molded scroll rim handles, stepped & domed cover w/pointed finial, decorated w/wide blue & white stripes, ca. 1850, 11" h. (chips) **385.00**

Vegetable dish, cov., flaring oval body raised on a flaring base, domed cover w/pine cone finial, h.p. w/colorful stylized floral bands in

Decorated Vegetable Dish

red, blue, teal, green & black, mid-19th c., chips, 9½" l. (ILLUS.) **82.50**

Vegetable dish, cov., Laurel patt., all-white, J. Wedgwood, 10" d. **65.00**

Wash bowl & pitcher, all-white, Hughes, Burslem, 2 pcs....................**95.00**

Wash bowl & pitcher, all-white, Royal Alcock, 2 pcs. **225.00**

TEA LEAF IRONSTONE

Apple bowl, round w/ruffled sides, Alfred Meakin....................................**225.00**

Apple bowl, round fluted bowl on low pedestal foot, Anthony Shaw **475.00**

Baker, rectangular, Alfred Meakin, 5 x 7"...**45.00**

Baker, oblong, Micratex by Adams, ca. 1960s, 10" l. **35.00**

Bone dish, scalloped crescent-shape, Johnson Bros. **45.00**

Bone dish, scalloped crescent shape, Mayer China Co., Beaver Falls, Pennsylvania **35.00**

Boston egg cup, Alfred Meakin (fine hairline inside foot)..........................**325.00**

Bowl, serving, 10" d., Mellor-Taylor **85.00**

Butter dish, cover & liner, square, Arthur Wilkinson..............................**110.00**

Butter pat, round, unsigned..................**8.00**

Cake plate, square, Bamboo patt., Alfred Meakin.....................................**55.00**

Cake plate, round w/molded scrolls at sides, Anthony Shaw (lustre wear) **90.00**

Cake plate, square, Mayer China Co., Beaver Falls, Pennsylvania **110.00**

Casserole, cov., round, Homer Laughlin's "Kitchen Kraft" line, ca. 1930s, 10" d. **40.00**

Chamberpot, cov., Cable patt., Anthony Shaw (hairline underside of cover) **175.00**

Chamberpot, cov., Chinese patt., Anthony Shaw................................**400.00**

Chamberpot, cov., W. & E. Corn (small rim chips).................................**75.00**

Chamberpot, cov. Peerless patt., John Edwards **300.00**

Chamberpot, cov., Square Ridged patt., Mellor-Taylor..........................**175.00**

Chamberpot, cov., Square Ridged patt., J. Wedgwood **175.00**

Coffeepot, cov., Fish Hook patt.,
Alfred Meakin.....................................**120.00**
Coffeepot, cov., Lily of the Valley
patt., Anthony Shaw..........................**500.00**
Coffeepot, cov., Sunburst patt.,
Arthur Wilkinson................................**130.00**
Compote, open, 7" d. round, ringed
pedestal base, Anthony Shaw (slight
discoloration)...................................**175.00**
Compote, open, 8" sq., Red Cliff, ca.
1960s...**110.00**
Compote, open, Square Ridged patt.,
Powell & Bishop, gold lustre.............**60.00**
Creamer, miniature, ovoid body
tapering to a flaring rim, Sterling
Pottery, gold lustre, 3½" h..................**45.00**
Cup, handleless, Lily of the Valley
patt...**90.00**
Cup & saucer, child's, Anthony Shaw
(hairline in saucer) **180.00**
Cup & saucer, handled, Chelsea
patt., Johnson Bros. (lustre wear)......**65.00**
Cup & saucer, handled, conical,
Alfred Meakin.....................................**45.00**
Cup plate, Alfred Meakin.....................**40.00**
Cuspidor, figural head spouts on
each side, 8" d., 4" h........................**595.00**
Cuspidor, round w/molded side
spouts, Anthony Shaw (upper part of
one spout cracked) **1,100.00**
Doughnut stand, square, Mayer
China Co., Beaver Falls,
Pennsylvania **130.00**
Egg cup, unmarked (small chip repair
on bottom)...**325.00**
Ewer, ornate footed shape w/scrolled
rim, decorated by Ruth Sayers, ca.
1980...**55.00**
Gravy boat, Cable patt., Anthony
Shaw...**90.00**
Gravy boat, Fish Hook patt., Alfred
Meakin...**90.00**
Gravy boat, Lily of the Valley patt.,
Anthony Shaw....................................**230.00**
Gravy boat, Simple Square patt.,
Arthur Wilkinson..................................**45.00**
Gravy boat, Square Ridged patt.,
Powell & Bishop, gold lustre..............**65.00**
Mixing bowl, Homer Laughlin
"Kitchen Kraft" line, ca.1930s,
10" d...**40.00**
Pie plate, Homer Laughlin "Kitchen
Kraft" line, 9½" d. (some wear)..........**40.00**
Pitcher, milk, Bamboo patt., Alfred
Meakin...**155.00**
Pitcher, water, Maidenhair Fern patt.,
Arthur Wilkinson (mild discoloration,
small chip repair) **275.00**
Plate, 6¾" d., Lily of the Valley patt......**37.50**
Plates, 9" d., Alfred Meakin, set of 6....**80.00**
Plates, 9" d., Anthony Shaw, set of 6
(mild crazing)......................................**60.00**
Plate, 9¾"d., Lily of the Valley patt.,
Anthony Shaw....................................**35.00**

Plates, 10" d., Micratex by Adams,
ca. 1960s, set of 8 ....**140.00**
Platter, 14" rectangle, Anthony
Shaw...**50.00**
Platter, 11½ x 16" rectangle, Arthur
Wilkinson **30.00**
Relish dish, footed, oval, Shaw 1856
- Fan patt., Anthony Shaw (shows
wear)...**400.00**
Relish dish, Sunburst patt., Arthur
Wilkinson **65.00**
Salt & pepper shakers, baluster-
shaped, Empress patt., Micratex by
Adams, ca. 1960s, pr......................**275.00**
Sauce dish, Anthony Shaw **10.00**
Sauce tureen, cov., Cable patt.,
Anthony Shaw....................................**230.00**
Sauce tureen, cov., Columbia patt.,
unmarked (lustre worn to green)......**150.00**
Sauce tureen, cover, undertray &
ladle, Bamboo patt., Alfred Meakin
(chips on inner lid rim, chip on
foot)..**285.00**
Shaving mug, Lily of the Valley patt.,
hotel room number on front in
copper lustre **135.00**
Soap dish, cov., Bamboo patt., Alfred
Meakin **190.00**
Soup plate, Lily of the Valley patt.,
Anthony Shaw....................................**55.00**
Soup tureen, cov., rectangular,
Square Ridged patt., Powell &
Bishop, gold lustre, 12" l. **70.00**
Sugar bowl, cov., Bamboo patt.,
Alfred Meakin.....................................**90.00**
Sugar bowl, cov., Fig Cousin patt.,
Davenport, pink lustre trim...............**450.00**
Sugar bowl, cov., Fish Hook patt.,
Alfred Meakin (crazing).....................**50.00**
Sugar bowl, cov., Simple Square
patt., J. Wedgwood **80.00**
Sugar bowl, cov., Simple Square
patt., Arthur Wilkinson (small nick on
inner rim)..**75.00**
Teapot, cov., Bamboo patt., Alfred
Meakin **140.00**
Teapot, cov., Empress patt.,
Micratex by Adams, ca. 1960s.........**180.00**
Teapot, cov., Simple Square patt.,
Henry Burgess **155.00**
Teapot, cov., Square Ridged patt.,
Red Cliff, ca. 1960s **80.00**
Tea set: cov. teapot, cov. sugar bowl
& creamer; Hexagon patt., Anthony
Shaw, 3 pcs. (chips & hairline in
creamer) **425.00**
Tea set: cov. teapot, cov. sugar bowl
& creamer; Square Ridged patt.,
Powell & Bishop, gold lustre,
3 pcs...**190.00**
Toothbrush vase, Bamboo patt.,
Alfred Meakin.....................................**120.00**
Vegetable dish, cov., square,

Bamboo patt., Alfred Meakin,
10" w. **90.00**

Vegetable dish, cov., rectangular,
Fish Hook patt., Alfred Meakin, 10" l.
(small inside rim chip) **85.00**

Vegetable dish, cov., square, Simple
Square patt., Arthur Wilkinson,
10" w. **90.00**

Vegetable dish, cov., rectangular,
Sunburst patt., Arthur Wilkinson,
10" l. **60.00**

Vegetable dish, open, oval, Lily of
the Valley patt., Anthony Shaw,
10" l. **230.00**

Wash pitcher, Square Ridged patt.,
Powell & Bishop, gold lustre **80.00**

Washbowl & pitcher, Bamboo patt.,
Alfred Meakin, 2 pcs. **275.00**

Washbowl & pitcher, Fish Hook
patt., Alfred Meakin, 2 pcs. (hairline
in bowl base)................................**225.00**

Washbowl & pitcher, squared shape
pitcher, Arthur Wilkinson (tiny spout
nick) **300.00**

Waste bowl, Mellor-Taylor.................**90.00**

TEA LEAF VARIANTS

Cake plate, porcelain, Cloverleaf
patt., unmarked................................**35.00**

Coffeepot, cov., Niagara shape,
Chelsea grape lustre patt., Edward
Walley **190.00**

Cup, handleless, Morning Glory patt.,
Elmore & Forster............................**65.00**

Cup & saucer, handleless, child's,
Teaberry patt., J. Clementson **425.00**

Cup & saucer, handleless, Ceres
patt., copper lustre trim, Elmore &
Forster **40.00**

Cup & saucer, handleless, Cinque-
foil patt., unmarked (slight glaze
flaw) **40.00**

Cup & saucer, handleless, Laurel
Wreath patt., copper lustre trim,
Elmore & Forster............................**125.00**

Cup & saucer, handleless, Pinwheel
patt., Edward Walley........................**65.00**

Cuspidor, Tobacco Leaf patt.,
unmarked....................................**650.00**

Demitasse set: cov. coffeepot, cov.
sugar bowl, creamer & 4 cups &
saucers; lustred triple leaf design
w/clusters of small dot blossoms,
Gray's Pottery, England, ca. 1930s,
the set..**120.00**

Mug, child's, Pepperleaf patt.,
Elmore & Forster............................**350.00**

Pitcher, 6" h., Morning Glory patt.,
Elmore & Forster............................**340.00**

Pitcher, 7½" h., Teaberry patt.,
J. Clementson................................**610.00**

Pitcher, 8¼" h., Gothic shape, lustre
band trim, Red Cliff, ca. 1960s **55.00**

Pitcher, milk, 9" h., Heavy Square
shape, Teaberry patt.,
J. Clementson................................**220.00**

Pitcher, 9½" h., Plain Round shape,
Teaberry patt., Clementson (bottom
spider).......................................**205.00**

Plates, 8½" w., Gothic shape,
Pinwheel patt., Edward Walley, set
of 4..**125.00**

Platter, 17" oval, Teaberry patt.,
J. Clementson................................**85.00**

Relish dish, mitten-shaped, Ceres
patt., copper lustre trim, Elmore &
Forster (base rim chip)....................**225.00**

Relish dish, mitten-shaped, Teaberry
patt., unmarked..............................**510.00**

Relish dish, oblong diamond-shaped,
Laurel Wreath patt., copper lustre
trim, Elmore & Forster....................**210.00**

Sauce tureen, cover & undertray,
Portland shape, Morning Glory patt.,
Elmore & Forster, 3 pcs. **445.00**

Shaving mug, Teaberry patt.,
J. Clementson, 3½" h....................**2,000.00**

Slop jar, Portland shape, Reverse
Teaberry patt., Elmore & Forster
(no cover, hairline) **775.00**

Teapot, cov., Crystal shape,
Pepperleaf patt., Elmore &
Forster **260.00**

Tea set: cov. teapot, cov. sugar bowl
& creamer; porcelain, Cloverleaf
patt., 3 pcs. **70.00**

Vegetable dish, cov., oval, Teaberry
patt., J. Clementson........................**350.00**

Vegetable dish, open, oval, Laurel
Wreath patt., copper lustre trim,
Elmore & Forster, 7" l....................**210.00**

Wash pitcher, Teaberry patt., J.
Clementson, 13" h. **300.00**

(End of Ironstone Section)

JASPER WARE
(Non–Wedgwood)

*Jasper ware is fine-grained exceedingly
hard stoneware made by including barium
sulphate in the clay and was first devised
by Josiah Wedgwood, who utilized it for
the body of many of his fine cameo blue-
and-white and green-and-white pieces. It
was subsequently produced by other potters
in England and Germany, notably William
Adams & Sons, and is in production at the
present. Also see WEDGWOOD - JASPER.*

Pitcher, 5⅞" h., tapering cylindrical
body, rope twist handle, white relief
dancing classical ladies on dark
blue, pale blue base band, glossy

finish, marked "Dudson Bros.
England," ca. 1900..........................**$55.00**
Plate, 5½" d., white relief bust of an
Indian Chief in full headdress on
green, white relief beaded swag
border, Germany................................**39.00**
Plate, 7½" d., white relief bust of an
Indian Chief in full headdress on
green, Germany **35.00**
Plaque, pierced to hang, oval, white
relief figure of Indian in full dress
taming horse, border decorated
w/white relief figures of hatchets,
feathers & headdress on blue
ground, signed, "Heubach,"
Germany, 6½ x 8½" **145.00**
Plaque, pierced to hang, white relief
figure of man w/mandolin
serenading lady on blue,
Germany, 6" w. **40.00**
Vase, handled, 3½" h., white relief
classical figures on blue....................**22.00**

LIMOGES

Limoges Cake Plate

*Numerous factories produced china in
Limoges, France, with major production in
the 19th century. Some pieces listed below
are identified by the name of the maker or
the mark of the factory. Although the
famed Haviland Company was located in
Limoges, wares bearing their marks are
not included in this listing. Also see
HAVILAND.*

An excellent reference is The Collector's
Encyclopedia of Limoges Porcelain, Second
Edition, *by Mary Frank Gaston (Collector
Books, 1992).*

Cake plate w/open handles, gently
scalloped rim, decorated on each
side w/clusters of pink & red & pink
& yellow roses & green leaves

against a creamy white ground, a
wide dark green border band w/gilt
rose sprigs on the inner edge,
10½" d. (ILLUS.) **$45.00**
Dessert set: cov. coffeepot, creamer
& sugar bowl, waste bowl, two cake
servers, eight cups & saucers, ten
dessert plates & twelve lemon
dishes; ornately molded shapes
w/gold floral decoration & raised
outlines, pale aqua shading to white
ground, 44 pcs. **475.00**
Dresser set: cov. footed hair receiver
& cov. footed box on 9½ x 12⅞"
tray; decorated w/pink flowers on
blue & cream pastel ground, gold
trimmed rim on tray, boxes w/gold
feet, handles & trim, the set **195.00**

Limoges Charger with Birds

Charger, round w/lightly scalloped rim
& molded long scrolls & dots around
the edge, decorated w/a pair of
partridges against a shaded green
to pale yellow ground, wild roses &
leaves above & below the birds,
artist-signed, 13¾" d.
(ILLUS.) **225.00**

Fine Limoges Coffee Service

Coffee service: tall ovoid cov.
coffeepot, matching cov. sugar &
creamer & eight cups & saucers;
each piece decorated near the rim
w/a purple, black & white continuous
scene of an owl & forest, gold

handles, spout & finials, marked,
coffeepot 9" h., the set (ILLUS.).......**595.00**
Fish set: platter & nine plates; h.p.
fish & underwater plants w/lavish
gold trim, 10 pcs. **1,895.00**

Game Plate with Ducks

Game plate, round w/scalloped &
scroll-molded gilt rim, decorated in
color w/a large flying duck & a
smaller duck landing in the water,
plants in the background, pale blue,
green & tan ground, artist-signed,
11¼" d. (ILLUS.) **225.00**
Game plates, pierced to hang, h.p.
colorful pheasants on one & a pair
of quail on the other, w/pastel
natural colored background, purple
berries & green leaves on border,
9½" d., pr. **265.00**

Game Plate with a Quail

Game plates, each w/scalloped gilt
border, each decorated w/a large
quail against a shaded pink to
yellow to green or orange to yellow

to green ground, artist-signed,
10⅛" d., Coronet - Limoges, pr.
(ILLUS. of one) **325.00**
Pitcher, 11" h., ribbed, decorated
w/colorful berries & grapes **295.00**

Limoges Plaque with Fruit

Plaque, pierced to hang, scalloped
scroll- and bead-molded gold
border, h.p. w/a grouping of
peaches & pear against a shaded
green to beige ground, artist-signed,
12½" d. (ILLUS.) **245.00**
Plaque, pierced to hang, "The Music
Lesson," h.p. medallion portrait of
two women sitting in the forest
playing a lute, a dog in the
foreground, dark green w/heavy
gold trim, ca. 1900, 10 x 14" **550.00**
Plates, 6½" d., gold reticulated
border, decorated w/garlands of
dainty pink flowers, set of 6 (Jean
Pouyat) **90.00**
Plates, 9" d., angled corners, each
decorated w/h.p. underwater scene
of different fish & seaweed, set of 4...**65.00**

Limoges Plate with Roses

Plate, 10⅜" d., pierced to hang, scalloped gold border, one h.p. w/a cluster of large yellow & red roses, the other w/large pink & red roses, green leaves & shaded, brown, blue & pale yellow ground, pr. (ILLUS. of one) **265.00**

Limoges Hanging Plate

Plate, 10¼" d., pierced to hang, scalloped & scroll-molded gold edge, h.p. w/a large cluster of pink & dark yellow roses & green leaves against a shaded green to pale yellow ground (ILLUS.) **110.00**

Ramekins w/underplates, decorated w/h.p. green flowers, gold border, ca. 1894-1930, set of 12 (Charles Ahrenfeldt - France) **250.00**

LIVERPOOL

Liverpool Creamware Pitcher

Liverpool is most often used as a generic term for fine earthenware products, usually of creamware or pearlware, produced at numerous potteries in this English city during the late 18th and early 19th centuries. Many examples, especially pitchers, were decorated with transfer-printed patriotic designs aimed specifically at the American buying public.

Bowl, 7" d., creamware, the interior w/a printed compass design in green, the exterior w/transfer-printed vignettes & verses including "From Rocks and Sands and every ill may God preserve the sailor still," early 19th c. (minor discoloration) **$1,380.00**

Pitcher, jug-type, 7½" h., transfer-printed w/a scene of a ship flying the American flag & "Success to the Trade;" on the reverse a man & woman flanking a shield & "the farmers arms;" flower motif under spout, the whole enhanced w/polychrome enamels & gilt, 19th c. (cracks around spout) **575.00**

Pitcher, jug-type, 7¾" h., transfer-printed in black on one side w/a scene of logging on a hill above shipbuilding at the water's edge within husk-bordered roundel surmounting a verse, on the reverse w/the naval battle between the French frigate L'Insurgent & the American frigate Constellation inscribed on its transom "CONSTALATION" (sic) above an inscription recording the encounter "Feby the 12th 1799," ca. 1800 (some discoloration, chip on spout, minor rim chips) **2,185.00**

Pitcher, jug-type, 8" h., creamware, transfer-printed w/hunting scene, inscribed "death of the fox from a much admired painting in the exhibition at the Royal Academy;" on reverse is a sly gentleman w/£20,000 bag above the inscription "twenty thousand I've got - how lucky's my lot." signed below "Thos Fletcher Shelton," early 19th c. (hairline & repaired spout)....**920.00**

Pitcher, jug-type, 8¼" h., creamware, transfer-printed w/wreathed portrait of Washington, reverse w/funeral urn, under spout "A man without example A patriot without reproach," early 19th c., restoration (ILLUS.) **1,495.00**

Pitcher, jug-type, 8⅞" h., black transfer-printed designs, one side w/an oval reserve of a seated figure of Columbia holding a staff & shield below the inscription "May Commerce Flourish," the reverse w/a grouping of Masonic emblems, the seal of the United States under the spout, early 19th c. (restoration to spout, hairline on foot) **2,475.00**

Pitcher, jug-type, 9" h., creamware, transfer-printed Washington map includes legend describing scene, reverse w/battle scene enclosed by a ribbon inscribed "Our country, extended our commerce, and laid the foundation of a great empire," early 19th c. **1,725.00**

Pitcher, jug-type, 9" h., one side w/a black transfer-printed design of the city of Washington, the reverse w/"Washington in Glory" (repairs, discoloration) **862.50**

Pitcher, jug-type, 9¼" h., one side w/a black transfer-printed three-masted ship flying an American flag & trimmed w/red, blue, yellow & green enamel, the reverse w/"Virtue & Valor," a gilt monogram under the spout & remains of gilt trim at the rim (imperfections) **1,092.50**

Pitcher, jug-type, 9½" h., black transfer-printed designs, the front w/"Washington Monument," the reverse w/"Washington in Glory - America in Tears" w/profile portrait facing right, American eagle under the spout, rim & body trimmed w/gilt (chip at spout & base) **1,725.00**

Pitcher, jug-type, 9½" h., decorated on one side w/a black transfer-printed design of "L'Insurgent and Constellation," the reverse w/a shipbuilding scene, "Success to the infant Navy of America" under the spout, trimmed w/gilt (repaired) **977.50**

Pitcher, jug-type, 9½" h., one side w/a black transfer-printed two-masted schooner flying the American flag trimmed w/red, blue, yellow & green enamel, the reverse w/"Independence" an American eagle under the spout, remains of gilt trim (repairs) **1,840.00**

Pitcher, jug-type, 11½" h., transfer-printed w/figures of Faith, Hope & Charity, monogram below spout dated "1792" (restored) **546.00**

Plate, 10" d., decorated w/a scene of a three-masted ship, 19th c. (rim chip) **86.00**

LLADRO

Spain's famed Lladro porcelain manufactory creates both limited and non-limited edition figurines as well as other porcelains. The classic simple beauty of the figures and their subdued coloring makes them readily recognizable and they have an enthusiastic following of collectors.

LLADRÓ

Abraham, No. 5169 ....**$1,000.00**	
Afghan, No. 1069, 12" h. **450.00**	
Angel with Clarinet, No. 1232 ....**400.00**	
Angel with Flute, No. 1233, 9½" h....**375.00**	
Angel with Lute, No. 1231, 8" h. ....**375.00 to 400.00**	
At Attention, No. 5407 ....**450.00**	
At the Circus, No. 5052 ....**1,500.00**	
Baby's First Christmas, 1992, No. LL5922 ....**100.00**	
Beagle puppy, sitting, No. L107I........................**200.00 to 250.00**	
Beagle puppy, lying, No. L1072.......................**200.00 to 250.00**	
Bear, brown, No. 1204 ....**100.00**	
Bear, brown, No. 1205 ....**100.00**	
Bear, brown, No. 1206 ....**100.00**	
Best Wishes, No. 5244......................**275.00**	
Birdwatcher, No. 4730, 6 x 8" **250.00**	
Blooming Roses, No. 1339...............**400.00**	
Blue Moon, No. 1435.........................**475.00**	
Boy Meets Girl, No. 1188 ....**225.00 to 275.00**	
Boy Soccer Player, No. 5135, 8½" h...**435.00**	
Boy with Baskets, No. 5055 (Apprentice Seaman)....................**350.00**	
Boy with Cymbal, No. 4613 ....**415.00**	
Boy with Double Bass, No. 4615 .....**435.00**	
Boy with Drum, No. 4616, 4½" h. **435.00**	
Bugler (The), No. 5406......................**450.00**	
Bunny Boy, No. 1507 ....**150.00**	
Cadet Captain, No. 5404...................**450.00**	
Charlie the Tramp, No. L5233 ....**1,200.00**	
Clown, lying on stomach, No. 4618, 6" l...**300.00**	
Clown with Clock, No. 5056 ....**735.00**	
Clown with Girl, No. 4605, matte finish **850.00**	
Cobbler, No. 4853 ....**537.50**	
Coveret jug, decorated, No. 5261 .....**275.00**	
Couple with Parasol, No. 4563......**1,600.00**	
Cycling to a Picnic, No. 5161 ....**3,000.00**	
Dentist, No. 4762, 15¾" h.................**450.00**	
Dog in basket, No. 1128 ....**250.00**	
Dog Playing Guitar, No. 1152...........**375.00**	
Domino Clown - Boy, No. 1179, 7½" h...**250.00**	
Donkey w/Daisy, matte finish, No. 4524 ....**362.50**	
Drummer Boy, No. 5403 ....**500.00**	
El Greco, No. 5359 ....**625.00**	

Eve, No. 1482.....................................**625.00**
Fifa Trophy, No. 5133 ....**575.00**
Flag Bearer (The), No. 5405 ....**475.00**
Flamenco Dancers on Horseback,
  No. 4647 ....**1,250.00**
Ford Fiesta, beige, No. 7017.............**800.00**
Free As A Butterfly, No. L1483 ....**417.00**
Gardener in Trouble, No. 4852.........**295.00**
Girl in White Nightgown Carrying
  Blue Towel & Grey Slippers,
  No. A30E, 10½" h. **65.00**
Girl Manicuring Nails, bisque finish,
  No. 1082, 7½" h. **183.00**
Girl Pot Seller, No. 5081 (Jugs for
  Sale) **500.00**
Girl Seated before a Scale
  Weighing her Cat, No. 5474,
  6½" h..**175.00**
Girl Seated with Flowers,
  No. 1088 ....**650.00**
Girl Soccer Player, No. 5134 ....**450.00**
Girl Tennis Player, No. 4798,
  12½" h...**195.00**
Girl with Brush, No. 1081 ....**275.00**
Girl with Calla Lily, bisque finish,
  No. 4650, 9" h..................................**85.00**
Girl with Child, No. 4636, 7½" h. **125.00**
Girl with Doll in Cart, No. 1083,
  10¾" h. **275.00**
Gossips, No. 4984.............................**735.00**
Great Dane, No. 1068.......................**280.00**
Heavenly Harpist, No. 5830..............**300.00**
Hebrew Student, No. 4684,
  10¾" h..**415.00**
Honey Lickers, No. 1248 ....**450.00**
Ironing Time, No. 4981 ....**300.00**
Jugs for Sale, girl w/parasol selling
  pottery, No. 5081, 12" h. **525.00**
Leilani, No. 1530...............................**345.00**
Lilly, No. 5119....................................**750.00**
Little Harlequin "B", No. 5076..........**335.00**
Little Harlequin "C", No. 5076..........**335.00**
Little Leaguer Exercising,
  No. L5289 ....**425.00**
Little Pals, No. S-7600 ....**2,500.00**
Little Red Riding Hood, No. 4965 ....**950.00**
Lost Love, No. 5128 ....**1,000.00**
Lullaby & Goodnight, No. 5083.....**1,500.00**
Male Equestrian, No. 5329...............**400.00**
Male Soccer Player, blue & white
  shirt, No. 5200.3 ....**500.00**
Male Soccer Player, red shirt,
  No. 5200 ....**500.00**
Male tennis player, No. L1426, matte
  finish **267.00**
Man on Horse, No. 4515 ....**1,000.00**
Moonlight, No. 1437..........................**550.00**
My Buddy, No. S-7609 ....**390.00**
Nude, No. 4511 ....**675.00**
Old Man with Violin, No. 4622.........**875.00**
Olympic Torch, No. 5870, Olympic
  Champion, No. 5871, & Olympic
  Pride, No. 5872, set of 3 ....**500.00**
Olympic Ball, No. 5945, 3½" h. **160.00**

Plates Satyr (Pan Right), No. 1006 ..**475.00**
Playful Dogs (poodles), No. 1367 ....**395.00**
Pondering Nymph, No. 1403............**500.00**
Predicting the Future, No. 5191.......**350.00**
Puppet Tennis Player, No. 4966 ......**410.00**
Rain in Spain, boy & girl under
  umbrella, No. 2077, matte finish,
  8" h...**400.00**
Reflections of Hamlet, No. 1455 ...**1,750.00**
Resting Nude, No. LL3025...............**725.00**
Rosalinda, No. 4836, matte finish,
  7½" h..**250.00**
Say "Cheese," No. 5195 ....**450.00**
School Days, No. S-7604..................**487.00**
Schoolgirl Olivia "O," No. 5148 ....**500.00**
Schoolgirl Ursula "U," No. 5149 .....**525.00**
School Marm, No. 5209 ....**675.00**
Sheriff Puppet, No. 4969 ....**762.50**
Soldier's Headvase, No. 1105,
  10" h...**485.00**
Spanish Soldier, No. 5255...............**425.00**
Star Gazing, No. 1477, 7½" h...........**368.00**
Studying in the Park, No. 5425 ....**875.00**
Summer Stroll, No. S7611................**339.00**
Teasing the Dog, girl w/ball & dog,
  No. 5078, 10" h.................................**500.00**
Teething, No. 5102, 4½" h.................**250.00**
Torch Bearer, No. 5251.....................**285.00**
Torso in White, No. 4512 ....**300.00**
Valencia Boy, No. 1400.....................**475.00**
Veterinarian, No. 4825......**425.00 to 450.00**
Victorian Girl on Swing, No. 1297,
  15½" h..**1,450.00**
Waltz Time, No. 4856........................**425.00**
Watchman, No. 5087.........................**900.00**
Windblown Girl (White),
  No. L4922.3 ....**750.00**
Wrath of Don Quixote, No. 1343,
  16½" h..........................**725.00 to 750.00**
Young Harlequin seated with Cat,
  No. 1229, 9" h. **350.00**
Young Mozart, No. LL5915,
  6¾" h...**1,525.00**

LOTUS WARE

Avidly sought by many collectors are these exquisite china wares made by Knowles, Taylor & Knowles of East Liverpool, Ohio, in the last decade of the 19th century. The firm also produced ironstone and hotel china.

Bowl-vase, slightly bulbous all-white
  body w/narrow undulating serrated
  rim, decorated w/relief vining florals
  & reticulated medallions, marked,
  4¼" h...**$357.50**
Creamer, fishnet design, clear mark,
  3½" h...**165.00**

Teapot, cov., silver finial, marked
"K.T.K. Co. Lotus Ware" **225.00**
Vase, 8" h., bulbous, handled, h.p.
floral decoration w/gold handles,
ca. 1896, artist-signed **550.00**

LUSTRE WARES

*Lustred wares in imitation of copper,
gold, silver and other colors were produced
in England in the early 19th century and
onward. Gold, copper or platinum oxides
were painted on glazed objects which were
then fired, giving them a lustred effect.
Various forms of lustre wares include plain
lustre – with the entire object coated to
obtain a metallic effect, bands of lustre
decoration and painted lustre designs.
Particularly appealing is the pink or
purple "splash lustre" sometimes referred
to as "Sunderland" lustre in the mistaken
belief it was confined to the production of
Sunderland area potteries. Objects
decorated in silver lustre by the "resist"
process, wherein parts of the objects to be
left free from lustre decoration were treated
with wax, are referred to as "silver resist."*

*Wares formerly called "Canary Yellow
Lustre" are now referred to as "Yellow-
Glazed Earthenwares." Also see YELLOW
GLAZED EARTHENWARES.*

COPPER

Copper Pitcher with Ballet Dancers

Goblet, tapering, cylindrical ringed
bowl on a ringed pedestal w/disc
foot, a wide pink body band
decorated w/orange & green
enameled florals, 3⅜" d., 5" h. **$85.00**
Pitcher, 4" h., decorated w/embossed
girl on cobalt band **30.00**

Pitcher, 4½" h., footed flaring
cylindrical body w/an angled
shoulder to the cylindrical neck
w/wide spout & embossed beaded
rim band, angled handle, the body
w/a wide yellow band decorated
w/black transfer-printed scenes, one
tirled "Lafayette" w/a bust portrait,
the other titled "Cornwallis
Resigning His Sword," w/a scene of
the surrender at Yorktown, ca. 1840
(tiny enamel flake) **1,100.00**
Pitcher, 5" h., 4½" d., blue band
around collar, dark copper color on
interior, ca. 1920-30, marked
"Gibbons" & "made in England" **185.00**
Pitcher, jug-type, 5" h., transfer-
printed w/"Tolls Taken at the Menai
Bridge," England, early 19th c. (chips
& hairline).....................................**230.00**
Pitcher, 6" h., embossed scene
decoration on blue band, ca.
1809..**135.00**
Pitcher, 6½" h., 4" d., footed tapering
cylindrical body w/widely arching rim
& C-scroll handle, embossed scene
of two female ballet dancers,
w/embossed scrolls & blue trim
(ILLUS.) **89.00**

Pitcher with Ballet Dancers

Pitcher, 7¼" h., 4⅝" d., footed
tapering cylindrical body w/widely
flaring rim & C-scrolled handle,
embossed scene of two female
ballet dancers, embossed scrolls
& blue trim (ILLUS.) **95.00**
Pitcher, 7¼" h., spherical body on a
short pedestal foot, the wide
cylindrical flaring neck w/molded fine
rings & a long rim spout, C-scroll
handle, the center w/a wide yellow
band reserved w/three oval panels
edged in brown & printed in black on
one side w/an inscribed bust portrait
of "LAFAYETTE" being crowned w/a

wreath held by two seated maidens amid clouds, on the reverse w/a scene of "Cornwallis resigning his Sword at York Town Oct! 19ᵗʰ 1781," & beneath the spout w/a cluster of fruit & a blossom, fine rings around the lower body, beadwork band around the rim, ca. 1825-35 (chipped spout, interior rim chip & handle cracked) **2,070.00**

Pitcher, 11½" h., footed wide bulbous body boldly molded w/large scrolls framing a round medallion, tapering to a lightly scalloped rim w/a wide, arched spout & ornate S-scroll handle, one medallion printed in pink w/a woman representing Faith holding a large cross, the other w/a printed clock face, ca. 1850 ....**605.00**

SILVER & SILVER RESIST

Jug-type Pitcher

Mug, child's, cylindrical, yellow-glazed ground w/vertical silver lustre stripes of small stars alternating w/leaf bands, ca. 1820, 2" h. (tiny repaired rim chip, faint hairline).....................**170.50**

Mug, child's, cylindrical, yellow-glazed earthenware w/a wide silver-resist band w/leaf sprigs, 2" h. (tiny rim chip) **148.50**

Pitcher, jug-type, 4⅜" h., silver lustre ground resisted on either side w/bird perched on two crossed leafy boughs beneath a berried vine border around the neck, probably Leeds, England, ca. 1815-20 (ILLUS.) **575.00**

Pitcher, jug-type, 4¾" h., the bulbous body & tapering neck decorated in silver resist w/large stylized blossoms & leafy bands, ca. 1820, short hairline at rim **176.00**

SUNDERLAND PINK & OTHERS

Bowl, 8½" d., polychrome floral

decoration within pink lustre arches, early 19th c. **259.00**

Condiment set, salt, pepper & mustard jar w/original china "shovel" spoons & matching footed holder, the set **135.00**

Dish, divided w/center handle, decorated w/flower sprays & gold trim, 14" l.....................................**145.00**

Mug, miniature, cylindrical w/molded base band, loop handle, overall pink Sunderland lustre w/copper lustre rim band, 3" h.................................**143.00**

Mug, transfer-printed scene of sailing vessel on one side, reverse w/"Here's to the Wind that Blows...," against a splashed pink lustre ground, 4½" h. (chips).....................**287.50**

Mug, 'Sailor's Return,' cylindrical body transfer-printed in black & enameled in iron-red, green & yellow on one side w/a sailor & his sweetheart before ships in a harbor between the inscription "The Token or Jack's Safe Return to his True Love," & "If You Love's I as I Love's You No Pair so Happy as We Two," the reverse w/a rhyming prayer within a floral oval panel, all surrounded by pink lustre squiggles between pink lustre borders around the rim & foot, the strap handle w/a pink lustre foliate device, ca. 1830-40, 5⅛" h. (discolored) **1,150.00**

Pitcher, 5⅞" h., footed bulbous body w/wide panels around the middle, C-scroll handle, the center panels on each side h.p. in pink lustre w/country houses, band of relief-molded flowers around the top trimmed w/pink lustre & pink lustre banding overall, ca. 1830................**275.00**

Pitcher, jug-type, 6¼" h., a large central oval reserve w/a pink transfer-printed English manor house scene, the surrounding borders in pink lustre resist w/overall floral & leaf designs, early 19th c. (overall staining, two small chips on rim, flake on spout) **192.50**

Pitcher, jug-type, 6½" h., angled handle, h.p. pink lustre decoration of a large cottage in a landscape on one side, a landscape on the other, oak leaf lustre rim band, early 19th c. (four reglued handle breaks, two chips on foot, small flake & repaired chip on rim) **110.00**

Pitcher, 7⅛" h., barrel-shaped body transfer-printed in black w/bust-length portrait of an American military or naval hero within trophies of war, one side depicting General Zebulon Montgomery Pike beneath

Sunderland Barrel-shaped Pitcher

the inscription "Be always ready to die for your country PIKE," & the reverse w/Captain Isaac Hull beneath inscription "Captain HULL of the Constitution," all surrounded by pink splash lustre, English, ca. 1815-20, small chips on spout (ILLUS.) **6,038.00**

Pitcher, jug-type, 7½" h., the body decorated w/a pink lustre landscape featuring a large house & tower, lustre Greek key neck band & trim on petaled spout, C-scroll handle, ca. 1830 (some wear & scratches) ..**302.50**

Plaque, pierced to hang, reeded border w/pink lustre trim forming a frame effect around a black transfer likeness of John Wesley "The Best of All God is With Us. The Revd. John Wesley A.M....," 6¾" w., 5¾" h. (minor stains) **286.00**

Plaque, pierced to hang, oval wreath around black transfer "Thou God, See'st Me," within a pink-trimmed molded reeded border, 6¾" w., 5¾" h. (minor wear & pinpoints) **220.00**

Plaque, pierced to hang, molded pink lustre rim enclosing a black transfer likeness of Adam Clark & "He that Believeth Shall be Saved, Adam Clark...," 6¾" w., 5¾" h. (minor stains) **302.50**

Plaque, pierced to hang, black transfer "Prepare to Meet Thy God" within a wreath w/angel Gabriel above, all within a molded pink lustre rim w/clusters of flowers at corners, 7¾" w., 6⅝" h. (minor wear) **231.00**

Plaque, pierced to hang, rectangular w/cove-molded scrolled self-frame, the center w/a black transfer-printed landscape w/ladies & a fisherman near a small bridge in the foreground, buildings in the

distance, the border frame trimmed in pink lustre, green, red & yellow w/a pink lustre edge band, ca. 1840, 7½ x 8¼" (small chip on back of one corner) **280.50**

Plaque, pierced to hang, scroll-molded pink lustre border trimmed in brown enamel enclosing a brown enamel inscription "In Memory of Michael Walton who died September 15th 1853 Aged 72," 8½" w., 7⅝" h. **550.00**

Plaque, pierced to hang, rectangular w/lightly scalloped flared border, black transfer-printed central floral wreath around "Behold GOD will not cast away a perfect man, neither will HE help the evil doers," Sunderland pink splash border & copper lustre rim, impressed "Dixon Co.," 8⅞" l. ...**550.00**

Plaque, pierced to hang, scroll-molded pink lustre rim w/polychrome flowers at corners framing a black transfer likeness of John Wesley & "The Best of All, God is with us, the Revd. John Wesley A.M....," 8¾" w., 8" h. (stains & wear).....................**1,320.00**

Plaque, pierced to hang, rectangular w/lightly scalloped flared border, black transfer-printed central floral wreath framing "PREPARE TO MEET THY GOD," Sunderland pink splash border & copper lustre rim, 8⅞" l. **495.00**

Plaque, pierced to hang, rectangular, depicting "La Bretagne," 140 guns, pink & copper lustre, ca. 1825, 8½ x 9½"..**150.00**

Plaque, pierced to hang, rectangular w/a flaring scroll-molded self-frame, the center w/a black transfer-printed scene of a British ship under full sail above a pair of flower-filled cornucopia flanking a scroll-bordered reserve inscribed "May Peace and Plenty on our Nation Smlle and Trade with Commerce Bless the British Isle," Sunderland lustre frame w/copper lustre trim on the molded scrolls, ca. 1840, 8½ x 9½" (professional restoration to back of two corners, few chips on back rim) **181.50**

Plate, 5½" d., scene of boys playing Rugby **35.00**

MAJOLICA

Majolica, a tin-enameled glazed pottery, has been produced for centuries. It

originally took its name from the island of
Majorca, a source of figuline (potter's clay).
Subsequently it was widely produced in
England, Europe and the United States.
Etruscan majolica, now avidly sought, was
made by Griffen, Smith & Hill, Phoenix-
ville, Pa., in the last quarter of the 19th
century. Most majolica advertised today is
19th or 20th century. Once scorned by most
collectors, interest in this colorful ware so
popular during the Victorian era has now
revived and prices have risen dramatically
in the past few years. Also see SARRE-
GUEMINES, MINTON, and WEDG-
WOOD.

Reference books which collectors will
find useful include: The Collector's
Encyclopedia of Majolica, by Mariann
Katz-Marks (Collector Books, 1992);
American Majolica, 1850-1900, by M.
Charles Rebert (Wallace-Homestead Book
Co., 1981); Majolica, American & Euro-
pean Wares, by Jeffrey B. Snyder & Leslie
Bockol (Schiffer Publishing, Ltd., 1994);
and Majolica, British, Continental and
American Wares, 1851-1915, by Victoria
Bergesen (Barrie & Jenkins, Ltd., London,
England, 1989).

ETRUSCAN

Sunflower Cuspidor

Mug, Pineapple patt. **195.00**
Pitcher, 8" h., Wild Rose w/Butterfly
  Lip patt. **207.50**
Plate, 8" d., Shell & Seaweed patt. **175.00**
Platter, 9 x 12", w/open twig handle,
  Oak Leaf patt. **195.00**

GENERAL

Heron Pattern Cheese Keeper

Asparagus server cradled on twig
  stand, nice color, Luneville,
  France, 6 x 9"...................................**595.00**
Bread tray, Grape patt., ivory ground,
  ca. 1880, Wedgwood, England........**200.00**
Butter pat, Basketweave w/Butterfly
  patt., Fielding, England **50.00**
Candlestick, figural tulip w/boy
  leaning against it..............................**185.00**
Charger, decorated w/red crab,
  mussels, rocks & seaweed, 13" d. **195.00**
Cheese keeper, cov., Heron patt.,
  cylindrical cover w/paneled sides
  w/heron clutching a fish in his beak,

Etruscan Cheese Keeper

Bowl, 7½" d., 3" h., Shell & Seaweed
  patt. **$450.00**
Bowl, Daisy patt. **225.00**
Cheese keeper, cov., Fern patt.,
  cover w/embossed ferns &
  wildflowers, blossom finial on
  cover (ILLUS.).............................**3,300.00**
Compote, Morning Glory patt. **495.00**
Creamer, Shell & Seaweed patt.........**225.00**
Cuspidor, Sunflower patt., 6" h.
  (ILLUS. top next column) **2,200.00**

framed w/bamboo, unknown maker, England, 11" h. (ILLUS.) **3,190.00**
Compote, open, 6" d., 9" h., Shell patt., attributed to Morley **350.00**
Creamer, Corn patt., 4½" h. **55.00**
Ewer, lattice & yellow basketweave body w/delicate floral decals on front, relief-molded scrolls & scroll handle, rim & spout, glossy grey, scrolls glazed in turquoise, olive & cobalt, England, 5" d. at shoulder, 12" h..**155.00**
Humidor, cov., decorated w/pig dressed topcoat, 6¼" h. **185.00**
Humidor, cov., model of a cat's head, Austria, 4½" h. **195.00**
Ice cream tray, Fan patt., Fielding, 14½" l...**200.00**

Majolica Scroll-Decorated Jardiniere

Jardiniere, bulbous ovoid body w/widely flaring rim & dragon handles, leaf & scroll decoration on royal blue ground, late 19th c., 10" h. (ILLUS.) **287.50**

George Jones Jardiniere

Jardiniere & undertray, cylindrical body w/arched panels w/pink iris

decoration & scattered leaf-shaped decoration, George Jones, various chips & hairline cracks (ILLUS.)....**1,430.00**

Model of Googly-Eyed Dog

Model of googly-eyed dog, white & brown w/green collar, wearing a blue hat w/yellow edging, 3" d., 6" h. (ILLUS.) **135.00**
Model of pair of woman's high-heel shoes on cushion w/applied flowers, maroon w/turquoise interior, sanded, 6" h...**130.00**

Majolica Oyster Plates

Oyster plate, crescent-shaped, Copeland (ILLUS. front) **660.00**
Oyster plate, five-well, decorated w/seashells & seaweed, Wedgwood (ILLUS. left)...................**412.50**
Oyster plate, six-well, mottled, Minton (ILLUS. right) **632.50**

George Jones Oyster Plates

Oyster plates, six wells divided by brown & green seaweed w/raised center figural shell, George Jones, 10" d., set of four (ILLUS. two of four) **4,400.00**

Pitcher, 4⅞" h., Raspberry patt., Avalon Faience line, Haynes & Co., Baltimore...**67.50**

Pitcher w/metal lid, 5½" h., basketweave design on base w/leaf decoration, original pewter lid (small lid split) **145.00**

Pitcher, 6" h., bird feeding young in nest **240.00**

Pitcher, 6" h., Wild Rose patt...............**75.00**

Pitcher, 6¾" h., Strawberry patt., Avalon Faience line, Haynes & Co., Baltimore..**127.00**

Pitcher, 7¼" h., floral decoration, France..**135.00**

Pitcher, 7¼" h., stork w/fish decoration above base bamboo decoration **265.00**

Pitcher, 7½" h., figural Pug dog.........**350.00**

Pitcher, 8" h., Wild Rose patt., tree bark background **157.50**

Pitcher, 8½" h., cylindrical body w/angled handle, a large pointed leaf w/a fern sprig against a brown tree bark ground ....**100.00 to 150.00**

Pitcher, 9¾" h., figural monkey in shades of red, brown & black (pinpoint flakes) **605.00**

Tankard-shaped Pitcher

Pitcher w/hinged pewter lid, tankard, 12½" h., 5¼" d., decorated w/raised decorative circles on mottled brown, gold & green background (ILLUS.) **245.00**

Planter, decorated w/twigs & branches, applied roses on front, turquoise interior **165.00**

Plaques, pierced to hang, relief-molded portrait of man's head on one & woman's head on the other, turquoise border w/red poppies,

impressed artist signature, 12½" d., pr...**450.00**

Italian Majolica Plaque

Plaques, polychrome decorated biblical scenes, wooden frames, Italy, early 19th c., 8½" d., four pcs. (ILLUS. one of four)..............**5,175.00**

Plaques, pierced to hang, a small center reserve of a flying bird framed by small oval reserves within a wide outer border of floral oval reserves w/openwork, probably French, 19th c., 13" d., pr. **615.00**

Plate, 6" d., figural maple leaf, "Zell," Baden, Germany............................**22.00**

Plate, 7¼" d., strawberry decoration, France..**45.00**

Plate, 7½" d., decorated w/raised strawberries & leaves, Portugal **110.00**

Plate, 8" l., Begonia Leaf patt., aqua ground..**75.00**

Plate, 8" l., figural maple leaf, "Zell," Baden, Germany...............................**40.00**

Plate, dessert, 8" d., strawberry leaves, fruit & flowers decoration on blue ground.......................................**15.00**

Plate, 8¼" d., Trenton-type bird patt., attributed to the Eureka Pottery Co., Trenton, N.J. **160.00**

Plate, 9" d., Begonia patt., lavender, yellow & green on brown ground **95.00**

Plate, 9" d., Maple Leaf Basketweave patt., good color, American..............**135.00**

Plate, 9" d., decorated w/scene of cherub on lion **95.00**

Plate, 9½" d., shell-shaped w/scalloped edge, mottled glaze........**80.00**

Plate, 10" d., Basketweave & Black-berry patt., brown background **135.00**

Plate, 11½" d., overall molded green leaves w/a sawtooth leaf rim, impressed "BRAMELED" **88.00**

Plate, 12" l., figural maple leaf, "Zell," Baden, Germany...............................**50.00**

Plate, 12" l., raspberries decora-tion **175.00**

Platter, 10½ x 13½", Picket Fence patt., pink floral decoration on cobalt blue **350.00**

Platter, 11" l., scalloped edge, molded center scene of a dog & doghouse, leaf border **140.00**

Sugar bowl, cov., brown to gold basketweave design w/green leaves & red roses decoration....................**145.00**

Syrup pitcher w/pewter lid, decorated w/begonia leaves around bulbous base, brown & yellow ground, 4" h. **160.00**

Teapot, cov., decorated w/dogwood & branches, tree bark spout & handle, blue ground.....................................**220.00**

Tray, oval w/open scroll end handles, embossed overall leafy scrolls, shaded green glaze, 11½" l. (rim chip) **143.00**

Majolica Umbrella Stand

Umbrella stand, slightly tapering cylindrical body decorated w/storks standing in rushes on cobalt ground, various hairline cracks, (ILLUS.) **990.00**

Vase, 5" h., limbs outlined in brown, Avalon Faience line, Haynes & Co., Baltimore..**75.00**

Vase, 8¾" h., polychrome leaves against a blue dot ground, Italy, 19th c. **230.00**

MC COY

Collectors are now seeking the art wares of two McCoy potteries. One was founded in Roseville, Ohio, in the late 19th century as the J.W. McCoy Pottery, subsequently becoming Brush-McCoy Pottery Co., later Brush Pottery. The other was founded also in Roseville in 1910 as Nelson McCoy Sanitary Stoneware Co., later becoming

Mammy Cookie Jar

Nelson McCoy Pottery. In 1967 the pottery was sold to D.T. Chase of the Mount Clemens Pottery Co. who sold his interest to the Lancaster Colony Corp. in 1974. The pottery shop closed in 1985. Cookie jars are especially collectible today.

    A helpful reference book is the Collector's Encyclopedia of McCoy Pottery *by the Huxfords (Collector Books), and* McCoy Cookie Jars From the First to the Latest, *by Harold Nichols (Nichols Publishing, 1987).*

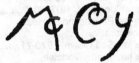

Coffee server, cov., El Rancho Bar-B-Que line **$110.00**

Cookie jar, Alpo Dog **50.00**

Cookie jar, Apples on Basketweave, 1957..**39.50**

Cookie jar, Aunt Jemima **75.00**

Cookie jar, Barn, red, 1963 ....**150.00**

Cookie jar, brown drip glaze, No. 7024 ....**25.00**

Cookie jar, Bugs Bunny, cylinder w/decal, 1971-72 ....**106.00**

Cookie jar, Burlap Sack, 1985............**28.00**

Cookie jar, Cookie Barrel **33.00**

Cookie jar, Coffeepot, blue "graniteware" finish, 1974-75 ....**25.00**

Cookie jar, Cookie Bank, 1961.........**135.00**

Cookie jar, Cookie Bell, 1963-66........**31.00**

Cookie jar, Cookie Boy, 1940-43.......**175.00**

Cookie jar, Corn (Ear of Corn), 1958-59 ....**125.00 to 150.00**

Cookie jar, Dog House, 1983, blue bird finial **200.00**

Cookie jar, Drum, 1959-60 ....**95.00**

Cookie jar, Duck, 1964 ....**33.00**

Cookie jar, Dutch girl...........................**85.00**

Cookie jar, Freddie the Gleep, green,
1974 ....**650.00**
Cookie jar, Frog on Stump, 1971 ....**57.00**
Cookie jar, Garbage Can, 1978-87 .....**27.00**
Cookie jar, Grandfather Clock,
1962-64 ....**64.00**
Cookie jar, Grandma, w/red skirt,
1972-73 ....**96.50**
Cookie jar, Kettle w/stationary bail
handle, 1961-67 ....**20.00**
Cookie jar, Kitten on Basketweave,
1956-69 ....**55.00**
Cookie jar, Lamb on Cylinder **185.00**
Cookie jar, Little Bo Peep **95.00**
Cookie jar, Mammy, all-white dress,
"Cookies" on front of dress, green
trim & red cap, 1948-57
(ILLUS.) ....**150.00 to 175.00**
Cookie jar, Milk Can (Early
American), silver, 1972-74 ....**33.00**
Cookie jar, Mother Goose, white,
1948-82 ....**85.00**
Cookie jar, Nabisco, red & tan, 1974 ...**70.00**
Cookie jar, Orange, 1970 ....**58.00**
Cookie jar, Owl, 1978-79 ....**15.00**
Cookie jar, Panda w/lollipop **140.00**
Cookie jar, Pelican, turquoise or
white, 1940-43, each **150.00**
Cookie jar, Pelican, yellow,
1940-43 ....**150.00**
Cookie jar, Pillsbury Doughboy **80.00**
Cookie jar, Pitcher (Blue Willow),
white w/blue decal, 1978-79 ....**40.00**
Cookie jar, Pontiac Indian Head,
commemorative **100.00**
Cookie jar, Sad Clown, 1970-71 ....**112.50**
Cookie jar, Timmy Tortoise,
1977-80 ....**28.50**
Cookie jar, Windmill (Dutch
Windmill), 1961 ....**97.50**
Creamer & open sugar bowl, Daisy
patt., pr. **15.00**
Dog feeding dish, embossed "To
Man's Best Friend, His Dog," green,
7" d., 2" h. **65.00**
Mug, El Rancho Bar-B-Que line,
1960 ....**20.00**
Mug, Happy Face decoration **10.00**
Pitcher, oil, 5" h., Olympia line,
ca. 1905 ....**275.00**
Planter, fan-shaped, w/bow, pink,
ca. 1956 ....**20.00**
Planter, pussy at the well, green
w/white & black cat on edge
of well, ca. 1956 ....**80.00**
Planter, model of the Liberty Bell,
dated "8th (sic) July 1776" **100.00**
Teapot, cov., Pine Cone patt. **35.00**
Tea set: cov. teapot, open sugar bowl
& creamer; Daisy patt., shaded pink
& green glaze, ca. 1942, 3 pcs. **51.00**
Tea set: cov. teapot, creamer & sugar
bowl; Ivy patt., 3 pcs. (ILLUS. top
next column) **80.00**

Ivy Pattern Tea Set

Vase, 13" h., Vesta line, ca. 1962 ....**30.00**

Mailbox Wall Pocket

Wall pocket, model of mailbox
(ILLUS.) **40.00**
Wall pocket, model of a pear against
green leaves **22.00**

MEISSEN

Meissen Figural Centerpiece

*The secret of true hard paste porcelain,
known long before to the Chinese, was*

discovered" accidentally in Meissen, Germany, by J.F. Bottger, an alchemist working with E.W. Tschirnhausen. The first European true porcelain was made in the Meissen Porcelain Works, organized about 1709. Meissen "crossed swords" marks have been widely copied by other factories. Some pieces listed here are recent.

Bowls, serving, 11¼" d., shaped round form, white ground w/overall raised new gold morning glory decoration, 19th c., pr. (gilt wear) ..**$126.50**

Candelabra, three-light, figural, each w/a male & female figure seated on a shell, supporting three foliate-scrolled candle branches centering a putto w/foliate-scrolled tripartite base headed by a putto playing a musical instrument, each within a glass domed cover, 20" h., pr. **6,900.00**

Carafe, stopper & undertray, teardrop-form body w/pierced floral sprays & gilt insects, flat stopper, early 20th c., 10" h., the set **467.50**

Centerpiece bowl, decorated w/center floral bouquet, relief-molded roses & heavy gilt gold in two shades, crossed swords mark, 12" d...**1,100.00**

Centerpiece, figural, three classical females centering a branch support-ing a pierced bowl, standing on turned wood plinth base, third quarter 19th c., 19¾" h. (ILLUS.) ..**2,875.00**

Centerpiece, figural, w/a free-form grape leaf-wrapped standard modeled w/two hunting putti, supporting a pierced latticework bowl w/scrolled ends modeled w/a female figure holding a cornucopia & putto, late 19th c., 27½" h. (losses) **10,925.00**

Charger, decorated overall w/raised gold flowers & foliage against a soft green ground, ca., 1890, blue crossed swords mark, 11" d. **225.00**

Cup & saucer, Blue Onion patt., crossed swords mark........................**85.00**

Dinner service: 42 dinner plates, 30 salad plates, 15 small bowls, 18 dessert plates, 17 cups, 11 serving bowls, a cov. tureen, three gravy boats, two figural master salt dips, a cov. entree dish, cov. teapot,

creamer, cov. sugar bowl, 12 serving spoons & 12 fruit knives; Blue Onion patt., late 19th - early 20th c., the set **8,625.00**

Figure of a chocolate maker, a putti draped only in a slender cloth seated beside a footed low brick stove mixing chocolate, colored enamel decoration, scroll-molded oval base, blue crossed swords mark, late 19th c., 4¼" h. **862.50**

Figure of a classical Muse, wearing a short floral-decorated robe & standing beside a short column & playing a pan pipe, polychrome decoration w/gilt trim, blue crossed swords mark, 15¼" h. **385.00**

Figure of young man, depicted in Colonial dress, seated & reading a book, a dog at his side, 19th c., 8⅝" h. (restoration) **1,092.50**

Figure of a woman holding a basket of flowers, lace work on bodice & edges of gown, ca. 1850, 6½" h. ..**1,050.00**

Figures, "Je les couronne," depicting a cupid w/column & flowers & "Je blesse et soulage," also depicting a cupid w/column & flowers, first half 19th c., each 5½" h., pr. (some damage)..**1,150.00**

Figures, model of a girl w/a kitten & a boy w/a dog, Marcolini star mark, late 18th - early 19th c., 4⅜" & 4½" h., pr. **402.50**

Figure group, three putti holding flowers, ca. 1890, 3½ x 4"................**795.00**

Courting Couple Figure Group

Figure group, male suitor kissing the hand of a seated female w/satyr boy by their side, enamel & gilt decorated, crossed-swords mark, Germany, late 19th c., 5¾" h. (ILLUS.) **1,092.50**

Figure group, depicting Pan, a maiden & a satyr child w/pan pipes, 19th c., 12⅜" h. (restoration) **1,380.00**

Meissen Fire Screen

Fire screen, composed of porcelain bobbin segments w/figural mounts at upper corners & center of cross bar, figural mounts at corners of trestle foot, suspending a cloth screen, 31" w., 42½" h. (ILLUS.)...**6,325.00**

Model of a large colorful parrot perched on a stump on a rockwork base, gilt trim, blue crossed swords mark & "Made in Germany," 10¾" h...**412.50**

Plate, 9" d., Blue Onion patt., ca. 1880-1925...**50.00**

Plate, 10" d., Blue Onion patt., crossed swords mark........................**95.00**

Plate, 10" d., gold leaf border, crossed swords mark.....................**100. 00**

Plates, 9¼" d., wide scalloped & reticulated basketweave border w/three solid panels each h.p. w/a different bird & trimmed w/gilt, a bird perched on a branch in the center, blue crossed swords mark, late 19th c., set of 11 (chips) **3,450.00**

Plates, 9¾" d., lightly scalloped rim, white w/a colorful cluster of h.p. fruit in the center, gilt rim band, blue crossed swords mark, late 19th c., set of 12 ....**2,300.00**

Platter, 12 x 15½", Blue Onion patt., ca. 1888-1924, crossed swords mark...**350.00**

Potpourri, stands & covers, figural panel & floral opposing sides surmounted by a pierced domed lid, raised on a bracket base, the whole encrusted w/flowers, fruit, scrolled handles & putti, late 19th c., 35" h., pr...**40,250.00**

Powder box, cov., decorated w/pink roses on white w/a rose bud handle on cover, crossed swords mark **175.00**

Shaving mug, scuttle-shaped, Blue Onion patt., ca. 1870, 3" d., 3¾" h..**140.00**

Soup tureen w/domed cover, Blue Onion patt., 10" h. **450.00**

Tea set: cov. teapot, creamer & cov. sugar bowl; each in a footed spherical shape, green ivy decoration w/gold trim, late 19th - early 20th c., teapot 5¾" h., the set..**402.50**

Tea & coffee service: cov. teapot, cov. coffeepot, cov. sugar bowl, creamer, 18 dessert plates, 18 cups & saucers & an oval tray; baluster-shaped coffeepot & creamer & spherical teapot, each piece in white decorated w/scattered small colorful flower sprays, gilt edge trim, late 19th - early 20th c., teapot 5½" h., the set....................................**1,725.00**

Vase, cov., 12½" h., enameled insects between applied leaves & florets, underglazed crossed swords mark, 19th c. **287.50**

Vegetable dish, cov., round, decorated w/the Indian Flower patt. in magenta, figural cherub w/cornucopia finial, underglaze-blue mark, 19th c., 10⅝" d., 8½" h. **230.00**

METTLACH

Ceramics with the name Mettlach were produced by Villeroy & Boch and other potteries in the Mettlach area of Germany. Villeroy and Boch's finest years of production are thought to be from about 1890 to 1910.

Beaker, bright floral branch w/birds incised, No. 1046, 4" h..................**$125.00**

Pitcher, 4¼" h., bulbous paneled body w/cylindrical neck, angled handle, Art Nouveau trees decoration rising from body panels to spout & rim, No. 1947, ¼ liter **195.00**

Plaque, pierced to hang, etched scene of a cavalier pouring wine, ca. 1903, No. 2621, 7½" d. **225.00**

Cameo of Classical Woman

Plaque, pierced to hang, oval, phanolith, white relief-molded bust portrait of classical woman w/her hair pulled into a bun, No. 7032, 7½ x 9" (ILLUS.) **395.00**

Man Raising Toasting Glass Plaque

Plaque, pierced to hang, etched scene of man raising toasting glass, No. 2622, 7¾" d. (ILLUS.) **275.00**

Plaque with Man Smoking

Plaque, pierced to hang, etched

scene of man smoking, No. 2624, 7¾" d. (ILLUS.) **275.00**

Castle on Rhine River Plaque

Plaque, pierced to hang, etched scene of a castle on the Rhine River w/gold edging, No. 1365, 17" d. (ILLUS.) **1,150.00**

Roman Lady with Servants Plaque

Plaque, pierced to hang, phanolith, white relief-molded scene of Roman lady w/servants in attendance, No. 2443, 18" d. (ILLUS.).............**1,150.00**

Plaque with Roman Soldiers

Plaque, pierced to hang, phanolith, white relief-molded scene of Roman soldiers in boat on a green ground, No. 2442, 18" d. (ILLUS.)..............**1,150.00**

Plaques, pierced to hang, etched ducks in flight, No. 1044/102A & 102 B, printed Mercury marks, 13¾" h., pr. **312.00**

MINTON

Minton Foxglove Jardiniere

The Minton factory in England was established by Thomas Minton in 1793. The factory made earthenware, especially the blue-printed variety and Thomas Minton is sometimes credited with invention of the blue "Willow" pattern. For a time majolica and tiles were also an imported part of production, but bone china soon became the principal ware. Mintons, Ltd., continue in operation today.

Bowl, fruit, footed, 8½ x 10½", 4" h., decorated w/green leaves & melons on interior & exterior, gold border & four gold feet, artist-signed **$395.00**

Charger, Secessionist Ware, decorated w/a squeeze-bag border of stylized white swirling flowers outlined in green against a burgundy ground w/a khaki green interior scalloped band, die-stamped "MINTONS LTD, NO. 13," 15" d. **935.00**

Coffee set: 8" h. cov. coffeepot & six cups & saucers and matching 7" h.

cov. chocolate pot; Cockatrice Pink patt., No. 9646, 14 pcs.....................**975.00**

Cup & saucer, Ancestral patt., No. S376...**30.00**

Dinner service, child's: a pair 3⅛," w. square vegetable dishes w/covers, 4⁵⁄₁₆" shaped oval sauce tureen & cover, ladle, two undertrays, a pair of 5¾" l. rectangular platters, a 4¾" l. rectangular platter, a 4³⁄₁₆" l. rectangular platter, three 4¼" l. rectangular open serving dishes, a 3½" square bowl, a pair of soup plates, 11 dinner plates, & ten dessert plates; each piece w/a medium-blue transfer-printed English landscape scene featuring various locales, some pieces w/impressed potter's mark, ca. 1825, 37 pcs. (some w/chips & hairlines) **2,645.00**

Dinner service: dinner, salad & bread & butter plates, bowl, cups & saucers, platters, cov. teapot, cov. sugar bowl, creamer & cov. serving dish; Ancestral patt., 20th c., 101 pcs. **920.00**

Figure group, "Naiomi and her Daughter in Law," a standing woman being embraced at one side by a young woman while another sits at her feet on the other side, marked "Minton," 19th c., 12¼" h. (minor edge damage) **181.50**

Jardiniere, majolica, squatty bulbous body w/flaring scalloped rim w/C-scrolled handles, decorated w/relief-molded ferns & leaves, Foxglove patt. (ILLUS.) **3,740.00**

Minton Pastille Burner

Pastille Burner, cov., ironstone, square body w/angled corners & a widely flaring rim sitting on four

claw-shaped feet, each side
w/panels depicting Oriental figures
in turquoise & orange detail on a
white ground, mid-19th c., 9" h.
(ILLUS.) **1,380.00**
Plate, bread & butter, Ancestral
patt...**16.00**
Plate, salad, 7¾" d., Ancestral patt. **20.00**

Minton Landscape Decorated Plate

Plates, 9¼" d., medallions decorated
w/a landscape scene against gold
trimmed white ground, rims
decorated w/gold bands & gold trim
alternating w/bands of raised gold
dots, pr. (ILLUS. one of two) **150.00**
Tea set: cov. teapot, creamer & sugar
bowl; Cockatrice patt, 3 pcs............**350.00**
Tray, torte, floral enamel design
w/blue border, ca. 1912, 12" l. **105.00**
Vase, bud, 7½" h., 5¼" d., Secessionist Ware, squatty bulbous
body tapering sharply to a small
cylindrical neck w/rolled rim,

Minton Coral Shell Urn

decorated w/stylized squeeze-bag
flowers in ivory outlined in green
against a burgundy ground under
a glossy glaze, die-stamped
"MINTONS LTD. No. 29" **440.00**
Urns, majolica, molded conch shell
sitting atop molded coral base, pr.
(ILLUS. one of two, bottom previous
column) **13,750.00**

MOCHA

Mocha Mug, Chamber Pot & Salt Dip

*Mocha decoration is found on basically
utilitarian creamware or yellowware
articles and is achieved by a simple
chemical reaction. A color pigment of
brown, blue, green or black is given an acid
nature by infusion of tobacco or hops.
When this acid nature colorant is applied
in blobs to an alkaline ground color, it
reacts by spreading in feathery seaweed
designs. This type of decoration is usually
accompanied by horizontal bands of light
color slip. Produced in numerous
Staffordshire potteries from the late 18th
until the late 19th centuries, its name is
derived from the similar markings found
on mocha quartz. In addition to the
seaweed decoration, mocha wares are also
seen with Earthworm and Cat's Eye
patterns or a marbleized effect.*

Bowl, 12" d., 5¾" h., rounded sides
w/slightly flaring rim, wide white
band w/blue seaweed decoration
within two black stripes on
yellowware **$412.50**
Bowl, 13½" d., 6½" h., widely flaring
rounded sides on footring & w/a
molded rim, yellowware w/a white
band flanked by thin brown stripes &
decorated w/scattered green
seaweed designs, East Liverpool,
Ohio (minor wear, chips on base,
old dark surface chip in center of
interior)...**154.00**
Chamber pot, miniature, yellowware,
bulbous body w/slightly tapering rim
& loop handle, decorated w/white
band, black stripes & blue seaweed
decoration East Liverpool, Ohio,
slight hairline crack, 3⅛" d. (ILLUS.
center)..**145.50**
Creamer, ovoid body w/rim spout, C-

scroll handle, beige w/olive green rim, white leaf handle & spout, black seaweed decoration in a band around the lower half, 4¼" h. (edge wear, small old chips, interior w/blob of adhered clay) **852.50**

Mug, applied handle, marbleized brown & pumpkin orange w/applied white swag design, England, early 19th c. (imperfections) **747.50**

Mug, cylindrical, alternating bands of dicing, brown & blue w/dark brown seaweed decoration, England, 19th c., 5¾" h. (restored, minor imperfections) **230.00**

Mocha Ware Earthworm Mug

Mug, cylindrical body w/molded foot & loop handle decorated w/*cafe-au-lait* slip border w/brown, blue & white Earthworm patt. between mocha brown bands beneath a cobalt blue glazed bead-edged rouletted hatchwork border, the rim & lower body w/brown plain & scalloped borders within further beadwork bands, ca. 1820-30, rim abrasion & star cracks at base, 5⅝" h. (ILLUS.) **1,610.00**

Mug, yellowware, cylindrical body on a molded foot w/loop handle, decorated w/white band, brown stripes & black seaweed decoration, East Liverpool, Ohio, 3⅛" h. (ILLUS. left)....................................**522.50**

Pitcher, jug-type, 5½" h., decorated w/a wide band of brown seaweed decoration on a pumpkin orange ground, dark blue bands & pinstripes around the top rim & base, early 19th c. (tiny hairline in spout, few small chips at base)........**977.50**

Salt dip, yellowware, squatty bulbous body slightly tapering to flat rim, decorated w/white band & blue seaweed decoration, East Liverpool,

Ohio, glazed over chips & stains, 3" d. (ILLUS. right)..............**275.00**

Tea set, miniature: cov. teapot, cov. coffeepot, cov. sugar bowl, creamer, & four cups & saucers; simple ovoid & spherical forms w/a pumpkin orange ground decorated w/black seaweed designs, early 19th c., teapot 3¾" h., the set (imperfections) **4,887.00**

MULBERRY

Mulberry or Flow Mulberry wares were produced in the Staffordshire district of England in the period between 1835 and 1855 at many of the same factories which produced its close "cousin," Flow Blue China. In fact, some of the early Flow Blue patterns were also decorated with the purplish mulberry coloration and feature the same heavy smearing or "flown" effect. Produced on sturdy ironstone bodies, quite a bit of this ware is still to be found and it is becoming increasingly sought-after by collectors although presently its values lag somewhat behind similar Flow Blue pieces. The standard reference to Mulberry wares is Petra Williams book, Flow Blue China and Mulberry Ware, Similarity and Value Guide. *Another fine reference is* Mulberry Ironstone, Flow Blue's Best Kept Little Secret, *by Ellen R. Hill, (Mulberry Hill, 1993).*

Creamer, Jeddo patt., W. Adams & Son, 7¼" h. **$245.00**

Creamer, Nin-Po patt., R. Hall & Co. **265.00**

Creamer, Sydenham patt., J. Clementson.....................................**275.00**

Creamer & cov. sugar bowl, Corean patt., Podmore, Walker & Co., pr. (professionally repaired) **200.00**

Cup & saucer, handleless, Jeddo patt., Wm. Adams & Sons............**57.50**

Cup & saucer, handleless, Pelew patt., Edward Challinor **50.00**

Cup & saucer, handleless, Rhone Scenery patt., T. J. & J. Mayer **65.00**

Cup & saucer, handleless, Washington Vase patt., Podmore, Walker & Co......................................**95.00**

Pitcher, 9⅞" h., Hong patt., Thomas Walker, 2 qt..............**495.00**

Plate, 7½" d., Corean patt., Podmore, Walker & Co. **60.00**

Plate, 8" d., Chinese Ching (Canton) patt., Gildea & Walker........................**40.00**

Plate, 8¾" d., Corean patt., Podmore, Walker & Co. **75.00**

Plate, 9" d., Corean patt., Podmore, Walker & Co. **46.00**

Plates, 9½" d., Jeddo patt., Wm. Adams & Sons, pr. **75.00**

Plate, 9¾" d., Corean patt., Podmore, Walker & Co. **64.00**

Plate, 9¾" d., Temple patt., Podmore, Walker & Co. **80.00**

Plate, 9¾" d., Washington Vase patt., Podmore, Walker & Co. **53.00**

Plate, 10" d., Moss Rose patt., Jacob Furnival & Co. **65.00**

Plate, 10" d., Pelew patt., Edward Challinor & Co. **75.00**

Plate, 10⅜" d., Chinese Ching (Canton) patt., Wm. Adams **55.00**

Plate, 10½" d., Bochara patt., John Edwards **70.00**

Platter, 12" l., "Indian Encampment on the St. Lawrence," Francis Morley & Co. **250.00**

Platter, 12½" l., Cyprus patt., Davenport **125.00**

Platter, 14 x 17¾", Pelew patt., Edward Challinor & Co. (tiny nick & hairline) **325.00**

Platter, 15" l., Castle Scenery patt., Jacob Furnival **175.00**

Platter, 15" l., Whampoa patt., Dilwyn Swansea **245.00**

Platter, 15½" l., Tavoy patt., Thomas Walker **235.00**

Platter, 15½" l., rectangular w/cut corners, Washington Vase patt., Podmore, Walker & Co. (light stain) **275.00**

Platter, 15¾" l., Jeddo patt., W. Adams & Sons **190.00**

Platter, 16" l., Corean patt., Podmore, Walker & Co. **225.00**

Platter, 16¼" l., Chinese Ching (Canton) patt. **150.00**

Platter, 18" l., Corean patt., Podmore, Walker & Co. **395.00**

Platter, 18" l., Cyprus patt., Davenport **275.00**

Platter, 18" l., Pelew patt, Edward Challinor & Co. **275.00**

Platter, 18¾" l., Chinese Ching (Canton) patt. **225.00**

Punch cups, Corean patt., Podmore, Walker & Co., set of six **425.00**

Sauce tureen, cov., Washington Vase patt., Podmore, Walker & Co. **475.00**

Sauce tureen, cover & underplate, Vincennes patt., Samuel Alcock, the set (finial reglued & professional restoration) **575.00**

Soup plate w/flanged rim, Madras patt. **35.00**

Soup plate w/flanged rim, Chinese Ching (Canton) patt., Gildea & Walker, 8⅞" d. **55.00**

Sugar bowl, cov., lion handles, Corean patt., Podmore, Walker & Co. (small lid edge chip) **175.00**

Sugar bowl, cov., Corean patt., Podmore, Walker & Co. (professional repair) **225.00**

Sugar bowl, cov., Jeddo patt., William Adams & Sons **325.00**

Teapot, cov., Corean patt., Podmore, Walker & Co. (finial reglued) **495.00**

Teapot, cov., Jeddo patt., W. Adams & Sons **387.50**

Teapot, cov., Pelew patt. **295.00**

Teapot, cov., Tavoy patt., Thomas Walker (flakes on lid edge) **375.00**

Teapot, cov., Tivoli patt., Charles Meigh & Sons **325.00**

Teapot, cov., Washington Vase patt., Podmore, Walker & Co. (chip under finial) **425.00**

Undertray for soup tureen, octagonal w/wide tab handles, the center w/a river landscape w/a large mansion & mountains in the distance, people in the foreground, the border w/vignettes of classical scenes, 14¼" w. (professional rim restoration) **220.00**

Vegetable bowl, cov., Vincennes patt., Samuel Alcock, 10" d. (nick) **495.00**

Vegetable bowl, cov., Washington Vase patt., Podmore, Walker & Co. (finial reglued) **375.00**

Vegetable bowl, open, octagonal, Corean patt., Podmore, Walker & Co., 9" d. **325.00**

Vegetable bowl, open, Temple patt., Podmore, Walker & Co., 6¼ x 8" **335.00**

Vegetable bowl, open, Washington Vase patt., Podmore, Walker & Co., 7¾ x 9¾" **325.00**

Wash bowl & pitcher, Corean patt., Podmore, Walker & Co., 2 pcs. (tiny nick on pitcher & ¾" fine hairline under bowl rim) **1,075.00**

Wash bowl & pitcher, Jeddo patt., W. Adams & Son, ca. 1845, 2 pcs. **675.00**

Wash bowl & pitcher, Washington Vase patt., Podmore, Walker & Co., 2 pcs. (small under rim chip on bowl) **1,075.00**

NIPPON

"Nippon" is a term which is used to describe a wide range of porcelain wares produced in Japan from the late 19th century until about 1921. It was in 1891 that the U.S. implemented the McKinley

Tariff Act which required that all wares exported to the United States carry a marking indicating the country of origin. The Japanese chose to use "Nippon," their name for Japan. In 1921 the import laws were revised and the words "Made in" had to be added to the markings. Japan was also required to replace the "Nippon" with the English name "Japan" on all wares sent to the U.S.

Many Japanese factories produced Nippon porcelains and much of it was hand-painted with ornate floral or landscape decoration and heavy gold decoration, applied beading and slip-trailed designs referred to as "moriage." We indicate the specific marking used on a piece, when known, at the end of each listing below. Be aware that a number of Nippon markings have been reproduced and used on new porcelain wares.

Important reference books on Nippon include: The Collector's Encyclopedia of Nippon Porcelain, Series One through Three, by Joan F. Van Patten (Collector Books, Paducah, Kentucky) and The Wonderful World of Nippon Porcelain, 1891-1921 by Kathy Wojciechowski (Schiffer Publishing, Ltd., Atglen, Pennsylvania).

Nippon Urn

Ashtray, center decoration of two relief-molded horse heads w/clover decoration around rim, shaded brown, 5¼" d. (green "M" in Wreath mark).................................**$350.00**

Ashtray w/matchbox holder, scenic decoration of trees w/shoreline, yellow ground (green "M" in Wreath mark).................................**75.00**

Basket w/overhead scrolled handle, large h.p. roses on pastel ground, lavish gold trim, 5" h. (green Maple Leaf mark).................................**85.00**

Bowl, 5¼" sq., mitered corners, interior decoration of h.p. semi-matte peaches & peach tree branch,

delicately outlined in black on pastel peach ground, ivory exterior, brown rim w/black jeweled tracery.............**65.00**

Bowl, 7" d., footed, relief-molded peanuts.................................**120.00**

Bowl, 7" d., 3¼" h., three-footed, hexagonal, center medallion, band of pink roses & green leaves separated by geometric designs, gold beading, gold feet ("RC" in Wreath mark).................................**48.00**

Bowl, 8" d., handled, scenic decoration, moriage trim.................**85.00**

Bowl, 8½" d., two-handled, relief-molded purple, red & green grapes & leaves around rim (green "M" in Wreath mark).................................**210.00**

Bowl, 9" d., gold handled, black & gold decoration on white ground (one handle worn).................................**45.00**

Bowl, 10" d., footed, floral decoration w/cobalt border.................................**225.00**

Candlesticks, squared baluster-form, overall decoration of lavender violets w/yellow tops & base trimmed in gold decoration, 4¼" d., 9" h., pr......**265.00**

Celery set: oval handled tray & six tiny oval dishes; decorated w/h.p. plums on branch in almond, greens & tans, Art Deco geometric border, 7 pcs. (green "M" Wreath mark).......**145.00**

Celery tray, decorated w/h.p. violets & leaves, geometric gold design & raised beading, 5 x 12" (blue Rising Sun mark).................................**48.00**

Chocolate set: cov. chocolate pot & six cups & saucers; upper & lower bands of small stylized roses outlined in gold, white ground, 13 pcs. (green "M" In Wreath mark)......**250.00**

Condensed milk jar, cover & under-plate, decorated w/h.p. floral medallions on black ground w/gold outlining, wide bands of rust w/black crisscross design & geometric gold borders, gold handles & finial (green "M" in Wreath mark), 3 pcs. **150.00**

Cup & saucer, demitasse, floral decoration w/heavy gild trim.............**120.00**

Cup & saucer, decorated w/h.p. red & orange roses & green leaves, gold outlines & jewels, gold jeweled rim, cup 3" d., 1¾" h., saucer, 4½" d. (green Crown mark).........................**15.00**

Cup & saucer, footed, gold trim (green "M" in Wreath mark)...............**80.00**

Dish, divided w/center basket handle, decorated w/pink flowers, green leaves, gold outlining, beading & trim, 7½ x 7¾" (red "M" in Wreath mark).................................**65.00**

Dish, leaf-shaped w/relief-molded acorns decoration, 8" l. **95 00**

Ewer, squatty bulbous body

decorated w/h.p. giant pink & red roses, green leaves on pastel ground, cobalt rim w/gold tracery, ornate gold handle, 6" d., 5⅜" h. (Maple Leaf mark)............................**140.00**

Hair receiver, cov., footed, scenic decoration, beaded edges, satin finish, 3½" h. **65.00**

Hatpin holder, hanging-type, cornucopia-shaped w/decoration of apple blossoms, gooseberries & other florals, lavish gold trim, artist-signed **275.00**

Humidor, cov., decorated w/h.p. yellow roses **115.00**

Humidor, cov., hexagonal, Indian head decoration, peace pipe on opposite side, applied Indian designs on lid (small chip inside lid).......................................**375.00**

Mayonnaise ladle, decorated w/pink flower on white ground, 4½" l. **18.00**

Nut set: footed master bowl & four individual footed dishes; moriage nuts & leaves decoration, scalloped rim, the set (green "M" in Wreath)....**120.00**

Nut set: footed master bowl & five individual footed dishes; decorated w/h.p. flowers & gold trim, 6 pcs. **125.00**

Pitcher, 8¼" h., floral decoration on cobalt blue ground, unmarked **185.00**

Pitcher, tankard, 12" h., overall decoration of irises & foliage, "Royal Kinran) **275.00**

Pitcher, tankard, 12¼" h., front decorated w/ornate large gold relief-molded scrolls, gold flowers & raised outlines & large pink poppies, back w/single flower on sprayed purple & grey pastel satin ground, ornate scroll handle (Royal Nishiki Nippon) **250.00**

Plaque, pierced to hang, pink & orchid floral decoration, 9½" d. **155.00**

Plaque, pierced to hang, scenic decoration, 9½" d., (green "M" in Wreath mark) **250.00**

Plaque, pierced to hang, bisque, scene of trees, meadow, 10" d. (green "M" in Wreath mark)..............**140.00**

Plaque, pierced to hang, decorated w/scene of trio of white swans, sun behind clouds, draped moriage border, 10" d. (green "M" in Wreath mark)...**275.00**

Plaque, pierced to hang, fall foliage scene w/house & meadow, brown rim, 10" d. (green "M" in Wreath mark)...**210.00**

Plaque, pierced to hang, scenic decoration of large tree by lake, brown & cream satin finish ground w/fine brown moriage border, 10¼" d., (green "M" Wreath mark) ...**125.00**

Plaque, pierced to hang, relief-molded bison, 10½" d. (green "M" in Wreath mark) **595 00**

Plate, child's, 5¾" d., molded Doll Face patt. **60.00**

Plate, 6½" d., pierced to hang, relief-molded boy's face (Rising Sun mark)...**90.00**

Plate, 7" d., decorated w/cranes **20.00**

Plate, 7" d., decorated w/violets...........**20.00**

Plate, 10¼" d., pierced to hang, scenic decoration of tree, lake & grass in brown satin finish on cream satin background, (green "M" in Wreath **195.00**

Plate, 10¼" d., center mountain scene w/trees & lake, border of alternating birds & flowers bordered w/black & beaded gold trim (blue Maple Leaf mark) **95.00**

Spoonholder, overall decoration of peonies on earthtone ground of tree bark...**85.00**

Tea set, child's: cov. teapot, creamer, cov. sugar bowl, two cups & saucers & two tea plates; decorated w/bouquets of pink roses & yellow birds, 9 pcs. (blue Rising Sun mark).........**155.00**

Tea set: cov. teapot, creamer & cov. sugar bowl, six cups & saucers & plates; decorated w/h.p. florals, 23 pcs. **425.00**

Toothpick holder, scenic sailboat decoration **90.00**

Urn, baluster-shaped body w/squared handles at shoulder sitting on complimentary base, decorated w/h.p. pastoral scene w/sheep, printed mark under base, 20th c., 27⅛" h. (ILLUS.) **1,840.00**

Vase, 4¾" h., footed bulbous body w/short cylindrical neck flanked by small angled handles on the shoulder, scenic landscape decoration on lower body w/cobalt upper body w/overall moriage trim (blue Maple Leaf mark) **150.00**

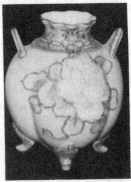

Melon-lobed Nippon Vase with Roses

Vase, 5½" h., 4" d., footed bulbous melon-lobed body tapering to a short ruffled neck flanked by small green loop handles on the shoulder, decorated w/pink roses & moriage trim, green feet, marked (ILLUS.) **75.00**

Vase, 6" h., hexagonal w/gold angled handles, decorated w/white peonies on taupe ground..**90.00**

Vase, 6½" h., bulbous footed body, ornate shoulder handles, short flaring scalloped mouth, moriage tree & mountain scenic decoration **435.00**

Vase, 6½" h., cylindrical body tapering to wide flared neck, angled stand-up shoulder handles, decorated w/a camel rider in a desert scene, blue ground w/gold trim (Maple Leaf mark).....................**225.00**

Vase, 6½" h., cylindrical body w/rounded shoulder to short neck w/molded flaring rim, small angled scroll shoulder handles, moriage Dragon patt. on a grey ground (green "M" in Wreath mark)...............**135.00**

Vase, 6½" h., tapering cylindrical body with a wide shoulder tapering to short wide cylindrical neck, cobalt blue w/heavy silver overlay, unmarked **345.00**

Vase, 7" h., decorated w/yellow roses & green leaves on light green ground, brown handles w/ beading...**80.00**

Vase, 10" h., 8" d., heavy gilded handles & lavish gilded designs around the center floral decoration, artist-signed, (blue Maple Leaf mark)..**300.00**

Vase, 12" h., four-sided, decorated w/pastel scenic panels, each site a different scene, gold trim (green "M" in Wreath mark) **325.00**

Vase, footed bulbous four melon-lobed body tapering to a short ruffled neck flanked by small loop handles on the shoulder, one lobe decorated w/h.p. water & shoreline scene, others w/h.p. flowers, lobes outlined in green & white jeweling, brick red feet w/gold trim, unmarked..**55.00**

Vases, 7⅜" h., 4" d., decorated w/h.p. large red poppies, white flowers & green leaves on pastel purple & laventer ground, lavish raised gold outlining, tracery & beading, gold feet & shoulder handles (blue Maple Leaf mark), pr...**295.00**

NORITAKE

Noritake china, still in production in Japan, has been exported in large quantities to this country since early in this century. Though the Noritake Company first registered in 1904, it did not use "Noritake" as part of its backstamp until 1918. Interest in Noritake has escalated as collectors now seek out pieces made between the "Nippon" era and World War II (1921-41). The Azalea pattern is also popular with collectors.

Ashtray, harlequin figure on rim, blue lustre ground **$195.00**

Ashtray, figural pelican, white on yellow & black ground....................**145.00**

Basket, Azalea patt., "Dolly Varden," No. 193, 2½ x 4⅜", 4" h. **147.00**

Basket, basketweave design w/relief molded acorns & blossoms, 6" l.........**60.00**

Berry set: master bowl & six sauce dishes; parrot on branch decoration, dark blue lustre finish w/cream lustre center, black trim, set of 7................**160.00**

Bowl, 5" d., Pattern No. 175, white & gold...**15.00**

Bowl, 5" d., Pattern No. 16034, white & gold...**15.00**

Bowl, fruit, 5¼" d., Azalea patt., No. 9 ....**9.50**

Bowl, cereal (oatmeal), 5½" d., Azalea patt., No. 55 ....**23.00**

Bowl, fruit, 5¼" d., Azalea patt., No. 9 ....**9.50**

Bowl, 6" d., Pattern No. 175, white & gold...**18.00**

Bowl, 6" d., Pattern No. 16034, white & gold...**18.00**

Bowl, 7½" d., Pattern No. 175, white & gold **20.00**

Bowl, 7½" d., Pattern No. 16034, white & gold **20.00**

Bowl, 7¾" d., decorated w/ship scene **80.00**

Bowl, salad, 10" d., handled, Azalea patt., No. 12 ....**40.00**

Bowl, cloverleaf-shaped, large scrolled handle, decorated w/woodland stream scene, detailed tree, gold rim...**58.00**

Cake plate, Azalea patt., No. 10, 9¾" d..**40.00**

Cake plate, Tree in Meadow patt., No. 45 ....**40.00**

Candy dish, cov., stylized floral decoration **85.00**

Casserole, cov., Tree in the Meadow patt. **90.00**

Casserole, cov., Pattern No. 175, white & gold **140.00**

Casserole, cov., Pattern No. 16034, white & gold **140.00**

Celery set: tray & six individual salt dips; decorated w/raised gold design on ivory ground, 7 pcs. **85.00**

Celery set: tray & six individual salt dips, Pattern No. 175, white & gold, 7 pcs. **125.00**

Celery set: tray & six individual salt dips, Pattern No. 16034, white & gold, 7 pcs. **125.00**

Chalice on pedestal base, curled handles, moriage trim, green marbleized ground **55.00**

Chocolate set: cov. tankard-type, chocolate pot, six cups & saucers; decorated w/lavender shaded irises & gold trim, 13 pcs. **245.00**

Compote, open, 6½" d., Art Deco style scene of lady in gondola & gondolier, tree & setting sun **150.00**

Compote, open, 6½" d., 2¾" h., Tree in Meadow patt., No. 175 ....**67.50**

Condiment set: salt & pepper shakers & cov. mustard jar w/spoon on handled tray; Azalea patt., No. 14, the set **47.00**

Condiment set: toothpick holder, cov. mustard jar, & salt & pepper shakers on handled tray; Tree in Meadow patt., brown & beige, the set **25.00**

Creamer, h.p. sunset, lakeside scene, 3" h. **7.00**

Creamer & open sugar bowl, demitasse, Azalea patt., No. 123, pr. **92.50**

Creamer & cov. sugar bowl, Morning Glory patt., blue w/gold trim, pr. **30.00**

Creamer & cov. sugar bowl, berry decoration, geometric lustre, pr. **75.00**

Cup & saucer, demitasse, Athlone patt. **10.00**

Cup & saucer, demitasse, Azalea patt., No. 183 ....**140.00**

Cup & saucer, demitasse, Pattern No. 175, white & gold **25.00**

Cup & saucer, demitasse, Pattern No. 16034, white & gold **25.00**

Cup & saucer, Pattern No. 175, white & gold **24.00**

Cup & saucer, Pattern No. 16034, white & gold **24.00**

Dish, lemon-shaped, Tree in the Meadow patt. **20.00**

Dish, relief-molded figural lemon & leaves, 5¾" d. **65.00**

Dish, shell-shaped, Tree in the Meadow patt. **350.00**

Dish w/three open handles, rounded triangular-shape decorated w/h.p. large pink daisies on pastel ground w/gold rim, artist-signed, 7" w. **22.00**

Gravy boat, Pattern No. 175, white & gold **65.00**

Gravy boat, Pattern No. 16034, white & gold..**65.00**

Gravy boat w/attached underplate, Azalea patt., No. 40 ....**47.00**

Jam jar, cov., basket-type w/overhead handle, molded red cherries finial on notched cover w/earthtone scenic decoration **68.50**

Jam jar, cov., basket-type w/overhead handle, Tree in the Meadow patt. **130.00**

Lemon plate, square, Art Deco style, decorated w/daisies on orange ground..**36.00**

Mustard jar w/handle, cover & spoon, Azalea patt., No. 191 ....**58.00**

Mustard jar, cov., handled, & spoon, Azalea patt., No. 191 (light gold wear on knob) **58.00**

Night Light, figural owl on tree branch, natural coloring **650.00**

Plate, bread & butter, Pattern No. 175, white & gold **15.00**

Plate, bread & butter, Pattern No. 16034, white & gold....................**15.00**

Plate, luncheon, Pattern No. 175, white & gold **22.00**

Plate, luncheon, Pattern No. 16034, white & gold **22.00**

Plate, dinner, Pattern No. 16034, white & gold..**24.00**

Plate, salad, Pattern No. 175, white & gold **17.00**

Plate, salad, Pattern No. 16034, white & gold..**17.00**

Plate, 7¾" d., Art Deco decoration of lady holding flower basket **195.00**

Plate, 8⅝" d., Tree in Meadow patt. **7.00**

Plate, dinner, 9¾" d., Tree in Meadow patt. **75.00**

Plate, dinner, pattern No. 175, white & gold..**24.00**

Platter, 9 x 12", Azalea patt., No. 56....**52.00**

Platter, 12" l., Tree in Meadow patt......**60.00**

Platter, 14" l., Pattern No. 175, white & gold **85.00**

Platter, 14" l., Pattern No. 16034, white & gold **85.00**

Platter, 16" l., Pattern No. 175, white & gold **95.00**

Platter, 16" l., Pattern No. 16034, white & gold **95.00**

Powder puff box, cov., disc-form, Art Deco style in orange & pale blue w/a figural blossom finial, 3¾" d. **200.00**

Refreshment set, Art Deco style,

kidney-shaped plate w/one open
handle & cup, cup interior decorated
w/face of Art Deco lady, orange,
plate 8½" w., 2 pcs. **175.00**
Relish dish, divided, two-compart-
ment, Tree in the Meadow patt. **50.00**
Salt shaker, gold self top, Tree in
Meadow patt., 2⅜" h. **6.00**
Salt & pepper shakers, Azalea patt.,
No. 11, pr. (gold top worn on
one)...**22.00**
Salt & pepper shakers, Azalea
patt., No. 14, pr. (gold wear) **10.00**
Salt & pepper shakers, individual
size, Tree in the Meadow patt.,
pr. **25.00**
Salt & pepper shakers, bulb-type,
Tree in the Meadow patt., pr. **25.00**
Sandwich plate w/center handle,
scenic decoration of couple fishing,
9¾" d. **150.00**
Server, handled, three-section, scene
of man on camel, cobalt &
gold, 8½" d. **100.00**
Sugar bowl, cov., Athlone patt. **15.00**

Azalea Pattern Sugar Bowl

Sugar bowl, cov., cylindrical body
w/molded squared handles, Azalea
patt., No. 7 (ILLUS.) **20.00**
Sugar shaker, Azalea patt.,
No. 19322 ....**90.00**
Syrup pitcher, cov., Azalea patt.,
No. 97, 4½" h. **75.00**
Tete-a-tete set, demitasse: cov. pot,
creamer, sugar bowl, two cups &
saucers & tray; decorated w/gold
birds & flowers on orange &
pearlized white ground, 8 pcs. **140.00**
Vegetable bowl, open, oval, Pattern
No. 175, white & gold **47.00**
Vegetable bowl, open, oval, Pattern
No. 16034, white & gold **47.00**
Wall pocket, decorated w/poppies **95.00**
Wall pocket, flared, colorful Art Deco
style landscape scene w/house,
7" h. **125.00**
Waste bowl, Tree in the Meadow
patt. **60.00**
Whipped cream set: 4½" d. bowl,

ladle & underplate; Azalea patt.,
No. 3, 3 pcs. **35.00**

OLD IVORY

*Old Ivory china was produced in
Silesia, Germany, in the late 1800s and
takes its name from the soft white
background coloring. A wide range of table
pieces was made with the various patterns
usually identified by a number rather than
a name.*

Berry set: master bowl & seven small
sauce dishes; No. 16, 8 pcs. **$200.00**
Bowl, master berry, 9½" d., No. 16 ......**75.00**
Cake plate, open-handled, No. 78,
10"d. **110.00**
Cake set: 10" d. pierced handle cake
plate & six 6¼" d. plates; No. 84,
7 pcs. **195.00**
Creamer & cov. sugar bowl, No. 84,
pr. **150.00**
Cup & saucer, No. 84 ....**55.00**
Plate, 6" d., Holly patt., artist-signed **65.00**
Plate, 7½" d., No. 82 ....**75.00**
Plate, 8" d., No. 28 ....**42.50**
Platter, open-handled, No. 16,
11½" l. **120.00**
Salt & pepper shakers, No. 75, pr. **85.00**
Sugar bowl, cov., No. 15 ....**50.00**
Waste bowl, No. 75 ....**110.00**

OLD SLEEPY EYE

Indian Head Stein

*Sleepy Eye, Minnesota, was named
after an Indian chief. The Sleepy Eye*

Milling Co. had stoneware and pottery premiums made at the turn of the century first by the Weir Pottery Company and subsequently by Western Stoneware Co., Monmouth, Illinois. On these items the trademark Indian head was signed beneath "Old Sleepy Eye," The colors were Flemish blue on grey. Later pieces by Western Stoneware to 1937 were not made for Sleepy Eye Milling Co. but for other businesses. They bear the same Indian head but "Old Sleepy Eye" does not appear below. They have a reverse design of tepees and trees and may or may not be marked Western Stoneware on the base. These items are usually found in cobalt blue on cream and are rarer in other colors. In 1952, Western Stoneware made a 22 oz. and 40 oz. stein with a chestnut brown glaze. This mold was redesigned in 1968. From 1968 to 1973 a limited number of 40 oz. steins were produced for the Board of Directors of Western Stoneware. These were marked and dated and never sold as production items. Beginning with the first convention of the Old Sleepy Eye Club in 1976, Western Stoneware has made a souvenir which each person attending receives. These items are marked with the convention site and date. It should also be noted that there have been some reproduction items made in recent years.

Pitcher, 9" h., blue on beige, ca. 1906-37...**$145.00**
Stein, chestnut brown, 1952, 22 oz. size **275.00**
Stein, Flemish blue on grey stoneware, Weir Pottery Co., 1903, 7¾" h. (ILLUS.)...............**500.00 to 550.00**

OYSTER PLATES

Union Porcelain Works Oyster Plate

Oyster plates intrigue a few collectors. Oysters were shucked and the meat served in wells of these attractive plates specifically designed to serve oysters. During the late 19th century they were made of fine china and majolica. Some plates were decorated in the realistic "trompe l'oeil" technique while others simply matched the pattern of a dinner service.

Haviland china, four-wells, decorated w/small yellow roses, brown foliage & gold edge trim, set of 8...............**$595.00**
Limoges porcelain, five-well, pastel-colored wells outlined w/gilt scrolls all on a white ground, marked "Limoges," 8½" d., set of 4...............**440.00**
Porcelain, delicate white pattern, good bas-relief scrollwork, 8" d..........**60.00**
Porcelain, five-well, cream w/gold trim, Germany, 8¼" d........................**70.00**
Porcelain, h.p. brown relief-molded oyster shell & two mussel shells in center for condiments, white swirled, scalloped blank w/gold trim, unmarked, 9" d. (under base collar flake) **40.00**
Union Porcelain Works, clam shell-shaped, cream colored, molded w/four black-edged concave oyster shells variously tinged, a gilt-edged concave scallop shell, red lobster claw, a small yellow & red crab, a blue or purple shaded black mussel shell & other small colorful shells amid seaweed differently colored in white, tan, turquoise, rose & yellow, the hinge of the rim edge in gilding, marked "U.P.W." & an eagle's head, printed in olive green "PAT JAN 4. 1881.," four marked in yellow "UNION PORCELAIN WORKS GREENPOINT N.Y.," three incised "V," "5," or "12," Greenpoint, New York, ca. 1881-1885, 8¼" to 8⁹⁄₁₆" l. (ILLUS. one of six) **920.00**

PARIAN

Parian is unglazed porcelain in the biscuit stage, and takes its name from its resemblance to Parian marble used for statuary. Parian wares were made in this country and abroad through much of the last century and continue to be made.

Busts of Apollo & Athena, each wearing helmets & armor, marked "Bavaria, Germany," 10¾" & 11" h., facing pr. **$132.00**
Creamer, ovoid body tapering to a flaring rim w/side spout, C-scroll

handle, the body relief-molded w/camping scenes, marked "Published by S. Alcock & Co., Burslem," ca. 1840, 4¼" h................**38.50**

Figure of barefoot female in peasant dress & scarf, holding a mandolin, shades of ivory, ca. 1885, marked in a lozenge on reverse "Robinson & Leadbeater," 16" h. **550.00**

Figure of a classical goddess standing beside a round column & leaning on a small globe & holding a calipers, 19th c., 15½" h. **110.00**

Figure of a young woman standing w/one leg raised, nude except for drape across the raised leg, 11½" h..**150.00**

Figure of Mercury, standing nude except for helmet & small drapery, holding a pan flute, marked "R & L" for Robinson & Leadbeater, late 19th c., 23" h. **357.50**

Figure group, a seated woman in peasant dress w/a large dog w/front paws across her lap, applied flowers at base, 13" h. (minor damage to flowers) **82.50**

Pitcher, 10¾" h., low foot, tapering sides, slightly flaring rim, orange handle, relief-molded decoration of bundled reeds & berries...................**192.50**

PARIS & OLD PARIS

China known by the generic name of Paris and Old Paris was made by several Parisian factories from the 18th through the 19th century; some of it is marked and some is not. Much of it was handsomely decorated.

Paris Porcelain Figural Vase

w/h.p. garden & field flowers, 19th c., 11⅝" d., 13¾" h. (ILLUS.) **$1,035.00**

Tea set: cov. teapot, cov. sugar bowl, creamer, waste bowl, seven tea cups, seven coffee cups & seventeen saucers; simple footed ovoid forms, each piece w/h.p. landscape scenes of buildings & ruins, gilt band trim, figural sphinx heads atop the handles of teapot, creamer & sugar bowl, dragon head spout on teapot, mid-19th c., the set (damages).....................................**2,300.00**

Vases, 11¼" h., 9" l., cornucopia-form w/widely flaring scalloped & scroll-molded rims & large, ornate leafy scrolls along the bottom, raised on rectangular scroll-molded plinths, the upper neck decorated w/colorful floral bouquets against a white ground above mauve & lower white scrolls trimmed w/gilt, Jacob Petit, Paris, 19th c., pr. (chips).................**862.50**

Bell-form Jardiniere

Jardiniere, bell-form, decorated

Two- Handled Old Paris Vase

Vase, 12" h., figural, enamel & gilt decorated, woman sitting on a pillow supporting a leaf-formed vase, 19th c. (ILLUS. top previous page)..**374.00**

Vase, 13½" h., paneled baluster-form body w/reticulated rim & base w/two bamboo-shaped handle at sides, h.p. scene of children in rectangular reserve on one side, on cerulean blue ground w/gold accents, marked w/raised sunburst "633" in oval, late 19th c., some rubbing (ILLUS. bottom previous page) **489.00**

PENNSBURY

Inspired by the long tradition of Pennsylvania Dutch style pottery in Pennsylvania, Henry and Lee Below founded their pottery near Morrisville in 1950 and named it for the nearby Pennsbury Manor.

Specializing in Pennsylvania Dutch and country-style decoration, Pennsbury Pottery was hand-painted in a variety of colorful designs. Although tablewares were the major products, special commemorative items and a line of bird figures also originated at this pottery until its closure in 1970.

Ashtray, motto-type, round, Amish boy & girl kissing w/"Such Schmootzers," 5" d. **$26.00**

Ashtray, motto-type, round, Amish mother & boy w/"What giffs? - What ouches you?," 5" d. **16.00**

Ashtray, motto-type, round, busts of Amish man & woman w/"Outen the light," 5" d. **25.00**

Ashtray, round, commemorative, "Bordentown Yacht Club," 8" d. **30.00**

Basket, desk-type, Eagle patt. **45.00**

Bowl, heart-shaped, decorated w/a bird..**30.00**

Bowl, heart-shaped, Yellow Rooster patt...**48.00**

Bread tray, oval, Wheat patt., "Give Us This Day..." motto around rim, 6 x 9"..**40.00**

Butter dish, cov., Hex patt....................**24.00**

Canister set: cylindrical jar w/flat wooden cover w/rooster finial, incised w/"Flour," "Sugar," "Tea," or "Coffee;" Black Rooster patt., graduated set of 4 ....**250.00**

Canister set: cylindrical jar w/flat wooden cover w/rooster finial, incised w/"Flour," "Sugar," "Tea," or "Coffee;" Red Rooster patt., graduated set of 4............................**365.00**

Christmas plate, "Tree Tops," 1961 ......**35.00**

Christmas plate, "Tree Tops," 1965........**35.00**

Christmas plate, "Tree Tops," 1971 Glenview...**25.00**

Christmas plate, 1970, Angel patt., Stumar Company, 8½" d.................**20.00**

Coffeepot, cov., Black Rooster patt. **40.00**

Creamer, Amish patt., 2½" h...............**17.00**

Creamer, Black Rooster patt., 2½" h. ..**28.00**

Creamer, Red Rooster patt., 4" h........**24.00**

Creamer, Hex patt., 4" h. **18.00**

Cruets, oil & vinegar, jug-shaped, the stopper for one in the form of an Amish woman's head, the other the head of an Amish man, 7" h., pr. **123.00**

Cup & saucer, Red Rooster patt. **27.00**

Model of Audubon's Warbler, No. 122, artist-signed.......................**175.00**

Mug, Amish patt., 5" h..........................**30.00**

Mug, Amish Fisherman patt. **25.00**

Mug, beer-type, Barber Shop Quartet patt...**22.50**

Mug, beer-type, "Swallow the Insult"....**37.50**

Pitcher, 4" h., Black Rooster patt.........**22.00**

Pitcher, 5" h., Hex patt.........................**38.00**

Pitcher, 6¼" h., Eagle patt., 1 qt..........**70.00**

Pitcher, 7¼" h., Black Rooster patt., 2 qt...**92.50**

Plaque, rectangular, commemorative, railroad series, relief-molded early train engine w/"Western & Atlantic R.R. 1855 - General," 5½ x 7½" **40.00**

Plaque, round, motto-type, "Outen the light," 4" d. **35.00**

Plaque, round, motto-type, "Papa's half et already," 4" d. **31.00**

Plaque, round, motto-type, "Such Schmootzers," 4" d. **22.00**

Plaque, round, "Walking to Homestead," pictures a family walking, 6" d....................................**50.00**

Plaque, rectangular, ship series, "The Flying Cloud," 7 x 9½"........................**80.00**

Plate, 8" d., Family Wagon patt............**38.00**

Plate, 10" d., Black Rooster patt. **15.00**

Pretzel bowl, oblong, Barber Shop Quartet patt., 8 x 12"........................**73.00**

Salt & pepper shakers, pitcher-shaped, Black Rooster patt., pr. **30.00**

Snack set: kidney-shaped plate & cup; Black Rooster patt., 2 pcs. **22.00**

Snack set: kidney-shaped plate & cup; Hex patt., 2 pcs. **28.00**

Snack set: kidney-shaped plate & cup; Red Rooster patt., 2 pcs. **24.00**

Sugar bowl, cov., Red Rooster patt., 4" h...**23.00**

Wall pocket, square w/cut corners, h.p., lady's head w/rose, 6½" w. **150.00**

Wall pocket, model of a fireplace bellows, embossed eagle on the front, 10" l..**67.50**

PHOENIX BIRD & FLYING TURKEY PORCELAIN

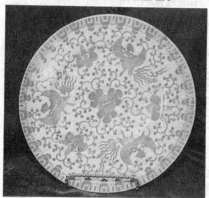

Phoenix Bird Plate

The Phoenix bird, a symbol of immortality and spiritual rebirth, has been handed down through Egyptian mythology as a bird that consumed itself by fire after 500 years and then rose again, renewed, from its ashes. This bird has been used to decorate Japanese porcelain designed for export for more than 100 years. The pattern incorporates a blue design of the bird, variously known as the "Flying Phoenix," the "Flying Turkey" or the "Ho-o," stamped on a white ground. It became popular with collectors because there was an abundant supply since the ware was produced for a long period of time. Pieces can be found marked with Japanese characters, with a "Nippon" mark, or a "Made in Japan" or "Occupied Japan" mark.Though there are several variations to the pattern and border, we have lumped them together since values seem to be quite comparable. A word of caution to the collectors, Phoenix Bird pattern is still being produced.

Bowl, 4¾" d., Phoenix Bird **$7.00**
Bowl, 6 x 7¾" oval, Phoenix Bird.........**20.00**
Creamer, hotel size, Phoenix Bird **10.00**
Creamer & cov. sugar bowl,
   Phoenix Bird, pr. **27.50**

Phoenix Bird Salt & Pepper Shakers

Cup & saucer, demitasse, Phoenix
   Bird **16.00**
Cup & saucer, Phoenix Bird..............**11.00**
Egg cup, Phoenix Bird **12.00**
Plate, 6" d., Phoenix Bird **5.00**
Plate, 7½" d., Phoenix Bird **8.50**
Plate, 8½" d., Phoenix Bird (ILLUS.)....**22.00**
Salt & pepper shakers, Phoenix
   Bird, 3" h., pr. (ILLUS. bottom
   previous column...............................**16.50**
Teapot, cov., Phoenix Bird..................**55.00**
Trivet, Phoenix Bird **75.00**

PICKARD

Pickard, Inc., making fine hand-colored china today in Antioch, Illinois, was founded in Chicago in 1894 by Wilder A. Pickard. The company now makes its own blanks but once only decorated those bought from other potteries, primarily from the Havilands and others in Limoges, France.

Ashtray & cigarette holder, gold
   overall, 2 pcs...................................**$35.00**
Berry set: 9½" d. master bowl & six
   5½" d. sauce dishes; h.p. blackberry
   decoration, artist-signed, the set......**895.00**
Bowl, boat-shaped, 5 x 7½",
   decorated w/nuts, artist-signed,
   ca 1905-10......................................**250.00**
Bowl, fruit, 6 x 10½", 4" h., footed,
   interior & exterior decorated w/
   green leaves & fruits, artist-
   signed **350.00**
Bowl, 7 x 8", footed, decorated
   w/nuts, artist-signed, ca. 1912-18....**220.00**
Bowl, 8¼" d., handled, decorated
   w/orange poppies & buds, gold &
   red tracery & lavish gold trim,
   pearlized iridescent w/pastel
   highlights, eight tri-scallops,
   ca. 1898-1904.................................**255.00**
Bowl, 8½" d., two-handled, decorated
   w/deserted garden scene around
   border & gold center, artist-signed...**155.00**
Bowl, 9" d., shallow, open handles,
   scenic decoration w/gold border,
   ca. 1912, artist-signed **225.00**
Bowl, 10" d., decorated w/red
   raspberries, artist-signed,
   ca. 1905-10......................................**160.00**

Bowl, 10" d., decorated w/swirl of
lilies, ca. 1903-05.............................**245.00**

Bowl, decorated w/gold & red
poppies, artist-signed, Limoges
blank **145.00**

Candy dish w/gold pinched loop
handles, center decoration of cerise
sunflowers, fluffy iridescent green
leaves, outlined in gold, gold cross-
hatch work & lavender & pink design
below sunflowers, wide gold border
w/three red bands, artist signed,
ca. 1910-12.....................................**170.00**

Centerpiece bowl, gold pedestal
base w/eight feet, decorated
w/orange & yellow figures w/white
triangles above, outlined by light &
dark green & overall gold, interior
center gold figure, eight multi-
petalled scallops rise above rim,
7½ x 8½"...**325.00**

Charger, decorated w/red poppies &
gold border, ca. 1910, 12½" d..........**225.00**

Compote, open, 7" d., 2¾" h.,violets
decoration, artist-signed, ca.
1912-18...**250.00**

Compote, open, 10½" d., handled,
decorated w/violet & pink flowers,
artist-signed, 1905 mark **345.00**

Creamer & cov. sugar bowl, broad
floral band w/plums & raspberries
overall on gold ground, artist-signed,
pr...**175.00**

Creamer & cov. sugar bowl,
decorated w/one inch band of
various blue shaded blossoms on
gold etched floral ground, ca. 1919,
pr...**145.00**

Creamer & cov. sugar bowl,
decorated w/Pilgrims & the sailing
ship Mayflower, matte finish, ca.
1912-19, pr. **225.00**

Mustard jar, cov., floral decoration,
gold trim, ca. 1912-19 ....**32.00**

Pitcher, cider, 4" h., decorated
w/violets, artist-signed,
ca. 1910-12.......................................**495.00**

Pitcher, milk, 4½" h., violets decoration, artist-signed, ca. 1905-10 .....**250.00**

Pitcher, cider, 5½" h., decorated
w/yellow poppies, artist-signed,
ca. 1905-10.......................................**500.00**

Pitcher, cider, 5½" h., gold etched
body w/wide band of pink roses,
artist-signed **395.00**

Pitcher, cov., milk, 5½" h., flower
basket decoration, gold ground,
artist-signed, ca. 1922-25 ....**325.00**

Pitcher, cider, 5¾" h., decorated
w/gold daisies & metallic brown
band on ivory ground, artist-signed,
ca. 1910-12.......................................**650.00**

Pitcher, cider, 6" h., decorated

w/currants, artist-signed,
ca. 1903-05.......................................**650.00**

Pitcher, cider, 6" h., lilies decoration,
artist-signed, ca. 1905-10 ....**650.00**

Pitcher, milk, 8" h., tulip decoration,
artist-signed, ca. 1905-10 ....**690.00**

Plate, 7" d., landscape scene, matte
finish, artist-signed.........................**250.00**

Plate, 7⅝" d., decorated w/acorns on
branch, green leaves, rose & light
green pastel ground, gold trim,
apple scallop gold narrow border,
artist-signed, ca. 1905-10 ....**75.00**

Plate, 8¼" d., decorated w/lavender &
pink lilies & huge highly detailed &
vari-colored green leaves & stems
on rosy pastel ground, gold border
w/wide & short scallops & fleur-de-
lis below each short gold scallop,
artist-signed, ca. 1905-10 ....**90.00**

Plate, 8¼" d., scenic decoration of
water, temple pillars, moon & trees,
matte finish, ca. 1912-19,
artist-signed **205.00**

Plate, 8½" d., overall decoration of
pink thistles, blue bells & gold oak
leaves w/Scotch plaid border, three
gold shields w/orange lions, gold
rim, artist-signed, ca. 1910-1912 .....**195.00**

Plate, 8½" d., Art Nouveau decoration
w/Dutch girls, windmills & tulips,
matte finish, artist-signed.................**145.00**

Plate, 8½" d., decorated w/flowers &
berries, artist-signed **225.00**

Plate, 8½" d., decorated w/lilies,
artist-signed **138.00**

Plate, 8½" d., decorated w/orchids,
artist-signed **138.00**

Plate, 8½" d., decorated w/pink
daffodils, artist-signed......................**125.00**

Plate, 8½" d., decorated w/poppies,
artist-signed **138.00**

Plate, 8½" d., scenic, "Yosemite,"
artist-signed,1905 mark **175.00**

Plate, 8⅝" d., center decoration of red
& purple berries & flowers, vari-
colored leaves & stems on pastel
& aqua ground, wide & narrow
scalloped border defined by red
scrolled tracery, artist signed,
ca. 1898-1904..................................**155.00**

Plate, 8¾" d., decorated w/maple leaf
& poinsettias, artist-signed..............**145.00**

Plate, 8¾" d., scenic decoration
w/stream & trees, pink & yellow
flowers & leaves & petals on grass
in foreground, purplish abstract
spires across water in background,
matte finish, artist-signed,
ca. 1912-19.......................................**215.00**

Plate, 8¾" d., decorated w/three large
sprays of flowers, leaves & buds,
iridescent green, violet & deep

melon, gold detailed & outlined, light
ground w/pastel tones, gold border,
outlined in red w/red tracery flower
& leaf groups, artist-signed,
ca. 1910-12 ....**105.00**

Plate, 8¾" d., Wildwood patt., artist-
signed **155.00**

Plate, 9" d., decorated w/gold
plaid & lions, artist-initialed,
ca. 1910-12......................................**95.00**

Plate, octagonal, 9¾" w., 10½" corner
to corner, depressed center
decorated w/pink roses & other
yellow & red florals & petals
w/balistrade & water in background,
cream ground, outlined by a circle
of gold, gold rim & 2" border w/
chains of light pink tea roses
alternating w/small blue flowers,
ca. 1912-19......................................**155.00**

Plate, 10" d., octagonal, center
decoration of fruits, artist-signed......**210.00**

Plate, 10¾" d., clover decoration in
center w/abstract border designs,
overall gold, lion & shield mark **65.00**

Relish dish, deep, decorated
w/nasturtiums, leaves & long trailing
stems on creamy ground, pale
green exterior, ca. 1898, 4 x 7"
oval **87.50**

Relish dish, open-handled, copper
lustre center w/matching stylized
florals on wide creamy border,
pealized exterior, 1905 mark,
5½ x 8"...**75.00**

Salt & pepper shakers, overall gold
decoration, pr.....................................**22.00**

Sign, advertising, triangular, free-
standing, decorated w/gold lion
w/shield & banner, reads "Pickard
China Made in USA," in gold letters,
5" each side, 4" base **95.00**

Tea set: cov. teapot, creamer & cov.
sugar bowl; deserted garden scene
decoration, artist signed, ca.
1912-18, 3 pcs. **950.00**

Tea set: cov. teapot, creamer & cov.
sugar bowl; violets decoration, artist-
signed, ca. 1910-12, 3 pcs...............**450.00**

Vase, 7" h., cylindrical body tapering
to a short cylindrical neck, decorated
w/moonlight scene of water & palm
trees, touch of pink in foreground
w/deep pink flowers, bisque finish
gold rim, artist-signed, gold maple
leaf mark **495.00**

Vase, 7½" h., palm trees decoration,
matte finish, artist-signed,
ca. 1912-18 ....**235.00**

Vase, 11½" h., cylindrical body
w/four-lobed gold rim, decorated
w/tropical sunset scene w/palm
trees & water, flowers in foreground,

bisque finish, artist-signed, gold
maple leaf mark **695.00**

PICTORIAL SOUVENIRS

Souvenir Vase of Albany, NY

*These small ceramic wares, expressly
made to be sold as a souvenir of a town or
resort, are decorated with a pictorial scene
which is usually titled. Made in profusion
in Germany, Austria, Bavaria, and
England, they were distributed by several
American firms including C.E. Wheelock &
Co., John H. Roth (Jonroth), Jones,
McDuffee & Co., Stratton Co., and others.
Because people seldom traveled in the early
years of this century, a small souvenir tray
or dish, picturing the resort or a town
scene, afforded an excellent, inexpensive
gift for family or friends when returning
from a vacation trip Seldom used and
carefully packed away later, there is an
abundant supply of these small wares
available today at moderate prices. Their
values are likely to rise.*

Dish, "Sheriff's Residence,
Cannelton, Ohio," ca. 1900.............**$22.00**

Plate, 10⅛" d., "Souvenir of
Zanesville (Ohio)," a large round
center scene of the "New Y Bridge,"
other scenes around the border,
blue & white, produced by Rowland
& Marsellus Co. for C.C. Aler Co. of
Zanesville, early 20th C. (age
crazing) **27.50**

Plate, "Astor Hotel," New York City,
Royal Rudolstadt blank.....................**59.00**

Plate, center picture of "Kingfisher
County Courthouse, Kingfisher,
Oklahoma," Germany **35.00**

Vase, 5" h., baluster-form body
w/double-loop handles & flared
base, color scene of "New Hotel

Ten Eyck, Albany, N.Y.," marked
"Made in Germany" (ILLUS.) **17.50**

POT LIDS

Collectible pot lids are decorated ceramic lids for commercial pots and jars originally containing soaps, shaving creams, hair pomade, and so on. The best-known lids were made by F. & R. Pratt in Fenton, England from about the middle of the 19th century.

**"Magda Toilet Cream Countie of
Boston,"** blue decoration on white
china **$85.00**
Pratt, Shakespeare birthplace,
pomade..**165.00**
Pratt, "Pegwell Bay...," color transfer-
printed harbor scene, 19th c.,
4" d..**77.00**

PRATT WARES

The earliest ware now classified as Pratt ware was made by Felix Pratt at his pottery in Fenton, England from about 1810. He made earthenware with bright glazes, relief sporting jugs, toby mugs and commercial pots and jars whose lids bore multicolored transfer prints. The F. & R. Pratt mark is mid-19th century. The name Pratt ware is also applied today to mid and late 19th century English ware of the same general type as that made by Felix Pratt.

Pitcher, jug-type, 5¼" h., embossed
portrait on one side of Lord
Wellington, on the other side
w/General Hill, ca. 1810 (glaze
wear) **$431.00**
Pitcher, jug-type, 7½" h., molded
design on one side of "Royal
Sufferers," & on the other w/the
Duke of York, impressed "Hawley"
at base, ca. 1795 (small chip at
base) **690.00**

Early Pratt Plaque

Plaque, pierced to hang, oval w/a
molded & pierced crest band, relief-
molded scene of two partially
draped figures near a tree, titled
"Paris and Oenone," decorated in
yellow, green & brown, ca. 1790-
1820, tiny enamel flakes, small
repaired rim chip. 6¼ x 7½"
(ILLUS.) **522.50**
Plate, 9½" d., a central polychrome
transfer-printed scene of schoolboys
fighting, an oak leaf & acorns border
w/gilt trim, marked "W. Mulready
R.A. Pinx.," Pratt, Fenton (minor
wear, crazing) **49.50**
Teapot, cov., long oval body, base &
top borders of molded acanthus
leaves flanking the center band
w/scenes of classical ladies, reeded
swan's-neck spout, entwined strap
handle, domed cover w/a band of
molded acanthus leaves & a small
recumbent lion finial, trimmed in
yellow ochre & loden green, early
19th c., 12" l., 7" h. (professional
repair to hairline in base, small chip
on spout tip & underside of cover) ...**550.00**

QUIMPER

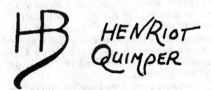

This French earthenware pottery has been made in France since the end of the 17th century and is still in production

today. Because the colorful decoration on this ware, predominantly of Breton peasant figures, is all hand-painted and each piece is unique, it has become increasingly popular with collectors in recent years. Most pieces offered today date from about the mid-19th century to the present. Modern potteries continue to operate today and contemporary examples are available in gift shops.

Plate, 12¼" d., peasant woman decoration, "Henriot L.F. 127" **$50.00**
Tray, 12¼" l., 6" w., blue floral decoration **60.00**
Vase, 10¼" h., portrait decoration of man on one side, woman on other side, brown rings, marked "HB France" **250.00**

REDWARE

Redware Beaker

Red earthenware pottery was made in the American colonies from the late 1600s. Bowls, crocks and all types of utilitarian wares were turned out in great abundance to supplement the pewter and handmade treenware. The ready availability of the clay, the same used in making bricks and roof tiles, accounted for the vast production. The lead-glazed redware retained its reddish color though a variety of colors could be obtained by adding various metals to the glaze. Interesting effects occurred accidentally through unsuspected impurities in the clay or uneven temperatures in the firing kiln which sometimes resulted in streaks or mottled splotches.

Redware pottery was seldom marked by the maker.

Apple butter jar, tapering rounded sides, everted rim, applied strap handle, mottled greenish amber & brown glaze, 6" d., 5" h. (small flakes) **$126.50**
Beaker, flaring cylindrical body w/a natural glaze, incised German lettering & tulip flower & vine decoration, Pennsylvania, 1703, 4⅛" h. (ILLUS.) **460.00**
Bowl, 6½" d., 3" h., cylindrical w/flared rim & small applied handles, rich amber glaze w/running splotches of dark brown (edge chips) **225.00**
Cookie board, rectangular w/six square embossed panels w/designs including a harp, stag, fruit, urn of flowers & bird, 5¾ x 8½" **440.00**
Cup, squatty w/slightly rounded sides & everted rim, rich amber glaze w/brown flecks, 4½" d., 3" h. (minor flakes) **82.50**
Flask, two-tone dark brown glaze, 6⅜" h. **110.00**
Flask, expanding cylinder tapering at the shoulder to a narrow neck w/flared rim, clear glaze w/rich reddish color w/dark brown splotches, 7¼" h. (chips on base) **170.50**

Redware Flowerpot

Flowerpot, flaring cylindrical body w/yellow glaze, applied decoration in two floral bands inscribed w/slip "APR 13 1877," flanked by two applied yellow-glazed handles above a ring of budding flowers, Pennsylvania, 1877, 8½" d., 9¼" h. (ILLUS.) **3,990.00**
Jug, globular w/strap handle rising from midsection to rim, rich dark olive green glaze w/orange spots, 6" h. (chips on base) **137.50**
Jug, cylindrical w/tapering shoulder & collared neck, applied strap handle, green glaze w/amber spots, 7⅞" h. (chips) **247.50**
Model of a lion, recumbent animal

w/large eyes, on an oblong base,
probably Pennsylvania, second half
19th c., 7½" l. (some chips) **3,737.00**

Preserving jar, cov, tapering cylinder
w/angled shoulder, cover w/knob
finial, greenish beige glaze w/brown
flecks & reddish highlights,
attributed to Morganville, N.Y.,
5¼" h. (minor chips) **258.50**

Preserving jar, cylindrical w/flared lip,
greenish beige glaze w/brown flecks
& reddish highlights, 6¼" h. (minor
glaze flakes on lip) **49.50**

RED WING

*Various potteries operated in Red Wing,
Minnesota from 1868, the most successful
being the Red Wing Stoneware Co.,
organized in 1878. Merged with other local
potteries through the years, it became
known as Red Wing Union Stoneware Co.
in 1894, and was one of the largest
producers of utilitarian stoneware items in
the United States. After a decline in the
popularity of stoneware products, an art
pottery line was introduced to compensate
for the loss and this was reflected in a new
name for the company, Red Wing Potteries,
Inc., in 1930. Stoneware production ceased
entirely in 1947, but vases, planters, cookie
jars and dinnerwares of art pottery quality
continued in production until 1967 when
the pottery ceased operation altogether.*

BRUSHED & GLAZED WARES

Vase, 6½" h., Modern style, rust
ground, No. B1418.........................**$68.00**

Vase, 9½" h., 7" d., wide ovoid body
w/a wide flat base, flat molded rim,
decorated w/an overall abstract
design in lustred pink, grey & yellow
interspersed w/random large black
'crystals,' die-stamped circular mark
"RED WING ART POTTERY"..........**880.00**

Vase, 10½" h., 6" d., ovoid body
tapering to a short cylindrical neck,
overall green & ochre mottled matte
glaze, die-stamped "RED WING
ART POTTERY" **275.00**

Vase, 10½" h., 6" d., footed squatty
bulbous base below a tall, wide &
gently tapering neck w/a rolled rim,
mottled green & ochre matte glaze,
die-stamped "RED WING ART
POTTERY - 186" **302.50**

Vase, 12 x 12", muted grey-blue, No.
M-3014......................................**130.00**

DINNERWARES & NOVELTIES

Lotus Pattern Cup & Saucer

Ashtray, wing-shaped, 1953
Anniversary....................................**100.00**

Beverage server, cov., Smart Set
patt..**92.50**

Bowl, 5" d., Magnolia patt. **5.00**

Bowl, 5¼" d., Lotus patt.........................**4.50**

Bowl, berry, Blossom Time patt.,
Concord shape **3.00**

Bowl, cereal, Bob White patt...............**10.00**

Bowl, 8½" d., Blossom Time patt.,
Concord shape **9.00**

Bowl, 8½" d., Lotus patt.........................**8.50**

Bowl, salad, 9 x 12", Tampico patt.......**35.00**

Bread tray, Bob White patt., 24" l. **55.00**

Butter dish, cov., Brocade patt............**15.00**

Casserole, cover & stand, Bob White
patt., 2 qt.....................................**45.00**

Casserole, cover & stand, Bob White
patt., 4 qt.....................................**60.00**

Casserole, cov., Smart Set patt.,
2 qt...**70.00**

Casserole, cov., white w/
"Compliments of Dyste & Dyste,
Forman ND" **100.00**

Console bowl w/standing deer
centerpiece **65.00**

Cookie jar, cov., figural French Chef,
yellow glaze **51.50**

Cookie jar, cov., figural pumpkin,
Jack Frost patt. **725.00**

Cookie jar, cov., King of Tarts **537.00**

Cookie jar, cov., model of a pear,
high-gloss turquoise glaze,
impressed "Red Wing U.S.A.".........**150.00**

Cookie jar, cov., figural rooster,
turquoise glaze **250.00**

Creamer, Zinnia patt. **6.00**

Creamer & cov. sugar bowl, Bob
White patt., pr. **40.00**

Creamer & cov. sugar bowl, Crazy
Rhythm patt., pr. **25.00**

Cup & saucer, Blossom Time patt.,
Concord shape, green or yellow,
each **4.50**

Cup & saucer, Lotus patt., chartreuse...**4.00**

Cup & saucer, Lotus patt., Concord
shape (ILLUS.).............................**8.00**

Cup & saucer, Magnolia patt. **10.00**

Cup & saucer, Round Up patt. **40.00**

Egg tray, cov., Lotus patt. **95.00**

Gravy boat w/attached liner,
Magnolia patt., chartreuse interior,
ivory exterior **10.00**

Mug, Bob White patt. **25.00**

Pitcher, Round Up patt **165.00**

Pitcher, scene of monk in cloister,
cobalt blue **200.00**

Plate, 4¼" sq., Lotus patt. **3.50**

Plate, 6" d., Blossom Time patt.,
Concord shape **2.00**

Plate, 6" d., Lotus patt. **2.50**

Plate, 6½" d., Capistrano patt. **3.00**

Plate, 6½" d., Round Up patt. **24.00**

Plate, 7" d., Blossom Time patt.,
Concord shape **3.50**

Plate, salad, 7½" d., Bob White patt. ...**8.00**

Plate, 10" d., Magnolia patt. **10.00**

Plate, 10½" d., Blossom Time patt.,
Concord shape **5.00**

Plate, 10½" d., Lotus patt. **5.50**

Plate, 11½" d., Bob White patt. **8.50**

Plate, dinner, Lute Song patt. **8.00**

Plate, dinner, Tampico patt. **10.00**

Platter, 12¾" l., Lotus patt. **10.00**

Platter, 13¼" l., Blossom Time patt.,
Concord shape **10.00**

Platter, 13½" l., Bob White patt. **24.00**

Relish tray, Tampico patt., 13" l **22.50**

Soup plate w/flanged rim,
Lotus patt., 7¼" d. **6.50**

Soup plate w/flanged rim, Magnolia
patt. **8.00**

Sugar bowl, cov., Lotus patt., brown **6.50**

Sugar bowl, cov., Morning Glory patt. ...**3.50**

Teapot, cov., figural lady, green...........**139.00**

Tidbit tray, two-tier, Normandy patt. **11.00**

Vegetable bowl, open, divided,
oval, Bob White patt., 9" l **20.00**

STONEWARE & UTILITY WARES

Bean pot, cov., wire bail handle,
white ribbed base, brown-glazed
top, marked "Red Wing Union
Stoneware Co.," 1 qt. **50.00**

Beater jar, Grey Line w/sponge band
decoration **130.00**

Bowl, 7" d., Saffron Ware, rust & blue
sponging on a creamy ground **125.00**

Bowl, 8" d., blue & grey Greek Key
patt., Iowa advertising....................**175.00**

Bowl, 8" d., pink & blue bands, "It

Pays to Mix With The Economy
Store, Emerson, Nebr." **100.00**

Crock, large wing mark, 1 gal. **340.00**

Fruit jar w/screw-on zinc lid, "Stone

Red Wing Fruit Jar

Mason Fruit Jar, Union Stoneware
Co., Red Wing, Minn." printed on
stoneware, half gal. (ILLUS.). **200.00**

Red Wing Jug

Jug, cylindrical sides, brown tapering
top, wing mark, 1 gal. (ILLUS.) **175.00**

"Koverwate" (crock cover-weight
designed to hold pickles under
brine), 5 gal. (crock) size **185.00**

Pitcher, 6" h., Cherry Band patt.,
blue & white **325.00**

Pitcher, 8¼" h., Cherry Band patt.,
blue at borders fading to white.........**235.00**

Salt box, cov., hanging-type, sponge
band decoration (No. 3 lid) **1,300.00**

Water cooler, cov., schoolhouse-
type, 5 gal. **500.00**

Water cooler, cov., w/advertising,
5 gal. **595.00**

RIDGWAYS

English potters, the firm J. & W.

Ridgway operated in Shelton from 1814 to 1930 and produced many pieces with scenes of historical interest. William Ridgway operated in Shelton from 1830 to 1865. Most wares marked Ridgway that have been offered in this country were made by one of these two firms, or by Ridgway Potteries, Ltd., still in operation. Also see HISTORICAL & COMMEMORATIVE WARES

Pitcher, 5½" h., Coaching Days & Ways series **$65.00**
Plates, 8" d., Coaching Days & Ways series, scenes in black on glossy caramel background, black rims, signed on back in large black shield, "Scenes from Coaching Days & Coaching Ways by Special Permission of MacMillian & Co." & "Ridgeways England," different scene on each plate, set of 6...........**150.00**
Teapot, cov., 7" h., Dickensware **135.00**
Tea set: cov. teapot, open handled sugar bowl & creamer; spherical bodies, rich deep caramel background w/scenes in black, silver lustre top bands & handle trim, scenes based on Dickens' Mr. Pickwick character, teapot 4" d., 4½" h., sugar bowl 5½" d., 2⅜" h., creamer 3⅛" d., 2⅝" h., 3 pcs..........**195.00**

Ridgway Earthenware Child's Tea Set

Tea set, child's: cov. teapot, cov. sugar bowl & creamer & seven tea cups & saucers; paneled bulbous bodies w/angled handles, handleless cups, each piece printed w/scene of man by a log cabin beneath a border of stars between foliate bands on a light blue ground, ca. 1840, teapot 4⅜" h., 17 pcs., various chips & discoloration (ILLUS.) **1,495.00**

ROCKINGHAM WARES

Rockingham Cat

An earthenware pottery was first established on the estate of the Marquis of Rockingham in England's Yorkshire district about 1745 and occupied by a succession of potters. The famous Rockingham glaze of mottled brown, somewhat resembling tortoiseshell, was introduced about 1788 by the Brameld Brothers, and was well received. During the 1820s, porcelain manufacture was added to the production and fine quality china was turned out until the pottery closed in 1842. The popular Rockingham glaze was subsequently produced elsewhere, including Bennington, Vermont, and at numerous other U.S. potteries. We list herein not only wares produced at the Rockingham potteries in England, distinguishing porcelain wares from the more plentiful earthenware productions, but also include items from other potteries with the Rockingham glaze. Also see BENNINGTON.

Bottle, figural, model of a mermaid w/a human head and chest & a long, curled-up scaly fish body below, mottled dark brown glaze, 8" l...**$302.50**
Bottle, figural, model of a flattened fish w/molded details & scales, mottled brown glaze, 11" h. (flakes from kiln adhesion) **385.00**
Bowl, 8½" d., 2¼" h., mottled brown glaze **60.50**
Bowl, 9⅝" d., 4¾" h., canted sides, molded rings under rim, mottled brown glaze (wear) **192.50**
Creamer, figural Mr. Toby, footed spherical body w/his hat forming the spout, strap handle, mottled dark brown glaze, 5" h. **93.50**
Dish, octagonal, shallow, mottled brown glaze **93.50**
Model of a cat, seated on oval base,

brown glaze w/streaks of green, chipped on base, 13¾" h. (ILLUS.) **3,300.00**

Model of a dog, seated Spaniel, well-molded fur & face w/heavily applied 'coleslaw' mane & tail, mottled brown glaze, 7¾" h. (chips on base & nose)...............................**935.00**

Model of a dog, seated Spaniel, well-molded fur & face details, closed front legs, redware w/rich mottled brown glaze, probably Cincinnati, Ohio, 12" h. (minor firing crack, chips on base) **247.50**

Model of a dog, seated Spaniel facing the viewer, well-molded fur & face w/open front legs, on a high rectangular platform base molded on the sides w/hunting dogs, mottled brown glaze w/bluish green highlights, attributed to East Liverpool, Ohio, late 19th c., 12½" h. (pinpoint flakes, hairline in base) **852.50**

Mug, ringed rim & base, C-scroll handle, mottled & drippy brown glaze, 3¾" h. (wear, minor base flake) **44.00**

Pitcher, 7¼" h., wide flat ring-molded base below tapering cylindrical sides w/a flat rim & pinched spout, applied C-scroll handle, mottled & streaky dark brown glaze on yellowware, attributed to Cincinnati, Ohio, 19th c. (hairline in base) **82.50**

Teapot, cov., "Rebecca at the Well" patt...**75.00**

Whistle, figural frog.............................**49.00**

Whistle, figural poodle **49.00**

ROOKWOOD

Considered America's foremost art pottery, the Rookwood Pottery Company was established in Cincinnati, Ohio in 1880, by Mrs. Maria Nichols Longworth Storer. To accurately record its development, each piece carried the Rookwood insignia, or mark, was dated, and, if individually decorated, was usually signed by the artist. The pottery remained in Cincinnati until 1959 when it was sold to Herschede Hall Clock Company and

moved to Starkville, Mississippi, where it continued in operation until 1967.

A private company is now producing a limited variety of pieces using original Rookwood molds.

Bowl-vase, squatty spherical body w/rolled rim pinched-in at two sides above incurved loop handles on the shoulder, decorated w/mushrooms in pink, grey & brown on a shaded dark brown to celadon green ground, No. 911, 1902, Carl Schmidt, 5" d., 3¾" h. **$2,750.00**

Bowl-vase, wide flat bottom below flaring squatty bulbous sides to a wide gently sloping shoulder to a wide rolled rim, the lower portion molded w/six wide panels, caramel over light yellowish green Matte glaze, No. 1893, 1910, 10½" d., 6" h...**660.00**

Lamp base, table model, slender baluster-form w/a widely flaring foot, overall molded pine cone & needle design, green Matte glaze, w/a modern widely flaring leather shade, 1918, overall 24" h. **770.00**

Plaque, rectangular, riverside landscape w/large green & blue trees & a pink path reflected in a river bend, the sky shades from blue to salmon, titled "Banks of the River," original frame & backing, Vellum glaze, ca. 1915, Fred Rothenbusch, 7 x 10".................**1,980.00**

Tile, rectangular, carved relief design of large dogwood blossoms & green leaves on a grey ground, Matte glaze, framed, 6 x 8" (few flakes).....**990.00**

Tile, rectangular, two-piece, carved & painted w/large poppies on slender stems & leaves in brown & green against a thick matte green ground, in a narrow dark wood frame, 6 x 12" (several minor chips) **880.00**

Vase, 5" h., broad ovoid body w/a wide flat mouth, molded around the base w/a band of pine cones & needles w/branches up the sides, pale greyish blue & bone white Carved Vellum glaze, No. 942D, 1904, John D. Wareham.................**825.00**

Vase, 5½" h., tapering cylindrical body w/slightly flaring rim, molded w/twisted panels w/stylized Greek key design at the base, pale green over pink Matte glaze, No. 2135, 1919...**231.00**

Vase, 7¾" h., 5" d., wide ovoid body w/a narrow angled shoulder to a short & wide cylindrical neck w/flaring rim, the body molded w/broad pointed leaves alternating

w/upright mistletoe berries,
mahogany brown Matte glaze,
No. 2413, 1928 ....**302.50**

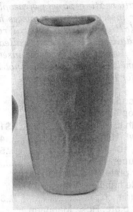

Simple Molded Rookwood Vase

Vase, 8½" h., simple ovoid body
tapering to a slightly shaped flat rim,
molded w/stylized leaves & pods on
broad stems, pale greyish green
over straw Matte glaze designed by
Kataro Shirayamadani, No. 1297,
1913 (ILLUS.) **715.00**

Vase, 8½" h., 5" d., gently flaring
cylindrical body w/a wide flat mouth,
molded w/large dragonflies in red on
a textured brown ground, Matte
glaze, No. 1661, 1912, William
Hentschel (some color run)..............**660.00**

Vase, 10" h., ovoid body tapering to a
short neck w/rolled rim, molded
w/broad leaves alternating w/stems
w/oval blossom buds around the
shoulder, pale green over blue
curdled Matte glaze, No. 2379,
1919..**660.00**

Vase, 11¼" h., 4½" d., baluster-form
w/a short cylindrical neck, modeled
sprigs of lavender & white bleeding
hearts w/green leafage against a
brownish orange ground, Vellum
glaze, No. 901, 1914, Sara
Sax...**2,750.00**

Vase, 12½" h., tall ovoid body
tapering to a short cylindrical neck,
overall reddish brown matte glaze
w/tiny flecks of reddish brown glossy
glaze, No. 940B, 1907 ....**605.00**

Vase, 13¾" h., 5¼" d., swelled
cylindrical body tapering to a flat
mouth, embossed w/large stylized
leaves, fine bluish grey & caramel
Matte glaze, No. 2997, 1928...........**660.00**

Vase, 14¾" h., 9" d., large wide
baluster-form body tapering to a
wide cylindrical neck flanked by
downswept loop handles, molded in
blue, purple & yellow w/large

stylized flowers w/green foliage
against a Matte blue ground, No.
1339B, 1918, C.S. Todd **1,540.00**

ROSEMEADE POTTERY

*Laura Taylor was a ceramic artist who
supervised Federal Works Projects in her
native North Dakota during the Depression
era and later demonstrated at the potter's
wheel during the 1939 New York World's
Fair. In 1940, Laura Taylor and Robert J.
Hughes opened the Rosemeade-Wahpeton
Pottery, naming it after the the North
Dakota county and town of Wahpeton
where it was located. Rosemeade Pottery
was made on a small scale for only about
twelve years with Laura Taylor designing
the items and perfecting colors. Her animal
and bird figures are popular among
collectors. Hughes and Taylor married in
1943 and the pottery did a thriving
business unitl her death in 1959. The
pottery closed in 1961 but stock was sold
from the factory salesroom until 1964.*

Ashtray, model of a chicken
w/DeKalb chick on front **$125.00**
Bank, model of a hippopotamus,
rose glaze **250.00**
Book end, model of a Wolfhound,
black **75.00**
Creamer, figural corn cob **35.00**
Figure group, Paul Bunyan & Babe **80.00**
Hors d'oeuvre server, model of a
pheasant...**40.00**
Jelly jar, cov., model of a turkey........**165.00**
Model of a bear, red, large.................**200.00**
Model of a buffalo, bronze glaze,
small **95.00**
Model of a buffalo, tan glaze, small **95.00**
Model of a mountain goat **200.00**
Model of an ox head, red glaze............**55.00**
Model of a pheasant, 12" h. **200.00**
Model of a pheasant, 14" h. **225.00**
Model of a pony, rose glaze, 5" h.......**125.00**
Model of a sea gull, wings open,
artist-signed, 12" l...........................**225.00**
Models of flamingoes, pr....................**85.00**
Models of pheasants, miniature, pr......**95.00**
Mug w/duck decal **65.00**

Plaque, pierced to hang, model of
a Mallard duck **45.00**
Relish dish, cov., model of a turkey,
w/original label **95.00**
Salt & pepper shakers, figural corn
cob, pr..**30.00**
Salt & pepper shakers, figure of
Egyptian woman & dog-headed
god, pr...**350.00**
Salt & pepper shakers, model of a
bear cub, pr.....................................**40.00**
Salt & pepper shakers, model of a
cactus, pr. **55.00**
Salt & pepper shakers, model of a
cat, black, pr. **37.50**
Salt & pepper shakers, model of a
chicken, pr. **35.00**
Salt & pepper shakers, model of a
Chihuahua, pr. **185.00**
Salt & pepper shakers, model of a
donkey head, pr. **45.00**
Salt & pepper shakers, model of a
duck, pink glaze, pr.........................**35.00**
Salt & pepper shakers, model of a
goat, pr...**85.00**
Salt & pepper shakers, model of a
Mallard duck, pr. **42.00**
Salt & pepper shakers, model of a
pelican, pr. **70.00**
Salt & pepper shakers, model of a
pheasant & hen, tail down, pr. **75.00**
Salt & pepper shakers, model of a
quail, pr. **40.00**
Salt & pepper shakers, model of a
turkey, pr. **47.00**
Spoon rest, model of a lily...................**35.00**
Toothpick holder, model of a
pheasant..**25.00**
Wall pocket, model of a fawn **45.00**

ROSE MEDALLION &
ROSE CANTON CHINA

Rose Mandarin Vase

*The lovely Chinese ware known as Rose
Medallion was made through the past
century and into the present one. It
features alternating panels of people and
flowers or insects with most pieces having
four medallions with a central rose or
peony medallion. The ware is called Rose
Canton if flowers and birds or insects fill
all the panels. Unless otherwise noted, our
listing is for Rose Medallion ware.*

Boullion cup, cover & saucer, cup
w/two loop handles, late 19th -
early 20th c. **$115.50**
Chop bowl, 19th c., 15½" d. **402.50**
Compote, 10" d., 5" h. **595.00**
Cup & saucer **45.00**
Hot water plate, shallow dished top,
small side handles, 19th c.,
10¼" d. (rim chip).........................**345.00**
Hot water plate, Rose Mandarin
variant, armorial design w/the arms
of Wight or Bradley, early 19th c.,
9⅜" d..**1,725.00**
Platter, 15¼" l. oval.........................**385.00**
Platter, 19" oval, well-and-tree type,
19th c. (rim chips) **747.50**
Platters, 14¾" l., Thousand Butterfly
patt. border, 20th c., pr. **690.00**
Punch bowl, deep rounded sides,
colorful panels around the sides,
19th c., 14¾" d. **1,035.00**
Punch bowl, deep rounded sides,
19th c., 15⅝" d. **1,380.00**
Punch bowl, slightly rounded sides,
19th c., 16" d................................**920.00**
Tazza, Rose Mandarin variant, round
slightly dished plate w/small scallops
around the rim, raised on a wide
funnel base, 19th c., 10" d., 4" h...**1,265.00**
Tea set: cov. teapot & two cups in a
wicker cozy, 6¾" h., the set **231.00**
Vase, 23½" h., Rose Mandarin,
paneled baluster body, the lower
panels decorated w/various Oriental
figures & landscape scenes, the
shoulder flanked by two applied
lizards & the neck flanked by two
Oriental figures,
19th century, chip (ILLUS.) **862.50**

ROSENTHAL PORCELAIN

*The Rosenthal porcelain manu-factuory
has been in operation since 1880 when it
was established by P. Rosenthal in Selb,
Bavaria. Tablewares and figure groups are
among its specialties.*

Figure of a Balinese dancer, shown
leaning against a Buddha, decorated

in polychrome w/gold accents, designed by C. Holzer-Defanti, glazed on base "C. HOLZER-DEFANTI" w/company's printed mark, impressed "H.566," early 20th c., 15¾" h. **$1,610.00**

Figure of a nude woman, seated & reclining on one arm, the other arm crossed across her chest, decorated in realistic colors, designed by M. H. Fitz, ca. 1930, impressed designer's name & green stamp mark, 8" l., 6½" h. **287.50**

Figure of nude, 17" h. **600.00**

Figure of nude w/blue drape **450.00**

Figure of a young man, seated nude except for a drape across his lap, one leg crossed under the other, holding an apple in one hand, decorated in realistic colors, designed by F. Heidenreich, ca. 1930, impressed designer's name "53," & green stamp, 6½" l, 8" h. **460.00**

Figure of a nude woman walking, on a square base, cream matte glaze, designed by O. Obennaien, 1931, stamped mark & impressed "1527-H," artist's signature & date, 17" h. **287.50**

Figure group, boy feeding a young fawn, all white, 6¼" h. **145.00**

Figure group, boy w/four birds, one in his hand, all white, 5" h. **130.00**

Figure group, boy w/lamp, No. 16665 ....**235.00**

Figure group, seated boy feeding a bird, all white, 4" h. **120.00**

Figure group, seated boy feeding a squirrel, all white, 4½" h. **125.00**

Figure group, depicting the two Hopfner Sisters dancing the Kaiser's Waltz w/bare feet & swirling gowns, decorated in shades of charcoal & orange, designed by Lona Fr. Crounau, decorated by L. Zimmermann, inscribed "Lona Fr. Cronau" & stamped "Hedi und

Margot Hopfner - Im. - 'Kaiserwalzer'" & "Rosenthal - GERMANY - KUNST-ABTEILUNG - SELB," numbered "16831 - I" & signed in enamel "Hand-gewaldt - L. Zimmermann," ca. 1925, 12" h. **3,162.00**

Model of an angelfish, yellow w/black stripes, artist-signed, 10 x 14".........**595.00**

Model of a beaver, all white, artist-signed, 15" l. **375.00**

Model of a dog, Dachshund, sitting, No. 1247, 6" h. **231.00**

Model of a dog, grey Poodle, No. 1211, artist-signed, "Karner," 7½ x 8½" (small flat flake under foot)...**150.00**

Model of a frog on a lily pad, artist-signed, 2⅛" d., 1¼" h. **50.00**

Model of a shorthaired cat, No. 3616 ....**200.00**

Model of two pigs, ca. 1918, artist-signed, 7½" h. **595.00**

Plates, 8" d., scalloped edges, decorated w/pears, grapes & berries, gold trim, set of 6 ....**125.00**

Tea set: 10" h. cov. teapot, 5¼" h. cov. sugar bowl & 5" h. creamer; Silver Overlay, 3 pcs. **395.00**

ROSEVILLE

Roseville Pottery Company operated in Zanesville, Ohio from 1898 to 1954 after having been in business for six years prior to that in Muskingum County, Ohio. Art wares similar to those of Owens and Weller Potteries were produced. Items listed here are by patterns or lines.

APPLE BLOSSOM (1948)

White apple blossoms in relief on blue, green or pink ground; brown tree branch handles.

Basket w/circular handle, blue ground, No. 309-8", 8" h. **$180.00**

Basket w/asymmetrical overhead handle, pink ground, No. 311-12", 12" h...**265.00**

Basket, hanging-type, green ground, 8" ....**125.00 to 150.00**

Bowl, 8" d., blue ground, No. 328-8"   **90.00**

Bowl, 10" d., pink ground,
No. 329-10" **98.00**
Candleholders, squatty, blue ground,
No. 351-2", 2" h., pr. **75.00**
Console bowl, pink ground,
No. 396-12", 12" l. **95.00**
Cornucopia-vase, pink ground,
No. 321-6", 6" h...............................**65.00**
Creamer, pink ground, No. 371-C **35.00**
Ewer, ovoid, green ground,
No. 316-8", 8" h..............................**110.00**
Flowerpot, blue ground, No. 356-5",
5" h. ....**100.00 to 125.00**
Jardiniere, two-handled, blue ground,
No. 342-6", 6" h...............................**85.00**
Vase, 6" h., two-handled, squatty
base, long cylindrical neck, pink
ground, No. 381-6"...........................**80.00**
Vase, 8¼" h., green ground,
No. 385-8" **125.00**
Vase, 9½" h., 5" d., asymmetrical
handles, cylindrical w/disc base,
pink ground, No. 387-9" **175.00**
Vase, 10" h., base handles, blue
ground, No. 388-10".........................**145.00**
Vase, 10" h., base handles, pink
ground, No. 389-10" ....**125.00 to 150.00**
Vase, 12" h., blue ground,
No. 369-12" **210.00**
Vase, 15½" h., double base handles,
short globular base, long cylindrical
neck, green ground,
No. 392-15"......................................**385.00**
Vase, 15½" h., double base handles,
short globular base, long cylindrical
neck, pink ground,
No. 392-15".....................................**395.00**
Wall pocket, conical w/overhead
handle, green ground, No. 366-8",
8" h. ....**200.00 to 225.00**
Window box, end handles, blue
ground, No. 368-8", 2½ x 10½"..........**95.00**

AUTUMN (before 1916)

*Shaded brown ground with printed forest
landscapes in dark green, black & brown.*

Chamber pot, cov., handled **200.00**
Jardiniere, bulbous ovoid body,
7" h...**400.00**
Shaving mug **300.00**
Soap dish ....**325.00 to 350.00**

AZUREAN (ca. 1902)

*Shaded blue and white with florals,
landscapes or ships; glossy glaze.*

Vase, 7½" h., white to medium blue
floral decoration, artist-signed..........**600.00**
Vase, 8⅞" h., pillow-type, two-
handled, ruffled rim, decorated w/a
portrait of a retriever w/a pheasant

in its mouth, base stamped "X
Azurean 88 2 RPCo," artist-
initialed..**1,210.00**

BANEDA (1933)

*Band of embossed pods, blossoms and
leaves on green or raspberry pink ground.*

Bowl, 8" d., 2½" h., two-handled,
raspberry pink ground.....................**245.00**
Console bowl, green ground, 13" l....**325.00**
Ewer, green ground, 5" h. **350.00**

Baneda Vase

Vase, 4" h., footed tapering ovoid
body w/tiny rim handles, green
ground, No. 587-4"
(ILLUS.) ....**225.00 to 250.00**
Vase, 4" h., footed tapering ovoid
body w/tiny rim handles, red ground,
No. 587-4".......................................**215.00**
Vase, 4½" h., tiny rim handles,
sharply canted sides, green ground,
No. 603-4".......................................**250.00**
Vase, 5½" h., rounded base w/sharply
canted sides w/two shell
handles at rim, green ground...........**265.00**
Vase, 6" h., two-handled, tapering
cylinder w/short collared neck,
raspberry pink ground......................**310.00**
Vase, 8" h., tapering conical body
w/loop handles at base, raspberry
pink ground, No. 593-8" **425.00**
Vase, 9" h., two-handled, footed
bulbous ovoid body, green
ground ....**550.00 to 575.00**
Vase, 9" h., two-handled, footed
bulbous ovoid body raspberry pink
ground..**650.00**
Vase, 12" h., expanding cylinder
w/small rim handles, raspberry pink
ground, No. 599-12"........................**475.00**

BANKS & BOTTLES (early 1900s)

Bank, model of an eagle, teal sponge
decoration **225.00**

Bank, model of a pig, large recumbent animal, spotted brown on white, 4 x 5½" **150.00**
Bank, model of Uncle Sam head, 4" h...**125.00**
Bottle, model of a monkey, spongeware.....................**175.00 to 200.00**

BITTERSWEET (1940)

Orange bittersweet pods and green leaves on a grey blending to rose, yellow with terra cotta, rose with green or solid green bark-textured ground; brown branch handles.

Basket, low overhead handle, shaped rim, green ground, No. 810-10", 10" h..**215.00**
Basket, hanging-type, green ground ....**175.00 to 225.00**
Cornucopia-vase, grey ground, No. 856-5", 5" h. **95.00**
Cornucopia-vase, green ground, No. 857-4", 4½" h. ....**50.00 to 75.00**
Cornucopia-vase, double, grey ground, No. 858-4", 8½" w., 4" h...**120.00**
Ewer, yellow ground, No. 816-8", 8" h..**70.00**
Planter, curved shaped sides, green ground, No. 828-10", 10½" l...............**90.00**
Teapot, cov., green ground, No. 871-P **225.00**
Urn, footed spherical body w/tiny loop handles, green or yellow ground, No. 842-7", 7" h.............................**125.00**
Vase, 8" h., curved handles rising from midsection to edge of flaring shaped rim, green ground, No. 884-8"...**90.00**
Wall pocket, curving conical form w/;overhead handles continuing to one side, grey ground, No. 866-7", 7" h. ....**175.00 to 225.00**

BLACKBERRY (1933)

Band of relief clusters of blackberries with vines and ivory leaves accented in green and terra cotta on a green textured ground.

Bowl, 4 x 9", 4" h. ....**400.00 to 450.00**
Console bowl, small pointed end handles, 13" l. **350.00**
Jardiniere, two-handled, 4" h............**200.00**
Vase, 4" h., two-handled, squatty.......**275.00**
Vase, 5" h., two tiny rim handles, tapering sides ....**300.00 to 330.00**
Vase, 8" h., handles at mid-section, slightly globular base & wide neck, original paper label..............................**450.00 to 550.00**

BLEEDING HEART (1938)

Pink blossoms and green leaves on shaded blue, green or pink ground.

Basket, hanging-type, two-handled, blue ground, No. 362-5", 8" w. **325.00**
Basket, hanging-type, two-handled, green ground, No. 362-5", 8" w. **290.00**
Cornucopia-vase, pink ground, No. 141-6", 6" h..............................**85.00**
Ewer, green ground, No. 963-6", 6" h...**85.00**
Ewer, green ground, No. 972-10", 10" h. ....**200.00 to 250.00**
Flower frog, pink ground, No. 40.........**65.00**

Bleeding Heart Jardiniere

Jardiniere & pedestal base, blue ground, 24" h., 2 pcs. (ILLUS.) **975.00**
Pitcher, 8" h., asymmetrical w/high arched handle, green ground, No. 1323 ....**400.00**
Pot, spherical footed body w/tiny side handles, No. 651-3", 3½" h. **82.00**
Rose bowl, blue ground, No. 377-4", 4" h...**150.00**
Vase, 6½" h., footed trumpet-form w/petal rim & base handles, pink ground, No. 964-6"............................**55.00**
Vase, bud, 7" h., green ground, No. 967-7"..**95.00**
Wall pocket, angular overhead handle rising from midsection, pink ground, No. 1287-8", 8½" h. **395.00**

BLENDED (late teens)

Simply forms with mottled streaky glossy glazes.

Jardiniere & pedestal base, iris floral at top, 28" h., 2 pcs. **450.00**

Pitcher, 7" h., wide waisted cylindrical body w/an angular handle...............**110.00**

Umbrella stand, panels of embossed flowers on sides, band of leaves at rim, No. 609, 20" h. **295.00**

Vase, 8" h..**75.00**

BURMESE (1950s)

Oriental faces featured on pieces such as wall plaques, book ends, candleholders and console bowls. Some plain pieces also included. Comes in green, black and white.

Candleholders-book ends combination, bust of woman w/long hair, black glaze, No. 70-B, pr. **420.00**

Planter, black glaze, No. 908-10", 10" l..**70.00**

Wall pocket, bust of a woman **195.00**

BUSHBERRY (1948)

Berries and leaves on blue, green or russet bark-textured ground; brown or green branch handles.

Ashtray, handled, russet ground, No. 26 ....**72.00**

Basket w/asymmetrical overhead handle, green ground, No. 371-10", 10" h..**175.00**

Basket, hanging-type w/original chains, russet ground, No. 465-5", 7" ....**300.00 to 350.00**

Book ends, russet ground, No. 9, pr...**165.00**

Bowl, 3" h., small side handles, globular, blue ground, No. 657-3" **45.00**

Bowl, 6" d., green ground, No. 412-6"...**110.00**

Bowl, 10" d., brown ground, No. 415-10"....................................**125.00**

Candleholders, large flaring handles, green ground, No. 1147, 2" h., pr. **70.00**

Console bowl, brown ground, No. 1-10", 10" l. ....**150.00 to 180.00**

Flower frog, green ground, No. 45 ....**125.00**

Jardiniere, blue ground, No. 657-3", 3" h..**165.00**

Jardiniere, two-handled, russet ground, No. 657-8", 8" h. **450.00**

Jardiniere & pedestal base, green ground, No. 657-8", jardiniere 8" h., 2 pcs...**850.00**

Pitcher w/ice lip, green ground, No. 1325, 8½" h. **250.00**

Pitcher w/ice lip, russet ground, No. 1325, 8½" h...............**300.00 to 325.00**

Vase, 6" h., asymmetrical side handles, cylindrical w/low foot, green ground, No. 29-6" **125.00**

Vase, 7" h., two-handled, russet ground, No. 31-7"............................**110.00**

Vase, bud, 7½" h., asymmetrical handles rising from base, slender cylindrical body, blue ground, No. 152-7"..**135.00**

Wall pocket, high-low handles, blue ground, No. 1291-8", 8" h. **175.00**

CAPRI (late line)

Various shapes depicting shells, leaves and overlapping petals, Sandlewood (sic) yellow or cactus green matte finishes and a metallic red semi-matte finish.

Basket w/center overhead branch handle, molded leaf design at terminal, pointed ends, cactus green, No. C-1012-10", 10" h............**95.00**

Basket, green ground, No. 509-8", 8" h...**140.00**

Vase, 6" h., grotesque free-form shape, metallic red, No. 580 ....**55.00**

Vase, bud, 9" h., free-form, glossy dark green exterior, chartreuse interior, No. 1004-9" **60.00**

CARNELIAN I (1910-15)

Matte glaze with a combination of two colors or two shades of the same color with the darker dripping over the lighter tone or heavy and textured glaze with inter-mingled colors and some running.

Console bowl, dark & light blue or pink & blue, 8" l., each **95.00**

Flower holder, fan-shaped w/elaborate scrolled handles from rim to slightly domed base, dark & light blue, 6" h **105.00**

Vase, 10" h., squatty bulbous base w/a tall slender slightly flaring neck, long angled handles at lower sides, heavy textured light green glaze......**125.00**

Wall pocket, ornate side handles, flaring rim, deep green & light green, 8" h...**120.00**

CARNELIAN II (1915)

Intermingled colors, some with a drip effect.

Vase, 6" h., purple & rose, No. 306-6"...**75.00**

Vase, 7" h., baluster-form w/large scroll handles, shades of rose & purple..**220.00**

Vase, 10" h., handles rising from squatty base to mid-section of cylindrical neck, intermingled shades of pink & purple **225.00**

Vase, 20" h., handled, shades of pink & purple **600.00**

Wall pocket, trumpet-form w/slender base & widely flaring rim, long side handles molded w/blossoms at the top, shades of green, 7" h. **165.00**

Carnelian II Wall Pocket

Wall pocket, ribbed fan-form w/long side handles, intermingled shades of green, 8" h. (ILLUS.) **195.00**
Wall pocket, plain trumpet-form w/long side handles, intermingled shades of green, 8" h. **300.00**

CHERRY BLOSSOM (1933)

Sprigs of cherry blossoms, green leaves and twigs with pink fence against a combed blue-green ground or creamy ivory fence against a terra cotta ground shading to dark brown.

Basket, hanging-type, terra cotta ground, 8" **595.00**
Bowl, 5" h., terra cotta ground **220.00**
Bowl, 6" d., two-handled, globular, terra cotta ground ....**250.00 to 265.00**
Jardiniere, shoulder handles, terra cotta ground, 8" d., 6" h. **275.00**
Jardiniere, two-handled, blue-green ground, 7" h. **465.00**
Jardiniere, shoulder handles, blue-green ground, 10" h. **1,200.00**
Urn-vase, large spherical body w/a short cylindrical neck flanked by small loop handles, terra cotta ground, 8" h. **450.00**
Vase, 5" h., two-handled, slightly ovoid, blue-green ground ....**250.00 to 300.00**
Vase, 7" h., jug-type, tall ovoid body w/small loop handles at the shoulder, blue-green ground............**285.00**
Vase, 7" h., slightly ovoid body, blue-green ground **325.00**
Vase, 7½" h., two-handled, cylindrical, terra cotta ground...........**310.00**
Vase, 10" h., two-handled, ovoid w/short wide neck, terra cotta ground...**412.50**

CLEMATIS (1944)

Clematis blossoms and heart-shaped green leaves against a vertically textured ground—white blossoms on blue, rose-pink blossoms on green and ivory blossoms on golden brown.

Basket w/ornate circular handles, green ground, No. 387-7", 7" h. ....**125.00 to 150.00**
Basket w/low overhead handle, footed, green ground, No. 388-8", 8" h...**95.00**
Basket w/overhead handle, pedestal base, brown ground, No. 389-10", 10" h...**110.00**
Basket, hanging-type, blue ground, No. 470-5", 5".......................**175.00**
Basket, hanging-type, brown ground, No. 470-5", 5".......................**140.00**
Basket, hanging-type, green ground, No. 470-5", 5".......................**135.00**
Bowl, 10" d., two-handled, blue ground, No. 459-10".........................**85.00**
Candleholders, bulbous w/tiny pointed handles, green ground, No. 1158-2", 2½" h., pr. **37.00**
Candlesticks, two-handled, brown ground, No. 1159-4½", 4½" h., pr. ....**75.00 to 115.00**
Console bowl, end handles, brown ground, No. 45-6", 9" l.....................**78.00**
Console bowl, end handles, green ground, No. 458-10", 14" l...............**110.00**
Console bowl, two-handled, blue ground, No. 460-12", 12"l...............**145.00**
Console bowl, brown ground, No. 461-14", 14" l...........................**125.00**
Cookie jar, cov., brown ground, No. 3-8", 8" h. ....**250.00 to 325.00**
Cornucopia-vase, brown ground, No.193-6", 6" h...............................**60.00**
Cornucopia-vase, brown ground, No. 101-8", 8" h. ....**50.00 to 75.00**
Ewer, brown ground, No. 101-8", 8" h.....................................**105.00**
Ewer, brown ground, No. 18-15", 15" h..**300.00**
Flower frog-triple vase, blue ground, No. 50 ....**45.00**
Jardiniere, blue ground, No. 667-4", 4" h..**85.00**
Jardiniere, blue ground, No. 667-5", 5" h...**135.00**
Jardiniere & pedestal base, brown ground, No. 667-8", jardiniere 8" h., 24½" h., 2 pcs......................**550.00 to 625.00**
Sugar bowl, open, green ground, No. 5-S ....**45.00 to 55.00**
Vase, 7⅞" h., 5½" d., bulbous body, low side handles, tall

neck, brown ground,
No. 106-7".......................................**70.00**
Vase, 9" h., green ground,
No. 110-9"..**90.00**
Vase, 12" h., two-handled, green
ground, No. 112-12".....................**165.00**
Vase, 15" h., brown ground,
No. 114-15" ....**195.00 to 225.00**

COLUMBINE (1940s)

*Columbine blossoms and foliage on shaded
ground—yellow blossoms on blue, pink
blossoms on pink shaded to green and blue
blossoms on tan shaded to green.*

Basket, elaborate handle rising
from midsection, blue ground,
No. 365-7",
7" h. ....**150.00 to 160.00**
Basket, pointed handle rising from flat
base, ovoid w/boat-shaped top
w/shaped rim, blue ground, No.
368-12", 12" h. **215.00**
Basket, hanging-type, pink ground,
No. 17-7", 7½"..............................**275.00**
Book end/planter combination,
pink ground, No. 8, 5" h.,
pr. ....**300.00 to 350.00**
Bowl, 6" d., two-handled, blue
ground, No. 401-6" ....**75.00 to 95.00**
Candlesticks, blue ground,
No. 1145-2½", 2½" h., pr. **135.00**
Console bowl, stepped handles
rising from rim, blue ground,
No. 404-10", 10" l. ....**125.00 to 135.00**
Ewer, sharply angled handle, pink
ground, No. 18-7", 7" h. **145.00**
Jardiniere & pedestal base, pink
ground, No. 655-8", jardiniere 8" h.,
30" h., 2 pcs. **950.00**
Rose bowl, two-handled, tan ground,
No. 400-6", 6" d................................**175.00**
Vase, 4" h., blue ground, No. 12-4" **70.00**
Vase, 6" h., blue or brown ground,
No. 14-6", each **80.00**
Vase, 7" h., blue ground, No. 16-7" **100.00**
Vase, 8" h., handles rising from base,
blue ground, No. 19-8"......................**95.00**
Vase, 8" h., footed cylinder w/small
angled handles, tan ground,
No. 20-8"..**95.00**

CORINTHIAN (1923)

*Deeply fluted ivory and green body below a
continuos band of molded grapevine, fruit,
foliage and florals in naturalistic colors,
narrow ivory and green molded border at
the rim.*

Basket, hanging-type w/chains,
8" d...**165.00**

Vase, double bud, 4½" h., 7" w.,
gate-form **110.00**

Corinthian Vase

Vase, 7" h., baluster-form (ILLUS.) **100.00**
Vase, 8" h., slightly rounded at
shoulder & base, collared
neck...................................**75.00 to 100.00**
Vase. 12" h., cylindrical w/flared
rim..**120.00**
Wall pocket, 12" h. **175.00**

CORNELIAN (early 1900s)

*Simple shapes with relief-molded designs
and overall sponged decoration.*

Pitcher, 5½" h., tapering cylindrical
body, molded wheat design **65.00**
Pitcher, tankard, 9" h., molded wild
rose design **75.00**

COSMOS (1940)

*Embossed blossoms against a wavy
horizontal ridged band on a textured
ground—ivory band with yellow and
orchid blossoms on blue, blue band with
white and orchid blossoms on green or tan.*

Basket w/overhead handle, tan
ground, No. 357-10",
10" h. ....**225.00 to 285.00**
Basket, hanging-type, handles rising
from midsection to rim, green
ground, No. 361-5", 7" **300.00**
Bowl, 6" h., globular w/small loop
handles at shoulder, green ground,
No. 376-6"..**135.00**
Ewer, blue ground, No. 957-15",
15" h..**395.00**
Flower frog, pierced globular body
w/asymmetrical overhead handle,
green ground, No. 39, 3½" h...........**135.00**
Jardiniere, blue ground, No. 649-3",
3" h..**65.00**
Jardiniere, green ground, No. 649-4",
4" h..**70.00**

Urn-vase, green ground, No. 135-8",
8" h..**145.00**
Vase, 9" h., handles rising from
midsection of ovoid body to neck,
green ground,
No. 952-9" ....**150.00 to 200.00**
Vase, 10" h., blue ground,
No. 954-10"......................................**275.00**
Vase, 12½" h., ovoid w/large loop
handles, blue ground,
No. 956-12"......................................**300.00**
Vase, 18" h., floor-type, trumpet-
shaped w/handles rising to flaring
rim, blue ground, No. 58-18"............**750.00**
Window box, blue ground,
No. 381-9", 9" l. ....**350.00 to 450.00**

CREMONA (1927)

*Relief-molded floral motifs including a tall
stem with small blossoms and arrowhead
leaves, wreathed with leaves similar to
Velmoss or a webb of delicate vines against
a background of light green mottled with
pale blue or pink with creamy ivory.*

Candleholders, squared flaring base,
baluster-form candle nozzle, green
ground, No. 10684", 4" h.,
pr. ....**75.00 to 100.00**
Console set: console bowl, flower
frog & pair of candleholders; green
ground, 4 pcs. **300.00**

DAHLROSE (1924-28)

*Band of ivory daisy-like blossoms and
green leaves against a mottled tan ground.*

Bowl, 10" oval, two-handled...............**250.00**
Console bowl, 10" d...........................**185.00**
Console set, console bowl & a pair of
candleholders, 3 pcs. ......**225.00 to 250.00**
Vase, 4" h., two-handled **65.00**
Vase, 6" h., square body w/flared
mouth...**88.00**
Vase, 10" h., slightly tapering square
shaped **175.00**
Wall pocket, green ground, 14" h.
(internal hairline) **185.00**
Window box, 6 x 11½".......**225.00 to 250.00**

DAWN (1937)

*Incised spidery flowers—green ground
with blue-violet tinted blossoms, pink or
yellow ground with blue-green blossoms,
all with yellow centers.*

Flower frog, cylindrical, pink ground,
No. 31-3 x 4", 3" d., 4" h. **100.00**
Vase, 6" h., cylindrical w/tab handles
below rim, square foot, yellow

ground, No. 826-6",
each...............................**100.00 to 120.00**
Vase, 6½" h., 11" w., spherical body
raised on square pedestal base, flat
mouth & short arms at rim each
w/ovoid candle socket, No. 319-6".....**95.00**
Vase, 8" h., slender cylinder w/tab
handles below rim, square foot, pink
ground, No. 818-8".........................**135.00**
Vase, 8" h., angled squatty base
tapering to a tall cylindrical neck
w/small tab handles, raised on a
square foot, No. 829-8"...................**150.00**
Vase, 10" h., ovoid w/square base &
tab handles, yellow ground, No.
832-10" **195.00**

DELLA ROBBIA, ROZANE (1906)

*Incised designs with an overall high-gloss
glaze in colors ranging from soft pastel
tints to heavy earthtones and brilliant
intense colors.*

Teapot, cov., wide foot supports a
wide squatty body w/a wide curving
angled shoulder tapering to a flat rim
w/inset domed cover w/ringed knob
finial, pointed angular handle & short
curved spout, the top half carved
w/stylized flowers & grasses in two
shades of green, a zigzag ribbon
band around the cover, base
marked "Rozane Ware" & artist's
initials "E.B.," ca. 1906, 5⅜" h.
(two small repaired flakes) **825.00**
Vase, 6½" h., 4¼" d., bulbous center
& pinched top & bottom, excised
peacock feathers in blue, yellow &
green enamels on a light blue
ground, unmarked (repaired
inside top chip, drilled bottom) **1,540.00**

Della Robbia Vase

Vase, 8¼" h., 5" d., swelled cylindrical

body tapering to a flat mouth,
excised & enameled bright yellow
chrysanthemums & green leaves on
a blue ground & sand-colored body,
wafer mark & incised "E. Dutro"
(ILLUS.) **7,700.00**

Bellflower Della Robbia Vase

Vase, 8½" h., 6" d., footed bulbous
ovoid body w/a wide shoulder
tapering to a short flaring neck,
excised w/a band of curled
bellflowers in white & green w/long
green stems & leaves against a
glossy brown center band w/matte
mustard yellow ground at top &
bottom, signed "KD" w/wafer
(ILLUS.) **6,050.00**

Three-Handled Della Robbia Vase

Vase, 9¼" h., 4" d., tapering
cylindrical body w/three short flat
handles to the rolled rim band,
deeply incised w/oak trees w/over-
sized acorns & leaves in brown &
green, small flat shallow chip on
side under base, signed "GB"
(ILLUS.) **9,350.00**
Vase, 10" h., slightly tapering
cylindrical body w/three short flat
handles at indented band near the

Unusual Della Robbia Vase

footed base, designed by Frederick
Rhead, deeply incised w/bands of
squared staggered stylized trees in
cream, yellow, green, blue, pink &
black (ILLUS.) **10,450.00**
Vase, 11¼" h., 7½" d., footed tall
slender conical body, overall
excised design of a stylized
landscape w/a rocky path winding
into a forest, in celadon & light
green, unmarked (repaired rim &
base chips) **2,310.00**

DOGWOOD (1916-18)

*White dogwood blossoms and brown
branches against a textured green ground.*

Basket, hanging-type, w/original
chains, 7" **180.00**
Bowl, 2½" h., 7" d., bulb-type..............**75.00**

DOGWOOD II (1928)

*White dogwood blossoms & black branches
against a smooth green ground.*

Vase, double bud, 8" h., cornucopia-
shaped **85.00**
Vase, 14½" h., openwork at top **295.00**
Wall pocket, conical w/tall openwork
branch & blossom top handle,
15" l..**275.00**

DONATELLO (1915)

*Deeply fluted ivory and green body with
wide tan band embossed with cherubs at
various pursuits in pastoral settings.*

Ashtray, w/three cigar rest
depressions **195.00**
Basket w/curved overhead handle,
flaring rim slightly pinched at ends,
7½" h..**250.00**

Bowl, 7" l., oval **75.00**
Bowl, 8½" d., 3½" h. **95.00**
Candlesticks, slightly domed base,
  gently flaring candle nozzle, No.
  1022-10", 10" h., pr........................**350.00**
Chamberstick, deep saucer base
  w/ring handle,
  No. 1011 ....**125.00 to 150.00**
Compote, 4" h., footed.......................**95.00**
Incense burner, shallow base
  w/conical pierced top, 3½" h.
  (minor nicks) ....**600.00 to 650.00**
Jardiniere, 5" h. **60.00**
Jardiniere, No. 575-7", 7" h. **100.00**
Powder jar, cov., 5" d., 2" h. (tiny
  inside nicks) **350.00**

Donatello Double Bud Vase

Vase, double bud, 5" h., gate-form
  (ILLUS.) **225.00**
Vase, bud, 6" h., flared, No. 116-6"....**110.00**
Vase, 12" h., expanding cylinder........**225.00**
Wall pocket, 10" h. **150.00**
Wall pocket, 11½" h. **175.00**

EARLAM (1930)

*Mottled glaze on various simple shapes.
The line includes many crocus or
strawberry pots.*

Console bowl, two-handled, square
  w/rounded corners, mottled lavender
  & tan glaze, No. 218-9", 9" l. **185.00**
Urn-vase, small rim handles, mottled
  tan & lavender glaze, No. 516-
  4½", 4½" h. **95.00**
Urn-vase, bulbous ovoid body
  w/small loop handles at rim,
  6" h. ....**250.00 to 300.00**
Vase, 6" h., two-handled, mottled tan
  experimental glaze..........................**170.00**

EARLY EMBOSSED PITCHERS (pre 1916)

*Utility pitchers with various embossed
scenes; high gloss glaze.*

The Bridge, 6" h..................................**85.00**
Decal decoration, 7" h., pendent fan
  devices..**145.00**
Poppy, 9" h. ....**150.00 to 175.00**

EGYPTO (1905)

*Classic shapes resembling those from
ancient Egypt; soft deep green matte glaze.*

Bowl, 9" d., 3½" h., three-handled **125.00**
Ewer, Mideastern oil lamp-form, a
  short pedestal foot supporting a wide
  squatty bulbous body w/a short upturned spout at one side & a thick
  ring handle at the other, tapering at
  the top to a short cylindrical neck w/a
  wide cupped rim, thick matte green
  glaze, wafer mark, 6" d., 5" h. **330.00**
Pitcher, 10½" h., 5½" d., base
  w/canted sides w/embossed
  geometric designs, long ribbed neck
  w/flaring rim, angular side handle,
  leathery matte green glaze **412.50**
Urn, footed wide squatty bulbous
  body w/a short, wide neck w/wide
  flat rim, small loop handles at the
  shoulder, rich organic green matte
  glaze, unmarked, 6⅜" h. **467.50**

FALLINE (1933)

*Curving panels topped by a semi-scallop
separated by vertical peapod decorations;
blended backgrounds of tan shading to
green and blue or tan shading to darker
brown.*

Large Falline Vase

Vase, 6" h., footed cylindrical body
  w/large loop handles, brown ground,
  No. 643-6" ....**275.00 to 325.00**
Vase, 7" h., two-handled, tan shading
  to brown ground...............................**375.00**
Vase, floor-type, 14" h., 7¼" d.,
  cylindrical body around at the
  bottom & tapering slightly at the top
  w/a short tapering neck flanked by
  small loop handles, green 'pods' on
  a light shaded to dark brown ground,
  unmarked, two flat chips under
  base (ILLUS.)..............................**1,210.00**

FERRELLA (1930)

Impressed shell design alternating with small cut-outs at top and base; mottled brown or mottled turquoise and red glaze.

Bowl w/attached flower frog, 10" d., 5" h., footed deep flaring sides, brown ground...................................**450.00**
Bowl, 12" d., 7" h., footed, brown ground, No. 212-12 x 7" ..**650.00 to 750.00**
Candlestick, goblet-form w/candle nozzle rising from center, brown ground, No. 1078-4", 4½" h. **200.00**
Compote, 5" d., 4" h., brown ground, No. 210-4"....................................**225.00**
Lamp base, footed spherical form w/small loop handles at rim, mottled turquoise ground............................**750.00**
Vase, 8" h., footed urn-form w/angled handles, No. 509-8" **600.00**
Vase, 12½" h., bulbous ring base w/loop handles below a swelled cylindrical body w/a closed rim **695.00**
Wall pocket, brown ground, No. 1266-6½", 6½" h.......................**850.00**

FLORANE I (1920s)

Terra cotta shading to either dark brown or deep olive green on simple shapes, often from the Rosecraft line.

Tray, brown ground, No. 395-9", 9" l..**115.00**
Vase, double bud, 5" h., gate-form.......**90.00**
Vase, bud, 7" h. **29.00**
Vase, 9" h., green ground, No. 82-9" .. **75.00**
Wall pocket, conical w/flaring rim, dark brown, 9" h.............................**150.00**
Wall pocket, two-handled, ovoid w/fan-shaped top, dark brown, 10½" h. ....**140.00 to 150.00**

FLORENTINE (1924-28)

Bark-textured panels alternating with embossed garlands of cascading fruit and florals; ivory with tan and green, beige with brown and green or brown with beige and green glaze.

Ashtray, shallow, brown, 5" d., ...**70.00**
Basket, hanging-type, beige, No. 339-5", 5" **140.00**
Basket, hanging-type, 9" d................**160.00**
Bowl, 6" d., brown...............................**60.00**
Bowl, 10" d...**75.00**
Candleholders, brown, No. 1062-4", 4" h., pr..............................**45.00**
Candlesticks, flaring base, baluster-form stem, brown, 10½" h., pr. ....**150.00 to 200.00**
Compote, 10" d., footed, beige **70.00**

Jardiniere, ivory, No. 602-5", 5½" h..**95.00**
Jardiniere, bulbous wide body w/short wide neck flanked by small angled handles, 5¾" d. base **185.00**
Vase, double bud, 4½" h., 9" w., gate-form, brown ....**85.00 to 100.00**
Vase, 8½" h., squared handles at rim, ovoid, brown, No. 231-8" **75.00**

Florentine Footed Vase

Vase, 10" h., footed baluster-form, beige, No. 232-10" (ILLUS.).............**125.00**
Vase, 10" h., footed baluster-form, brown, No. 232-10" **150.00**
Wall pocket, overhead handle, ivory, No. 1238-8", 8½" h...........................**125.00**

FOXGLOVE (1940s)

Sprays of pink and white blossoms embossed against a shaded matte finish ground.

Foxglove Jardiniere

Basket, hanging-type, pink ground, No. 466-5", 6½"...............................**230.00**
Candleholders, pink ground, No. 1149, 1½" h., pr. **89.00**
Candleholders, green ground, No. 1150-4½", 4½" h. **175.00**
Cornucopia-vase, blue ground, No. 163-6", 6" h. **95.00**

Cornucopia-vase, green ground, No. 166-6", 6" h. **85.00**

Cornucopia-vase, pink ground, No. 166-6", 6" h. **80.00**

Ewer, green ground, No. 4-6½", 6½" h............................**175.00**

Flower frog, cornucopia-form, blue ground, No. 46 ....**65.00**

Jardiniere & saucer, two-handled, blue ground, No. 659-5", 5" h. (ILLUS.) ....**50.00 to 60.00**

Rose bowl, two-handled, pink ground, No. 418-6", 6" h. **175.00**

Tray, open rim handles, shaped oval, green ground, 11" l. **110.00**

Urn-vase, two-handled, pink ground, No. 161-6", 6" h............................**58.00**

Urn-vase, blue or green ground, No. 162-8", 8" h., each **225.00**

Vase, 3" h., wide cylindrical body w/small angled handles & tapering at the base, pink ground, No. 659-3"............................**40.00**

Vase, 4" h., cylindrical w/long angular side handles, blue ground, No. 42-4"............................**60.00**

Vase, double bud, 4½" h., gate-form, blue ground, No. 160-4".........**135.00**

Vase, 6" h., blue ground, No. 43-6"......**85.00**

Vase, 7" h., two-handled, green ground, No. 45-7"............................**100.00**

Vase, 7" h., two-handled, green ground, No. 46-7" **110.00**

Vase, 8½" h., fan-shaped, handles rising from base to midsection, pink ground, No. 47-8"............................**125.00**

Vases, 9" h., green ground, No. 49-9", pr. ....**100.00 to 150.00**

Vase, 10" h., angular handles rising from base to below flaring rim, blue ground, No. 51-10" ....**200.00 to 210.00**

Vase, 15" h., two-handled, pink ground, No. 54-15"............................**350.00**

Vase, 16" h., two-handled, pink ground, No. 55-16"............................**495.00**

Vase, 18" h., floor-type, green ground............................**1,450.00**

Wall pocket, two-handled, green ground, No. 1292-8", 8" h. **425.00**

Wall pocket, two-handled, pink ground, No. 1292-8", 8" h. ....**350.00 to 375.00**

FREESIA (1945)

Trumpet-shaped blossoms and long slender green leaves against wavy impressed lines - white and lavender blossoms on blended green; white and yellow blossoms on shaded blue or terra cotta and brown.

Basket w/overhead handle, green ground, No. 391-8", 8" h. **150.00**

Basket w/pointed overhead handle, high shaped sides, flaring base, green ground, No. 392-10", 10" h. ...**225.00**

Basket, hanging-type, green ground, No. 471-5", 5" ....**175.00 to 200.00**

Basket, hanging-type, terra cotta ground, No. 471-5", 5" **220.00**

Bowl, 8½" d., two-handled, blue ground, No. 464-6"............................**75.00**

Bowl, 14" d., blue ground, No. 468-12" **85.00**

Candlesticks, disc base, cylindrical w/low handles, blue ground, No. 1161-4½", 4½" h., pr. **65.00**

Candlesticks, disc base, cylindrical w/low handles, terra cotta ground, No. 1161-4½", 4½" h., pr. **75.00**

Cornucopia-vase, green ground, No. 197-6", 6" h................................**65.00**

Freesia Ewer

Ewer, squatty, blue ground, No. 19-6", 6" h. (ILLUS.) **130.00**

Ewer, squatty, terra cotta ground, No. 19-6", 6" h................................**125.00**

Ewer, green ground, No. 20-10", 10" h................................**180.00**

Jardiniere, rim handles, blue ground, No. 669-6", 6" h................................**75.00**

Jardiniere, terra cotta ground, No. 669-8", 12" d., 8" h. **200.00**

Teapot, cov., terra cotta ground, No. 6-T............................**155.00**

Tea set: cov. teapot, creamer & open sugar bowl; terra cotta ground, No. 6, 3 pcs............................**300.00**

Urn-vase, blue ground, No. 196-8", 8" h............................**115.00**

Urn-vase, terra cotta ground, No. 196-8", 8" h................................**90.00**

Vase, 8" h., two-handled, blue ground, No. 121-8"............................**100.00**

Vase, 8" h., two-handled, terra cotta ground, No. 121-8"............................**125.00**

Vase, 8" h., globular base & flaring rim, handles at midsection, terra cotta ground, No. 122-8".................**130.00**

Vase, 9½" h., pointed handles at midsection, blue ground, No. 123-9" ....**140.00 to 180.00**

Vase, 9½" h., pointed handles at midsection, green ground, No. 123-9"......................................**175.00**

Vase, 10" h., terra cotta ground, No. 126-10".....................................**140.00**

Vase, 10½" h., expanding cylinder w/handles rising from raised base, terra cotta ground, No. 125-10" ....**150.00 to 175.00**

Vase, 12" h., two-handled, green ground, No. 127-12"........................**150.00**

Vase, 18" h., terra cotta ground, No. 129-18"......................................**375.00**

Wall pocket, angular handles, blue ground, No. 1296-8", 8½" h. ....**160.00 to 190.00**

Window box, two-handled, blue ground, No. 1392-8", 10½" l..............**90.00**

FUCHSIA (1939)

Coral pink fuchsia blossoms and green leaves against a background of blue shading to yellow, green shading to terra cotta or terra cotta shading to gold.

Basket, hanging-type, blue ground, No. 359-5", 5" h............................**385.00**

Basket, hanging-type, terra cotta ground, No. 359-5", 5" h. **425.00**

Bowl, 4" d., urn-form, two-handled, blue ground, No. 346-4" **75.00**

Bowl, 4" d., urn-form, two-handled, green ground, No. 346-4" **75.00**

Bowl, 5" d., two-handled, blue ground, No. 348-5"............................**110.00**

Bowl, 6" d., two-handled, blue ground, No. 347-6"............................**350.00**

Bowl, 8" d., two-handled, blue ground, No. 349-8"............................**155.00**

Console bowl, two-handled, blue ground, No. 351-10", 12½" l., 3½" h...**250.00**

Fuchsia Cornucopia-Vase

Cornucopia-vase, terra cotta ground, No. 129-6", 6" h. (ILLUS.) **110.00**

Flower frog, terra cotta ground, No. 37 ....**130.00**

Jardiniere, two-handled, green ground, No. 645-3", 3" h. **70.00**

Pitcher w/ice lip, 8" h., green ground, No. 1322-8" **220.00**

Vase, 6" h., two handles rising from bulbous base to neck, blue ground, No. 891-6"......................................**150.00**

Vase, 6" h., two-handles rising from bulbous base to neck, green ground, No. 891-6"......................................**125.00**

Vase, 6" h., footed swelled cylindrical body w/long loop handles, blue ground, No. 893-6"............................**135.00**

Vase, 7" h., two-handled, globular base w/slightly flaring rim, blue ground, No. 895-7" ....**225.00 to 275.00**

Vase, 7" h., two-handled, globular base w/slightly flaring rim, green ground, No. 895-7".........................**275.00**

Vase, 8" h., footed bulbous base w/tapering cylindrical neck, loop handles, terra cotta ground, No. 898-8".......................................**250.00**

Vase, 8½" h., pillow-type w/handles rising from base to midsection, terra cotta ground, No. 896-8"................**185.00**

Vase, 9" h., two-handled, terra cotta ground, No. 899-9"..........................**275.00**

Vase, 10" h., two-handled, green ground, No. 901-10"........................**300.00**

Vase, 15" h., green ground, No. 904-15"...**495.00**

Vase, 18" h., floor-type, green ground, No. 905-18" ....**1,100.00 to 1,350.00**

Vase, 18" h., floor-type, terra cotta ground, No. 905-18".......................**600.00**

Wall pocket, two-handled, blue ground, No. 1282-8", 8½" h. ....**450.00 to 475.00**

Wall pocket, two-handled, terra cotta ground, No. 1282-8", 8½" h. ....**350.00 to 375.00**

FUDJI or FUJIYAMA (1906)

This Rozane line features slip-trailed designs, often florals, against a bisque ground of grey or beige.

Vase, 9" h., 3¾" d., gently tapering cylindrical body swelled at the top w/a molded mouth, decorated w/incised & enameled spider-like thistles in gold on a pricked bisque buff ground, ink-stamped "Fujiyama"......................................**990.00**

Vase, 11" h., 3¼" d., tall slender ovoid body w/a swelled neck w/cylindrical tip, Art Nouveau style florals w/yellow, brown & caramel swirling leafy flowers against a shaded buff to dark brown ground, ink-stamped "Fujiyama" (ILLUS. top next page)....................................**4,125.00**

Roseville Fudji Vase

FUTURA (1928)

Varied line with shapes ranging from Art Deco geometrics to futuristic. Matte glaze is typical although an occasional piece may be high gloss.

Futura Pillow-Shaped Vase

Basket, hanging-type, wide sloping shoulders, sharply canted sides, terra cotta & brown w/embossed stylized pastel foliage, No. 344-5", 5" **300.00**

Bowl, 3½" h., round stepped base, sharply folded sides, sandy beige, No. 187-8".............**325.00 to 375.00**

Candlesticks, conical base w/square handles, widely flaring shallow socket, No. 1072-4", 4" h., pr. ....**375.00 to 450.00**

Jardiniere, angular handles rising from wide sloping shoulders to rim, sharply canted sides, terra cotta & brown w/embossed stylized pastel foliage, No. 616-6", 6" h. **350.00**

Pot, square mounted cone-shaped bowl w/four vertical supports extending down from mid-point of sides to corners of square disc base, striated blue, green & yellow, 4" h...**400.00**

Vase, 4½" h., 6½" w., straight handles rising from sharply canted low base to rim, upper portion square w/cut corners & canted sides, low-relief curving design on sides & base, terra cotta, No. 85-4".......................**350.00**

Vase, 5" h., flaring squared footed & slightly flaring squared sides, No. 421-5"......................................**350.00**

Vase, 6" h., fan-shaped, No. 82-6" ....**325.00 to 375.00**

Vase, 6¼" h., rectangular pillow-shape, No. 81-5 x 1½ x 5" (ILLUS.) **350.00**

Vases, 6" h., 3½" d., cylindrical body swelling to wider bands at the top & base, long pierced angled handles down the sides, apricot w/green bands & handles, one w/paper label, No. 381-6", pr. ....**275.00 to 350.00**

Vase, 7" h., 3¼" w., square slightly tapering body twisting toward the rim, embossed floral decoration, brown & green **295.00**

Vase, 7" h., footed ringed-ovoid body w/short flaring wide mouth, No. 424-7".......................................**425.00**

Vase, 7½" h., square wedge-shaped base, globular body w/short neck, relief-molded stylized tapering bluish green leaf design rising from base to shoulder against a light bluish green ground, No. 387-7"..........................**795.00**

Vase, 8" h., footed spherical body w/stepped stick neck, No. 384-8".....**475.00**

Vase, 8" h., upright rectangular form on rectangular foot, stepped neck, long square handles, No. 386-8" **580.00**

Vase, 8" h., pyramidal base w/buttress legs supporting a spherical body w/small trumpet neck, green ground, No. 404-8".......**850.00**

Vase, bud, 10" h., slender stick-form body composed of stepped, tapering cones on a disc foot, brown ground, No. 390-10"....................................**425.00**

Vase, 10" h., large spherical body on a small footring, the neck composed of stepped bands, flame-form molded design around the lower half, No. 391-10".............**550.00 to 650.00**

Vase, 12" h., wide ovoid body on a footring, the neck composed of tapering bands, smooth sides, No. 394-12"....................................**895.00**

GARDENIA (1940s)

Large white gardenia blossoms and green leaves over a textured impressed band on a shaded green, grey or tan ground.

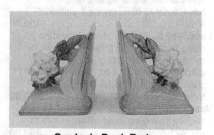

Gardenia Book Ends

Basket w/overhead handle, shaped
rim, grey ground, No. 608-8",
8" h...**150.00**
Basket w/circular handle, green
ground, No. 609-10", 10" h. **185.00**
Basket w/overhead handle, grey
ground, No. 610-12", 12" h. **275.00**
Basket, hanging-type, green
ground, 6" **200.00**
Basket, hanging-type, grey
ground, 6" **175.00**
Book ends, tan ground, No. 659,
5" h., pr. (ILLUS.) **165.00**
Candleholders, green ground,
No. 651-2", 2" h., pr. **115.00**
Vase, 6" h., grey ground, No. 682-6"....**65.00**
Vase, 10" h., tall ovoid body w/fanned
rim, base handles, grey ground,
No. 685-10"......................................**125.00**
Vase, 14½" h., floor-type, two handles
rising from midsection to below rim,
grey ground, No. 689-14"................**450.00**

IMPERIAL (1924)

*Brown pretzel-twisted vine, green grape
leaf and cluster of blue grapes in relief on
green and brown bark-textured ground.*

Basket, hanging-type,
8" h. ....**125.00 to 150.00**
Bowl, 7" d., pierced rim handles,
rounded sides, No. 71-7".....**70.00 to 90.00**
Flower frog...**25.00**
Jardiniere, 10" d., 8" h.......................**155.00**
Jardiniere & pedestal base, overall
28" h., 2 pcs..................................**675.00**
Vase, 8" h., slightly tapering
cylindrical body w/rim handles **70.00**
Wall pocket, peanut-shaped, 10" h. ..**125.00**

IMPERIAL II (1924)

*Varied line with no common character-
istics. Many of the pieces are heavily
glazed with colors that run and blend.*

Ashtray, blue glaze..........................**225.00**
Bowl, 4½" d., deep upright sides,
closed rim **120.00**
Bowl, 12½" d., 5" h., deep widely
flaring sides ringed around the lower

half, on a short foot, mottled blue
ground, No. 207 ....**425.00**
Vase, 5" h., bulbous ovoid body
tapering to a small flat mouth...........**160.00**
Vase, 5½" h., tapering cylinder
w/horizontal ribbing above base,
mottled mauve & turquoise,
No. 468-5"......................................**175.00**
Vase, 7" h., hemispherical w/sloping
shoulder & short collared neck,
mottled turquoise & yellow glaze,
No. 474-7".......................................**350.00**
Vase, 8" h., tapering ovoid body
w/wide flat mouth,
No. 480-8" ....**250.00 to 275.00**

IRIS (1938)

*White or yellow blossoms and green leaves
on rose blending with green, light blue
deepening to a darker blue or tan shading
to green or brown.*

Basket w/pointed overhead handle,
compressed ball form, tan ground,
No. 354-8", 8" h..............................**325.00**
Basket w/semicircular overhead
handle, tan ground, No. 355-10",
9½" h..**250.00**
Basket, hanging-type, handled, tan
ground, 8" d. **240.00**
Basket, hanging-type, handled, rose
ground, 8" d. **295.00**
Bowl, 4" d., blue ground, No. 357-4"....**95.00**
Bowl, 4" d., rose ground,
No. 357-4".......................................**110.00**
Bowl, 5" d., two-handled, footed, blue
ground, No. 359-5"............................**75.00**
Bowl, 6" d., blue ground,
No. 360-6".......................................**120.00**
Console bowl, oval, rose ground,
No. 361-8", 8" l., 3" h. ......**125.00 to 175.00**
Console bowl, oval, rose ground,
No. 362-10", 10" l. ....**125.00 to 175.00**
Ewer, bulbous body, cut-out rim, rose
ground, No. 926-10", 10" h. **300.00**
Flower frog, rose ground,
No. 38.............................**125.00 to 145.00**
Jardiniere, two-handled, rose
ground, No. 647-3", 3" h. ......**50.00 to 75.00**
Urn-vase, rose ground, No. 130-4",
4" h..**65.00**
Vase, 4" h., base handles, blue
ground, No. 914-4"............................**65.00**
Vase, 6" h., blue ground, No. 916-6"....**90.00**
Vase, 6½" h., two handles rising from
shoulder of globular base to
midsection of wide neck, tan ground,
No. 917-6"...**95.00**
Vase, bud, 7" h., two-handled, blue
ground, No. 918-7"..........................**120.00**
Vase, 8" h., urn-form w/pedestal
base, blue ground,
No. 923-8" ....**125.00 to 175.00**

Vase, 8" h., urn-form w/pedestal
base, tan ground, No. 923-8" **150.00**
Wall pocket, two handles rising from
base to below flaring rim, rose
ground, No. 1284-8", 8" h. **550.00**

IVORY II (1937)

*White matte-glazed shapes from earlier
lines such as Orian, Velmoss, Donatello
and others. Also included are figurines of a
draped mule and a sleeping dog.*

Model of a dog, sleeping, 6½" l........**250.00**
Urn-vase, footed spherical body
w/loop side handles, No. 274-6",
6½" h...**39.00**
Wall pocket, double, pine cone
decoration, 8½" h. ....**250.00 to 295.00**

IXIA (1930s)

*Embossed spray of tiny bell-shaped flowers
and slender leaves - white blossoms on
pink ground; lavender blossoms on green
or yellow ground.*

Basket, hanging-type, yellow
ground, 7" d. **225.00**
Bowl, 6" d., pink ground,
No. 387-6"...**130.00**
Rose bowl, pink ground, No. 327-6",
6" d..**110.00**
Urn-vase, green ground, No. 640-5",
5" h...**80.00**
Vase, 7" h., footed ovoid body w/small
tab handles flanking the short neck,
green ground, No. 855-7" **120.00**
Vases, 8½" h., tall cylindrical body
w/stepped buttress handles up the
sides from the round foot,
No. 856-8", pr...................................**200.00**
Vase, 9½" h., No. 860-9" **85.00**
Vase, 15" h., floor-type, pink ground,
No. 865-15" **525.00**

JONQUIL (1931)

*White jonquil blossoms and green leaves in
relief against textured tan ground; green
lining.*

Bowl, 9" d., 3½" h., two-handled,
canted sides.....................................**225.00**
Bowl, 6 x 10" oval, 3½" h., two-
handled, No. 220 ....**195.00**
Bowl-vase, two-handled, tapering
cylindrical sides, 4" d.......................**125.00**
Jardiniere, No. 621-5", 5½" h. **195.00**
Strawberry pot, bulbous body w/four-
spout rim, No. 95-6½", 6½" h...........**395.00**
Urn-vase, baluster-form w/widely
flaring rim & base handles,
4" h. ....**100.00 to 125.00**

Urn-vase, spherical w/small angled
shoulder handles, 5½" h. **135.00**
Vase, 4" h., two-handled, globular,
No. 524-4"..**115.00**
Vase, wide ovoid body tapering to a
wide, flat mouth, shoulder handles,
6½" h., 5½" d. **135.00**
Vase, 7" h., ovoid body w/small
shoulder handles, No. 527-7" **200.00**
Vase, 8" h., ovoid body tapering to a
flaring neck, down-turned shoulder
handles, No. 529-8" **268.00**
Wall pocket, open handles rising
from pointed base & extending
above flaring rim to form a pointed
top, 8½" h..**475.00**

JUVENILE (1916 on)

*Transfer-printed and painted on
creamware with nursery rhyme characters,
cute animals and other motifs appealing to
children.*

Bowl, cereal, 6" d., ducks w/boots **150.00**
Feeding dish w/rolled edge, duck
w/hat, 8" d. **110.00**
Feeding dish w/rolled edge, nursery
rhyme, "Little Bo-Peep," 8" d............**135.00**
Feeding dish w/rolled edge, nursery
rhyme, "My Black Hen," 8" d. **185.00**
Feeding dish w/rolled edge, nursery
rhyme, "Old Woman....," 8" d. **130.00**
Feeding dish w/rolled edge,
Sunbonnet girl, 8" d. **125.00**
Mug, sitting rabbit, 3" h........................**75.00**
Pitcher, 3" h., chicks **75.00**
Pitcher, 3" h., side pour, chicks **200.00**
Pitcher, 3" h., standing rabbit..............**85.00**
Pitcher, 3½" h., sitting rabbit...............**85.00**
Plate, 8" d., standing
rabbit ....**125.00 to 150.00**

LA ROSE (1924)

*Swags of green leaves & red roses on a
creamy ivory ground.*

Basket, hanging-type, No. 338-6",
6" **166.00**
Console set: bowl & pr. of
candleholders; 3 pcs........................**225.00**
Umbrella stand................................**650.00**
Vase, 6" h, cylindrical w/small rim
handles, No. 238-6" **70.00**
Wall pocket, fan-shaped, No. 1234,
7½" h...**150.00**
Wall pocket, long teardrop-form,
No. 1235, 12" h. **275.00**

LAUREL (1934)

*Laurel branch and berries in low-relief
with reeded panels at the sides. Glazed in*

deep yellow, green shading to cream or terra cotta.

Vase, 6" h., tapering cylinder w/wide mouth, closed angular handles at shoulder, green, No. 667-6" ....**185.00 to 200.00**
Vase, 6" h., angular shoulder handles, deep yellow, No. 668-6" **135.00**
Vase, 10" h., footed trumpet-form body w/tapering tab handles, deep yellow, No. 676-10" **250.00**
Vase, 12¼" h., tall trumpet-form w/base handles, deep yellow, No. 677-12¼" **385.00**

LOTUS (1952)

Stylized lotus petals in relief.

Candlesticks, maroon & beige, No. L5, 2½" h., pr. **75.00**
Planter, maroon & beige, glossy finish, No. L9-4", 4" sq., 3½" h. **65.00**
Vase, 10" h., cylindrical, maroon & beige, glossy finish, No. L3-10" **120.00**
Vase, pillow-type, 10½" h., blue & ivory, No. L4-10" **175.00**
Vase, pillow-type, 10½" h., maroon & beige, glossy finish, No. L4-10" **125.00**
Vase, pillow-type, 10½" h., green ground, No. L4-10" **195.00**
Wall pocket, blue & ivory, glossy finish, No. L8-7, 7½" h. **285.00**
Wall pocket, maroon & beige, glossy finish, No. L8-7, 7½" h. ....**300.00 to 325.00**

LUFFA (1934)

Relief-molded ivy leaves and blossoms on shaded brown or green wavy horizontal ridges.

Candlesticks, two-handled, bell-shaped base, green ground, 5" h., pr. **275.00**
Console bowl, 8 x 12", 4" h. **250.00**
Jardiniere, green ground, 5" h. **180.00**
Jardiniere, brown ground, 9" h. **325.00**
Vase, 6" h., two-handled, cylindrical, green ground **115.00**
Vase, 9" h., two-handled, green ground ....**350.00 to 375.00**
Vase, 13" h., two-handled, trumpet-form w/flaring foot, green ground..**495.00**

MAGNOLIA (1943)

Large white blossoms with rose centers and black stems in relief against a blue, green or tan textured ground

Ashtray, two-handled, low bowl form, blue ground, No. 28, 7" d. **125.00**

Ashtray, two-handled, low bowl form, green ground, No. 28, 7" d................**75.00**
Basket w/fan-shaped overhead handle, green ground, No. 384-8", 8" h..**95.00**
Basket w/low overhead handle, footed, blue ground, No. 385-10", 13" w., 10" h....................................**150.00**
Basket w/low overhead handle, footed, green ground, No. 385-10", 13" w., 10" h. ....**125.00 to 150.00**
Basket, hanging-type, tan ground, No. 469-5" **135.00**
Book ends, green ground, No. 13, pr...**165.00**
Bowl, 6" d., two-handled, green ground, No. 447-6"..........................**90.00**
Bowl, 8" d., two-handled, brown ground, No. 448-8"........................**100.00**
Bowl, 12" d., two-handled, blue ground, No. 451-12"........................**150.00**
Bowl, 14" d., tan ground, No. 452-14" ..**165.00**
Cookie jar, cov., shoulder handles, blue ground, No. 2-8", overall 10" h...**495.00**

Magnolia Cookie Jar

Cookie jar, cov., shoulder handles, tan ground, No. 2-8", overall 10" h. (ILLUS.)................**400.00 to 450.00**
Jardiniere, two-handled, blue ground, No. 665-5", 5" h...............................**70.00**
Model of a conch shell, blue ground, No. 453-6", 6½" w...............**60.00 to 80.00**
Planter, shell-form, w/angular-base handles, blue ground, No. 183-6", 6" l...**95.00**
Tea set: cov. teapot, creamer & open sugar bowl; green ground, Nos. 4, 4C & 4S, 3 pcs. ....**400.00 to 425.00**
Vase, 6" h., footed squatty bulbous body w/short cylindrical neck & angled handles, blue ground, No. 180-6"..**75.00**
Vase, bud, 7" h., blue ground, No. 179-7"...**80.00**
Vase, 8" h., globular w/large angular handles, tan ground, No. 91-8" **170.00**

Vase, 10" h., two-handled, blue
ground, No. 95-10"............................**175.00**
Vase, 12" h., blue ground,
No. 96-12".......................................**255.00**
Vase, 12" h., green ground,
No. 96-12".......................................**275.00**
Vase, 14" h., floor-type, tan ground,
No. 97-14".......................................**395.00**
Vase, 18" h., floor-type, blue ground,
No. 100-18".....................................**485.00**
Wall pocket, overhead handle
w/pointed ends, tan ground,
No. 1294-8½", 8½" h......................**250.00**

MATT COLORS (late 1920s)

*Simple paneled forms in colors of light
blue, turquoise, yellow and pink. Reissued
later with a glossy glaze.*

Basket, hanging-type, aqua glaze,
No. 364-5", 5" h................................**80.00**
Bowl, 3" d., squatty bulbous form
w/closed rim, No. 15, pink glaze........**40.00**
Bowl, 4" d., compressed globular
form w/handles at shoulder, low
foot, aqua glaze, No. 550-4"..............**75.00**
Bowl, 5½" d., 4" h., footed squatty
bulbous body w/wide flaring mouth,
small handles at shoulder, blue
ground, No. 550-4"............................**45.00**
Flowerpot, incised geometric design,
pink glaze, No. 549-4", 4" h..............**40.00**
Vase, 4" h., angular handles, tapering
sides w/embossed geometric
design, collared neck, pink glaze,
No. 607-4".......................................**30.00**

MATT GREEN (before 1916)

*Dark green matt finish. Some pieces plain;
others decorated with various embossed
designs such as leaves or children's faces.*

Matt Green Umbrella Stand

Basket, hanging-type, everted
scalloped rim, embossed design **175.00**

Jardiniere, No. 550-4", 4" d. **98.00**
Umbrella stand, slightly waisted
cylindrical form w/slender ribs
alternating w/panels of tall stylized
flowers, small glaze nick at rim,
11½" d., 23" h. (ILLUS.)...................**550.00**
Wall pocket, smooth conical form,
10" h...**130.00**

MAYFAIR (late 1940s)

*Utilitarian line with various embossed
designs; glossy glaze.*

Bowl, 10" w., model of a shell, green
& lime glaze, No. 1119-9" **58.00**
Cornucopia-vase, brown glaze,
No. 1013-6", 6" h..............................**37.00**
Pitcher, 5" h., globular base &
collared neck, green glaze,
No. 1102-5".......................................**45.00**
Pitcher, 10" h., brown glaze,
No. 1106-10".....................................**75.00**
Vase, 7" h., burgundy glaze,
No. 557-7"...**30.00**
Vase, 7" h., stylized lily-form w/stalk
of leaves to one side, on
asymmetrical base, dark green
glaze, No. 1104-9" **68.00**
Vase, 8" h., dark brown glaze,
No. 1003-8".......................................**40.00**
Wall pocket, corner-type, fluted
sides, dark brown exterior, creamy
beige interior, No. 1014-8", 8" h.........**55.00**

MING TREE (1949)

*Embossed twisted bonsai tree topped with
puffy foliage—pink-topped trees on mint
green ground, green tops on white ground
and white tops on blue ground; handles in
the form of gnarled branches.*

Basket w/overhead branch handle,
blue ground, No. 509-12", 13" h.......**190.00**
Book ends, blue, No. 559,
5½" h., pr. **140.00**
Book ends, white, No. 559,
5½" h., pr. **145.00**
Console bowl, end handle,
asymmetrical rim, blue ground,
No. 528-10", 10" l..............................**60.00**
Ewer, blue ground, No. 516-10",
10" h..**135.00**
Vase, 10½" h., cylindrical w/narrow
shoulder, asymmetrical, branch
handles, white ground,
No. 583-10" ....**100.00 to 110.00**
Vase, 12½" h., curving body w/two
handles at midsection, green
ground, No. 584-12"..........................**190.00**
Wall pocket, overhead branch
handle, white ground,
No. 566-8", 8½" h. ....**250.00 to 300.00**

MODERNE (1930s)

Art Deco style rounded and angular shapes trimmed with an embossed panel of vertical lines and modified swirls and circles—white trimmed with terra cotta, medium blue with white and turquoise with a burnished antique gold.

Compote, open, 5" d., 6" h., deep round bowl raised on an open U-form support above the disc foot, No. 295-6" **125.00**

Compote, open, 6" d., wide shallow bowl raised on a slender pedestal flanked by buttress supports, wide flaring foot, terra cotta ground, No. 297-6" **125.00**

Vase, 6" h., short & wide cylindrical bowl raised on a short flaring foot & two open supports, white ground, No. 789-6" **40.00**

Vase, 7" h., baluster-form w/wide flat mouth & small loop handles at the shoulders, terra cotta ground, No. 793-7" **80.00**

MONTACELLO (1931)

White stylized trumpet flowers with black accents on a terra cotta band—light terra cotta mottled in blue or light green mottled and blended with blue backgrounds.

Montacello Handled Vase

Basket w/pointed overhead handle, tall collared neck, blue ground, No. 332-6", 6½" h. **225.00**

Basket w/pointed overhead handle, tall collared neck, terra cotta ground, No. 332-6, 6½" h. **450.00**

Urn-vase, ovoid w/shoulder handles, green ground, No. 564-9", 9" h. **365.00**

Vase, 4" h., sharply compressed globular base, handles rising from shoulder to rim, terra cotta ground, No. 555-4" **130.00**

Vase, 5" h., ovoid w/shoulder handles, blue ground, No. 557-5" **225.00**

Vase, 5" h., ovoid w/shoulder handles, terra cotta ground, No. 557-5" **195.00**

Vase, 7" h., two-handled, slightly ovoid, wide mouth, blue ground, No. 561-7" **345.00**

Vase, 7" h., two-handled, slightly ovoid, wide mouth, terra cotta ground, No. 561-7" (ILLUS.) **325.00**

MORNING GLORY (1935)

Stylized pastel morning glory blossoms and twining vines in low relief against a white or green ground.

Basket w/high pointed overhead handle, globular body, white ground, 10½" h. **350.00**

Candlesticks, flaring base, small angular handles at midsection, green ground, 5" h., pr. **450.00**

Vase, 6" h., two-handled, waisted cylinder, green ground, No. 6-6" **340.00**

Vase, 7" h., pillow-shaped, base handles, green ground ....**200.00 to 250.00**

Vase, 8" h., two-handled, ovoid, white ground **350.00**

Vase, 15" h., shoulder handles, slightly expanding cylinder, white ground **1,210.00**

Wall pocket, double, green ground, 8½" h. **1,300.00**

MOSS (1930s)

Spanish moss draped over a brown branch with green leaves against a background of ivory, pink or tan shading to blue.

Basket, hanging-type, pink ground, No. 353-5" **425.00**

Bowl, 4" d., blue or green ground, No. 289-4", each **90.00**

Jardiniere, pink ground, No. 635-8", 8" h. **395.00**

Pedestal base, blue ground, 17" h. ....**475.00 to 525.00**

Vase, 8" h., pillow-type w/small angular handles rising from midsection to rim, green ground, No. 781-8" **155.00**

Vase, 12" h., floor-type, pink & green, No. 785-12" **475.00**

Wall pocket, bucket-shaped, blue ground, No. 1279, 10" h. **575.00**

MOSTIQUE (1915)

Incised Indian-type design of stylized flowers, leaves or geometric shapes glazed in bright glossy colors against a heavy, pebbled ground.

Bowl, 5½" d., geometric design, tan
ground...**70.00**
Jardiniere, canted sides, geometric
design, grey ground w/brown & red,
8" h...**165.00**
Jardiniere, geometric floral design
w/arrowhead leaves, tan
ground, 10" h. ....**150.00 to 200.00**
Vase, 5" h., grey ground......................**60.00**
Vase, 10" h., waisted cylindrical body,
arrowhead leaves design,
grey ground......................................**195.00**
Vase, 12" h., waisted cylinder
w/flaring mouth, two handles rising
from base to midsection, arrowhead
leaves design, grey ground,
532-12" **250.00**

ORIAN (1935)

*Art Deco-style shapes, blade-like slender
leaf-shaped handles; glossy glaze, often in
a two-tone color combination.*

Basket, hanging-type, yellow ground,
7" h...**148.00**
Compote, 10½" d., 4½" h., glossy
turquoise w/tan lining...........**75.00 to 85.00**
Vase, 6" h., cylindrical body w/bulging
top & wide mouth, slender handles
rising from low foot to shoulder,
glossy green ground, No. 733-6" **110.00**
Vase, 8" h., two handles rising from
semi-globular base to middle of
tapering cylindrical neck,
blue ground......................................**175.00**
Vase, 10" h., two-handled, turquoise
blue w/orange lining.........................**110.00**
Wall pocket, straight sides, rounded
bottom, slightly flared rim, stylized
florals, dark green ground, 9" h........**175.00**

PANEL (1920)

*Recessed panels decorated with embossed
naturalistic or stylized florals or female
nudes.*

Bowl, 9" d...**125.00**
Urn-vase, bulbous ovoid body on low
flaring foot, flat closed rim, 8" h........**195.00**
Vase, double bud, 5½" h., waisted
cylinders joined by floral panel, dark
brown ground....................................**150.00**
Vase, 6" h., pillow-type, small rim
handles, brown ground **95.00**
Vase, 8" h., fan-shaped, female
nudes, dark brown ground **400.00**
Vase, 8" h., fan-shaped, female
nudes, dark green ground.................**525.00**
Wall pocket, rectangular openwork
handles, scalloped edge, female
nudes, dark green ground, 7" h. **425.00**

Wall pocket, conical, stylized
blossoms, dark brown ground,
9" h..**165.00**

PAULEO (1914)

*Classic shapes similar to ancient Oriental
vases decorated in over two hundred
different color combinations in either a
lustre or marbleized glaze.*

Vase, 16" h., 6" d., baluster-form,
decorated in a lustre glaze w/large
undulating red blossoms on sinewy
stems against a beige ground..........**660.00**
Vase, 16½" h., 7½" d, wide ovoid
body tapering to a flaring neck,
decorated w/a landscape w/large
trees in orange, brown & green,
unmarked......................................**1,760.00**
Vase, floor-type, 24⅜" h., a short
pedestal foot supporting a
compressed cushion body tapering
to a tall cylindrical neck w/flaring
flattened rim, rich organic yellowish
green matte glaze, unmarked **1,540.00**

PEONY (1942)

*Peony blossoms in relief against a textured
swirling ground—yellow blossoms against
rose shading to green, brown shading to
gold or gold with green; white blossoms
against green.*

Peony Cornucopia-Vase

Basket, hanging-type, gold ground,
No. 467-5"..**150.00**
Basket, hanging-type, rose ground,
No. 467-5"...**170.00**
Candleholder, gold ground,
No. 1152-4½", 4½" h...........................**55.00**
Console bowl, green ground,
No. 4-10", 10" l................................**125.00**
Console set: bowl & pair of
candleholders; green ground,
3 pcs..**150.00**

Cornucopia-vase, gold ground, No. 170-6", 6" h. (ILLUS.). **80.00**

Cornucopia-vase, gold ground, No. 171-8", 8" h. **150.00**

Creamer, gold ground, No. 3-C, 3" h. **52.00**

Ewer, green ground, No. 7-6", 6" h. **95.00**

Model of a conch shell, green ground, No. 436, 9½" l. ....**150.00 to 200.00**

Mug, green ground, No. 2-3½", 3½" h. **65.00**

Mug, rose ground, No. 2-3½", 3½" h. **79.00**

Pitcher w/ice lip, 7½" h., gold ground, No. 1326-7½" **95.00**

Pitcher w/ice lip, 7½" h., green ground, No. 1326-7½" **200.00**

Planter, rectangular w/angular end handles, slightly canted sides, gold ground, No. 387-8", 10" l. **100.00**

Teapot, cov., green ground, No. 3 .....**200.00**

Tea set: cov. teapot, sugar bowl & creamer; gold ground, Nos. 3, 3C & 3S, 3 pcs. **325.00**

Vase, 4" h., base handles, gold ground, No. 57-4" **25.00**

Vase, 6" h., gold ground, No. 59-6" **69.00**

Vase, bud, 7" h., gold ground, No. 173-7" **60.00**

Vase, bud, 7" h., green ground, No. 173-7" **115.00**

Vase, 9" h., gold ground, No. 65-9" **110.00**

Vase, 15" h., floor-type, gold ground, No. 69-15" **325.00**

Vase, 18" h., gold ground, No. 70-18" **285.00**

Wall pocket, two-handled, gold ground, No. 1293-8", 8" h. **175.00**

PINE CONE (1931)

Realistic embossed brown pine cones and green pine needles on shaded blue, brown or green ground. (Pink extremely rare.)

Pine Cone Mug

Ashtray, brown ground, No. 499, 4½" l. **90.00**

Basket w/overhead branch handle, asymmetrical body, green ground, No. 408-6", 6" h. ....**150.00 to 200.00**

Basket w/overhead branch handle, boat-shaped, brown ground, No. 410-10", 10" h. ....**350.00 to 400.00**

Basket w/overhead branch handle, boat-shaped, green ground, No. 410-10", 10" l. **375.00**

Basket w/overhead branch handle, blue ground, No. 339, 13" l., 9" h. **600.00**

Basket, hanging-type, blue ground, No. 352-5", 5" **400.00**

Basket, hanging-type, brown ground, No. 352-5", 5" ....**300.00 to 350.00**

Basket, hanging-type, green ground, No. 352-5", 5" ....**300.00 to 350.00**

Bowl, 4½" h., asymmetrical handles, irregular rim, green ground, No. 457-7" ....**125.00 to 150.00**

Bowl, 6" d., brown ground, No. 354-6" **225.00**

Bowl, 4 x 11", two-handled, brown ground, No. 279-9" **165.00**

Bowl, 4 x 11", two-handled, green ground, No. 279-9" **125.00**

Candleholders, flat disc base supporting candle nozzle in the form of a pine cone flanked by needles on one side & branch handle on the other, green ground, No. 112-3", 3" h., pr. **125.00**

Console bowl, end handles, blue ground, 11" l. **330.00**

Console bowl, end handles, brown ground, silver paper label, 11" l. **295.00**

Dish, blue ground, No. 497-7", 7" d. **115.00**

Dish, brown ground, No. 497-7", 7" d. **75.00**

Dish, brown ground, No. 428-8", 8" d. **250.00**

Ewer, green ground, No. 909-10", 10" h. ....**325.00 to 375.00**

Ewer, brown ground, No. 880-18", 18" h. **850.00**

Flower frog, No. 20-5¼", 5¼" h. **120.00**

Jardiniere, two-handled, globular, brown ground, No. 632-3", 3" h. **85.00**

Jardiniere, blue ground, No. 632-4", 4" h. **180.00**

Jardiniere, green ground, No. 632-4", 4" h. ....**100.00 to 125.00**

Jardiniere, green ground, No. 401-6", 6" h. **155.00**

Jardiniere & pedestal base, brown ground, No. 405-8", jardiniere 8" h., 2 pcs. ....**1,500.00 to 1,850.00**

Match holder, green ground, No. 498-3", 3" h. **200.00**

Mug, brown ground, No. 960-4", 4" h. (ILLUS.). ....**200.00 to 250.00**

Mug, green ground, No. 960-4", 4" h. **225.00**

Pitcher, 9" h., blue ground, No. 415-9" ....**750.00 to 775.00**

Pitcher, 9½" h., ovoid, small branch
handle, green ground, No. 708-9"....**750.00**
Planter, blue ground,
No. 456-6", 6" l. ....**100.00 to 150.00**
Plate, wall-type, green
ground ....**350.00 to 400.00**
Rose bowl, blue ground, No. 278-4",
4" h. ....**200.00 to 250.00**
Rose bowl, brown ground,
No. 278-4", 4" h............................**150.00**
Sand jar, green ground, No. 776-14",
14" h...**1,650.00**
Tray, rectangular, brown ground,
No. 430-12", 12" l...........................**300.00**
Umbrella stand, brown ground,
No. 777-20", 20" h. **1,800.00**
Urn-vase, footed spherical body,
small twig handle, blue ground,
5" h..**275.00**
Urn-vase, footed, small branch
handles, blue ground,
No. 121-7", 7" h..............................**225.00**
Urn-vase, footed, small branch
handles, green ground,
No. 121-7", 7" h. ....**125.00 to 150.00**
Vase, 6" h., fan-shaped w/single
handle, brown ground, No. 472-6" ...**225.00**
Vase, 6" h., brown ground,
No. 748-6" ....**100.00 to 150.00**
Vase, 6" h., green ground,
No. 748-6" **95.00**
Vase, 6" h., two-handled, brown
ground, No. 839-6"..........................**200.00**
Vase, 6" h., two-handled, green
ground, No. 839-6" ....**120.00 to 140.00**
Vase, 7" h., blue ground,
No. 840-7" ....**185.00 to 200.00**
Vase, bud, 7½" h., single handle
rising from disc base to mid-section,
brown ground, No. 479-7" **195.00**
Vase, triple bud, 8" h., blue ground,
No. 113-8".......................................**265.00**
Vase, 8" h., green ground,
No. 842-8".......................................**160.00**
Vase, 8" h., blue ground, cone-
shaped, handled, four cut-outs in
top, No. 843-8" **385.00**
Vase, 8" h., blue ground,
No. 844-8".......................................**350.00**
Vase, pillow-type, 8" h., brown
ground, No. 845-8"..........................**225.00**
Vase, 9" h., blue ground,
No. 705-9".......................................**325.00**
Vase, 9" h., brown ground,
No. 705-9".......................................**250.00**
Vase, 9" h., brown ground,
No. 847-9".......................................**350.00**
Vase, 10" h., blue ground,
No. 648-10"......................................**495.00**
Vase, 10" h., blue ground,
No. 747-10"......................................**490.00**
Vase, 10" h., brown ground,
No. 747-10".....................................**425.00**

Vase, 10" h., green ground,
No. 747-10".....................................**225.00**
Vase, 10" h., brown ground,
No. 849-10".....................................**200.00**
Vase, 14½" h., expanding cylinder
w/branch handles at shoulder, blue
ground, No. 850-14".........................**650.00**
Vase, 14½" h., expanding cylinder
w/branch handles at shoulder,
green ground, No. 850-14" **750.00**
Vase, 15" h., floor-type, green
ground, No. 912-15".....................**1,200.00**
Wall bracket, brown ground,
No. 1-5" x 8" **475.00**

Pine Cone Double Wall Pocket

Wall pocket, double, blue ground,
No. 1273-8", 8½" h. (ILLUS.) **450.00**
Wall pocket, triple, brown ground,
No. 466, 8½" w. **595.00**
Window box, brown ground,
No. 430-12", 12" l............................**350.00**
Window box, brown ground,
No. 469-12", 12" l............................**325.00**

POPPY (1930)

*Embossed full-blown poppy blossoms, buds
and foliage—yellow blossoms on green,
white blossoms on blue or soft pink
blossoms on a deeper pink.*

Basket, wide trumpet-form w/high &
wide arched handle, pink ground,
No. 347-10", 10" h............................**425.00**
Basket w/pointed overhead handle,
slender ovoid body on disc base,
blue ground, No. 348-12", 12" h.......**400.00**
Ewer, green ground, No. 880-18",
18" h...**550.00**
Flower frog, brown ground, No. 35 ...**110.00**
Jardiniere, tiny handles at rim,
globular, green ground,
No. 642-5", 5" h...............................**185.00**
Vase, 6½" h., two-handled, ovoid,
pink ground, No. 867-6"...................**140.00**
Vase, 7½" h., wide baluster-form

w/small handles at neck, blue
ground, No. 868-7"..........................**125.00**

Vase, 7½" h., footed gently flaring
cylindrical body w/small handles
near rim, pink ground,
No. 869-7" ....**175.00 to 200.00**

Large Poppy Vase

Vase, 15" h., squatty footed bottom
w/loop handles, tall cylindrical sides
w/a rolled rim, green ground,
No 878-15" (ILLUS.) **425.00**

PRIMROSE (1932)

*Cluster of long-stemmed blossoms and
pod-like leaves in relief on blue, pink or tan
ground.*

Basket, hanging-type, two-handled,
globular, blue ground, No. 354-5",
5" h.,..**250.00**

Cornucopia-vase, tan ground,
No. 125-6", 6" h...................................**80.00**

Rose bowl, blue ground, No. 284-4",
4" d...**95.00**

Vase, 6" h., a wide flat mouth flaring
to a tapering cylindrical body flanked
by long angled handles, blue
ground, No. 760-6"..............................**90.00**

Vase, 8" h., pink ground,
No. 766-8" ....**160.00 to 180.00**

Vase, 12" h., blue ground,
No. 771-12"..**375.00**

Vase, 12" h., pink ground,
No. 771-12"..**400.00**

RAYMOR (1952)

Modernistic design oven-proof dinnerware.

Baker, Terra Cotta, No. 156................**39.00**

Bean pot, cov., Avocado green,
No. 193, 3 qt. **100.00**

Bowl, soup, lug-type, Terra Cotta,
No. 155 ....**22.00**

Butter dish, cov., Avocado green,
No. 181, 7½" **200.00**

Casserole, cov., individual size,
Autumn brown, No. 199, 7½"............**45.00**

Casserole, cov., Terra Cotta, medium
size, No. 183, 11" d..........................**95.00**

Celery & olive dish, Terra Cotta,
No. 177, 15½" l..................................**90.00**

Corn server, individual, Autumn
brown, No. 162, 12½" l. **16.00**

Cup & saucer, Terra Cotta, Nos. 150
& 151, set. **20.00**

Gravy boat, Terra Cotta, No. 190,
9½" l...**45.00**

Jam jar, cov., Autumn brown,
No. 172 ....**165.00**

Mug, Autumn brown, No. 179 ....**30.00**

Mug, Terra Cotta, No. 179 ....**50.00**

Pitcher, water, 10" h., Autumn brown,
No. 189 ....**225.00**

Plate, dinner, Terra Cotta, No. 152 ......**20.00**

Plate, luncheon, Terra Cotta,
No. 153 ....**20.00**

Plate, chop, Autumn brown, No. 164 ...**60.00**

Platter, rectangular, Autumn brown,
No. 163 ....**52.00**

Ramekin, cov., individual, Avocado
green, No. 156....................................**65.00**

Sugar bowl, cov., Autumn brown,
No. 157 ....**25.00**

Shirred egg dish, Terra Cotta,
No. 200 ....**40.00**

Teapot, cov., Autumn brown,
No. 174 ....**175.00**

Trivet, Beach grey, No. 159................**20.00**

Vegetable bowl, Autumn brown,
No. 160, 9" l.......................................**32.00**

Vegetable bowl, divided, Terra Cotta,
No. 165, 13" l.....................................**45.00**

ROSECRAFT (1916)

Untrimmed classic shapes; glossy glazes.

Basket, hanging-type, glossy blue **125.00**

Basket, hanging-type, glossy yellow....**95.00**

Bowl, 8½" d., 2" h., incurved sides,
glossy black **70.00**

Candleholders, flat base, baluster-
form stem, flaring rim, glossy black,
No. 1029-3¾", 3¾" h., pr. **120.00**

Vase, bud, 8½" h., glossy black,
No. 44-8½"...**85.00**

Vase, 12" h., 9" d., ovoid w/handles
rising from shoulder to ringed neck,
glossy black, No. 338-12" **357.50**

Wall pocket, teardrop-shaped,
Azurine glaze...................**125.00 to 150.00**

Wall pocket, conical w/flared rim,
glossy black, No. 1236-9", 9" h., ...**195.00**

SILHOUETTE (1952)

Recessed shaped panels decorated with

floral designs or exotic female nudes against a combed background.

Silhouette Fan-Shaped Vase

Basket, flaring cylinder w/pointed overhead handle, florals, rose ground, No. 708-6", 6" h. **115.00**

Basket, flaring cylinder w/pointed overhead handle, florals, white ground, No. 708-6", 6" h. **75.00**

Basket w/curved rim & asymmetrical handle, florals, turquoise blue ground, No. 710-10", 10" h. ....**120.00 to 140.00**

Basket, hanging-type, florals, rose ground...**120.00**

Basket, hanging-type, florals, white ground...**100.00**

Bowl, 10" d., florals, turquoise blue ground, No. 730-10"..........................**60.00**

Console set: bowl & pair of candleholders; white ground w/turquoise blue panel, 3 pcs. **175.00**

Cornucopia-vase, tan ground, No. 722-6", 6" h................................**75.00**

Ewer, bulging base, florals, white w/turquoise blue panel, No. 716-6", 6" h...**45.00**

Ewer, sharply canted sides, florals, tan ground, No. 717-10", 10" h. **165.00**

Planter, footed narrow rectangular form, green ground, No. 731-14", 14" l..**115.00**

Planter, double, No. 757-9", 9" l., 5½" h.. **50.00**

Rose bowl, female nudes, turquoise blue ground, No. 742-6", 6" h...........**290.00**

Vase, 6" h., rectangular curved body on wedge-shaped base, tan ground, No. 781-6"...**55.00**

Vase, 7" h, fan-shaped, female nudes, rose ground, No. 737-7".......**300.00**

Vase, 7" h., fan-shaped, female nudes, turquoise blue ground, No. 737-7" **275.00**

Vase, 7" h., fan-shaped, female nudes, tan ground, No. 783-7" (ILLUS.) ....**225.00 to 275.00**

Vase, 9" h., double, base w/canted sides supporting two square vases w/sloping rims, joined by a stylized branch-form center post, florals, turquoise blue ground, No. 757-9" ...**110.00**

Vase, 9" h., florals, white ground, No. 786-9" **85.00**

Wall pocket, bullet-shaped, florals, rose ground, No. 766-8", 8" h. ....**165.00 to 195.00**

SNOWBERRY (1946)

Clusters of white berries on brown stems with green foliage over oblique scalloping, against a blue, green or rose background.

Snowberry Ewer

Ashtray, round, shaded blue ground, No. 1AT...**78.00**

Basket, w/asymmetrical overhead handle, shaded blue ground, No. IBK-8", 8" h. ....**180.00 to 200.00**

Basket w/asymmetrical overhead handle, shaded rose ground, No. 1BK-8", 8" h..............................**195.00**

Basket w/curved overhead handle, disc base, shaded blue ground, No. 1BK-10", 10" h..........................**130.00**

Basket, hanging-type, shaded blue ground, No. 1 HB-5", 5" h. **200.00**

Basket, hanging-type, shaded green ground, No. 1 HB-5", 5" h. **185.00**

Bowl, 10" d., footed, shaded rose ground, No. IFB-10".........................**115.00**

Console bowl, pointed end handles, shaded rose ground, No. 1BL-8", 11" l...**85.00**

Creamer & sugar bowl, angular side handles, shaded green ground, Nos. 1C & 1S, pr. **60.00**

Ewer, shaded rose ground, No. 1TK-6", 6" h. (ILLUS.)................**125.00**

Ewer, sharply compressed base w/long conical neck, shaded green ground, No. 1TK-10", 10" h. **150.00**

Ewer, sharply compressed base

w/long conical neck, shaded rose
ground, No. 1TK-10",
10" h. ....**150.00 to 175.00**
Jardiniere, two-handled, shaded blue
ground, No. 1J-4", 4" h......................**82.00**
Jardiniere, two-handled, shaded blue
ground, No. 1J-6", 6" h....................**150.00**
Jardiniere, shaded green ground,
No. 1J-8", 8" h. ....**400.00 to 475.00**
Tea set: cov. teapot, open sugar bowl
& creamer; shaded rose ground,
Nos. 1TP, 1S, & 1C, the set............**350.00**
Urn-vase, two-handled, shaded blue
ground, No. 1UR-8", 8½" h. **80.00**
Vase, 6½" h., pillow-type, shaded
rose ground, No. 1FH-6".....................**55.00**
Vase, bud, 7" h., single base handle,
asymmetrical rim, shaded blue
ground, No. 1BV-7"..........................**60.00**
Vase, 7½" h., globular base w/high
angular handles, long slender neck,
shaded blue ground, No. 1V2-7"........**75.00**
Vase, 9" h., shaded blue ground,
No. 1V2-9".......................**125.00 to 130.00**
Vase, 9" h., shaded green ground,
No. 1V2-9" **150.00**
Vase, 9" h., shaded rose ground,
No. 1V2-9" **125.00**
Vase, 12" h., shaded blue ground,
No. 1V2-12" **235.00**
Vase, 12½" h., angular handles at
mid-section, ovoid w/flaring mouth,
shaded green ground,
No. 1V1-12" **225.00**
Wall pocket, angular handles rising
from base, shaded blue ground,
No. 1WP-8", 8" w., 5½" h. **125.00**
Wall pocket, angular handles rising
from base, shaded green ground,
No. 1WP-8", 8" w.,
5½" h. ....**150.00 to 175.00**
Wall pocket, angular handles rising
from base, shaded rose ground,
No. 1WP-8", 8" w., 5½" h................**140.00**

SUNFLOWER (1930)

*Long-stemmed yellow sunflower blossoms
framed in green leaves against a mottled
green textured ground.*

Bowl, 4" h., canted sides, low collared
neck **275.00**
Jardiniere, 8" h., decorated w/spiders
on base **695.00**
Urn-vase, globular w/small mouth,
5½" h. **485.00**
Urn-vase, globular, 7" h. **1,000.00**
Vase, 6" h., angular rim handles,
cylindrical **250.00**
Vase, 6" h., tiny rim handles, slightly
tapering cylinder **522.50**
Vase, 9½" h., 7" d., two-handled,
bulbous **880.00**

Vase, 10" h., globular base & short
collared neck w/small handles **585.00**

TEASEL (1936)

*Gracefully curving long stems and delicate
pods.*

Bowl, 4" h., closed handles at
midsection, shaded blue,
No. 342-4"..**55.00**
Rose bowl, beige shading to tan,
No. 342-5", 5".................................**75.00**
Vase, 8" h., closed handles at
shoulder, low foot, beige shading to
tan, No. 884-8"................................**125.00**

THORN APPLE (1930s)

*White trumpet flower and foliage one side,
reverse with thorny pod and foliage
against shaded blue, brown or pink
ground.*

Bowl, 4" d., No. 304-4"........................**45.00**
Bowl, 6" d., pointed handles, shaded
pink ground, No. 307-6"....................**95.00**
Bowl, 8" d., uneven rim, small angular
handles, No. 309-8".......................**165.00**
Candlesticks, figural thorn apple on
leaf base, No.1117, 2½" h., pr. **160.00**
Centerpiece, bowl flanked by tall
slightly conical vases, on shaped
base, shaded blue ground,
No. 312 ....**185.00**
Ewer, shaded blue ground,
No. 825-15", 15" h...........................**350.00**
Flowerpot w/saucer, shaded blue
ground, No. 639-5", 5" h. **215.00**
Flowerpot w/saucer, shaded brown
or pink ground, No. 639-5", 5" h.,
each **150.00**
Urn, stepped handles, disc foot,
shaded brown ground, No. 305-6",
6" h..**400.00**
Vase, 4" h., squatty body w/short
narrow neck, angular pierced
handles rising from midsection,
shaded pink ground, No. 808-4" **87.00**
Vase, 6" h., shaded pink ground,
No. 810-6"......................................**120.00**
Vase, double bud, 5½" h.,
No. 1119 ....**135.00**
Vase, 8" h., shaded blue ground,
No. 818-8".......................................**135.00**
Vase, 10" h., shaded brown
ground, No. 821-10" ....**250.00 to 300.00**
Vase, 15" h., floor-type, shaded
brown ground, No. 824-15"..............**410.00**

TOPEO (1934)

*Four evenly spaced vertical garlands
beginning near the top and tapering gently
down the sides.*

Console bowl, oval, blue glaze,
13" l., 4" h......................................**225.00**
Jardiniere, Artcraft shape, red glaze,
7" h...**200.00**
Urn-vase, spherical, blue glaze,
6" h...**280.00**
Vase, 6½" h., ovoid w/short flaring
neck, blue glaze..............................**185.00**
Vase, 9" h., ovoid w/short cylindrical
neck, blue glaze..............................**325.00**
Vase, 9½" h., ovoid w/tapering sides
& short collared neck, glossy
red glaze **250.00**

TOURMALINE (1933)

*Produced in various simple shapes and a
wide variety of glazes including rose and
grey, blue-green, brown or azure blue with
green and gold, and terra cotta with
yellow.*

Bowl, 13¼" d., 4¾" h., molded
ribbing, low foot, mottled blue,
No. 241-12" ....**70.00 to 90.00**
Console set: 8" d. console bowl & pr.
of 4" h. candlesticks; pink &
turquoise, 3 pcs. **300.00**
Ginger jars, cov., mottled terra cotta
& yellow, 12" h., pr. **375.00**
Planter, footed ribbed oval form,
mottled blue, No. 241-12", 12½" l.,
5" h...**120.00**
Urn-vase, compressed globular
base w/short collared neck,
mottled blue, No. A-200-4",
4½" h. ....**50.00 to 100.00**
Vase, 6" h., pillow-type, two-handled,
horizontally ribbed lower half,
mottled gold, No. A-65-6"..................**80.00**
Vase, 6" h., pillow-type, two-handled,
horizontally ribbed lower half,
mottled turquoise, No. A-65-6"...........**75.00**
Vase, 7½" h., square, tapering slightly
towards base, embossed design
around rim, mottled blue,
No. 612-7".......................................**75.00**
Vase, 9" h., tall trumpet-form w/flaring
foot & four short columns around the
base, mottled blue **95.00**

TUSCANY (1927)

*Simple forms with gently curving handles
ending in leaf and grape clusters. Mottled
finish found in shiny pink with pale blue-
green leaves, overall greyish blue or dull
turquoise.*

Basket, hanging-type, mottled pink....**155.00**
Candleholder, domed base w/open
handles rising from rim to beneath
the candle socket, mottled greyish
blue, 3" h. **20.00**

Candlesticks, domed base w/open
handles rising from rim to beneath
the candle socket, mottled dull
turquoise, 4" h., pr..............................**78.00**
Console set: bowl w/flower frog & pr.
3" h. candleholders; mottled pink,
4 pcs. **195.00**
Vase, 6" h., squared form w/large
handles rising from the low foot to
the flaring rim, mottled
dull turquoise **70.00**
Vase, 10" h., shoulder handles,
bulbous body, mottled
greyish blue **135.00**
Vase, 12" h., tall swelled cylindrical
body tapering to a short neck
flanked by small handles,
mottled pink **325.00**
Wall pocket, long open handles,
rounded rim, mottled
greyish blue, 8" h............**140.00 to 150.00**
Wall pocket, long open handles,
rounded rim, mottled dull
turquoise, 8" h................................**325.00**

VELMOSS (1935)

*Embossed clusters of long slender green
leaves extending down from the top and
crossing three wavy horizontal lines. Some
pieces reverse the design with the leaves
rising from the base.*

Planter, pointed end handles,
rectangular w/shaped sides, mottled
green, No. 266-12", 12" l.................**225.00**
Vase, double bud, 8" h., mottled
green, No. 116-8".............................**95.00**
Vase, 10" h., cylindrical w/angular
handles rising from disc base,
mottled blue, No. 720-10" **150.00**

VELMOSS SCROLL (1916)

*Incised stylized red roses and green leaves
on a creamy ivory matte glaze.*

Basket, hanging-type.........**350.00 to 375.00**
Bowl, 9" d., 2½" h., incurved sides **75.00**
Candlestick, flat base, slender
standard w/flaring rim, No. 1044-8",
8" h...**82.50**
Candlesticks, slender swelled
standard w/flaring base,
10" h., pr. ....**175.00 to 200.00**
Vase, 10" h., footed slender baluster-
form w/gently flaring flat mouth,
No. 203-10".....................................**150.00**
Wall pocket, elongated oviform,
No. 1226-11", 11" h..........................**395.00**
Wall pocket, conical w/pointed
bottom, pointed hanging tab,
No. 1227-12", 11½" h.......................**395.00**

VENETIAN (early 1900s)

Utilitarian crockery ware with blue or yellow exteriors and white interiors.

Baking bowl, 7" d....................................49.00
Pudding crock w/bail handles,
  9" d..110.00

VICTORIAN (1924)

Simple shapes with a band of lightly embossed slip decorated designs.

Urn-vase, wide tapering rounded
  sides, grey ground, No. 132-4",
  4" h...300.00
Vase, 6" h., shouldered ovoid body,
  soft violet blue ground, No. 256-6"...250.00
Vase, 7½" h., 6" d., sharply canted
  sides, flat shoulder, band of scarabs
  & birds in blue & green against a
  matte bluish grey ground,
  No. 258-7"...412.50
Vase, 11" h., 7½" d., tapering ovoid
  body, band of yellow & blue fruit
  w/green foliage around shoulder
  against a bluish grey ground............412.50

VISTA (1920s)

Embossed green coconut palm trees and lavender blue pool against grey ground.

Basket w/high overhead handles,
  6" h..195.00
Basket w/high overhead handle,
  9½" h..495.00
Vase, 12" h., tapering cylindrical body
  w/flaring base......................................395.00
Vase, 15" h., cylindrical w/small
  pointed rim handles, No. 121-15" 675.00
Vase, 18" h., slightly swollen cylinder,
  rim handles ....900.00 to 1,100.00

WATER LILY (1940s)

Water lily blossoms and pads against a horizontally ridged ground. White lilies on green lily pads against a blended blue ground, pink lilies on a pink shading to green ground or yellow lilies against a gold shading to brown ground.

Basket w/pointed overhead handle,
  cylindrical w/flaring rim, blended
  blue ground, No. 380-8",
  8" h. ....125.00 to 175.00
Basket w/pointed asymmetrical
  overhead handle & pleated rim, gold
  shading to brown ground,
  No. 381-10", 10" h...........................115.00
Basket w/asymmetrical overhead
  handle, curved & sharply scalloped

rim, blended blue ground,
  No. 382-12", 12" h.............................275.00
Basket w/asymmetrical overhead
  handle, curved & sharply scalloped
  rim, pink shading to green ground,
  No. 382-12", 12" h.............................250.00
Basket, hanging-type, pink shading to
  green ground, No. 468-5" 180.00
Bowl, 6" d., gold shading to brown
  ground, No. 439-6"..............................45.00
Candleholders, gold shading to
  brown ground, No. 1154-2",
  2" h., pr. 75.00
Flowerpot w/saucer, blended blue
  ground, No. 664-5", 5" h. 150.00
Jardiniere, gold shading to brown
  ground, No. 663-10", 10" h. 450.00
Jardiniere & pedestal base, gold
  shading to brown ground, 8" h.
  jardiniere, 2 pcs. 695.00
Urn-vase, gold shading to brown
  ground, No. 175-8",
  8" h. ....110.00 to 120.00
Vase, novelty-type, 6" h., gold
  shading to brown ground,
  No. 174-6"...75.00
Vase, 7" h., blended blue ground,
  No. 74-7"...80.00
Vase, 8" h, two-handled, pink shaded
  to green ground, No. 76-8" 70.00
Vase, 8" h., two-handled, blended
  blue ground, No. 77-8" 199.00

Water Lily Vase

Vase, 9" h., two large handles at midsection, low foot, shaded blue
  ground, No. 78-9" (ILLUS.) 95.00
Vase, 9" h., pink shaded to green
  ground, No. 79-9"...........................110.00
Vase, 15" h., two-handled, blended
  blue ground, No. 83-15"...................225.00

WHITE ROSE (1940)

White roses and green leaves against a vertically combed ground of blended blue, brown shading to green or pink shading to green.

Basket, brown shading to green ground, No. 362-8", 8" h. **145.00**

Basket w/sweeping handle rising from base to rim at opposite side, brown shading to green ground, No. 364-12", 12" h.....................**165.00**

Book ends, brown shading to green ground, No. 7, pr. **165.00**

Bowl, 6" d., handled, blended blue ground, No. 389-6"......................**80.00**

Bowl, 8" d., pink shading to green ground, No. 390-8" ....**100.00 to 130.00**

Bowl-vase, spherical, two-handled, brown shading to green ground, No. 653-3", 3" h................................**85.00**

Bowl-vase, spherical, two-handled, pink shading to green ground, No. 653-3"....................................**75.00**

Bowl-vase, spherical, two-handled, blended blue ground, No. 653-4", 4" h...**115.00**

Candleholders, two-handled, low, blended blue ground, No. 1141, pr. ...**80.00**

Candleholders, double, pink shading to green ground, No. 1143, 4" h., pr. **175.00**

Console bowl, blended blue ground, No. 391-10", 10" l.............................**160.00**

Console bowl, pink shading to green ground, No. 391-10", 10" l................**150.00**

Console bowl, elongated pointed handles, blended blue ground, No. 393-12", 16½" l....................**135.00**

Cornucopia-vase, double, blended blue ground, No. 145-8", 8" h.............**79.00**

Cornucopia-vase, double, pink shading to green ground, No. 145-8", 8" h................................**95.00**

Flower frog, basket-shaped w/overhead handle, blended blue ground, No. 41 ....**70.00**

Flowerpot & saucer, blended blue ground, No. 654-5", 5" h. **110.00**

Jardiniere & pedestal base, brown shading to green ground, No. 654-8", 2 pcs. ...**900.00 to 950.00**

Pitcher, blended blue ground, No. 1324 ....**200.00 to 225.00**

Rose bowl, brown shading to green ground, No. 342-4", 4" h. **75.00**

Tea set: cov. teapot, sugar bowl & creamer; blended blue ground, Nos. 1T, 1S & 1C, 3 pcs. ....**350.00 to 400.00**

Urn-vase, spherical, two-handled, blended blue ground, No. 388-7", 7" h. ....**120.00 to 140.00**

Urn-vase, two-handled, globular w/wide neck, footed, blended blue ground, No. 147-8", 8" h. **95.00**

Urn-vase, spherical, two-handled, brown shading to green ground, No. 653-6", 6" h................................**125.00**

Urn-vase, spherical, two-handled,

pink shading to green ground, No. 653-10", 10" h............................**230.00**

Vase, 7" h., trumpet-form w/asymmetrical handles, pink shading to green ground, No. 982-7".................................**129.00**

Vase, 9" h., fan-shaped, handles rising from base to mid-section, blended blue ground, No. 987-9" **175.00**

Vase, 10" h., brown shading to green ground, No. 988-10".........................**185.00**

Vase, 12½" h., ovoid, angular handles at rim, blended blue ground, No. 991-12"....................................**395.00**

Vase, 15½" h., two-handled, shaped rim, brown shading to green ground, No. 991-15"....................................**395.00**

Wall pocket, swirled handle, flaring rim, brown shading to green ground, No. 1288-6", 6½" h.........................**150.00**

Wall pocket, conical w/flaring rim w/overhead handle continuing to one side, pink shading to green ground, No. 1289-8", 8½" h. ....**325.00 to 350.00**

WINCRAFT (1948)

Shapes from older lines such as Pine Cone, Cremona, Primrose and others, vases with an animal motif, and contemporary shapes. High gloss glaze in bright shades of blue, tan, yellow, turquoise, apricot and grey.

Ashtray, glossy blue ground, No. 240-T.....................................**35.00**

Basket w/low overhead handle, shaped rim, berries & foliage in relief on glossy brown ground, No. 209-12", 12" h........................**125.00**

Book ends, glossy brown ground, No. 259, 6½" h., pr. **150.00**

Bowl, 8" d., glossy green ground, No. 226-8".....................................**65.00**

Bowl, 10" l., canoe-form w/high shaped ends, glossy mottled yellow w/grasses in relief around base, No. 231-10".....................................**60.00**

Coffee set: 9½" h. cov. coffeepot, creamer & sugar bowl; glossy green ground, Nos. 250P, 271C & 271S, 3 pcs. **350.00**

Console set: 12" l. bowl & pair of candleholders; glossy blue ground, Nos. 228-12" & 252, 3 pcs. **125.00**

Planter, two-handled, geranium blossoms & leaves in relief on shaded chartreuse ground, No. 268-12", 12" l.............................**75.00**

Tea set: cov. teapot, creamer & sugar bowl; glossy brown ground, Nos. 271P, 271C & 271S, 3 pcs. **195.00**

Vase, 8" h., flowing lily form

w/asymmetrical side handles, tulip &
foliage in relief on glossy blue
ground, No. 282-8" ....**80.00 to 100.00**
Vase, 10" h., cylindrical w/flat disc
base, relief arrowroot leaf & blossom
decoration on glossy turquoise
ground, No. 285-10" **110.00**
Vase, 10" h., cylindrical, tab handles,
black panther & green palm trees in
relief on glossy shaded turquoise
ground, No. 290-10" **350.00**
Vase, 12" h., fan-shaped, glossy blue
ground, No. 287-12" **120.00**
Vase, 12" h., fan-shaped, glossy tan
ground, No. 287-12" **100.00**
Wall pocket, globular, green ivy vine
in relief on glossy apricot ground,
No. 267-5", 5" h...............................**160.00**
Wall pocket, globular, green ivy vine
in relief on glossy blue ground, No.
267-5", 5" h. **165.00**
Wall pocket, glossy blue ground, No.
266-4", 8½" h. **160.00**

WINDSOR (1931)

*Stylized florals, foliage, vines and ferns on
some, others with repetitive band
arrangement of small squares and
rectangles, on mottled blue blending into
green or terra cotta and light orange
blending into brown.*

Basket, footed fan-shape w/low long
handle looping under the rim,
mottled brown ground, No. 330-5",
5" h..**415.00**
Bowl, 10" d., 3" h., two-handled,
stylized florals against mottled blue
ground, paper label **260.00**
Vase, 5" h., ovoid body w/short wide
neck, two handles rising from midsection to below rim, geometric
design against mottled terra cotta
ground..**190.00**
Vase, 7" h., bulbous ovoid body
w/short flaring neck, loop handles
from shoulder to rim, fern decoration
on a brown ground,
No. 551-7" ....**350.00 to 375.00**
Vase, 8" h., cylindrical w/narrow
shoulder to a short rolled neck, long
& low side handles, blue flowers,
No. 552-8"......................................**295.00**
Vase, 10" h, tall ovoid body tapering
to a wide trumpet neck, loop
handles from neck to shoulder,
mottled blue ground, No. 554-10" **650.00**

WISTERIA (1933)

*Lavender wisteria blossoms and green
vines against a roughly textured brown
shading to deep blue ground, rarely found
in only brown.*

Basket, hanging-type, blue ground,
7½" **700.00**
Bowl, 4" h., angular rim handles, blue
ground, No. 242-4" ....**300.00 to 325.00**
Bowl-vase, wide squatty bulbous
form tapering to a flat mouth flanked
by tiny angled loop handles, vines in
purple & green around the shoulder
against an ochre & brown ground,
paper label, No. 637-6½", 7½" d.,
6¾" h...**412.50**
Candleholders, high domed base
w/angular pointed handles, blue
ground, No. 1091-4", 4" h., pr. **525.00**
Console bowl, small angular end
handles, blue ground,
No. 243, 12" l. ....**400.00 to 450.00**
Jardiniere, small rounded handles
beneath rim, rounded sides,
12½" d., 9" h. (small flat chip at
base, glaze nick on one flower) **440.00**
Vase, 6" h., ovoid w/small handles at
shoulder, No. 630-6" **295.00**
Vase, 8½" h., ovoid w/angular
handles from shoulder to rim, brown
ground..**325.00**
Vase, 9" h., cylindrical ovoid body
w/angular handles rising from
shoulder to mid-section of slender
cylindrical neck, brown ground,
No. 638-9".......................................**398.00**
Vase, 10" h., cylindrical w/angular
handles at top, brown ground,
No. 639-10".....................................**450.00**
Vase, 12" h., two-handled, expanding
cylinder w/flaring rim, brown ground,
No. 640-12".....................................**695.00**
Wall pocket, flaring rim, brown
ground, 8" h. **1,000.00**

WOODLAND (1905)

*A Rozane line w/stippled creamy bisque
backgrounds incised with naturalistic
flowers and leaves decorated in glossy
enamel colors.*

Vase, 6½" h., 3½" d., slender
corseted body w/a wide shoulder &
small short cylindrical neck,
enameled around the sides w/tulips
in gold w/green stems on a buff
bisque ground, wafer mark (minute
glaze nick at rim).............................**660.00**
Vase, 9" h, iris decoration..................**800.00**
Vase, 10" h., 4¼" w., tall tapering
squared body decorated w/incised
stylized flowers in brown & green on
a creamy ground ....**550.00 to 600.00**
Vase, 10½" h., 3" w., tall squared &
swelled slender body w/shaped &
lobed foot & rim, decorated
w/stylized brown blossoms on
scrolling green stems against

a bisque ground,
wafer mark......................**660.00 to 700.00**

ZEPHYR LILY (1946)

*Deeply embossed day lilies against a swirl-
textured ground. White and yellow lilies on
a blended blue ground; rose and yellow
lilies on a green ground; yellow lilies on
terra cotta shading to olive green ground.*

Zephyr Lily Pillow-Type Vase

Basket w/asymmetrical overhead
  handle & rim, blue ground,
  No. 394-8", 8" h. ....**150.00 to 200.00**
Book ends, terra cotta ground,
  No. 16, pr. **200.00**
Bowl-vase, small shoulder handles,
  terra cotta ground, No. 671-4", 4" h. ...**90.00**
Bowl-vase, small shoulder handles,
  green ground, No. 671-6", 6" h. **139.00**
Candleholders, two-handled, terra
  cotta ground, No. 1162-2", 2" h., pr. ..**78.00**
Candlesticks, blue ground,
  No. 1163-4½", 4½" h, pr. **65.00**
Console bowl, green ground,
  No. 8-10", 10" l..............................**225.00**
Console bowl, raised shaped sides,
  blue ground, No. 475-10", 10" l........**125.00**
Console bowl, brown ground,
  No. 478-12", 12" l............................**80.00**
Console set: 10" bowl & pair of 2" h.
  candleholders; blue ground,
  No. 475-10" & 1162-2", 3 pcs. **185.00**
Creamer, green ground, No. 7C **35.00**
Ewer, blue ground, No. 23-10",
  10" h...**145.00**
Sugar bowl, green ground, No. 7S......**35.00**
Tray, leaf-shaped, green ground,
  14½" l...**145.00**
Vase, 7" h., blue ground, No. 132-7"....**85.00**
Vase, 7" h., terra cotta ground,
  No. 132-7" **80.00**
Vase, 7" h., pillow-type w/base
  handles, blue ground,
  No. 206-7" ....**100.00 to 125.00**
Vase, 7" h, pillow-type w/base handle,

green ground, No. 206-7"
  (ILLUS.) **110.00**
Vase, bud, 7½" h., handles rising from
  conical base, green ground,
  No. 201-7".......................................**72.00**
Vase, 8" h., two-handled, blue
  ground, No. 134-8"..........................**195.00**
Vase, 9" h., blue ground,
  No. 136-9".....................................**150.00**
Vase, 9½" h., waisted cylindrical body
  w/flaring rim & handles at mid-
  section, blue ground, No. 135-9" **135.00**
Vase, 12" h., conical w/base handles,
  blue ground, No. 139-12"................**275.00**
Vase, 12" h., conical w/base handles,
  terra cotta ground, No. 139-12" **125.00**
Vase, 12½" h., handles rising from
  shoulder of compressed globular
  base to middle of slender neck
  w/flaring mouth, green ground,
  No. 140-12".....................................**295.00**
Vase, 15" h., two-handled, green
  ground, No. 141-15" ....**300.00 to 400.00**
Wall pocket, two handles at base,
  blue ground, No. 1297-8", 8" h.........**185.00**
Wall pocket, two handles at base,
  green ground, No. 1297-8", 8" h. **170.00**
Wall pocket, two handles at base,
  terra cotta ground, No. 1297-8",
  8" h..**140.00**

ROYAL BAYREUTH

*Good china in numerous patterns and
designs has been made at the Royal
Bayreuth factory in Tettau, Germany, since
1794. Listings below are by the company's
lines, plus miscellaneous pieces. Interest in
this china remains at a peak and prices
continue to rise. Pieces listed carry the
company's blue mark except where noted
otherwise.*

CORINTHIAN
Creamer, classical figures on green
  ground..**$40.00**
Creamer & cov. sugar bowl,
  classical figures on black ground,
  pr...**60.00**
Loving cup, three-handled, classical
  figures on black ground **110.00**

Pitcher, milk, classical figures on green ground **95.00**

Planter, classical figures on red ground..**75.00**

DEVIL & CARDS

Mug, 4¾" h...**300.00**

Salt dip, master size **295.00**

Sugar bowl, cov...............................**350.00**

MOTHER-OF-PEARL

Ashtray, Murex Shell patt. **80.00**

Bowl, 3½" octagonal, white w/green highlights, pearlized finish.................**65.00**

Cake plate, decorated w/roses, 10½" d..**125.00**

Compote, open, decorated w/roses, pearlized finish, small **39.00**

Compote, open, 4½" d., 4½" h., reticulated bowl & base, decorated w/delicate roses, pearlized finish **125.00**

Creamer & cov. sugar bowl, grape cluster mold, pearlized yellow, colorful foliage, pr. **275.00**

Dish, cov., Murex Shell patt., large **125.00**

Mustard pot, cov., Murex Shell patt..**107.50**

Nappy, handled, poppy decoration, pearlized satin finish **35.00**

Sugar bowl, cov., Murex Shell patt....**100.00**

Toothpick holder, Murex Shell patt. ...**90.00**

ROSE TAPESTRY

Rose Tapestry Planter

Basket, miniature, rope handle, tiny pink roses frame the rim, small bouquet of yellow roses on each side & yellow roses on the interior, shadow green leaves, 2½ x 4¼ x 4½"..**325.00**

Bowl, 10½" d., shell- & scroll-molded rim, three-color roses......................**995.00**

Box, cov., three-color roses, 2½ x 4½", 1¾" h. **295.00**

Box w/domed cover., three-color roses, 4½" d., 2¾" h...............**400.00**

Box, cov., two-color roses, 1½ x 2½"..**165.00**

Creamer, pinched spout, two-color roses **355.00**

Creamer & sugar bowl, pink & white roses, pr..**650.00**

Dish, leaf-shaped, three-color roses, 5" l...**195.00**

Dish, three-color roses, 2" w., 4½" l., 1⅛" h...**195.00**

Nappy, tri-lobed leaf shape, decorated w/orange roses, 4½" l..**175.00**

Pitcher, 5" h., wide cylindrical body tapering slightly toward rim, three-color roses, 24 oz. **350.00**

Planter, squatty bulbous base below wide gently flaring sides w/a ruffled rim, small loop handles near the base, three-color roses, 2¾" h. (ILLUS.) **280.00**

Salt & pepper shakers, three-color roses, pr...**495.00**

Salt dip, ruffled rim, 3" d. **280.00**

Vase, 4¼" h., footed swelled base tapering to cylindrical sides, two-color roses **345.00**

Vase, 4¾" h., slightly tapering cylindrical body w/a short flared neck, three-color roses in pink, yellow & white **287.50**

Rose Tapestry Vase

Vase, 4¾" h., slightly swelled slender cylindrical body w/a short rolled neck, three-color roses in pink, yellow & white (ILLUS.) **287.50**

Wall pocket, three-color roses, 5 x 9"..**1,100.00**

SUNBONNET BABIES

Candlestick, babies washing, 5" d., 1¾" h...**225.00**

Dish, diamond-shaped.....................**175.00**

Dish, heart-shaped...........................**175.00**

Saucer, babies fishing.........................**45.00**

Vase, 3" h., babies fishing.................**215.00**

TOMATO ITEMS

Tomato bowl, berry 40.00
Tomato bowls, 5¾" d., set of 4 ....105.00
Tomato box, cov., w/green & brown
finial, 3" d. 25.00
Tomato creamer & cov. sugar bowl,
pr...109.00
Tomato mustard jar, cover & figural
leaf spoon, 3 pcs..............................92.00
Tomato plate, 4¼" d., ring-handled,
figural lettuce leaf...........................18.50
Tomato plate, 5½" d., ring-handled,
figural lettuce leaf w/molded yellow
flowers 28.50
Tomato plate, 7" d., ring-handled,
figural lettuce leaf w/molded yellow
flowers 33.00
Tomato tea set, cov. teapot, creamer
& cov. sugar bowl, 3 pcs. 245.00

MISCELLANEOUS

Figural Poppy Creamer

Ashtray, stork decoration, artist-
signed, 4½" l. 48.00
Ashtray, scenic decoration of Dutch
lady w/basket, 5½" d. 48.00
Ashtray, figural shell, 4½ x 4½" 45.00
Basket, handled, boy & donkey
decoration, artist-signed, 5¾" h. 150.00
Basket, miniature, scene w/cows,
unmarked..59.00
Bell, peacock decoration, 2½" d.,
3" h..245.00
Bell, w/original wooden clapper,
decorated w/scene of ocean liner
being brought into harbor by
tugboats 235.00
Bowl, 5¾" d., nursery rhyme scene
w/Jack & Jill 110.00
Bowl, 6" d., figural conch shell.............60.00
Bowl, 6⅞" d., 2½" h., footed, shallow
slightly scalloped sides, Cavalier
Musicians decoration, gold
trim on feet..110.00
Bowl, 9½" d., figural poppy 102.00
Box, cov., figural turtle, 2¾ x 5" 1,200.00

Box, cov., four-footed ring base,
scenic decoration of Dutch
children 110.00
Candlestick, elks scene, 4" h. 125.00
Candlestick, figural bassett hound 450.00
Candlestick, figural clown, red, 4½"
x 6½"...525.00
Candlestick w/match holder, figural
clown, 7" h. 1,096.00
Celery dish, figural lobster................118.00
Creamer, Arab scene decoration 75.00
Creamer, crowing rooster & hen
decoration, 4¼" h............................125.00
Creamer, figural clown, green,
3½" h...350.00
Creamer, figural crow, black,
4¾" h. ....200.00 to 225.00
Creamer, figural eagle, grey 245.00
Creamer, figural elk............................65.00
Creamer, figural girl w/pitcher, red.....695.00
Creamer, figural grape cluster, yellow
(unmarked) 165.00
Creamer, figural lamplighter, green,
4½" h...225.00
Creamer, figural oak leaf, white
w/orchid highlights 225.00
Creamer, figural pansy, purple...........225.00
Creamer, figural pig, blue...................650.00
Creamer, figural poppy, peach
iridescent (ILLUS.) 375.00
Creamer, figural seashell, boot-
shaped, 3¾" h...................................170.00
Creamer, figural snake.......................800.00
Creamer, cobalt blue, Babes in
Woods decoration (unmarked) 175.00
Creamer, pasture scene w/cows &
trees, 3¼" h......................................55.00
Creamer, pinched spout, "tapestry,"
goats decoration, 4" h. 295.00
Creamer, "tapestry," Scottish
highland goats scene.......................355.00
Creamer, decorated w/man in fishing
boat scene 145.00
Creamer, miniature, "tapestry" scene
of girl & horse...................................275.00
Creamer & cov. sugar bowl, figural
apple, pr..298.00
Creamer & cov. suger bowl, figural
rooster, pr. 250.00
Creamer & open sugar bowl, figural
poppy, white satin finish, pr. 475.00
Creamer & open sugar bowl, figural
rooster, creamer w/multicolored
feathers & sugar bowl in black, pr....950.00
Creamer & open sugar bowl,
"tapestry," barrel-shaped, the
creamer w/a long pinched spout,
creamer w/goose girl scene, sugar
w/Alpine village scene, sugar bowl
3⅞" h., creamer 4¼" h., pr. 575.00
Cup & saucer, demitasse, Castle
scene decoration, artist-signed........100.00
Cup & saucer, demitasse, figural
orange..125.00

Cup & saucer, scene of man w/turkeys.............................**100.00**

Ewer, scene of hunter w/dog, 4½" h.......................................**180.00**

Ewer, cobalt blue, Babes in Woods decoration, 6" h....................**585.00**

Gravy boat & underplate, figural poppy, satin finish, 2 pcs **175.00**

Gravy boat w/attached liner, decorated w/multicolored floral sprays, gadrooned border, gold trim cream ground.................................**18.50**

Hair receiver, cov., "tapestry," scene of farmer w/turkeys **265.00**

Humidor, cov., figural elk.................**850.00**

Match holder, hanging-type, figural elk **485.00**

Match holder, hanging-type, figural shell ....**200.00 to 250.00**

Mint dish, ruffled, w/Dutch girl decoration, 4½" d.........................**110.00**

Model of a man's high top slipper **225.00**

Mustard jar, cov., figural grape cluster, yellow **150.00**

Mustard jar, cov., figural rose...........**445.00**

Mustard jar, cover & spoon, figural poppy, red, green spoon, 3 pcs. **213.00**

Nappy, handled, figural poppy **100.00**

Pincushion, figural elk head.............**325.00**

Pitcher, 2½" h., scene w/cows..........**170.00**

Pitcher, 3½" h., scenic decoration of Arab on horse **75.00**

Pitcher, 3¾" h., corset-shaped, Colonial Curtsey scene w/a couple **165.00**

Pitcher, miniature, 4½" h., scene of a skiff w/sail **110.00**

Pitcher, 5" h., scene of an Arab on white horse w/brown horse nearby ..**125.00**

Pitcher, squatty, 5" h., 5" d., decorated w/hunting scene...............**75.00**

Pitcher, 5¼" h., pinched spout, "tapestry," scene of train on bridge over raging river.............................**480.00**

Pitcher, 5" h., figural crow.................**165.00**

Lobster Milk Pitcher

Pitcher, milk, figural lobster (ILLUS.) ....**200.00 to 225.00**

Pitcher, milk, figural poppy **295.00**

Pitcher, milk, Goose Girl decoration ..**110.00**

Pitcher, water, 7¾" h., 6" d., figural lobster, red shaded to orange w/green handle **470.00**

Plate, 5¼" d., leaf-shaped, decorated w/small yellow flowers on green ground, green curved handle...**37.50**

Plate, 7" d., decorated w/scene of girl walking dog..................................**75.00**

Plate, 7½" d., nursery rhyme scene w/Little Bo Peep.............................**55.00**

Plate, 8" d., scene of man hunting **78.00**

Plate, 8½" d., scene of man fishing......**95.00**

Plate, 8½" d., scene of man hunting **95.00**

Plate, 9" d., figural ear of corn............**495.00**

Plate, 9½" d., scroll-molded rim, "tapestry," toasting Cavalier scene **700.00**

Powder box, cov., Cavalier Musicians scene **175.00**

Salt & pepper shakers, figural conch shell, unmarked, pr. **75.00**

Salt shaker, figural elk......................**125.00**

Stamp box, cov., "tapestry," Cottage by Water Fall scene **150.00**

Sugar bowl, cov., Brittany Girl decoration **85.00**

Sugar bowl, cov., figural lemon (small finial flake) **160.00**

Sugar bowl, cov., figural lobster.........**145.00**

Teapot, cov., figural poppy, red **275.00**

Toothpick holder, ball-shaped w/overhead handle, "tapestry," lady w/horse scene...............................**410.00**

Toothpick holder, figural Murex Shell...**150.00**

Toothpick holder, man hunting turkeys scene.................................**175.00**

Toothpick holder, three-handled, scene of horse & wagon **95.00**

Toothpick holder, two-handled, four-footed, scene of horsemen, unmarked......................................**50.00**

Tray, club-shaped, scene of hunter w/dog **90.00**

Tray, "tapestry," scene of train on bridge over raging river, 7¾ x 11"......................................**700.00**

Trivet, Snow Babies scene, sledding...**95.00**

Vase, 3" h., scene of children w/St. Bernard dog **85.00**

Vase, 3½" h., Cavalier Musicians decoration **85.00**

Vase, 4" h., ovoid body w/a tiny, short flaring neck, "tapestry," scene of two cows, one black & one tan..............**400.00**

Vase, 4½" h., "tapestry," courting couple decoration **475.00**

Vase, 5" high, ovoid body w/a tiny, short flaring neck, "tapestry," scene of castle by lake **350.00**

Vase, 5½" h., decorated w/brown &

white bust portrait of lady on dark
green ground, artist-signed..............**395.00**

Vase, 6" h., "tapestry," decorated w/a
scene of an elk & three hounds in a
river...**285.00**

Vase, 11½" h., polar bear scene........**800.00**

Vase, double-bud, ovoid body w/two
angled short flaring necks joined by
a small handle, scene of Dutch
children **105.00**

Vase, miniature, 2¾" h., conical body
on three tab feet, tapering to a short
flaring neck, small knob handles at
shoulders, decorated w/a scene of
cows..**105.00**

Wall pocket, figural grape cluster,
purple..**275.00**

Wall pocket, figural grape cluster,
yellow..**260.00**

ROYAL BONN & BONN

Floral Decorated Royal Bonn Vase

*Bonn and subsequently Royal Bonn
china were produced in Bonn, Germany, in
a manufactory established in 1755. Later
wares made there are often marked
Mehlem or bear the initials FM or a castle
mark. Most wares were of the hand-
painted type. Clock cases were also made
in Bonn.*

Cheese dish, cov., wedge-shaped,
floral decoration, 6" h. **$395.00**

Ewer, decorated w/large rose & pink
flowers & multicolored leaves front &
back, raised gold veining & outlining,
ornate handle, ca. 1900, red crown
mark, Franz Anton Mehlem
Porcelain Factory.............................**125.00**

Vase, 6¼" h., decorated w/portrait of
two Dutch women, "The
Gleaners" series, artist-signed.........**595.00**

Vase, 8" h., 5" d., cylindrical
w/rounded shoulder & tiny neck
w/slightly flared rim, decorated
w/gold & orange flowers, brown &
yellow background (ILLUS.)..............**95.00**

Vase, 8½" h., double gourd-shape,
large spherical base, small bulbous
top, roses decoration on green
ground...**275.00**

Vase, 11" h., four-handled, portrait of
"Woman with Shawl," green ground
w/gold overlay base & neck, artist-
signed...**875.00**

Vase, 11¼" h., decorated w/pink &
yellow roses on green & yellow
ground, gold trim, ca. 1900, Red
Crown mark, Germany.......................**250.00**

Vase, 20" h., 5" d. at widest point,
footed, greenish gold band at base
& rim band decorated w/raised gold
flowers, link-style neck handles, h.p.
giant multicolored floral sprays on
front & back, pre-1890, Red
Crown mark **310.00**

ROYAL COPENHAGEN

*This porcelain has been made in
Copenhagen, Denmark, since 1715. The
ware is hardpaste.*

Coffeepot, cov., No. 48, blue,
fluted..**$195.00**

Creamer, No. 60, blue, fluted..............**45.00**

Figure, Goat Girl, No. 2180, 8" h. **225.00**

Figure, Goose Girl, No. 528,
7½" h...**270.00**

Figure, Goose Girl, No. 527,
9½" h...**225.00**

Figure, girl knitting, No. 1314,
6" h. ....**325.00 to 340.00**

Figure, girl w/doll, No. 1938,
5" h. ....**315.00 to 325.00**

Figure, girl w/Teddy bear, No. 1879,
5⅛" h..**442.50**
Figure group, boy & girl kissing, No.
2162, 8" h.....................................**175.00**
Figure group, children playing, No.
1568, 4½" h. ....**180.00 to 200.00**
Figure group, children reading, Nc
1567, 3⅞" h..................................**150.00**
Model of a baby robin, No. 2238,
1¾" h...**25.00**
Rose jar, cov., Raphael-type cherubs
decoration on front & back, blue
ground, 8" h. to top of finial.............**275.00**
Sugar bowl, cov., No. 424, blue,
fluted..**95.00**
Vase, 8" h., narcissus decoration on
pale blue ground.............................**85.00**
Vase, 8½" h., floral decoration, No.
5381..**185.00**
Vase, 10⅛" h., two-handled,
decorated w/country villa scenes
against an orchid ground, 19th c. **374.00**

scroll gestures to seated woman, a
fan beside her on corner bench,
green & brown w/gold trim, pink
triangle mark, 7¾ x 10¾" base,
12½" h.......................................**1,130.00**
Figure group, a standing man &
lady in 18th c. attire, No. 3802,
9" h...**195.00**
Figure group, a standing man &
lady in 18th c. attire, No. 3803,
9" h...**195.00**
Model of a doe, standing animal in
low stance w/head lowered, on a
log-molded base, ivory w/brown
decoration & gold trim, triangle
medallion mark & impressed "0177 -
43," 3⅜ x 10⅜", 8⅛" h. **172.50**
Vases, 17½" h., figural, bulbous
vessel molded w/waves & flowers, a
young woman standing on the
shoulder & leaning on the mouth,
ca. 1900, drilled & mounted as table
lamps, pr. **230.00**

ROYAL DUX

*This factory in Bohemia was noted for
the figural porcelain wares in the Art
Nouveau style which were exported around
the turn of the century. Other notable
figural pieces were produced through the
1930s and the factory was nationalized
after World War II.*

Centerpiece, figural, oblong shell-
form shallow bowl w/Art Nouveau
maiden, No. 1776, 12" h. **$495.00**
Ewers, white ground w/lavish cobalt
& gold decoration, 12" h., pr. **275.00**
Figure, "Michele," seated nude young
woman, polychrome glaze, green
base, triangular wafer impressed
marks, ca. 1900, 18" h. (base
damage & restoration) **632.50**
Figurines, peasant couple, the
woman carrying a kettle, the man
carrying grain, Nos. 2445 & 2446,
13" h., pr. **575.00**
Figure group, lady seated in sedan
chair, two couriers & hound, lavish
detail & gold trim, artist-signed,
8½ x 14", 15½" h...........................**970.00**
Figure group, man & woman in
classic clothing, the man holding a

ROYAL RUDOLSTADT

*This factory began as a faience pottery
established in 1720. E. Bohne made hard
paste porcelain wares from 1852 to 1920,
when the factory became a branch of
Heubach Brothers. The factory is still
producing in the former East Germany.*

Cheese dome & tray, decorated
w/rose sprays, Prussia mark...........**$95.00**
Cracker jar, cov., fluted body, pastel
floral decoration on cream matte
ground, gold trim & detail, artist-
signed, 7" h. **195.00**
Dish, leaf-shaped, multicolored,
mother-of-pearl finish w/lavish
gold trim, 6" l. **14.00**
Dresser tray, decorated w/h.p. roses,
8 x 11½"..**60.00**
Hatpin holder, hexagonal, decorated
w/roses, pearlized finish **145.00**
Vase, 9½" h., reticulated front in pale
pink w/gold center design, cream
ground w/purple flowers,
gold handles, ca. 1887.....................**95.00**

ROYAL VIENNA

Large Royal Vienna Urn

The second factory in Europe to make hard paste porcelain was established in Vienna in 1719 by Claud Innocentius de Paquier. The factory underwent various changes of administration through the years and finally closed in 1865. Since then, however, the porcelain has been reproduced by various factories in Austria and Germany, many of which have reproduced also the early beehive mark. Early pieces, naturally, bring far higher prices than the later ones or the reproductions.

Figure group, two classical ladies, one w/long pink floral dress lined in yellow, holding a tiny bird, other in green flowered gown lined in lavender, flowers in her hair & at her feet, molded, footed base, blue beehive mark **$595.00**
Plate, 9¾" d., portrait design of a young woman, w/lavish gold trim on rim, artist-signed, titled on the reverse "Ruth" **1,195.00**
Urn, cov., bulbous baluster-form body w/continuous panel depicting allegorical figures within cobalt blue borders flanked by loop handles ending in masks, raised on square base painted w/figural panels, signed "Selle," pseudo-shield marks in blue enamel, third-quarter 19th century, 24" h. (ILLUS.) **4,313.00**

Vase, 9¾" h., decorated w/a portrait of a lady w/long black hair, maroon & gold lustre ground w/raised turquoise beading, red beehive mark & "#511," artist-signed **1,050.00**

ROYAL WORCESTER

Beige Satin Finish Ewer

This porcelain has been made by the Royal Worcester Porcelain Co. at Worcester, England, from 1862 to the present. For earlier porcelain made in Worcester, see WORCESTER. Royal Worcester is distinguished from those wares made at Worcester between 1751 and 1862 that are referred to as only Worcester by collectors.

Bowl, pedestal base, 4" h., reticulated border at top w/flowers & butterflies, artist-signed **$295.00**
Creamer & cov. sugar bowl, pink & blue gilt outlined floral decoration w/green gilt outlined leaves, No. 1253, artist-signed, 3¼" h., pr..........**225.00**
Cup & saucer, pierced & scrolled leafy vine body w/turquoise enamel jeweling on rims, printed Grainger - Worcester marks, late 19th C., saucer 4½" d. **402.50**
Cup & saucer, Serenade patt.............**40.00**
Dish, shell-shaped, artist-signed, No. 1274, ca. 1890, 9" d. **125.00**
Ewer, bulbous body tapering to a tall slender neck, dragon handle,

decorated w/blue flowers & tan leaves all outlined & detailed in gold, beige satin finish ground, gold trim on handle, ca. 1887, 4⅝" d., 9¼" h. (ILLUS.) **495.00**

Ewer, bulbous bottom tapering to tall, slender neck, gold serpent handle, decorated w/owl in branch before amoonlit sky, ca. 1885, 11¼" h...**935.00**

Royal Worcester Ewer

Ewer, bulbous bottom tapering to tall, slender neck, bronze salamander handle, decorated w/overall gold flowers & blue leaves on glossy cream background, ca. 1883, 6" d., 11½" h. (ILLUS.) **650.00**

Figure, "April," designed by F. Doughty, No. 3416, 1947 ....**225.00**

Figure, "Boy with Paroquet," designed by F. Doughty, No. 3087, 1935, 6¾" h................................**126.50**

Figure, "Cairo Water Carrier," kneeling female, artist-signed, No. 637, 1877, 5½" h....................**275.00**

Figure, "December," signed F. Doughty, No. 3458, 1949, 6½" h......**175.00**

Figure, "Dutch Boy," blue hat & pants, carrying baskets of flowers, designed by F. M. Gertner, No. 2923, ca. 1931, 2⅝" d., 5½" h......................................**215.00**

Figure, "First Dance," lady w/lavender dress & pink shawl, designed by F. Doughty, No. 3629, 1957, 4" d., 7½" h. (ILLUS. right top next column) **165.00**

Figure, "Fortune Teller," designed by F. Doughty, No. 2924, 1931.............**295.00**

Figure, "Grandmother's Dress," designed by F. Doughty, No. 3081, ca. 1935 ....**146.00**

Figure, "Happy Days," designed by F. Doughty, No. 3435, 1948..........**1,250.00**

Figure, "Michael," designed by F. Doughty, No. 2912, 1931, 3" d., 2½" h..**110.00**

"First Dance" & "Sister" Figures

Figure, "Mischief," little girl picking flowers, designed by F. Doughty, No. 2914, ca. 1931 ....**240.00**

Figure, "Noel," miniature, designed by Sybil V. Williams & Jessamine S. Bray, No. 2905, 1931 ....**150.00**

Figure group, model of three foxes, designed by D. Lindner, No. 3131, 1936..**350.00**

Figure group, "Sister," girl in pink dress w/arm around little blonde boy, designed by F. Doughty, No. 3149, 1936, 4" d., 7" h. (ILLUS. left)....................................**175.00**

Model of a cat, short-furred, designed by F. Doughty, No. 3616, 1957, 3⅓" h...**75.00**

Model of a dog, Bulldog, No. 2945, 1931...**250.00**

Model of a dog, Bull Terrier, white w/pearlized eyes, natural colored ears, nose, mouth, sitting on pale blue base, designed by D. Lindner, No. 2931, 1931, 2½ x 4" **350.00**

Model of a kingfisher w/fish, designed by E. Soper, No. 3235, 1935 ....**65.00**

Mug, decorated w/pink & yellow roses on peach ground, 1½" h....................**95.00**

Pitcher, jug-type, 10¼" h., w/bamboo-type handle, decorated w/pink & blue flowers & gold trim, artist-signed **250.00**

Plate, bread & butter, Serenade patt...**10.00**

Plate, 10½" d., three shell feet, reticulated edge, center floral decoration, Grainger **765.00**

Plate, dinner, Serenade patt. **40.00**

Plate, salad, Serenade patt.................**20.00**

Potpourri jars, cov., decorated w/chrysanthemums on a white ground, further gilt detailing & three gilt scrolling handles, late 19th c., 7" h., pr. **862.00**

Vase, bud, 4" h., decorated w/raised
gilt florals on ivory ground,
artist-signed **30.00**

Vase, 4" h., pedestal base, floral
decoration on cream ground, green
reticulated border & jeweling at
base, artist-signed **350.00**

Vase, 5" h., 7¾" d., a band of pierced
scrolls around the top collar, the
lower body decorated w/five
swallows in flight, No. 703, ca.
1879...**965.00**

Vase, cov., 6" h., egg-shaped body
w/three hooved feet, reticulated
openwork on cover & upper two-
thirds of body, ca. 1910 ....**565.00**

Royal Worcester Vases

Vase, 9½" h., bulbous ovoid body
tapering to tall thin cylindrical neck,
h.p. w/enamel decorated butterflies
& gilt tall grass on an ivory ground,
late 19th c. (ILLUS. right) **230.00**

Vase, 14" h., lobed form, decorated in
the Oriental taste w/birds & flowers,
now mounted as a lamp, late
19th c. **862.00**

Vases, 6" h., bulbous bodies tapering
to thin cylindrical necks w/enamel
decorated portraits of "King Charles
the First" & "James Graham,
Marquis of Montrose" on blue
ground, w/satyr mask handles,
printed marks, ca. 1862, pr.
(ILLUS. left).....................................**632.50**

Vases, 14" h., globular form w/a tall
cylindrical neck & elephant head
handles, decorated in the Oriental
taste w/stylized florals, late 19th c.,
now mounted as lamps, pr............**1,725.00**

Vegetable bowl, open, oval,
Dunrobin patt. **60.00**

R.S. PRUSSIA &
RELATED WARES

*Ornately decorated china marked "R. S.
Germany" and "R.S. Prussia" continues to*
grow in popularity. According to Clifford
J. Schlegelmilch in his book, Handbook of
Erdmann and Reinhold Schlegelmilch—
Prussia—Germany and Oscar
Schlegelmilch—Germany, Erdmann
Schlegelmilch established a porcelain
factory in the Germanic provinces at Suhl,
in 1861. Reinhold, his younger brother,
worked with him until 1869 when he
established another porcelain factory in
Tillowtiz, upper Silesia. China bearing the
name of this town is credited to Reinhold
Schlegelmilch. It also customarily bears
the phrase "R.S. Germany." Now collectors
seek additional marks including E.S.
Germany, R.S. Poland and R.S. Suhl.
Prices are high and collectors should
beware the forgeries that sometimes find
their way to the market. Mold names and
numbers are taken from Mary Frank
Gaston's books on R.S. Prussia.

We illustrate three typical markings,
however, there are several others. The "R.S.
Prussia" mark has been reproduced in
decal form so buy with care.

R.S. GERMANY

Bowl, 9¼" d., decorated w/lilies **$65.00**

Bowl, 10" d., twelve-sided, decorated
w/roses **75.00**

Bowl, 10¼" d., Mold 91, six oval dome
shapes outlined by beaded border,
center decoration of crimson & pink
roses & leaves, sapphire blue &
chartreuse to white ground **255.00**

Chocolate set: 11" h. footed, cov.
chocolate pot w/ring-type finial & five
cups & saucers: Mold 644, floral
decoration on pale yellow, ivory &
white ground w/apple green to

turquoise shading, all pieces
footed w/flaring rims, 11 pcs. **625.00**

Creamer & cov. sugar bowl,
decorated w/roses, pr. **185.00**

Mayonnaise bowl w/underplate &
spoon, Cabbage or Lettuce mold
(Mold 126), 3 pcs. **125.00**

Plate, 6¼" d., decorated w/large
red & yellow roses on pastel
green & tan ground, elaborate gold
trim **12.00**

Plate, 7½" d., floral decoration **35.00**

Plate, 8¼" d., decorated w/long ivory &
white roses, green leaves &
brown stems **27.00**

Plate, 8½" d., decorated w/pink
roses on cream & tan ground **37.50**

Plate, 8½" d., rococo border,
decorated w/turquoise, green & white
dogwood on moss ground,
gold trim **21.00**

Plate, 9" d., floral decoration **40.00**

Plate, 9" d., gold (hand-painted R. S.
Germany) **150.00**

Plate, 9½" d., handled, rococo border,
decorated w/dogwood on
cocoa iridescent tinged ground **31.00**

Plate, 11¼" d., decorated w/lilacs on
white, green & pink ground
w/green & gold trim, gold border **110.00**

R.S. PRUSSIA

R.S. Prussia Dresser Tray

Bell, ruffled edge, decorated w/small
purple flowers, green leaf & twig
handle, white ground, 3½" h. **285.00**

Berry set: master bowl & five sauce
dishes; Carnation mold (Mold 28),
pink & yellow roses on white &
turquoise ground, 6 pcs. **495.00**

Berry set: 9" d. master bowl & six 5"
d. sauce dishes; Leaf mold, pink
roses decoration w/raised lily of the
valley buds, 7 pcs. **495.00**

Berry set: master bowl & six sauce
dishes; Mold 329, decoration
w/roses & carnations, 7 pcs. **775.00**

Bowl, 7⅝" d., Hidden Image Mold,
decorated w/purple pansies, yellow

flowers & leaves, pink ground,
unmarked **266.00**

Bowl, 8" d., Icicle mold (Mold 7), fruit
decoration **275.00**

Bowl, 6 x 8", Iris mold (Mold 25),
carnation blue ground **230.00**

Bowl, 8½" d. (Mold 91), decorated
w/yellow roses w/pink highlights **150.00**

Bowl, 9" d., Plume or Feather mold
(Mold 16), Easter lily decoration **250.00**

Bowl, 9¼" d., Lily mold (Mold 29),
Lebrun portrait center, bronze
iridescent Tiffany finish **822.50**

Bowl, 9½" d., Mold 182, decorated
w/white lilies & dogwoods **150.00**

Bowl, 10" d., Carnation mold (Mold
526), decorated w/pink & white roses
on cream & teal green ground **495.00**

Bowl, 10" d., Ripple mold (Mold 259),
large decoration of crimson roses &
leaves in autumn colors, overall
green shading w/shadow daisies in
white over darker ground, deep sides
have "Quilted" look & eight raised
outline channels **250.00**

Bowl, 10½" d., Mold 55, high gold
floral decoration w/yellow trim..........**140.00**

Bowl, 10½" d., Mold 82, floral
decoration **200.00**

Bowl, 10¼" d., Mold 91, decorated w/crimson & pink roses,
multicolored leaves, border of
myriads of flower forms, six single
oval dome shapes, beaded outline,
sapphire blue w/white shadow floral,
fine line embossing white to
chartreuse between domes **255.00**

Bowl, 10¼" d., scrolled border, gold
over beige, shaded red raised floral
decoration & gold tracery on apple
green ground w/interior decoration of
crimson & pink poppies & smaller
flowers, leaves & fronds..................**315.00**

Bowl, 3 x 10½", Carnation mold (Mold
526), pink poppies decoration..........**350.00**

Bowl, 10½" d., Mold 182, decorated
w/roses, twelve scallops, crinkle
embossed, gold edged & separated
by Fleur-de-lis forms & leaf chain
under scallops, shaded pinks to white
ground...**235.00**

Bowl, 10¾" d., Mold 116, center
decoration of purple, yellow & green
grapes, peaches & leaves on
raspberry colored ground, gold
trim **385.00**

Bowl, 11" d., Mold 82, center
decoration pink & yellow rose w/gold
highlights, rose decoration
around sides **220.00**

Bowl, 11" d., Mold 207, decorated
w/hanging basket of roses in blue,
brown & green & jewels **275.00**

Bowl, 3 x 11", Fishscale mold,
elaborated double scalloped rim,
purple & orange lustre, center of
interior decorated w/large white lilies
& green foliage, vertical scalloping,
ca. 1880 ....**395.00**

Bowl, 11" d., Mold 401, h.p. blue floral
decoration, much enameling, dark
blue & gold trim on border,
unmarked......................................**245.00**

Bun tray, Mold 78, decorated
w/roses, 15" l., 6¾" w.......................**300.00**

Cake plate, Sunflower mold (Mold
626), decorated w/red, white & yellow
roses on ground of grey &
green tones, 6" d., unmarked...........**250.00**

Cake plate, open-handled, Mold 304,
decorated w/pink roses, purples &
lavenders, satin finish, 9" d. **350.00**

Cake plate, open-handled, Mold 305,
white lilies of the valley decoration
w/red highlights, satin finish,
9" d..**275.00**

Cake plate, open-handled, Mold 251,
poppies decoration, 9¼" d. **225.00**

Cake plate, open-handled, decorated
w/white irises & pink flowers on deep
turquoise ground w/center decoration
of pink & red roses, buds & leaves,
9¾" d..**250.00**

Cake plate, open-handled, Medallion
mold (Mold 14), pheasant & pine
scene, lavender tones, 10½" d. **795.00**

Cake plate, open-handled, Mold 155,
center floral decoration, six hanging
baskets of flowers w/green ribbon
alternate w/clusters of red flowers,
aqua beaded border, 10½" d. **175.00**

Cake plate, open-handled, Mold 182,
decorated w/dogwood sprigs, petals
& leaves on white satin ground,
10½" d...**85.00**

Cake plate, open-handled, Mold 341,
decorated w/violet pansies, mauve
florals & tiny flowers & leaves,
10¾" d..**145.00**

Cake plate, open-handled, "Hidden
Images" mold (Mold 5), relief-molded
lady w/green hair & yellow
band, 11" d.....................................**450.00**

Cake plate, open-handled, Iris mold,
decorated w/scattered pink
poppies, lavender & peach
ground..**600.00**

Cake plate, Lily mold, center
decoration of multi-colored floral
clusters, 11" d. **200.00**

Cake plate, open-handled, Point &
Clover mold (Mold 82), floral
decoration, 11¼" d., unmarked..........**85.00**

Cake plate, open-handled, Mold 208,
California poppy decoration, satin
finish, 11½" d. **165.00**

Cake plate, open-handled, Mold 256,
decorated w/pink & crimson roses,
leaves & shadow leaves on shaded
turquoise ground, 11½" d................**210.00**

Cake plate, open-handled, decorated
w/white, yellow & orange flowers
w/raised gold centers, pastel green &
orange satin finish, scalloped edge,
gold trimmed, 11½" d......................**275.00**

Cake plate, Mold 404, decorated
w/pansies, 10" d. (unmarked) **175.00**

Cake plate, open-handled, Mold 208,
California poppy decoration, satin
finish **165.00**

Cake plate, open-handled, Sawtooth
mold, decorated w/cottage scene,
brown ground...................................**895.00**

Celery tray, Mold 98, center
decoration of mixed florals w/gold
stenciled designs inner border, lavish
gold trim, 5¾ x 12½", unmarked......**195.00**

Centerpiece bowl, Mold 278,
decorated w/poppies on shaded soft
green satin ground, 7¾" d.,
3½" h..**200.00**

Chocolate pot, cov., decorated w/pink
roses on green ground, ornate
handle **295.00**

Chocolate pot, cov., Mold 521, floral
decoration w/gold trim, 10½" h. **350.00**

Chocolate pot, cov., Mold 643,
decorated w/pink roses & white
chrysanthemums, green leaves on
white & blue ground, 11" h..............**600.00**

Chocolate set: cov. chocolate pot &
five cups & saucers; Mold 207,
decorated w/white star flowers &
green surreal dogwood, pearlized
lustre finish, 11 pcs. **475.00**

Chocolate set: cov. chocolate pot & 6
cups & saucers: Mold 644, decorated
w/figural scene of lady w/dog on
turquoise background on ivory, gold
trim & edging, 13 pcs. (one cup
w/hairline inside, professional
restoration of finial) **625.00**

Coffee set: cov. demitasse coffeepot
& six cups & saucers; Mold 641,
decorated w/baskets of red, pink &
white flowers, tinged w/turquoise,
13 pcs...**875.00**

Cracker jar, cov., Mold 632, decorated
w/multicolored roses, white
ground...**399.00**

Cracker jar, cov., Mold 509A,
poppies decoration **300.00**

Creamer, hummingbird decoration,
brown shades..................................**350.00**

Creamer, Mold 601, pink & white
roses on vivid blue, green & lime
green background, 4½" h.................**60.00**

Creamer & cov. sugar bowl, Mold
502, decorated w/roses, pr. **150.00**

**Creamer & cov. two-handled sugar
bowl,** pedestal scalloped bases
w/egg-shaped body decorated
w/buds, fronds & leaves in
varicolored greens & red, gold
upper borders w/tracery below,
glossy white ground w/shaded
lavender & green, 4" h., pr. **195.00**
Cup & saucer, demitasse, decorated
w/red roses on green ground............**95.00**
Cup & saucer, Mold 704...................**130.00**
Dessert set: two 9¾" handled plates,
eleven 7¼" plates, nine cups &
saucers, oversized creamer & sugar
bowl; all pieces decorated w/pink
poppies w/aqua, yellow & purple
tints, plain mold, pedestal-based
cups, saucers, creamer &
sugar bowl, 33 pcs. **1,950.00**
Dresser tray, Stippled Floral mold
(Mold 23), rectangular shape w/white
embossed stippled border w/small
yellow flowers, center decorated
w/pink roses & shadow flowers on
soft green & deeper green ground,
red mark, 7 x 10¾" (ILLUS.) **175.00**
Dresser tray, Lily mold, blue floral
decoration, unmarked, 11¾"............**165.00**
Hair receiver, cov., Mold 182,
decorated w/mauve & red flowers &
multi-colored leaves on white to
ivory ground **95.00**
Hatpin holder w/attached rectangular
open trinket box, embossed shape
w/decoration of pink roses
w/powder blue & gold trim **125.00**
Inkwell, footed, decorated w/blue
daisies & purple flowers, 2½" h..........**50.00**
Mustache cup, Mold 502, lavender
neck, blue base, raised gold leaves
decoration **255.00**
Mustard pot, cov., Point & Clover
mold (Mold 82), bowl of flowers
decoration **235.00**
Pin box, cov., Mold 833, hexagonal,
sheepherder decoration...................**395.00**
Pin tray, Daffodil Rim mold, center
decoration of peach & pink roses,
gold trim, 3¼" x 5¼" **95.00**
Pitcher, lemonade, 8¾" h., Carnation
mold (Mold 526), decorated w/pink &
yellow roses, white poppies **795.00**
Pitcher, tankard, 10¼" h., Fleur-de-lis
mold, footed, baby blue decor
w/mixed flowers of lavender, pink,
orange & white, unmarked..............**425.00**
Pitcher, tankard, 13" h., Carnation
mold (Mold 526), decorated w/pink
poppies **795.00**
Pitcher, tankard, 13" h., Carnation
mold (Mold 526), decorated w/pink &
yellow roses on a teal green &
cream ground (ILLUS. top next
column) **1,100.00**

Carnation Mold Tankard Pitcher

Pitcher, tankard, 13" h., Mold 584,
hanging basket decoration, satin
finish **900.00**
Pitcher, tankard, 13½" h., Carnation
mold, decorated w/red & yellow
roses **895.00**
Pitcher, tankard, 13¼" h., Stippled
Floral mold (Mold 23), decorated
w/vivid red & yellow roses on blue
& green background, unmarked **495.00**
Plate, 6½" d., Mold 202, decorated
w/roses, pearlized finish **30.00**

Lily Mold Plate

Plate, 7½" d., Lily mold (Mold 29),
Lebrun   portrait (ILLUS.) **185.00**
Plate, 8½" d., Mold 92, eight dome
sections, turkey & evergreens scenic
decoration w/gold trim, high
glaze finish......................................**525.00**
Plate, 10" d., open-handled, Hidden
Image mold, decorated w/red,
chartreuse & white mums, gold
trim, unmarked................................**575.00**
Plate, 10½" d., open-handled, Point &
Clover mold (Mold 82), Melon Eates
decoration **795.00**
Plates, 8¾" d., Rope Edge mold, Dice
Throwers scene on one, Melon

Eaters scene on other, dark green tinted ground, unmarked, pr.......................................**1,550.00**

Relish tray, Point & Clover mold, Melon Eaters decoration, green, 8½" l.....................................**695.00**

Relish tray, Point & Clover mold, Melon Eaters decoration, 4½ x 9½"...............................**695.00**

Sugar bowl, cov., two-handled, footed, Mold 342, decorated w/red, orange & mauve roses & leaves w/lavish gold trim on ivory ground w/pastel shaded satin finish..............**45.00**

Two Unmarked R.S. Prussia Teapots

Teapot, cov., egg-shaped on round pedestal foot decorated w/dainty white flowers & green leaves on pastel white, green, pink & beige ground, unmarked, 7" d., 6¼" h. (ILLUS. left)....................................**135.00**

Teapot, cov., angular bulbous body on square pedestal foot decorated w/pink roses & green leaves on a pastel green ground, unmarked, 7½" d., 5¾" h. (ILLUS. right)............**135.00**

Tea set, child's: cov. teapot & four cups & saucers; decorated w/pink & white roses, 9 pcs. ....**600.00 to 650.00**

Toothpick holder, Iris mold, pink poppies decoration **310.00**

Toothpick holder, Stippled Floral Mold (Mold 23) decorated w/pink roses **155.00**

Toothpick holder, three-handled, Mold 627, decorated w/house scene, molded petal feet, 2½" h. **395.00**

Toothpick holder, three-handled, Mold 627, Old Man of the Mountain scene, molded petal feet, 2½" h. **395.00**

Toothpick holder, urn-shaped, Stippled Floral mold, 2¼" h..............**155.00**

Tray, portrait medallion, center decoration of roses w/cobalt ground, 5 x 10"..................................**695.00**

Urns, cov., decorated w/mill scene & castle scene, 11¾" h., pr. **3,475.00**

Vase, 5½" h., two-handled, pale green ground w/white lily decoration............**95.00**

Vase, 6½" h., decorated w/cottage scene in brown tones.......................**495.00**

Vase, 6½" h., Mold 910, cottage scene, brown & gold ground w/lavender highlights **599.00**

Vase, pillow-type, 7" h., Dice Throwers scene, shaded green ground w/lavender highlights w/jewels......**2,400.00**

Vase, 7½" h., footed, decorated w/pink roses & portrait of Colonial couple **550.00**

Vase, 8" h., Mold 932, Melon Eaters, shaded green ground w/lavender highlights, exceptional looking pedestal mold w/sixteen jewels **2,100.00**

Vase, 9" h., 6" d., pedestal base, graceful handles, mill scene decoration, jeweled bottom & top **475.00**

Vase, 10" h., decorated w/mill scene, green & yellow w/jeweled pedestalled base............................**775.00**

Vase, 10" h., two-handled, jeweled pedestal base, mill scene decoration **795.00**

Vase, 11" h., large handles, rare double of Diana & reclining lady, iridescent Tiffany w/heavy gold stenciling, scalloped top, unmarked......................................**950.00**

Vegetable bowl, open-handled, Mold 182, center decoration of three yellow & red apples, leaves & branches, glossy turquoise w/lavender to ivory tints, 12⅜" d., unmarked..**190.00**

OTHER MARKS

Basket, handled, maiden & cherub scene on iridescent ground w/gold trim, artist-signed, 6⅜" h. (E.S. Germany - Royal Saxe) **125.00**

Bowl, 3 x 6 x 8" oval, double pierced ends & four molded feet, decoration w/open white roses, leaves & gold trim on shaded turquoise & grey ground (R.S. Tillowitz) **95.00**

Bowl, 10" d., handled, decorated w/lilies of the valley (R.S. Silesia) **125.00**

Cake plate, open-handled, Mold 302, decorated w/lavender poppies & large mauve & yellow flowers & shadow flowers on white to light green ground, Steeple mark, 11" d...**145.00**

Celery tray, portrait scene of two women & a man, reading a book, gold stenciled designs, 1½ x 5 x 10" (E.S. Germany - Prov. Saxe) **225.00**

Chocolate set: 10" h. cov. chocolate pot & eight cups & saucers; decorated w/pink roses on lavender & baby blue ground, gold trim, the set (E.S. Prussia) **495.00**

Planter, wide bulbous body on a short pedestal foot, decorated w/a wide

band of pink flowers trimmed
w/gold, 6½" d., 6¾" h. (R.S.
Poland) **235.00**

Plate, 9" d., decorated w/h.p. roses
w/gold thorns, cobalt raised gold
border, Steeple mark **225.00**

Sachet holder, decorated w/tiny pink
roses, 5" h. (Prov. Saxe - E.S.
Germany)...................................**95.00**

Sandwich server, center handle,
scalloped rim, lavender & pink roses
w/gold trim, 11" d., 8" to top
of handle (R.S. Poland) **515.00**

Server, center-handled, scene of
robin, 6" d., (E.S. Germany)..............**48.00**

Sugar bowl, cov., decorated w/pink &
white poppies, 4" d., 2½" h. (R.S.
Poland) **45.00**

Urn, three-footed base, decorated
w/two victorian women & a cherub,
heavy gold beading on cobalt blue
ground, 6¾" h. (E.S. Germany) **195.00**

Vase, 6½" h., Mold 915, "Rembrandt
Scene" w/musket, grey & brown
ground (R.S. Suhl) **599.00**

Vase, 8¾" h., "Lady with Doves,"
portrait decoration, maroon
w/turquoise jewelling (Prove.
Saxe - E.S. Germany)....................**525.00**

Vase, 9" h., ovoid body w/tall
cylindrical neck, floral decoration
outline in gold, cobalt ground,
Steeple mark.................................**600.00**

Vase, 9¼" h., portrait of "Goddess of
the Sea," turquoise "tapestry"
decoration, Tiffany shading (Prov.
Saxe - E.S. Germany)....................**575.00**

Vase, 10" h., decorated on front
w/scene of lady w/peacock, reverse
has scene of lady w/doves,
(E.S. Germany -Prov. Saxe) **850.00**

Vase, 11¾" h., two-sided figural scene
of woman w/letter, teal background
(E.S. Germany - Prov. Saxe) **795.00**

RUSSEL WRIGHT DESIGNS

*The innovative dinnerwares designed
by Russel Wright and produced by various
companies beginning in the late 1930s
were an immediate success with a society
that was turning to a more casual and
informal lifestyle. His designs, with their
flowing lines and unconventional shapes,
were produced in many different colors
which allowed the hostess to arrange a
creative table. Although not antique, these
designs, which we list below by line and
manufacturer, are highly collectible. In
addition to dinnerwares, Wright was also*

*known as a trend-setter in the design of
furniture, glassware, lamps, fabric and a
multitude of other household goods.*

AMERICAN MODERN (Steubenville Pottery Company)

Ashtray, coaster-type, chartreuse **$11.00**

Ashtray, coaster-type, coral................**10.00**

Bowl, fruit, lug handle, granite grey **12.00**

Bowl, salad, black chutney (deep
brown)..**40.00**

Bowl, salad, incurved sides, seafoam
blue **38.00**

Bowl, soup, lug handle, black
chutney......................................**18.50**

Butter dish, cov., cedar green...........**265.00**

Butter dish, cov., chartreuse..............**195.00**

Butter dish, cov., granite grey...........**175.00**

Carafe w/stopper, coral....................**120.00**

Carafe w/stopper, seafoam blue **165.00**

Casserole, cov., stick handle, bean
brown...**75.00**

Casserole, cov., stick handle, granite
grey **25.00**

Celery tray, slender oblong shape
w/asymmetrical incurved sides,
cantaloupe, 13" l..........................**50.00**

Celery tray, slender oblong shape
w/asymmetrical incurved sides,
glacier blue, 13" l.........................**50.00**

Coffeepot, cov., demitasse,
cantaloupe **125.00**

Coffeepot, cov., demitasse, glacier
blue **117.50**

Coffeepot, cov., demitasse, granite
grey **110.00**

Coffeepot, cov., cedar green.............**125.00**

Creamer, black chutney.....................**10.00**

Creamer, granite grey........................**10.00**

Creamer & cov. sugar bowl,
chartreuse, pr.............................**22.00**

Cup & saucer, demitasse, cedar
green...**35.00**

Cup & saucer, demitasse, seafoam
blue **20.00**

Cup & saucer, chartreuse **9.00**

Cup & saucer, coral..........................**10.00**

Hostess plate, avocado......................**75.00**

Hostess plate, black chutney **75.00**

Hostess plate, cedar green..................**45.00**

Hostess plate, chartreuse...................**75.00**

Hostess plate, coral..........................**75.00**

Pitcher, water, 12" h., cantaloupe......**225.00**

Pitcher, water, 12" h., cedar green **95.00**

Pitcher, water, 12" h., white...............**195.00**

Plate, bread & butter, 6¼" d.,
granite grey..................................**4.50**

Plate, bread & butter, 6¼" d.,
seafoam blue **2.00**

Plate, child's, coral **95.00**
Plate, dinner, 10" d., cantaloupe **20.00**
Plate, dinner, 10" d., chartreuse.............**5.00**
Plate, dinner, 10" d., granite grey...........**7.50**
Plate, dinner, 10" d., seafoam blue **6.00**
Plate, dinner, 10" d., white **16.00**
Platter, 13¾" l., oblong, black
  chutney...**20.00**
Platter, 13¾" l., oblong, chartreuse......**18.50**
Platter, 13¾" l., oblong, granite
  grey...**25.00**
Refrigerator jar, cov., coral **187.50**
Relish dish, divided, chartreuse **135.00**
Relish dish, divided w/raffia handle,
  chartreuse..**175.00**
Relish rosette, granite grey.............**150.00**
Salt & pepper shakers, chartreuse,
  pr..**12.50**
Sugar bowl, cov., chartreuse..............**15.00**
Sugar bowl, cov., coral.......................**15.00**
Sugar bowl, cov., granite grey.............**14.00**
Teapot, cov., chartreuse **32.50**
Tidbit tray, coral, 13" l. **22.00**
Tumbler, cedar green **90.00**
Tumbler, chartreuse **75.00**
Vegetable bowl, open, oval,
  chartreuse, 10" l................................**15.00**
Vegetable bowl, open, oval, granite
  grey, 10" l..**18.50**
Vegetable bowl, open, coral, 11" d. **28.00**
Vegetable dish, cov., black chutney,
  12" l..**55.00**

**CASUAL CHINA (Iroquois China
Company)**
Bowl, cereal, 5" d., lemon yellow **6.00**
Bowl, cereal, 5" d., nutmeg brown **5.00**
Bowl, cereal, 5" d., sugar white..............**8.00**
Bowl, fruit, 5½" d., avocado yellow **4.00**
Bowl, fruit, 5½" d., ice blue **4.00**
Bowl, fruit, 5½" d., lettuce green **15.00**
Bowl, fruit, 5½" d., nutmeg brown **5.50**
Bowl, fruit, 5½" d., sugar white **8.00**
Butter dish, cov., charcoal **95.00**
Butter dish, cov., sugar white.............**110.00**
Butter dish, cov., restyled, avocado
  yellow, ¼ lb. **275.00**
Carafe, cov., charcoal, 10" h. **200.00**
Carafe, cov., nutmeg brown, 10" h.....**125.00**
Carafe, cov., pink sherbet, 10" h. **105.00**
Casserole, cov., divided, avocado
  yellow...**35.00**
Casserole, cov., divided, ripe apricot...**40.00**
Casserole, cov., ice blue, 2 qt. **29.00**
Casserole, cov., lemon yellow,
  2 qt. (scuff).......................................**15.00**
Casserole, cov., nutmeg brown, 2 qt...**18.00**
Casserole, cov., ripe apricot, 2 qt. **18.00**
Casserole, cov., ice blue, 4 qt. **42.50**
Casserole, cov., divided, redesigned,
  ripe apricot..**50.00**
Creamer, stack-type, parsley green.......**5.00**
Creamer, stack-type, lemon yellow......**10.00**

Creamer, stack-type, ripe apricot.........**12.00**
Creamer, restyled, lemon yellow..........**15.00**
Creamer, restyled, lettuce green..........**15.00**
Creamer, restyled, ripe apricot.............**20.00**
Creamer, stack-type, sugar white **8.00**
Creamer & sugar bowl, stack-type,
  avocado yellow, family size, pr. **75.00**
Creamer & sugar bowl, stack-type,
  avodado yellow, pr.............................**12.00**
Creamer & sugar bowl, stack-type,
  chartreuse, pr....................................**22.00**
Creamer & sugar bowl, stack-type,
  ripe apricot, pr...................................**35.00**
Cup & saucer, demitasse, avocado
  yellow..**100.00**
Cup & saucer, tea, charcoal..................**9.00**
Cup & saucer, tea, ice blue **7.00**
Cup & saucer, tea, lemon yellow...........**7.00**
Cup & saucer, tea, nutmeg brown.........**6.00**
Cup & saucer, tea, parsley green..........**7.00**
Cup & saucer, tea, ripe apricot.............**6.00**
Cup & saucer, tea, sugar white **10.00**
Gumbo soup bowl, handled, avocado
  yellow, 21 oz......................................**28.50**
Gumbo soup bowl, handled, ripe
  apricot, 21 oz. **27.50**
Mug, avocado yellow, 13 oz.................**45.00**
Mug, oyster grey, 13 oz.......................**45.00**
Mug, parsley green, 13 oz....................**45.00**
Mug, pink sherbet, 13 oz......................**65.00**
Mug, ripe apricot, 13 oz.......................**50.00**
Mug, restyled, cantaloupe...................**150.00**
Mug, restyled, lemon yellow................**65.00**
Mug, restyled, sugar white **65.00**
Mug, restyled, ripe apricot...................**65.00**
Pitcher, cov., water, ripe apricot **65.00**
Plate, bread & butter, 6" d., avocado
  yellow..**3.00**
Plate, bread & butter, 6" d., charcoal **3.00**
Plate, bread & butter, 6" d., ice blue.......**3.50**
Plate, bread & butter, 6" d., lemon
  yellow..**3.00**
Plate, bread & butter, 6" d., nutmeg
  brown..**3.50**
Plate, bread & butter, 6" d., pink
  sherbet..**3.00**
Plate, bread & butter, 6" d., ripe
  apricot **3.00**
Plate, bread & butter, 6" d., sugar
  white **6.00**
Plate, salad, 7½" d., avocado yellow......**6.00**
Plate, salad, 7½" d., ice blue................**7.00**
Plate, salad, 7½" d., nutmeg brown **7.00**
Plate, salad, 7½" d., sugar white..........**10.00**
Plate, luncheon, 9" d., avocado yellow ..**5.00**
Plate, luncheon, 9" d., nutmeg brown **6.00**
Plate, dinner, 10" d., lemon yellow.........**8.00**
Plate, dinner, 10" d., nutmeg brown.......**8.00**
Plate, chop, 14" d., lettuce green **32.00**
Platter, 12¾" oval, avocado yellow......**12.00**
Platter, 12¾" oval, ice blue **15.00**
Platter, 12¾" l., oval, pink sherbet.......**15.00**
Platter, 14½" l., avocado yellow...........**16.00**

Platter, 14½" l., ice blue 18.00
Platter, 14½" l., parsley green.............25.00
Platter, 14½" l., oval, pink sherbet 22.00
Platter, 14½" l., ripe apricot.................18.00
Platter, 14½" l., sugar white................30.00
Salt shaker, tall, redesigned,
  nutmeg brown 100.00
Salt & pepper shakers, stack-type,
  avocado yellow, pr. 8.00
Salt & pepper shakers, stack-type,
  oyster grey, pr. 25.00
Salt & pepper shakers, stack-type,
  parsley green, pr. 20.00
Salt & pepper shakers, stack-type,
  pink sherbet, pr. 10.00
Sugar bowl, cov., restyled, ripe
  apricot 30.00
Teapot, cov., nutmeg brown 165.00
Teapot, cov., restyled, oyster grey.....150.00
Vegetable bowl, open, avocado
  yellow, 36 oz., 8" d. 14.00
Vegetable bowl, open, ice blue,
  36 oz., 8" d. 15.00
Vegetable bowl, open, nutmeg
  brown, 36 oz., 8" d. 15.00
Vegetable bowl, open, sugar white,
  36 oz., 8" d. 20.00
Vegetable bowl, open, avocado,
  10" d. 16.00
Vegetable bowl, open, ice blue,
  10" d. 16.00
Vegetable bowl, open, sugar white,
  10" d. 35.00
Vegetable bowl, open, divided,
  avocado yellow, 10" d. 18.00
Vegetable bowl, open, divided, ice
  blue, 10" d. 18.00
Vegetable bowl, open, divided,
  lemon yellow, 10" d. 78.00
Vegetable bowl, open, divided,
  nutmeg brown, 10" d. 18.00
Vegetable bowl, open, divided,
  parsley green, 10" d. 22.00
Vegetable bowl, open, divided,
  oyster grey 35.00
Vegetable bowl, open, divided, pink
  sherbet, 10" d. 30.00
Vegetable bowl, open, divided, ripe
  apricot, 10" d. 18.00

SALTGLAZED WARES

This whitish ware has a pitted surface
texture, which resembles an orange skin as
a result of salt being thrown into the hot
kiln to produce the glaze. Much of this
ware was sold in the undecorated state, but
some pieces were decorated. Decorative
pieces have been produced in England and
Europe since at least the 18th century with
later production in the United States. Most
pieces are unmarked.

"Good Samaritan" Pitcher

Pitcher, 7" h., 4½" d., footed tapering
  cylindrical body w/flaring lip &
  angled C-scroll handle, relief-
  molded w/biblical scene of the Good
  Samaritan, light grey, marked "1841"
  & "Jones & Walley" on base,
  ca. 1841 (ILLUS.)...........................$225.00

Tan Relief-Molded Pitcher

Pitcher, 8" h., 5½" d., footed tapering
  cylindrical body w/flaring lip &
  branch-shaped C-scroll handle,
  relief-molded w/figures of ranger
  w/gun, his dog & horse, grapes &
  leaves top border, tan, black registry
  mark on base, either Walley or
  Alcock, ca. 1847 (ILLUS.) 235.00

SARREGUEMINES

This factory was established in Lorraine, France, about 1770. Subsequently
Wedgwood-type pieces were produced as

was Mocha ware. In the 19th century, the factory turned to pottery and stoneware.

Sarreguemines Garden Seat

Garden seat, tree trunk-form, the seat molded as a blue cushion w/four hanging tassels, the trunk w/green ivy & oak leaves, the whole glazed in natural colors, impressed "MAJOLICA - SARREGUEMINES," late 19th c., minor wear to glaze, minute chips (ILLUS.) **$1,093.00**
Oyster plate, grey & coral..................**130.00**
Pitcher, 12" h., 3½" d., flat stepped foot, slender expanding cylindrical body w/sloping shoulder & slender neck, squared handle, shimmering metallic silvery crystalline glaze on a brown ground, ink mark "SARREGUEMINES FRANCE" **192.50**
Plate, 7½" d., majolica, pears decoration **30.00**
Vase, 11¼" h., bulbous base tapering to a cylindrical neck, celadon green glaze w/a crazed effect, impressed mark..**220.00**

SATSUMA

These decorated wares have been produced in Japan since the end of the 18th century. The early pieces are scarce and high-priced. Later Satsuma wares are plentiful and, with prices rising, are highly collectible as earlier pieces.

Incense burner, foo dog finial &

handles, heavily enameled florals on cobalt ground, ca. 1900, 10" h..**$125.00**

Satsuma Globular Vase

Vase, 3½" h., globular body tapering to short, narrow flared rim sitting on three scrolled feet, decorated w/figures in shaped cartouches on brocade patterned ground, signed under foot, 19th c. (ILLUS.) **715.00**
Vase, 24" h., tall ovoid body tapering to a short neck w/rolled rim, decorated w/four long panels w/detailed landscapes (minor wear) **2,640.00**

Ovoid Satsuma Vase

Vases, 12¼" h., slender ovoid body tapering to short flat rim, decorated w/bijin & landscapes in circular panels, keyfret band, lappets at neck & butterflies to the bottom of body, sealed under foot, 19th c., pr. (ILLUS. one of two) **1,650.00**

SCHAFER & VATER

Two Schafer & Vater Ashtrays

Founded in Rudolstadt, Thuringia, Germany in 1890, the Schafer and Vater Porcelain Factory specialized in decorative pieces of porcelain usually in white or colored bisque. They produced many novelty figural items such as creamers, toothpick holders, boxes and hatpin holders and also produced a line of jasper ware with white-relief decoration in imitation of the famous Wedgwood jasper wares. The firm also decorated whiteware blanks.

The company ceased production in 1962 and collectors now seek out their charming pieces which may be marked with a crown over a starburst containing the script letter "R."

Ashtray, figural, bisque, little boy & little girl w/green hair ribbon, white rabbits on one corner, white doves on other, inscribed on front "Everybody's Doing it," 3¼" d., 3¼" h. (ILLUS. left) $150.00

Ashtray & match holder, figural, bisque, couple w/their heads under a lavender hat, she wearing a blue dress & he wearing a black coat & green pants, holes in top of hat for matches, ashtray in front, inscribed in front "Hidden Fire," 2⅞" d., 3¾" h. (ILLUS. right) 175.00

Bottle, jasper ware, handled, white relief scene of troubadour & lady toasting each other, light green ground, 6½" h. 175.00

Bottle w/original stopper, decorated w/white relief figure of Egyptian woman kneeling on pedestal w/jug on shoulder, 9" h. (small chip on neck on back) 185.00

Candleholder, handled, w/embossed owls decoration, 4¾" h. 135.00

Figurine, girl dressed in pink standing next to pink basket, 6" h. 125.00

Model of a bear in coat w/muff, 6¼" h. 185.00

Pitcher, 5" h., jasper ware, white relief woman w/sheep, blue ground 70.00

Schafer & Vater Novelty Vase

Vase, 4½" h., 3" d., bulbous body w/brown squared fence-like handle that forms two bud vases, decorated w/slightly embossed white relief lions on cobalt blue ground (ILLUS.) 85.00

SEVRES & SEVRES-STYLE

Sevres Ormolu-Mounted Bowl

Some of the more desirable porcelain ever produced was made at the Sevres factory, originally established at Vincennes, France, and transferred, through permission of Madame de

Pompadour, to Sevres as the Royal Manufactory about the middle of the 18th century. King Louis XV took sole responsibility for the works in 1759 when production of hard paste began. Between 1850 and 1900, many biscuit and soft-paste porcelains were again made. Fine early pieces are scarce and high-priced. Many of those available today are late productions. The various Sevres marks have been copied and pieces listed as "Sevres-Style" are similar to actual Sevres wares, but not necessarily from that factory. Three of the many Sevres marks are illustrated below.

Bowl, 7" h., deep rounded bowl decorated w/vignette of colorful exotic birds on blue ground w/gold trim w/ormolu basketweave rim & vine handles, resting on four Oriental figures who sit on chairs atop a square base, 18th c. (ILLUS.) **$3,680.00**

Sevres Gilt-Bronze Mounted Box

Box, cov., Sevres-Style, rectangular, gilt-bronze frame mounted w/four rectangular sides & top adorned w/panels depicting pastoral scenes, on cobalt blue ground w/gilt trim,

signed "W. Rosner," 19th c., 9½" l. (ILLUS.) **6,900.00**

Bust of Napoleon

Bust of Napoleon, unglazed porcelain, inscribed "NAPOLEON" on front base, impressed marks, 18th c., firing imperfections & edge chips, 11⅝" h. (ILLUS.) **2,070.00**

Centerpiece, Sevres-Style, Louis XV style, a figural panel & an opposing landscape panel surrounded by gilt-bronze decoration, fitted w/scrolled handles & a pierced rim, all on a celeste blue ground, 18" h. **9,200.00**

Sevres Charger

Charger, round, h.p. battle scene of men on horses & others on foot, within a gilt enhanced cobalt blue border, printed marks, ca. 1844, 20" d. (ILLUS.) **2,760.00**

Figure, bisque, the nude female draped in a wide mantle & holding out her arms, wearing a tricorner hat w/a mask on top & bowed slippers, base impressed "M. GUIRAURI-VIERE" & "SEVRES," ca. 1900, 22" h...**1,035.00**

Figure group, bisque, depicting lovers in an outdoor setting, on a gilt carved wood base, 9" h. **345.00**

Plate, 9½" d., Sevres-Style, center portrait of Mme. DuBarry, signed "Robert" on front **250.00**

Plates, dinner, 9½" d., blue ground w/central cartouches of putti flanking a central gilt monogram of Louis-Philippe, printed marks, mid-19th c., set of 12 ....**920.00**

Tete-a-tete set: cov. teapot, cov. sugar bowl, creamer, tray, & two cups & saucers; each decorated w/a blue ground w/enameled putti flanking gilt monograms w/cartouches, printed marks, ca. 1846, tray 11½" l., the set **1,495.00**

Floral-decorated Sevres Vase

Sevres-Style Urn

Urn, cov., Sevres-Style, baluster shaped body w/satyr head handles at shoulder, decorated w/oval panels of colorful enamel flowers on cobalt ground, sitting on metal octagonal base, France, late 19th c., 24¾" h. (ILLUS.) **2,415.00**

Urns, cov., Sevres-Style, each w/opposing oval panels depicting Napoleonic battle scenes, flanked by gilt-bronze winged female terms surmounted by a domed top headed by an eagle, raised on a domed & gilt-bronze base, pseudo interlacing "L's" mark in blue enamel, 4' 8" h., pr. **28,750.00**

Vase, 41" h., paneled baluster-shaped body painted w/prunus blossoms & leafage in shades of grey, pink & brown, mounted on bronze base, printed factory marks, artist-signed in underglaze "E. Drouet," ca. 1907 (ILLUS. top next column) **20,700.00**

Hand-painted Sevres Vase

Vases, 12¾" h., h.p. footed bottle-form body w/a slender ringed & slightly flaring neck, decorated w/oval reserves of 18th c. couples in landscapes against a turquoise blue ground, round red Republic mark, ca. 1872-99, pr. (ILLUS. one of two) **862.50**

Pair of Sevres-Style Vases

Vases, 16¼" h., Sevres-Style, classical trumpet-shaped body w/handles at shoulder on flared square base w/paw feet, ornate gilt decoration on brown ground, signed "'Schoelcher' factory, Paris, Fauborg Saint-Denis," 19th c., gilt wear, foot repair, lids missing, pr. (ILLUS. bottom previous page) **3,450.00**

Vase, 22½" h., shouldered ovoid body elaborately painted w/a continuous band of flowers, gilt foot & neck, mounted as a lamp **977.00**

SHELLEY CHINA

Members of the Shelley family were in the pottery business in England as early as the 18th century. In 1872 Joseph Shelley formed a partnership with James Wileman of Wileman & Co. who operated the Foley China Works. The Wileman & Co. name was used for the firm for the next fifty years, and between 1890 and 1910 the words "The Foley" appeared above conjoined "WC" initials.

Beginning in 1910 the Shelley family name in a shield appeared on wares, although the firm's official name was still Wileman & Co. The company's name was finally changed to Shelley in 1925 and then Shelley China Ltd. after 1965. The firm changed hands in the 1960s and became part of the Doulton Group in 1971.

At first only average quality earthenwares were produced but in the late 1890s new shapes and better quality decorations were used.

Bone china was introduced at Shelley before World War I and these fine dinnerwares became very popular in the United Sates and are increasingly popular today with collectors. Thin "eggshell china" teawares, miniatures and souvenir items were widely marketed during the 1920s and 1930s and are sought-after today.

Shelley
CHINA
ENGLAND

Bell, Regency patt............................**$200.00**
Bowl, fruit, Bridal Rose patt. **30.00**
Bowl, fruit, Rose Spray patt. **30.00**
Bowl, soup, Bridal Rose patt...............**40.00**

Bowl, soup, Rose Spray patt. **40.00**
Butter dish, cov., Lily of the Valley patt...**125.00**
Batter pat, Blue Rock patt. **30.00**
Cake plate, handled, Crochet patt., yellow..**105.00**
Cake plates, Crochet patt., multicolored, set of 6......................**169.00**
Cake stand, footed, Regency patt., Dainty White shape...........................**95.00**
Candy dish, Forget-Me-Not patt., 4" d...**35.00**
Candy dish, Pansy patt., 4" d. **37.50**
Candy dish, Rosebud patt., 4" d..........**37.50**
Coffeepot, cov., demitasse, Lily of the Valley patt.......................................**155.00**
Coffeepot, cov., individual, Begonia patt., Dainty shape, 5 1/2" h............**295.00**
Coffeepot, cov., Bridal Rose patt.......**195.00**
Coffeepot, cov., Colonial Bouquet patt...**359.00**
Coffeepot, cov., Lily of the Valley patt...**225.00**
Coffeepot, cov., Pansy patt. **349.00**
Coffeepot, cov., Regency patt. **210.00**
Coffeepot, cov., Rosebud patt...........**349.00**
Coffeepot, cov., Wildflowers patt.......**369.00**
Coffee server, Rose Spray patt.........**250.00**
Compote, footed, Dainty Blue patt.....**255.00**
Creamer, Bridal Rose patt. **45.00**
Creamer, Rose Spray patt. **38.50**
Creamer & cov. sugar bowl, Dainty Blue patt., pr. **75.00**
Creamer & sugar bowl, Forget-Me-Not patt., pr. **115.00**
Creamer & sugar bowl, Georgian patt...**99.00**
Creamer & sugar bowl, Mixed Flowers patt., pr...............**125.00 to 150.00**
Creamer & sugar bowl, Pansy patt., pr...**110.00**
Creamer & sugar bowl, Rosebud patt., pr...**110.00**
Creamer & sugar bowl, Stocks patt., pr. ....**125.00 to 150.00**
Creamer & cov. sugar bowl, Violets patt., pr...**85.00**
Creamer & sugar bowl, Wildflowers patt., pr...**115.00**
Creamer, sugar bowl & undertray, Blue Rock patt., miniature, 3 pcs. **210.00**
Creamer, sugar bowl & undertray, Rose Spray patt., 3 pcs...................**150.00**
Cup & saucer, demitasse, Georgian patt., T.M. James **50.00**
Cup & saucer, demitasse, Dainty Green patt......................................**75.00**
Cup & saucer, demitasse, Pansy patt...**62.50**
Cup & saucer, demitasse, Rosebud patt...**62.50**
Cup & saucer, demitasse, Violets patt...**60.00**

Cup & saucer, demitasse, Wild Rose
patt...**35.00**
Cup & saucer, demitasse, Wild Rose
patt., six-flute shape.............................**55.00**
Cup & saucer, demitasse,
Wildflowers patt. **67.50**
Cup & saucer, Begonia patt., six-flute
shape...**50.00**
Cup & saucer, Blue Rock patt. **54.00**
Cup & saucer, Bridal Rose patt............**45.00**
Cup & saucer, Charm patt....................**57.50**
Cup & saucer, Dahlia patt. **55.00**
Cup & saucer, Dainty White patt. **30.00**
Cup & saucer, Forget-Me-Not patt. **48.00**
Cup & saucer, Harebell patt. **45.00**
Cup & saucer, Heather patt. **45.00**
Cup & saucer, Lily of the Valley patt. ..**50.00**
Cup & saucer, Maytime patt..................**47.50**
Cup & saucer, Montrose patt. **45.00**
Cup & saucer, Pansy patt. **51.50**
Cup & saucer, Pansy patt., Dainty
shape...**75.00**
Cup & saucer, Red Daisy patt.,
Dainty shape...**65.00**
Cup & saucer, Rock Garden patt. **52.00**
Cup & saucer, Rose patt. **48.00**
Cup & saucer, Rose patt., Dainty
shape...**65.00**
Cup & saucer, Rosebud patt. **48.00**
Cup & saucer, Rose Spray patt............**47.50**
Cup & saucer, Stocks patt., six-flute
shape...**40.00**
Cup & saucer, Summer Glory patt. **48.00**
Cup & saucer, Violets patt....................**55.00**
Cup & saucer, Wild Anemone patt......**48.00**
Cup & saucer, Wildflowers patt. **55.00**
Cup & saucer, Woodland patt., junior
size..**65.00**
Cup & saucer, Yellow Rose patt.,
large..**60.00**
Dessert set: cup & saucer & dessert
plate; Dainty Blue patt., 3 pcs. **120.00**
Dessert set: cup & saucer & dessert
plate; Lily of the Valley patt., 3 pcs. ...**85.00**
Dessert set: cup, saucer & dessert
plate; Regency patt., 3 pcs. **75.00**
Dessert set: cup & saucer & dessert
plate; Rosebud patt., 3 pcs. **75.00**
Dessert set: cup & saucer & dessert
plate; Rose Spray patt., 3 pcs............**75.00**
Dessert set: handled cake plate & six
serving plates; Charm patt., 7 pcs. ..**239.00**
Dish, small, Blue Rock patt. **35.00**
Dish w/gold center handle, three-
compartments, Regency patt. **210.00**
Egg cup, Harebell patt. **39.00**
Egg cup, Violets patt.............................**50.00**
Gravy boat, Bridal Rose patt. **165.00**
Gravy boat, Rose Spray patt. **165.00**
Jam jar, cov., Rosebud patt., six-flute
shape...**110.00**
Mustard jar, cov., Campanula patt. ...**110.00**
Plate, 5" d., Forget-Me-Not patt. **32.50**

Plate, 5" d., Pansy patt..........................**32.50**
Plate, 5" d., Rosebud patt. **32.50**
Plate, 8" d., Rose Spray patt. **30.00**
Plate, bread & butter, Bridal Rose
patt...**25.00**
Plate, bread & butter, Rose Spray
patt...**25.00**
Plate, dinner, Bridal Rose patt. **45.00**
Plate, dinner, Rose Spray patt. **45.00**
Plate, salad, Bridal Rose patt. **35.00**
Plate, salad, Rose Spray patt................**35.00**
Plate, 8" d., Begonia patt. **160.00**
Platter, 12½" l., Bridal Rose patt.......**135.00**
Platter, 12½" l., Rose Spray patt.......**135.00**
Platter, 14½" l., Bridal Rose patt.......**185.00**
Platter, 14½" l., Rose Spray patt.......**185.00**
Platter, 17" l., Blue Rock patt.............**200.00**
Snack tray, Harebell patt. **52.00**
Sugar bowl, demitasse, Harebell
patt...**50.00**
Sugar bowl, cov., Bridal Rose patt. **45.00**
Sugar bowl, cov., Rose Spray patt......**45.00**
Teapot, cov., Blue Rock patt. **220.00**
Teapot, cov., Harebell patt. **159.00**
Teapot, cov., Regency patt. **195.00**
Tea set: cov. teapot, creamer & sugar
bowl, six cups & saucers, & six 8"
plates; Dainty Blue patt., six-flute
shape, 21 pcs. **695.00**
Toothpick holder, Stocks patt.............**50.00**
Tray, 14" l., Dainty Blue patt..............**175.00**
Vegetable bowl, open, oval,
Wildflowers patt. **199.00**

SLIPWARE

Slipware Jar with Flowers

*This term refers to ceramics, primarily
redware, decorated by the application of
slip, or semi-liquid paste made of clay.
Such wares were made for decades in
England and Germany and elsewhere on
the Continent, and in the Pennsylvania
Dutch country, and elsewhere in the
United States. Today, contemporary copies*

*of early Slipware items are featured in
numerous decorator magazines and offered
for sale in gift catalogs.*

Bean pot, wide ovoid body tapering
to a wide galleried mouth, deeply
grooved loop handles at the
shoulders, redware w/a large triple
cluster of yellow slip tulips & green
leaves alternating w/large stylized
blossoms, Montgomery County,
Pennsylvania, late 18th c., 5¾" h.
(minor chipping) **$13,800.00**

Bowl, 15⅞" d., wide shallow sides,
redware decorated w/concentric
bands of yellow & green slip, the
yellow band squiggled, stylized
yellow & green floral cluster in the
center, possibly by John Leidy I,
1765-1846, Hillstown Township,
Bucks County, Pennsylvania, 1797-
1800 ....**2,530.00**

Charger, large shallow round redware
dish w/the top glazed in yellow slip &
daubs of green & decorated
w/sgraffito designs of a slender tree
issuing branches w/leaves or large
tulip-like blossoms & w/a bird
perched on each, possibly Bucks
County, Pennsylvania, late 18th -
early 19th c., 11" d. (repaired rim
chip) **7,475.00**

Charger, coggled edge, central
inscription in yellow slip "Charles
Murvin" with a squiggle border,
Pennsylvania, 19th c., 13½" d.
(hairline crack & some glaze
flakes) **575.00**

Charger, yellow slip "David" in script
between two rows of yellow slip
squiggles above & below, on
redware, American-made, 19th c.,
14" d...**2,750.00**

Charger, redware w/a coggled rim,
the interior glazed w/yellow slip
w/overall finely combed horizontal
bands centered by a squiggled small
rectangle, American-made, 19th c.,
13½" d...**920.00**

Dish, round w/deeply canted sides,
redware w/sgraffito decoration
w/yellow slip interior incised w/a tall
tapering tree issuing slender
branches w/leaves & stylized
blossoms & trimmed w/green
splotches, Pennsylvania, ca. 1800,
11¼" d. (some minor flakes) **1,840.00**

Flask, flattened ovoid body w/small
molded lip & small loop shoulder
handles, redware w/mottled green &
yellow slip decoration overall, New
England, 18th c., 8½" h. (chips).......**115.00**

Jar, cylindrical body w/flaring rim,

redware glazed w/yellow daubs of
green slip & decorated w/sgraffito
designs of notched tulips & vines
alternating w/budding flowers,
possibly Conrad Mumbouer, 1761-
1845, Haycock Township, Bucks
County, Pennsylvania, 1794-1844,
5⅜" d., 6" h. (ILLUS.) **18,400.00**

Pennsylvania Slipware Jug

Jug, redware, ovoid footed body
w/flaring lip above four pieced
carrying handles, inscribed "WA
1744" in yellow slip on each side,
Pennsylvania, ca. 1774, 8" h.
(ILLUS.) **1,610.00**

Slipware Loaf Dish

Loaf dish, rectangular w/cogglewheel
rim, redware decorated w/"Mary's
Dish" in yellow slip, Pennsylvania,
19th century, 9⅛ x 12½"
(ILLUS.) **4,830.00**

Milk bowl, interior decorated w/yellow
slip stripes & wavy lines, 12" d.,
3¾" h. (minor wear & small chips) ...**247.50**

Pie plate, redware w/coggled rim,
three bands of squiggled triple-band
yellow slip across the interior, 8" d.
(wear)...**357.50**

Pie plate, oval w/crimped edge, redware w/the interior decorated w/triple green slip bands alternating w/triple yellow slip squiggled bands down the length, probably Connecticut, first half 19th c., 11⅞" l. **4,025.00**

Conrad Mumbouer Plate

Plate, 10¼" d., circular, redware decorated w/incised pinwheel-budding flowers on a glazed yellow ground w/green & red daubs, possibly Conrad Mumbouer, 1761-1845, Haycock Township, Bucks County, Pennsylvania, 1794-1844 (ILLUS.) **12,650.00**

Plate, 12" d., yellow slip "APPLE" center between a straight yellow slip line above & below, on redware, American-made, late 19th c. (imperfections) **935.00**

Slipware Serving Bowl

Serving bowl, circular, redware, the dished rim w/deep brown squiggle decoration, the interior w/alternating vertical bands of brown & yellow slip, possibly Bucks County,

Pennsylvania, late 18th - early 19th century, 12⅞" d. (ILLUS.) **7,130.00**

SPATTERWARE

This ceramic ware takes its name from the "spattered" decoration, in various colors, generally used to trim pieces hand-painted with rustic center designs of flowers, birds, houses, etc. Popular in the early 19th century, most was imported from England.

Related wares, called "stick spatter," had free-hand designs applied with pieces of cut sponge attached to sticks, hence the name. Examples date from the 19th and early 20th century and were produced in England, Europe and America.

Some early spatter-decorated wares were marked by the manufacturers, but not many. 20th century reproductions are also sometimes marked, including those produced by Boleslaw Cybis in the 1940s which sometimes have 'CYBIS' impressed.

Cow creamer, model of a cow w/brown & black stripes of spatter, on an oval green spatter base, 5" h...**$467.50**

Cups & saucers, blue transfer-printed center design of a spread-winged eagle before a United States shield, purple spatter borders, 2 sets (small chips on rims of cups, chips on one saucer)................................**440.00**

Pitcher, 9¾" h., footed waisted cylindrical paneled sides w/leaf sprig rim spout & angled handle, overall red spatter stripes (wear, minor flakes & hairlines) **247.50**

Plate, 8⅜" d., Schoolhouse patt., green, red & brown school, blue spatter border (stains, wear, old rim chips) **330.00**

Plate, 8½" d., Rose patt., free-hand flower in red, green & black, blue spatterware border, impressed "Walker" (stains, minor crazing & short rim hairline) **275.00**

Platter, 12⅜" l., red transfer scene of cowboys & wild horses, blue spatter rim (wear, stains, glaze flakes & hairlines) **192.50**

Platter, 14⅝" l., octagonal, Rose patt., free-hand flower in red, green & black, red spatter rim band (minor wear)...**935.00**

Platter, 15½" l., rectangular w/cut corners, blue transfer-printed center design of a spread-winged American eagle before a United States shield,

Spatter Platter with Eagle

blue spatter border, unseen chip on
extreme rim (ILLUS.) **330.00**
Sugar bowl, cov., squatty bulbous
footed body tapering to a flaring rim,
low domed cover w/knop finial,
vertical bands of blue & green
spatter, ca. 1830, 4½" h. (small
chip on cover rim) **575.00**

Child's Peafowl Tea Set

Tea set, child's: cov. teapot, cov.
sugar bowl & creamer; squatty ovoid
bodies decorated w/stylized peafowl
on spatter decorated ground, 19th
century, repairs, teapot 4¼" h.
(ILLUS.) **632.50**

STICK & CUT SPONGE
Bowl, 9¼" d., the center w/h.p.
rounded & petalled flowers w/pairs
of small cut-sponge blossoms in
purple, pink, green & blue, wide pink
cut-sponge border band, 19th c.
(light stain) **77.00**
Bowl, 18½" d., 2¾" h., decorated
w/free-hand flowers in blue, red &
green interspersed w/cut-sponge
blossoms, center decorated w/free-
hand sprig surrounded by cut-
sponge blossom border, all within
cut-sponge blossom outer border,
crazing w/chips & hairline
(ILLUS. top next column) **594.00**

Gaudy Stick Spatter Shallow Bowl

Cup & saucer, cut-sponge floral
decoration in blue, black & green,
red spatter border **203.50**
Plate, 7½" d., large free-hand colored
florals in the center w/small cut-
sponge blossoms, black cut-sponge
border band, marked "Made
in Holland," 20th c. **27.50**
Plate, 8¾" d., cut-sponge foliate
designs in green, purple & black
within blue stripes, impressed
"Elsmore & Forster" (stains)............**220.00**
Plate, 9¼" d., Rabbit patt., brown
transfer-printed center scene of four
rabbits trimmed in yellow, free-hand
border band w/large fanned red
blossoms, green leaves & triple
clusters of small blue cut-sponge
blossoms (minor bubbles in red)......**495.00**
Plate, 9⅜" d., Rabbit patt., black
transfer-printed border band
w/rabbits & fronts trimmed in green
& yellow, free-hand decorated
center w/a ring of large cut-sponge
blue blossoms w/green & red
leaves, center circle w/small cut-
sponge blue blossoms (chip on back
rim edge)...**440.00**
Plate, 9½" d., Rabbit patt., wide
border band w/h.p. large leaf-form
red blossoms, green leaves & cut-
sponge clusters of blue blossoms,
center w/brown transfer-printed
scene of three rabbits & frog
trimmed in green & yellow **495.00**
Plate, 10½" d., the center w/a large
h.p. blossom flanked by four large
half-leaves & small leaf sprigs
w/scattered cut-sponge blossoms in
pink, purple, blue & green, purple
cut-sponge wide border band **77.00**
Soup plate, h.p. large central stylized
blossoms framed by leaf sprigs &
small cut-sponge blossoms in pink,

blue, purple & green, purple cut-sponge border band, marked "Made in Holland," 20th c., 8¾" d. **55.00**

SPONGEWARE

Spongeware Water Cooler with Lid

Spongeware's designs were spattered, sponged or daubed on in colors, sometimes with a piece of cloth. Blue on white was the most common type, but mottled tans, browns and greens on yellowware were also popular. Spongeware generally has an overall pattern with a coarser look than Spatterwares, to which it is loosely related. These wares were extensively produced in England and America well into the 20th century.

Beater jar, green & brown on cream **$125.00**

Bowl, 8½" d., blue sponging on yellow **45.00**

Bowl, dough-rising-type, metal rim on top & bottom, blue on white, large ...**400.00**

Casserole, rust sponging on white **55.00**

Custard cup, blue on white **20.00**

Maple syrup jug, bulbous ovoid beehive-form, short spout at top of one side, wire bail handle w/wooden grip, overall blue on white, marked on front "Grandmother's Maple Syrup of 50 Years Ago," maker's mark on bottom "F. H. Weeks, Akron, O.," 5½" h. (chips) **660.00**

Mustard pot, cov., baluster-shaped w/low-domed cover w/small knop & spoon notch, C-scroll handle, overall blue sponging on white & a double blue band around the middle, England, early 19th c., 3½" h. (hairlines) **316.00**

Pie plate, blue on white, marked "Sanitary, The Pure Food" **140.00**

Pitcher, 6¾" h., bulbous body tapering to a short & slightly scalloped rim, C-scroll handle, heavy dark blue on white **165.00**

Pitcher, tankard, 9" h., blue on white **385.00**

Platter, 11¼" oval, canted edges, heavy dark blue on white **93.50**

Water cooler, cov., tall ovoid body tapering to slightly flaring rim, stoneware w/applied blue spongeware decoration overall, stenciled "No. 7" on side, brass spigot at base, ca. 1880-1890, 13" h. (ILLUS.) **357.50**

STAFFORDSHIRE FIGURES

"Tam O'Shanter & Sooter Johnny"

Small figures and groups made of pottery were produced by the majority of the Staffordshire, England potters in the 19th century and were used as mantel decorations or "chimney ornaments," as they were sometimes called. Pairs of dogs were favorites and were turned out by the carload, and 19th century pieces are still available. Well-painted reproductions also abound and collectors are urged to exercise caution before investing.

Bust of George Washington, polychrome trim, 19th c., 8¼" h. **$489.00**

Calf, recumbent animal in front of a small tree, on a rockwork base, the calf in yellow w/tiny brown spots, green base, 19th c., 3" h. (several foot chips & flakes, piece of tree missing) **302.50**

Cottage, two-story w/side wing, two round-topped windows flank the center door, polychrome decoration, 4½" h. **148.50**

Cottage-bank, model of a house w/two tall wings w/pointed roofs &

chimneys flanking the lower center section w/door, polychrome decoration, 4½" h. **148.00**

Cottage pastille burner, model of a tall building w/multiple dormers & bay windows & a side tower, pierced w/various small openings, polychrome decoration, mid-19th c., 6¾" h. **220.00**

Dog, Pug in seated position on a quilted rectangular pillow base w/corner tassels, the dog in tan w/brown details & black collar, green & orange pillow w/gold tassels, 19th c., 4½" h. (tiny flake on ear & face, tiny enamel flakes on pillow) **1,100.00**

Dog, Spaniel in seated position, molded curly hair, painted facial details, white w/black spots, 3¾" h. **71.50**

Dog, Spaniel in seated position, white w/brown muzzle, 10" h. **440.00**

Dogs, Poodle, standing on rectangular base & holding a basket in its mouth, "coleslaw" trim on shoulders & head, white w/polychrome & gilt trim, 3⅜" h., pr. (crazing) **198.00**

Dogs, Spaniel in seated position, white w/painted faces & gold lustre accents, 19th c., 12⅜" h., pr. (hairlines) **431.00**

Dogs, Spaniel in seated position, molded & painted collar & long chain looped from neck to back, white w/polychrome & gilt, 12¾" h., facing pr. (wear, crazed finish, stains, height varies slightly) **440.00**

Equestrian groups, a Scottish Highlander on a white prancing steed, colored trim only on the faces & details, flesh-colored face w/black trim & hair, faint gold highlights, 19th c., 14½" h., facing pair (glaze rubs, short hairline in one horse's neck) ...**385.00**

Figure of a girl holding a basket, mottled yellow & brown glaze, early 19th c., 4⅜" h. **115.00**

Figure of "The Archeress," a standing lady wearing a hat & a striped dress & holding a bow, a leafy tree behind her, on a mound atop a square base, brightly decorated in yellow, green, pink & blue, 19th c., 8¼" h. **176.00**

Figure of Diana, a classical lady standing holding a bow & reaching for a quiver of arrows on her back, her long pale yellow robe trimmed in blue & orange floral sprigs, on a square foot, possibly by Ralph Wood the Younger, ca. 1780-90, 11¾" h. (restoration to base & her arm) **275.00**

Figure of a girl standing holding a

basket of fish, crudely modeled, polychrome decoration, 19th c., 4" h. **214.50**

Figure of a lady, pearlware, a standing figure wearing a long classical gown, a yellow & purple jeweled band in her light brown hair, her light green gown w/purple floral sprigs & dots & lined in pink w/an orange sash at her waist, bare-footed on a green mound above a square base, ca. 1800, 10½" h. (small areas of restoration, few minor chips on edges of base) **220.00**

Figure of a lady titled "Old Age," standing wearing a bonnet & cape, leaning on a cane & carrying a basket of flowers, polychrome decoration, early 19th c., 7" h. (restoration to cane, tiny chip on base) **192.50**

Figure of a man seated on a cabriole-legged chair playing a flute, wearing jacket, waistcoat & kneebreeches, his music in his lap & the instrument case under the chair, polychrome decoration, octagonal base, 19th c., 5" h. (minor restoration to flute, tiny chips) **176.00**

Figure of a young girl seated on a tree stump reading a book, raised on a footed rectangular platform base titled "The Villec Made" (The Village Maid?), polychrome decoration, Obadiah Sherratt, early 19th c., 10¾" h. (bocage missing, feet & head reattached, small chip on stump) **852.50**

Figure of a young woman seated on a tree stump reading a book, early 19th c., 10⅜" h. (glaze chips) **402.50**

Figure group, a circus group w/a standing bear trainer & his bear on a leash to the left & an organ grinder standing to the right, all before a small spread-branched tree, decorated in green, red, light blue, grey, black, dark blue, purple, yellow & orange, ca. 1800, 6½" h. (restoration to tree & scroll-molded oval base) **1,650.00**

Figure group, a courting couple, standing side by side w/a small dog reclining at their feet, she holds an umbrella, he holds a basket, polychrome decoration, ca. 1810, 6½" h. (restoration to his coat & hat, her hat, face & neck, small chips on base, few enamel chips) **440.00**

Figure group, a king wearing a long robe seated before an arched & draped canopy, a small child standing to either side, on an oblong base, white trimmed w/black, gold, orange & blue, some "coleslaw" trim, 12¾" h. (few tiny enamel flakes) **412.50**

Figure group, "Highland Mary and Bobby Burns," a Scottish man & lady in costume seated atop a round molded clock dial framed by a leafy wreath, on an oblong base, trimmed in green, blue, pink, orange & gold, 19th c., 14½" h. (short hairline on base, flake on tip of her nose) **165.00**

Figure group, a lady & gentleman gardener stand in front of a large flowering tree, she holds a watering can, her skirt filled w/flowers, he stands on the other side of a small central stream, polychrome decoration, oval rockwork base, possibly by Ralph Salt, ca. 1830, 6½" h. (small chips off the bocage, tip of watering can broken, few touched up areas on bocage) **715.00**

Figure group, a man riding a large goat, armed w/two pistols & a knife, carrying a basket w/two sheep on his back, holding on to the goat's horns, the standing goat w/a flatiron in its mouth, polychrome decoration, possibly Scotland or Europe, early, 8" h. (chips to applied flowers, barrel of one pistol & one of the ram's ears missing) **412.50**

Figure group, "Returning from Egypt," Joseph leading the donkey carrying Mary & Jesus, a leafy tree behind them, on an oval base painted w/the title & trimmed w/"cole slaw," polychrome decoration, ca. 1820, 7¼" h. (restoration to donkey's rope & ears, Joseph's hand, Jesus' feet, small chips in bocage, several enamel chips) **990.00**

Figure group, "Romulus & Remus," a large wolf recumbent before a bocage, two small naked boys at the side of the wolf, wave-like molded scrolls on the rectangular base, polychrome decoration, ca. 1790-1815, probably Obadiah Sherratt, 7¼" l, 6½" h. (two reglued breaks, several small chips in bocage, two partially restored base chips, restoration to child's feet) **1,540.00**

Figure group, "Prince & Princess," a young boy wearing a large feathered hat & seated astride a pony pulling a two-wheeled cart w/a young girl also wearing a large feathered hat, on an oval base, decorated in orange, black, blue, red, green & gold, 7½" h. (wheel of carriage broken, Prince broken & reglued) **385.00**

Figure group, a Scottish lass wearing a feathered hat & a flounced skirt stands beside an oversized sheep w/sanded coat, polychrome detailing, 8" h. (stains, chips on base) **385.00**

Figure group, "Tam O'Shanter & Sooter Johnny," two men sitting on either side of a barrel, inscribed on front base "Tam O'Shanter & Sooter Johnny," all in natural colors & gold trim, 9½" d., 13" h. (ILLUS.) **450.00**

Figure group, "The Tithe Pig," figures of a man holding a small pig, a lady holding a baby & a clergyman, all in 18th c. attire, standing before a large-leafed tree, a small pig at the foot of each person, raised on a scroll-molded mound base, decorated in green, brown, orange, tan, black, blue & red, ca. 1800, 6½" h. (several enamel flakes, restoration to tree & her basket handle) **825.00**

Figure group, The Vicar & Moses, polychrome decoration, early 19th c., 9¾" h. **345.00**

Figure group, pearlware, Venus & Cupid, the partially draped standing goddess holding a comb to her head while a small Cupid stands at her feet reaching upward, a large dolphin behind her, above an ornate shell-cast mound raised on a square footed base titled "Venus," decorated in flesh tones, green, orange, grey, yellow, blue, purple & black, ca. 1800, 10" h. (few enamel flakes & restoration to Cupid's arm) **2,200.00**

Figure group, a young girl seated in a high-backed armchair holding a smiling cat, polychrome decoration, ca. 1830-60, 3⅛" h. (small glaze flakes) **412.50**

Lion, pearlware, the black beast standing w/his front left paw balancing on a ball, on a rectangular waisted base, the top w/a green glaze, attributed to the Wood Family, impressed "32," ca. 1780, 11¼" l. (lower base edges restored, minor edge chips) **1,380.00**

Lion, creamware, the ochre beast standing w/his head to the right, his right front paw balancing on a yellow ball, raised on a rectangular sponged-black base w/a yellow waist, ca. 1810, minor chips to edge of base, small nick on nose, 11⅜" l. (ILLUS. top next page) **1,955.00**

Lions, recumbent animal on oval base, tan w/gilt trim & glass eyes, 12½" l., facing pr. **330.00**

Model of a cottage, a turreted & multi-

Staffordshire Figure of a Lion

roofed building w/applied "cole slaw" trim & framed by a pierced & arched foliage wreath, decorated in light orange, green, orange, gold, black & pink, 19th c., 9½" h. (small chip on back) **275.00**

Ram, pearlware, recumbent animal on an oval mound base, decorated in two shades of green enamel & black horns & hooves, 4¾" h. (repairs) **192.50**

Ram & lamb, pearlware, a large spotted ram standing on a rocky tier w/a small recumbent lamb below, a flowering bocage behind them, decorated in orange, grey, turquoise blue & dark blue, early 19th c., 5½" h. (several chips to bocage, some enamel flakes).......................**467.50**

Staffordshire Figural Spill Vase

Spill vase, figural, pearlware, a bull-baiting scene w/a brown-spotted bull & dog in front of a large three-stump tree, in brown & ochre, early 19th c., professional restoration, 8" h. (ILLUS.) **660.00**

Spill vases, figural, one w/a woman seated petting a dog in front of a tall, wide tree trunk-form vase, the other w/a man reclining asleep, a small dog trying to awaken him w/a matching vase, polychrome

decoration, marked "Walton," ca. 1825-50, 5¾" h., pr. (one of her arms restored, chip on his hat & tree) **770.00**

Spill vases, figural, each realistically modeled & painted as elephants standing before hollow tree trunk vases, oblong base, mid-19th c., 5¾" h., pr. (one crack & w/nick to rim of tree, other w/minor staining & repair) **230.00**

Squirrel, seated dark orange animal w/a large bushy tail, holding a brown nut, fine detailing, 19th c., 3½" h. (several tiny glaze flakes, ear restored) **1,045.00**

Vase, 8½" h., figural, milkmaid seated beside large spotted cow standing in front of vase, polychrome glaze, 8½" h. (wear & hairlines)..................**577.50**

Vase, 10" h., figural, standing shepherd holding his crook, his dog seated beside him, in front of a front tall tree stump vase, white w/polychrome & gilt **192.50**

Vase, 12" h., figural, cow & nursing calf standing in front of a slender low tree trunk vase, on a grassy rectangular base, green, white & red enamel w/polychrome & gilt trim (wear & hairlines in bottom) **396.00**

Vase, 12½" h., figural, a woodsman standing & wearing a short skirted tunic & leaning on his ax beside a tall tree trunk vase, his seated dog on opposite side, decorated w/green, orange, black, pink & brown enamel **176.00**

Vase, 12¾" h., a seated Spaniel dog in front of a tree trunk vase, brown, green, orange & yellow enamel trim, black trim & lustre trim on dog (areas of stain) **275.00**

STAFFORDSHIRE TRANSFER WARES

The process of transfer-printing designs on earthenwares developed in England in the late 18th century and by the mid-19th century most common ceramic wares were decorated in this manner, most often with romantic European or Oriental landscape scenes, animals or flowers. The earliest such wares were printed in dark blue but a little later light blue, pink, purple, red, black, green and brown were used. A majority of these wares were produced at various English potteries right up till the turn of the century but French and other

*European firms also made similar pieces
and all are quite collectible. The best
reference on this area is Petra Williams'
book* Staffordshire Romantic Transfer
Patterns - Cup Plates and Early Victorian
China *(Fountain House, East, 1978). Also
see HISTORICAL & COMMEMORATIVE
WARES and ABC PLATES.*

Basket, oval w/flanged rim & loop end
handles, center pastoral scene
w/horse, cows & sheep, floral
border, embossed latticework
around exterior, dark blue, 13" l.,
3½" h...**$660.00**

Basket & undertray, oval, basket
w/reticulated border & loop end
handles, Mosque and Fishermen
patt., medium blue, Davenport, ca.
1840, undertray 9½" l., basket 11" l.,
4½" h., 2 pcs. (tiny chips & faint
hairline in basket, spot of stain on
undertray) **825.00**

Bowl, 3½" d., Kenilworth Priory patt.,
probably by Minton, ca. 1830,
blue (stained around rim)................**203.50**

Bowl, 15" d., 5" h., Surrey patt.,
border band w/blocks of diamond
lattice & florals w/three oval
reserves w/castle vignettes, light
blue, Hanley......................................**44.00**

Cake plate, low pedestal base,
Asiatic Pheasants patt., blue,
Podmore, Walker & Co., ca. 1850,
10" d., 2½" h. **165.00**

Coffeepot, cov., tapering octagonal
body, Ailanthus patt., light blue, by
Harvey, ca. 1840, 9½" h. (tiny spout
chip, inside rim, base & lid
chips, finial reglued) **247.50**

Coffeepot, cov., decorated w/a bird &
floral design, green, 19th c.,
10½" h..**402.50**

Compote, open, pedestal base, two-
handled, oblong, Canova patt.,
blue **375.00**

Creamer, Antelope patt., Quadruped
series, dark blue, Hall, ca. 1830,
5" h. (few tiny glaze flakes & other
chips) **209.00**

Cup & saucer, handleless,
polychrome, Canella patt.,
E. Challinor **55.00**

Cup & saucer, handleless, Eagle
patt., large eagle flying above
crossed flags over a seascape
w/sailing ships, brown, Hall, ca.
1830 (pinpoint rim flake on
saucer)..**110.00**

Cup & saucer, handleless, Geneva
patt., light blue, Heath, ca. 1840........**88.00**

Cup & saucer, handleless, horse-
drawn sleigh scenes, dark blue,
impressed "Wood," ca. 1830 (minor
pinpoint in cup) **330.00**

Cup & saucer, handleless, Neptune
patt., by Alcock, ca. 1830 (some
stain) **88.00**

Cup & saucer, handleless, Palestine
patt., pink **60.00**

Cup & saucer, handleless, Swans
patt., floral border, dark blue, ca.
1830 (small chip on saucer rim,
restored hairline in cup) **88.00**

Cup plate, Sheep patt., single
recumbent sheep in the center, wide
floral border, dark blue, Stevenson,
3¾" d. (overall stain, hairline at
rim)...**159.50**

Egg stand & egg cups, the circular
low-footed stand printed w/an
overall Oriental landscape w/small
figures, sampans & pagodas w/a
river scene, the top edge & center
pierced w/seven holes supporting
goblet-form egg cups, the low
galleried rim printed w/a Fitzhugh-
type border of patterned panels,
butterflies & floral sprigs, ca. 1810-
15, stand 8⅝" d., seven egg cups
1¾" to 1⅞" h. (various chips &
hairlines) **805.00**

Gravy boat, boat-shaped, oval
reserve w/large clusters of fruit &
bird, flowers border, dark blue, ca.
1830, 4" h. (light overall stain, some
pinpoint rim flakes) **220.00**

Gravy boat, Oriental patt., blue,
Ridgway **95.00**

Knife rests, narrow rectangular form
w/rounded top w/a notched section,
scene of a woman at a water pump,
dark blue, ca. 1840, 4⅜" l., pr.
(tiny base chip on one) **253.00**

Ladle, The Beemaster patt., medium
blue, ca. 1840, 6⅝" l. (tiny glaze
flake on rim) **275.00**

Ladle, round bowl w/a towered
building in a scroll vignette, floral
border, light blue, 4¼" l. (pinpoint
handle flake) **88.00**

Mug, applied leaf handle, scene of
children on teeter-totter, black,
2½" h. (pinpoint flakes & minor
stains) **93.50**

Mug, cylindrical, scene of two men
fighting a man on horseback, castle
in distance, floral border, light blue,
ca. 1830, 3⅛" h. (in-the-making
base separation) **55.00**

Mug, scene entitled "Kilchurn Castle,"
light blue, 4" h. **110.00**

Mug, child's, motto-type, black
transfer-printed scene illustrating
"Dr. Franklin - Poor Richard" maxim
"Constant dropping wears away
stones..." **140.00**

Pepper pot, Bosphorus patt., Robert Jamieson, blue....................................**200.00**

Pitcher, jug-type, miniature, 2⅜" h., the body printed in maroon on the front w/a commemorative inscription "Conflagration CITY OF NEW YORK - 16th of Dec. 1835 - 700 Houses burnt, Amount Property destroyed - 25,000.000 DOLLARS - did not affect Public Credit," the rim w/a brown band border, ca. 1836 (hairlines at rim, handle a composition reconstruction)..........**1,035.00**

Pitcher, jug-type, 6½" h., angled handle, overall large white blossoms w/long pointed & serrated leaves, dark blue, ca. 1830 (faint star crack in base)....................................**440.00**

Pitcher, 6½" h., decorated w/scenes titled "Werter going to shoot himself" & "Charlotte weeping at Werter's tomb," early 19th c. (small rim chips & glaze wear)..............................**460.00**

Pitcher, 7" h., the obverse decorated w/a tavern scene above the verse "From night till morn I take my glass, in hopes to forget my Chloe...," the reverse w/a flutist serenading a lady above the verse "The softest ones his flute can give...," early 19th c. (hairlines)....................................**374.00**

Pitcher, 8" h., footed bulbous body w/flaring rim & wide spout, molded scroll handle, Palestine patt., light blue, Wm. Adams (two tiny internal hairlines)..............................**247.50**

Pitcher, 11½" h., Begonia patt., brown....................................**45.00**

Plate, 3¼" d., Asiatic Birds patt., light blue....................................**33.00**

Plate, 3⅝" d., Kenilworth Priory patt., probably by Minton, blue.........**170.50**

Plate, 5¼" d., center design of a standing ass w/name below, green, embossed floral border, ca. 1850 (glaze rubs at rim)..........................**170.50**

Plate, 5¼" d., creamware, embossed blue feather-edge design, the center w/a dark brown transfer of a maiden in a landscape titled "HOPE," early 19th c. (light stain)..........................**302.50**

Plate, 5¾" d., center scene of hunter & two dogs in a landscape, ribbon-style border, medium blue, ca. 1830 (small chip under rim, tiny flake on outer rim)..............................**143.00**

Plate, 6¼" w., paneled edges, center floral spray w/an American flag & Liberty Cap, floral clusters around the border, light blue trimmed in red & yellow....................................**121.00**

Plate, 6½" d., center scene of a couple at a bridge w/a castle in the distance, medium blue w/pink lustre rim trim, ca. 1840..............................**49.50**

Plate, 6¾" d., Field Sports patt., center scene of a seated hunter & two dogs, flowers border, dark blue, Herculaneum Pottery, ca. 1830 (light overall stain, chip on rim)................**187.00**

Plate, 7" d., Flensburg patt., polychrome decoration in pink, green, yellow & light blue, J. Edwards, ca. 1840........................**38.50**

Plate, 7" w., octagonal, pearlware, embossed blue feather edge design, the center w/a large black transfer-printed Seal of the United States below "Arms of the United States," a banner below reading "May Success Attend Our Agriculture Trade and Manufactures," early 19th c. (faint star crack)....................................**1,045.00**

Plate, 8" d., depicts scene from "Uncle Tom's Cabin," ca. 1860........**265.00**

Plate, 8¼" d., Wild Rose patt., John Heath....................................**70.00**

Plate, 8⅝" d., Otter patt., Quadrupeds series, dark blue, ca. 1830...............**275.00**

Plate, 8¹¹⁄₁₆" d., pearlware, lightly scalloped rim w/a molded gadroon band, the center printed in russet w/a bust portrait of Andrew Jackson inscribed "General Jackson the Hero of New Orleans" against a background of clouds encircled by a pink lustre roundel, the rim w/a pink lustre S-and-dot border, lustre edge band, ca. 1829 (some scratching)....................................**1,035.00**

Plate, 8¾" d., Genevese patt., light blue, Clews....................................**33.00**

Plate, 9" d., Camel patt., dark blue, J & R Riley, ca. 1814-28..................**120.00**

Plate, 9" d., Clyde Scenery patt., pink, ca. 1840....................................**55.00**

Plate, 9¼" d., Canova patt., light blue, T. Mayer, Longport..................**100.00**

Plate, 9¼" d., Canova patt., pink & green....................................**65.00**

Plate, 9½" d., Vignette patt., light blue, Dimmock & Co., ca. 1850.........**33.00**

Plate, 9¹¹⁄₁₆" d., creamware, printed in black w/a central roundel depicting a classical lady allegorical portrait of 'Peace' holding an olive branch & a sixteen-starred & striped shield, running before a Washington memorial obelisk toward an eagle & shield on a shore before a distant ship, the rim w/six striped ovals bordered w/sixteen stars, ca. 1810 (some rim abrasions)....................**1,380.00**

Plate, 9¾" d., Millennium patt., pink, Stevenson, ca. 1830....................**170.50**

Plate, 10" d., The Festoon patt., dark blue, ca. 1850....................................**49.50**

Plate, 10" d., center landscape scene w/deer, floral border, blue (faint hairline, rim flake) **99.00**

Plate, 10" d., the center w/an Oriental river scene framed w/a rose border, blue **195.00**

Plate, 10" d., center reserve w/large clusters of fruit w/a bird, wide flowers & scrolls border, dark blue, ca. 1830 ....**330.00**

Plate, 10" d., Lion patt., Quadrupeds series, dark blue, Hall, ca. 1830 ......**330.00**

Plate, 10¼" d., Palestine patt., pink & green **104.50**

Plate, 10½" d., Cambrian patt., black, Edward Phillips........................**65.00**

Plate, 10½" d., Millennium patt., brown, R. Stevenson & Son.............**110.00**

Plate, 10½" d., Oriental scenery decoration, black, impressed "T. Mayer - Stoke - 9" **65.00**

Plate, 10½" d., Palestine patt., blue **75.00**

Plates, 9" d., Castle Scenery patt., Furnival, ca. 1850, set of 6 ....**198.00**

Plates, 9" d., Venus patt., light blue, Podmore, Walker & Co., set of 3 ....**93.50**

Plates, 9¾" d., Warwick Vase patt., medium blue, E. Wood, set of 7 (one w/tiny rim chip) **159.50**

Plates, 10½" d., Antiques patt., light blue, ca. 1850, pr. **77.00**

Plates, 10¾" d., Bologna patt., brown, Wm. Adams, set of 3..............**77.00**

Albany Restaurant Platter

Platter, 8 x 10½", oval, Venetian Star patt., w/fancy floral border, overall blue pattern on front, printed in blue right in the pattern "The Albany Restaurant - 190 Picadilly" (ILLUS.) **75.00**

Platter, 11" l., oval, "Quadrupeds" patt., a central oval reserve of horses grazing, scroll-framed border reserves w/a horse in each, dark blue, John Hall, second quarter 19th c. **862.50**

Platter, 13¼" l., octagonal, Ontario Lake Scenery patt., light blue, Heat, ca. 1850 (light stain) **115.50**

Platter, 13½" l., octagonal, Priory patt., light blue, J. & G. Meakin, ca. 1850s (four tiny rim chips) **93.50**

Platter, 14½" l., oval, Venetian Scenery patt., light blue, E. Wood (overall stain, small glaze flake at rim)..**143.00**

Platter, 15" l., oval, floral decoration, blue, 19th c. (imperfections) **345.00**

Platter, 15¾" l., octagonal, Baronial Halls patt., light blue, Mayer, ca. 1850 (two face scratches, small border chip)..**99.00**

Platter, 16½" l., oval, lightly scalloped rim, the center w/an oval reserve w/an Oriental landscape w/temple & tower, a wide floral border, dark blue, Ralph Clews, second quarter 19th c. (minor rim chips) **517.50**

Platter, 16¾" l., oval, large center scene of a polar bear hunt w/a sailing ship in the distance, ornate scrolls & flowers border, marked "Enoch Wood & Sons Burslem," dark blue, second quarter 19th c. (imperfections) **862.50**

Platter, 20½" l., oval, Hospitality patt., landscape scene w/lady & children w/elderly man, cottage in background, dark blue, ca. 1830 (several deep scratches, light overall stain & edge wear)..............................**605.00**

Sauce dish, Lozere patt., blue, Challinor..**50.00**

Sauce tureen, cov., squatty bulbous body on pedestal foot, flared rim supporting domed cover w/large knop, loop end handles, Quadrupeds patt., vignette of dog on one side, rabbit on the other, dark blue, Hall, ca. 1830, 6½" h. (light interior stain, short hairline & two repaired chips on foot, small chip under cover) **550.00**

Sauce tureen undertray, oblong, Chinoiserie High Bridge patt., medium blue, Davenport, ca. 1830, 8⅛" l. (light overall stain, tiny glaze flakes, chip on foot rim).....................**99.00**

Soap dish, cover & liner, Cleopatra patt., purple polychrome, 3 pcs........**150.00**

Soup plate w/flanged rim, Caladonia patt., red, Adams, 10½" d. **89.00**

Soup plate, Italian patt., medium blue, John Mare, 10" d.....................**44.00**

Soup plate, Shells patt., large cluster of shells in the center, shells border, dark blue, Stubbs, ca. 1830 ....**357.50**

Soup plate, Palestine patt., purple, 10½" d...**75.00**

Soup tureen, cover, ladle & undertray, Lucano patt., squatty round body raised on a pedestal foot, loop end handles, stepped domed cover w/loop handles, dark blue, Clews, 13¼" d., 11" h., the set **990.00**

Soup tureen, cov., Polish Views patt., blue **495.00**

Soup tureen undertray w/open twig end handles, oval, large seashell center reserve, bold florals & scrolls border, dark blue, Stubbs, 15" l. (restored hairline, one handle replaced) **720.50**

Sugar bowl, cov., toy-size, squatty oval body w/slightly domed cover w/knob finial, Salopian ware, black transfer-printed pastoral landscape w/a man playing a musical instrument & a lady w/a bucket on her head, decorated in green, blue, yellow & pink polychrome, ca. 1810, 3" h. (unseen hairline in cover) **330.00**

Sugar bowl, cov., footed octagonal form, Rhone Scenery patt., light blue, Mayer, 7⅛" h. (few areas of light stain) **148.50**

Sugar bowl, cov., footed squatty paneled shape, Panama patt., light blue, 7½" h. (stain in base, hairline in foot) **159.50**

Teapot, cov., boat-shaped w/high flanged rim, angled handle & swan's-neck spout, continuous rural landscape w/ruins, dark blue, Wood, marked "Stone China," ca. 1830, 6" h. (tiny chip on cover, large chip on inner base rim, small spout chip) **302.50**

Teapot, cov., oval boat-shaped body w/rolled rim, C-scroll handle & thick swan's-neck spout, landscape scene w/sheep shearer kneeling beside a sheep, medium blue, ca. 1820, 6" h. (professional restoration to cover & base).............................**330.00**

Toddy plate, "Moral Maxims," purple, 5⅞" d. (edge flakes & minor stains) **71.50**

Tureen, cov., oblong body w/wide flanged rim, stepped domed cover w/a large acanthus & fruit finial, decorated w/an arbored surround opening to a Romantic architectural landscape, dark blue, ca. 1830, 9 x 12", 6" h......................................**345.00**

Undertray, octagonal w/molded scroll handles, Medina patt., blue, 8¼" w. (some stain, chip on back rim) **33.00**

Vegetable dish, cov., square w/cut corners, domed cover, Lechlade

Bridge patt., probably by Minton, ca. 1840, blue, 3⅞" w., 3" h. **247.50**

Staffordshire Pearlware Veilleuse

Veilleuse (night light), pearlware, cylindrical body printed in medium underglaze-blue on the front & reverse w/floral & foliate sprigs issuing from a cluster of crystals interrupted on the front by a pattern of piercing above the spirit burner aperture, the rims & loop handles w/dotted-cross & foliate-scroll borders repeated on the compressed spherical spirit burner & cover within, the deep hot water bowl & spouted broth bowl above, marked "CRYSTAL" above a beehive & "FLORENTINE CHINA" & the numeral "7" printed in underglaze-blue, ca. 1830, water bowl cracked & both bowls discolored, hair cracked, chipped & cover missing, 8¼" h., 4 pcs. (ILLUS.) **374.00**

Wash pitcher, paneled sides, footed squatty bulbous body w/a tall neck & high, wide arched spout & angled handle, Marino patt., green, Phillips, ca. 1850, 11½" h. **192.50**

Waste bowl, Geneva patt., light blue, Heath, ca. 1840, 5¼" d., 3½" h. (light staining, faint base star crack) **49.50**

STANGL POTTERY

Johann Martin Stangl, who first came to work for the Fulper Pottery in 1910 as a ceramic chemist and plant superintendent, acquired a financial interest and became president of the company in 1926. The name of the firm was changed to Stangl Pottery in 1929 and at that time much of

the production was devoted to a high grade dinnerware to enable the company to survive the Depression years. One of the earliest solid-color dinnerware patterns was their Colonial line, introduced in 1926. In the 1930s it was joined by their Americana pattern. After 1942 these early patterns were followed by a wide range of hand-decorated patterns featuring flowers and fruits with a few decorated with animals or human figures.

Around 1940 a very limited edition of porcelain birds, patterned after the illustrations in John James Audubon's "Birds of America," was issued. Stangl subsequently began production of less expensive ceramic birds and these proved to be popular during the war years, 1940-46. Each bird was handpainted and each was well marked with impressed, painted or stamped numerals which indicated the species and the size.

All operations ceased at the Trenton, New Jersey plant in 1978.

Two reference books which collectors will find helpful are The Collectors Handbook of Stangl Pottery by Norma Rehl (The Democrat Press, 1979), and Stangl Pottery by Harvey Duke (Wallace-Homestead, 1994).

BIRDS

Audubon Warbler, No. 3755-S,
4¼" h.....................................**$350.00**
Bird of Paradise, No. 3408, 5½" h. **97.50**
Black-Throated Warbler, No. 3814 ....**85.00**
Bluebird, No. 3276, 5" h.........**85.00 to 95.00**
Bluebird (Double), No. 3276-D,
8½" h. **161.50**
Blue-Headed Vireo, No. 3448,
4¼" h. ....**60.00 to 70.00**
Blue Jay, No. 3715, 10¼" **587.50**
Blue Jay, No. 3716, 10¼" h. **575.00**
Canary facing right, rose flower,
No. 3746, 6¼" h. **265.00**
Cerulean Warbler, No. 3456,
4¼" h. **70.00**
Chestnut-Sided Warbler, No. 3812,
4" h. **85.00**
Cockatoo, No. 3405-S, 6" h...........**55.00**
Cockatoo, No. 3484, 11⅜".........**265.00**
Cockatoo, medium, No. 35808,
8⅞" h. **132.50**
Cockatoo, No. 3584, 15" h. **200.00**
Cock Pheasant, No. 3492, 6¼" x
11"...**142.50**

Drinking Duck, No. 3250-E, 3¾" h......**35.00**
European Finch, No. 3722...............**650.00**
Feeding Duck, No. 3250C, 1¾" h........**70.00**
Flying Duck, No. 3443, green, 9" h. ..**285.00**
Golden Crowned Kinglet, No. 3848,
4" h...**85.00**
Grey Cardinal, No. 3596, 4¾" h. **73.00**
Grosbeak, No. 3813 ....**95.00 to 120.00**
Group of Chickadees, No. 3581,
5½ x 8½"................................**190.00**
Group of Goldfinches, No. 3635,
4 x 11½"..................................**195.00**
Hen, No. 3446, 7" h. **145.00**
Hen Pheasant, No. 3491, 6¼ x
11"...**200.00**
Kentucky Warbler, No. 3598, 3" h. **49.00**
Key West Quail Dove, No. 3454,
9" h.......................................**240.00**
Kingfisher, No. 3406, 3½" h. **77.00**
Love Bird, No. 3400, 4" h. **65.00**
Magpie-Jay, No. 3758 ....**770.00**
Nuthatch, No. 3593, 2½" h. **43.00**
Oriole, No. 3402, 3¼" h. **60.00**
Oriole, No. 3402-S, 3¼" h. (beak
down) **125.00**
Painted Bunting, No. 3452, 5" h. **95.00**
Pair of Cockatoos, No. 3405-D,
9½" h......................................**107.50**
Pair of Hummingbirds, No. 3599-D,
8 x 10½".................................**300.00**
Pair of Kingfishers, No. 3406-D,
5" h..**139.00**
Pair of Orioles, No. 3402-D,
5½" h......................................**112.00**
Pair of Parakeets, No. 3582, 7" h. **181.00**
Pair of Redstarts, No. 3490-D,
9" h..**182.00**
Pair of Wrens, No. 3401-D, 8" h........**120.00**
Parula Warbler, No. 3583, 4¼" h. **48.00**
Penguin, No. 3274, 5½" h **550.00**
Preening Duck, No. 3250-B, 2¼" h. **37.50**
Red-Headed Woodpecker,
No. 3751-S, 6¼" h. **20.00**
Red-Headed Woodpecker (Double),
No. 3752-D, 7¾" h......................**475.00**
Rooster, grey, No. 3445, 9" h. **175.00**
Running Duck, No. 3432, 5" h. **425.00**
Scarlet Tanager (Double),
No. 3750-D, 8" h. **65.00**
Standing Duck, No. 3431, 8" h..........**110.00**
Summer Tanager, No. 3868, 4" h. **450.00**
Titmouse, No. 3592, 2½" h. **57.00**
Turkey, No. 3275, 3½" h. **550.00**
Wilson Warbler, No. 3597, 3½" h........**50.00**
Wren, No. 3401, 3½" h. **60.00**
Wren, No. 3401-S, 3½" h. **200.00**
Yellow Warbler, No. 3447, 5" h. **80.00**
Yellow Warbler, No. 3850 ....**82.00**

DINNERWARES & ARTWARES
Ashtray, Golfer patt., Sportsmen's
Giftware Line, No. 3926 ....**95.00**
Ashtray, Tulip patt. **16.00**

Ashtray, oval, Canadian Goose patt., Sportsmen's Giftware line, No. 3926, 10⅝" l. **22.00**

Ashtray, oval, Mallard Duck patt., Sportsmen's Giftware line, No. 3926, 10⅝" l. **22.00**

Ashtray, oval, Pheasant patt., Sportsmen's Giftware line, No. 3926, 10⅝" l. **22.00**

Ashtray, oval, Wood Duck patt., Sportsmen's Giftware line, No. 3926, 10⅝" l. **42.00**

Ashtray, pheasant decoration, No. 39280 ....**55.00**

Bank, model of a pig, h.p. tulips............**80.00**

Bowl, cereal, 5½" d., Fruit & Flowers patt. **15.00**

Bowl, soup, 5½" d., w/lug handles, Blueberry patt. **15.00**

Bowl, soup, 5½" d., w/lug handles, Orchard Song patt. **12.00**

Bowl, soup or cereal, 5¾" d., Town & Country patt., green, 15 oz. **17.50**

Bowl, soup or cereal, 5¾" d., Town & Country patt., yellow, 15 oz. **15.00**

Bowl, 8" d., Country Garden patt. **25.00**

Bowl, pear-shaped, 8" l., Town & Country patt., yellow & white **35.00**

Bowl, salad, 10" d., Fruit & Flowers patt. **50.00**

Bowl, salad, 10" d., Country Life patt., pig at fence decoration **175.00**

Bowl, salad, 12" d., Golden Harvest patt. ....**35.00 to 40.00**

Bowl, berry, Orchard Song patt. **6.00**

Bowl, soup, flat, Orchard Song patt. **7.00**

Bowl, Pony Trail patt., Kiddieware line **125.00**

Bread tray, Orchard Song patt. **25.00**

Butter dish, cov., Maize-Ware............**18.00**

Butter dish, cov., Orchard Song patt.....**3.00**

Candle warmer, No. 3412, terra cotta **10.00**

Casserole w/handle, Fruit & Flowers patt., 8" d. **40.00**

Cigarette box, cov., w/two ashtrays, rosebud decoration, the set **70.00**

Coffeepot, cov., Apple Delight patt......**35.00**

Coffeepot, cov., Town & Country patt. **130.00**

Coffee warmer, Golden Harvest patt...**12.00**

Creamer, Cherry patt. **6.00**

Creamer, Country Life patt.....................**80.00**

Creamer, Fruit & Flowers patt. **10.00**

Creamer & cov. sugar bowl, Orchard Song patt., pr. **12.00**

Cup, ABC, Kiddieware line...................**60.00**

Cup, Country Life patt., pig decoration **100.00**

Cup, Humpty Dumpty patt., green, Kiddieware line **125.00**

Cup, Little Bo Peep patt., Kiddieware line **65.00**

Cup, Little Boy Blue patt., Kiddieware line **80.00**

Cup, Little Quackers patt., Kiddieware line **72.50**

Cup, Our Barnyard Friends patt., Kiddieware line **60.00**

Cup, Peter Rabbit patt., Kiddieware line **135.00**

Cup & saucer, Amber Glo patt. **7.00**

Cup & saucer, Dahlia patt. **4.50**

Cup & saucer, Fruit & Flowers patt. **12.00**

Cup & saucer, Garland patt.................**14.00**

Cup & saucer, Golden Harvest patt. ...**11.00**

Cup & saucer, Holly patt. **40.00**

Cup & saucer, Orchard Song **8.00**

Cup & saucer, White Dogwood patt. ...**17.00**

Dessert mold, ribbed, Town & Country patt., green, 7½" d...............**45.00**

Deviled egg tray, Rooster patt. **100.00**

Dish, divided, Kitten Capers patt., Kiddieware line **70.00**

Egg cup, Cherry patt............................**12.00**

Egg cup, double, Thistle patt. **12.00**

Gravy boat, Fruit & Flowers patt.........**20.00**

Gravy boat & undertray, Blue Daisy patt., 2 pcs. **16.50**

Model of a buffalo, bronze & gold **350.00**

Model of a duck, gold...........................**50.00**

Mug, low, Holly patt. **35.00**

Mug, Holly patt., 2 cup size **45.00**

Lamp base, bird decoration, No. 3452 ....**175.00**

Oyster plate, turkey decoration, white glaze, artist-signed **175.00**

Pitcher, Colonial patt., No. 1388, white **50.00**

Pitcher, Country Garden patt., 1 qt. **42.00**

Pitcher, Provincial patt. **25.00**

Planter, Terra Rose line, model of a stallion head, No. 3611, 13" h..........**495.00**

Plate, 6" d., Amber Glo............................**4.00**

Plate, 6" d., Blueberry patt. **7.00**

Plate, 6" d., Colonial patt., yellow...........**1.50**

Plate, 6" d., Fruit & Flowers patt............**3.00**

Plate, 6" d., Golden Harvest patt...........**6.00**

Plate, 6" d., Orchard Song patt. **5.00**

Plate, 6" d., Starflower patt....................**2.00**

Plate, 6" d., Town & Country patt., brown & white **6.00**

Plate, 6" d., Town & Country patt., yellow & white **6.00**

Plate, 8" d., Country Life patt., pig decoration **100.00**

Plate, 8" d., Fruit & Flowers patt............**7.00**

Plate, 8" d., Garland patt. **10.00**

Plate, 8" d., Holly patt. **35.00**

Plate, 8" d., White Dogwood patt. **10.00**

Plate, dinner, 9" d., Fruit & Flowers patt. **12.00**

Plate, 9" d., Humpty Dumpty patt., green, Kiddieware line **165.00**

Plate, 9" d., Little Bo Peep patt., Kiddieware line **125.00**

Plate, 9" d., Little Boy Blue patt.,
Kiddieware line **135.00**
Plate, 9" d., Little Quackers patt.,
Kiddieware line **112.50**
Plate, 9" d., Peter Rabbit patt.,
Kiddieware line **185.00**
Plate, 9" d., Peter Rabbit patt.,
Kiddieware line, Lunning marking....**200.00**
Plate, 10" d., Amber Glo.......................**10.00**
Plate, 10" d., Blue Daisy patt..................**8.00**
Plate, 10" d., Golden Harvest patt........**12.00**
Plate, 10" d., Magnolia patt. **12.00**
Plate, 10" d., Town & Country patt. **45.00**
Plate, 10" d., White Dogwood patt. **15.00**
Plate, 11" d., Canadian Goose, patt.,
bronze & gold, Sportsmen's
Giftware line, No. 3774 ....**45.00**
Plate, chop, 12½" d., Amber Glo
patt...**20.00**
Plate, chop, 12½" d., Country Life
patt., farmhouse decoration **225.00**
Plate, chop, 12½" d., Fruit &
Flowers patt. **27.50**
Plate, chop, 12½" d., Holly patt. **75.00**
Plate, chop, 12½" d., Orchard Song
patt...**25.00**
Plate, chop, 12½" d., Town &
Country patt. **65.00**
Plate, chop, 14½" d., Country Life
patt., barn w/farm name
decoration **300.00**
Plate, chop, 14½" d., Thistle patt. **24.00**
Plate, chop, 14½" d., Tulip patt. **30.00**
Plate, three compartments, oval,
Kitten Capers patt., Kiddieware
line **125.00**
Plate & cup, Ducky Dinner,
Kiddieware line, 2 pcs. **80.00**
Plates, 8" d., Fruit patt., set of 6...........**56.00**
Platter, oval, 14¾" l., White
Dogwood patt....................................**35.00**
Relish dish, Bittersweet patt...............**24.00**
Relish, Country Garden patt. **30.00**
Relish tray, Orchard Song, patt..........**18.00**
Relish tray, Wild Rose patt..................**18.00**
Salt & pepper shakers, Country
Garden patt., pr..................................**12.00**
Salt & pepper shakers, Orchard
Song patt., pr......................................**8.00**
Server, center handle, Antique Gold
patt., Giftware Line, 22 carat gold
over satin green glaze, 10" d. **15.00**
Server, center-handled,
Country Garden patt. **12.00**
Server, center-handled, Orchard
Song patt. **14.00**
Server, center-handled, Sgraffito
patt...**12.00**
Shaving mug, Town & Country patt. ...**18.00**
Spoon rest, Town 'n Country patt........**50.00**
Stoby mug w/ashtray lid, Parson,
6½" h., No. 1675................................**145.00**
Sugar bowl, cov., Country Life patt. ..**125.00**
Teapot, cov., Americana (No. 2000)

patt., decorated w/h.p. field daisies
on blue background **75.00**
Teapot, cov., Star Flower patt.,
8¾" h..**45.00**
Tumbler, Town & Country patt., 9 oz...**18.00**
Vase, 7" h., three-handled, Rainbow
Ware, brown w/yellow rim, green &
yellow interior, impressed mark **125.00**
Vase, 9½" h., decorated w/leaping
fish, No. 3618....................................**125.00**
Vegetable bowl, open, divided,
Country Garden patt. **18.00**
Vegetable bowl, open, divided,
Golden Harvest patt...........................**35.00**
Vegetable bowl, open, Country Life
patt., 8" d...**125.00**
Vegetable bowl, open, Fruit &
Flowers patt., 8" d. **25.00**
Vegetable bowl, open, Holly patt.,
8" d...**75.00**
Vegetable bowl, open, Magnolia
patt., 8" d..**23.00**
Vegetable bowl, open, divided,
Orchard Song patt. **15.00**
Wig stand, stylized lady's head,
blonde hair **260.00**
Wig stand, stylized lady's head,
brown hair, No. 5168, w/wooden
base, 15" h. **300.00**

STONEWARE

New York Churn

*Stoneware is essentially a vitreous
pottery, impervious to water even in its
unglazed state, that has been produced by
potteries all over the world for centuries.
Utilitarian wares such as crocks, jugs,
churns and the like, were the most common
productions in the numerous potteries that
sprang into existence in the United States
during the 19th century. These items were
often enhanced by the application of a
cobalt blue oxide decoration. In addition to
the coarse, primarily salt-glazed*

stonewares, there are other categories of stoneware known by such special names as basalt, jasper and others.

Butter churn w/cover & wooden dasher, semi-ovoid body w/eared handles, slip-quilled cobalt blue "6" above a 'bull's-eye' squiggle, ca. 1850-70, 6 gal., 17" h. (two minor chips on handles) **$187.00**

Butter churn, slightly tapering cylindrical form, the front decorated w/brushed cobalt blue bunch of grapes w/leaves & tendrils, impressed maker's name, A. K. Ballard, Burlington, Vermont, ca. 1860, 17" h., (hairline crack to rim & minor flakes) **345.00**

Butter crock, slightly waisted cylinder w/molded rim, cobalt blue stenciled label "A. Conrad, New Geneva, Pa.," 9" d., 6" h. (hairlines) **181.50**

Butter crock, blue band design, 9¼" h...**78.00**

Churn, ovoid body w/eared handles, cobalt decorated w/stylized bird & flowers & leaves, impressed "White & Wood, Binghamton, New York," 1883-87, 5 gal., 17½" (ILLUS.) **4,600.00**

Crock, cov., cylindrical w/eared handles, flat cover w/button finial, brushed cobalt blue curved leaf sprigs around the rim, impressed "R.C.R. Phila.," 19th c., 8" d., 8" h. (chips) **495.00**

Crock, cylindrical w/molded rim & eared handles, cobalt blue stenciled label below a squiggled free-hand top band, marked "Hamilton & Jones, Greensboro, Pa. 2," 2 gal. 10" d., 8" h. **330.00**

Crock, straight-sided w/eared handles, decorated w/a brushed cobalt blue squatting quail, impressed "N. Clark Jr., Athens, NY, 2," ca. 1860, 2 gal., 9" h...**690.00**

Crock, straight sided w/eared handles & heavy rim, cobalt blue slip-quilled floral decoration & impressed label "J. Burger, Rochester, N.Y.," ca. 1860, 3 gal., 9½" h. **316.00**

Crock, cylindrical w/applied eared handles, cobalt blue slip-quilled stylized floral decoration, impressed label "O. Whittemore, Havana, N.Y. 3," 3 gal., 10" h. (hairlines) **203.50**

Crock, very wide ovoid body w/molded rim & eared handles, large slip-quilled bird looking back over its shoulder, impressed circular mark "N. Clark, Lyons, N.Y.," 1822-55, 10½" h. (minor stains, small flakes & short hairlines) **1,155.00**

Crock, cylindrical w/heavy molded rim & eared handles, cobalt blue slip-quilled foliate decoration & impressed label "West Troy N.Y. Pottery 3," 3 gal., 10¾" h. **247.50**

Crock, straight-sided w/eared handles, the front decorated w/a brushed cobalt blue paddle-tailed bird perched on a branch, impressed "N.A. White & Son, Utica, NY, 4," ca. 1880, 4 gal., 11" h. **460.00**

Crock, slightly tapering cylindrical body w/eared handles, slip-quilled cobalt blue crude stylized thistle blossoms & leaves, ca. 1860-80, 3 gal., 12" h. **88.00**

Pottery Works Crock

Crock, cylindrical body w/eared handles, the front decorated w/a soldier wearing a hat w/plume dressed in full regalia, playing a drum, a similarly dressed standing figure opposite playing a recorder, a key of victual w/two mugs in the foreground, the impressed inscription "W. A. MacQuoid & CO. POTTERY WORKS, Little Wst 12th ST,., NY. 6," 1873-79, rim w/two hairline cracks & some minor flakes, 13" (ILLUS.) **13,800.00**

Crock, semi-ovoid w/eared handles, brushed cobalt blue decoration of three scattered tulip-like flowers & two feathered leaves below a large "3," ca. 1850-70, 3 gal., 14" h. **385.00**

Crock, elephant ear leaves, 5 gal., Union Stoneware **225.00**

Jar, ovoid w/applied ear handles, cobalt blue slip-quilled stylized floral & foliate decoration & cobalt blue stenciled label "A. Conrad, New Geneva, Pa.," 8¼" h. (hairlines in base) **330.00**

Jar, slightly ovoid w/molded rim, cobalt blue stenciled marking "Weyman & Bros. - Pittsburgh, PA," late 19th c., 2 gal., 9¼" h.................................**165.00**

Jar, slightly ovoid w/molded rim, cobalt blue stenciled marking "Hamilton & Jones - Greensboro - PA," late 19th c., 2 gal., 10¼" h. **165.00**

Jar, cylindrical w/rounded shoulder & rolled rim, applied eared handles, cobalt blue slip-quilled polka dot floral design & impressed label, "C.L. & A.K. Ballard, Burlington, Vt. 2," 2 gal., 10½" h. **275.00**

Jar, applied shoulder handles, slip-quilled cobalt blue stylized floral decoration, impressed label "New York Stoneware Co. 2," 2 gal., 11" h. (small flakes) **99.00**

Jar, cobalt blue stenciled label "Jas Hamilton & Co. Greensboro, Pa. 2," 2 gal., 11¾" h. **165.00**

Jar, ovoid w/applied shoulder handles, decorated w/a brushed cobalt blue flower, 12¾" h. (hairline, small rim chips) **242.00**

Jar, cylindrical w/eared handles & heavy rimmed neck, brushed stripes w/vining garlands of stylized foliage between, impressed label, "Pough-ner, Greensboro, Pa. 4," 4 gal., 15" h. (professional repair).............**1,430.00**

Jar, cylindrical w/applied eared handles, tooled lines at shoulder & heavily molded rim, cobalt blue brushed fern-like leaves above stenciled label "C.L. Williams and Company, Best Blue Stoneware, New Geneva, Pa. 10," 10 gal., 20¾" h. (very minor edge chips) **1,100.00**

Jug, miniature, ovoid, slip-quilled cobalt blue decoration, late 19th c., 3" h. **1,725.00**

Cobalt Decorated Jug

Jug, miniature, bulbous ovoid body tapering to a short thin cylindrical neck, decorated w/incised cobalt blue stylized bird & branch w/leaves, impressed "S.D.R.," 19th century, America, 4½" h. **6,325.00**

Jug, applied strap handle, cylindrical w/rounded shoulder, cobalt blue

stenciled label "C. B. Somerville & Co. Staunton, VA.," 11" h. **275.00**

19th Century Stoneware Jug

Jug, baluster form w/incised cobalt decorated bird & tree, 19th c., 12" h. (ILLUS.) **1,150.00**

Jug, semi-ovoid, slip-quilled cobalt blue bird on a branch below the incised mark "West Troy Pottery," West Troy, New York, ca. 1870-80, 12" h...**302.50**

Jug, applied strap handle, cobalt blue slip-quilled flourish & im-pressed label "Haxton & Co. Fort Edward N.Y., 2," 2 gal., 13¾" h. **88.00**

Jug, ovoid, brushed cobalt blue stylized tulip blossom & leaf sprig below the impressed label "Cowden & Wilcox - Harrisburg, PA - 22," 1870-81, 2 gal., 14" h. **231.00**

Jug, slightly ovoid, cobalt blue slip-quilled bird on a branch decoration & impressed label "Ottman Bros. & Co. Fort Edward, N.Y. 2," 2 gal., 14" h...**385.00**

Jug, ovoid, small attached handle, cobalt blue slip-quilled flower & foliage & "2," impressed label "Burger & Lang, Rochester, N. Y.," 2 gal., 14⅞" h. **165.00**

Jug, ovoid w/wide flat bottom, slip-quilled cobalt blue pair of birds w/a scrolling flourish below a "3," impressed mark "S. Hart, Fulton," Fulton, New York, 1840-76, 3 gal., 14" h...**825.00**

Jug, semi-ovoid, applied strap handle, slip-quilled cobalt blue bird on branch, impressed "3" on shoulder, 3 gal., 15⅝" h. (minor hairlines) **440.00**

Jug, baluster form body w/reeded neck & strap handle above a molded circular base, the body centering an incised & cobalt blue decorated

New York Stoneware Jug

figure of a woman looking backwards between through her legs, her arms extended & a pair of eyes incised into her posterior, probably New York, 1810-1815, 17" h. (ILLUS.) **10,350.00**

Jug, ovoid, slip-quilled cobalt blue stylized flower, ca. 1820-40, 1 gal., 20" h..**176.00**

Model of a dog, seated Spaniel, molded fur & facial details w/closed front legs, white glaze w/overall blue dots & facial details & neck collar & chain, attributed to Williams Pottery, Texas, 9⅛" h. (minor base chips) **880.00**

Models of dogs, spaniels, each seated w/an incised collar & leash, brown metallic glaze, one initialed "M E P" on the head, probably Ohio, 19th c., 7⅛" h., pr. (minor flakes on base) **403.00**

Mug, miniature, ovoid w/molded rim & applied strap handle, splotch of cobalt blue on the front shoulder, 4¾" h. (surface flakes) **335.50**

Pitcher, 7½" h., bulbous ovoid body tapering to a slightly flared rim w/pinched spout, applied ribbed strap handle, bold brushed cobalt blue upright floral sprig on front & long 'comma' devices around the neck **1,017.50**

Pitcher, 7½" h., very ovoid body tapering to a flared rim, short tubular spout, small strap handle, band of triangular tooled designs around the shoulder high-lighted in cobalt blue (edge chips)................**2,145.00**

Pitcher, 7¾" h., ovoid w/flaring rim & pinched spout, tan w/brushed floral design in brown Albany slip, attributed to New Geneva, Pennsylvania **522.50**

Pitcher, 8½" h., brushed cobalt blue

doe & fawn, orange peel texture..**175.00**

Pitcher, 11¼" h., bulbous ovoid body tapering to a flat rim w/pinched spout, applied strap handle, bold brushed cobalt blue vertical feather leaves up the front & band of large horizontal forked leaves around the neck, Albany slip interior **770.00**

Pitcher, 11¼" h., bulbous ovoid body tapering to a cylindrical neck w/pinched spout, applied strap handle, slip-quilled cobalt blue finely done floral sprig w/scrolls on front, Albany slip interior, impressed "1" **715.00**

Pitcher, blue w/relief-molded ducks & geese on sides....................................**99.00**

Pitcher, cobalt apricot decoration **140.00**

Stoneware Planter

Planter, underplate, bulbous ovoid body decorated w/incised & cobalt blue Masonic & patriotic symbols, birds, fish & a gentleman w/top hat, probably Pennsylvania/Ohio, 19th c., cracks, 10½" h. (ILLUS.) **13,800.00**

Preserving jar, cylindrical w/knob handles near rim, incised decoration highlighted in cobalt blue, designs include two stags, stars & one almond-shaped reserve w/"H.L.," & another on the reverse w/"1844," 6" h. (hairlines, chips) **715.00**

Preserving jar, cylindrical w/applied eared handles & heavily molded neck, cobalt blue stenciled label "Wm. R. Beall & Co. Groceries, Cumberland, Md.," 8¼" h. **170.50**

Preserving jar, slightly tapering cylindrical body w/molded rim, stenciled cobalt blue label w/a central pear framed by "Palantine Pottery Co. - Palantine, Va.," late 19th c., 8½" h. (ILLUS. top next page)..**165.00**

Preserving jar, cylindrical, cobalt blue stenciled label "Excelsior Works,

Palantine Preserving Jar

Isaac Hewitt, Jr. Rices Landing, Pa.,"
8¾" h. (minor flakes) **357.50**
Preserving jar, cylindrical w/rolled rim,
cobalt blue slip-quilled single fruit
w/long stem decoration, 9½" h **330.00**
Snuff jar, embossed horse head,
blue & grey, 4¾" d., 4" h., NYS **150.00**
Water cooler, barrel-shaped, decorated w/a cobalt blue slip-quilled
flourish & "5," w/wooden
spigot, 5 gal., 14¼" h. **55.00**

SUMIDA GAWA WARES

*Contrary to some popular stories heard
in the collecting world, these heavy
porcelain wares were not produced in
Korea nor on a mythical island of Poo.
They were Japanese products made in the
Tokyo region where the Sumida River
(gawa = river) flows.*

*It was in the late 1890s that these wares
apparently were first decorated with thick,
often drippy-looking, "flambé" glazes and
applied with small molded figures around
the sides. Earliest wares usually had red,
green or black grounds but later, in the
1920s, orange, brown, blue, and lavender
appeared. These unique and charming
pieces are today highly collectible. For
further information, see Sandra Andacht's
Oriental Antiques & Art, An Identification
and Value Guide (Wallace-Homestead).*

Mug, enamel drip glaze at top
w/applied monkey, 4½" h. **$90.00**
Mug, applied bearded elder seated &
kneeling woman, 5" h......................**375.00**
Mug, applied child about to throw a
ball w/dog watching, 5" h. **225.00**
Mug, relief-molded scene of a man
w/large plant on front, enameled
handle & interior, enamel drip
around border, 5¼" h. **225.00**
Mug, applied wise man at center,
enameled border & handle, black
ground, seal signature, 5½" h. **150.00**
Mug, applied young man walking
w/backpack, 5" h............................**275.00**

TOBY MUGS & JUGS

Staffordshire "Hearty Good Fellow" Mug

*The Toby is a figural jug or mug
usually delineating a robust, genial
drinking man. The name has been used in
England since the mid-18th century.
Copies of the English mugs and jugs were
made in America.*

*For listings of related Character Jugs
see DOULTON & ROYAL DOULTON.*

Bennington Ben Franklin Toby,
seated figure w/pipe & wine goblet,
mottled brown Rockingham glaze,
1849-58, 6⅜" h. **$550.00**
Pratt ware Toby, seated Mr. Toby
holding a jug, wearing a tricorner
hat, jacket, vest, & kneebreeches,
decorated in manganese, soft
green, brown ochre, yellow &
orangish ochre, 18th c., 9⅛" h. (pipe
bowl by chair missing, small
flake on one hand) **1,540.00**
**Staffordshire pearlware, "Hearty
Good Fellow" Toby,** full-figure man
wearing a tricorner hat, coat,
waistcoat & knee breeches &
carrying a pitcher & ale glass, on a
rockwork base, decorated in
manganese, green, pale blue,
brownish tan, brown-ochre & olive
green, probably Ralph Wood,
18th c., professional restoration
to minor hat chips & cover,
11½" h. (ILLUS.) **3,575.00**
Staffordshire Toby, seated Mr. Toby
wearing tricornered hat, decorated
in polychrome glaze w/lustre trim,
5¼" h..**192.50**
Staffordshire Sailor Toby, seated
man wearing a tricorner hat &
holding a jug in one hand & pipe in
the other, 19th c., 10½" h.
(repair) **345.00**

Staffordshire Toby, seated Mr. Toby
wearing tricornered hat, decorated
in underglaze-blue & green, red,
black & brown enamel w/pink flesh
colors, original lid, 11¼" h. (repair
to hat)...**220.00**

VERNON KILNS

 The story of Vernon Kilns Pottery
begins with the purchase by Mr. Faye
Bennison of the Poxon China Company
(Vernon Potteries) in July 1931. The Poxon
family had run the pottery for a number of
years in Vernon, California, but with the
founding of Vernon Kilns the product lines
were greatly expanded.

 Many innovative dinnerware lines and
patterns were introduced during the 1930s,
including designs by such noted American
artists as Rockwell Kent and Don
Blanding. In the early 1940s items were
designed to tie in with Walt Disney's
animated features "Fantasia" and
"Dumbo." Various commemorative plates,
including the popular "Bits" series, were
also produced over a long period of time.
Vernon Kilns was taken over by Metlox
Potteries in 1958 and completely ceased
production in 1960.

DINNERWARES
Bouillon cup, Anytime patt................**$10.00**
Bouillon cup, Shadows patt................**12.00**
Bowl, fruit, 5½" d., Homespun patt. **4.00**
Bowl, 5½" d., Organdie patt. **4.00**
Bowl, 5¼" d., deep, Tam O'Shanter
 patt...**14.00**
Bowl, 8¾" d., Organdie patt. **10.00**
Bowl, 8¾" d., Tam O'Shanter patt. **23.00**
Bowl, 9" d., coupe-shape, Brown
 Eyed Susan patt. **18.00**
Bowl, 9" d., open, Dolores patt. **25.00**
Bowl, 9" d., Gingham patt. **11.00**
Bowl, open, 10" oval, Dolores patt......**25.00**
Bowl, salad, 10½" d., Barkwood
 patt...**20.00**
Butter dish, cov., Frontier Days
 (Winchester 73) patt. **200.00**
Butter dish, cov., Homespun patt........**20.00**
Butter pat, Barkwood patt...................**10.00**
Carafe & stopper, Brown Eyed
 Susan patt..**37.50**

Carafe & stopper, Calico patt.............**95.00**
Carafe & stopper, Homespun patt. **24.00**
Carafe & stopper, Modern patt. **20.00**
Carafe & stopper, Tam O'Shanter
 patt...**60.00**
Carafe & stopper, Tweed patt.............**95.00**
Casserole, cov., individual, Barkwood
 patt., 4" d...**12.00**
Casserole, cov., Brown Eyed Susan
 patt...**45.00**
Casserole, cov., chicken pie,
 individual, stick handle, Barkwood
 patt., San Marino shape.....................**35.00**
Casserole, cov., chicken pie,
 individual, stick handle, Gingham
 patt...**40.00**
Casserole, cov., Homespun patt.
 8" d..**32.00**
Casserole, cov., Tam O'Shanter
 patt., 8" d...**49.00**
Chowder bowl, Brown Eyed Susan
 patt...**10.00**
Chowder bowl, lug-handled, Dolores
 patt...**12.50**
Chowder bowl, lug-handled, Early
 California line **10.00**
Chowder bowl, lug-handled,
 Gingham patt., 6" d. **12.00**
Chowder bowl, lug-handled,
 Homespun patt., 6" d. **7.00**
Chowder bowl, lug-handled, May
 Flower patt., Melina shape, 6" d. **10.00**
Coaster, Organdie patt. **18.00**
Coffeepot, cov., demitasse, Bouquet
 patt...**95.00**
Coffeepot, cov., May Flower patt........**59.00**
Coffee server & stopper, Barkwood
 patt., 10 cup **20.00**
Coffee server w/stopper, Montecito
 shape, Milkweed Dance patt............**850.00**
Creamer, Anytime patt. **8.00**
Creamer, Frontier Days
 (Winchester 73) patt., 5" h. **45.00**
Creamer, Shadows patt. **8.00**
Creamer & cov. sugar bowl,
 Barkwood patt., pr.............................**14.00**
Creamer & cov. sugar bowl, Brown
 Eyed Susan patt., pr. **35.00**
Creamer & cov. sugar bowl, Early
 California line, pr. **18.00**
Creamer & cov. sugar bowl,
 Organdie patt., pr. **15.00**
Cup & saucer, coupe-shape, Brown
 Eyed Susan patt. **10.00**
Cup & saucer, Dolores patt. **20.00**
Cup & saucer, Gingham patt. **8.50**
Cup & saucer, Homespun patt. **6.00**
Cup & saucer, May Flower patt. **15.00**
Cup & saucer, Organdie patt. **8.50**
Cup & saucer, Raffia patt., green &
 brown **5.00**
Cup & saucer, Tam O'Shanter patt. **9.00**
Custard cup, Homespun patt. **25.00**
Egg cup, double, Barkwood patt...........**9.50**

Egg cup, Organdie patt........................18.00
Gravy boat, Early California line.........10.00
Gravy boat, Gingham patt. 25.00
Gravy boat, Homespun patt. 10.00
Gravy boat, Organdie patt. 10.00
Mixing bowl, Organdie patt., 7" d. 30.00
Mug, Early California line, bulbous
   w/applied handle, turquoise 25.00
Mug, coffee, Frontier Days
   (Winchester 73) patt. 75.00
Mug, Homespun patt.............................9.00
Mug, Modern California line, aqua 12.00
Mug, Modern California line, brown 12.00
Mug, Modern California line, cobalt......12.00
Nappy, Gingham patt.............................18.00
Pepper shaker, May Flower patt.,
   Melinda shape 8.00
Pitcher, 7" h., Anytime patt. 12.00
Pitcher, 8½" h., Gingham patt.............38.00
Pitcher, Brown Eyed Susan patt.,
   2 qt...30.00
Pitcher, Organdie patt., 2 qt.............32.50
Pitcher, 9" h., streamlined style,
   Organdie patt., 2 qt...........................40.00
Pitcher, water, 11" h., Mexicana
   patt..40.00
Pitcher, Raffia patt., 1 qt. 22.00
Pitcher, water, Rose-A-Day patt. 38.00
Plate, 6" d., coupe shape, Brown
   Eyed Susan patt. 5.00
Plate, 6" d., Early California line............6.00
Plate, 6" d., Raffia patt. 2.00
Plate, bread & butter, 6½" d.,
   Dolores patt. 15.00
Plate, bread & butter, 6½" d.,
   Gingham patt. 4.00
Plate, bread & butter, 6½" d.,
   Homespun patt. 2.50
Plate, bread & butter, 6½" d.,
   Organdie patt. 3.00
Plate, bread & butter, 6½" d., Tam
   O'Shanter patt......................................4.50
Plate, 7" d., Early California line............8.00
Plate, salad, 7½" d., May Flower
   patt., Melinda shape 10.00
Plate, salad, 7½" d., Tam O'Shanter
   patt..7.00
Plate, 9" d., Early California line...........10.00
Plate, luncheon, 9½" d., Casa
   California line, No. T632
   decoration 45.00
Plate, luncheon, 9½" d., Dolores
   patt..15.00
Plate, luncheon, 9½" d., Homespun
   patt...6.00
Plate, luncheon, 9½" d., Tam
   O'Shanter patt.......................................4.50
Plate, 9¾" d., coupe shape, Brown
   Eyed Susan patt. 10.00
Plate, dinner, 10" d., Desert Bloom
   patt..15.00
Plate, dinner, 10" d., Harvest patt. 45.00
Plate, dinner, 10" d., Raffia patt. 6.00

Plate, dinner, 10" d., Tickled Pink
   patt...7.00
Plate, dinner, 10¼" d., Dolores patt. 15.00
Plate, dinner, 10½" d., Gingham
   patt...8.00
Plate, dinner, 10½" d., Homespun
   patt...6.00
Plate, dinner, 10½" d., May Flower
   patt..16.00
Plate, dinner, 10½" d., Organdie
   patt..10.00
Plate, chop, 12" d., Dolores patt...........30.00
Plate, chop, 12" d., May Flower patt.,
   Melinda shape 38.00
Plate, chop, 12⅜" d., coupe shape,
   Brown Eyed Susan patt. 20.00
Plate, chop, 12½" d., Ultra line, aster
   blue 15.00
Plate, chop, 14" d., Blossom Time
   patt..55.00
Plate, chop, 14" d., Frontier Days
   (Winchester 73) patt. 145.00
Plates, 9½" d., Rippled patt.,
   lavender, set of 8 ....320.00
Platter, 12" l., Organdie patt................17.50
Platter, 12" l., oval, Tam O'Shanter
   patt..22.00
Platter, 13" l., Raffia patt. 12.00
Platter, 14" l., Chintz patt. 30.00
Platter, 14" l., Gingham patt..................40.00
Platter, 14" l., Organdie patt..................32.00
Platter, 16" l., Vernon's 1860 patt. 40.00
Relish dish, leaf-shaped, two-part,
   Cosmos patt.......................................60.00
Relish dish, leaf-shaped, four-part,
   Cosmos patt.......................................95.00
Salt & pepper shakers, Anytime
   patt., pr...10.00
Salt & pepper shakers, Barkwood
   patt., pr...10.00
Salt & pepper shakers, Homespun
   patt...9.00
Salt & pepper shakers, Organdie
   patt., pr...8.00
Salt & pepper shakers, Tickled Pink
   patt., pr...10.00
Salt & pepper shakers, Vernon's
   1860 patt., pr....................................24.00
Salt shaker & pepper mill,
   Homespun patt., pr. 145.00
Soup bowl w/flanged rim, Gingham
   patt..15.00
Soup bowl w/flat rim, Early California
   line 12.00
Sugar bowl, cov., Homespun patt. 12.00
Sugar bowl, cov., San Marino shape,
   Mojave patt. 12.00
Syrup pitcher w/metal top,
   Barkwood patt....................................30.00
Syrup pitcher w/metal top,
   Homespun patt...................................30.00
Syrup pitcher w/metal top,
   Organdie patt. 35.00

Teapot, cov., Barkwood patt.,
eight-cup, 11" l. **25.00**
Teapot, cov., Chintz patt. **60.00**
Teapot, cov., May Flower patt., six
cup, pestle **40.00**
Teapot, cov., Organdie patt. **65.00**
Teapot, cov., Raffia patt......................**25.00**
Tidbit tray, Arcadia patt......................**30.00**
Tidbit tray, two-tier, Brown Eyed
Susan patt......................................**25.00**
Tumbler, Barkwood patt., No. 5,
14 oz. **12.00**
Tumbler, Brown Eyed Susan patt.,
5½" h., 14 oz....................................**16.00**
Tumbler, water, Homespun patt. **20.00**
Tumbler, Organdie patt., No. 5,
5" h...**21.00**
Tumbler, Rose-A-Day patt..................**20.00**
Tureen, cover & underplate, Vernon's
1860 patt., 3 pcs. **275.00**
Vegetable bowl, open, Early
California line, orange, 8½" l. **15.00**
Vegetable bowl, open, Chatelaine
patt., bronze, 9" w.............................**45.00**
Vegetable bowl, open, May Flower
patt., Melinda shape, 9" d. **20.00**
Vegetable bowl, open, Organdie
patt., 9" d..**9.00**
Vegetable bowl, open, oval, Vernon's
1860 patt., 10" l................................**25.00**
Vegetable bowl, open, oval, divided,
Gingham patt., 11½" l, ...**18.00**
Vegetable bowl, open, oval, divided,
Homespun patt., 11½" l. **15.00**
Vegetable bowl, open, oval, divided,
Organdie patt., 11½" l. **13.00**
Vegetable bowl, open, oval, divided,
Tweed patt., 11½" l. **60.00**

"BITS" SERIES
Plate, 8½" d., Bits of Old New
England, "The Whaler,"
multicolored **6.50**
Plate, 8½" d., Bits of the Old South,
"Cypress Swamp" **30.00**
Plate, 12" d., Bits of the Old
Southwest **85.00**
Platter, 14" l., Bits of the Old South,
"Down on the Levee" **75.00**

CITIES SERIES
Plate, "Davenport, Iowa - Tri Cities,"
red..**13.00**
Plate, "Lincoln, Nebraska"....................**15.00**
Plate, "Moline, Illinois - Tri Cities,"
red..**13.00**
Plate, "Rock Island, Illinois - Tri
Cities," red **13.00**
Plate, Ft. Worth Texas Centennial,
1849-1949...**28.00**
Plate, 10½" d., "Greenville, South
Carolina," blue **13.00**
Plate, "Long Beach, California," blue ...**13.00**
Plate, "Washington, D.C." **14.50**

DISNEY "FANTASIA" & OTHER ITEMS

Oriental Mushroom
Salt & Pepper Shakers

Bowl, 7 x 12" rectangle, Mushroom
design, pink, No. 120 ....**277.00**
Bowl, 10½" d., 3" h., Sprite design,
light green, No. 125 ....**380.00**
Figure of a centaurette, No. 22,
8½" h..**800.00**
Figure of Dumbo, 5" h., No. 41 ....**155.00**
Figure of an elephant w/trunk raised,
No. 26, American Pottery, 6" h. **375.00**
Figure of satyr, from Disney's
"Fantasia," No. 5, 4½" h...................**325.00**
Figure of a sprite, reclining, No. 8,
3" h...**375.00**
Figure of a sprite, No. 9, 4½" h.........**445.00**
Figure of a sprite, No. 10, 4½" h........**445.00**
Figure of a unicorn, rearing, No. 15,
6" h...**347.50**
Plate, chop, 12" d., Nutcracker patt....**325.00**
Salt & pepper shakers, model of a
mushroom, tan glaze, 3½" h., pr.
(ILLUS.) **159.00**
Vase, , 7½" h., 12" l., rectangular
w/rounded ends, Pegasus patt.,
blue, No. 127 ....**1,175.00**
Vase, 10½" h., Goddess patt., pink,
No. 126 ....**1,325.00**

DON BLANDING DINNERWARES
Bowl, fruit, 5½" d., Leilani patt. **23.50**
Bowl, 8½" d., coupe soup, Leilani
patt..**28.00**
Bowl, 11", Hawaiian Flowers patt.,
maroon..**135.00**
Chowder bowl, lug-type, Leilani patt.,
San Marino shape.............................**45.00**
Creamer, Leilani patt.,
San Marino shape.............................**24.00**
Cup & saucer, demitasse, Leilani
patt., maroon & blue **65.00**
**Dinner service for four w/serving
pieces,** Leilani patt., 32 pcs...........**1,000.00**
Plate, 6½" d., Leilani patt. **20.00**
Plate, 7½" d., Leilani patt. **30.00**
Plate, 9" d., Leilani patt. **36.00**
Plate, dinner, 10½" d., Hawaiian
Flowers patt., blue **40.00**
Plate, dinner, 10½" d., Leilani patt. **65.00**
Plate, chop, 12" d., Leilani patt. **95.00**
Plate, chop, 17" d., Leilani patt. **250.00**
Platter, 14" l., Hawaiian Flowers patt.,
maroon..**140.00**

Platter, 17" l., Hawaiian Flowers patt.,
maroon...**195.00**
Salt shaker, Leilani patt. **20.00**
Soup bowl w/flanged rim, Leilani
patt...**65.00**
Vegetable bowl, open, Hawaiian
Flowers patt., blue, 9" d. **65.00**

MUSIC MASTERS
Plate, Ludwig Van Beethoven **35.00**
Plate, Frederic Chopin **35.00**
Plate, Edvard Grieg...............................**35.00**
Plate, Felix Mendelssohn **35.00**
Plate, Ignace Paderewski.....................**35.00**

ROCKWELL KENT DESIGNS
Bowl, chowder, Moby Dick patt............**62.50**
Cup & saucer, demitasse, Moby Dick
patt., brown.......................................**100.00**
Dinner service: five dinner plates,
five cups & saucers, four 5¾" d.
bowls, four 6½" plates, 13" d. chop
plate; Moby Dick patt., brown,
24 pcs. **850.00**
Plate, bread & butter, 6½" d., Moby
Dick patt...**25.00**
Plate, 7" d., Salamina patt...................**95.00**
Plate, 9½" d., Moby Dick patt. **47.50**
Plate, 10½" d., Moby Dick patt.,
brown...**45.00**
Plate, 10½" d., "Our America" **95.00**
Plate, chop, 12" d., Moby Dick patt.,
blue **110.00**
Plate, chop, 12" d., Moby Dick patt.,
brown...**122.50**
Platter, 12" l., Moby Dick patt.,
maroon...**175.00**

STATES SERIES - 10½" d.
Plate, "California," blue............................**7.00**
Plate, "California," brown.......................**7.00**
Plate, "California," multicolored............**11.00**
Plate, "Idaho," multicolored **13.00**
Plate, "Indiana"....................................**10.50**
Plate, "Kentucky," blue **20.00**
Plate, "Louisiana," blue **27.50**
Plate, "South Carolina,"
brown...**13.00**
Plate, "Tennessee," blue **8.00**
Plate, "Texas, Lone Star State,"
maroon...**20.00**
Plate, "Utah," red.................................**13.00**
Plate, "Vermont," red............................**12.00**
Plate, "Vermont - The Green
Mountain State," blue........................**20.00**
Plate, "Washington - The Evergreen
State," maroon **16.00**
Plate, "Washington - The Evergreen
State," red **13.00**
Plate, "Wisconsin," multicolored...........**20.00**

MISCELLANEOUS COMMEMORATIVES
Plate, 8½" d., "Court House Battle
Monument," blue **11.00**

Plate, 8½" d., "Old Shot Tower,"
blue **11.00**
Plate, 10" d., Capitol of California
Centennial 1849-1949, white &
brown **8.50**
Plate, 10" d., "Indianapolis, Indiana,"
red, race cars around border **30.00**
Plate, 10½" d., "Grand Canyon
National Park," red.............................**13.00**
Plate, 10½" d., Noah's Ark, ark in
center w/references to Bible verses
& seven multicolored biblical
scenes, 1953 ....**75.00**
Plate, "1949 Chicago Rail Road Fair" ..**25.00**
Plate, "New Hampshire Aerial Tram" ...**12.00**
Plate, "Mission San Rafael
Archangel," brown, Eugena Brady.....**45.00**
Plate, 10½" d., "Will Rogers"...............**15.00**

WARWICK

Numerous collectors have turned their attention to the productions of the Warwick China Manufacturing Company that operated in Wheeling, West Virginia, from 1887 until 1951. Prime interest would seem to lie in items produced before 1914 that were decorated with decal portraits of beautiful women, monks and Indians. Fraternal Order items, as well as floral and fruit decorated items, are also popular with collectors.

IOGA

Beer set: tankard pitcher & one mug;
transfer scene of a man playing a
guitar, 2 pcs. **$300.00**
Pitcher, 9½" h., scrolled relief-molded
base & spout, ornate scrolled
handle, decorated w/poppies &
leaves on shaded brown ground,
IOGA mark...**98.00**
Plates, Sunbonnet Girl & Overall Boy,
pr...**85.00**
Vase, 9" h., hibiscus decoration,
IOGA mark...**125.00**
Vase, 10½" h., 4" d., base flares to
5½" d., scrolled scalloped rim,
twisted side handles, gold trim, red
poppies & green leaves on gold
shading to dark brown **185.00**

WATT POTTERY

Starflower Pattern Canister Set

Founded in 1922, in Crooksville, Ohio, this pottery continued in operation until the factory was destroyed by fire in 1965. Although stoneware crocks and jugs were the first wares produced, by 1935 sturdy kitchen items in yellowware were the mainstay of production. Attractive lines like Kitch-N-Queen (banded) wares and the hand-painted Apple, Cherry and Pennsylvania Dutch (tulip) patterns were popular throughout the country. Today these hand-painted utilitarian wares are "hot" with collectors.

A good reference book for collectors is Watt Pottery, An Identification and Value Guide, *by Sue and Dave Morris (Collector Books, 1933).*

Apple bowl, Double Apple patt., No. 73, 9½" d., 4" h.......................**$112.50**

Apple bowl, Starflower patt. (four petals), No. 73, 9½" d., 4" h. **75.00**

Baker, cov., Apple patt., No. 96, w/advertising, 8½" d., 5¾" h. **80.00**

Baker, cov., Apple patt. (three leaf) No. 96, 8½" d., 5¾" h.......................**35.00**

Baker, cov., Double Apple patt., No. 96, 8½" d., 5¾" h.......................**215.00**

Baking dish, rectangular, Rooster patt., 10" l., 2¼" h.........................**1,050.00**

Bean server, individual, Apple patt., No. 75, 3½" d., 2¼" h.....................**362.50**

Bean pot, cov., Starflower patt., No. 76 ....**160.00**

Bowl, 4" d., Starflower patt. (four-petal), No. 04 ....**45.00**

Bowl, 5" d., 2½" h., ribbed, American Red Bud (Tear Drop) patt., No. 05.............................**200.00 to 250.00**

Bowl, 5" d., individual salad or cereal, American Red Bud (Tear Drop) patt., No. 68 ....**67.50**

Bowl, 5½" d., 2" h., individual cereal,

American Red Bud (Tear Drop) patt., No. 74 ....**40.00**

Bowl, 5½" d., individual salad or cereal, Apple patt., No. 74 ...**57.50**

Bowl, 5¾" d., individual salad or cereal, Cherry patt., No. 23..**66.50**

Bowl, 6" d., 3" h., Starflower patt., No. 06 ....**50.00**

Bowl, 6" d., cereal or salad, Autumn Foliage patt., No. 94 ....**45.00**

Bowl, 6¾" d., ribbed, Apple patt., No. 604 ....**110.00**

Bowl, 7" d., 3¾" h., ribbed, Apple patt., No. 07 ....**60.00**

Bowl, cov., 7½" d., 5½" h., American Red Bud (Tear Drop) patt., No. 66...**225.00**

Bowl, cov., 7½" d., Rooster patt., No. 66 ....**110.00**

Bowl, 8" d., Tulip patt., No. 110 ....**130.00**

Bowl, cov., 8½" d., Apple patt., No. 96..**125.00**

Bowl, cov., 8¾" d., 8½" h., ribbed, Apple patt., w/advertising, No. 601 ....**75.00**

Bowl, salad, footed, 10¾" d., Apple patt., No. 106 (very small nick on rim).....................................**250.00**

Bowl, 11¾" d., Cherry patt., No. 55 ....**295.00**

Canister, cov., American Red Bud (Tear Drop) patt., No. 72, 7" d., 9½" h.................................**550.00**

Canister, cov., Apple patt., No. 72, 7" d., 9½" h. ....**450.00 to 550.00**

Canister set: flour, sugar, coffee & tea; Starflower patt., set of 4 (ILLUS.) **1,500.00**

Casserole, cov., individual, tab-handled, Apple patt., No. 18, 5" d., 4" h. ....**250.00 to 300.00**

Casserole, cov., Starflower patt., No. 3/19, 8½" d. **125.00**

Casserole, cov., Apple patt., No. 54, 8½" d., 6" h. **77.50**

Casserole, cov., Starflower patt., No. 54, 8½" d., 6" h...........................**60.00**

Casserole, cov., Dutch oven-type, American Red Bud (Tear Drop) patt., No. 73, 9½" d., 6" h.................**150.00**

Casserole, cov., Dutch oven-type, Double Apple patt., No. 73, 9½" d., 6" h...**75.00**

Cookie jar, cov., Apple patt., No. 503 ....**400.00 to 450.00**

Cookie jar, cov., Green & Brown, No. 21 ....**110.00**

Cookie jar, cov., Green Swirl-Sided line, No. 21, 7½" h. ....**80.00 to 90.00**

Cookie jar, cov., Raised Pansy patt., No. 21, 7½" h.......................**225.00**

Cookie jar, cov., Starflower patt., No. 21, 7½" h.......................**170.00**

Cookie jar, cov., Tulip patt., No. 503 ....**350.00 to 400.00**

Cookie jar, cov., Woodgrain Cookie
Barrel, No. 617W **140.00**
Creamer, Apple patt., No. 62,
4¼" h. **100.00**
Creamer, Double Apple patt.,
No. 62, 4¼" h. **525.00**
Creamer, Apple (two leaf) patt.,
No. 62, 4¼" h. **98.50**
Creamer, cov., Raised Pansy patt.,
No. 62, 4¼" h. **250.00**
Creamer, Rooster patt., No. 62,
w/advertising, 4¼" h. **295.00**
Creamer, Starflower patt., No. 62,
w/advertising, 4¼" h. **75.00**
Creamer, Tulip patt., blue, No. 62,
w/advertising, 4¼" h. **185.00**
Creamer & cov. sugar bowl, Apple
patt., w/advertising, creamer, No.
62, cov. sugar bowl, No. 98, pr. **310.00**
Grease jar, cov., Autumn Foliage,
No. 01, 5½" h. **225.00**
Grease jar, cov., Starflower patt.,
No. 47, 5" h. **277.50**
Grease jar, cov., Starflower patt., pink
on green, No. 47, 5" h. **150.00**
Ice bucket, cov., Apple (two leaf)
patt., 7¼" h. ....**250.00 to 350.00**
Mixing bowl, ribbed, Apple (two leaf)
patt., No. 5, 5" d., 2¾" h. **60.00**
Mixing bowl, Apple patt., No. 6,
6" d. **47.50**
Mixing bowl, American Red Bud
(Tear Drop) patt., No. 7, 7" d., 4" h. ...**60.00**
Mixing bowl, Apple patt., No. 7,
7" d. **258.00**
Mixing bowl, Apple (two-leaf) patt.,
ribbed, No. 7, 7" d., 4" h. **60.00**
Mixing bowl, Dutch Tulip patt., No. 8,
w/advertising, 8" d. **165.00**
Mixing bowl, Raised Pansy patt.,
No. 8, 8" d., 3¾" h. **60.00**
Mixing bowl, Morning Glory patt.
(yellow), No. 9, 9" d., 4½" h. **120.00**
Mixing bowl, ribbed, pink & blue
bands, No. 9, 9" d. **65.00**
Mixing bowl, Rooster patt., No. 9,
9" d. **80.00**
Mixing bowl, pink & blue bands,
12" d. **30.00**
Mixing bowl, Apple patt., No. 64,
7½" d., 5" h. **45.00**
Mixing bowl, Apple (two leaf) patt.,
No. 64, 7½" d., 5" h. **35.00**
Mixing bowl, Dutch Tulip patt.,
No. 65, 8½" d. 5¾" h. **60.00**
Mixing bowl, Rooster patt., No. 65,
8½" d., 5¾" h. **90.00**
Mixing bowls, nesting-type, Apple
patt., Nos. 6, 7 & 8, set of 3 ....**150.00**
Mixing bowls, nesting-type, Apple
patt., Nos. 63, 64 & 65, 6½", 7½", &
9" d., set of 3 ....**195.00**
Mixing bowls, nesting-type, Apple

(two leaf) patt., Nos. 63, 64 & 65,
6¼", 7½" & 9" d., set of 3 ....**210.00**
Mixing bowls, nesting-type,
Basketweave, set of 5 ....**120.00**
Mixing bowls, nesting-type, Morning
Glory patt., Nos. 6 & 8, set of 2 ....**285.00**
Mug, Esmond line, grape cluster
decoration, No. 31, 3½" h.,
3½" d. **52.50**
Mug, waisted shape, Apple patt.,
No. 121, 3" d., 3¾" h. **230.00**
Mug, waisted shape, Autumn Foliage
patt., No. 121, 3" d., 3¾" h. **150.00**
Pepper shaker, barrel-shaped,
Rooster patt. **205.00**
Pepper shaker, hourglass shaped,
Apple patt., w/raised letter, 2½" d.
4½" h. **100.00**
Pie plate, Apple patt., No. 33,
9" d. ....**100.00 to 150.00**
Pie plate, Old Pansy (Cross-Hatch
Pansy patt.), No. 33, 9" d. **295.00**
Pitcher, 5½" h., Apple patt., No. 15
w/advertising **75.00**
Pitcher, 5½" h., Apple (two-
leaf) patt., No. 15 ....**73.50**
Pitcher, 6¾" h., Autumn Foliage
patt., No. 16 ....**90.00 to 120.00**
Pitcher, 6¾" h., Apple patt.,
No. 16 ....**100.00 to 125.00**
Pitcher, 6¾" h., Tulip patt., No. 16,
w/advertising **175.00**
Pitcher w/ice lip, 8" h., Pansy patt.,
No. 17 ....**175.00**
Pitcher, Woodgrain series,
No. 614W **48.00**
Plates, salad, 7½" d., Pansy patt.,
set of 4 ....**160.00**
Platter, 12" d., Apple patt., No. 49 .....**400.00**
Platter, 12" d., Starflower patt.,
No. 49 ....**195.00**
Salt shaker, Apple patt., hourglass-
shaped **175.00**
Salt Shaker, barrel-shaped,
Starflower patt. ....**100.00 to 135.00**
Salt & pepper shakers, hourglass-
shaped, Apple patt., matte finish,
pr. ....**65.00 to 100.00**
Salt & pepper shakers, barrel-
shaped, American Red Bud (Tear Drop)
patt., No. 194, pr. **300.00**
Serving bowl, Bullseye patt., (Cut-
Leaf Pansy), 15" d. **120.00**
Spaghetti bowl, Apple (two
leaf) patt., No. 39, 13" d. **113.00**
Spaghetti bowl, Tulip patt., No. 39,
13" d. **665.00**

WEDGWOOD

*Reference here is to the famous pottery
established by Josiah Wedgwood in 1759*

in England. Numerous types of wares have been produced through the years to the present.

WEDGWOOD

BASALT
Figure of Shakespeare at podium, full
figure, marked "W.W.," ca. 1850,
16" h...**$1,200.00**
Jar, cov., modeled w/classical figures,
marked "Wedgwood - Made in
England," 4½" h. **110.00**
Model of a cat, ca. 1913, 3½" h. **550.00**

JASPER WARE

Jasper Ware Mug

w/small white medallion at the front
showing two soldiers, on blue,
marked "Wedgwood" only,
3¾" d., 5" h. (ILLUS.) **125.00**
Pin tray, white relief classical figures
on bleeding green ground, 2⅜ x
5⅞", marked "Wedgwood -
England" **50.00**
Pitcher, miniature, 2" h., 1¼" d.,
cylindrical, white relief classical
figures & grapevine on light blue **135.00**
Pitcher, tankard, 3" h., 2" d., white
relief classical figures on lavender,
raised white grapes & leaves border,
marked "Wedgwood - England" **75.00**

Wedgwood Match Striker

Cracker jar, cov., barrel-shaped,
white relief classical figures on dark
blue, silver plate rim, cover & bail
handle, marked "Wedgwood" only,
5" d., 6" h. **198.00**
Cracker jar, cov., bulbous ovoid
body, white relief classical figures on
dark blue, flat silver plate cover, rim
& twisted bail handle, marked
"Wedgwood" only, 6¼" h...................**220.00**
Cracker jar, cov., cylindrical, white
relief classical figures on blue, flat
silver plate cover, lid, bail handle &
base ring on ball feet, marked
"Wedgwood England," 7" h. **165.00**
Dish, heart-shaped, white relief
classical figures on red, ca. 1920,
4½" w., marked "Wedgwood
England" **395.00**
Match striker, cov., cylindrical body
w/place in finial to place a candle,
white relief classical figures on blue ,
marked "Wedgwood England,"
2⅜" d., 3¾" h. (ILLUS.) **225.00**
Mug, cylindrical body w/rope twist
handle & silver top rim, white relief
classical ladies & cupids on sides

Green Jasper Pitcher

Pitcher, 3¾" h., 3⅞" d., cylindrical
body w/C-scroll handle, decorated
w/white relief molded scrolls &
heads of Washington & Franklin on
bleeding green ground, marked
"Wedgwood England" (ILLUS.) **325.00**
Pitcher, 5¼" h., white relief classical
figures on red, marked "Wedgwood
England" **725.00**
Pitcher, tankard, 6⅜" h., 3¾" d.,
cylindrical body decorated w/white
relief classical ladies & cupids,
border of relief molded grapes on

Sage Green Jasper Ware Pitcher

sage green, marked "Wedgwood England" (ILLUS.) **155.00**
Portland vase, 4⅞" h., white relief classical figures on dark blue, ca. 1840..**185.00**
Portland vase, 5½" h., white relief classical figures on dark blue, ca. 1840..**250.00**
Portland vase, 7¾" h., white relief classical figures on dark blue, ca. 1840..**395.00**
Sugar bowl, cov., white relief mythological figures on light blue, 4⅜" d., 4" h., marked "Wedgwood" only **110.00**
Urn, cov., campana-form, tall flaring body w/loop handles near the base, raised on a ringed pedestal on a square foot, a stepped & domed cover w/a knob finial, white relief classical figures & leaf bands on

Jasper Ware Vase

lavender, marked "Wedgwood" only, 9¼" h..**1,190.00**
Vase, miniature, 5" h., two-handled, white relief classical figures on dark blue, marked "Wedgwood England" **425.00**
Vase, 6¼" h., 3" d., angled baluster-shaped body w/handles at shoulder, white relief classical figures on blue ground, marked "Wedgwood England" (ILLUS. bottom previous column) **225.00**

MISCELLANEOUS
Pitcher, jug-type, 7⁹⁄₁₆" h., pearlware, the body transfer-printed in black on one side w/a ship w/a yellow hull, flying a red, white & blue American flag & pennant above a green sea & the black-enameled inscription "The Amazon, A.H. Burrows, Commander," on the reverse w/an oval scene of a ship in distress on a stormy sea, its figurehead picked out in red & blue & under the spout an eagle beneath thirteen stars & above a banderole inscribed "E PLURIBUS UNUM," the rim edged in worn gilding, impressed "WEDGWOOD," ca 1810 (small spout chip)..........................**2,300.00**
Plate, salad, Appledore patt. **22.00**
Plate, 10" d., blue, Ivanhoe series, "Black Knight Exchanges with Friar" **65.00**
Plate, 10½" d., Dominion of Canada Coat of Arms, serrated edge w/brilliant orange border design, Etruria, England (glaze flake on rim)...**200.00**
Plate, 10½" d., Dominion of Canada Coat of Arms, light blue border depicting the Provinces' Coat of Arms, Etruria, England....................**150.00**
Plate, 10½" d., Montreal Coat of Arms, serrated edge w/brilliant orange border design, Etruria, England...**225.00**
Plate, 10½" d., Vancouver, British Columbia Coat of Arms, serrated edge w/brilliant orange border design, Etruria, England **225.00**
Plate, commemorative, "Harvard University," blue transfer on white, ca. 1927 ....**38.00**
Plate, commemorative, "Harvard University," rose transfer on white, ca. 1941 ....**34.00**
Plate, commemorative, "University of Pennsylvania," rose transfer on white, ca. 1940.................................**28.00**
Plate, commemorative, "Swathmore College," rose transfer on white.........**24.00**
Plates, majolica, seashell-shaped, pr...**250.00**

Plates, 10¼" d., commemorative, "Massachusetts Institute of Technology," scenes of different buildings, blue transfer on white, ca. 1930, set of 12 ....**550.00**

WELLER

The Weller Pottery was established by Samuel A. Weller in 1872 and operated until 1945. Originally located in Fultonham, Ohio, the factory moved to Zanesville in 1882. A wide range of lines, both of art pottery and commercial quality, were produced over the years and we list a sampling here.

Reference books on Weller include The Collectors Encyclopedia of Weller Pottery, by Sharon & Bob Huxford (Collector Books, 1979) and All About Weller by Ann Gilbert McDonald (Antique Publications, 1989)

WELLER

Weller Pottery

ARDSLEY (1928)

Various shapes molded as cattails among rushes with water lilies at the bottom. Matte glaze.

Candleholders, 3" h., bulbous lotus-blossom shape, on petal base, pr. **85.00**
Console set, 9 x 15" oblong irregular console bowl w/iris flower frog and pair of 2" h. candleholders, 3 pcs.....**325.00**
Console set: 16" d., 3½" h. console bowl, figural kingfisher flower frog & a pair of candleholders; the wide shallow bowl molded on the interior w/narrow green cattails, the candleholders w/a lily pad & blossom disc base centered by a flaring blossom-form socket, black ink kiln mark, the set **522.50**

AURELIAN (1898-1910)
Similar to Louwelsa line but brighter colors and a glossy glaze.

Lamp, kerosene table-type, a wide baluster-form body on small knob feet, the deep shoulder w/a wide short molded neck supporting a collar w/a kerosene burner & glass globe shade, the body decorated w/bold grape clusters & leaves on a fiery gold, green & mahogany ground, decorated by Eugene Roberts, incised "Aurelian" on the base, electrified, base only 9½" d., 11" h. **660.00**
Plaque, rectangular, decorated w/life-sized red apples hanging on leafy branches against a streaky brown, orange & yellow background, decorated by Frank Ferrell, ca. 1898, w/old metal framework & hanging chain, 10⅞ x 16½" (several glaze scratches, small patch of glaze loss, some bubbles in glaze) **935.00**
Vase, 5½" h., 5¾" d., spherical w/pinched neck, decorated w/yellow, brown & green roses on a fiery yellow & brown ground **467.50**
Vase, 7" h., bulbous ovoid body tapering to a trumpet neck, decorated w/yellow & orange rose blossoms & green leaves against a dark brown ground, the neck & rim mounted w/a foliate-cast sterling silver mount, decorated by Hattie Mitchell, artist-initials & impressed "WELLER - 838 - 6," silver impressed "STERLING - 634" w/hallmark, ca. 1900-10................**1,840.00**

BALDIN (about 1915-20)

Baldin Jardiniere & Pedestal

Rustic designs with relief-molded apples and leaves on branches wrapped around each piece.

Bowl, 4" d., blue **150.00**
Jardiniere & pedestal base,
  overall 39" h., 2 pcs. (ILLUS. bottom
  previous page) **1,800.00**
Vase, 6" h., bulbous base taper-
  ing to a cylindrical neck....................**85.00**
Vase, 7" h., bulbous base **82.00**
Vase, 11" h., wide cylindrical body
  swelling at base, blue ground **395.00**
Vase, 19" h., floor-type, apple
  decoration w/closed twig handles,
  turquoise high glaze w/blue, red and
  yellow drip.....................................**650.00**

BRIGHTON (1915)

Various bird or butterfly figurals colorfully decorated and with glossy glazes.

Kingfisher flower frog,
  9" h. ....**350.00 to 375.00**

Model of a Parakeet

Model of a parakeet, on tapering
  cylindrical pedestal perch, bird in
  polychrome colors of pink, yellow &
  blue, on a green perch, 5¾" d.,
  7½" h., unmarked (ILLUS.) **825.00**

Pair of Brighton Parakeets

Model of parakeets, perched on a

curving branch, birds brightly
colored in red, yellow &
blue, brown perch, glossy
finish (ILLUS.) **1,100.00**

Brighton Parrot

Model of a parrot, bright raspberry
  red & blue, yellow & green, on a tall
  swirled brown upright perch, die-
  stamped mark, 9" w., 14" h.
  (ILLUS.) **1,760.00**

Model of a Woodpecker

Model of a woodpecker, perched on
  a base of entwined branches, blue &
  orange bird on a green perch,
  glossy glaze, unmarked, 3½" d.,
  6¼" h. (ILLUS.)...............**125.00 to 175.00**
Name card holder w/figural but-
  terfly & attached bud vase **395.00**

BURNT WOOD (1910)

Etched designs on a light tan ground with dark brown trim. Similar to Claywood but no vertical bands.

Basket, hanging-type **150.00**

Burntwood 'Dechiwo' Vase

Vase, 6½" h., early 'Dechiwo' line,
ovoid body tapering to a thick rolled
rim, incised decoration of children
blowing bubbles on one side &
playing ball on the other, band of
flowering trees branches around the
shoulder (ILLUS.)..........................**1,900.00**
Vase, 8" h., birds decoration **175.00**
Vase, 9" h., 4½" d., ovoid w/short
neck, overall stylized floral
decoration, light beige on
a chocolate brown ground **220.00**

COPPERTONE (late 1920s)

*Various shapes with an overall mottled
green glaze. Some pieces with figural frog
or fish handles. Models of frogs also
included.*

Bowl, 9" d., 3¾" h., two raised open
square handles on flat rim, mottled
green & brown matte glaze (two
pinhead glaze nicks to rim) **66.00**
Bowl, 9¾" l., 5½" h. deep rounded
sides w/an undulating oblong
molded rim molded at one side w/a
frog, each side embossed w/a carp,
rich mottled green & brown glaze,
ink kiln mark "191-G" **935.00**
Candleholder, model of a turtle w/lily
blossom, 3" h..................**175.00 to 200.00**
Card tray, in the form of a lily pad leaf
w/shallow dished sides, molded at
one side w/a crouching frog on the
rim, ink kiln mark, 6" l., 2¼" h..........**247.50**
Center bowl, deep w/irregular rim,
frog perched on one edge, mottled
green & brown glaze, 5½" h.,
10½" w..**385.00**
Cigarette stand, model of a
frog, 5" h. **155.00**
Console bowl, long narrow oblong
form w/undulating rim, molded at
one end w/a small figural frog & at
the opposite end w/a water lily &
leaves, ink kiln mark, 15½" l.,
3½" h..**990.00**
Console bowl w/figural lily pad &
frog flower frog, oblong bowl,
8 x 10½", 2 pcs. **475.00**

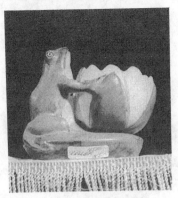

Coppertone Flower Frog

Flower frog, model of a lily pad
bloom w/seated frog, 5½" w.,
4½" h. (ILLUS.) **330.00**

Weller Fishing Boy Fountain

Fountain, tall boy holding fishing pole
standing on pedestal surrounded by
four upright fish on flared base, all
on round pedestal base, rich mottled
green and brown semi-gloss finish
glaze, boy and fish are fitted w/water
nozzles (ILLUS.) **4,125.00**
Model of a frog, 2" h. ....**150.00 to 200.00**
Model of a frog, 4" h. ....**275.00 to 300.00**
Model of a frog, the large stylized
animal w/a hole at its mouth & on a
round base, mottled green & brown
glaze, probably used as a fountain,
6½" d., 5¼" h. (short tight line at
factory hole in base) **605.00**
Model of a frog, large animal w/a
hole in its mouth to accommodate a
sprinkler, dark mottled green &
brown w/ivory chest, 10¼" l.,
8½" h. (ILLUS. top next page) **2,860.00**

Coppertone Frog Model

Vase, bud, 9" h., 3¼" d., slender body
w/flaring irregular rim, frog crawling
up the side, mottled green & brown
glaze **357.50**
Vase, 10" h., trumpet-shaped
w/molded lily pads **325.00**
Vase, 14" h., tall baluster-form body
w/angled shoulder & molded rim, C-
form handles at the shoulder **550.00**
Vase, 19" h., floor-type **750.00**

**DICKENSWARE 2nd Line
(early 1900s)**

*Various incised "sgraffito" designs usually
with a matte glaze.*

Mug, bust portrait of American Indian
"Tame Wolf," artist-signed, 6¼" h. ...**625.00**
Mug, monk drinking ale scene,
5½" h. ....**225.00 to 275.00**
Mug, scene of a deer **175.00**
Pitcher, 10½" h., portrait of monk,
blue & white, marked "X"
(experimental) **625.00**
Vase, 5¼" h., 5¼" w., pocket-form,
flattened bulbous ovoid sides
tapering to a short flaring rim
pinched together at the center,
sgraffito marsh scene w/a duck &
reeds by a lake in shades of brown
& green, die-stamped "Dickensware
- Weller - X352"...............................**220.00**
Vase, 9¼" h., golfer decoration,
unmarked.......................................**1,500.00**
Vase, 16" h., etched scene
w/hunting dogs.............................**1,400.00**
Vase, 17⅞" h., very tall slender
cylindrical body w/a narrow rounded
shoulder to the short rolled neck,
decorated w/a standing monk
tasting wine, in browns & yellow
against a shaded brown to gold

ground, glossy glaze, decorated by
Mary Gellier, ca. 1900, marked
& artist-signed **1,650.00**

Two Tall Dickensware Vases

Vase, tall slender cylindrical body
raised on four slender pillars
flanking a pedestal base on a
stepped flaring foot, incised scene of
man on a branch from "Barnaby
Rudge" (ILLUS. left) **950.00**
Vase, 12½" h., tall cylindrical body
w/a narrow shoulder to the short
rolled rim, continuous landscape
scene of white mounted knights
in deep woods, blue sky above,
glossy glaze (ILLUS. right)............**3,100.00**

**EOCEAN and Eocean Rose
(1898-1925)**

*Early art line with various hand-painted
flowers on shaded grounds, usually with a
glossy glaze.*

Vase, miniature, 5⅛" h., squared
shape, pink, white & blue flowers on
slate blue ground, ca. 1910 ....**165.00**
Vase, bud, 5½" h., slip-painted florals
on shaded pale blue to grey ground ..**75.00**
Vase, wide short cylindrical body w/a
wide rounded shoulder to a short
conical neck w/a closed rim,
decorated w/a bust portrait of a
greyish white kitten against a
shaded charcoal grey to white
ground...**1,500.00**
Vase, 5" h., 7½" d., squatty bulbous
low base w/the wide shoulder
tapering to a wide short cylindrical
neck, the shoulder decorated w/rose

& pale pink blossoms w/yellow, white & green centers on long twisting stems & greyish green leaves against a yellow matte ground, artist-initialed, impressed mark..**385.00**

Vase, 6" h., 5" d., swelled cylindrical body w/a wide flat shoulder to the short cylindrical neck, decorated w/dogwood branches in white & purple against a shaded dark blue to ivory ground, glossy glaze, marked, Eocean Rose **330.00**

Vase, 6½" h., 3" d., simple cylindrical body, decorated w/a large polychrome stork standing on one leg against a shaded dark grey to white ground, incised "Eosian - Weller" (crazed) **495.00**

Vase, 8" h., 2½" d., slender cylindrical body w/a narrow round shoulder & short rolled neck, decorated w/purple & green lily-of-the-valley against a shaded black to light green ground, die-stamped circle mark **412.50**

Vase, 10½" h., decorated w/daisies on grey ground.................**150.00**

Vase, 10⅝" h., wide slightly tapering cylindrical body w/a wide shoulder to the compressed incurved short neck, decorated w/a band of swimming green fish against a shaded dark green to cream ground, signed, ca. 1905, Eocean Rose....**2,420.00**

Vase, 12¾" h., 4¾" d., slender tapering body w/six open handles rising from narrow shoulder to flared rim, decorated w/large green & violet leaves against a shaded pale pink & dark green ground **880.00**

Vase, 12⅝" h., tall slender slightly waisted cylindrical body, decorated around the top w/large mauve Virginia creeper leaves w/the green vines down the sides, against a black to pale green ground, decorated by Levi J. Burgess, ca. 1905, stamped "801 - 10," incised "F" **880.00**

ETNA (1906)

Similar to Eocean line but designs are molded in low-relief and colored.

Lemonade set: a 14" h. tankard pitcher & two cylindrical mugs, each w/an angled handle; decorated w/a large cluster of deep reddish purple grapes & green leaves at the top against a shaded grey to pink ground, signed, 3 pcs. (hairline in one mug)..**220.00**

Vase, 6½" h., footed angular bulbous body tapering to a wide cylindrical neck w/slightly flaring rim, slip-painted floral design.........................**125.00**

Vase, 7" h., cylindrical, decorated w/yellow dandelions on grey ground..**165.00**

Vase, 11" h., tall ovoid body w/bulbous short neck w/closed rim flanked by short twisted strap handles, low-relief floral bouquet in rosy red & pale green leafy stems against a shaded grey ground **300.00**

Vase, 14⅝" h., tall gently flaring cylindrical body w/a wide rounded shoulder tapering to a flat mouth, decorated around the top w/a large cluster of purple grapes & green leaves & vines on a shaded blue to pale lavender ground, marked (two flat chips on the base)......................**412.50**

FOREST (mid-Teens -1928)

Realistically molded and painted forest scene

Basket, hanging-type, 9" d.................**295.00**
Jardiniere, full kiln mark, 6½" d. **150.00**

Forest & Ivory Jardinieres & Pedestals

Jardiniere & pedestal, 26" h., tapering jardiniere bowl, on waisted cylindrical pedestal (ILLUS. left) **990.00**
Pitcher, 5¼" h., 6¼" d., cylindrical body slightly flared at the base & rim, molded forest landscape in browns & greens against a creamy ground, marked...............................**220.00**
Vase, 10¼" h. **250.00**
Vase, 12" h., waisted cylindrical form ....**200.00 to 225.00**

HUDSON (1917-34)

Underglaze slip-painted decoration.

Pair of Hudson Vases

Vase, 7" h., swelled cylindrical body w/a flaring base & widely flaring rim, decorated around the top w/a pink, yellow & blue blossom against a group of pale green leaves all against a shaded white to pale green ground, decorated by Sara Timberlake, ca. 1920, marked (ILLUS. left).....................................**220.00**

Vase, 7" h., 3½" d., ovoid, decorated w/white & pink dogwood blossoms against a blue shading to cream to pink ground, artist-signed **302.50**

Vase, 8¼" h., 3½" d., baluster-form, decorated w/slip-painted trefoil blossoms in dark & light blue w/green leaves on a blue to cream ground, die-stamped "WELLER"......**357.50**

Vase, 8⅞" h., swelled cylindrical body w/a short molded mouth, decorated w/large white jonquils on pale green leafy stems against a green to pale cream ground, stamped "Weller" in block letters.............................**467.50**

Vase, 9⅜" h., swelled cylindrical shouldered body w/a short rounded neck w/flat rim, decorated around the top half w/large creamy white nasturtium blossoms & green leaves & vines against a shaded blue to pale green ground, decorated by Sarah McLaughlin, ca. 1920, artist-signed & marked (ILLUS. right) **522.50**

Vase, 9½" h., 5" d., swelling cylindrical body w/a wide shoulder tapering to a short wide mouth, decorated around the upper half w/large white & blue morning glories & green leaves against a shaded blue to green ground, decorated by Hester Pillsbury, artist's initials on side, black kiln mark on base...........**605.00**

Vase, 11" h., 'Hudson Light,' tall slender ovoid body tapering to a molded rim, decorated w/large pastel pink & white iris blossoms w/pale green leaves & stems against a shaded dark to light green ground, signed (few small glaze imperfections in the making)............**385.00**

Vase, 13½" h., bulbous ovoid body tapering to a short cylindrical neck w/rolled rim, strap handles from the sides of the neck to the shoulder, decorated w/large quince & blackberries in red, pink & blue on leafy branches against a shaded blue to pink ground, decorated by Hester Pillsbury, ca. 1925, signed (two very tight lines at the rim) **1,320.00**

Vase, 13½" h., urn-form, the wide ovoid body tapering to a short cylindrical neck w/rolled rim, wide strap handles from neck to shoulder, decorated w/a scenic design of a large peacock resting near a large wrought-iron gate & stone fence in shades of blue, white, yellow, green & black against a mottled blue-green to tan ground, attributed to Mae Timberlake, the base marked w/a letter "A" in black slip **5,060.00**

IVORY (1910 to late 1920s)

Ivory-colored body with various shallow embossed designs with rubbed-on brown highlights.

Jardiniere & pedestal, tapering jardiniere bowl on scrolled feet w/molded Art Nouveau women and scrolling on sides, on matching pedestal (ILLUS. right with Forest) **2,090.00**

Vase, 11" h., decorated w/molded peacocks design **80.00**

Vase, 12" h., decorated w/pea-cocks..**110.00**

Window box, embossed Victorian nudes, 7 x 13"...................**295.00**

LASA (1920-25)

Various landscapes on a banded reddish and gold iridescent ground.

Vase, 7¼" h., wide disc foot supporting a slender trumpet-form body, decorated w/a landscape of bare trees (small nick on base)........**137.50**

Vase, 7⅝" h., slender trumpet-shaped body w/widely flaring foot, decorated w/landscape done in gold, reddish & green gold, iridescent metallic glaze (ILLUS. top next page)....................**402.50**

Lasa Trumpet-shaped Vase

LOUWELSA (1896-1924)

Hand-painted underglaze slip decoration on dark brown shading to yellow ground; glossy glaze.

Candlestick, decorated w/pansies, 10" h. **225.00**

Louwelsa Table Clock

Clock, table model, scalloped case decorated w/yellow daffodils, artist-signed, tiny base repair (ILLUS.) **650.00**

Lamp base, wide squatty baluster-form body on scrolled tab feet, decorated w/large yellow iris & green leaves on a shaded dark brown to yellow ground, early 20th c., original oil font & burner adapted for electricity, marked on the base, 10⅞" h. **880.00**

Mug, slightly tapering cylindrical body w/a thick D-form handle, decorated w/a bust portrait of an American Indian in dark brown & rust against a dark brown ground, decorated by Levi J. Burgess, ca. 1898, stamped on base "562 - 5," 5⅞" h. **825.00**

Mug, slightly tapering cylindrical body w/a thick D-form handle, decorated w/the bust portrait of a smiling monk in dark brown, rust & blue against a dark brown ground, decorated

by Levi J. Burgess, ca. 1898, marked, 5⅞" h. (very minor glaze scratches) **247.50**

Vase, 5½" h., globular body w/stick neck, decorated w/wild rose, artist-signed **250.00**

Vase, 6⅝" h., 'Blue Louwelsa,' plain cylindrical body decorated in shades of dark blue w/large poppies, base stamped "Louwelsa Weller" & "X 516", & incised "7," ca. 1900............**605.00**

Louwelsa Vase with Cavalier

Vase, 13½" h., tall slender cylindrical body w/a narrow flat shoulder to a short rolled neck, h.p. bust portrait of a Cavalier in brown, black, tan & cream against a black shaded to green shaded to brown ground (ILLUS.) **3,300.00**

Louwelsa Floor Vase

Vase, 24" h., 8¾" d., floor model, baluster-shaped body w/a tall flaring neck, decorated w/yellow & orange carnations w/green foliage, on a shaded brown ground, decorated by Eugene Roberts, artist's initials (ILLUS. bottom previous page) **1,210.00**

Louwelsa Vase with Fish

Vase, tall very slender cylindrical body w/a slightly flaring foot, the narrow shoulder tapering to a short flaring neck, decorated w/a long swirled school of grey & white fish down the sides against a shaded black to dark green to pale yellowish green ground (ILLUS.) **4,000.00**

MATT GREEN (ca. 1904)

Various shapes with slightly shaded dark green matte glaze and molded with leaves and other natural forms.

Matt Green Jardiniere

Ewer, spherical body molded w/a lizard around the sides below a cylindrical neck w/pinched spout & long angled handle, rich mottled matte greenish blue glaze, die-stamped "WELLER," 3¼" d., 5" h..**605.00**

Jardiniere, bulbous ovoid body w/a wide molded mouth flanked by four small ribbon handles, molded around the shoulder w/stylized florals, unmarked, 7¼" h. (ILLUS.)...**522.50**

Jardiniere, decorated w/embossed hosta leaves, 8" h. **250.00**

Large Matte Green Jardiniere

Jardiniere, wide cylindrical body w/molded rim flanked by four small loop handles, four wide ribs down the sides to the rounded bottom edge, embossed w/a wide center band of repeating herringbone, unmarked 11" d., 8¼" h. (ILLUS.) **357.50**

Lamp base, Art Nouveau design, slender swelled cylindrical body above a flaring shaped base w/four wide strap handles, a band of molded fleurettes around the top, w/brass mount, 7" d., 14" h. (bottom missing) **935.00**

Lamp base, wide bulbous multi-lobed gourd-form body tapering sharply to a slender cylindrical neck w/a molded rim, em-bossed on each side of the base w/grotesque 'devil' heads, raised on a narrow flaring base w/four 'knob' feet, smooth matte green glaze, complete w/original gas fittings, unmarked, 8½" d., 14½" h. (ILLUS. top next page)..**440.00**

Vase, 11" h., 10" d., compressed globular lower section on a low foot, broad stovepipe neck, covered in a leathery green to terra cotta matte glaze **275.00**

Vase, 11¾" h., footed tall slender cylindrical body w/a wide flattened

rim overhanging small square
loop handles, dark green blaze,
marked.. **880.00**

Matt Green Lamp Base

MUSKOTA (1915-late 1920s)

*Figural pieces with human figures, birds,
animals or frogs. Matte glaze.*

Figure, Fishing Boy, boy seated
on rockwork, 6½" h. **225.00**
Flower frog, figural, a small nude boy
kneeling on a large green rock base,
unmarked, 4¼" w., 4¼" h.................**275.00**
Flower frog, figural frog half
immersed in water lily,
4½" h. ....**200.00 to 250.00**
Flower frog, model of a king-
fisher, 9" h.......................................**375.00**

Muskota Southern Belle Powder Jar

Powder jar, cov., figural, modeled as
a lady standing wearing a wide hoop
skirt, her arms down touching the
front of the skirt, her torso & upper
half of dress forming the cover,
decorated w/red roses & blue bows
on a glossy yellow ground, marked
only "27," 5" d., 7½" h. (ILLUS.).......**302.50**
Vase, 7½" h., boy fishing...................**200.00**

SICARDO (1902-07)

*Various shapes with iridescent glaze of
metallic shadings in greens, blues,
crimson, purple or coppertone decorated
with vines, flowers, stars or free-form
geometric lines.*

Jardiniere, very wide bulbous body
raised on short arcaded feet, the
sides boldly embossed w/large
Moorish arabesques, tapering to a
wide short flaring scalloped neck,
iridescent purple, gold & green
glaze, painted "Weller SICARD" on
the side, 14½" d., 12½" h..............**1,650.00**
Vase, 3¼" h., 5¾" d., footed wide &
low cushion-form body centered by
a short widely flaring trefoil neck,
bright satiny decoration of gold
arabesques against a lustred green
& burgundy ground, signed on the
side **715.00**
Vase, 5" h., baluster-form, a
multicolored iridescent glaze
decorated w/mistletoe branch-
es, signed **437.00**
Vase, 5½" h., 3" d., cylindrical, Art
Nouveau design of swirled
arabesques under a green & purple
iridescent glaze, script marks on
body "Weller" & "Sicard," impressed
on base "7"......................................**495.00**
Vase, 6½" h., 4¼" d., tapering ovoid
body w/a bulbous compressed &
closed neck flanked by small loop
handles, iridescent gold flowers on a
deep purple ground, unmarked.....**1,017.50**

Tri-lobed Sicardo Vase
Vase, 7" h., tall tri-lobed upright

undulating body, floral designs on sides, covered in iridescent glaze in shades of green & gold (ILLUS.) ..**1,150.00**

Ovoid Sicardo Vase

Vase, 7" h., 3¾" d., ovoid body tapering to a short thick rim, decorated w/swirling mistletoe, iridescent gold & lavender glaze (ILLUS.) **605.00**

Tall Sicardo Vase

Vase, 13" h., 5¾" d., bulbous top w/closed small mouth above tapering cylindrical sides, embossed w/large, tall irises, rich burgundy & gold lustre glaze, unmarked (ILLUS.) **7,700.00**
Vase, 19½" h., 13" d., Art Nouveau style, ovoid body on scroll-molded feet, the sides tapering to a bulbous, pierced rim molded w/whiplash swirls above large pendent blossoms above the relief-molded figures of two swirling Art Nouveau maidens flanked by long scrolls, the body flanked by large, long pierced scrolling handles continuing down to the scrolled feet, gold, green, blue & purple iridescent glaze, signed "Weller - Sicard" **7,700.00**

Vase, pillow-type, wide squatty double-gourd form w/long double-loop handles down the sides, decorated w/overall three-leaf scroll sprigs in dark gold on a bluish green lustre ground **2,200.00**

SILVERTONE (1928)

Various flowers, fruits or butterflies molded on a pale purple-blue matte pebbled ground.

Candleholders, pr. **285.00**
Console bowl w/flower frog, 12" l......**325.00**
Flower frog.....................................**100.00**
Jardiniere, 10" **350.00**
Vase, 5½" h., molded irises ....**125.00 to 175.00**
Vase, 7" h., ...**250.00 to 295.00**
Vase, 8½" h., footed, bulbous body w/heavy loop handles below a short neck w/ruffled rim, decorated w/molded pink & yellow flowers, green leaves & brown branches.........................**395.00 to 475.00**
Vase, 10" h., molded calla lilies (in-the-making base chip).........................**250.00 to 300.00**
Vase, 12" h., decorated w/poppies & butterflies (two professional chip repairs)..**395.00**
Vase, 15" h., molded calla lilies..........**500.00**

WOODCRAFT (1917)

Rustic designs simulating the appearance of stumps, logs and tree trunks. Some pieces are adorned with owls, squirrels, dogs and other animals.

Candlestick, double, modeled as an owl perched at the top of an apple tree between candle nozzles, 8" w., 13½" h...**357.50**
Flower frog, figural lobster **120.00**
Jardiniere, slightly tapering cylindrical tree trunk form w/molded branch, acorns & leaves, figural squirrel on one side & figural woodpecker on other side, 9½" h.............................**675.00**
Lawn ornament, figural, model of a large squirrel seated & holding an acorn, mottled brown & green, stamped "WELLER POTTERY," 11½" w., 11¾" h. (restoration to ears, tight hairline in tail).............**2,530.00**
Planter, "Cats on Fence," w/flower-pots **795.00**
Planter, log-form w/molded leaf & narrow strap handle at top center, 11" l....................................**95.00**
Vase, 12" h., smooth tree trunk form w/molded leafy branch around rim

& down sides w/hanging purple
plums **195.00**
Vase, 13" h., waisted cylindrical tree
trunk form w/relief-molded branch,
apple & leaves down the front **395.00**
Vase, double bud, 13½" h., tall
slender tree trunks flanking apple
blossom branch topped by small
owl ....**450.00 to 550.00**
Vase, 15¼" h., 7" d., tall cylindrical
tree trunk-form, pierced w/a large
hole on one side, a large figural owl
to one side of the hole & a cluster of
apples & leaves above, polychrome
matte glaze, die-stamped
"WELLER"................................**1,045.00**
Wall hanging, model of a large
climbing squirrel, matte brown &
green glaze, black ink kiln
mark, 4¾" w., 13½" h. **935.00**
Wall pocket, conical tree trunk form
w/relief-molded branch down front
& figural squirrel seated at base,
9" h. ....**300.00 to 350.00**
Wall pocket, smooth tree trunk form
w/molded leaves & hanging purple
plums at base, 9" h. **400.00**
Wall pocket, conical, molded
owl head in trunk opening,
10" h. ....**250.00 to 350.00**

ZONA (about 1920)

*Red apples and green leaves on brown
branches all on a cream-colored ground;
some pieces with molded florals or birds
with various glazes.*
*A line of children's dishes was also
produced featuring hand-painted or
molded animals. This is referred to as the
"Zona Baby Line."*

Pitcher, 8" h., kingfisher decoration, green glaze..............**130.00 to 150.00**

Zona Child's Plate

Plate w/rolled edge, Juvenile line,
decorated w/ducks, 7" d. (ILLUS.) **85.00**

Zona Umbrella Stand

Umbrella stand, 10" d., 20" h., tall
cylindrical slightly flaring body,
decorated w/women in purple
dresses holding long garlands of red
flowers under grapevines, white
ground (ILLUS.) **715.00**

(End of Weller Section)

WILLOW WARES

This pseudo-Chinese pattern has been
used by numerous firms throughout the
years. The original design is attributed to
Thomas Minton about 1780 and Thomas
Turner is believed to have first produced
the ware during his tenure at the Caughley
works. The blue underglaze transfer print
pattern has never been out of production
since that time. An Oriental landscape
incorporating a bridge, pagoda, trees,
figures and bird, supposedly tells the story
of lovers fleeing a cruel father who wished
to prevent their marriage. The gods,
having pity on them, changed them into
birds enabling them to fly away and seek
their happiness together.
Also see BUFFALO POTTERY.

BLUE
Ashtray, "Please don't burn our
home," oval, unmarked, 6" l. **$40.00**
Ashtray, oval, unmarked, 7¼" l............**30.00**
Bowl, 5¼" d., Homer Laughlin **4.00**
Bowl, fruit, 5½" d., Royal China Co.
Sebring, Ohio.....................................**3.50**
Bowl, fruit, 5½" d., Allerton,
England...**15.00**

Bowl, cereal, 6½" d., Flair, Japan **5.00**
Bowl, cereal, 6½" d., Homer
  Laughlin **7.00**
Bowl, 9" d., Royal, Sebring, Ohio........**13.00**
Bowl, fruit, large, Wedgwood, Etruria,
  England, ca. 1944, ...**200.00**
Cake lifter, Moriyama, Japan.............**150.00**
Cake plate, round, Moriyama, Japan...**90.00**
Cheese dish, cov., Wadrus & Sons,
  Staffordshire, England **150.00**
Coffeepot, cov., demitasse,
  cylindrical, recessed lid w/finial,
  Pountney & Co., Ltd., England,
  6¼" h..**85.00**
Cookie jar, cov., Japan......................**100.00**
Cruet, oil, w/original stopper,
  unmarked...**45.00**
Cup & saucer, demitasse, Allerton,
  England..**56.00**
Cup & saucer, Allerton, England.........**31.00**
Cup & saucer, large, Allerton,
  England..**38.00**
Cup & saucer, Booth's, England **12.00**
Cup & saucer, interior design & on
  handle, Japan **12.00**
Cup & saucer, Old Japan......................**8.50**
Cup & saucer, Homer Laughlin **5.00**
Cup & saucer, stacking-type, USA........**2.50**
Gravy boat, unmarked..........................**25.00**

Blue Willow Hot Water Dish

Hot water dish w/original stopper &
  two 10" dinner plates, dish
  w/printer's mark in underglaze-blue
  & impressed "Y," plates
  w/"MASON'S PATENT
  IRONSTONE CHINA" banner marks
  printed in underglaze-blue, dish
  w/central star crack & small rim chip,
  plates worn, water dish 11⅜" d.,
  3 pcs. (ILLUS.) **201.00**
Lamp, hurricane-type, complete,
  unmarked...**95.00**
Lamp, kerosene-type, 8½" h.,
  Japan..**125.00**
Mug, interior design & on handle,
  Japan..**13.50**
Pitcher, figural toby, William Kent,
  England, unmarked, 5½" h. **795.00**
Plate, 3¾" d., Occupied Japan.............**12.50**
Plate, 4⅞" d., light blue w/pink lustre
  rim, England, early 19th c.
  (hairline at rim) **44.00**

Plate, 6" d., Allerton, England **14.50**
Plate, 6" d., Royal China Co.,
  Sebring, Ohio..**2.00**
Plate, 6⅜" d., Royal................................**3.00**
Plate, 6½" d., Booth's, England...........**18.00**
Plate, 7" d., Allerton, England **16.00**
Plate, 7⅝" d., Booth's, England...........**18.00**
Plate, 8¼" d., Ridgway, England..........**25.00**
Plate, 8" d., Allerton, England **20.00**
Plate, 9" d., Allerton, England **26.00**
Plate, 9" d., Royal China Co..................**5.50**
Plate, 9½" d., Japan.............................**10.00**
Plate, grill, 9¾" d., Homer Laughlin........**5.00**
Plate, grill, 9¾" d., Japan **12.00**
Plate, 10" d., w/rolled edge **5.00**
Plate, grill, 10¾" d., divided,
  Japan..**10.00**
Plate, 12¼" d., Royal China Co............**15.00**
Plate, dinner, Ridgway, England **22.00**
Plate, grill, Shenango China Co. **15.00**
Plate, luncheon, Adams, England........**15.00**
Plate, luncheon, Ridgway, England **20.00**
Plate, salad, Adams, England **12.00**
Plate, salad, Japan.................................**8.00**
Plates, luncheon, Carter & Hall,
  England, set of 8...............................**200.00**
Platter, child's, 5" l., oval, Clews, ca.
  1825-50..**115.50**
Platter, 6¼" l., Occupied Japan **30.00**
Platter, 8½ x 10½", England **175.00**
Platter, 12" l., Japan.............................**22.00**
Platter, 13" l., U.S.A.............................**29.00**
Platter, 7 x 14", England **225.00**
Platter, 14 x 17", England **300.00**
Platter, 18" l., Allerton,
  England ....**125.00 to 150.00**
Platter, 18½" oval, impressed on
  back "18," England, ca. 1820..........**198.00**
Platter, small, Allerton, England...........**65.00**
Platter, medium, Allerton, England **125.00**
Salt & pepper shakers, pr...................**55.00**
Salt & pepper shakers w/wooden
  tops & bottoms, unmarked, pr...........**20.00**
Soup plate w/flanged rim, Dunn
  Bennett Co., Ltd., Burslem,
  England, 7½" d. **13.00**
Soup plate w/flanged rim, Maddocks
  & Sons Ltd., England, 8⅞" d..........**22.00**
Soup plate w/flanged rim, 9½" d.,
  Ridgway, England **26.00**
Sugar shaker, Japan **45.00**
Teapot, cov., Sadler, England...........**150.00**
Toaster, electric **1,795.00**
Toothpick holder, unmarked **25.00**
Toothpick holder, Wedgwood,
  England..**60.00**
Trinket box, domed cover, round **89.50**
Tumbler, 5" h., Homer Laughlin.............**9.00**
Vegetable bowl, cov., Allerton,
  England..**140.00**
Vegetable bowl, open, oval,
  Grindley, England, 7 x 9" **30.00**
Vegetable bowl, Royal China
  Co., 9" d. **12.00**

Vegetable bowl, open, round,
Japan **20.00**

OTHER COLORS

Baker, black, Japan **35.00**
Bowl, 5" d., red, Homer Laughlin **4.00**
Cup & saucer, black, Japan **12.00**
Plate, 6" d., red, Homer Laughlin **2.50**
Plate, 7" d., red, Homer Laughlin **3.00**
Plate, 9¾" d., red, Homer Laughlin **7.00**
Platter, 11½" l., red, Homer
Laughlin **18.00**
Platter, 13½" l., red, Homer
Laughlin **16.00**
Pudding molds, red, England,
set of 3 ....**75.00**
Soup plate w/flanged rim, black,
Japan **15.00**
Tile, sepia tone, 6" d **28.00**

YELLOW-GLAZED EARTHENWARE

Yellow-Glazed Earthenware Pitcher

*In the past this early English ware was
often referred to as "Canary Lustre," but
recently a more accurate title has come into
use.*

*Produced in the late 18th and early
19th centuries, pieces featured an overall
yellow glaze, often decorated with silver or
copper lustre designs or black, brown or
red transfer-printed scenes.*

*Most pieces are not marked and today
the scarcity of examples in good condition
keeps market prices high.*

Basket, openwork wrapped lattice
type w/the side slats interlaced
w/stringing & a string-wrapped rolled
rim, basketweave bottom, trimmed
w/black, brown & dark orange, ca.
1790, 9" d., 3¼" h. (one rim crack,
one hairline in stringing, faint hairline

across the base, few enamel
flakes) **$2,200.00**
Bowl, 6¼" d., 3⅛" h., deep rounded
sides on a thick footring, decorated
w/a band of h.p. band & green
leaves w/black curling tendrils,
orange rim band (some light
wear, chip on foot rim) **412.50**
Cup & saucer, child's, handled, each
decorated w/large round orange
flowers & green leaves, early 19th c.
(overall stain, restoration to foot rim
of cup, tiny flake on foot of
saucer) **385.00**
Mug, child's, cylindrical, decorated
w/black transfer-printed oval portraits of Lafayette & Washington below a spread-winged eagle w/a ban-
ner in its beak, ca. 1820s, 2¾" h. ...**1,092.50**
Pitcher, 6⅛" h., ovoid body tapering
to a short cylindrical flat rim, printed
in black on one side w/an eagle
perched on a wreath entwined w/a
ribbon inscribed "New Jersey,
Boston, Kentucky, South Carolina,
North Carolina, Virginia, Maryland,"
& in an oval at the top "New York," &
enclosing the inscription "PEACE
PLENTY *and* INDEPENDENCE,"
flanked by maidens allegorical of
Peace & Plenty beneath a sixteen-
star American flag & on the reverse
w/a further flag beneath a cartouche
inscribed on a ribbon "SUCCESS to
the UNITED STATES of AMERICA"
above "E PLURIBUS UNUM"
between an Indian maiden & an
eagle, both within silver lustre
roundels, a sliver lustre sunburst
beneath spout & the handle, neck,
rim & lower body w/silver lustre
bands, England, 1812-15, chip &
three hair cracks (ILLUS.) **2,070.00**
Pitcher, jug-type, 8½" h., decorated
w/a large scrolling bouquet of
orange, black & blue flowers &
leaves, early 19th c. (some
scratches & flakes, restored chip on
spout) **1,210.00**
Plate, 8" w., octagonal, the wide
border band embossed w/small
flowerheads trimmed in orange, blue
& green, the center w/a black
transfer-printed zoo landscape
w/figures titled "Zoological Gardens
- Otter House" (transfer slightly
faded, professional restoration at
rim) **291.50**
Salt dip, footed, round wide bowl
decorated w/a pair of thin blue
stripes, short pedestal base, 3" d.,
2⅛" h. (pinpoint flakes, stains) **220.00**

(End of Ceramics Section)

CHALKWARE

Chalkware Bank & Model of a Rooster

So-called chalkware available today is actually made of plaster of Paris, much of it decorated in color and primarily in the form of busts, figurines and ornaments. It was produced through most of the 19th century and the majority of pieces were originally quite inexpensive when made. Today even 20th century "carnival" pieces are collectible.

Bank, hollow-molded in the form of a perched dove decorated w/a gold beak on a base w/coin slot & gold-painted tree w/green leaves & red fruit, Pennsylvania, 19th c., 11⅓" h. (ILLUS. left) **$1,150.00**

Figure of a Buddha, incense burner, large..**115.00**

Figure of a Drum Majorette, carnival-type, 13" h. **60.00**

Figure of a Kewpie, wearing a feather dress & top hat & holding a cane, carnival-type, 4½" h. **12.50**

Goblets, slightly flaring cylindrical bowl w/a swelled rib-molded base tapering to a ringed pedestal base w/swirled ribbing, stars molded in the cup, stars, ribbing, rim & base trimmed in brown, Pennsylvania, mid-19th c., 5¾" h., pr...................**1,840.00**

Mantel garniture, hollow-molded piece depicting an arrangement of vegetables, fruit & leaves painted w/gold, red & black highlights, on a pedestal, Pennsylvania, 19th c., 13½" h. (ILLUS. top next column) **1,610.00**

Model of a cat, hollow-molded seated animal, black w/red ears & mouth, highlighted w/olive green & black spots, white whiskers & claws, on a black rectangular base, Pennsylvania, mid-19th c., 5½" h...**2,070.00**

Chalkware Mantel Garniture

Model of a cat, the animal in an alert seated position w/paint-decorated ears, eyes, whiskers & claws, on a high rectangular base, 19th c., 7¼" h. (imperfections) **770.00**

Model of a cat, the seated animal painted w/a striped coat, whiskers & eyes, on a low oval base, 19th c., 9¼" h. (some wear)......................**3,960.00**

Model of a cat, seated, molded & painted features & a ribbon around its neck, on a round base, 19th c., 9¾" h. (retouch) **431.00**

Model of a cat, the reclining animal w/black markings on a white ground w/traces of yellow & red, 10" l..........**715.00**

Model of a cat, in reclining position w/head up, original black & yellowed white paint w/faded red, 10" l. (minor wear)......................................**165.00**

Model of a cat, hollow-molded seated animal, painted yellow w/black spots & red collar, circular base, Pennsylvania, mid-19th c., 10½" h...**1,265.00**

Model of a cat, large reclining animal w/head down, original painted red & blue ribbon around neck & black & white coat, 12" l. (wear, crazing, punched hole in bottom & chips on ear) **165.00**

Model of a cat, curled up in sleeping position, original paint w/black stripes on yellowed white w/red, blue & green, 12¼" l. (wear & crazing) **110.00**

Model of a compote of fruit, well-detailed colorful fruit against a background of foliage, arranged in a low bowl w/a square base, 19th c., 13" h. (imperfection).....................**2,090.00**

Model of a dog, seated facing viewer, crudely modeled w/black-sponged white body & black ears, red trim, 5½" h. (wear, old shallow chip on base) **165.00**

Model of a Pekinese dog, carnival-type, 6 x 10" **45.00**

Model of a dog, Spaniel in a seated position, on a low square base, original paint w/black stripes on yellowed white w/red, black & yellow, 7¾" h. (wear & possible paint touch-up on face) **159.50**

Model of a dog, Spaniel in seated position, original paint w/black spots on yellowed white w/orange & green, 8¾" h. (some wear & minor flakes) **165.00**

Model of a Spaniel

Model of a dog, Spaniel, the hollow-molded animal in a seated position w/articulated fur & gold-painted eyes, black ears & red collar, Pennsylvania, 19th c., 10⅜" h. (ILLUS.) **115.00**

Model of a dove, worn painted decoration, late 19th c., 10" h...**115.00**

Model of a lion, the standing animal w/its right front foot on a ball, on a stepped rectangular base w/rounded corners, worn polychrome paint, green base w/pencil inscription, 10" l...**93.50**

Model of a poodle, standing hollow-molded animal w/articulated curly coat around neck highlighted w/orange, red & blue dots, ears & tail in brown, on a stepped rectangular base, Pennsylvania, 19th c., 8" h......................................**518.00**

Model of a rabbit, nodding-type, the reclining animal w/paint-decorated

ears, eyes & whiskers, further trimmed w/a painted ring around the neck, on a low shaped rectangular base, 19th c., 3¼" h. (imperfections) **1,100.00**

Model of a rabbit, hollow-molded seated animal w/red ears, gold eyes & black eyebrows, on a rectangular base, Pennsylvania, 19th c., 5¼" h..**1,150.00**

Model of a rooster, hollow-molded in the form of a rooster w/yellow-painted body, black legs & red, black & green highlight decoration, on a circular base, Pennsylvania, 19th c., 6⅜" h. (ILLUS. right with bank) **1,840.00**

Model of a squirrel, seated animal eating an acorn, articulated tail, traces of red, black & green decoration, oval base, Pennsylvania, 19th c., 6¼" h..**230.00**

Model of a stag, reclining animal w/bent antlers & one foreleg arched, decorated w/gold, olive & black trim, on rectangular base w/cut corners, Pennsylvania, mid-19th c., 4¼ x 7⅞", 7½" h. **1,840.00**

Model of a stag, reclining animal w/short pointed antlers, raised ears & one foreleg arched, hollow full-bodied style w/golden brown antlers & ears, on an oblong molded green-painted base, Pennsylvania, 19th c., 10" l., 10¼" h...................................**518.00**

CHARACTER COLLECTIBLES

Andy Gump Roadster

Numerous objects made in the likeness of or named after comic strip and comic book personalities or characters abounded from the 1920s to the present. Scores of these are now being eagerly collected and prices still vary widely.

Alley Oop (comic strips) original art, pen & ink on paper, a four-panel daily strip dated August 6, 1939, 5½ x 21".............................**$460.00**

Andy Gump toy, cast iron, Andy seated in his red, green & white roadster w/doughnut-style tires, "348" embossed on the front grille, Arcade, ca. 1923, 7" l. (ILLUS.) **2,990.00**

Barney Google figure, pressed wood, Multi Products of Chicago, 4" h. ....**75.00 to 85.00**

Barney Google & Spark Plug Dolls

Barney Google & Spark Plug dolls, wood & cloth, Barney w/a wooden head, large painted black & white eyes, single stroke brows, painted mustache, wooden ears, painted hair, wooden body jointed at shoulders & hips & wearing his original white shirt, black & white checked pants, black felt jacket & wooden hat, Spark Plug w/a jointed wooden body, painted facial features & replaced leather ears, Schoenhut, early 20th c., Spark Plug repainted, tail missing & no blanket, Barney 7½" h., Spark Plug 9" l., 6" h. at shoulders, pr. (ILLUS.) **375.00**

Barney Google & Spark Plug game, by Milton Bradley, King Features Syndicate, 1923, complete & mint in colorful original box, 18" ....**100.00 to 150.00**

Barney Google & Spark Plug toy, pull-type, lithographed tin, featuring Spark Plug w/jockey on a green base w/Barney Google on a sep- arate yellow base interconnected to a four-wheel superstructure, when

Barney Google & Spark Plug Toy

pulled the figures bob up & down alternately as if dashing ahead, ca. 1924, 8" l. (ILLUS.).................**6,270.00**

Barney Rubble (Flintstones comics) Christmas tree ornament, 1976, 4" d., mint in box **25.00**

Betty Boop & Bimbo ashtray, china, lustre trim, Japan..................**225.00**

Blondie game, "Blondie Goes to Leisureland," Westinghouse premium, 1940, in original envelope **28.00**

Blondie paint box, tin, American Crayon Co., 1946, 4½ x 5¾".............**25.00**

Blondie & Dagwood letter holder, ceramic, 1940s **110.00**

Bonny Braids (Dick Tracy) pin-back button, figural, on original card....**45.00**

Bringing Up Father comic book, No. 4, ca. 1921 ....**45.00**

Bringing Up Father original comic art, hand-colored ink & mixed media on paper, colorful Sunday comic page w/title box for "Rosie's Beau," dated "7/5/36," signed by George McManus, 16½ x 21" **1,725.00**

Buck Rogers Atomic Pistol, No. U-235, steel finished metal, adapted from prewar disintegrator pistol, Daisy Mfg. Co., w/original yellow box, ca. 1946, 9" l. **425.00**

Buck Rogers badge, "Solar Scout," Cream of Wheat premium, 1934, mint......................................**175.00**

Buck Rogers book, pop-up type, "Spidership Adventures," 1935 ....**175.00**

Buck Rogers booklet, Kellogg's premium, 1933...............................**200.00**

Buck Rogers helmet, child's, leather, w/metal goggles w/plastic lens, metal side tabs embossed w/"Buck Rogers 25th Century" & a scene, ca. 1930s, leather dry & cracked, minor rust (ILLUS. top next page)....**247.50**

Buck Rogers pencil box, thick red cardboard w/snap-open closure, each side w/a colorful scene of Buck

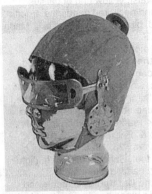

Buck Rogers Child's Helmet

in action, American Lead Pencil Co.,
1936, 6 x 10" (slight edge wear) **98.00**
Buck Rogers ring, "Ring of Saturn,"
w/red stone, glow in the
dark crocodile base, 1940s **750.00**
Buck Rogers spaceship w/secret
bomb sight, "Morton Salt" premium,
the Umbrella Girl on the sight,
complete in original package **75.00**
Buck Rogers toy, "Battle Cruiser
Rocket Ship," cast metal, red &
yellow, Tootsietoy, Dowst Mfg.
Co., 1937, 4¾" l. **495.00**
Buck Rogers toy, "Flash Blast
Attack Ship," cast metal, Tootsietoy,
1930s **135.00**
Buck Rogers toy, "Buck Rogers
Midget Caster Set," nicely
lithographed box w/comic colorful
illustrations of Buck & Wilma,
contents include handles, scooper,
paints, metal piece & two Buck
figures, 1934, box 7½ x 18½" (part
of side panel missing, missing the
molds, some edge wear, some
paint stains on box)........................**375.00**
Buck Rogers toy, "Strato-Kite,"
w/envelope, 1946-50,
mint in box ....**100.00 to 150.00**
Casper, the Friendly Ghost game,
battery-operated, 1959 ....**32.00**
Dagwood puzzle, jigsaw-type,
100-piece puzzle titled "Dag-wood's
in Trouble," features Blondie,
Dagwood, Mr. Dithers & neighbors,
Jaymar, 1960, box 8 x 10" **22.00**
Daisy Mae (Li'l Abner comic) mug,
ceramic, light tan w/a
picture of Daisy Mae, 1940s **35.00**
Dennis the Menace game,
lithographed tin, baseball game
w/three balls..**60.00**
Dennis the Menace napkins,
1954, in original box...........................**30.00**
Dennis the Menace tumbler, clear
glass w/frosted band printed in black

Dennis the Menace Tumbler

w/a cartoon scene, the caption
reads "This is my mother,
Tommy. Isn't she pretty," 5½" h.
(ILLUS.) **44.00**
Dick Tracy coloring book,
Saalfield, ca. 1940s **45.00**
Dick Tracy "Crimestopper" kit,
w/badge, whistle, flashlight, etc.,
1961 ....**95.00**
Dick Tracy game, board-type, "Dick
Tracy Master Detective Game,"
Selchow & Righter, 1961, complete
in 10 x 20" box (light shelf wear on
box)...**32.00**
Dick Tracy handcuffs, on original
card **52.00**
Dick Tracy hand puppet, Ideal,
1961 ....**75.00**
Dick Tracy puzzle, jigsaw-type, 100-
piece puzzle features Tracy viewing
a police line-up w/Flat top, Stooge,
Villa & The Mole, Jaymar,
1961, 8 x 10" box **22.00**
Dick Tracy pistol, "siren" type, tin,
Louis Marx & Co., 1934, boxed,
7" l. **77.00**
Dick Tracy ring, enameled bust
portrait of Dick Tracy, radio
premium ....**185.00 to 195.00**
Dick Tracy suspenders, from
Detective set, boxed **75.00**
Dick Tracy toy, Squad Car #1,
friction-type, lithographed green
w/various Tracy characters, battery-
operated roof light, plated grille &
bumper, Marx,
mint, 11" l. ....**300.00 to 350.00**
Dick Tracy tumbler, clear w/printed
scene of Tracy in black, reds &
fleshtones, Domino's Pizza
series, 16 oz. **95.00**
Dick Tracy wrist watch, round dial
depicts a half-length portrait of Tracy
w/yellow fedora & blue overcoat,
subsidiary seconds dial shaped as a
gun, weathered brown leather band,

Dick Tracy Wrist Watch

insert & box showing Dick Tracy
& Junior, New Haven, 1948
(ILLUS.) **368.00**
Dionne Quintuplets book, "Going
On Three," 1936 ....**40.00 to 50.00**
Dionne Quintuplets book, "Soon
We'll Be Three Years Old," 1936 ......**30.00**
Dionne Quintuplets calendar,
1940, "Quints in School Days" **35.00**
Dionne Quintuplets calendar,
1941, "All Dressed Up" **35.00**
Dionne Quintuplets calendar,
1944, feeding baby birds **30.00**
Dionne Quintuplets handkerchief,
pictures the Quints...........................**48.00**
**Dionne Quintuplets magazine
cover,** "Life," September 2, 1940,
pictures the Quintuplets receiving
First Communion **18.00**

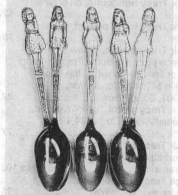

Dionne Quintuplets Teaspoons

Dionne Quintuplets teaspoons,
silver plate, full figure handles
w/names, Carlton, set of 5
(ILLUS.) **150.00**
Elsie the Cow doll, velveteen
w/painted brown eyes, painted
upper lashes, multi-stroke brows,
accented nostrils, closed smiling
mouth, applied ears & horns, stiff
neck, body jointed at shoulders only,
black velveteen hooves, applied
wire-covered tail, dressed in original
blue pinafore lettered "Elsie" above

the waist, yellow ring of daisies
around neck, red bandanna around
head, blue bow on end of tail, "Made
in U.S.A." tag on left side, 13" h.
(few moth holes) **325.00**
Felix the Cat figure, jointed wood,
wooden character head w/painted
eyes, wooden nose, closed smiling
mouth, applied leather ears, jointed
wooden body & segmented tail in
black, marked "Felix" on front of
torso & "Felix, Pat. 1922, 1924...
Sullivan,...23, 1925" on bottom of
right foot, Schoenhut, 3½" h. (light
wear, needs restringing) **230.00**
Felix the Cat figure, jointed wood,
jointed wood head w/painted black
intaglio eyes w/white around them,
wooden nose, closed smiling mouth,
leather ears, black wooden body
w/jointed wooden arms & legs, feet
& segmented tail, marked "Felix" on
the chest, "Felix - Copyright 1922,
1924 by Pat. Sullivan Pat. Applied
For" on bottom of foot, 7½" h. (ears
replaced, fine crazing & some
flaking, old repair to right foot) **350.00**
Felix the Cat Ginger Ale bottle **100.00**
Felix the Cat yarn winder,
England, ca. 1930............................**65.00**
Flash Gordon book, pop-up-type,
"Tournament of Death," w/three pop-
up pictures, Pleasure Books, Inc.,
King Features Syndicate,
1935, hard covers **316.00**
Flash Gordon kite, paper, decorated
w/a picture of Flash's head,
wrapped in paper tube w/his
name on it, 1950s, 17 x 21" **45.00**

Gloria Tumbler

Gloria (Little Lulu comic) tumbler,
clear w/printed figure w/cat in blue
& dark yellow (ILLUS.) **88.00**
Harold Teen ukulele, red-painted
wood, Harold's head at the top &
other strip characters at the bottom

w/various sayings like "Boop-Boop-Ah Doop" scattered about, mother-of-pearl neck, 1930s, 21" l. (paint flakes on back, minor edge wear) **145.00**

Jiggs Ashtray & Match Holder

Jiggs (Bringing Up Father comic) ashtray & match holder, wood & metal, a silhouetted cut-out figure of Jiggs in a black suit, green vest, red bow tie & green, white & black top hat, holding a round metal ashtray w/a match box holder on the rim, on a round wooden base, minor scratches, ca. 1930s, 35" h. (ILLUS.) **385.00**

Joe Palooka lobby cards, color cards featuring scenes from "Humphrey Takes A Chance," 1950s, each 11 x 14", set of 8 ....**95.00**

Katzenjammer Kids toy, seesaw pull-type, cast iron, consisting of a cast three-wheeled platform on which Hans & Fritz seesaw together, colorfully painted, N.N. Hill Brass Company, ca. 1900, 7½" l................**575.00**

Li'l Abner color decal, "Orange Crush" premium, in illustrated envelope, 1940s **16.00**

Li'l Abner mug, ceramic, light tan w/a picture of Li'l Abner, 1940s..........**35.00**

Li'l Abner tumbler set: includes illustrations of Daisy Mae, Li'l Abner, Lonesome Polecat, Mammy Yokum, Marryin' Sam/Sadie Hawkins, Pappy Yokum, Shmoos, Unwashable Jones; clear glass, United Features Syndicate, 1949, 4¾" h., set of 8 .....**195.00**

Little King pinback button, Kellogg's Pep Cereal premium ....**20.00 to 25.00**

Little King toy, pull-type, colorful wooden figure of the Little King on wheeled base, 1940s, in original box, 4" h...**85.00**

Little Nemo (early comics) toy, bell-type, cast iron & steel, both Little Nemo & his friend sway side-to-side

causing three bells on the platform base to ring, raised on four metal wheels w/heart-shaped spoke openings, ca. 1905, 10½" l. **345.00**

Maggie & Jiggs (Bringing Up Father) Christmas card, 1930s **28.00**

Marvel Bunny (Captain Marvel comics) figure, hand-painted plastic, standing on a base, original "Plastics" decal on bottom, R.W. Kerr Co., 1946, in original box & original packing, 5½" h. **3,450.00**

Max & Moritz plate, china, illustrates Max & Moritz & other characters, marked "Kaiser W. Germany," 7½" d. ....**100.00 to 125.00**

Olive Oyl pinback button, Kellogg's Pep Cereal premium **25.00**

Orphan Annie decoder, 1937, Ovaltine premium ....**35.00 to 45.00**

Orphan Annie decoder, "Tele-matic," 1938, Ovaltine premium ......**30.00 to 40.00**

Orphan Annie doll, molded & painted composition head & arms, cloth body & legs, wearing original outfit, head marked "Famous Artists Synd.," 1930s, 14½" h. (some paint wear) **80.50**

Orphan Annie game, "Treasure Hunt," Ovaltine premium, 1933, Wander Co...**65.00**

Orphan Annie's Song Sheet Music

Orphan Annie sheet music, "Little Orphan Annie's Song," 1931 (ILLUS.) **20.00**

Orphan Annie tea set, child's, china w/tan lustre finish, ca. 1930s, 17 pcs. **300.00**

Orphan Annie & Sandy dolls, Annie made of oilcloth w/circles for eyes, single stroke brows, nose indicated w/a line, closed mouth, painted hair, oilcloth body jointed at shoulders only, painted shoes & stockings, dressed in original blue dress w/white polka dots, matching pants,

Orphan Annie & Sandy Dolls

Sandy made of gold velveteen w/a few darker areas to indicate spots, glass eyes, black floss nose & mouth, marked "Little Orphan Annie by Harold Gray, Patent Applied For" on belt of dress, Annie 16" h., pr. (ILLUS.) **95.00**

Peanuts game, board-type, Selchow & Righter, 1959, complete in 10 x 20" box **79.00**

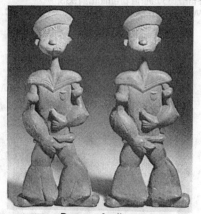

Popeye Andirons

Popeye andirons, cast metal, half-round figure of standing Popeye, one incised "ARK" on his arm, missing billet bars, early 20th c., 14¼" h., pr. (ILLUS.) **1,380.00**

Popeye mechanical pencil, 1929, w/original box....................................**45.00**

Popeye paint set, "Popeye Paints," tin, The American Crayon Co., Sandusky, Ohio, 1933, unused.........**75.00**

Popeye pencil coloring set, contains 12 color pencils, pencil sharpener & 12 pre-numbered sketches in two different sizes, Hasbro, 1950, unused, box 10 x 13" **89.00**

Popeye postcard, patriotic-type, 1940s...**30.00**

Popeye toy, pop-up type, "Popeye Spinach" can, plastic & metal, Popeye's head comes up when the can is opened, Mattel, 1957.......**100.00**

Popeye Tumbler

Popeye tumbler, clear glass w/a printed design of Popeye in boxing trunks throwing a punch, late 1930s (ILLUS.) **50.00**

Popeye & Olive Oyl toy, windup tin, Popeye & Olive Oyl tossing a beach ball back & forth, Line Mar, ca. 1940s, w/original box, 19" l. **1,265.00**

Shmoo (Li'l Abner comic) tumbler, clear glass w/orange enamel illustration, Al Capp series, 1949 ......**35.00**

Smokey the Bear head scarf **10.00**

Snoopy toy, "My Friend Snoopy," pull the arms back & it will knock all the bowling pins down, United Features Syndicate, 1955-66, w/original box....................................**35.00**

Spider-man game, target-type, 1981, mint in box **35.00**

Steve Canyon game, board-type, Lowell, 1959, complete in 10 x 20" box...**59.00**

Steve Canyon model kit, ⅛ scale all-plastic, depicts Canyon wearing a jet fighter pilot uniform, Aurora, 1959, unassembled in 5 x 13" box......................................**249.00**

Superman belt, brown leather embossed w/illustrations of Superman breaking a chain, landing from flight & taking off, gold metal buckle w/embossed bust of Superman breaking his chains, his name embossed to the side, 1940s (minor wear) **125.00**

Superman card set, a different color scene on each card, produced for Superman Gum by Gum Inc., ca. 1940, set of 72 (ILLUS. of part, top next page)..............................**2,990.00**

Superman Gum Cards

Superman figure, chalkware,
carnival-type, 15" h. **125.00**
Superman game, "Horseshoes," in
original box **130.00**
Superman Kryptonite rock, 1977,
in original box....................................**14.00**
Superman ring, "Jet Airplane"...........**275.00**
Superman secret code folder,
"Action Comics" premium **29.00**
Superman toy, quoit set, "Junior
Quoits," two bases & two pegs
w/Superman's insignia embossed
on the bases, box illustrated
w/Superman w/his logo on the side,
1950s, the set (tape marks
on box, edge & surface wear) **65.00**
Terry & the Pirates coloring book,
1946, unused **40.00**
Toonerville Trolley toy, cast iron,
painted green & orange, the Skipper
at the controls, w/"Tooner-ville"
embossed on each side, attributed
to Dent Hardware, early 20th c.,
5½" h..**575.00**
Uncle Wiggily game, board-type,
Parker, 1971 ....**65.00**
Wonder Woman cookie jar, cov.,
ceramic, silver, marked "USA 847,
copyright, D.C. Comics Inc.,
1978"..**1,000.00**

Woody Woodpecker Animation Cel

Woody Woodpecker animation cel,
gouache on full celluloid applied to a
non-matching production background from the same era, a green-
eyed Woody flies & pecks, from the
main title sequence in which he
pecks out his name, signed by
Walter Lantz, 1952, overall 10½ x
13" (ILLUS.) **1,840.00**
Woody Woodpecker puppet, hand-
type, w/talking mechanism, Mattel,
Inc. (Hawthorne, California),
1963 ....**50.00 to 60.00**
Woody Woodpecker handkerchief,
full-color images, authorized by
"Walter Lantz Productions, Inc.,"
9" sq...**30.00**

Yellow Kid Pinback Buttons

**Yellow Kid (early comics) pinback
buttons,** each w/a different color
picture of the Yellow Kid, numbered
41 through 94, ca. 1900, set of 39
(ILLUS. five of 39) **2,990.00**

CHILDREN'S BOOKS

*The most collectible children's books
today tend to be those printed after the
1850s and, while age is not completely
irrelevant, illustrations play a far more
important role in determining the values.
While first editions are highly esteemed, it
is the beautiful illustrated books that most
collectors seeks. The following books, all in
good to fine conditions, are listed
alphabetically. Also see BLACK AMERI-
CANA, BIG LITTLE BOOKS, CHARAC-
TER COLLECTIBLES, COMIC BOOKS,
DISNEY COLLECTIBLES, RADIO &
TELEVISION MEMORABILIA, SPACE
AGE COLLECTIBLES and WESTERN
CHARACTER COLLECTIBLES.*

**"All About the Little Small Red
Hen,"** by Beatrix Potter, illustrated
by John Gruelle, 1917....................**$25.00**
"All About the Three Little Pigs," by
Beatrix Potter, illustrated by Dick
Harley, 1914 ....**25.00**
"Alphabet," Wet the Brush & Bring
Out Colors-type, Saalfield
Publishing Co., Akron, Ohio, 1940,
7 x 9"..**6.00**
"Answer The Riddles," follow the
dots-type, Saalfield Publishing Co.,
Akron, Ohio, 1938, 6⅜ x 7½" **9.00**
"Bambi's Children," by Felix Salten,
1950..**15.00**

"Child's Garden of Verses," by Robert Louis Stevenson, 1905, w/12 full color pen & ink illustrations by Jessie Willcox Smith **125.00**

"Christmas Time in Action," pop-up type, 1949 ....**48.00**

"Christopher Robin Story Book," by A.A. Milne, illustrated by Shepard, 1957 ....**20.00**

"Fairy Tale Pictures, Hansel & Gretel," Pasting Without Paste-type, illustrated by Martha E. Miller, Saalfield Publishing Co., Akron, Ohio, 1939, 9 x 11" **10.00**

"Good Times," Push Out & Paste Without Paste-type, Saalfield Publishing Co., Akron, Ohio, 1946, 8¾ x 11" **11.00**

"Green Eggs & Ham," by Dr. Seuss, 1960 ....**25.00**

"Hans Brinker or The Silver Skates," by Mary Mapes Dodge, illustrations by C.M. Burd, 1925 ....**30.00**

"Horses & Colts," by Frances Montgomery, 1911 ....**20.00**

"How the Grinch Stole Christmas," by Dr. Seuss, 1957 ....**125.00**

"I Like My Toys," Push Out & Paste Without Paste-type, Saalfield Publishing Co., Akron, Ohio, 1946, 8¾ x 11" **15.00**

"I Like to Play Aviator," Wet the Brush & Bring Out Colors-type, Saalfield Publishing Co., Akron, Ohio, 1943, 7 x 9" **10.00**

"I Like to Play Sailor," Wet the Brush & Bring Out Colors-type, Saalfield Publishing Co., Akron, Ohio, 1943, 7 x 9" **10.00**

"Just So Stories," by Rudyard Kipling, 1935, illustrated by Bramson **27.50**

"Life Begins For Andy Panda," story & illustrations by Walter Lantz, 1940 ....**35.00**

"Marvelous Land of Oz," by L. Frank Baum, 1st edition, 1904 ....**270.00**

"Mother Goose," Pasting Without Paste-type, illustrated by Martha E. Miller, Saalfield Publishing Co., Akron, Ohio, 1939, 9 x 11" **15.00**

"The Night Before Christmas," colorful linen, 1935, Whitman **25.00**

"Nursery Rhymes," Wet the Brush & Bring Out Colors-type, Saalfield Publishing Co., Akron, Ohio, 1940, 7 x 9" **10.00**

"Oz Man Tales, Once Upon A Time," by L. Frank Baum, 1st edition, 1916 ....**140.00**

"Peter Rabbit & Jimmy Chipmunk," by Saalfield, 1918, w/original dust jacket **27.00**

"Play House," Wet the Brush & Bring Out Colors-type, Saalfield Publishing Co., Akron, Ohio, 1940, 7 x 9" **9.00**

"Playmates," Pasting Without Paste-type, illustrated by Martha E. Miller, Saalfield Publishing Co., Akron, Ohio, 1939, 9 x 11" **10.00**

"Puddinhead Wilson," by Mark Twain, 1894 ....**40.00**

"River Motor Boat Boys on the Rio Grande," 1915 ....**18.00**

"Skeezix & Uncle Walt," by F. King, 1924 (fair) **50.00**

"Stories of Little Brown Koko," American Colortype, 1940, hard cover **28.00**

"Tale of Rusty Wren," by Arthur S. Bailey, "Tuck Me In Tales," 1917 ......**25.00**

"The Bambam Clock," 30 illustrations, copyright 1920 ....**25.00**

"The Bird's Christmas Carole," by Kate D. Wiggin, illustrations by Jessie Gillespie (chip out of cover) **19.00**

"The Busy Bears," eight color illustrations, 1907 ....**50.00**

"The Calico Pup," by Lupprian, 1939 ....**25.00**

"The Circus," Pasting Without Paste-type, illustrated by Martha E. Miller, Saalfield Publishing Co., Akron, Ohio, 1939, 9 x 11" **20.00**

"The King's Stilts," by Dr. Seuss, 1939 ....**95.00**

"This Little Pig," Push Out & Paste Without Paste-type, Saalfield Publishing Co., Akron, Ohio, 1946, 8¾ x 11" **15.00**

"Through the Looking Glass," by Lewis Carroll, 1897, w/linen covers ...**35.00**

"Toys," Wet the Brush & Bring Out Colors-type, Saalfield Publishing Co., Akron, Ohio, 1940, 7 x 9" **8.00**

"Uncle Wiggly and His Friends," by Howard Garis, Platt & Munk, 1955, dust jacket..............................**22.00**

"Uncle Wiggily and the Troublesome Boys" by Howard Garis, 1943, soft cover, contains ten stories **40.00**

"Watty Piper's Folk Tales Children Love," by Dr. Seuss, 1955 ....**48.00**

"Welcome to Our Baby," illustrated by Charlotte Becker, mint in box........**35.00**

"Wee Miss Violet," illustrated by Willie Pogany **30.00**

CHILDREN'S DISHES

During the reign of Queen Victoria, dollhouses and accessories became more popular and as the century progressed, there was greater demand for toys which would subtly train a little girl in the art of homemaking. Also see CHARACTER COLLECTIBLES and DISNEY COLLECTIBLES and, under Glass, AKRO AGATE, DEPRESSION GLASS and PATTERN GLASS.

Bowls, individual berries, pressed glass, Nursery Rhyme patt., clear, set of 6 ....**$150.00**

Bowls, individual berries, pressed glass, Wheat Sheaf patt., clear, set of 6 ....**75.00**

Breakfast set: bowl, plate & milk pitcher; ceramic, reads "The Cat & The Fiddle," 3 pcs. **150.00**

Butter dish, cov., pressed glass, Button Panel patt., clear **90.00**

Butter dish, cov., pressed glass, Diamond Panels patt., blue **45.00**

Butter dish, cov., pressed glass, Diamond Panels patt., clear...............**30.00**

Butter dish, cov., pressed glass, Doyle's 500 patt., amber **55.00**

Butter dish, cov., pressed glass, Nursery Rhyme patt., clear **85.00**

Butter dish, cov., pressed glass, Sawtooth patt., clear **50.00**

Butter dish, cov., pressed glass, Stippled Vines & Beads patt., clear **90.00**

Butter dish, cov., pressed glass, Sweetheart patt., clear.......................**37.50**

Butter dish, cov., pressed glass, Thumbelina patt., clear **35.00**

Butter dish, cov., pressed glass, Tulip & Honeycomb patt., clear........**60.00**

Butter dish, cov., pressed glass, Wild Rose patt., milk white.................**60.00**

Cake set: handled master cake plate, four cake plates, cov. teapot, sugar bowl, creamer & four cups & saucers; china, decorated w/bouquets of roses.......................**135.00**

Canister set, porcelain, decorated w/flowers & gold trim, early 1900s, Germany, 14 pcs. **350.00**

Canister & spice set: 3⅛" h. cov. canisters marked "Tea," "Flour," "Sugar," "Oatmeal," "Coffee," & "Rice;" 2⅜" h. cov. canisters marked "Ginger," "Cloves," "Cinnamon," "Pepper," "Allspice" & "Nutmeg;" cov. salt box & two cruets w/original stoppers; ceramic, green lustered ground w/gold decoration, 15 pcs. **295.00**

Castor set, a footed pewter stand w/a ring for bottles & a center tall scrolled loop handle, holds two clear glass cruets w/stoppers, one glass

shaker w/metal lid & one glass jar w/metal lid & condiment spoon, late 19th c., 9½" h., the set......................**150.00**

Creamer, china, Blue Willow patt.........**15.00**

Creamer, porcelain, decorated w/three-quarter length portrait of two girls surrounded by flowers, Germany, 4" h......................................**22.50**

Creamer, pressed glass, Block patt., opaque blue **40.00**

Creamer, pressed glass, Bucket patt., amber...**75.00**

Creamer, pressed glass, Buzz Star patt., clear **20.00**

Creamer, pressed glass, Cambridge Colonial patt., emerald green............**25.00**

Creamer, pressed glass, Doyle 500 patt., clear **35.00**

Creamer, pressed glass, Drum patt., clear **58.00**

Creamer, pressed glass, Fernland patt., clear **15.00**

Creamer, pressed glass, Grapevine w/Ovals patt., amber **50.00**

Creamer, pressed glass, Grapevine w/Ovals patt., blue **65.00**

Creamer, pressed glass, Grapevine w/Ovals patt., clear **40.00**

Creamer, pressed glass, Hobnail w/Thumbprint Base patt., amber.......**65.00**

Creamer, pressed glass, Hobnail w/Thumbprint Base patt., blue **45.00**

Creamer, pressed glass, Lamb patt., clear **55.00**

Creamer, pressed glass, Menagerie patt., figural owl, clear.....................**125.00**

Creamer, pressed glass, Michigan patt., decorated w/flowers & yellow stain **55.00**

Creamer, pressed glass, Pointed Jewel patt., clear **55.00**

Creamer, pressed glass, Stippled Vine & Beads patt., amber................**65.00**

Creamer, pressed glass, Stippled Vine & Beads patt., clear **50.00**

Creamer, pressed glass, Style patt., clear **15.00**

Creamer, chocolate glass, Sultan patt....................................**225.00**

Creamer, pressed glass, Sunbeam patt., clear **75.00**

Creamer, pressed glass, Tulip & Honeycomb patt., clear **15.00**

Creamer, pressed glass, Whirling Star patt., clear **20.00**

Creamer, pressed glass, Wabash patt., clear **25.00**

Creamer, pressed glass, Wee Branches patt., clear.........................**40.00**

Creamer & sugar bowl, pressed glass, Sawtooth patt., clear, pr. **59.00**

Cup, pressed glass, embossed head of a boy, blue, Findlay.......................**45.00**

Cup, pressed glass, embossed head of a boy, clear, Findlay......................**32.00**

Cup, pressed glass, embossed head of a girl, blue, Findlay.........................**45.00**

Cup, pressed glass, embossed head of a girl, clear, Findlay.......................**32.00**

Cup & saucer, china, Blue Willow patt., Japan, 3¼" d. saucer, 2¼" h. cup...............................**15.00**

Cup & saucer, earthenware, medium blue transfer-printed central landscape of a horseman near a cottage, floral border, Staffordshire, England, ca. 1830, cup 2" h. (two short hairlines in saucer).................**121.00**

Cup & saucer, pressed glass, chickens w/ABC border & gold trim, clear.......................................**65.00**

Dinner set: service for six & covered dishes, platter & salt & pepper shaker; china, Moss Rose patt., w/gold trim, the set..................**145.00**

Dinner set: cov. teapot, cov. sugar bowl, creamer, six cups & saucers, six plates, two small plates, two platters & soup tureen; graniteware, simple ovoid forms in white w/a band of staggered green florettes around the tops & edges of each piece, late 19th - early 20th c., the set (some chipped edges & touch-up).......................................**155.00**

Dinner service: a pair 3½" l. oval sauce tureens & covers, a pair of rectangular vegetable dishes & covers, a 2⅞" w. square bowl, a pair of sauceboats, a 4½" l. chamfered rectangular platter, a 3¾" l. chamfered rectangular platter, a 3⅜" l. chamfered rectangular platter, eight dinner plates & four dessert plates; each piece transfer-printed in blue w/a profusion of flowering branches on a fishroe-patterned ground, Staffordshire, England, ca. 1825, 22 pcs. (various damages).......................................**1,150.00**

Dinner set, tin, lithographed Blue Willow patt., Ohio Art, 19 pcs. in original box, the set........................**90.00**

Dish, china, oval boat-shaped, Oriental landscape scene w/a butterfly border, medium blue, attributed to Davenport, ca. 1850, 3½" l. **66.00**

Epergne, blown glass, single-lily, base w/deeply ruffled rim on a squatty bowl raised on a pedestal w/a cushion foot, the trumpet-form lily w/deeply ruffled rim, clambroth decorated w/white florals, 7¼" h., 2 pcs. (tiny unseen separation on one ruffle).............................**65.00**

Kitchen set: seven canisters & a cruet w/original stopper; china, tan lustre glaze w/gold trim, marked "Germany," 8 pcs. **90.00**

Mug, china, mother, child & cat near open hearth on one side, verse for February on other side, Staffordshire, England **135.00**

Mug, porcelain, decorated w/triple bust portraits of "Brundage Girls," Germany, 2¾" h...............................**25.00**

Mug, porcelain, three-quarter length portrait of two girls surrounded w/flowers, Germany **25.00**

Mug, pressed glass, Diamond Peg patt., ruby-stained, 2⅜" h. **22.00**

Mug, pressed glass, Squirrel patt., clear **59.00**

Mug, pressed glass, Swan patt., milk white **35.00**

Mug, pressed glass, Wolf patt., amber..**45.00**

Pepper bottle, pressed glass, English Hobnail patt., green **15.00**

Pitcher, china, jug-type, the front w/a black transfer-printed picture of a dog titled "Pompey," 2¼" h. (light overall stain, tiny spout chip)...**143.00**

Pitcher, water, pressed glass, Fancy Cut (or Rex) patt., clear **75.00**

Pitcher, water, pressed glass, Galloway patt., clear w/gold **35.00**

Pitcher, pressed glass, Oval Star patt., clear...................................**52.50**

Pitcher, water, pressed glass, Pattee Cross patt., clear.........................**50.00**

Plate, china, Oriental landscape w/a butterfly border, medium blue, attributed to Davenport, ca. 1850, 2¼" d..**44.00**

Plate, china, sepia transfer-print scene of two children, sepia rim band, impressed "Wood," early 19th c., 3½" d. **140.00**

Plate, china, Franklin Flying Kite patt., dark blue, ca. 1830, 2⅞" d. **66.00**

Plate, china, Blue Willow patt., 3¾" d...**10.00**

Plate, porcelain, decorated w/three-quarter length portrait of two girls surrounded w/flowers, 5¼" d...**8.50**

Plate, pressed glass, head of a cat, clear, Findlay, 6" d..........................**50.00**

Plate, pressed glass, head of a dog, clear, Findlay, 6" d. **50.00**

Plate, dessert, china, pink lustre w/scene of children playing soccer ...**35.00**

Platter, china, Blue Willow patt., 6" l. ...**40.00**

Platter, china, oval, Oriental landscape w/a butterfly border, medium blue, attributed to Davenport, ca. 1850, 3¾" l. **66.00**

Platter, oval, china, Franklin Flying a

Kite patt., faded blue on white, early 19th c., 4½" l. **55.00**

Punch cups, pressed glass, Wild Rose patt., milk white, set of 6 ....**150.00**

Punch set: punch bowl & two matching cups; Nursery Rhyme patt., milk white, 3 pcs. **295.00**

Punch set: punch bowl & three matching cups; Nursery Rhyme patt., blue, 4 pcs. **275.00**

Punch set: punch bowl & six cups; pressed glass, Nursery Rhyme patt., clear, 7 pcs. **300.00**

Punch set: bowl & six cups; pressed glass, Whirligig patt., clear, 7 pcs. **67.50**

Sauce dish, pressed glass, Nursery Rhyme patt., clear, 2¼" d. **18.00**

Soup tureen, cov., china, Oriental landscape design w/a butterfly border, medium blue, attributed to Davenport, ca. 1850, 3½" h. **148.50**

Spooner, pressed glass, Button Panel patt., clear...............................**50.00**

Spooner, pressed glass, Cambridge Colonial patt., emerald green.............**30.00**

Spooner, pressed glass, Horizontal Threads patt., clear...........................**30.00**

Spooner, pressed glass, Mardi Gras patt., clear **40.00**

Spooner, pressed glass, Menagerie patt., figural fish, blue......................**150.00**

Spooner, pressed glass, Menagerie patt., figural fish, clear.....................**125.00**

Spooner, pressed glass, Michigan patt., clear **50.00**

Spooner, pressed glass, Stippled Diamond patt., clear...........................**75.00**

Spooner, pressed glass, Stippled Vine & Beads patt., clear **50.00**

Spooner, pressed glass, Sweetheart patt., clear **30.00**

Spooner, pressed glass, Twin Snow-Shoes patt., clear....................**45.00**

Spooner, pressed glass, Twist patt., clear **32.00**

Spooner, pressed glass, Wabash patt., clear **30.00**

Spooner, pressed glass, Wee Branches patt., clear.........................**40.00**

Spooner, pressed glass, Whirling Star patt., clear **18.00**

Spooner, pressed glass, Wild Rose patt., milk white **40.00**

Sugar bowl, cov., china, Blue Willow patt. **20.00**

Sugar bowl, cov., pressed glass, Button Panel patt. **125.00**

Sugar bowl, cov., pressed glass, Hobnail patt., clear, Northwood Glass Co. **200.00**

Sugar bowl, cov., pressed glass, Michigan patt., clear w/gold rim **80.00**

Sugar bowl, cov., pressed glass, Oval Star patt., clear **35.00**

Sugar bowl, cov., pressed glass, Pert patt., clear **50.00**

Sugar bowl, cov., pressed glass, Tappan patt., blue.............................**25.00**

Sugar bowl, cov., pressed glass, Wee Branches patt., clear **25.00**

Sugar bowl, cov., pressed glass, Whirling Star patt., clear **22.50**

Table set: creamer, spooner & cov. sugar bowl; pressed glass, Stippled Vine & Beads patt., clear, 3 pcs.......**145.00**

Table set, pressed glass, Sweetheart patt., Cambridge, clear, 4 pcs. **85.00**

Teapot, cov., china, Blue Willow patt. ...**30.00**

Tea set: cov. teapot, cov. sugar bowl & creamer; flow blue china, footed squatty bulbous bodies w/flared rim & domed covers w/button finials, free-hand blue decoration of tight scrolls & leaves, mid-19th c., teapot 4⅜" h., 3 pcs. (chips) **2,035.00**

Tea set, china, features elephants & bunnies, Japan, service for two, mint in box **55.00**

Tea set: cov. teapot, cov. sugar bowl, creamer, four plates & four cups & saucers; porcelain, each piece decorated w/colorful transfer-printed nursery rhyme scenes including Higgledy Piggledy, My Black Hen, Hickory, Dickory, Dock, etc., late 19th - early 20th c., the set (one cup w/a chip, one cracked, one saucer w/short crack, one w/edge roughness) **90.00**

Tea set: cov. teapot, cov. sugar bowl, four cups & saucers; china, decorated w/pink & white roses w/gold accents, unmarked, R.S. Prussia, 10 pcs. **595.00**

Tea set: cov. teapot, cov. sugar bowl, five handleless cups & six saucers; Staffordshire transfer-printed earthenware, Beehive patt., purple, William Adams, ca. 1840, the set (various damages & repairs)............**467.50**

Tea set: cov. teapot & six cups & saucers; china, Fun-loving Children also Tease a Kitten decoration, 13 pcs. **155.00**

Tea set: cov. teapot, creamer, four cups & saucers & four tea plates; china, Dutch children decoration, 14 pcs. (tiniest roughness on teapot spout) **165.00**

Tea set: cov. teapot, sugar bowl, creamer & four plates, cups & saucers; china, white w/gold trim, marked "Noritake, M, Handpainted, Made in Japan," in original decorated box, together w/four each metal knives, forks & spoons marked "Germany," the set (teapot w/crack on handle & small flake inside edge of lid, light wear on some gold) **85.00**

Tea set: cov. teapot, cov. sugar bowl, creamer, three plates, cups & saucers; china, decorated w/decal scenes of children at various activities, Germany, the set (teapot w/repair on rim w/hairline, creamer & sugar w/inherent dark spots, one saucer w/fine hairline) **275.00**

Tea set: cov. teapot, cov. sugar bowl, creamer, four plates, four off-size cups & saucers & one correct size cup; china, Gaudy Oyster patt., marked "Staffordshire, England," 19th c., the set (some hairlines, crazing, discoloration & small chip on lid of teapot) **360.00**

Tea set: cov. teapot, cov. sugar bowl, waste bowl, five cups & saucers & two plates; china, "gaudy" decoration in orange & dark blue w/gold design, Minton, the set (chip on rim of sugar, flake on one saucer, tiny air bubbles on one cup & plate) **210.00**

Tea set: cov. teapot, cov. sugar bowl, creamer, waste bowl, five cups & saucers & six plates; china, tapering cylindrical bodies, each piece in white h.p. w/blue & green leaf sprigs, late 19th - early 20th c., the set (some damages & discoloration) **200.00**

Tea set: cov. teapot, creamer & sugar bowl, waste bowl, six cups & saucers; china, Chintz patt. in black on white, Ridgway, 16 pcs. **360.00**

Tea set: cov. teapot, creamer & sugar bowl, waste bowl, three cups & saucers, four 3¾" plates, two 5 x 5½" serving plates; china, blue on white, Animals patt., Copeland, 16 pcs. **415.00**

Staffordshire Children's Tea Set

Tea set: cov. ovoid teapot, cov. sugar bowl, pear-shaped creamer, waste bowl, six teabowls & saucers; pearlware, each piece printed in underglaze-blue w/a checkered pattern of solid & dotted-X squares beneath a florette-guilloche border around the rim, Staffordshire, ca.

1810, teapot 4⅝¹⁶" h., 16 pcs. (ILLUS.) **1,150.00**

Tea set, tin, Blue Willow patt., includes tray & muffin dome w/base, unmarked, 30 pcs., the set (minor wear)....................................**350.00**

Tray, pressed glass, Doyle's 500 patt., blue.....................................**45.00**

Tray, pressed glass, Doyle's 500 patt., clear **50.00**

Tumble-up set, blown glass, citrus green pitcher w/black handle, tumbler fitting inside the neck, 5" h...**110.00**

Tureen, cov., china, Blue Willow patt.....**45.00**

Vegetable dish, open, oval, transfer-printed center scene of a building in a landscape, vining scroll border band, green, ca. 1850, 4⅜" l. (some glaze flakes)............................**49.50**

Vegetable dish, cov., oval, china, Oriental landscape w/a butterfly border, medium blue, attributed to Davenport, ca. 1850, 2" h. **88.00**

Water set: pitcher & three tumblers; pressed glass, Rex patt., clear, 4 pcs. **195.00**

Water set: pitcher & four tumblers; pressed glass, Oval Star patt., clear w/gold edges, 5 pcs. **100.00**

Water set: pitcher & six tumblers; pressed glass, Nursery Rhyme patt., clear, 7 pcs. **150.00**

CHILDREN'S MUGS

Yellow-Glazed Earthenware Mug

The small sized mugs used by children first attempting to drink from a cup appeal to many collectors. Because they were made of such diverse materials as china, glass, pottery, graniteware, plated silver and sterling silver, the collector can assemble a diversified collection or single out a particular type around which to base a collection. Also see CHILDREN'S DISHES, PATTERN GLASS, and YELLOW-GLAZED EARTHENWARE under Ceramics.

China, design of children & animals

playing w/hoop & toys, marked
"Royal Rudolstadt" & dated 1915.....**$50.00**
Pressed glass, Baby Animals patt.,
clear...**34.00**
Pressed glass, Bleeding Heart patt.,
clear, medium size............................**45.00**
Pressed glass, Cord & Tassel patt.,
clear **85.00**
Pressed glass, Cupid & Venus patt.,
clear, medium size............................**30.00**
Pressed glass, Divided Block
w/Sunburst patt., clear, medium
size **18.00**
Pressed glass, Doyle's No. 500 patt.,
clear...**20.00**
Pressed glass, Drum patt., clear,
2½" h..**95.00**
Pressed glass, embossed "In Fond
Remembrance," amber......................**20.00**
Pressed glass, Good Girl patt., clear,
3 x 3½"...**40.00**
Pressed glass, embossed w/Little
Red Riding Hood, clear......................**85.00**
Pressed glass, Robin patt., amber......**25.00**
Pressed glass, Robin patt., blue
opaque..**42.00**
Pressed glass, Shell & Tassel patt.,
clear, 2¼" h..**65.00**
Pressed glass, Still & Running
Rabbits patt. w/pressed Lamb patt.
in base, clear **50.00**
Staffordshire pearlware, cylindrical,
transfer-printed in black on the front
w/the displayed American eagle
beneath an aura of stars & between
the inscription "REPUBLICANS ARE
NOT Always UNGRATEFUL - R.ᵈ
Hall & Son," flanked on each side by
an oval bust portrait, one of George
Washington & inscribed
"WASHINGTON HIS COUNTRY'S
FATHER," the other of General
Lafayette & inscribed "FAYETTE
(sic) THE NATIONS GUEST," the
reverse w/a strap handle, the rim
edged in black enamel, ca. 1825,
Ralph Hall & Son, 2⁷⁄₁₆" h. (minor
chips, some discoloration) **920.00**
Staffordshire pottery, cylindrical,
purple transfer-printed "Prosper
Freedom," 19th c., 2½" h. **172.50**
Staffordshire pottery, cylindrical,
black transfer-printed decoration of
American eagles flanking a scroll-
bordered rectangular plaque w/the
script inscription "The Land of
Liberty," early 19th c., 2⅜" h. **431.00**
Staffordshire pottery, cylindrical,
green transfer-printed design w/
"Prosper Freedom" within a flower &
scroll cartouche, an eagle on a shell
on either side of the handle, ca.
1840, 2½" h. (tiny flake on
foot)...**412.50**

Staffordshire pottery, cylindrical,
brown transfer-printed oblong
reserve printed "A Gift For Charles"
on one side & w/three people
gathering branches on the other, ca.
1830, 2½" h. (light overall stain,
flake on rim) **275.00**
Staffordshire pottery, cylindrical,
green transfer-printed design of
children around a maypole, enamel
trim in pink, yellow, green & blue,
ca. 1830, 2½" h................................**126.50**
Staffordshire pottery, cylindrical,
black transfer-printed comic scene
of a black man & boy, titled
"Subtraction," 2¾" h. (stains, edge
flakes) **192.50**
Staffordshire pottery, cylindrical,
black transfer-printed design of two
boys playing marbles w/buildings in
the distance, titled "The Game at
Marbles," another scene on the
reverse titled "Fare Thee Well," ca.
1840, 3" h. (blurred transfer)...........**302.50**
Staffordshire pottery, cylindrical
w/molded base, angled handle, dark
blue transfer-printed design w/a
wide band of floral & fruit blocks
around the top above scattered
flowers below, ca. 1850, 3½" h.
(small chip on rim) **126.50**
Staffordshire pottery, motto, "For A
Gift" in gold on front flanked by h.p.
florals, thin gold, red & blue bands
on white, 2" h. **125.00**
Staffordshire pottery, transfer-
printed scene of child in nightcap &
gown & rhyme about the sugar plum
tree...**70.00**
Yellow-glazed earthenware,
cylindrical, black transfer-printed
oval reserve of a seated girl & dog
below "A Present For My Dear Girl,"
silver lustre rim, 2" h. (tiny rim chip &
hairline) **330.00**
Yellow-glazed earthenware,
cylindrical body printed in black on
the front w/two bust-portraits within
laurel-edged ovals beneath a
banderole inscribed "LA FAYETTE,"
& "WASHINGTON," suspended from
the beak of a spread-winged eagle
under an aura of stars, the strap
handle on the reverse w/foliate
terminals, ca. 1825, some abrasions
& a tiny chip, 2⁹⁄₁₆" h.
(ILLUS.) **1,265.00**

CHRISTMAS TREE ORNAMENTS

The German blown glass Christmas

tree ornaments and other commercially-made ornaments of wax, cardboard and cotton batting were popular from the time they were first offered for sale in the United States in the 1870s. Prior to that time, Christmas trees had been decorated with homemade ornaments that usually were edible. Now nostalgic collectors who seek out ornaments that sold for pennies in stores across the country in the early years of this century are willing to pay some rather hefty prices for unusual or early ornaments.

Angel w/long wings, blown glass **$95.00**
Banana, blown glass, 5" l. **50.00**

Clown Christmas Ornament

Clown, cotton w/plaster face & crepe paper collar, minor soiling, 7" h. (ILLUS.) **55.00**
Clown boy, cotton batting body, arms & legs, molded plaster mask face w/painted features & a conical crepe paper hat & collar, 7½" h. (minor soiling) **55.00**
Ear of corn, blown glass, 5" l. **75.00**
Girl, cotton batting long coat & legs,

Masquerade Girl Ornament

crepe paper sleeves & ruffled collar, cotton bonnet head w/molded plaster face w/painted features & side-glancing eyes, 6" h. (minor soiling) **60.50**
Horn, blown glass **35.00**
Kugel, blue, brass hanger, 4¼" d.......**104.50**
Mandolin, Dresden-type, silver w/floral accents, 3⅜" l. (some silver loss on back) **201.00**
Masquerade girl, cotton w/plaster face, crepe paper collar, body in orange & cream, minor soiling, 4¼" h. (ILLUS. bottom previous column) **77.00**
Pickle, blown glass **75.00**

Santa Christmas Ornament

Santa Claus, cotton w/plaster face, minor soiling & fading, 7" h. (ILLUS.) **71.50**
Santa Claus, cotton batting long coat w/white piping trim & black belt, black legs extend at bottom, pointed cotton cap w/white piping above the molded plaster face w/painted laughing features & a white cotton beard, 7" h. (very minor soiling & fading) **82.50**
Santa Claus, white cotton batting long coat w/orange trim & a black belt, black legs extend at bottom, pointed white cotton hat on head w/molded plaster face w/painted features & white cotton beard, 7" h. (very minor soiling & fading) **82.50**
Strawberry, blown glass **30.00**

HALLMARK KEEPSAKE ORNAMENTS

Note: these must be "Mint in box" to bring top prices.

A Christmas Treat, "Handcrafted" ornaments, 1979..............................**60.00**
Angel Delight, "Little Trimmers" ornaments, 1979..............................**75.00**

Baroque Angel, "Handcrafted"
ornaments, 1982..............................**71.50**
Betsey Clark, "Christmas 1976" ball
ornament, "Property" ornaments,
seventh edition, 1976......................**22.00**
Betsey Clark, "Musicians" ball
ornament, "Property" ornaments,
second edition, 1974......................**24.00**
British, "Clothespin Soldiers
Collectibles" series, 1982..................**85.00**
Calico Mouse, "Handcrafted"
ornaments, 1978.............................**95.00**
Candle, "Colors of Christmas"
ornaments, 1977.............................**30.00**
Cardinalis, Cardinalis, "Holiday
Wildlife" series, first edition, 1982 ....**250.00**
Chris Mouse, "Keepsake Magic"
series, 1985 ....**52.50**
Christmas Owl, "Holiday Humor"
ornaments, 1984.............................**27.00**
Cinnamon Bear, "Porcelain Bear"
series, fourth edition, 1986 ....**22.00**
Cinnamon Bear, "Porcelain Bear"
series, seventh edition, 1989............**12.00**
Cinnamon Teddy, "Porcelain Bear"
series, second edition, 1984 ....**35.00**
Classical Angel, "Limited Edition"
ornaments, 1984.............................**42.00**
Clothespin Drummer Boy, "Little
Trimmers" ornaments, 1981 ....**30.00**
Cowboy Snowman, "Handcrafted"
ornaments, 1982.............................**40.00**
Cycling Santa, "Handcrafted"
ornaments, 1982.............................**90.00**
Dancer, "Reindeer Champs," 1987 ......**55.00**
Dasher, "Reindeer Champs," 1986....**110.00**
Della Robia Wreath, "Twirl-About"
collection, 1977 ....**80.00**
Elfin Artist, "Handcrafted" ornaments,
1982..**35.00**
Engineering Mouse, "Holiday
Humor" ornaments, 1985..................**30.00**
Frosty Friends, "Frosty Friends"
series, second edition, 1981 ....**250.00**
Frosty Friends, "Frosty Friends"
series, fourth edition, 1983 ....**145.00**
Frosty Friends, "Frosty Friends"
series, fifth edition, 1984 ....**40.00**
Frosty Friends, "Frosty Friends"
series, sixth edition, 1985 ....**40.00**
Frosty Friends, "Frosty Friends"
series, seventh edition, 1986............**30.00**
Heavenly Trumpeter, "Limited
Edition" ornaments, 1985..................**42.00**
Holiday Scrimshaw, "Handcrafted"
ornaments, 1979 ....**100.00**
House, "Yesteryears" collection,
1977...**90.00**
Jolly Trolley, "Here Comes Santa"
ornaments, Fourth Edition, 1982 ....**75.00**
Joy, "Colors of Christmas" ornaments,
1977...**25.00**
Locomotive, "Nostalgia Ornaments,"
1975...**140.00**

Madonna & Child & St. John, "Art
Masterpiece" ornaments, 1984 ....**15.00**
Madonna of the Pomegranate, "Art
Masterpiece" ornaments,
1985...**20.00**
Mele Kalikimaka, "Windows of the
World" series, third edition, 1987 ....**14.00**
Merry Mistletoe Time, "Mr. and Mrs.
Claus" series, first edition, 1986 ....**85.00**
Mouse in a thimble, "Thimble" series,
first edition, 1978 ....**195.00**
Napping Mouse, "Holiday Humor"
ornaments, 1984.............................**30.00**
Nativity, "Nostalgia Collection"
ornament, 1977...............................**75.00**
Nutcracker Ballet, "Christmas
Classics" series, 1986.......................**40.00**
Old-Fashioned Toy Shop, "Nostalgia
Houses & Shops" series, second
edition, 1985 ....**80.00**
Partridge in a Pear Tree, "Twelve
Days of Christmas" series, first
edition, 1984 ....**275.00**
Peace on Earth, "Nostalgia"
Ornaments, 1975 ....**140.00**
Peppermint Penguin, "Handcrafted"
ornaments, 1983.............................**30.00**
Perky Penguin, "Little Trimmers"
ornaments, 1981.............................**30.00**
Porcelain Doll, Diana, "Handcrafted"
ornaments, 1983.............................**20.00**
Postman and Kids, "Norman
Rockwell" series, sixth edition,
1985...**25.00**
Raccoon Surprise, "Handcrafted"
ornaments, 1982...........................**115.00**
Ring-Necked Pheasant, "Holiday
Wildlife" series, third edition, 1984 .....**35.00**
Rocking Horse, "Nostalgia
Collection" ornaments, 1976............**125.00**
Rocking horse, Black, "Rocking
Horse" series, second edition,
1982 ....**200.00 to 250.00**
Rocking horse, Pinto, "Rocking
Horse" series, fifth edition, 1985 ....**35.00**
Santa and Friends, "Carrousel"
series, sixth edition, 1983 ....**37.50**
Santa Express, "Here Comes Santa"
series, fifth edition, 1983 ....**200.00**
Santa's Deliveries, "Here Comes
Santa" series, sixth edition, 1984.......**62.50**
Santa's Fire Engine, "Here Comes
Santa" ornaments, seventh edition,
1985...**40.00**
Santa's Sleigh, "Brass" ornaments,
1982...**30.00**
Santa's Woody, "Here Comes Santa"
ornaments, ninth edition, 1987 ....**45.00**
Santa's Workshop, "Handcrafted"
ornaments, 1982.............................**52.00**
Scottish Highlander, "Clothespin
Soldiers Collectibles" series, 1985.....**21.00**
Skaters, "Carrousel" series, fourth
edition, 1981 ....**71.00**

Skiing Fox, "Handcrafted"
ornaments, 1983................................**25.00**
Snowgoose, "Property" ornaments,
1974..**35.00**
Snowman in Snowflake, "Twirl-
About" collection, 1977 ....**45.00**
Snowmobile Santa, "Holiday Humor"
ornaments, 1984.................................**25.00**
Snowshoe Penguin, "Holiday
Humor" ornaments, 1984...................**30.00**
Soccer Beaver, "Holiday Humor"
ornaments, 1985.................................**30.00**
Space Santa, "Handcrafted"
ornaments, 1981.................................**60.00**
Star Swing, "Handcrafted"
ornaments, 1981.................................**35.00**
The Spirit of Christmas,
"Handcrafted" ornaments, 1982.........**65.00**
Thimble Angel, "Thimble" series,
fourth edition, 1981 ....**45.00**
Thimble Elf, "Thimble" series, third
edition, 1980 ....**175.00**
Thimble Elf, "Thimble" series, sixth
edition, 1983 ....**60.00**
Thimble Soldier, "Thimble" series,
second edition, 1979.........................**100.00**
Tin Locomotive, "Tin Locomotive"
series, second edition, 1983 ....**200.00**
Tin Locomotive, "Tin Locomotive"
series, fourth edition, 1985 ....**55.00**
Tin Locomotive, "Tin Locomotive"
series, fifth edition, 1986...................**50.00**
Tin Locomotive, "Tin Locomotive"
series, sixth edition, 1987 ....**50.00**
Tin Locomotive, "Tin Locomotive"
series, eighth edition, 1989................**38.00**
Touchdown Santa, "Holiday Humor"
ornaments, 1986.................................**20.00**
Tree Treats - Angel, "Handcrafted"
ornaments, 1976.................................**95.00**
Two Turtle Doves, "Twelve Days of
Christmas" series, second edition,
1985..**55.00**
Unicorn, "Handcrafted" ornaments,
1983..**40.00**
Victorian Dollhouse, "Nostalgia
Houses & Shops" series, first
edition, 1984 ....**167.00**
Wooden and Woven Straw,
"Miniature Creche" series, first
edition, 1985 ....**25.00**
Wreath, "Colors of Christmas"
ornaments, 1977.............................. **25.00**

CIRCUS COLLECTIBLES

*The romance of the "Big Top," stirred by
memories of sawdust, spangles, thrills and
chills, has captured the imagination of the
American public for over 100 years.
Though the heyday of the traveling circus
is now past, dedicated collectors and fans*

*of all ages eagerly seek out choice
memorabilia from the late 19th and early
20th centuries, the "golden age" of circuses.*

Invitation, Barnum & Bailey Madison
Square Garden opening night,
1911..**$30.00**
Program, "Ringling Bros. and Barnum
& Bailey Circus," 1954 ....**30.00**
Side show circus banner, painted
canvas "Human Volcano—
Something Never Seen Before,"
depicts a fire eater & another
performer, 1930s, 5 x 7'..............**1,495.00**
Side show circus banner, painted
canvas "Human Fishman—World's
Most Unusual Curiosity Alive,"
depicts a suave merman &
awestruck fisherman, 1930s, 7 x 8'
(some wear) **1,150.00**

"Midget Horse" Side Show Banner

Side show circus banner, painted
canvas "Midget Horse," depicts two
clowns & small brown midget horse,
early 20th c., 10 x 12'
(ILLUS.) **1,380.00**

CLOCKS

Gilt Bronze Carriage Clock

Animated, Happy Days, Lux............**$350.00**

Carriage clock, gilt bronze, the case set w/stylized foliate motifs, one button hour repeater, late 19th c., 7" h. (ILLUS.) **2,070.00**

Carriage clock, L. Vrard & Co., brass upright rectangular case w/glass front, molded base & top, loop swing handle at the top, white enamel dial w/Roman numerals & lower seconds dial, hour repeating movement w/alarm, France, late 19th c., 7¼" h..**1,150.00**

Carriage clock, brass, brass upright rectangular case w/an ogee-molded base on bracket feet & a deep ogee-molded top w/a fixed angular loop handle, reeded pilasters down the front sides flanking the white enamel dial w/Arabic numerals & a subsidiary seconds dial, France, late 19th c., 8" h. **546.00**

Chadwick Classical Mirror Clock

Joseph Chadwick, Boscawen, New Hampshire, Classical giltwood & ebonized, w/ring-turned columnar sides & corner carved rosettes, top section w/stenciled floral decoration surrounding white dial w/Roman numerals above rectangular mirror-plate, ca. 1820, 4½ x 14", 30" h. (ILLUS.) **4,600.00**

Grandfather, Colonial Clock Co., Mission style (Arts & Crafts movement), the flat top hood overhanging arched corbels above a beveled glass door opening to floral-decorated gilded face w/Arabic numerals, above beveled glass door exposing brass pendulum & three cylindrical weights, on short legs formed by corner stiles, 15 x 27", 7' 1" h. (ILLUS. top next column) **3,300.00**

Grandfather, William Cummens, Roxbury, Massachusetts, Federal style satinwood-inlaid mahogany

Colonial Clock Co. Grandfather Clock

case, the hood w/pierced crest surmounted by a central brass eagle finial flanked by a pair of brass ball-and-steeple finials, the white-painted dial below painted w/flowers & birds w/phases of the moon, also depicting a ship at sea & a gentleman fishing, seconds & calendar date registers below, centering the inscription "WARRENTED by Wm. Cummens," brass stop-fluted colonnettes flanking, the waisted case below w/fan-inlaid door flanked by brass stop-fluted quarter-columns, the fan-inlaid base on ogee bracket feet, 9¾ x 19", 8' ½" h. **48,875.00**

Grandfather, John Davis, New Holland, Pennsylvania, Chippendale style carved walnut case, the molded broken scroll pediment terminating in carved rosettes above a pierced & shaped tympanum over an arched glazed door opening to a white-painted dial w/Roman & Arabic chapter rings enclosing a sweep seconds hand & calendar day aperture surmounted by a floral reserve, the gilt spandrels painted w/strawberries & flowers, inscribed "John Davis New Holland," flanked by fluted square columns & above a beaded molding & punched dentils over a waisted case w/thin pierced arched cupboard door flanked by fluted quarter columns w/lambrequin terminus above a pierced dentil molding over a box base w/shaped panel flanked by rounded quarter columns w/lambrequin terminus, on cyma-curved bracket feet w/spur returns, 1805-07, 12 x 21⅝", 7' 11½" h. (rear feet replaced) **12,650.00**

Grandfather, Harris Fritwell, England, George III black & gilt-japanned case, the pagoda hood w/ball & eagle finial above arched glazed door flanked by columnar uprights, the case w/arched door & plinth base, decorated overall w/foliage & chinoiserie scenes, the arched dial w/brass chapter ring w/date aperture & seconds dial, pierced foliate chased spandrels, the movement w/anchor escapement striking the hour on bell, 7' 9½" h. (redecorated) **5,175.00**

Grandfather, Abel Hutchins, Concord, New Hampshire, Federal style cherry case, the arched crest w/pierced fretwork & three block finials supporting brass urn finials above the arched glazed doors over a painted dial w/Roman numerals below a 'rocking ship' scene, floral decorated spandrels, the case w/a long door flanked by fluted quarter-round columns, boxed base w/rounded center apron drop & short bracket feet, old finish, ca. 1790, 7' 7½" h. (minor imperfections) **9,200.00**

Grandfather, J. & J. Kohn, Austria, Modern style beechwood case, a tall flat backboard forming a rounded crest above the outset case w/door over the dial w/Arabic numerals & supported at the front by tall slender pointed posts extending to bottom of the case, a panel in the backboard at the center of the case above an outset rounded lower cabinet w/paneled door, metal feet, designed by Josef Hoffmann, original manufacturer's label, ca. 1906, 19" w., 6' 4" h. **5,175.00**

Grandfather, New Jersey, Federal inlaid mahogany & cherry case, the swan's-neck crest ending in diamond-inlaid terminals, centering three brass ball-and-steeple finials, the arched glazed door below opening to a white-painted dial w/Roman numerals, phases of the moon, seconds & calendar date registers, the waisted case below w/line-inlaid door flanked by reeded quarter-columns, the inlaid base raised on French feet, ca. 1805, 9¾ x 19¼", 7' 5½" h. (minor veneer repairs) **8,050.00**

Grandfather, regulator, Richard Orpwood, London, England, George III style mahogany case, designed w/architectural pediment & fluted chamfered angles above a square glazed door opening to a silvered

dial signed "Richard Orpwood, London," w/a minute ring, date aperture & subsidiary seconds dial, over a trunk door & paneled plinth on scalloped skirt, the movement w/Graham-type deadbeat escapement & Harrison maintaining power & pendulum, 6' 8" h. (alterations to case) **3,680.00**

Victorian Rosewood Grandfather Clock

Grandfather, Victorian inlaid rosewood case, the hood w/arched crest flanking a scroll-cut palmette, the inlaid frieze over arched panel, the silver dial w/Arabic numerals on silver répoussé & floral motifs, the tall waisted case w/elaborate foliate & scrolling motifs flanked by thin columns, on pedestal w/ornate inlaid decoration, 17 x 24", 8' 4" h. (ILLUS.) **17,250.00**

Grandfather, Jonathan Wait, Gun Dock, Wopping, England, George II style mahogany case, the broken-arched crest w/ball & eagle brass finials above an arched glazed door over the dial signed on a cartouche "JN. Wait Gundock, Wapping," w/calendar aperture, subsidiary seconds & urn & bird spandrels, a strike/silent dial in the arch, rack & bell striking movement w/anchor escapement, the lower case w/fluted, canted corners flanking a long arch-topped door above the stepped-out paneled base w/a molded & scalloped apron, ca. 1770, 9½ x 20¼", 7' 7" h. **4,888.00**

Schoolhouse wall clock, Ansonia Clock Co., walnut veneer case w/ebonized trim, octagonal frame around the round dial w/Roman numerals, box base w/pointed bottom, glass door marked in gold

"Regulator," large brass pendulum, late 19th c., 32" h. (face worn, veneer damage)...............................**302.50**

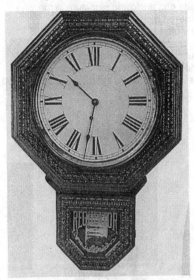

Schoolhouse Regulator Clock

Schoolhouse wall clock, oak case, octagonal frame w/stamped egg-and-dart trim around the round glazed door opening to a replaced dial w/Roman numerals, box base w/egg-and-dart trim & angled bottom & glass panel stenciled in gilt "Regulator," brass pendulum, ca. 1900, 17" w., 24¾" h. (ILLUS.) **247.50**

Shelf or mantel, Arts & Crafts style, L. & J. G. Stickley, the tapered rectangular oak case w/a beveled foot, a small rectangular window on the lower front exposing the pendulum, a round dial w/Arabic numerals, rectangular top w/widely flaring cornice, Model No. 85, w/key, ca. 1912, 8 x 16", 22" h. (hour hand missing) **8,625.00**

Shelf or mantel, Birge & Fuller, Bristol, Connecticut, mahogany Gothic-style double-steeple case w/glass door, fusé movement, ca. 1840, 27½" h. **1,210.00**

Shelf or mantel, J. C. Brown, Bristol, Forestville Mfg. Co., Connecticut, Acorn mahogany & laminated wood case, the triple line-inlaid hinged door w/acorn-shaped upper & bombé-shaped lower églomisé section w/conforming case & sidearms w/gilt acorn finial terminal, the painted dial w/Roman numerals & floral decoration, dial signed "Forestville Manufg. Co., Bristol,

CT., U.S.A.," the lower églomisé panel w/painted landscape scene w/Victorian gingerbread house & sailboat, on a stepped line-inlaid base, the interior labeled "Eight Day Spring clocks, Manufactured by J. C. Brown, Bristol, Connecticut," ca. 1847, 15" w., 24½" h. (losses to églomisé) **19,500.00**

J. C. Brown Shelf or Mantel Clock

Shelf or mantel, J. C. Brown, Bristol, Connecticut, rosewood & mahogany, the serpentine pitched pediment surmounted by four pointed finials, the circular white-painted dial enclosed by a circular glazed door, the lower églomisé panel painted w/a building surrounded w/etched floral decoration, 1855, 3¾ x 11¾", 20" h. (ILLUS.) **2,300.00**

Eastlake Shelf or Mantel Clock

Shelf or mantel, Victorian Eastlake style, elaborately scroll-cut walnut case surrounding ornately painted glass door w/angular arched top opening to white face w/Arabic numerals, on angled pedestal base w/bubble level, 15" w., 24" h. (ILLUS.) **220.00**

Shelf or mantel, Filon, Paris, France, ormolu & red marble, the central enamel dial signed "Filon A Paris," similarly signed flat-bottom circular plated movement w/verge escapement, silk suspension & outside countwheel bell striking, the elaborate case surmounted by a stag & swathed in ribbon-tied garlands of berried leaves flanked by armorial trophies, on a rectangular breakfront red marble base faced w/a frieze depicting putti playing musical instruments, stag hoof feet, ca. 1790, 9" deep, 27" w., 29½" h. **10,350.00**

Shelf or mantel, Kartel, Paris, France, ormolu-mounted ebony, portico-style, rectangular tablet w/projecting cornice above a 4½" gilt engine-turned dial signed "Kartel a Paris" w/aperture for moon phase, the outside countwheel bell striking movement w/deadbeat escapement & 9-rod pendulum, the ebony veneered case w/plain pillars & ormolu capitals, the front faced w/ormolu leaf mounts, ca. 1810, 6" deep, 11½" w., 22½" h. **6,325.00**

Samuel Terry Shelf or Mantel Clock

Shelf or mantel, Samuel Terry, Plymouth, Connecticut, Federal mahogany pillar & scroll case, the hood w/scroll pediment above glass door opening to white dial w/floral painted corners & Roman numerals, above lower glass panel painted w/scene of a house & trees, on scroll-cut base, minor imperfections, 4½ x 17½", 30" h. (ILLUS.) **2,990.00**

Shelf or mantel, Thomas Wagstaffe, London, England, George III style mahogany case, the inverted belltop case w/carrying handles at the

sides, the door w/foliate scroll fretwork, the dial w/silvered strike/silent ring in the arch above a silvered chapter ring incorporating date ring enclosing signature in the silvered center, the movement w/triple fusee w/wire lines, verge escapement w/knife edge suspension to bob pendulum striking the hour & chiming the quarters on a nest of eight bells, 21" h...............**7,475.00**

Willard Shelf or Mantel Clock

Shelf or mantel, Aaron Willard, Federal mahogany, slightly curved hood w/scroll-cut crest flanking an eagle finial, above a rectangular door w/arched & slightly tapering glass opening to scroll-painted face w/Roman numerals, all above rectangular base on scroll-cut feet, ca. 1810, imperfections, 5½ x 12¼", 32¼" h. (ILLUS.) **31,050.00**

Mahogany Vienna Regulator Clock

Vienna regulator, mahogany, the flat top hood tapering to a long glass door opening to an enamel dial

w/Roman numerals, time & strike
weight driven movement, three
weights, above tapering base foot,
late 19th c., 42½" h. (ILLUS.)........**3,850.00**

CLOISONNÉ & RELATED WARES

Japanese Cloisonné Charger

*Cloisonné work features enameled
designs on a metal ground. There are
several types of this work, the best-known
utilizing cells of wire on the body of the
object into which the enamel is placed. In
the plique-a-jour form of cloisonné, the
base is removed leaving translucent
enamel windows. The champlevé technique
entails filling in, with enamels, a design
which is cast or carved in the base. "Pigeon
Blood" (akasuke) cloisonné includes a type
where foil is enclosed within colored
enamel walls. Cloisonné is said to have
been invented by the Chinese and brought
to perfection by the Japanese.*

CLOISONNÉ

Box, cov., decorated overall
w/multicolored lotus blooms borne
on & encircled by continuous
scrolling leafy vine tendrils reserved
on a turquoise ground, the
underside w/cloud scrolls, Kangxi
period China, 5¾ x 9½" **$3,162.00**
Charger, decorated w/pink, green,
blue & gold flowers in profusion,
leaves & bird in flight on turquoise
blue background w/multicolored
border, Japan, 11⅞" d.
(ILLUS.) **325.00**
Jardinieres, wide trumpet forms on
short cylindrical bases, decorated on
each side w/birds perched & soaring
amid seasonal flowering branches,
including peony, chrysanthemum &

Chinese Cloisonné Jardiniere

prunus, all above a band of lappets
encircling the feet, w/band of keyfret
further repeated at the rims & on the
everted rims, China, late 18th - early
19th c., 6½" h., typical pitting, pr.
(ILLUS.) **4,888.00**
Plaque, rectangular, colorfully
decorated w/a bottle-form vase filled
w/prunus branches, ginko, berried
stems, bamboo & other flowering
branches, & a *shuixianpen*
w/narcissus & *lingzhi,* amid fruits,
hand-scrolls, books, double fish & a
ruyi sceptre, 15½ x 18¾" (typical
pitting) **4,025.00**

Cloisonné Potpourri Jar

Potpourri jar, cov., squatty bulbous
body w/oval & rounded panels
around the sides w/bird, flowers &
butterflies, background panels are
blue, green & brown w/bits of
goldstone, Japan, 4⅜" d., 4¼" h.
(ILLUS.) **265.00**
Tazza, the small shallow circular dish
supported on a knopped cylinder &
raised on a tiered base, decorated
overall w/multicolored lotus blooms
amid foliate vines, the underside
case w/a six character seal marking
of Qianlong, of the period, China,
4½" h...**2,300.00**
Teapot, cov., miniature, globular body
w/loop handle, four rounded panels
in green, turquoise & two in royal
blue foil w/flowers in color & butterfly
panels surrounded by black, navy &

Japanese Cloisonné Miniature Teapot

dark green, Japan, 3" d., 4" h.
(ILLUS.) **125.00**

Vase, footed baluster-form, a
polychrome dragon around the sides
on a black ground, florals around the
neck & rounded lappets around the
base, marked "China," 8¾" h. **71.50**

Vase, baluster-form body w/flaring
neck, decorated overall w/large
polychrome flowers on a deep red
ground, China, 20th c., 10½" h. **143.00**

Cloisonné Double Gourd Vase

Vase, double gourd-shaped body,
brightly colored overall w/*shou*
medallions amid continuously
scrolling foliate vines issuing varying
colorful exotic lotus & other blooms,
beneath three tapered angular
scrollwork blades, minor chips,
Quinlong period, China, 14⅝" h.
(ILLUS.) **5,175.00**

Vases, decorated w/creamy white
flowers & red bird on turquoise
ground, 8½" h., pr. **150.00**

Vases, baluster-form w/angled
shoulders, decorated w/white mums,
lavender mums, green leaves &
small brick red flowers, on blue
ground w/green interior, Japan,
3¼" d., 8¾" h., pr. (ILLUS. top
next column) **595.00**

Pair of Cloisonné Vases

Cloisonné *Fu* Lion Wine Pot

Wine pot, cov., cast as a seated *fu*
lion, the paws outstretched grasping
a brocade ball issuing an upright
curved spout, w/clenched jaws,
broad snout & beady eyes framed
by a curly shaggy mane forming a
cover & trailing down the back,
applied scroll-form handle, Qianlong
period, China, typical pitting, 4¾" h.
(ILLUS.) **2,300.00**

RELATED WARES

Champleve clock garniture: clock &
two urns; the dial painted w/cherubs
& floral swags & surrounded by
paste 'jewels,' set in an architectural
case w/colorful floral decoration,
raised on an onyx base,
w/complimentary baluster-shaped
urns on pedestal base, retailed by
Tiffany & Co., France, height of
clock 20½" (ILLUS. clock &
one urn, top next page)..................**6,900.00**

Plique-a-jour pin, modeled in the
form of a butterfly w/articulated
wings, worked in shades of blue,

Champleve Clock Garniture

yellow & green w/a textured gold
body & ruby eyes **201.00**

CLOTHING

18th Century Men's Shoes

Recent interest in period clothing, uniforms and accessories from the 18th, 19th and through the 20th century compels us to include this category in our compilation. While style and fabric play an important role in the values of older garments of previous centuries, designer dresses of the 1920s and '30s, especially evening gowns, are enhanced by the original label of a noted courturier such as Worth, or Adrian. Prices vary widely for these garments which we list by type, with infant's and children's apparel so designated. Also see MOVIE MEMORA-BILIA.

Bloomers, cotton edge w/lace,
1890s **$125.00**
Bloomers, gym-type, blue wool,
early 1900s **40.00**

Bloomers, white cotton, pintucks &
crocheted lace trim, early 1900s **125.00**
Boating outfit, lady's, blue plaid,
1910, 2 pcs. **115.00**
Boots, child's, lace-up type, brown
leather, early 1900s, pr. **200.00**
Camisole, crocheted yoke, early
1900s **50.00**
Cape, lady's, Arts & Crafts style,
embroidered wool, w/shawl collar &
pockets, embroidered in silver &
gold silk on the grey ground w/tall
stylized arching round designs, fully
lined, early 20th c., size 4 (minor
holes) **330.00**
Christening dress, sheer batiste,
dainty overall embroidery w/band of
embroidery around hem, 41" l.........**165.00**
Dress w/original bustle, midnight
blue silk & velvet, Victorian, 1870s ..**255.00**
Dress w/original bustle, two-tone
grey, beaded w/pinwheel pleated
trim, Victorian, 1870s **255.00**
Evening gown, black velvet w/white
ermine collar, 1940s **30.00**
Galoshes, lady's fur-trimmed
overshoe-type, rubber, 1940s, pr.......**45.00**
Gloves, gauntlet length, black bear
fur, pr. **80.00**
Gown, "Delphos" style, pleated grey
silk, sleeveless trimmed to side
seams w/white striped clear
Venetian glass beads, w/grey
printed silk belt, Fortuny, Italy (some
staining & small tears) **1,150.00**
Hat, lady's, beaver w/long plumed
"bird," w/wide brim, Edwardian **98.00**
Hat, lady's, black velvet, Gibson Girl
style, early 1900s............................**100.00**
Hat, lady's, flapper-style, black
w/rhinestone trim **23.00**
Hat, lady's, brown velvet w/berry trim,
ca. 1870s **68.00**
Hat, lady's, straw, laden w/flowers,
w/wide brim, Edwardian...................**110.00**
Hat, man's, beaver top hat w/leather
case **125.00**
Hat, man's, top hat, beaver w/feather
trim, 1890s **150.00**
Jacket, lace & satin, black w/jet
beads overall, turn-of-the-century......**75.00**
Mourning shawl, wool, black,
8' long **75.00**
Muffler, beaver, large.........................**25.00**
Opera cape, black velvet, early
1900s **175.00**
Pantaloons, white cotton trimmed
w/embroidered edges **125.00**
Petticoat, white, full gathering in the
back & one row of beautiful lace,
early 1900s **125.00**
Petticoat, woman's, full-length, lacy
trim, Victorian....................................**30.00**

Shoes, child's, high button-type, red
leather, 5" l., pr. **68.00**
Shoes, lady's, high-top, white leather,
pr. **125.00**
Shoes, lady's, leather w/ribbon ties,
1890s **100.00**
Shoes, men's, black leather,
traditional form w/a buckle at the
front above scroll-decorated arch &
a band of narrow ribs across the
toes, 1720-70, 11¾" l., pr.
(ILLUS.) **1,380.00**
Shoes, men's, gangster-type, black &
white, size 10, pr. **25.00**
Skirt hoops, wire & tape, for full
Victorian skirt **85.00**
Suit, child's, linen, 1910, 2 pcs. **56.00**
Wedding gown, ivory satin, size 5/6,
ca. 1950 ....**500.00**

COCA-COLA ITEMS

Coca-Cola Advertisement

*Coca-Cola promotion has been achieved
through the issuance of scores of small
objects through the years. These, together
with trays, signs, and other articles
bearing the name of this soft drink, are
now sought by many collectors.*

Advertisement, lithograph on
cardboard, a B-52 Bomber bombing
enemy objectives, Coca-Cola bottle
& button at bottom corner, 1943,
corners w/minor wear, small cut at
top, large crease at bottom left
corner, 13 x 15" (ILLUS.) **$110.00**
Ashtray, foil, 1940s **45.00**
Ashtray set, ruby glass, each in the
form of a card suit (diamond,
heart, spade & club), 1950s,
set of 4 ....**600.00**
Baseball scorekeeper, "Perpetual
Calendar," for runs, hits & errors,
1906 ....**50.00**
Blotter, 1937, bottle superimposed

across "COLD refreshment"
w/"Coca-Cola" in diamond **42.50**
Blotter, 1938, pictures a policeman,
"Stop for a pause-Go refreshed" &
"Drink Coca-Cola" **30.00**
Blotter, 1944, "How about a Coke,"
three girls w/bottles of Coca-Cola **10.00**
Blotter, 1951, Sprite Boy behind
bottle, "Delicious and Refreshing" **18.50**
Blotter, 1953, Sprite Boy w/bottle,
"Good" **15.00**
Blotter, 1956, Santa, "Twas the Coke
before Christmas" **15.00**
Booklet, "Our America," 1940 ....**175.00**
Bookmark, 1906, celluloid, owl
holding book, 1 x 3½" **680.00**
Bottle, 1909, amber, straight-sided
w/"Coca-Cola" & embossed arrow **75.00**
Bottle carrier, wooden w/rope
handle, 6-pack, 1940s **100.00**
Bottle carton-carrier, cardboard,
1937, 6-pack **30.00**
Bottle holder for automobile,
cardboard, ca. 1950 ....**18.00**
Bottle opener, "Drink Coca-Cola,"
bottle-shaped, 1950s **35.00**
Bottle opener, wall-type, cast iron,
"Star X," 1925, w/box **24.00**
Bowl, pretzel, aluminum, three bottle-
shaped legs, 1936, 8¼" d. **250.00**
Calendar, 1918, distributor's, w/June
Caprice, full pad, 5 x 9" **275.00**
Calendar, 1921, young lady seated in
garden holding glass, framed **175.00**
Calendar, 1935, boy & dog fishing
from stump, Norman Rockwell
illustration, full page **300.00**
Calendar, 1938, pretty girl in summer
dress & hat holding a bottle of
Coca-Cola, full pad **475.00**
Calendar, 1960, ski couple **100.00**
Calendar, 1962, prom scene **22.00**
Calendar, 1963, girl in front of
mirror **22.00**
Calendar, 1977 ....**25.00**
Cigarette lighter, figural bottle **18.00**
Clock, counter-type, electric, square
face, lights up, 1950s **450.00**
Clock, electric wall-type, square
plastic & metal, white w/green
Arabic numerals & embossed red
lettering in the upper left corner
reading "Things go better with
Coke," embossed red logo button in
the bottom right corner w/silver
lettering, 16" sq. (minor scratches,
hands bent) **66.00**
Clock, wall-type, electric, rectangular,
plastic, "Drink Coca-Cola" at bottom,
1960s **162.50**
Clock, wall-type, electric, square,
wooden frame, "Drink Coca-Cola in
Bottles," 1939, 16 x 16" **400.00**

Coasters, aluminum, embossed bottle & "Drink Coca-Cola," 1960s, set of 8 ....**25.00**

Coca-Cola Cooler

Cooler, metal, embossed "ICE COLD Coca-Cola SOLD HERE," w/bottle on side, 22 x 29", 32½" h., rust & paint chipping overall (ILLUS.)......**1,045.00**

Doll, Buddy Lee w/original striped uniform, 12" h., 1950s......................**265.00**

Doll, Santa Claus standing holding bottle of Coca-Cola, cloth-stuffed body, ca. 1970 ....**60.00**

Festoon, die-cut cardboard, "Petunia," five-part, two small sections w/green leaves & large pink blossoms, two long leaf & flower sections w/round reserves w/a bust profile portrait of a pretty lady drinking from a glass w/"Coca-Cola" below, & a round silver center circle w/a brown glass of Coca-Cola & "Thirst Stops Here" above, 1939, 41" l., center circle 13½" d. **1,100.00**

Game, Chinese Checkers, wood & heavy paperboard playing board, 1940s **100.00**

Knife, pocket-type, bone handle, 1908 ....**475.00**

Mirror, pocket-type, 1906, young lady drinking from glass, "The Whitehead & Hoag Co." etc., on rim, oval..........**362.50**

Needle case, pictures pretty girl w/bottle of Coke on front, glass back, 1924 ....**55.00**

Playing cards, 1943, Autumn Girl, original box, unopened **200.00**

Playing cards, 1943, World War II service woman, mint, unopened......**225.00**

Radio, model of a bottle, 1930, 24" h..**4,125.00**

Ruler, wooden, trademark in tail of "C", ca. 1937, 1 foot **25.00**

Salesman training program kit, "Knowledge is Power," includes six large records, 10 film reels & a 20 x

20" carrying case, 1940 copyright, the set **595.00**

Sewing kit, World War II, gold "US Army" & American Eagle on khaki-colored leatherette kit, w/thread, buttons & needles, 1940s **35.00**

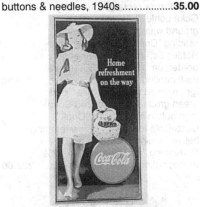

Home Refreshment Sign

Sign, cardboard, rectangular, green ground w/yellow lettering "Home refreshment on the way," to the right of a woman dressed in cream carrying a tan basket w/food & Coca-Cola, framed, bottom left corner missing, very minor scratches & watermarks, 24½ x 50" (ILLUS.) **276.00**

Hospitality Coca-Cola Sign

Sign, cardboard, rectangular, red background w/pretty girl w/white flower in her hair lighting a candle, reads "Hospitality - Coca-Cola," one bottom corner missing, water stains along edges, minor scratches, 30 x 59" (ILLUS.) **770.00**

Coca-Cola Metal Sign

Sign, painted metal, red & white

w/white lettering, reads "ENJOY
Coca-Cola," to the left of a
bottle of Coke, 11¾ x 32"
(ILLUS.) **121.00**
Sign, painted tin, embossed lettering,
long narrow rectangle, an early
Coke bottle at the left end, red
ground w/large yellow lettering
reading "Drink - Coca-Cola - in
Bottles 5¢," narrow green edge
border, ca. 1908, 12 x 36" (overall
rust, denting & soiling) **412.50**
Sign, painted tin, rectangular, dark
green ground w/a large red Coke
logo button at the top w/"Drink
Coca-Cola Ice-Cold," yellow lettering
below reading "Delicious and
Refreshing," ca. 1941, 19½ x 27½"
(minor fading, pitting of paint) **220.00**

Tin Coca-Cola Sign

Sign, painted tin, round, red w/green
& yellow borders, white letters read
"Coca-Cola" across a Coke bottle,
marked "Made in U.S.A./AAW 10-
37," touched up overall, minor
crazing, 45" d. (ILLUS.) **440.00**
Sign, paper, rectangular, a large tilted
Coke bottle & a red logo button
above an iceberg w/the word "Cold"
spelled out as icebergs in light blue
& green, ca. 1939, framed, 58½" l.,
20" h. (very minor crease marks
& soiling) **660.00**
Sign, porcelain, rectangular, "Coca-
Cola - Sold Here Ice Cold," red &
white w/green border, 12 x 29",
1940s **300.00**
Sign, porcelain, round "button"
w/arrow, red button w/"Drink Coca-
Cola - Sign of Good Taste," 1950,
16" d. w/arrow **675.00**
Sign, porcelain, rectangular, white
ground w/green pinstripes
overprinted w/a red "fishtail" reserve
printed in yellow w/"Coca-Cola -
Sign of Good Taste," ca. 1963,

46" l., 16" h. (rust spot in upper left
& under "taste") **176.00**
Sign, porcelain, round "button"
w/arrow, white button w/Coca-
Cola bottle, 1950, 23" d.
w/arrow **750.00**
Sign, porcelain, round "button"
w/arrow, red button w/"Drink
Coca-Cola - in Bottles," 1950s,
36" d. **675.00**
Sign, tin, bottle-shaped, "Coca-Cola,
Trade Mark Registered, Bottle
Pat'd Dec. 25, 1923," 1933, 3' h. **650.00**
Sign, tin, rectangular, "fishtail" logo,
"Coca-Cola - Sign of Good Taste,"
ca. 1960, 20 x 28" **210.00**
Sign, tin, rectangular, "Fountain
Service" & "Drink Coca-Cola,"
1950s, 12 x 28" **150.00**

Coca-Cola Fountain Syrup Can

Syrup can, metal, red w/silver
highlights, red & white lettering,
manufactured by The Coca-Cola
Company Principal Office New York,
N.Y., minor scratches overall, top of
can missing, minor denting, 6" d.,
8¾" h. (ILLUS.) **60.50**
Thermometer, tin, bottle-shaped,
1950s, 17" h. **185.00**
Thermometer, tin, bullet-shaped,
w/silhouette portrait of girl drinking
from bottle at bottom, 1939,
6½" w., 16" h. **350.00**
Thermometer, tin, embossed bottle
shape, ca. 1958, 8½" w.,
30" h. **135.00**
Thimble, aluminum, dated
1920 ....**30.00**
Trade card, 1942, illustration of glass
of "Coke," free Coca-Cola coupon
on reverse side **22.00**
Tray, change, 1903, "bottle tray,"
5½" d. **2,000.00**
Tray, change, 1907, young lady
holding up a glass w/"Relieves
Fatigue," 4½ x 6¼" oval...**700.00 to 750.00**

Tray, change, 1913, Hamilton King
Girl in a picture hat holding a glass,
4¼ x 6" oval.....................**350.00 to 400.00**
Tray, change, 1914, Betty, 4¼ x 6"
oval **269.00**
Tray, change, 1916, girl under tree
holding glass, 4¼ x 6" oval **151.00**
Tray, change, 1920, Garden Girl,
4¼ x 6" oval **500.00**

1908 Coca-Cola Tray

Tray, 1908, "Wherever Ginger Ale,
Seltzer or Soda is Good - Coca-Cola
is better - Try It," printed around a
topless sitting girl, all surrounded by
scrolling design on
border, 12¼" d. (ILLUS.).............**13,200.00**
Tray, 1913, Hamilton King Girl,
10½ x 13¼" oblong..........................**400.00**
Tray, 1914, Betty, 10½ x 13¼"
rectangle **350.00**
Tray, 1914, Betty, 12½ x 15¼"
oval **237.50**
Tray, 1922, Summer Girl, 10½ x
13¼" oblong.....................................**250.00**
Tray, 1923, Flapper Girl, 10½ x
13¼" rectangle ....**400.00 to 425.00**
Tray, 1926, Golfer & pretty lady, 10½
x 13¼" rectangle **1,298.00**
Tray, 1927, Curb Service, 10½ x
13¼" rectangle ....**800.00 to 1,200.00**
Tray, 1927, Girl with Bobbed Hair,
10½ x 13¼" oblong............................**75.00**
Tray, 1928, girl sipping a bottle of
Coke, 10½ x 13¼" rectangle.........**1,275.00**
Tray, 1930, Bathing Beauty in Swim
Cap, 10½ x 13¼" oblong **290.00**
Tray, 1931, Farm Boy with Dog, by
Norman Rockwell, 10½ x 13¼"
oblong **467.00**
Tray, 1935, Madge Evans, 10½ x
13¼" rectangle.................................**247.50**
Tray, 1936, Hostess, 10½ x 13¼"
rectangle **172.50**
Tray, 1939, Springboard Girl, artwork
by Haddon Sundblom, 10½ x
13¼" oblong.....................................**257.00**

Tray, 1940, Girl Fishing, 10½ x
13¼" rectangle ....**300.00 to 350.00**
Tray, 1942, Two girls at Car, 10½ x
13¼" rectangle.................................**283.00**
Tray, 1950-52, Girl w/Bottle of Coke,
10½ x 13¼" rectangle **75.00**
Tray, 1958, Picnic Basket in Cart,
10½ x 11¼" oblong............................**25.00**
Tray, 1961, Pansy Garden.................**20.00**
Tray, 1961, TV tray - Thanksgiving
scene **20.00**
Vending machine, Vendo model 33,
original condition, working **1,950.00**
Vending machine, "Vendo 39," 6 oz.
bottle size, original condition w/eight
cases ....**1,200.00 to 1,500.00**

COFFEE GRINDERS

Fisher Lap-type Grinder

Clamp-on table type, cast iron, "L.F.
& C. No. 1".......................................**$75.00**
Lap-type, cherry dovetailed case
w/nailed drawer, iron hopper,
branded label "J. Fisher Warranted,"
6¼" h. plus handle (ILLUS.).............**192.50**
Lap-type, cherry dovetailed case,

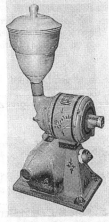

Royal Store Counter Coffee Grinder

pewter cup, signed "Celsor Cook
& Co., Pat.," 7 x 7½ x 9½" **250.00**
Store counter model, two-wheel,
cast iron, "Enterprise
No. 2"...............................**600.00 to 650.00**
Store counter model, two-wheel,
cast iron, "Enterprise No. 2," rare
small size, 7" w., 9" h. (soiled, minor
paint loss) **550.00**
Store counter model, cast iron, red
w/black & gold motif overall, marked
"Royal," some paint loss & rust,
9½ x 15½", 34" h. (ILLUS. bottom
previous page) **159.00**
Store floor model, cast iron, two-
wheel, "Enterprise No. 18," patent-
dated 1873, over 5' h. **950.00**

COMIC BOOKS

Plastic Man #1

*Comic books, especially first, or early
issues of a series, are avidly collected
today. Prices for some of the scarce ones
have reached extremely high levels. Prices
listed bleow are for copies in fine to mint
condition.*

Action Comics, November, 1939
(cover loose, complete) **$350.00**
**Adventures of Krazy Kat & Ignatz
Mouse in Koko Land,** Herriman,
No. 1056, 1934, very good
condition **95.00**
Amazing Fantasy #15, Marvel
Comics, 1962, first appearance
of Spider-Man, very fine..............**16,100.00**
Batman, No. 110................................**85.00**
Batman, No. 112................................**85.00**
Ben Bowie and His Mountain Men,
Dell Publishing No. 10 ....**10.00**

Bonanza, Dell Publishing Co. (Gold
Key) No. 1221 ....**48.00**
Buffalo Bill, Jr., Dell Publishing Co.
No. 38 ....**14.00**
Cisco Kid, Dell Publishing
Co. No. 24, 1954...............................**15.00**
Daniel Boone, No. 96.........................**10.00**
Dobie Gillis, National Periodical
Publications No. 24...........................**10.00**
Flintstones, Dell Publishing Co.
No. 37 ....**9.00**
Flying A's Range Rider, Dell
Publishing Co. No. 17.........................**9.00**
Golden West Rodeo Treasury, Dell
Giant Comics No. 2............................**45.00**
Goofy, Dell Publishing Co.
No. 747 ....**7.00**
Gun Smoke, Dell Publishing Co.
(Gold Key) No. 73...............................**5.00**
King of the Royal Mounted, Dell
Publishing Co. No. 26........................**12.00**
King of the Royal Mounted, Dell
Publishing Co. No. 27........................**10.00**
Lone Ranger, Dell Publishing Co. No.
13, mint condition.............................**50.00**
Lone Ranger, Dell Publishing Co.
No. 107 ....**25.00**
Lone Ranger, Dell Publishing Co.
No. 120 ....**25.00**
Lone Ranger, Dell Publishing Co.
No. 122, mint condition **50.00**
Lone Ranger, Dell Publishing Co.
No. 125 ....**12.00**
Lone Ranger, Dell Publishing Co.
No. 134 ....**20.00**
Mutt & Jeff, All American/National
No. 33 ....**30.00**
Mutt & Jeff, All American/National
No. 34 ....**30.00**
Nancy & Sluggo, Dell Publishing Co.
No. 175 ....**7.00**
Pixie & Dixie & Mr. Jinks, Dell
Publishing Co. (Gold Key)
No. 1112..**8.00**
Plastic Man #1, unnumbered, Vital
Publications, 1943
(ILLUS.) **1,380.00**
Red Ryder, Dell Publishing Co.,
No. 104 ....**15.00**
Red Ryder, Dell Publishing Co.
No. 147, April-June 1957 ....**5.00**
Rin Tin Tin, Dell Publishing Co.
No. 23 ....**16.00**
Roy Rogers Comics, Dell Publishing
Co., No. 32..**20.00**
Roy Rogers Comics, Dell Publishing
Co., No. 51..**12.00**
Showcase #4, DC Comics, 1956, Joe
Kubert's personal file copy, first
appearance of The Flash
(ILLUS. top next page)................**3,450.00**
Tarzan, Marvel Comics Group
No. 25 ....**15.00**

Showcase #4

Tarzan, Marvel Comics Group
No. 92 ....**10.00**
Tom & Jerry, Dell Publishing Co.
No. 193 ....**4.00**
Uncle Scrooge, Dell Publishing Co.
No. 7 ....**5.00**
Uncle Scrooge, Dell Publishing Co.
No. 30 ....**25.00**

COMMEMORATIVE PLATES

Limited editions commemorative and collector plates rank high on the list of collectible items. The oldest and best-known of these plates, those of Bing & Grondahl and Royal Copenhagen, retain leadership in the field, but other companies are turning out a variety of designs, some of which have been widely embraced by the growing numbers who have made plate collecting a hobby. Plates listed below are a representative selection of fine porcelain, glass and other plates available to collectors.

BAREUTHER
1967, Stiftskirche **$50.00**
1968, Kappl **14.00**
1969, Christkindlesmarkt.....................**17.00**
1970, Chapel in Oberndorf **8.50**
1971, Toys for Sale (ILLUS.
top next column) **8.00**
1972, Christmas in March.....................**18.50**
1973, Christmas Sleigh Ride **7.00**
1974, Church in the Black Forest **9.50**
1975, Snowman.....................................**22.00**
1976, Chapel in the Hills.......................**19.00**
1977, Story Time **13.00**
1978, Mittenwald **9.50**

1971 Bareuther Christmas Plate

1979, Winter Day.................................**10.00**
1980, Miltenberg..................................**21.00**
1981, Walk in the Forest......................**16.00**
1982, Bad Wimpfen **25.00**
1983, The Night Before Christmas **25.50**
1984, Zeil on the River Main................**24.50**
1985, Winter Wonderland.....................**27.50**
1986, Market Place in Forchheim.........**26.50**
1987, Decorating the Tree....................**21.00**
1988, St. Coloman Church **43.50**
1990, The Old Forge in Rothenburg.....**27.00**

Thanksgiving
1972, Harvest......................................**13.50**
1978, Apple Harvest.............................**19.50**
1982, Autumn **17.00**

BING & GRONDAHL

Christmas

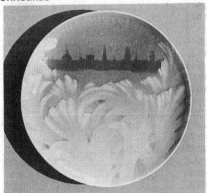

1895 Bing & Grondahl Christmas Plate

1895 (ILLUS.) **5,171.00**
1896..**1,571.00**
1897..**1,410.50**
1898...**623.50**
1899..**1,212.00**
1900...**802.50**
1901...**347.50**
1902...**284.50**

1903	280.00
1904	114.50
1905	128.50
1906	67.00
1907	94.00
1908	64.00
1909	77.00
1910	76.00
1911	72.00
1912	77.00
1913	77.00
1914	65.50
1915	111.00
1916	66.00
1917	64.00
1918	64.00
1919	57.00
1920	64.50
1921	57.00
1922	56.00
1923	53.50
1924	63.00
1925	63.00
1926	63.00
1927	94.50
1928	57.00
1929	61.00
1930	78.00
1931	75.50
1932	75.00
1933	61.00
1934	58.00
1935	57.00
1936	62.00
1937	74.00
1938	110.00
1939	152.00
1940	152.00
1941	193.00
1942	163.00
1943	137.00
1944	79.00
1945	116.00
1946	68.00
1947	91.50
1948	74.00
1949	71.00
1950	101.00
1951	85.00
1952	84.00
1953	82.00
1954	83.00
1955	89.00
1956	108.50
1957	116.00
1958	80.00
1959	103.00
1960	114.00
1961	85.00
1962	53.00
1963	65.00
1964	27.00
1965	31.00
1966	27.00

1967	26.00
1968	21.00
1969	15.00
1970	14.00
1971	11.00
1972	11.00
1973	14.00
1974	14.00
1975	13.00
1976	15.00
1977	14.50
1978	15.00
1979	17.00
1980	18.00
1981	22.00
1982	29.00
1983	29.00
1984	28.00
1985	28.00

Mother's Day

1969, Dog & Puppies	305.00
1970, Birds & Chicks	11.00
1971, Cat & Kitten	8.00
1972, Mare & Foal	9.50
1973, Duck & Ducklings	13.50
1974, Bear & Cubs	16.00
1975, Doe & Fawns	14.00
1976, Swan Family	15.00
1977, Squirrel & Young	15.00
1978, Heron	16.00
1979, Fox & Cubs	35.20
1980, Woodpecker & Young	25.00
1981, Hare & Young	25.50
1982, Lioness & Cubs	26.50
1983, Raccoon & Young	28.00
1984, Stork & Nestlings	39.00
1985, Bear with Cubs	28.50
1986, Elephant with Calf	29.00
1987, Sheep with Lambs	56.00

Jubilee

1915, Frozen Window	114.00
1920, Church Bells	45.00
1925, Dog Outside Window	83.00
1930, The Old Organist	109.00
1935, Little Match Girl	568.00
1940, Three Wise Men	1,525.00
1945, Royal Guard Amalienborg Castle	117.00
1950, Eskimos	122.00
1955, Dybbol Mill	123.00
1960, Kronborg Castle	89.00
1965, Churchgoers	53.00
1970, Amalienborg Castle	10.00
1975, Horses Enjoying Meal	27.00
1980, Happiness over Yule Tree	26.00
1985, Lifeboat at Work	38.00

FRANKOMA

1965, Goodwill Toward Men	201.00
1966, Bethlehem Shepherds	89.00
1967, Gifts for the Christ Child	60.00
1968, Flight into Egypt	25.00

1969 Laid in a Manger Christmas Plate

1969, Laid in a Manger (ILLUS.) 31.00
1970, King of Kings 20.00
1971, No Room in the Inn....................13.00
1972, Seeking the Christ Child.............15.00
1973, The Annunciation.........................9.00
1974, She Loved & Cared 12.00
1975, Peace on Earth...........................14.00
1976, Gift of Love 18.00
1977, Birth of Eternal Life.....................18.50
1978, All Nature Rejoiced.....................22.50
1979, Star of Hope 15.00
1980, Unto Us a Child Is Born..............12.50
1981, O Come Let Us Adore Him........15.00
1982, Wise Men Rejoice......................13.00
1983, Wise Men Bring Gifts.................14.00
1984, Faith, Hope & Love.....................14.50
1985, The Angels Watched 13.50
1986, For Thee I Play My Drum 15.50
1987, God's Chosen Family 16.00

HAVILAND & CO.

Christmas

1970 Haviland & Co. Christmas Plate

1970, A Partridge in a Pear Tree
(ILLUS.) 42.50
1971, Two Turtle Doves 34.50
1972, Three French Hens....................24.00
1973, Four Colly Birds 23.00

1974, Five Golden Rings.....................20.50
1975, Six Geese A'Laying 24.00
1976, Seven Swans A'Swimming.........24.00
1977, Eight Maids A'Milking 25.00
1978, Nine Ladies Dancing 50.50
1979, Ten Lords A'Leaping 27.50
1980, Eleven Pipers Piping 60.00
1981, Twelve Drummers Drumming.....42.00
12 Days of Christmas, set 314.00

HUMMEL (GOEBEL WORKS)

Annual
1971, Heavenly Angel 477.00
1972, Hear Ye, Hear Ye 56.00
1973, Globe Trotter 77.00
1974, Goose Girl 77.00
1975, Ride into Christmas 48.00
1976, Apple Tree Girl 46.00
1977, Apple Tree Boy...........................57.00
1978, Happy Pastime 37.00
1979, Singing Lesson 24.50
1980, School Girl 43.50
1981, Umbrella Boy 45.00
1982, Umbrella Girl..............................91.00
1983, The Postman 138.00
1984, Little Helper 50.00
1985, Chick Girl...................................61.00
1986, Playmates..................................103.00
1987, Feeding Time..............................179.00

LALIQUE (GLASS)

Annual

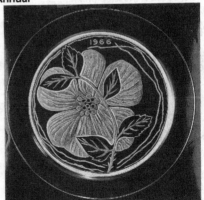

1966 Lalique Plate

1965, Deux Oiseaux (Two Birds)........**797.00**
1966, Rose de Songerie (Dream
Rose) (ILLUS.) ....75.00 to 100.00
1967, Ballet de Poisson (Fish
Ballet)...107.50
1968, Gazelle Fantaisie (Gazelle
Fantasy)...79.50
1969, Papillon (Butterfly) 73.00
1970, Paon (Peacock) 75.00
1971, Hibou (Owl)................................67.50
1972, Coquillage (Shell) 55.00

1973, Petit Geai (Jayling) **93.00**
1974, Sous d'Argent (Silver Pennies)...**73.50**
1975, Dou de Poisson (Fish Duet) **100.00**
1976, Aigle (Eagle) **85.00**

LENOX

Boehm Bird Series
1970, Wood Thrush **98.00**
1971, Goldfinch **80.00**
1972, Mountain Bluebird.....................**48.50**
1973, Meadowlark **42.00**
1974, Rufous Hummingbird.................**59.50**
1975, American Redstart......................**53.00**
1976, Cardinals **51.50**
1977, Robins **53.50**
1978, Mockingbirds **62.00**
1979, Golden-Crowned Kinglets..........**85.00**
1980, Black-Throated Blue Warblers....**95.00**
1981, Eastern Pheobes **95.00**

PORSGRUND

Christmas
1968, Church Scene............................**55.00**
1969, Three Kings **7.50**
1970, Road to Bethlehem......................**7.50**
1971, A Child is Born............................**8.00**
1972, Hark, the Herald Angels Sing **7.00**
1973, Promise of the Savior **9.00**
1974, The Shepherds **6.00**
1975, Jesus on the Road to the
Temple...**9.00**
1976, Jesus & the Elders.......................**7.00**
1977, Draught of the Fish **8.00**

RED SKELTON

Freddie the Freeloader Series (Crown Parian)
1979, Freddie in the Bathtub **145.00**
1980, Freddie's Shack...........................**65.00**
1981, Freddie on the Green **55.50**
1982, Love That Freddie **46.00**

Famous Clowns Series (Fairmont)
1976, Freddie the Freeloader.............**348.00**
1977, W.C. Fields...............................**59.00**
1978, Happy **63.00**
1979, The Pledge **56.50**

Freddie's Adventures Series (Crown Parian)
1981, Captain Freddie **51.50**
1982, Bronco Freddie **45.00**
1983, Sir Freddie **46.00**

RORSTRAND
1968, Bringing Home the
Tree ....**300.00 to 350.00**
1969, Fisherman Sailing Home **13.00**
1970, Nils with His Geese
(ILLUS. top next column) **13.00**
1971, Nils in Lapland...........................**19.00**

1970 Rorstrand Christmas Plate

1972, Dalecarlian Fiddler.....................**11.50**
1973, Farm in Smaland **46.00**
1974, Vadstena **40.00**
1975, Nils in Vastmanland...................**16.00**
1976, Nils in Uppland **13.00**
1977, Nils in Varmland **10.50**
1978, Nils in Fjallbacka.......................**20.50**
1979, Nils in Vaestergoetland..............**25.00**
1980, Nils in Halland...........................**30.00**
1981, Nils in Gotland **28.00**
1982, Nils at Skansen in Stockholm **33.00**
1983, Nils in Oland **32.00**
1984, Nils in Angermanland **37.00**
1985, Nils in Jamtland **40.00**
1986, Nils in Karlskrona......................**39.00**

ROSENTHAL

1930 Rosenthal Christmas Plate

1910...**370.00**
1911...**104.00**
1913...**106.00**
1915...**119.00**
1916...**123.00**
1923...**75.00**
1926...**108.00**
1927...**108.00**
1928...**110.00**
1929...**135.00**
1930 (ILLUS.).....................................**63.00**

1931	108.50
1933	125.00
1934	125.00
1935	85.00
1936	83.50
1937	110.00
1938	97.00
1939	110.00
1942	200.00
1944	176.00
1945	240.00
1946	150.00
1949	110.00
1950	110.00
1951	250.00
1952	95.00
1953	120.00
1954	120.00
1955	118.00
1956	124.00
1957	115.00
1958	115.00
1959	110.00
1960	115.00
1961	83.00
1962	81.00
1963	76.50
1964	80.00
1965	69.00
1966	88.00
1967	75.00
1968	88.00
1969	77.00
1970	60.00
1971	52.00
1972	52.00
1973	48.50
1974	37.00
1975	49.00
1976	38.00
1977	50.00
1978	47.50
1979	72.00
1980	99.00
1981	110.00
1982	133.00
1983	147.50
1984	147.50

ROYAL COPENHAGEN

Christmas
1908	2,932.00
1909 (ILLUS. top next column)	148.00
1910	99.00
1911	122.00
1912	122.00
1913	117.00
1914	130.00
1915	138.50
1916	96.50
1917	84.00
1918	83.00
1919	83.00

1909 Royal Copenhagen Christmas Plate

1920	70.00
1921	78.00
1922	70.00
1923	67.00
1924	96.50
1925	78.00
1926	69.00
1927	115.50
1928	78.00
1929	78.00
1930	102.50
1931	98.00
1932	105.00
1933	130.00
1934	126.00
1935	174.00
1936	158.00
1937	201.00
1938	246.00
1939	329.00
1940	329.50
1941	293.00
1942	285.00
1943	456.00
1944	195.00
1945	341.00
1946	152.50
1947	204.00
1948	176.00
1949	187.00
1950	138.50
1951	284.00
1952	108.50
1953	116.00
1954	110.00
1955	153.00
1956	133.00
1957	101.00
1958	93.00
1959	98.50
1960	105.00
1961	115.00
1962	157.00
1963	63.00
1964	43.00
1965	40.00

1966	22.00
1967	22.00
1968	18.00
1969	20.00
1970	25.00
1971	13.00
1972	12.00
1973	15.00
1974	17.00
1975	14.00
1976	17.50
1977	18.00
1978	17.00
1979	32.00
1980	27.00
1981	23.00
1982	32.00
1983	37.00
1984	33.50
1985	46.50
1986	44.50
1987	47.00

Mother's Day

1971, American Mother	78.00
1972, Oriental Mother	39.00
1973, Danish Mother	37.50
1974, Greenland Mother	30.00
1975, Bird in Nest	34.50
1976, Mermaids	33.00
1977, The Twins	25.00
1978, Mother & Child	26.20
1979, A Loving Mother	8.00
1980, An Outing with Mother	14.00
1981, Reunion	14.50
1982, Children's Hour	13.50

ROYAL DOULTON

Mother & Child Series

1973, Colette & Child	278.00
1974, Sayuri & Child	71.00
1975, Kristina & Child	39.00
1976, Marilyn & Child	47.50
1977, Lucia & Child	39.50
1978, Kathleen & Child	51.00

WEDGWOOD

Christmas

1969, Windsor Castle	76.00
1970, Christmas in Trafalgar Square	41.00
1971, Picadilly Circus, London	35.00
1972, St. Paul's Cathedral	46.00
1973, Tower of London	61.50
1974, Houses of Parliament	22.00
1975, Tower Bridge	51.50
1976, Hampton Court	19.00
1977, Westminster Abbey	22.00
1978, Horse Guards	24.00
1979, Buckingham Palace	32.00
1980, St. James Palace	29.00
1981, Marble Arch	26.00
1982, Lambeth Palace	59.00

1983, All Souls, Langham Palace	55.00
1984, Constitution Hill	45.00
1985, The Tate Gallery	53.00
1986, Albert Memorial	135.00
1987, Guildhall	75.00
1988, The Observatory, Greenwich	70.00

(End of Commemorative Plates Section)

COMPACT & VANITY CASES

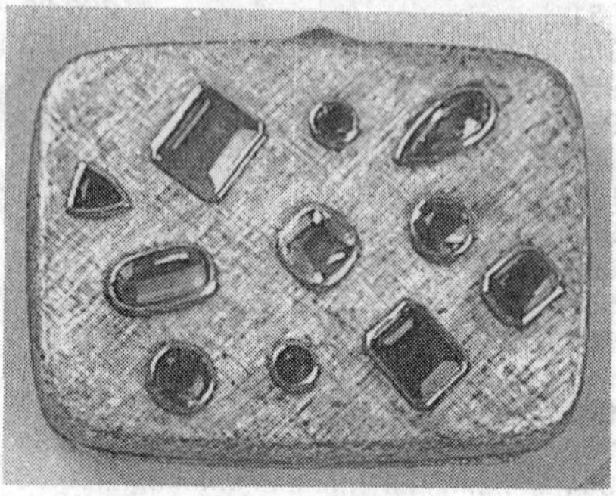

Gold Gem-set Compact

Enameled goldtone vanity case, rectangular, white w/gold crown, Prince Matchabelli ... **$50.00**

Gold (18kt yellow) & enamel compact, centered by a jade quatrefoil within a reeded case w/blue enamel borders, accented by a jade & diamond closure, French hallmarks (some enamel loss) ... **1,035.00**

Gold (14kt yellow) gem-set compact, rectangular Florentine finish w/various shaped collet-set semi-precious stones, opening to mirror & powder, 2 x 2¾" (ILLUS.) ... **546.00**

Gold (14kt yellow) vanity case, rectangular w/engraved floral design & four oval cabochon sapphire push-pieces opening to reveal a mirror & a powder compartment, attached to a gold chain ... **1,265.00**

Goldtone compact, "American Beauty" by Elgin ... **25.00**

Goldtone compact, John Deere promotional piece ... **46.00**

Silver compact w/enameled orange & green design, w/finger ring ... **45.00**

Sterling silver compact, flap jack-form, decorated w/engraved pink & yellow flowers ... **75.00**

Sterling silver compact, flap jack-form, decorated w/engraved blue flowers, "Rex of 5th Avenue" ... **85.00**

Sterling silver compact, flap jack-
form, pinwheel design, "Rex of 5th
Avenue" **70.00**

Sterling silver compact, pendant-
type, round w/floral decoration,
ca. 1905, Codding Bros. **95.00**

Sterling silver compact w/floral
engraving, marked "Elgin,"
3½" d..**95.00**

Sterling silver compact w/applied
sterling flowers decoration, "Reed &
Barton" **60.00**

Sterling silver (950), overall
engravings of birds, flowers &
foliage, marked "T MUTO
Silversmith" **125.00**

Ladies' Home Journal, 1960, first
edition **20.00**
"McCall's," 1963 ....**8.00**
"The Modern Family Cookbook,"
Meta Given **8.00**
**"Salads, Sandwiches & Chafing
Dish Dainties,"** Hill's, 1919..............**25.00**
"The World's Modern Cookbook,"
1932..**15.00**

COOKBOOKS

*Cookbook collectors are usually good
cooks and will buy important new
cookbooks as well as seek out notable older
ones. Many early cookbooks were published
and given away as advertising premiums
for various products used extensively in
cooking. While some rare, scarce first
edition cookbooks can be very expensive,
most collectible cookbooks are reasonably
priced. We list our advertising cookbooks
alphabetically by the names of the
companies which produced them.*

Advertising, "Columbine Condensed
Milk," can-shaped **$10.00**
Advertising, "Cottolene Cooking Oil
Recipes"..**8.00**
Advertising, "Indianapolis Brewing
Company," 1912 ....**65.00**
Advertising "Jello," 'Polly Put the
Kettle On,' illustrated by
Maxfield Parrish, 1924 ....**55.00**
Advertising, "Jewel Tea Cookbook,"
by Mary Dunbar, 1933 ....**20.00**
**"A Thousand Ways to Please a
Husband,"** 1917..............................**75.00**
**"Betty Crocker Cookbook for Boys
& Girls,"** 1957, first edition................**95.00**
**"Betty Crocker's Cookbook from
Sears,"** 1972 ....**8.00**
"Better Homes & Gardens," 1953 ....**8.00**
"Cook Is In the Parlor," McCarthy's,
1947...**14.95**
"Double Quick Cooking," Allen's,
1943...**10.00**
"Good Housekeeping Cookbook,"
1944...**15.00**
"Household Searchlight,"
1946...**20.00**
"House Maker's Guide," by Marjorie
Mills, 1929.......................................**12.00**
"Joy of Cooking," 1946........................**6.00**

COOKIE CUTTERS

Man with Outstretched Hand Cutter

*Recently there has been an accelerated
interest in old tin cookie cutters. For the
most part, these were made by tinsmiths
who shaped primitive designs of tin strips
and then soldered them to a backplate,
pierced to allow air to enter and prevent a
suction from holding the rolled cookie
dough in the form. Sometimes an
additional handle was soldered to the
back. Cookie cutters were also
manufactured in great quantities in an
outline form that could depict animals,
birds, stars and other forms, including the
plain round that sometimes carried
embossed advertising for flour or other
products on the handle. Aluminum cookie
cutters were made after 1920. All cutters
listed are tin unless otherwise noted.*

Dancing Dutchman, flat backplate
pierced w/two holes, 7¾" h. **$159.50**
Multiple design, round w/twelve
interior shapes including a star,
heart, diamond, crescent & other
designs, 6¾" d. **99.00**
Horse, flat backplate pierced w/two
holes, 5¼" l. **27.50**
Horse, realistic standing animal
w/full tail & slightly pointed
muzzle, backplate conforms to
the outline & punched w/a single
hole, 7¾" l. **104.50**
Man w/outstretched hand,
rectangular backplate w/two finger
holes, 9¾" h. (ILLUS.)......................**385.00**

COOKIE JARS

All sorts of charming and whimsical cookie jars have been produced in recent decades and these are increasingly collectible today. Many well known American potteries such as McCoy, Hull and Abingdon, produced cookie jars and their products are included in those listings. Below we are listing cookie jars produced by other companies.

Current reference books for collectors include: The Collectors Encyclopedia of Cookie Jars, by Fred and Joyce Roerig (Collector Books, 1991); Collector's Encyclopedia of Cookie Jars, Book II by Fred and Joyce Roerig (Collector Books, 1994) and The Complete Cookie Jar Book by Mike Schneider (Schiffer, Ltd. 1991).

AMERICAN BISQUE

Davy Crockett Standing in the Woods

After School Cookies	$40.00
Blackboard Hobo	307.00
Boy Bear	95.00
Boy Pig	75.00
Bow Bear	92.50
Butter Churn	19.00
Cat with Bow	60.00
Churn Boy	203.00
Clown	65.00
Clown w/chalkboard	185.00
Clown with Raised Arms	70.00
Cookie Clock, gold trim	150.00
Cookie Pail	19.00
Cow	47.00
Cow/Bull Turnabout	205.00
Davy Crockett, standing in the woods (ILLUS.)	950.00 to 1,000.00
Deer	150.00
Dog in Basket	65.00
Girl & Lamb	82.50
Horse, sitting	1,500.00
Jack-in-the-box	102.00
Little Girl Lamb	80.00
Peasant Girl	750.00
Popeye	1,122.00

Rabbit in Basket	30.00
Sailor Elephant	102.00
Santa Head, winking	550.00 to 575.00
Sea Bag	153.00
Seal on Igloo	388.00
Spool of Thread w/thimble finial	210.00
S. S. Kookie Elephant	227.50
Teddy Bear w/feet together	110.00
Wilma on the Telephone	1,200.00

AMERICAN POTTERY

Clown w/patches	35.00
Miniature Bear	35.00
Pig in overalls	40.00

BRAYTON - LAGUNA

Elephant	1,500.00
Gingerbread House	175.00
Gypsy Lady	562.50
Mammy, red apron	600.00
Mammy, yellow	750.00
Plaid Dog	650.00
Swedish Maiden	506.00

BRUSH - MC COY

Bunny, grey	275.00
Crock w/cat finial	35.00
Dog w/Basket	546.00
Hobby Horse	1,500.00
Little Angel	900.00
Little Boy Blue, gold trim, large	770.00
Little Red Riding Hood, small	795.00
Old Clock	275.00
Owl, green	95.00
Peter Pumpkin Eater	356.00
Raggedy Ann	695.00
Santa Head	350.00
Sitting Hippo, w/hat, green glaze	433.00
Teddy Bear, feet apart	175.00

CALIFORNIA ORIGINALS

Airplane w/pilot	385.00
Baseball Boy	45.00
Bear, brown w/blue eyes	60.00
Bert & Ernie, No. 515 MC	675.00
Big Bird on Nest, No. 971	45.00
Clown	57.50
Cookie Bakery	30.00
Cookie Crock	75.00
Fire Truck, red	375.00
Humpty Dumpty	135.00
Indian w/lollipop	115.00
Lion	300.00
Lioness & Cub	195.00
Little Girl	225.00
Little Red Riding Hood	650.00
Noah's Ark	75.00
Old Radio	117.50
Owl, large	150.00
Owl, small	40.00
Rooster	20.00
Scarecrow Turnabout (sad side/happy side), No. 858	150.00
Scarecrow, No. 871	152.50

Sitting Turtle 15.00
Space Cadet.....................................70.00
Superman, w/phone booth, brown.....462.50
Superman, w/phone booth, silver 525.00
Taxi 85.00
Wonder Woman, silver 800.00

CARDINAL
Cookieville Bus...............................487.00
French Chef, bust..............................92.00
Pig Head 65.00

DORANNE OF CALIFORNIA
Chef..150.00
Clown w/drum 175.00
Green Dragon 65.00
Hound Dog 62.50
Lunchbox 49.00
Monkey 75.00
Mother Goose, red 193.00
Old Woman in the Shoe.......50.00 to 75.00
Sitting Rabbit, yellow 49.00

METLOX
Ballerina Bear 77.00
Bear w/sweater 59.00
Beaver..247.50
Bell Pepper, white, small 39.00
Blue Bird on Stump 250.00
Black Santa 995.00
Bluebird on Pine Cone 225.00
Bouquet 75.00
Broccoli 175.00
Cat, Katy 225.00
Chef Pierre 95.00
Clown, blue & white 495.00
Clown, yellow 200.00
Cow w/Butterfly, yellow 291.00
Drum 225.00
Drummer Boy.................................837.50
Egg Basket 225.00
Feathered Friends 650.00
Ferdinand Calf 1,187.50
Fido 175.00
Flamingo......................................1,350.00
Flowerpot 50.00
Frog (w/label) 245.00
Frog Prince......................................135.00
Fruit Basket 55.00
Gingham Dog, blue 326.00
Hen, blue 445.00
Hippopotamus, "Bubbles," yellow 850.00
Lamb, lying down 350.00
Little Red Riding Hood 1,569.00
Lucy Goose 133.00
Mammy, blue dots...........................480.00
Mother Goose 351.00
Noah's Ark 221.00
Owl 70.00
Pescado Fish 310.00
Pineapple..75.00
Pinocchio, bust...............................348.00
Pretty Ann 187.50

Rabbit, clover bud finial 375.00
Santa Claus, white, standing 895.00
Scottie Dog, white 250.00
Teddy Bear w/Cookie 35.00
Walrus, white w/blue scarf & hat.......225.00
Whale, white....................................297.50

NAPCO
Miss Cutie-Pie Head, blue 235.00
Nestle Toll House Cookies 122.00
Woody Woodpecker on Barrel 317.00

REGAL CHINA
Alice in Wonderland (minor
    damage)....................................1,850.00
Baby Pig w/diaper, gold trim............462.50
Cat, gold 475.00
Cookie Jarrin's Little Angel 722.50
Majorette, bust................................292.50
Oriental Lady, green 775.00
Peek a Boo 1,166.00
Poodle "Fifi"....................................560.00
Wolf (Little Red Riding Hood
    Series) 900.00

SIERRA VISTA
House, 9" h. 75.00
Pirate on Chest 400.00
Poodle...385.00
Spaceship..625.00
Stagecoach 242.00
Train 72.50
Tuggles...165.00

TREASURE CRAFT
Cookieville, house...........................35.00
Dog w/Cookie Keg 40.00
Juke Box (Wurlitzer), 11½" h............65.00
Katrina 900.00
Mexican Boy.....................................30.00
Monk...48.00
Mouse, brown 45.00
Professor Snail 650.00
Squirrel on Stump, matte finish 48.00

TWIN WINTON
Child in Shoe, grey............................65.00
Collegiate Owl 125.00
Cookie Sack, gold label.....................36.00
Dobbin 123.00
Happy Bull 95.00
Lion...85.00
Little Lamb 40.00
Mother Goose 162.50
Noah's Ark..76.50
Potbelly Stove, red............................50.00
Puppy in Basket..............................100.00
Smiling Bear w/Badge ....50.00 to 75.00
Squirrel w/nut 45.00

VANDOR
Betty Boop head 147.50
Court Jester 395.00

Cowboy...................84.50
Fred Flintstone, standing................195.00
Fred Flintstone & Pebbles.............342.00

WISECARVER
Cookie Jar Mammy.....................125.00
Cookstove Mammy.....................152.50
Beauty & The Beast, gold trim..........125.00
Black Miss America.....................225.00
Indian Chief w/gold trim................110.00
Indian Maiden, gold trim...................110.00
Milk Churn Mammy.....................125.00
Mammy Bust................125.00
Pappy Bust................125.00
Quilting Mammy, gold w/mother-of-
  pearl................350.00
Saturday Bath.....................150.00
Snow White, gold trim.....................125.00
Teepee................110.00
Three Kittens.....................150.00
Veggie Mammy................125.00

MISCELLANEOUS COMPANIES
Albert Apple, Pittman-Dreitzer
  & Co., Inc......................90.00
Archway Cookie Bus.....................40.00
Aunt Jemima (plastic), F&F Mold
  Co....................337.50
Bear, Josef Originals.....................60.00
Betsy Ross, Enesco.....................160.00
Big Bird, Demand Marketing.............65.00
Boy/Girl Bear Turnabout, Ludowici
  Celadon................75.00
Brown Cow, Otagari.....................25.00
Cadillac, pink, Expressive Design.......20.00
Century 21 House.....................975.00
Chef, Japan................50.00
Chef, Sigma................150.00
Clown, DeForest of California.............45.00
Clown, Hirsch................65.00
Clown, Lane................300.00
Clown head, Schmid.....................65.00
Colonial Lady................95.00
Dachshund, DeForest of
  California................135.00
Dennis the Menace, Starnes.............695.00
Dog, Alpo advertising.....................70.00
Emmett Kelly, Japan.....................150.00
Fat Cat, Fitz & Floyd.....................35.00
Fox, San Joaquin................125.00
Friar Tuck, Goebel................460.00
Gangster Car, Starnes.....................180.00
Halo Boy, DeForest of California.......744.00
Harley Davidson gas tank, blue.........95.00
Human Bean, Enesco.....................110.00
Indian Head, Southeast Pottery.........90.00
Keebler Tree House, Haeger Pottery..75.00
Kitty Santa, Hoan................95.00
Little Red Riding Hood, Weiss,
  Portugal................287.50
Merlin Magician, Alfano Art Pottery..350.00
Monk, DeForest of California,
  1964................75.00

Neal the Frog, Sears................22.50
Owl, Goebel................106.00
Peter Pumpkin Eater, Vallona Starr
  Design................309.00
Pig Head, DeForest of California.........65.00
Pig, pink & white, Terrace Ceramics....44.00
Pig w/apple in mouth, Starnes.........175.00
Pinocchio, W. H. Hirsch Mfg. Co.,
  L.A. California................525.00 to 575.00
Plaid Teddy, Fitz & Floyd.................105.00
Polka Dot Witch, Fitz & Floyd...........375.00
Poodle, DeForest of California............95.00
Prayer Lady, pink, Enesco................295.00
Precious Moments Bear, Enesco....35.00
Rolls Royce Santa, Fitz & Floyd.......925.00
Rooster, Gilner & Gonder...................89.50
Santa Claus, combination cookie &
  candy jar, Howard Holt, 8½" h.........145.00
Santa with Toy Bag, Alberta's Molds,
  Inc................175.00
School House, Gilner......................250.00
Sheriff, Fitz & Floyd.....................325.00
Sheriff, Gonder, green................1,000.000
Southwest Santa, Fitz & Floyd..........820.00
Squirrel, Starnes................150.00
Stan Laurel, Cumberland Ware.........900.00
Sylvester Head, Applause..................42.00
Tasmanian Devil, Applause...............42.00

CORKSCREWS

Anheuser Busch Corkscrew

Advertising, "Anheuser Busch,"
  metal, very minor wear, 2¾" h.
  (ILLUS.)................$44.00
Nickel plated, clamp-on type, hand
  lever, "The Modern"................100.00
Sterling silver, stag handle,
  hallmarked, 8" l................125.00

COUNTRY STORE COLLECTIBLES

Shopkeeper's Bag Sorter

Bag sorter, counter type, wooden, quarter-fan form, painted on yellow ground w/black star decoration, the graduated bag slats identifying rail numbered ¼ through 10, painted at top "PAT. MAY 20 '84," late 19th c., 7⅞ x 15", 16" h. (ILLUS.) **$863.00**

Buggy whip store display rack, metal, cross-form flat bars w/upturned & notched edges for securing whips, suspended by four slender chains, 18" w. **49.50**

Butcher block, all-wood construction, 30 x 30" cutting surface, 450 lbs......**675.00**

Humphrey's Remedies Cabinet

Cabinet, counter-type, "Humphrey's Veterinary Remedies," wooden, the arched top crest printed w/"Humphrey's Specific Remedies," the glass door w/molded edging lined w/a colorful tin panel showing various farm animals & listing the various medications & the ailments they treat, flared molded base, late 19th - early 20th c. (ILLUS.)..........**3,685.00**

Christie's Biscuit Display Case

Case, counter-type, "Christie's Biscuits," wood w/painted front panels, ca. 1900, 47 x 12", 54" h. (ILLUS.) **1,210.00**

Card Seed Company Display

Rice Seeds Display

Display, counter-type, "Card Seed Company," wood w/paper label, various colorful seed packets, minor wear & soiling, 24¼" w., 15" h. (ILLUS. previous page) **302.50**

Display, counter-type, "Rice Seeds," wood w/metal front, various seed packets, vibrant colors on seed packets, blue lettering on golden yellow, minor denting & scratching to metal front, soiling, 18 x 21¾", 27¾" h. (ILLUS. bottom previous page)...**522.50**

COW CREAMERS

Staffordshire Cow Creamer & Cover

These silver or earthenware cream jugs were modeled in the form of that beautiful bovine animal, the original source of their intended contents. The most desirable versions are the early silver and Dutch Delft faience creations turned out in the 18th century, as well as those produced in the Staffordshire potteries before the mid-19th century. However, traditional style cow creamers, made in the late 19th or in the 20th centuries, are also deemed collectible.

China, covered, Blue Willow, England..**$445.00**

Red clay, decorated w/dark brown sponging & gilt horns, 7½" l. (small edge chips) **165.00**

Staffordshire pottery, modelled as a cow w/brown slip eyes, curly horns, an open mouth forming the spout, a looped tail forming the handle & standing forsquare above a suckling calf on a shaped rectangular base w/ an incised border & impressed trefoil motifs at the upper edge, the square cover surmounted by a flowerhead knop, & the whole w/a cream colored body in manganese & splashed

in grey & ochre, late 19th c., horn & cover repaired, 5⅞" l. (ILLUS.) **1,438.00**

Staffordshire pottery, the standing animal on a rectangular base w/a suckling calf standing beside her, decorated overall w/a tortoiseshell glaze of sponged manganese & splashed green & ochre, late 18th - early 19th c., 6⅛" l. (teat missing, tail, cover & one horn repaired) **805.00**

CURRIER & IVES PRINTS

American Country Life, Pleasures of Winter

This lithographic firm was founded in 1835 by Nathaniel Currier with James M. Ives becoming a partner in 1857. Current events of the day were portrayed in the early days and the prints were hand-colored. Landscapes, vessels, sport, and hunting scenes of the West all became popular subjects. The firm was in existence until 1906. All prints listed are hand-colored unless otherwise noted.

American Country Life, Pleasures of Winter, after F. F. Palmer, large folio, N. Currier, 1855, framed (ILLUS.) **$1,265.00**

American Fruit Piece, small folio, undated, in old molded frame w/gilt liner **165.00**

American Homestead—Summer, small folio, dated 1868 & American Homestead—Autumn, small folio, 1869, framed, pr. (minor toning & staining, several small holes to margins) **402.50**

American Railroad Scene— Snowbound, small folio, 1871, framed (some ink staining on reverse)......................................**2,530.00**

American Whaler, small folio, undated, framed (pale scattered fox marks, pale mat staining) **1,150.00**

Among the Pines—A First Settlement, small folio, undained, framed (stains) **176.00**

Arkansaw (sic) Traveler, small folio, 1870, framed (dark stains, some paper damage) **165.00**

Battle of Waterloo, N. Currier, small folio, undated, framed light- & mat staining, laid down) **115.00**

Beach Snipe Shooting, medium folio, 1869, framed (very pale staining) **4,025.00**

Bound Down the River, small folio, 1870, framed (occasional creases, very pale light- & mat staining, small tear bottom margin) **1,380.00**

Capturing the Whale, small folio, undated, framed (margins trimmed, long horizontal crease through image, surface soiling) **690.00**

Central Park in Winter, small folio, undated, framed (two pinholes in image & one in lower margin, small repaired loss & tiny necks in top sheet edge) **1,610.00**

Central Park, Winter—The Skating Carnival, small folio, undated, framed (tear to lower margin, toning & foxing) **57.50**

Champion Pacer Johnston (The), large folio, 1884, framed (few fox marks, discoloration in the sheet edges, laid down) **1,035.00**

City of New York (The), large folio, 1876, framed (faint light stain, minor soiling & foxing, slight abrasions, small loss in edge, backed w/a sheet of wove) **8,625.00**

Clipper Ship "Flying Cloud," large folio, 1852, later impression, framed **489.00**

Clipper Yacht "America" (The), small folio, undated, framed (some fox marks, pale light-staining, bottom margin corner reattached) **920.00**

Cottage Life—Summer, medium folio, 1856, framed (stains, two bleached spots) **275.00**

Express Train (The), N. Currier, small folio, undated, framed (two tiny margin tears, very pale mat staining) **3,220.00**

Fruit Girl (The), N. Currier, 1845, framed, 10 x 14 ....**265.00**

Garden, Orchard & Vine, after F. F. Palmer, medium folio, 1867, framed **345.00**

Gen. George Washington—The Father of His Country, N. Currier, small folio, undated, framed (stains) **49.50**

Getting Out (soldier hiding under shelf), N. Currier, small folio,

undated, matted & framed (stains, edge tears) **82.50**

Grand National Democratic Banner, "Press Onward," Lewis Cass & Wm. D. Butler Jugate busts, hand-colored, 1848, small folio, N. Currier **525.00**

Grand National Whig Banner, horizontal Jugate busts of Zachary Taylor & Millard Fillmore, hand-colored, 1848, small folio by N. Currier **650.00**

Great Conflagration at Pittsburgh, PA, N. Currier, small folio, undated, framed (pale staining, bottom margin corner made-up) **1,610.00**

Great International Boat Race Aug. 27th 1869 (The), small folio, undated, framed (staining, small loss in top margin) **2,530.00**

Hunting on the Plains, small folio, 1871, framed (pale staining, tiny margin tear) **2,185.00**

Killeries (The)—Connemara, small folio, undated, matted, unframed (stains) **66.00**

Life & Age of Woman (The), small folio, N. Currier, 1850, framed (stains, some paper damage & margins slightly trimmed) **258.50**

Lightning Express (The), small folio, undated, framed (very pale staining & foxing, soft crease bottom margin) **2,070.00**

Loading Cotton, small folio, 1870, framed (pale staining, tiny margin hole) **1,380.00**

Mansion of the Olden Time (A), small folio, undated, matted, unframed **77.00**

Moosehead Lake, small folio, undated, framed (stains, margin tear) **60.50**

Night Express (The)—The Start, small folio, undated, framed (pale staining, repaired margin tears) **2,070.00**

Nipped in the Ice, small folio, undated, framed (pale staining) **1,610.00**

Old Blandford Church, Petersburgh, Virginia, small folio, undated, framed (cleaned) **110.00**

Old Homestead (The), after F. F. Palmer, N. Currier, medium folio, 1855, matted & framed (cleaned, some paper damage & edge tears) **220.00**

Old Oaken Bucket (The), small folio, 1872, framed (minor damage in margins) **137.50**

O'Sullivan's Cascade—Lake of Killarney, small folio, undated, framed (minor stains) **60.50**

Paron's Colt (The), small folio, 1879, framed (worn, faded, crinkled paper) **104.50**

Pennsylvania Rail Road Scenery, small folio, undated, framed (two creases through image, small margin split, pale staining) **920.00**
Pointing a Bevy, after F. F. Palmer, large folio, 1866, framed (unobtrusive soiling & staining) **1,380.00**
Quails, N. Currier, small folio, undated, framed (pale staining) **575.00**
Raspberries, small folio, 1870, framed (stains & tear in top margin)............**192.50**
Route to California (The), small folio, 1871, framed (trimmed margins, staining, colors somewhat faded).................................**1,610.00**
Sale of the Pet Lamb (The), after William Collins, Esp. R. A., small folio, N. Currier, undated, framed 10 x 14"...**175.00**

Snipe Shooting

Snipe Shooting, N. Currier, after F. F. Palmer, large folio, 1852, skillful repairs in margin, crease in bottom margin, pale staining on reverse (ILLUS.) **1,150.00**
South Sea Whale Fishery, small folio, undated, framed (pale mat staining) **633.00**
Sperm Whale (The)—"In a Flurry," small folio, 1852, framed (trimmed margins, pale staining)....................**920.00**
Steam-Boat Knickerbocker, N. Currier, small folio, undated, framed (pale staining, soft creases) **1,380.00**
Sunnyside—On the Hudson, small folio, undated, framed (pale staining) **115.00**
Through Express (the), small folio, undated, framed (few repaired margin tears, margin corner made-up, minor soiling on margin & reverse)......................................**2,070.00**
Two Watchers (The), small folio, undated, framed (stains) **192.50**
Whale Fishery—Sperm Whale—"In a Flurry," small folio, undated, framed (some staining, several creases, thin margin losses) **1,035.00**
Whale Fishery (The)—"Laying On," small folio, 1852, framed (pale

staining, surface scuff in lower image, tiny margin tears) **1,035.00**
William Tell, small folio, undated, Victorian criss-cross frame **38.50**
Winter in the Country, The Old Grist Mill, after G. H. Durrie, large folio, 1864 (slight foxing, 1½" repaired tear in left margin, water stains & discoloration in sheet edges) **4,313.00**

CUSPIDORS

Chinese Export Cuspidor

The cuspidor, or spittoon, is a bowl-shaped vessel into which tobacco chewers could spit. These containers were a necessity in an era when much of the male population chewed tobacco and even some ladies were known to "take a chew." Made of metal, earthenware pottery, china and glass, they ranged in size from the large barroom floor models to small glass cuspidors designed for the ladies.

Brass, saloon-style, marked "Goldfield Hotel, Goldfield, Nevada" **$275.00**
Cast iron, model of a turtle, tin shell top lifts when head stepped on **195.00**
Chinese Export porcelain, spherical base applied w/green branches bearing pink & gold chrysanthemums, rose-centered blue & yellow-centered aubergine blossoms, rose & yellow buds & green, gold & turquoise leaves, the flaring trumpet-shaped rim w/a wide salmon-ground border on the interior patterned w/iron-red & gold peony blossoms & scrolling leafage, China, ca. 1740, minor chips, hairline in rim, 4⅜" h. (ILLUS.) **1,495.00**
Graniteware, blue speckled................**75.00**
Stoneware, molded beading around top & Greek key band at bottom separated by a white band flanked by blue stripes, Albany slip interior, 13¾" d..**1,155.00**

DECOYS

Crowell Mallard Decoy

Decoys have been utilized for years to lure flying water fowl into target range. They have been made of carved and turned wood, papier-maché, canvas and metal, and some are in the category of outstanding folk art and command high prices.

American Widgeon Drake, attributed to Tom Wilson, Ipswich, Massachusetts, carved wood w/inset glass eyes, retains original paint (minor crazing to the head, breast & underside of tail area, minor chips & loss of paint)........**$1,610.00**

Black-breasted Plover, attributed to Tom Wilson, Ipswich, Massachusetts, carved wood w/inset glass eyes, relief-carved wings & split tail, retains original paint (stress crack on left side of neck, minor crazing to paint on head, lifting of filler on top of head)...**1,380.00**

Black-bellied Plover, carved wood w/original worn paint, on driftwood base, 11¾" h. (bill replaced) **192.50**

Black Duck, by Swan B. Brewster, Connecticut, carved wood w/hollow two-piece construction, relief-carved wings, old working repaint, made in 1925, 16¼" l. (wear, old chip on tail) **165.00**

Black Duck, by Gus Wilson, South Portland, Maine, full-carved body w/attached carved wings in an outstretched position, the head in a swimming position, appears to retain original paint, ca. 1920 (minor loss to one wing tip, crack in base) **11,500.00**

Bluebill Drake, by Ira Hudson, Chincoteague, Virginia, carved & painted wood, ball foot, body w/fluted tail, second quarter 20th c., 13" l., 7" h. (imperfections)............**1,870.00**

Bluebill Drake, carved wood, original paint w/shot scars, glass eyes, branded mark "W.J.F.," from Michigan, down river carver, 15" l....**110.00**

Bluebill Drake, carved wood, old working repaint, glass eyes, attributed to Ben Schmidt, 14¾" l. (age cracks & shot scars) **220.00**

Bluebill Hen, Mason factory, worn original paint & glass eyes, Detroit, Michigan, 15" l. (slight paint touch-up, age cracks in block & head).......**192.50**

Blue Wing Teal Drake, Mason Premium Grade, carved wood, original paint, ca. 1915, 13" l., 6" h. (imperfections) **1,760.00**

Brant, carved & painted wood, hollow body, impressed "E.B. Cobb" & "E," Cobb's Island, Virginia, late 19th c., 18" l., 7½" h. (some age cracks, worn repaint) **17,600.00**

Brandt Goose swimmer, by Bill Geonne, King City, California, original paint, branded "W.R.G.," 24" l...**71.50**

Bufflehead Drake, by F. J. Dubbins, Jonesport, Maine, carved wood w/original paint, signed, 10½" l. **165.00**

Canada Goose, by Joe Lincoln, Accord, Massachusetts, carved wood, original paint, stamped "Joe Lincoln, Accord, Massachusetts," on a base, 14" l., 5" h. (minor wear) **3,105.00**

Canada Goose, attributed to Madison Mitchell, carved wood w/old paint, 21½" l. (minor paint wear, age cracks in block & head)...................**385.00**

Canada Goose, by Tom Humberstone, New York, carved wood w/original paint & glass eyes, 23½" l...**192.50**

Canada Goose, attributed to Tom Wilson, Ipswich, Massachusetts, carved wood w/inset glass eyes, retains original paint (minor structural crack to base, minor loss of paint where head meets body) **8,050.00**

Canvasback Drake, by Joe Begin, Clinton River, Mt. Clemens, Michigan, sleeping position, balsa w/old sanded paint & glass eyes, 11¾" l..**88.00**

Canvasback Drake, by Mike Bonnet, Wisconsin, carved wood w/oversized head, original paint & glass eyes, 15½" l...........................**104.50**

Canvasback Drake, by Dave Hodgman, Niles, Michigan, carved wood w/carved & combed feather detail, original paint, glass eyes, 15¼" l...**104.50**

Canvasback Hen, carved wood, old working repaint & glass eyes, attributed to Dobson, 16½" l. (wear, shot scars) **159.50**

Curlew, by William Bowman, Long Island, New York, carved wood full-bodied bird in low-head position, inset eyes, relief-carved wing, retaining most of the original paint, ca. 1870-80 (partial tips of wings missing, ½" of bill missing, lightly scarred by shot) **90,500.00**

Eider Duck Drake, hollow-carved cedar construction w/glass eyes, original paint, a wood mussel grasped in its bill, 20th c. (some loss on the back) **575.00**

Eider Duck Hen, primitive carved wood w/hollow body, flipped-up tail, tack eyes, old brown & black paint, branded "C.L. Richards," from Maine, 18¾" l. (old bill repair) **165.00**

Fish, "Yellow Perch," by Miles Smith, Marine City, Michigan, carved wood w/metal fins & tack eyes, original paint, 9¼" l. **137.50**

Fish, carved wood w/tin fins, original folky brown & yellow paint w/white, red & black spots, 14" l. (glued repair to tail) **148.50**

Goldeneye Drake, Mason's 'Challenge' grade, rare early 'slope-breasted' style, traces of original paint w/old touch-up, glass eyes, possibly pre-1900, 14½" l. (age crack in bottom of block & at neck) **302.50**

Goldeneye Hen, carved & painted wood, attributed to George Huff, Delaware River, New Jersey, 13" l., 6½" h...**330.00**

Greenwing Teal Drake, by Paul Arness, California, initialed "P.A.," original paint & glass eyes, branded "Hall," 12½" l. **110.00**

Hooded Merganser Drake, full-carved wooden body w/applied wing carving, inset painted eyes, natural feet, original crazed paint, mounted on a paint-decorated base w/snail shells, probably New England, late 19th c. (minor neck separation)...**11,500.00**

Lesser Sandpiper, attributed to Obadiah Verity, Seaford, Long Island, full-carved body w/relief wing carving & carved eyes, retains original paint & bill, ca. 1870 (some loss to paint, minor shot scarring) **4,026.00**

Long Bill Curlew, hollow-carved cedar construction, glass eyes, original paint, 20th c........................**345.00**

Mallard Drake, by T.J. Hooker, Illinois, carved wood w/nestled head, glass eyes, carved wing detail & original paint, branded "T.J.'s Rig," 14" l. **165.00**

Mallard Drake, by Elmer Crowell, East Harwich, Massachusetts, carved wood w/fine original paint,

twice marked in rectangle, 13½" l. (ILLUS.) **1,840.00**

Mallard Drake, by Wm. E. Pratt Co., Chicago, Illinois, carved wood w/original paint in unused condition, glass eyes, ca. 1920-39, 17" l. (age crack in block) **220.00**

Mallard Hen, preening position, carved balsa wood body & hardwood head, good old paint, glass eyes, Illinois River, 11½" l. (glued crack in neck).......................**220.00**

Merganser Drake, attributed to Tom Wilson, Ipswich, Massachusetts, carved wood w/inset glass eyes, retains original paint (minor loss of paint on left side, crazing on the breast area & some on the sides) **6,612.00**

Mourning Dove, carved wood, original paint, nail beak, glass eyes, on modern base, from Maryland, 11¾" h. (minor shot scar)................**275.00**

Owl, papier-maché confidence-type, original paint & glass eyes, marked "Boales Swisher, Decatur, Illinois," 12¾" h. plus stand (minor wear) **275.00**

Red Breasted Merganser Hen, carved & painted, initialed "J.D.," Delaware River area, early 20th c., 18" l., 6" h....................................**14,300.00**

Redhead Drake, back-preening position, carved wood w/stylized detail, original paint & glass eyes, possibly from Maine, 13¼" l. **187.00**

Ringneck Drake, by Bill Goenne, King City, California, carved wood, original paint, initialed & branded "W.R.G.," 15" l...................................**104.50**

Shorebird, tin, folding-type, worn original paint, interior label, "Pat. Oct. 27, 1874," 11½" l. **165.00**

Snipe, by A. Elmer Crowell, East Harwich, Massachusetts, full-carved body w/inset eyes, raised wing carving, retaining original paint, mounted on a painted base, branded oval mark "A. Elmer

John Lewark Swan

Crowell East Harwich Mass. Decoy," ca. 1930 (minor paint loss to top of head & tip of tail) **9,200.00**

Swan, by John T. Lewark, Sea Gull, North Carolina, carved wood body, repainted, age cracks, 22" l., 24" h. (ILLUS. bottom previous page)...**1,840.00**

Swan, by Miles Smith, Michigan, folky style carved wood w/nearly straight upright neck, original white paint w/black trim & glass eyes, 20¾" h. (some wear) **275.00**

Willet, by Charles Thomas, Assinippi, Massachusetts, oversized, carved wood, inset glass eyes & original nail bill, retains its original paint (minor paint loss, few shot holes on underside of breast, minor loss where nail joins the head) **4,887.00**

Yellowleg, attributed to Tom Wilson, Ipswich, Massachusetts, carved wood w/inset glass eyes, relief-carved wings & split tail, retains original paint (minor staining to underside, minor stress crack to the neck) **2,300.00**

Yellowleg, attributed to Tom Wilson, Ipswich, Massachusetts, carved wood w/inset glass eyes, relief-carved wings & split tail, retains original paint (minor rub to top right head, stress crack to left side of wing) **1,380.00**

DISNEY COLLECTIBLES

Bambi Planter

Scores of objects ranging from watches to dolls have been created showing Walt Disney's copyrighted animated cartoon characters, and an increasing number of collectors now are seeking these, made primarily by licensed manufacturers.

Alice In Wonderland calendar, 1951, illustrates over 30 characters, Walt Disney Productions, opens to 6 x 16"...**$125.00**

Alice in Wonderland movie cel, gouache on trimmed celluloid applied to a gouache production background, a scene of Alice & the March Hare sitting at the table enjoying tea as the Dormouse floats down between them w/the aid of his umbrella, inscribed "To Jim Lawlor, Best Wishes, Walt Disney" on lower right mat, 1951, 9½ x 11½".........**10,925.00**

Alice in Wonderland movie cel, gouache on trimmed multi-cel set-up applied to a water-color production background, Alice sprawled on the grass as the Queen of Hearts swings a flamingo & the King of Hearts looks on, 1951, 10½ x 13¼".................**11,500.00**

Alice in Wonderland planter, figural, ceramic, Leeds China Co. **95.00**

Bambi face mask, uncut cardboard, from the back of a Wheaties box, 1950s, 10 x 12".................................**15.00**

Bambi layout drawing, graphite on paper, depicting Bambi falling on a reed as a field mouse watches from its nest, w/a Bambi production stamp & notes in lower right corner, full margins, 1942, 10 x 12".............**920.00**

Bambi movie cel, gouache on celluloid applied to a water-color preparation background, Bambi stands & looks out from a cave into the forest, 1942, 8½ x 11"..............**8,280.00**

Bambi planter, ceramic, tan, pink & green on beige, glossy, marked "Bambi, Walt Disney Productions" on bottom, Leeds China Co., 7" l., 7" h. (ILLUS.) **40.00**

Bambi "Soaky" container, near mint...**27.50**

Bambi wall pocket, ceramic, Leeds China Co...**45.00**

Bull fighter (from Ferdinand the Bull feature) doll, cloth, dressed in a blue hat, red cape, yellow coat & blue pants, Ideal Novelty and Toy Co., ca. 1940, 20" h. **460.00**

Captain Hook (from "Peter Pan") hand puppet, Gund, excellent condition **25.00**

Captain Hook (from "Peter Pan") marionette, Peter Puppet Playthings, ca. 1952 ....**195.00**

Cinderella bank, tin, dime register-type **150.00**

Cinderella planter, ceramic, pastel blue, pink, green & yellow, impressed WDP, Leeds China Co., 6½" l., 6½" h. (ILLUS. top next page)..**100.00**

Cinderella Planter

Davy Crockett bank, metal, dime
register-type **75.00**

Davy Crockett billfold, vinyl, picture
of Davy on the front & The Alamo on
the back, probably non-Disney,
1950s **40.00**

Davy Crockett bracelet, "Davy
Alamo ID," w/raised figure of Davy,
mint in box **45.00**

Davy Crockett cookie jar, cov.,
figural, Davy holding a rifle,
American Bisque, base marked
"USA" **395.00**

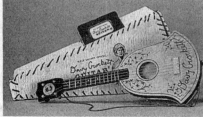

Davy Crockett Guitar

Davy Crockett guitar, wood, in
original box labeled "Walt Disney's
Official Davy Crockett Guitar"
w/picture of Davy, 25" l., 2 pcs.
(ILLUS.) ....**45.00 to 65.00**

Davy Crockett knife, pocket-type,
three-blade, Walt Disney
Productions **48.00**

Davy Crockett moccasin kit, boxed
set w/leather soles, Play-Learn, non-
Disney, 1950s **40.00**

Davy Crockett socks, children's
ankle-type, grey & white, complete
w/sticker & wrapper band showing
Davy & reading "Davy Crockett
Going to Congress," mint condition,
1950s **20.00**

Davy Crockett string tie, clip-on-
style, original package **23.00**

Davy Crockett suspenders, original
card...**67.00**

Davy Crockett wastebasket,
metal....................................**75.00 to 95.00**

Disney characters toy, "Disney
Television Playhouse," tinplate, a
large lithographed tinplate stage,
several set pieces & figures from
Snow White, Alice in Wonderland,
Peter Pan, Pinocchio, Mickey
Mouse, Dumbo & Donald Duck,
Louis Marx, ca. 1955, 3 x 11 x
28½", the set.....................................**138.00**

Disney characters toy, wind-up tin
"Disneyland Express" train,
characters pictured, Louis Marx &
Co., original box ....**125.00 to 150.00**

Disneyland map, heavy stock paper,
dated 1968, folded, near mint
condition, 30 x 45" **35.00**

Disneyland tea set, lithographed tin,
J. Chein Co., 1950s, in original box,
7 pcs. **195.00**

Disneyland toy, windup tin,
"Disneyland Ferris Wheel," J. Chein
& Co., New York, New York, 1939,
w/original box, 17" h.........................**805.00**

Donald Duck bank, cast metal, early
long-billed Donald w/painted white
shirt, orange scarf, blue outfit & gold
coins, ca. 1930s, 6" h. (some stress
wear, trap missing) **575.00**

Donald Duck book, "Donald Duck &
His Friends," first edition, hard
cover, 1939 ....**45.00**

Donald Duck cookie jar, cov.,
ceramic, Donald seated & reaching
into the cookie jar between his legs,
HOAN **125.00**

Donald Duck cookie jar, cov.,
ceramic, w/pumpkin, Disney
Productions **385.00**

Donald Duck figure, bisque, riding a
tricycle, 1930s, 3" h.........................**150.00**

Donald Duck figure, bisque, long-
billed, marked "Walt Disney," 1930s,
3¼" h..**95.00**

Donald Duck Chalkware Figure

Donald Duck figure, chalkware, 13½" h. (ILLUS. bottom previous page)...**68.00**

Donald Duck pinback button, color picture of the early 'long-billed' Donald in a fighting pose & titled "Wanna Fight," original back paper, ca. 1930s, 1¼" d. **1,265.00**

Donald Duck poster, die-cut cardboard, "Donald Duck Cola," very colorful, 22 x 25" **145.00**

Donald Duck Sign

Donald Duck sign, painted tin, "RPM Motor Oil," a round color scene in light blue, white & light grey showing Donald throwing a snowball at an angry snowman, Donald wearing a blue shirt w/yellow-trim & red bow tie, black & white lettering reads "A Knockout For Winter - RPM Motor Oil," marked at the bottom "Copyright 1940 Walt Disney Productions L-301 Made in U.S.A.," minor soiling, 23¼" d. (ILLUS.) **1,725.00**

Donald Duck store display, cardboard, "Whistling Flashlite," nice color lithograph of Donald standing by a stoplight blowing a whistle,

Donald Duck Windup Toy

1950s, 10½ x 14" (minor surface & edge wear) **50.00**

Donald Duck toy, pull-type, Donald the engineer w/locomotive front, on a wheeled cart, Model 450, Fisher-Price, Inc., 1942...........................**225.00**

Donald Duck toy, windup composition, Donald walks & waddles when wound, w/original illustrated box, 1930s (ILLUS. bottom previous column) **1,092.00**

Donald Duck & nephews wall mirror, the group carrying a large bass drum, the center of which is a mirror plate, overall 25" **65.00**

Dumbo the Elephant creamer, ceramic, Walt Disney Productions, Leeds China Co., 6" h.......................**62.00**

Dwarf Bashful figure, Enesco, w/foil labels, 5" h. **38.00**

Dwarf Dopey Animation Cel

Dwarf Dopey animation cel, from *Snow White and The Seven Dwarfs,* gouache on celluloid applied to an airbrushed Courvoisier background, Dopey happily sweeps up diamonds, w/the 'Walt Disney Enterprises' label on back, 7 x 7" (ILLUS.) **6,037.00**

Dwarf Dopey bank, tin, dime register-type, dated "1939" **150.00**

Dwarf Dopey doll, composition shoulder-head w/painted eyes, open-closed mouth & molded ears, a cloth body jointed at shoulders only, wearing original green pants, orange flannel coat & hat, oval paper tag on clothing reads "Walt Disney's - "Dopey" - Madame Alexander's Creation - All Rights Reserved by Madame Alexander," small paint flake on right eye, rust spots w/holes in coat, spots of discoloration on back, ca. 1940, 12" h. (ILLUS. top next page) **155.00**

Dwarf Dopey lamp, table model, figural standard on a round base w/name incised at front, electric socket at top **225.00**

Dwarf Dopey Doll

Dwarf Dopey movie cel, gouache on
partial celluloid, a close-up of
Dopey's head showing diamonds in
his eyes, 1937, 8¾ x 9¾"...............**5,750.00**
Dwarf Dopey planter, ceramic,
Leeds China Co. **55.00**
Dwarf Dopey toothbrush holder,
figural, china, 1937, England **195.00**

Dwarf Grumpy Movie Cel

Dwarf Grumpy movie cel, gouache
on trimmed cel applied to a
Courvoisier wood veneer
background, shows Grumpy sitting
on top of a barrel, 1937, unframed,
5½ x 7½" (ILLUS.) **2,990.00**
Dwarf Grumpy soap figure, Castile,
Lightfoot Schultz, 1930s, boxed.........**40.00**
Dwarf Happy figure, bisque, 1930s,
4" h...**60.00**
Fantasia movie cel, gouache on
celluloid applied to an airbrushed
Courvoisier background, from The
Nutcracker Suite sequence, showing
Hop Low waddling between two

rows of fellow mushroom dancers,
"WDP" stamp in lower right,
Courvoisier Galleries label on back,
1950, 10½ x 11".........................**2,875.00**
Fantasia movie cel, from the
Sorcerer's Apprentice segment,
gouache on celluloid, two-cel set-up,
depicting Mickey Mouse leading a
bucket-laden broom, 1940, framed,
10 x 13½".................................**12,650.00**
Fantasia movie program,
1940 ....**50.00 to 60.00**

Ferdinand the Bull Movie Cel

Ferdinand the Bull movie cel,
gouache on trimmed celluloid
applied to a wood veneer
Courvoisier background, shows the
angry matador approaching
Ferdinand who dangles flowers from
his tail, 1938, 8½ x 9½"
(ILLUS.) **3,162.00**

Ferdinand the Bull Tumbler

Ferdinand the Bull tumbler, clear
glass w/picture of Ferdinand sniffing
a flower, his name across the
bottom, ca. 1938 (ILLUS.).................**39.00**
Figaro (Pinocchio's cat) planter,
ceramic, Royal Copley **60.00**
Flower the Skunk (Bambi) figure,
ceramic, American Pottery Co. **45.00**

Flower the Skunk (Bambi) planter,
ceramic, Leeds China Co. **85.00**

**Flower the Skunk & Thumper
(Bambi) wall pockets,** marked
"Sidney Pottery," pr. **450.00**

Gepetto (Pinocchio) mask, paper,
Gillette Blue Blades advertising
premium, 1939....................................**20.00**

Jiminy Cricket (Pinocchio) figure,
ceramic, marked "National Porcelain
Co.," 3" h..**55.00**

**Jiminy Cricket (Pinocchio)
marionette,** Gund, 12½" h. **75.00**

Joe (Jose) Carioca pencil sharpener,
celluloid...**55.00**

Joe (Jose) Carioca toy, balancing-
type, lithographed paper on metal
Joe Carioca balances on a metal
base finished in black, France,
1940s, 12" h....................................**165.00**

Johnny Appleseed book, "Walt
Disney's Johnny Appleseed," first
edition **12.00**

Johnny Appleseed record album,
1949..**18.00**

Ludwig Von Drake pencil case,
"Ludwig Von Drake Wonderful World
of Color Pencil Case," thick red
cardboard w/snap closure, color
paper lid decal of Ludwig Von Drake
instructing Huey, Duey & Luey,
Hasbro, 1961, unused, sealed
contents, 4 x 9" **32.00**

Maleficent Movie Cel

**Maleficent (evil fairy from Sleeping
Beauty) movie cel,** gouache on
celluloid, a large full image of an
angry Maleficent, 1959, 12½ x
15" (ILLUS.) **3,163.00**

Mary Poppins billfold,
1964 ....**25.00 to 35.00**

Mary Poppins paper doll set,
includes three magic dolls & a 64-
piece wardrobe, in box.......................**45.00**

Mary Poppins tea set, tin, in original
colorful box, 13 pcs.........................**250.00**

Mickey Mouse baby spoon, silver
plate, Wm. Rogers & Son
(ILLUS. top next column) **29.00**

Mickey Mouse Baby Spoon

Mickey Mouse book, "Mickey Mouse
ABC Story," 1936, published by
Whitman Publishing Co. & Walt
Disney Enterprises...........................**125.00**

Mickey Mouse bowl, cereal,
Beetleware, Post Grape-Nuts
premium, marked "W.D. Ent.," ca.
1930s................................**40.00 to 50.00**

Mickey Mouse card game, "Canasta
Junior," two sealed decks, plastic
tray & box, 1950, set..........................**45.00**

Mickey Mouse card game, "Old
Maid," Whitman, ca. 1935,
w/original box ....**75.00 to 100.00**

Mickey Mouse cookie jar, cov.,
"Birthday Cake," produced for
Mickey's 50th birthday, Walt Disney
Productions ....**700.00 to 800.00**

Mickey Mouse cookie jar, cov.,
pottery, leather-ear Mickey bust,
marked "Copyright Walt Disney
Prod.," w/paper label
marked "Enesco"............**450.00 to 550.00**

Mickey Mouse cookie jar, cov.,
ceramic, circle w/"Gourmet Mickey"
& a color picture of Mickey & Minnie,
Treasure Craft ....**40.00 to 50.00**

Mickey Mouse doll, stuffed cloth,
leather cloth applied eyes, mustard
yellow gloves, greyish green short
pants w/mother-of-pearl buttons
front & back, rust shoes, metal
button in left ear & original
cardboard tag on chest, Steiff,
Germany, early 1930s,
6" h...**1,955.00**

Mickey Mouse doll, stuffed cloth, red
& black body w/yellow hands & red
composition shoes, a paper "Mickey
Mouse" label for Knickerbocker, ca.
1930s, 11" h.....................................**518.00**

Mickey Mouse drawing, animation
sketch, graphite on paper, from
"Touchdown Mickey," 1932, showing

Mickey Mouse Animation Drawing

Mickey successfully avoiding getting
tackled, 8½ x 11" (ILLUS.) **1,150.00**
Mickey Mouse figure, hand-carved
wood, painted red & black w/yellow
hands & feet, a "Mickey Mouse
Corp. Walt Disney" label on his
chest, ca. 1940s, 7" h. (one
cardboard ear missing) **207.00**
Mickey Mouse game, "Pin the Tail on
Mickey," in original envelope, 1960s,
Hallmark...**45.00**
Mickey Mouse magazine, "Modern
Mechanix," January 1937 issue,
color cover picture of Mickey,
Donald Duck & Pluto, w/inside story
(wear by spine) **20.00**
Mickey Mouse magazine, "Theatre
Arts," January 1941 issue, black &
white cover picture of Mickey in
Fantasia, w/inside story **25.00**
Mickey Mouse pencil box, blue &
yellow cardboard w/snap-open
closure, Mickey, Minnie Mouse &
Donald Duck in jalopy on the top,
Mickey & Donald in a boat fishing on
the bottom, Dixon, 1930s, 6 x 10"
(light top wear) **89.00**

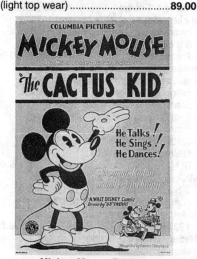

Mickey Mouse Poster

Mickey Mouse poster, "The Cactus
Kid" cartoon, printed in black & white
on a red background, shows a
likeness of Mickey in the foreground
w/a small Mickey & Minnie at the
piano in the lower right, reads
"Columbia Pictures presents -
Mickey Mouse - The World's
Funniest Cartoon Character in "The
Cactus Kid - He Talks! - He Sings! -
He Dances! - The Laugh Riot in
Sound & Synchrony - A Walt Disney
Comic - Drawn by "UB" Iwerks -
Recorded by Powers Cinephone,"
one-sheet, 1930, linen-
backed, 27 x 41" (ILLUS.
bottom previous column) **29,900.00**
Mickey Mouse puzzle, jigsaw-type,
"Greatest Show on Earth," 1933,
mint in box **375.00**
Mickey Mouse tea set: cov. teapot,
creamer, cov. sugar bowl, six plates,
cups & saucers; china w/tan lustre
finish, several different scenes of
Mickey & Minnie,
21 pcs.............................**425.00 to 475.00**
Mickey Mouse toy, battery-operated,
"Mickey Mouse Krazy Car," Marx,
mint in box **175.00**
Mickey Mouse toy, "Magic Lantern,"
a black tinplate lantern w/original
partial label featuring a pie-eyed
Mickey, w/loop & 22 slides depicting
various adventures of Mickey
Mouse, in original boxes, the set
(lantern box lid missing) **230.00**

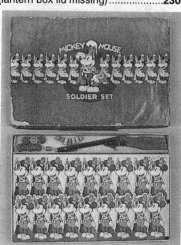

Mickey Mouse Soldier Set

Mickey Mouse toy, "Mickey Mouse
Soldier Set," contains 16 full-color
cardboard figures of Mickey wearing
a soldier's uniform, w/gun on
shoulder & w/a cork-shooting gun
included, w/original box w/Mickeys

on the top, England, ca. 1935, box
13 x 20" (ILLUS.) **1,150.00**
Mickey Mouse toy, windup tin,
balloon vendor man holding a small
figure of Mickey Mouse in one hand
& a bunch of balloons behind him,
the hand w/Mickey lifts up & down
when wound, not a licensed Disney
product, Germany **575.00**
Mickey Mouse toy, windup tin,
Mickey standing playing the
xylophone, Line Mar, Japan,
ca. 1950, 6½" h., mint
condition ....**700.00 to 900.00**

Mickey Ventriloquist Doll

Mickey Mouse ventriloquist doll,
vinyl & cloth, Mickey w/vinyl head &
hands, wearing a red jacket, white
shirt, black pants & shoes, by
Horsman (ILLUS.) **675.00**

Mickey Mouse Wrist Watch

Mickey Mouse wrist watch,
rectangular dial, leather band,
Ingersoll (U.S. Time), 1947,
mint in box (ILLUS.).........**350.00 to 450.00**
Mickey Mouse wrist watch, oblong
dial w/Mickey in a top hat, red band,
Deluxe model, Ingersoll, 1947, in
original box w/instructions...............**460.00**
Mickey Mouse & friends lunch pail,

lithographed tin, oblong shaped
w/metal strap closure & oval wire
bail handle on lid, a colorful parade
of Silly Symphony characters
around the sides, in orange, black &
yellow on pale green, silvered metal
lid, Walt Disney Enterprises, 1930s,
5 x 8½", 4⅞" h. (lid wear, minor
dent)..**402.50**
Mickey & Minnie Mouse pillow top,
stamped for embroidery, Vogue
Needlecraft No. 98, 1931
copyright.........................**125.00 to 150.00**
Mickey & Minnie Mouse tea set,
lithographed tin, Chein, mint in box,
9 pcs. **385.00**
Mickey & Minnie Mouse tea set,
lithographed tin, Ohio Art, 9 pcs. **395.00**
**Mickey & Minnie Mouse toothbrush
holder,** bisque, names impressed
on back, 1930s, 1¾ x 3½ x
4½" ....**250.00 to 300.00**

Mickey & Minnie Mouse toy

Mickey & Minnie Mouse toy, pull-
type, a rectangular long tinplate
platform lithographed in yellow,
black & orange w/circus scene
w/Mickey & Minnie, platform on solid
wood green wheels & supporting
raised bars each w/a wooden figure
of Mickey or Minnie w/composition
ears, pulling toy activates paper

Rare Mickey & Pluto Toy

bellows which causes the figures to flip on their bars, Nifty Toys, ca. 1935, 11½" l. (ILLUS. previous page)..**3,450.00**

Mickey Mouse & Pluto toy, windup celluloid, "Running Mickey on Pluto," Mickey seated astride Pluto who runs on three wheels, front wheel holds keywind mechanism, w/original illustrated box also marked "Made in Occupied Japan," Masudaya, Japan, ca. 1950, mint, 5½" l. (ILLUS. bottom previous page)..**6,325.00**

Minnie Fun-E-Flex Figure

Minnie Mouse figure, jointed wood, "Fun-E-Flex," original label on her chest, 3¾" h. (ILLUS.)......................**132.00**

Minnie Mouse toy, battery-operated, plastic, figure of Minnie pushing a shopping cart, "Bump 'N Go Action," w/original box...................................**150.00**

Minnie Mouse toy, windup tin, lithographed Minnie rocks to & fro while "knitting" on a piece of cloth, Line Mar, Japan, w/box, 7" h. ....**450.00 to 550.00**

Pinocchio & Jiminy Cricket Cel

Pinocchio animation cel, gouache on trimmed celluloid applied to a preliminary water-color background, a publicity cel of Pinocchio w/Jiminy Cricket perched on his toe, w/a Walt Disney signature on the mat in the

lower right & a Courvoisier Galleries label on the back, 1940, 8 x 10" (ILLUS.) **18,400.00**

Pinocchio cookie jar, cov., modeled as Pinocchio sitting & holding a fishbowl between his legs, Cleo, the fish, forms the finial, California Originals, new in box, 12" h. **80.00**

Pinocchio doll, composition & wood, Ideal, 11" h.....................................**265.00**

Pinocchio figure, chalkware, carnival-type, 10" h.............**55.00 to 65.00**

Pinocchio game, board-type, 1939, Walt Disney Enterprises **45.00**

Pinocchio magazine, "Screen Romances;" 1939, cover picture as well as an illustrated inside story **25.00**

Pinocchio Movie Cel

Pinocchio movie cel, gouache on trimmed celluloid applied to an airbrushed Courvoisier background, a scene w/Pinocchio looking unsure as a Dutch girl puppet dances in front of him, 1940, 8½ x 12" (ILLUS.) **6,900.00**

Pluto figure, wood & fiber, yellow ochre-painted wood body, head & feet w/dark green collar w/decal, twisted fiber legs & tail, yellow felt ears, Geo. Borgfeldt & Co., w/original box, 5¾" l. **747.50**

Pluto Tumbler

Pluto tumbler, clear glass w/a black

picture of Pluto & his name, first dairy series, 1936, 4½" h. (ILLUS.)....**44.00**

Silly Symphony Record Set

Silly Symphony record set, four picture records including "Who's Afraid of the Big Bad Wolf" and "Mickey Mouse and Minnie's in Town," w/green & red paper sleeves, Victor Records, early 1930s, the set (ILLUS.)................**1,266.00**

Sleeping Beauty movie cel, gouache on celluloid applied to a pan water-color production background w/production overlays, a long scene showing Briar Rose & Prince Phillip in a lush, green forest, 11½ x 28½" **11,500.00**

Sleeping Beauty puzzles, jigsaw-type, mint in box, 1959, 9 x 11", set of 3 ....**28.00**

Snow White figure, chalkware, carnival-type, 14" h. ....**45.00 to 65.00**

Snow White ironing board, lithographed tin, Wolverine, mint...................................**125.00 to 150.00**

Snow White jigsaw-puzzle, Jaymar, w/original box **35.00**

Snow White Movie Cel

Snow White movie cel, gouache on celluloid applied to an airbrushed Courvoisier background, a scene

showing Snow White dressed in rags & clogs (w/eyes closed) dreamily carrying a bucket to wash steps as doves fly around her, 1937, 6 x 8" (ILLUS.) **5,462.00**

Snow White movie cel, gouache on full celluloid applied to a Courvoisier airbrush & water-color background, scene of Snow White w/a small bird perched on her finger & singing to the forest birds, 1937, 9 x 9½"..**4,600.00**

Snow White Valentine, pull-tab, Walt Disney Enterprises, 1938...................**30.00**

Snow White & the Seven Dwarfs bank, dime register-type, square lithographed tin, Walt Disney Enterprises, ca. 1939 ......**150.00 to 175.00**

Snow White & the Seven Dwarfs handkerchief, Walt Disney enterprises, 9" sq................**25.00 to 35.00**

Snow White & the Seven Dwarfs sheet music, "Whistle While You Work," dated 1937 ....**20.00**

Snow White & the Seven Dwarfs tea set, china, white w/blue trim, 21 pcs. **450.00**

Song of the South game, bagatelle-type, Uncle Remus & black figures, 1946, in colorful box.........................**225.00**

Three Little Pigs mug, ceramic, Patriot China **65.00**

Three Little Pigs plate, Patriot China....................**125.00 to 175.00**

Three Little Pigs toothbrush holder, bisque, figures of three pigs in front of holder, colored trim, Japan, 4 x 4"....................**125.00 to 175.00**

The Three Little Pigs & Big Bad Wolf coloring pencils, w/illustrated cardboard box, the set **38.00**

Tigger Cookie Jar

Tigger (from Winnie-the-Pooh) cookie jar, cov., ceramic, California Originals, 12" h. (ILLUS.) ....**200.00 to 250.00**

Wendy Movie Cel

Wendy (from Peter Pan) movie cel,
gouache on full celluloid applied to a
hand-prepared background, Wendy
about to tell the children a story,
1953, 7½ x 9½" (ILLUS.) **863.00**
Zorro costume: hat, mask & gun;
Marx, on original display card,
1960s................................**90.00 to 125.00**
Zorro lamp, table-type, porcelain,
figural of Zorro holding a sword,
8" h...**195.00**
Zorro puzzle, jigsaw-type, 1950s,
boxed **14.00**

(End of Disney Section)

DOLL FURNITURE & ACCESSORIES

Bamboo-Trimmed Doll Armoire

Armoire, arched pierce-carved crest
on rectangular top above door
w/rectangular mirror that opens to
reveal shelves, above rectangular
drawer, surrounded by bamboo trim,
France, 7½" w., 12½" h.
(ILLUS.) **$195.00**

Bed, hard- & softwood, half-tester
style, very ornate pierced carving,
w/hidden drawer, old finish,
European, 12½ x 18", 20" h.
(some edge damage)........................**165.00**
Carriage, wicker, the body & frame of
wood, w/metal springs & wooden
handle & wheels w/metal rims, the
sides in wicker, w/original faded
upholstery, piece of old carpeting on
the front floor, metal bracket for an
umbrella, 23" h. (umbrella missing,
some excelsior stuffing missing)......**300.00**
Chamber set: washbowl & pitcher,
cov. chamber pot w/bail handle, cov.
hair receiver, open dish & cov.
powder jar; porcelain, each piece
w/worn gold floral decoration, late
19th c., the set (hairline in chamber
pot)...**175.00**
Chest of drawers, stenciled maple,
the tall superstructure w/a wide flat-
topped crest w/a reeded band above
a ropetwist band over the rounded
lower corners overhanging a large
rectangular mirror flanked by reeded
bands over a small shelf above a
black-stenciled sprig above the
rectangular top w/reeded edge
overhanging the case w/two long
drawers w/wooden knobs & each
decorated w/a black-stenciled sprig,
ca. 1890, 10" w., 17½" h. (fine crack
in wood at left of replaced
mirror) **235.00**
Chest of drawers, oak, a wide
scalloped crestrail above a
rectangular top over a case of six
narrow, long drawers each w/a
turned wood knob, each drawer w/a
reeded front, late 19th - early
20th c., 11" w., 19" h. **80.00**
Chest of drawers, walnut, burl walnut
& cherry, an upright rectangular
molded frame holding a mirror
above the rectangular top above a
case w/four reverse-graduated long
drawers flanked by bold burl sides,
flat base, ca. 1900, 17" w.,
33½" h. (mirror damaged) **250.00**
Clothespins w/original box,
wooden, box reads "For Dolly's
Clothes" **16.00**
Cradle, cherry, angled hood above
flat upright dovetailed sides w/small
hanging knobs, on rockers, old
mellow refinishing, 16¾" l. (some
hood damage)..................................**660.00**
Cradle, poplar, hood w/canted top at
one end above low flat sides & a
rounded footboard, short curved
rockers, old dark finish, 25" l. **440.00**
Cradle, walnut, low stepped sides
w/rounded end boards, dovetailed

construction, on long slender rockers, old mellow refinishing, 22½" l. (some added nails) **275.00**

Cupboard, walnut, two doors, attached scalloped backboard w/enclosed original mirror, gold stenciling overall, three shelves, Victorian, 6¼ x 13 x 24" **275.00**

Cupboard, stained poplar, scalloped crestrail on the superstructure above a rectangular top over a pair of glazed cupboard doors over a pair of drawers above the recessed pie shelf over the stepped-out rectangular work surface over a pair of drawers over a cupboard door w/ amethyst glass panel beside a flour bin, white porcelain knobs, late 19th - early 20th c., 16" w., 32½" h. **325.00**

Cupboard, tin w/wood lining, Hoosier-type, rectangular top over two doors over stepped-out work area over cupboard door on left & two drawers on right, painted bright yellow decorated w/Dutch children at top & windmills on lower section, Daily Reminder grocery list inside left door, Helpful Hints for the Kitchen inside right door, together w/cov. teapot, sugar bowl, creamer, two each cups, saucers & plates, a bread box & four canisters, 7 x 18", 25" h., the set..................................**180.00**

Dollhouse bathroom fixtures, cast iron w/cream enamel, vanity, lavatory, lift-lid toilet & four-leg table, largest piece 1⅝ x 2¾", probably Arcade, 4 pcs. **135.00**

Dollhouse, lithographed paper on wood, two-story Victorian house w/red, yellow & green paper on three sides, glass windows w/original curtains, a wide porch w/baluster-form posts at the front, front opens to reveal one room upstairs & one down, original floor paper, original paper on walls, late 19th c., 11 x 17", 21" h. (light wear)...........**1,550.00**

Dollhouse, one-story bungalow-style, painted wood, grey wooden base & wooden frame w/fiberboard walls & roof, multi-paned windows on three sides w/one beside the front door, roof lifts for access to the attic, sides painted yellow w/white trim & green shutters, red roof, right side opens to one large room, Schoenhut, unmarked, early 20th c., 12¼ x 14", 11" h. (light wear)...........**360.00**

Dollhouse, wood & fiberboard on wooden base, two-story, exterior painted yellow w/white window frames, green shutters & window

boxes w/flowers, white door, red fiberboard roof, front half of roof folds back for access to attic, front of house lifts off for access to four rooms, wooden staircase to second floor, marked "Schoenhut Doll Houses, Made in U. S. A.," 12 x 18 x 19" **310.00**

Dresser, oak, tall superstructure w/cut-out scalloped sides & a wide pointed crest framing a rectangular long mirror, two banks of two small drawers on sides of base flank a center well above a single long drawer across the base, ca. 1880-90, 10" w., 14" h. (flaking on mirror) **260.00**

Sideboard, painted poplar, the high superstructure w/a scalloped crest above a narrow shelf over a rectangular mirror above the oblong top overhanging the case w/a long drawer w/a pierced band of scrolls & leaves & white porcelain knobs above a pair of double-panel cupboard doors flanked by half-round ring-turned columns, the upper door panel w/a large raised cut-out S-scroll, lower panel w/a C-scroll, low scalloped apron, reddish brown paint, late 19th c., 19½" w., 31½" h. (light wear, mirror replaced) **235.00**

Wall cupboard, step-back type, walnut, one-piece construction, flat rectangular top w/carved design above pair of cut-out cupboard doors opening to two shelves, the stepped-out lower section w/two short drawers over pair of cupboard doors, ornate hardware on doors, ca. 1920, 13 x 20", 35" h.................**190.00**

Wash day set consisting of 8½ x 15½ x 17" folding washstand (legs unscrew for folding), lined w/blue corrugated metal, detachable wringer, No. 4 zinc tub, washboard w/same blue corrugated metal, decorated w/painted red scrollwork, the set...**325.00**

Washstand, oak, cut-out towel bar support above rectangular top w/slightly bowed front above a conforming case w/three drawers above a cut-out base, 9 x 22¼", 30" h..**200.00**

Washstand, oak, a wishbone towel bar above the rectangular top over a round-fronted long drawer over a pair of cupboard doors w/wooden knobs, heavy red stain finish, ca. 1900, 13" w., 17½" h. (finish checked) **155.00**

DOLLS

Madame Alexander "Madelaine"

Also see BARBIE DOLLS & COLLECTIBLES and STEIFF TOYS & DOLLS.

A.B.G. (Alt, Beck & Gottschalck) china head lady marked "1008 (crosshatch) 7," painted blue eyes w/red accent lines, single stroke brows, accented nostrils, closed mouth, molded & painted hair, cloth body w/china lower arms & legs w/molded & painted boots, dressed in red satin dress trimmed in black, antique underclothing, 19" (small flake off top of head, original fabric on legs recovered, lower china legs replaced) **$260.00**

A.B.G., bisque head girl marked "ABG, 1362, Made in Germany, 5," brown sleep eyes, painted upper & lower lashes, feathered brows, accented nostrils, open mouth w/four upper teeth, pierced ears, replaced wig, jointed wood & composition body, dressed in antique white eyelet dress, underclothing, new socks & shoes, 29" (numerous wig pulls, touch-up at all joints on lower right leg, toes & heels, lower right leg is old replacement & color does not match other leg parts)...............................**450.00**

Alexander (Madame) Amy marked "Alex" on head, hard plastic head, blue sleep eyes w/real lashes, painted lower lashes, single stroke brows, closed mouth, synthetic hair in original set, five-piece hard plastic body jointed at shoulders & hips, dressed in lavender taffeta dress trimmed w/white organdy w/tag "Louisa M. Alcott's Little Women,

'Amy,' by Madame Alexander, N.Y., U.S.A., All Rights Reserved," attached slip, pants, socks & shoes, velvet ribbons in her hair, 14" (plastic has slight odor).............**245.00**

Alexander (Madame) Dionne Quintuplets, composition heads & bodies, dressed in pastel rompers & bonnets, each w/a name pendant necklace, original pamphlet & carton w/label, in a cream-colored kiddie-car, ca. 1936, 7", set of 5 (Marie's necklace & one sock missing, some soiling) **1,150.00**

Alexander (Madame) Dr. Dafoe, composition character head, painted blue eyes, single stroke brows, closed smiling mouth, grey mohair wig, five-piece jointed composition body w/bent right arm, wearing tagged doctor suit, hat, original socks & shoes, 14" **1,400.00**

Alexander (Madame) Madelaine, composition head w/brown sleep eyes w/real lashes & painted lower lashes, single stroke brows, closed mouth, original h.h. (human hair) wig, five-piece composition body, dressed in original tagged red & blue flower print dress, attached slip, pantaloons, socks & shoes, blue ribbon & flowers in hair, clothing has aged, 11" (ILLUS.) **345.00**

A. M. (Armand Marseille) bisque flange head "Tee-Wee Head Babe," marked "A. M. Germany 341/2," blue sleep eyes, softly blushed brows, closed mouth w/accent line, softly blushed hair, cloth puppet body attached to blue pillow, celluloid hands, wearing original top part of gown, blue lace-trimmed pillow, in original marked box, 8½" circumference head, 13" (box heavily patched, minor color flaw on back of head) **210.00**

A. M. bisque socket head mulatto girl marked "A.M. - DEP - Germany - 10/0" on back of head, set black pupilless eyes, single stroke brows, caracul wig, open mouth w/four upper teeth, jointed wood & composition body, dressed in red & gold flowered dress, underclothing, new socks & shoes, light brown rub, color wear on lower lip, few wig pulls, crack on lower left seam, minor repair to left knee, 9" (ILLUS. top next page)...................**175.00**

A. M. bisque head 'Just Me' character girl marked "Just Me 310 7/0," blue glass "googlie" eyes looking left, closed pursed mouth, replaced brown h.h. wig, straight-leg

Armand Marseille Mulatto Girl

five-piece composition body,
wearing a silk dress w/pleated chine
silk short skirt, socks, shoes &
matching handbag, ca. 1929,
9½"...**1,380.00**

A. M. bisque head Oriental baby
marked "353 - 10," brown sleep
eyes, closed mouth, painted dark
hair, straight-leg fabric body
w/composition hands, wearing
Oriental outfit w/tan satin pants,
black brocade tunic & gold silk vest,
9¾" (vest fragile)..............................**805.00**

A. M. bisque socket head boy
marked "Germany, 550, A 3/0," blue
sleep eyes, painted upper & lower
lashes, single stroke brows,
accented nostrils, closed mouth,
original mohair wig, jointed wood &
composition body, dressed in
original Scottish outfit,
underclothing, socks & shoes, 10"
(tiny inherent black speck in
forehead, stringing loose, paint strip
off upper right leg).........................**1,000.00**

A. M. bisque socket head
"Florodora" marked "Made in
Germany - Florodora - A 3/0 XM,"
brown sleep eyes, open mouth
w/four upper teeth, original blonde
mohair wig, crude five-piece jointed
composition body, wearing original
factory clothing, straw hat, socks &
shoes, in original box, 14" (tiny flake
inside corner right eye)...................**250.00**

A. M. bisque socket head child
marked "Made in Germany - 390, A.
6. M.," blue sleep eyes, painted
upper & lower lashes, molded &
feathered brows, accented nostrils,
open mouth w/accented lips & four
upper teeth, red mohair wig, jointed

wood & composition body,
redressed in rust colored silk dress
& matching coat, underclothing,
socks & shoes, 21" (inherent chip in
right side of neck opening, several
minor cracks in finish, right
forefinger broken w/half missing).....**335.00**

Arranbee "Nancy," composition
head w/painted blue eyes, single
stroke brows, closed mouth, molded
& painted hair, five-piece jointed
composition child body w/bent right
arm, wearing original tagged green
dress, matching underclothing & hat,
original shoes & socks, 12" (pale
face color, light hair wear)...............**145.00**

Bahr & Proschild bisque head
character girl marked "686 3/0,"
brown glass weighted "googlie" eyes
looking to the left, closed slightly
smiling mouth, old brown mohair
wig, five-piece straight-limb
composition body w/starfish hands,
wearing original printed gauze dress
w/pleated front, lace & ribbon trim,
socks, brown leather shoes & later
peach silk bonnet, 10" (wig
sparse) **1,955.00**

Bartenstein two-face wax baby, first
face w/set brown eyes, feathered
brows, open-closed smiling mouth
w/six upper teeth indicated, second
face w/set brown eyes, feathered
brows, open-closed screaming
mouth w/molded tongue, h.h.
attached to molded hood, cloth body
w/cryer, composition lower arms &
legs, torso marked "...in
Deutschland," wearing probably
original white baby dress,
underclothing & diaper, 14" (first
face w/flattened nose, soil on top of
head, second face w/fine crack at
nose, chip on nose, hair mostly
gone)...**700.00**

Bergmann (C. M.) bisque socket
head girl marked "S & H CMB 10,"
brown sleep eyes, molded &
feathered brows, pierced ears,
blonde mohair wig, open mouth
w/accented lips & four upper teeth,
jointed wood & composition body,
wearing blue & white dotted dress,
off-white apron & bonnet,
underclothing, socks & shoes, 23"
(hands & ball at left knee replaced
w/old parts, repair at hip joint &
right lower arm)..............................**350.00**

Bergmann (C. M.) bisque socket
head girl marked "C. M. Bergmann,
Waltershausen, 1916, 9," set blue
eyes, painted upper & lower lashes,
feathered brows, accented nostrils,
open mouth w/accented lips & four

upper teeth, synthetic wig, jointed wood & composition body, dressed in old gold dress, underclothing, socks & shoes, 26" (inherent uneven coloring back of head, minor cracks in finish at neck socket, arm sockets) **450.00**

Bergmann (C. M.) bisque socket head girl marked "C. M. Bergmann, Simon & Halbig 14½," set blue eyes, molded & feathered brows, brown h.h. wig, pierced ears, open mouth w/four upper teeth, jointed wood & composition body, wearing a white dress w/lace inserts, underclothing, socks & shoes, 31½" (small firing lines behind ears, body repainted, some wear & flaking on body) **600.00**

Bierschenk (Fritz) bisque head character lady marked "FB 616," well-modeled face w/blue intaglio eyes, open-closed mouth w/molded & painted upper teeth, five-piece straight-limb shapely body, arms slightly bent, brown h.h. wig, appropriately redressed in peach pink satin & net long gown w/matching ribbon trim, old white leather lace-up ankle boots, underwear & straw hat, ca. 1910, 13" **2,875.00**

Bisque baby, pink bisque head w/stiff neck, painted blue eyes w/red accent line, single stroke brows, open-closed mouth w/white space, painted blond hair, all-bisque body jointed at shoulders & hips, wearing possibly original blue organdy dress trimmed in lace, 6½" (firing flaw on back of head) **85.00**

Bisque boy, swivel head, painted blue eyes, single stroke brows, accented nostrils, closed mouth, molded & painted blond hair, all bisque body jointed at shoulders & hips, molded & painted socks & black boots, dressed in original light brown felt suit stitched on, 4" **115.00**

Bisque character girl marked "34/12," stiff neck, tiny blue sleep eyes, open-closed smiling mouth w/four upper teeth, blonde mohair wig, all-bisque body jointed at shoulders & hips, molded & painted white socks w/blue garters & black one-strap shoes, wearing lace dress & panties, 5".....................................**480.00**

Bisque Oriental socket head baby marked "4/0, Germany," brown sleep eyes, painted upper & lower lashes, softly blushed brows, accented nostrils, closed mouth, painted hair, five-piece composition baby body, dressed in new red

Oriental-type outfit w/gold pattern, trimmed in green, fastened w/pink Oriental frogs, 9" (few minor chips at neck opening of head, tiny inherent flaw low on front of neck socket, tiny firing flaws under each ear, chip on big toe of left foot) **525.00**

Bisque "Princess" girl, marked "150" on head, bisque head w/stiff neck, brown sleep eyes, single stroke brows, brown mohair wig, open mouth w/four upper teeth, all-bisque body jointed at shoulders & hips, molded & painted socks w/blue garters & black one-strap shoes, label on stomach reads "Princess, Made in Germany," wearing pink two-piece outfit & underclothing, 7" (minor flaw in rear torso, minor firing lines in feet) **150.00**

Black Fashion Lady marked "F 1 G," black bisque shoulder head, set black eyes, painted upper & lower lashes, multi-stroke brows, accented nostrils, closed mouth, original wig, black kid body w/individually stitched fingers, gussets at elbows, hips & knees, dressed in antique red wool dress, white blouse, pinafore & ruffled bonnet, underclothing, socks & shoes, 13" (light rub on end of nose, light wear on lip color, black finish on body is worn & white showing through, sawdust has settled in gussets at hips & knees) **2,800.00**

Borgfeldt Character Doll

Borgfeldt (George), bisque head 'Gladdie' character boy, incised "Gladdie, Copyriht (sic) Helen W. Jensen," weighted brown eyes, molded & painted hair, open smiling mouth w/four upper teeth & tongue, fabric body w/celluloid hands, brown leather integral boots, in old white shirt & blue short pants, ca. 1929, 17½" (ILLUS.) **2,587.00**

Bru bisque swivel head girl marked "2," fixed blue paperweight eyes, closed pale mouth, pierced ears, blonde mohair wig, kid body w/bisque lower arms, kid lower legs, redressed in a period style maroon & cream satin frock, underwear, socks, brown leather shoes & matching hat, 11½" **6,325.00**

Bru bisque swivel head Fashion lady marked "D," fixed pale blue eyes, painted closed mouth, pierced ears, blonde mohair wig over cork pate, gusseted kid body, delicate bisque hands, in original *eau de nil* & maroon wool two-piece day dress, green jacket, full maroon skirt w/underwear including a large hoop bustle, straw hat, socks, old light brown leather lace-up ankle boots, ca. 1875, 14½"................................**4,025.00**

Bru bisque head girl marked "Bru Jne 5," brown fixed paperweight eyes outlined in black & w/plum shaded lids, closed mouth, pierced ears, blonde mohair wig over cork pate, jointed kid body w/bisque lower arms & composition legs, redressed in pale green satin frock w/lace trim at front & yoke, socks & old marked Bru brown leather shoes, furry hat w/ostrich feather plume & green satin trim, muff & holding a small metal mesh bag, decorative parasol w/blue satin, 16½" (left pinky restored)...........**13,800.00**

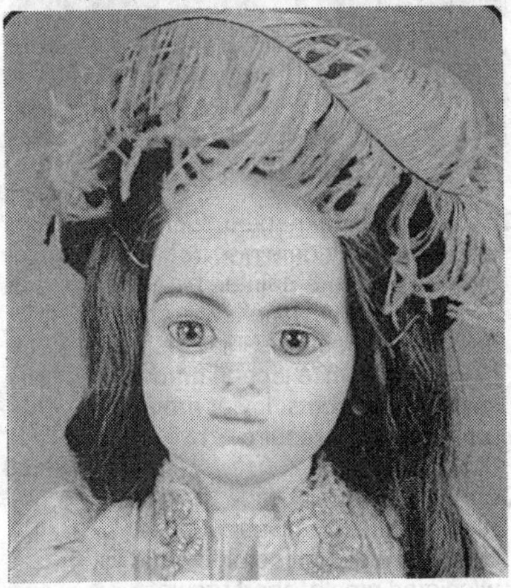

Bru Girl Doll

Bru bisque socket head girl marked "Bru Jne, 10" on back of head, "Bru Jne" on left shoulder, "No. 8" on right shoulder & "9" on top of arms, blue paperweight eyes w/mauve blush over them, painted lashes, feathered brows, h.h. wig, accented nostrils, closed mouth w/accented lips w/a hint of tongue, kid body w/bisque lower arms & wooden lower legs, dressed in original French dress made of ecru silk trimmed w/lace; shoes marked "Bru Jne" on soles, inherent 'pimple' on back of head, slight wear or age discoloration, 21½" (ILLUS.) **9,100.00**

Buddy Lee, hard plastic boy marked "Buddy Lee" on back, stiff neck, large painted eyes to side, painted upper lashes, single stroke brows, closed smiling mouth, molded & painted hair, hard plastic body jointed at shoulders, dressed in original denim shirt, red bandanna, Lee overalls & Lee hat, 13" (three small spots of discoloration on face, light wear on back of hair, spots of discoloration or glue on chest, lower torso, back of left leg & rear torso, light wear on black boots) **175.00**

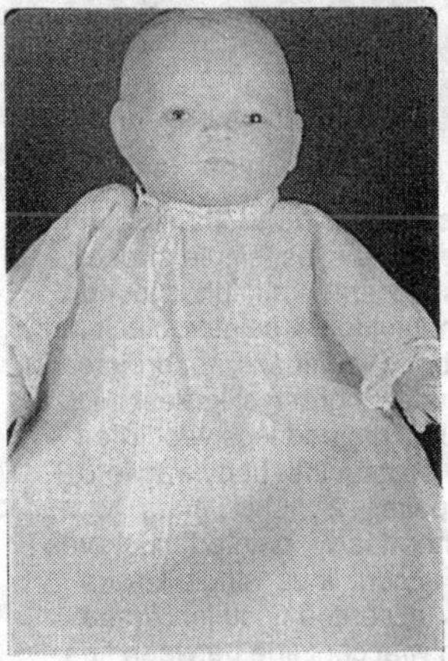

Bye-Lo Baby

Bye-Lo Baby, bisque head marked "Copr. Grace S. Putnam" on back of head, "Bye-Lo Baby, Pat Appl'd., Copy... (rest illegible)" on body, blue sleep eyes, painted upper & lower lashes, softly blushed brows, closed mouth w/accent line between lips, accented nostrils, cloth body w/celluloid hands & "frog" legs, dressed in original baby dress, slip, no underclothing, few minor age spots, 11" (ILLUS.)..........................**300.00**

Bye-Lo Baby, bisque flange head marked "Copr. by Grace S. Putnam, Made in Germany," brown sleep eyes, softly blushed brows, painted upper & lower lashes, accented nostrils, closed mouth, molded & painted hair, cloth body w/"frog" legs, celluloid hands, dressed in original tagged dress, slip, diaper, socks & bonnet, 12" circumference head, 13" (very faint rub on nose & back of head, non-working crier) **450.00**

Bye-Lo Baby, bisque head w/brown sleep eyes, closed mouth, cloth body, celluloid hands, marked "Copr. by Grace S. Putnam, Made in Germany...," 14½".......................**374.00**

'Flat-Top' China Head Doll

China shoulder head 'flat-top' lady, painted blue eyes, single stroke brows, accented nostrils, closed mouth, molded & painted black hair, cloth body w/china arms, dressed in antique dark green silk dress, slip & no pants, molded legs w/painted green boots, cloth body fragile & leg repairs, 12" (ILLUS.) **135.00**

China head lady, painted blue eyes w/red accent lines, single stroke brows, accented nostrils, closed mouth w/accent line between lips, molded & painted hair w/exposed ears, homemade cloth body w/leather hands w/individually stitched fingers, dressed in antique maroon print dress, slip, socks & replaced shoes, 21" (few minor rubs on back of head, light damage on leather hands) **200.00**

China "covered wagon" lady, painted blue eyes w/red accent lines, single stroke brows, closed mouth, molded & black-painted center-part hair w/ten vertical curls each side, cloth body w/kid lower arms, wearing a white print dress trimmed in black, underclothing & socks, 22" (light nose rub, arms probably old replacements, some repair to left leg, no shoes) **375.00**

China head lady, black center-part "covered wagon" hairdo, brown eyes & painted features, cloth body, redressed in a bronze fabric outfit & purse, 23½" (hands damaged) **368.00**

China head lady, "covered wagon-type," painted brown eyes, small painted mouth, center-parted black hair molded in short side curls, fabric body w/leather lower arms w/separately stitched fingers, wearing original white cotton gown w/lace trim at neck & sleeves, layers of white underwear, original high brown leather boots w/four button closure, mid-19th c., 25" (kiln flaws on face)..**805.00**

China head lady, painted blue eyes w/red accent lines, single stroke brows, accented nostrils, closed mouth w/white space between lips, molded & painted black hair, cloth body w/china lower arms, dressed in antique clothing, underclothing, socks & shoes, 32" **450.00**

China Head Man

China head man marked "Germany B10," painted blue eyes, closed mouth, molded & painted blonde hair, kid body w/china lower arms, gussets at knees, wearing replaced boy's suit w/white lace-trimmed shirt, leather boots, lower arms replaced, body repaired, 13" (ILLUS.) **180.00**

Composition mask-face "Hug Me Kiddies" girl, fixed blue "googlie" eyes looking right, painted head w/painted mouth, short brown mohair wig, tan felt body, wearing original outfit w/floral printed cotton dress w/lace-trimmed yoke, collar & sleeves, socks & pink cloth shoes, pink straw hat, ca. 1915, 11"........**1,150.00**

Composition Smoker Lady

Composition smoker lady,
composition uplifted head, painted
brown eyes w/brown eyeliner &
bluish grey shadow, feathered
brows, mohair wig, open mouth
w/cigarette, long lanky composition
body jointed at neck, shoulders,
elbows, hips & knees, unusual pin
joints at elbows & knees, dressed in
original orange felt two-piece pant
suit trimmed in black, molded high
heels go through oilcloth shoes,
original necklace, shoes & cigarette,
ca. 1920s, light paint flaking on torso
at neck edge, finish of upper leg
cracked & lifting w/some flaked off,
left upper leg w/some cracks &
lifting, cracks in finish on bottom of
feet, 25" (ILLUS.) **525.00**

Dressel (Cuno & Otto) bisque head
lady marked "1469," blue sleep
eyes, closed mouth, brown mohair
wig, adult-form jointed composition
body w/molded bust, long limbs,
shaped feet w/original white leather
low-heeled shoes, wearing a floral-
printed chiffon-trimmed dress, 14"
(dress frail) **1,725.00**

Dressel (Cuno & Otto) bisque
socket head child marked "made in
Germany, +, 1912 4," blue sleep
eyes w/real lashes, painted upper &
lower lashes, feathered brows, open
mouth w/four upper teeth, synthetic
wig, jointed wood & composition
body, dressed in white eyelet dress,
underclothing, new socks & shoes,
22" (finish on eyelids chipped,
touch-up on torso, thighs & lower
legs, hands repainted, minor repair
on toes) **250.00**

Effanbee "Mickey," marked
"Effanbee, Made in U.S.A.,"
composition flange head, blue flirty
sleep eyes w/real lashes, painted
lower lashes, multi-stroke brows,
accented nostrils, closed mouth, h.h.
wig, cloth body w/composition arms
& lower legs, dressed in original pink
& white romper, replaced socks &
shoes, 16" (small crack over left
eye, fine crack from corner of right
eye, light crazing on arms & legs,
couple tiny flecks of
paint off mouth) **225.00**

Effanbee "Mae Starr" marked "Mae
Starr Doll" on back & "Effanbee Doll,
Finest & Best, Made in U.S.A." on
dress tag, composition head w/blue
tin sleep eyes w/real lashes, painted
upper & lower lashes, feathered
brows, accented nostrils, open
mouth w/two upper teeth & metal
tongue, original h.h. wig, cloth body
w/talk-mechanism, composition
arms & lower legs, dressed in
tagged pink dress, original
underclothing, replaced socks &
shoes, w/one record, "Little Boy
Blue," 29" (general light crazing on
composition, few light flakes off lip
color, hair reset, light flaking on
fingers, light touch-up on legs, left
arm & edge of shoulder plate,
mechanism works but does
not talk) **500.00**

Effanbee "Patricia Kin," marked
"Effanbee Patricia Kin" on head,
"Effanbee Patsy Jr. Doll" on body,
composition head w/blue tin sleep
eyes w/real lashes, closed mouth,
red h.h. wig, five-piece jointed
composition child body, wearing
original blue & white checked dress
w/white bodice & bolero jacket, blue
felt hat, underclothing, original socks

Effanbee "Patsy Ann"

& shoes, 11" (minor crazing & flaking) **260.00**

Effanbee "Patsy Ann," composition head w/blue tin sleep eyes w/real lashes, closed rosebud mouth, molded & painted hair, five-piece composition child body, wearing possibly original multicolored striped dress, matching hat, underclothing old socks & shoes, 18" (face pale, lower lashes missing, most left eyelashes missing, minor crazing) **240.00**

Effanbee "Patsy Ann," composition head w/blue tin sleep eyes w/real lashes, closed mouth, molded & painted hair, five-piece composition child body, wearing original white dress w/pink & green design, matching underclothing, green felt coat trimmed in green velvet, original socks & shoes, flaking on arm sockets & hands, small crack in right leg & left arm, 19" (ILLUS. bottom previous page) **225.00**

Effanbee "Patsyette," composition head w/painted brown side-glancing eyes, single stroke brows, closed mouth, molded & painted hair, five-piece composition jointed child body, wearing original white organdy dress trimmed in red on collar, matching hat, underclothing, socks & shoes, 9" (small flake off right eye, light crazing on body) **250.00**

Effanbee "Patsy Joan," composition head w/green sleep eyes & real lashes, single stroke brows, closed mouth, molded & painted hair, five-piece jointed composition child body, wearing a tagged blue & white floral design dress & matching underclothing, replaced socks & shoes, w/metal heart bracelet, w/original box, 16" (face pale, left eye clouded, light crazing on arms & legs) **475.00**

Effanbee "Patsyette" George & Martha Washington, marked "Effanbee Patsyette" on backs of both dolls, "This is Patsyette, The Lovable Imp with tiltable head and movable limb, An Effanbee Durable Doll" on paper tag of Martha, "Effanbee Durable Doll" on metal heart bracelet of George, composition heads, painted brown eyes to side, single stroke brows, painted upper lashes, original mohair wigs, closed rosebud mouths, five-piece composition child bodies w/bent right arms, Martha wearing original organdy long dress w/pink felt overjacket w/original

Effanbee "Patsyette" George & Martha

underclothing, George wearing original gold felt vest, felt pants, blue jacket & hat, socks & shoes, Martha's clothes are fading & George has craze lines on bridge of nose & a few paint flakes on nose & right eyebrow, 9", pr. (ILLUS.) **290.00**

Emma Clear George & Martha Washington, both marked "Clear" on back of bisque shoulder plate, George w/set blue glass eyes, painted lashes, single stroke brows, accented nostrils, closed mouth, molded & painted hair, cloth body w/bisque lower arms & legs w/molded & painted buckle shoes, dressed in black velvet suit w/short pants, white vest & print ascot; Martha w/set brown glass eyes, painted lashes, single stroke brows, accented nostrils, closed mouth, molded & painted hair & cap w/decorative band, cloth body w/bisque lower arms & legs w/painted flat-soled shoes, dressed in dark green & gold velvet dress, pants, both made w/pink slip, the hands & legs modeled especially for each figure, pr. (tiny flake of black off his right shoe, spot on her rear torso taped w/adhesive tape, middle finger on left hand broken & well repaired) **400.00**

French Fashion, bisque swivel head w/blue fixed glass eyes, closed mouth, red h.h. wig, pierced ears, gusseted kid body, kid hands w/separately stitched fingers, redressed in period-style two-piece day dress w/plum silk jacket, blue brocaded silk full skirt, underclothes, socks & later suede shoes, ca. 1875, 17" **1,840.00**

Blonde French Fashion Doll

French Fashion, bisque shoulder head, stationary paperweight eyes, pierced ears, original blonde mohair wig, closed mouth, cloth body & limbs, composition hands, original champagne satin ball gown w/train, French white kid boots, ca. 1880, paint missing on hands, minor fabric wear & staining, 23" (ILLUS.)........**1,955.00**

Frozen Charlie, all-china, painted blue eyes w/red accent line, two-tone brows, accented nostrils, closed mouth w/accent line between lips, molded & painted hair, body w/stiff neck, unjointed arms & legs, arms out to front, fists clenched, overall pink tint, 15" (light nose rub, short minor firing line on back of neck) **270.00**

Frozen Charlotte, all-china, painted blue eyes w/grey accent line, single stroke brows, accented nostrils, closed mouth w/accent line between lips, molded & painted blonde hair, neck & head have pink tint, arms extended to the front, hands in fists, large flat feet, dressed in original linen dress & pinafore, underclothing, 13" (no pants)...........**320.00**

Frozen Charlotte w/Alice hairstyle, stiff figure w/painted blue eyes w/red accent line, single stroke brows, closed smiling mouth, molded & painted blonde Alice hairstyle w/black band, unjointed china body w/arms extended, 3¼" (small inherent black line on left side of head, tiny pick mark end of right eye)...**45.00**

Gaultier (Francois) bisque head girl marked "F 1 G," pale blue paperweight eyes outlined in black & shadowed in pink, molded & painted

closed mouth, pierced ears, replaced blonde skin wig over old cork pate, jointed wood & composition body, redressed in a red wool drop-waist dress, flannel & cotton underwear, black socks & brown leather lace-up boots w/brown silk rosettes on toes, 16½" (hands flaking) **4,025.00**

Grace Drayton "Captain Kiddo," stuffed cloth boy, cloth head w/painted blue side-glancing eyes, single stroke brows, painted nose & smiling mouth w/chubby cheeks, brown mohair wig, cloth body jointed at shoulders & hips, wearing original red & white checked romper w/red belt, oversized straw hat, 7" (overall soiling, straw hat fragile) **350.00**

Grace Drayton "Chocolate Drop," stuffed cloth black girl, character head w/painted black & white side-glancing eyes, single stroke brows, painted nose & smiling mouth w/chubby cheeks, painted black curly hair w/three braids, cloth body w/non-working crier, jointed shoulders & hips, wearing old white dress & underclothing, 11½" (light overall soil, small stain at left arm)...**400.00**

Handwerck (Heinrich) bisque socket head child marked "119 13, Handwerck, 5, Germany," blue sleep eyes, painted upper & lower lashes, molded & feathered brows, accented nostrils, open mouth w/accented lips & four upper teeth, pierced ears, synthetic wig, jointed wood & composition body marked "Heinrich Handwerck, Germany, 5," dressed in antique white dress, underclothing, socks & shoes, 28" (stain on right front torso, second finger missing from left hand) **600.00**

Handwerck (Heinrich) bisque socket head girl marked "Germany, Heinrich Handwerck, Simon & Halbig, 8, W," set blue eyes w/real lashes, painted lower lashes, molded & feathered brows, pierced ears, synthetic wig, jointed wood & composition body marked "Heinrich Handwerck, Germany, 8," dressed in new satin dress trimmed w/lace & ribbons, pants, socks & shoes, 37" (fine minor crack in finish rear lower torso, hands touched-up, touch-up around neck opening) **1,300.00**

Hartman (Karl) bisque socket head girl marked "K inside large H, 3, Germany," brown sleep eyes w/real lashes, painted lower lashes, feathered brows, open mouth w/accented lips & four upper teeth,

synthetic wig, jointed wood &
composition body, dressed in
antique blue & white dress, underclothing, new socks & shoes, 25"
(few minor chips at neck opening,
light rub on left cheek, several areas
of wear & minor cracks in finish,
wear on hands & one finger missing
on each hand)................................**335.00**

Hertel, Schwab & Co., bisque head
"Our Fairy" girl marked "222/22,"
fixed brown "googlie" side-glancing
eyes, open-closed broadly smiling
mouth w/molded upper teeth, old
light brown mohair wig, bisque body
w/straight limbs, jointed legs, hands
w/fingers spread, wearing a blue silk
belted jacket & matching short puff
shirt, 8½" (right pinky missing)......**1,840.00**

Hertel, Schwab & Co., bisque
socket head baby marked "2/0,
151," painted blue eyes w/red
accent line, feathered brows,
accented nostrils, open mouth
w/molded tongue & two painted
upper teeth, molded & brush-stroked
hair, five-piece bent limb baby body,
dressed in undershirt, sweater &
diaper, 9" (light rub on right cheek,
light color wear on neck socket,
body repainted w/areas of wear on
front torso) **275.00**

Heubach-Koppelsdorf Character Baby

Heubach (Ernst) - Koppelsdorf
bisque head character baby marked
"Heubach-Koppelsdorf - 399 • 6/0 -
Germany - D.R.G.M." on back of
head, brown sleep eyes, softly
blushed brows, painted upper &
lower lashes, accented nostrils,
pierced ears, painted hair, closed
mouth, composition five-piece body,
dressed in original brown grass skirt
& ankle bracelet, celluloid necklace

& metal bracelet, minor rubs on hair,
earrings missing, tiny rub on lips,
normal wearing & aging on body,
little finger repaired on left hand,
13" (ILLUS.) **475.00**

Heubach (Gebruder) all-bisque
character girl marked "10490 - 3,"
slightly side-tilted head w/intaglio
brown side-glancing eyes, open-
closed mouth w/two painted teeth,
molded curly brown hair w/three
molded blue hair ribbons, straight
limb all-bisque body w/molded &
painted white socks & brown shoes,
bent arms, wearing original off-white
cotton dress w/matching ribbon
trim & underwear, 9" **2,070.00**

Heubach (Gebruder) bisque head
"Baby Stuart" baby marked "7977,"
blue intaglio eyes, closed mouth,
molded bonnet decorated
w/transfers of flowers, five-piece
curved-limb composition body, long
white cotton baby dress, 9" (body
worn) **805.00**

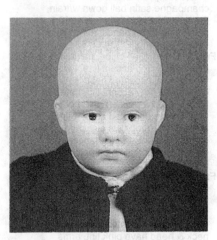

Gebruder Heubach Bisque Boy

Heubach (Gebruder) bisque
shoulder plate boy, marked "5/0 -
Germany (sunburst) DEP - 6688" on
shoulder plate, blue intaglio eyes,
single stroke brows, painted hair &
closed pouty mouth, pink cloth body
w/bisque lower arms, jointed at hips
& knees, dressed in blue two-piece
suit, white shirt, striped socks & new
shoes, minor inherent flaw front
shoulder plate & rear left side of
shoulder plate, bisque arms
probably replaced, 10"
(ILLUS.) **245.00**

Heubach (Gebruder) bisque
shoulder head character baby
marked "2/OD Heubach (in square)

8306 Germany," blue intaglio eyes w/white highlight, single stroke brown, open-closed grinning mouth w/upper teeth, molded & painted hair, gauze-type cloth body w/composition lower arms & legs, wearing antique white baby dress, underclothing, 10½" (light forehead rub, top of body filled w/cotton, worn finish on arms & legs) **225.00**

Horsman "Jo-Jo" toddler marked "Jo-Jo, © 1937 Horsman," composition head, blue tin sleep eyes w/real lashes, painted lower lashes, eye shadow, single stroke brows, accented nostrils, closed mouth, original mohair wig in braids, chubby five-piece composition body, dressed in original pink dress trimmed in blue, underclothing, socks & shoes, 12" (very light crazing, bottom of torso not painted) **210.00**

Jumeau (E.) bisque head girl marked "Depose E 3#J," blue paperweight eyes, closed mouth, pierced ears, blonde mohair wig over cork pate, eight-ball jointed wood & composition body w/blue Jumeau stamp on back, redressed in a purple satin dress w/vertically pleated front panel, pink ribbon & lace trim, cotton underwear, pink silk hat, old black socks & old brown leather shoes, 11" (slightly grainy bisque) **4,600.00**

Jumeau (E.) bisque socket head girl marked "Depose, Tete Jumeau, Bte S.G.D.G.," blue eyes that sleep by a lever in back of head, painted upper & lower lashes, feathered brows, accented nostrils, closed mouth w/accented lips & white space between lips, pierced ears, original mohair wig & cork pate, jointed composition body w/jointed wrists marked "Jumeau, Medaille d'Or, Paris," dressed in pink factory chemise, underclothing, socks & French shoes, 15" (very light nose rub, general wear on arms & legs, especially at joints, wear on hands & fingers, hip joints, ball on right knee joints reglued) **3,800.00**

Jumeau (E.) bisque head 'portrait' girl marked "6x - L," fixed pale blue paperweight eyes, closed well-painted mouth, pierced ears, goatskin wig, eight-ball jointed wood & composition body w/straight wrists, buttocks stamped "Jumeau Medaille d'Or," wearing an old sailor suit w/blue wool pants & cream wool skirt w/blue embroidered details,

blue wool cap, old two-tone leather shoes, 14¼" **5,750.00**

Jumeau (E.) bisque head girl marked "7," fixed brown paperweight eyes, closed mouth, pierced ears, blonde mohair wig over skin base & cork pate, eight-ball jointed wooden body w/oval paper label from "Grand Bazar Mahaut, Cherbourg," straight wrists, redressed in pink silk & net dress w/matching ribbon trim socks & marked "Depose" brown leather shoes & matching bonnet, 15¾" (one shoe sole missing) **5,175.00**

Jumeau Bisque Head Girl

Jumeau (E.) bisque socket head girl marked "Depose - E 9 J" on back of head, "Bebe Jumeau Depose" on sole of left shoe, "Depose (bee) Paris" on sole of right shoe, bulbous blue paperweight eyes w/mauve blush over them, heavy feathered brows, painted lashes, accented nostrils, pierced & applied ears, h.h. wig, closed mouth w/accented lips & white space between lips, jointed wood & composition body w/straight wrists, dressed in teal & white striped silk antique dress, underclothing, socks, shoes & hat, minor firing line on mold line below left ear, slight color imperfection on lower right cheek, tiny firing line inside corner left eye, minor flake left earring hole, normal wear at joints & on fingertips, 20" (ILLUS.) **5,400.00**

Jumeau, (E.) poured bisque head girl marked "Depose Tete Jumeau Bte. S.G.D.G. 9," large brown fixed glass eyes, closed mouth, applied pierced ears, blonde mohair wig over cork pate, jointed wood & composition body w/blue Jumeau stamp on buttocks, pull-string "mama" mechanism (inoperative), redressed in a maroon velvet coat, underwear, old brown leather shoes w/maroon rosettes, lacy bonnet, 20" (fingers rubbed) **4,312.00**

Jumeau (E.) bisque head girl marked "11," blue paperweight eyes, h.h. wig w/cork pate, open mouth w/six teeth, fully-jointed composition body, wearing period clothes w/original shoes & box, 24" h........**2,300.00**

Jumeau (E.) bisque socket head girl marked "Depose, Tete Jumeau, Bte S.G.D.G., Medaille d'Or, Paris," brown paperweight eyes, long painted lashes, feathered brows, accented nostrils, closed mouth w/accented lips & white space between lips, pierced ears, replaced h.h. wig, jointed wood & composition body w/jointed wrists, redressed in mauve & ecru lace dress, bonnet, underclothing, socks & pink silk baby shoes, 26" (minor wig pulls, several chips at neck opening, minor flake at left earring hole, small scuff mark on right eye, body repainted w/some peeling at joints & on torso) **2,300.00**

Jutta bisque head baby marked "10, Jutta, 1914, 12½," blue sleep eyes w/real lashes, feathered brows, painted upper & lower lashes, accented nostrils, open mouth w/accented lips & two upper teeth, h.h. wig, bent-limb baby body w/jointed wrists, dressed in antique white long baby dress & short slip, 21" (wear & cracks at neck socket of body) **800.00**

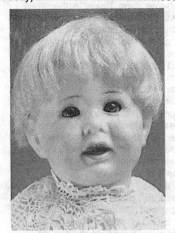

K ★ R Character Baby

K (star) R (Kammer & Reinhardt) bisque head character baby marked

"116A - 28," weighted blue eyes, replaced blonde mohair wig, open/closed mouth w/painted upper teeth, five-piece curved limb composition body, redressed in black velvet shorts, white shirt, maroon socks, black shoes, one thumb repaired, slight wear to hands, 10¾" (ILLUS.) **1,495.00**

K (star) R bisque head character girl marked "K ★ R - Simon & Halbig - 30 - 101," blue painted eyes, closed mouth, replaced blonde wig, jointed wood & composition body, wearing original white gauze dress w/lace yoke & trim on sleeves, underwear, cream socks & brown leather boots, 11½" (one thumb repaired) **2,587.00**

K (star) R bisque head character boy marked "K ★ R - Simon & Halbig - 115 - 38," dome head w/blue sleep eyes, closed pouty mouth, dimpled chin, painted brown hair, jointed wood & composition body, redressed in white corded cotton jacket w/large collar & short pants, white socks, black shoes, 15" (slight rubbing on hands) **4,887.00**

K ★ R Character Girl

K (star) R bisque socket head character girl marked "K ★ R - 101 - 39" on back of head, painted blue eyes, single stroke brows, h.h. wig, accented nostrils, closed pouty mouth, jointed wood & composition stick-type body w/straight wrists, dressed in antique blue sailor-type dress, underclothing, socks & shoes, neck socket of head professionally repaired, firing lines behind both ears, minor kiln dirt on face, few wig pulls near crown, lower rear torso repaired, toes chipped, doll not on correct body, 15½" (ILLUS.) **750.00**

K (star) R bisque head character
boy marked "101 - 46," painted blue eyes, closed mouth, replaced brown synthetic wig, redressed in white shirt, maroon velvet jacket & black velvet pants, 18" **4,312.00**

K (star) R bisque socket head baby
marked "K ★ R, Simon & Halbig, Germany, 126 - 46," brown flirty sleep eyes, painted upper & lower lashes, feathered brows, accented nostrils, open mouth w/two upper teeth & wobble tongue, replaced wig, five-piece French-type composition baby body, dressed in antique long white baby dress, underclothing & lace-trimmed bonnet, 19" (deep crazing on torso, arms & back, left forefinger & little finger missing, minor crazing on right leg) **425.00**

K (star) R bisque head character girl marked "112 - 49," painted blue eyes looking slightly to the right, open-closed mouth w/two painted upper teeth, replaced blonde mohair wig, jointed wood & composition body, wearing a white gauze dress, 21" (hairline at back of head, hands repainted) **5,175.00**

K (star) R bisque socket head child
marked "K ★ R, Simon & Halbig, Germany, 76," blue sleep eyes w/real lashes, painted upper & lower lashes, accented nostrils, open mouth w/four upper teeth, original mohair wig, jointed composition body w/rubber bands, high knee joints & diagonal hip joints, dressed in original organdy dress trimmed in blue, matching bonnet, slip, panties, socks & shoes, 29" (large piece broken out of neck socket of head by opening, rubber hands are misshapen w/fingers bent & deteriorating).....................................**450.00**

Kestner (J.D.) bisque socket head
girl marked "b - made in Germany 3, 143," blue sleep eyes, painted upper & lower lashes, feathered brows, accented nostrils, open mouth w/two upper teeth, original plaster pate & mohair wig, jointed Kestner composition body w/straight wrists, dressed in white flowered nylon dress, underclothing, socks & shoes, 9½" (tiny rub on nose, finish of body yellowed) **900.00**

Kestner (J.D.) bisque socket head
baby marked "J.D.K., made in 7 Germany," solid dome head, painted blue eyes w/red accent lines, feathered brows, accented nostrils, open-closed mouth w/accented lips, molded & brush-stroked hair, composition Kestner bent-limb baby body, dressed in antique white long baby dress, slip, diaper & socks, 10" (light wear to body, wear on right heel, repair on right toe, craze line on front torso & top of rear torso).....**355.00**

Kestner "Gibson Girl" Doll

Kestner (J.D.) bisque shoulder
head "Gibson Girl" lady, marked "6/0 - 172 - 10/0 made in Germany" on back of shoulder plate, brown sleep eyes, feathered brows, painted upper & lower lashes, accented nostrils & ear canals, original mohair wig up in Gibson Girl style, closed smiling mouth w/accent line between lips, cloth body w/bisque lower arms & legs w/molded & painted stockings & boots, dressed in white w/lace inserts & tucks, underclothing, normal aging on body, 10" (ILLUS.) **550.00**

Kestner (J.D.) bisque head
character baby marked "255, 7, O. I. C., Made in Germany," tiny set blue eyes, softly blushed brows, accented nostrils, open-closed mouth in wide open scream, painted hair, cloth body, dressed in antique white baby dress, slip, diaper & socks, 8½" circumference, 11" (quite a bit of color worn off mouth & tongue, light nose & cheek rubs, cloth body probably old replacement) **800.00**

Kestner (J.D.) bisque head
character boy marked "221," weighted brown glass "googlie" eyes, smiling mouth, original brown mohair cropped wig over plaster pate, jointed wood & composition

body, wearing original outfit w/an off-white side button cotton jacket & matching short pants, white belt w/large buckle, socks, silk shoes, wide-brimmed straw hat w/brown grosgrain ribbon, 11" (hands rubbed, right index finger broken off) **4,887.00**

Kestner (J.D.) bisque shoulder head girl marked "Dep. 154, Made in Germany," brown sleep eyes, painted upper & lower lashes, feathered brows, accented nostrils, open mouth w/four upper teeth, synthetic wig, kid body w/gussets at hips & knees, bisque lower arms, dressed in antique navy blue dress, underclothing, replaced socks & shoes, 12" (few tiny kiln specks on face, some wear on torso, small chip inside of fourth finger tip of right hand)..**300.00**

Kestner (J.D.) bisque head baby marked "J. D. K. 235," brown sleep eyes, painted upper & lower lashes, feathered brows, accented nostrils, open mouth w/accented lips & two lower teeth, original mohair wig on original plaster pate, pin-jointed kid baby body w/label "J.D.K., Germany, ½ cork stuffed," composition lower arms & legs, dressed in antique embroidered dress & diaper, 12" (hairline from left rear shoulder plate to side of shoulder, tiny rub on end of nose, rust from doll stand on torso) **640.00**

Kestner (J.D.) bisque head "Wunderkind" character girl w/four separate interchangeable heads, one head marked "182," w/brown weighted eyes, closed mouth, original brown mohair wig; second head marked "179," w/blue weighted eyes, open-closed mouth w/molded tongue, original blonde mohair wig; third head marked "183," w/blue weighted eyes, open-closed mouth w/molded teeth, original blonde mohair wig; fourth head marked "171," w/weighted blue eyes, open mouth w/upper teeth, brown mohair wig; wearing a floral-printed cream gauze dress w/lace & pink ribbon trim, socks & shoes, in original maroon paper-covered cardboard box w/lithographed label on cover, ca. 1910, 14½", the set **12,650.00**

Kestner (J.D.) bisque head 'Bru-type' girl marked "10," brown sleep eyes, open-closed mouth w/molded & painted upper teeth, blonde mohair wig over replaced pate, jointed wood & composition

Kestner 'Bru-type' Girl

body w/straight wrists, redressed in a pink & cream satin frock w/pink hair ribbons, cotton underwear, socks, old brown leather shoes, holding a tiny all-bisque baby, minor repairs, retouching to hands & body joints, 15" (ILLUS.) **3,450.00**

Kestner (J.D.) bisque shoulder head child, blue sleep eyes, painted upper & lower lashes, feathered brows, accented nostrils, open-closed mouth w/accented lips & four upper teeth, synthetic wig, kid body w/bisque lower arms, gussets at elbows, hips & knees, dressed in probably original white dress, underclothing, socks & shoes, 17" (couple fingers chipped on right hand, firing line on left hand) **275.00**

Kestner (J.D.) bisque head "Hilda" character baby marked "Hilda - J D K Jr 1914 Gs Gesch N. 1010 Made in 16 Germany," fixed blue glass eyes, dome head w/brushstroked hair, open mouth w/two upper teeth, five-piece curved limb composition baby body, wearing a simple white cotton baby dress, 20" (fingers & hands slightly worn) **4,312.00**

Kewpie, all-bisque w/movable arms, impressed mark on feet, ca. 1920s, 6½" h. (needs restringing)................**172.50**

Kley & Hahn bisque socket head character boy marked "Germany, K & H (in banner), 525, 0½," blue intaglio eyes, feathered brows, accented nostrils, open-closed mouth w/accented lips, molded & brushstroked hair, jointed wood & composition body, redressed in cream wool suit, socks & shoes, 15" (minor inherent flaw on bottom of neck socket & on back of head, wear, flaking on left upper & lower arm, repair & repaint on right hand)..**1,200.00**

Kling & Co. bisque head boy marked "186, K (in bell), 6," turned head, painted vivid blue eyes w/red accent line, one-stroke brows, accented nostrils, closed mouth w/accent line between lips, molded & painted hair, heavy kid body w/bisque lower arms, gussets at elbows, hips & knees, dressed in antique white night shirt, underclothing & socks, 15" (minor wear on back of head, minor repair at hip & knee gussets) **285.00**

Kling & Co. bisque head girl marked "123.3," solid dome head, brown paperweight eyes, painted upper & lower lashes, feathered brows, accented nostrils, closed mouth w/accent line between lips, original mohair wig w/ornate small braids, kid body w/gussets at elbows & knees, dressed in ecru organdy dress w/embroidered lace over it, underclothing & new high button boots, 15" (light nose rub, tiny flake inside corner of right eye, kid body deteriorating & flaking on top of torso, replaced kid arms w/individually stitched fingers) **300.00**

Kruse (Kathe) baby, molded cloth, painted brown eyes & hair, jointed cloth body w/wide hips, five-section legs, hands w/separately stitched thumbs, wearing original blue cotton short-sleeved dress w/matching cap, socks, underwear, marked on foot, ca. 1920, 16½" (small scratch on left cheek, rubbing on face & end of nose) **1,610.00**

Kruse (Kathe) child, marked "Kathe Kruse, Made in U.S. Zone Germany, Mariellchen, IX" on paper tag w/"Wilh. Heiges Nachf., AM Postmichelbrunnen, Esslingen A.N., Mariellchen, 52.60" on sticker on back of tag, oil-painted cloth head, painted brown eyes, single stroke brows, accented nostrils, closed mouth, h.h. wig, jointed cloth body, dressed in original dress, apron, panties, socks, shoes & hat, in original box, 14" **1,300.00**

Kruse (Kathe) character girl marked "Kathe Kruse" on bottom left foot, "MRZ 86" on bottom of right foot, "Original Kathe Kruse Stoffpuppe - Made in Germany" on paper tag, hard plastic head, painted brown eyes, single stroke brows, accented nostrils, h.h. wig, closed mouth, cloth body jointed at shoulders &

Kathe Kruse Character Girl

hips, dressed in original pink & white dress, white embroidered pinafore, underclothing, socks & shoes, 18" (ILLUS.) **185.00**

Lenci 'Fascist' Boy

Lenci 'Fascist' boy, pressed felt head, painted brown eyes, multi-stroke brows, accented nostrils, applied ears, mohair wig, two-tone lips w/highlight dots on lower lip, felt body jointed at shoulders & hips dressed in original felt Fascist boy's outfit of black jacket w/pockets & covered buttons & emblem on sleeve, grey shorts, grey knit socks, black leather shoes, black felt hat w/tassel, blue felt kerchief around neck, light rub on right cheek, nose & chin, tiny hole in left thumb, tiny hole in back of shorts & on right shoulder of clothing, button showing through felt covering on left sleeve, 13" (ILLUS.)....................**1,100.00**

Lenci baseball player, pressed felt

head w/brown side-glancing eyes,
medium brown inserted hair,
wearing a bright pink felt shirt, beige
short pants, knitted socks, brown
leather shoes, beige cap w/blue
brim, complete w/wood baseball bat
w/leather-bound grip & leather
catcher's mitt, late 1920s, 17½"
(some moth damage to shirt &
socks) **3,450.00**

Lenci Italian Soldier, pressed felt
head, painted brown eyes to side,
painted upper & lower lashes to
side, single stroke brows, accented
nostrils, closed mouth, applied ears,
mohair wig, felt body jointed at
shoulders & hips, dressed in original
detailed Italian soldier's uniform for
division that marched through Italian
Alps, grey wool w/canvas knapsack
& tent, ropes, pick, two leather
pockets strapped around chest,
brown leather shoes, felt wine
bottle, 16" **2,200.00**

Limoges French Character Lady

Limoges bisque French character
lady marked "J. E. Masson - SC. -
Lorraine - No. 0 - AL & Co." on back
of head, bisque socket head, set
blue eyes, molded & feathered
brows, painted upper & lower
lashes, accented nostrils, mohair
wig, open-closed mouth w/six upper
teeth, jointed composition body w/
unusual shape, jointed at shoulders,
elbows, hips & knees, straight
wrists, hands w/fingers all molded
together, dressed in old fabrics in
regional-type outfit, molded &
painted heeled black shoes, bisque
head w/ruddy coloring, composition
body shows overall light soil & wear,
especially at joints & on feet, lower
legs painted white to indicate
stockings, 16½" (ILLUS.) **600.00**

Madame Hendren composition
'Mama' child marked "Genuine
Madame Hendren Doll, C/16, Made
in U.S.A." & "Genuine Madame
Hendren Waukantauk Doll (Lloyd's
Patent Voice)," w/instructions for
operation, blue tin sleep eyes w/real
lashes, painted lower lashes,
feathered brows, accented nostrils,
open mouth w/two upper teeth,
metal tongue, mohair wig, cloth
body w/working crier, composition
lower arms & legs, dressed in
original pink dress, matching
bonnet, underclothing, socks &
shoes, 16" (light paint wear on upper
lip, minor wear on tips of fingers,
small crack in finish on
right ankle) **165.00**

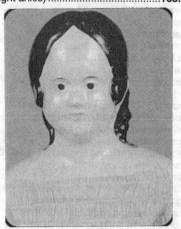

Papier-maché "Milliner's Model" Lady

Papier-maché "Milliner's Model"
papier-maché shoulder head,
painted brown eyes, single stroke
brows, accented nostrils, molded &
painted hair w/long curls on neck &
shoulders, exposed ears, closed
mouth, kid body w/wooden lower
limbs, jointed at shoulders only,
dressed in original dress,
underclothing & painted shoes, tiny
rub on nose, minor crack in finish of
back shoulder plate, some paint
strips off arms, left ankle reglued,
16" (ILLUS.) **775.00**

Papier-maché head lady, black
center-part hairdo pulled to the
back, molded & painted features, on
a kid body w/simple carved wooden
arms & legs, wearing early knee-
length dress & pantaloons, small
celluloid fan attached to one hand,
ca. 1840, w/glass dome, 17½"
(wear, fabric damage) **1,045.00**

Papier-maché lady, shoulder head
w/painted brown eyes w/white

Papier-maché Lady

Volland Raggedy Ann Doll

highlight, feathered brow, molded &
painted black hair, closed mouth,
cloth body w/leather lower arms,
dressed in antique floral two-piece
taffeta outfit, underclothing, socks &
shoes, deep rub on nose & chin,
lighter wear on cheeks & forehead,
general wear on shoulder plate &
hair, finish is shiny, leather lower
arms repaired, needs repair to
fingers, torso covered w/old
stockinette, pants fragile, 29"
(ILLUS.) **350.00**
Parian head man, painted blue eyes
w/red accent line, single stroke
brows, closed mouth w/accent line,
exposed ears, molded & painted
brown man's hair style w/brush
strokes at temples, cloth body
w/squeaker in torso, wooden lower
arms & legs, wearing antique man's
nightshirt, 6" h. (small chip on edge
of shoulder plate, body patched on
upper torso) **400.00**
Raggedy Ann, cloth head w/unjointed
neck, black shoe button eyes, single
stroke brows, red triangle nose
w/black border, closed smiling
mouth, original brown yarn hair,
cloth body w/cardboard heart,
jointed at shoulders & hips, wearing
original print dress, white bloomers
& red & white striped socks w/black
shoes, Volland, face worn, some
clothing stains, apron missing,
15"..**1,050.00**
Raggedy Ann, cloth head w/unjointed
neck, black shoe button eyes, dash
brows, painted dot lower lashes, red
triangle nose outlined in black,
single black line for smiling mouth,
red cheeks, brown yarn hair, cloth
body w/cardboard heart, stitch-

jointed shoulders & hips, lower legs
w/red & white striped socks, black
shoes form feet, wearing original
blue sprigged calico dress, white
pinafore & white bloomers, Volland,
back marked "Patented Spt. 7,
1915," small wear holes on
forehead, general soil & discoloration, hair worn & partially
missing, 16" (ILLUS.) **850.00**
Raggedy Andy, cloth head
w/unjointed neck, black shoe button
eyes, single stroke brows, red
triangle nose, closed smiling mouth,
original reddish brown yarn hair,
cloth body jointed at shoulders &
hips, wearing original red & white
checked shirt, blue pants, blue &
white hat, red & white striped socks
& black shoes, Volland, somewhat
worn & faded, 15" **650.00**
Raggedy Andy, cloth head
w/unjointed neck, embroidered
eyes, single stroke stitched brows,
floss lower lashes, red triangle
stitched nose, closed smiling mouth
w/red stitched lips & outer corners of
mouth, original reddish brown yarn
hair, cloth body stitch-jointed at
shoulders & hips, wearing a
yellowish brown checked shirt, tan
corduroy suspender pants w/one
suspender, black shoes part of the
doll, some floss missing, clothes
worn & faded, unmarked, 20" **130.00**
Raggedy Ann & Andy, stuffed cloth,
made by Mollye Goldman, all-
original, Andy w/original cardboard
wrist tag, early 1920s, 18", pr. (some
fading & discoloration, left leg on
Ann split at ankle) **747.50**
Ravca (Bernard) man & woman
marked "Made in France" on cloth
tag of man's pant leg, "Original
Ravca, Paris, Brittany, B. Ravca

(signature), Saks 5th Ave., 1944" on paper wrist tag of man, "Made in France" cloth tag on woman's skirt, both w/sculptured stockinette faces, painted blue eyes, multi-stroke brows, accented nostrils, closed smiling mouths, mohair wigs, padded wire armature bodies, dressed in original regional attire, celluloid shoes, 9½", pr...........**95.00**

Scherf (Peter) bisque socket head girl marked "Made in Germany, P. Sch., 2," set blue eyes, painted upper & lower lashes, heavy feathered brows, open mouth w/four upper teeth, original mohair wig, jointed wood & composition body w/straight wrists, dressed in plaid taffeta dress w/blue overdress, matching bonnet, pants, socks & shoes, 16" (minor firing line on crown, color flow on back of head)...**300.00**

Schmidt (Bruno) bisque head "Wendy" character girl marked "2033 BSW" in heart, brown sleep eyes, closed mouth, brown mohair wig, jointed wood & composition body, wearing a floral-printed dress, cotton underwear, socks, pink shoes & a straw hat, 11" (old hairline in forehead, hands flaking) **3,450.00**

Schmidt (Bruno) "Tommy Tucker" bisque socket head boy marked "2048, 4," blue sleep eyes, painted upper & lower lashes, feathered brows, accented nostrils, open mouth w/two upper teeth, molded & painted hair, jointed wood & composition body, redressed in black velvet suit, white shirt trimmed w/eyelet, socks, black high button boots, 17" (light rub on hair high up in back, light nose rub, first fingers on both hands repaired, upper legs not matching) **900.00**

Schoenau & Hoffmeister bisque socket head girl marked "S PB (in star) H, 1906, 12, Germany," brown sleep eyes, synthetic wig, open mouth w/accented lips & four upper teeth, painted upper & lower lashes, molded feathered brows, accented nostrils, jointed wood & composition body, dressed in white dress made from antique fabric, underclothing, new socks & shoes, 25".................**425.00**

Schoenhut baby, socket head marked "H. E. Schoenhut © 1911," wooden, painted blue eyes, closed mouth, painted hair, spring-jointed five-piece wooden baby body, wearing old white baby dress & bonnet, underclothing & diaper, 13"

(face pale, wear to hair, some head crazing & small chip above right eye, paint flaking on body) **385.00**

Schoenhut character girl #105, wooden, blue intaglio eyes, feathered brows, accented nostrils, closed pouty mouth, molded & painted bobbed hair w/blue band, spring-jointed wooden body jointed at shoulders, elbows, wrists, hips, knees & ankles, dressed in blue & white plaid dress w/white collar, replaced underclothing, new socks, replaced shoes, 14" (small ding on right cheek, light nose rub, general wear on finish of hair, light wear on lip color, body repainted & flaking, light wear on toes) **950.00**

Schoenhut girl marked "Schoenhut Doll, Pat. Jan. 17, '11, U.S.A. & Foreign Countries," wooden socket head, brown intaglio eyes, faded brows, accented nostrils, open-closed mouth w/six upper teeth, molded & painted hair w/red bow on right side, spring-jointed wooden body, dressed in old red plaid dress, original knit underclothing, replaced shoes & socks, 14" (facial coloring pale, few paint flakes off in two places on forehead & right cheek, color worn off hair w/some wood showing in back, paint off tops of both feet, wear on edges of feet w/bare wood showing) **1,000.00**

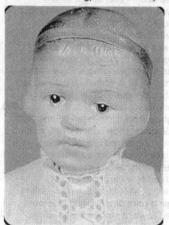

Schoenhut Girl

Schoenhut girl marked "Schoenhut Doll - Pat Jan. 17th - 1911, U.S.A." on black oval label on back, wooden head, blue intaglio eyes w/white highlights, feathered brows, accented nostrils, molded & painted hair w/blue ribbon, closed mouth, spring-jointed body dressed in antique white dress, underclothing, knit underclothing, socks & old shoes, light wear on hair & blue band, light wear on body, paint chip on heel & ankle of right foot, 16" (ILLUS.) **2,700.00**

Schoenhut girl marked "Schoenhut Doll, Pat. Jan. 17 - '11 - U.S.A. & Foreign Countries" impressed on back, wooden socket head, blue intaglio eyes w/white highlight, feathered brows, accented nostrils, closed mouth, molded & painted hair & bonnet w/yellow flowers, green leaves, gold trim, spring-jointed wooden body, dressed in yellow cotton dress w/white trim, underclothing, socks & shoes, 16" (face repainted from eyes down, paint flaking in semicircle between eyebrows & on brows, light wear & flaking on hands, light wear on legs & feet)....................................**4,500.00**

Schoenhut manikin marked "Schoenhut Doll, Pat. Jan. 17, '11, U.S.A. & Foreign Countries," figure of a man w/wooden head, blue intaglio eyes w/white highlights, single stroke brows, accented nostrils, closed mouth, carved & painted hair, spring-jointed wooden body, dressed in grey & white striped shirt, white pants, replaced socks & shoes, 19" (touch-up around nose, eyes, mouth & ears, color wear on carved hair on back of head)..**2,500.00**

Schoenhut priest, wooden, the carved wood head w/brown intaglio eyes w/white highlights, molded eyelids, closed smiling mouth, molded & painted brown hair, spring-jointed wooden body, wearing original priest's outfit w/black taffeta shirt, black wool pants & long robe, original socks & shoes, black four-cornered hat w/tassel, 22" (shoes deteriorating, face washed) **2,500.00**

Schoenhut toddler girl, wooden, carved wood head w/round label reading "H. E. Schoenhut © 1913," socket head w/painted blue eyes, single stroke brows, closed mouth, original brown mohair wig, spring-jointed wooden body, wearing original white organdy baby dress, slip, knit shirt, diaper, socks & high button shoes, label on back reads "Schoenhut Doll, Pat. Jan. 17th 1911, U.S.A.," 11" (very fine crazing on face, wig sparse, holes in soles of shoes) **625.00**

S.F.B.J. (Societe Francaise de Fabrication de Bebes & Jouets) bisque head girl marked "3," fixed blue glass eyes, open mouth w/teeth, pierced ears, original brown mohair wig, jointed wood & composition body, wearing a factory cotton chemise, old blue socks, & blue leather shoes w/size 3 bee mark, 12"..**805.00**

S.F.B.J. bisque socket head girl marked "5 Depose S.F.B.J.," brown paperweight eyes, feathered brows, pierced ears, blonde h.h. wig, open smiling mouth w/four upper teeth, jointed wood & composition body, redressed in a black & gold French-style dress, matching bonnet, underclothing, socks & shoes, 17" (inherent line under chin, hands probably replaced, some hand & knee flaking) **400.00**

S.F.B.J. bisque socket head "Laughing Jumeau" marked "S.F.B.J. 236 Paris - 8," brown sleep eyes w/real lashes, feathered brows, open-closed mouth w/two upper teeth, original blonde mohair wig, jointed wood & composition toddler body w/jointed wrists, wearing factory chemise, pants, black socks & shoes, 18" (body lightly repainted, some finish flaking on body, left foot toes repaired)........................**1,400.00**

S.F.B.J. bisque socket head child, blue paperweight eyes, painted lower lashes, feathered brows, accented nostrils, open mouth w/accented lips & four upper teeth, pierced ears, h.h. wig, jointed wood & composition body, dressed in French-style dress made w/antique fabrics, matching hat, pants, socks & antique shoes, 21" (tiny flaw on left cheek, minor firing line behind & above left ear, hands probably old replacements) **800.00**

S.F.B.J. bisque socket head girl marked "S.F.B.J. Paris 10," blue paperweight eyes, feathered brows, pierced ears, open mouth w/four upper teeth, brown synthetic wig, jointed wood & composition body w/jointed wrists, wearing antique style dress & cap, 23½" (flaking on hands & left arm) **400.00**

S.F.B.J. bisque head girl marked "Depose S.F.B.J. 8," bluish grey paperweight eyes, pierced ears, replaced synthetic wig, open mouth w/four teeth, French composition body w/straight knees, redressed in black velvet, 24".............................**805.00**

S.F.B.J. bisque head child marked "S.F.B.J., 230, Paris (in circle), 10," blue paperweight eyes, painted upper & lower lashes, feathered brows, accented nostrils, open mouth w/accented lips & six upper teeth, pierced ears, full mohair wig, jointed wood & composition body, dressed in antique white dress, underclothing, socks & shoes, 24" (tiny flake at right earring hole, hands repainted & flaking, finish worn on lower left arm) **1,700.00**

S.F.B.J. Character Boy

S.F.B.J. bisque head character boy, model 238, glass eyes, brown h.h. wig, smiling open mouth w/upper teeth, joined composition body, wearing hat, white shirt w/bow tie & vest, knee breeches, socks & shoes (ILLUS.) **3,800.00**

Shirley Temple Doll & Trunk

Shirley Temple, composition head w/hazel sleep eyes w/real lashes, feathered brows & painted lower lashes, accented nostrils, original mohair wig, open mouth w/six upper teeth, composition five-piece child body dressed in original blue & white dress & matching hat, underclothing, socks & shoes, w/original Shirley Temple trunk w/decals from her movies, an original pink organdy Shirley dress trimmed in blue, three other dresses & red flannel pajamas, light crazing overall, hair has been combed & restyled, ribbon replaced in hair & around waist, trunk damaged on top, some fading & water damage, 13", the set (ILLUS.)................................**450.00**

Shirley Temple, marked "Shirley Temple" on head, "Shirley Temple, 13" on body, composition head w/hazel sleep eyes w/real lashes, painted lower lashes, single stroke brows, accented nostrils, open mouth w/six upper teeth, original blonde mohair wig in original set, five-piece composition child body, dressed in original tagged (NRA) blue knife-pleated organdy dress w/white organdy embroidered collar, original one-piece underclothing, socks & shoes, original Shirley Temple picture button, in original box w/label "Shirley Temple, Genuine Shirley Temple Doll," etc. stamped "blue 2013" & "102-2013" w/J.C. Penney Co. price tag for $2.95, 13".....................................**2,000.00**

Shirley Temple, marked "Ideal Doll, ST-15-N," vinyl head, hazel sleep eyes w/real lashes, feathered brows, painted lower lashes, synthetic rooted hair in original set, open-closed mouth w/six upper teeth, five-piece vinyl child body, dressed in original pink nylon dress, replaced panties, possibly original socks, blue vinyl shoes, black vinyl purse w/"Shirley Temple" in script & original script pin, 15"......................**125.00**

Shirley Temple, composition, hazel sleep eyes w/real lashes, original blonde mohair wig in original set, open mouth w/six upper teeth, five-piece composition child body, wearing original tagged blue organdy pleated dress from "Baby Take A Bow," original underclothing, shoes & socks & w/original Shirley Temple button, unplayed-with condition, 16" (eyes cracked, fine lines around eyes & on torso & left arm) **600.00**

Shirley Temple, composition head marked "Shirley Temple, Cop. Ideal N & T Co.," hazel sleep eyes w/real

lashes, feathered brows, open
mouth w/six upper teeth, blonde
curly mohair wig, five-piece jointed
composition child body, wearing
tagged pink organdy dress w/blue &
white flowers, original underclothing,
socks & shoes, 1930s, 18" (two fine
lines below right eye, one line below
left eye, one fine chin craze,
one eye crazed & oiled) **1,700.00**

Shirley Temple, composition head
w/hazel sleep eyes w/real lashes,
single stroke brows, open mouth
w/six upper teeth & molded tongue,
original curly blonde mohair wig in
original set, five-piece jointed
composition child body, wearing
tagged blue organdy dress trimmed
in pink, original underclothing, socks
& shoes, 22" (tiny flake off
composition below left eye, eyes
cracked, light finger crazing) **525.00**

Simon & Halbig bisque head girl
marked "979," fixed blue glass eyes,
open mouth w/upper teeth, pierced
ears, replaced red wig, jointed wood
& composition body w/straight
wrists, redressed in gown of old
cream silk, w/underwear & matching
bonnet, 9".......................................**920.00**

Simon & Halbig bisque socket head
girl marked "S & H 1079, DEP,
Germany, 14½," brown sleep eyes,
painted upper & lower lashes,
molded & feathered brows,
accented nostrils, open mouth
w/four upper teeth, pierced ears,
original h.h. wig, jointed composition
body, dressed in antique white
eyelet dress, underclothing, socks &
shoes, 30" (light firing line over right
ear, minor wear on left shoulder,
light touch-up on hands, both hips,
knee joints & right lower leg)...........**850.00**

Simon & Halbig bisque socket head
girl marked "S H 1079 - DEP, 15,"
blue sleep eyes, dark painted upper
& lower lashes, heavy feathered
brows, accented nostrils, open
mouth w/accented lips & four upper
teeth, pierced ears, original h.h. wig,
jointed wood & composition body,
dressed in antique white dress,
underclothing, socks & high button
shoes, 32" (wear at hip sockets &
left little toe, tip off little finger on
right hand).....................................**1,200.00**

Springfield lady marked "Patented
April 29, 1879, Dec. 7, 1880, May
31, 1881" on black paper band
around waist, composition over
wood head w/painted blue eyes
w/red accent line, single stroke
brows, accented nostrils, closed

mouth, molded & painted blonde
hair, stiff neck, wooden body jointed
at shoulders, elbows, hips & knees,
metal hands & feet, wearing antique
white trimmed w/red clothing
w/matching underclothing, 12" (fine
crack across eyes to side seam,
finish of head yellowed, paint flaked
off spots of metal hands & feet) **1,200.00**

Steiner (Jules) bisque socket head
girl marked "J. Steiner Bte. S.G.D.G.
Paris Fre A 19," blue paperweight
eyes, feathered brows, pierced ears,
antique black h.h. wig w/long curls,
closed mouth, jointed composition
body w/straight wrists, wearing an
antique white dress w/eyelet trim,
underclothing, shoes & socks, 29"
(firing lines in front & behind left ear,
tiny flake at right earring hole) **3,400.00**

Steiner poured bisque head lady
marked "J. Steiner Bte. S G D G
Paris Fi re A 6," blue fixed
paperweight eyes, closed mouth,
pierced ears, remains of original
skin wig, replaced blonde mohair
ringletted wig, jointed wood &
composition body w/straight legs &
Steiner label on back, redressed in
aqua silk gown w/cream lace trim &
edge piping, matching hat, cotton
underwear, socks & old brown
leather shoes **3,162.00**

Stuffed cloth, black woman
w/embroidered features & a wool
twill body w/oilcloth limbs, w/a note
reading "this is Pompey given to
John Adams Paine in 1889, when
he was two years old...," late 19th c.,
18"..**1,380.00**

Unis France Girl

Unis France bisque girl marked
"Paris - France (in oval) - 71-301-
140" on back of head, bisque socket

head, painted blue eyes, single stroke brows, accented nostrils, mohair wig, closed mouth, five-piece composition body dressed in original regional costume of France, molded & painted shoes, fine crack front & back of left leg, 5" (ILLUS.) **100.00**

Vogue "Ginny," marked "Vogue" on back of head, "Vogue Doll" on body, hard plastic head, painted blue eyes, painted upper lashes, single stroke brow, original mohair wig, hard plastic body jointed at shoulders & hips, dressed in tagged white taffeta dress w/blue flowers, matching panties, socks & center snap shoes, blue flowers in hair, in box labeled "Vogue Dolls, Inc., Medford, Mass., Fashion Leaders in Doll Society," 7½" **350.00**

Vogue "Toddles," marked "Vogue" on back of head, "Doll Co.," on back & "Toddles" on bottom of left shoe, composition head, painted blue eyes to side, painted upper lashes, single stroke brows, closed mouth, mohair wig in braids, composition body jointed at shoulders & hips, dressed in white dress w/red & blue flowers & pinafore, panties attached to dress, original socks & shoes, in box labeled "Vogue Toddles, Red, Braids, 052," 7½" (paint scratch left front torso from stand, small paint flaw lower front torso)..............**270.00**

Wax over composition lady, "Sonneberg Taufling" type, large weighted dark glass eyes, painted eyebrows, closed mouth, black painted center-part hair w/buns above each ear, Motschmann-style body w/jointed composition lower arms & hands, composition hips, fabric thighs, composition lower legs jointed at ankles, several layers of old flannel & cotton underwear, old long gown w/pintucked skirt, bodice w/ayreshire-work front panel, short puff sleeves & matching cotton cap, Germany, ca. 1875, 20½" (tip of nose slightly rubbed)....................**1,150.00**

Wax over papier-maché shoulder head lady, brown pupilless wire eyes, single stroke brows, accented nostrils, original mohair wig, closed smiling mouth, cloth body w/leather arms dressed in possibly original white dress w/eyelet, underclothing, socks, high button boots & bonnet, wire to operate eyes protrudes from lower abdomen, finish on shoulder cracked w/dirt in the cracks, wax lid on left eye damaged, wig sparse,

Wax Over Papier-Maché Doll

some wear & stains on body, right arm partially replaced, thumb on right hand & two fingers on left hand damaged, 27" (ILLUS.) **425.00**

(End of Dolls Section)

DOORSTOPS

Bobby Blake Doorstop

All doorstops listed are flat-back cast iron unless otherwise noted. Most names are taken from Doorstops - Identification & Values, *by Jeanne Bertoia (Collector Books, 1985).*

Ally Sloper, comic standing man w/bulbous nose, wearing top hat & leaning on umbrella, one hand on hip, small dog at his feet, England, old worn polychrome repaint, 11¼" h...**$165.00**

Aunt Jemima, Hubley, full figure, original polychrome paint w/green

dress & old repaint white apron &
collar, 12¼" h. (wear & light rust) **275.00**

Bear, standing on open feet, upper
paws together, old red & brown
repaint, 15" h..................................**715.00**

Bobby Blake, young boy standing on
oval base holding a Teddy bear,
Hubley, 5¼" l., 9½" h. (ILLUS.) **220.00**

Cat - kitten, seated animal w/ribbon &
bow around neck, Hubley & National
Foundry, marked "Gray Iron Works
Pats. Pend. 1925," original paint,
original label, 7" h. **90.00**

Cats, Twin, one black & one white,
dressed as a little boy & little girl,
standing on a grassy mound base,
Hubley & National Foundry,
5¼" w., 7" h..................................**200.00**

Charleston Dancers, worn original
polychrome paint, marked "© Fish"
& "Hubley," 8⅞" h..........................**1,400.00**

Cockatoo, full figure, bright
polychrome paint, 14" h. **375.00**

Dog, English Bulldog, full figure,
repainted, 7" h..............................**104.50**

Dog, German Shepherd, flat-bodied
profile-style on a bar base w/shoe
feet, old dark red paint, 12½" h........**110.00**

Dog, Scottie, full figure, standing
facing forward, black paint, 11" l. **195.00**

Dog, Scottie (large), full figure, sitting
animal, black, Hubley, 12 x 16"........**800.00**

Dog, Terrier, sitting sideways w/head
turned toward viewer, sad
expression, oblong base, back
marked "Made in England," 8½" w.,
14¾" h. (very minor wear).................**55.00**

Dog, Whippet, white animal w/brown
markings standing on rectangular
grassy base, 6¾" l., 7½" h. **400.00**

Flower Basket, poppies &
cornflowers, Hubley, 7¼" h. **165.00**

Flower Basket, roses, daisies & other
flowers in stave-constructed basket
w/flared foot & shaped overhead
handle, on stepped base, original
polychrome paint, 5¾ x 6½" **235.00**

Flower Pot, red poppies in
Southwest-style pot, marked
"Hubley 300," 6⅛" w., 7" h. **180.00**

Giraffe, standing animal w/tall grass
behind its legs, rectangular base,
6½" w., 12" h. (minor wear).............**165.00**

Gnome with keys, full figure, carrying
lantern in one hand & keys in other,
10" h...**475.00**

Horse, full figure, standing animal
w/original bay paint, black mane &
tail, Hubley, 10½ x 12".....................**150.00**

Jack, large model of a four-armed toy
jack, cream colored paint, 8½" w.,
7" h. (rust, overall paint loss) **71.50**

Lion, full figure, standing w/head

turned & tail to left side, old gold &
silver repaint, 8¾" l. **170.50**

Lion, seated, flat back, bronze finish,
BS Co. **125.00**

Napoleon on rearing stallion, cast
brass, 6" d., 6½" l **75.00**

"Old Salt," full figure, man wearing
yellow slicker & black rain hat,
original polychrome paint, 11" h.......**250.00**

Punch, profile view of seated figure
w/dog seated at side, old black
paint, marked "Kenrick," England,
9" w., 12" h....................................**325.00**

Rooster, head raised, arched tail,
wide S-scrolls support body, on
oblong base, 5½" w., 7" h. (minor
rust, overall paint wear) **165.00**

Squirrel, seated on naturalistic
ground holding nut in paws, marked
"Blodgett Studio, Lake Geneva,"
8¼" h. (worn old paint).....................**220.00**

Squirrel, seated on log holding nut in
paws, 9½ x 11" **350.00**

Woman w/hatbox, 5¼" w.,
6¾" h..**110.00**

DRUGSTORE & PHARMACY ITEMS

*The old-time corner drugstore, once a
familiar part of every American town, has
now given way to the modern, efficient
pharmacy. With the streamlining and
modernization of this trade many of the
early tools and store adjuncts have become
outdated and now fall into the realm of
"collectibles." Listed here are a variety of
tools, bottles, display pieces and other
ephemera once closely associated with the
druggist's trade.*

Apothecary jar, cov., heavy lead
crystal, paneled & cut, remnants of
old label, 7 x 16" **$225.00**

Apothecary jar, cov., clear pressed
glass, slender cylindrical body on
slightly domed foot, inset w/flattened
knob top, 24" h................................**302.50**

Apothecary jar, cov., clear pressed
glass, tall cylindrical body on slightly
domed foot, inset top w/pressed
swirl design, filled w/colored glass
shards, 33" h. (rim chip)...................**330.00**

Business card holder, clear pressed
glass w/white porcelain insert
w/black lettering "A. H. Smith & Co.
Druggist, San Francisco" & an 1895
calendar, base embossed "1889
Patent" **145.00**

Show globe, glass w/stopper & Art
Deco metal stand, 24" h..................**175.00**

EGG REPLICAS

Pennsylvania Decorated Chicken Egg

Chicken egg, dyed deep red w/sgraffito decoration of tulips & inscribed "1816," Pennsylvania, 1816, 2½" l. (ILLUS.) **$1,955.00**

Enamel on silver, model of an Easter egg w/colorful stylized foliage w/geometric border, hinged at the center, Dmitri Nicholaev, Moscow, Russia, ca. 1900, 2¾" h. **1,380.00**

Gold & translucent enamel, vinaigrette, egg-shaped, steel blue enamel over a *guilloche* ground w/a border of diamonds, the interior grill pierced w/the Cyrillic initials "A.N.," marked w/the Cyrillic name of Workmaster Michael Perchin & the 56 standard, Fabergé, St. Petersburg, ca. 1890, 1½" h. **7,475.00**

Gold, enamel & jewels, the pendant enameled translucent pale pink over a *guilloché* ground & set w/colored stones in a swirl pattern, opening to reveal a hinged cover enameled translucent red & set w/a diamond-set ribbon-bow, containing a powder puff, Continental, 19th c., 1¾" h..**9,775.00**

Porcelain, peachbloom glaze gilded w/the Imperial monogram of the Dowager Empress Marie Feodorovna, Imperial Porcelain Manufactory, St. Petersburg, Russia, late 19th c., 4" h. **1,955.00**

Nephrite & diamond miniature Easter egg pendant, the egg inlaid w/gold scrolls set w/diamonds, marked w/Cyrillic initials of Workmaster Michael Perchin, & 56 standard, Fabergé, St. Petersburg, Russia, ca. 1900, ⅝" l. **6,037.00**

Silver-gilt & enamel, enameled w/colorful foliage on a gilded stippled ground, opening to reveal an icon of the Guardian Angel,

Grachov Bros., St. Petersburg, Russia, ca. 1900, 3" h...................**3,335.00**

Tin Easter egg w/lithographed image of two children playing w/an egg, 2" l..**65.00**

ENAMELS

Oval Inscribed Enamel Box

Enamels have been used to decorate a variety of substances, particularly metals. The best-known small enameled wares, such as patch and other small boxes and napkin rings, are the Battersea Enamels made by the Battersea Enamel Works in the last half of the 18th century. However, the term is often loosely applied to other English enamels. Russian enamels, usually on a silver or gold base, are famous and expensive. Early 20th century French enamel on copper wares and those items produced in China at the turn of the century in imitation of the early Russian style are also drawing dealer and collector attention.

Bowl, low foot, rounded sides delicately painted & shaded in tones of mauve, ruby & blue w/four large open lotus blooms, on & encircled by fleshy green stems bearing leaves, multicolored vine tendrils & further smaller blooms of pale yellowish green & blue, all reserved on a rich yellow ground, above an overlapping lappet collar encircling the foot, the interior turquoise, the underside white w/a pair of confronted foliate dragons in rose framing a central *jing zhi* mark in blue Kangxi, China, 5" d. (hairline cracks, chips) **$10,350.00**

Bowl, silver-gilt & shaded enamel, the lobed body enameled on the interior w/colorful flower sprays against pink, red, set green, dark blue &

pale blue grounds, the exterior of the bowl also w/enameled reserves, the circular foot similarly enameled, w/cable border at rim & foot, Fyodor Rucker, Moscow, Russia, ca. 1900, 5" d. **7,475.00**

Bowl, *base taille* decoration on copper, Limoges-style florals in yellow & pink w/green leaves, highlighted w/gold-painted leaves on a tortoiseshell enamel ground, purple exterior, signed "C. Faure," France, ca. 1900, 6" d. **330.00**

Bowl, long narrow oval-form, the long sides designed w/pairs of fan devices flanking a large upright oval panel decorated w/courting peasant couples in rustic settings, similar designs at the ends, raised on a base ring on four double-scroll legs, dark blue & gilt fans & pastel scenes, Vienna, Austria, ca. 1880, 7½" l. **1,725.00**

Box, cov., miniature, Battersea-type, deep pink w/scene on cover outlined w/tiny white dots & reading "Esteem The Giver," mirror in cover, ¾ x 1 x 1½" **275.00**

Box w/hinged cov., oval, bearing inscription "May no laws invade - Our American Trade," enclosing a mirror & opening to a conforming oval compartment w/cobalt blue enamel exterior & white enamel interior, Staffordshire, late 18th - early 19th c., hinge broken, 1¼ x 1½", 1" h. (ILLUS.) **1,540.00**

Box, cov., square silver-gilt form decorated on the cover w/colored rings & stylized foliage between geometric borders, further florals & scrolls around the sides, handles at the sides in the form of blue & white roosters, raised on four silver-gilt claw-and-ball feet, Ovchinnikov, Moscow, Russia, 1880, 2½" w. **1,495.00**

Box, cov., heart-shaped, depicting a three-masted ship w/floral border & lettered "Success to the Fleet," England, 19th c., 2¾" h. **522.50**

Box, cov., trunk-form, the curved top enameled *en plein* w/flowers within a border of blue beads, the sides enameled w/colorful stylized foliage, each end w/a carrying handle, Maria Semyonova, Moscow, Russia, ca. 1900, 2¾" l. **3,220.00**

Candlesticks, Battersea-type, h.p. floral decoration, England, 18th c., 9⅝" h., pr. (restoration) **412.50**

Charger, Limoges-style, decorated w/a colorful scene of the 'Rape of the Sabines,' 19th c., 16" d. **1,380.00**

Coffee set, miniature: cov. coffeepot, open sugar bowl, creamer, three cups & saucers, three spoons & an oval tray; footed bulbous shapes, each w/a gilt-decorated red ground decorated w/colored figural landscape scenes, France, 19th c., tray 4" l., coffeepot 2" h., the set......**862.50**

Creamer & sugar bowl, silver-gilt & shaded enamel, jug-shaped creamer & rounded sugar bowl w/swing handle enameled w/colorful stylized foliage on a gilded stippled ground between borders of blue beads, Moscow, Russia, ca. 1900, creamer 3⅛" h., pr. **805.00**

Kovsh **(boat-shaped cup),** silver-gilt deep oval bowl w/a fin-shaped prow at one end & an angled handle at the other, decorated overall w/colorful flowering scrolling foliage on grounds of cream & deep green, handle w/an aubergine reserve, The Sixth Artel, Moscow, Russia, ca. 1910, 6" l. **1,495.00**

Necessaire, tapered oval form, the yellow ground painted w/reserves depicting rustic scenes, gilt-metal mounts, the interior fitted w/various implements, South Staffordshire, ca. 1770, 3⅞" l. **1,840.00**

Plaque, rectangular, decorated w/a Biblical scene w/figures in a landscape, Limoges, France, 19th c., 5½ x 7" (chips) **489.00**

Plaque, rectangular, painted w/an allegorical scene, Vienna, Austria, late 19th c., 3 x 3½" **460.00**

Plaque, rectangular, painted w/a portrait of a woman, foil-backed decoration, Limoges, France, late 19th c., 5 x 7½" **805.00**

Snuff box, cov., realistically formed as a fan-shaped shell, delicately painted in pastel *famille rose* enamels following the flutes of the hinged lobed cover, w/a miniature crab & hermit crab above varying floral sprigs, the box underside painted in bands following the lines of the fluted shell, the interior cover w/a scene depicting a hermit crab, two mollusks & a conch shell on a sandy water bank, w/tall grasses & a blooming stem, Qianlong period, China, 3" l. (hairline cracks, minute chips) **4,600.00**

Stein, cov., silver gilt & enamel, tapering cylindrical form w/a domed lid, the body worked w/birds & animals surrounded by stylized foliate & floral designs, Russia, 8" h. (ILLUS. top next page).................**5,225.00**

Russian Silver & Gilt Enamel Stein

Steins, cov., miniature, slightly
tapering cylindrical body w/flared
silver foot w/embossed knobs, the
domed silver cover w/matching
design & figural finial & an S-Scroll
silver handle, the body decorated
w/an enameled classical figure
landscape scene, France, 19th c.,
4½" h., pr. **1,265.00**

Sugar basket, round silver-gilt sides
on a base ring, decorated w/colorful
stylized foliage on a gilded stippled
ground, w/geometric borders, silver-
gilt silver handle, Ovchinnikov,
Moscow, Russia, 1889, 4¼" d. **1,610.00**

Vase, silver-gilt & shaded enamel,
two-handled, bulbous, enameled
w/flowers & foliage on a cream, blue
& purple ground, each handle set
w/a cabochon amethyst,
Ovchinnikov, Moscow, Russia,
ca. 1900, 4½" h. **3,450.00**

Vase, enamel-on-copper, a wide
squatty bulbous form tapering
slightly to a small top opening,
raised on a metal footring, enameled
w/large stylized flowerheads in
raised frosty white w/deep cobalt
blue centers against a leaf-
decorated ground in crimson & pink,
signed in black enamel "C. Fauré -
Limoges," France, ca. 1920s,
4⅞" h. **2,875.00**

Vase, baluster-form, copper ground,
decorated w/four dancing children
in polychrome on dark blue
background, brass trim, artist-
signed, Limoges, France, 8⅛" h. **522.50**

Vase, waisted splayed foot, barrel-
shaped body w/angled shoulders &
tall neck w/scroll-form handles,
finely decorated on each side w/a

shaped panel enclosing a playful
dog & a European gentleman in a
bucolic watery landscape, grasping
a tricorn hat in one hand & a cane in
the other, all reserved on a pale sky-
blue ground finely stippled &
decorated w/a continuously scrolling
vine tendril bearing numerous
colorful blooms, between narrow
rope-twist bands, the shoulders &
neck w/matching decoration, the
underside w/Qianlong seal mark,
Canton, China, Qianlong period,
8⅞" h. (small chips, restored
chips) **8,625.00**

Vase, enamel on copper, bulbous
ovoid body tapering to a small flat
mouth, incised & enameled w/a
stylized geometric design of
overlapping pointed waves in
shades of maroon, orange, yellow &
gold, signed in enamel "C. Fauré -
Limoges - France," ca. 1925,
9¼" h. **2,645.00**

EPERGNES

Blue Overlay Epergne

Blue overlay glass, single lily,
trumpet-form lily w/blue ruffled rim &
interior of lower wide blue ruffled
bowl decorated w/green & maroon
flowers & lacy foliage, white
underside, 10½" d., 16" h.
(ILLUS.) **$425.00**

Cranberry glass, single lily, ruffled
top lily w/fancy crystal applied spiral
trim w/brass connector to ruffled
bowl base, 7½" d., 12" h.
(ILLUS. top next page)....................**195.00**

Cranberry glass, two-lily, embossed
swirling ribbed design w/scalloped
rim lily, similar large bowl,
15½" h...**910.00**

Pink-rimmed clear & frosted glass,

Cranberry Glass Epergne

single-lily in footed bowl, cut &
wheel-cut decoration, attributed to
the Boston & Sandwich Glass Co.,
19th c., 17¼" h. **747.50**

Opalescent Glass Epergne

**Opalescent glass w/rich purple
trim,** single lily, ruffled vase lifts out
of ruffled lower bowl, nickel plated
foot & vase holder, 10½" d.,
14½" h. (ILLUS.) **265.00**

Sterling Silver Epergne

Sterling silver epergne, four basket,
central lily on scroll-cut rim sitting on
domed scroll-cut base w/four floral-
stem C-scrolled arms suspending
four scroll-cut footed baskets,
monogrammed & dated, Roger
Williams, ca. 1900, 14½" h.
(ILLUS. bottom previous
column) **5,175.00**

FABERGÉ

Gold & Enamel Compact

*Carl Fabergé (1846-1920) was gold-
smith and jeweler to the Russian Imperial
Court and his creations are recognized as
the finest of their kind. He made a number
of enamel fantasies, including Easter eggs,
for the Imperial family and utilized
precious metals and jewels in other work.*

Bell push, silver & hardstone,
cylindrical, the hardstone drum
applied w/a silver frieze of swans
w/outstretched wings, raised on three
bun feet, Cyrillic initials of Workmaster Anders Nevalainen & 88
standard, St. Petersburg,
ca. 1900, 1¾" d. **$4,313.00**
Brooch, gold & jewels, in the form of a
folded bow, one half reeded & set
w/a cabochon sapphire, the other
part set w/diamonds, marked w/the
initials of Workmaster Wilhelm
Reimer & 56 standard, St.
Petersburg, ca. 1900, 1⅛" w.........**2,070.00**
Card case, lady's, gold-mounted
carved nephrite, of upright
rectangular form, the gold mount at
the hinged opening enameled white
& translucent red, the hinges & clasp
set w/diamonds, marked w/initials of
Workmaster August Hollming,
"Fabergé" in Cyrillic & 56 standard
(14k), St. Petersburg, ca. 1900,
3½" h. **5,175.00**
Compact, gold & enamel, square
w/translucent enamel pale blue over
a *guilloché* ground, the cover chased

w/patera set w/a moon-stone cabochon, the borders chased w/leaf-tips, the compart-mented interior fitted w/a powder puff & two other implements, marked "K. Fabergé" in Cyrillic w/Imperial warrant & 56 standard, Moscow, ca. 1900, 1⅞" w. (ILLUS.) **9,200.00**

Fabergé Silver-gilt & Enamel Compact

Compact, silver-gilt & enamel, rectangular, enameled translucent blue over a *guilloché* ground, the cover w/three compartments & three hinged covers, the central compartment mirrored, w/diamond-set thumbpieces, marked w/Cyrillic initials of Andrei Gorianov & 88 standard, St. Petersburg, ca. 1910, 3⅞" l. (ILLUS.) **4,600.00**

Cuff links, gold, enamel & jewels, a white-enameled oval ring set w/four small rubies surrounded a large oval faceted aquamarine, suspended on rings from a white-enameled bar, Cyrillic initials of Workmaster Andrei Gorianov, St. Petersburg, ca. 1900, ¾" l., pr...**4,312.00**

Cuff links, gold, nephrite & enamel, the nephrite discs applied w/the cross of St. George in white enamel centered by a red stone cabochon, marked w/initials of workmaster Wilhelm Reimer & 56 standard, St. Petersburg, ca. 1890, ⅞" d., pr..**5,520.00**

Decanter w/silver stopper, clear glass w/silver neck, ovoid glass body w/heavy pebbled design, fitted w/a cylindrical silver neck w/flaring rim & an embossed design of water flowers, bulbous silver stopper w/swirls, marked "K. Fabergé" in Cyrillic, w/Imperial warrant & 84 standard, ca. 1900, 9⅜" h.............**2,875.00**

Fruit knives & forks, silver-gilt & mother-of-pearl, plain mother-of-pearl handles w/rounded ends, silver-gilt three-tined forks & knife blades w/curved ends, marked w/Cyrillic initials of workmaster Julius Rappoport, "Fabergé" in Cyrillic w/Imperial warrant & 88 standard, Moscow, ca. 1900, set of 6 ....**1,150.00**

Match case, silver-gilt & translucent enamel, rectangular form enameled translucent blue over a *guilloché* ground, w/diamond-set thumbpiece, marked w/initials of workmaster Henrik Wigstrom, "Fabergé" in Cyrillic & 88 standard, also w/London import marks for 1910, St. Petersburg, ca. 1910, 1¾" l. **6,900.00**

Model of an elephant, carved bowenite, the animal in standing position w/curled under trunk, red stone eyes, St. Petersburg, ca. 1900, 1½" l. **4,025.00**

Model of a samovar, miniature, gold, of fluted vase shape w/reeded scroll handles, the square base supported on four bun feet, marked w/the Cyrillic initials of Workmaster Michael Perchin, also "Fabergé" in Cyrillic & the 56 standard (14k), St. Peters-burg, ca. 1890, 3½" h.................**17,825.00**

Photograph frame, silver & enamel, the round frame enameled translucent pale blue over a *guilloché* ground, the border chased w/acanthus leaves, surmounted by a ribbon-bow, Cyrillic initials of Workmaster Johan Victor Aarne, "Fabergé" in Cyrillic & 88 standard, St. Petersburg, ca. 1900, 3¾" d...**11,500.00**

Pin, gold & enamel, navette shape enameled translucent pale blue over a *guilloché* ground & applied w/the Imperial Eagle set w/a diamond, marked w/initials of Workmaster August Hollming & 56 standard, St. Petersburg, ca. 1913, 1¼" l. **3,163.00**

Pocket knife & cigar cutter, the handle of each enameled white & chases w/foliage & scrolls, both w/diamond borders & w/cabochon rubies, marked w/Cyrillic initials of Workmaster Johan Victor Aarne & 56 standard, St. Petersburg, ca. 1900, 2¾" & 2¼" l., 2 pcs......................**4,025.00**

Scent flask, rock crystal, gold & enamel, slightly bulbous swirled base, paneled neck w/gold mount chased leafage at neck, the domed cover enameled translucent royal blue over a *guilloché* ground, moonstone thumbpiece, marked w/initials of Workmaster Henrik Wigstrom, 72 standard & w/incised signature of Fabergé in Cyrillic, St. Petersburg, ca. 1910, 2¼" h...**4,888.00**

Thermometer, silver & marble, the red marble base applied w/swags of leafage, the borders chased w/leaves of ribbon-tied acanthus leaves, raised

on four bun feet, w/pine cone finial,
Cyrillic initials for the First Artel, "K.
Fabergé" in Cyrillic w/Imperial
warrant & 91 standard, Moscow,
ca. 1900, 8¼" h. **12,650.00**
Watch & pin, gold & jewels, the pin
set w/a blue-grey chalcedony
cabochon bordered by diamonds &
surmounted by a diamond-set ribbon-
bow, the matching watch similarly
mounted w/a chalcedony cabochon
bordered by a diamond-set wreath,
marked w/initials of Workmaster
August Holmstrom & 56 standard,
the watch Swiss, St. Petersburg,
ca. 1900, contained in original
fitted holly wood case, 2¾" l. **20,700.00**

FANS

Advertising, printed cardboard,
beautiful color image of 1920s
"flapper" in bathing suit **$65.00**
Decorated & painted paper, the
paper-covered blades h.p. in water-
colors w/harbor scenes of Canton,
China w/the Hongs, intricate &
delicate pierce carving at base of
the blades, China, 19th c., opens to
17" w. (paper & blade damage &
some tape stains on the
paper) **1,320.00**
Gold frame w/burgundy velvet, h.p.
florals in gouache, cream silk leaf
w/h.p. pastoral scene of French
women & highly hand-decorated
w/sequins & netting, tortoiseshell
sticks & guards, ca. 1850 (minor
repair to one guard) **100.00**
Ivory, ornate pierced carving on the
blades forming a scene of a girl
feeding doves, tied w/ivory satin
ribbon **145.00**
Ostrich feather, dark blue **55.00**
Wood & voile, 29 tiny wood sticks
support an 8½" l. oval voile panel
h.p. w/a detailed landscape scene
w/Colonial figures, trimmed
w/flowers & violins **60.00**

FARM COLLECTIBLES

Branding iron, wrought iron,
w/branding letters "AH" **$70.00**
Flax hatchels, fine nails mounted on
tin 3 x 7" block & 4 x 18" wooden
board, pr. **70.00**
Implement seat, cast iron, half-round,

pierced stars & "Stoddard,"
5 x 13½ x 16" **200.00**
Ox yoke, single-calf training-type,
pine w/hickory bow, painted red,
early 19th c., 16 x 17½", 4" thick......**140.00**
Rope making machine, cast iron,
mechanical, crank-operated, marked
"The Wonder Rope Maker,"
12" h..**350.00**
Sod plow, all-oak frame, one-horse,
two-shank model.............................**195.00**
Windmill weight, cast iron, model of
a short-tailed horse, Dempster
No. 4 ....**225.00**

FIREARMS

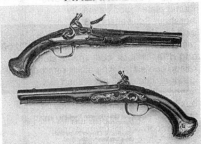

18th Century French Pistols

Carbine rifle, Gwyn & Campbell,
percussion-type, .52 caliber, walnut
stock w/inspector's mark, blue barrel
& traces of case coloring on
hammer & frame, serial No. 3891
(few small spots of pitting) **$1,320.00**
Carbine rifle, Joslyn Model 1862, butt
stock carved "L.M.," lock & breech
block w/bold stamped signature,
brass hardware & faint inspector's
marks, serial No. 1672.................**1,265.00**
Carbine rifle, Maynard second
model, .50 caliber percussion-type,
dated "1865" on trigger plate, very
good condition w/bold inspector's
marks, serial No. 25199...............**1,100.00**
Carbine rifle, Palmer bolt action-type,
.50 caliber, lock stamped "U.S." &
"E. G. Lamson & Co., Windsor, VT.,"
inspector's stamp on stock (few
small areas of light pitting) **1,595.00**
Carbine rifle, Sharps New Model
1859, .52 caliber, walnut stock, iron
hardware w/patchbox, round barrel,
serial No. 65731, barrel 22" l. (stock
w/age cracks & wear at toe) **1,375.00**
Carbine rifle, Sharps & Hankins 1862
model, .52 caliber Navy-type
w/leather-covered barrel, brass butt
plate, serial No. 10779 (leather
worn but complete) **1,100.00**

Carbine rifle, Spencer, .52 caliber, walnut stock w/good inspector's marks & faint carving "C. Scott" in several places, serial No. 39778, barrel w/light brown finish, barrel 22" l. (two minor hairlines in forearm where it meets the frame) **1,485.00**

Carbine rifle, Starr, percussion-type, .54 caliber, walnut stock w/good dark patina, lock & tang w/stamped signature, serial No. 12337, barrel 21" l. (nailed split at toe, small chip behind the breech plug w/putty)....**1,045.00**

Long rifle, flintlock, .45 cal., relief-carved curly maple stock, engraved New York City patchbox w/drooping feather design & three piercings, ten silver inlays including a man in the moon over the check piece & oval thumb plate, good patina, by Abraham Schweitzer, 43" l. octagonal barrel, 49" l. (some edge restoration, lock restored) **9,625.00**

Long rifle, flintlock, curly maple stock, raised carved molding along ramrod channel, fine scroll decoration along bottom of stock butt, brass patch box w/simple engraving & daisy finial, two silver inlays including man in the moon & oval thumbpiece, signed "Samuel Galbreath," Allegheny County, Pennsylvania (pinned repair in wrist & other small repairs)........................**3,300.00**

Long rifle, percussion-type, maple stock w/some figure, brass patch box & silver inlays finely engraved w/an eagle, barrel & lock signed "A. Kopp," Blair County, Pennsylvania (old plate repairs, small inlay missing, minor age cracks) **2,090.00**

Pistol, flintlock, walnut stock fitted w/brass hardware & "115" trigger guard, lock engraved "H. Nock," England, round barrel tapered & flared, barrel 9" l. (light pitting in barrel, crack in tang, age cracks).....**605.00**

Pistol, I.N. Johnson "1853," percussion-type, .54 caliber, walnut stock stamped "Ohio" on left side of grip strap & shows inspector's markings, brass hardware, lock w/good signature & "U.S.," 14" l.......**605.00**

Pistol, Kentucky flintlock, approximately .50 cal., refinished curly maple stock w/brass hardware, lock stamped "Rogers, Slocomb & Co., New Orleans," octagonal barrel, barrel 5¼" l., overall 9½" l. (old pieced repair at lock mortise, short age crack at fore end & lock bolt area) **1,375.00**

Pistol, Watters Model 1836, flintlock,

.54 caliber, lock stamped "1837" w/signature & eagle head, bright finish on steel hardware, very good condition, 14" l. **880.00**

Pistols, flintlock, French officer's, silver-mounted walnut, each w/gilt-decorated barrel & walnut stock w/a relief panoply of arms on the butt, relief-carved behind the tang & entry pipe, signed "M. Morizeau AParis Rue Des Sts. Peres," Paris, France, third quarter 18th c., original condition, 14½" l. pr. (ILLUS.) **20,700.00**

Pistols, flintlock, swamped octagonal barrel & steel hardware w/ornate engraving, walnut stock w/checkered grip & raised carving, locks signed "Chaillot, Dyon," probably France, pair in fitted mahogany case w/metal powder flask, cleaning rod, cap box & mold, the set...............................**1,430.00**

Revolver, Colt 1849 Pocket Model, .31 caliber, percussion action, cylinder shows faint engraved scene, brass trigger guard w/traces of silver plate, in original mahogany case w/an early metal powder flask, Colt mold & tin of caps, barrel 5" l. (crack in case lid) **1,210.00**

Revolver, Colt Model 1878 "Frontier" double action, .44 caliber, faint etching on barrel "Colt Frontier six shooter," areas of original blued finish, hard rubber grips, serial No. 13861, barrel 7½" l **632.50**

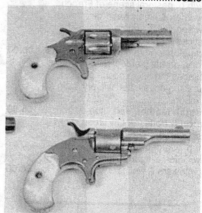

Colt Revolvers

Revolver, Colt New Line Model, .22 caliber, white pearl grips, serial No. 18061, ca. 1875 (ILLUS. top)...........**247.50**

Revolver, Colt "Open Top" model, rim-fire, .22 caliber, white pearl grips, possibly renickled at the factory, serial No. 32057, frame

serial No. 32157, ca. 1875
(ILLUS. bottom) **220.00**
Rifle, Bedford City percussion-type,
maple stock w/bold stripes, brass
hardware w/engraved four-piece
patch box & five piercings, lock &
barrel signed "J.S." for Jacob
Stoudenour, octagonal barrel 43" l.
(some repairs at fore end) **1,705.00**
Rifle, early flintlock fowling-type, curly
maple stock w/good patina,
engraved brass butt plate, thumb
guard & side plate, Ketland-marked
lock, tapering round barrel marked
"London," 60" l. (age crack at toe,
old square nail repair) **1,980.00**
Rifle, flintlock, figured maple stock
w/old varnished finish, engraved &
pierced patch box w/a peacock &
"C. Wever," engraved palm plate
dated "1834" w/an eagle & toe plate
extending up to trigger guard
w/scroll engraving, Lehigh Valley
origin, 41½" l., smooth barrel (minor
age cracks at toe, short hairline
ahead of lock) **6,160.00**
Rifle, Kentucky full-stock, curly maple
stock, percussion lock stamped
"R.W. Booth, Cincinnati," Ohio,
early 19th c., barrel 36" l.,
overall 52" l. **687.50**
Rifle, Kentucky w/relief-carved curly
maple stock, scrolled leaf carving
around cheek piece & above brass
patch box, brass hardware
w/engraving w/scrolls & fans on
patch box, signed "G. Kettering,"
Westmoreland County,
Pennsylvania (some pieced
restoration & lock repairs) **6,380.00**
Rifle, Pennsylvania full-stock, .40 cal.
percussion-type, curly maple stock
w/nineteen engraved silver inlays
including an eagle over the
beavertail cheek piece, brass patch
box w/fine engraving & eleven
piercings, octagonal barrel, stock
signed "J.D. McKahan," Washington
City, Pennsylvania, barrel 41½" l.
(old crack in wrist) **3,410.00**
Rifle w/bayonet, flintlock, Hall Model
1819, walnut stock w/old dark finish,
original brown lacquer finish on all
metal except bayonet, second
production w/boldly stamped
signature & date "1837," breech
block shows signs of case coloring,
probably unfired (few dents in
stock) **2,640.00**
Rifle w/bayonet, Springfield 1863,
type I, .58 caliber, walnut stock
w/inspector's marks, bright finish on
metal, blued rear sight (steel

w/traces of old packing
grease)..**1,925.00**
Shotgun, 18 ga. double-barrel
percussion-type, quality walnut
stock, damascus barrels & steel
hardware w/ornate engraving,
signed "Mortimer," in brass-bound
mahogany case w/original paper
label & fold-away lid handle,
complete w/12 accessories..............**770.00**

Parker 20 Ga. Shotgun

Shotgun, Parker 20 ga., DHE grade,
walnut stock, engraved
hardware (ILLUS.) **8,800.00**

FIRE FIGHTING COLLECTIBLES

Miniature Fire Bucket & Helmet

Badge, fireman's, Reading,
Pennsylvania, hand-chased nickel-
plated brass, depicts a steamer, hat,
hose, etc., 1870 ....**$225.00**
Bucket, miniature, painted leather,
cylindrical form painted red w/scroll-
enclosed cartouche depicting a
burning building over the inscription
"Charles W. Elliot," America, 19th c.,
8½" h. (ILLUS. right) **747.00**
Bucket, painted leather, slightly
swelled cylindrical form w/swing bail
handle, old worn green repaint
w/sunburst design & "A. Fish No.-,"
12½" h. (old repair on handle) **385.00**
Buckets, leather, Charlestown,
Massachusetts, swelled cylindrical
form w/swing handle, a painted
eagle w/its wings spread above

Pair of Charlestown Fire Buckets

banner reading "JEFFERSON FIRE SOCIETY - S. SWEETSER - 1807," w/original stenciled carrying bag, pr. (ILLUS.) **9,000.00**

Pair of New England Fire Buckets

Buckets, painted leather, tapering cylindrical form w/stitched rim & base, the fronts painted w/small eagle perched on an urn surrounded by a ribbon inscribed "S. Frothingham Ex. Flammis Resurgo 1794," all over a pale olive green ground, each w/a leather covered rope swing handle, probably New England, 1794, 11¼" h., pr. (ILLUS.) **1,840.00**

Fire extinguisher, brass & copper, "The Captain," w/fire captain shown wearing old fire hat & rubber hose, brass nozzle...................................**150.00**

Fire extinguisher, clear glass, "W.D. Allen Manufacturing Company, Chicago, Illinois," melon-ribbed body tapering to a cylindrical neck w/ringed rim, ca. 1885-90, qt., 8¼" h. (stress crack on one section of the base)....................................**154.00**

Fire extinguisher, electric blue glass, "Hayward's Hand Fire Grenade - Patented Aug. 8, 1871 - S.F. Hayward, 407 Broadway, N. Y.," squared body w/domed shoulder & slender neck w/tooled shoulder & slender neck w/tooled lip & original embossed foil neck seal & contents, ca. 1871-80, pt., 6¼" h....................**165.00**

Fire extinguisher, golden yellowish amber glass, "Pat Nov 28, 1884," squared body w/domed shoulder & cylindrical neck w/ringed rim, Canadian, ca. 1884-90, pt., 6⅛" h...**522.50**

Fire extinguisher, sapphire blue glass, "Star (inside star) Harden Hand Grenade - Fire Extinguisher," globular w/wide ring at midsection & vertical ribbing, smooth base, long cylindrical neck w/ringed rim, ca. 1875-85, pt., 6⅜" h.....................**88.00**

Fire Extinguisher, long slender metal cylinder, "Phoenix Fire Extinguishing Compound," painted label in red, black & gold, 22" l. (scratches, paint chips)..**55.00**

Fireman's belt, leather, black w/red & white trim, inscribed "31" & "South Penn," 47" l. (very worn).................**110.00**

Fireman's belt, leather, white & red, inscribed "Hercules," 19th c. **90.00**

Helmet, miniature, leather, inscribed "RESCUE" above the numeral one w/crossed hook & ladder within a shield, inscribed "FD" below, mounted on black metal stand, New York, ca. 1850, 4" h. (ILLUS. left)..................................**3,162.00**

FIREPLACE & HEARTH ITEMS

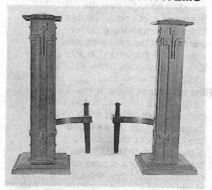

Prairie School Andirons

Andirons, brass, Chippendale, an urn-form finial decorated w/swags, the conforming shaped log guard behind on spurred arched supports ending in claw-and-ball feet, ca. 1785, 18¾" l., 24" h., pr. $3,220.00

Andirons, brass, Federal style, a heavy ring-turned tapering front post supporting a large ball finial, connected by a heavy angled bar to a shorter matching post fronting the iron log bar, singed "Hunneman Boston," ca. 1825, 11" h., pr. **690.00**

Andirons, brass, Federal style, the ball-and-ring shaped finial above a reeded sphere over a tapering & flaring cylindrical support above a rectangular molded plinth chased & engraved w/urns, swags & rosettes, over a shaped base on arched spurred legs w/ball feet, attributed to William or Richard Wittingham, New York, ca. 1791-1821, 19½" h., pr..**9,200.00**

Andirons, brass, Federal style, a faceted pointed spire & ring-turned ball capital above a ring-turned & faceted cylindrical support over a circular plinth on spurred arched legs w/ball feet, stamped "Bailey," New York, New York, early 19th c., 26¼" h., pr. **4,025.00**

Andirons, brass, Prairie School style, each heavy four-sided shaft mounted w/a long strap w/a three-branch top, on a square base & w/an overhanging top, the strap design affixed w/brass screws, original patina, unmarked, early 20th c., 7¼" w., 19½" h., pr. (ILLUS.) **1,760.00**

Fiddle-Head Andirons

Andirons, cast iron, cast in the half-round in the form of a large tightly curled fiddle-head curving down to widely flaring legs, Bradley & Hubbard Mfg. Co., Meriden, Connecticut, late 19th c., 12" h., pr. (ILLUS.) **575.00**

Andirons, cast iron, modeled in the half-round in the form of an owl on a tree branch base, inset glass eyes,

American-made, 20th c., 15" h., pr. **1,869.00**

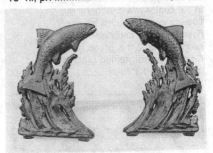

Leaping Trout Andirons

Andirons, cast iron, cast in the half-round as a leaping trout above curled tall water plants, early 20th c., facing pr. (ILLUS.)...........................**600.00**

Andirons, cast iron, cast in the half-round as marching Hessian soldiers, their costumes painted red, white & blue w/black hats & boots, American-made, late 19th c., 19" h., pr..**230.00**

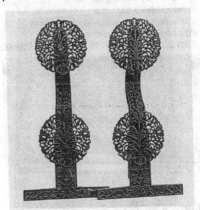

Aesthetic Movement Andirons

Andirons, cast iron, Aesthetic Movement style, a large curving upright decorated w/delicate cast scrolls & mounted w/two large round scroll-pierced medallions, scroll-cast cross-bar base, unmarked, late 19th c., 11¾" w., 23" h., pr. (ILLUS.) **660.00**

Fireboard, painted wood, rectangular, decorated in the *trompe l'oeil* technique with a small vase holding long leafy flowering branches & set within a recessed fireplace opening surrounded by a band of tiles, each painted w/a leafy tree, in shades of sepia, brown & black, New England, early 19th c., 34 x 50" **20,700.00**

Fireplace fans, hand-held, painted &

decorated wood, rectangular form w/ornately scroll-cut edges, painted in the center w/a cartouche of flowers w/ornate scroll border & flower clusters in upper corners, painted in cream & green on a black & brown wood-grained ground, mid-19th c., 13" l., pr. **632.00**

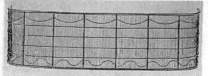

Brass Fireplace Fender

Fireplace fender, brass & iron wire, of bracket form w/a brass railing above an iron wire screen decorated at the top w/a repeating swag & at the bottom w/a serpentine scroll, early 19th c., 46" l., 12¼" h. (ILLUS.) **1,955.00**

Fireplace fender, brass & iron, the low bracket-form w/a brass railing centering three ring-turned & faceted finials above an interlocking iron wire screen, all on a conforming iron base, American-made, early 19th c., 18 x 51", 13" h.................**1,035.00**

Federal Fireplace Set

Fireplace set, brass, Federal style, andirons w/bulbous knob finial above an ornate ring-turned standard, on arched spurred legs w/ball feet, w/matching tongs & shovel, New York, ca. 1825, andirons 15" h., the set (ILLUS.) **322.00**

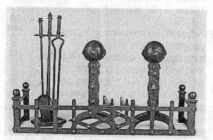

Arts & Crafts Fireplace Set

Fireplace set, wrought iron, Arts & Crafts style, the andirons w/large rough knob finials above heavy square standards mounted w/knobs & a diamond above arched legs, picket fence-form fender w/knob finials at the corner posts & a diamond device at the front center, w/a four-piece matching tool set, unmarked Bradley & Hubbard, early 20th c., andirons 24" h., the set (ILLUS.) **1,320.00**

Fire screen, brass, fan-style, composed of nine long rounded pierced blades opening to form a half-round fan, central arched pierced & scroll-decorated frame on a rectangular foot, early 20th c., 26" h..**302.50**

Fire screen, brass & wire, Louis XV-style, a large oval cartouche brass frame composed of leafy scrolls & w/a scroll loop handle at the top, resting on tall scroll legs & enclosing a fine wire mesh centered by a ribbon & leaf cluster, based on 18th c. French design, early 20th c., 31¾" h..**522.50**

Fire screen, mahogany, Federal pole-style, the shield-shaped framed panel enclosing a silk embroidery depicting a full standing female figure supported by an anchor w/trees & foliage in the background, the border decorated w/polychrome flowers tied w/bowknots, the whole sliding on a rod w/urn finial, the ring-turned standard below continuing to a tripod base w/downcurving scrolled legs, New England, ca. 1800, 17⅛" w., 5' 4½" h. (repairs to two legs) **1,265.00**

Classical Fire Screen

Fire screen, mahogany, Classical style, the rectangular screen w/sliding extendible panel centering

a pair of uprights on molded
downcurving legs ending in brass
toe-caps on brass casters, ca. 1830,
minor repairs, 22½" w., 41" h.
(ILLUS.) **575.00**

FISHER (Harrison) GIRLS

The Fisher Girl, that chic American girl whose face and figure illustrated numerous magazine covers and books at the turn of the century, was created by Harrison Fisher. A professional artist who had studied in England and was trained by his artist father, he was able to capture an element of refined, cultured elegance in his drawings of beautiful women. They epitomized all that every American girl longed to be and catapulted their creator into the ranks of success. Harrison Fisher, who was born in 1877, worked as a commercial artist full time until his death in 1934. Today collectors seek out magazine covers, prints, books and postcards illustrated with Fisher Girls.

Book, "A Checked Love Affair," 1903,
    illustrated by Harrison Fisher, first
    edition **$75.00**
Book, "A Dream of Fair Women," 20
    full pages of color illustrations of
    lovely women by Harrison Fisher,
    New York, 1908 ....**182.50**
Book, "A Six-Cylinder Courtship," by
    Edward Salisbury Field, 1907,
    illustrated by Harrison Fisher **40.00**
Book, "A Song of Hiawatha," by
    Henry Wadsworth Longfellow, 1906,
    illustrated by Harrison Fisher,
    Bobbs-Merrill Co. **75.00**
Book, "Bachelor Belles," 1908,
    illustrated by Harrison Fisher, 21
    illustrations, published by Grosset &
    Dunlap **195.00**
Book, "The Day of the Dog,"
    illustrated by Harrison Fisher,
    1904..**31.50**
Book, "Fair Americans," 1911, 23
    color illustrations by Harrison Fisher,
    first edition **155.00**
Book, "Love Finds the Way," by Paul
    Leicester Ford, 1904, first book
    illustrated by Harrison Fisher, fine
    condition **75.00**
Print, "Stages of a Girl's Life,"
    w/original frame **79.00**

FISHING COLLECTIBLES

BOOKS & PAPER ITEMS

Book, "Atlantic Salmon Fishing," by
    C. Phair, 1937................................**$550.00**
Book, "Lake & Stream Fishing," 1917,
    first edition **22.00**
Book, "The Salmon Fishing Fly," by
    G. M. Kelson, 1895 ....**990.00**
Catalog, "Abercrombie & Fitch,"
    1910..**130.00**
Catalog, "Edw. Vom Hofe," 1938.......**275.00**
Catalog, "South Bend," 1937 ....**38.00**
Catalog, "William Mills," 1932, tackle...**42.00**

LURES

Haskell Hollow Brass Minnow Lure

Charmer Minnow Co. "Charmer,"
    wooden w/nose-mounted propeller
    w/tail propeller mounted to a rotating
    rear section of the body painted
    w/corkscrew stripe, patented
    1910..**360.00**
Creek Chub Bait Co. "The Beetle,"
    wooden, catalog series No. 3800,
    2½" l., set of 10 ....**715.00**
**Creek Chub Bait Co. "Fin Tail
    Shiner,"** wooden, catalog series
    No. 2100, 4" l. **385.00**
Creek Chub Bait Co. "Jigger,"
    wooden, 1933, in original box **495.00**
Creek Chub Bait Co.
    "No-Weed-O" **990.00**
Creek Chub Bait Co. "Weed Bugs,"
    wooden, catalog series No. 2800,
    2" l., pr...**690.00**
Creek Chub Bait Co. "Wee Dee,"
    wooden, catalog series No. 4800,
    2½" l., set of 3 ....**690.00**
Haskell Hollow, minnow, brass,
    ca. 1859 (ILLUS.).......................**7,480.00**
Heddon "Dummy Double,"
    w/"football" style side hook, No.
    1500 series **880.00**
Heddon "Dummy Double," L-rig
    hanger, No. 1500 series **360.00**
Heddon "Punkinseed," wooden, 2"
    size **660.00**
Heddon "Walton Feather Tail,"
    No. 40 series................................**330.00**
Immell Bait Co. "Chippewa,"
    wooden, patented 1910 ....**300.00**
Oliver & Gruber "Glowurms,"
    wooden, painted, double-jointed
    w/three body sections w/metal plate
    protruding slightly below head,
    forming a diving lip, original wooden
    box, pr...**550.00**

**Pepper (Joseph E.) "Roman
Spider,"** wooden, painted eyes.......**385.00**
Pflueger "Kent Frog," wooden.........**220.00**
Pflueger "Neverfail," wooden,
catalog series No. 3100...................**215.00**
Pflueger "Pal-O-Mine," wooden,
catalog series 5000.........................**145.00**
Real Lure No. 9202, Springfield,
MO...**75.00**
"Sam-bo," plastic, black man in a
barrel, w/original box, 3½" l..............**135.50**
Shakespeare "Revolution Bait,"
acorn-type body, aluminum **195.00**
Shakespeare "Revolution Bait,"
round end body style, aluminum **220.00**
**South Bend Bait Co. "Truck-
Oreno,"** No. 936 series, 9" l. **910.00**
Wilson "Winged Wobbler," wooden
w/metal wing, two belly trebles &
trailing treble hook, patented 1914,
original box **440.00**

REELS

Fowler Hard Rubber Fly Reel

Bodan (Stan), "Baby" trout reel **1,210.00**
Conroy & Bissett trout reel, ca.
1882..**385.00**
Conroy, Bissett & Malleson trout
reel, ca. 1878 ....**440.00**
Cox Coronet No. 25N.........................**90.00**
Fin-Nor No. 1 trout reel.....................**400.00**
Flegel "Spooler," bait casting reel,
1912..**330.00**
Follett trout reel, ca. 1885.................**800.00**
Fowler GEM fly reel, hard
rubber, ca. 1872 (ILLUS.) **4,400.00**
Hardy Bros. "Perfect," 3⅛" **250.00**
Hardy Bros. "Perfect," 3⅜" **250.00**
Hardy Bros. "Saint George Junior,"
1928-64...**525.00**
Horton Mfg. Co., "Meek No. 55," in
original box **300.00**
Humphreys Model 3-A, boxed............**35.00**
Meek & Sons (B.F.) "No. 3 Free
Spool Tournament," Horton Mfg.
Co. **385.00**
Meek & Sons (B.F.) "No. 5
Bluegrass," Horton Mfg. Co. **540.00**

Meek & Sons (B.F.) "No. 7," Horton
Mfg. Co. **450.00**
Meek & Sons (B.F.) "No. 8,"
Frankfort, Kentucky.......................**3,190.00**
Orvis trout reel, ca. 1874 ....**415.00**
Pflueger No. 1893, mint in box...........**48.00**
Red River No. 7345.............................**35.00**
South Bend No. 1131A........................**75.00**
"Spike reel," unsigned **495.00**
Thumezy (Benjamin) bait casting
reel...**440.00**
Edward Vom Hofe, "Griswold,"
salmon, 1926 ....**1,210.00**
Edward Vom Hofe, "Restigouche,"
salmon reel, 4/0 size......................**715.00**
Edward Vom Hofe trout reel, metal,
1/0 size "Perfection"....................**4,400.00**
Henry Walker, salmon reel,
1/0 size **880.00**

RODS

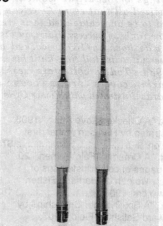

Pair of Sam Calson Trout Rods

C.W. Jenkins, bamboo, 8½' l............**495.00**
Sam Calson, trout rods, 6½' l., pr.
(ILLUS.) **13,750.00**
Hiram L. Leonard "Model 66,"
bamboo, 8' l. **770.00**
Orvis "Battenkill" fly rod, bamboo,
serial No. 70, 355, one tip, 3⅞ oz.,
HDG/6 line, original cloth rod sack &
metal rod tube, 7½' l. **650.00**
Charles F. Orvis "Flea," bamboo,
6½' l...**415.00**
Henry John Thomas "Dirigo,"
bamboo, 9' l. **440.00**

MISCELLANEOUS
Creel, "Hardy Perfect" **500.00**
Creel, leather-bound, by F. Mariner,
Seattle, Washington........................**855.00**
Flies, lake trout, by F. Stearns,
framed...**350.00**
Flies, salmon, by Frances Stearns,
framed (ILLUS. top next page) **500.00**

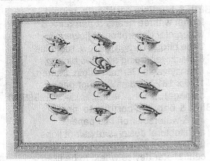

F. Sterns Salmon Flies

Flies, trout, by Dette, framed..............**715.00**
Minnow, articulated brass, once
  owned by Lord Carmichael,
  recovered from the wreck of the SS
  Medina...**715.00**
Painting, oil, of a hanging brook trout
  by B. Bishop, 1871...........................**880.00**
Painting, oil, of a salmon by W.M.
  Brackett, 1901..............................**2,420.00**

FLUE COVERS

*These decorative, round disks were used
to cover the stove pipe holes left in walls
when wood or coal-burning heating stoves
were taken down and stored during warm
weather months. Most were stamped tin or
heavy cardboard with stamped metal rims.*

Fruit, 7" d. **$30.00**
Girl, 7¾" d. **47.00**
Glass, figure of a young lady wearing
  a blue dress & holding a cat, circular
  metal frame....................................**80.00**
Gorgeous Moorish-dressed lady,
  ca. 1910...**75.00**
Men & boat scene, 6¼" d....................**35.00**
Oriental girl, 9½" d. **52.00**
Scene of two girls, 5¼" d....................**25.00**
Scene w/two girls, 9½" d. **60.00**

FOOT & BOOT SCRAPERS

Cast iron, foliate detail set within a
  rectangular pan, 11¾ x 14¾"...........**$22.00**
Cast iron, model of a full-bodied
  dachshund dog, black paint w/red
  trim, 20½" l.....................................**77.00**
Cast iron, a pair of griffins back to
  back w/joined wings & tails, on a
  white marble block base, overall
  18" h. (edge damage on base) **880.00**
Wrought iron, stylized model of a

dragon, arc-welded w/good detail,
old pitted surface, 12¾" l. **214.50**

FRAKTUR

Birth Announcement for Lidia Jegle

*Fraktur paintings are decorative birth
and marriage certificates of the 18th and
19th centuries and also include family
registers and similar documents.
Illuminated family documents, birth and
baptismal certificates, religious texts and
rewards of merit, in a particular style, are
known as "fraktur" because of the
similarity to the 16th century type-face of
that name. Gay water-color borders,
frequently incorporating stylized birds,
angels, animals or flowers, surrounded the
hand-lettered documents, which were
executed by local ministers, school masters
or itinerant penmen. Most are of
Pennsylvania Dutch origin.*

Birth Announcement for Lidia Jegle,
  pen & ink & watercolor on paper, the
  rectangular multiple sawtooth border
  decorated in red, yellow & green
  pigments all enclosing the birth
  information of Lidia Jegle, born to
  Johannes & Elizabeth Jegle of
  Schwatara Township, Lebanon
  County, on 28 September 1825, the
  whole surrounded by stylized yellow,
  red & green acanthus leaves, tulips,
  grape bunches & a foliate draped
  urn, w/the later inscribed below "Died
  September 13th 1889. Aged 63 years
  and 17 day," attributed to Abraham
  Huth, 1807-1830, Lebanon County,
  Pennsylvania, ca. 1825, 11½ x 15½"
  (ILLUS.) **$6,900.00**
Birth Announcement for Lydia Hoff,
  pen & ink & watercolor on paper, a
  rectangular border consisting of
  alternating red & white & blue & white
  hearts headed by flowers & enclosing
  the large inscription "Lydia Hoff Was

born Jany 2nd, 1789," above a facing
pair of red & blue birds flanking a
central large red, blue, yellow & black
flower, southeastern Pennsylvania,
ca. 1789, 7¾ x 10¾" **4,025.00**

Birth Announcement Fraktur

Birth Announcement for Samuel
Eschleman, pen & ink & watercolor
on paper, the central announce-ment
pertaining to the birth of Samuel
Eschleman on 17 August 1800 to
Christian & Rosina (Ziegler)
Eschleman enclosed by a printed
heart surrounded by birds & flowers
& flanked by two smaller hearts
w/print filled inscriptions centering
two profile mermaids & flanked by
two elaborately costumed women, in
red, yellow, green, pink & blue,
printed by Friedrich Speyer, 1780-
1803, southeastern Pennsylvania,
ca. 1800, 13¾ x 16" (ILLUS.)........**8,050.00**

Birth & baptism certificate for Maria
Gerhart, pen & ink & watercolor on
paper, a large central circle enclosing
the long German inscription
concerning the birth on January 17,
1818 & baptism on April 12, 1818,
circle flanked in the corners by large
birds on scrolling floral vines in blue,
red, yellow & sepia, all within a blue
& yellow rectangular border,
southeastern Pennsylvania
ca. 1818, 13 x 15¾" **2,530.00**

Birth & baptism certificate for Mary
Meiser, pen & ink & watercolor on
paper, a circle of hearts flanked by
large-leafed floral sprigs above a
large central heart w/the English
inscription relating to the birth on
February 18, 1839 & the baptism, the
heart flanked by long flowering vines
topped by yellow birds, a lady w/a
bird on ring & a flowering tree w/four
large birds at the bottom, in shades
of green, yellow & red, signed by
Francis Portzline, southeastern
Pennsylvania, ca. 1840,
11¾ x 15¾" **6,000.00**

Birth & baptism certificate, printed
format w/three hearts & pen & ink &
watercolor decoration of flowers &
three birds in green, yellow, red, blue
& black, regarding an 1805 birth,
Pennsylvania German origin, framed,
15½ x 18½" (stains & minor paper
damage)..........................**385.00**

Birth & baptism certificate, pen &
ink & watercolor on laid paper,
architectural design w/a pair of lions
flanking a crown above a wall w/a
central star device w/text to be filled
in w/birth information, names &
dates, in bright shades of orange,
red, blue, yellow, olive & black,
signed "Beigen," unused, 18¼" w.,
15¾" h. (wear, taped tears & paper
damage)..........................**4,840.00**

Birth record for Mahlon B. Spang, pen
& ink & watercolor on wove paper,
overall floral design in the top half
above a round reserve w/the
inscription in English, bright colors of
red, yellow, green, orange, blue &
black, dated "May 30, 1840," Oley
Township, Berks County, Pennsylvania, modern curly maple frame,
9⅝ x 11⅝" (minor damage on
fold line) **1,210.00**

Birth record for Mary Linzenbigler,
watercolor & pen & ink on paper,
a central ink-drawn & watercolor
decorated heart inscribed
w/information of the birth on
December 29, 1789 in New Hanover,
Montgomery County, Pennsylvania,
decorated above by a purple &
yellow flower & flanked by red, yellow
& green tulips & flowers above a red
& green mermaid in each lower
corner flanking two large purple, red
& yellow flowers, attributed to
Friederich Krebs, ca. 1789,
7¾ x 12¾" **3,220.00**

Birth record, printed & hand colored,
large heart surrounded by flowers,
foliage & birds enclosing information
concerning an 1812 birth in Dolphin
County, Pennsyl-vania, printed in
Ephrata by Baumann, good color,
framed 18⅛" w., 15⅝" h. (minor
creases) **302.50**

Book plate, pen & ink & water-
color on paper, double page
w/"Johannes Jungten" & single
sheet w/"Abraham Jungten 1788,"
stylized floral design in reds, blues,
yellow, brown & black, attributed to
Eastern Bible artist Johann Ernst,
Spangenberg, Lebanon County,
Pennsylvania, matted & framed
together in shadowbox frame,

21¾" w., 17¼" h. (stains & bleeding color, old rebacking & repair)...........**495.00**

Drawing, pen & ink & watercolor on paper, a large central vase flanked by smaller vases, each issuing a tall branched vine w/large stylized tulip blossoms on each branch & large starbursts & a hex sign at the top, all in red & black, 19th c., framed, 12 x 15".......................................**3,450.00**

Drawing & penmanship book, pen & ink & watercolor on paper, the handsewn paper booklet is interspersed w/schoolboy watercolor drawings of birds, human figures & decorative elements along w/a series of penmanship exercises & the name "Jacob Arnold," American school, dated 1836, 6¼ x 8".....................**2,300.00**

Family record, pen & ink & water-color on paper, "John Dodds Family Record...done by John Dodds April 1806," architectural design & listing of births from 1777 to 1806 in black, green, red, blue & brown, in a grained frame, 14½" w., 18½" h. (wear, stains, tears & paper damage)...**797.50**

Vorschrift, pen & ink & watercolor on paper, a rectangular border defined by crossed bands of straight flowering & foliate vines w/large stylized tulips facing in toward the text, the inscription in three registers, the third inscribed at base "Written in the Year of Our Lord 1806, the 17th of February," & concluding below w/a German inscription translating to "This Vorschrift belongs to me Judith Buchwalter," School of the Huber Artist, Lancaster County, Pennsyl-vania, ca. 1806, 12¾ x 15¼" **5,175.00**

Vorschrift, pen & ink & watercolor on paper, rectangular, the center panel w/German inscription framed by a wide border band of flowering vines in red, green, blue & black, signed & dated "P.W.J. Brown 1792," framed 15¾ x 18" (damage at fold lines, stains, water damage & old edge repair) **550.00**

FRAMES

Bronze, Zodiac patt., rectangular wide-sided table-top model w/rounded corners, rectangular opening w/rounded corners, cast around the sides w/signs of the zodiac, copper finish, impressed

Tiffany Studios mark & "942," 7 x 8"...**$1,150.00**

Bronze & glass, rectangular, the amber glass within a rectangular frame, stamped "LOUIS C. TIFFANY FURNACES, INC. 54," 13" h..**4,370.00**

Bronze & slag glass, rectangular w/wide flat sides pierced w/overall delicate florals backed by green & white mottled glass, rectangular opening, original patina, marked "REVERE STUDIOS NEW YORK," early 20th c., 9 x 11½" **440.00**

Ornate Cast Metal Frame

Cast metal, rectangular w/ornate scroll decoration w/cabinet photo marked "W H Ernsberger Photograph Parlors 83 Genesee Street, Auburn, N.Y.," signed, easel-backed frame, 8 x 11½" (ILLUS.) **49.50**

Gilt-bronze, Venetian patt., rectangular, stamped "TIFFANY STUDIOS NEW YORK 1682," 12" h..**1,495.00**

Silver-gilt, table model, Art Deco style, upright rectangular narrow frame raised on short square posts upon a rectangular platform base w/angled sides on top, the top & bottom rim, legs & rim of the base lined w/rows of calibré-cut amethysts, France, maker's mark "PB," ca. 1930-40, sliding back panel, 12¾" h...............................**4,600.00**

FRATERNAL ORDER COLLECTIBLES

B.P.O.E. (Benevolent & Protective Order of Elks) hand towel holder, brass finished cast metal **$110.00**

G.A.R. (Grand Army of the Republic) badge w/ribbon, mint in original box, Joseph K. Davison's, Inc. **60.00**

G.A.R. canteen, miniature, stoneware, flattened round form w/side tabs for string handle & small top spout, embossed "26th Annual Encampment of Iowa G.A.R. Davenport, June 1900," trimmed in cobalt blue, labeled "Hinrichs Crockery Co. Davenport, Iowa," 3¼" h. (pinpoint flakes) **192.50**

G.A.R. encampment schedule, Boston & Maine Railroad, 1904 ....**25.00**

Masonic books, "History of Freemasonry," 1906, 5 vols. **45.00**

Masonic table piece, crocheted w/Masonic emblem w/"G" in the center, cream colored, 15 x 17" **42.00**

Masonic pitcher, early Liverpool earthenware jug-type, the ovoid body decorated on the obverse w/Masonic symbols including pillars, pavement, etc., the reverse w/a wreath of symbols centering the verse "The world is in pain our secrets to gain...," wreath of symbols under spout & inscribed "Nath. L. Otis," early 19th c., 10¾" h. (base cracks) **1,150.00**

Shrine tumbler, milk white glass, photos of "Ben & Bill" & inscribed "Atlantic City, June 4, 1918"............**135.00**

FRUIT JARS

ARS (in script), glass stopper (embossed) "A. Kline," smooth base, applied collared mouth, ca. 1860-80, aqua, qt. **$66.00**

Atlas E-Z Seal, smooth base, smooth mouth w/golden amber glass lid & wire bail, ca. 1920-40, golden amber, qt. (flakes on mouth) **55.00**

Ball Perfect Mason, smooth base, smooth mouth w/zinc lid, 1910-30, yellowish amber, qt. **66.00**

Ball Perfect Mason, smooth base, smooth mouth w/zinc lid, ca. 1910-30, yellowish green, qt. **44.00**

Banner (encircled by) Patd Feby 9th 1864 Reisd Jan 22d 1867, smooth base, ground mouth, ca. 1865-80, clear, qt. (no closure) **88.00**

Canton (The) Fruit Jar, smooth base, ground mouth w/glass lid, 1880-1900, clear, qt. **115.50**

C J Co, smooth base, smooth mouth w/zinc lid, ca. 1900-10, ½ gal. **44.00**

Clarke Fruit Jar Co., Cleveland O., ground lip, glass-domed lid & metal cam lever & wire, aqua, qt. **49.50**

Commonwealth (angled up) "Fruit" above & "Jar" below, smooth base, smooth mouth, glass lid & wire bail, Australian, 1900-30, clear w/pale yellowish green tint, qt. **71.50**

Dandy (The) below arched "Trade Mark," wire bail handle, ground lip, ca. 1885-1900, light yellowish amber, qt. (no glass lid) **115.50**

Dexter (encircled by fruit & vegetables), smooth base, ground mouth w/glass lid & zinc screw band, ca. 1865-80, aqua, qt. **55.00**

Dillon Glass Co., Fairmont, Ind (embossed on base), groove ring wax sealer, 1860-80, light green, ½ gal. **33.00**

Eagle, unmarked glass lid & iron yoke clamp, aqua, qt. **55.00**

Electric Fruit Jar (around globe) w/glass lid & clamp, aqua, qt. **143.00**

Empire (The), ground mouth, smooth base, greenish aqua, qt. (no closure) **55.00**

Fahnestock Albree & Co. (on base), pontil scar, applied mouth, ca. 1850-60, aqua, pt. **121.00**

Flaccus Bros. Steers Head Fruit Jar (steer's head), pale greyish aqua, pt. (no closure) **49.50**

Franklin Fruit Jar, smooth base, ground mouth w/glass lid & metal screw-on band, 1862-80, aqua, qt. **27.50**

Gilberds (embossed star) Jar, glass lid, wire clamp, smooth base, ground lip, ca. 1883-1900, aqua, ½ gal. (reproduction wire clamp, some wear & stain on lid) **242.00**

GJCo monogram (Gilchrist Jar Co.), unlined aluminum lid marked "The Keystone Jar," aqua, qt.....................**26.50**

Globe, glass lid, wire & iron clamp, metal band around neck, smooth base, ground lip, ca. 1886-1900, light yellowish amber, qt. **115.50**

Haller (Mrs. G.E.) Patd. Feb. 25.73, glass stopper, aqua, qt. **66.00**

Hero (above cross), smooth base, glass lid w/wire bail, ca. 1895-1900, aqua, ½ gal. **38.50**

Imperial Pat. April 20th 1886 (on base), smooth base, ground mouth, glass lid, 1885-90, clear, pt. **99.00**

Independent Jar, glass lid embossed "Pat. Oct. 4, 1882," ground mouth, ca. 1880-1900, clear, qt. **44.00**

Lafayette (in script) below profile of Lafayette, smooth base, tooled mouth w/three piece glass & metal stopper, ca. 1890-1900, aqua, ½ gal. **154.00**

Lafayette, (in script) below profile of Lafayette, aqua, qt. 632.50

Lightning below arched "Trade Mark," smooth base, amber glass lid w/wire bail, 1882-1900, yellowish amber, pt...**55.00**

Lyman (W.W.) 28 - Patd Feb. 9th 1864, ground lip, metal lid, smooth base, ca. 1864-80, aqua, qt. **49.50**

Mascot (The) Trade Mark Pat'd Improved, smooth base, smooth mouth w/milk glass lid & metal screw band, 1890-1910, clear, qt. **264.00**

Mason SWG, smooth base, smooth mouth w/zinc lid, ca. 1900-20, pale sun-colored amethyst, ½ gal. (incorrect lid) **99.00**

Mason's (Cross) CFJCo Patent Nov 30th 1858, smooth base, ground lip, zinc lid, ca. 1880-1900, clear w/amethyst tint, qt. **198.00**

Mason's (Cross) CFJCo Patent Nov 30th 1858 (reproduction jar), smooth base, screw-on metal lid, 1970-75, cobalt blue, ½ gal...........................**55.00**

Mason's (Cross) Patent Nov 30th 1858, smooth base, ground lip, zinc lid, golden amber, qt. **148.50**

Mason's Patent Nov 30th 58 (known as the Christmas Mason because of the style of lettering), smooth base, ground mouth w/glass lid & metal screw band, 1880-1900, aqua, pt. **71.50**

Mason's Patent Nov 30th 1858, ground lip, zinc lid, yellowish amber, pt...**632.50**

Mason's Patent Nov 30th 1858, ground lip, zinc lid, yellowish amber, qt..**330.00**

Mason Patent Nov 30th 1858 (reproduction jar), smooth base, old screw-on zinc lid, 1970-75, cobalt blue, midget pint **66.00**

Mason's (shield) Union, smooth base, ground lip, ca. 1865-90, aqua, qt. (zinc lid missing) **82.50**

My Choice, smooth base, applied collared mouth, ca. 1888-1900, aqua, qt. (no closure, some minor interior stain in base) **137.50**

Myers Test Jar, ground lip, metal lid w/attached brass clamp, aqua, ½ gal. **110.00**

Paragon w/"New" embossed above & "3" below, glass lid & metal band, smooth base, ca. 1870-80, aqua, ½ gal. **88.00**

Patent June 9, 1863, Cin. O. (base embossed), ground mouth w/screw on lid, metal lid w/wrench lugs, deep aqua, ½ gal. **110.00**

Patent Sept. 18, 1860, smooth base, ground wax sealer mouth, ca. 1860-80, deep aqua, qt. **522.50**

Queen (The) CFJCo., glass lid & zinc band, aqua, qt. **34.00**

Rau's Improved Pat Applied For Grove Ring, smooth base, applied wax sealer mouth, 1860-80, light sun-colored amethyst, qt. **33.00**

Safety, smooth base, ground mouth w/glass lid & wire clamp, ca. 1870-90, yellowish amber, ½ gal. **187.00**

Safety Valve Patd May 21, 1895 w/monogram (on base), glass lid w/metal band clamp, aqua, ½ gal. **55.00**

Spencer's (C.F.) Patent Rochester N.Y., applied mouth w/metal stopper w/finger ring for lifting, smooth base, ca. 1863-80, aqua, qt. **132.00**

Standard - W. McC & Co. (on reverse heel), smooth base, applied wax sealer mouth, 1860-86, aqua, qt. **33.00**

Stark Jar & embossed "K" within a star, smooth lip, glass lid, metal clamp & spring, smooth base, 1900-20, clear, qt. **165.00**

Sun (within circle & radiating lines) Trade Mark, cast-iron clamp w/patent dates in the 1890s, aqua, pt...**132.00**

Sun (within circle & radiating lines) Trade Mark, cast-iron clamp w/patent dates in the 1890s, greenish aqua, ½ gal. **176.00**

Union No. 1, smooth base, applied wax sealer mouth, ca. 1860-80, deep aqua, qt. **55.00**

Valve (The) Jar Co. - Philadelphia, smooth base, ground lip w/glass lid & wire coil clamp, 1868-1880, aqua, ½ gal. (small chip on lid) **165.00**

Victor (The) Patented 1899 (encircles "M" in diamond), smooth lip, glass lid & metal buckle clamp, smooth base, ca. 1899, clear, pt. **66.00**

Victory 1 (encircled by) Patd Feby 9th 1864 Reisd June 11d 1867, smooth base, ground lip w/glass lid & metal screw band, 1867-90, aqua, qt. **60.50**

Whitmore's Patent Rochester, N.Y., ground lip, glass lid w/wire bail, smooth bottom aqua, qt. **385.00**

Wilcox (B.B.) - 18 - (below arched) Pat'd March 26th 1867, ground mouth, glass lid & wire bail, brilliant aqua, qt...**82.50**

Winslow (The) Improved Valve Jar, smooth base, ground mouth, ca. 1870-90, greenish aqua, pt. (no closure) **385.00**

Woodbury & WGW monogram, Woodbury Glass Works, Woodbury N.J. on base, glass lid & zinc band, aqua, ½ gal. **38.50**

FURNITURE

Furniture made in the United States during the 18th and 19th centuries is coveted by collectors. American antique furniture has a European background, primarily English, since the influence of the Continent usually found its way to America by way of England. If the style did not originate in England, it came to America by way of England. For this reason, some American furniture styles carry the name of an English monarch or an English designer. However, we must realize that, until recently, little research has been conducted and even less published on the Spanish and French influences in the areas of the California missions and New Orleans.

After the American revolution, cabinetmakers in the United States shunned the prevailing styles in England and chose to bring the French styles of Napoleon's Empire to the United States and we have the uniquely named "American Empire" style of furniture in a country that never had an emperor.

During the Victorian period, quality furniture began to be mass-produced in this country with its rapidly growing population. So much walnut furniture was manufactured, the vast supply of walnut was virtually depleted and it was of necessity that oak furniture became fashionable as the 19th century drew to a close.

For our purposes, the general guidelines for dating will be:

Pilgrim Century - 1620-85
William & Mary - 1685-1720
Queen Anne - 1720-50
Chippendale - 1750-85
Federal - 1785-1820
  Hepplewhite - 1785-1820
  Sheraton - 1800-20
American Empire (Classical) - 1815-40
Victorian - 1840-1900
  Early Victorian - 1840-50
  Gothic Revival - 1840-90
  Rococo (Louis XV) - 1845-70
  Renaissance - 1860-85
  Louis XVI - 1865-75
  Eastlake - 1870-95
  Jacobean & Turkish Revival - 1870-95
  Aesthetic Movement - 1880-1900
Art Nouveau - 1890-1918
Turn-of-the-Century - 1895-1910
Mission (Arts & Crafts movement) - 1900-15
Art Deco - 1925-40

All furniture included in this listing is American unless otherwise noted. Also see MINIATURES (Replicas), ROYCROFT ITEMS and SHAKER COLLECTIBLES.

BEDROOM SUITES

Eastlake Bed

Victorian Eastlake substyle: bed & chest of drawers; carved maple, each piece w/a flat serrated crestrail flanked by long carved blocks, the bed w/a long dentil band above & below a pair of narrow raised panels above two long burl panels, the lower footboard w/serrated & beaded banding & two large rectangular burl panels, ca. 1880, 2 pcs. (ILLUS. bed) **$2,750.00**

Large Eastlake Wardrobe

Victorian Eastlake substyle: half-tester bed, chest of drawers, washstand, nightstand & wardrobe; carved burl walnut, each piece w/a raised crown-form gallery cornice w/pierced lattice designs flanking the raised central panel w/floral designs & round-topped blocks, an ornately carved frieze band below the cornice, the wardrobe w/a pair of tall mirrored doors flanked by colonettes above a pair of burl panel drawers, molded base w/corner blocks, ca. 1875, the set (ILLUS. wardrobe) **13,200.00**

Renaissance Revival Bed

Victorian Renaissance Revival substyle: bed, dresser, washstand, nightstand & wardrobe; bird's-eye maple & mahogany, the bed w/a high arched headboard w/a carved shell crest above a long button-carved cartouche flanked by scrolls all in mahogany above a bird's-eye maple panel, the heavy round side posts w/large flat ring- and ball-turned finials flanking a large raised mahogany rectangular frame around a maple panel, the lower footboard w/an arched crest tapering down to side scrolls centered by a recessed panel, on short rounded legs on casters, possibly by Seignouret, New Orleans, Louisiana, ca. 1870-80, the set (ILLUS. bed) **13,200.00**

Victorian Rococo substyle: bed, chest of drawers & washstand; carved mahogany, the chest & washstand w/white marble tops, the chest w/a tall arched mirror swiveling in a scroll-carved frame w/a high scroll-carved crest above side columns ending in large C-scrolls, the rectangular white marble top w/a serpentine front & outset canted corners above a conforming case w/four long graduated drawers w/leafy scroll-carved pulls, the outset corners w/large carved scrolls, molded serpentine apron, the bed w/a shaped high back

Victorian Rococo Chest of Drawers

cresting w/a shell carving & a central carved head of a maiden, the side posts terminating in trefoils, New Orleans or New York, ca. 1860, 3 pcs. (ILLUS. chest of drawers) **6,050.00**

BEDS

Art Nouveau Single Bed

Art Nouveau single beds, mahogany & burled maple, each head- and footboard framed w/carved clematis vines, leafage & blossoms, the shaped panels in burled maple w/applied carved poppy blossoms & leafage, the siderails also carved w/vines, France, ca. 1900, 45 x 81", 4' 6" h., pr. (ILLUS. one of two) **6,900.00**

Chippendale country-style tall poster bed, cherry & maple, the headboard w/tall slender turned tapering posts above square block legs flanking a low shaped headboard, the footboard w/tall slender tapering turned posts above square block legs w/stepped feet, probably Connecticut, ca. 1780, old refinish, 47½ x 77", 7' 2" h. **4,025.00**

Classical (American Empire) country-style tall poster bed, maple, the head- and footposts w/baluster-turned finials above a plain column above an urn-turned base on square posts ending in tapering turned short legs, the headboard w/a scroll-cut board above a band of short spindles, the footboard w/a knob-turned blanket roll bar above a narrow shaped board bar, old varnish finish, original rails, first half 19th c., mattress size 53 x 70", 6' 8" h. (replaced canopy frame) ...**1,485.00**

Classical Youth Beds

w/tall slender head- and footposts w/baluster-turned finials, the headboard w/an arched & scalloped crestrail above a band of five slender baluster-turned spindles, the lower footboard w/an arched & scalloped crestrail, on baluster-turned legs w/turned bell-form feet, two spindles missing in one headboard, ca. 1850, pr. (ILLUS.) **825.00**

Country-style low poster "cannon ball" rope bed, curly maple, the headboard w/a scroll-cut crest centered by a raised block w/half-round spindle finial, baluster-turned posts w/large cannon ball finials, the footboard w/a boldly knob-turned rail above a low arched board & knob rail, turned tapering heavy legs, old mellow refinishing, original siderails, 51 x 68", 47½" h. (one post w/glued flange break) **1,100.00**

Classical "Sleigh" Bed

Classical (American Empire) "sleigh" bed, mahogany, the serpentine head- and footboard each w/scrolling crestrail terminating in swans' heads, on sabre legs w/hairy paw feet on casters, Philadelphia, ca. 1820-40, 49½ x 78", 44½" h. (ILLUS.) **4,600.00**

Classical (American Empire) tall tester bed, mahogany, the rectangular tester raised on tall head- and footposts w/ring-turnings, a spiral-turned section & a baluster- and ring-turned section, the headboard w/a long acanthus-carved crest bar w/scroll ends above a wide panel, raised on heavy baluster-turned legs, ca. 1830, 51" w., 7' 4" h. **2,310.00**

Classical (American Empire) tall poster tester bed, stained sycamore, the rectangular tester above heavy cylindrical posts flanking a shaped headboard, blocked sections above the heavy ring-turned cylindrical legs, probably Chappell Hill, Texas, ca. 1850, 54⅓" w., 8' h..................**1,840.00**

Classical (American Empire) tall poster youth beds, walnut, each

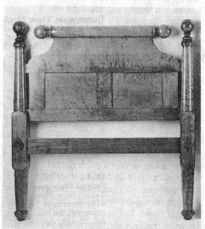

Low Poster "Cannon Ball" Bed

Country-style low poster "cannon ball" rope bed, curly maple, the headboard w/a large round bar crest w/ball end finials above tapering shaped sides above a pair of rectangular panels flanked by the tapering round posts w/ring- and ball-turned finals, tapering turned legs w/button feet, original siderails fitted w/angle irons, refinished, some loss, ca. 1835, 43¾ x 78", 47" h. (ILLUS. bottom previous page) **1,380.00**

Country-style tall poster tester bed, painted, the rectangular tester above octagonal tapering headposts centering a shaped headboard w/scalloped crest above a row of 15 spindles, the footposts similarly chamfered & centering a rectangular footboard, on square tapering legs, painted red, Texas, mid-19th c., 52½ x 76", 7' 2" h. **3,910.00**

Country-style tall poster bed, walnut, the octagonal tapering posts w/acorn-form finials flanking a shaped headboard w/cylindrical turned crest, w/baluster-turned footbar above rectangular footboard, on square legs w/cylindrical feet, Texas, 19th c., 60¼ x 83¾", 7' 7" h. **1,150.00**

Federal Child's Bed

Federal child's bed, figured mahogany, the low baluster-turned head- and footposts flanking an arched & stepped reeded & figured mahogany headboard & matching footboard, bulbous baluster-turned short legs on casters, probably New York, ca. 1820, 42 x 75", 31" h. (ILLUS.) **1,955.00**

Federal tall poster bed, carved & inlaid mahogany, the headboard w/a low gently arched board between pencil posts, the footboard w/tall slender reeded baluster-turned posts on plain turned & tapering legs w/swelled feet, original rails,

refinished, New England, ca. 1800, 54" w., 7' 3" h. (replaced testers, restoration) **2,645.00**

Federal tall poster canopy bed, maple, the headboard w/a low gently arched board flanked by plain turned tapering posts & baluster-turned legs, the footboard w/baluster- and ring-turned reeded tapering posts & baluster-turned legs, New England, ca. 1820, 47 x 72", 6' h. (restoration) **920.00**

Federal tall poster canopy bed, tiger stripe maple, the headboard w/a wide gently arched board flanked by tall baluster- and ring-turned posts & legs w/knobbed ankles, matching footposts, New England, ca. 1820, assembled 48 x 72", 6' h. (refinished, restoration) **1,610.00**

Federal Canopy Bed

Federal tall poster canopy bed, birch, the arched canopy frame supported on square tapering plain headposts flanking a low arched headboard & reeded baluster-turned footposts above turned tapering legs, stained red, original finish, New England, ca. 1815, 54 x 70", 6' 5" h. (ILLUS.) **4,025.00**

Federal tall poster tester bed, inlaid mahogany, flat rectangular tester frame, square tapering plain headposts flanking the low arched headboard, baluster-turned & reeded footposts above turned tapering reeded legs w/baluster-turned feet, the footposts w/checkered line-inlaid reserves at the juncture w/the rails, headboard replaced, some alteration to rails, Massachusetts, ca. 1800, 61 x 81" 6' 11" h. (ILLUS. top next page) **3,450.00**

Inlaid Federal Tester Bed

Georgian-Style Canopy Bed

Federal Carved Mahogany Tester Bed

Gothic Revival Child's Bed

Federal tall poster tester bed,
carved mahogany, flat rectangular
tester frame, plain baluster-turned
headposts flanking the rectangular
plain headboard, the footposts
baluster-turned & reeded & w/a leaf-
carved segment above a chamfered
block segment, on turned tapering
legs w/knob feet on casters, some
restorations, headboard reshaped,
Middle Atlantic States, ca. 1815,
63 x 79", 7' 6" h. (ILLUS.) **3,105.00**

**Georgian-Style tall poster canopy
bed,** carved mahogany, the low
arched & flaring canopy frame
supported on baluster-turned &
reeded posts w/rice-carved
segments above square legs
w/block feet, a wide plain
rectangular headboard w/rounded
top corners, England, early 20th c.
(ILLUS. top next column) **1,980.00**

Victorian child's crib-bed, Gothic
Revival substyle, walnut, the heavy
square pointed pillar cornerposts
joined by slatted sides forming
pointed Gothic arches, on square
legs w/block feet, New York, 1840-
60, 29¼ x 43", 45" h. (ILLUS.) **1,495.00**

Victorian half-tester bed, Aesthetic
Movement substyle, carved walnut,
the arched half-tester w/scalloped
button band trim supported on long
scroll-cut brackets above the tall
headboard w/a band of round
flowerheads above an arched
beaded panel filled w/scrolling
flowers, leaves & berries above two
large rectangular burl panels
w/beaded framing & separated by a
band of florettes, the whole
headboard flanked by blocks of
carved herringbone above pairs of
slender colonnettes, the low
footboard w/a flat top flanked by

Aesthetic Movement Half-Tester Bed

round sunbursts above a band of florettes above a rectangular burl panel w/a beaded frame, ca. 1885 (ILLUS.) **3,025.00**

Renaissance Revival Half-tester Bed

Victorian half-tester bed, Renaissance Revival substyle, walnut, the half-tester frame w/a serpentine front & a scroll-cut crest flanked by knob-turned corner finials, the tall headboard w/a tall pierced scroll-cut crest above an arched & paneled crestrail w/a roundel above a pair of tall arched panels, scroll brackets support the half-tester above the flattened & shaped headposts decorated w/half-round turned spindles, the low arched footboard w/rounded

corners & centered by a large ringed roundel, ca. 1860 (ILLUS.) **2,420.00**

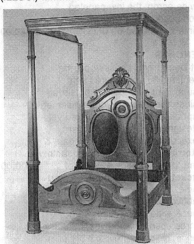

Renaissance Revival Tester Bed

Victorian tester bed, Renaissance Revival substyle, walnut & burl walnut, the deep rectangular molded tester above molded tapering posts w/applied mid-molding, the high headboard w/a carved scroll crest above an arched & paneled crestrail above a band of shaped raised panels & a ringed roundel over two large oval burl panels, the low arched footboard w/two shaped raised panels flanking a ringed roundel, octagonal block feet, Southern U. S., ca. 1860, 65 x 88", 8' 10" h. (ILLUS.)...........................**3,220.00**

Victorian Rococo High Back Bed

Victorian bed, Rococo substyle, mahogany, the high headboard w/an arched & stepped crestrail decorated w/pierced scroll carvings above an arched panel above three tall arched panels, paneled & ring-turned headposts w/ring-turned pointed finials, the siderails w/scroll-carved corner brackets above the wide apron, the low paneled footposts w/bulbous ring-turned finials, ca. 1850-60 (ILLUS.) **3,740.00**

BENCHES

Art Deco bench, rosewood, the rectangular upholstered seat supported by curved upholstered sides continuing to rectangular legs, upholstered in camel-colored velvet, designed by Eugene Schoen, executed by Schmeig, Hungate & Kotzian, ca. 1935, stamped factory marks & numbers, 49½" l..............**2,300.00**

Bucket (or water) bench, painted pine, a long rectangular board top above one-board tall sides curving out & widening at the lower half, three open long shelves, bootjack ends, old worn greyish ivory paint over earlier darker grey, 17½" x 36", 4' 10½" h. (minor edge damage)......................................**1,650.00**

Early Bucket Bench

Bucket (or water) bench, painted pine, one-board ends w/large round finials flanking two open shelves, traces of red paint, New England, early 19th c., imperfections, 22½" x 47½", 30½" h. (ILLUS.) **1,725.00**

Mission-style (Arts & Crafts movement) bench, oak, rectangular long seat on end legs w/a short slat above a cross-brace, the legs joined by a long stretcher, medium-dark finish, remnant of the paper label of J. M. Young, Camden, New York, early 20th c., 12 x 38", 20⅛" h. (refinished) **1,035.00**

Regency bench, giltwood, the rectangular slightly curved upholstered seat raised on four scroll-carved legs w/animal paw feet, rails stamped "T.G." three times, England, first quarter 19th c.,

Regency Bench

flaking finish, 18 x 26¼", 19" h. (ILLUS.) **5,750.00**

Victorian "Prie Dieu"

Victorian "prie dieu" (praying bench), Rococo substyle, carved mahogany, a scroll-carved crest w/crucifix on the upholstered handrail above a large pierce-carved panel w/crucifix flanked by slender spiral-turned spindles, the upholstered kneeler w/rounded corners & raised on tiny turned legs, covered w/Aubusson tapestry upholstery, ca. 1860 (ILLUS.) **990.00**

BOOKCASES

Arts & Crafts bookcase, oak, the rectangular top w/a pointed backboard & galleried sides above a solid back & three open shelves flanked by arched braces, arched apron, paper label of L. & J.G. Stickley, Model No. 345, ca. 1910, 12 x 19", 45" h..............................**1,955.00**

Classical bookcase, gilt, grain-painted & ormolu-mounted rosewood, breakfront-form, the rectangular top w/a stepped-out center section above a paneled

English Classical Bookcase

frieze band w/ormolu rosette mounts, one deep center shelf flanked by narrow end sections w/two shelves, each section separated w/ormolu-mounted columns, raised on bulbous baluster-turned legs, old finish, England, ca. 1825, imperfections, 14½ x 42", 34⅛" h. (ILLUS.) **2,415.00**

Classical (American Empire) "breakfront" bookcase, mahogany, three-part construction: the upper section w/rectangular top w/overhanging flared cornice & knife-edged molding; the central section w/four geometrically glazed Gothic arch doors w/brass edging opening to reveal four moveable shelves each w/a beaded edge; the lower stepped-out section w/a central hinged writing surface above three narrow drawers over three pairs of setback paneled cupboard doors w/brass edging opening to shelved compartments, the doors flanked by columns w/carved Ionic capitals, on carved lion's-paw feet w/acanthus leaves, the conical rear feet turned, apparently original

Classical "Breakfront" Bookcase

round rosette & ring drawer pulls, New England, 1815-25, 21 x 80⅛", 8' 8" h. **14,950.00**

Classical "breakfront" bookcase, mahogany, the rectangular top w/a stepped-out center section w/a pair of tall glazed doors flanked by a glazed tall door at each end, four scroll brackets across the top front, on a molded base, ca. 1850 (ILLUS. bottom previous column) **2,090.00**

Fine Federal Bookcase

Federal bookcase, inlaid mahogany, two-part construction: the upper section w/a molded & dentil-carved cornice above a pair of cupboard doors w/12 arched panes each opening to adjustable shelves; the projecting lower section w/a pull-out writing section opening to small drawers over pigeonholes centering a prospect door inlaid w/a basket of flowers & opening to a valance drawer & a small drawer, the lower case w/three long line-inlaid drawers, on bracket feet, New York, ca. 1800, 22¼ x 47", 7' 7" h. (ILLUS.) **10,925.00**

George III bookcase, mahogany, two-part construction: the upper section w/a wide swan's-neck scrolled crest on the rectangular top above a pair of wide geometrically-glazed doors opening to three shelves; the lower section w/a molded medial band over a pair of paneled doors, plinth base, England, third quarter 18th c., 18 x 52", 7' 11½" h. **10,350.00**

George III-Style bookcases, mahogany & satinwood inlay, rectangular top w/molded cornice above a pair of geometrically-glazed

George III-Style Bookcase

doors opening to three shelves, molded base, England, late 19th c., 13½ x 62", 4' 6" h., pr. (ILLUS. one of two) **2,645.00**

Georgian-Style Bookstand

Georgian-Style bookstand, revolving-type, the round galleried top above a stepped cylindrical case w/arched opening alternating w/rectangular openings in two tiers, on a baluster-turned pedestal w/a tripod base w/cabriole legs ending in pad feet, England, late 19th - early 20th c. (ILLUS.) **412.50**

Mission-style (Arts & Crafts movement) bookcase, oak, a deep three-quarter gallery on the rectangular top over a pair of 6-pane glazed cupboard doors opening to shelves, flat apron, through tenons w/keys in the sides which continue to form low arched feet, original medium finish & black-finished metal hardware, red decal mark of Gustav Stickley, Model No. 525, ca. 1901, two panes replaced, interior molding strip repair, 11¾ x 39", 45" h.........**6,900.00**

Mission-style (Arts & Crafts movement) bookcase, oak, a rectangular top w/a low gallery above a pair of tall 8-pane glazed cupboard doors opening to shelves, wrought-iron escutcheons & circular pulls, red decal mark of Gustav Stickley, Model No. 542, ca. 1902, 12¼ x 36", 4' 8" h. **6,325.00**

Gustav Stickley Bookcase

Mission-style (Arts & Crafts movement) bookcase, oak, a rectangular top w/a low gallery above a pair of wide 16-pane glazed doors opening to three shelves, flat base, the sides w/beveled through-tenons, fully chamfered back, original dark brown finish, large early red decal mark of Gustav Stickley, 12¼ x 62", 4' 8" h. (ILLUS.) **9,075.00**

Mission-style (Arts & Crafts movement) bookcase, three-quarter open gallery above a rectangular top over three glazed cupboard doors w/metal pulls opening to a shelved interior, the sides w/exposed key tenons, L. & J. G. Stickley, Model No. 331½, ca. 1905, 12 x 72", 4' 8" h. **16,100.00**

Mission-style (Arts & Crafts movement) bookcase, oak, rectangular top w/a low three-quarter gallery above a pair of long 4-pane glazed doors each w/two small over two long panes, slightly arched apron, dark finish, original copper hardware, eight adjustable shelves, branded Limbert Furniture mark, Model No. 376, ca. 1907, 14 x 42¾", 5' h. (some refinish) **2,185.00**

Turn of the century bookcase, oak, stacking-type, a rectangular top w/low gallery above five stacking units w/long glazed lift-front doors, the lower cabinet taller than the upper four, raised on short ogee bracket feet, Globe-Wernicke, ca. 1910 .... **440.00**

Gothic Revival Bookcase

Victorian bookcase, Gothic Revival substyle, rosewood, rectangular top w/a deep flaring ogee cornice above a pair of wide glazed doors w/double arches at the top opening to four shelves, double-arch glazed sides, molded base on bun feet, Anglo-Indian, mid-19th c. (ILLUS.) **880.00**

Victorian bookcase, Renaissance Revival substyle, mahogany, inverted-breakfront form, the rectangular top w/stepped-out end sections above a deep cornice & conforming case w/stepped-out end sections w/tall arched & glazed cupboard doors opening to shelves & flanking an inset pair of matching cupboard doors, flat molded base, ca. 1880, 18 x 89", 7' h. **2,200.00**

Ornate Renaissance Revival Bookcase

Victorian bookcase, Renaissance Revival substyle, walnut, "breakfront" style, the outset center section w/a tall arched bead-carved crestrail w/a crest carved w/two seated figures flanking a shell & w/floral-carved urn finials above a wide arched frieze band carved in full-relief w/a bust of Shakespeare framed by scrolls above tall arched glazed door w/carved dogs at the upper corners & a rectangular panel at the bottom w/a large carved button cartouche, the door flanked at the top w/male caryatids & half-round carved drops, the set-back side sections w/scroll-carved crests & corner finials above narrow frieze bands each w/a different bust carving above the arched glazed door w/carved flying dragons at the top corners & cartouche panels at the bottom, each canted outside corner carved at the top w/a caryatid, molded base w/carved scrolls & center blocks w/carved busts, on short stepped block feet, Europe, second half 19th c., 17½ x 113½", 11' h. (ILLUS. bottom previous column) **19,550.00**

BUREAUX PLAT

Louis XV-Style Bureau Plat

Louis XV-Style, ormolu-mounted kingwood, the rectangular top w/outset round corners above an apron w/a center drawer w/ormolu banding & a scroll ormolu pull flanked by scroll ormolu mounts & a pair of ormolu-banded drawers w/scroll mounts & keyhole escutcheons, figural ormolu mounts at each corner above the cabriole legs ending in paw feet w/*sabots,* France, late 19th - early 20th c., 25 x 42", 30" h. (ILLUS.) **1,650.00**

Louis XV-Style, gilt bronze-mounted kingwood, the shaped rectangular top w/inset tooled leather writing surface, above three frieze drawers w/scroll-trimmed ormolu banding & pulls, raised on cabriole legs w/ormolu figural mounts & *sabots,* France, 19th c., 38 x 68", 31" h.....**5,462.00**

Napoleon III Bureau Plat

Napoleon III, Sèvres plaque-mounted ebonized wood, the leather-inset rectangular top above a frieze band w/two drawers, mounted all around w/round Sèvres china plaques, on tapering ring-turned & reeded legs joined by paired long C-scroll flat stretchers centered by an ormolu urn finial, on casters, ca. 1860 (ILLUS.) **3,850.00**

CABINETS

Oak Baker's Cabinet

Baker's cabinet, turn-of-the-century, oak, two-piece construction: the upper section w/a rectangular top above a case w/a pair of tall double-paneled cupboard doors beside a small paneled door over a stack of three small drawers; the stepped-out lower section w/a zinc-lined dry sink well beside a work surface above a wide pull-out work surface faced to look like two drawers & beside

another drawer, all above three paneled cupboard doors at the base, on square feet extending from stiles (ILLUS.) **1,100.00**

Cellerettes (wine cabinets), Classical (American Empire), mahogany veneer, the rectangular top w/a raised center pale w/gadroon edge above the gadroon edge on the top lifting to a deep well, paneled sides w/crotch grain veneer & tiny beaded edging w/similar edging down the outside corners, gadroon band along base of case, raised on a ring-turned pedestal above a gadroon knob on a cross-form plinth raised on four boldly carved paw feet, Middle Atlantic States, 1825-35, 13½ x 15", 27½" h., pr. (refinished, imperfections) **4,025.00**

China cabinet, Mission-style (Arts & Crafts movement), a low shaped crestrail on the D-form top above curved glass sides & a wide flat front w/a single-pane door opening to shelves, original medium brown finish, Lifetime Furniture, signed "Grand Rapids Chair Co.," early 20th c., 17½ x 45", 5' 1" h. **1,100.00**

China cabinet, Mission-style (Arts & Crafts movement), oak, a low crestrail on the rectangular top above a single 12-pane glazed cupboard door opening to three shelves & flanked by 4-pane glazed sides, corner stiles continue to form square legs, printed decal label of Gustav Stickley & indistinct paper label, Model No. 820, ca. 1905, 15 x 36", 5' 2⅜" h.........................**3,450.00**

Gustav Stickley China Cabinet

China cabinet, Mission-style (Arts & Crafts movement), oak, a rectangular top w/low gallery above a pair of 10-pane glazed doors opening to fixed shelves, arched apron, original hammered copper pulls, original reddish brown finish, middle period red Gustav Stickley decal & remnants of original paster, Model No. 815, 15 x 40", 5' 3½" h. (ILLUS.) **7,975.00**

Turn-of-the-Century China Cabinet

China cabinet, turn-of-the-century, oak, D-form top above curved side moldings & carved front molding over curved glass sides & a curved glass door flanked by scroll-carved drops & narrow incised bands, on heavy animal paw front feet & tall block rear feet, ca. 1890 (ILLUS.) **1,760.00**

China Cabinet-Secretary

China cabinet-secretary, turn-of-the-century, mahogany veneer, the crestrail w/a long oval mirror flanked by pierce-carved griffins & centered

by a small round shelf above the two-part base w/a china cabinet on the left w/a curved-glass door opening to shelves & a desk unit on the right w/a shaped shelf w/a slender scroll leg support above an oblong mirror over a tiny drawer & shelf over a wide slant-front w/embossed scroll-carved oval cartouche opening to a fitted interior over an ogee-front drawer above two flat drawers all w/simple brass bail pulls, on short cabriole front legs w/animal paw feet, ca. 1890-1900 (ILLUS.) **1,430.00**

Display cabinet, Victorian Aesthetic Movement substyle, rosewood & marquetry, two-part construction: the upper section w/a rectangular top w/a low bobbin-turned gallery w/turned corner finials above a frieze band w/three light panels separated by carved leaf sprigs above a pair of 5-pane glazed cupboard doors opening to four shelves, the doors w/pointed strap hinges & metal thumblatch; the lower section slightly stepped-out w/a pair of cupboard doors w/a carved panel w/a central blossom flanked by leaf bands above a glass panel in each, pointed strap hinges & latch, a galleried apron w/tiny turned spindles, small turned feet, third-quarter 19th c., 20½ x 54½", 9' 1" h. **2,415.00**

Hoosier Kitchen Cabinet

Hoosier kitchen cabinet, hardwood, the superstructure w/a three-quarter gallery above a row of eight various sized small drawers above shaped sides & a tall opening above the wide rectangular top over a case w/pull-out work shelves at the front

& one end, the left end w/an arrangement of six small drawers over a long drawer, the front w/an arrangement of a drawer over two small angled bins beside a large angled bin, white porcelain knobs & handles, on short ring-turned legs on casters, ca. 1910-20 (ILLUS.) **770.00**

Liquor cabinet, Art Deco, burlwood, the arched top above a molded case w/two pairs of doors composed of vertical strips, the upper doors opening to a fitted interior, the lower doors opening to a fitted bottle shelf, raised on curved flat supports joining a stepped plinth base, England, ca. 1930, 18 x 48½", 5' 4" h. **2,070.00**

Map or surveyor's cabinet, oak, a low flat crestboard on the long rectangular top above a short case w/two rows of six long, shallow drawers each w/two metal name brackets w/pulls, flat base, early 20th c., 17 x 41", 15½" h. (overall wear) **330.00**

Modern cabinet on stand, Formica & painted wood, the rectangular cabinet covered in blond wood finish Formica w/sliding doors painted black & orange, raised on a simple low base painted black, Charles Eames, w/original manufacturer's label, ca. 1950, 14 x 72", 32¼" h...**920.00**

Music cabinet, Art Nouveau, marquetry inlaid mahogany, the carved & pierced foliate rear rail above a shaped rectangular top w/molded edge, above a single door w/inverted glazed heart-shaped cut-out, flanked by open shelves, above two drawers inlaid w/a grass-hopper, moths in flight & trumpet blossoms, around a distant turreted village in a landscape, the lower section w/vertical shaped dividers, the sides inlaid in various woods w/trumpet blossoms & leafage, signed in marquetry "Gallé," ca. 1895, 12¼ x 24", 4' 5½" h.............**4,888.00**

Music cabinet, Edwardian, inlaid mahogany, a low rectangular crestrail w/cornice band & decorated w/inlaid swags above the rectangular top w/ogee sides over a tall narrow case of six long drawers w/band inlay & bail pulls, on tall slender square tapering legs w/corner brackets, England, ca. 1910 (ILLUS. top next column) **770.00**

Edwardian Music Cabinet

Rosewood Music Cabinet

Music cabinet, Edwardian, rosewood & marquetry, a rectangular top w/a narrow pierced brass gallery above a coved band w/leafy scroll marquetry above a molded cornice above a long rectangular door w/a diamond-form mirror flanked by leafy scroll marquetry corner panels above a long narrow drawer w/urn & leafy scroll marquetry & two bail pulls above four open shelves, on slender turned & tapering legs w/button feet, w/a metal label for W.J. Mansell, cabinetmaker, upholsterer, 266 Fulham Rd., London, England, ca. 1900, 16 x 23", 45½" h. (ILLUS.) **805.00**

Pier cabinet, Classical (American Empire), carved & figured

mahogany, the rectangular top
above a pair of hinged paneled
doors opening to shelves, tapered
pilasters w/acanthus-carved capitals
flanking, on acanthus-carved gilt-
and verte-painted animal paw feet,
New York, ca. 1815,
16½ x 46½", 41¼" h.....................**8,050.00**

Portfolio cabinet, Art Deco,
lacquered wood & brass,
rectangular top w/rounded edges
above a pair of wide doors opening
to six narrow, sliding shelves, the
exterior painted in chartreuse, dark
blue & silver w/large brass demilune
hardware on the doors w/ring pulls,
metal tag on back w/"Skyscraper
Furniture - Frankl Galleries - 4 East
48th St., New York," ca. 1930,
28¼ x 42", 47⅜" h.....................**19,500.00**

Side cabinet, Art Deco, rosewood,
rectangular top w/very low flat
gallery & rounded front above a pair
of tall curved cabinet doors, the
closure set w/carved strapwork &
opening to a shelved interior,
France, ca. 1935, 25 x 51⅜",
5' 2¾" h. **2,588.00**

Side cabinet, Art Nouveau, fruitwood
marquetry, the top rectangular shelf
w/carved & pierced rail depicting
stylized dragonflies supported by
scrolling foliate brackets above a
larger rectangular shelf, the
backboard inlaid in various woods
w/a landscape, above a cabinet
section w/short drawers carved
w/whiplash devices & centered by a
bronze escutcheon of conforming
design, above a small cabinet door
inlaid w/various fungi & flanked by a
larger cabinet door inlaid in various
woods w/leafage & two dragonflies
in flight, continuing to a lower open
shelf pierced & inlaid w/ blossoms
raised on animal-form feet, signed in
marquetry "Gallé" & inscribed "E.
GALLÉ," France, ca. 1900, w/key,
15½ x 26", 5' 4" h......................**31,625.00**

Side cabinet, Oriental, cypress,
tapered-form, rectangular beaded
top above a pair of long doors
opening to an interior w/a single
shelf & a pair of short drawers, the
sides tapering out, raised on
tall legs, China, 18th c.,
16¾ x 28¾", 41¾" h.....................**3,738.00**

Side cabinet, Victorian Renaissance
Revival substyle, inlaid & ebonized
rosewood, the superstructure
centered by a later added bisque
plaque, the scrolled top w/berried &
foliate finials above a central

pedestal, the lower section w/two
cupboard doors carved w/foliate
swags, the canted sides fitted
w/rectangular panels, headed by a
gilt-bronze bust & ending in paw
feet, the whole inlaid w/anthemia,
interlacing ribbons & incised scrolls,
New York, third quarter 19th c.,
78½" w., 7' 4" h. (losses &
additions) **5,463.00**

Side cabinet, Victorian Rococo
substyle, rosewood, the rectangular
top w/serpentine edges above a flat
case w/a long drawer w/incised oval
banding & a roundel above a pair of
cupboard doors w/oval mirrors
flanked by chamfered front corners
w/scroll carved drops at the top, the
serpentine apron w/shell carving at
the center, ca. 1860 ....**1,320.00**

Victorian Rococo Side Cabinet

Side cabinet, Victorian Rococo
substyle, mahogany, two-part
construction: the upper section w/a
tall pierced & scroll-carved arched
cornice above the arched top
w/rounded front corners & molded
cornice above an arched cupboard
door w/a large round mirror flanked
by chamfered front corners w/carved
leafy scroll bands; the stepped-out
lower section w/serpentine molded
edges above a long drawer over two
cupboard doors w/oval panels
flanked by chamfered front corners
w/carved scroll bands, molded base
on short bulbous tapering front feet,
ca. 1850 (ILLUS.).....................**1,210.00**

Smoker's cabinet, Mission-style (Arts
& Crafts movement), oak,
rectangular top slightly overhanging

the case w/a narrow drawer w/two wooden knobs above a single cupboard door, arched apron, original medium dark brown finish, Gustav Stickley red decal mark, Model No. 89, 15 x 20", 29" h. (minor top staining, veneer repair on door) **1,650.00**

Vitrine cabinet, Art Nouveau, fruitwood & glass, gently curved & shaped rectangular cornice above glass walls w/sinuously carved glazing bars, the frame carved w/whiplash motifs, w/side doors opening to two glass shelves, raised on four curved legs, Edward Colonna, France, 1900, 21 x 42½", 5' 9" h. **32,200.00**

Louis XV-Style Vitrine Cabinet

Vitrine cabinet, Louis XV-Style, marquetry inlaid ormolu-mounted, the rectangular top w/swelled edges & a low pierced brass gallery above a case w/long curved glass panels over urn & scroll marquetry panels, the front w/a long curved door w/a large panel of glass opening to two glass shelves & above a rectangular urn & scroll marquetry panel, on simple cabriole legs w/ormolu bands, ormolu chain banding on the apron & forming a front scroll pendant, France, late 19th c. (ILLUS.) **1,320.00**

Vitrine cabinet, Louis XVI-Style, ormolu-mounted mahogany, a D-form top w/curved sides & flat front section above conforming curved glass sides & a central flat glass door opening to a burgundy velvet-lined interior w/two glass shelves,

narrow openwork brass gallery on the top & an ormolu decorative band at the top frieze, ormolu mounts at the top & bottom of the stiles separating the door from the sides, on very simple slender cabriole legs, late 19th - early 20th c., 4' 7½" h. **770.00**

Neoclassical Vitrine Cabinet

Vitrine cabinet, Neoclassical style, walnut, the rectangular top w/deep coved cornice flanked by stepped-back side wing panels w/matching cornice, the central cabinet section w/a frieze band w/dentil carving over a floral-carved band flanked by scroll-carved corner blocks above a long glass door w/a lower panel w/an oval floral-carved panel & latticework all flanked by slender reeded columns, the tall side wings w/overall lattice-carved panels & vining floral-carved edging fitted w/quarter-round shelves above quarter-round side cabinets w/curved doors w/oval floral-carved & lattice-carved panels, wide molded apron on short peg feet, Europe, late 19th - early 20th c., 15 x 50", 5' 9" h. (ILLUS.) **2,530.00**

CHAIRS
Art Deco armchair, gold leaf, the curved back frame w/stepped arms & short legs in gold leaf, upholstered in coral & gold fabric w/a geometric pattern, designed by Paul T. Frankl, ca. 1927, 27" w., 29" deep, 34" h...**4,370.00**

Art Deco armchair, mahogany & parquetry, the arched padded upholstered back w/outcurved arms

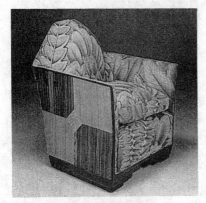

Art Deco Armchair

& padded seat on bracket feet, the
exterior of the rectangular arms
w/geometric parquetry designs,
American-made, 29" h.
(ILLUS.) **1,840.00**

Art Deco armchairs, birch &
upholstery, the rounded back above
deep outswept arms w/curved wood
facings continuing to the wooden
base frame raised on short reeded
S-scroll front legs & tapering curved
square rear legs, upholstered in tan
striped silk, France, ca. 1925, pr...**2,875.00**

Art Deco armchairs, *ebene-de-
Macassar,* wide rectangular straight
upholstered back flanked by slender
flat square open wooden arms
above curved cut-out sides, deep
upholstered seat, heavy block feet,
original celadon green mohair
upholstery, Leon Jallot, France,
ca. 1930, pr. **8,050.00**

Art Deco 'gondola' side chairs,
carved mahogany, the low back
w/tapering stiles to the backswept
rolled bar crestrail continuing in a
ribbed fanned carved back panel,
tufted upholstered back & rounded
tufted upholstered seat on a molded
seatrail & shaped squared legs w/a
tassel carved at the knees & block
feet, Sue et Mare, France,
ca. 1925, set of 6 ....**27,600.00**

Art Deco side chairs, painted wood,
the rectangular overscrolling padded
back & seat on square tapering
slightly splayed legs, American-
made, 30½" h., pr. **1,093.00**

Art Nouveau *bergere* **(armchair),**
giltwood, the gently curved crestrail
continuing to flattened curved
armrests, on divided carved legs
w/out-turned feet, the backrest
divided into three panels &
upholstered in needlepoint w/an Art

Nouveau floral design, Louis
Majorelle, France, 28" deep,
34¾" w., 45" h. **7,475.00**

Art Nouveau dining chairs, carved
fruitwood, each w/a flower-carved
concave crestrail above a pierced &
oblong padded back w/molded arms
centering an over-upholstered seat
raised on square tapering legs
w/scrolling toes, Italy, ca. 1900,
two arm & six side chairs,
set of 8 ....**2,875.00**

Arts & Crafts armchair, oak & woven
straw, the tall winged concave
woven straw back continuing to
shaped wood arms on turned
supports, straw seat, square wood
legs joined by flat stretchers,
England, early 20th c. **5,175.00**

Arts & Crafts side chair, oak, the
slab back w/rectangular hand-hold,
resting against the crestrail, joining
two stiles, w/leather-covered drop-in
seat, on square legs joined by
stretchers, designed by Frank Lloyd
Wright for the Francis Little House,
Peoria, Illinois, 1902, 30" h. **5,750.00**

Bentwood armchair, the curved
backrail above three horizontal
supports, the upholstered seat
raised on four round section feet
conjoined by a horseshoe-form
base, designed by Josef Hoffmann,
probably made by J. & J. Kohn,
Austria, early 20th c., 29" h. **230.00**

Bentwood Armchairs

Bentwood armchairs, the U-form
crestrail continuing to form armrests
& front legs, bentwood stretchers,
upholstered back & seat, paper
label, designed by Gustav Siegel,
Austria, ca. 1905, reupholstered,
29¾" h., pr. (ILLUS.) **715.00**

Bentwood rocking chairs w/arms,
painted finish, unusual sculptural
form w/curled branch-form sides &
arms centering a slat-mounted seat
& back, on rockers, painted green,
Pennsylvania, early 20th c., pr......**1,380.00**

Bentwood rocking chair w/arms, the scrolled branch-form stiles & arms centering a bentwood pierced back & seat, on rockers, probably Pennsylvania, early 20th c. **1,380.00**

Chippendale armchair, carved walnut, the shaped crestrail centering a carved shell above a pierced volute-carved vase-form splat, the shaped arms ending in scrolled handholds w/incurvate arm supports below, the molded shell-carved seatrail enclosing a slip seat, on cabriole legs ending in claw-and-ball feet, Philadelphia, ca. 1760 (patch to front section of shoe & other repairs) **19,550.00**

Chippendale corner chair, maple, the U-shaped crestrail & shaped backrail continuing to form outscrolled handholds above heart-pierced splats, the seatrail below enclosing a removable rush seat, on square legs joined by ring- and block-turned stretchers, probably Rhode Island, ca. 1785 (old repair to crestrail) **2,300.00**

Chippendale side chair, carved mahogany, the arched crest w/carved ruffle flanked by scrolled & carved acanthus leaves & scrolled & carved ears above a pierced splat over a carved tassel, ruffled & pierced flared trefoil flanked by scroll-carved acanthus leaves & volutes above original slip seat & front rail w/applied carved gadrooning, on acanthus-carved cabriole legs w/ball-and-claw feet, incised Roman numeral III on slipseat & chair frame, New York, 1760-80, 38¼" h. (repair to seatrail at joint w/front rail) **10,350.00**

Chippendale side chair, carved mahogany, the carved & shaped crest above a volute-carved vase-form splat & over-upholstered seat, on punchwork-decorated acanthus-carved cabriole legs joined by turned stretchers ending in claw-and-ball feet, Boston-Salem, Massachusetts, ca. 1770 ....**3,450.00**

Chippendale side chair, mahogany, the shaped crest above a pierced Gothic splat, the molded seatrail enclosing a slip seat, on square molded legs joined by stretchers, Philadelphia, Pennsylvania, ca. 1770 ....**1,265.00**

Chippendale side chair, walnut, ox-yoke crest centered by a shell carving above shaped stiles flanking a vase-form splat, upholstered balloon-seat on cabriole front legs

Chippendale Walnut Side Chair

w/shell- and bellflower-carved knees & ending in claw-and-ball feet, baluster-turned H-stretcher, Newport, Rhode Island, ca. 1750, old refinish, imperfections, 39" h. (ILLUS.) **8,050.00**

Chippendale side chair, walnut, ox-yoke crestrail w/carved shell & scrolled ears above a vasiform splat, molded edge seat frame w/slip seat, cabriole legs w/trifid feet, 39¾" h. (inside of seat frame has old added strips of wood that probably supported a commode seat, new brace to inside back of seat frame under splat rail) **8,250.00**

Chippendale side chairs, maple, serpentine arch & carved ears above a pierced vase-shaped splat & stay-rail over a reeded balloon seat w/exposed front corners, on block- and vase-turned legs w/front Spanish feet joined by square side stretchers & ball- and ring-turned front stretcher, New England, 1760-80, 37½" h., pr. **3,450.00**

Chippendale-Style corner chair, carved hardwood w/old mahogany finish, the curved crestrail w/carving above three ring-turned supports & two ornately pierce-carved vase-form splats, needlepoint-upholstered seat, on three cabriole legs w/scroll-carved knees & ending on ball-and-claw feet, round turned back leg, late 19th - early 20th c., 31" h. (some wear & edge damage) **467.50**

Chippendale-Style side chairs, carved mahogany, scroll-carved oxbow crestrail above a pierced vase-form splat w/a latticework oval at the center, over-upholstered seat w/tack trim, cabriole front legs w/scroll-carved knees & ending in claw-and-ball feet, dark finish, England, late 19th - early 20th c., pr. (age cracks, minor repairs) **605.00**

Chippendale-Style wing chair, arched upholstered wingback above outward scrolled arms above the wide seat, on cabriole front legs w/shell-carved knees & claw-and-ball feet, old floral tapestry upholstery, 20th c. reproduction, 46" h..**1,100.00**

Child's highchair, Pilgrim Century, cherry, the back surmounted by lemon-form finials, the back & arm rails comprised of vase- and ring-turned cross members, the arms fitted w/mushroom-form handhold, the plank seat on turned legs joined by turned stretchers, New England, probably coastal Connecticut, ca. 1685, 40½" h. (old splice to lower 1" of right rear leg, front seatrail replaced & lacks footrest) **19,550.00**

Classical Gondola Dining Chair

Classical (American Empire) dining chairs, mahogany, gondola-form, arched & scroll-molded crestrail above vase-form splat on scalloped cross stretcher, slightly curved caned seat, simple front sabre legs joined by a flat stretcher, simple turned stretcher at sides & back, Southern U.S., ca. 1835, set of 6 (ILLUS. one of six) **495.00**

Classical (American Empire) side chairs, brass inlaid rosewood, each w/slightly bowed scrolling crestrail w/brass rosette terminals above a pierced foliate splat inset w/circular brass medallions flanked by molded sloping stiles over trapezoidal slip seat, on molded sabre legs, one stamped on seatrail "WS," attributed to William Seavers, Boston,

Classical Rosewood Side Chair

slip seat, shaped front sabre legs, Philadelphia or New York, ca. 1825, 31¼" h., set of 6 (ILLUS. one of six) **1,380.00**

Classical Maple Side Chairs

Classical (American Empire) country-style side chairs, curly maple, the shaped crest above a vase-form splat, the curved stiles continuing to a caned seat on sabre-legs, joined by stretchers, first quarter 19th c., pr. (ILLUS.) **402.00**

Classical (American Empire) country-style side chairs, painted wood, a flat curved crestrail above slightly curved stiles flanking a lower gently arched slat above the square caned seat, flat shaped front legs joined by a flat curved stretcher & round side & back stretchers, simulated overall rosewood graining & gold striping, old surface w/over-varnish, New York State or New

England, ca. 1830, set of 6
(replaced cane seats) **546.00**

Country-Style Weaver's Chair

Country-style weaver's chair, birch
& ash, the back w/three slats, the
arms & rush seat below on turned
legs joined by stretchers, ca.
1800-20 (ILLUS.) **1,955.00**
Danish Modern folding side chairs,
oak & rush, the folding cross-legged
chair w/organically carved stretcher,
the back & seat in woven rush,
designed by Hans J. Wegner,
branded "JOHANNES HANSEN
COPENHAGEN DENMARK,"
ca. 1949, 29¼" h., pr....................**2,530.00**

Edwardian Corner Chair

Edwardian corner chair, painted
satinwood, two upright square back
panels, each w/flat-curved paint-
decorated crestrail over a half-round
caned back panel, square
upholstered seat on turned &
tapering legs, ca. 1900 (ILLUS.) ...**1,320.00**

Federal armchair, carved mahogany,
shield-shaped back carved w/wheat-
ears, a kylix & a basket of fruit &
leaves, shaped arms on curved
arm supports above the over-
upholstered bowed seat w/a brass-
tacked border, on square molded
tapering legs joined by stretchers,
original black horsehair upholstery,
appears to retain original patina,
attributed to Samuel McIntire,
Salem, Massachusetts, ca. 1800
(lacks two small sections of
splat) **21,850.00**

Painted Federal Armchair

Federal armchair, painted, the
slightly bowed tablet crest painted
w/country river landscape depicting
a farmhouse & figures in a rowboat
above two rod-and-reel horizontal
slats flanked by chamfered stiles &
scrolled arms over rush seat, on
turned tapering legs joined by
stretchers, w/compressed ball feet,
the entire surface painted green
& embellished w/gilt highlights,
probably New York, ca. 1800,
33¾" h. (ILLUS.) **805.00**
Federal "barrel-back" wingchair,
the rounded barrel-back above
out-swept upright arms over a
loose cushion seat, square tapering
legs, upholstered in brocade, New
York or New England, ca. 1800 ....**3,738.00**
Federal "fancy" side chairs,
painted, a flat crestrail above three
arrow slats between tapering stiles,
shaped plank seat, canted bamboo-
turned legs joined by box stretchers,
each painted yellow w/brown
& black trim, the tablet crestrail
painted w/a shell & foliage, New
England, early 19th c., 32½" h.,
pr..**575.00**

Federal country-style "fancy"
chairs, painted & decorated,
horizontal crestrail above four
bamboo-turned slats w/a central
arrow back slat flanked by slightly
splayed stiles, the shaped plank
seat on tapering bamboo-turned
legs joined by similarly turned
stretchers, w/red & green floral
decoration on a black ground
heightened w/yellow foliage &
piping, probably Pennsylvania,
ca. 1820, set of 6 ....**14,950.00**

Federal "Lolling" Chair

Federal "lolling" armchair,
mahogany, the tall back
w/serpentine crest canted &
continuing to downcurving arms
on square tapering legs, joined by a
recessed stretcher, Massachusetts,
ca. 1800, lacks medial stretcher
(ILLUS.) **4,025.00**

Federal Side Chairs

Federal side chairs, carved
mahogany, each w/slightly
bowed rectangular crestrail above
reeded stiles & stayrail centered

three reeded uprights flaring at
the top to form four Gothic arches,
over balloon-shaped over-
upholstered seat, on reeded
tapering legs w/tapering splayed
feet, Baltimore, Maryland, ca. 1815,
31¾" h., pr. (ILLUS.) **3,450.00**

Federal side chairs, mahogany,
each w/shield-shaped back
w/carved uprights & upholstered
seat on square tapering legs joined
by stretchers, possibly Maryland,
ca. 1800, formerly w/slip seats,
now over-upholstered w/leather,
some repairs, pr. **805.00**

Federal side chairs, carved
mahogany, each having a shield-
shape back centering bellflower-
and-leaf carved uprights, the over-
upholstered seat below on reeded
square tapering legs, ending in
spade feet, New York, ca. 1800,
one armchair & nine side chairs,
some w/repairs, set of 10............**33,350.00**

George III Library Chair

George III library armchairs,
painted pine, each w/serpentine
padded back & seat upholstered
in beige silk damask, w/foliated
scrolled armrests, the shaped
seatrail centering a foliate clasp,
on foliate-carved cabriole legs
ending in scrolled toes, England,
ca. 1760, possibly from Thomas
Chippendale's workshop, partly
rerailed, pr. (ILLUS. one of
two) **63,000.00**

George III side chairs, mahogany,
each w/shaped foliate-carved
crestrail & pierced splat above
an upholstered drop-in seat, on
foliate-carved cabriole legs ending
in claw-and-ball feet, England, mid-

George III Side Chair

18th century, pr. (ILLUS. one of
two) **3,680.00**
George III side chairs, mahogany,
a scalloped narrow crestrail above
three wavy-edged slats between
wavy-edged stiles over the drop-in
seat upholstered in striped silk, on
square chamfered legs joined by
stretchers, England, late 18th c.,
pr...**4,025.00**
George III tub chair, mahogany, the
arched crestrail continuing to form
arms enclosing a rounded back
over a serpentine seat covered in
green leather, serpentine arm
supports continuing to form square
tapered legs w/spade feet, England,
late 18th century (ILLUS. top next
page)...**3,680.00**

George III Tub Chair

Louis XVI-Style *fauteuils* (open-arm
armchairs), beech, the oval
upholstered back w/a molded frame

above padded open arms w/curved
arm supports above the upholstered
seat, curved molded seatrail, on
turned reeded & tapering front legs,
peach wool upholstery, France,
19th c., 34½"h., set of 4 ....**380.00**
Mission-style (Arts & Crafts
movement) armchair, oak, thick
crestrail above six back slats flanked
by gently canted stiles continuing to
form the back legs, narrow flat arms
w/brackets attached to straight arm
supports forming the front legs,
original box cushion, medium finish,
unsigned L. & J.G. Stickley, Model
No. 422, ca. 1910, 38" h. **690.00**
Mission-style (Arts & Crafts
movement) child's rocking chair
w/arms, oak, three horizontal slats
flanked by square stiles continuing
to form the back legs, flat arms on
square set-back arm supports
continuing to form front legs, single
wide stretcher at front & back, two
narrow side stretchers, square dark
leather seat, Gustav Stickley red
decal mark, Model No. 343, ca.
1909, 25½" h..............................**1,035.00**
Mission-style (Arts & Crafts
movement) dining chairs, oak, wide
curve-topped crestrail above five
back splats between rectangular
stiles, raised above the rectangular
seat w/upholstered insert, double
rungs at front & sides, original light
to medium finish, branded Limbert
Furniture Co. mark, Model No. 1851,
ca. 1907, 36½" h., set of 6 ....**2,185.00**
Mission-style (Arts & Crafts
movement) "H-back" dining chairs,
oak, each back w/a broad vertical
slat notched at the top & bottom
edge, above drop-in leather seats,
square legs joined by box
stretchers, original medium dark
brown finish, Gustav Stickley red
decal marks, Model No. 394,
40" h., set of 10 (minor wear)........**4,400.00**
Mission-style (Arts & Crafts
movement) Morris armchair, oak,
slated adjustable back above wide
flat arms above five wide slats,
through-tenons in front & on sides,
original medium-dark brown finish,
new leather cushion, Gustav
Stickley red decal mark, Model
No. 332, 39" h. **5,500.00**
Mission-style (Arts & Crafts
movement) Morris armchair, oak,
the canted back w/four slats above
flat drop-arms over five wide slats,
arched corbels & through-tenons in
the top & sides, drop-in spring seat,
original reddish brown finish,

Stickley Morris Chair

branded Gustav Stickley mark,
Model No. 369, 32½ x 37½",
41" h. (ILLUS.) **6,875.00**

Mission-style (Arts & Crafts
movement) Morris armchair, oak,
adjustable back w/five horizontal
slats, five slats below each arm &
drop-in rope support for cushion,
w/green upholstered seat cushions,
small red decal mark of Gustav
Stickley, Model No. 2342,
ca. 1903, 36" deep......................**6,325.00**

Mission-style (Arts & Crafts
movement) rocking chair w/arms,
oak, a wide V-form crestrail over five
vertical slats between stiles & raised
above the seat, flat, shaped arms
w/through tenons & arched corbels,
rectangular stretchers, replaced
leatherette seat, original dark finish,
red decal mark of Gustav Stickley,
Model No. 312½, 26 x 27",
34½" h...**550.00**

Mission-style (Arts & Crafts
movement) rocking chair w/arms,
oak, a wide curved-top crestrail
above six narrow slats pierced w/a
narrow slit between stiles above the
flat shaped arms above four slats,
leather-upholstered spring cushion,
gently curved arm supports continue
to form front legs, red paper label of
the Harden Co., Camden, New
York, ca. 1910, 37¾" h. **862.50**

Mission-style (Arts & Crafts
movement) sewing rocker, the tall
back w/four slightly curved
horizontal slats, rope seat
foundation, short square legs joined
by box stretchers, original black
finish, Gustav Stickley red decal
mark, 19 x 24½", 33" h.....................**495.00**

Mission-style (Arts & Crafts
movement) "ladder-back" side chair,
oak, the tall back w/three wide
gently curved slats between square

stiles, new woven rush seat, square
slender legs w/a wide flat front &
back stretcher & narrow side
stretchers, original medium brown
finish, Gustav Stickley red decal
mark, Model No. 306½, 36" h. **467.50**

Mission-style (Arts & Crafts
movement) side chair, oak, a
curved-top crestrail above five back
slats, square seat w/spring cushion,
single rungs at front & back &
double rungs at sides, medium
finish, unsigned L. & J.G. Stickley,
Model No. 820, 36" h. **259.00**

Mission-style (Arts & Crafts
movement) side chair, oak, the tall
back w/a slightly arched crestrail
above three tall slats in the back, the
center one inlaid in various woods,
pewter & copper w/a stylized
blossom, replaced upholstered seat,
square legs joined by rungs, original
finish, designed by Harvey Ellis for
Gustav Stickley, ca. 1904 (repair
to inlay & frame)............................**8,338.00**

Modern style armchair, leather &
laminated wood, the arched
laminated arms continue down to
form the legs framing the long
continuous curved black leather
back & seat, designed by Marcel
Breuer for the Geller House, Long
Island, executed by Theodore
Schwamb Co., Cambridge,
Massachusetts, ca. 1945 ....**3,163.00**

Modern style armchair & ottoman,
'Kurva' style, laminated plywood, the
laminated plywood frame w/beige
upholstery supported by four
laminated plywood legs, w/a
matching oblong ottoman, designed
by Yngve Ekstrom, each branded
'SWEDESE DESIGN YNGVE
EKSTROM MADE IN SWEDEN,"

Modern Armchair

ca. 1945, chair 27½ x 29",
39¾" h., 2 pcs. **1,265.00**

Modern style armchairs, chrome &
leather, rectangular leather back
panel between chrome stiles
continuing to form back legs,
chrome U-form padded arms
continue down to form legs, leather
upholstered seat, early 20th c., set
of four (ILLUS. one of four, bottom
previous page) **920.00**

Modern style side chair, birch, the
rear stiles fitted w/rectangular blocks
at the top & bottom, the slab back
descending to the back stretcher &
pierced for attachment of back
cushion, w/drop-in upholstered seat,
designed by Frank Lloyd Wright, for
the Avery Coonley Playhouse,
Illinois, ca. 1912, 31" h. **4,600.00**

Modern style "womb" chair &
ottoman, upholstered deep cupped
form w/outswept arms, low back &
seat cushions, raised on slender
chromed steel tubular frame & legs,
matching ottoman w/cushion,
original yellow woven upholstery,
designed by Eero Saarinen in 1948
for Knoll Associates, Knoll
International upholstery label,
35" h., 2 pcs. **977.50**

Queen Anne armchair, cherry,
shaped ox-yoke crest above a vase-
form splat & shaped scrolled arms
on curved arm supports, shaped
seatrail enclosing a slip seat, on
cabriole legs joined by turned
stretchers & ending in pad feet,
possibly retains original finish,
Hartford County, Connecticut,
ca. 1760 ....**26,450.00**

Queen Anne "ladder-back"
armchair, painted finish, the
cylindrical stiles w/turned finials
centering six graduated arched
slats, the flattened shaped arms
w/scrolled handholds above vase-
turned arm supports over a
trapezoidal rush seat w/double cyma
seatrails, on cabriole legs w/squared
feet joined by double cylindrical side
& single rear stretchers w/double
ball-and-ring turned front stretcher
w/flared terminals, painted black,
Delaware Valley, 1740-60,
16¾" deep, 23" w., 44" h. **2,760.00**

Queen Anne wing armchair, maple,
the arched crest flanked by ogival
wings continuing to scrolled arms,
the balloon-shaped seat on cabriole
legs joined by turned stretchers &
ending in pad feet, New England,
ca. 1760 ....**14,950.00**

Queen Anne Corner Chair

Queen Anne corner chair, painted
maple, the U-shaped back rail
above two vase-form splats
centering ring-turned uprights, the
serpentine seatrail centering a
leather-covered seat cushion lifting
to reveal a pine board pierced for a
commode, on a frontal cabriole leg
ending in a pad foot, the rear legs
tapering & ending in pad feet,
Massachusetts, ca. 1760, three rear
feet extended approximately two
inches & repair to one hand-hold
(ILLUS.) **2,070.00**

Queen Anne "banister-back" side
chair, maple, surmounted by acorn
finials centering a gilt leaf- and
volute-carved crest above four split-
baluster uprights, the rush seat on
vase- and block-turned legs joined
by a frontal bulbous stretcher,
New England, 1740-70 ....**2,300.00**

Queen Anne side chair, paint-
decorated maple, the shaped crest
above a vase-form splat & white-
painted rush seat on vase- and ring-
turned legs joined by a bulbous
stretcher, ending in pad feet, the
splat painted w/flowers & leaves in
polychrome on a green ground,
New York, 1760-90 ....**3,737.00**

Queen Anne side chair, maple, ox-
yoke crest above a solid vase-
shaped splat flanked by tapering
stiles over a trapezoidal rush seat
w/corner blocks above block-and-
baluster turned legs w/ball feet
joined by baluster- and ring-turned
front stretcher & double side
stretchers, lower rear stretcher
similarly turned, Connecticut,
1730-50, 40" h. **1,265.00**

Queen Anne side chair, walnut, the
upswept crestrail centering a

scalloped shell above cyma-curved stiles & a conforming pierced vase-shaped splat over a balloon-shaped slip seat, on shell-carved cabriole legs w/trifid feet, the seat marked "VI," the seat framed marked "IV," Philadelphia, 1749-1760, 41½" h. (two minor loses on splat) **27,600.00**

Queen Anne side chair, walnut, the shaped crest above a vase-form splat & slip seat on shell-carved cabriole legs, ending in paneled pad feet, Philadelphia, Pennsylvania, ca. 1745 (minor repair to crest) **3,162.00**

Queen Anne side chairs, veneered walnut, shaped crest above a vase-form splat, the veneered molded balloon-shaped seatrail enclosing a slip seat, on volute-carved cabriole legs ending in trifid feet, Philadelphia, 1725-45, pr. (patches to veneers & splats, some leg returns replaced) **24,150.00**

"RAR" rocking chair, greyish blue fiberglass shell on wire base w/curved birch rockers, designed by Charles & Ray Eames for Herman Miller, 1950, impressed marks & paper label, 25" w., 28" h. (minor blemish) **357.50**

Shaker Slat-back Chair

Shaker "slat-back" chair, maple, rounded button finials above swelled cylindrical stiles flanking two rod slats above a trapezoidal clothe-tape woven seat on tapering cylindrical legs joined by double box stretchers, stenciled "Shaker's - Mt. Lebanon, NY. - No.____ - Trademark," early 20th c., 13½ x 17¼", 27½" h. (ILLUS.) **1,610.00**

Turn of the century office chair, oak, the wide curved crestrail above a back w/square spindles above the

square seat swiveling on a pedestal w/four arched thick legs on casters, labeled by Heywood-Wakefield Co., ca. 1910 ....**137.50**

Victorian country-style high-back rocking chair w/arms, painted & decorated, a wide slightly shaped crestrail above a very wide scroll-cut splat w/a top keyhole cut-out flanked by round stiles, S-form arms on turned supports, wide plank seat on canted turned legs joined by front & back stretchers, worn original green paint w/black & gold striping & stenciled fruit in the crestrail, ca. 1860, 41" h. **550.00**

Gothic Revival Armchair

Victorian armchair, Gothic Revival substyle, carved mahogany, the arched pierced crest above a splat carved w/pointed arches centering a pierced flower & quatrefoils flanked by turned stiles & upholstered arm supports w/rounded hand grips over an upholstered seat, on ring-turned tapering cylindrical legs, New York, 1850-75, 4' 8¾" h. (ILLUS.) **4,025.00**

Victorian side chairs, Gothic Revival substyle, mahogany, the horizontal splat pierced w/three trefoils above four vertical slats forming pointed arches over an over-upholstered bowed seat, on sabre legs, attributed to J. & J.W. Meeks, 1836-1859, New York, set of 6 ...**10,350.00**

Victorian armchair, Rococo substyle, carved & laminated rosewood, balloon back carved at the crest w/fruit & flowers, over a serpentine seat, cabriole front legs & arched & splayed rear legs on casters, "Rosalie" patt., John Henry Belter, New York, ca. 1850 (ILLUS. top next page) **2,750.00**

Belter "Rosalie" Pattern Armchair

"Stanton Hall" Armchair

Upholstered Victorian Side Chair & Armchair

Victorian armchair, Rococo substyle, rosewood, barrel-back form, the high upholstered barrel back above rolled upholstered arms over the broad upholstered seat w/long front fringe, on four cabriole legs, brass front casters, probably New Orleans, ca. 1860, pr. (ILLUS. right, one of two) **522.50**

Victorian armchair, Rococo substyle, rosewood, the high balloon back w/an arched crestrail centered by a rose- and fruit-carved finial flanked by rope-twist bands over a pierced scroll-carved & serpentine back frame around the tufted upholstered back, padded open arms on curved molded arm supports over the wide upholstered seat w/serpentine seatrail carved w/a scroll cartouche, demi-cabriole front legs, square tapering canted back legs, all on casters, "Stanton Hall" patt., by J. & J.W. Meeks, New York, ca. 1850 (ILLUS. top next column) **4,125.00**

Belter Victorian Armchair

Victorian armchairs, Rococo substyle, carved & laminated rosewood, tall balloon back w/oval upholstered panel framed by wide pierced carved crestrail & sides w/a large fruit- and floral-carved crest & vine-carved sides, shaped open arms on curved arm supports over the upholstered seat, serpentine seatrail w/floral-carved center continuing to demi-cabriole legs, on casters, John Henry Belter, New York, ca. 1850, pr. (ILLUS. one of two) **38,500.00**

Victorian "patent" side chair, Renaissance Revival substyle, mahogany, "lollipop" form, round slightly curved crestrail above slender canted stiles, flanking three "lollipop"-form turned spindles joined at the base by a turned ring, angled front legs framing round upholstered

Hunzinger "Patent" Side Chair

seat, turned front supports on turned front stretcher, Hunzinger patent, ca. 1875 (ILLUS.) **192.50**

Rococo Side Chair

Victorian side chair, Rococo substyle, laminated & carved rosewood, tall balloon back w/tufted upholstered panel framed by ornate pierced scroll carving, oval upholstered seat w/scroll-carved seatrail continuing to demi-cabriole front legs on casters, "Stanton Hall" patt., Meeks, New York, ca. 1850 (ILLUS.) **2,200.00**

Victorian side chairs, Rococo substyle, rosewood, balloon back w/thumb molded frame around upholstered panel over rounded upholstered seat w/thumb molded serpentine seatrail continuing to demi-cabriole legs on casters, probably New Orleans, ca. 1860, set of 4 (ILLUS. one of four, left w/upholstered armchair) **770.00**

"Henry Clay" Pattern Side Chair

Victorian side chairs, Rococo substyle, laminated rosewood, rose-centered arched crest over C-scroll shaped upholstered back over balloon-shaped upholstered seat, rose-carved frieze on cabriole legs ending in French scroll feet, "Henry Clay" patt., by John Henry Belter, ca. 1850, pr. (ILLUS. one of two) **2,750.00**

Embossed Victorian Side Chair

Victorian side chairs, Rococo substyle, silver-covered rosewood, tall arched ballooned back w/upholstered panel framed by scroll-embossed silver framing, rectangular cushioned seat w/deep embossed seatrail, thick cabriole front legs, Anglo-Indian, mid-19th c., pr. (ILLUS. one of two)....................**412.50**

Wallace Nutting signed Windsor
"bow-back" armchair, the bowed
crestrail above seven spindles
above the armrail ending in
knuckled-handholds over baluster-
turned spindles & canted baluster-
& reel-turned arm supports, shaped
oblong seat on canted baluster- and
reel-turned legs joined by a turned
H-stretcher, original dark brown
finish, original paper label, early
20th c.. 38½" h. (some wear &
over-varnish) **935.00**

Wallace Nutting signed Windsor
"bow-back" side chair, the bowed
backrail over eight baluster-turned
spindles & two brack-back spindles,
shaped saddle seat on canted
baluster- and reel-turned legs joined
by a turned H-stretcher, original dark
finish, original paper label,
38½" h..**550.00**

Stickley, Model No. 64, ca. 1909,
31½" h., pr. **12,650.00**

Wicker side chairs, oval medallion
back w/tight caning framed by a
band of tight round spirals, raised
above an open arch over the round
caned seat, cabriole legs w/tapering
wicker scroll bands, painted white,
late 19th c., 40½" h., pr....................**316.00**

Pair of Wicker Side Chairs

Wicker side chairs, tall balloon back,
w/a central oval panel w/diamond
design framed by ornate scrolls &
latticework, slender skirt guards
from back to round woven seat,
slender curved front legs w/tightly
woven sections at the knees
flanking the initials "C.W.," late
19th c., 38½" h., pr. (ILLUS.) **5,175.00**

Wicker Armchair

Wicker armchairs, the back w/a
large tightly woven oval panel
framed by a ring of tight scrolls
between turned and wrapped stiles,
bentwood arms on ball-turned
supports above rectangular solid
seat, slender turned front legs
w/ornate wicker scroll brackets,
painted white, late 19th c., matching
gentlemen's & lady's, 42" h. &
45½" h., pr. (ILLUS. gentlemen's
chair) **575.00**

Wicker armchairs, willow, a low flat
square back of tightly woven bands
above an open diamond-lattice
lower section flanked by broad flat
tightly woven arms over latticework
sides, the seatrail w/a tightly woven
band above a diamond-lattice skirt,
pale moss green finish, w/canvas
cushion, attributed to Gustav

William & Mary Rush-seat Armchair

William & Mary armchair, black-
painted maple, the back w/four
arched & graduated slats flanked by
turned knop-form finials on sausage-
turned stiles continuing to turned

arms, the arm supports w/mushroom finials & supported on sausage-turned legs joined by conforming stretchers, New England, early 18th c., once fitted w/rockers (ILLUS.) **4,312.00**

William & Mary "Great" chair, painted wood, w/scrolled & heart-pierced crown crest above four vertical molded banisters flanked by balusters and ring-turned stiles & scrolled arms w/underarm stretcher over a rushed seat, on turned legs w/double stretchers, painted red, Connecticut, 1735-1745, 46½" h. (restorations to crest) **2,760.00**

William & Mary Side Chair

William & Mary side chairs, ox-yoke crest continuing to molded stiles flanking a vase-form splat, old woven rush seat, baluster-, ring-, and block-turned front legs ending in Spanish feet & joined by a knob- and ring-turned front stretcher, box stretcher at sides & back, old brown stain, New England, late 18th c., 42" h., pr. (ILLUS. one of two) **1,955.00**

Windsor "arrow-back" rocking chair w/arms, painted pine & maple, flat crestrail above fiddle-shaped splats over a narrow horizontal rail above four arrow-form uprights, flanked by slightly flared & bowed stiles continuing to downcurving shaped arms, the shaped seat on bamboo-turned legs joined by front & back stretchers on shaped rockers, the crestrail painted w/green oak leaves & acorns all on a mustard yellow ground highlighted by black & brown pinstriping, New England, ca. 1820 (some wear & paint loss) **1,725.00**

Windsor "bow-back" armchair, molded bowed crestrail above slender spindles, a shaped saddle seat on splayed baluster- and ring-turned legs joined by turned H-stretcher, New England, late 18th c., 35" h.,(refinished)............**3,190.00**

Windsor Child's Rocker

Windsor child's rocker, grain-painted & stenciled, the rectangular crestrail above five spindles, the seat w/incised edge on raking bamboo-turned legs joined by stretchers, painted & grained overall to simulate rosewood, the crestrail stenciled w/flowers & leaves, stenciled paterae flanking, ca. 1820-29, right arm repaired (ILLUS.) **1,150.00**

Windsor "comb-back" rocking chair w/arms, painted & decorated, a wide short crestrail w/canted ends raised on four arrow slats above the wide crestrail over four larger arrow slats, turned & flaring stiles above curved arms over bamboo-turned supports, thick plank seat w/rounded front on turned front legs w/inset rockers joined by a turned front stretcher & plain side & back stretchers, old worn & yellowed white repaint w/a stenciled vintage design on the crestrails & black & green striped trim, arms w/old natural finish, early 19th c., 43¾" h..**550.00**

Windsor "comb-back" & "brace-back" armchair, the shaped crestrail w/volute-carved ears above five tapered spindles, two supporting spindles behind, the ring-turned stiles flanking, continuing to shaped arms ending in scrolled knuckle handholds, the elliptical peaked plank seat below on vase- and reel-turned legs joined by turned stretchers, decorated w/gilt highlights on the legs, arm supports & stiles, branded C. Chase, Nantucket, Massachusetts, 1765-90, w/incised inscription on underside of seat "The Brigadier, 1794" (minor repairs) **28,750.00**

Windsor "continuous arm" & "brace-back" armchair, arched crestrail braced w/slender spindles above nine turned spindles, crest continues to form shaped arms on baluster- and ring-turned supports, shaped seat on splayed baluster- and ring-turned legs joined by a turned H-stretcher, old black paint, Rhode Island, 18th c., 38" h..........**1,595.00**

Windsor "fan-back" armchair, the serpentine crestrail above seven slender spindles on a medial rail continuing to form curved handgrips above heavy turned spindles above a shaped seat, raised on splayed baluster- and ring-turned legs joined by a turned H-stretcher, New England, ca. 1780, 41" h...........**2,310.00**

Windsor "fan-back" side chair, painted, the arched crestrail w/rounded ears above six spindles flanked by bamboo-turned stiles, shaped saddle seat on canted bamboo-turned legs joined by H-stretcher, old Spanish brown paint, Connecticut River Valley, 1790-1810, 36" h. (imperfections) **747.50**

Windsor "fan-back" & "brace-back" side chair, maple & ash, serpentine crestrail braced w/slender spindles above five spindles, shaped plank seat on splayed baluster- and ring-turned legs, turned H-stretcher, refinished, 37½" h. **1,320.00**

Fan-back Windsor Side Chair

Windsor "fan-back" side chairs, each w/serpentine crestrail above

seven tapering spindles flanked by baluster-turned stiles over a shaped plank seat, on baluster-turned tapering legs joined by swelled H-stretcher, New England, 19th c., 37½" h., pr. (ILLUS. one of two) ...**1,035.00**

Windsor "sack-back" armchair, painted, the bowed crestrail above seven tapering spindles, the U-shaped back rail continuing to form scrolled knuckle handholds, one arm w/incised inscription "IIA 1830," the peaked plank seat on vase- and reel-turned splayed legs joined by a turned medial stretcher, ending in elongated vase-form feet, green paint, Pennsylvania, ca. 1785.....**31,050.00**

Windsor "sack-back" armchair, the bow-back above seven spindles over a continuous arm w/mitten hand-holds above swelled arm supports over a thick incised shaped plank seat, on triple-swelled legs joined by a swelled H-stretcher, painted red, Connecticut, 1790-1810, 36½" h. **1,840.00**

Windsor "Sack-back" Armchair

Windsor "sack-back" armchair, painted brown, the arching crestrail above five spindles & U-shaped armrail w/out-turned handgrips over baluster-turned supports & a shaped seat, on ring- and baluster-turned legs joined by a swelled H-stretcher, the entire surface painted brown w/gilt highlights, Pennsylvania, ca. 1790, 37¾" h. (ILLUS.) **1,955.00**

Windsor "sack-back" child's highchair, painted, the arched crestrail above five plain spindles over a U-shaped backrest over seven swelled turned spindles & canted baluster-turned arm supports, shaped seat on tall baluster- and ring-turned raking legs joined by an H-stretcher, painted bottle green w/yellow striping, New England, late 18th c. **7,188.00**

Windsor "step-down" side chairs, painted & decorated, shaped & stepped crest above a six-spindle back flanked by slightly splayed stiles, the shaped plank seat w/incised edge on bamboo-turned tapering legs joined by conforming stretchers, the crest w/red & green stylized foliage, the whole painted salmon red heightened w/green & black pinstriping, Daniel Stewart, Farmington, Maine, ca. 1820, set of 6 ....**32,200.00**

CHESTS & CHESTS OF DRAWERS

Chinese Apothecary Chest

Apothecary chest, painted & decorated, shaped shelf above 32 graduated small drawers & one long drawer, on shaped feet, one side fitted w/an unusual fold-out shelf on a single folding leg used as a table to mix the medicinal products, the whole grain-painted brown, over an ochre ground, New England, early 19th c., 12 x 35", 5' 7½" h. **$25,300.00**

Apothecary chest on stand, hardwood, rectangular top w/upturned ends above a tall case w/36 small square drawers each w/a Chinese inscription, paneled sides, molded stand base w/scroll-cut apron & curved legs joined by end floor stretchers, China, 19th c. (ILLUS. top next column) **935.00**

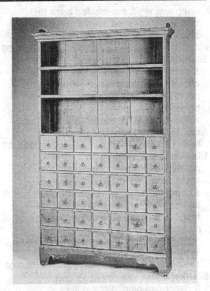

Rare Early Apothecary Chest

Apothecary chest & cupboard, painted pine, the rectangular top w/a deep cornice above two open shelves above a case w/42 small square molded drawers, molded front base w/scroll-cut bracket feet & shaped center pendant, overall bluish green paint, Massachusetts, ca. 1770-90, 10¼ x 41½", 6' 2" h. (ILLUS.) **151,000.00**

Child's Blanket Chest

Blanket chest, child's, painted pine, rectangular hinged top w/heavy molded edge opening to a well w/till, the front & sides of the case paneled & decorated w/stylized blossom heads in red on a yellow ground, singed by Jonathan Matiz, Pennsylvania, dated 1871, 13½ x 26¾", 16" h. (ILLUS.) **12,650.00**

Blanket chest, country-style, painted pine, the rectangular hinged lid w/wrought-iron hinges opening to a deep well w/till, the molded base on trestle feet, painted overall in red & black swirls, New England, early 19th c., 15¾ x 39", 17½" h...........**5,175.00**

Blanket chest, country-style, painted & decorated, molded rectangular top above conforming rectangular case decorated w/blue w/gold & copper floral foliate & geometric designs w/initials "W.B." in center, above molded rectangular base w/cut-out feet, 17 x 40", 18" h......................**1,265.00**

Blanket chest, country-style, grain-painted, the rectangular hinged top w/cleated molded edges opening to a compartment w/two drawer facade above two long drawers, on bracket feet, the drawers sponge-grained & mustard colored, the case sponge-grained & red, New England, 1760-1780, 43¾ x 44¾", 18¾" h....................................**6,900.00**

Blanket chest, country-style, painted & decorated pine, rectangular top w/molded edge opening to a deep well w/till, original reddish brown graining on a yellow ground, green compressed ball feet, 18½ x 36", 22½" h.....................................**2,200.00**

Blanket chest, late Federal country-style, painted wood, rectangular top w/molded edge opening to a well w/covered till, dovetailed case boldly decorated w/large fern-like leaves across the front in original brown flame graining, molded base on short baluster-turned feet, found in Archibold, Ohio, early 19th c., 19¾ x 45¾", 25" h........................**660.00**

Grain-Painted Blanket Chest

Blanket chest, country-style, grain-painted, rectangular top w/molded edge opening to a well, the dove-tailed case w/two long & one short drawers across the bottom decorated overall w/bold swirled grain paint in gold & old brown, on bracket feet, probably Pennsylvania, early 19th c., replaced brasses, imper-fections, 24 x 48", 29½" h. (ILLUS.) **1,840.00**

Blanket chest, Pilgrim Century, oak, rectangular top opening to a well above a case w/three molded panels centering a geometric coffered panel & split baluster-form appliqués flanked by broken-arch-molded panels, the skirt w/two molded panels centering split appliqués, the stiles continuing to form block feet, Essex County, Massachusetts, 1660-90, 21 x 45¼", 30½" h....................**63,000.00**

Blanket chest, Pilgrim Century, scratch-carved pine, the rectangular top opening to a well, the front of the case decorated w/incised pinwheel & geometric designs centering the initials "A S," Connecticut River Valley, 1690-1710, 16¾ x 39", 21¼" h. (right rear foot repaired, probably during the 18th c.) **2,875.00**

Chippendale "bow-front" country-style chest of drawers, painted maple, the rectangular top w/a bowed front above a conforming case w/four long drawers w/simple ball pulls & brass keyhole escutcheons, molded base on tall bracket feet, old Spanish brown paint, probably Massachusetts, ca. 1790, 18 x 37", 36" h. (imper-fections) **2,990.00**

Chippendale "Bow-Front" Chest of Drawers

Chippendale "bow-front" chest of drawers, mahogany, the rectangular thumbmolded top w/bowed front above a conforming case w/four cockbeaded graduated long drawers flanked by fluted quarter columns, over a molded base on ogee bracket feet, Philadelphia, ca. 1785, 23¼ x 43", 36⅞" h. (ILLUS.) **12,650.00**

Bird's-Eye Maple Chest of Drawers

Chippendale chest of drawers, bird's-eye maple & birch, rectangular top above a case of four long graduated drawers w/butterfly brasses & keyhole escutcheons, molded base w/tall bracket feet, old & possibly original finish, New England, ca. 1780, 20 x 38¾", 34" h. (ILLUS.) **4,025.00**

Chippendale chest of drawers, cherry, the rectangular molded top above four long graduated molded drawers, fluted quarter-columns flanking, on ogee bracket feet, Pennsylvania, ca. 1795, 22 x 41", 37" h. (minor repairs to feet) **3,162.00**

Chippendale chest of drawers, maple, rectangular top w/a molded edge above a case w/four long drawers w/original oval brass pulls, molded base on ogee bracket feet, old refinish, southeast New England, ca. 1790, 18 x 36", 35" h...............**4,600.00**

Chippendale "Serpentine-Front" Chest

Chippendale "serpentine-front" chest of drawers, cherry, the oblong thumb-molded top w/serpentine front above a conformingly-shaped case w/four long serpentine-front drawers, each w/incised edges, the gadrooned molded skirt below continuing to ogee bracket feet, Upper Connecticut River Valley, ca. 1785, 19½ x 36⅛" h., 32½" h. (ILLUS.) **10,350.00**

Chippendale "serpentine-front" chest of drawers, carved mahogany, oblong thumb-molded top w/reverse serpentine front above a conforming case w/four long graduated drawers, each w/cockbeaded surrounded, the molded skirt w/shaped center pendant, on claw-and-ball feet, possibly original rich warm brown patina, Boston area, Massachusetts, ca. 1770, 21⅛ x 36¼", 33" h...................**63,000.00**

Chippendale "serpentine-front" chest of drawers, mahogany, the rectangular thumbmolded top w/serpentine & reverse serpentine front above a conforming case fitted w/a leather lined writing slide over four graduated long drawer each w/cockbeaded surrounds & a molded base on short cabriole legs w/ball-and-claw feet, Boston, 1765-1775, 22¼ x 41", 35" h. **19,550.00**

Chippendale Tall Chest of Drawers

Chippendale tall chest of drawers, curly maple, rectangular top w/molded cornice above a row of three small drawers over a pair of drawers above three long graduated drawers, all w/simple bail pulls, molded base on tall scroll-cut bracket feet, probably Pennsylvania, ca. 1800, probably original brasses,

21½ x 39½", 4' 1⅞" h.
(ILLUS.) **6,900.00**

Chippendale tall chest of drawers,
curly walnut, rectangular top w/deep
flaring coved cornice above a row of
three arch-topped drawers over a
pair of long drawers above four long
graduated drawers all flanked by
quarter-columns, molded base on
large, tall scroll-cut bracket feet,
some original brass butterfly pulls,
old mellow refinishing, late 18th c.,
cornice 23½ x 42", 5' 1¼" h. (one
back foot old replacement, repaired
breaks in front feet, minor edge
repair & age cracks).......................**9,900.00**

Chippendale chest-on-chest, carved
maple, two-part construction: the
upper section w/a molded broken
scroll pediment terminating in carved
rosettes w/carved flame finials
surmounting fluted plinths above a
molded arched tympa-num over
three conforming thumbmolded
drawers, the central drawer carved
w/fans, above three long graduated
thumbmolded drawers; the lower
section w/mid-molding above four
long graduated thumbmolded
drawers, the bottom drawer carved
w/a fan, drawers flanked by fluted
pilasters surmounted by carved fans,
on cyma-curve bracket feet,
apparently original brasses,
attributed to Moses Nazen,
New Hampshire, 1800-15,
21½ x 43¼", 7' 3½" h. **17,250.00**

**Chippendale country-style chest of
drawers**, painted pine, rectangular
top slightly overhanging the case
w/four long overlapping drawers
w/replacement turned wooden knobs,
molded base on simple bracket feet,
old red repaint, late 18th c., 17½ x
39", 38" h. (old repairs to feet) **852.50**

**Chippendale country-style tall chest
of drawers**, maple, rectangular top
w/a deep coved molding above a
case w/six long graduated drawers
w/simple bail pulls and oval brass
keyhole escutcheons, molded base
w/shaped center apron drop & tall
scrolled bracket feet, New England,
ca. 1780, 17½ x 35½", 4' 3½" h.
(refinished) **4,312.50**

**Chippendale Revival "bow-front"
chest of drawers**, mahogany, a
small scroll-cut splashboard on the
rectangular top w/a bowed front
above a conforming case w/three
long drawers, on legs ending in claw-
and-ball feet, labeled by the Cowan
Company of Chicago, Illinois, early
20th c. **357.50**

**Classical (American Empire) chest
of drawers**, mahogany, the
rectangular top fitted w/a small case
of two small hanky drawers w/wood
knobs, the lower case w/four long
reverse-graduated drawers w/large
turned wood knobs, on short
bulbous inverted pear-shaped legs,
ca. 1840, 18 x 36½", 40¼" h...........**275.00**

Danish Modern Vanity Chest

Danish Modern vanity, walnut,
rectangular top above a drop-front
top long drawer opening to an
interior fitted w/a central retractable
mirror flanked on one side by small
drawers & on the other by slots, all
above two long drawers, simple
wood pulls, on round slightly
tapering legs, metal tag & stamped
mark of Illums Bolighus, Copenhagen, Denmark, mid-20th c.,
18⅛ x 39½", 34⅛" h. (ILLUS.) **431.00**

Dower chest, painted pine, the
rectangular molded hinged lid
opening to a well, the case w/mid-
molding above three short drawers,
the molded base on scroll-carved
bracket feet on pads, the whole
painted in red & black to simulate
rosewood, Pennsylvania,
early 19th c., 21 x 43", 27½" h. ...**6,900.00**

Dower chest, painted & decorated,
the rectangular molded top opening
to a deep well w/till, the case
w/waisted lower sections fitted
w/two small drawers, raised on
circular turned tapering legs, the
whole grain-painted in orange &
yellow, the front w/simulated owl's
eye & the sides w/stylized tulip
motifs, Pennsylvania, ca. 1830,
23 x 46", 29" h. (some wear
& loss to paint) **12,650.00**

**Federal "bow-front" chest of
drawers**, cherry, the rectangular top
w/bowed front above a conformingly

shaped case w/four graduated long drawers flanked by engaged quarter columns, raised on slightly splayed bracket feet, replaced brasses, old refinish, Connecticut, 1800-20, 23¾ x 42", 36¼" h. (imperfections) **2,420.00**

Federal "bow-front" chest of drawers, flamed birch- & mahogany-veneered birch, the oblong thumbmolded top w/bowed front above four reverse graduated mahogany cross-banded drawers, each comprising two book-matched flamed birch rectangular panels, the shaped skirt below centering a rectangular inlaid reserve, on bracket feet, Northeastern Shore, New England, possibly Portsmouth, ca. 1810, 21 x 41", 38½" h. (minor repairs to inlay) **6,325.00**

Federal "Bow-Front" Chest

Federal "bow-front" chest of drawers, mahogany w/satinwood inlay, rectangular top w/bowed front & ovolu front corners above a conforming case w/four long drawers w/wooden knobs flanked by outset reeded corner columns w/ring-turned tops & ending in baluster-turned reeded legs w/peg feet, New England, probably Rhode Island, ca. 1810, 22¼ x 43¼", 40" h. (ILLUS.) **9,775.00**

Federal chest of drawers, birch & bird's-eye maple, rectangular top w/outset rounded corners above a case w/four long graduated drawers each edged w/mahogany crossbanding centering an oval flame birch reserve flanked by rectangular bird's-eye maple panels flanked by reeded columns, on turned tapering legs w/ring-turned ankles, Spooner and Fitch, Athol,

Massachusetts, 1800-10, 20½" deep, 42⅞" h. **10,350.00**

Federal chest of drawers, inlaid applewood, rectangular top above two small drawers over three graduated long drawers, the sides w/inlaid canted corners, wooden pulls & escutcheons, shaped skirt w/a fan-inlaid central drop, on tapering French feet, Haddam, Connecticut, early 19th c., 18½ x 39½", 41" h. (imperfections).........**4,400.00**

Federal chest of drawers, inlaid cherry, rectangular top above a case w/four long graduated drawers outlined w/stringing & cockbeading, inlaid escutcheons & inlay along the skirt, replaced brasses, refinished, Vermont, early 19th c., 19 x 40", 40" h..**2,310.00**

Federal chest of drawers, inlaid walnut, the rectangular top w/cross-banded edge above four graduated cockbeaded long drawers, the shaped skirt inlaid w/diamonds & centering a demi-lune reserve inlaid w/sprigs, on splayed bracket feet, Pennsylvania, ca. 1820, 17⅝ x 35½", 38½" h. **4,313.00**

Federal chest of drawers, mahogany, a rectangular top fitted w/a raised rectangular case of two small hanky drawers w/wooden knobs (one knob missing), the top above a long drawer overhanging three long graduated drawers flanked by spiral-turned columns, on tall ring-turned legs w/peg feet, simple wood knobs, early 19th c. **495.00**

Federal Walnut Chest of Drawers

Federal chest of drawers, walnut, rectangular top w/a molded edge above a pair of drawers over three long graduated drawers each w/simple bail pulls & oval brass keyhole escutcheons, scalloped

apron & French feet, southeastern
United States, early 19th c., old
refinish, 18 x 33", 32½" (imper-
fections) (ILLUS.) **1,495.00**

Federal tall chest of drawers, carved
& painted wood, the rectangular top
w/molded cornice over six molded
& graduated drawers, the fronts
w/oval medallions simulating inlay,
on scroll-cut bracket feet, painted
& grained in shades of yellow & red,
retaining the original chased brass
mounts, stamped "H.J.," signed
"Elijah Royce," & dated "1788,"
northern New England,
19½ x 37½", 4' 10¾" h. **28,750.00**

George II chest-on-chest, walnut,
two-part construction: the upper
section w/a rectangular top w/a
deep flaring cornice w/a band of
dentil carving above a lattice-carved
frieze band above a pair of small
drawers over three long graduated
drawers all flanked by canted &
reeded front edges; the lower
section w/a mid-molding over three
long graduated drawers, molded
base & cut-out bracket feet, simple
brass bail pulls, England, mid-
18th c., 21½ x 39", 6' 2" h.,
(losses, damage) **2,300.00**

George III Chest of Drawers

George III chest of drawers,
mahogany, the rectangular
thumbmolded top above a case
w/cockbeaded dressing slide over
four cockbeaded long graduated
drawers on a molded base w/later
bracket feet, England, third quarter
18th century, 35" w., 19¾" d.,
32¼" h. (ILLUS.) **4,025.00**

**George III "serpentine front" chest
of drawers**, satinwood, rectangular
top w/serpentine front above a
conforming case w/four long

graduated drawers, each w/round
brass ring pulls, later bracket feet,
late 18th c., 23 x 45", 37¼" h. (top
drawer now w/divides, some pulls
missing) **1,610.00**

George III-Style chest-on-chest,
mahogany, two-part construction:
the upper section w/an angled
pediment scroll-cut in the center w/a
central finial platform above a wide
molded cornice above a pair of
drawers over three long graduated
drawers flanked by chamfered front
corners; the lower section w/a
medial molding over three long
drawers flanked by slightly bombé
side styles, each drawer w/pierced
butterfly brasses & inlaid edge
banding, on a molded base
w/bracket feet, England, late 19th c.,
20 x 44½", 6' 10" h. **2,990.00**

**Hepplewhite country-style chest of
drawers**, cherry, rectangular top
above a case w/four long drawers
w/replaced oval brass pulls,
serpentine apron & French feet,
late 18th-early 19th c., 19 x 42",
39⅜" h. (refinished, minor foot
repairs) **1,485.00**

Jacobean Oak Chest

Jacobean chest, oak, rectangular
three-panel lid opening to a deep
well above a case w/a scroll-carved
front band above three molded
panels each w/cartouche & florette
carving, molded stile legs, England,
late 17th c., 23 x 55½", 29" h.
(ILLUS.) **1,092.50**

**Mission-style (Arts & Crafts
movement) chest of drawers**,
oak, rectangular top w/low backrail
above a pair of drawers over
three long graduated drawers all
w/wooden knobs, slightly curved
apron, paneled sides, original dark
brown finish, L. & J. G. Stickley
red decal mark, Model No. 97,
16 x 38", 39" h............................**1,760.00**

**Mission-style (Arts & Crafts
movement) chest of drawers**, oak,
a rectangular framed mirror

swiveling between tapering uprights above the rectangular top overhanging a case w/two short drawers over three long drawers, hammered strap hardware w/large round pulls, butterfly joints on the mirror, original finish, branded mark of Gustav Stickley, Model No. 905, ca. 1910, 22 x 48", 5' 5" h. **4,950.00**

Mission-style (Arts & Crafts movement) tall chest of drawers, oak, a rectangular top over a pair of paneled doors opening to cedar-lined cabinets over a pair of small drawers over three long graduated drawers, all w/painted wrought-iron plates & ring pulls, red decal mark of Gustav Stickley, Model No. 614, ca. 1902, 23½ x 46", 5' 1⅞" h. **24,150.00**

Mule chest (box chest w/one or more drawers below a storage compartment), Chippendale country-style, pine & poplar, rectangular top lifting above a well, the tall case w/two fake drawers above three long dovetailed drawers all w/bail pulls, molded base on tall scroll-cut bracket feet, old dark finish, late 18th c., top 19 x 38¾", 4' ¼" h. (two bails missing, one back foot reattached, age cracks) **1,595.00**

Early Mule Chest

Mule chest, cherry & pine, rectangular top w/applied molded edge opening to a deep well w/till, the case w/three molded long graduated drawers, the molded base on shortened bracket feet, bears a red-painted date on the back "1793," New England, 16¼ x 39", 38" h. (ILLUS.) **2,185.00**

Mule chest, Pilgrim Century, pine, the rectangular lid lifting above a deep well, the front of the case w/three

vertical rectangular raised panels above two long, paneled drawers at the bottom, raised on short, turned feet, old refinish, western Massachusetts, 17th c., 19½ x 41½", 43" h. **4,125.00**

Queen Anne chest of drawers, burr walnut, rectangular top inlaid w/a lobed oval panel above two short & three long drawers each w/figured burr walnut, boxwood & ebony lines, molded base w/bracket feet, England, early 18th c., 22 x 37", 35½" h. **9,200.00**

Queen Anne Chest-on-Frame

Queen Anne chest-on-frame, walnut, two-part construction: the upper section w/a rectangular top & molded cornice above a row of three short drawers above four long graduated drawers; the lower section w/a mid-molding above a deep scroll-cut apron on cabriole legs ending in trifid feet, warm brown color, Pennsylvania, ca. 1765, 22 x 41½", 5' 2¼" h.(ILLUS.)..........................**9,200.00**

Shaker sugar chest, maple, pine & oak, rectangular top w/bread-board ends & hinged lid opening to a conforming interior enclosed by raised panels over two drawers & a paneled cupboard door enclosing a single compartment interior, all on tapering cylindrical feet, Ohio, late 19th century, 25½ x 46¾", 43" h. **4,025.00**

Sheraton country-style chest of drawers, inlaid cherry, rectangular top above a case w/a pair of drawers w/line inlay above three long drawers w/line inlay, round brass drawer pulls, inlaid keyhole

escutcheons, cross-banded inlay
down front posts, simple ring-turned
legs w/ball feet, signed on the back
"Wm. McCormack, Cadiz, OH.,"
early 19th c., 20½ x 41", 43½" h.
(replaced brasses) **1,320.00**

Decorated Storage Chest

Storage chest, country-style, painted
pine, rectangular top w/molded ends
lifting above a deep well, the top,
front & sides decorated overall w/a
red wash w/mustard yellow & black
stippling, probably New England,
early 19th c., 24 x 54", 24" h.
(ILLUS.) **862.50**

Labeled New Orleans Chest of Drawers

Victorian chest of drawers, Rococo
substyle, carved mahogany, a tall
cartouche-form mirror w/scroll- and shell-
carved crest swiveling between scroll-
carved upright supports on the rectangular
white marble top above a long scroll-carved
drawer flanked by leaf-carved corner blocks
over three matching long drawers flanked
by chambered front corners w/rope twist &
baluster-turned bands, deep molded base
w/leaf-carved band & corner blocks on
compressed block feet on casters, bears the
label of Joseph Hubbard of New Orleans,
ca. 1850, 21½ x 45", 5' 4" h.
(ILLUS.)....................................**2,420.00**

Victorian Rococo Rosewood Chest

Victorian chest of drawers, Rococo
substyle, carved rosewood, a tall
arched mirror w/ornate pierced &
scroll-cut crest swiveling between
scroll-carved upright supports on a
rectangular white marble top
w/serpentine sides & front above a
serpentine band & three long flat-
front graduated drawers w/scroll-
carved banding & shell-carved pulls
& flanked by chamfered front corners
w/pierced scroll carving, serpentine
molded base on casters, incised
signature on the back "Belter," New
York, ca. 1860 (ILLUS.) **1,650.00**

CRADLES

Fine Biedermeier Cradle

Biedermeier cradle, mahogany, the rectangular cradle w/deep rounded sides w/slats & a brass liner suspended by columnar uprights, one fitted w/a swan's head w/ring, raised on a trestle base w/double baluster- and ring-turned stretchers & down-scrolled legs, Europe, second quarter 19th c., 21¼ x 41", 4' 7¾" h. (ILLUS. bottom previous page)......................................**2,300.00**

Country-style low cradle on rockers, pine, arched & canted headboard joined by low shaped sides to the shorter footboard, small heart cut-outs on each side, old worn dark finish, 42½" l...................**165.00**

Early Windsor Cradle

Windsor cradle, the sides w/thin turned rails above tall slender turned spindle sides, a stepped high end opposite a low gently curved end, solid rectangular bottom on solid shaped rockers, retains old brown over bluish green paint, New England, ca. 1810, imperfections, 17½ x 38", 24" h. (ILLUS.) **2,300.00**

CUPBOARDS

Corner cupboard, Chippendale, walnut, two-part construction: the upper section w/a molded & dentil-carved cornice above a pair of geometrically-glazed tall cupboard doors opening to a white-painted interior w/three shelves; the lower section w/a mid-molding above a pair of paneled cupboard doors opening to a white-painted interior w/shelves, molded base on ogee bracket feet, probably Pennsylvania, ca. 1780, 26½ x 52", 8' 1¼" h. (ILLUS. top next column) **3,450.00**

Corner cupboard, Chippendale, walnut, two-part construction: the upper section w/a molded shaped cornice above a pair of arched 11-pane glazed cupboard doors opening to shelves & flanked by fluted pilasters; the lower section

Chippendale Walnut Corner Cupboard

w/mid-molding above a pair of drawers over a pair of paneled cupboard doors flanked by fluted pilasters & opening to shelves, on bracket feet, Southern, ca. 1780, 28 x 5' 2", 8' 6" h. **6,325.00**

Corner cupboard, country-style, cherry, one-piece construction, a wide shaped & flaring cornice above a pair of long, raised panel cupboard doors, gently arched apron & simple cut-out feet, old finish, probably Ohio, 19th c., 62" w., 7' ½" h. (some water damage to feet, one door stile w/age cracks) **990.00**

Corner cupboard, country-style, cherry & poplar, one-piece construction, the flat top w/a narrow molded cornice above a pair of eight-pane glazed tall cupboard doors opening to shelves above a medial band over a pair of paneled cupboard doors, low molded bracket feet, 48" w., 7' 2¼" h. (hardware missing from doors, edge damage on cornice) **2,035.00**

Corner cupboard, country-style, painted poplar, two-part construction: the upper section w/a narrow cove-molded cornice over a very wide side & top panels framing a pair of six-pane glazed cupboard doors opening to serpentine shelves w/spoon cut-outs; the lower section w/a medial molding above a pair of paneled cupboard doors, flat base w/stubs of old feet, old red repaint, 19th c., 55" w., 6' 5¾" h. (replaced cast-iron door latches, one pane cracked) **770.00**

Small Corner Cupboard

Corner cupboard, country-style, painted pine, small size w/a flat top w/molded cornice above a long single molded door w/original wrought-iron "heart" strap hinges, opening to three shelves, on tapered bracket feet, original red w/white striping on the moldings & corners, feet painted black, ca. 1770-1800, 12 x 22", 5' 2" h. (ILLUS.) **3,450.00**

Corner cupboard, country-style, pine, two-part construction: the upper section w/a cove-molded cornice over a single 9-pane cupboard door; the lower section w/a pair of paneled cupboard doors, short turned feet, cupboard door frames w/beaded edge, cornice 44½" w., 6' 2½" h. (cornice ends replaced) **2,090.00**

Corner cupboard, country-style, walnut, two-piece construction: the upper section w/a flat flaring cornice above a pair of 6-pane glazed doors opening to two shelves; the lower section w/a medial molding above two small drawers above a pair of paneled cupboard doors, base molding & tall block feet, old dark alligatored finish, original brass thumb latches on the doors, western Pennsylvania, early 19th c., cornice 51½" w., 6' 9½" h. (brass pulls replaced, minor edge damage, corner crack in one glass)............**4,070.00**

Corner cupboard, Federal "bonnet-top" style, cherry, two-part construction: the upper section w/a swan's-neck scroll crest flanking an urn- and-acorn-turned finial w/matching corner finials above a long rope-turned arched frieze band

Federal "Bonnet-top" Corner Cupboard

issuing from ring- and rope-turned half-round pilasters flanking a pair of tall geometrically-glazed cupboard doors opening to three shelves; the lower section slightly stepped-out w/a mid-molding over a row of three small beaded drawers w/early pressed glass knobs above a pair of molded & raised-panel cupboard doors, molded base w/low gently curved apron & bracket feet, signed by Peter Levengood, Shop of William Royer, Douglas Township, Montgomery County, Pennsylvania, dated 1832, 55½" w., 7' 11" h. (ILLUS.) **5,750.00**

Corner cupboard, Federal, inlaid cherry, two-part construction: the upper section w/molded cornice above a dentil-inlaid tympanium & 12-pane glazed hinged door, opening to a white-painted shelved interior w/plate grooves, the door frame inlaid w/quarter fans; the lower section w/two bird's-eye maple drawers & a pair of line- and fan-inlaid cupboard doors, on bracket feet, Pennsylvania, first quarter 19th c., 28" deep, 44¾" w., 7' 4" h. **10,925.00**

Corner cupboard, Federal, inlaid walnut, two-part construction: the upper section w/molded cornice & tympanium inlaid w/line-inlaid swags above a pair of 8-pane glazed doors opening to shelves; the lower section w/a pair of line-inlaid hinged doors opening to shelves, pilasters inlaid w/columns flanking, the shaped skirt continuing to bracket

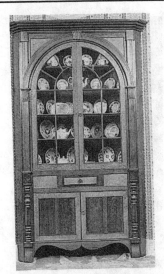

Fine Federal Corner Cupboard

feet, Southern, ca. 1800, 27½ x
49¼", 7' 11" h.............................**8,625.00**
Corner cupboard, Federal, curly
maple & cherry, one-piece
construction, a wide stepped cornice
above a paneled & arched frieze
over a pair of tall arched 10-pane
glazed cupboard doors opening to
four shelves above a small drawer
flanked by curly maple panels above
a pair of double-paneled cupboard
doors flanked by ring- and rod-
turned half-round pilasters,
serpentine apron & bracket feet,
ca. 1800, 22 x 54", 8' 4" h.
(ILLUS.) **9,625.00**
Corner cupboard, Federal country-
style, walnut, two-part construction:
the upper section w/a narrow coved
cornice above a pair of 8-pane
glazed cupboard doors opening to
three shelves; the lower section w/a
pair of paneled cupboard doors
opening to a shelf, old surface,
Southern States, early 19th c.,
22½ x 46½", 7' 4½" h.
(replaced pulls, imperfections) **3,162.50**
Corner cupboard, painted &
decorated pine, two-part
construction: the upper section
w/molded cornice w/fluted frieze
above an open cupboard w/butterfly
shelves; the lower section w/double
paneled door over simple base
molding, old red graining w/worn
blue interior, found in New England,
44½" w., 7' 4" h. **3,520.00**
Corner cupboard, Queen Anne,
carved cherry, one-piece
construction, the molded cornice &

surround centering a molded
serpentine pinwheel-carved
cupboard frame revealing three
open shaped shelves w/plate
grooves, a cupboard door below w/a
pair of arched panels over a
rectangular panel, fluted pilasters
flanking the door, Connecticut,
1750-70, 20 x 37", 6' 6" h. (some
patches to lower section, lower
backboards replaced) **8,050.00**

Early Hanging Wall Cupboard

Hanging wall cupboard, painted
pine, a rectangular top w/deep
molded cornice above a case w/a
long raised panel door w/wooden
knob & wooden thumb latch opening
to two shelves, molded base,
painted green, New England, late
18th c., 11½ x 19¾", 29" h.
(ILLUS.) **7,475.00**

Grain-painted Hanging Cupboard

Hanging wall cupboard, painted &
decorated pine, rectangular top
w/molded cornice above a pair of
raised panel cupboard doors
opening to an interior fitted w/eight

divided sections, the back side of
the right door w/a metal shield
painted in black & gold "N. J. Lord's
Office," the exterior painted &
grained in red & black & fitted
w/hinges for hanging, New England,
late 18th c., 12 x 37½", 31" h.
(ILLUS.) **1,495.00**
Jelly cupboard, poplar, rectangular
top above two short drawers in
beaded frames above pair of
paneled cupboard doors, old iron
thumb latch, simple cut-out feet,
refinished, 19¼ x 44",
4' 4¾" h. **715.00**

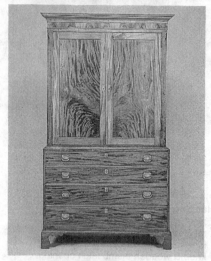

Chippendale Linen Press

Linen press, Chippendale,
mahogany, two-part construction:
the upper section w/a rectangular
top above a flaring coved cornice
above a pair of tall paneled doors
opening to shelves; the lower
section w/a mid-molding above four
long graduated cockbeaded
drawers, molded base on scroll-cut
bracket feet, New York, ca. 1795,
20¾ x 47", 6' 11" h. (ILLUS.) **11,500.00**
Linen press, Federal, cherry, two-
part construction: the upper section
w/a rectangular top w/a molded
cornice w/dentil frieze above a pair
of astragal-paneled cupboard doors
flanked by fluted quarter columns
opening to a compartment w/three
fitted shelves flanked by fluted
quarter columns; the lower section
w/mid-molding above two short
thumb-molded drawers over two
long thumb-molded drawers, on high
bracket feet w/spur returns, New
Jersey, 1790-1810, 19⅞ x 52½",

Federal Linen Press

6' 4½" h. (lower portion of right rear
foot replaced; upper cornice
missing) **7,475.00**
Linen press, Federal, inlaid & figured
mahogany, three-part construction:
the removable cornice above a midsection w/a pair of tall crotch-figured
& line-inlaid doors opening to two
adjustable shelves; the lower
section w/three long cockbeaded
graduated line-inlaid drawers,
shaped skirt continuing into tall
slender French feet, labeled by
Slover & Taylor, New York,
ca. 1800, w/original oval brasses,
21½ x 48", 7' 2" h. (ILLUS.) **8,625.00**

Early Texas Linen Press

Linen press, Victorian country-style,
yellow pine, the rectangular top w/a

narrow stepped cornice above a paneled frieze band w/arched corner blocks above a pair of arched raised-panel tall cupboard doors opening to shelves & flanked by fluted pilasters, two drawers in the base w/raised scalloped edging & flanked by scroll-cut corner blocks, on square tapering feet, Texas, mid-19th c., 22½ x 60", 6' 10½" h. (ILLUS.) **2,300.00**

Linen press, Victorian country-style, carved yellow pine, a low arched & pierced crestrail above a molded cornice w/canted corners over a conforming case centering two long lozenge-form recessed panels & inlaid ivory keyhole escutcheons, opening to shelved interior, on tall French feet, Texas, ca. 1870, 19¾ x 50", 6' 11" h. **1,610.00**

Pewter cupboard, painted poplar, one-piece construction, the rectangular top w/a narrow molded cornice above an open cupboard w/two shelves & molded framing, the lower half slightly stepped-out w/a pair of long cupboard doors w/white porcelain knobs & wooden thumb latch, low simple bracket feet, one-board ends, old light green repaint, probably from New York State, ca. 1850, cornice 10½ x 49½", 6' 3½" h. **5,720.00**

Pie safe, yellow pine, rectangular top above a pair of tall three-panel doors w/pierced tin inserts decorated w/Masonic designs, three pierced tin panels in each end, on tall square tapering legs, found in La Grange, Georgia, 17 x 41½", 4' 3" h. **990.00**

Step-back wall cupboard, Chippendale, walnut, two-part construction: the upper section w/molded cornice above a pair of 6-pane glazed doors opening to shelves; the projecting lower section w/a pair of short drawers above a pair of paneled hinged doors, on bracket feet, Pennsylvania, first quarter 19th c., 19½ x 51½", 6' 9" h. (feet replaced, patches to doors & drawers) **4,600.00**

Step-back wall cupboard, Classical country style, painted poplar, two-part construction: the upper section w/a rectangular top above a cove-molded cornice over a pair of 6-pane glazed doors w/curved top rails opening to shelves above an open pie shelf; the lower section w/three ogee-front drawers in a

conforming ogee-curved case over a pair of paneled doors, cut-out pilasters & front feet, turned back feet, old dark red & white repaint over earlier red, found in Mahatango Valley, Pennsylvania, 47½" w., 6' 10¾" h. **880.00**

Grain-Painted Step-back Cupboard

Step-back wall cupboard, Federal, painted & decorated poplar, two-part construction: the upper section w/a molded & reeded cornice above a pair of hinged 8-pane glazed doors opening to shelves fitted w/plate grooves & pierced for cutlery; the projecting lower section w/a row of two long & a short chamfered drawers over a pair of raised-panel cupboard doors opening to a shelf & centered by reeded pilasters, molded base w/slender French feet, painted & grained overall in reddish orange & black to simulate mahogany, the mullions painted yellow, the lower section incised to simulate line-inlay & crossbanding, original glass, Pennsylvania, ca. 1810, 19¼ x 50¾", 6' 11½" h. (ILLUS.) **29,900.00**

Step-back wall cupboard, country-style, cherry, two-part construction: the upper section w/a crown-molded cornice over double 6-pane glazed cupboard doors & a center stationary glazed panel; the stepped-out lower section w/a pair of drawers flanking a small center drawer over a pair of paneled cupboard doors, turned feet, 66" w., 7' 4½" **5,060.00**

Step-back wall cupboard, country-style, painted, two-part construction:

the upper section w/a rectangular top w/a deep stepped flaring molding above a pair of 6-pane glazed doors opening to two shelves; the stepped-out lower section w/a pair of paneled cupboard doors w/raised notch-cornered panels, deeply scalloped apron & bracket feet, overall ochre & raw sienna comb-graining, probably Ohio, ca. 1860, 20 x 47½", 6' 5" h. (top possibly different origin) **2,415.00**

Step-back wall cupboard, country-style, painted pine, one-piece construction, rectangular top w/flaring molded cornice above a pair of long four raised-panel doors w/a cast-iron latch w/porcelain knob above a mid-molding over a pair of short double-paneled doors w/matching latch, old refinish w/some traces of old red paint, New England, early 19th c., 17½ x 57", 7' 5" h. **1,955.00**

Federal Pine Step-back Cupboard

Step-back wall cupboard, Federal, pine, two-part construction: the upper section w/a rectangular top w/a molded cornice above a pair of 6-pane glazed cupboard doors opening to a red-painted shelved interior above an open pie shelf; the projecting lower section w/a pair of drawers above a pair of paneled cupboard doors opening to shelves, molded base w/bracket feet, Pennsylvania, ca. 1810, some repairs, 18¾ x 59", 7' 2½" h. (ILLUS.) **3,737.00**

Step-back wall cupboard, Federal country-style, cherry, two-part

construction: the upper section w/a rectangular top over a cove-molded cornice above a pair of 6-pane glazed doors opening to shelves above an arched open pie shelf; the stepped-out lower section w/a rectangular top above a row of three drawers w/wood knobs above a pair of paneled cupboard doors w/brass thumb latches, scalloped apron & short bracket feet, early 19th c., 15 x 56½", 6' 11½" h. (hardware replaced, some pieced repairs & one drawer overlap glued) **4,345.00**

Early Texas Step-back Cupboard

Step-back wall cupboard, Federal country-style, yellow pine, two-part construction; the upper section w/a rectangular top above a deep, widely flaring flat cornice above a pair of tall 8-pane glazed cupboard doors opening to three shelves; the projecting lower section w/a long drawer w/wooden knobs above a pair of raised-panel cupboard doors opening to a shelf, molded base on bracket feet, La Grange, Texas, ca. 1840, 19¼ x 50", 7' 6" h. (ILLUS.) **7,475.00**

Step-back wall cupboard, Sheraton, cherry, two-part construction: the upper section w/cove-molded cornice w/three-quarter gallery above double glazed doors each w/eleven panes in a Gothic arch design; the stepped-out lower section w/two short drawers w/applied edge beading above a pair of paneled cupboard doors, on high turned feet, old dark varnish stain finish, found in Massachusetts,

16½ x 44¾", 7' 11½" h. (some edge damage & damage to mullions) **1,870.00**

Wall cupboard, country-style, walnut, one-piece construction, the upper section w/a rectangular top w/a narrow molded cornice above a pair of square paneled cupboard doors above a tall pie shelf w/scalloped ends & a set-back narrow shelf above the slightly stepped-out lower section w/two deep drawers flanking a shorter deep drawer above a pair of paneled cupboard doors, low slightly arched apron, worn original finish, 19th c., cornice 12½ x 47½", 6' 2½" h. (minor edge damage, repaired split in one drawer front) **4,950.00**

Wall cupboard, Federal country-style, cherry, two-part construction: the upper section w/a rectangular top w/a narrow molded cornice above a pair of 6-pane glazed cupboard doors opening to shelves above an open pie shelf; the slightly stepped-out lower section w/a row of three drawers above a pair of raised-panel cupboard doors, the panels w/notched corners, molded base on simple bracket feet, mellow old refinishing, old brass thumb latch, early 19th c., cornice 14½ x 56" (some edge damage & age cracks, one pane cracked) **6,050.00**

Wall cupboard, Federal country-style, maple, two-part construction: the upper section w/a rectangular top w/a widely flaring cove-molded cornice above a pair of 9-pane glazed doors opening to three shelves above an open pie shelf; the lower stepped-out section w/a pair of small square end drawers flanking two long drawers which flank a smaller central drawer all w/original oval brass pulls above a pair of square paneled doors w/brass ring pulls, gently undulating apron & short bracket feet, good old cherry-colored finish, found in Chester County, Pennsylvania, early 19th c., cornice 15 x 67½", 6' 11¼" h. (minor edge damage, age cracks) **16,500.00**

Wall cupboard, Victorian country-style, painted pine, rectangular top w/narrow flaring flat cornice above a pair of tall raised panel cupboard doors opening to three shelves, deep scallop-cut apron, square

Painted Texas Wall Cupboard

tapering legs, painted red, Texas, mid-19th c., 20¾ x 50", 6' 4½" h. (ILLUS.) **2,300.00**

Georgian Welsh Cupboard

Welsh cupboard, Georgian, elm & fruitwood, two-part construction: the upper section w/a rectangular top w/a molded cornice above corner drops over three long open shelves w/racks; the stepped-out lower section w/a wide rectangular top over a deep apron w/three drawers w/brass butterfly pulls, on cabriole front legs ending in snake feet, England, late 18th - early 19th c., restorations, 62" w., 5' 8" h. (ILLUS.) **1,485.00**

Welsh cupboard, George III, elm, two-part construction: the upper section w/a rectangular top w/a scallop-cut frieze apron above three

George III Welsh Cupboard

open-backed shelves; the stepped-out lower section w/a rectangular top over two deep drawers above a tiny center lower drawer, double-arch apron, cabriole front legs ending in pad feet, England, late 18th c., 18½ x 52½", 6' 4" h. (ILLUS.) **2,990.00**

DESKS

Fine Art Nouveau Desk

Art Deco desk & chair, lacquered wood, kidney-shaped top on a conforming pedestal base w/a frieze drawer flanked by side drawers, lacquered in mottled reddish brown, w/a shaped glass top, w/an upholstered side chair similarly lacquered, Europe, ca. 1930-40, 39 x 72", 31" h., 2 pcs. **8,050.00**

Art Nouveau desk, mahogany marquetry, an upright superstructure w/a curved crestrail w/long lobed ends over a stepped upper shelf before the scale-design inlay over a lower shelf above a pair of drawers w/gilt-bronze loop pulls, the kidney-shaped writing surface over a long drawer w/foliate scroll-cast gilt-bronze pull, curved molded supports from edge of corners taper down to the gently outswept curved legs w/pointed pad feet, Louis Majorelle, France, ca. 1900, 30½ x 50", 4' h. (ILLUS.).............................**23,000.00**

Art Nouveau partner's desk, fruitwood marquetry & mahogany, H-form top w/outset corners, inset w/three green leather panels above a single kneehole w/drawer flanked by pedestals, each w/a cabinet door opening to an arrangement of shelves & a single short drawer, the side panels of each pedestal hinged at the bottom & opening to form a broad shelf; the panels inlaid in various woods w/scenic landscapes w/iris blossoms in the foreground, France, early 20th c., 54" l., 29¾" h..**1,840.00**

Chippendale "Block-Front" Desk

Chippendale "block-front" slant-front desk, mahogany, narrow rectangular top over a hinged rectangular slant lid opening to an interior w/valanced pigeonholes & small drawers centering a pull-out prospect section w/hinged door & three secret drawers behind, above four long graduated drawers w/blocking, the skirt w/a shaped pendant continuing to scroll-cut bracket feet, Boston, Massachusetts, ca. 1755, lower feet replaced, 23¼ x 41¾", 44" h. (ILLUS.) **9,775.00**

Boston "Block-Front" Desk

Chippendale "block-front" slant-front desk, mahogany, narrow rectangular top above w/rectangular hinged lid opening to an interior fitted w/pigeonholes over serpentine small drawers centering a valance drawer carved w/winged beasts above a fan-carved prospect drawer, above four long graduated blocked drawers, molded base w/front claw-and-ball feet, Boston, Massachusetts, ca. 1760, extensively restored, 20¾ x 38", 45" h. (ILLUS.) **6,037.00**

Chippendale slant-front desk, curly maple, a narrow rectangular top above the wide hinged slant-lid opening to an interior fitted w/pigeonholes & small drawers flanking a prospect door, above four long graduated drawers, molded base w/center drop & scroll-cut bracket feet, old refinish, probably Massachusetts, ca. 1780, 19½ x 38¾", 39¾" h. (imperfections).......**2,415.00**

Chippendale slant-front desk, carved mahogany, the rectangular hinged molded lid opening to an interior fitted w/shell- and fretwork-carved small drawers & pigeonholes over serpentine small drawers centering an arched chip-carved document door opening to a fitted interior flanked by document drawers, four graduated molded long drawers below, on ogee bracket feet, Philadelphia, ca. 1765, 21½ x 38½", 42" h. (feet replaced, lid possibly replaced, patches to drawer fronts) **9,775.00**

Chippendale slant-front desk, carved walnut, narrow rectangular top above a hinged slant lid opening to reveal a fitted interior w/two concave central prospect doors, the upper drawer carved, flanked by figured fluted pilaster document drawers flanked by four valanced pigeonholes over serpentine short drawers above a molded base, all above a long thumb-molded drawer flanked by short box drawers above three long graduated thumb-molded drawers, on ogee bracket feet w/squared pads, Lancaster County, Pennsylvania, 1760-80, 22¼ x 40⅛", 46½" h. (splits in feet) **10,925.00**

Chippendale-Style writing desk, walnut, cherry & mahogany w/flame veneer, rectangular top w/molded edge above a long drawer over a pair of short drawers flanking the kneehole fitted w/scroll-carved corner brackets, on cabriole legs w/leafy scroll-carved knees & ending in claw-and-ball feet, refinished, early 20th c., 21¾ x 42¼", 30¼" h. (minor repair) **715.00**

Chippendale-Style Writing Desk

Chippendale-Style writing desk, walnut, rectangular top w/molded carved edges above two pairs of small burled drawers w/leaf-carved pulls & beaded edging flanking a longer burl center drawer w/pulls over a kneehole w/scroll-carved brackets, on four cabriole legs w/leafy scroll-carved knees & hairy paw feet, American-made, ca. 1875 (ILLUS. **935.00**

Classical (American Empire) *secrétaire à abbatant* (fall-front secretary-desk), carved mahogany & satinwood, a rectangular top w/reeded edges above a long flush drawer over a flat rectangular fall-front opening to a baize-lined writing surface & an interior fitted w/satinwood valanced pigeonholes & small drawers, above a pair of hinged doors, half-round columns w/acanthus-carved capitals down

Classical *Secrétaire à Abbatant*

the side, on carved paw feet, New York, ca. 1815, foot damage, 19 x 39", 4' 10" h. (ILLUS.) **5,175.00**

Classical Slant-Front Desk

Classical country-style slant-front desk, painted, a narrow top shelf w/an arched & notched three-quarter gallery above a wide rectangular paneled fall-front decorated w/scrolls & dots & a cartouche inscribed "The Flower and the Fern" & opening to an interior fitted w/cubbyholes, on a projecting rectangular top over a long drawer w/wooden knobs raised on rod- and knob-turned legs ending in knob feet, overall painted red, ca. 1840 (ILLUS.)..............................**605.00**

Classical country-style "plantation" desk, mahogany, the superstructure w/a rectangular top w/a deep ogee cornice above a pair of large paneled cupboard doors over a

drawer flanking a central rack of letter file slots, the wide stepped-out & gently sloping writing surface above a pair of long drawers, on ring-, rod- and baluster-turned legs on casters, ca. 1845 ....**2,200.00**

Classical "Plantation" Desk

Classical country-style "plantation" desk, walnut, the tall narrow superstructure w/a scroll-cut cornice above a pair of glazed cupboard doors w/beaded edging opening to two shelves above a wide rectangular fall-front writing surface opening to an interior fitted w/pigeonholes & letter slots, the projecting base w/a long drawer w/beaded edging, on tapering chamfered legs w/baluster-turned sections & peg feet, Southern U.S., ca. 1850, 23 x 37½", 7' 2½" h. (ILLUS.) **935.00**

Edwardian "Kidney-Shaped" Desk

Edwardian "kidney-shaped" desk, satinwood-inlaid mahogany, oblong kidney-shaped top above a conforming case w/stacks of three rounded drawers w/delicate leafy scroll inlay at each end flanking a long incurved center drawer w/similar inlay above the kneehole opening w/paneled inset back w/fan inlay, on square tapering line-inlaid legs w/spade feet on knobs, a bookcase at the rear, England, early 20th c. (ILLUS.).............................**4,675.00**

New York Butler's Desk

Federal butler's desk, mahogany, the rectangular top w/outset rounded corners above a cockbeaded long drawer over a hinged drawer opening to reveal an interior fitted w/central prospect door flanked by a long drawer above three valanced pigeonholes before a baize-lined writing surface over an arched shaped apron flanked by reeded colonnettes, on reeded cylindrical tapering legs w/brass sockets & ball feet, New York, 1810-25, 23¼ x 43", 46⅜" h. (ILLUS.) **4,600.00**

George II writing table, the long leather-lined rectangular top w/a molded edge above a pair of long divided frieze drawers mounted w/foliate-cast gilt-bronze pulls, on cabriole legs w/acanthus-carved knees & ending in hairy paw feet, England, mid-18th c., 28 x 55½", 31¾" h...**18,400.00**

George III-Style partner's desk, decorated wood, rectangular top w/molded edge above a double pedestal base w/two stacks of four short drawers each flanking a central long drawer over the kneehole, the drawers each decorated w/a chinoiserie landscape scene w/figures & birds on a dark

Gustav Stickley Mission Desk

ground, bail pulls, England, late 19th c., 47 x 60", 30⅛" h..............**5,175.00**

Mission-style (Arts & Crafts movement) desk, oak, rectangular top w/leather covering trimmed along the edges w/large brass tacks above a case w/stacks of two short drawers flanking a central drawer over the kneehole, brass loop pulls, on square legs, original dark brown finish, Gustav Stickley large red decal mark, Model No. 710, 24 x 42", 29" h. (ILLUS.) **2,530.00**

Mission-style (Arts & Crafts movement) drop-front desk, oak, thin rectangular top overhanging a wide three-paneled fall-front, each narrow panel inlaid w/a stylized round blossom on a thin stem in copper, pewter & rare woods, iron hinges, the closed base w/an open shelf, slightly tapering one-board sides ending in bootjack legs, recent dark finish & interior gallery, designed by Harvey Ellis for Gustav Stickley, after a Baillie Scott design, unmarked, 11 x 30¼", 44" h..........................**16,500.00**

Modern style desk, lacquered walnut, birch & brass, the long narrow rectangular walnut top above a black lacquered base w/square tapering legs at one end joined by a cross stretcher to square canted legs at the other end w/an attached arrangement of two drawers, brass feet on the legs & a brass center section on the stretcher, Gio Ponti, ca. 1953, 23½ x 60¼", 30½" h..**7,187.00**

Regency writing desk, brass-mounted rosewood, the rectangular leather-inset top w/a low pierced brass gallery above two drawers w/round brass knobs over a thin brass-beaded border opposed by false drawers, raised on ring-turned & reeded round tapering legs

Fine Regency Writing Desk

w/brass feet & casters, England, first
quarter 19th c., 23 x 44", 31" h.
(ILLUS.) **11,500.00**

Victorian Counting House Desk

Victorian counting house desk,
walnut & mahogany, surmounted by
a cabinet w/square paneled door
opening to a divided well above a
small drawer, the right-hand side
fitted w/a shaped backboard over
a long canted canvas-lined writing
surface opening to a well, two small
drawers in the apron at one end
beside the arched kneehole
opening, on ring-, baluster- and
rod-turned tapering legs w/cushion
feet, New Bedford, Massachusetts,
ca. 1850, 25 x 50", 48½" h.
(ILLUS.) **1,495.00**
William & Mary slant-front desk,
walnut, a narrow rectangular top
above a rectangular hinged slant lid
opening to an interior fitted
w/valanced pigeonholes above
small drawers centering a hinged
prospect door opening to two

William & Mary Slant-Front Desk

prospect drawers w/document
drawers flanking, all above two short
& two long drawers, molded base on
ball feet, Long Island, New York,
ca. 1730, feet replaced, 20 x 34¼",
40" h. (ILLUS.) **4,025.00**

William IV "Davenport" Desk

William IV "Davenport" desk,
carved mahogany, a narrow top
shelf w/low gallery beside the wide
slant lift-top w/an old tooled brown
leather inset writing surface
supported on two faceted tapering
columns, one side w/faux short
drawers, the other w/four working
drawers, the incurvate platform base
on brass casters, England,
ca. 1830, 24 x 24", 33½" h.
(ILLUS.) **2,090.00**

DINING ROOM SUITES
Art Nouveau: table & six side chairs;
carved mahogany, the rectangular
table w/rounded corners & a shaped

apron, raised on four molded legs & center pedestal conjoined by gently arched X-form stretchers, the chairs w/a gently arched pierced crestrail & stiles flanking a rectangular padded back, upholstered seat, on molded square legs joined by high, gently arched stretchers, Abel Landry, France, ca. 1900, together w/two modern leaves, table 43½ x 51", 29" h., the set.............................**13,225.00**

Baroque-Style Dining Table

Baroque-Style: dining table, large sideboard, small server, large china cabinet, small curved-front china cupboard, six side chairs & two armchairs; ebonized oak, each case piece w/an ornate pierced & scroll-carved crestrail centered by a grotesque mask, the sides w/baluster-form & ropetwist columns, scroll-carved panels & figural carved winged griffin supports, each chair w/a crown-form crestrail centered by a grotesque mask above a rectangular upholstered back panel flanked by ropetwist stiles, the armchairs w/lion head carved handgrips, on cabriole front legs w/paw feet, the rectangular dining table opening for leaves, the gadrooned edge above a deep scroll-carved apron, raised on heavy reeded baluster-turned supports & full-figure carved winged griffins at each corner, possibly by Horner, New York, ca. 1880, 13 pcs. (ILLUS. table)............................**26,400.00**

Baroque-Style: round dining table, three-tier sideboard, tall china cupboard, rectangular server on cabriole legs, eight side chairs & four armchairs; oak, the round dining table opening for leaves, the gadrooned edge above a deep gadrooned apron & raised on a pedestal w/four heavy S-scroll legs w/fruit & nut carving, the sideboard w/a high superstructure w/two open serpentine shelves & ornate pierced & scroll-carved backboards & S- &

Baroque-Style China Cupboard

C-scroll supports above the serpentine top above a pair of long drawers overhanging a recessed paneled front flanked by cabriole legs, the chairs w/simple arched crestrails above tall backs w/upholstered panels, the tall rectangular china cupboard w/scroll- and fruit-carved banding framing a pair of tall glazed cupboard doors opening to two shelves above a long drawer at the bottom & raised on trumpet-form legs, ca. 1880, 16 pcs. (ILLUS. china cupboard)..............**8,800.00**

GARDEN & LAWN
(Cast iron unless otherwise noted.)

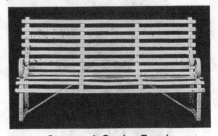

Strapwork Garden Bench

Armchair, the arched crestrail curving down to form the arms above spreading fern leaves, leafy scroll pierced seat, fern frond legs, 35½" h. (rusted, pitted) **550.00**

Bench, strapwork, the S-form back & seat composed of thin long straps of iron, low scroll arms, strapwork legs & thin iron bar braces under the seat, painted white, early 20th c., 67½" l. (ILLUS.) **302.50**

Gothic Design Settee

Settee & two armchairs, Gothic
design, each piece with shaped
scroll-cast crestrail above a back
composed of band of small rounded
arches, scrolled arms w/long C-
scrolls above the pierced scroll-cast
seat, on S-scroll cabriole front legs
& pierced aprons, 19th c., 3 pcs.
(ILLUS. settee)..............................**1,870.00**
Tree surround bench, a tall upright
circle of cast pierced grapevine
design above a narrow pierced
round bench seat raised on flared
narrow pierced grapevine legs,
mid-19th c. **742.50**

HALL RACKS & TREES

Classical Hall Rack

Hall rack, Victorian Classical
substyle, mahogany, the tall narrow
superstructure w/a pierced fan-
shaped finial above long S-scroll
ears above an arch-topped
rectangular mirror above a wide
vase-form backboard over the

rectangular white marble top above
a pierced & galleried apron w/tiny
drops, a forked scroll-carved back
support behind two shaped open
shelves between pierced & scroll-cut
ends w/modified scroll feet, ca.
1840-50 (ILLUS.) **1,210.00**

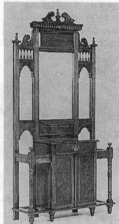

Renaissance Revival Hall Rack

Hall rack, Victorian Renaissance
Revival substyle, mahogany, the tall
three-panel back w/the tallest center
panel topped w/a broken-scroll
crestrail centering a turned finial
over a long gadrooned band over a
raised panel & long rectangular
mirror, the lower side panels w/a
scroll-carved crest & corner finial
over a band of short spindles over a
tall narrow arched panel over similar
lower arched open panel flanking a
rectangular center cabinet w/a
drawer over a pair of paneled scroll-
carved cupboard doors flanked by
umbrella racks, raised on short
tapering ring-turned front legs,
England, late 19th c. (ILLUS.)..........**605.00**
Hall tree, Victorian, cast iron, in the
form of intertwined naturalistic
branches & foliate vines, w/six
extended arms each mounted w/an
S-shaped hook, the base mounted
w/an umbrella holder & removable
drip tray, ca. 1870, 14¼ x 26¼",
6' 6½" h. **978.00**

HIGHBOYS & LOWBOYS

Highboys
Chippendale "bonnet-top" highboy,
walnut, two-part construction: the
upper section w/a molded swan's-
neck pediment centering three
turned urn-and-flame finials, eight
short & three long molded graduated

drawers below, fluted quarter-columns flanking; the lower section w/one long & three short drawers flanked by fluted quarter-columns, on shell-and-volute-carved cabriole legs ending in claw-and-ball feet, alteration to upper section of bonnet, Pennsylvania, ca. 1765, 23½ x 43", 7' 8" h. **$14,950.00**

Connecticut Cherry Highboy

Queen Anne "bonnet-top" highboy, cherry, two-part construction: the upper section w/a molded swan's-neck crest centering three bird- and spirally-twisted finials over a row of three drawers, the center one fan-carved, over four long graduated drawers; the lower section w/a mid-molding over a long narrow drawer over a row of three drawers, the center one fan-carved, a shaped apron w/two pendent drops, angular cabriole legs ending in pad feet, Connecticut, ca. 1765, legs replaced, other repairs, 19½ x 40", 6' 10¾" h. (ILLUS.) **8,080.00**

Queen Anne "flat-top" highboy, gumwood, two-part construction: the upper section w/a flat rectangular top w/a deep flaring molded cornice w/a convex secret drawer over a pair of drawers over three long graduated drawers; the lower section w/a molded edge over a row of two deep & one shallow drawers, arched shaped spur above angular cabriole legs ending in pad feet, New York, 1750-70, repairs to three legs, appears to retain original brasses, 20 x 39", 5' 5" h. (ILLUS. top next column) **5,175.00**

Queen Anne "Flat-Top" Highboy

Queen Anne "flat-top" highboy, carved maple, two-part construction: the upper section w/molded cornice above four graduated molded long drawers; the lower section w/two long drawers, the lower drawer faced to simulate three working drawers, the center panel fan-carved, the shaped skirt below hung w/turned pendants, continuing to volute-carved cabriole legs ending in shod pad feet, New Hampshire, ca. 1770, 20½ x 39½", 5' 10½" h. **10,350.00**

Queen Anne "flat-top" highboy, figured maple, two-part construction: the upper section w/molded cornice above a secret drawer faced to simulate a molding, two short & three long graduated drawers below; the lower section w/five short drawers, the shaped cockbeaded skirt hung w/turned acorn pendants continuing to cabriole legs, ending in pad feet, Massachusetts, probably Salem or Ipswich, 1730-50, 21½ x 37½", 5' 8" h. **41,400.00**

Queen Anne "flat-top" highboy, mahogany, maple & pine, two-part construction: the upper section w/a rectangular top w/a widely flaring molded cornice above a pair of drawers above three long graduated drawers; the lower section w/a mid-molding above a pair of deep drawers flanking a shallower center drawer above the deeply arched apron w/a pair of turned drops, on cabriole legs ending in pad feet, Boston area, Massachusetts, 1730-60, 20½ x 36⅜", 5' 4¾" h. (some repairs to feet)..................**11,500.00**

William & Mary "flat-top" highboy,
burl-veneered walnut, two-part
construction: the upper section
w/molded cornice above two short &
three long graduated drawers; the
lower section w/three short drawers,
the shaped cock-beaded skirt below
on trumpet-turned legs joined by
shaped stretchers ending in ball
feet, Boston, Massachusetts, 1720-
60, 20½ x 36½", 5' 2" h. (minor
repairs)......................................**32,200.00**

Lowboys

Queen Anne Mahogany Lowboy

Chippendale lowboy, walnut,
rectangular thumb-molded top
w/notched front corners above one
long & three short thumb-molded
drawers, the shaped skirt below
continuing to cabriole legs ending in
claw-and-ball feet, Pennsylvania,
ca. 1760, overall 20¼ x 32⅝",
28½" h. **23,000.00**

Chippendale-Style lowboy, walnut,
rectangular top w/a molded edge
above a pair of small drawers
flanking a longer drawer above two
deep drawers, deeply scalloped
apron, on cabriole legs w/shell-
carved knees & ending in ball-and-
claw feet, old finish, 20 x 37½",
29¾" h. (reconstructed from old
parts)...**880.00**

Queen Anne lowboy, carved
mahogany, rectangular top w/a
thumb-molded edge & notched
corners overhanging a case w/a
long drawer above a row of three
small drawers, the center one fan-
carved, the shaped skirt hung w/two
turned pendant drops, on cabriole
legs ending in pad feet, butterfly
brasses, Boston, Massachusetts,
ca. 1760, 19¾ x 34¼", 29" h.
(ILLUS.) **20,700.00**

Queen Anne lowboy, figured walnut,
the oblong thumb-molded top
w/canted corners above one long &
two short molded drawers, the
shaped skirt below continuing to
cabriole legs, ending in trifid feet,
Philadelphia, ca. 1745, 19½ x
29⅞", 28¾" h. **9,200.00**

Queen Anne Walnut Lowboy

Queen Anne lowboy, figured walnut,
the rectangular top w/molded edges
& notched front corners over a long
drawer over a row of two deep &
one shallow drawers flanked by
fluted canted corners, scalloped
apron & shell-carved cabriole legs
ending in trifid feet, Delaware River
Valley, 1740-60, top probably
replaced, 19⅞ x 34¼", 29¼" h.
(ILLUS.) **8,625.00**

LOVE SEATS, SOFAS & SETTEES

Sleigh-style Daybed

Day bed, Classical (American
Empire) country-style sleigh-form,
walnut, the short ends w/an S-form
outline & a top crossbar & a medial
bar above short baluster-turned
spindles, plain siderails, an
adjustable backrest at one end, old

mellow finish, fitted w/cushions, early 19th c., 80" l. **440.00**

Daybeds, Empire style, mahogany, sleigh-form, each w/outscrolled headboard above rectangular rails w/short rounded footrests raised on block feet, Europe, early 19th c., interior length 74", pr. (ILLUS. one of two) **3,737.00**

Yellow Pine Daybed

Daybed, country-style, yellow pine, rectangular w/outwardly flaring ends, each w/three horizontal slats, on square tapering chamfered legs, Texas, mid-19th c., retains traces of original blue paint, 29½ x 77½", 31½" h. (ILLUS.) **518.00**

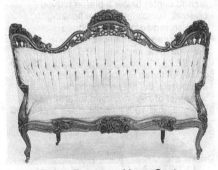

Belter Rosewood Love Seat

Love seat, Victorian Rococo substyle, carved & laminated rosewood, ornately pierce-carved crestrail continuing to arms enclosing a tufted-upholstered rounded back & upholstered seat cushion over a floral-carved seatrail on demi-cabriole legs on casters, "Fountain Elms" patt., by John Henry Belter, New York, ca. 1850-60, 36 x 67", 47" h. (ILLUS.) **35,750.00**

Ottoman, Victorian Turkish Revival substyle, cylindrical tufted-upholstered center column w/wooden cap above wide tufted -upholstered circular seat w/fringe trim, ca. 1860 (ILLUS. top next column) **880.00**

Turkish Revival Ottoman

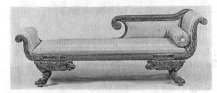

Classical Recamier

Recamier, Classical, (American Empire), carved mahogany, the scrolled acanthus-carved crest w/rosette termini flanked by similarly carved scrolled acanthus supports, above a bolection-molded & gadrooned seatrail, on cornucopia-carved hairy paw feet fitted w/brass casters, probably New York, ca. 1825-35, 25½ x 82¾", 30" h. (ILLUS.) **8,050.00**

Recamier, Classical (American Empire), ebonized mahogany, the scrolled & molded crestrail above molded scrolled arm supports continuing to form a molded exposed seatrail, now w/loose cushion & bolster, on molded downcurving legs ending in brass animal paw feet, on brass & leather casters, attributed to William Camp, Baltimore, Maryland, 1815-18, 83" l. (minor repair to feet) **17,250.00**

Settee, bentwood, rectangular bentwood frame, the back & arm supports centered w/a diamond-shaped design, the back & seat upholstered, designed by Josef Hoffmann, probably executed by J. & J. Kohn, Austria, ca. 1909, 21 x 49", 29" h...............................**403.00**

Settee, Edwardian, painted satinwood, double chair-back style, double crestrail w/oval panel flanked by oval openings above diamond-pierced splat on lower rail between curved stiles, curved open arms on baluster-turned supports, caned

Edwardian Twinback Settee

seat w/gently curved seatrail,
slender tapering turned front legs,
England, ca. 1900 (ILLUS.) **1,760.00**

Settee, Federal country-style, painted
wood, double-back style, the long
wide crestrail divided w/scroll-cut
end sections above a central stile
& end stiles above a lower rail
above short knob-turned spindles,
S-scroll end arms above knob-
turned spindles above the shaped
plank seat, on eight slightly canted
rod- and ring-turned legs joined by
turned stretchers, old blue repaint,
ca. 1825-50, 72" l. **935.00**

George I Settee

Settee, George I double chair-back
style, walnut, the scroll-carved
crestrail above pierced vase-form
backsplats, the drop-in seat flanked
by shepherd's crook armrests, on
cabriole legs ending in pad feet,
joined by stretchers, England, first
quarter 18th c., minor repairs, 55" l.
(ILLUS.) **11,500.00**

Settee, Mission-style (Arts & Crafts
movement), oak, the long flat
crestrail above six wide vertical
slats, wide flat arms w/front legs
through-tenoned above two wide
slats, flat seatrail & slatted

foundation for the long pillow
seat, thin overcoat on original
medium finish, Stickley Brothers
branded mark, 30 x 73",
37" h. **2,090.00**

Settee, Mission-style (Arts & Crafts
movement), oak, a long crestrail
slightly curved along the top above
three lower rails between the square
stiles, narrow shaped flat arms, rope
seat foundation w/cushion, original
medium brown finish, large Gustav
Stickley red decal mark, Model
No. 161, 27 x 51", 38" h. **3,575.00**

Rococo Walnut Settee

Settee, Victorian Rococo substyle,
carved walnut, double-back style
w/two balloon backs flanking slightly
arched center below a pierce-carved
crestrail, upholstered arms flanking
upholstered seat cushion above
carved seatrail, continuing to front
demi-cabriole legs, ca. 1850
(ILLUS.) **990.00**

Settee, Victorian Rococo substyle,
mahogany, the serpentine back
w/a crest of pierce-carved foliate
designs, mid-19th c., 64" l...............**690.00**

Windsor Rocking-style Settee

Settee, Windsor rocking-style, cherry,
the wide S-form crestrail above
twenty simple turned spindles
flanked by S-scroll end arms above
three simple turned spindles, S-
scroll plank seat above ring-turned
front legs joined by a wide flat
stretcher, early 19th c. (ILLUS.) **990.00**

Settee, Windsor, painted wood, the
slender turned crestrail on the
canted back above seventeen

tapering bamboo-turned spindles above the oblong plank seat, bamboo-turned arms above three turned spindles, six bamboo-turned splayed legs joined by bamboo-turned stretchers, later green paint, ca. 1805, 45¼" l. **6,900.00**

Settee, Windsor, the horizontal crestrail above fifty-three bamboo-turned spindles flanked by shaped arms on supports over a shaped plank seat, on bamboo-turned legs joined by swelled stretchers, early 19th century, 24 x 109", 33⅓" h....**6,900.00**

Settle, country-style, painted pine, tall flat back continuing to the floor, shaped sides forming arms, long plank seat, cut-out feet, old red paint, New England, ca. 1790, 47½" h. (imperfections)................**1,495.00**

Settle, Mission-style (Arts & Crafts movement), oak, even-arm style, flat even crestrails above numerous vertical slats in the back & arms, heavy corner posts continue to form legs, attributed to Charles Stickley, drop-in spring seat, early 20th c., 28 x 36", 78" l..............................**1,430.00**

Settle, Mission-style (Arts & Crafts movement), oak, flat molded crestrail over eight vertical slats, molded even arms each over three vertical slats, w/fabricoid covered spring seat, red decal mark of Gustav Stickley, Model No. 208, ca. 1904, 32" deep, 76" l., 29" h. **9,775.00**

Sofa, Chippendale, mahogany, curving crest flanked by outswept rolled arms, serpentine seatrail & square molded tapering legs joined by stretchers, upholstered in 20th c. green silk floral striped fabric, Massachusetts, ca. 1780, 86" w., 36½" h. (imperfections) **7,700.00**

Sofa, Classical, (American Empire) mahogany, the serpentine crestrail centered by a raised curved base w/scrolled ends & a narrow veneer band above the upholstered back flanked by outswept scroll arms w/leafy scroll- and fruit-carved arm supports continuing into the flat seatrail carved w/florettes, cushion seat, paw feet supporting fruit-filled cornucopia forming the legs on casters, old refinish, possibly Boston, ca. 1825, 21 x 84", 35¼" h...**2,300.00**

Sofa, Classical, carved mahogany, the arched rounded crest terminating in foliate-carved volutes above an upholstered back & seat flanked by cornucopia-carved scrolling arms above a bolection-

Classical Carved Mahogany Sofa

molded apron on stylized foliate-carved legs w/scrolled returns, w/paw feet & casters, possibly Boston, ca. 1815-30, 24½ x 86¾", 38¼" h. (ILLUS.) **2,185.00**

Sofa, Federal, cherry, the arched upholstered back continuing to form scrolled handholds above reeded baluster-turned supports, the slightly bowed over-upholstered seat on molded square tapering legs, the rear legs on casters, ca. 1805, 67½" l..**9,200.00**

Sofa, Federal, carved mahogany, the molded crest centering a rectangular reserve carved w/waterleaves & fans, the downcurving molded arms continuing to flowerhead-carved handholds, the over-upholstered bowed seat on circular reeded tapering legs ending in vase-form feet, on brass casters, attributed to Slover & Taylor, New York, ca. 1805, 71¾" l. **10,350.00**

Sofa, Federal, carved mahogany, paneled crestrail centering three reserves, the central one carved w/bow-knotted arrows flanked by wheat ears, the flanking reserves w/bow-knotted drapery swags, the downcurving reeded arms continuing to ring-turned & reeded supports, the bowed seat on reeded tapering legs ending in brass casters, New York, ca. 1800, 64½" l. **16,100.00**

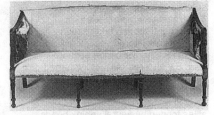

Maple-inlaid Mahogany Sofa

Sofa, Federal, figured maple-inlaid mahogany, the arched upholstered back flanked by downcurving arms & reeded arm supports, the slightly bowed seat below flanked by figured maple rectangular dyes, on reeded tapering legs ending in flattened-ball feet, Northeast Coast, New England, ca. 1810, appears to retain its original finish, 77¾" l. (ILLUS.) **5,462.00**

Sofa, George II, the long serpentine padded back continuing to form the sides, the crestrail w/a central anthemion crest draped w/husk chains, the loose cushioned seat above a fluted seatrail, on turned tapering fluted legs headed by flowerheads & w/gadrooned feet, upholstered in powder blue patterned silk, England, ca. 1770, 78" l. **16,100.00**

Louis XVI-Style Sofa

Sofa, Louis XVI-Style, giltwood, the long, low oblong back w/arched ends tapering to low center & surrounding an upholstered back, open padded arms on dolphin supports, oblong upholstered seat w/carved seatrail w/floral-carved drops all on scroll-carved feet w/floral swags, Europe, late 19th c., 72" l., 38¾" h. (ILLUS.) **4,600.00**

Sofa, Mission-style (Arts & Crafts movement), oak, long flat crestrail above numerous slats flanked by square stiles over the shaped flat arms w/corbels, drop-in spring seat over a straight apron, normal wear to original medium-dark finish, L. & J.G. Stickley "Handcraft" decal, 29¼ x 76¾", 36" h.........................**2,200.00**

Sofa, Victorian Renaissance Revival substyle, ormolu-mounted rosewood & marquetry, a triple-back form w/two round-topped end sections w/tufted upholstered backs flanking a long rectangular center section w/an upholstered crest roll w/turned finial ends, above a tufted upholstered back, the three sections divided by two ormolu-mounted stiles topped by figural sphinx heads above padded arms w/curved arm supports each fitted at the top front w/an oval painted mount, rounded ends & a curved seatrail above an apron of swagged upholstery on short legs, late 19th c., 95" l. 40" h......................**3,450.00**

Rococo Rosewood Sofa

Sofa, Victorian Rococo substyle, laminated rosewood, the pierce-carved serpentine crestrail continuing to closed upholstered arms ending in scrolled supports & enclosing tufted-upholstered back & seat above serpentine seatrail, all on demi-cabriole legs on casters, "Stanton Hall" patt., J. & J.W. Meeks, New York, ca. 1850 (ILLUS.) **5,225.00**

Country-style Wagon Seat

Wagon seat, country-style, double back w/two pairs of arched slats flanked by cylindrical turned stiles over a splint seat on turned cylindrical legs joined by double box stretchers, 19th c., refinished, seat replaced, 33¾" w., 28" h. (ILLUS.) **187.00**

MIRRORS

Art Deco wall mirror, wrought iron, the rectangular frame wrought w/scrolling devices enclosing a rectangular mirror plate, France, ca. 1925, 29¼" w., 35¼" h............**1,610.00**

Chippendale wall mirror, mahogany, the scrolled crest above a rectangular mirror plate, a shaped pendant below, labeled "John Elliott & Sons," Philadelphia, ca. 1780, 23" w., 4' h. (minor repairs) **1,840.00**

Chippendale wall mirror, parcel-gilt mahogany veneer, surmounted by a ribbed urn-form finial flanked by scrolled wires terminating in flowers & leaves, the swan's-neck pediment flanking, the oblong mirror plate flanked by fruit- and flowerhead-carved gilt fillets, a pierced shaped pendant below, incised overall, ca. 1765, 23¼" w., 4' ½" h. **3,738.00**

Fine Chippendale Mirror

Chippendale wall mirror, parcel-gilt walnut, the swan's-neck crest w/leaf-carved finials centering a spread-winged phoenix, a rectangular mirror plate below, gilt border band & berry & leaf bands down the sides, shaped base, repairs, losses, 18th c., 30" w., 4' 8½" h. (ILLUS.)..........................**3,737.00**

Classical Shaving Mirror

Classical (American Empire) shaving mirror, carved mahogany,

the rectangular mirror frame pivoting between pierced & scroll uprights, the bowed support below on scrolled feet, Boston, Massachusetts, ca. 1830, 10 x 27", 29" h. (ILLUS.) **2,587.00**

Classical double-light convex wall mirror, ebonized & giltwood, surmounted by an ebonized spread-winged eagle perched on the circular molded slip mounted w/spherules centering an ebonized slip & a convex mirror plate, acanthus-carved pendant below, the front w/two projecting candle arms ending in clear Waterford glass vase-form candlecups, first quarter 19th c., overall 35½" w., 36" h. (ebonized slip restored) **13,800.00**

Courting mirror, walnut & églomisé, the rectangular mirror plate within a cushion-molded frame surmounted by a trapezoidal églomisé floral panel, all within a rectangular box-form frame, mid-18th c., 6¼" w., 9½" h. (loss to mirror plate & veneers) **805.00**

Federal "girandole" wall mirror, giltwood, surmounted by a spread-winged eagle on a rockwork base flanked by leafage, the convex round mirror below w/spherule-mounted & ebonized slip & projecting scroll candle arms ending in gilt metal candle sockets, a shaped pendant below, ca. 1815, 22" w., 38" h.................................**5,750.00**

Federal Mirror with America

Federal wall mirror, giltwood, the narrow crest w/stepped-out ends above a band of spherules over flat pilasters flanking the églomisé tablet decorated w/a figure of America holding an American flag & flanked by flower-filled urns above the rectangular mirror plate, probably Massachusetts, ca. 1815, 16" w., 33" h. (ILLUS.) **9,775.00**

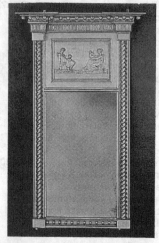

Federal Mirror with Figural Panel

Federal wall mirror, giltwood, the cove-molded broken cornice hung w/gilt spherules above a rectangular frieze w/a relief-molded panel depicting two women w/children wearing Empire-style dresses & seated in Greek klysmos chairs, above the rectangular mirror plate flanked by spiral-turned pilasters over a molded base, New England, ca. 1815, 44" h. (ILLUS.) **1,725.00**

Federal wall mirror, inlaid mahogany & giltwood, surmounted by a giltwood finial in the form of an urn w/a spray of wheat & flowers, the incised swan's-neck crest above a shell-inlaid tympanum, the rectangular mirror plate below flanked by flower- and leaf-form gilt fillets, a shaped pendant at the base, New York, ca. 1800, 17½" w., 45" h. (repairs) **3,163.00**

Federal wall mirror, giltwood & églomisé, the molded broken pediment hung w/gilt spherules above a frieze punctuated w/acanthus leaves over an églomisé panel depicting a house in a landscape within an oval w/scrolling foliate surround above a rectangular mirror plate flanked by reeded pilasters over a molded base, New York, 1790-1810, 26" w., 4' 5" h. ..**1,265.00**

Federal wall mirror, inlaid & parcel-gilt mahogany, the swan's-neck crest centering a finial in the form of an urn w/flowers & leaves, a rectangular mirror plate below flanked by gilt fruit & leaf fillets above a shaped pendant, probably New York, ca. 1800, 26" w., 5' 1¾" h. (finial replaced & other repairs)..**3,738.00**

French-style overmantel mirror, gilt gesso, the egg-and-dart outer border enclosing a high-relief border of scrolling leaves & a wide concave border enclosing the mirror plate, late 19th c., 37½" w., 4' 1" h. **357.50**

George II overmantel mirror, parcel-gilt mahogany, the long low narrow rectangular frame w/shaded ends w/outset corners & gilt pendant fruit, the whole w/narrow gilt leaf-carved outer & inner edge bands, w/a later rectangular beveled mirror, ca. 1740, 64" l., 21½" h.................**1,725.00**

Mission-style (Arts & Crafts movement) wall mirror, oak, simple rectangular arched framed, Model No. 98, L. & J.G. Stickley, 35" w., 26" h..**2,070.00**

Queen Anne pier mirror, parcel-gilt mahogany, the scrolled crest w/a pierced circular reserve w/a gilt phoenix & leafage, above a cushion-molded surround w/inner gilt border centering a two-part beveled & shaped rectangular mirror plate w/scrolled pendant below, second quarter 18th c., 24¼" w., 4' 9½" h. (some repairs to gilding) **6,325.00**

Queen Anne wall mirror, parcel-gilt, the shaped crest centering a volute-carved gilt shell, the rectangular mirror plate below w/gilt slip above a shaped pendant, ca. 1760, 12¼" w., 27¾" h. (minor repairs)..**1,150.00**

Queen Anne wall mirror, parcel-gilt walnut veneer, the shaped scrolled crest centering a gilt foliate appliqué above a two-part oblong beveled mirror plate, 1730-60, 14" w., 33¾" h. **4,888.00**

Queen Anne wall mirror, parcel-gilt walnut, the scroll-cut crest centered by a concave gilt shell pressed w/bellflower designs above the molded frame enclosing a two-section beveled mirror, ca. 1745, 17¼", 4' 1½" h. (ILLUS. top next page)..**32,200.00**

Queen Anne wall mirror, parcel-gilt walnut, the shaped cresting pierced w/shell above a rectangular mirror plate within gilded slip, 18th c., 22" w., 4' 4" h. **3,162.00**

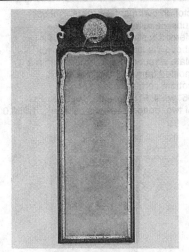

Rare Queen Anne Wall Mirror

Regency Wall Mirror

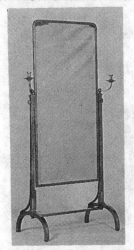

Victorian Brass Cheval Mirror

Regency wall mirror, giltwood, a large spread-winged eagle finial over pierced leafy scrolls over the round convex mirror framed by a molded band w/spherules, a fan-shaped bottom base drop, England, ca. 1825 (ILLUS. middle previous column) **825.00**

Victorian cheval mirror, brass, the tall rectangular mirror plate w/rounded top corners swiveling between slender square uprights fitted w/two candlearms, on a trestle base w/arched legs, ca. 1860, 6' h. (ILLUS. bottom previous column) **770.00**

Unusual Mahogany Cheval Mirror

Victorian cheval mirror, mahogany, the tall oval mirror w/ribbon-carved crest swivels between slender ropetwist-turned uprights above a trestle base w/flaring shaped ends on metal claw feet w/glass balls & joined by a ropetwist stretcher & angled ropetwist braces, ca. 1870, 6' 6" h. (ILLUS.)............................**1,210.00**

Victorian cheval mirror, bamboo-turned maple, the tall rectangular mirror w/rounded top corners in a bamboo-turned frame & swiveling between bamboo-turned uprights w/beehive-turned finials, a bamboo-turned stretcher at the top w/double stretchers flanking small spindles at the bottom, on canted legs on casters, late 19th c., 36" w., 6' 5" h. (ILLUS. top next page)..................**1,150.00**

Victorian overmantel mirror, Rococo substyle, giltwood, the tall oval mirror w/a molded frame w/a wide border of pierced leafy scrolls, berries & ribbons, mid-19th c., (ILLUS. middle next page) **1,430.00**

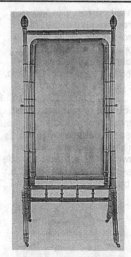

Bamboo-Turned Cheval Mirror

Ornate Overmantel Mirror

Victorian Overmantel Mirror

Victorian overmantel mirrors, Rococo substyle, gilt gesso, an ornate pierced & scroll-carved crestrail above the large rectangular mirror plate w/rounded top corners within a molded frame w/scrolls at the bottom corners, mid-19th c., 36" w., 4' 9" h., pr. (ILLUS. one of two, bottom previous column)...**1,650.00**

Victorian Rococo Pier Mirror

Victorian pier mirror, Rococo substyle, giltwood, the high arched & pierced scroll-carved crest w/grape clusters above a tall narrow arched mirror within a molded frame decorated w/leafy scrolls at the base above the narrow serpentine-front white marble shelf above the deep scroll-carved apron on leafy scroll legs, mid-19th c. (ILLUS.) **1,540.00**

Renaissance Revival Mirror

Victorian wall mirror, Renaissance Revival substyle, giltwood, an arched crest above the wide coved crestrail molded w/leafy scrolls & flanked by blocked ears w/finials over the tall rectangular mirror plates flanked by narrow paneled sides, the base band molded w/roundels, ca. 1875, 4' 8" h. (ILLUS. bottom previous page) **440.00**

PARLOR SUITES

Victorian Gentleman's & Lady's Chairs

Art Nouveau: settee, two side chairs & two armchairs; carved fruitwood, each piece w/a shaped crestrail carved w/delicate lilac blossoms & leaves, the settee w/three upholstered panels & the seat flanked by square molded closed arms, slender molded cabriole legs, Louis Majorelle, France, ca. 1900, settee 50" l., the set **6,037.00**

Bentwood: settee, armchair & six side chairs; the settee & armchair w/curved open back, the arms enclosing oval bentwood splats, the upholstered rounded seats raised on four tapering legs, by Thonet, Austria, late 19th - early 20th c., settee, 20 x 42", 35" h., the set **1,150.00**

Empire-Style: sofa, two open-arm armchairs, two closed-arm armchairs & a bench; mahogany, each piece w/a wide flat crestrail above the upholstered back & long S-scroll arms above a cushion seat over the flat & slightly bowed seatrail on square tapering & slightly curved legs, green mohair upholstered w/a gold star design, France, late 19th c., sofa 70" l., 38" h., the set (restoration) **8,050.00**

Louis XVI-Style: settee, armchair & two side chairs, rose & chain design, newly reupholstered, pegged construction, 4 pcs. **900.00**

Modern style: bench, four matching chairs & a table; the bench

w/hammered copper rectangular backrest above three circular parchment-covered back splats, the parchment-covered seat above elaborately inlaid apron on four angular legs; the table w/a square top above four columnar legs joined by an arched inlaid wood & parchment-covered support, by Carlo Bugatti, Italy, early 20th c., bench 27 x 64", 42" h., the set **3,450.00**

Victorian Renaissance Revival: armchair & two side chairs; walnut w/upholstered backs & seats, carved throughout w/oak leaves & acorns, last quarter 19th c., 37" h., 3 pcs. **1,150.00**

Victorian Renaissance Revival substyle: settee & two armchairs; the chairs w/flat crestrails w/carved circular portrait medallions & carved ears over rectangular upholstered backs w/closed padded curved arms flanking upholstered seat cushions over carved trumpet-form legs on casters, third quarter 19th c., the chairs: 42" h. & 34½" h., the set (ILLUS. two of three)....................**1,725.00**

Carved Rosewood Parlor Suite

Victorian Renaissance Revival substyle: settee, two armchairs & four side chairs; carved rosewood, each w/carved crestrails centered by central carved classical head, open padded arms ending in the carved busts of a classical lady, all on carved trumpet-form legs, attributed to J.E. Jelliff, New York, ca. 1875, the set (ILLUS.)............................**6,050.00**

Victorian Rococo substyle: settee & two armchairs; silvered embossed metal over wood, the settee w/an undulating arched crestrail above the scroll-pierced back w/three large oval upholstered panels flanked by tapering lattice-pierced arms, cushion seat, tapering heavy square front legs w/thick cushion feet, the armchairs matching, Anglo-Indian, 19th c., settee 5' 1" l., 36" h., 3 pcs. **990.00**

Victorian Rococo substyle: settee, four armchairs & four side chairs; carved rosewood, the settee w/a long gently arched crestrail w/scroll-carved crest continuing down to frame the upholstered back above padded open arms, serpentine scroll-carved seatrail on demi-cabriole legs, the chairs w/matching crestrail on the squared balloon backs, attributed to Siebrecht, New Orleans, Louisiana, ca. 1850, 9 pcs. **4,950.00**

Victorian Rococo Sofa

Victorian Rococo substyle: triple-back sofa, a pair of armchairs & a pair of side chairs; carved rosewood, each piece w/a scalloped rest topped by crisply carved sprays of various flowers, out-curved shaped armrests, serpentine seatrails w/floral- and scroll-carved scalloped seatrail, on cabriole front legs w/acanthus carving, on brass casters, all covered in old gold woven tapestry upholstery, ca. 1850-60, sofa 58½" l., the set (ILLUS. sofa)................................**5,500.00**

SCREENS

Victorian Aesthetic Fire Screen

Fire screen, Art Deco style, painted wrought iron & mesh, long rectangular frame arched in the center & enclosing a wire mesh applied w/silhouetted stylized opposing rearing gazelles flanked by lean racing wolf-like hounds, painted black, in the manner of Wilhelm Hunt Diederich, American-made, ca. 1925, 68" l, 29" h. (holes in mesh edge) **4,600.00**

Fire screen, three-panel, a hinged brass framework featuring three leaded panels, each w/a central bull's-eye, the central one in red, the side ones in blue, each framed by a diamond & other geometric pieces in pale yellow, amethyst, pale green & amber, unsigned, Boston, ca. 1910, overall 29" w., 25½" h. **2,185.00**

Fire screen, Victorian Aesthetic Movement substyle, mahogany & glass, the flat crest w/a pierced bobbin-turned band between corner blocks w/turned finials above a tall rectangular panel composed of small colored glass panes w/a central double pane depicting a medieval maiden in a garden in yellow & white on a blue ground, a bobbin band across the base, on stepped shoe feet, England, late 19th c., 41½" h. (ILLUS.) **715.00**

Elizabethan Revival Fire Screen

Fire screen, Victorian Elizabethan Revival substyle, walnut, a flat crestrail mounted w/three spheres w/pointed finials above a rectangular glazed box flanked by barley-twist uprights above a trestle base w/barley-twist stretcher & downswept legs w/carved cartouches on casters, the glazed box holding a small tree mounted w/stuffed hummingbirds, England, third quarter 19th c., 32" w., 45" h. (ILLUS.) **3,450.00**

Louis XVI-Style Screen

Folding screen, three-fold, Louis XVI-Style, giltwood, the center panel crested by a ribbon & foliate wreath above a floral urn issuing fanned arrows, the side panels w/down-curved crests above lattice panels over the gold floral fabric panels, within a leaf-carved frame, late 19th c., separation at lower inside corner of one side panel, 48¾" l., 5' 2¾" h. (ILLUS.)..............................**880.00**

Folding screen, three-fold, painted wood, each framed panel divided equally above fielded panels over arched lower panels, painted over silver leaf on one side w/a fanciful underwater scene w/schools of fish & aquatic plants, on the reverse w/fantastic birds & butterflies perching & fluttering amid stylized flowers & foliage, probably American-made, early 20th c., 79½" l, 6' 4¼" h. **3,910.00**

Folding screen, four-fold, painted panels, the four forming a continuous scene of various yachts & pleasure boats in open seas w/a large white house, formal gardens, green lawns & the figure of a woman wearing a kimono & carrying a parasol accompanied by dogs in the foreground, signed "Victoria White," New York, ca. 1920, each panel 22" w., 6' h. **4,600.00**

Folding screen, four-fold, Regency style, painted wood, each panel w/a long central panel decorated in color

English Regency Screen

w/chinoiserie figures in foliate landscapes, each panel flanked above & below w/square panels of floral bouquets against a deep red ground, border framing in black, the reverse w/floral sprays, England, 19th c., each panel 23" w., 6' 6" h. (ILLUS.) **7,475.00**

Folding screen, six-fold, painted paper, each arch-shaped panel depicting an active fishing village *en grisaille* within green beaded border, raised on hexagonal & rosette-shaped border above a *faux* porphyry base, France, early 19th c., each panel 21¾" w., 6' 7" h. (water damage, minor tears).........**2,875.00**

Folding screen, six-fold, lacquered, each panel incised & lacquered to form a continuous jungle scene in shades of gold, green, red & brown, inscribed "Max Kuehne," ca. 1930, 10' 6" l., 8' 3" h. **6,900.00**

SECRETARIES

Chippendale 'block-front' & 'bonnet-top' secretary-bookcase, cherry, two-part construction: the upper section w/molded swan's-neck crest centering a dentil-carved spirally-twisted finial, a pair of arched paneled doors below w/stop-fluted pilasters opening to an interior w/adjustable shelves over valanced pigeonholes; the lower section w/hinged rectangular slant lid opening to an interior comprising two fan-carved blocked tiers of drawers centering valanced pigeonholes & a shell-carved prospect door opening to a fan-carved drawer, stop-fluted document drawers flanking, the case below w/an upper frieze drawer carved

Rare Chippendale Secretary

w/two convex shells centering a concave shell, two blocked drawers below, the blocked & molded base continuing to ogee bracket feet, Connecticut, ca. 1760, minor repairs, 20⅛ x 42", 7' 10½" h. (ILLUS.) **35,650.00**

Fine Classical Secretary

Classical (American Empire) secretary-bookcase, carved mahogany, two-part construction: the upper section w/a rectangular top above a flaring stepped cornice over an inset arched frieze band above a pair of Gothic arch-glazed cupboard doors opening to three shelves & flanked by slender colonnettes w/carved Corinthian capitals; the stepped-out lower section w/two small drawers above a fall-front panel opening to a fitted interior w/baize-lined writing surface overhanging a pair of paneled cupboard doors flanked by columns w/carved Corinthian capitals, on lion's paw front feet headed by acanthus leaf carving, New York, ca. 1820-30, 23 x 46½", 8' 6" h. (ILLUS.) **6,325.00**

Classical Mahogany Secretary

Classical secretary-bookcase, mahogany, two-part construction: the upper section w/a low pointed pediment over a wide flat & flaring cornice above a pair of tall 6-pane glazed cupboard doors w/triple pointed top panes opening to two shelves above two drawers w/wooden knobs; the stepped-out lower section w/a fold-down writing leaf above a long ogee drawer above two long drawers w/wooden knobs flanked by long S-curve pilasters, tall heavy C-scroll front legs & baluster-turned rear legs, ca. 1840 (ILLUS.)............................**990.00**
Federal secretary-bookcase, mahogany, two-part construction: the upper section w/a swan's-neck pediment w/reeded blocks above a pair of short cupboard doors w/double arched glazed panes opening to a shelf & small drawers above a pair of drawers w/brass knobs; the lower stepped-out section w/a fold-down writing leaf above a long drawer flanked by pull-out supports above two long drawers all w/round brass knobs & brass keyhole escutcheons, on baluster- and ring-turned legs w/peg feet, New England, ca. 1825, imperfections, 18 x 37½", 5' 4" h. (ILLUS. top next page).................**1,495.00**

Short Federal Secretary

Fine Federal Secretary

Federal secretary-bookcase, inlaid mahogany, two-part construction: the upper section w/a shaped cornice centering a carved giltwood finial in the form of a spread-winged American eagle flanked by brass ball-form finials over a pair of diamond-glazed cupboard doors opening to an interior fitted w/three shelves & pigeonholes; the stepped-out lower section w/a baize-lined fold-down writing flap above a long drawer flanked by pull-out supports over two long drawers, all w/round brass pulls, shaped apron & baluster- and ring- turned legs w/peg feet, Massachusetts, ca. 1805, 18 x 40", 6' 7" h. (ILLUS.) ...**5,175.00**

George III-Style secretary-bookcase, mahogany, two-part construction: the upper section w/a

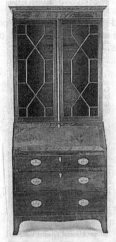

George III-Style Secretary

rectangular top w/narrow flaring cornice above a pair of tall geometrically-glazed cupboard doors opening to shelves; the lower section w/a rectangular slant-lid opening to a fitted interior above three long graduated drawers w/oval brass pulls, shaped apron & tall French feet, England, mid-19th c., minor veneer damage, 18 x 36", 7' ¼" h. (ILLUS.)...........................**2,415.00**

English Queen Anne Secretary

Queen Anne secretary-bookcase, walnut, two-part construction: the upper double-dome arched top fitted w/three gilt urn- and flame-turned finials above a pair of arched 8-pane glazed cupboard doors opening to three shelves; the lower section w/a rectangular slant-lid opening to a fitted interior over a long narrow drawer franked by slide supports over a mid-molding above three long graduated drawers, molded base on squatty ball feet, glazing of later date, England, ca. 1720 (ILLUS.) **7,425.00**

Fine Dutch Secretary

Rococo style secretary-bookcase, burl walnut, two-part construction: the upper section w/a domed cornice above a frieze band w/a scroll-pierced brass mount over a pair of arched cupboard doors fitted w/shaped oblong mirrors; the lower section w/a molded top over an ogee long fold-down slant-lid opening to a fitted interior above a serpentine molding over three long graduated serpentine drawers w/scroll-cast brass pulls & keyhole escutcheons, a serpentine apron w/scroll-carved mount & bracket feet w/brass mounts, Holland, ca. 1800, 6' 6" h. (ILLUS.)..........................**17,000.00**

Victorian country-style secretary- bookcase, fruitwood, two-part construction: the upper section w/a rectangular molded cornice w/canted corners above a conforming case w/two glazed cupboard doors w/molded surrounds & applied foliate & acorn escutcheons opening to two shelves; the lower section w/a hinged fall-front w/two applied octagonal reserves opening to a baize-lined writing surface & interior fitted w/two banks of drawers centering an open shelved compartment all above a pair of cupboard doors w/applied octagonal reserves opening to a single shelf,

Early Texas Secretary

shaped apron & short bracket feet, attributed to Paul Maureaux, San Antonio, Texas, ca. 1855-75, 19 x 44", 8' h. (ILLUS.).................**3,680.00**

Renaissance Revival Secretary

Victorian Renaissance Revival secretary-bookcase, carved rosewood, two-part construction: the upper section w/an arched & angled crestrail w/a carved fruit cluster & raised panels flanked by small turned finials above the flaring ogee cornice over a pair of tall glazed cupboard doors w/scroll-pierced corner brackets opening to two shelves over two small drawers w/two oblong applied reserves & a round keyhole reserve; the lower section w/a rectangular hinged slant lid w/two oval applied reserves opening to a fitted interior above a case w/three long graduated drawers w/half-oval applied reserves & round central reserves & leaf- and cartouche-carved pulls, all flanked by canted front corners w/raised block reserves, a narrow base drawer w/applied reserves, ca. 1860-70 (ILLUS.) **1,760.00**

Unusual Rococo Secretary

Victorian Rococo substyle
secretary-bookcase, carved mahogany, two-part construction: the upper section w/an ornate pierced-scroll crest above a rectangular cornice w/canted corners above scroll blocks over a pair of arched cupboard doors w/mirrors & beaded banding; the lower stepped-out section w/a serpentine front above a conforming fold-down writing surface on tall S-scroll carved supports & a double arch-paneled backboard w/beaded banding, the incurved platform base raised on disc- and ball-turned feet, ca. 1850 (ILLUS.) **2,200.00**

Victorian Rococo substyle
secretary-bookcase, carved rosewood, two-part construction: the upper section w/an arched shell- and foliate-carved scrolled crest flanked by gadrooned urn finials over a scroll-carved frieze band above a pair of glazed arched doors w/scroll-carved corner details opening to shelves; the lower section w/a row of three small drawers w/wooden knobs over a fall-front writing flap opening to an interior fitted w/small drawers & pigeonholes above a pair of shaped-panel cupboard doors, scalloped apron w/scroll carving, curved

Fine Rococo Secretary

bracket feet, old polished surface, ca. 1850, 21 x 48", 8' 10" h. (ILLUS.) **12,375.00**

William & Mary-Style Secretary

William & Mary-Style secretary-
bookcase, oak, two-part construction: the upper section w/a flat rectangular top above a pair of tall raised panel cupboard doors w/ornate pierced brass hinges & oval keyhole escutcheons & opening to shelves; the lower section w/a rectangular hinged slant-lid opening to a fitted interior w/letter slots over pull-out supports over a pair of paneled doors over two long drawers all w/small brass knobs & brass keyhole escutcheons, flaring molded base on block feet, England, 19th c., 22 x 36¾", 7' ½" h. (ILLUS.) **1,840.00**

SIDEBOARDS

Art Deco Sideboard

Art Deco sideboard, mahogany & brass, the long rectangular top w/a bowed center section above a conforming case w/two center doors opening to a storage area w/two lower drawers, flanked by two side doors opening to three shelves, raised on a low platform base w/short tapering legs, France, ca. 1935, 20½ x 91½", 38" h. (ILLUS.) **7,475.00**

Classical (American Empire) server, mahogany, the rectangular top w/canted front corners above a conforming case w/a row of three small drawers above a pair of deep drawers over a pair of paneled cupboard doors, on acanthus-carved scroll front legs & baluster-form back legs, ca. 1825..................**880.00**

New York Classical Sideboard

Classical sideboard, carved mahogany, the rectangular top surmounted by a paneled backboard mounted w/two turned corner finials, the case w/a row of two short & one long drawers overhanging a pair of cupboard doors flanked by single end doors flanked by four columns, leaf-carved animal front feet, appears to retain original finish & pulls, New York, ca. 1830, 22¼ x 69", 4' 9" h. (ILLUS.) **2,070.00**

Classical sideboard, mahogany, a superstructure w/a crestrail centered by scrolling flanking a shell carving above a pair of narrow shelves w/beaded front edges & flanked by long S-scroll end supports all backed by a mirror above the rectangular top w/rounded front corners above a round-fronted border w/drawers above four paneled cupboard doors, molded base on flattened bun front feet & block rear feet, Southern U.S., ca. 1830 ....**2,530.00**

Ornate Classical Sideboard

Classical sideboard, mahogany & bird's-eye maple, a high galleried top w/a paneled backboard topped by a row of short spindles & four bulbous turned finials above rows of spindles at each end, the rectangular top above a row of two short & one long drawers w/bird's-eye maple panels & round glass pulls overhanging two maple-trimmed end doors flanking a pair of matching central doors all flanked by four spiral-turned columns over a gadrooned apron band & bulbous spiral-turned feet, New England, ca. 1830 (ILLUS.)...........................**1,760.00**

Birch Federal Server

Federal server, birch, the rectangular top above a narrow long desk drawer over a long deeper drawer over a pair of small bow-fronted cupboard doors flanked by concave panels, oval brass pulls & keyhole escutcheons, on square tapering legs, New England, ca. 1800, refinished, minor imperfections, 22 x 36", 39" h. (ILLUS.) **3,737.50**

Cherry Federal Server

Federal server, inlaid cherry, a rectangular top above a thin pull-out writing surface over a deep drawer flanked by narrow bottle drawers above three long graduated drawers, banded trim, oval brasses & inlaid diamond keyhole escutcheons, scalloped apron & tall French feet, possibly Massachusetts, ca. 1810, old refinish, imperfections, 20 x 40½", 45½" h. (ILLUS.) **2,990.00**

Maryland Federal Sideboard

Federal sideboard, inlaid mahogany, the rectangular top w/line-inlaid edge above a pair of hinged end doors centering a frieze drawer & a pair of recessed convex hinged doors on line- and bellflower-inlaid square tapering legs ending in crossbanded cuffs, Baltimore, Maryland, ca. 1805, patches, repairs, 23¾ x 66", 43½" h. (ILLUS.) **6,325.00**

Federal "serpentine-front" sideboard, mahogany & satinwood inlay, long rectangular top w/ serpentine front w/alternating line inlays above a conforming case centering a bowed, cockbeaded & line-inlaid long drawer flanked by in-swept cockbeaded & line-inlaid short drawers over full serpentine-shaped cockbeaded & line-inlaid central cupboard doors flanked by lozenge-inlaid panels flanked by inswept bottle drawers, on pendent flower & line-inlaid tapering square legs, Massachusetts, 1790-1810, 27¼ x 66¼", 41⅛" h....................**21,850.00**

New York Federal Sideboard

Federal "serpentine-front" sideboard, inlaid mahogany, the oblong top w/rounded center over a conforming case w/four frieze drawers above a pair of recessed center cupboard doors flanked by concave bottle drawers, all w/line-inlaid banding & oval reserves, on line-inlaid square tapering legs w/cross-banded cuffs, New York, ca. 1800, repairs to inlay, 26¾ x 72½", 40⅛" h. (ILLUS.) **8,050.00**

Middle Atlantic Federal Sideboard

Federal "serpentine-front" sideboard, inlaid mahogany, the oblong top w/bowed center section above a conforming case w/a pair of small drawers flanking a pair of small square drawers flanking a long center bowed drawer all above tall end doors flanking a pair of small doors flanking the central pair of convex doors, the center section w/curved corner brackets w/fan inlay, doors & drawers w/line-inlaid panels, on turned reeded legs w/knob feet, probably Middle Atlantic States, ca. 1815, old refinish, minor imperfections, 25¾ x 78¼", 45" h. (ILLUS.) **4,025.00**

George III sideboard, inlaid mahogany, rectangular top w/bowed front above a central drawer over a recessed arched drawer flanked to one side w/two short drawers & the other side w/a swiveling cupboard door inlaid to resemble two drawers, the whole w/banded inlay, on square tapering legs w/spade feet, England, late 18th c., 26¾ x 56", 36½" h..**6,670.00**

George III-Style sideboard, inlaid mahogany, the rectangular top w/bowed front above a conforming case w/pairs of end drawers flanking a longer central drawer above an arched opening, on square tapering legs, inlaid line banding, round brass pulls, England, late 19th - early 20th c. **1,980.00**

Mission-style (Arts & Crafts movement) server, oak, the rectangular top w/a low backrail over an apron w/a blind drawer, raised on square legs joined by a medial shelf, original medium brown finish, conjoined L. & J.G. & Gustav Stickley mark, 16 x 32", 32" h. **660.00**

Gustav Stickley Sideboard

Mission-style (Arts & Crafts movement) sideboard, rectangular top w/a low gallery above a pair of drawers over a long drawer above a pair of long rectangular doors w/long pointed strap hinges, squared iron pull plates & drawer knobs, red decal mark of Gustav Stickley, Model No. 967, ca. 1902, 24 x 60", 43" h. (ILLUS.) **9,200.00**

Mission-style (Arts & Crafts movement) sideboard, oak, a tall plate rail crest above the rectangular top overhanging the case w/a pair of

square cupboard doors w/long spearpoint hammered copper hinges flanking three graduated central drawers all above a single long drawer across the bottom, on square legs, hammered copper pull plates w/ring pulls, original medium to dark brown finish enhanced on the top only, paster & red decal Gustav Stickley mark, Model No. 814, 24 x 66", 4' h..................**5,500.00**

Mission Sideboard with Plate Rail

Mission-style (Arts & Crafts movement) sideboard, oak, the tall gently arched backboard w/a plate rail above the rectangular top overhanging a case w/a long narrow drawer over a pair of paneled cupboard doors flanking a stack of three drawers, all w/metal plates & bails, on square legs joined by end stretchers, Stickley-signed (ILLUS.) **1,705.00**

Turn-of-the-Century Oak Sideboard

Turn of the century sideboard, oak, a tall crestboard w/a long leafy scroll crest on a flat molded crestrail over a wide panel w/scroll-carved ends above a narrow shelf supported on columns w/small shelves flanking a rectangular mirror in the tall back, the rectangular top w/serpentine front over a conforming case w/a pair of drawers over a long drawer above a pair of flat cupboard doors w/applied scroll carving, wooden knobs, applied S-scrolls at the front bottom corners above the animal paw front feet, on casters, ca. 1890-1910 (ILLUS.) **660.00**

Baroque-Style Sideboard

Victorian Baroque-Style sideboard, carved oak, the superstructure w/a wide ornately carved crestrail w/a large urn of fruit flanked by two recumbent griffins between flaring block finials over a long narrow panel flanked by grotesque mask-carved blocks above the rectangular "break-front" top w/stepped-out corner blocks above a row of three drawers carved w/leafy branches over three paneled cupboard doors carved w/oval reserves, two w/large baskets of fruit & the center one w/a coat of armor & scrolls, the outset corners w/barley-twist columns above carved apron band, on squatty bulbous lobed feet, late 19th c., 22½ x 72", 5' h. (ILLUS.) **880.00**

Victorian Renaissance Revival substyle sideboard, carved walnut, the tall superstructure w/a high winged palmette finial above an oval boss & an arched crestrail over burl panels flanked by scrolled corners above two long narrow serpentine open shelves w/scroll bracket supports, an oval mirror w/banded frame between the shelves, an oval panel in the lower panel above the rectangular white marble top, the lower case w/a pair of paneled drawers recessed above a pair of paneled cupboard doors w/carvings of dead game, reeded angular block

Renaissance Revival Sideboard

bands down the front & sides, flat molded base, ca. 1875 (ILLUS.) **2,310.00**

Alexander Roux Sideboard

Victorian Rococo substyle sideboard, carved rosewood, the tall superstructure w/a scalloped crest centered by a relief-carved fox head amid fruited garlands & foliate scrollwork over two long D-form shelves w/long rectangular mirrors flanked by pierce-carved scrolling end brackets, the long white marble D-form top above a conforming case w/a band of four small drawers w/carved fruit pulls above two carved end doors w/floral- and scroll-carved reserves flanking a pair of flat paneled center doors, one carved w/a reserve of dead game, the other w/a reserve of hunting trophies, molded base on flat block feet, original label of Alexander Roux, New York, ca. 1850-60, 24 x 80", 8' ½" h. (ILLUS.) **13,200.00**

STANDS

Federal Cherry Candlestand

Book stand, Mission-style (Arts & Crafts movement), oak, four rectangular open shelves between slated sides, arched front & back apron on the lowest shelf, original medium finish, retail tag of Frederick Loeser & Co., New York, ca. 1910, 12 x 19½", 42⅛" h. **402.50**

Candlestand, Chippendale country-style, painted hardwood, a round top fixed above a simple baluster-turned pedestal above a tripod base w/cabriole legs ending in snake feet, old red repaint, 19½" d., 27½" h. (age cracks) **715.00**

Candlestand, Chippendale tilt-top, mahogany & cherry, the circular dished cherry top tilting & revolving above a birdcage support & vase-form standard on cabriole legs ending in snake feet, 18½" d., 28" h...**4,600.00**

Candlestand, Federal, inlaid cherry, the oblong top w/wide rounded corners inlaid in the center w/an oval central reverse in flame birch outlined w/carving, tilting above a baluster-and ring-turned standard on a tripod base w/spider legs, Connecticut River Valley, early 19th c., imperfections, 13⅜ x 18⅛", 30½" h. (ILLUS.) **4,400.00**

Candlestand, Federal tilt top, carved mahogany, the oblong octagonal top tilting above an acanthus-carved ring-turned standard on acanthus-carved cabriole legs ending in brass

animal paw feet, on brass casters, possibly Charles Honoré Lannuier, ca. 1815, 20⅞ x 26", 28" h. (one foot repaired) **5,175.00**

Federal Mahogany Candlestand

Candlestand, Federal tilt top, mahogany, the squared top w/serpentine edges tilting above a ring- and urn-turned shaft over a tripod base w/cabriole legs ending in slipper feet, New England, late 18th - early 19th c., 19½ x 19¾", 27¼" h. (ILLUS.) **3,565.00**

Candlestand, Federal tilt top, mahogany, oval tilting top above a baluster-turned pedestal & chip-carved incised base, on three spider legs w/spade feet, New England, 1790-1810, 15⅛ x 21", 28¼" h. **863.00**

Candlestand, Federal tilt top, mahogany, the oblong shaped top tilting above a reeded & ring-turned standard on reeded downcurving legs, New York, ca. 1820, 18¾ x 25", 29" h............................**2,195.00**

Two Early Candlestands

Candlestand, Federal country-style, painted birch, the oval top tilting above a vase-form turned standard on a tripod base w/spider legs, New England, ca. 1810, 15 x 20", 29½" h. (ILLUS. left) **4,025.00**

Candlestand, primitive country-style, maple & birchwood, the circular top swiveling & adjustable on a threaded standard, the molded square medial shelf on a tripod base, New England, 1770-80, 28½" h. (ILLUS. right) **690.00**

Candlestand, Queen Anne, cherry, the circular top above a duo-directional drawer & vase-form standard, on cabriole legs ending in snake feet, Connecticut, ca. 1770, 15¼" d., 26" h. **4,888.00**

Candlestand, Queen Anne tilt-top, cherry, the circular dished top tilting above an urn-form standard, on cabriole legs ending in snake feet, probably Connecticut, ca. 1785, 18½" d., 26½" h. **4,313.00**

Country Queen Anne Candlestand

Candlestand, Queen Anne country-style, cherry, the round top w/a molded rim above a ring- and baluster-turned pedestal on a tripod base w/cabriole legs & snake feet, New England, 1750-60, two feet pieced, 15½" d., 26" h. (ILLUS.) **460.00**

Candlestand, Queen Anne country-style, tiger maple, a round top above an urn-form standard above a tripod base w/cabriole legs ending in snake feet, honey color finish, Massachusetts, ca. 1790, 21" d., 27" h. **2,300.00**

Dumbwaiter (three-tier stand), Chippendale, mahogany, three dished round graduated tiers each above a reeded urn-turned pedestal, on a tripod base w/peaked pad feet on casters, Mid-Atlantic States, 1760-80, 43½" h. (ILLUS. top next column) **3,220.00**

Chippendale Dumbwaiter

Classical Music Stand

Music stand, Classical (American Empire), carved mahogany, rectangular top w/molded edges above a case w/five open & shaped tall pigeonholes, the acanthus-carved pedestal above a plinth base w/four animal paw feet on casters, retains old finish, New York, ca. 1830, 13⅛ x 23", 35" h. (ILLUS.) **3,450.00**

Music stand, Mission-style (Arts & Crafts movement), oak, four wide rectangular open shelves, each w/a low, gently arched gallery, four square legs slightly tapering at the top, arched toeboard at the bottom shelf, original medium dark brown finish, Gustav Stickley paper label, Model No. 670, 14½ x 22", 39" h. **3,520.00**

Nightstand, Art Nouveau, carved mahogany & marble, the rectangular variegated marble top resting on a carved mahogany stand, fitted

w/one long drawer, an open shelf &
a lower drawer opening to reveal a
ceramic-lined storage space,
w/carved mahogany backsplash,
13¼ x 19", 40" h..............................**748.00**

Oriental stand, carved teak, a round
top w/soapstone insert above a wide
pierce-carved flaring apron above
four carved inward-curving legs
above a round faux marble small
shelf w/a carved flaring apron above
four curved animal paw feet joined
by cross-stretchers, China, late
19th - early 20th c., 28" h.................**401.50**

Oriental stand, carved teak,
octagonal top w/soapstone insert
above a deep pierce-carved
conforming apron raised on four
pierce-carved slender legs joined by
low stretchers above the outswept
paw feet, China, late 19th - early
20th c., 31¾" h. **522.50**

Plant stand, beech bentwood, a thin
square top raised on four tall square
tapering legs joined by two pairs of
narrow bentwood stretchers,
mahogany stain, designed by Josef
Hoffmann, probably produced by
J. & J. Kohn, Austria, ca. 1906,
12" w., 42½" h..............................**1,150.00**

Plant stand, Mission-style (Arts &
Crafts movement), chestnut, four
square tapering tall legs joined at
the top by heavy stretchers just
above a boxed shelf, no finish, dark
color, attributed to Gustav Stickley,
12" sq., 28½" h...............................**385.00**

Shaving stand, Chippendale-Style,
mahogany, a stepped-back top shelf
over a lower shelf above two frieze
drawers & two deeper drawers, all
on tapering legs joined by a lower
cut-out shelf, by Mahon of New
York, early 20th c., 17¾" w.,
47" h...**165.00**

Classical Shaving Stand

Shaving stand, Classical, mahogany,
squared top w/serpentine edges
overhanging a case w/two
graduated drawers w/inset round
brass pulls, the scalloped aprons
w/molded scrolls & corner drops,
raised on a tapering octagonal
pedestal on a shaped square
platform raised on four short
cabriole legs w/paw feet, slight
damages, Southern U.S., ca. 1830
(ILLUS. bottom previous column) **440.00**

Mission Oak Telephone Stand

Telephone stand, Mission-style (Arts
& Crafts movement), oak, square
top raised on tall square legs joined
by a medial shelf w/apron, original
dark brown finish, Gustav Stickley
red decal mark, Model No. 605,
14" w., 30" h. (ILLUS.) **1,210.00**

Umbrella stand, cast iron, a nautical
design w/a central anchor
supporting ropes above a shell-
form base, Victorian,
29" h..**575.00**

Umbrella stand, Mission-style (Arts &
Crafts movement), oak, four tall
tapering square posts joined at
the top by stretchers & w/a square
boxed base, original medium-dark
finish, unmarked Gustav Stickley,
Model No. 54, 11½" w., 33" h.
(water damage, base liner
missing) **467.50**

Washstand, Classical, figured
mahogany, the hinged rectangular
top opening to a panel pierced for
a basin w/molded receptacle holders
flanking, the case w/a single arched
drawer, the hinged crossbanded
door flanked by free-standing
acanthus-carved Ionic columns,
on acanthus-carved paw feet,
New York, ca. 1825, 16½ x 21",
33½" h. (ILLUS. top next page) **4,600.00**

New York Classical Washstand

Washstand, Federal, mahogany, the rectangular top above a sub-top pierced for basins, the shaped skirt below above a medial shelf fitted w/a drawer, reeded dies flanking on reeded tapering legs, ending in flattened ball feet, Boston, Massachusetts, ca. 1815, 19⅛ x 22½", 34½" h......................**2,070.00**

Federal "Tambour" Washstand

Washstand, Federal, mahogany, the top w/two hinged box-form supports opening to a panel pierced for a basin, a cockbeaded drawer below w/a tambour slide, on ring-turned legs ending in tapered feet, appears to retain original lion's mask brass handles, Boston area, Massachusetts, ca. 1805, minor repairs, 15 x 20", 35½" h. (ILLUS.) **2,875.00**

Washstand, Federal country-style, pine, the rectangular top w/a three-quarter scroll-cut gallery above a single long drawer w/two wooden knobs raised on slender ring- and baluster-turned supports to a rectangular medial shelf on ring- and

Federal Country-style Washstand

knob-turned feet, Mid-Atlantic States, ca. 1820, 17¼ x 24⅝", 37¼" h. (ILLUS.) **715.00**

Washstand, Victorian Renaissance Revival substyle, chestnut, an arched backsplash w/two small candle shelves above the rectangular top w/beveled edges above a case w/three long drawers w/fruit-and-leaf-carved pulls, ca. 1880, 16 x 30½", 38½" h...........**275.00**

Washstand, Victorian Rococo substyle, mahogany, rectangular white marble top w/serpentine front & chamfered front corners above a conforming case w/a long drawer over a pair of paneled cupboard doors flanked by chamfered corners w/scroll blocks at the top & base, scroll-carved serpentine apron, rounded block feet, ca. 1860, 19½ x 36", 28½" h...........................**715.00**

Federal one-drawer stand, cherry, the rectangular top w/line-inlaid edge above a cock-beaded drawer, on square tapering legs, Connecticut, 1790-1820, 13⅜ x 19", 24¾" h...........................**690.00**

Federal country-style one-drawer stand, painted pine, square top above an apron w/a single drawer w/wooden knob raised on slender turned & slightly tapering legs w/cylindrical feet, original red & black graining, yellow striping & gold stenciled top decoration, 16¾" sq., 29" h. (wear & top scratches)...........**852.50**

Federal country-style one-drawer stand, painted & decorated pine, the rectangular top w/notched corners overhanging a case fitted w/a single drawer, on square tapering legs, the top & legs painted & finger-dabbed in shades of dark bluish green, the drawer front in shades of yellow &

Federal Country-style Stand

brown, New England, ca. 1800,
15¾ x 16⅝", 28" h. (ILLUS.) **9,200.00**
Federal two-drawer stand,
mahogany, the rectangular top
above two graduated drawers, on
spirally turned legs joined by a
shaped medial shelf, on vase-form
feet ending in brass casters, New
York, ca. 1825, 15¾ x 22¼",
30" h...**3,738.00**
Hepplewhite country-style one-
drawer stand, curly maple, the
nearly square one-board top
overhanging a shallow apron w/a
single drawer w/a lacy glass pull,
raised on tall slender square
tapering legs, old worn finish, early
19th c., 17 x 17¾", 26" h. (pull an
old replacement) **1,980.00**

STOOLS

Classical Caned-Top Footstool

Classical (American Empire)
footstools, mahogany, concave
caned top edged w/reeded rails on
four reeded sabre legs w/ebonized
side medallions, Duncan Phyfe,
New York, 1810-33, 9¼ x 13",
7¾" h., pr. (ILLUS. one of two) **4,830.00**

Classical Mahogany Piano Stool

Classical piano stool, carved
mahogany, the circular seat
revolving above a conforming
molded base, on reeded cylindrical
tapering legs w/ebonized ball-turned
capitals & feet, Boston, ca. 1830,
14½" d., 21½" h. (ILLUS.) **920.00**

Classical Rosewood Piano Stool

Classical piano stool, rosewood, the
round needlework-covered top
above an octagonal frame, the fluted
standard on a shaped triangular
base ending in flattened ball feet,
probably New England, ca. 1840,
15¼" d., 19½" h. (ILLUS.) **402.00**
Footstool, country-style, cherry &
poplar, the rectangular top covered
w/a hooked cushion depicting a
flower with a striped border & w/a
shaped felt skirt, raised on slightly
swelled tapering legs, first half
19th c., 15½" l., 6¾" h.....................**690.00**
Footstool, country-style, thick oval
plank top on four turned, slightly
splayed legs, old dark worn paint,
8 x 11½", 6" h....................................**71.50**

Footstool, painted & parcel-gilt, rectangular upholstered slip seat within a molded frame on reeded tapering legs hung w/carved drapery & ending in scrolling toes, France, early 20th c., 19½ x 23½", 17" h. (chips, paint losses) **1,955.00**

Painted Decorated Pine Footstool

Footstool, miniature, paint-decorated pine, the rectangular form w/deeply scalloped apron & bootjack legs, apron containing a single small drawer painted w/sprays of stylized flowers & leafage in red, yellow & green on a white ground, the drawer inscribed in pencil on the reverse "Tobias K. Nice - 1859," probably Mahantango Valley, Schuykill County, Pennsylvania, dated 1859, 6 x 8¾", 5¾" h. (ILLUS.) **2,875.00**

Louis XVI *tabourets,* giltwood, rectangular upholstered top, the reeded rails raised on circular tapered stop-fluted legs headed by paterae, signed by C. Chevigny, France, last quarter 18th c., 17" w., 16½" h., pr. **8,625.00**

Stickley Footstool

Mission-style (Arts & Crafts movement) footstool, oak, square leather top w/tack trim above the deep arched aprons, on four tall square legs, L. & J.G. Stickley red & yellow decal mark, Model No. 311, 16" h. (ILLUS.) **345.00**

Regency stools, curule-type, verdigris-painted & parcel-gilt, each w/rectangular padded upholstered top above scrolling X-form legs carved w/stiff leaves & starbursts, resting on ball feet, England, early 19th c., one signed "George Boxall" & dated "1815," 21" l., pr. **5,225.00**

Victorian Rococo Footstool

Victorian footstool, Rococo substyle, carved mahogany, the round upholstered top above a deep shaped apron w/line-incised branching scrolls & carved rose cluster & scroll bosses at the top of the four spearpoint-carved legs, mid-19th c., 15½" d., 14½" h. (ILLUS.) **770.00**

William & Mary Stool

William & Mary stool, turned & black-painted oak, the rectangular molded top above a plain skirt on ring- and baluster-turned legs joined by a box stretcher, 13½ x 21½", 21" h. (ILLUS.) ....**3,??**

William & Mary Walnut Stool

William & Mary stool, walnut, rectangular seat covered in ivory & red silk, raised on trumpet-form square channeled legs joined by flattened cross stretchers, England, late 17th c., 15½ x 18", 16½" h. (ILLUS.) **4,600.00**

TABLES

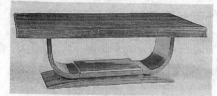

Art Deco Dining Table

Adams-Style console table, painted wood, the long D-shaped top above a segmented apron w/a long drawer in the center section flanked by curved end sections, each section painted w/a diamond & sprig design in polychrome on the ivory ground, four square, tapering legs, England, 20th c., 17 x 43½", 30" h. (minor wear, edge damage) **770.00**

Art Deco center table, parcel-silver & gilt-mahogany, oval polished figured top w/a carved dentil border above a wide frieze band carved w/four panels of very stylized geometric flowerheads trimmed in gilt & parcel-silver, on slender swelled & finely ribbed tapering turned legs joined by S-form stretchers centered by a carved domed stylized flower cluster, gilt & parcel-silver, Paul Follot, ...ce, ca. 1925, 22 x 28½", ...h. **10,350.00**

...dining table, rosewood, the ...ngular top w/draw-leaf ...rted by a wide U-shaped ...n a rectangular base,

includes two leaves, attributed to Jules Leleu, France, ca. 1925, 43 x 81¾", 27" h. (ILLUS.) **2,300.00**

Art Deco dressing table & stool, rosewood, tortoiseshell, gilt-bronze & ivory, the circular mirror swiveling above a top inset w/a central panel of inlaid tortoiseshell & ivory, central drawer flanked by a column, three short drawers w/ivory knobs, the legs inlaid w/an ivory stripe, ending in ivory *sabots,* the rosewood stool upholstered in olive green cut velvet, dressing table impressed "DESSINE PAR RUHLMANN - EDITE PAR PORTENEUVE," stool impressed "A. Portenueve," ca. 1934, dressing table 20 x 36", 30" h. plus mirror...................................**17,250.00**

Chippendale country-style drop-leaf dining table, maple, rectangular top flanked by two wide drop leaves w/cut-out corners, raised on square molded legs w/swing-leg supports, old worn dark brown finish, top 14½ x 46", each leaf 14¼" w., 27" h. (small corner repair to rule joint) **1,045.00**

Chippendale drop-leaf dining table, carved cherry, rectangular top flanked by two hinged rectangular leaves above a plain apron on round tapering legs ending in claw-and-ball feet, New York, ca. 1765, open 41¼ x 50½", 28" h.......................**2,875.00**

Chippendale Dining Table

Chippendale drop-leaf dining table, carved mahogany, the rectangular top flanked by two hinged rectangular drop leaves above a cyma-shaped apron continuing to angular cabriole legs ending in claw-and-ball feet, Massachusetts, ca. 1765, 36 x 36½" extended, 27½" h. (ILLUS.) **10,062.00**

Chippendale Pembroke table, mahogany, rectangular top w/bowed ends flanked by serpentine-shaped drop leaves above a conforming case fitted w/a single drawer, on molded square legs w/pierced brackets, appears to retain original brasses, Massachusetts, ca. 1770, 33¼ x 35⅝", 27½" h.....................**5,175.00**

Chippendale Pembroke Table

Chippendale Pembroke table, mahogany, the rectangular top flanked by two short hinged drop leaves above a frieze w/a single end drawer, the pierced leg brackets below continuing to square molded legs joined by a pierced X-form stretcher, New England, ca. 1785, pierced brackets restored, 29½ x 36½", 28" h. (ILLUS.) **6,900.00**

Chippendale Serving Table

Chippendale serving table, mahogany, the rectangular molded top above a plain frieze w/projecting skirt, acanthus- and C-scroll-carved pierced leg brackets on square legs, possibly Southern U.S., ca. 1775, 25 x 48", 32" h. (ILLUS.) **4,600.00**

Chippendale tea table, carved mahogany, the circular 'piecrust' dished top tilting & revolving above a birdcage support & ring-turned columnar standard, on a tripod base w/acanthus-carved cabriole legs

Chippendale 'Piecrust' Tea Table

ending in claw-and-ball feet, feet once fitted w/casters, Philadelphia, ca. 1760, upper section of standard extended, 37½" d., 29¾" h. (ILLUS.) **6,900.00**

Chippendale-Style Miniature Table

Chippendale-Style country-style miniature tea table, mahogany, the circular top above a ring- and vase-turned standard on a tripod base w/cabriole legs ending in snake feet, signed by Samuel Newman, North Andover, Massachusetts, ca. 1880, 11½" d., 11½" h. (ILLUS.) **1,265.00**

Classical (American Empire) card table, mahogany, the rectangular patera-veneered top w/canted corners above a foliate-carved pedestal & quadripartite base, on molded downswept legs w/foliate carved knees & brass hairy paw casters, New York, 1815-25, 18 x 35¾", 29½" h........................**1,840.00**

Classical card tables, mahogany, the rectangular hinged top w/rounded corners above a straight apron over a ring-turned & reeded baluster-form pedestal on a

Classical Card Table

quadripartite base w/sabre legs ending in brass hairy paw feet & casters, Boston, 1820-30, 16⅝ x 33¾", 30" h., pr. (ILLUS. one of two) **4,600.00**

Classical center table, carved mahogany & marble, the circular veined black marble top above a figured frieze w/brass border, the columnar standard w/gilt-metal base, the shaped plinth base on scrolled & gilt feet, Boston, Massachusetts, ca. 1830, 36¼" d., 29¼" h. **8,625.00**

Fine Classical Center Table

Classical center table, stenciled & ormolu-mounted mahogany, the circular top w/segmented radiating figured veneer w/leaf-stenciled border tilting above a ribbed leaf-carved gilt standard w/an ormolu ring below, the tripartite plinth base on acanthus-carved paw feet on brass casters, attributed to Anthony Quervelle, Philadelphia, ca. 1830, 47" d., 33" h. (ILLUS.) **13,800.00**

Classical dining table, double-pedestal, carved mahogany,

rectangular top w/rounded corners above a conforming apron, each end w/bolection molding & gadrooning over two flaring cylindrical pedestals each above a shaped plinth, on quadripartite acanthus-carved legs w/paw feet, on casters, probably Philadelphia, 1820-35, 59 x 108" extended, 29½" h...**3,220.00**

Classical 'Drum' Table

Classical 'drum' table, mahogany, the segmented round top above an apron fitted w/two drawers, on a ring-turned & acanthus leaf-carved pedestal on a tripod base w/leaf-scrolled legs ending in paw feet w/brass casters, probably Philadelphia or Baltimore, ca. 1830, 23¾" d., 30¼" h. (ILLUS.) **3,300.00**

Classical Work Table

Classical work table, mahogany, the rectangular top w/beaded edge above a wide ogee apron w/a hidden drawer, raised on scroll-carved lyre-form end supports w/flaring scroll legs joined by a ring- and baluster-turned stretcher, probably Philadelphia, ca. 1830, 16¼ x 25", 29½" h. (ILLUS.) **1,210.00**

Early Painted Side Table

Country-style side table, painted
pine, rectangular top w/breadboard
ends overhanging a deep apron on
slender turned legs, base w/old
Spanish brown paint, the top
scrubbed, New England, ca. 1800,
imperfections, 19¼ x 27¾",
28" h. (ILLUS.) **1,092.50**

Early Texas Side Table

Country-style side table, fruitwood,
rectangular top w/applied edge
widely overhanging a straight apron
w/one end drawer, on square
tapering legs, Texas, mid-19th c.,
25½ x 33¼" h., 28" h. (ILLUS.) **575.00**
Federal card table, flame birch-inlaid
mahogany, the oblong top
w/conformingly shaped hinged leaf
above a flame birch-inlaid frieze
centering an oval reserve, on
reeded circular tapering legs ending
in slightly bulbous feet,
Massachusetts, probably Salem, ca.
1805, 17¾ x 36½", 30½" h. (patches
to leaf where hinges broke out) **8,625.00**
Federal card table, inlaid mahogany,
the oblong D-form table w/inlaid
edge & conformingly shaped hinged
leaf above a crotch-figured frieze

Fine Federal Inlaid Card Table

w/diamond-inlaid edge centering
spring-inlaid dyes, on dot- and
bellflower-inlaid square double-
tapering legs ending in crossbanded
cuffs, warm brown color, attributed
to Jacob Forster, Charlestown,
Massachusetts, ca. 1805, repair to
upper section at one leg, patch to
top at hinge, 17⅞ x 35¾", 29" h.
(ILLUS.) **3,450.00**

New York Federal Card Table

Federal card table, mahogany, the
rectangular top w/crossbanded edge
& canted corners & a conforming
hinged leaf swiveling to reveal a
baize-lined well, raised on ring- and
drum-turned reeded pedestal on a
quadripartite base w/four
downcurving reeded legs ending in
carved paw feet on casters, deep
reddish brown color, New York,
ca. 1815, 18 x 36", 29½" h.
(ILLUS.) **4,600.00**
Federal card table, painted & gilt-
metal mounted mahogany, the
oblong top w/reeded edge &
conformingly shaped hinged leaf
swiveling above a well, the frieze
below mounted w/gilt-metal lion's

masks centering a gilt-metal mount decorated w/a wreath & foliage, the double lyre-form standard below on a figured mahogany plinth continuing to gilt acanthus-leaf-painted cabriole legs ending in brass animal paw feet on brass casters, Boston, Massachusetts, ca. 1810, 17½ x 35½", 30½" h....................**5,750.00**

Federal Dining Table

Federal dining table, two-part, mahogany, composed of two D-shaped end sections, each w/a wide hinged leaf above a plain apron, on square tapering legs, ca. 1810, patched & repaired, extended 47½ x 101½", 28" h. (ILLUS.) **4,312.00**

Baltimore Federal Dining Table

Federal dining table, two-part, mahogany, composed of two D-form end sections, each w/reeded edges above an apron w/turned corner pendants, on wide urn-form & reeded standards w/quadripartite bases w/downcurving reeded legs ending in paw feet w/brass casters, w/seven leaves, Baltimore, Maryland, ca. 1830, extended 54 x 130", 28¾" h. (ILLUS.) **4,312.00**
Federal dressing table, painted & decorated pine, the shaped splashboard above a narrow shelf incorporating two drawers above a shaped apron, the case on ring-turned tapering legs ending in ball feet, overall yellow ground painted

Rare Federal Dressing Table

w/clusters of red roses & green leaves, round repoussé brass pulls, probably Massachusetts or Maine, ca. 1825-28, bears a penciled inscription in drawers "September 12th, 1828," 17½ x 33¼", 38" h. (ILLUS.) **11,500.00**
Federal country-style "harvest" table, pine & maple, long narrow rectangular top flanked by long drop leaves, on square tapering legs, old refinish, probably Massachusetts, ca. 1800, 35½ x 114", 26½" h. (minor imperfections) **3,737.50**

Federal Library Table

Federal library table, mahogany, the rectangular top flanked by two D-form drop leaves above an apron w/a single end drawer & acorn corner drops, raised on shaped end supports joined by two turned medial stretchers, on pairs of downswept reeded legs ending in brass casters in the form of recumbent lions, Baltimore, Maryland, ca. 1825, three corner drops replaced, 42 x 45", 28" h. (ILLUS.) **1,495.00**

Federal Pembroke Table

Federal Pembroke table, curly maple, the rectangular top w/slightly pointed ends flanked by shaped hinged drop leaves above a plain apron, on square tapering legs, extended 35 x 35", 28" h. (ILLUS.) **1,610.00**

Federal pier table, birch-inlaid mahogany, rectangular white marble top above a frieze inlaid w/rectangular flame birch panels, the line-inlaid square tapering legs ending in crossbanded cuffs, early 19th c., 22 x 48", 4' 1" h. **2,300.00**

Federal Seamstress Table

Federal seamstress table, hardwood, the rectangular top above pairs of folding slender ring-turned legs on casters, dimensions incised on the top, 19th c., 22 x 36" (ILLUS.) **747.00**

Federal side table, ebony-inlaid cherry, the rectangular top inlaid w/four quarter-fans & central stellar inlay above a line-inlaid frieze drawer, on almond-inlaid legs ending in crossbanded cuffs, Rhode Island or Connecticut, ca. 1805, 15½ x 15⅞", 27½" h. **5,463.00**

Federal work table, mahogany & satinwood, the square top w/canted corners w/inset carved disks above a conforming case fitted w/two short cockbeaded drawers, the canted corners w/ring- and baluster-turned pilasters over ring-turned & reeded tapering round legs w/turned feet, pairs of small brass knobs on the drawers, Massachusetts, 1780-1800, 16 x 16¼", 27½" h..............**5,175.00**

Fine Federal Work Table

Federal work table, two-drawer, mahogany & bird's-eye maple, the nearly square top w/notched corners above a case w/two small drawers faced w/bird's-eye maple & w/bird's-eye maple sides, on slender turned & tapering reeded legs w/slender peg feet, ca. 1810 (ILLUS.)...........**6,050.00**

Federal work table, carved mahogany, rectangular hinged top opening to reveal a fitted interior w/compartments & a hinged writing surface opening to a well, above a case fitted w/two drawers flanked by stop-fluted pilasters, over reeded turned legs & a shelf, on vase-turned feet & socket casters, New England, 1800-10, 15½ x 21½", 28¾" h...**1,840.00**

Federal work table, three-drawer, mahogany-veneered cherry, the rectangular top above a case of three long graduated drawers, on rod- and ring-turned supports to the shaped medial shelf on ring-turned tapering legs w/ball feet, Pennsylvania or Middle Atlantic States, ca. 1820, 19½ x 33", 37" h. (ILLUS. top next page) **3,737.00**

Federal country-style work table, pine & birch, a wide rectangular one-board top widely overhanging an apron w/one long drawer

Federal Mahogany Work Table

w/turned wood knob, on baluster-
and ring-turned legs, old mellow
refinishing, 26½ x 42",
29¾" h..**1,320.00**

Federal country-style work table,
walnut & curly maple, rectangular
top w/narrow drop leaf at the back
overhanging a deep apron w/two
curly maple drawers w/replaced
wooden knobs, turned legs w/ring-
turned sections, old mellow finish,
19th c., top 21¾ x 36¾" plus 11½"
leaf, 29" h.....................................**1,210.00**

"Harvest" table, pine & poplar, long
rectangular top widely overhanging
a canted apron & four canted
baluster- and block-turned legs
joined by a long flat stretcher &
baluster-turned end rungs, New
England, 19th c., 72½" l................**2,250.00**

Hutch (or chair) table, painted, a
wide round top lifting above a boxed
seat w/deep apron w/scroll-cut lower
edge, on shoe feet joined by a flat
shaped stretcher, scrubbed top over
old red base, northern New York
state, late 18th c., 32 x 43½",
26" h. (imperfections)..................**3,737.00**

Mission Oak Center Table

Mission-style (Arts & Crafts
movement) center table, oak,
hexagonal top overhanging a

conforming base w/slightly arched
apron above heavy rectangular legs
joined by a "wagon wheel" style
stretcher joined at the center by a
hexagonal block, the legs w/key
exposed tenons, branded mark of L.
& J.G. Stickley, 48" w., 29" h.
(ILLUS.) **9,775.00**

Mission-style (Arts & Crafts
movement) dining table, oak, round
divided top raised on a central
standard composed of four square
pedestals resting upon four everted
feet, L. & J.G. Stickley white decal
mark, w/two leaves, 48" d.,
27" h..**3,680.00**

Mission-style (Arts & Crafts
movement) dining table, oak, round
divided top above a heavy slightly
tapering square pedestal w/four
curved 'feet,' mostly original medium
to dark brown finish, w/five original
leaves, Gustav Stickley red decal
mark, Model No. 656, 54" d., 29" h.
(color enhanced on top, some
veneer chipping on edges of feet
& apron) **4,125.00**

Mission-style (Arts & Crafts
movement) dining table, oak,
rectangular top widely overhanging
canted heavy legs on shaped trestle
feet, L. & J.G. Stickley, Model No.
548, ca. 1910, 44¼ x 84",
29¼" h..**7,475.00**

Mission-style (Arts & Crafts
movement) dressing table, oak, a
long rectangular mirror swiveling
between two uprights w/hammered
wrought-iron candle sconces above
a wide rectangular top over a row of
three drawers over two drawers
flanking a rounded kneehole
opening, on square slightly tapering
legs, red decal mark of Gustav
Stickley, Model No. 632, ca. 1902,
21¾ x 54", 4' 10" h.......................**5,520.00**

Mission-style (Arts & Crafts
movement) library table, oak,
rectangular top slightly overhanging
an apron w/two drawers over arch
corbels above a lower tenoned
stretcher shelf, original medium
brown finish, L. & J.G. Stickley
"Handcraft" decal mark, Model
No. 520, 28 x 42", 29" h. **770.00**

Pietra dura center table, the top
w/stone floral sprays within an
ebonized border, raised on a
knopped standard resting on a
shield-shaped base, Italy,
late 19th c., 33" d., 30" h..............**2,990.00**

Queen Anne breakfast table, walnut,
the rectangular narrow top

Rare Queen Anne Breakfast Table

w/rounded ends flanked by D-
shaped drop leaves, the whole w/a
molded edge above a cyma-shaped
apron, on cabriole legs ending in
pad feet, Boston, Massachusetts,
1740-60, extended 27" d., 26" h.
(ILLUS.) **19,550.00**
Queen Anne tea table, birchwood,
the rectangular top w/molded dished
edge above a shaped skirt on
cabriole legs, New England,
ca. 1760, 19⅞ x 26⅞", 24⅞" h. **3,162.00**

Queen Anne Painted Tea Table

Queen Anne tea table, grain-painted
cherry, the rectangular top w/molded
edge above an apron of double
cyma-curved outline continuing to
bracketed slightly angular cabriole
legs ending in delicate pad feet, the
top painted & veined in shades of
ochre to simulate marble, the frame
& legs painted in shades of
brownish yellow on a grey ground,
New England, ca. 1730, top reset,
old repair to one leg, 18½ x 26¾",
26½" h. (ILLUS.) **40,250.00**

"Porringer-top" Tea Table

Queen Anne "porringer-top" tea
table, mahogany, the oblong top
w/rounded outset corners above a
cyma-shaped apron, on circular
tapering legs ending in pad feet,
reddish brown color, attributed to
John Goddard, Newport, Rhode
Island, 1740-60, 25¼ x 34",
26½" h. (ILLUS.) **28,750.00**
Regency game table, mahogany,
long D-form fold-over top w/cross-
banded edges, above an ebony-
inlaid frieze, above a reeded
pedestal on four leaf-carved
downswept & reeded legs w/cast
brass toe mounts & casters,
England, ca. 1820, 21 x 40",
30" h..**3,450.00**

Regency Sofa Table

Regency sofa table, brass-inlaid
rosewood, the long rectangular top
flanked by crossbanded end drop
leaves above an apron w/two brass
band-inlaid drawers, on lyre-form
end supports on arched scrolled
legs joined by a double-S-scroll
stretcher, England, second quarter
19th c., extended 23¾ x 51¾",
29¼" h. (ILLUS.) **4,887.50**

Shaker Work Table

Shaker work table, pine, the top
fitted w/a detachable long
compartmented double shelf unit
above the rectangular top
w/breadboard ends over a plain
apron above four square tapering
legs, the underside signed in pencil
"Anderson," New York, early
20th c., 22 x 29¾", 35" h.
(ILLUS.) **1,725.00**

Renaissance-Style center table,
walnut, oblong top w/molded frieze,
raised on fruit-carved scrolling
trestle supports joined by a
balustrade, ca. 1920, 30 x 70½",
29" h..**1,840.00**

New England Tavern Table

Tavern table, painted & turned maple
& pine, the oval top above a molded
apron raised on vase- and reel-
turned legs joined by a box
stretcher, on turned flared feet, the
base painted black, scrubbed top,
New England, ca. 1730-70, 23 x 32",
25" h. (ILLUS.) **6,900.00**

Tavern table, painted maple & pine,
the rectangular top above a plain

frieze on turned legs joined by a box
stretcher, painted yellowish tan,
New England, 1760-1800,
19½ x 23¾", 28" h........................**1,955.00**

Pennsylvania Tavern Table

Tavern table, painted poplar, the
removable rectangular top above a
deep apron w/a single deep drawer
w/oval brass pulls, on ring- and
baluster-turned legs joined by a
stretcher, on turned feet, painted
red, Pennsylvania, first quarter
19th c., 24 x 69", 28" h.
(ILLUS.) **1,610.00**

Aesthetic Movement Side Table

Victorian Aesthetic Movement side
table, carved walnut, the square top
over a florette- and roundel-carved
trelliswork apron, on slender ring-
and rod-turned legs joined by a
galleried medial shelf, on
downcurved brass feet, unrestored
surface, New York, late 19th c.,
19¾", 30¼" h. (ILLUS.) **550.00**

Victorian Gothic Revival center
table, mahogany, the hexagonal top
inset w/ochre marble above an
arcaded apron, raised on three
tapering columnar legs on a tripartite
incurvate base on down-scrolled
feet on brass casters, restoration to
marble, ca. 1840, 29¼" d., 29¾" h.
(ILLUS. top next page)..................**2,860.00**

Gothic Revival Center Table

Oak Renaissance Revival Dining Table

Victorian Renaissance Revival
dining table, oak, the round divided top w/a narrow carved edge above a deep apron, on a heavy acanthus-carved pedestal & column issuing four legs headed by griffin heads & w/fruit clusters & paw feet on casters, w/three leaves, late 19th c., 51½" d., 30" h. (ILLUS.) **1,760.00**

Walnut Victorian Dining Table

Victorian Renaissance Revival
dining table, walnut, the round divided top w/a molded edge over an apron w/a line-incised Greek key design, raised on a squared pedestal w/four long scroll- and leaf-carved legs on casters, ca. 1880, w/one leaf (ILLUS.) **1,600.00**

Victorian Renaissance Revival
substyle folding table, cherry, "patent rotary" model w/folding adjustable top w/two drawers, raised on an adjustable support on four paw feet, each drawer w/the paper label of the Gates Manufacturing Company, Philadelphia, patented in 1877 ....**460.00**

Renaissance Revival Games Table

Victorian Renaissance Revival
games table, gilt-incised rosewood, the rectangular top w/rounded corners opening to a red felt-lined gaming surface, the apron w/incised geometric designs, on four slender fluted turned columns on a cross-form platform w/urn finial raised on four down-curved reeded legs w/paterae & scroll feet on wooden casters, polished surface, original gilt paint, ca. 1865, 18⅝ x 38", 29" h. (ILLUS.) **1,430.00**

Oval Renaissance Revival Table

Victorian Renaissance Revival
parlor table, walnut, the oval top inset w/marble, a deep molded apron w/scroll-cut side drops, raised on four molded S-scroll legs joined by scroll-carved cross stretchers centered by a large urn finial, on casters, ca. 1860-70 (ILLUS.) **715.00**

Rectangular Renaissance Revival Table

Victorian Renaissance Revival
parlor table, walnut, the rectangular
white marble top w/molded edges &
notched corners above a conforming
apron w/raised burl panels & a
flaring edge w/half-round drops,
raised on four baluster- and ring-
turned columns raised on upcurved
brackets centering a large turned
urn finial & raised on four
downswept legs w/burl panels, on
casters, ca. 1870 (ILLUS.) **880.00**

Belter-Attributed Parlor Table

Victorian Rococo substyle parlor
center table, carved rosewood, the
round white marble top w/gadrooned
edge over a pierced & scroll-cut
apron w/carved roundels raised on
three long S-scroll pierced supports
joined at a tripartite paneled plinth
w/a turned urn finial & raised on
three double-C-scroll-carved legs on
casters, attributed to John Henry
Belter, New York, ca. 1850, 28" d.
(ILLUS.) **5,225.00**
Victorian Rococo substyle "turtle-
top" parlor center table, rosewood,
the oblong shaped top above a
conforming apron w/a fitted drawer

on one side, on four heavy S-scroll
legs w/carved acanthus & scrolls &
joined by slender S-scroll stretchers
centered by a squatty urn turning,
ca. 1850 ....**1,980.00**

Ornate "Turtle-top" Parlor Table

Victorian Rococo substyle "turtle-
top" parlor center table, carved
walnut, the shaped ochre & rouge
variegated marble top over a
conforming apron carved w/scrolled
cartouches, raised on heavy
cabriole legs headed by male masks
over C-scrolls & floral swags, the
curvate scrolled stretchers centered
by a shaped marble shelf, on brass
casters, dark finish, ca. 1850,
28½ x 42¾", 29¼" h. (ILLUS.) **5,225.00**

Simple "Turtle-top" Parlor Table

Victorian Rococo substyle "turtle-
top" parlor center table, walnut, the
shaped white marble top above a
conforming molded apron w/fan-
carved drops, on simple slender S-
scroll legs headed by carved
acanthus leaves & joined by arched
cross-stretchers centered by an urn-
form finial, on casters, ca. 1850-60
(ILLUS.) **495.00**
Victorian Rococo substyle "turtle-
top" parlor center table, carved
rosewood, the shaped white marble

top above a deep conforming apron ornately carved overall w/leafy scrolls & fruit & flower clusters, on ornate S-scroll legs carved w/fruit & flower clusters & large scrolls, slender S-scroll stretchers centered by a large floral-carved urn, ca. 1850, 60" l. **6,050.00**

"Turtle-top" Table with Drawer

Victorian Rococo substyle "turtle-top" parlor center table, carved mahogany, the shaped wood top above a plain conforming apron, on a bulbous gadrooned urn-form pedestal raised on four downswept S-scroll legs on casters, w/a drawer in the apron, ca. 1850 (ILLUS.) **550.00**

William & Mary drop-leaf "gate-leg" dining table, maple, the oblong top w/two hinged D-shaped leaves above a single-drawer frieze on vase- and block-turned legs joined by turned stretchers, ending in turned feet, New England, ca. 1760, 40" l., extended 51" w., 28" h. (feet replaced & other repairs) **2,588.00**

Decorated William & Mary Table

William & Mary drop-leaf "gate-leg" dining table, painted & turned maple & pine, a narrow rectangular top flanked by two D-shaped drop-leaves above a plain apron, on slender baluster-turned legs joined by rectangular stretchers, on turned feet, the top decorated w/19th c. grain-painted decoration in shades of orange & brown, the base painted dark red, probably Windsor, Connecticut, ca. 1760, extended 24¼ x 33½", 26½" h. (ILLUS.) **19,550.00**

WARDROBES & ARMOIRES

American Classical Armoire

Armoire, child's, American French Provincial, mahogany, rectangular top w/flaring coved cornice above a pair of tall paneled doors, scallop-cut apron, on short cabriole legs, Louisiana, ca. 1790, 5' h.....**1,540.00**

Armoire, Art Moderne, gilt-bronze mounted figured maple, stepped rectangular top above a slightly arched front over a pair of wide cabinet doors veneered w/a diamond pattern & set at the center w/a gilt-bronze escutcheon, opening to a fitted interior, raised on short shaped legs w/gilt-bronze *sabots*, France, possibly by Leleu, ca. 1940, 21 x 70", 5' 4¾" h. **4,025.00**

Armoire, Classical (American Empire), mahogany, the rectangular top w/a narrow cornice above a pair of tall three-panel doors w/oblong brass keyhole escutcheons, flat base on bulbous turned & tapering feet, ca. 1830, 19¼ x 47¼", 6' 8¾" h. (ILLUS.) **2,530.00**

Armoire, Classical (American Empire), mahogany, rectangular top w/deep beveled cornice above a flat frieze band above a pair of long double-paneled doors w/a long panel over a short panel, reeded brass edging & brass cornucopia keyhole escutcheons, opening to two compartments, the left w/three sliding galleried shelves above a single drawer over two sliding galleried shelves; the other half an open compartment & both compartments above a long single drawer w/original oval brasses stamped w/acorns, doors flanked by columns w/ormolu capitals, platform base on carved waterleaf & paw feet, Duncan Phyfe, New York, 1815-25, 28¼ x 66¾", 7' 3½" h. **32,200.00**

Continental Provincial Armoire

Armoire, Continental Provincial, carved walnut & pine, the rectangular top w/flaring ogee cornice above a pair of tall triple-paneled cupboard doors w/large diamonds & small blocks in the upper & lower panels & a stylized blossomhead in the center panel, a single long drawer across the base, a gently scalloped apron & bracket feet, Europe, mid-19th c., 18¾ x 53½", 6' 9" h. (ILLUS.)......**1,870.00**

Armoire, French Provincial, carved oak, a rectangular top w/an arched crestrail carved w/flowers, ribbons & leafy scrolls above a carved frieze band over a pair of tall double-paneled doors w/scroll-carved trim & a half-length winged putto at the top of one door, the doors flanked by half-length putti at the upper corners of the case, a long narrow drawer at the base flanked by leafy scrolls & raised on shoulder scroll feet,

French Provincial Armoire

France, 19th c. (ILLUS.)......................................**3,025.00**

Kas (American version of the Netherlands *Kast* or wardrobe), cherry, wide molded cornice, over pair of double paneled doors opening to interior w/shelf & wooden hooks, simple cut-out feet, old worn finish, 22½ x 58¼", 6' 6" h. (mismatched wooden knobs on doors, overlapping edge strip missing from one door) **2,090.00**

William & Mary Kas

Kas, William & Mary, gumwood, the elaborately molded projecting cornice above square pilasters flanking & dividing a pair of molded & raised panel doors opening to an interior fitted w/three shelves & an under-hung drawer; the lower section w/mid-molding above a long drawer w/central diamond-molded reserve flanked by applied moldings to give the appearance of two drawers, flanked by diamond-molded reserves, on a molded base on turned ball front feet & rectangular rear feet, New York state, 1730-1780, old refinish, restoration, repair, overall 75½" w., 27" d., 6' 5½" h. (ILLUS.).....................................**3,450.00**

Schrank (massive Germanic wardrobe), painted pine, in several parts, a rectangular top w/a widely flaring carved, painted & dentil-carved deeply double-molded cornice above a paneled case w/a large single door w/six panels flanked by side panels of three panels each, opening to shelves, the slightly stepped-out base w/two drawers above the widely flaring molded base, painted bluish green w/the panels in a mottled red-strippled finish, Pennsylvania, ca. 1770, 26 x 69", 7' 3" h. **31,050.00**

German Rococo Schrank

Schrank, Rococo, walnut, an arched crestrail continuing to rounded corners above a conforming frieze over a pair of double-panel arched & molded cupboard doors, round-cornered base molding on large flattened bun feet, Germany, late 18th c., 22 x 60", 7' 5" h. (ILLUS.).......................................**2,760.00**

Wardrobe, Classical country-style, cherry & walnut, the rectangular top w/no cornice above a pair of tall paneled doors, raised on tall heavy ring- and baluster-turned legs, the interior w/a central support w/hanging space on left & shelves on right, Louisiana, ca. 1830.........**1,320.00**

Wardrobe, Classical country-style, walnut, a rectangular top w/a scallop-cut cornice w/a band of large beads above a pair of tall double-panel doors opening to three shelves, scalloped apron continuing to bracket feet, probably Louisiana, ca. 1820 ....**550.00**

Wardrobe, Edwardian, mahogany & mahogany veneer, in three sections; the outset center section w/an arched crest above a molded cornice over a pair of tall arched doors w/raised conforming banding opening to pull-out shelves & two drawers above a long drawer below; the stepped-back end sections w/flat tops over molded cornices above a single long door w/arch-top raised banding & opening to long compartments, molded base, England, early 20th c., 28½ x 99½", 7' 7" h. (wear, veneer & edge damage)..**990.00**

Wardrobe, Victorian country-style, painted poplar, rectangular top above a wide stepped cornice over a pair of tall narrow double-paneled doors flanked by wide front boards, simple cut-out apron, old red refinishing, interior of doors w/old yellow graining, 19¾ x 54½", 6' 1¾" h. (minor edge damage)........**522.50**

Wardrobe, Victorian Eastlake substyle, walnut, the geometric cornice above a pair of mirrored long doors on a stepped-out base w/two drawers w/carved shell & leaf pulls, ca. 1880, 20½ x 50", 6' 11" h. **990.00**

Gothic Revival Wardrobe

Wardrobe, Victorian Gothic Revival substyle, bird's-eye maple, the rectangular top w/flattened flaring wide cornice above a pair of tall Gothic arch-paneled doors opening to interior drawers & shelves in the right side, flat base on C-scroll front legs, ca. 1835, original surface, in four sections (ILLUS.) **4,620.00**

Wardrobe, Victorian Renaissance Revival substyle, walnut & burl veneer, rectangular top w/flaring, molded cornice above a pair of narrow panels w/a small square burl panel above a tall burl panel, each separated by carved scrolls, the panels flanking a tall center door w/arch-topped mirror, a pair of drawers over a single long drawer at the bottom, each w/burl veneering, molded base, labeled "Manufactured by the Scottish Co-operative Wholesale Society Ltd.," late 19th - early 20th c., 21¼ x 52½", 6' 10¼" h. **495.00**

Renaissance Revival Wardrobe

Wardrobe, Victorian Renaissance Revival substyle, walnut, the arched & deeply molded crest w/a central carved block & urn-form corner finials above an arched frieze band boldly carved w/leafy scrolls framing a large cartouche above a pair of tall mirrored doors w/arched tops above a pair of drawers at the bottom w/applied oval reserves & leaf-carved pulls, paneled sides, molded base on thin block feet, ca. 1860 (ILLUS.).......................................**2,420.00**

Wardrobe, Victorian Renaissance Revival substyle, bird's-eye maple, the tall central section w/a high arched & scroll-carved crest centered by a carved roaring griffin's head

Ornate Renaissance Revival Wardrobe

above the widely flaring molded cornice over a block-carved frieze band above a tall mirrored door flanked by blocked & reeded pilasters, the central case flanked by shorter side cabinets each w/a galleried top w/finials above an open shelf w/a curved back above two small paneled drawers over a stepped-out case w/blocked corners & three paneled drawers flanked by blocks & raised on short columns to an open shelf above the flaring deeply molded base on squatty feet, attributed to Herter Brothers, New York, ca. 1875, 90" w., 9' 6" h. (ILLUS.).......................................**13,100.00**

Wardrobe, Victorian Rococo substyle, oyster burl walnut, the rectangular top w/rounded front corners over a flaring curved cornice above a pair of full-length arched panel doors, England, ca. 1850............................**880.00**

Wardrobe, Victorian Rococo substyle, mahogany, triple-door, the stepped & arched top w/a high ornate pierced vine-carved crestrail centered by large flower-filled urns & flanked by squatty gadrooned finials above the deeply molded cornice & arched case w/an arched mirrored center door w/scroll-carved banding flanked by solid side doors w/scroll-carved reserves, a long paneled drawer across the bottom above a beaded band over the scroll-carved apron on ringed cylindrical feet, Prudent Mallard, New Orleans, ca. 1850, veneer damages (ILLUS. top next page)..**18,700.00**

Prudent Mallard Wardrobe

WHATNOTS & ETAGERES

Classical-Style Etagere

Etagere, Classical-Style, ormolu-mounted mahogany, the white marble square top above a frieze drawer w/brass ring pulls raised on columnar supports joined by medial shelves above a cupboard door w/ring handle, thin block feet, Europe, late 19th c., 20¼ x 20½", 4' 11¼" h. (ILLUS.)......................**6,900.00**

Etagere, Federal, mahogany, three square open shelves w/knob finials at the top & raised on slender baluster-turned posts, the base shelf w/a narrow drawer in the apron, on short turned legs on casters, New York, 1790-1810, 17½" sq., 4' 5" h. (ILLUS. top next column) **6,670.00**

Federal Mahogany Etagere

Fine Renaissance Revival Etagere

Etagere, Victorian Renaissance Revival, carved walnut, the tall back w/a high fanned finial above a flaring scroll cartouche centered by the head of a man flanked by high quarter-round pierce-carved brackets above a flat molded crestrail above a raised arched scroll-incised panel centered by a grotesque mask & flanked by carved corner scrolls, a tall oblong mirror flanked on each side by three quarter-round shaped graduated shelves backed by recessed shaped mirrored or plain panels all above a D-form white marble shelf on a deep apron w/a paneled drawer w/a carved lion's head pull, on stepped block feet, ca. 1850, 50" w., 8' 7" h. (ILLUS.) **2,750.00**

Victorian Rococo Etagere

Etagere, Victorian Rococo substyle,
carved rosewood, the tall tapering
superstructure w/a tall pointed &
pierce-carved scrolling crest above
two graduated serpentine shelves
on S-scroll & C-scroll supports &
backed by shaped mirrors above the
red marble serpentine top above a
deep conforming scroll-carved apron
raised on tall scroll-carved S-scroll
legs joined by two reverse-
graduated serpentine open shelves,
ca. 1850 (ILLUS.)..........................**1,540.00**

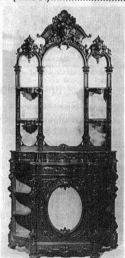

Ornate Walnut Etagere

Etagere, Victorian Rococo substyle,
carved & figured walnut, the tall
superstructure w/an arched &
fanned central crest w/shell-carved
finials above a carved cartouche

w/scrolls above a tall oblong central
mirror flanked by arched side units
w/cartouche-carved finials over
oblong mirrors behind two scroll-
carved half-round small shelves; the
serpentine top w/three small scroll-
carved drawers above a wider
serpentine stepped-out top over a
long drawer over a cupboard door
w/oval mirror & scroll-carved corners
all flanked by the canted corner
shelves at the sides, scalloped &
scroll-carved apron on squatty
bulbous feet, ca. 1850, 47½" w.,
7' 4¾" h. (ILLUS.).........................**7,975.00**

Rare & Ornate Meeks Etagere

Etagere, Victorian Rococo substyle,
carved & laminated rosewood, the
tall superstructure w/a swan's-neck
crest centered by an urn finial over
scroll-carved panels, the arched
central crestrail flanked by urn-form
finials & corner scrolls, the three-
section back w/a wide arched
central mirror flanked by rectangular
mirrors backing on each side two
shaped open shelves w/pierced
scroll trim & suspended between
ring-turned slender columns
w/further matching columns &
pierced scrolls at the outer edges of
the case, the wide serpentine top
w/a scroll-carved center drawer over
a stepped-out serpentine apron
w/deeply carved scrolls & a large
central fruit- and scroll-carved
reserve, on four cabriole legs
w/carved knees backed by a central
arched mirror flanked by graduated
corner shelves, all joined by a
serpentine base w/scroll-carved

apron, J. & J.W. Meeks, New York,
ca. 1850 (ILLUS.).......................**10,450.00**
Whatnot, Victorian Rococo substyle,
walnut, corner-type, four shaped
graduated open shelves backed
w/pierce-carved galleries &
supported by ring-turned spindles,
ca. 1870-80, 18 x 24", 45½" h..........**275.00**

GAMES & GAME BOARDS

German Mother-of-Pearl Game Box

African Bridge game, w/dice cage,
Rott Games, New York City.............**$95.00**
Archie Bunker card game, 1972........**19.00**
Checkerboard, h.p. oilcloth on
wooden frame, black w/finely
detailed floral design in several
colors, Pennsylvania, 21 x 23"
(some wear & small holes) **522.50**
Checkerboard, painted pine, black &
natural squares, old patina,
17¾ x 18"..........................**137.50**
Checkerboard, painted wood,
painted red, black, grey & brown,
reverse painted for backgammon,
raised buttons around edge,
17¾ x 18¾".........................**440.00**
Checkerboard, inlaid wood w/two
tones of hardwood w/old varnish
finish, narrow edge molding,
17 x 29½" (age cracks) **220.00**
Cribbage board, walrus tusk ivory,
the flattened tusk carved w/various
arctic scenes & animals including a
reindeer pulling a sled, sea gulls, a
polar bear & a seal, Eskimo-carved,
early 20th c., 30" l. **1,430.00**
Down You Go game, based on TV
game show, 1954, complete.............**25.00**
Famous Authors game, Parker
Bros., 1943, complete......................**18.00**
Game board, painted wood, one side
w/a wide cross design centered by a
lacy medallion w/"Home," large lacy
medallions at each corner, all in
brown, orange, green, blue, white &
goldenrod, the reverse w/a

checkerboard, applied gallery edge,
21" sq................................**605.00**
Game box, wooden, checkerboard on
exterior & backgammon in the
interior, old worn green paint
w/black & red, 8 x 16½", opens to
16 x 16½" (some edge wear)..........**165.00**
Game of Dr. Busby (The) card game,
the cards each w/a figure including
Dr. Busby, Mrs. Busby, Dr. Busby's
son & several others, each inscribed
underneath the picture w/a name,
the right hand corner w/a symbol
representing the figure, in original
box inscribed w/"The Game of Dr.
Busby," America, late 19th c., 2½ x
4" (some losses to cover & minor
staining) **1,380.00**
Gold & mother-of-pearl games set
comprising: four rectangular mother-
of-pearl boxes, w/covers mounted
w/gold foliate decoration w/birds &
fountains, each cover w/a revolving
wheel & a viewing window, each
inlaid in gold w/respective suites,
spades, hearts, diamonds & clubs,
each box containing counters of
three different designs, circular,
rectangular & pale shaped, each
box w/gold hinges, contained in
original fitted kingwood parquetry
box, Germany, ca. 1720-30, overall
7½" l., the set (ILLUS. one of
four) **34,500.00**
LaVerne & Shirley board game **25.00**
Lotto, Parker Bros., illustration of
Sunbonnet Twins on cover, ca.
1910......................................**45.00**
Lone Ranger board game, 1938,
excellent condition **75.00**
Mah-Jongg, Bakelite tiles, in original
carrying case **195.00**
Maypole Game, paper-on-wood, four
lithographed children appear to
dance around a tall maypole, each
holding on to a ribbon attached to
the pole, directions & marbles
attached, attributed to Bliss,
ca. 1900, 12 x 12 x 13" **2,530.00**
The Piggeries Game, painted tinplate
pigs race, mint in box......................**245.00**
Puss in Boots game, board-type,
wooden box w/lithographed paper
decoration, box bottom forms
playing board, w/two wooden
playing pieces, McLoughlin Bros.,
1897, the set **747.50**
Rummy Royal, Whitman, 1937 ....**25.00**
Skittle set, stuffed cloth, consisting of
three Japanese ladies, three Piey
Dogs, & three cats, together w/the
original wooden ball, Europe, ca.
1895, tallest 8¾" h., the set **690.00**
Swingeroo marble game....................**20.00**

Tales of Wells Fargo board game,
1959..**32.00**

GARDEN FOUNTAINS & ORNAMENTS

*Ornamental garden or yard fountains,
urns and figures often enhanced the formal
plantings on spacious lawns of mansion-
sized dwellings during the late 19th and
early 20th century. While fountains were
usually reserved for the lawns of estates,
even modest homes often had a latticework
arbor or cast-iron urn in the yard. Today
garden enthusiasts look for these
ornamental pieces to lend an aura of
elegance to their landscaping.*

Lead Figure of Nike

Figure of a woman, bronze, the
lovely Oriental woman wearing a
kimono & traditional headdress
looking at her reflection in a hand
mirror, 40½" h. **$2,588.00**
Figure, bronze, depicting the
Winged Victory, standing on an
orb, mounted on a circular
sandstone base, patinated finish,
late 19th c., 42" h. plus base........**8,250.00**
Figures of Nike, lead, classical
goddess w/long curls, holding one
wreath in each hand, standing on
a square pedestal, ca. 1900,
set of four (ILLUS. one of four) ...**27,600.00**
Font, stone, the circular standard
supporting a gadrooned font,
32" d., 35" h. **1,840.00**
Fountain, cast iron, three-tier, a wide
shallow round base w/the edge cast
w/flowers, foliage & frogs, centered

by a tall pedestal, the base cast
as three egrets supporting three
graduated bowls each w/rolled &
fluted edges cast w/foliage, a crown
finial at the top, traces of old paint,
from a Zanesville, Ohio home &
sold w/an early lithograph of the
home showing the fountain in the
yard, some rust damage, flange for
largest bowl welded, late 19th c.,
70" d., 6' 8" h................................**7,975.00**
Fountain, lead, three-tiered, shallow
dish-form in graduating diameters,
the tri-form base cast w/swans,
42" h...**2,588.00**
Fountain, lead, designed w/two
graduating lily pad cast tiers, the
upper tier fitted w/four frogs
incorporating nozzles, centered
by a young boy, 4' 6" h.................**3,788.00**

Lead Figural Fountain

Fountain, lead, figural, the tri-form
standard depicting three swans
surmounted by a well centering a
child caressing a duck incorporating
a nozzle, further raised on a
conforming plinth set within shaped
rectangular fountain basin decorated
w/flowerheads, alterations, 5' 1" h.
(ILLUS.) **2,760.00**
Fountain, marble, depicting a young
child riding a hound, raised on a
naturalistic base, late 19th c.,
32" h..**6,325.00**
Fountain, wall-type, marble, figural, in
three parts, the upper w/a winged
dolphin, the mouth formed for a
nozzle above a shell-formed basin,
19th c., 43" h. (ILLUS. top next
page)..**44,850.00**

Marble Wall Fountain

Zinc Figural Fountain

Fountain, zinc, figural, two frolicking nude putti's on a round pedestal in a shell-shaped basin, 42½" w., 33" h. (ILLUS.) **1,495.00**

Jardiniere, marble, decorated w/two rows of leaftips, 17" h....................**1,265.00**

Jardinieres, stone, decorated w/mask medallions surrounded by foliage, 29" l., 17" h., pr.................**1,380.00**

Model of a horse's head, terra cotta, life-like depiction w/well modeled features, 22" h.............................**2,300.00**

Model of a rabbit, cast iron, full-bodied animal in seated position w/ears up, old white repaint, 11½" h..**275.00**

Model of a rabbit, cast iron, in seated position w/ears up, old worn white repaint, 12" h.....................................**220.00**

Models of lions, cast iron, recumbent animal w/head resting on extended paws, one sleeping, one awake, each on a rectangular black-painted base & painted overall w/mottled

gold, American-made, second half 19th c., 16 x 43", 17" h., pr............**8,050.00**

Panel, marble, carved w/a central figure of Quan Yin flanked by a smaller figure on either side, ornately carved background, 41" h..**1,380.00**

Pedestal, clay, circular top above a tri-shaped standard depicting griffins, on a conforming stepped base, 59½" w., 20" h. **1,495.00**

Planters, stone, rectangular form, decorated on each w/putti, 27" h., set of 8 ....**2,530.00**

Urn, marble, designed after the antique "Warwick" urn w/a continuous band carved w/busts in lion pelts, the rim carved w/berried vines flanked by intertwining handles, raised on a circular fluted socle & low flat base, 19th c., 23" h..**7,475.00**

Urn & pedestal base, clay, Neoclassical style, the urn w/a continuous band depicting putti in various pursuits within gadrooned borders, the pedestal w/a continuous allegorical band, w/an impressed Rome foundry mark, 5' h. **3,220.00**

Urn on stand, cast iron, the lattice-form urn resting on the head of a stag & flanked by the horns, raised on a terra cotta tree-form pedestal, urn stamped "Janes Beebe & Co., N.Y.," overall 46" h. **4,600.00**

Cast Iron Urn on Stand

Urn on stand, painted cast iron, wide campana-form cast w/flowers & leaftips, raised on a plinth, stamped "J.L. Mott," by J.L. Mott Iron Works, New York, late 19th c., 47½" h. (ILLUS.) **1,350.00**

Urns, cast iron, cast on the exterior w/a band of scrolling vines above a ribbed band, the lower portion cast w/blossoms, raised on a square foot & stepped base, foliate scroll eared handles, base labeled, "Mfg. by the Kramer Bros. Fdy. Co, Dayton, O," white repaint, 21½" d., 29½" h. plus handles, overall 35" h., pr........**550.00**

Urns, cast iron, cast w/fluted & foliate detail, large scrolled ears, base labeled "Mfg. by the Kramer Bros. Fdy. Co. Dayton, Ohio," white repaint, 21½" d., 36" h. plus handles, overall 43" h. (minor damage & handles welded) **770.00**

Urns, cast iron, slender campana-form w/a gadrooned base & reeded pedestal foot, high arched scroll handles flanking the rolled rim, raised on a tall square pedestal w/paneled sides, traces of paint, 4' 1" h., pr. (rusted) **2,200.00**

Urns, cast iron, wide campana-form raised on a slender short ringed pedestal foot, the upper sides cast w/scrolling florals centered by a buffalo head medallion, flowering leafy scroll handles, raised on a short square pedestal w/scroll-cast panels, base labeled "Mfg. by the Kramer Bros. Fdy. Co., Dayton, O.," 36½" d., overall 5' 3" h., pr. (rusted, some bolts replaced) **7,920.00**

GLASS

AKRO AGATE

This glass was made by the Akro Agate Company in Clarksburg, West Virginia between 1932 and 1951. The company was famous for their marble production but also produced many novelty items in various colors of marbleized glass and offered a popular line of glass children's dishes in plain colors and marbleized glass. Most articles bear the company mark of a crow flying through a capital letter A.

Akro Agate Trademark

GENERAL LINE

Ashtray, ellipsoid, marbleized blue & white **$10.00**

Powder jar, Scottie Dog cover, powder blue opaque **75.00**

Powder jar, Scottie Dog cover, marbelized blue **150.00**

CHILDREN'S DISHES

Bowl, cereal, Concentric Ring patt., red...**6.00**

Bowl, cereal, Chiquita patt., red............**7.00**

Pitcher, 2⅞", Interior Panel patt., transparent green **12.00**

Plate, dinner, Chiquita patt., green.........**4.00**

Plate, dinner, Chiquita patt., transparent cobalt blue **8.00**

Plate, dinner, small, Concentric Ring patt., green.................................**5.00**

Plate, dinner, 4¼" d., Interior Panel patt., yellow...................................**10.00**

Teapot, cov., Chiquita patt., cobalt blue..**20.00**

Saucer, Interior Panel patt., green, 2¾"...**3.00**

Saucer, Interior Panel patt., transparent green, 3¼" d. **5.00**

AMBERINA

Amberina was developed in the late 1880s by the New England Glass Company and a pressed version was made by Hobbs, Brockunier & Company (under license from the former). A similar ware, called Rose Amber, was made by the Mt. Washington Glass Works. Amberina-Rose Amber shades from amber to deep red or fuchsia and cut and plated (lined with creamy white) examples were also made. The Libbey Glass Company briefly revived blown Amberina, using modern shapes, in 1917.

Amberina Label

Bowl, 6⅞", 3¼" h., low body w/ruffled rim, lustre iridescence lightly applied to glaze (ILLUS. top next page) **$125.00**

Bowl 10" w., oblong diamond shape, pressed Daisy & Button patt. **400.00**

Butter dish, cov., Inverted Thumbprint patt., 5" h. **220.00**

Butter pat, square, pressed Daisy & Button patt. **125.00**

Celery vase, Diamond Quilted patt., New England Glass Co., 6½" h. **310.00**

Ruffled Amberina Bowl

Celery vase, scalloped rim, in ornate
silver pate frame marked "Pairpoint,"
4" d., 6½" h. celery insert w/original
Mt. Washington Glass Co.
seal, overall 11¼" h. **795.00**
Cruet w/original stopper, Inverted
Thumbprint patt., Mt. Washington
Glass Co. **325.00**
Cruet w/original amber facet-cut
stopper, applied amber handle,
bulbous body supported on a
pedestal base, polished pontil **265.00**
Finger bowl, square, Hobnail patt.,
Mt. Washington Glass Co. **225.00**

Inverted Thumbprint Finger Bowl

Finger bowl, squatty bulbous body
w/closed, slightly ruffled rim,
Inverted Thumbprint patt., 4⅜" d.,
2" h. (ILLUS.) **175.00**
Mug, barrel-shaped body, amber
applied handle, Swirled Optic Rib
patt., 2⅞" d., 4⅞" h. (ILLUS. top
next column) **58.00**
Pitcher, 9" h., melon-ribbed body
w/clear applied reeded handle,
decorated w/h.p. enameled
flowers **550.00**
Plate, cheese, 9½" d., twelve-
paneled, optic design........................**315.00**
Punch cup, Diamond Quilted patt.,
New England Glass Co....................**120.00**
Punch cup, Diamond Quilted patt. **160.00**

Amberina Barrel-shaped Mug

Tumbler, Diamond Quilted patt.,
Mt. Washington Glass Co.,
3¾" h...**135.00**
Tumbler, Diamond Quilted patt.,
New England Glass Co.,
3¾" h...**200.00**

Amberina Tumbler

Tumbler, footed, Inverted Thumbprint
patt., 2½" d., 3⅞" h. (ILLUS.) **69.00**
Tumbler, Inverted Thumbprint
patt..**100.00**

Amberina Jack-in-the-Pulpit Vase

Tumbler, mold-blown, large blown-
out ribs **85.00**
Tumbler, Reverse Amberina, Optic
Rib patt. **100.00**
Vase, 12" h., 5¼" d., jack-in-the-pulpit
style, Swirled Optic Rib patt. (ILLUS.
bottom previous page) **225.00**

ANIMALS

Heisey Balking Pony

*Americans evidently like to collect glass
animals and, for the past sixty years,
American glass manufacturers have
turned out a wide variety of animals to
please the buying public. Some were
produced for long periods and some were
later reproduced by other companies, while
others were made for only a short period of
time and are rare. We have not included
late productions in our listings and have
attempted to date the productions where
possible. Evelyn Zemel's book,* American
Glass Animals A to Z, *will be helpful to the
novice collector. Another helpful book is*
Glass Animals of the Depression Era *by
Lee Garmon and Dick Spencer (Collector
Books, 1993).*

Angelfish book end, clear, American
Glass Co., 8¼" h. (single) **$45.00**
Asiatic Pheasant, clear, A.H. Heisey
& Co., 1944-45, 7¼" l., 10¼" h.,......**295.00**
Bird, Happiness Bird, Rosalene,
Fenton Art Glass Company, 1950-
present, 6½" l......................................**24.00**
Donkey standing, clear, A.H. Heisey
& Co., 1944-53, 4¼" l. base,
6½" h..**260.00**
Donkey standing, frosted, Duncan &
Miller Glass Co., 4½" l., 4½" h. **105.00**
Dove, on pedestal base, clear,
Duncan & Miller Glass
Co....................................**175.00 to 200.00**
Duck ashtray, ruby, Duncan & Miller
Glass Co., 5" l **125.00**
Duck (Mallard) w/wings down, clear,
A.H. Heisey & Co., 1942-53,
5¾" h. ....**200.00 to 250.00**

Duck (Mallard) w/wings half up,
clear, A.H. Heisey & Co., 1942-53,
4½" h...**145.00**
Duck (Mallard) w/wings half up,
caramel slag, Imperial Glass Co.
(Heisey mold).....................................**45.00**
Duck (Mallard) w/wings up, clear,
A.H. Heisey & Co., 1942-53,
6½" h...**140.00**
Duck (Mallard) w/wings up, clear,
Imperial Glass Co. (Heisey mold) **135.00**
Duck, No. 1317, orange, Viking Glass
Company,1960s, 5" h. **29.00**
Eagle book ends, clear, Cambridge
Glass Co., 4" base d., 6" w. wing
spread, 6" h., pr. **225.00**
Eagle book ends, clear, Fostoria
Glass Co., 1938-44, 3 x 4½" base,
7¼" h., pr. **225.00**
Elephant book ends, clear, New
Martinsville Glass Mfg. Co., prior to
1945, 3¼ x 5¼" base, 6¼" l.,
5¼" h., pr. **185.00**
Elephant book ends, clear, Fostoria
Glass Co., 1938-44, 5¾ x 3" base,
7¾" h., pr. **95.00**
Elephant w/long trunk extended,
clear, A.H. Heisey & Co., 1944-53,
medium, 6¾" l. **291.00**
Fish book ends, clear, Heisey & Co.,
1942-52, 5" l., 6½" h., pr. **235.00**
Fish match holder, Sunshine Yellow,
Imperial Glass Co. (Heisey mold),
1982, on wave base, 3½" h. **40.00**
Giraffe w/head straight, clear, A.H.
Heisey & Co., 1942-52,
11¼" h. ....**175.00 to 200.00**
Goose (The Fat Goose), clear,
Duncan & Miller Glass Co., 6" l.,
6½" h..**239.00**
Goose, wings half up, clear, A.H.
Heisey & Co., 1942-53, 8¾" l.,
4½" h...**81.00**
Goose, pale blue, Paden City Glass
Co., ca. 1940, 5" h. **95.00**
Hen, clear, New Martinsville Glass
Mfg. Co., 2¾" base d., 5" h. **52.00**
Heron standing, clear, Duncan &
Miller Glass Co., 2¾" base d.,
7¼" h...**95.00**
Horse, Colt sitting, clear, Fostoria
Glass Co., 1938-44, 1 x 3" base,
2¾" w., 2¼" h......................................**37.50**
Horse, Colt Standing, clear, Fostoria
Glass Co., 1938-44, 1 x 2¼" base,
2½" w., 4" h..**42.50**
Horse, Colt standing, clear, A.H.
Heisey & Co., 5" h. **55.00**
Horse, Pacemaker ashtray, clear,
Knox Glass Co., 1940s, 5½" d.,
3½" h...**22.00**
Horse, Plug (Sparky), Pink, Imperial
Glass Co. (Heisey mold), marked
HCA-IG-78, 1978, 4" h......................**45.00**

Horse, Pony balking, clear, A.H.
Heisey & Co., 1941-45,
1½ x 3⅛" base, 4" h. (ILLUS.) **174.00**

Horse, Pony kicking, clear, A.H.
Heisey & Co., 1941-45,
1½ x 2¼" base, 3" l., 4" h.................**172.00**

Horse, Pony sitting, clear, Fostoria
Glass Co., 1938-44,
1 x 3", 2¾" h.....................................**30.00**

Horse, Pony standing, clear, Fostoria
Glass Co., 1938-44, 1 x 2¼", 4" h......**30.00**

Horse, Pony standing, chocolate
(caramel slag), Imperial Glass Co.
(Heisey mold)...................................**100.00**

Horse, Pony standing, clear, Paden
City Glass Mfg. Co., 3 x 5½" base,
12" h..**95.00**

Horse set: 3¾" h. Pony Balking,
4⅛" h. Colt kicking & 5" h. Colt
standing; Horizon Blue, Imperial
Glass Co. (Heisey mold), set of 3 ....**200.00**

Horse rearing book end, clear,
Fostoria Glass Co., 3 x 5" base,
6" l., 7½" h...**55.00**

Horse rearing book end, dark blue,
L.E. Smith, 1940s, 3 x 5½" base,
5¾" l., 8" h...**48.00**

Horse rearing book end, dark green.
L.E. Smith, 1940s, 3 x 5½" base,
5¾" l., 8" h...**45.00**

Horse rearing book ends, clear,
New Martinsville Glass Mfg. Co.,
5¼ x 3¼" base, 5¾" l., 8" h.,
pr..**175.00**

Horse Head book ends, frosted, A.H.
Heisey & Co., 1937-55,
2¾ x 4¾" base, 7¼" h., pr................**275.00**

Pheasant w/turned head, clear,
Paden City Glass Mfg. Co.,
2½ x 2¾" base, 12" l., 7" h.................**82.50**

Pouter Pigeon, clear, A.H. Heisey &
Co., 1947-49, 6½" h. ....**450.00 to 500.00**

Rabbit paperweight, clear, A.H.
Heisey & Co., 1¾ x 3¾" base,
2¼" h...**165.00**

Ringneck Pheasant, clear, A.H.
Heisey & Co., 1942-53, 11" l.,
4¾" h. ....**100.00 to 125.00**

Rooster, clear, New Martinsville
Glass Mfg. Co., 8" l., 8" h...................**76.00**

Rooster, frosted, New Martinsville
Glass Mfg. Co., 8" l., 8" h...................**65.00**

Rooster (Chanticleer), clear, Paden
City Glass Mfg, Co., 9¼" h.................**65.00**

Rooster vase (Chanticleer), clear,
A.H. Heisey & Co., ca. 1939-48,
6½" w., 6½" h. ....**50.00 to 75.00**

Scottie Dog book ends, clear,
Cambridge Glass Co., 6½" h.,
pr...**100.00**

Scottie Dog book end, clear, A.H.
Heisey & Co., 1941-46, 3½" l.,
5" h..**85.00**

Seal w/ball, clear, New Martinsville
Glass Mfg. Co., 7¼" h........................**50.00**

Sparrow, clear, A.H. Heisey & Co.,
1942-45, 4" l., 2¼" h. at raised
tail. **67.50**

Swan candleholders, ruby, Janice-S
Line, New Martinsville Glass Mfg.
Co., 4¼" h., pr....................................**45.00**

Swan dish, pink opalescent, Sylvan
patt., Duncan & Miller Glass Co.,
6½" l..**55.00**

Swan dish w/spread wings, blue
opalescent, Duncan & Miller Glass
Co., 12" w., 11" h...............................**150.00**

Swan dish w/spread wings, ruby,
Duncan & Miller Glass Co., 12" w.,
11" h...**77.50**

Swan figure, Pall Mall patt., ruby red,
Duncan & Miller Glass Co.,
7" l..**48.00**

Swan figure, Pall Mall patt., green,
Duncan & Miller Glass Co.,
10½" l...**47.50**

Swordfish, opalescent blue, Duncan
& Miller Glass Co., 3¾ x 4" h.,
base, 4" h..**249.00**

Wolfhound (Russian) book end,
clear, New Martinsville Glass Mfg.
Co., 1920s, 9" l., 7¼" h. **50.00**

APPLIQUED

Appliqued Transparent Orange Bowl

Simply stated, this is an art glass form with applied decoration. Sometimes master glass craftsmen applied stems or branches to an art glass object and then added molded glass flowers or fruit specimens to these branches or stems. At other times a button of molten glass was daubed on the object and a tool pressed over it to form a prunt in the form of a raspberry, rosette or other shape. Always the work of a skilled glassmaker, applied decoration can be found on both cased (two-layer) and single layer glass. The English firm of Stevens and Williams is renowned for the appliqued glass they produced. Also see STEVENS & WILLIAMS.

Bowl, 4⅞" d., 4¼" h., transparent orange body w/applied clear rigaree around top, applied crystal ruffled leaf, all on three applied clear feet. (ILLUS.) **$135.00**

Mahogany Red Appliqued Bowl

Bowl, 7½" d., 6¼" h., mahogany red ovoid bulbous body tapering to flared edge comprised of applied clear shells, two more rows of clear shells below rim, all on applied clear shell base, probably Webb (ILLUS.) **495.00**

Appliqued Creamer & Sugar Bowl

Creamer & sugar bowl, orange bodies, both w/fancy crystal applied ruffled tops, clear rigaree below, creamer w/clear applied handle, creamer 2¾" d., 4⅜" h., sugar bowl 5¼" d., 2¾" h., the set (ILLUS.) **160.00**

Vase, 3¾" h., 3" d., orange spherical body w/five rows of crystal overlapping leaves applied around the body, amber applied leaf feet. ...**145.00**

Vase, 4¼" h., 5¾" d., squatty bulbous body w/tri-lobed rim, alternating olive green & sapphire blue stripes of Aventurine w/appliqued clear icicle rigaree down the sides, on three applied clear feet, probably Webb **225.00**

Heavenly Blue Appliqued Vase

Vase, 5⅜" h., 3½" d., baluster-form body w/angled shoulders w/widely ruffled rim, heavenly blue shaded interior w/off-white exterior w/applied green, amber & cranberry ruffled leaves, Stevens & Williams (ILLUS.) **125.00**

Vase, 5½" h., 4½" d., cream squatty bulbous body tapering to a widely flaring ruffled rim w/crystal applied edging around the top, large crystal applique ruffled leaf, heavenly blue interior, Webb **145.00**

Vase, 5¾" h., 4" d., off-white opalescent ovoid bulbous body tapering to widely flaring ruffled rose

Opaque & Amber Appliqued Vase

rim, applied amber leaves curving around body to form three feet..**165.00**

Vase, 6⅞" h., 4½" d., bulbous white opaque body w/amber-edged ruffled & flaring mouth, on three amber petal feet, applied amber acorn & cranberry leaf (ILLUS. bottom previous page) **135.00**

Vase, 8¾" h., 4½" d., waisted cylindrical body tapering to a flaring neck w/crimped rim, deep amethyst body w/applied clear icicles from the rim to the center of the body & applied ornate clear feet. **880.00**

ART GLASS BASKETS

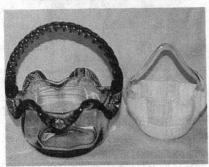

Two Art Glass Baskets

Cased, pink exterior, white interior, applied amber rigaree edge trim & applied amber thorn handle, 7 x 8"...**$150.00**

Lemon yellow opaque, ruffled rim, embossed beaded band & swirls, applied clear handle, 5" d., 5¾" h. (ILLUS. right) **88.00**

Golden amber, widely ruffled blue rim w/applied rope handle, 6½" d., 7½" h. (ILLUS. left) **135.00**

Green Ruffled basket

Green, ruffled rim, paneled sides, embossed Diamond Quilt patt., clear applied handle, 5½" d., 5½" h. (ILLUS. bottom previous column) **85.00**

Spangled, amber w/cream & brown spatter & gold mica flecks, lightly ruffled rim, applied amber twist handle, 4½" d., 6½" h.......................**355.00**

Spangled, lemon yellow & pale pomegranate w/clear cased exterior, white interior, paneled sides flare to eight pulled-out points, applied clear twisted thorn handle, 5¾" d., overall 8½" h. **260.00**

BACCARAT

"Rose Teinte" Cologne Bottle

Baccarat glass has been made by Cristalleries de Baccarat, France, since 1765. The firm has produced various glassware of excellent quality and paperweights. Baccarat's Rose Teinte is often referred to as Baccarat's Amberina.

Cologne bottle w/matching stopper, cylindrical body w/deep shoulder, short cylindrical neck w/flat flaring rim, Rose Teinte Swirl patt., 2½" d., 6¼" h. (ILLUS.) **$70.00**

Vase, 6¼" h., 3¾" d., footed, flared rim, overall floral & vine etching, signed **85.00**

Vase, 10¼" h., inverted bell-form, etched w/five urns issuing tall scrolling branches, printed factory mark, 20th c. **805.00**

BLOWN THREE MOLD

This type of glass was entirely or partially blown in a mold and was popular from about 1820 to 1840. The object was formed and the decoration impressed upon it by blowing the glass into a metal mold, usually of three but sometimes more sections, hinged together. Mold-blown glass actually dates back to ancient times. Recent research reveals that certain geometric patterns were reproduced in the 1920s and collectors are urged to read all recent information available. Reference numbers are from George L. and Helen McKearin's book, American Glass.

Bird cage fountain, geometric, ribbed sides w/an applied "chicken" finial, factory-ground drinking trough, atttributed to the Boston & Sandwich Glass Co., clear, 5⅞" h. (GI-12) **$550.00**

Bowl, 4¼" d., 1¼" h., geometric, folded rim, thick rayed base w/pontil, clear (GII-33, shape D-2) **77.00**

Bowl, 4⅞" d., 1⅛" h., geometric, folded rim, plain base w/pontil, clear (GIII-13, shape D-4) **66.00**

Bowl, 5¼" d., 1⅞" h., geometric, deep flaring sides w/a folded rim, 16-diamond base w/pontil, clear (GII-21) **88.00**

Caster set: two ribbed bottles w/solid pressed steeple stoppers, a ribbed shaker w/brass cap & a ribbed mustard jar w/pressed cover, all in a pewter frame; smooth bases w/pontils, clear, the set (GI-10) **275.00**

Cologne bottle w/original "Tam O'Shanter" stopper, geometric, ovoid ribbed body w/flanged lip & rayed base w/pontil, deep colbalt blue, 6¼" h. (GI-7) **302.50**

Creamer, geometric, small ovoid body w/a widely flaring neck w/pinched spout, applied strap handle, clear, 3¹⁄₁₆" h. (GII-21) **550.00**

Creamer, geometric, wide ovoid body tapering to a short neck w/a widely flaring rim w/pinched spout, applied strap handle w/end curl, ringed base w/pontil, clear, 3¾" h. (GIII-26) **440.00**

Decanter w/original bulbous ringed stopper, cylindrical ribbed sides & ringed shoulders, flanged lip, petal base, clear, quart (GI-15) **214.50**

Decanter w/original swirled rib hollow stopper, geometric, a band of ribs around the base below a triple ring band around the center & swirled ribs up the three-ring neck, clear, quart, GI-27 (rim possibly lightly ground) **132.00**

Decanter w/pressed wheel stoppper, barrel-shaped, diamond point w/wide ribbed center band, Keene,

New Hampshire, clear, pint (GII-7) **228.00**

Decanter w/pressed "umbrella" stopper, miniature, geometric, clear, ¼ pint (GII-18) **302.50**

Decanter w/original pressed "wheel" stopper, geometric, clear w/faint bluish tint, GIII-5 (lip ground)................................**154.00**

Decanter w/original swirled rib bulbous stopper, baroque, clear, quart, GV-14 (small pontil chip, interior haze on bottom) **187.00**

Blown Three Mold Decanter

Decanter, no stopper, geometric, slightly tapering cylindrical body to a tall cylindrical neck w/flattened rim, yellow-moonstone, pint, GII-6 (ILLUS.) **13,200.00**

Decanter, no stopper, miniature, geometric, flared lip, clear, 3⅞" h., GII-18 (minor interior residue).........**247.50**

Decanter, no stopper, geometric, diamond band & ribbing, square w/beveled shoulders to short neck & flattened flaring rim, probably Keene Marlboro Street Glassworks, Keene, New Hampshire, medium bluish green, pint, GII-28 (interior bubble w/a star crack).....................**825.00**

Decanter, no stopper, geometric, diamond point band w/starburst panels, Keene, New Hampshire, bright olive green, pint (GIII-16) **467.50**

Dish, geometric, folded rim, rayed base w/pontil, clear, 4⅜" d., ⅞" h. (GII-1, shape D-3) **88.00**

Dish, round, geometric, narrow folded rim & 17-diamond base w/pontil, clear, 6⅜" d., 1¼" h. (GII-16) **77.00**

Dish, round, geometric, folded rim & rayed base, clear, 5¼" d., 1⅛" h. (GIII-21) **88.00**

Flip glass, cylindrical, geometric, 18-diamond base w/tubular pontil, clear, 4⅜" d., 5½" h. (GII-18) **181.50**

Inkwell, geometric, cylindrical
w/rounded edge, deep amber,
Keene, New Hampshire, 2" d.
(GII-18) **110.00**
Model of a top hat, geometric,
unrecorded variant, clear, 2" h.
(GII-13) **165.00**
Model of a top hat, geometric, cobalt
blue, 2⅜" h. (GIII-3) **412.50**
Model of a top hat, geometric, wide
folded rim, ringed base w/pontil,
sapphire blue, 2¼" h. (GIII-25).........**467.50**
Mug w/applied strap handle w/curled
end, geometric, slightly tapering
cylindrical body, smooth base
w/pontil, clear, 3½" h. (GII-4) **412.50**
Tumbler, cylindrical, geometric, clear,
3½" h. (GII-16) **99.00**
Tumbler, barrel-shaped, geometric,
ringed base w/pontil, clear, 3½" h.,
GIII-25 (rim lightly ground) **77.00**
Wine glass, geometric, applied
ringed stem & disc foot, clear,
3⅞" h. (GI-6) **247.50**
Wine taster, geometric, slightly
tapering cylindrical form w/tooled rim
& plain base w/pontil, clear w/slight
bluish cast, 3⅛" h. (GI-20) **220.00**

BRIDE'S BASKETS & BOWLS

Cream Color Bride's Bowl

*These berry or fruit bowls were popular
late Victorian wedding gifts, hence the
name.*

Blue opalescent bowl, Reverse Swirl
patt., ornate silver plate frame **$395.00**
Cased bowl, pink shaded to white
satin interior decorated w/apricot
mums, leaves & dots, ornate silver
plate frame decorated w/applied
flowers & insects, made by Mt.
Washington Glass Company &
decorated by Smith Brothers **475.00**

Cased bowl, white interior, apricot
satin mother-of-pearl Diamond
Quilted patt. exterior decorated
w/yellow coralene branches, S-
shaped bowl w/pleated rim, ornate
silver plate frame, bowl signed
Webb **1,050.00**
Cranberry opalescent bowl, Ribbed
Opal Lattice patt., square bowl
w/ruffled rim, ornate footed Simpson
silver plate frame decorated
w/strawberries & leaves, 6" w.,
9½" h..**595.00**
Cream bowl, white exterior, cream
interior w/maroon leaf-like rim,
raised embossed designs,
decoration of tiny pink flowers &
green leaves, base 2⅞" d., 11" d.,
3" h. (ILLUS.) **195.00**
Honey amber bowl, pressed, Daisy
& Button patt., ornate footed silver
plate frame, 12" d., 12½" h. **100.00**

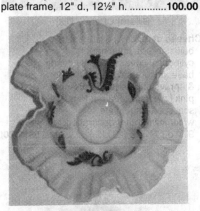

Pink Satin Bride's Bowl

Pink satin bowl, white exterior w/pink
interior decorated w/flowers &
leaves in colors of blue, red, green,
lavender & yellow, base 3⅛" d.,
9¼ x 10⅞", 4½" h. (ILLUS.) **225.00**
Peach Blow bowl, decorated
w/enameled flowers & a spider,
signed Webb, bronze base w/figural
lion's head......................................**495.00**
White bowl, tightly pleated rim,
enameled bird & floral decoration,
ornate frame, 10" w., 10" h. **245.00**

BRISTOL

*A number of glasshouses operated in
Bristol, England over the years and they
produced a variety of wares. Today,
however, the generic name Bristol refers to
a type of semi-opaque glass, often accented
with ornate enameling. Such wares were*

produced in England, Europe and America in the 19th and early 20th centuries.

Bristol Cheese Dish

Cheese dish, cov., white satin, baluster-form finial handle, cylindrical cover w/slightly flaring base, decorated w/daisy-like flowers & sprays of blue forget-me-nots, pink flowers & blue dot trim, scalloped-edge plate w/complimentary decoration, 9½" d., 7¾" h. (ILLUS.) **$195.00**

Bristol Perfume Bottle

Perfume bottle w/matching stopper, baluster-shaped body w/tapering cylindrical stopper decorated w/white & green leaves w/pink flowers on a turquoise blue ground, 2¼" d., 5½" h. (ILLUS.) **98.00**

Vase, 2¾" h., 2¼" d., squatty baluster-shaped body w/flat rim, opaque glossy turquoise decorated w/pink florals, gold scallops & gold trim (ILLUS. top next column) **35.00**

Squatty Baluster-shaped Bristol Vase

Decorated Bristol Vase

Vase, 5⅞" h., 2½" d., squatty bulbous ovoid body w/long thin cylindrical neck w/flat rim, decorated w/sanded gold decoration, gold trim & cream colored dainty flowers all on a turquoise blue ground (ILLUS.)..........**45.00**

White Satin Bristol Vase

Vase, 11¾" h., 3⅜" d., white satin baluster-shaped body decorated w/heavy gold trim & pink glass jewels set into the design & larger red jewels in centers of gold stars (ILLUS.) **195.00**

Pair of Bristol Vases

Vases, 6⅛" h., 2½" d., baluster-form body w/flat rim, handles at shoulders, glossy turquoise blue & decorated w/elaborate gold designs w/white trim & small pink roses, pr. (ILLUS.) **125.00**

BURMESE

Miniature Burmese Rose Bowl

Burmese is a single-layer glass that shades from pink to pale yellow. It was patented by Frederick S. Shirley and made by the Mt. Washington Glass Co. A license to produce the glass in England was granted to Thomas Webb & Sons, which called its articles Queen's Burmese. Gundersen Burmese was made briefly about the middle of this century, and the Pairpoint Crystal Company is making limited quantities at the present time.

Bowl, 4¼" d., 3½" h., scalloped rim, pedestal base, polished pontil, satin finish **$330.00**

Bowl, 5½" w., 2¼" h., rectangular w/slightly folded rim, polished pontil, satin finish **200.00**
Plate, 9" d., Mt. Washington Glass Co. **150.00**
Rose bowl, miniature, eight-crimp rim, unsigned Webb, 2¼" d., 2¼" h. (ILLUS.) **175.00**

Floral-Decorated Burmese Rose Bowl

Rose bowl, crimped rim, floral decoration & applied glass at rim, marked by Thomas Webb, 6¼" d., 3¾" h. (ILLUS.) **1,110.00**
Sugar shaker w/original metal top, decorated w/h.p. daisies, Mt. Washington Glass Co., 4¼" h. **425.00**
Toothpick holder, waisted cylindrical form, polished pontil, satin finish, 2½" h...**140.00**
Toothpick holder, bulbous body w/six-sided collared rim, polished pontil, satin finish, 3" h. **275.00**
Toothpick holder, tricorner rim, Diamond Quilted patt., Mt. Washington Glass Co. **395.00**

Spherical Burmese Vase by Webb

Vase, 3" h., 2⅝" d., spherical body tapering to ruffled rim, satin finish, Thomas Webb (ILLUS.) **200.00**
Vase, 4" h., 2⅞" d., squatty bulbous base tapering to flared rim w/folded over ruffles, unsigned Webb (ILLUS. top next page)....................**200.00**

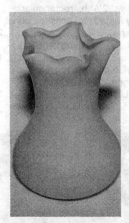

Burmese Vase Attributed to Webb

Baluster-Shaped Burmese Vase

Vase, 4¼" h., ribbed baluster-form
   w/scalloped flaring rim (ILLUS.).......**475.00**
Vase 5" h., urn-form w/applied
   handles, Mt. Washington Glass
   Co. **350.00**
Vase, lily-form w/jack-in-the-pulpit rim,
   6½" h., Gundersen-Pairpoint **172.50**

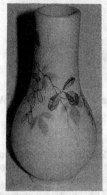

Floral-Decorated Vase by Webb

Vase, 8⅛" h., 3⅞" d., bulbous body
   on short foot tapering to thin
   cylindrical neck w/flat rim, decorated
   w/coral-colored flower buds w/green
   & tan foliage, unsigned Webb
   (ILLUS. bottom previous column) **695.00**
Vase, 8¼" h., h.p. floral decoration, in
   silver plate handled frame,
   Thomas Webb & Sons.....................**515.00**

CAMBRIDGE

Rose Point Goblet

   *The Cambridge Glass Company was
founded in Ohio in 1901. Numerous pieces
are now sought, especially those designed
by Arthur J. Bennett, including Crown
Tuscan. Other productions included
crystal animals, "Black Amethyst," "blanc
opaque," and other types of colored glass.
The firm was finally closed in 1954. It
should not be confused with the New
England Glass Co., Cambridge,
Massachusetts.*

Various Cambridge Marks

Ashtray, Statuesque line, Moonlight
   bowl, clear Nude Lady stem **$559.00**
Ashtray, Statuesque line, Pistachio
   bowl, clear Nude Lady stem **499.00**
Ashtray, No. 1314, Amethyst..............**55.00**

Banana bowl, pressed Caprice patt.,
Moonlight **295.00**
Bonbon, handled, etched Apple
Blossom patt., Topaz, 5½" **22.00**
Bonbon, footed, etched Wildflower
patt., Crystal w/gold trim, 7" h. **33.00**
Bowl, salad, 10" d., pressed Caprice
patt., Moonlight **250.00**
Bowl, 11" oval, footed, pressed
Caprice patt., Topaz **45.00**
Bowl w/ram's head handles,
Rubina **750.00**
Cake plate, No. 731, pink (Rosalie),
signed **185.00**
Candlestick, one-light, pressed
Caprice patt., Dianthus **125.00**
Candlesticks, three-light, pressed
Caprice patt., Crystal, pr. **50.00**
Candlesticks, Martha Washington
line, Carmen, pr. **79.00**
Candy dish, cov., pressed Caprice
patt., Dianthus................................**129.00**
Champagne, short, etched Daffodil
patt., Crystal....................................**27.50**
Champagne, Statuesque line, Smoke
bowl, clear Nude Lady stem **450.00**
Cigarette box, cov., Dolphin & Sea
Shell patt., green..............................**65.00**
Cigarette holder, round, No. 1337,
Amethyst..**20.00**
Cigarette holder, round, No. 1337,
Royal Blue **29.00**
Cocktail, Caprice patt., blue **55.00**
Compote, open, 7" d., pressed
Caprice patt., Dianthus **159.00**
Compote, open, 8" d., Statuesque
line, Smoke bowl, clear Nude Lady
stem **559.00**
Compote, open, cheese, etched Apple
Blossom patt., Peach-Blo/Dianthus
Pink w/gold trim **30.00**
Cordial, etched Rose Point patt.,
w/pulled stem, clear **95.00**
Creamer & sugar bowl, both
w/scrolled handles, etched Diane
patt., Crystal, pr. **24.00**
Creamer, sugar bowl & Farber chrome
undertray, etched Chantilly
patt., Crystal, the set........................**12.00**
Crown Tuscan bowl, 8" d., footed,
Shell & Dolphin patt. **75.00**
Crown Tuscan compote, open,
Seashell line, 4½" d. **40.00**
Crown Tuscan model of a conch
shell, 7" **35.00**
Crown Tuscan model of a swan,
4½" l...**75.00**
Crown Tuscan relish, three-part,
footed, handled, Gadroon (No.
3500/64) line, 10" d. **95.00**
Crown Tuscan relish dish, footed,
handled, three-part, Gadroon line,
10" d.,...**495.00**

Crown Tuscan vase, 8½" h.,
footed, Sea Shell line.........................**55.00**
Crown Tuscan vase, 13" h................**135.00**
Cup & saucer, etched Daffodil patt.,
Crystal..**47.50**
Goblet, pressed Caprice patt.,
Moonlight, 7½" h. **42.50**
Goblet, etched Diane patt., Crystal,
9 oz. **25.00**
Goblet, Rose Point patt., Crystal
(ILLUS.) **32.50**
Goblet, Statuesque line, Smoke,
clear Nude Lady stem **559.00**
Goblet, sq., No. 3797, clear "crackle" ...**77.00**
Ice bucket, etched Rose Point patt.,
No. 3400/851, Carmen **75.00**
Ivy ball, Statuesque line, Smoke
bowl, clear Nude Lady stem **499.00**
Liqueur set: ball-shaped, 12 oz.
decanter w/stopper & six liqueurs;
Amethyst, w/Farberware holder &
tray, 8 pcs. **429.00**
Mayonnaise set: bowl, underplate
& ladle, pressed Caprice patt.,
Moonlight, 3 pcs...............................**100.00**
Model of a swan, milk white, 3" l. **60.00**
Oyster cocktail, etched Candlelight
patt., Crystal.....................................**49.00**
Pitcher, high-handled, Doulton-style,
etched Rose Point patt., Crystal **345.00**
Pitcher, martini, etched Rose Point
patt., Crystal....................................**495.00**
Plate, 6" d., two-handled, etched Apple
Blossom patt., Peach-
Blo/Dianthus Pink **15.00**
Plate, 6½" d., etched Diane patt.,
Crystal..**7.00**
Plate, 8" d., etched Candlelight patt.,
Crystal..**25.00**
Plate, 8" d., etched Daffodil patt.,
Crystal..**29.00**
Plate, 8" d., etched Diane patt.,
Crystal..**9.00**
Plate, cabaret, 13¾" d., pressed
Caprice patt., Moonlight....................**85.00**
Punch set: bowl, base & twelve cups
(four w/applied green handles, four
w/applied amethyst handles & four
w/applied amber handles); Tally Ho
line, Crystal, 14 pcs. **160.00**
Relish dish, etched Apple Blossom
patt., Peach-Blo/Dianthus Pink,
9" l..**18.00**
Relish dish, three-part, pressed
Caprice patt., Moonlight....................**40.00**
Salad set: 13" d. bowl & 16" d.
underplate; pressed Caprice patt.,
Moonlight, 2 pcs. **499.00**
Salt shaker w/original silver plate top
& base, etched Chantilly patt.,
Crystal..**18.00**
Sandwich server w/center handle,
etched Rose Point patt., Crystal,
11" d..**95.00**

Seafood cocktail w/liner, etched
  Rose Point patt., Crystal **72.50**
Sherbet, tall, etched Chantilly patt.,
  Crystal...**14.00**
Sherbet, No. 1401, Mandarin Gold
  (medium yellow) **9.00**
Sherry, etched Rose point, Crystal,
  2 oz...**60.00**
Sherry, Wheat Sheaf patt., clear,
  3 oz. **6.00**
Shot glass, Caprice patt., clear **15.00**
Tumbler, footed, etched Candlelight
  patt., Crystal, 5 oz. **45.00**
Tumbler, juice, three-footed, etched
  Daffodil patt., Crystal **39.00**
Tumbler, footed, etched Diane patt.,
  Crystal, 5 oz. **18.00**
Tumbler, juice, etched Versailles
  patt., Moonlight **47.50**
Tumbler, water, No. 3035, Heather-
  bloom **175.00**
Vase, 8" h., Caprice patt., blue...........**215.00**
Vase, 8¼" h., No. 79, decorated
  w/enameled black trim, Primrose.......**68.00**
Vase, 9¾" h., Block Optic patt.,
  Forest Green, original sticker.............**65.00**
Vase, bud, 10" h., etched Wildflower
  patt., gold encrusted **30.00**
Vase, pressed Caprice patt.,
  Amethyst.......................................**95.00**
Wine, etched Candlelight patt.,
  Crystal...**69.00**
Wine, Caprice patt., blue, 2½ oz. **55.00**
Wine, sq., No. 3797, clear, "crackle"......**66.00**

CARNIVAL GLASS

Earlier called Taffeta glass, the Carnival glass now being collected was introduced early in this century. Its producers gave it an iridescence that attempted to imitate that of some Tiffany glass. Collectors will find available books by leading authorities Donald E. Moore, Sherman Hand, Marion T. Hartung and Rose M. Presznick.

ACORN (Fenton)

Bowl, 3½" d., marigold **$50.00**
Bowl, 5" d., milk white
  w/marigold overlay **322.00**
Bowl, 6" d., aqua...............................**128.00**
Bowl, 6" d., blue..............................**45.00**
Bowl, 6" d., ruffled, sapphire blue **90.00**
Bowl, 6" d., vaseline..........................**125.00**
Bowl, 7" d., ruffled, amber..................**98.00**
Bowl, 7" d., aqua...............................**82.50**
Bowl, 7" d., ice blue **150.00**
Bowl, 7" d., lime green........................**55.00**
Bowl, 7" d., marigold..........................**35.00**
Bowl, 7" d., peach opalescent **185.00**

Bowl, 7" d., ruffled, peach
  opalescent **300.00**
Bowl, 7" d., purple..............................**45.00**
Bowl, 7" d., red..................................**537.50**
Bowl, 7" d., ruffled,
  vaseline ....**100.00 to 125.00**
Bowl, 7" d., vaseline...........................**170.00**
Bowl, 7½" d., aqua...............................**475.00**
Bowl, 7½" d., blue **50.00**
Bowl, 7½" d., ruffled, blue **105.00**
Bowl, 8" to 9" d., blue.........................**55.00**
Bowl, 8" to 9" d., ice blue **350.00**
Bowl, 8" to 9" d., marigold....................**41.00**
Bowl, 8" to 9" d., ribbon candy rim,
  purple...**115.00**
Bowl, 8" to 9" d., ruffled,
  red ....**700.00 to 750.00**
Bowl, ice cream shape, aqua.............**125.00**
Bowl, ice cream shape, blue................**50.00**
Bowl, ice cream shape, green **65.00**
Bowl, ice cream shape, ice blue
  w/marigold overlay **75.00**
Bowl, ice cream shape, moonstone...**185.00**
Bowl, ice cream shape, red slag........**650.00**
Bowl, ice cream shape, teal blue **75.00**
Bowl, ruffled, aqua opalescent............**125.00**
Bowl, ruffled, green............................**70.00**
Bowl, ruffled, sapphire blue **675.00**

ACORN BURRS (Northwood)

Acorn Burrs Creamer

Berry set: master bowl & 5 sauce
  dishes; purple, 6 pcs. **415.00**
Berry set: master bowl & 6 sauce
  dishes; green, 7 pcs.........................**350.00**
Bowl, master berry, 10" d., green **80.00**
Bowl, master berry, 10" d., marigold....**78.00**
Bowl, master berry, 10" d., purple......**175.00**
Butter dish, cov., green ....300.00 to 375.00**
Butter dish, cov., marigold **178.00**
Butter dish, cov., purple....175.00 to 200.00**
Creamer, marigold **100.00**
Creamer, purple (ILLUS.)..................**220.00**
Pitcher, water, marigold......................**325.00**
Pitcher, water, purple..........................**550.00**
Punch bowl & base, purple,
  2 pcs. **1,100.00**

Punch cup, aqua opalescent..........1,800.00
Punch cup, blue 85.00
Punch cup, green..................40.00
Punch cup, ice blue.......................100.00
Punch cup, ice green 97.00
Punch cup, marigold 21.00
Punch cup, purple 30.00
Punch cup, white.................80.00
Punch set: bowl, base & 5 cups;
    green, 7 pcs. 1,800.00
Punch set: bowl, base & 6 cups;
    ice blue, 8 pcs. 7,000.00
Punch set: bowl, base & 6 cups;
    marigold, 8 pcs. 1,000.00
Punch set: bowl, base & 6 cups;
    purple, 8 pcs ....1,200.00 to 1,500.00
Punch set: bowl, base & 6 cups;
    white, 8 pcs 4,000.00
Sauce dish, green 37.50
Sauce dish, marigold.......................31.00
Sauce dish, purple.......................55.00
Spooner, green.................................150.00
Spooner, marigold 88.00
Spooner, purple...............250.00 to 275.00
Sugar bowl, cov., purple...................290.00
Table set: cov. sugar bowl, creamer,
    spooner & cov. butter dish;
    marigold, 4 pcs. 900.00
Table set, purple, 4 pcs 1,000.00
Tumbler, green 88.00
Tumbler, marigold.................................55.00
Tumbler, purple 55.00
Water set: pitcher & 4 tumblers;
    marigold, 5 pcs. ....600.00 to 650.00
Water set: pitcher & 6 tumblers;
    green, 7 pcs. 1,200.00
Water set: pitcher & 6 tumblers;
    purple, 7 pcs....................800.00 to 850.00

ADVERTISING & SOUVENIR ITEMS

Basket, "Feldman Bros. Furniture,
    Salisbury, Md.," open edge,
    marigold..............................50.00 to 75.00
Basket, "John H. Brand Furniture Co.,
    Wilmington, Del.," marigold................60.00
Bell, souvenir, BPOE Elks, "Atlantic
    City, 1911," blue.....................2,250.00
Bell, souvenir, BPOE Elks,
    "Parkersburg, 1914," blue 1,250.00
Bowl, "Isaac Benesch," 6¼" d.,
    purple (Millersburg)..........................400.00
Bowl, "Bernheimer Brothers,"
    blue...................................1,000.00
Bowl, "Dreibus Parfait Sweets,"
    ruffled, smoky lavender....................400.00
Bowl, "Horlacher," Peacock Tail patt.,
    green.................................95.00
Bowl, "Horlacher," Thistle patt.,
    green.................................100.00
Bowl, "Sterling Furniture," purple 600.00
Bowl, souvenir, BPOE Elks, "Atlantic
    City, 1911," blue, one-eyed Elk........657.00
Bowl, souvenir, BPOE Elks, "Detroit,
    1910," blue, one-eyed Elk...............550.00

Bowl, souvenir, BPOE Elks, "Detroit,
    1910," green, one-eyed Elk 1,000.00
Bowl, souvenir, BPOE Elks, "Detroit,
    1910," ruffled, green 250.00
Bowl, souvenir, BPOE Elks, "Detroit,
    1910," marigold...............................845.00
Bowl, souvenir, BPOE Elks, "Detroit,
    1910," purple, one-eyed Elk.............385.00
Bowl, souvenir, BPOE Elks, "Detroit,
    1910," purple, two-eyed Elk
    (Millersburg) ....775.00 to 825.00
Bowl, souvenir, "Brooklyn Bridge,"
    marigold..........................400.00 to 425.00
Bowl, souvenir, "Brooklyn Bridge,"
    unlettered, marigold.........475.00 to 550.00
Bowl, souvenir, "Millersburg
    Courthouse," purple 655.00
Bowl, souvenir, "Millersburg
    Courthouse," unlettered, purple 1,000.00
Card tray, "Isaac Benesch," Holly
    Whirl patt., marigold ....50.00 to 70.00
Hat, "Arthur O'Dell," green..................75.00
Hat, "General Furniture Co.," 1910,
    Peacock Tail patt., green 75.00
Hat, "Horlacher," Peacock Tail patt.,
    green.................................70.00
Hat, "John Brand Furniture,"
    open edge, marigold 45.00
Paperweight, souvenir, "BPOE Elks,"
    green.................................625.00
Paperweight, souvenir, "BPOE Elks,"
    purple (Millersburg) ....600.00 to 700.00
Plate, "Ballard, California," purple
    (Northwood) 900.00
Plate, "Brazier Candies," w/handgrip,
    6" d., purple ....500.00 to 600.00
Plate, "Campbell & Beesley,"
    w/handgrip, purple 1,250.00
Plate, "Dreibus Parfait Sweets,"
    6¼" d., purple 400.00
Plate, "Eagle Furniture Co.,"
    purple 750.00
Plate, "Fern Brand Chocolates,"
    6" d., purple......................................800.00
Plate, "Gervitz Bros., Furniture &
    Clothing," w/handgrip, 6" d.,
    purple ....1,400.00 to 1,600.00
Plate, "Jockey Club," w/handgrip,
    6" d., purple 500.00
Plate, "Old Rose Distillery," Grape &
    Cable patt., stippled, 9" d., green.....370.00
Plate, "Spector's Department Store,"
    Heart & Vine patt., 9" d., mari-
    gold 450.00
Plate, "Utah Liquor Co.," w/handgrip,
    6" d., purple......................................1,800.00
Plate, souvenir, BPOE Elks, "Atlantic
    City, 1911," blue ....800.00 to 900.00
Plate, souvenir, BPOE Elks, "Par-
    kersburg, 1914," 7½" d., blue........1,050.00
Vase, "Howard Furniture," Four Pillars
    patt., green..65.00

APPLE BLOSSOMS

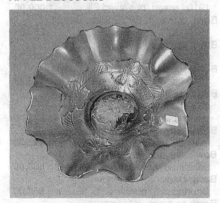

Apple Blossom Bowl

Bowl, 5½" d., purple **42.50**
Bowl, 6" d., marigold **22.00**
Bowl, 6" d., deep, purple......................**30.00**
Bowl, 7" d., collared base, marigold
  (ILLUS.) **33.50**
Bowl, 7" d., ribbon candy rim,
  marigold **25.00**
Bowl, 7" d., ribbon candy rim,
  white **135.00**
Bowl, 9" d., three-in-one edge, peach
  opalescent **130.00**
Rose bowl, marigold............................**65.00**
Tumbler, enameled, blue...................**120.00**
Water set: pitcher & 1 tumbler;
  enameled, blue, 2 pcs.....................**300.00**

APPLE BLOSSOM TWIGS
Banana boat-shaped bowl, ruffled,
  peach opalescent...........................**175.00**
Banana boat-shaped bowl, ruffled,
  purple......................................**155.00**
Bowl, 8" to 9" d., marigold .....**55.00 to 75.00**
Bowl, 8" to 9" d., peach
  opalescent.......................**180.00 to 185.00**
Bowl, 8" to 9" d., purple .....**155.00 to 200.00**
Bowl, 9" d., ice cream shape,
  white ....**150.00 to 175.00**
Plate, 9" d., blue **265.00**
Plate, 9" d., ruffled, blue...................**210.00**
Plate, 9" d., marigold.........................**100.00**
Plate, 9" d., ruffled, marigold.............**107.50**
Plate, 9" d., peach
  opalescent **400.00**
Plate, 9" d., purple ....**200.00 to 300.00**
Plate, 9" d., flat, smooth edge,
  purple.......................................**900.00**
Plate, 9" d., white..............**200.00 to 225.00**
Plate, 9" d., ruffled, white...**200.00 to 225.00**

APPLE TREE
Pitcher, water, marigold....................**115.00**
Tumbler, blue..................................**70.00**
Tumbler, marigold.............................**42.00**
Tumbler, white **250.00**

Water set: pitcher & 4 tumblers;
  white, 5 pcs. ....**1,100.00 to 1,250.00**
Water set: pitcher & 6 tumblers;
  blue, 7 pcs. ....**1,000.00 to 1,250.00**
Water set: pitcher & 6 tumblers;
  marigold, 7 pcs. ....**500.00 to 550.00**

AUTUMN ACORNS (Fenton)
Bowl, 8" to 9" d., blue...........................**70.00**
Bowl, 8" to 9" d., marigold...................**80.00**
Bowl, 8" to 9" d., purple **45.00**
Bowl, 8½" d., three-in-one edge,
  green..**80.00**
Bowl, 8½" d., ribbon candy rim,
  green..**35.00**
Bowl, 8½" d., ribbon candy rim,
  marigold **30.00**

BASKET or BUSHEL BASKET (Northwood)

Northwood Basket

Aqua, 4½" d, 4¾" h **425.00**
Aqua opalescent, 4½" d, 4¾" h **500.00**
Blue...**150.00**
Celeste blue **1,900.00**
Cobalt blue ....**150.00 to 200.00**
Blue w/electric iridescence..............**160.00**
Green **520.00**
Honey amber ....**400.00 to 500.00**
Horehound, variant......................**1,250.00**
Ice blue **750.00**
Ice green..**400.00**
Lavender..**190.00**
Lime green **350.00**
Lime green opalescent................**2,350.00**
Marigold (ILLUS.) **100.00**
Olive green....................................**500.00**
Purple **90.00**
Sapphire blue **1,750.00**
Smoky...**750.00**
Teal blue **450.00**
Vaseline **2,600.00**
White ....**150.00 to 175.00**

BEADED CABLE (Northwood)
Bowl, 7" d., three-footed, green...........**50.00**

Bowl, 7" d., three-footed, ruffled,
 marigold **35.00**
Candy dish, green **50.00**
Candy dish, marigold **30.00**
Candy dish, purple **55.00**
Rose bowl, aqua **350.00**
Rose bowl, aqua opale-
 scent ....**325.00 to 350.00**
Rose bowl, blue ....**125.00 to 150.00**
Rose bowl, blue w/electric
 iridescence **300.00**
Rose bowl, green **90.00**
Rose bowl, ice blue ....**800.00 to 825.00**
Rose bowl, ice green .....**950.00 to 1,300.00**
Rose bowl, lime green opale-
 scent **1,200.00**
Rose bowl, marigold **75.00**
Rose bowl, ribbed interior,
 marigold **120.00**
Rose bowl, purple **108.00**
Rose bowl, white ....**500.00 to 525.00**

BEAUTY BUD VASE
Purple, 6½" h. ....**75.00 to 100.00**
Marigold, 8" h. **30.00**
Purple, 8" h. **40.00**
Marigold, 9½" h. **35.00**

BIRDS & CHERRIES
Bonbon, blue **80.00**
Bonbon, green **75.00**
Bonbon, marigold **38.00**
Bonbon, purple **75.00**
Bowl, 8" to 9" d., blue **440.00**
Bowl, 10" d., blue **425.00**
Compote, blue **65.00**
Compote, green **60.00**
Compote, lavender **60.00**
Compote, marigold **40.00**
Compote, purple **71.00**

BLACKBERRY BRAMBLE
Compote, ruffled, green **52.00**
Compote, ruffled, lavender **50.00**
Compote, ruffled, marigold **45.00**
Compote, ruffled, purple **46.00**

BLACKBERRY MINIATURE COMPOTE

Blackberry Miniature Compote

Blue (ILLUS.) **108.00**
Blue, flat top **325.00**
Blue, w/red stem **350.00**
Green **200.00**
Marigold **93.00**
Purple **80.00**
White **448.00**

BLACKBERRY WREATH (Millersburg)
Bowl, 5" d., green **65.00**
Bowl, 5" d., marigold **43.00**
Bowl, 5" d., ruffled,
 marigold ....**100.00 to 125.00**
Bowl, 5" d., purple **57.50**
Bowl, 5" d., ribbon candy edge,
 purple ....**75.00 to 100.00**
Bowl, 7" d., green **62.00**
Bowl, 7" d., marigold **51.00**
Bowl, 7" d., purple **66.00**
Bowl, 7½" d., ruffled, purple **115.00**
Bowl, 7½" d., three-in-one edge,
 clambroth **75.00**
Bowl, 8" to 9" d., green **196.50**
Bowl, 8" to 9" d., marigold **57.00**
Bowl, 8" to 9" d., purple **97.50**
Bowl, 10" d., blue ....**850.00 to 900.00**
Bowl, 10" d., green **82.00**
Bowl, 10" d., marigold **76.00**
Bowl, 10" d., purple **165.00**
Bowl, ice cream, large, green **70.00**
Bowl, ice cream, large, marigold **68.00**
Bowl, ice cream, large,
 purple ....**200.00 to 225.00**

BLOSSOM TIME COMPOTE

Blossom Time Compote
Green **400.00**
Marigold **175.00**
Purple (ILLUS.) **225.00**

BUTTERFLIES (Fenton)
Bonbon, blue **50.00**
Bonbon, green **52.00**
Bonbon, marigold **40.00**
Bonbon, purple **69.00**

BUTTERFLY (Northwood)
Bonbon, threaded exterior,
 blue ....**250.00 to 270.00**

Bonbon, handled, threaded exterior, blue w/electric iridescence...............**425.00**

Bonbon, threaded exterior, emerald green...**575.00**

Bonbon, threaded exterior, ice blue...**2,200.00**

Bonbon, threaded exterior, purple ....**225.00 to 275.00**

Bonbon, green ....**125.00 to 150.00**

Bonbon, marigold **50.00**

Bonbon, purple **72.00**

Bonbon, smoky.................................**350.00**

BUTTERFLY & TULIP

Bowl, 9" w., 5½" h., footed, marigold...............................**350.00 to 375.00**

Bowl, 10½" square flat shape, footed, marigold...........................**500.00 to 550.00**

Bowl, 10½" square flat shape, footed, purple ....**1,600.00 to 1,650.00**

Bowl, 12" d., upturned sides, footed, marigold **354.00**

CAPTIVE ROSE

Captive Rose Bowl

Bonbon, two-handled, blue, 7½" d. **90.00**

Bonbon, two-handled, green, 7½" d. **57.50**

Bowl, 6" d., blue.....................................**35.00**

Bowl, 8" d., three-in-one edge, purple...**112.50**

Bowl, 8" to 9" d., blue.............................**77.00**

Bowl, 8" to 9" d., green **77.50**

Bowl, 8" to 9" d., marigold....................**99.00**

Bowl, 8" to 9" d., purple **39.00**

Bowl, 8" to 9" d., ribbon candy rim, green...**70.00**

Bowl, 8" to 9" d., ribbon candy rim, marigold...**66.00**

Bowl, 8" to 9" d., ribbon candy rim, purple (ILLUS.) **68.00**

Bowl, 8" to 9" d., ruffled rim, blue.........**80.00**

Bowl, 8" to 9" d., ruffled rim, green **127.50**

Bowl, 8" to 9" d., ruffled rim, marigold...**35.00**

Compote, blue **75.00**

Compote, ice blue ....**125.00 to 150.00**

Compote, marigold **55.00**

Compote, white.................................**125.00**

Compote, ribbon candy rim, purple ...**100.00**

Plate, 6" d., marigold............................**65.00**

Plate, 9" d., blue.................**425.00 to 525.00**

Plate, 9" d., green ....**800.00 to 825.00**

Plate, 9" d., marigold **350.00**

Plate, 9" d., purple ....**500.00 to 550.00**

CHERRY (Dugan)

Berry set: master bowl & 4 sauce dishes; marigold, 5 pcs. **310.00**

Bowl, 5" d., Jeweled Heart exterior, purple...**45.00**

Bowl, 6" d., clambroth opalescent.......**30.00**

Bowl, 6" d., Jeweled Heart exterior, purple...**42.50**

Bowl, 6" d., purple................................**67.50**

Bowl, 7" d., three-footed, crimped rim, peach opalescent................................**150.00**

Bowl, 8" to 9" d., three-footed, marigold...**120.00**

Bowl, 8" to 9" d., three-footed, peach opalescent.............................**285.00**

Bowl, 8" to 9" d., three-footed, purple...**142.00**

Bowl, 10" d., Jeweled Heart exterior, purple...**260.00**

Bowl, large, peach opalescent...........**240.00**

Dish, ruffled, marigold, 6" d.................**80.00**

Dish, ruffled, purple, 6" d.....................**50.00**

Plate, 6" d., ruffled, purple, ...**150.00**

Plate, 6½" d., ribbon candy rim, purple ....**225.00 to 250.00**

Plate, 6½" d., ruffled, Jeweled Heart exterior, purple **95.00**

Sauce dish, peach opalescent **65.00**

Sauce dish, Jeweled Heart exterior, ruffled, peach opalescent...................**75.00**

Sauce dish, purple **45.00**

CHERRY CHAIN (Fenton)

Bonbon, two-handled, marigold...........**36.00**

Bowl, 5" d., blue...................................**42.50**

Bowl, 5" d., Orange Tree exterior, marigold...**30.50**

Bowl, 5" d., white **56.00**

Bowl, 5" d., blue...................................**65.00**

Bowl, 6" d., ruffled, emerald green.......**85.00**

Bowl, 6" d., marigold............................**30.00**

Bowl, 6" d., white **75.00**

Bowl, 7" d., marigold............................**25.00**

Bowl, 8" to 9" d., blue...........................**47.00**

Bowl, 8" to 9" d., clambroth..................**70.00**

Bowl, 8" to 9" d., marigold .....**55.00 to 65.00**

Bowl, 8" to 9" d., Orange Tree exterior, purple.............................**225.00**

Bowl, 8" to 9" d., white.........................**75.00**

Bowl, 8" d., ice cream shape, clambroth...**35.00**

Bowl, 9½" d., ice cream shape, clambroth...**50.00**

Bowl, 10" d., ice cream shape, Orange Tree exterior, white **100.00**

Bowl, 10" d., clambroth........................**75.00**

Bowl, 10" d., Orange Tree exterior, marigold...**65.00**

Bowl, 10" d., Orange Tree exterior, red..**235.00**

Bowl, 10" d., ribbon candy rim, vaseline...**125.00**

Bowl, 10" d., three-in-one edge,
  blue **245.00**
Bowl, 10½" d., blue **45.00**
Bowl, 10½" d., ruffled,
  white ....**100.00 to 125.00**
Bowl, ruffled, large, green **300.00**
Plate, 6" d., Orange Tree exterior,
  blue **145.00**
Plate, 6" d., Orange Tree exterior,
  marigold **87.00**
Plate, 6" d., white **225.00**
Plate, 6" to 7" d., blue **102.00**
Plate, 6" to 7" d., marigold **78.00**

CHRYSANTHEMUM or WINDMILL & MUMS

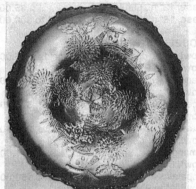

Chrysanthemum Bowl

Bowl, 8" to 9" d., three footed,
  blue.....................**125.00 to 130.00**
Bowl, 8" to 9" d., three footed,
  green..**76.50**
Bowl, 8" to 9" d., three footed,
  marigold **46.00**
Bowl, 9" d., ruffled, blue **115.00**
Bowl, 9" d., ruffled,
  green ....**175.00 to 200.00**
Bowl, 9" d., marigold **62.00**
Bowl, 9" d., ruffled, marigold **120.00**
Bowl, 9" d., ruffled, purple **162.50**
Bowl, 9" d., red w/amber center **4,100.00**
Bowl, 10" d., three-footed, blue
  (ILLUS.) **130.00**
Bowl, 10" d., three-footed, marigold.....**92.00**
Bowl, 10" d., collared base, red **5,000.00**
Bowl, 11" d., three-footed,
  blue.........................**250.00 to 300.00**
Bowl, 11" d., three-footed, green **250.00**
Bowl, 11" d., three-footed, marigold.....**48.50**
Bowl, 12" d., three-footed, ruffled,
  black amethyst...................................**575.00**
Bowl, 12" d., three-footed, vaseline ...**275.00**
Bowl, collared base, green **238.00**
Bowl, collared base, marigold **62.00**
Bowl, collared base,
  purple ....**300.00 to 350.00**

COBBLESTONES BOWL (Imperial)
Marigold, 7" d. **81.00**

Green, 9" d. **87.50**
Purple, 9" d. **89.00**
COIN SPOT (Dugan)
Compote, 7" d., marigold....................**35.00**
Compote, 7" d., peach opalescent.......**57.50**
Compote, 7" d., fluted, peach
  opalescent **91.00**
Compote, 7" d., fluted, purple **65.00**
Vase, 10" h., purple **25.00**
Water set: lemonade pitcher & 4
  tumblers; marigold, 5 pcs................**365.00**

CORINTH (Westmoreland)
Bowl, 7" d., shallow, purple.................**35.00**
Bowl, milk white w/marigold overlay ..**100.00**
Bowl, aqua **45.00**
Dish, banana, amber...........................**42.50**
Dish, banana, marigold **35.00**
Dish, banana, purple **38.00**
Rose bowl, ice blue **110.00**
Vase, 7½" h., jack-in-the-pulpit, peach
  opalescent **100.00**
Vase, 7½" h., purple **20.00**
Vase, 7½" h., smoke **28.00**
Vase, 7½" h., teal blue **65.00**
Vase, 8" h., jack-in-the-pulpit,
  amber **165.00**
Vase, 8" h., jack-in-the-pulpit, purple....**46.00**
Vase, 8" h., blue opalescent..............**200.00**
Vase, 9" h., jack-in-the-pulpit,
  purple..**60.00**
Vase, 9½" h., amber...........................**125.00**
Vase, 9½" h., jack-in-the-pulpit,
  marigold **42.50**
Vase, 9½" h., jack-in-the-pulpit, teal
  blue **80.00**
Vase, blue opalescent **195.00**
Vase, jack-in-the-pulpit, aqua..............**80.00**

CORN VASE (Northwood)

Northwood Corn Vase

Aqua w/light marigold overlay **1,975.00**
Green (ILLUS.) ....**900.00 to 925.00**
Ice blue **1,750.00**
Ice green ....**350.00 to 375.00**
Marigold ....**800.00 to 850.00**
Pastel marigold...............................**475.00**

Purple 615.00
White...292.00

COSMOS & CANE (U.S. Glass Co.)

Bowl, 6" d., ice cream shape, honey
amber...50.00
Bowl, 7" d., Headdress interior,
purple...175.00
Bowl, 8" d., Headdress interior,
white 85.00
Bowl, 8" to 9" d., marigold...................40.00
Bowl, 8" to 9" d., white 155.00
Bowl, 10" d., marigold...........................86.00
Bowl, 10" d., white 120.00
Butter dish, cov., amber....................158.50
Butter dish, cov., marigold 325.00
Butter dish, cov., white......................300.00
Compote, marigold 160.00
Compote, purple 350.00
Compote, white....................................587.50
Creamer, honey amber......100.00 to 125.00
Creamer, marigold 93.50
Cuspidor, honey amber..................7,000.00
Pitcher, honey amber 1,500.00
Rose bowl, pedestal footed, honey
amber..1,300.00
Sauce dish, honey amber......................55.00
Sauce dish, honey amber, squat.......225.00
Sauce dish, marigold.............................35.00
Sauce dish, white 50.00
Sugar bowl, cov., marigold................150.00
Tumbler, amber 110.00
Tumbler, honey amber 61.00
Tumbler, marigold..................................70.00
Tumbler, marigold, w/advertising.......137.50
Tumbler, white...................150.00 to 200.00

DAHLIA (Dugan or Diamond Glass Co.)

Berry set: master bowl & 1 sauce
dish; white, 2 pcs. 400.00
Bowl, master berry, 10" d., footed,
white 190.00
Butter dish, cov., marigold 275.00
Butter dish, cov., white......................300.00
Creamer, white.....................................177.00
Pitcher, water, marigold......................650.00
Pitcher, water, purple ....675.00 to 700.00
Pitcher, water, white ....1,000.00 to 1,100.00
Sauce dish, purple.................................50.00
Sauce dish, white 60.00
Sugar bowl, cov., marigold..................65.00
Table set, purple, 4 pcs. 1,200.00
Table set, white, 4 pcs. 1,150.00
Tumbler, purple 131.00
Tumbler, white...................125.00 to 150.00
Water set: pitcher & 6 tumblers; white
w/blue flowers, 7 pcs. 2,000.00

DAISY & LATTICE BAND or LATTICE & DAISY

Tumbler, blue...50.00
Tumbler, marigold..................................32.50
Water set: pitcher & 6 tumblers;
blue, 7 pcs. 450.00

Water set: pitcher & 6 tumblers;
marigold, 7 pcs. 366.00

DIAMOND POINT COLUMNS

Vase, 6" h., green...................................42.00
Vase, 7" h., green.................................125.00
Vase, 7" h., purple.................................41.00
Vase, 7½" h., white ....150.00 to 200.00
Vase, 8" h., green...................................40.00
Vase, 9" h., purple.................................97.50
Vase, 10" h., green.................................80.00
Vase, 10" h., purple 73.50
Vase, 11" h., green.................................30.00
Vase, 11" h., ice blue 240.00
Vase, 12" h., marigold...........................28.00
Vase, 12" h., purple 35.00
Vase, 16" h., blue...............250.00 to 300.00

DOUBLE STEM ROSE

Bowl, 7" d., dome-footed, marigold......35.00
Bowl, 8" to 9" d., dome-footed,
aqua...450.00
Bowl, 8" to 9" d., dome-footed,
celeste blue...................................575.00
Bowl, 8" to 9" d., dome-footed,
lavender...200.00
Bowl, 8" to 9" d., dome-footed,
marigold 71.00
Bowl, 8" to 9" d., dome-footed, peach
opalescent ....125.00 to 150.00
Bowl, 8" to 9" d., dome-footed,
purple...75.00
Bowl, 8" to 9" d., dome-footed,
white 94.00
Bowl, 10" d., peach opalescent 175.00
Plate, dome-footed, purple.................145.00
Plate, dome-footed, white 150.00

DRAPERY (Northwood)

Candy dish, tricornered, ice
blue 139.00
Candy dish, tricornered, ice
green ....150.00 to 200.00
Candy dish, tricornered, purple.........400.00
Candy dish, tricornered, white...........135.00
Rose bowl, aqua opalescent 325.00
Rose bowl, blue ....250.00 to 300.00
Rose bowl, blue w/electric
iridescence....................................600.00
Rose bowl, ice blue........800.00 to 1,000.00
Rose bowl, lavender...........................110.00
Rose bowl, marigold ....325.00 to 375.00
Rose bowl, purple ....250.00 to 300.00
Rose bowl, white...............275.00 to 375.00
Vase, 7" h., blue 67.50
Vase, 7" h., ice green 95.00
Vase, 7" h., marigold 68.00
Vase, 8" h., blue 50.00
Vase, 8" h., ice blue 60.00
Vase, 8" h., ice green 150.00
Vase, 8" h., marigold 42.00
Vase, 8" h., white................................100.00
Vase, 9" h., blue 95.00

Vase, 9" h., marigold 57.00
Vase, 9" h., purple 150.00
Vase, 10" h., ice blue 425.00
Vase, 10" h., ice green 180.00
Vase, 10" h., marigold 90.00

FEATHERED SERPENT
Bowl, 8" to 9" d., green 60.00
Bowl, 8" to 9" d., marigold..................40.00
Bowl, 8" to 9" d., purple 70.00
Bowl, 10" d., ruffled, blue....................65.00
Bowl, 10" d., fluted, green...................55.00
Bowl, 10" d., marigold..........................60.00
Bowl, 10" d., flared, purple..................55.00
Bowl, 12½" d., ruffled, blue..................95.00
Sauce dish, blue..................................27.50
Sauce dish, green 24.00
Sauce dish, marigold............................15.00
Sauce dish, purple...............................35.00
Whimsey, tricornered, marigold...........45.00

FIELD FLOWER (Imperial)
Pitcher, water, amber 350.00
Pitcher, water, green 325.00
Pitcher, water, marigold....................230.00
Pitcher, water, purple ....400.00 to 425.00
Tumbler, amber 39.00
Tumbler, blue......................................100.00
Tumbler, green 70.00
Tumbler, marigold................................44.00
Tumbler, purple 55.00

FINECUT & ROSES (Northwood)
Candy dish, three-footed, aqua
    opalescent ....400.00 to 450.00
Candy dish, three-footed, blue
    w/electric iridescence.........................67.50
Candy dish, three-footed, green........107.50
Candy dish, three-footed, ice
    blue.................................300.00 to 350.00
Candy dish, three-footed,
    ice green 175.00
Candy dish, three-footed,
    marigold...57.50
Candy dish, three-footed, purple.........50.00
Candy dish, three-footed, white 159.00
Rose bowl, amber 550.00
Rose bowl, aqua opales-
    cent........................1,000.00 to 1,300.00
Rose bowl, green 186.00
Rose bowl, ice blue 252.50
Rose bowl, ice green.........................800.00
Rose bowl, marigold.............................88.00
Rose bowl, purple...............................124.00
Rose bowl, white..............425.00 to 450.00
Rose bowl/whimsey, straight top,
    lavender 650.00
Rose bowl/whimsey, purple 195.00

FISHERMAN'S MUG
Black amethyst 195.00
Marigold...195.00
Pastel marigold ....200.00 to 250.00
Peach opalescent 1,233.00

Fisherman's Mug
Purple (ILLUS.) **164.00**

FOUR SEVENTY FOUR (Imperial)

Four Seventy Four Pitcher

Compote, green....................................95.00
Goblet, water, marigold.......................52.50
Pitcher, milk, green.............................400.00
Pitcher, milk, marigold 162.00
Pitcher, water, marigold....................177.00
Pitcher, water, purple (ILLUS.) 725.00
Punch cup, green.................................60.00
Punch cup, marigold 25.00
Punch cup, purple 50.00
Punch cup, teal blue............................40.00
Punch set: bowl, base & 6 cups;
    marigold, 8 pcs. 425.00
Tumbler, blue......................................200.00
Tumbler, marigold................................35.00
Tumbler, purple 75.00
Water set: pitcher & 6 tumblers;
    marigold, 7 pcs. 385.00

GOOD LUCK (Northwood)
Bowl, 8" d., ruffled, blue.....275.00 to 300.00
Bowl, 8" d., ruffled, stippled, blue.......374.00
Bowl, 8" d., ruffled, blue w/electric
    iridescence..285.00
Bowl, 8" d., ruffled, stippled, blue
    w/electric iridescence.......................405.00
Bowl, 8" d., ruffled, green.................281.50

Bowl, 8" d., ruffled, Basketweave
exterior, green ....**250.00 to 300.00**
Bowl, 8" d., ruffled, marigold..............**125.00**
Bowl, 8" d., ruffled, Basketweave
exterior, marigold............**200.00 to 225.00**
Bowl, 8" d., ruffled, stippled,
marigold **160.00**
Bowl, 8" d., ruffled,
purple ....**200.00 to 225.00**
Bowl, 8" d., ruffled, Basketweave
exterior, purple ....**275.00 to 300.00**
Bowl, 8" to 9" d., piecrust rim, aqua
opalescent **1,800.00**
Bowl, 8" to 9" d., piecrust rim, blue **376.50**
Bowl, 8" to 9" d., piecrust rim, blue
w/electric iridescence................**795.00**
Bowl, 8" to 9" d., piecrust rim,
stippled, blue................**321.00**
Bowl, 8" to 9" d., piecrust rim,
green ....**375.00 to 400.00**
Bowl, 8" to 9" d., piecrust rim,
marigold **205.00**
Bowl, 8" to 9" d., piecrust rim,
stippled, marigold................**190.00**
Bowl, 8" to 9" d., piecrust rim,
purple **322.00**
Bowl, 8" to 9" d., piecrust rim,
teal blue ....**2,500.00 to 3,000.00**
Bowl, 8" to 9" d., ruffled, aqua opales-
cent................**1,300.00**
Bowl, 8" to 9" d., ruffled, green **650.00**
Bowl, 8" to 9" d., ruffled, ice blue **4,200.00**
Bowl, 8" to 9" d., ruffled, lav-
ender ....**200.00 to 250.00**
Bowl, 8" to 9" d., ruffled, marigold......**168.00**
Bowl, 8" to 9" d., ruffled, purple **297.00**
Bowl, 8" to 9" d., ruffled,
teal blue ....**1,200.00 to 1,500.00**
Bowl, aqua................**1,200.00**
Bowl, piecrust rim, stippled, ribbed
exterior, blue w/electric irides-
cence **775.00**
Bowl, ruffled, sapphire blue **1,300.00**
Bowl, stippled, marigold irides-
cence **385.00**
Plate, 9" d., blue w/electric
iridescence ....**1,250.00 to 1,275.00**
Plate, 9" d., green................**1,350.00**
Plate, 9" d., marigold................**500.00**
Plate, 9" d., purple................**475.00**
Plate, 9" d., stippled, purple **600.00**
Plate, 9" d., Basketweave exterior,
purple................**525.00**

GRAPE & CABLE
Banana boat, blue............**475.00 to 500.00**
Banana boat, banded rim, stippled,
blue................**1,000.00 to 1,200.00**
Banana boat, green................**331.00**
Banana boat, ice blue ......**550.00 to 600.00**
Banana boat, ice green **750.00**
Banana boat, marigold **135.00**
Banana boat, stippled,
marigold................**300.00 to 350.00**

Banana boat, purple................**375.00**
Banana boat, white ....**650.00 to 685.00**
Berry set: master bowl & 6 sauce
dishes; green, 7 pcs................**300.00**
Berry set: master bowl & 6 sauce
dishes; purple, 7 pcs. ......**300.00 to 375.00**
Bonbon, two-handled, stippled, aqua
opalescent **3,900.00**
Bonbon, two-handled, blue................**95.00**
Bonbon, two-handled, stippled,
blue................**225.00**
Bonbon, two-handled, green **58.00**
Bonbon, two-handled, stippled,
green ....**100.00 to 125.00**
Bonbon, two-handled, marigold..........**75.00**
Bonbon, two-handled, stippled,
marigold................**45.00**
Bonbon, two-handled, purple **69.00**
Bonbon, two-handled,
white ....**650.00 to 750.00**
Bowl, 5" d., blue (Fenton) **50.00**
Bowl, 5" d., green................**92.50**
Bowl, 5" d., marigold................**38.00**
Bowl, 5" d., purple................**78.50**
Bowl, 6" d., ruffled, purple................**40.00**
Bowl, 6½" d., marigold................**38.00**
Bowl, 7" d., ice cream shape, aqua
(Fenton) **300.00**
Bowl, 7" d., ice cream shape, ice
green................**315.00**
Bowl, 7" d., ice cream shape,
marigold (Fenton) **125.00**
Bowl, 7" d., ice cream shape, milk
white w/marigold overlay
(Fenton) ....**150.00 to 250.00**
Bowl, 7" d., ice cream shape, purple
(Fenton) **50.00**
Bowl, 7" d., ice cream shape,
red (Fenton) **750.00**
Bowl, 7" d., blue (Fenton) **40.00**
Bowl, 7" d., ice blue **750.00**
Bowl, 7" d., red (Fenton) **500.00**
Bowl, 7" d., ruffled, green (Fenton) **65.00**
Bowl, 7" d., ruffled, purple................**42.50**
Bowl, 7" d., ruffled, teal blue **250.00**
Bowl, 7" d., ruffled, vaseline
(Fenton) **47.50**
Bowl, 7" d., spatula-footed, green
(Fenton) **85.00**
Bowl, 7½" d., ball-footed, amber
(Fenton) **90.00**
Bowl, 7½" d., ball-footed, blue
(Fenton) **65.00**
Bowl, 7½" d., ball-footed, green
(Fenton) **42.00**
Bowl, 7½" d., ball-footed, marigold
(Fenton) **40.00**
Bowl, 7½" d., ball-footed, purple
(Fenton) **92.50**
Bowl, 7½" d., ball-footed, red
(Fenton) **550.00**
Bowl, 7½" d., ball-footed, vaseline
(Fenton) **82.50**

Bowl, 7½" d., ruffled, blue **28.00**
Bowl, 7½" d., flat, green......................**38.00**
Bowl, 7½" d., ruffled, green...............**102.50**
Bowl, 7½" d., flat, marigold **72.00**
Bowl, 7½" d., flat, purple **40.00**
Bowl, 7½" d., ruffled, ice
    blue...............................**750.00 to 850.00**
Bowl, 7½" d., ruffled, red ...**825.00 to 850.00**
Bowl, 7½" d., ruffled, vaseline.............**80.00**
Bowl, 7½" d., ruffled, vaseline
    w/marigold overlay **150.00**
Bowl, 7½" d., spatula-footed, green
    (Northwood) **75.00**
Bowl, 7½" d., spatula-footed,
    marigold (Northwood) **46.00**
Bowl, 7½" d., spatula-footed, purple
    (Northwood) **69.00**
Bowl, 8" d., ice cream shape, footed,
    blue (Fenton) **65.00**
Bowl, 8" d., ice cream shape,
    stippled, blue..................................**130.00**
Bowl, 8" d., ice cream shape, footed,
    green (Fenton) **58.00**
Bowl, 8" d., red (Fenton) **550.00**
Bowl, 8" d., ruffled, green....................**65.00**
Bowl, 8" d., ruffled, vaseline................**65.00**
Bowl, 8½" d., crimped edge,
    scalloped, green **85.00**
Bowl, 8½" d., ruffled, stippled, ribbed
    back, green **495.00**
Bowl, 8½" d., scalloped, purple
    (Northwood) **75.00**
Bowl, 8¾" d., ruffled, purple................**94.00**
Bowl, 8" to 9" d., piecrust rim, aqua
    opalescent (Northwood)...............**3,900.00**
Bowl, 8" to 9" d., piecrust rim, blue
    w/electric iridescence......................**300.00**
Bowl, 8" to 9" d., piecrust rim,
    stippled, blue..................................**312.50**
Bowl, 8" to 9" d., piecrust rim,
    green..**143.00**
Bowl, 8" to 9" d., piecrust rim,
    Basketweave exterior, green **177.00**
Bowl, 8" to 9" d., piecrust rim, ice
    blue...**1,000.00**
Bowl, 8" to 9" d., piecrust rim,
    marigold...**100.00**
Bowl, 8" to 9" d., piecrust rim,
    purple ....**175.00 to 200.00**
Bowl, 8" to 9" d., piecrust rim,
    Basketweave exterior,
    purple...**167.50**
Bowl, 8" to 9" d., ball-footed, blue
    (Fenton) **85.00**
Bowl, 8" to 9" d., ball-footed, green
    (Fenton) **75.50**
Bowl, 8" to 9" d., ball-footed, pastel
    marigold (Fenton) **55.00**
Bowl, 8" to 9" d., ball-footed, purple
    (Fenton) **50.00**
Bowl, 8" to 9" d., ball-footed, smoky
    (Fenton) **275.00**
Bowl, 8" to 9" d., ball-footed, teal
    blue...**275.00**

Bowl, 8" to 9" d., spatula-footed, blue
    (Northwood) **65.00**
Bowl, 8" to 9" d., spatula-footed,
    clambroth (Northwood) **90.00**
Bowl, 8" to 9" d., spatula-footed,
    marigold (Northwood) **57.50**
Bowl, 8" to 9" d., spatula-footed,
    ruffled, purple
    (Northwood)......................**75.00 to 100.00**
Bowl, 8" to 9" d., stippled, blue **360.00**
Bowl, 8" to 9" d., stippled, ruffled,
    w/Basketweave exterior, marigold ...**300.00**
Bowl, 8" to 9" d., stippled, green........**325.00**
Bowl, 8" to 9" d., stippled, ice
    blue **1,000.00**
Bowl, 8" to 9" d., stippled, marigold ..**125.00**
Bowl, 8" to 9" d., stippled, purple **225.00**
Bowl, berry, 9" d., clam-
    broth ....**75.00 to 100.00**
Bowl, berry, 9" d., green **105.00**
Bowl, berry, 9" d., ice green...........**1,100.00**
Bowl, berry, 9" d., marigold................**95.00**
Bowl, berry, 9" d., purple....................**82.00**
Bowl, 9" d., Basketweave exterior,
    green..**77.50**
Bowl, orange, 10½" d., banded,
    marigold...........................**400.00 to 425.00**
Bowl, orange, 10½" d., footed,
    Persian Medallion interior, blue
    (Fenton) ....**225.00 to 250.00**
Bowl, orange, 10½" d., footed,
    Persian Medallion interior, green
    (Fenton) ....**225.00 to 250.00**
Bowl, orange, 10½" d., footed,
    Persian Medallion interior, marigold
    (Fenton) **146.00**
Bowl, orange, 10½" d., footed,
    Persian Medallion interior, purple
    (Fenton) **271.00**
Bowl, orange, 10½" d.,
    footed, blue......................**450.00 to 500.00**
Bowl, orange, 10½" d., footed,
    clambroth **350.00**
Bowl, orange, 10½" d., footed,
    stippled, blue w/electric iridescence
    (Northwood)....................**800.00 to 825.00**
Bowl, orange, 10½" d., footed,
    green................................**300.00 to 350.00**
Bowl, orange, 10½" d., footed, ice
    blue...**1,250.00**
Bowl, orange, 10½" d., footed, ice
    green ....**950.00 to 1,150.00**
Bowl, orange, 10½" d., footed,
    marigold...**213.50**
Bowl, orange, 10½" d., footed,
    stippled, marigold...........................**300.00**
Bowl, orange, 10½" d., footed,
    purple...**337.50**
Bowl, orange, 10½" d., footed,
    white..**1,250.00**
Bowl, orange, 10½" d., lavender........**395.00**
Bowl, 10½" d., ruffled, Basketweave
    exterior, green................................**200.00**

Bowl, 10½" d., ruffled, Basketweave
exterior, marigold.................**65.00 to 75.00**
Bowl, 10½" d., ruffled, Basketweave
exterior, purple ....**100.00 to 125.00**
Bowl, 10½" d., ruffled, white **145.00**
Bowl, 11" d., ice cream shape,
blue **700.00**
Bowl, 11" d., ice cream shape,
green ....**750.00 to 850.00**
Bowl, 11" d., ice cream shape,
Basketweave exterior, green **1,250.00**
Bowl, 11" d., ice cream shape,
ice blue ....**2,100.00 to 2,750.00**
Bowl, 11" d., ice cream shape,
ice green ....**1,200.00 to 1,500.00**
Bowl, 11" d., ice cream shape,
marigold...................................**417.50**
Bowl, 11" d., ice cream shape,
Basketweave exterior,
marigold...........................**150.00 to 200.00**
Bowl, 11" d., ice cream shape,
purple **357.00**
Bowl, 11" d., ice cream shape,
Basketweave exterior, purple **450.00**
Bowl, 11" d., ice cream shape,
white ....**350.00 to 400.00**
Bowl, footed, Meander exterior,
purple **350.00**
Bowl, footed, Meander exterior,
white **712.50**
Breakfast set: individual size
creamer & sugar bowl; purple,
pr.................................**200.00 to 250.00**
Bride's basket, purple **2,975.00**
Butter dish, cov., amber **155.00**
Butter dish, cov., green...................**180.00**
Butter dish, cov., ice green **250.00**
Butter dish, cov., marigold **165.00**
Butter dish, cov., purple **328.00**
Candle lamp, green..........**650.00 to 700.00**
Candle lamp, marigold.....**500.00 to 550.00**
Candle lamp, purple.........**500.00 to 600.00**
Candlestick, green **135.00**
Candlestick, marigold........................**72.00**
Candlestick, purple ....**125.00 to 150.00**
Candlesticks, blue, pr **275.00**
Candlesticks, marigold, pr. **235.00**
Card tray, green.................................**350.00**
Card tray, horehound..........................**80.00**
Card tray, marigold **50.00**
Card tray, purple **80.00**
Centerpiece bowl, green....................**775.00**
Centerpiece bowl, ice blue **825.00**
Centerpiece bowl, ice green **910.00**
Centerpiece bowl, marigold..............**255.00**
Centerpiece bowl, purple...................**412.50**
Centerpiece bowl, white **653.50**
Cologne bottle w/stopper,
green ....**225.00 to 250.00**
Cologne bottle w/stopper,
ice blue **950.00**
Cologne bottle w/stopper,
marigold..........................**200.00 to 250.00**

Cologne bottle w/stopper, purple......**315.00**
Cologne bottle w/stopper, sapphire
blue **795.00**
Cologne bottle w/stopper,
white ....**625.00 to 650.00**
Compote, cov., large, green **425.00**
Compote, cov., large, marigold.......**1,450.00**
Compote, cov., small,
purple ....**325.00 to 350.00**
Compote, cov., large, purple **450.00**
Compote, open, large, green.............**795.00**
Compote, open, large, mari-
gold...............................**300.00 to 350.00**
Compote, open, small, purple...........**237.50**
Compote, open, large,
purple ....**425.00 to 525.00**
Cracker jar, cov., ice green **800.00**
Cracker jar, cov., marigold **425.00**
Cracker jar, cov., purple **612.50**
Cracker jar, cov., white.....................**875.00**
Creamer, green **125.00**
Creamer, marigold **90.00**
Creamer, purple **88.00**
Creamer, individual size, green **65.00**
Creamer, individual size, marigold.......**68.00**
Creamer, individual size, purple...........**65.00**
Creamer & cov. sugar bowl, purple,
pr. **278.00**
Cup & saucer, blue............................**275.00**
Cup & saucer, marigold.....................**250.00**
Cup & saucer, purple **450.00**
Cuspidor, purple **3,000.00**
Decanter w/stopper, whiskey,
marigold..........................**575.00 to 600.00**
Dresser set, purple, 7 pcs. **2,500.00**
Dresser tray, blue.............................**250.00**
Dresser tray, green ....**250.00 to 275.00**
Dresser tray, ice blue **1,500.00**
Dresser tray, marigold.......................**150.00**
Dresser tray, purple ....**275.00 to 300.00**
Fernery, ice blue.............................**1,300.00**
Fernery, purple ....**650.00 to 700.00**
Hatpin holder, blue.........................**1,000.00**
Hatpin holder, green **290.00**
Hatpin holder, ice blue **2,500.00**
Hatpin holder, ice green................**3,000.00**
Hatpin holder, lavender ....**400.00 to 450.00**
Hatpin holder, marigold....................**315.00**
Hatpin holder, purple ....**300.00 to 350.00**
Hatpin holder, white **1,800.00**
Hat shape, green...............**225.00 to 250.00**
Hat shape, marigold............................**50.00**
Hat shape, purple ....**50.00 to 60.00**
Humidor (or tobacco jar), cov.,
blue **1,000.00**
Humidor, cov., stippled, blue **1,500.00**
Humidor, cov., marigold ....**375.00 to 400.00**
Humidor, cov., stippled, marigold......**160.00**
Humidor, cov., purple **800.00**
Ice cream set: master bowl & 1
individual dish; marigold, 2 pcs. **425.00**
Ice cream set: master bowl & 6
individual dishes; white, 7 pcs. **1,500.00**

Nappy, single handle, green 75.00
Nappy, single handle, ice blue 600.00
Nappy, single handle, marigold...........47.00
Nappy, single handle, purple 130.00
Nappy, cup whimsey, hairpin, purple ...50.00
Perfume bottle w/stopper,
    marigold...........................525.00 to 550.00
Perfume bottle w/stopper,
    purple ....650.00 to 675.00
Pin tray, green 225.00
Pin tray, ice blue 900.00
Pin tray, marigold.............................196.00
Pin tray, purple ....300.00 to 325.00
Pitcher, water, 8¼" h., green 412.50
Pitcher, water, 8¼" h., marigold..........205.00
Pitcher, water, 8¼" h., purple 370.00
Pitcher, tankard, 9¾" h., marigold 540.00
Pitcher, tankard, 9¾" h., purple 600.00
Plate, 5" to 6" d., purple (North-
    wood).........................140.00 to 150.00
Plate, 7½" d., turned-up handgrip,
    green...95.00
Plate, 7½" d., turned-up handgrip,
    marigold......................100.00 to 125.00
Plate, 7½" d., turned-up handgrip,
    purple 114.00
Plate, 8" d., clambroth........................850.00
Plate, 8" d., footed, green (Fenton) 185.00
Plate, 8" d., green (Northwood)..........140.00
Plate, 8" d., footed, marigold...............92.00
Plate, 8" d., footed, purple...................84.00
Plate, 8" d., purple ....225.00 to 275.00
Plate, 9" d., spatula-footed, blue 150.00
Plate, 9" d., stippled, blue...................600.00
Plate, 9" d., green ....300.00 to 400.00
Plate, 9" d., marigold.........................250.00
Plate, 9" d., spatula-footed, green......155.00
Plate, 9" d., spatula-footed,
    ice green ....850.00 to 875.00
Plate, 9" d., marigold 109.00
Plate, 9" d., spatula-footed,
    marigold...85.00
Plate, 9" d., purple 128.00
Plate, 9" d., spatula-footed, purple.....125.00
Plate, 9" d., Basketweave exterior,
    green..150.00
Plate, 9" d., Basketweave exterior,
    marigold.........................100.00 to 125.00
Plate, 9" d., Basketweave exterior,
    purple..189.50
Plate, 9" d., stippled, green 302.00
Plate, 9" d., stippled, green,
    variant............................775.00 to 800.00
Plate, 9" d., stippled, marigold,
    variant 750.00
Plate, 9" d., stippled, purple 525.00
Plate, 9" d., stippled, sapphire
    blue.........................3,500.00 to 3,800.00
Plate, 9" d., stippled, teal...............2,700.00
Plate, chop, 12" d., white 5,000.00
Plate, olive green 900.00
Plate, pastel marigold.........................300.00
Powder jar, cov., blue........................600.00

Powder jar, cov., green 160.00
Powder jar, cov., marigold.................155.00
Powder jar, cov., purple ....200.00 to 225.00
Punch bowl & base, green, 11" d.,
    2 pcs. 600.00
Punch bowl & base, marigold, 11" d.,
    2 pcs. 250.00
Punch bowl & base, purple, 11" d.,
    2 pcs. 450.00
Punch bowl & base, purple, 14" d.,
    2 pcs. ....500.00 to 525.00
Punch bowl & base, marigold, 17" d.,
    2 pcs. 100.00
Punch cup, aqua opalescent 895.00
Punch cup, blue 50.00
Punch cup, stippled, blue......50.00 to 75.00
Punch cup, green 41.50
Punch cup, stippled, green...................45.00
Punch cup, ice blue...............................90.00
Punch cup, ice green 80.00
Punch cup, lavender 25.00
Punch cup, marigold..............................30.00
Punch cup, purple..................................27.00
Punch cup, white ....60.00 to 75.00
Punch set: 11" bowl & 6 cups; blue,
    7 pcs. 1,500.00
Punch set: 11" bowl & 6 cups; white,
    7 pcs. 1,750.00
Punch set: 14" bowl & 10 cups; ice
    green, 11 pcs. 2,300.00
Punch set: 14" bowl, base & 5 cups;
    purple, 7 pcs. 895.00
Punch set: 14" bowl, base & 6 cups;
    marigold, 8 pcs. 585.00
Punch set: 14" bowl, base & 6 cups;
    white, 8 pcs. 3,500.00
Punch set: 14" bowl & 8 cups;
    blue, 10 pcs. 2,300.00
Punch set, master: 17" bowl, base &
    6 cups; purple, 8 pcs.....................2,000.00
Punch set, master: 17" bowl, base &
    8 cups; green, 10 pcs. 3,800.00
Punch set, master: 17" bowl, base &
    10 cups; white, 12 pcs. 6,000.00
Punch set, master: 17" bowl, base &
    12 cups; marigold, 14 pcs. 2,500.00
Sauce dish, green 25.00
Sauce dish, marigold............................45.00
Sauce dish, purple................................30.00
Sherbet or individual ice cream
    dish, ice green...............................175.00
Sherbet or individual ice cream
    dish, marigold.................................27.50
Sherbet or individual ice cream
    dish, purple 35.00
Sherbet or individual ice cream
    dish, white.....................175.00 to 200.00
Spooner, green...................................125.00
Spooner, marigold 52.00
Spooner, purple..................................100.00
Sugar bowl, cov., green 85.00
Sugar bowl, cov., marigold..................85.00

Sugar bowl, cov., purple....................**149.50**
Sugar bowl, individual size, green.......**60.00**
Sugar bowl, individual size,
marigold..**35.00**
Sugar bowl, individual size, purple......**68.00**
Sweetmeat jar, cov., marigold........**1,800.00**

Grape & Cable Sweetmeat

Sweetmeat jar, cov.,
purple (ILLUS.) **250.00**
Table set: cov. sugar bowl, creamer
& spooner, purple, 3 pcs.................**450.00**
Table set: cov. sugar bowl, creamer
& spooner, cov. butter dish; green,
4 pcs. **525.00**
Tumbler, green......................**55.00 to 65.00**
Tumbler, ice green ....**700.00 to 800.00**
Tumbler, marigold...............................**41.00**
Tumbler, stippled, marigold **60.00**
Tumbler, purple **56.00**
Tumbler, stippled, purple **50.00**
Tumbler, tankard, blue........................**72.00**
Tumbler, tankard, green....**200.00 to 225.00**
Tumbler, tankard, marigold.................**48.00**
Tumbler, tankard, stippled,
marigold **65.00**
Tumbler, tankard, purple ....**45.00 to 55.00**
Tumbler, tankard, stippled, purple **89.00**
Water set: pitcher & 2 tumblers; blue,
3 pcs. **450.00**
Water set: pitcher & 2 tumblers;
purple, 3 pcs. **675.00**
Water set: pitcher & 6 tumblers;
green, 7 pcs..............**1,050.00 to 1,075.00**
Water set: pitcher & 6 tumblers;
marigold, 7 pcs. ....**500.00 to 550.00**
Water set: tankard pitcher
& 5 tumblers; marigold,
6 pcs. **1,650.00**
Whimsey compote (sweetmeat
base), purple **135.00**
Whimsey punch cup, green **100.00**
Whimsey punch cup, marigold.........**125.00**
Whimsey teacup, purple...**100.00 to 125.00**
Whiskey shot glass, marigold **165.00**
Whiskey shot glass, purple **173.00**

GREEK KEY (Northwood)
Bowl, 8" to 9" d., blue........................**500.00**
Bowl, 8" to 9" d., fluted, green **180.00**
Bowl, 8" to 9" d., ruffled, marigold........**85.00**
Bowl, 8" to 9" d., purple **118.00**
Bowl, 8" to 9" d., ruffled,
purple ....**150.00 to 200.00**
Bowl, eight-sided, 6½" w., 4" h.,
purple...**75.00**
Bowl, dome-footed, green...................**55.00**
Bowl, piecrust rim, blue w/electric
iridescence..................................**1,950.00**
Bowl, piecrust rim, green **400.00**
Pitcher, water, green...**1,300.00 to 1,400.00**
Pitcher, water, marigold.....................**600.00**
Pitcher, water, purple ....**500.00 to 700.00**
Plate, 9" d., blue............................**2,800.00**
Plate, 9" d., green..........................**1,100.00**
Plate, 9" d., marigold.......................**825.00**
Plate, 9" d., purple ....**300.00 to 400.00**
Tumbler, green...................**75.00 to 100.00**
Tumbler, marigold...............................**84.00**
Tumbler, purple ....**100.00 to 110.00**
Water set: pitcher & 4 tumblers;
purple, 5 pcs. **1,250.00**
Water set: pitcher & 6 tumblers;
marigold, 7 pcs. **1,125.00**

HEAVY IRIS (Dugan or Diamond Glass)
Pitcher, water, marigold ....**300.00 to 350.00**
Pitcher, water, tankard, mari-
gold..................................**300.00 to 350.00**
Tumbler, clambroth.............................**65.00**
Tumbler, marigold...............................**74.00**
Tumbler, pastel lavender **350.00**
Tumbler, purple **72.50**
Tumbler, white...................**200.00 to 250.00**
Water set: pitcher & 5 tumblers;
marigold, 6 pcs. ....**750.00 to 800.00**
Water set: pitcher & 6 tumblers;
purple, 7 pcs. **2,000.00**

**HOLLY WHIRL or HOLLY SPRIG
(Millersburg, Fenton & Dugan)**
Bowl, 6" w., tricornered, amethyst **125.00**
Bowl, 6" w., tricornered, green.............**85.00**
Bowl, 6" w., tricornered, marigold **295.00**
Bowl, 6" w., tricornered, purple..........**125.00**
Bowl, 6" d., ruffled, marigold...............**95.00**
Bowl, 6" d., ruffled, purple..................**92.50**
Bowl, 7" d., green...............................**60.00**
Bowl, 7" d., marigold **55.00**
Bowl, 7" d., ruffled, purple .....**55.00 to 60.00**
Bowl, 7" w., tricornered, marigold **160.00**
Bowl, 8" d., ice cream shape,
marigold, variant................................**68.00**
Bowl, 8" d., ice cream shape,
white...**110.00**
Bowl, 8" to 9" d., ruffled, blue..............**50.00**
Bowl, 8" to 9" d., green..........**75.00 to 85.00**
Bowl, 8" to 9" d., marigold...................**55.00**
Bowl, 8" to 9" d., peach opalescent **75.00**
Bowl, 8" to 9" d., purple ....**75.00 to 100.00**

Bowl, 10" d., ruffled, marigold 50.00
Bowl, 10" d., ruffled,
  purple ....100.00 to 125.00
Card tray, two-handled, marigold 65.00
Hat shape, green, 6" 38.00
Nappy, single handle, marigold............45.00
Nappy, single handle, peach
  opalescent (Dugan) 62.00
Nappy, single handle, purple
  (Dugan) ....75.00 to 100.00
Nappy, tricornered, green (Dugan) 110.00
Nappy, tricornered, marigold
  (Millersburg) 110.00
Nappy, tricornered, purple (Dugan) ...100.00
Nappy, tricornered, purple
  (Millersburg) ....175.00 to 200.00
Nappy, two-handled, amethyst
  (Millersburg) 68.00
Nappy, two-handled, green
  (Dugan) ....75.00 to 100.00
Nappy, two-handled, green
  (Millersburg) 80.00
Nut dish, two-handled, green 75.00
Nut dish, two-handled, marigold..........64.00
Nut dish, two-handled, purple.............72.50
Rose bowl, blue...................................300.00
Rose bowl, small, marigold 325.00
Sauceboat, peach opalescent
  (Dugan) 135.00
Sauce dish, green, 6½" d.
  (Millersburg) ....100.00 to 125.00
Sauce dish, deep, purple...................350.00

INVERTED STRAWBERRY (Cambridge)
Bowl, 6½" d., green, marked "Near-
  Cut"..52.00
Bowl, 7" d., green..............................125.00
Bowl, master berry, 10" d.,
  purple ....200.00 to 225.00
Candlestick, marigold........................128.00
Compote, open, 5" d., 6" h., mari-
  gold..225.00
Compote, open, giant,
  marigold............................225.00 to 250.00
Creamer, blue 300.00
Creamer, marigold.............300.00 to 350.00
Cuspidor, green............................1,000.00
Cuspidor, marigold............800.00 to 850.00
Pitcher, tankard, marigold.................950.00
Powder jar, cov., green .....150.00 to 200.00
Powder jar, cov., marigold..................100.00
Sherbet w/flared sides, blue 625.00
Spooner, purple..................................140.00
Sugar bowl, cov., green 250.00
Table set, marigold, 4 pcs...............1,000.00
Table set, purple, 4 pcs. 1,500.00
Tumbler, green 275.00
Tumbler, marigold ....125.00 to 150.00
Tumbler, purple ....175.00 to 200.00
Water set: pitcher & 1 tumbler;
  green, 2 pcs. 1,500.00
Water set: pitcher & 6 tumblers;
  marigold, 7 pcs. 1,700.00

Water set: pitcher & 6 tumblers;
  purple, 7 pcs. 3,750.00
Whimsey, made from two-handled
  nappy, marked "Near-Cut,"
  green...1,400.00

KITTENS (Fenton)

Kittens Dish

Bowl, cereal, blue ....450.00 to 500.00
Bowl, cereal, marigold 181.00
Bowl, ruffled, blue 775.00
Bowl, ruffled, marigold.......100.00 to 125.00
Bowl, four-sided, blue 350.00
Bowl, four-sided, ruffled, marigold 168.00
Bowl, six-sided, ruffled, mari-
  gold..................................175.00 to 200.00
Cup, blue 675.00
Cup, marigold 140.00
Cup & saucer, blue.........................2,600.00
Cup & saucer, marigold.....................225.00
Dish, turned-up sides, blue 550.00
Dish, turned-up sides, mari-
  gold (ILLUS.) ....150.00 to 200.00
Dish, turned-up sides, purple 525.00
Plate, 4½" d., marigold.......150.00 to 200.00
Spooner, blue 280.00
Spooner, marigold 150.00
Toothpick holder, blue .....400.00 to 475.00
Toothpick holder, marigold................177.00
Vase, marigold 225.00
Vase, child's, ruffled, marigold 145.00

LEAF & BEADS (Northwood)
Candy bowl, footed, green....65.00 to 70.00
Candy bowl, footed, marigold.............60.00
Candy bowl, footed, purple 55.00
Nut bowl, aqua opalescent................575.00
Nut bowl, handled, green 60.00
Nut bowl, handled, mari-
  gold..82.00
Nut bowl, handled, purple...................95.00
Rose bowl, aqua................................300.00
Rose bowl, aqua opales-
  cent..................................475.00 to 525.00
Rose bowl, blue..................................195.00

Rose bowl, blue w/electric irides-
cence ....**200.00 to 250.00**
Rose bowl, green **114.00**
Rose bowl, interior pattern,
green ....**75.00 to 85.00**
Rose bowl, ice blue **1,400.00**
Rose bowl, lime green.....................**450.00**
Rose bowl, marigold.........................**105.00**
Rose bowl, interior pattern, mari-
gold **80.00**
Rose bowl, olive green......**225.00 to 275.00**
Rose bowl, pastel marigold **50.00**

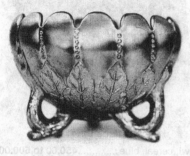

Leaf & Beads Rose Bowl

Rose bowl, purple (ILLUS.) **110.50**
Rose bowl, purple w/smooth
rim ....**350.00 to 375.00**
Rose bowl, interior pattern, purple **150.00**
Rose bowl, interior pattern, teal
blue **1,000.00**
Rose bowl, white **900.00**

LEAF RAYS NAPPY
Marigold...**30.00**
Peach opalescent................**45.00 to 50.00**
Purple **40.00**
Purple, "Souvenir of Cedar City,
Michigan" **60.00**
White..**52.50**

LITTLE FISHES (Fenton)

Little Fishes Bowl

Bowl, 6" d., three-footed, marigold.......**62.50**
Bowl, 8" to 9" d., three-footed, blue ...**245.00**
Bowl, 8" to 9" d., three-footed, mari-
gold **145.00**
Bowl, 10" d., three-footed,
blue (ILLUS.) ....**225.00 to 250.00**
Bowl, 10" d., three-footed,
marigold **147.50**
Bowl, 10" d., three-footed,
white **1,000.00**
Sauce dish, three-footed, aqua,
5" d..**210.00**
Sauce dish, three-footed, blue,
5" d..**90.00**
Sauce dish, three-footed, marigold,
5" d..**59.00**
Sauce dish, three-footed, purple,
5" d..**100.00**
Sauce dish, three-footed, vaseline,
5" d..**95.00**

MAPLE LEAF (Dugan)
Berry set: master bowl & 6 small
berry bowls; pedestaled, purple,
7 pcs. **300.00**
Bowl, 6" d., small berry, marigold **25.00**
Bowl, 6" d., small berry, purple **30.00**
Bowl, master berry or fruit, purple......**100.00**
Bowl, ice cream, footed, marigold........**35.00**
Butter dish, cov., blue **82.50**
Butter dish, cov., marigold **175.00**
Butter dish, cov., purple **195.00**
Creamer, marigold **42.00**
Creamer, purple **58.00**
Pitcher, water, blue...........................**277.50**
Spooner, blue **70.00**
Spooner, marigold **43.00**
Spooner, purple **60.00**
Table set, blue, 4 pcs.......................**295.00**
Tumbler, amber **75.00**
Tumbler, blue.....................................**65.00**
Tumbler, lavender..............................**150.00**
Tumbler, marigold...............................**26.00**
Tumbler, pastel marigold **75.00**
Tumbler, purple **38.00**
Water set: pitcher & 6 tumblers;
marigold, 7 pcs. ....**375.00 to 400.00**
Water set: pitcher & 6 tumblers;
purple, 7 pcs. ....**600.00 to 650.00**

NESTING SWAN (Millersburg)
Bowl, 9" d., green...............................**525.00**
Bowl, 9" d., marigold.........................**450.00**
Bowl, 10" d., amber...........................**325.00**
Bowl, 10" d., green ....**300.00 to 325.00**
Bowl, 10" d., marigold........**200.00 to 225.00**
Bowl, 10" d., purple ....**300.00 to 350.00**

OPEN ROSE (Imperial)
Berry set: master bowl & 6 sauce
dishes; purple, 7 pcs........................**290.00**
Bowl, 5" d., amber..............................**28.00**
Bowl, 5" d., blue................................**125.00**

Bowl, 5" d., marigold............................37.00
Bowl, 5" d., purple..............................45.00
Bowl, 7" d., amber...............................30.00
Bowl, 7" d., footed, blue.......................55.00
Bowl, 7" d., footed, marigold.................35.00
Bowl, 7" d., footed, purple....................64.00
Bowl, 7" d., footed, white 65.00
Bowl, 8" to 9" d., amber 65.00
Bowl, 8" to 9" d., aqua.........................45.00
Bowl, 8" to 9" d., green 40.00
Bowl, 8" to 9" d., marigold...................28.00
Bowl, 8" to 9" d., purple 72.00
Bowl, 8" to 9" d., smoky 62.50
Bowl, 8" to 9" d., footed, vaseline 150.00
Bowl, 8" to 9" d., white 95.00
Bowl, 10" d., amber ....175.00 to 200.00
Bowl, 10" d., marigold..........................85.00
Bowl, 11" d., marigold..........................35.00
Bowl, 11" d., smoky 75.00
Fernery, three-footed, blue 45.00
Fernery, three-footed, smoky............110.00
Plate, 9" d., amber..............................195.00
Plate, 9" d., clambroth........................145.00
Plate, 9" d., green ....100.00 to 125.00
Plate, 9" d., marigold..........................100.00
Plate, 9" d., purple..............................850.00
Rose bowl, amber 65.00
Rose bowl, green 50.00
Rose bowl, marigold.............................48.00
Spooner, marigold 28.00
Sugar bowl, open, aqua 85.00

ORIENTAL POPPY (Northwood)
Pitcher, water, green 1,250.00
Pitcher, water,
   marigold.........................475.00 to 500.00
Pitcher, water, purple.......................950.00
Tumbler, blue.....................................200.00
Tumbler, green 57.50
Tumbler, ice blue...............................155.00
Tumbler, ice green ....375.00 to 425.00
Tumbler, lilac 39.00
Tumbler, marigold...............................42.00
Tumbler, pastel marigold 45.00
Tumbler, purple 57.50
Tumbler, white..................150.00 to 175.00
Water set: pitcher & 1 tumbler;
   white, 2 pcs. 1,900.00
Water set: pitcher & 6 tumblers;
   green, 7 pcs. 1,850.00
Water set: pitcher & 6 tumblers;
   ice blue, 7 pcs..............................5,000.00
Water set: pitcher & 6 tumblers;
   marigold, 7 pcs. ....825.00 to 850.00
Water set: pitcher & 6 tumblers;
   purple, 7 pcs. 1,550.00

PANSY and PANSY SPRAY
Bowl, 8" to 9" d., amber 50.00
Bowl, 8" to 9" d., green 70.50
Bowl, 8" to 9" d., marigold...................37.50
Bowl, 8" to 9" d., purple .....100.00 to 125.00
Bowl, 9" d., fluted, marigold.................65.00

Pansy Bowl

Bowl, 9" d., fluted, purple (ILLUS.).......75.00
Bowl, 9" d., stippled, purple 100.00
Bowl, 9" d., ruffled, smoky 95.00
Breakfast set: individual size
   creamer & sugar bowl; purple, pr.......35.00
Creamer, amber...................................85.00
Creamer, green....................................44.00
Creamer, marigold 25.00
Creamer, purple 38.00
Creamer & sugar bowl, marigold, pr. ...60.00
Creamer & sugar bowl, purple,
   pr. ....100.00 to 125.00
Dresser tray, amber ....150.00 to 200.00
Dresser tray, marigold ....50.00 to 75.00
Nappy, green 45.00
Nappy, marigold...................................25.00
Nappy, purple......................................60.00
Plate, 9" d., ruffled, marigold................75.00
Plate, 9" d., ruffled, purple...................85.00
Spooner, green....................................35.00
Sugar bowl, aqua 110.00
Sugar bowl, green 55.00
Sugar bowl, marigold 18.00

PEACOCK & GRAPE (Fenton)
Bowl, 8" d., collared base, amber 120.00
Bowl, 8" d., collared base, blue............53.00
Bowl, 8" d., collared base, ruffled,
   green..92.50
Bowl, 8" d., collared base, ruffled,
   ice green...225.00
Bowl, 8" d., collared base, marigold.....40.00
Bowl, 8" d., collared base, purple 76.00
Bowl, 8" d., collared base, ruffled,
   red...1,200.00
Bowl, 8" d., collared base, smoky 585.00
Bowl, 8" d., collared base, vaseline ...275.00
Bowl, 8" d., collared base, ribbon
   candy rim, blue 80.00
Bowl, 8" d., collared base, ribbon
   candy rim, lavender 75.00
Bowl, 8" d., spatula-footed, blue 50.00
Bowl, 8" d., spatula-footed, green........72.00
Bowl, 8" d., spatula-footed, ice green
   opalescent ....350.00 to 375.00

Bowl, 8" d., spatula-footed, lavender............................**150.00 to 200.00**
Bowl, 8" d., spatula-footed, marigold ...**60.00**
Bowl, 8" d., spatula-footed, milk white w/marigold overlay...........................**360.00**
Bowl, 8" d., spatula-footed, peach opalescent.........................**325.00 to 350.00**
Bowl, 8" d., spatula-footed, purple.......**68.00**
Bowl, 8" d., spatula-footed, red....................................**800.00 to 850.00**
Bowl, 8" d., spatula-footed, smoky.......**90.00**
Bowl, 8" d., spatula-footed, vaseline opalescent......................**450.00 to 550.00**
Bowl, ice cream shape, Amberina **650.00**
Bowl, 8" d., ice cream shape, green **82.50**
Bowl, 8" d., ice cream shape, marigold...**91.50**
Bowl, 8" d., ice cream shape, red ...**1,475.00**
Bowl, 9" d., ice cream shape, red **695.00**
Bowl, ice cream shape, collared base, vaseline...............................**185.00**
Bowl, 9" d., ruffled, collared base, blue................................**100.00 to 150.00**
Bowl, 9" d., ruffled, ice blue w/marigold overlay............................**195.00**
Bowl, 9" d., ruffled, ice blue w/smoky overlay...............................**395.00**
Bowl, 9" d., ruffled, purple....................**75.00**
Bowl, 9" d., ruffled, red.........................**300.00**
Bowl, fluted, aqua...............................**135.00**
Bowl, ruffled, iridized moonstone......**325.00**
Plate, 9" d., collared base, blue..........**325.00**
Plate, 9" d., collared base, marigold...**287.50**
Plate, 9" d., flat base, marigold **525.00**
Plate, 9" d., collared base, berry exterior, smoky ice blue...................**800.00**
Plate, 9" d., spatula-footed, green ....**150.00 to 175.00**
Plate, 9" d., spatula-footed, marigold...**350.00**
Plate, 9" d., spatula-footed, purple...**225.00**

PEACOCK & URN (Millersburg, Fenton & Northwood)
Berry set: master bowl & 5 sauce dishes; purple, 6 pcs. ......**750.00 to 850.00**
Bowl, 5½" d., ruffled, blue (Millersburg)....................................**1,240.00**
Bowl, 5¾" d., ice cream shape, purple, variant.................................**550.00**
Bowl, 6" d., ice cream shape, blue, stippled **175.00**
Bowl, 6" d., ice cream shape, green (Millersburg)...................................**325.00**
Bowl, 6" d., ice cream shape, ice green..**315.00**
Bowl, 6" d., ice cream shape, marigold (Millersburg)...............................**75.00**
Bowl, 6" d., ice cream shape, marigold (Northwood)..............................**50.00**
Bowl, 6" d., ice cream shape, purple..**87.50**

Bowl, 6" d., ice cream shape, purple (Millersburg)...................**300.00 to 325.00**
Bowl, 6" d., ice cream shape, purple satin **195.00**
Bowl, 6" d., ice cream shape, white...**150.00**
Bowl, 7" d., ruffled, blue (Millersburg)..**400.00**
Bowl, 7" d., ruffled, green (Millersburg)..**250.00**
Bowl, 7" d., ruffled, marigold (Millersburg)...................................**395.00**
Bowl, 7" d., ruffled, purple (Millersburg)..**350.00**
Bowl, 8" d., collared base, moonstone (Fenton) **1,825.00**
Bowl, 8" d., ice cream shape, green (Fenton)..........................**250.00 to 300.00**
Bowl, 8" d., ice cream shape, ice blue **350.00**
Bowl, 8" d., ice cream shape, marigold (Fenton) **108.00**
Bowl, 8" d., ice cream shape, Beaded Berry exterior, purple **275.00**
Bowl, 8" d., ice cream shape, white **350.00**
Bowl, 8" to 9" d., blue (Fenton) **250.00**
Bowl, 8" to 9" d., green (Fenton).......**300.00**
Bowl, 8" to 9" d., green (Millersburg)...........................**400.00 to 425.00**
Bowl, 8" to 9" d., marigold (Fenton) ...**123.50**
Bowl, 8" to 9" d., ruffled, marigold (Millersburg)...................**200.00 to 250.00**
Bowl, 8" to 9" d., purple (Fenton).......**180.00**
Bowl, 8" to 9" d., purple (Millersburg)...........................**275.00 to 300.00**
Bowl, 8" to 9" d., white (Fenton) **250.00**
Bowl, 9" d., ruffled, blue ....**175.00 to 200.00**
Bowl, 9" d., ruffled, purple (Fenton) **400.00**
Bowl, 9" d., ruffled, purple (Millersburg) **3,500.00**
Bowl, 9" d., ruffled, vaseline..............**675.00**
Bowl, 9½" d., berry, purple (Millersburg) **525.00**
Bowl, 10" d., fluted, green (Millersburg) **400.00**
Bowl, 10" d., fluted, lavender (Millersburg) **600.00**
Bowl, 10" d., fluted, marigold (Millersburg) **275.00**
Bowl, 10" d., ruffled, marigold...........**150.00**
Bowl, 10" d., ruffled, pastel marigold (Northwood) **650.00**
Bowl, 10" d., ruffled, purple ....**400.00 to 450.00**
Bowl, ice cream shape, 10" d., aqua opalescent (Northwood).............**25,000.00**
Bowl, ice cream shape, 10" d., blue (Northwood) **625.00**
Bowl, ice cream shape, 10" d., blue, stippled **1,250.00**
Bowl, ice cream shape, 10" d., blue w/electric iridescence (Northwood) **1,450.00**

Bowl, ice cream shape, 10" d., green
(Northwood) **2,500.00**

Bowl, ice cream shape, 10" d., green,
w/bee (Millersburg) **935.00**

Bowl, ice cream shape, 10" d., ice
blue (Northwood) ....**900.00 to 1,000.00**

Bowl, ice cream shape, 10" d., ice
green (Northwood) ....**1,200.00 to 1,300.00**

Bowl, ice cream shape, 10" d., mari-
gold (Millersburg) **375.00**

Bowl, ice cream shape, 10" d.,
marigold (Northwood) ......**450.00 to 500.00**

Bowl, ice cream shape, 10" d., pastel
marigold (Northwood) ......**650.00 to 700.00**

Bowl, ice cream shape, 10" d.,
stippled, pastel marigold
(Northwood) **485.00**

Bowl, ice cream shape, 10" d.,
periwinkle blue (Northwood) **4,000.00**

Bowl, ice cream shape, 10" d., purple
(Millersburg) **465.00**

Bowl, ice cream shape, 10" d., purple
(Northwood) ....**650.00 to 700.00**

Bowl, ice cream shape, 10" d., smoky
(Northwood) **900.00**

Bowl, ice cream shape, 10" d., white
(Northwood) ....**575.00 to 600.00**

Bowl, 10½" d., ruffled, green (Millers-
burg) ....**350.00 to 400.00**

Bowl, 10½" d., ruffled, marigold (Millers-
burg) **250.00**

Bowl, 10½" d., ruffled,
purple ....**250.00 to 300.00**

Bowl, 10½" d., ruffled, purple (Millersburg) ....**400.00 to 450.00**

Compote, 5½" d., 5" h., aqua
(Fenton)............................**200.00 to 225.00**

Compote, 5½" d., 5" h., blue
(Fenton) **100.00**

Compote, 5½" d., 5" h., green
(Fenton) **230.00**

Compote, 5½" d., 5" h., ice green
(Fenton) **135.00**

Compote, 5½" d., 5" h., marigold
(Fenton) **61.00**

Compote, 5½" d., 5" h., marigold over
ice blue (Fenton) **85.00**

Compote, 5½" d., 5" h., red
(Fenton) **800.00**

Compote, 5½" d., 5" h., vaseline
(Fenton) **150.00**

Compote, 5½" d., 5" h., white
(Fenton) ....**250.00 to 300.00**

Compote, green (Millersburg
Giant).............................**1,350.00 to 1,400.00**

Compote, marigold (Millersburg
Giant)...**1,900.00**

Compote, purple (Millersburg
Giant) **3,000.00**

Goblet, Marigold (Fenton) **50.00**

Ice cream dish, purple, 5¾" d.
(Millersburg) ....**350.00 to 400.00**

Ice cream dish, aqua opalescent,
small (Northwood)..........................**1,500.00**

Ice cream dish, stippled, blue, small
(Northwood) **145.00**

Ice cream dish, blue, small (North-
wood) **82.50**

Ice cream dish, blue w/electric
iridescence......................................**175.00**

Ice cream dish, ice blue, small **600.00**

Ice cream dish, ice green, small **425.00**

Ice cream dish, lavender, small
(Northwood) **225.00**

Ice cream dish, marigold, small **85.00**

Ice cream dish, purple, small **86.00**

Ice cream dish, white, small **200.00**

Ice cream set: large bowl & 6 small
dishes; purple, 7 pcs. (Millers-
burg) ....**800.00 to 1,000.00**

Plate, 6½" d., green (Millersburg)....**3,600.00**

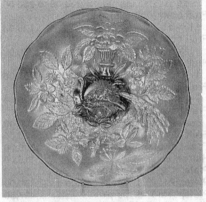

Peacock & Urn Plate

Plate, 6½" d., marigold, Millersburg
(ILLUS.) **275.00**

Plate, 6½" d., purple (Millersburg)......**500.00**

Plate, 9" d., blue
(Fenton) ....**500.00 to 525.00**

Plate, 9" d., marigold (Fenton) **408.00**

Plate, 9" d., white
(Fenton) ....**450.00 to 500.00**

Plate, chop, 11" d., marigold
(Millersburg) **2,200.00**

Plate, chop, 11" d., marigold
(Northwood) **995.00**

Plate, chop, 11" d., purple
(Millersburg) **3,500.00**

Plate, chop, 11" d., purple
(Northwood) ....**1,200.00 to 1,400.00**

Sauce dish, blue (Millersburg) **250.00**

Sauce dish, blue (Northwood) **120.00**

Sauce dish, green (Millersburg) **75.00**

Sauce dish, ice blue (Northwood) **200.00**

Sauce dish, ice blue, 6" d. **70.00**

Sauce dish, ice green, 6" d. (North-
wood) **415.00**

Sauce dish, lavender (Millersburg)......**45.00**

Sauce dish, marigold (Millersburg).....**65.00**

Sauce dish, purple (Millersburg)........**125.00**

Sauce dish, purple (Northwood) **100.00**

Sauce dish, white (Northwood) **185.00**

Whimsey sauce dish, marigold, 5¼" d.
(Millersburg) 175.00
Whimsey sauce dish, purple,
5¼" d. ....275.00 to 300.00

PERSIAN GARDEN (Dugan)
Bowl, 5" d., peach opalescent.............45.00
Bowl, 5" d., white 81.50
Bowl, ice cream shape, 6" d., white.....65.00
Bowl, 9" d., ruffled, marigold...............150.00
Bowl, ice cream shape, 11" d.,
lavender tint 345.00
Bowl, ice cream shape, 11" d.,
peach opalescent ....850.00 to 900.00
Bowl, ice cream shape, 11" d.,
purple 800.00
Bowl, ice cream shape, 11" d.,
white ....225.00 to 250.00
Fruit bowl (no base), marigold,
11½" d...125.00
Fruit bowl (no base), peach
opalescent, 11½" d..........................350.00
Fruit bowl (no base), white,
11½" d..250.00
Fruit bowl & base, marigold,
2 pcs. 225.00
Fruit bowl & base, peach
opalescent, 2 pcs. 650.00
Fruit bowl & base, purple, 2 pcs. 800.00
Fruit bowl & base, white, 2 pcs.........500.00
Hair receiver, blue 115.00
Plate, 6" to 7" d., marigold..................80.50
Plate, 6" to 7" d., pastel marigold 50.00
Plate, 6" to 7" d., purple 487.50
Plate, 6" to 7" d., white 188.00
Plate, chop, 11" d., purple 5,500.00

QUESTION MARKS
Bonbon, footed, marigold,
6" d., 3¾" h. 38.00
Bonbon, footed, peach opalescent,
6" d., 3¾" h. 80.00
Bonbon, footed, purple, 6" d.,
3¾" h..47.50
Bonbon, footed, white, 6" d.,
3¾" h...130.00
Bonbon, stemmed, marigold 38.50
Bonbon, stemmed, peach
opalescent 45.00
Bonbon, stemmed, purple 60.00
Bonbon, stemmed, white.....................48.00
Compote, crimped edge, marigold 47.50
Compote, crimped edge, peach
opalescent 83.00
Plate, dome-footed, Georgia Peach
exterior, purple................................250.00
Plate, stemmed, marigold 80.00
Plate, stemmed, white.......................325.00

RASPBERRY (Northwood)
Pitcher, milk, green.............................250.00
Pitcher, milk, ice blue ..1,900.00 to 2,100.00
Pitcher, milk, marigold 180.50

Pitcher, milk, purple 290.00
Pitcher, milk, white ......1,000.00 to 1,200.00
Pitcher, water, green ....295.00 to 355.00
Pitcher, water, ice blue 2,100.00
Pitcher, water, marigold.....................125.00
Pitcher, water, purple ....225.00 to 250.00
Sauceboat, green 225.00
Sauceboat, marigold............................70.00
Sauceboat, purple 80.00
Tumbler, aqua 295.00
Tumbler, green 51.00
Tumbler, ice blue...............275.00 to 300.00
Tumbler, ice green ....550.00 to 650.00
Tumbler, marigold.................................32.00
Tumbler, purple 41.00
Tumbler, white....................................675.00
Water set: pitcher & 4 tumblers;
marigold, 5 pcs. 400.00
Water set: pitcher & 5 tumblers;
green, 6 pcs. 675.00
Water set: pitcher & 5 tumblers;
purple, 6 pcs. 490.00
Water set: pitcher & 6 tumblers;
blue, 7 pcs. 850.00

ROSE SHOW

Rose Show Plate

Bowl, 9" d., aqua ....650.00 to 750.00
Bowl, 9" d., aqua opalescent 1,400.00
Bowl, 9" d., blue 566.00
Bowl, 9" d., blue opales-
cent.........................1,500.00 to 1,950.00
Bowl, 9" d., blue w/electric irides-
cence 1,250.00
Bowl, 9" d., green............................3,400.00
Bowl, 9" d., ice blue.........................1,600.00
Bowl, 9" d., ice green...1,500.00 to 2,000.00
Bowl, 9" d., ice green opalescent....2,150.00
Bowl, 9" d., lavender.......................3,500.00
Bowl, 9" d., marigold.........................552.00
Bowl, 9" d., purple 1,275.00
Bowl, 9" d., sapphire blue 3,200.00
Bowl, 9" d., smoky 1,100.00
Bowl, 9" d., white..............400.00 to 450.00
Plate, 9" d., aqua opalescent 8,000.00
Plate, 9" d., blue ....1,200.00 to 1,400.00

Plate, 9" d., clambroth......................1,350.00
Plate, 9" d., custard.........................4,500.00
Plate, 9" d., electric green...............7,500.00
Plate, 9" d., green (ILLUS.)............3,600.00
Plate, 9" d., ice blue.....1,800.00 to 2,000.00
Plate, 9" d., marigold.........600.00 to 650.00
Plate, 9" d., moonstone...................7,000.00
Plate, 9" d., pastel mari-
  gold..........................1,000.00 to 1,500.00
Plate, 9" d., purple...........................1,500.00
Plate, 9" d., vaseline.......................3,400.00
Plate, 9" d., white..............425.00 to 475.00

SHELL & JEWEL
Creamer, cov., green.........................40.00
Creamer, cov., marigold......................30.00
Creamer & cov. sugar bowl, green,
  pr...90.00
Sugar bowl, cov., green.....................65.00
Sugar bowl, cov., marigold..................35.00

SINGING BIRDS (Northwood)

Singing Birds Water Set

Berry set: master bowl & 3 sauce
  dishes; green, 4 pcs..........................132.00
Berry set: master bowl & 6 sauce
  dishes; purple, 7 pcs. 325.00
Bowl, ice cream shape, green.............48.00
Bowl, ice cream shape, marigold.........48.00
Bowl, master berry, blue...................225.00
Butter dish, cov., purple...................350.00
Creamer, green...............................150.00
Creamer, marigold.............................52.00
Creamer, purple.................125.00 to 150.00
Mug, aqua
  opalescent.................1,000.00 to 1,550.00
Mug, blue.......................................194.00
Mug, stippled, blue............................575.00
Mug, blue w/electric irides-
  cence............................200.00 to 250.00
Mug, green.......................................262.50
Mug, stippled, green..........................424.00
Mug, ice blue.....................750.00 to 800.00
Mug, lavender...................................400.00
Mug, marigold....................125.00 to 150.00
Mug, stippled, marigold......................139.50
Mug, purple......................................151.00
Mug, purple, w/advertising, "Amazon
  Hotel"...125.00
Mug, white..585.00

Pitcher, green....................275.00 to 325.00
Pitcher, marigold...............250.00 to 275.00
Pitcher, purple..................................545.00
Sauce dish, blue................................65.00
Sauce dish, blue w/electric irides-
  cence.............................200.00 to 250.00
Sauce dish, green..............................28.00
Sauce dish, marigold..........................32.00
Spooner, green................................150.00
Spooner, marigold..............................62.00
Sugar bowl, cov.,
  marigold..........................90.00 to 100.00
Table set, purple, 4 pcs. 750.00
Tumbler, amber.................................60.00
Tumbler, green..................................80.00
Tumbler, green w/marigold overlay.....60.00
Tumbler, marigold.................40.00 to 45.00
Tumbler, purple.................................62.50
Water set: pitcher & 6 tumblers;
  green, 7 pcs. (ILLUS.)...................1,045.00
Water set: pitcher & 6 tumblers;
  purple, 7 pcs. 795.00

STAR OF DAVID (Imperial)

Star of David Bowl

Bowl, 7" d., ruffled, purple.................140.00
Bowl, 8" to 9" d., collared base, blue ...75.00
Bowl, 8" to 9" d., collared base, green
  (ILLUS.) 105.00
Bowl, 8" to 9" d., collared base,
  marigold..48.00
Bowl, 8" to 9" d., collared base,
  purple...85.00
Bowl, 9" d., flat, ruffled,
  purple ....80.00 to 100.00

STIPPLED RAYS
Bonbon, two-handled, celeste blue ...325.00
Bonbon, two-handled, green...............46.50
Bonbon, two-handled, lime green......200.00
Bonbon, two-handled, marigold..........37.50
Bonbon, two-handled, purple.............47.00
Bonbon, two-handled, red.................350.00
Bowl, 5" d., Amberina.......................175.00
Bowl, 5" d., blue................................50.00

Bowl, 5" d., green..............................33.00
Bowl, 5" d., marigold........................20.00
Bowl, 5" d., purple............................30.00
Bowl, 5" d., red ....350.00 to 400.00
Bowl, 6" d., Amberina 225.00
Bowl, 6½" d., ruffled, red...................410.00
Bowl, 6½" d., ruffled, reverse
  Amberina 295.00
Bowl, 7" d., dome-footed, green 32.00
Bowl, 7" d., red................................250.00
Bowl, 7" d., ruffled rim, red.................450.00
Bowl, 8" to 9" d., blue.......................225.00
Bowl, 8" to 9" d., green.......................60.00
Bowl, 8" to 9" d., ribbon candy rim,
  green..75.00
Bowl, 8" to 9" d., marigold...................32.00
Bowl, 8" to 9" d., purple 46.00
Bowl, 8" to 9" d., ribbon candy rim,
  purple..70.00
Bowl, 8" to 9" d., red 605.00
Bowl, 10" d., green..............................65.00
Bowl, 10" d., ruffled, green.................110.00
Bowl, 10" d., ruffled, lavender 75.00
Bowl, 10" d., ruffled, marigold.............40.00

Stippled Rays Bowl

Bowl, 10" d., piecrust rim, purple
  (ILLUS.) 51.00
Bowl, 10" d., white............150.00 to 200.00
Bowl, 10" w., tricornered, crimped
  rim, green.......................................85.00
Bowl, 11" d., Basketweave exterior,
  ruffled, marigold 60.00
Bowl, 11" sq., dome-footed, ribbon
  candy rim, green 115.00
Bowl, dome-footed, Greek Key &
  Scales exterior, purple 90.00
Bowl, Wild Rose exterior, green 75.00
Bowl, Wild Rose exterior, purple........110.00
Creamer, blue 25.00
Creamer & sugar bowl, marigold,
  pr...45.00
Plate, 6" to 7" d., green 95.00
Plate, 6" to 7" d., marigold..................42.00
Plate, 6" to 7" d., red 1,250.00
Rose bowl, green..............................80.00

Rose bowl, purple..............................65.00
Sherbet, Amberina............................275.00
Sugar bowl, individual size,
  marigold...10.00
Sugar bowl, open, blue 25.00
Sugar bowl, open, marigold 18.00

THIN RIB VASE
7" h., ice blue (Northwood) 500.00
8" h., green 30.00
9" h., aqua opalescent 85.00
9" h., blue...35.00
9" h., green 40.00
9" h., jack-in-the-pulpit shape, green ...75.00
9" h., teal blue.................................105.00
9½" h., green (Northwood)..................45.00
10" h., blue..35.00
10" h., green (Northwood)...................40.00
10" h., marigold..................................40.00
10" h., purple (Northwood)..................32.50
10" h., white.......................................70.00
10½" h., peach opalescent 40.00
11" h., aqua opalescent 125.00
11" h., green 75.00
11" h., pastel olive............................60.00
12" h., aqua 75.00
12" h., blue..40.00
12" h., green 92.50
12" h., purple.....................................45.00
13" h., aqua opalescent
  (Northwood) 1,100.00
13" h., green ....100.00 to 125.00
13" h., purple....................................100.00
13" h., funeral, white 200.00
14" h., funeral, green (Northwood).....100.00
14" h., funeral, purple........................135.00
16½" h., green 135.00

TIGER LILY (Imperial)

Tiger Lily Pitcher

Pitcher, water, green
  (ILLUS.) ....150.00 to 200.00
Pitcher, water, purple........................365.00
Tumbler, blue....................................250.00
Tumbler, clambroth............................65.00
Tumbler, green 45.00
Tumbler, marigold...............................30.00

Tumbler, olive green............................115.00
Tumbler, purple 80.00
Water set: pitcher & 2 tumblers;
   green, 3 pcs. 390.00
Water set: pitcher & 4 tumblers;
   marigold, 5 pcs. 310.00
Water set: pitcher & 6 tumblers;
   aqua, 7 pcs. 2,205.00

TWO FLOWERS (Fenton)

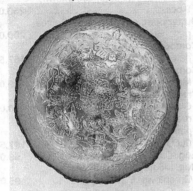

Two Flowers Large Bowl

Bonbon, stemmed, blue 85.00
Bowl, 6" d., footed, blue.......................75.00
Bowl, 6" d., footed, lime green.............45.00
Bowl, 6" d., footed, marigold...............38.00
Bowl, 6" d., footed, purple....................75.00
Bowl, 6" d., footed,
   vaseline ....100.00 to 125.00
Bowl, 7" to 8" d., footed, blue...............60.00
Bowl, 7" to 8" d., footed, clambroth......90.00
Bowl, 7" to 8" d., footed,
   green..82.50
Bowl, 7" to 8" d., footed, marigold........55.00
Bowl, 7" to 8" d., footed, fluted,
   purple...47.00
Bowl, 7" to 8" d., footed, red 2,247.00
Bowl, 8" d., footed,
   Amberina...................1,500.00 to 1,900.00
Bowl, 8" d., collared base,
   marigold.........................100.00 to 125.00
Bowl, 8" d., collared base, ice cream
   shape, marigold 140.00
Bowl, 8½" d., footed, blue....................99.00
Bowl, 9" d., footed, marigold...............75.00
Bowl, 9" d., footed, ice cream shape,
   marigold 115.00
Bowl, 9½" d., ruffled, purple...............150.00
Bowl, 10" d., footed, scalloped rim,
   blue 85.00
Bowl, 10" d., footed, scalloped rim,
   green..75.00
Bowl, 10" d., footed, scalloped rim,
   marigold (ILLUS.)...............................62.50
Bowl, 10" d., footed, scalloped rim,
   purple...135.00
Bowl, 10" d., footed, blue ..100.00 to 125.00
Bowl, 10" d., footed, marigold..............90.00

Bowl, 10" d., ruffled, footed, red......2,000.00
Bowl, 10" d., footed, vaseline.............350.00
Bowl, 10" d., footed, white 750.00
Bowl, 10½" d., ruffled, blue 162.00
Bowl, 11" d., aqua.............................650.00
Bowl, 11" d., green..........................1,050.00
Bowl, 11" d., footed, ruffled, purple....750.00
Bowl, 11" d., ice cream shape, blue...125.00
Bowl, 11" d., ice cream shape, mari-
   gold 40.00
Bowl, 11½" d., footed, blue 125.00
Bowl, 11½" d., ball footed, marigold 55.00
Plate, 6½" d., marigold......................125.00
Plate, 9" d., footed, marigold.............425.00
Plate, chop, 11½" d., three-footed,
   marigold...350.00
Plate, chop, 13" d., three-footed,
   marigold...575.00
Rose bowl, three-footed,
   blue...............................190.00 to 200.00
Rose bowl, three-footed,
   marigold...........................50.00 to 75.00
Rose bowl, three-footed, purple 257.00

WAFFLE BLOCK

Basket w/tall handle, clambroth,
   10" h...55.00
Basket w/tall handle, marigold,
   10" h...51.00
Basket w/tall handle, pastel marigold,
   10" h...145.00
Basket w/tall handle, teal, 10" h..........95.00
Bowl, 7½" sq., marigold 36.00
Bowl, 8½" d., clambroth.......................55.00
Compote, clambroth 135.00
Creamer, clambroth 35.00
Pitcher, water, marigold.....................102.50
Punch bowl & base, mari-
   gold.................................150.00 to 175.00
Punch cup, marigold 12.00
Sugar bowl, clambroth 30.00
Tumbler, marigold 215.00

WILD ROSE

Wild Rose Bowl

Bowl, 5½" d., three-footed, open
   heart rim, green 47.00

Bowl, 7" d., three-footed, open
heart rim, green, Northwood
(ILLUS.) ....**65.00 to 75.00**
Bowl, 7" d., three-footed, open heart
rim, marigold (Northwood) **52.00**
Bowl, 7" d., three-footed, open heart
rim, purple (Northwood).......**50.00 to 70.00**
Bowl, 8" to 9" d., marigold
(Northwood) **32.50**
Bowl, 8" to 9" d., green (Northwood) ...**38.00**
Candy dish, open edge, blue,
5¾" d..**150.00**
Candy dish, open edge, green............**70.00**
Candy dish, open edge, purple **90.00**
Lamp, three portrait medallions,
w/original burner & etched chimney
shade, green, small (Millersburg) **850.00**
Lamp, w/original burner & etched
chimney shade, green, medium
(Millersburg) ....**1,250.00 to 1,450.00**
Lamp, w/original burner & etched
chimney shade, marigold, medium
(Millersburg) ....**1,100.00 to 1,300.00**
Lamp, w/original burner & etched
chimney shade, purple
(Millersburg) **1,400.00**
Syrup pitcher, marigold ....**750.00 to 850.00**

ZIPPERED LOOP LAMP (Imperial)
Hand, marigold, 4½" h.....................**1,200.00**
Hand, marigold, medium....**625.00 to 650.00**
Sewing, marigold, small.....................**325.00**
Sewing, marigold,
medium...........................**600.00 to 675.00**
Sewing, smoky,
medium...........................**925.00 to 975.00**
Sewing, marigold,
large ....**550.00 to 575.00**

(End of Carnival Glass Section)

CHOCOLATE

Leaf Bracket Cruet

*This glass is often called Caramel Slag.
It was made by the Indiana Tumbler and
Goblet Company of Greentown, Indiana,
and other glasshouses, beginning at the
turn of this century. Various patterns were
produced, highly popular among them
being Cactus and Leaf Bracket.*

Berry set: master bowl & 8 sauce
dishes; Cactus patt., Greentown,
9 pcs. **$250.00**
Butter dish, cov., flat base, Cactus
patt., Greentown **200.00**
Compote, open, 5¼" d., Cactus
patt., Greentown **167.50**
Compote, jelly, Geneva patt.,
McKee..**129.00**
Creamer, Leaf Bracket patt.,
Greentown **80.00**
Cruet w/original stopper, Leaf Bracket
patt., Greentown
(ILLUS.) **187.50**
Mug, Cactus patt., Greentown **50.00**
Mug, Indoor Drinking Scene,
Greentown, 5" h................................**95.00**
Mug, Outdoor Drinking Scene,
Greentown **134.00**
Nappy, triangular, handled, Leaf
Bracket patt., Greentown **49.00**
Pitcher, water, 9" h., Racing Deer
and Doe patt., Greentown...............**622.50**
Pitcher, 6" h., Shuttle patt.,
Greentown **160.00**
Pitcher, water, Squirrel patt.,
Greentown **615.00**
Plate, 6¼" d., Serenade (or
Troubadour) patt., McKee...............**185.00**
Salt shaker w/original top, Cactus
patt., Greentown **57.50**
Sauce dish, Cactus patt.,
Greentown **50.00**
Spooner, Geneva patt. **115.00**
Sugar bowl, cov., Leaf Bracket patt.,
Greentown **85.00**
Syrup jug w/original metal top,
Cactus patt., Green-
town ....**175.00 to 225.00**
Toothpick holder, Cactus patt.,
Greentown **58.00**
Tumbler, Leaf Bracket patt.,
Greentown **58.00**
Tumbler, finely ribbed band around
the bottom, Greentown **95.00**

CONSOLIDATED
*The Consolidated Lamp and Glass
Compony of Coraopolis, Pennsylvania was
founded in 1894 and for a number of years
was noted for its lighting wares but also
produced popular lines of pressed and*

blown tablewares. Highly collectible glass patterns of this early era include the Cone, Cosmos, Florette and Guttate lines.

Lamps and shades continued to be good sellers but in 1926 a new "art" line of molded decorative wares was introduced. This "Martelé" line was developed as a direct imitation of the fine glasswares being produced by René Lalique of France and many Consolidated patterns resembled their French counterparts. Other popular lines produced during the 1920s and 1930s were "Dancing Nymph," the delightfully Art Deco "Ruba Rombic," introduced in 1928, and the "Catalonian" line, imitating 17th century Spanich glass, which debuted in 1927.

Although the factory closed in 1933, it was reopened under new management in 1936 and prospered through the 1940s. It finally closed in 1967. Collectors should note that many later Consolidated patterns closely resemble wares of other competing firms, especially the Phoenix Glass Company. Careful study is needed to determine the maker of pieces from the 1920-40 era.

A recent book which will be of help to collectors is Phoenix & Consolidated Art Glass, 1926-1980, by Jack D. Wilson (Antique Publications, 1989).

Florette Cracker Jar

LATER LINES
Lamp, table model, brass base & shade cap, Foxglove patt., Martelé line, satin custard ground.................**170.00**
Vase, 6" h., Screech Owls patt., Martelé line, gold decoration on a milk white ground............................**300.00**

CORALENE

Orange Coralene Creamer

Coralene is a method of decorating glass, usually satin glass, with the use of a beaded-type decoration customarily applied to the glass with the use of enamels, which were melted. Coralene decoration has been faked with the use of glue.

Creamer, spherical body tapering to a cylindrical neck, applied amber handle, orange body decorated w/amber rigaree around neck,

Consolidated Martelé Label

BULGING LOOPS
Creamer, cased pink.........................**$65.00**
Sugar bowl, cov., cased pink **115.00**
Syrup pitcher w/original top, cased pink......................................**245.00**
Toothpick holder, green, opaque **75.00**

CONE
Salt shaker w/original top, green opaque, tall **60.00**
Sugar shaker w/original top, blue opaque, tall **60.00**
Sugar shaker w/original top, green, opaque, glossy finish **190.00**
Sugar shaker w/original top, cased pink **245.00**

FLORETTE
Cracker jar w/original glass cover, cased pink, Regent line, ca. 1940s (ILLUS. top next column) **198.00**

colored enamel water lilies & leaves decoration covered w/coralene beading, enamelled, marked "Patent," 3¾" d., 6½" h. (ILLUS.) **$225.00**

Blue Coralene Vase

Vase, 4½" h., 3⅞" d., bulbous body on a round foot, tapering to a slightly flaring cylindrical neck w/gold trim, heavenly blue ground w/yellow "seaweed" coralene beading overall, white interior (ILLUS.) **375.00**

Vase, 4½" h., squatty bulbous body tapering to a cylindrical neck, pink mother-of-pearl Diamond Quilted patt. satin exterior w/"seaweed" coralene beading, white interior **350.00**

Vase, 7½" h., Peach Blow exterior w/yellow "seaweed" coralene beading, gold trim, white lining, "PATENT" incised on base **675.00**

CRANBERRY

Candle Lamp with Brass Holder

Gold was added to glass batches to give this glass its color on reheating. It has been made by numerous glasshouses for years and is currently being reproduced. Both blown and molded articles were produced. A less expensive type of cranberry was made with the substitution of copper for gold.

Bottle w/cut faceted stopper, squatty bulbous body tapering to a long thin cylindrical neck flaring to a ruffled rim, decorated w/dot flowers & gold trim, 3½" d., 7¼" h. **$135.00**

Candle lamp w/nickle plated brass holder, cylindrical glass shade sits in brass holder w/scroll-cut decorations, loop handle & embossed cupid heads around base, 4¾" d., 6¾" h. (ILLUS.) **235.00**

Cranberry Centerpiece Bowl

Centerpiece, deeply ruffled cranberry opalescent bowl atop jewelled brass plated base, embossed irises & red jewels on base, 9½" d., 9" h. (ILLUS.) **225.00**

Cologne bottle w/original clear cut faceted stopper, squatty ovoid body tapering to a cylindrical widely flaring rim, decorated w/gold flowers & leaves & lattice, 3½" d., 5¼" h. **145.00**

Cruet w/clear cut faceted stopper, bulbous body tapering to a tall thin cylindrical neck w/flared rim & lip all on a clear glass foot, crystal applied handle, decorated w/gold scrolls & basket of flowers, 4" d., 9½" h. **195.00**

Liqueur set: 8½" h., 3" d. liqueur bottle w/faceted stopper, six - 1⅞" h., 1¼" d. shot glasses, 8¼" d. undertray; slightly flaring cylindrical bottle tapering to thin cylindrical neck w/flat rim, all pieces decorated w/lacy gold bands & flowers, the set (ILLUS. top next page)....................**275.00**

Cranberry Liqueur Set

Salt dip, individual size, insert w/applied rigaree on top in metal tri-legged base **125.00**

Salt dip, folded leaves on top, applied pedestal base, 2¾" d. **60.00**

Salt dip, master size, threaded top, applied clear petal type base, 2¾" d...**50.00**

Sugar shaker w/original top, tapered shape, Inverted Thumbprint patt.........**97.50**

Syrup pitcher w/original top, Coin Spot patt. **125.00**

Toothpick holder, in a ball-footed, filigree silver plate holder marked Derby **150.00**

Inverted Thumbprint Tumbler

Tumbler, Inverted Thumbprint patt., 2¾" d., 3¾" h. (ILLUS.) **25.00**

Vase, 6" d., 9½" h., bulbous body tapering to slightly flaring neck w/applied fancy crystal handles, elaborately decorated w/white, green & blue enamelled flowers, gold fan & leaves, all on a clear wafer foot (ILLUS. top next column) **425.00**

Fancy Decorated Cranberry Vase

CROWN MILANO

Crown Milano Creamer & Sugar Bowl

This glass, produced by Mt. Washington Glass Company late last century, is opal glass decorated by painting and enameling. It appears identical to a ware termed Albertine, also made by Mt. Washington.

Printed Crown Milano Mark

Creamer & cov. sugar bowl, squatty bulbous ribbed bodies decorated w/molded scrolls & florals trimmed w/gilt, silver plate scroll-edged rim & handle on creamer & scroll-edged

rim, cover & bail handle on sugar,
sugar lid incised "M.W. 2040," sugar
6" h., pr. (ILLUS.) **$385.00**
Dish, triangluar w/two rolled in edges,
decorated w/multicolored
flowers & heavy gold trim, signed 475.00
Rose bowl, decorated overall w/h.p.
daisies & roses on a soft ivory
ground, 3½ x 4½"............................**250.00**
Sweetmeat jar, cov., melon-ribbed
body, pink shaded to opaque white
body decorated w/ornate gold
scrolling on upper portion &
multicolored flowers on the lower
sections, ornate silver plate cover,
rim & bail handle, marked
5¼" d., 4" h. **830.00**
Sweetmeat jar, cov., creamy satin
ground decorated w/enameled gold
designs, silver plate rim, cover & bail
handle, cover marked "M.W." &
numbered...**450.00**
Vase, 3¾" h., 4⅜" d., flat-sided body
w/flared rim, creamy satin ground
decorated w/light peach & light
yellow stylized maple leaves in
background, light peach apricot &
greenish charcoal five-petal flowers
in the center ground & large rust &
gold maple leaves & barren
branches in the foreground..............**695.00**
Vase, 5¾" h., wide squatty bulbous
body below a squatty bulbous short
neck, heavy gilt enameled overall
leaf design over a gold & pink
scrolling & double eagle medallion
ground, unsigned **805.00**
Vase, 6¼" h., spherical body w/a tiny
cylindrical neck, decorated overall
w/blue-centered pink & white
blossoms on a pastel beige & yellow
foliate background, unsigned...........**517.50**
Vase, 7" h., baluster-form body w/a
narrow neck & widely flaring
flattened rim, the body lightly
molded w/swirled ribs & decorated
w/large white blossoms & buds
outlined in gold against a ground of
blue scrolls, label on base reads "M
& W G Co. Crown Milano" **977.50**
Vase, 8" h., tall cylindrical body w/flat
rim, decorated in pastel coloring w/a
distant desert city, palm trees &
birches in foreground, dotted & gold
rim border, unsigned, some dots
missing (ILLUS. top next column) **747.50**
Vase, 8" h., wide ovoid body tapering
sharply to a small flat mouth,
decorated w/large branches of gold
& silver enamel apple blossoms &
leaves w/applied bead 'jewels' in the
blossom centers, against a pastel
yellow & pink floral background,
unsigned (gilt worn at rim) **805.00**

Scenic Crown Milano Vase

Vase, 9" h., footed ovoid body
tapering to a tiny cylindrical neck,
decorated overall w/green leafy
maidenhair fern design w/three
delicate gold medallions & a scroll-
decorated neck, unsigned................**460.00**
Vase, 11½" h., cream ground
decorated w/gold spider mums
w/shadow medallions, signed **875.00**

CRUETS

Art Glass Cruets

Amethyst, mold-blown, Tiny Optic
patt., enamel decoration, original
stopper..**$95.00**
Cornflower blue, mold-blown,
embossed inner vertical paneled
spherical body tapering to a
cylindrical neck, decorated w/a
seaweed design & two pink

blossoms, applied opaque blue
handle, original stopper **285.00**
Cranberry, blown, cylindrical body
w/deep shoulder & a cylindrical
neck, encased in metal base
w/handle, clear facet-cut stopper
w/metal band, 3" d., 8½" h. **165.00**
Cranberry crackle, blown spherical
body tapering to thin cylindrical neck
w/pinched spout & clear applied
handle all on a clear wafer base,
w/clear bubble stopper, 4¼" d.,
7¾" h. (ILLUS. right) **135.00**
Emerald green, blown, ovoid body
tapering to cylindrical neck
w/pinched lip & spun rope applied
handle, decorated w/pink scrolls &
peach, white & blue flowers,
w/matching green stopper,
4" d., 8½" h. (ILLUS. left) **295.00**
Light sapphire blue, blown, tapering
cylindrical body w/a slender
cylindrical neck, decorated w/white
flowers w/yellow centers, white
foliage & gold trim, applied amber
handle, original amber ball stopper,
3" d., 8½" h. **165.00**

Decorated Orange Cruet

Sapphire Blue Cruet

Sapphire blue, blown, ovoid body
tapering to a cylindrical neck,
decorated w/small lavender flowers,
green leaves & gold foliage, applied
clear handle, original clear ball
stopper, 4" d., 9" h. (ILLUS.) **165.00**
Yellow satin, blown, tricorner rim,
decorated w/white bird & foliage,
w/original stopper **345.00**

Lime Green Cruet

Lime green, blown, bulbous body w/a
slender cylindrical neck w/pinched
lip, decorated w/white daisies &
green leaves, applied green handle
& original green ball stopper,
3¼" d., 7¾" h. (ILLUS.) **110.00**
Orange, blown, tapering cylindrical
body w/deep shoulder, a short
cylindrical neck w/flaring ruffled rim,
decorated w/white flowers w/yellow
centers & white branches, applied
clear handle, original clear ball
stopper, 3" d., 8½" h.
(ILLUS. top next column) **165.00**

CUP PLATES

*Produced in numerous patterns
beginning some 170 years ago, these little
plates were designed to hold a cup while
the tea or coffee was allowed to cool in a
saucer. Cup plates were also made of
ceramics. Where numbers are listed below,
they refer to numbers assigned these plates
in the book,* American Glass Cup Plates, *by
Ruth Webb Lee and James H. Rose. Plates
are of clear glass unless otherwise noted. A
number of cup plates have been
reproduced.*

L & R-95, 10-sided, Shield patt., opaque white (two points lightly tipped)................................**$115.50**

L & R-129, round, star & leaf sprigs in center, stars & diamonds border, clear...**44.00**

L & R-133, round, Thistle patt., clear (several bull's-eyes lightly tipped, mold roughness) **99.00**

L & R-134, round, six-petal florette w/bull's-eyes in center, bull's-eye rim band, clear (fin roughness) **77.00**

L & R-159A, round w/petaled rim, Thistle patt., clear (small slightly disfiguring rim chip)...........................**27.50**

L & R-160B, round, six-petal florette in center, zig-zag border, clear **49.50**

L & R-162B, round, large four-point center star w/four tiny blossoms, tiny leaftip border band, clear **44.00**

L & R-200A, round, six-ray fan & lancet center, spearpoint & fan border, clear (small areas of roughness) **38.50**

L & R-265, round, four-branch rose sprigs in center, dainty scrolls in border, fiery opalescent (several tipped & rough scallops) **220.00**

L & R-285, round, Hairpin border w/diamond-lattice center, clear (one point tipped, mold roughness) **38.50**

L & R-334A, round w/small rim scallops, large florette in center, leaf band in rim, opalescent (three scallops lightly tipped, mold roughness) **176.00**

L & R-439C, hearts alternating w/small diamonds w/stars in border, pinwheel in center, 57 rim scallops, clear, 3½" d. **45.00**

L & R-465F, round w/small rim scallops, Heart patt., deep opalescence (four scallops lightly tipped, mold roughness) **77.00**

L & R-465, round, Thirteen Heart patt., opal opaque (three tipped scallops)...**165.00**

L & R-465j, round, Thirteen Heart patt., fiery opalescent (scallop roughness) **110.00**

L & R-549, round, starburst center, ringed rim, opalescent (scallop roughness) **121.00**

L & R-550, sunburst patt., round w/tiny scallops on rim, fiery opalescent (three tipped scallops, slight mold roughness)..................**132.00**

L & R-564, round, Henry Clay patt., light fiery opalescence (several scallops lightly tipped, mold roughness) **275.00**

L & R-565B, Henry Clay patt., round, peacock blue (three scallops tipped, usual mold roughness) **110.00**

L & R-571, round, Queen Victoria patt., clear (trace of mold roughness) **132.00**

L & R-580, round, Victoria & Albert patt., clear (trace of mold roughness) **247.50**

L & R-585C, round, Major Ringgold patt., clear (slight underfill & fin roughness) **550.00**

L & R-593, round, Log Cabin patt., clear (small roughness & flaking on foot rim) **99.00**

L & R-619, Benjamin Franklin ship patt., scalloped rim, light opal **275.00**

L & R-656, round, Eagle patt., clear (two tipped scallops, mold roughness) **330.00**

L & R-694, Beehive patt., round, clear (several lightly tipped beads, mold roughness) **121.00**

L & R-697, round, Marriage patt., clear (three tipped scallops)...............**77.00**

CUSTARD GLASS

This ware takes its name from its color and is a variant of milk white glass. It was produced largely between 1890 and 1915 by the Northwood Glass Co., Heisey Glass Company, Fenton Art Glass Co., Jefferson Glass Co., and a few others. There are 21 major patterns and a number of minor ones. The prime patterns are considered Argonaut Shell, Chrysanthemum Sprig, Inverted Fan and Feather, Louis XV and Winged Scroll. Most custard glass patterns are enhanced with gold and some have additional enameled decoration or stained highlights. Unless otherwise noted, items in this listing are fully decorated.

Northwood Script Mark

ARGONAUT SHELL (Northwood)
Bowl, master berry or fruit, 10½" l., 5" h. ....**$185.00 to 225.00**
Butter dish, cov. **282.00**
Compote, jelly, 5" d., 5" h. **124.00**
Creamer...**145.00**
Cruet w/original stopper **850.00**
Pitcher, water....................................**433.00**
Sauce dish (ILLUS. top next page) **57.00**
Spooner...........................**125.00 to 150.00**
Sugar bowl, cov................................**205.00**
Table set: cov. butter dish, cov. sugar bowl, creamer & spooner, 4 pcs. **550.00**

Argonaut Shell Sauce Dish

Toothpick holder ....300.00 to 325.00
Tumbler 110.00
Water set, pitcher & 6 tumblers,
   7 pcs. 900.00

BEADED SWAG (Heisey)

Beaded Swag Souvenir Goblet & Wine

Butter dish...95.00
Goblet.................................55.00 to 65.00
Goblet, souvenir (ILLUS.) 70.00
Sauce dish...25.00
Sauce dish, souvenir 45.00
Sugar bowl, open 45.00
Wine..48.50
Wine, souvenir (ILLUS. left) 65.00

CHRYSANTHEMUM SPRIG
(Northwood's Pagoda)

Berry set, master bowl & 6 sauce
   dishes, 7 pcs. 520.00
Bowl, master berry or fruit, 10½"
   oval, decorated 165.00
Bowl, master berry or fruit, 10½"
   oval, undecorated 199.00
Butter dish, cov. 297.00
Celery vase...755.00
Compote, jelly, decorated..................112.50
Compote, jelly, undecorated................65.00
Condiment tray 562.50
Creamer..117.00

Chrysanthemum Sprig Cruet

Cruet w/original stopper (ILLUS.).......385.00
Pitcher, water, decorated...................457.00
Pitcher, water, undecorated...............225.00
Salt & pepper shakers w/original
   tops, pr...187.50
Sauce dish...64.00
Sauce dish, blue trim.........................140.00
Spooner..125.00
Sugar bowl, cov., decorated..............216.00
Sugar bowl, cov., undecorated..........150.00
Toothpick holder w/gold trim & paint,
   signed 260.00
Toothpick holder, undecorated 175.00
Tumbler 82.00
Water set, pitcher & 6 tumblers,
   7 pcs. 800.00

GENEVA (Northwood)

Geneva Cruet

Banana boat, four-footed, 11"
   oval....................................95.00 to 125.00
Banana boat, four-footed, green
   stain, 11" oval 145.00
Bowl, master berry or fruit, 8½"
   oval, four-footed.................................90.00
Bowl, master berry or fruit, 8½"
   oval, four-footed, green stain 85.00
Bowl, master berry or fruit, 8½" d.,
   three-footed 135.00

Butter dish, cov. 171.00
Compote, jelly..75.00
Creamer...............................80.00 to 100.00
Cruet w/original stopper
  (ILLUS.) ....250.00 to 350.00
Pitcher, water.....................................223.00
Salt & pepper shakers w/original
  tops, pr. 241.00
Sauce dish, oval..................................38.00
Sauce dish, round 40.00
Spooner...92.00
Sugar bowl, open 75.00
Syrup pitcher w/original top 275.00
Table set, 4 pcs. ....450.00 to 500.00
Toothpick holder, decorated 125.00
Toothpick holder, decorated, green
  stain, goofus trim 237.50
Tumbler 55.00

GRAPE & GOTHIC ARCHES
(Northwood)

Grape & Gothic Arches Goblet

Berry set, master bowl & 6 sauce
  dishes, 7 pcs. 550.00
Goblet (ILLUS.).....................................67.50
Sugar bowl, cov., blue stain 195.00
Table set, 4 pcs. 375.00
Tumbler 57.50
Vase, 10" h. ("favor" vase made from
  goblet mold) 75.00
Vase, ruffled hat shape 55.00

INTAGLIO (Northwood)
Berry set, 9" d. footed compote & 6
  sauce dishes, 7 pcs. 391.50
Bowl, fruit, 7½" d. footed compote.....127.00
Bowl, fruit, 9" d., footed compote 325.00
Butter dish, cov. 263.00
Creamer & cov. sugar bowl, pr. 275.00
Cruet w/original stopper 310.00
Pitcher, water.....................................373.00
Salt shaker w/original top 98.00
Salt & pepper shakers w/original
  tops, pr. 205.00
Table set, green stain, 4 pcs..............540.00
Tumbler (ILLUS. top next column).......77.00

Intaglio Tumbler

RING BAND (Heisey)

Ring Band Water Pitcher

Berry set, master bowl & 6 sauce
  dishes, 7 pcs. 482.00
Butter dish, cov. 222.50
Compote, jelly ....145.00 to 175.00
Condiment tray 150.00
Pitcher, water (ILLUS.) 322.50
Salt shaker w/original top,
  undecorated...50.00
Sauce dish..37.50
Spooner...120.00
Sugar bowl, cov. ....150.00 to 175.00
Syrup pitcher w/original top 365.00
Toothpick holder, decorated 115.00
Toothpick holder, undecorated 85.00
Toothpick holder, souvenir.................75.00
Tumbler, decorated 75.00
Tumbler, undecorated 70.00
Water set, pitcher & 6 tumblers 550.00

WINGED SCROLL or IVORINA
VERDE (Heisey)
Berry set, master bowl & 4 sauce
  dishes, undecorated, 5 pcs. 275.00
Berry set, master bowl & 5 sauce
  dishes, 6 pcs. 445.00
Bowl, fruit, 8½" d., undecorated.........120.00
Butter dish, cov. 185.50

Celery vase	350.00
Cigarette jar	160.00
Creamer, decorated	102.00
Cruet w/original stopper, undecorated	100.00
Match holder	190.00 to 225.00
Pitcher, water, 9" h., bulbous	230.00
Pitcher, water, tankard, decorated	337.50
Pitcher, water, tankard, undecorated	230.00
Salt & pepper shakers w/original tops, pr.	150.00
Sauce dish, 4½" d.	36.00
Spooner	82.00
Sugar bowl, cov., decorated	135.00
Sugar bowl, cov., undecorated	95.00
Table set, cov. butter dish, creamer & spooner, 3 pcs.	250.00
Toothpick holder	129.00
Tumbler	69.00

Winged Scroll Water Set

Water set, tankard pitcher & 6 tumblers, 7 pcs. (ILLUS.) ....**700.00 to 750.00**

CUT GLASS

Cut glass most eagerly sought by collectors is American glass produced during the so-called "Brilliant Period" from 1880 to about 1915. Pieces listed below are by type of article in alphabetical order.

Hawkes, Hoare, Libbey and Straus Marks

BOTTLES
Ketchup, overall hobstars, tri-pour lip, sterling silver stopper **$125.00**
Liquor, bottom half Harvard patt., plain upper half, cut shoulder, rayed base, cut stopper, square, 9½" h. **110.00**
Whiskey, Cornell patt., hobstar, strawberry diamond & prism, matching stopper, qt. **325.00**

BOWLS

Cut Glass Center Bowl

Banana, Hunt's Royal patt., Russian motif w/hobstar button, five-sided strawberry diamond lozenge & large hobstars, 11" l. **475.00**
Banana, Straus' Imperial patt., chain of hobstars alternating w/strawberry diamond, serrated rim, Napoleon's hat shape, 5 x 12" **475.00**
Blackmer Cut Glass Co., hobstars, fan, crosshatching & hobnail, 9½" d. **302.50**
Centerbowl, oval, navette form, the sides cut overall w/diamond patt., early 20th c., chips to rim, 7¼ x 14¾", 5½" h. (ILLUS.) **192.50**

Harvard Pattern Bowl

Egginton's Marquise patt., chain of hobstars, fan, flashed fan, star & strawberry diamond, low, 9" d................**200.00**

Harvard patt. variant, scalloped top, 24-point hobstar in bottom, 9" d., 2" h. (ILLUS. bottom previous page)................**275.00**

Hawkes signed, puffy blossoms & leafy polished design, flared compote form w/low foot, scalloped rim, marked "Hawkes Gravic Glass," 8" d., 5" h. **330.00**

Hoare signed, miters, cross-hatching & hobstars around a central star, low, 7" d. **154.00**

Hoare signed, Gladys patt., chain of hobstars, fan & strawberry diamond, low, 8" d., pr. **450.00**

Sterling Silver Rimmed Bowl

Hobstars & diamonds, bulbous body deeply cut w/hobtars & diamonds, flaring flat sterling rim w/scrollwork by Gorham, late 19th c., 11" d., 4½" h. (ILLUS.) **495.00**

Hunt signed, Royal patt., Russian motif w/hobstar button, five-sided strawberry diamond lozenge & large hobstars, 8" d................**121.00**

Orange, cane, hobstars, diamond point & fan, step-cut open base, 10" w., 9" h................**950.00**

Pinwheel, hobstar & fan, 8½" d. **150.00**

Prima Donna patt. (Triple Square), checkerboard design w/square enclosed in two other squares, chain of hobstars on serrated edge, Clark signed, 8" d................**400.00**

Straus signed, hobstars, hobnail & miters, serrated rim, 9" d................**330.00**

Tuthill signed, intaglio-cut w/large chrysanthemum blossoms & leaves, 9" d., 4½" h **345.00**

BOXES

Powder, Harvard patt. overall, 4" d. **250.00**

Handkerchief, hinged square lid cut w/hobstars & miters, 6¾" sq. **352.00**

CANDLESTICKS & CANDLEHOLDERS

Hawkes, baluster-form, engraved w/a floral design, 12" h., pr. **357.50**

Libbey, faceted baluster stem w/controlled air bubble, the circular foot cut w/a hobstar, 9" h., pr. **319.00**

CARAFES

Clarke signed, Yolande patt., 8½" h..**170.00**

Empire's Peerless patt., 7¾" h.........**121.00**

Pairpoint's Cambridge patt., ovals & miters, 7½" h. **220.00**

CELERY TRAYS

Clark signed, Prima Donna (Triple Square) patt., chain of hobstars, square enclosed within two other squares, right angle serrated edge, 4 x 12½"................**425.00**

Hawkes signed, overall eight-point star cutting, oval, 11" l................**50.00**

CLOCKS

Cut Glass Mantel Clock

Boudoir, Fry signed, Princess patt................**350.00**

Mantel, domed case cut in Harvard patt. above a rectangular tablet of intaglio-cut flower & foliage, rectangular base w/thumbprint edge, w/reversible face, eight-day movement, 8¼" h. (ILLUS.) **600.00**

COMPOTES

Cane cut deep flaring bowl on a faceted zipper-cut stem & star-cut foot, 8¼" d., 9½" h. (ILLUS. top next page)................**431.00**

Chain of hobstars beneath 1½" h. gallery cut w/single stars, notched stem, star-cut foot, 6¾" d., 10" h. (ILLUS. middle next page) **465.00**

Foliage w/feathered edges, serrated rim, hexagonal notched stem, step-cut scalloped base, 6¼" d., 5½" h. **75.00**

Hoare's Monarch patt., cross-cut vesicas w/split, hobstar, fan & other cutting, teardrop stem, scalloped foot, 8" d., 7" h. **375.00**

Cane Cut Compote

Chain of Hobstars Compote

Hobstars, fan & other cutting,
  notched prism stem w/teardrop,
  6" d., 7½" h., pr. **550.00**
Hobstars, fan & other cutting, stem
  w/teardrop & cut w/a band of
  honeycomb, 7" d., 9" h. **345.00**
Libbey signed, Lovebirds (Wisteria)
  patt., intaglio-cut birds &
  foliage, 7" d., 4½" h. **975.00**

CREAMERS & SUGAR BOWLS
Blackmer Cut Glass Company's
  Ruby patt., 4" d., pr. **143.00**
Chain of hobstars separated by field
  of squared cross-cut diamond & fan
  w/two hobstars on each side,
  double-cut handles, pr. **225.00**
Drape & Pinwheel patt., footed,
  pr. **135.00**
Hawkes signed, hobstars, cane &
  fan, notch-cut & zipper handles,
  pedestal base, 4½" h., pr. **750.00**

Hoare signed, hobstars, fan & bands
  of crosshatching, sides & bottoms
  cut in pattern, double-
  notched handles, pr. **250.00**
Hoare's Pluto patt., chain of
  hobstars, beading, strawberry
  diamond & fan, creamer w/triple-
  notched handle, 4" w., 3½" h.,
  pr. **395.00**
Hobstar & fan cutting overall,
  double-notched handles, pedestal
  base, 3½" h., pr. **425.00**
Libbey signed, hobstars & other
  cutting, pr. **125.00**
Pinwheel surrounded by nailhead
  diamond & crosshatching, hobstar
  base, sugar handle to handle
  7" w., each 4" h., pr. **425.00**
Tuthill's Primrose patt., intaglio-
  cut blossoms & foliage, pr. **175.00**

CRUETS
Bull's-eye, strawberry diamond &
  star **150.00**
Hobstar, strawberry daimond, fan &
  hobstar, slender, pedestal base,
  9" h. **275.00**

DECANTERS
Green cut to clear, Dorflinger,
  diamond point & oval cutting, two
  applied green neck rings, original
  cut mushroom-shaped stopper **295.00**
Hoare signed, Gladys patt., chain of
  hobstars, fan & strawberry diamond,
  faceted stopper, 11" h. **495.00**
Libbey's Kimberly patt., cross-cut
  diamond, fan & hobstar, double
  gooseneck, conformingly cut
  stopper, 12½" h. **895.00**

DISHES, MISCELLANEOUS
Relish, hobstar, hobnail, strawberry
  diamond & fan, S-shaped dish
  raised on a notched prism stem
  w/rayed foot, 4¼ x 7¼", 7¾" h. **275.00**
Relish, Hunt signed, Royal patt.,
  Russian motif w/hobstar button, five-
  sided strawberry diamond
  lozenge & large hobstars **80.00**

ICE TUBS
Harvard patt., 10½" d., 7¾" h. **150.00**
Hoare signed, Hindu patt. variant **225.00**

JARS
Sweetmeat, cov., hobstar, strawbery
  diamond, cane & fan, rayed base,
  16-point hobstar mushroom-shaped
  stopper, 3¼" d., 6" h. **350.00**
Tobacco jar, cov., hobstar & notched
  prism, rayed base, 24 point hobstar
  mushroom-shaped stopper, base 6",
  9½" h. (ILLUS. top next page) **800.00**

Cut Glass Tobacco Jar

LAMPS

Cut Glass Parlor Lamp

Parlor, mushroom-shaped shade, pinwheels, diamonds, hatching, conforming baluster-shaped shaft on domed foot, metal rim w/prisms, electrified, early 20th c., 21½" h. (ILLUS.) **1,400.00**

Table, mushroom-shaped shade, chain of hobstars, fan, crosshatching & other cutting, matching cylindrical stem bulging near slightly domed foot, silver rim w/notch-cut spear prisms, 21" h..**2,640.00**

Table, Gone-With-the-Wind type, the globes cut in Persian (Russian patt. w/hobstar button) patt., lower globe 8" d., upper globe 7" d., on a silver plate base w/four legs, silver plate font, overall including chimney 22" h. **5,250.00**

Table, Hawkes signed, 12" d. mushroom shade cut w/a swirling

Newport starred design, on a matching base w/a slender horizontally step-cut shaft above a domed cut foot, 23" h....................**2,415.00**

Table, mushroom-shaped shade, hobstar, diamond, fan & shield, conforming baluster-form shaft, brass rim w/prisms, 29" h..............**5,300.00**

MISCELLANEOUS

Beer stein w/sterling silver top, cranberry cut to clear w/hobstars & crosshatching, hobstar base, cut handle **850.00**

Bell, table-type, strawberry diamond & fan, 7" h. **450.00**

Bell, table-type, hobstar & split vesica, cut handle, original clapper **165.00**

Berry set: master bowl & ten individual dishes; strawberry diamond, 11 pcs. **595.00**

Brandy warmer, Monarch patt., hobstar, crosshatching, fan, pyramidal star & cross-cut vesicas w/split, notch-cut stem, rayed base, 5½" d., 7" h..........................**200.00**

Cake plate, Harvard patt., "X" in center, four-footed, 10" d **475.00**

Candy stand, Hawkes signed, Devonshire patt., fan, hobstar, star & strawberry diamond, pedestal base **245.00**

Celery vase, hobstar intersected by triangle of crosshatching & strawberry diamond, 4½" d., 6½" h...**275.00**

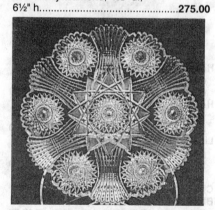

Cut Glass Charger

Charger, six hobstars alternating w/six notched prism flairs, centered by 24-point hobstar surrounded by 12-point strawberry diamond, 14¾" d. (ILLUS.) **2,300.00**

Flower center, Libbey, Empress patt., 15½" d., 8¾" h. (ILLUS. top next page)......................................**4,700.00**

Empress Pattern Flower Center

Hair receiver, Harvard patt.
overall **295.00**
Ice cream set: 15" d. tray & six
7½" d. plates; Festoon patt. variant,
outer ring of thirty-two point hobstars
around a square superimposed on
another square forming an eight-
point star centering a large hobstar,
7 pcs. **5,000.00**
Ice cream set: 10 x 18" tray & six
7" d. plate; Libbey signed, Marcella
patt., cluster of hobstars
around hexagon center, 7 pcs. **6,000.00**
Mayonaisse set: 6½" d. bowl &
7" d. underplate; Propeller patt.,
Harvard, hobstar & cane, 2 pcs. **525.00**
Napkin ring, hobstar & strawberry
diamond **65.00**
Napkin ring, deeply cut swirls w/tiny
cut buttons & finecut,
notched edges **95.00**
Paperweight, book-form, the front cut
w/a large diamond cut into four
small diamonds each w/a cut flower,
all within diamond point cutting,
back cut in diamond point,
2½ x 3" **165.00**
Paperweight, hobstars, buttons,
crosshatching & other cutting,
heart-shaped, 3½ x 3½"...................**195.00**
Picture frame, satin-cut tulips &
deeply cut leaves, notching
around edge, 7 x 9"..........................**275.00**
Salad set: 9" d. bowl & 11" d.
undertray; Sterling's Arcadia patt.,
five-sided strawberry diamond figure
w/hobstar & single star, 2 pcs..........**900.00**
Sauceboat & underplate, hobstars &
strawberry diamond rayed base,
sauceboat 3¼" w., overall 7¼" l.,
underplate 4½" w., 8⅛" l., 2 pcs. **375.00**
Sugar shaker, hobstars overall,
breakfast size, bulbous, silver
plate top, 4" h.....................................**95.00**
Urn, hobstars, cane, strawberry
diamond & fans, square rayed base,
7½" d., 11¼" h. (ILLUS. top next
column) **2,500.00**

Cut Glass Urn

Wine set: double gooseneck handled
decanter w/teardrop stopper & eight
wines w/double teardrop stems;
hobstars, strawberry diamond & fan,
decanter w/hobstar base, wines
w/rayed bases, decanter 13¾" h.,
the set **1,200.00**

PERFUME & COLOGNE BOTTLES
Perfume, overall cane cutting
w/matching stopper, 2½" d.,
6½" h...**100.00**
Perfume, hobstars overall, lapidary-
cut stopper, 4½" d., 6½" h................**250.00**

PITCHERS

Cut Tankard Pitcher

Champagne, strawberry diamond &
fan, 12" h..**350.00**
Milk, Middlesex patt., chain of
hobstars, fan & other cutting,
5¼" d., 6¼" h. **150.00**
Tankard, vertical bands of large
hobstars alternating w/crosses,
notched handle, sterling silver rim &

spout w/chased floral collar,
9⅞" h...**402.50**

Tankard, clusters of hobstars, nine in
each cluster, two clusters on each
side, strawberry diamond,
24-point hobstar base, 7¼" d.,
16" h. (ILLUS.) **1,400.00**

Water, Dorflinger's Marlboro patt.,
chain of hobstars, strawberry
diamond & fan, triple-notched
handle, 7½" d., 8" h..........................**625.00**

Water, large thirty-two point hobstars
on each side, further cut w/large
cane & fan, hobstar base,
11" h...**4,200.00**

Water, large thirty-two point hobstar
each side surrounded by hobnail
vesicas, strawberry diamond fields &
smaller hobstars surrounded by
hobnail vesicas on upper portion,
pedestal base w/twenty-four point
hobstar notched foot, 5" base d.,
2½" top d., 14" h. **3,250.00**

Water, Libbey signed, Comet patt.,
cylindrical, 10" h.............................**775.00**

PLATES

6" d., strawberry diamond & fan, set
of 12..**500.00**

7" d., Dorflinger signed, cranberry cut
to clear, strawberry diamond
w/rayed center **295.00**

9" d., Corinthian patt. variant, hobstar
center w/figures of hobnail &
strawberry diamond alternating
w/hobstars, two fans on each
figure...**225.00**

PUNCH BOWLS & SETS

Cut Glass Punch Set

Libbey signed, scalloped bowl
w/repeating hobstar & zipper cutting,
on conforming base, 12" d., 11" h.,
2 pcs. **632.50**

Punch set: 14" d. bowl, eight 4½" h.,
cups; Ribbon Star patt. variant,
9 pcs. (ILLUS.) **2,325.00**

ROSE BOWLS

Hunt's Royal patt. variant, hobstars
w/strawberry diamond centers,
three-footed, 7½" d., 6½" h. **600.00**

Pairpoint's Nevada patt., 3" h. **95.00**

Straus' Encore patt., fan, star &
strawberry diamond **100.00**

TRAYS

Egginton Tray

Egginton signed, hobstars & clear
tusk vesicas radiating out from strips
of clusters of six hobstars w/the
center of the plate cut in the small
hobstars, 14½" d. (ILLUS.) **8,000.00**

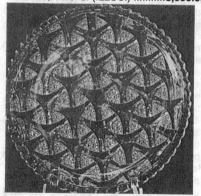

Rare Hawkes Tray

Hawkes signed, Concentric Circle
patt., six hobstars in each circle
separated by a triangle beveled
area, 11" d. (ILLUS.) **13,500.00**

Hawkes signed, four intersecting
chains of hobstars across the
bottom w/fans in adjoining areas &
fans between each hobstar, 32
hobstars around raised edge w/fans
in bow ties between each
hobstar, 10¼" w., 15½" l. **3,250.00**

Hawkes signed, Lattice & Rosette
patt., 15¼" d. (ILLUS. top next
page)...**20,000.00**

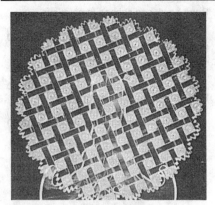

Lattice & Rosette Pattern Tray

Hawkes' Venetian patt., chain of
hobstars, fan, star, & strawberry
diamond split vesica, 13" d. **1,300.00**
Ice cream, Bergen's Progress patt.,
hobstar vesicas extending into
strawberry diamond vesicas
w/polished almond shapes as splits
in the vesicas, 10¼" w.,
17¾" l...**1,500.00**
Ice cream, cut in eight cane bars
extending out from center of tray to
hobnail & strawberry diamond fields,
separated w/split vesicas of
strawberry diamond, hobstars at
each end, 10¼" w., 17½" l. **1,100.00**
Ice cream, Clark signed, Quatrefoil
Rosette patt., rose-cut diamond
surrounded by hobstars & fine
hobnail w/prism & chains of
hobstars separating the sections,
10¾" w., 15¼" l. **4,600.00**
Ice cream, clusters of hobstars
divided by vesicas of hobnail & six-
sided Kohinoor star, large hobstars
at each end, 10½" w., 17¼" l. **1,900.00**
Ice cream, cut in a fine feathering
expanding from center to a chain of
hobstars around the edge w/uncut
centers, hobstar center,
10½" w., 17¾" l.............................**2,500.00**
Ice cream, Libbey's Imperial patt.,
cane, fan, hobstar & star, 10½" w.,
17½" l..**1,300.00**
Ice cream, Libbey's Stratford patt.,
hexagon of hobstars w/strawberry
diamond, 10½" w.,18" l. **1,500.00**
Libbey signed, Somerset patt.,
hobstar, strawberry diamond, large
beaded vesicas w/diamond fields of
crosscut squares, 14" d. **1,400.00**
Relish tray, Lattice & Rosette patt.
variant, 6 x 12" (ILLUS. top next
column) **2,100.00**
Pin, Persian (Russian w/clear
button) patt., 3¾ x 7".......................**200.00**

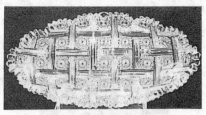

Cut Glass Relish Tray

Tuthill signed, intaglio-cut vintage
center, geometric hobstar border,
oval, 5 x 7½" **425.00**

VASES

Brilliant Butterfly Vase

Engraved daisy-like blossoms &
butterflies w/pressed leafy stems on
the large bulbous trumpet-form bowl
above a large facet-cut knob & a flat
scalloped foot, 14½" h. (ILLUS.) **690.00**
Engraved large daisy-like blossoms
at the flaring rim of the tall slender
cylindrical body, presses long leafy
stems down the sides, on a round
foot, 24" l...**402.50**

Hawkes Wild Turkey Vase

Hawkes signed, ruby cut to clear,
overall cutting centering wild turkey,
12½" h. (ILLUS.) **920.00**

Hunt signed, butterflies & foliage,
12" h...**150.00**
Libbey signed, bull's-eye & cross-cut
diamond, corset-shapet, 5" h. **100.00**

Pair of Hawkes Vases

Hawkes signed, engraved iris
blossoms on leafy stems, long
baluster form, on sterling silver
bases, pr. (ILLUS.)........................**2,695.00**

(End of Cut Glass Section)

CUT VELVET

*This mold-blown, two-layer glassware
is usually lined in white with a colored
exterior with a molded pattern. Pieces have
a satiny, acid finish, giving them a
'velvety' appearance. The Mt. Washington
Glass Company was one of several firms
which produced this glass.*

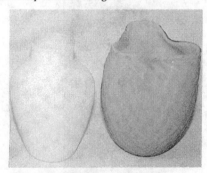

Cut Velvet Rose Bowl & Vase

Rose bowl, egg-shaped, three-crimp
rim, rose red satin Diamond Quilted
patt., white lining, 3½" d.,
4½" h. (ILLUS. right) **$165.00**

Rose bowl, egg-shaped three-crimp
rim, deep blue satin Diamond Quilt
patt., white lining, 3⅝" d., 4¼" h.......**135.00**
Rose bowl, spherical, six-crimp rim,
deep blue satin Diamond Quilted
patt., white lining, 3⅜" d.,
3¾" h..**145.00**
Rose bowl, clear applied rigaree on
ruffled rim, pink shaded to white
satin Rib patt., white lining **250.00**

Diamond Quilted Tumbler

Tumbler, glossy blue Diamond
Quilted patt., white lining (ILLUS.) **70.00**
Vase, 4¾" h., 3" d., ovoid body
tapering to short flat cylindrical neck,
lemon yellow Diamond Quilted patt.,
white lining (ILLUS. left)...................**118.00**
Vase, 6¼" h., 3½" d., bulbous body
tapering to a cylindrical stick neck,
blue satin Diamond Quilted
patt., white lining **295.00**
Vase, 6¼" h., 2⅞" d., gourd-shaped
body on short base, heavenly blue
satin Diamond Quilted patt.,
white lining **118.00**

Heavenly Blue Diamond Quilted Vase

Vase, 6⅛" h., 3⅛" d., squatty bulbous
body tapering to a tall thin cylindrical
neck, shaded heavenly blue
Diamond Quilted patt., white
lining (ILLUS.) **110.00**

DAUM NANCY

Daum Nancy Cameo Table Lamp

This fine glass, much of it cameo, was made by Auguste and Antonin Daum, who founded a factory in 1875 in Nancy, France. Most of their cameo and enameled glass was made from the 1890s into the early 20th century.

Daum Nancy Marks

Bowl, 16" d., wide-mouthed form w/low sides, pale green, deeply acid-etched w/inner rings & a wide outer band of repeating loops, ca. 1930, inscribed "DAUM - NANCY - FRANCE" w/a cross of Lorraine **$690.00**

Cameo box w/silver-gilt domed cover, squatty bulbous round body in frosted pink overlaid w/clear & cut w/water lilies & pads highlighted in gold enamel, the hinged cover cast w/a bough of holly, box inscribed "DAUM NANCY" w/the cross of Lorraine in enamel, ca. 1920, 5½" d..**1,265.00**

Cameo center bowl, a wide rectangular flat-sided fan-shaped body in grey streaked w/strawberry & lemon yellow, overlaid in chocolate brown & cut w/flower & garden tool-filled baskets pendent from ribbon-tied floral festoons, gilt-

bronze to edge band & large rim end ring handles, raised on a rectangular stepped gilt-bronze base, signed in cameo, ca.1910, overall 13½" l...**2,588.00**

Cameo ewer, tall slender double-gourd form raised on a disc foot, an applied amber handle from the rim to the side, grey mottled w/yellow, orange & purple, overlaid in mottled deep green & cut w/orchid blossoms, buds & leafage, enameled in ochre yellow, green & brown, signed in intaglio, ca. 1910, 13" h...**6,325.00**

Cameo lamp, table-type, spherical body tapering to short cylindrical neck w/silvered metal domed cap w/three light sockets, all on a stepped base w/scrolled feet, the heavy textured colorless glass overlaid in emerald green & acid-etched w/Art Deco-style blossoms, lighted within, engraved mark "Daum Nancy France" on side, 11½" d., 28" h. (ILLUS.)...............**2,587.50**

Cameo vase, 3¾" h., footed squatty bulbous ovoid body tapering to a wide closed mouth, opalescent *martelé* sides shaded w/violet, overlaid w/emerald green & cut w/cornflowers & leafage, signed in intaglio, ca. 1900..........................**4,312.00**

Cameo vase, 6½" h., 6¾" d., wide squatty baluster-form body tapering to a wide slightly flared mouth flanked by loop handles, mottled yellow shading to reddish burgundy overlaid in maroon, acid-etched & wheel-carved w/exotic blossoms on leafy stems, maroon handles, cameo signature **4,025.00**

Cameo vase, 8" h., bulbous ovoid body tapering to a wide short rolled neck, raised on a widely flaring socle base, grey shaded w/pale teal blue mottled w/yellow, overlaid in dark aubergine & cut w/a river landscape w/leafy trees, signed in cameo, ca. 1900 ....**2,587.00**

Cameo 'marqueterie-sur-verre' vase, 12" h., squatty bulbous base tapering to a tall swelled cylindrical neck w/flat rim, grey internally decorated w/lavender, pale yellow & purple, overlaid in deep mottled green, purple & orange & finely wheel-carved w/crocus blossoms & leaves reserved against a *martelé* ground, signed in cameo, ca. 1900 ....**23,000.00**

Ewer, grey walls cut w/branches of leafy berries & three crosses of

Lorraine, enameled in shades of charcoal, gold & red, the whole heightened in gilding, signed in enamel "DAUM - NANCY" w/cross of Lorraine, ca. 1900, 10" h..........**3,163.00**

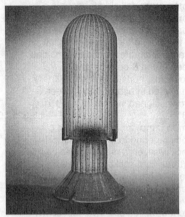

Daum Bullet-shaped Lamp

Lamp, table-type, bullet-shaped shade above flared base tapering to cylindrical neck w/wrought-iron mount, greyish white acid-etched in furrows, base & shade inscribed "DAUM - NANCY - FRANCE" w/cross of Lorraine, ca. 1925, 20¼" h. (ILLUS.) **10,062.00**

Pitcher, 7¾" h., clear ovoid body w/overall irregular design of airtrap bubbles, the short straight neck continuing to a tiny spout & applied w/an opaque orange loop handle, etched "DAUM NANCY" w/cross of Lorraine, ca. 1925 ....**345.00**

Plate, 14" d., wide dished circular form w/upturned rim, frosted & clear, acid-etched on the exterior w/panels of geometric design, the cavetto set w/three rows of *millefleurs* half-spheres, molded "DAUM - NANCY - FRANCE" w/a cross of Lorraine, ca.1925-30.....................................**1,265.00**

Vase, miniature, 1⅝" h., flattened ovoid sides, acid-etched grey shaded w/pink & grass green at the base, overlaid & enameled *en grisaille* w/trees bending in a rainstorm, signed in enamel "DAUM - NANCY" w/cross of Lorraine, ca. 1910 ....**2,587.00**

Vase, 5¼" h., "marqueterie-sur-verre" style, ovoid body tapering to wide slightly ruffled rim, grey decorated in *marqueterie* w/four red tulip blossoms in deep crimson above stems & leafage in mottled amber, the ground in mottled ochre, amber, red, purple & green enamel, lime

"Marqueterie-Sur-Verre" Daum Vase

green trim, inscribed "DAUM - NANCY" w/cross of Lorraine, ca. 1915 (ILLUS.)........................**31,050.00**

Vase, 5⅞" h., paneled bowl raised on a low foot, pale grey decorated w/a band of wheel-carving below the rim, inscribed "DAUM - NANCY - FRANCE" w/a cross of Lorraine, ca.1930 ....**690.00**

Daum Nancy Vase

Vase, 9⅝" h., flaring cylindrical form w/wide shoulders tapering to flat rim, decorated w/mottled yellow-green & blue frosted ground, etched & enamel painted in sunny waterfront riverscape w/tall trees in foreground, purple mountains beyond, inscribed "Daum Nancy" w/cross of Lorraine (ILLUS.) **7,475.00**

Vase, 11½" h., "verre parlant," tall cylindrical body w/trefoil rim, opalescent w/etched borders above & below an enameled garden scene *en grisaille* within scroll borders above the etched inscription "Les Fleurs de L'Imperatrice - Compiegne 1901," enameled in gold w/red blossoms & a black coat-of-arms,

inscribed on base "Daum Nancy"
w/cross of Lorraine **6,325.00**
Vases, 3¾" h., upright square form,
grey mottled w/white shading to
purple at the base, cut w/violets &
leaves & enameled in purple &
green, signed in cameo, ca. 1910,
pr...**5,175.00**

DEPRESSION GLASS

The phrase "Depression Glass" is used by collectors to denote a specific kind of transparent glass produced primarily as tablewares, in crystal, amber, blue, green, pink, milky-white, etc., during the late 1920s and 1930s when this country was in the midst of a financial depression. Made to sell inexpensively, it was turned out by such producers as Jeannette, Hocking, Westmoreland, Indiana and other glass companies. We compile prices on all the major Depression Glass patterns. Collectors should consult Depression Glass references for information on those patterns and pieces which have been reproduced.

ADAM, Jeannette Glass Co.,
1932-34 (Process-etched)

Adam Candy Jar with Cover

Ashtray, green, 4½" sq. **$22.00**
Ashtray, pink, 4½" sq.........................**25.00**
Bowl, dessert, 4¾" sq., green.............**15.00**
Bowl, dessert, 4¾" sq., pink................**14.00**
Bowl, cereal, 5¾" sq., green...............**36.00**
Bowl, cereal, 5¾" sq., pink.................**39.00**
Bowl, nappy, 7¾" sq., green...............**23.00**
Bowl, nappy, 7¾" sq., pink..................**20.50**
Bowl, cov., 9" sq., green **68.00**
Bowl, cov., 9" sq., pink.......................**55.00**
Bowl, 9" sq., pink **19.50**
Bowl, 10" oval vegetable, green **25.00**
Bowl, 10" oval vegetable, pink.............**31.50**
Butter dish, cov., green......................**270.00**

Butter dish, cov., pink **76.50**
Cake plate, footed, green, 10" sq. **23.00**
Cake plate, footed, pink, 10" sq...........**22.00**
Candlestick, green, 4" h......................**42.00**
Candlestick, pink, 4" h........................**38.00**
Candlesticks, green, 4" h., pr..............**96.00**
Candlesticks, pink, 4" h., pr. **83.00**
Candy jar, cov., green **93.00**
Candy jar, cov., pink (ILLUS.).............**86.00**
Coaster, clear, 3¼" sq. **13.50**
Coaster, pink, 3¼" sq..........................**20.00**
Creamer, green..................................**18.60**
Creamer, pink **17.00**
Cup, pink **20.00**
Cup & saucer, green **25.50**
Cup & saucer, pink.............................**27.00**

Adam Green Pitcher

Pitcher, 8" h., 32 oz., cone-shaped,
green (ILLUS.) **42.50**
Pitcher, 8" h., 32 oz., cone-shaped,
pink **34.00**
Pitcher, 32 oz., round base, pink **45.00**
Plate, sherbet, 6" sq., green.................**7.00**
Plate, sherbet, 6" sq., pink...................**7.00**
Plate, salad, 7¾" sq., green **13.00**
Plate, salad, 7¾" sq., pink....................**14.00**
Plate, dinner, 9" sq., green..................**22.00**
Plate, dinner, 9" sq., pink **28.00**
Plate, grill, 9" sq., green **16.00**
Plate, grill, 9" sq., pink.........................**19.00**
Platter, 11¾" l., green.........................**23.00**
Platter, 11¾" l., pink............................**26.00**
Salt & pepper shakers, footed,
green, 4" h., pr. **88.00**
Salt & pepper shakers, footed, pink,
4" h., pr. **68.00**
Sherbet, green, 3" h............................**32.00**
Sherbet, pink, 3" h..............................**26.00**
Sugar bowl, cov., green **38.00**
Sugar bowl, cov., pink **40.00**
Tumbler, cone-shaped, green,
4½" h., 7 oz...**24.00**
Tumbler, cone-shaped, pink,
4½" h., 7 oz...**26.00**
Tumbler, iced tea, green, 5½" h.,
9 oz..**44.00**
Vase, 7½" h., green.............................**50.50**

AMERICAN SWEETHEART, MacBeth - Evans Glass Co., 1930-36 (Process-etched)

American Sweetheart Cup & Saucer

Bowl, berry, 3¾" d., pink.....................**41.00**
Bowl, cream soup, 4½" d.,
  Monax..**135.50**
Bowl, cream soup, 4½" d., pink **77.50**
Bowl, cereal, 6" d., Monax...................**11.00**
Bowl, cereal, 6" d., pink **14.00**
Bowl, berry, 9" d., Monax.....................**59.00**
Bowl, berry, 9" d., pink.........................**37.50**
Bowl, soup w/flanged rim, 9½" d.,
  Monax..**73.00**
Bowl, soup w/flanged rim, 9½" d.,
  pink..**62.00**
Bowl, 11" oval vegetable, Monax.........**72.00**
Bowl, 11" oval vegetable, pink.............**57.00**
Creamer, footed, Monax........................**9.50**
Creamer, footed, pink **14.00**
Creamer, footed, ruby red.....................**86.50**
Cup & saucer, Monax............................**12.00**
Cup & saucer, pink................................**19.50**
Cup & saucer, ruby red (ILLUS.).........**91.50**
Lamp shade, Monax.............................**560.00**
Plate, bread & butter, 6" d., Monax **4.50**
Plate, bread & butter, 6" d., pink **5.00**
Plate, salad, 8" d., blue **74.50**
Plate, salad, 8" d., Monax **9.00**
Plate, salad, 8" d., pink.........................**13.00**
Plate, salad, 8" d., ruby red...................**48.00**
Plate, luncheon, 9" d., Monax **10.50**
Plate, dinner, 9¾" d., Monax.................**23.00**
Plate, dinner, 9¾" d., pink **35.00**
Plate, dinner, 10¼" d., Monax...............**19.50**
Plate, dinner, 10¼" d., pink **32.00**
Plate, chop, 11" d., Monax....................**14.50**
Plate, salver, 12" d., Monax..................**18.50**
Plate, salver, 12" d., pink......................**27.00**
Platter, 13" oval, Monax........................**63.00**
Platter, 13" oval, pink............................**47.00**
Salt & pepper shakers, footed,
  Monax, pr..**236.00**
Salt & pepper shakers, footed, pink,
  pr...**217.50**
Sherbet, footed, pink, 3¾" h. **20.00**
Sherbet, footed, Monax, 4¼" h. **18.00**
Sherbet, footed, pink, 4¼" h. **15.00**
Sherbet, metal holder, clear.................**14.00**
Sugar bowl, open, Monax **7.00**
Sugar bowl, open, pink...........................**12.00**

Sugar bowl, open, ruby red **90.00**
Tidbit server, two-tier, Monax **63.00**
Tumbler, pink, 3½" h., 5 oz..................**72.00**
Tumbler, pink, 4¼" h., 9 oz..................**69.00**

AUNT POLLY, U.S. Glass Co., late 1920s

Bowl, 4¾" d., 2" h., blue....................**18.00**
Bowl, 4¾" d., 2" h., green **8.00**
Bowl, 7¼" d., oval, handled pickle,
  blue..**39.50**
Bowl, 7⅞" d., large berry, blue.............**40.00**
Butter dish, cov., blue **192.50**
Butter dish, cov., green.......................**195.00**
Plate, sherbet, 6" d., blue.....................**12.00**
Plate, sherbet, 6" d., iridescent **13.00**
Sherbet, blue **11.00**
Sherbet, iridescent...............................**13.00**
Sugar bowl, cov., green.........................**45.00**
Tumbler, water, blue, 3⅝" h., 8 oz.......**29.50**
Vase, 6½" h., blue **38.00**

BLOCK or Block Optic, Hocking Glass Co., 1919-33 (Press-mold)

Bowl, berry, 4¼" d., green **7.00**
Bowl, 4½" d., green................................**25.00**
Bowl, cereal, 5¼" d., green...................**12.00**
Bowl, cereal, 5¼" d., pink **20.00**
Bowl, salad, 7" d., green.......................**32.00**
Bowl, large berry, 8½" d., green **25.00**
Bowl, large berry, 8½" d., pink............**22.00**
Candlesticks, amber, 1¾" h., pr.........**88.50**
Candlesticks, green, 1¾" h., pr..........**91.00**
Candlesticks, pink, 1¾" h., pr. **66.00**
Candy jar, cov., green, 2¼" h. **44.00**
Candy jar, cov., yellow, 2¼" h. **50.00**
Candy jar, cov., clear, 6¼" h...............**23.00**
Candy jar, cov., green, 6¼" h. **49.00**
Candy jar, cov., pink, 6¼" h...............**110.00**
Creamer, various styles, green............**12.50**
Creamer, various styles, pink................**9.50**
Creamer, various styles, yellow............**12.50**
Cup & saucer, green **15.00**
Cup & saucer, pink................................**12.00**
Goblet, cocktail, clear, 4" h. **13.00**
Goblet, cocktail, pink, 4" h. **30.00**
Goblet, wine, green, 4½" h. **39.00**
Goblet, clear, 5¾" h., 9 oz....................**14.00**
Goblet, pink, 5¾" h., 9 oz.....................**28.50**
Goblet, yellow, 5¾" h., 9 oz.................**31.00**
Goblet, green, 7¼" h., 9 oz...................**18.00**
Goblet, pink, 7¼" h., 9 oz.....................**18.00**
Goblet, yellow, 7¼" h., 9 oz. **31.00**
Ice bucket, w/metal bail handle,
  clear...**18.00**
Ice bucket, w/metal bail handle,
  green..**36.00**
Ice tub, tab handles, green **39.50**
Ice tub, tab handles, pink......................**76.50**
Mug, green...**29.00**
Pitcher, 8" h., 80 oz., green **69.00**
Pitcher, 8½" h., 54 oz., green **47.00**
Pitcher, 8½" h., 54 oz., pink.................**38.00**
Plate, sherbet, 6" d., green....................**3.00**

Plate, sherbet, 6" d., pink 3.00
Plate, sherbet, 6" d., yellow..................3.00
Plate, luncheon, 8" d., green.................4.00
Plate, luncheon, 8" d., pink...................5.00
Plate, luncheon, 8" d., yellow................5.00
Plate, dinner, 9" d., green....................19.00
Plate, dinner, 9" d., pink 20.50
Plate, dinner, 9" d., yellow....................34.00
Plate, grill, 9" d., yellow 45.00
Plate, sandwich, 10¼" d., green...........25.50
Salt & pepper shakers, squat, green,
    pr...72.00
Salt & pepper shakers, footed,
    green, pr. 35.00
Sandwich server w/center handle,
    green...51.00
Sandwich server w/center handle,
    pink 44.00

Green Cone-Shaped Sherbet

Sherbet, cone-shaped, footed, green
    (ILLUS.) 4.00
Sherbet, cone-shaped, footed,
    yellow...9.00
Sherbet, stemmed, clear, 3¼" h.,
    5½ oz. 4.00
Sherbet, stemmed, green, 3¼" h.,
    5½ oz. 5.00
Sherbet, stemmed, pink, 3¼" h.,
    5½ oz. 7.00
Sherbet, stemmed, green, 4¾" h.,
    6 oz. 12.50
Sherbet, stemmed, pink, 4¾" h.,
    6 oz. 14.00
Sherbet, stemmed, yellow, 4¾" h.,
    6 oz. 14.00
Sugar bowl, open, various styles,
    green...11.00
Sugar bowl, open, various styles,
    pink 13.00
Sugar bowl, open, various styles,
    yellow...10.50
Tumbler, whiskey, clear, 2¼" h.,
    2 oz. 8.00
Tumbler, whiskey, green, 2¼" h.,
    2 oz. 20.50
Tumbler, footed, green, 2⅝" h.,
    3 oz. 20.00

Tumbler, footed, pink, 2⅝" h.,
    3 oz..25.50
Tumbler, juice, green, 3½" h., 5 oz......16.00
Tumbler, juice, pink, 3½" h., 5 oz. 20.00
Tumbler, footed, pink, 9 oz. 16.00
Tumbler, green, 3⅞" h., 9½ oz. 15.50
Tumbler, pink, 3⅞" h., 9½ oz. 13.00
Tumbler, iced tea, footed, green,
    6" h., 10 oz. 25.00
Tumbler, iced tea, footed, pink, 6" h.,
    10 oz. 22.00
Tumbler, green, 5" h., 10 to 11 oz. 17.00
Tumbler, pink, 5" h., 10 to 11 oz.........15.00
Tumbler, green, 4⅞" h., 12 oz. 20.00
Tumbler, pink, 4⅞" h., 12 oz...............21.00
Tumbler, yellow, 4⅞" h., 12 oz. 16.50
Tumbler, green, 5¼" h., 15 oz. 28.00
Tumbler-up bottle, green...................17.00
Tumble-up set: bottle & 3" h.
    tumbler; green, 2 pcs. 59.00

BUBBLE, Bullseye or Provincial,
Anchor-Hocking Glass Co.,
1940-65 (Press-mold)

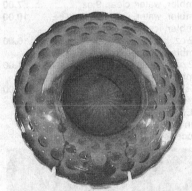

Bubble Pattern Bowl

Bowl, berry, 4" d., blue.........................14.00
Bowl, berry, 4" d., clear.......................3.50
Bowl, fruit, 4½" d., blue 10.00
Bowl, fruit, 4½" d., clear......................4.00
Bowl, fruit, 4½" d., green.....................6.50
Bowl, fruit, 4½" d., ruby red..................8.00
Bowl, cereal, 5¼" d., blue 12.00
Bowl, cereal, 5¼" d., green.................12.00
Bowl, soup, 7¾" d., blue 14.00
Bowl, soup, 7¾" d., clear 8.50
Bowl, soup, 7¾" d., pink 9.00
Bowl, 8⅜" d., blue 14.50
Bowl, 8⅜" d., clear 7.50
Bowl, 8⅜" d., green 14.00
Bowl, 8⅜" d., ruby red (ILLUS.) 19.00
Candlesticks, clear, pr. 13.50
Creamer, blue 32.00
Creamer, clear 6.50
Creamer, green 11.00
Cup & saucer, blue..............................6.00
Cup & saucer, clear..............................4.00

Cup & saucer, green **11.50**
Cup & saucer, ruby red **14.00**
Dinner service, 4 dinner plates, 4
cups & saucers, 4 5½" d., bowls,
creamer & sugar bowl,
18 pcs., green **190.00**
Dinner service for 4 w/serving
pieces, blue, 31 pcs. **200.00**
Pitcher w/ice lip, 64 oz., ruby red........**53.00**
Plate, bread & butter, 6¾" d., blue **5.00**
Plate, bread & butter, 6¾" d., clear **1.50**
Plate, dinner, 9⅜" d., blue......................**7.00**
Plate, dinner, 9⅜" d., clear....................**4.00**
Plate, dinner, 9⅜" d., green...................**17.00**
Plate, dinner, 9⅜" d., ruby red..............**17.00**
Plate, grill, 9⅜" d., blue.........................**18.00**
Platter, 12" oval, blue............................**14.00**
Sugar bowl, open, blue **16.00**
Sugar bowl, open, green **10.00**
Sugar bowl, open, milk white **4.50**
Tumbler, juice, clear, 6 oz. **7.00**
Tumbler, juice, ruby red, 6 oz. **9.00**
Tumbler, old fashioned, ruby red,
3¼" h., 8 oz.......................................**14.00**
Tumbler, water, clear, 9 oz. **7.00**
Tumbler, water, ruby red, 9 oz.............**10.00**
Tumbler, iced tea, clear, 4½" h.,
12 oz. **16.00**
Tumbler, iced tea, ruby red, 4½" h.,
12 oz. **11.00**
Tumbler, lemonade, ruby red,
5⅞" h., 16 oz.....................................**16.00**

CHERRY BLOSSOM,
Jeanette Glass Co., 1930-38
(Process-etched)

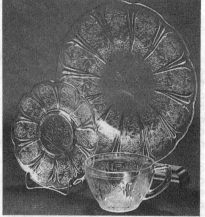

Cherry Blossom Pattern

Bowl, berry, 4¾" d., green **16.00**
Bowl, berry, 4¾" d., pink......................**16.00**
Bowl, cereal, 5¾" d., green...................**32.50**
Bowl, cereal, 5¾" d., pink **31.50**
Bowl, soup, 7¾" d., green......................**55.00**
Bowl, soup, 7¾" d., pink **62.00**
Bowl, berry, 8½" d., green **42.00**

Bowl, berry, 8½" d., pink......................**42.50**
Bowl, 9" d., two-handled, Delphite.......**27.50**
Bowl, 9" d., two-handled, pink.............**36.00**
Bowl, 9" oval vegetable, green **37.00**
Bowl, 9" oval vegetable, pink..............**36.00**
Bowl, fruit, 10½" d., three-footed,
green..**76.00**
Bowl, fruit, 10½" d., three-footed,
pink **81.00**
Butter dish, cov., green.........................**84.00**
Butter dish, cov., pink **75.50**
Cake plate, three-footed, green,
10¼" d..**24.50**
Cake plate, three-footed, pink,
10¼" d..**26.00**
Coaster, green **12.00**
Coaster, pink **16.00**
Creamer, Delphite.................................**18.00**
Creamer, green **16.00**
Creamer, pink **17.50**
Cup & saucer, Delphite **22.00**
Cup & saucer, green **22.00**
Cup & saucer, pink (ILLUS. front) **23.00**
Mug, green, 7 oz. **167.50**
Pitcher, 6¾" h., 36 oz., overall patt.,
Delphite..**83.50**
Pitcher, 6¾" h., 36 oz., overall patt.,
green..**55.00**
Pitcher, 6¾" h., 36 oz., overall patt.,
pink **54.00**
Pitcher, 8" h., 36 oz., footed, cone-
shaped, patt. top, green.....................**51.50**
Pitcher, 8" h., 36 oz., footed, cone-
shaped, patt. top, pink **54.00**
Pitcher, 8" h., 42 oz., patt. top,
green..**53.00**
Pitcher, 8" h., 42 oz., patt. top, pink.....**57.00**
Plate, sherbet, 6" d., green.....................**6.00**
Plate, sherbet, 6" d., pink **9.00**
Plate, salad, 7"d., green........................**24.00**
Plate, salad, 7" d., pink **23.00**
Plate, dinner, 9" d., Delphite.................**19.00**
Plate, dinner, 9" d., green......................**21.00**
Plate, dinner, 9" d., pink (ILLUS.
back) **21.00**
Plate, grill, 9" d., green **24.00**
Plate, grill, 9" d., pink............................**24.00**
Platter, 11" oval, green **35.00**
Platter, 11" oval, pink **41.00**
Platter, 13" oval, pink **60.00**
Platter, 13" oval, divided, pink..............**62.00**
Sandwich tray, handled, Delphite,
10½" d..**25.50**
Sandwich tray, handled, green,
10½" d..**25.00**
Sandwich tray, handled, pink,
10½" d..**21.00**
Sherbet, green **14.50**
Sherbet, pink..**15.50**
Sugar bowl, cov., green **33.50**
Sugar bowl, cov., pink **29.00**
Sugar bowl, open, Delphite **18.00**
Sugar bowl, open, green **14.00**
Sugar bowl, open, pink.........................**11.50**

Tumbler, patt. top, green, 3½" h.,
4 oz. **23.00**
Tumbler, patt. top, pink, 3½" h.,
4 oz. **20.00**
Tumbler, juice, footed, overall patt.,
green, 3¾" h., 4 oz. **16.50**
Tumbler, juice, footed, overall patt.,
pink, 3¾" h., 4 oz. **15.00**
Tumbler, footed, overall patt.,
Delphite, 4½" h., 8 oz. **19.00**
Tumbler, footed, overall patt., green,
4½" h., 8 oz. **32.00**
Tumbler, footed, overall patt., pink,
4½" h., 8 oz. **24.00**
Tumbler, patt. top, green, 4¼" h.,
9 oz. **21.00**
Tumbler, patt. top, pink, 4¼" h.,
9 oz. **20.00**
Tumbler, footed, overall patt.,
Delphite, 4½" h., 9 oz. **22.00**
Tumbler, footed, overall patt., green,
4½" h., 9 oz. **30.50**
Tumbler, footed, overall patt., pink,
4½" h., 9 oz. **30.00**
Tumbler, patt. top, pink, 5" h., 12 oz.....**56.00**
Water set: pitcher & 6 tumblers; pink,
7 pcs. **126.00**

Junior Set:
Creamer, Delphite.................................**40.00**
Creamer, pink **36.50**
Cup & saucer, Delphite **40.00**
Cup & saucer, pink...............................**40.00**
Plate, 6" d., Delphite.............................**12.00**
Plate, 6" d., pink **9.00**
Sugar bowl, Delphite **38.00**
14 pcs. set, Delphite **284.00**

**CLOVERLEAF Hazel Atlas Glass
Co., 1931-35 (Process-etched)**

Cloverleaf Open Sugar Bowl

Bowl, dessert, 4" d., green...................**19.00**
Bowl, cereal, 5" d., green......................**23.00**
Bowl, salad, 7" d., deep, green............**31.00**
Bowl, 8" d., green..................................**47.00**
Candy dish, cov., green **47.00**
Creamer, footed, black, 3⅝" h. **16.00**

Creamer, footed, green, 3⅝" h..............**9.00**
Cup & saucer, black **18.00**
Cup & saucer, green **10.50**
Cup & saucer, pink...............................**10.00**
Plate, sherbet, 6" d., black **31.00**
Plate, sherbet, 6" d., green....................**6.00**
Plate, sherbet, 6" d., yellow...................**7.00**
Plate, luncheon, 8" d., black.................**16.00**
Plate, luncheon, 8" d., green..................**8.00**
Plate, luncheon, 8" d., pink....................**7.00**
Plate, luncheon, 8" d., yellow **13.00**
Plate, grill, 10¼" d., green.....................**20.00**
Salt & pepper shakers, black, pr. **75.00**
Salt & pepper shakers, green, pr. **32.00**
Sherbet, footed, black, 3" h..................**17.00**
Sherbet, footed, green, 3" h...................**7.00**
Sherbet, footed, pink, 3" h. **6.00**
Sherbet, footed, yellow, 3" h...............**11.00**
Sugar bowl, open, footed, black,
3⅝" h..**16.00**
Sugar bowl, open, footed, green,
3⅝" h. (ILLUS.) **8.50**
Sugar bowl, open, footed, yellow,
3⅝" h..**14.00**
Tumbler, flared, green, 3¾" h.,
10 oz. **34.00**
Tumbler, footed, green, 5¾" h.,
10 oz. **22.00**
Tumbler, footed, yellow, 5¾" h.,
10 oz. **29.00**

**COLONIAL or Knife & Fork,
Hocking Glass Co., 1934-39
(Press-mold)**

Green Colonial Bowl

Bowl, berry, 3¾" d., pink.....................**52.50**
Bowl, berry, 4½" d., green **14.00**
Bowl, cream soup, 4½" d., green.........**56.00**
Bowl, soup, 7" d., clear **15.00**
Bowl, soup, 7" d., green.......................**57.00**
Bowl, 9" d., clear.................................**17.50**
Bowl, 9" d., green.................................**25.00**
Bowl, 10" oval vegetable, green
(ILLUS.) **34.00**
Bowl, 10" oval vegetable, pink.............**28.00**
Butter dish, cov., clear (ILLUS. top
next page)..**33.00**
Butter dish, cov., green.......................**50.50**
Celery or spooner, green...................**113.00**

Colonial Butter Dish

Celery or spooner, pink **112.00**
Creamer or milk pitcher, clear, 5" h.,
  16 oz. **15.00**
Creamer or milk pitcher, green,
  5" h., 16 oz. **24.00**
Cup & saucer, clear..............................**9.50**
Cup & saucer, green **15.00**
Cup & saucer, pink **15.50**
Goblet, cordial, clear, 3¾" h., 1 oz.......**15.00**
Goblet, cordial, green, 3¾" h.,
  1 oz. **27.00**
Goblet, wine, clear, 4½" h.,
  2½ oz. **14.50**
Goblet, wine, green, 4½" h.,
  2½ oz. **23.00**
Goblet, cocktail, clear, 4" h., 3 oz. **13.00**
Goblet, cocktail, green, 4" h., 3 oz.......**23.00**
Goblet, claret, clear, 5¼" h., 4 oz.........**15.00**
Goblet, claret, green, 5¼" h., 4 oz........**23.00**
Goblet, clear, 5¾" h., 8½ oz. **16.00**
Goblet, green, 5¾" h., 8½ oz. **26.00**
Goblet, pink, 5¾" h., 8½ oz...................**18.00**
Pitcher, ice lip or plain, 7" h., 54 oz.,
  clear **30.50**
Pitcher, ice lip or plain, 7¾" h.,
  68 oz., clear **27.00**
Pitcher, ice lip or plain, 7¾" h.,
  68 oz., green.......................................**63.00**
Pitcher, ice lip or plain, 7¾" h.,
  68 oz., pink **44.00**
Plate, sherbet, 6" d., clear **4.00**
Plate, sherbet, 6" d., green.....................**6.00**
Plate, sherbet, 6" d., pink.......................**5.50**
Plate, luncheon, 8½" d., clear **4.50**
Plate, luncheon, 8½" d., green...............**9.00**
Plate, dinner, 10" d., clear **24.50**
Plate, dinner, 10" d., green....................**55.00**
Plate, dinner, 10" d., pink......................**47.00**
Plate, grill, 10" d., green........................**23.00**
Plate, grill, 10" d., pink..........................**21.50**
Platter, 12" oval, clear...........................**16.00**
Platter, 12" oval, green **23.00**
Platter, 12" oval, pink............................**28.50**
Sherbet, green, 3⅜" h............................**13.00**
Sherbet, pink, 3⅜" h. **10.00**
Sugar bowl, cov., clear..........................**23.50**
Sugar bowl, cov., green.........................**32.00**
Sugar bowl, cov., pink...........................**60.00**
Tumbler, whiskey, clear, 2½" h.,
  1½ oz. **8.00**

Tumbler, whiskey, green, 2½" h.,
  1½ oz. **13.50**
Tumbler, whiskey, pink, 2½" h.,
  1½ oz. **11.00**
Tumbler, cordial, footed, clear,
  3¼" h., 3 oz...**12.00**
Tumbler, cordial, footed, green,
  3¼" h., 3 oz...**23.00**
Tumbler, cordial, footed, pink,
  3¼" h., 3 oz...**16.00**
Tumbler, juice, green, 3" h., 5 oz.........**23.00**
Tumbler, juice, pink, 3" h., 5 oz. **15.00**
Tumbler, footed, clear, 4" h., 5 oz........**13.00**
Tumbler, footed, pink, 4" h., 5 oz.........**21.00**
Tumbler, water, clear, 4" h., 9 oz..........**13.50**
Tumbler, water, green, 4" h., 9 oz. **20.50**
Tumbler, water, pink, 4" h., 9 oz..........**18.50**
Tumbler, footed, clear, 5¼" h.,
  10 oz. **23.00**
Tumbler, footed, pink, 5¼" h.,
  10 oz. **36.50**
Tumbler, clear, 5⅛" h., 11 oz.............**17.00**
Tumbler, pink, 5⅛" h., 11 oz. **34.50**

COLUMBIA, Federal Glass
Co., 1938-42 (Press-mold)
Bowl, cereal, 5" d., clear **14.00**
Bowl, soup, 8" d., clear **17.00**
Bowl, salad, 8½" d., clear **16.00**
Bowl, 10½" d., ruffled rim, clear...........**18.00**
Butter dish, cov., clear **17.00**
Cup & saucer, clear..............................**10.00**
Plate, bread & butter, 6" d., clear **3.00**
Plate, luncheon, 9½" d., clear **8.50**
Plate, luncheon, 9½" d., pink................**32.00**
Plate, chop, 11" d., clear **10.00**
Snack plate, handled, clear **35.00**
Snack plate, handled, w/cup, clear......**40.00**
Tumbler, juice, 2⅞" h., 4 oz., clear **13.50**

DAISY or Number 620,
Indiana Glass Co., 1933-40,
1960s-80s (Press-mold)

Daisy Bowl

Bowl, berry, 4½" d., amber **8.00**
Bowl, cream soup, 4½" d., amber..........**9.00**
Bowl, cereal, 6" d., amber (ILLUS.) **25.00**

Bowl, cereal, 6" d., clear 9.00
Bowl, berry, 7⅜" d., amber 14.00
Bowl, berry, 9⅜" d., amber 29.00
Bowl, 10" oval vegetable, amber 16.00
Creamer, footed, amber.........................6.00
Cup & saucer, amber 7.00
Plate, sherbet, 6" d., amber...................2.50
Plate, salad, 7⅜" d., amber...................9.00
Plate, luncheon, 8⅜" d., amber.............5.00
Plate, dinner, 9⅜" d., amber..................8.00
Plate, grill, 10⅜" d., amber..................13.00
Plate, grill, 10⅜" d., clear 6.00
Plate, 11½" d., amber (cake or
   sandwich)...14.00
Plate, 11½" d., clear (cake or
   sandwich)..9.50
Plate, 10¾" l., amber...........................14.00
Relish dish, three-part, amber,
   8⅜"...27.00
Relish dish, three-part, clear, 8⅜" 8.00
Sherbet, footed, amber..........................8.00
Sugar bowl, open, footed, amber 6.00
Tumbler, footed, amber, 9 oz. 16.00
Tumbler, footed, amber, 12 oz. 43.00

FLORAL or Poinsettia,
Jeannette Glass Co., 1931-35
(Process-etched)
Bowl, berry, 4" d., green 17.00
Bowl, salad, 7½" d., green...................19.00
Bowl, salad, 7½" d., pink......................24.00
Bowl, cov. vegetable, 8" d., green 40.50
Bowl, cov. vegetable, 8" d., pink..........39.00
Bowl, 9" oval vegetable, green 17.00
Bowl, 9" oval vegetable, pink...............17.00
Butter dish, cov., pink 83.00
Candlesticks, green, 4" h., pr..............27.00
Candy jar, cov., green 37.00
Candy jar, cov., pink 37.00
Coaster, green, 3¼" d 10.00
Coaster, pink, 3¼" d. 14.00
Creamer, green.....................................14.50
Creamer, pink 14.50
Cup & saucer, green 11.00
Cup & saucer, pink................................22.00
Pitcher, 5½" h., 24 oz., green 615.00
Pitcher, 8" h., 32 oz., cone-shaped,
   green...36.00
Pitcher, 8" h., 32 oz., cone-shaped,
   pink...33.50
Plate, sherbet, 6" d., green....................7.00
Plate, sherbet, 6" d., pink 6.50
Plate, salad, 8" d., green......................10.50
Plate, salad, 8" d., pink.........................11.00
Plate, dinner, 9" d., green.....................18.00
Plate, dinner, 9" d., pink.......................16.00
Platter, 10¾" oval, green 16.50
Platter, 10¾" oval, pink.........................18.00
Relish, two-part, oval, green 15.00
Relish, two-part, oval, pink...................15.50
Salt & pepper shakers, footed,
   green, 4" h., pr. 50.00
Salt & pepper shakers, footed, pink,
   4" h., pr. 44.00

Salt & pepper shakers, flat, pink,
   6" h., pr. 52.00
Sherbet, green......................................15.00
Sherbet, pink...15.00
Sugar bowl, cov., green 28.00
Sugar bowl, cov., pink...........................23.00
Tumbler, juice, footed, green, 4" h.,
   5 oz. 18.50
Tumbler, juice, footed, pink, 4" h.,
   5 oz. 21.00
Tumbler, water, footed, green,
   4¾" h., 7 oz. 19.50
Tumbler, water, footed, pink,
   4¾" h., 7 oz. 18.00
Tumbler, green, 4½" h., 9 oz. 167.50
Tumbler, lemonade, footed, green,
   5¼" h., 9 oz. 45.00
Tumbler, lemonade, footed, pink,
   5¼" h., 9 oz. 44.00

GEORGIAN or Lovebirds,
Federal Glass Co., 1931-36
(Process-etched)

(All items in green only)

Bowl, berry, 4½" d..................................7.50
Bowl, cereal, 5¾" d 16.00
Bowl, berry, 7½" d.................................58.50
Bowl, 9" oval vegetable........................60.00
Creamer, footed, 3" h...........................10.00
Creamer, footed, 4" h...........................13.00
Cup & saucer 12.50
Plate, sherbet, 6" d.................................5.00
Plate, luncheon, 8" d..............................8.50
Plate, dinner, 9¼" d 24.00
Sherbet 12.00
Sugar bowl, cov., footed, 3" h. 45.00
Sugar bowl, open, footed, 3" h. 8.00
Tumbler, 4" h., 9 oz. 53.00

HOLIDAY or Buttons and Bows,
Jeannette Glass Co., 1947-mid '50s
(Press-mold)

Holiday Milk Pitcher

(All items in pink unless otherwise indicated)

Bowl, berry, 5⅛" d...............................**12.50**
Bowl, flat soup, 7¾" d. **49.00**
Bowl, berry, 8½" d...............................**25.00**
Bowl, 9½" oval vegetable...................**26.00**
Butter dish, cov. **42.50**
Candlesticks, 3" h., pr. **101.00**
Console bowl, 10¾" d. **111.00**
Creamer, footed..................................**9.00**
Cup & saucer, plain or rayed base......**11.00**
Pitcher, milk, 4¾" h., 16 oz., pink
     (ILLUS.) **60.00**
Pitcher, 6¾" h., 52 oz. **36.50**
Plate, sherbet, 6" d................................**6.00**
Plate, dinner, 9" d................................**15.00**
Plate, chop, 13¾" d..............................**21.00**
Platter, 8 x 11⅜" oval, pink..................**22.00**
Sandwich tray, 10½" d. **19.00**
Sherbet..**6.00**
Sugar bowl, cov...................................**25.00**
Sugar bowl, open **8.50**
Tumbler, footed, pink, 4" h., 5 oz.........**30.00**
Tumbler, footed, 6" h., 9 oz. **134.00**
Tumbler, 4" h., 10 oz. **19.50**

IRIS or Iris & Herringbone, Jeannette Glass Co., 1928-32 (Press-mold)

Iris Tumbler

Bowl, berry, 4½" d., beaded rim,
     amber iridescent **9.00**
Bowl, berry, 4½" d., beaded rim,
     clear **36.00**
Bowl, cereal, 5" d., clear **122.00**
Bowl, sauce, 5" d., ruffled rim, amber
     iridescent **23.00**
Bowl, sauce, 5" d., ruffled rim, clear **9.50**
Bowl, soup, 7½" d., amber
     iridescent **62.00**
Bowl, soup, 7½" d., clear **165.00**
Bowl, berry, 8" d., beaded rim, amber
     iridescent **26.00**
Bowl, berry, 8" d., beaded rim, clear....**82.50**
Bowl, salad, 9½" d., amber
     iridescent **13.00**
Bowl, salad, 9½" d., clear **11.00**
Bowl, fruit, 11½" d., ruffled rim,
     amber iridescent **15.00**

Bowl, fruit, 11½" d., ruffled rim,
     clear **13.50**
Butter dish, cov., amber iridescent **39.50**
Butter dish, cov., clear **47.00**
Candlesticks, two-branch, amber
     iridescent, pr. **43.50**
Candlesticks, two-branch, clear, pr.....**38.00**
Candy jar, cov., clear..........................**142.50**
Creamer, footed, amber iridescent **12.00**
Creamer, footed, clear **11.00**
Cup & saucer, demitasse, clear **185.50**
Cup & saucer, amber iridescent..........**25.00**
Cup & saucer, clear............................**24.00**
Goblet, wine, amber iridescent,
     4¼" h., 3 oz......................................**29.00**
Goblet, wine, clear, 4¼" h., 3 oz. **15.00**
Goblet, cocktail, clear, 4¼" h.,
     4 oz. **25.00**
Goblet, clear, 5¾" h., 4 oz. **21.50**
Goblet, clear, 5¾" h., 8 oz. **24.00**
Lamp shade, blue................................**64.50**
Lamp shade, clear frosted...................**89.00**
Lamp shade, pink................................**66.00**
Nut set: 11½" d. ruffled bowl in metal
     holder, w/nutcracker & picks;
     clear, the set **68.00**
Pitcher, 9½" h., footed, amber
     iridescent **39.00**
Pitcher, 9½" h., footed, clear **35.00**
Plate, sherbet, 5½" d., amber
     iridescent **13.00**
Plate, sherbet, 5½" d., clear **14.00**
Plate, dinner, 9" d., amber iridescent ...**39.00**
Plate, dinner, 9" d., clear **52.00**
Plate, sandwich, 11¾" d., amber
     iridescent **31.00**
Plate, sandwich, 11¾" d., clear............**31.00**
Sherbet, footed, amber iridescent,
     2½" h. **14.00**
Sherbet, footed, clear, 2½" h. **25.00**
Sherbet, footed, amber iridescent,
     4" h. **12.00**
Sherbet, footed, clear, 4" h. **21.00**
Sugar bowl, cov., footed, clear............**23.00**
Sugar bowl, open, footed, amber
     iridescent **10.00**
Sugar bowl, open, footed, clear **11.00**
Tumbler, footed, amber iridescent,
     6" h. **17.00**
Tumbler, footed, clear, 6" h.
     (ILLUS.) **18.00**
Tumbler, footed, clear, 6½" h. **31.50**
Vase, 9" h., amber iridescent **24.00**
Vase, 9" h., clear **27.00**
Water set: pitcher & 6 tumblers;
     amber iridescent, 7 pcs......................**94.50**
Water set: pitcher & 6 tumblers; clear,
     7 pcs. **136.50**

LACE EDGE or Open Lace, Hocking Glass Co., 1935-38 (Press-mold)
Bowl, cereal, 6½" d., pink **$17.00**

Bowl, salad or butter dish bottom,
 7¾" d., pink **28.50**
Bowl, 9½" d., plain or ribbed, pink **22.00**
Butter dish or bonbon, cov., clear **25.00**

Lace Edge Butter Dish

Butter dish or bonbon, cov., pink
 (ILLUS.) **67.00**
Candlesticks, pink, pr........................**322.50**
Candy jar, cov., ribbed, pink, 4" h........**43.00**
Compote, cov., 7" d., footed, clear **28.00**
Compote, cov., 7" d., footed, pink........**44.00**
Compote, open, 7" d., footed, pink **20.50**
Console bowl, three-footed, pink,
 10½" d...**193.00**
Cookie jar, cov., pink, 5" h..................**80.00**
Creamer, pink **21.00**
Cup, pink **22.00**
Cup & saucer, pink...............................**33.00**
Flower bowl w/crystal block, pink........**22.50**
Flower bowl without crystal block,
 pink **17.00**
Plate, salad, 7¼" d., clear **4.50**
Plate, salad, 7¼" d., pink.....................**19.00**
Plate, luncheon, 8¾" d., pink...............**22.00**
Plate, dinner, 10½" d., clear.................**17.00**
Plate, dinner, 10½" d., pink **28.00**
Plate, grill, 10½" d., pink......................**18.00**
Plate, 13" d., solid lace, pink **36.00**
Platter, 12¾" oval, pink.......................**34.50**
Platter, 12¾" oval, five-part, pink **29.00**
Relish dish, three-part, deep, pink,
 7½" d...**63.00**
Relish plate, three-part, pink,
 10½" d...**24.00**
Relish plate, four-part, solid lace,
 pink, 13" d. **55.00**
Saucer, pink **14.00**
Sherbet, footed, pink............................**85.00**
Sugar bowl, open, pink........................**20.00**
Tumbler, pink, 4½" h., 9 oz..................**15.00**
Tumbler, footed, pink, 5" h.,
 10½" oz. **71.00**
Vase, 7" h., pink frosted **49.50**

**LORAIN or Basket or Number 615,
Indiana Glass Co., 1929-32
(Process-etched)**
Bowl, cereal, 6", green.........................**38.00**
Bowl, cereal, 6" , yellow.......................**52.50**
Bowl, salad, 7¼", green........................**41.00**
Bowl, salad, 7¼", yellow **55.00**

Bowl, berry, 8", green **86.00**
Bowl, berry, 8", yellow.......................**155.00**
Bowl, 9¾" oval vegetable, green **45.00**
Bowl, 9¾" oval vegetable, yellow.........**45.50**
Creamer, footed, green........................**14.00**
Creamer, footed, yellow **22.00**
Cup, green **10.00**
Cup, yellow...**14.50**
Cup & saucer, green **15.00**

Lorain Cup & Saucer

Cup & saucer, yellow (ILLUS.) **17.00**
Plate, sherbet, 5½", green......................**7.00**
Plate, sherbet, 5½", yellow...................**10.50**
Plate, salad, 7¾", clear **9.00**
Plate, salad, 7¾", green.......................**11.00**
Plate, salad, 7¾", yellow **11.50**
Plate, luncheon, 8⅜", green **15.00**
Plate, luncheon, 8⅜", yellow **25.00**
Plate, dinner, 10¼", clear **36.00**
Plate, dinner, 10¼", green....................**36.00**
Plate, dinner, 10¼", yellow...................**49.00**
Platter, 11½", green.............................**25.50**
Platter, 11½", yellow **40.00**
Relish, four-part, clear, 8" **14.00**
Relish, four-part, yellow, 8"..................**31.00**
Saucer, green **5.00**
Saucer, yellow.......................................**4.50**
Sherbet, footed, green.........................**20.00**
Sherbet, footed, yellow **29.00**
Sugar bowl, open, footed, yellow **18.00**
Tumbler, footed, green, 4¾" h.,
 9 oz. **22.00**
Tumbler, footed, yellow, 4¾" h.,
 9 oz. **24.00**

**MADRID, Federal Glass Co., 1932-
39 (Process-etched)**
Ashtray, amber, 6" sq..........................**264.00**
Bowl, cream soup, 4¾" d., amber........**14.50**
Bowl, sauce, 5" d., amber **5.00**
Bowl, sauce, 5" d., blue **35.00**
Bowl, sauce, 5" d., green **8.50**
Bowl, sauce, 5" d., pink.......................**10.00**
Bowl, soup, 7" d., amber......................**14.00**
Bowl, soup, 7" d., blue **20.00**
Bowl, soup, 7" d., clear **6.00**
Bowl, soup, 7" d., green **15.50**
Bowl, salad, 8" d., amber.....................**14.00**

Bowl, salad, 8" d., clear 9.50
Bowl, salad, 8" d., green.................15.50
Bowl, large berry, 9⅜" d., amber 22.00
Bowl, salad, 9½" d., deep, amber 30.50
Bowl, 10" oval vegetable, amber 15.00
Bowl, 10" oval vegetable, blue.............33.50
Bowl, 10" oval vegetable, green 18.50
Butter dish, cov., amber.....................67.00
Butter dish, cov., clear 57.00
Butter dish, cov., green......................78.00
Cake plate, amber, 11¼" d. 14.00
Cake plate, pink, 11¼" d 12.00
Candlesticks, amber, 2¼" h., pr..........18.50
Candlesticks, clear, 2¼" h., pr. 14.50
Candlesticks, iridescent, 2¼" h.,
    pr..21.50
Candlesticks, pink, 2¼" h., pr. 13.50
Console bowl, flared, amber, 11" d.....13.00
Console bowl, flared, iridescent,
    11" d...16.00
Console set: bowl & pair of
    candlesticks; amber, 3 pcs. 37.00
Console set: bowl & pair of
    candlesticks; iridescent, 3 pcs. 32.00
Console set: bowl & pair of
    candlesticks; pink, 3 pcs. 36.00

Madrid Cookie Jar

Cookie jar, cov., amber (ILLUS.) 43.00
Cookie jar, cov., pink 34.50
Creamer, amber.....................................7.50
Creamer, blue 14.00
Creamer, clear 7.00
Creamer, green.....................................10.50
Cup & saucer, amber 9.00
Cup & saucer, blue................................22.50
Cup & saucer, clear.................................8.00
Cup & saucer, green 12.00
Cup & saucer, pink.................................11.50
Gelatin mold, amber, 2⅛" h. 12.00
Gravy boat & platter, amber 1,575.00
Gravy boat platter, amber.................500.00
Hot dish coaster, amber, 5" d. 39.50
Hot dish coaster, clear, 5" d. 23.00

Hot dish coaster w/indentation,
    amber...35.00
Hot dish coaster w/indentation,
    clear...27.50
Hot dish coaster w/indentation,
    green..36.50
Jam dish, amber, 7" d...........................19.00
Jam dish, blue, 7" d..............................33.00
Jam dish, clear, 7" d.............................10.00
Jam dish, green, 7" d............................25.00
Pitcher, juice, 5½" h., 36 oz.,
    amber...34.00
Pitcher, 8" h., 60 oz., square,
    amber...44.00
Pitcher, 8" h., 60 oz., square, blue 147.50
Pitcher, 8" h., 60 oz., square, clear......22.00
Pitcher, 8" h., 60 oz., square,
    green...132.50
Pitcher, 8½" h., 80 oz., jug-type,
    amber...59.00
Pitcher, 8½" h., 80 oz., jug-type,
    green...188.50
Pitcher w/ice lip, 8½" h., 80 oz.,
    amber...55.50
Plate, sherbet, 6" d., amber....................4.00
Plate, sherbet, 6" d., blue.....................12.00
Plate, sherbet, 6" d., clear.....................4.00
Plate, sherbet, 6" d., green.....................4.50
Plate, salad, 7½" d., amber...................10.00
Plate, salad, 7½" d., blue......................17.00
Plate, salad, 7½" d., green......................9.00
Plate, salad, 7½" d., pink........................9.00
Plate, luncheon, 8⅞" d., amber 7.00
Plate, luncheon, 8⅞" d., blue 18.50
Plate, luncheon, 8⅞" d., clear 5.50
Plate, luncheon, 8⅞" d., green 10.00
Plate, dinner, 10½" d., amber..............37.00
Plate, dinner, 10½" d., blue.................54.50
Plate, dinner, 10½" d., clear 21.00
Plate, dinner, 10½" d., green...............34.00
Plate, grill, 10½" d., amber.....................9.00
Plate, grill, 10½" d., green....................16.00
Platter, 11½" oval, amber 16.00
Platter, 11½" oval, blue.........................29.00
Platter, 11½" oval, green 16.00
Relish plate, amber, 10½" d. 14.50
Relish plate, clear, 10½" d. 7.00
Relish plate, pink, 10½" d 12.00
Salt & pepper shakers, amber,
    3½" h., pr. 44.00
Salt & pepper shakers, green,
    3½" h., pr. 56.00
Salt & pepper shakers, footed,
    amber, 3½" h., pr. 61.00
Salt & pepper shakers, footed,
    green, 3½" h., pr. 81.00
Sherbet, amber.....................................7.00
Sherbet, clear 6.50
Sherbet, green.......................................9.50
Sugar bowl, cov., amber.......................40.00
Sugar bowl, cov., clear.........................32.50
Sugar bowl, cov., green........................48.00
Sugar bowl, open, amber........................7.00
Sugar bowl, open, blue 15.00

Sugar bowl, open, green 9.00
Tumbler, juice, amber, 3⅞" h.,
   5 oz. 13.50
Tumbler, juice, blue, 3⅞" h., 5 oz. 32.50
Tumbler, footed, amber, 4" h., 5 oz. 21.00
Tumbler, amber, 4½" h., 9 oz. 14.00
Tumbler, blue, 4½" h., 9 oz.................25.00
Tumbler, green, 4½" h., 9 oz. 23.50
Tumbler, pink, 4½" h., 9 oz.................15.00
Tumbler, footed, amber, 5¼" h.,
   10 oz. 23.00
Tumbler, footed, clear, 5¼" h.,
   10 oz. 14.00
Tumbler, footed, green, 5¼" h.,
   10 oz. 33.50
Tumbler, amber, 5½" h., 12 oz. 20.00
Tumbler, blue, 5½" h., 12 oz...............39.00
Tumbler, clear, 5½" h., 12 oz..............20.00
Tumbler, green, 5½" h., 12 oz. 32.00

**MANHATTAN or Horizontal Ribbed,
Anchor Hocking Glass Co., 1938-43
(Press-mold)**
Ashtray, clear, 4" d. 10.00
Ashtray, clear w/gold trim, 4½" sq. 16.50
Bowl, sauce, 4½" d., two-handled,
   clear 8.50
Bowl, berry, 5⅜" d., two-handled,
   pink 15.00
Bowl, 8" d., two-handled, clear...........17.00
Bowl, salad, 9" d., clear......................20.50
Bowl, cereal, 5½" d., clear 23.00
Bowl, large berry, 7½" d., clear..........15.00
Bowl, fruit, 9½" d., clear 32.00
Bowl, fruit, 9½" d., pink 46.50
Candleholders, clear, 4½" sq., pr......14.00
Candy dish, cov., clear........................33.00
Candy dish, open, three-footed,
   pink 10.50
Coaster, clear, 3½" d. 14.00
Compote, 5¾" h., clear 27.00
Compote, 5¾" h., pink 29.00
Creamer, oval, clear............................9.50
Creamer, oval, pink............................10.50
Cup, clear...15.00
Cup & saucer, clear............................23.00
Pitcher, juice, 42 oz., ball tilt-type,
   clear 30.00
Pitcher w/ice lip, 80 oz., ball tilt-
   type, clear 41.00
Plate, sherbet or saucer, 6" d., clear 6.00
Plate, salad, 8½" d., clear...................11.00
Plate, dinner, 10¼" d., clear 17.00
Plate, sandwich, 14" d., clear 22.50
Relish tray, four-part, clear, 14" d......15.00
Relish tray, five-part, clear w/clear
   inserts, 14" d. 44.00
Relish tray, five-part, clear w/ruby
   inserts, 14" d. 45.50
Relish tray insert, clear........................5.00
Relish tray insert, ruby.........................5.50
Salt & pepper shakers, square,
   clear, 2" h., pr..................................24.00

Salt & pepper shakers, square,
   pink, 2" h. pr. 55.00
Sherbet, clear......................................6.50
Sherbet, pink.....................................12.00
Sugar bowl, open, oval, pink 10.00
Tumbler, footed, clear, 10 oz. 14.00
Tumbler, footed, pink, 10 oz. 17.00
Vase, 8" h., clear................................17.00
Water bottle, cov., clear.....................15.00
Wine, clear, 3½" h. 6.00

**MOONSTONE, Anchor Hocking
Glass Corp., 1941-46 (Press-mold)**

(All items clear to opalescent only.)

Bonbon, heart-shaped, w/handle,
   6½" w. 11.00
Bowl, berry, 5½" d...............................16.00
Bowl, dessert, 5½" d., crimped rim 9.00
Bowl, 6" w., three-part, cloverleaf-
   shaped 9.50
Bowl, 6½" d., two-handled, crimped
   rim 12.00
Bowl, 7¾" d., flat...............................12.00
Bowl, 9½" d., crimped rim 20.00
Candleholder.......................................7.50

Moonstone Candleholders

Candleholders, pr. (ILLUS.) 17.00
Candy dish, cov., two-handled,
   6" d...25.00
Cigarette box, cov., rectangular 22.50
Creamer, footed 7.00
Cup & saucer 12.00
Dinner set, service for four,
   23 pcs. 275.00
Goblet, 10 oz. 18.50
Plate, sherbet, 6¼" d...........................6.50
Plate, luncheon, 8" d. 15.00
Plate, sandwich, 10" d., crimped rim 27.00
Puff box, cov., 4¾" d. 23.00
Relish bowl, divided, 7¾" d. 11.00
Sherbet, footed 7.50
Sugar bowl, footed 9.00
Vase, bud, 5½" h..................................10.50

**MOROCCAN AMETHYST, Hazel
Ware, Division of Continental Can,
1960s - (not true Depression)**
Ashtray, 3¾" triangle 6.50
Ashtray, 6" triangle 10.00
Ashtray, 6⅞" triangle 12.00
Bowl, fruit, 4¾" w., octagon 7.00
Bowl, cereal, 5¾" sq., deep 10.00
Bowl, 6" d. 11.00
Bowl, 7¾" oval 16.00
Bowl, 7¾" oval w/center handle 17.00
Bowl, 7¾" rectangle 13.00
Bowl, 9½" oval, low 11.50
Bowl, 9½" oval, w/metal center
  handle 40.00
Bowl, 10¾" 33.00
Candy jar, cov., short 26.00
Candy jar, cov., tall 28.50
Celery dish, 9½" 11.50
Chip & dip set, w/metal holder
  (5¾ x 10¾" bowls) 41.50
Cocktail shaker w/chrome lid,
  32 oz. 25.00
Cocktail stirrer, w/pouring lip,
  6¼" h., 16 oz. 24.00
Cup & saucer 8.00
Goblet, wine, 4" h., 4½ oz. 10.00
Goblet, juice, 4⅜" h., 5½ oz. 9.00
Goblet, water, 5½" h., 10 oz. 11.00
Plate, 5¾" w. octagon 5.50
Plate, salad, 7¼" w. 8.50
Plate, sandwich, w/center handle,
  8" oval 8.00
Plate, dinner, 9¾" w. 10.00
Plate, sandwich, 12" w. 19.00
Punch set, bowl, base & 12 cups,
  14 pcs. 140.00
Relish server, two 7¾" l.
  rectangular bowls in metal frame 24.00
Sandwich server, w/metal center
  handle, 12" 18.50
Sherbet, footed, 4¼" h. 6.50
Tidbit server, two-tier 20.00
Tidbit server, three-tier 28.50
Tumbler, juice, 2½" h., 4 oz. 9.00
Tumbler, Old Fashioned, 3¼" h.,
  8 oz. 13.50
Tumbler, water, crinkled bottom,
  4¼" h., 11 oz. 11.00
Tumbler, water, 4⅝" h., 11 oz. 11.00
Tumbler, iced tea, 6½" h., 16 oz. 15.50
Vase, 8½" h., ruffled 35.00

**NORMANDIE or Bouquet and
Lattice, Federal Glass Co., 1933-40
(Process-etched)**
Bowl, berry, 5" d., amber 6.00
Bowl, berry, 5" d., pink 5.50
Bowl, berry, 5" d., Sunburst
  iridescent 4.00
Bowl, cereal, 6½" d., amber 17.00
Bowl, cereal, 6½" d., Sunburst
  iridescent 7.00
Bowl, large berry, 8½" d., amber 17.00

Bowl, large berry, 8½" d., pink 36.50
Bowl, large berry, 8½" d., Sunburst
  iridescent 16.00
Bowl, 10" oval vegetable, Sunburst
  iridescent 13.00
Creamer, footed, amber 7.50
Creamer, footed, Sunburst iridescent 7.00
Cup & saucer, amber 11.00
Cup & saucer, pink 10.00
Cup & saucer, Sunburst iridescent........7.50
Luncheon set: 4 each 8" d., plates,
  cups & saucers plus creamer &
  sugar bowl; amber, 14 pcs. 80.00
Pitcher, 8" h., 80 oz., amber 70.00
Plate, sherbet, 6" d., amber 4.50
Plate, sherbet, 6" d., pink 4.50
Plate, sherbet, 6" d., Sunburst
  iridescent 2.50
Plate, salad, 8" d., amber 8.50
Plate, salad, 8" d., pink 12.00
Plate, luncheon, 9¼" d., amber 10.00
Plate, luncheon, 9¼" d., pink 13.50
Plate, luncheon, 9¼" d., Sunburst
  iridescent 15.00
Plate, dinner, 11" d., Sunburst
  iridescent 13.00
Plate, grill, 11" d., amber 13.50
Plate, grill, 11" d., Sunburst
  iridescent 7.00
Platter, 11¾" oval, amber 18.50
Salt & pepper shakers, amber, pr. 44.00
Salt & pepper shakers, pink, pr. 88.00
Sherbet, amber 6.00
Sherbet, clear 6.00
Sherbet, pink 8.00
Sherbet, Sunburst iridescent 6.00
Sugar bowl, cov., amber 81.00
Sugar bowl, open, amber 7.00
Sugar bowl, open, Sunburst
  iridescent 6.00
Tumbler, juice, pink, 4" h., 5 oz. 37.50
Tumbler, water, amber, 4½" h.,
  9 oz. 15.00
Tumbler, water, pink, 4½" h., 9 oz. 43.00
Tumbler, iced tea, amber, 5" h.,
  12 oz. 19.00
Tumbler, iced tea, pink, 5" h.,
  12 oz. 114.50

**PATRICIAN or Spoke,
Federal Glass Co., 1933-37
(Process-etched)**
Bowl, cream soup, 4¾" d., amber 11.00
Bowl, cream soup, 4¾" d., clear 13.00
Bowl, cream soup, 4¾" d., pink 18.50
Bowl, berry, 5" d., green 10.00
Bowl, berry, 5" d., pink 11.00
Bowl, cereal, 6" d., amber 20.50
Bowl, cereal, 6" d., clear 21.00
Bowl, large berry, 8½" d., amber 39.50
Bowl, large berry, 8½" d., pink 26.00
Bowl, 10" oval vegetable, clear 29.00
Bowl, 10" oval vegetable, green 29.00
Butter dish, cov., amber 78.00

Butter dish, cov, green.........................92.00
Butter dish, cov., pink 213.50
Cookie jar, cov., amber 82.00
Cookie jar, cov., clear..........................72.50
Creamer, footed, amber...........................8.00
Creamer, footed, clear 10.00
Creamer, footed, pink 12.00

Patrician Cup & Saucer

Cup & saucer, amber (ILLUS.).............18.00
Cup & saucer, clear..............................15.00
Pitcher, 8" h., 75 oz., molded handle,
   clear...97.00
Pitcher, 8" h., 75 oz., molded handle,
   green...166.00
Pitcher, 8" h., 75 oz., molded handle,
   pink...118.50
Pitcher, 8¼" h., 75 oz., applied
   handle, clear 127.50
Plate, sherbet, 6" d., amber.....................9.00
Plate, sherbet, 6" d., green......................7.00
Plate, salad, 7½" d., amber.................14.00
Plate, luncheon, 9" d., amber...............10.00
Plate, luncheon, 9" d., clear 11.00
Plate, dinner, 10½" d., amber.................6.00
Plate, dinner, 10½" d., pink 32.00
Plate, grill, 10½" d., amber..................12.00
Platter, 11½" oval, amber 28.00
Platter, 11½" oval, green 23.00
Salt & pepper shakers, amber, pr. 66.00
Salt & pepper shakers, clear, pr...54.00
Salt & pepper shakers, pink, pr. 79.00
Sherbet, amber 11.00
Sherbet, clear 12.00
Sherbet, green....................................12.00
Sugar bowl, cov., amber 58.00
Sugar bowl, open, amber 8.00
Sugar bowl, open, green.......................9.00
Sugar bowl, open, pink.........................10.00
Tumbler, amber, 4" h., 5 oz. 28.00
Tumbler, footed, amber, 5¼" h.,
   8 oz..45.00
Tumbler, amber, 4½" h., 9 oz. 25.00
Tumbler, green, 4½" h., 9 oz. 24.00
Tumbler, iced tea, amber, 5½" h.,
   14 oz...40.00
Tumbler, iced tea, pink, 5½" h.,
   14 oz...37.00

**PETALWARE, MacBeth-Evans
Glass Co., 1930-40 (Press-mold)**
Bowl, cream soup, 4½" d., plain
   Cremax or Monax 11.00
Bowl, cream soup, 4½" d.,
   decorated Cremax or Monax 10.50
Bowl, cream soup, 4½" d., pink 17.50
Bowl, cereal, 5¾" d., clear 4.50
Bowl, cereal, 5¾" d, plain Cremax
   or Monax...7.00
Bowl, cereal, 5¾" d., decorated
   Cremax or Monax 7.00
Bowl, cereal, 5¾" d., Florette...............11.00
Bowl, cereal, 5¾" d., pink 10.50
Bowl, large berry, 9" d., plain Cremax
   or Monax..17.00
Bowl, large berry, 9" d., decorated
   Cremax or Monax 26.00
Bowl, large berry, 9" d., Florette 25.00
Bowl, large, berry, 9" d., pink 21.00
Creamer, footed, plain Cremax or
   Monax 9.00
Creamer, footed, decorated Cremax
   or Monax...8.50
Creamer, footed, Florette.....................11.00
Creamer, footed, pink 11.50
Cup & saucer, clear...............................4.00
Cup & saucer, plain Cremax or
   Monax 11.00
Cup & saucer, decorated Cremax or
   Monax 9.00
Cup & saucer, Florette 11.50
Cup & saucer, pink...............................10.50
Lamp shade, Monax, 11" h...................15.50
Plate, sherbet, 6" d., plain Cremax or
   Monax 3.00
Plate, sherbet, 6" d., decorated
   Cremax or Monax 6.00
Plate, sherbet, 6" d., pink 5.00
Plate, salad, 8" d., clear 2.50
Plate, salad, 8" d., plain Cremax or
   Monax 6.00
Plate, salad, 8" d., decorated Cremax
   or Monax...10.50
Plate, salad, 8" d., Florette....................8.50
Plate, salad, 8" d., Red Trim Floral 6.00
Plate, salad, 8" d., pink.........................6.50
Plate, dinner, 9" d., plain Cremax or
   Monax 8.50
Plate, dinner, 9" d., decorated
   Cremax or Monax 13.50
Plate, dinner, 9" d., pink 8.00
Plate, salver, 11" d., plain Cremax or
   Monax 10.50
Plate, salver, 11" d., decorated
   Cremax or Monax 17.00
Plate, salver, 11" d., Florette...............16.00
Plate, salver, 11" d., pink.....................15.00
Plate, salver, 12" d., decorated
   Cremax or Monax 12.50
Plate, salver, 12" d., Red Trim
   Floral...40.00

Platter, 13" oval, plain Cremax or
  Monax **17.00**
Platter, 13" oval, pink...........................**15.00**
Sherbet, low foot, plain Cremax or
  Monax, 4½" h.....................................**9.00**
Sherbet, low foot, decorated Cremax
  or Monax, 4½" h................................**11.00**
Sugar bowl, open, footed, plain
  Cremax or Monax **5.50**
Sugar bowl, open, footed, decorated
  Cremax or Monax **10.00**
Sugar bowl, open, footed, Florette **10.00**
Sugar bowl, open, pink........................**10.00**
Tumbler, pink, 4¾" h.............................**27.00**

**PINEAPPLE & FLORAL or Number
618 or Wildflower, Indiana Glass
Co., 1932-37 (Press-mold)**
Ashtray, clear, 4½" l. **14.50**
Bowl, berry, 4¾" d., clear......................**42.00**
Bowl, cream soup, 4⅝" d, amber.........**17.00**
Bowl, cereal, 6" d., clear.......................**24.00**
Bowl, salad, 7" d., clear **4.00**
Bowl, 10" oval vegetable, clear............**24.00**
Compote, diamond-shaped, clear **4.00**
Creamer, diamond-shaped, amber........**9.50**
Creamer, diamond-shaped, clear **5.50**
Cup & saucer, amber **10.50**
Cup & saucer, clear..............................**14.50**
Plate, sherbet, 6" d., amber....................**4.00**
Plate, sherbet, 6" d., clear **3.00**
Plate, salad, 8⅜" d., amber **7.00**
Plate, salad, 8⅜" d., clear **7.50**
Plate, dinner, 9⅜" d., amber.................**12.00**
Plate, dinner, 9⅜" d., clear...................**18.00**
Plate, sandwich, 11½" d., amber..........**15.50**
Plate, sandwich, 11½" d., clear **14.50**
Plate, 11½" d., w/indentation,
  clear **14.00**
Platter, 11", closed handles, clear **16.00**
Relish, divided, clear, 11½" **18.00**
Sherbet, footed, clear **18.00**
Sugar bowl, open, diamond-shaped,
  clear...**7.00**
Tumbler, clear, 4¼" h., 8 oz.................**33.00**
Tumbler, iced tea, clear, 5" h., 12 oz...**41.00**

**SAILBOATS or Ships or Sportsman
Series, Hazel Atlas Glass Co.,
late 1930s**

*(All items in cobalt blue with white
decoration)*

Ashtray **25.00**
Cocktail mixer w/stirrer **26.00**
Ice bowl **34.00**
Plate, bread & butter, 5⅞" d. **20.00**
Plate, salad, 8" d. **28.00**
Plate, dinner, 9" d., ...**33.00**
Saucer...**15.00**
Tumbler, whiskey, 2¼" h., 2 oz............**12.00**
Tumbler, juice, 3¾" h., 5 oz. **9.00**
Tumbler, roly poly, 6 oz. **9.00**

Tumbler, Old Fashioned, 3⅜" h.,
  8 oz...**15.00**
Tumbler, water, straight sides,
  3¾" h., 9 oz...**10.50**
Tumbler, water, 4⅝" h., 9 oz...............**12.50**
Tumbler, iced tea, 4⅞" h.,
  10½ oz...**14.00**
Water set, water pitcher & six 9 oz.
  tumblers, 7 pcs. **95.00**

**SHARON or Cabbage Rose, Federal
Glass Co., 1935-39 (Chip-mold)**

Sharon Tumblers

Bowl, berry, 5" d., amber **8.00**
Bowl, berry, 5" d., green **12.50**
Bowl, berry, 5" d., pink.........................**11.50**
Bowl, cream soup, 5" d., amber..........**26.00**
Bowl, cream soup, 5" d., pink **40.00**
Bowl, cereal, 6" d., amber....................**19.00**
Bowl, cereal, 6" d., pink.......................**20.00**
Bowl, soup, 7½" d., pink **44.50**
Bowl, berry, 8½" d., amber **5.00**
Bowl, berry, 8½" d., pink......................**29.00**
Bowl, 9½" oval vegetable, amber **20.00**
Bowl, 9½" oval vegetable, green **28.00**
Bowl, fruit, 10½" d., amber...................**23.00**
Bowl, fruit, 10½" d., green....................**30.50**
Bowl, fruit, 10½" d., pink......................**35.00**
Butter dish, cov., amber......................**44.00**
Butter dish, cov., green.......................**81.50**
Butter dish, cov., pink.........................**50.00**
Cake plate, footed, amber,
  11½" d...**25.00**
Cake plate, footed, clear, 11½" d.,.......**15.00**
Cake plate, footed, pink, 11½" d..........**38.00**
Candy jar, cov., amber **42.00**
Candy jar, cov., green **141.00**
Candy jar, cov., pink **51.00**
Creamer, amber....................................**13.00**
Creamer, pink.......................................**15.00**
Cup & saucer, amber **11.00**
Cup & saucer, green **28.00**
Cup & saucer, pink..............................**23.00**
Jam dish, amber, 7½" d., 1½" h. **64.00**
Pitcher, 9" h., 80 oz., amber **110.00**

Pitcher w/ice lip, 9" h., 80 oz.,
  amber...**125.00**
Pitcher w/ice lip, 9" h., 80 oz., pink....**139.50**
Plate, bread & butter, 6" d., amber.........**4.00**
Plate, bread & butter, 6" d., green..........**6.50**
Plate, bread & butter, 6" d., pink **7.00**
Plate, salad, 7½" d., amber..................**15.00**
Plate, salad, 7½" d., green..................**20.00**
Plate, dinner, 9¼" d., amber................**10.00**
Plate, dinner, 9¼" d., pink **17.00**
Platter, 12¼" oval, amber **15.00**
Platter, 12¼" oval, green **24.00**
Platter, 12¼" oval, pink.......................**27.00**
Salt & pepper shakers, amber, pr. **37.00**
Salt & pepper shakers, green, pr. **64.00**
Salt & pepper shakers, pink, pr. **49.00**
Sherbet, footed, amber.......................**12.00**
Sherbet, footed, green........................**31.50**
Sherbet, footed, pink...........................**13.50**
Sugar bowl, cov., amber **31.00**
Sugar bowl, cov., pink **40.00**
Sugar bowl, open, pink.........................**13.00**
Tumbler, amber, 4" h., 9 oz. **24.00**
Tumbler, pink, 4" h., 9 oz....................**38.00**
Tumbler, pink, 5¼" h., 12 oz.
  (ILLUS. left)......................................**41.50**
Tumbler, footed, pink, 6½" h.,
  15 oz. (ILLUS. right).........................**46.00**

**SIERRA or Pinwheel, Jeannette
Glass Co., 1931-33 (Press-mold)**
Bowl, cereal, 5½" d., green..................**13.00**
Bowl, cereal, 5½" d., pink **12.50**
Bowl, berry, 8½" d., green **26.50**
Bowl, berry, 8½" d., pink......................**29.00**
Bowl, 9½" oval vegetable, green **72.50**
Bowl, 9½" oval vegetable, pink............**39.50**
Butter dish, cov., green.......................**67.50**
Butter dish, cov., pink **49.00**
Creamer, green....................................**21.00**
Cup & saucer, green **16.50**
Cup & saucer, pink **16.50**
Pitcher, 6½" h., 32 oz., pink................**84.00**
Plate, dinner, 9" d., green....................**18.00**
Plate, dinner, 9" d., pink......................**17.00**
Platter, 11" oval, pink..........................**36.00**
Salt & pepper shakers, pink, pr. **37.00**
Serving tray, two-handled, green........**16.50**
Serving tray, two-handled, pink...........**21.00**
Sugar bowl, cov., green **32.50**
Sugar bowl, cov., pink **25.00**
Tumbler, footed, green, 4½" h.,
  9 oz...**82.00**

(End of Depression Glass Section)

DUNCAN & MILLER

*Duncan & Miller Glass Company, a
successor firm to George A. Duncan & Sons
Company, produced a wide range of*
*pressed wares and novelty pieces during
the late 19th century and into the early
20th century. During the Depression era
and after, they continued making a wide
variety of more modern patterns, including
mold-blown types and also introduced a
number of etched and engraved patterns.
Many colors, including opalescent hues,
were produced during this era and
especially popular today are the graceful
swan dishes they produced in the Pall Mall
and Sylvan patterns. The numbers after
the pattern name indicate the original
factory pattern number. The Duncan
factory was closed in 1955. Also see
ANIMALS and PATTERN GLASS in
Glass section.*

Ashtray, flared rim, Canterbury patt.
  (No. 115), clear, 3½"..........................**$7.00**
Candelabra, w/etched shades &
  prisms, etched First Love patt.,
  clear, pr...**425.00**
Champagne, saucer-type, Mardi Gras
  patt. (No. 42), clear **42.00**
Claret, Mardi Gras patt., clear.............**40.00**
Cocktail, Canterbury patt., clear...........**8.00**
Condiment set w/glass tray, Early
  American Sandwich patt., (No. 41),
  clear, the set **82.50**
Cornucopia-vase, Three Feathers
  patt. (No. 117), blue opalescent,
  8" h..**90.00**
Cruet w/original stopper, Caribbean
  patt. (No. 112), clear..........................**30.00**
Dresser bottles w/original stoppers,
  Hobnail patt. (No. 118), green,
  6½" h., pr...**130.00**
Goblet, footed, Spiral Flutes patt.
  (No. 40), green, 6¼" h. **17.00**
Mayonnaise bowl & underplate,
  Teardrop patt. (No. 301), clear,
  2 pcs..**20.00**
Model of a swan, Sylvan patt. (No.
  122), pink opalescent, 7" l................**75.00**
Mustard pot, cov., Teardrop patt.,
  clear...**31.00**
Nut dish, Spiral Flutes patt., clear **7.00**
Oyster cocktail, etched Language
  of Flowers patt., clear, 4½ oz.............**20.00**
Pitcher, tankard, Mardi Gras patt.,
  clear...**75.00**
Plate, 9" d., Canterbury patt., clear **12.00**
Plate, 12" d., Early American
  Sandwich patt., clear **25.00**
Plate, hostess, 16" d., Early American
  Sandwich patt., amber **105.00**
Punch cup, Mardi Gras patt.,
  clear...**10.00**
Punch set: bowl, base & twelve cups;
  Mardi Gras patt., clear, 14 pcs.........**395.00**
Sherbet, low, Spiral Flutes patt.,
  green...**12.00**

Sherry, flared rim, Mardi Gras patt.,
  clear **45.00**
Toothpick holder, Mardi Gras patt.,
  clear **27.00**
Tumbler, whiskey, footed, Ripple
  patt. (No. 101), ruby, 2 oz. **65.00**
Tumbler, Mardi Gras patt., clear..........**45.00**
Vase, 4½" h., violet-type, crimped
  rim, Canterbury patt., clear **15.00**
Wine, Caribbean patt., clear,
  4¼" h., 3 oz..**22.00**

FENTON

Hobnail Pattern Fenton Bowl

*Fenton Art Glass Company began
producing glass at Williamstown, West
Virginia, in January 1907. Organized by
Frank L. and John W. Fenton, the
company began operations in a newly built
glass factory with an experienced master
glass craftsman, Jacob Rosenthal, as their
factory manager. Fenton has produced a
wide variety of collectible glassware
through the years, including Carnival.
Still in production today, their current
productions may be found at finer gift
shops across the country. William
Heacock's three-volume set on Fenton,
published by Antique Publications, is the
standard reference in this field.*

Modern Fenton Mark

Basket, Gold Crest, 6¼" h. **$85.00**
Basket, Spiral Optic patt., topaz
  opalescent, 4½" d., 9½" h. **165.00**
Basket, No. 192, Peach Crest,
  10" h..**125.00**
Basket, Silver Crest, 13" h. **105.00**

Bonbon, Blackberry Spray patt., blue
  opalescent, ca. 1915........................**50.00**
Bowl, 8" d., footed, Hobnail patt.,
  green opalescent (ILLUS.) **38.50**
Bowl, 10" d., shallow, Flame
  Crest **200.00**
Candleholders, No. 848, Chinese
  Yellow, pr. **70.00**
Candlesticks, Hobnail patt., No.
  3674, milk white, 6" h., pr.................**22.00**
Compote, open, 7" d., Topaz Stretch
  glass **20.00**
Console bowl, flared rim, No. 1663,
  Chinese Yellow, 12" d.......................**85.00**

Hobnail Pattern Fenton Cruet

Cruet w/original stopper, Hobnail
  patt., cranberry opalescent
  (ILLUS.) **70.00**
Cruets w/original stoppers,
  HangingHeart patt., No. 8969,
  custard ground, 1976, pr...................**95.00**
Epergne, three-lily, Hobnail patt.,
  green opalescent, signed................**275.00**
Ferner, round, footed, Vintage patt.,
  Chocolate glass, ca. 1910 ....**220.00**
Goblet, water, Plymouth patt., ruby **18.00**
Lamp, hurricane-type, Emerald
  Crest **85.00**
Lamp, kerosene-type, cranberry
  opalescent Hobnail patt. shade &
  font, painted white base..................**259.00**
Match holder, Lincoln Inn patt.,
  clear **15.00**
Novelty, top hat, Spiral Optic patt.,
  French Opalescent, 3" h. **95.00**
Perfume bottle w/original stopper,
  Hobnail patt., white opalescent,
  6¼" h..**30.00**
Pitcher, 6" h., Daisy & Fern patt., lime
  green opalescent **50.00**
Pitcher, 8½" h., Coin Dot patt.,
  white opalescent **150.00**
Pitcher, water, Daisy & Fern patt.,
  canary yellow opalescent................**195.00**

Plate, 12½" d., Silver Crest 32.00
Plate, luncheon, Lincoln Inn patt.,
   Jade Green 35.00
Punch set: bowl, twelve cups &
   matching ladle; Hobnail patt., milk
   white, 14 pcs. 595.00
Salt & pepper shakers w/original
   tops, Hobnail patt., cranberry
   opalscent. 47.50
Tidbit tray, three-tier, Aqua Crest........75.00
Vase, 4" h., bulbous base w/crimped
   rim, Hobnail patt., cranberry
   opalscent ....40.00 to 60.00
Vase, 4½" h., Hobnail patt.,
   cranberry opalescent 40.00
Vase, 5" h., Gold Crest.......................45.00
Vase, 6" h., fan-shaped, No. 847,
   Mandarin Red 50.00
Vase, 6¼" h., Polka Dot patt.,
   cranberry opalescent 50.00
Vase, 7½" h., Aqua Crest.....................35.00
Vase, 7½" h., Emerald Crest................95.00
Vase, 7½" h., Rose Crest 35.00
Vase, 8½" h., Hobnail patt., blue
   opalescent 75.00
Vase, 8½" h., Hobnail patt., Topaz
   opalescent 85.00
Vase, 10" h., Hanging Heart design,
   turquoise iridescent, Robert Barber
   Collection, signed 265 of 600,
   1975...195.00
Water set: pitcher & six tumblers;
   Hobnail patt., Aqua opalescent;
   7 pcs. 200.00

FOSTORIA

Fostoria Glass company, founded in 1887, produced numerous types of fine glassware over the years. Their factory in Moundsville, West Virginia closed in 1986.

Fostoria Label

Ashtray, hat shape, American patt.,
   clear $15.00
Ashtray, Coin patt., frosted blue,
   7½" d..35.00
Bonbon, Brocaded Acorns etching,
   6" d., clear.......................................30.00
Bonbon, three-footed, American
   patt., clear 20.00
Bonbon, three-footed, Century patt.,
   clear, 7½" d. 13.00
Bottle, bitters, American patt., clear.....65.00

Bouillon cup & saucer, Versailles
   patt., blue 55.00
Bowl, 4⅝" w., tri-cornered,
   handled, Baroque patt., blue..............22.00
Bowl, tri-cornered, Century patt.,
   clear 12.00
Bowl, 5½" d., two-handled, Colony
   patt., clear 8.00
Bowl, grapefruit, Trojan patt., yellow....37.50
Bowl, 6½" d., w/handles, June
   etching, blue 25.00
Bowl, salad, 7½" d., Meadow Rose
   etching, clear 15.00
Bowl, 8" d., American patt., clear.........45.00
Bowl, oval, Coin patt., azure 60.00
Bowl, 10" d., footed, American patt.,
   clear 23.00
Bowl, 10" d., flared, Colony patt.,
   clear 28.00
Bowl, fruit, 11" d., w/pedestal base,
   Vesper etching, green........................35.00
Bowl, wedding, cov., Coin patt.,
   amber...65.00
Cake plate, three-footed, American
   patt., clear, 12" d...............................18.00
Cake plate, Baroque patt., clear,
   10" d...15.00
Cake plate, two-handled, Colony
   patt., clear, 10" d...............................20.00
Cake plate, handled, Navarre
   etching, clear, 10" d. 39.50
Cake stand, Century patt., clear 50.00
Candleholder, Navarre patt.,
   No. 2496, clear 24.00
Candleholder, two-light, Morning
   Glory etching, No. 6023, clear 40.00
Candleholders, Arlington decoration,
   opaque blue, pr..................................30.00
Candleholders, seascape deco-
   ration, blue opalescent, pr. 40.00

American Candlestick

Candlestick, square, American patt.,
   clear, 7" h. (ILLUS.) 92.50
Candlestick, Baroque patt., topaz,
   5½" h..35.00
Candlestick, Vesper etching, blue,
   3¼" h..30.00

Candlesticks, Coin patt., frosted red, 8" h., pr. **105.00**

Candlesticks, No. 2620, blue green opaque, pr. (original labels) **35.00**

Candy dish, cov., triangular, two-part, American patt., clear **65.00**

Celery dish, Wedding Bells patt., clear w/gold.......................................**87.00**

Celery tray, oval, American patt., clear **18.00**

Centerpiece bowl, Trojan etching (No. 2375) yellow **25.00**

Champagne, Buttercup etching, clear **12.00**

Champagne, Chintz etching, clear **17.50**

Champagne, saucer-shaped, Romance etching, clear **17.50**

Champagne, Versailles etching, clear **35.00**

Cheese & cracker server, Meadow Rose etching, clear **65.00**

Cheese & cracker server, Navarre etching, clear **49.50**

Claret, Navarre etching, blue, 6½" h....**47.50**

Claret, Versailles etching, yellow **45.00**

Clock w/pr. of matching candlesticks, No. 2299, topaz, 3 pcs. **395.00**

Cocktail, Buttercup etching, clear........**18.75**

Cocktail, Century patt., clear **8.00**

Cocktail, Colony patt., clear...................**8.00**

Cocktail, Hermitage patt., blue **8.00**

Cocktail, June etching, pink, 3 oz......**50.00**

Cocktail, No. 6016, azure bowl, clear stem **17.50**

Cologne bottle w/original stopper, American patt., clear...........................**70.00**

Compote, 4½" d., Century patt., clear **16.00**

Compote, cov., American patt., clear, 9" h..**30.00**

Condiment set: vinegar & oil bottle; Navarre etching, clear, 2 pcs. **325.00**

Console bowl, footed, Vesper etching, blue, 10⅜" d. **88.00**

Console bowl, footed, No. 2324, green, plain, 10" d.............................**25.00**

Console set: bowl & pr. of candle-sticks; Baroque patt., Lido etching, 3 pcs. **98.50**

Cordial, Chintz etching, clear..............**48.00**

Cordial, Fairfax patt., clear, ¾ oz.........**10.00**

Cordials, Navarre etching, clear, set of 4 ....**200.00**

Creamer, American patt., clear 9½ oz. **10.00**

Creamer, Century patt., clear................**9.00**

Creamer, Colony patt., clear **5.00**

Creamer, Versailles patt., clear............**12.00**

Creamer & sugar bowl, Colony patt., clear, 2¾" h., pr.................................**10.00**

Creamer & sugar bowl, footed, June Rose etching, clear, pr. **38.00**

Creamer & sugar bowl, Versailles etching, green, small, pr. **55.00**

Creamer, sugar bowl & undertray, individual size, Century patt., clear, 3 pcs. **22.00**

Cruet w/original stopper, American patt., clear, 5 oz. **32.00**

Cruet, oil, w/original stopper, Century patt., clear **40.00**

Cruet, oil, w/original stopper, Heather patt., clear, 5 oz. **45.00**

Cruet w/original stopper, Plantation patt., clear **95.00**

Cup, coffee, Century patt., clear **8.00**

Cup, footed, Fairfax patt., pink **7.00**

Cup & saucer, Buttercup etching, clear **22.50**

Cup & saucer, Century patt., clear......**11.00**

Decanter set: one rye decanter, one decanter w/center lip & metal undertray; American patt., clear, 3 pcs. **250.00**

Float bowl, Century patt., (Lily Pond) clear, 11¼" d.......................................**32.00**

Goblet, American patt., clear, 5½" h. **7.50**

Goblet, Century patt., clear.................**20.00**

Chintz Etching Goblet

Goblet, water, Chintz etching, clear, 9 oz. (ILLUS.)....................................**25.00**

Goblet, Jamestown pat., red...............**26.00**

Goblet, Seville patt., amber, 4½" h., 3½ oz. **15.00**

Goblet, Spiral Optic patt. (No. 5082), green..**10.00**

Hurricane lamp base, American patt., clear **45.00**

Ice bucket, American patt., clear, large...**40.00**

Ice bucket, Century patt., clear...........**50.00**

Ice bucket, Sunray patt., clear............**28.00**

Ice cream saucer, American patt., clear **60.00**

Ice dish, American patt., clear **35.00**

Icer, American patt., clear (no liner) **20.00**

Lamp, oil, courting-type, Coin patt., amber..**120.00**

Lemon dish, cov., American patt., clear **20.00**

Mayonnaise bowl & underplate,
  Colony patt., clear, 2 pcs. **35.00**
Mayonnaise bowl w/underplate &
  spoon, American patt., clear,
  3 pcs. **32.00**
Mint dish, Colony patt., clear................**9.00**
Nappy, footed, Coin patt., clear,
  4½" d...**18.50**
Nappy, handled, three-cornered,
  Meadow Rose etching, clear, 5" **17.00**
Oyster cocktail, Rogene etching,
  clear **22.00**
Parfait, Versailles etching, pink...........**27.50**
Pin tray, Jenny Lind, milk white,
  6" d..**45.00**
Pitcher, Century patt., clear, 16 oz. **60.00**
Pitcher, Fairfax patt. (No. 5084),
  amber...**95.00**
Pitcher, Hermigate patt., yellow,
  3 pts. **65.00**
Plate, 6" d., American patt., clear...........**9.50**
Plate, 6" d., June etching, yellow **12.00**
Plate, dessert, 6½" d., American
  patt., clear **10.00**
Plate, 7" d. w/indentation, American
  patt., clear **7.00**
Plate, 8" d., Colony patt., clear..............**8.00**
Plate, luncheon, Jamestown patt.,
  red...**9.00**
Plate, dinner, 9½" d., Century patt.,
  clear **20.00**
Plate, torte, 13" d., Colony patt. **20.00**
Plates, 7½" d., Romance etching,
  clear, set of 12 ....**100.00**
Platter, 14" l., Romance etching,
  clear **40.00**
Punch bowl, Baroque patt., clear **350.00**
Punch set: bowl, base & seven cups;
  Coin patt., clear, 9 pcs. **475.00**
Punch set: bowl, twenty cups &
  ladle; Coin patt., clear, 22 pcs. **750.00**
Relish dish, American patt., clear,
  11" l...**25.00**
Relish dish, divided, Century patt.,
  clear, 11" l..**22.00**
Relish dish, three-part, Century patt.,
  clear **17.00**
Rose bowl, 5" d., American patt.,
  clear **20.00**
Salt dip, American patt., clear.............**12.50**
Salt & pepper shakers w/original
  tops, American patt., emerald
  green, pr. **90.00**
Salt & pepper shakers w/original
  tops, Buttercup etching, clear, pr. **50.00**
Sandwich server w/center handle,
  Cleo patt., blue..................................**55.00**
Sandwich server w/center handle,
  Coronet patt., clear **25.00**
Sherbet, high, Jamestown patt.,
  blue **16.00**
Sherbet, Seville etching, amber...........**13.00**
Sherbets, American patt., clear, low,
  set of 4 ....**32.00**

Sugar bowl, cov., Century patt.,
  clear **9.00**
Sugar bowl, open, Romance etching,
  clear **18.00**
Tidbit tray, two tier, American patt.,
  clear **85.00**
Tidbit tray, footed, Colony patt.,
  clear, 7" d...**45.00**
Tumbler, iced tea, low, American
  patt., clear, 5¾" h...............................**12.00**
Tumbler, juice, Buttercup etching,
  clear **12.00**
Tumbler, footed, Century patt., clear,
  5 oz. **15.00**
Tumbler, iced tea, Colony patt.,
  clear, 12 oz. **15.50**
Tumbler, water, footed, Navarre
  etching, blue **40.00**
Urn, American patt., clear, 11" h. **30.00**
Urn, cov., Coin patt., frosted red **110.00**
Vase, bud, 6" h., footed, Heather
  patt., No. 6021, clear **45.00**
Vase, 6½" h., straight-sided,
  American patt., clear...........................**25.00**
Vase, 12" h., deep etching, clear,
  No. 300 ....**65.00**
Vegetable bowl, two-part, American
  patt., clear, 10" d................................**18.00**
Whipped cream pail, Trojan etching,
  yellow...**160.00**
Wine, Century patt., clear....................**25.00**
Wine, Jamestown patt., blue **24.00**

FRY

Numerous types of glass were made by the H.C. Fry Company, Rochester, Pennsylvania. One of its art lines was called Foval and was blown in 1926-27. Cheaper was its milky-opalescent ovenware (Pearl Oven Ware) made for utilitarian purposes but also now being collected. The company also made fine cut glass.

Collectors of Fry Glass will be interested in the recent publication of a good reference book, The Collector's Encyclopedia of Fry Glassware, *by The H.C. Fry Glass Society (Collector Books, 1990.)*

Creamer, clear w/deeply engraved
  floral decoration **$60.00**
Creamer w/underplate, deep cut
  flower design, clear............................**75.00**
Lemonade mugs, Foval w/applied
  green handles, set of 4 ....**260.00**
Lemonade set: pitcher & eight mugs;
  Foval w/delft blue trim,
  9 pcs. **1,000.00**
Pie plate, Pearl Oven Ware, 9" d. **5.00**
Reamer, ruffled rim, kitchenware line,
  opalescent **100.00**

Vase, 14" h., bird & flower cut
design, signed..................................**319.00**

GALLÉ

Pair of Cameo Wall Sconces

*Gallé glass was made in Nancy,
France, by Emile Gallé, a founder of the
Nancy School and a leader in the Art
Nouveau movement in France. Much of his
glass, both enameled and cameo, is
decorated with naturalistic motifs. The
finest pieces were made in the last two
decades of the 19th century and the
opening years of the present one. Pieces
marked with a star preceding the name
were made between 1904, the year of
Gallé's death, and 1914.*

Various Gallé Marks

Bowl-vase, cov., the flattened bulbous
body w/wide swirled ribs, smokey
grey internally decorated w/grey
streaks, finely enameled w/flowering
tulips & a Dutch seascape in the
distance, trimmed w/gilt, enameled
"Emile Gallé fecit," 6" h. **$3,450.00**
Cameo bowl, 7½" d., wide squatty
bulbous body raised on a small, short
pedestal foot, w/a wide flat rolled rim,
milky white overlaid w/deep greyish
green U cut w/swirling leafy fruiting
branches, signed in cameo,
ca. 1900 ....**805.00**

Cameo box, cov., squatty cushion-
form body w/a wide, low domed
cover, frosted clear lined w/pink &
overlaid in amber & yellow, acid-
etched & carved w/nasturtium
blossoms & leaves on top & base,
cover signed in cameo, 5" d.
2½" h..**1,150.00**
Cameo lamp, table model, 10¾" d.,
pointed conical shade on a matching
spherical base, grey shaded w/lemon
yellow, overlaid in red & crimson &
cut w/flowering prunus branches,
buds & leafage, simple bronze
mounts, shade & base signed in
cameo, ca. 1900, 11" h. **23,000.00**
Cameo lamp, table model, 14" d.,
domical shade raised above a
matching slender cylindrical base
encased in elaborate scrolling foliate
bronze mounts & four large scrolling
bronze leaf-form feet, grey splashed
w/pink & olive green, overlaid in lime
green, rust & maroon & cut
w/unfurling fern fronds & grasses, the
whole fire-polished, the shade
supported on bronze flowerhead
arms, shade & base signed in
cameo, ca. 1900, 31" h. **36,800.00**
Cameo vase, miniature, 3⅜" h., wide
baluster-form body w/a short rolled
neck, yellow overlaid in pale blue
& aubergine & cut w/violets
& leaves, signed in cameo,
ca. 1900 ....**690.00**
Cameo vase, 5⅝" h., "Les Roses
de France" series, internally-
decorated & applied, footed broad
squatty bulbous body tapering to a
flaring neck, transparent lime green
splashed w/opalescence, overlaid in
pale green & cut all around w/an
impressionistic verdant summer
landscape, the skies above *martelé*,
the obverse applied in high-relief w/a
dusty pink rose, slender rose stems
& three leaves in lime green, lime
green over rose & lavender over
white, the surfaces finely wheel-
carved, signed in intaglio,
ca. 1902 ....**200,500.00**
Cameo vase, 6" h., compressed
cushion base below a tall cylindrical
neck, mottled green layered in
brownish amber & acid-etched
w/berries & leaves, signed
in cameo **690.00**
Cameo vase, 8¾" h., slightly swelled
cylindrical body tapering at the top
to a widely flaring, deeply ruffled
rim, clear splashed w/grey & puce,
overlaid in puce & cut w/morning
glory blossoms, buds & leafage,

the whole fire-polished, signed in cameo, ca. 1900 ....**2,875.00**

Cameo vase, 9¾" h., tall slender tapering cylindrical body w/a flaring rim, frosted pastel yellow layered in amethyst & dark purple & acid-etched & wheel-cut w/large iris blossoms & spiked leaves, came signature "Gallé" & paper label on base reading "Emile Gallé Nancy Paris" **3,450.00**

Cameo vase, 10½" h., shouldered ovoid body w/a short lobed neck, the base tapering sharply to a double-ring foot, pale amber overlaid in caramel at the base & cut w/ascending leaf ends, enameled around the shoulder w/dahlias & leafage in shades of crimson, mint green, yellow, orange & brown, signed in intaglio, ca. 1900 ....**17,250.00**

Cameo vase, 12¾" h., wide ovoid body tapering up to a thick molded wide mouth, tapering sharply down to a flared foot, grey shaded w/pale yellow, overlaid in amber & molded in low-, medium- & high-relief w/plum branches laden w/fruit, signed in cameo, ca. 1900 .... **23,000.00**

Cameo vase, 16¾" h., tall slender ovoid body tapering to a short slightly flared neck, grey mottled w/bubblegum pink, overlaid in white, yellow, pink & olive green, cut w/large clusters of chestnuts & leaves, faintly signed in cameo, ca. 1900 ....**4,887.00**

Cameo vase, 17¼" h., thick squatty cushion base tapering to a very tall cylindrical neck, grey shading to lavender at the base, overlaid w/lavender & green & cut down the neck w/wisteria, signed in cameo, ca. 1900 ....**1,840.00**

Cameo vase, 19½" h., disc foot, expanding cylinder w/narrow neck & flared mouth, grey walls shaded w/yellow, overlaid w/burnt sienna & cut w/falling maple leaves, signed in cameo "Gallé," ca. 1900............**3,163.00**

Cameo vase, 20" h., classic baluster-form body w/a short flaring neck & applied pedestal base, grey mottled w/yellow, overlaid w/pale olive green & brown, cut w/a tranquil river landscape, signed in cameo, ca. 1900 (chips at rim) **8,337.00**

Cameo vase, 24¾" h., baluster-form, grey walls shaded w/yellow, overlaid in purple & cut w/wisteria blossoms & leafage, signed in cameo "Gallé," ca. 1900 ....**60,250.00**

Cameo veilleuse (night light), grey walls w/orange mottling overlaid

w/dark amber & cut w/crocus blossoms & leaves, w/pierced gilt-metal mounts, signed in cameo, electrified, ca. 1900, 6½" h. **1,840.00**

Cameo wall sconces, each in grey shaded w/lemon yellow, overlaid in red & deepest burgundy & cut w/flowering leafy rose branches, simple gilt-bronze foliate mounts, signed in cameo "Gallé," ca. 1900, 7 x 11¼", pr. (ILLUS.) **16,100.00**

Decanter w/stopper, flask-form w/flattened Gothic arch-form sides, smokey grey etched w/heraldic shields on both sides, one side w/medieval monks seated around a table, the other w/monks picking flowers, enameled in colors of red, grey, dusty ivory & pale blue, framed w/an acanthus scroll motif, surmounted by lozenge-shaped stopper, overall gilt trim, enameled signature "E. Gallé," 1889, 9½" h..**9,200.00**

Enameled Gallé Decanter & Tumblers

Decanter w/stopper, ovoid ribbed transparent amber body w/slightly flared neck, applied handle & stopper rigaree, decorated in polychrome enamel painted blossoms & leaves w/gold embellishments, inscribed "E. Gallé Nancy," 7¼" h. (ILLUS. left) **2,300.00**

Dresser set: trumpet-form tumbler, footed squatty bulbous cov. box, baluster-form cruet w/stopper & a round dished tray w/notched rim; pale amber enameled w/stylized blossoms & geometric devices in shades of blue, black, pink, white, cream, red & pale yellow, trimmed w/gilt, various enamel signatures, tray 11⅞" d., cruet 6¼" h. **6,325.00**

Scent bottle w/flattened disc stopper, footed spherical body in pale amber decorated w/stylized blossoms & insects of pale pink, cram, blue & yellow, trimmed w/gilt, signed in enamel "E. Gallé - Nancy," ca. 1890, 6⅛" h. **2,587.00**

Tumblers, transparent ribbed glasses, enamel painted w/whimsical peasants & motto decorations, four signed on base "E. Gallé," 4½" h., the set (ILLUS. right).......................**977.50**

Vase, 4¾" h., 7¼" l., flattened spherical body w/convex sides, clear enameled w/sprays of spider chrysanthemums & foliage in shades of white, cobalt blue, rust & black heightened w/gilding, further finely intaglio carved w/two dragonflies in flight on the obverse & one dragonfly on the reverse, each delicately enameled in transparent shades of crimson, wintergreen, ochre & lavender, the side panels conformingly enameled w/spider chrysan-themums between scrolling black & gilt foliage, one side panel w/an applied clear frog in full-relief, the other w/a clear squirrel in full-relief, signed in enamel "E. Gallé - a Nancy," ca. 1890.....................**12,650.00**

Vase, 5¼" h., footed thick cylindrical form w/cupped rim, heavy large loop handles at the sides, clear deeply cut w/lozenges & swirls, enameled *en grisaille* w/two landscapes & two floral sprays enameled in pink, mauve & blue, trimmed w/gilt, signed in red enamel "E. & G. déposé Emile Gallé a Nancy," ca. 1890 ....**5,750.00**

Vase, 6¼" h., swirling floriform in pale amber, finely enameled w/delicate blossoms & leaves in natural colors, etched signature "E. Gallé a Nancy," ca. 1900...........**805.00**

Vase, 7" h., nautilus shell-form, clear, finely enameled w/sprays of thistles & leafage in shades of rust, puce, dusty rose, lemon yellow, black, grey, & chocolate brown trimmed w/gilt, signed in intaglio "E. Gallé - déposé," ca. 1890 ....**5,175.00**

Vase, 7¾" h., footed squatty bulbous body tapering to a trumpet neck flanked by three loop handles, clear w/the sides enameled w/rondels enclosing fantastic animals reserved against a gilt coral ground within Islamic borders in shades of turquoise, rust, lime green & white trimmed w/gilt, signed in intaglio "E. Gallé - Nancy," ca. 1890 ....**4,600.00**

Vase, 11½" h., broad cushion-form base tapering to a tall slender cylindrical neck, lightly ribbed transparent amber w/two applied cabochon 'jewel' flower centers integrated w/large blossoms & leafy

vines up the sides, inscribed on the base "Emile Gallé Cris-tallerie Nancy - modele et decor Déposés" **2,185.00**

Vase, 22¼" h., very tall & slender waisted cylindrical body in translucent yellow shaded to honey-red amber w/silver mica & gold inclusions, three etched medial, top & base border designs & elaborate polychrome enamel foliate designs up the sides, engraved on entire base around central blossoms "Cyrstallerie Gallé - Nancy Model et Decor Déposés".......................**11,500.00**

GREENTOWN

Greentown glass was made in Greentown Indiana, by the Indiana Tumbler & Goblet Co. from 1894 until 1903. In addition to its famed Chocolate and Holly Amber glass, it produced other types of clear and colored glass. Miscellaneous pieces are listed here. Also see PATTERN GLASS and CHOCOLATE GLASS.

Goblet, Austrian patt., clear **$60.00**
Pitcher, water, Heron patt., clear.......**275.00**
Sugar bowl, cov., Austrian patt.,
   clear...**52.00**
Tumbler, Pleated Band patt., clear
   w/engraved decoration **55.00**
Wine, Austrian patt., canary **85.00**

HANDEL

Handel Cameo Vase

Lamps, shades and other types of glass by Handel & Co., which subsequently became The Handel Co., Inc., were produced in Meriden, Connecticut, from

1893 to 1941. Also see LIGHTING DEVICES.

Cameo vase, 10" h., flaring cylindrical body w/shoulders tapering to flared rim, amber overlaid acid-cut back floral design on frosted colorless ground, artist-signed at side "Rouchett" & "4242 Handel" on base, small chips at top inner rim (ILLUS.) **$1,495.00**

Compote, 7½" d., deep green w/orange floral decoration **425.00**

Humidor, cov., opal, decorated w/a horse & dog, signed "Kelsey"...........**800.00**

Pin tray, opal, decorated w/h.p. Terrier dog, signed "Kelsey" **136.00**

Vase, 9¾" h., "Teroma," slightly tapering cylindrical body w/a wide short flaring neck, frosted textured ground h.p. w/a wooden riverside landscape, naturalistic colors, signed "Bedigie," oval mark on base (worn, base edge chip) **1,207.50**

Handel Scenic Vase

Vase, 10½" h., "Teroma," slightly bulbous ovoid body w/shoulders tapering to flared rim, h.p. landscape of trees & three birds, signed "Bedigie" & on base "Handel Teroma" in oval (ILLUS.) **1,955.00**

Vase, 11¼" h., "Teroma," slightly swelled cylindrical body w/a narrow shoulder to the wide flaring short neck, h.p. woodland scene w/birds perched & in flight, natural shades of green, brown & yellow, signed

"Bedigie" on back, base marked "Handel Lednah 4217" **1,840.00**

HEISEY

Numerous types of fine glass were made by A.H. Heisey & Co., Newark, Ohio, from 1895. The company's trade-mark - an H enclosed within a diamond - has become known to most glass collectors. The company's name and molds were acquired by Imperial Glass Co., Bellaire, Ohio, in 1958, and some pieces have been reissued. The glass listed below consists of miscellaneous pieces and types. Also see ANIMALS and PATTERN GLASS under Glass.

Heisey Diamond "H" Mark

Ashtray, Empress patt., clear **$250.00**

Ashtray, Queen Ann patt., clear **20.00**

Basket, Lariat patt., clear, 7½" h..........**80.00**

Basket, Double Rib & Panel patt., Moongleam (green) **195.00**

Basket, Garland etching, 15" h. **300.00**

Berry set: master berry bowl & four sauce dishes; Beaded Swag patt., clear; 5 pcs. **90.00**

Bonbon, two-handled, Hawthorne patt., clear **30.00**

Bowl, 5¼" d., Colonial patt., clear..........**6.00**

Bowl, 7" d., Quaker patt.......................**20.00**

Bowl, floral, 10" d., Empress patt., deep gently rounded sides, four paw feet, four lion's head handles, Sahara (yellow), ...**695.00**

Bowl, floral, 12" oval, Ridgeleigh patt., Zircon (blue-green) **350.00**

Bowl, cream soup, Yeoman patt., Marigold (deep yellow)....................**24.00**

Butter dish, cov., Waverly patt., clear **115.00**

Butter dish w/metal lid, Plantation patt., clear, ¼ lb. **45.00**

Cake stand, Plantation patt., clear.....**235.00**

Cake stand, Prince of Wales Plumes patt., clear, 10" d...............................**89.00**

Candelabrum, three-light, Crystolite patt., clear **35.00**

Candleholders, two-light, Waverly patt., Orchid etching, clear, pr.........**110.00**

Candleholders, Whirlpool (Provincial) patt., round, clear, pr.........................**40.00**

Candlesticks, three-light, Lariat patt.,
w/Moonglo cutting, clear, pr. **125.00**
Candlesticks, Empress patt.,
Flamingo (pink), 6" h., pr.................**295.00**
Celery dish, Fancy Loop patt., clear....**52.00**
Celery tray, Lodestar patt., Dawn (light
grey), 10" l.......................................**95.00**
Centerpiece bowl, Ridgeleigh patt.,
clear...**25.00**
Champagne, Carcassone patt., clear
stem w/cobalt bowl **55.00**
Champagne, Duquesne patt.,
Tangerine (deep orangish red) **175.00**
Cigar holder, Winged Scroll patt.,
green..**145.00**
Cigarette holder, Bethel patt., clear **45.00**
Cigarette holder, footed, Crystolite
patt., clear......................................**17.00**
Coaster, Ridgeleigh patt.,
Zircon, 3½" d...................................**40.00**
Cocktail, Provincial patt., clear,
3½" oz...**12.00**
Compote, cov., 6" d., Wabash patt.,
Moongleam foot & knob on cover **135.00**
Compote, open, 5" d., Orchid etching,
clear...**18.00**
Compote, open, 5" h., Pleat & Panel
patt., Flamingo **65.00**
Console bowl, Ipswich patt., clear **95.00**
Cordial, figural goose stem, frosted,
1 oz. **175.00**
Cordial, Oxford patt., clear.................**25.00**
Cordial, figural rose stem, Rose
etching, clear **160.00**
Cordial, Spanish patt., Cobalt blue.....**225.00**
Creamer, Continental patt., clear **65.00**
Creamer, Minuet etching, clear...........**35.00**
Creamer, Winged Scroll patt., green....**50.00**
Creamer & sugar bowl, individual-
size, Colonial patt., clear, pr. **25.00**
Creamer & sugar bowl, large,
Crystolite patt., clear, pr....................**40.00**
Creamer & sugar bowl, Lariat patt.,
clear, pr...**18.00**
Cruet w/original stopper, Colonial
patt., clear, 8¼" h.............................**45.00**
Cup & saucer, Empress patt., clear **38.00**
Cups & saucers, Twist patt.,
Flamingo, 5 sets, 10 pcs...................**175.00**
Decanter w/stopper, Victorian patt.,
clear, in chrome stand, 27 oz...........**125.00**
Goblet, Carcassone patt., clear stem
w/Sahara bowl, short **22.50**
Goblet, Symphone patt., Crinoline
etching, clear, 9 oz...........................**25.00**
Goblet, Crystolite patt., clear, 10 oz.....**24.00**
Goblet, Kimberly patt., Sungate
cutting, clear **65.00**
Goblet, Spanish patt., Killarney
cutting, clear **38.00**
Ice bucket, Fancy Loop patt.,
clear...**195.00**
Jar, cov., Ipswich patt., amethyst,
signed **150.00**

Heisey Lemon Dish

Lemon dish, cov., Narrow Flute patt.,
5" d. (ILLUS.) **36.50**
Pitcher, Banded Flute patt., clear,
1 pt..**130.00**
Pitcher, Narrow Flute patt.,
Flamingo **195.00**
Pitcher, water, w/ice lip, Plantation
patt., clear **295.00**
Plate, 7" d., Narrow Flute patt.,
clear **5.50**
Plate, 7½" d., Ridge & Star patt.,
Flamingo **9.00**
Plate, 9" d., Colonial patt., clear..........**45.00**
Plate, torte, 14" d., Orchid etching,
clear **45.00**
Powder box, cov., Crystolite patt.,
clear, 4¾" d......................................**50.00**
Punch cup, Crystolite patt., clear **4.00**
Punch cup, Fandango patt., clear **25.00**
Punch set: punch bowl, underplate,
12 cups & ladle; Lariat patt.,
clear, 15 pcs. **350.00**
Relish dish w/loop handle, three-part,
Teardrop patt., clear, 8½" d. **25.00**
Salt & pepper shakers w/original
tops, Cohasset cutting, clear, pr. **75.00**
Sandwich tray w/center handle,
Lariat patt., clear, 21" d...................**125.00**
Sherbet, Saxony patt., Sahara............**25.00**

Heisey Victorian Sherbet

Sherbet, Victorian patt., clear, 5 oz. (ILLUS. bottom previous page) **15.00**

Toothpick holder, Fandango patt., clear **69.00**

Tumbler, iced tea, footed, Orchid etching, clear **51.00**

Tumbler, soda, footed, Ridgeleigh patt., clear, 5½ oz. **45.00**

Tumblers, Lariat patt., clear, 9 oz., set of 12 ....**120.00**

Vase, 6" h., Lariat patt., Orchid etching, clear **139.00**

Vase, 10" h., dolphin-footed, Queen Ann patt., w/etching, clear **125.00**

Water set, child's: 4" h. scalloped-rim pitcher & 8 tumblers; Colonial patt., clear, 9 pcs. **65.00**

Water set: pitcher & 7 tumblers; Puritan patt., clear, 8 pcs. **150.00**

Whiskey set: decanter & 6 shot glasses; Ridgeleigh patt., clear, 7 pcs. **450.00**

Wine, Gascony patt., Tangerine, 3" h..**375.00**

Wine, Priscilla patt., clear, 2 oz. **14.00**

HISTORICAL & COMMEMORATIVE

Reference numbers are to Bessie M. Lindsey's book, American Historical Glass.

Knights of Labor Platter

American Flag platter, clear, 8 x 11", No. 51 ....**$230.00**

Bates (General J.C.) plate, handled, scalloped edge, clear, 8" d., No. 375.....................................**65.00**

Battleship Maine plate, transfer of battleship, circle & fan border, clear, 5½" d., No. 464 ....**25.00**

Bunker Hill cup plate, "Bunker Hill Battle fought June 17, 1775 - Cornerstone laid by Lafayette, June

17, 1825 - Finished by the Ladies, 1841 - From the Fair to the Brave," clear, 3¾" d., No. 45........**90.00**

Bunker Hill platter w/Bunker Hill monument shown in center, inscribed above, "Birthplace of Liberty," border carries the inscription "Prescott 1776 Stark," "Warren 1876 Putnam," "The Heroes of Bunker Hill," "The Spirit of Seventy-Six," shield-shaped handles, showing stars & stripes, clear, 9 x 13¼", No. 44..........**60.00**

Centennial Drape goblet, clear, stippled drape design w/"Centennial" & "1876," 6½" h..................**40.00**

Cleveland-Hendricks tray, bust portraits all-frosted center, stippled ivy leaves border, 8½ x 11½", No. 314 ....**262.50**

Columbia bread tray, shield-shaped, Columbia superimposed against 13 vertical bars, amber, 9½ x 11½", No. 54 ....**150.00**

Columbia bread tray, shield-shaped, Columbia superimposed, against 13 vertical bars, clear, 9½ x 11½", No. 54 ....**125.00**

Columbus lamp chimney, medallion portrait w/florals, inscribed "Columbus," clear, 7¼" h., No. 9......**900.00**

Columbus paperweight, clear w/frosted portrait center, "World's Columbian Exposition, 1492-1892," 3⅛" d. **125.00**

Crying Baby bread plate, Royal, pale amber, 8¾ x 13¼" **127.50**

Dewey (Admiral) dish, cov., boat-like base, milk white, 5½" l., 5" h., No. 391 ....**98.00**

Dewey (Admiral) plate, bust portrait of Dewey, clear, 5½" d., No. 392 ....**65.00**

Emblem creamer, vertical bars & thickly studded w/stars, two curving legs unite the shield-shaped body w/a flat, circular base, clear, 5¾" h..**165.00**

Emblem spooner, clear............**137.50**

Flat iron dish, cov., amber **85.00**

Flat iron dish, cov., blue....................**95.00**

Garfield Memorial mug, handled, embossed bust of Garfield, date of birth & death, clear, 2⅝" h., No. 294 ....**72.00**

Garfield Memorial plate, Garfield center, laurel wreath against stippled ground border, clear, 10" d., No. 302 ....**62.00**

Garfield Monument plate, leaf border, milk white, 7¼" d., No. 306 ....**50.00**

Grand Army of the Republic platter, insignia medal "Grand Army of the Republic Veteran - 1861-66" center, decorative border w/further inscriptions, 7⅝ x 11⅛", No. 505 ....**295.00**

Grant Memorial plate, portrait of Grant center, laurel wreath on stippled border, clear, 10" d., No. 288 ....**53.00**

Grant "Patriot and Soldier" plate, bust portrait of Grant center, decorative border, deep rim, amber, 9½" sq., No. 291 ....**65.00**

Grant spill holder, boldly embossed bust portrait of General Grant titled "GN GRANT," fiery opalescent, ca. 1870, 5" h. **275.00**

Hemple (Freda) plate, bust portrait of Hemple center, one-o-one border, clear, 5½" d., No. 431 ....**38.00**

Independence Hall platter, "The Nation's Birthplace," w/bear paw handles, clear, 8½ x 12", No. 29 ....**82.50**

Knights of Labor platter, clear, 11¾" l., No. 512 (ILLUS.) **200.00**

Lee (Major General Fitzhugh) plate, portrait transfer against a flag background, club border, milk white, 7¼" d., No. 379 ....**51.00**

Liberty Bell goblet, "Declaration of Independence" & "1776-1876" one side, "100 Years Ago" reverse, 6¼" h., No. 35 ....**57.50**

Lincoln (Abraham) paperweight, clear, 3 x 4½" rectangle, No. 275 ....**85.00**

Lind (Jenny), so-called, match safe, Pat'd. June 13, 1876," frosted, pierced to hang, 4½" l., No 426 ....**80.00**

Old Abe (eagle) butter dish, cov., clear, No. 478 ....**117.50**

Old Statehouse tray, shows Independence Hall above "Old Statehouse, Philadelphia, Erected 1735," clear, round, No. 32 ....**83.00**

Plymouth Rock paperweight, "A rock in the wilderness, etc.," & "Providence Inkstand Co., 1876," clear, 3¾" l., No.18 ....**65.00**

Plymouth Rock paperweight, "Mary Chilton was, etc." & "Inkstand Co., Prov., R.I.," clear, No. 19 ....**92.00**

Roosevelt (Theodore) platter, portrait center, Teddy bears, etc., border, clear, 7¾ x 10", No. 357 ......**145.00**

The Reaper Platter, oval, clear, 8 x 13", No. 119 ....**185.00**

Three Presidents platter, frosted bust portraits of Washington, Lincoln & Garfield framed in medallion settings, clear, stippled leaves on border, inscribed on border, "In Remembrance," inscribed beneath medallions, "God Reigns," "First in Peace," "Charity for All," 10 x 12½", No. 249 ....**57.50**

Volunteer plate, army camp scene center w/lonely volunteer stand-ing guard, border w/crossed muskets & cannon, clear, 10" d., No. 101 ....**285.00**

HOLLY AMBER

Holly Amber, originally marketed under the name "Golden Agate," was produced for only a few months in 1903 by the Indiana Tumbler and Goblet Company of Greentown, Indiana. When this factory burned in June 1903 all production of this ware ceased, making it very rare today. The same "Holly" pressed pattern was also produced in clear glass by the Greentown factory. Collectors should note that the St. Clair Glass Company has reproduced some Holly Amber pieces.

Cruet w/original stopper, 6¼" h. **$825.00**
Parfait, 6" h. **575.00**
Tumbler, set of 6 ....**2,000.00**

IMPERIAL

Imperial Glass Company, Bellaire, Ohio, was organized in 1901 and was in continuous production, except for very brief periods, until its closing in June 1984. It had been a major producer of Carnival Glass earlier in this century and also produced other types of glass, including an Art Glass line called "Free Hand Ware" during the 1920s and its "Jewels" about 1916. The company acquired a number of molds of other earlier factories, including the Cambridge and A.H. Heisey compa-nies, and reissued numerous items through the years. Also see CARNIVAL GLASS and ANIMALS under glass.

Imperial Nucut Mark

Early Imperial Cross Mark

Later Imperial Marks

CANDLEWICK PATTERN

Basket, No. 400/73/0, clear, 12" h. ..**$190.00**
Bowl, cream soup, 5", two-handled,
  No. 400/50, clear w/gold beads **45.00**
Bowl, 8½" d., two-handled, No.
  400/72B, clear.....................................**32.00**
Bowl, fruit, 10" d., footed, pedestal
  base, ruffled rim, No. 400/103C,
  milk white **75.00**
Bowl, 10½" d., bell-shaped,
  No. 400/63B, clear **50.00**
Bowl, 14" oval, No. 400/131B,
  clear **279.00**
Butter dish, cov., oblong,
  No. 400/161, clear, ¼ lb.....................**24.00**
Candleholder, flower (epergne inset),
  No. 400/CV, clear, 5" h. **85.00**
Candleholders, No. 400/80, clear,
  3½", pr. **13.00**
Candy box, cov., partitioned,
  No. 400/110, clear, 7" d. **65.00**
Celery tray, 13½" l., clear,
  No. 400/105 ....**40.00**
Cigarette set: three No. 400/19
  individual ashtrays, cigarette holder
  No. 400/19 & an undertray
  No. 400/29; the set No. 400/1919,
  clear, 5 pcs. **65.00**
Ice tub, No. 400/63, clear, 8" d.,
  5½" h...**113.00**
Marmalade set: footed jar w/dome-
  shaped beaded cover & ladle;
  No. 400/1989, clear, the set...............**30.00**
Oil & vinegar set w/undertray,
  No. 400/7796, clear, 3 pcs................**82.00**
Parfait, No. 3400, clear, 6 oz. **46.50**
Punch set: bowl, underplate &
  12 cups; No. 400/20, clear,
  14 pcs. **250.00**
Relish dish, two-part, No. 400/234,
  clear, 7" sq. **175.00**
Relish dish, five-part, No. 400/56,
  clear, 10½" d. **10.00**
Relish dish, two-part, No. 400/256,
  clear, 11" oval **17.50**
Salt & pepper shakers, individual,
  No. 400/19, clear, pr. **11.50**
Sugar bowl, open, domed foot,
  No. 400/18, clear **55.00**
Vase, 6" h., footed, flared rim,
  No. 400/138B, clear **245.00**
Vase, 8½" h., beaded foot, flared
  rim, No. 400/21, clear **250.00**

CAPE COD PATTERN

Bowl, 10" oval, No. 160/221, clear.......**80.00**
Claret, stemmed, No. 1602, clear,
  5 oz. **9.50**
Pepper mill, No. 160/236, clear...........**25.00**
Pitcher w/ice lip, No. 160/19, clear,
  40 oz. **61.00**
Plate, 13" d., birthday w/72 candle
  holes, No. 160/72, clear...................**265.00**

Relish, three-part, No. 160/55, clear,
  9½" oval **27.00**
Salt & pepper shakers w/original
  tops, footed, No. 160/116, clear,
  pr..**25.00**
Tumbler, double old fashioned, clear,
  No. 160, 14 oz. **15.00**
Tumbler, juice, footed, No. 1602,
  clear, 6 oz. **7.00**
Vase, 6¼" h., footed, No. 160/22,
  clear..**38.00**
Vase, 8½" h., flip-type, clear,
  No. 160/143, clear **45.00**

FREE HAND WARE

Vase, 8¼" h., hourglass shape,
  iridescent cobalt blue w/orange
  threading..**135.00**
Vase, 8½" h., white opal body w/navy
  blue pulled feather
  decoration **415.00**

MISCELLANEOUS

Animal covered dish, lion on lacy
  base, purple slag **118.00**
Punch set: bowl & ten cups;
  Monticello patt., clear, 11 pcs. **95.00**

JACK-IN-THE-PULPIT VASES

Glass vases in varying sizes and resembling in appearance the flower of this name have been popular with collectors since the 19th century. They were produced in various solid colors and in shaded wares.

Cased White & Pink Vase

Cased, white exterior, pink interior,
  decorated inside & out
  w/multicolored enamelled flowers,
  leaves & small butterflies, 4½" d.,
  5⅝" h. (ILLUS.) **$79.00**

Cased, opaque off-white exterior, shaded green to paler green interior, spherical body, applied clear feet, 5¾" d., 6½" h. **79.00**

Cased, opaque off-white exterior, shaded green interior, spherical body w/clear applied feet, 5" d., 7" h...**79.00**

Cranberry Opaque Vase

Cranberry shaded to lavender pink opaque, squatty bulbous base w/thin cylindrical neck w/clear edging around ruffled top, 4¼" d., 7¾" h. (ILLUS.) **165.00**

LACY

Acanthus Leaf & Eagle Pattern Bowl

Lacy Glass is a general term developed by collectors many years ago to cover the earliest type of pressed glass produced in this country. "Lacy" refers to the fact that most of these early patterns consisted of scrolls and geometric designs against a finely stippled background which gives the glass the look of fine lace. Formerly this

glass was often referred to as "Sandwich" for the Boston & Sandwich Glass Company of Sandwich, Massachusetts which produced a great deal of this ware. Today, however, collectors realize that many other factories on the East Coast and in the Pittsburgh, Pennsylvania and Wheeling, West Virginia areas also made lacy glass from the 1820s into the 1840s. All pieces listed are clear unless otherwise noted. Numbers after salt dips refer to listings in Pressed Glass Salt Dishes of the Lacy Period, 1825-1850, *by Logan W. and Dorothy B. Neal. Also see SANDWICH GLASS.*

Bowl, 6⅛" d., shallow, bands of circles & diamonds, acanthus leaves & scrolls (mold roughness) **$137.50**

Bowl, 6½" d., shallow, "Industry" patt. (eight tipped rim scallops).......**126.50**

Bowl, 7" w., octagonal, Acanthus Leaf & Eagle patt., two scallops lightly tipped, overall scallop roughness (ILLUS.) **330.00**

Bowl, 8½" l., 1½" h., oblong, Gothic Arch & Palm Leaf patt. (mold roughness) **93.50**

Bowl, 9" d., a large cross w/scrolls in two arms & strawberry diamonds in the others, a large florette in the center & diamond point design between each arm, clear w/an amethystine tint (three tipped scallops).....................................**203.50**

Bowl, 9" d., Peacock Feather & Scrolled Eye patt. (five tipped scallops)....................................**55.00**

Bowl, 9¼" d., bands of S-scroll, zig-zag & floral & shell designs w/a bull's-eye rim band (one bull's-eye missing, others lightly tipped) **247.50**

Bowl, 9¼" d., 1¾" h., Heart & Lyre border, large eight-point star at center framed by a wide band of strawberry diamond (four tipped scallops)....................................**220.00**

Bowl, 9½" d., 1½" h., wide flat base w/a large eleven-petal diamond point florette, lacy scrolls around the border (three flakes on rim).....................................**165.00**

Bowl, 10" l., 1¾" h., oblong, Gothic Arch & Pineapple patt. (mold roughness) **335.50**

Bowls, 9⅜" d., the center w/a large six-petal florette, the wide border w/six-point stars flanked by scrolled acanthus leaves, pr. (each w/a missing scallop & some tipped) **357.50**

Bowls, 9½" d., Zig-Zag & Quatrefoil patt., pr. (several flaked scallops, one missing) **143.00**

Lacy Compote

Compote, open, 9¼ x 12¼", 8" h., the ruffled shallow rectangular bowl w/notched corners in the Crossed Peacock Feather & Strawberry Diamond patt., attached by thick graduated wafers to the triple C-scroll pressed stem on a round domed lacy base, Boston & Sandwich Glass Co., ca. 1830, large chip at tip of one point, two shallow spalls on top rim (ILLUS.) **22,000.00**

Dish, round, Eagle patt., plain smooth edges w/scalloped rim, 4⅛" d. (one scallop chipped, overall scallop roughness) **132.00**

Plate, 5⅞" d., Pine Tree & Shield patt., pointed scallops at rim, fiery opalescent **390.50**

Plate, 6" d., intricate design of scrolls, leaves & fleur-de-lis (several lightly tipped scallops) **99.00**

Plate, 6⅜" w., octagonal, diamond band over Gothic arches border, starburst center (chips) **88.00**

Plate, 6¾" w., 12-sided, Shell patt. (three tipped scallops, mold roughness) **148.50**

Plate, 7¼" w., octagonal, Eagle & Stars patt., scrolls & cartouches in border (one scallop gone, overall scallop roughness)...........................**154.00**

Salt dip, casket-shaped w/scrolled ends & feet, crown patt., attributed to the Boston & Sandwich Glass Co., opalescent, mold roughness (CN 1a) **247.50**

Salt dip, casket-shaped w/scrolled ends, attributed to the Providence Flint Glass Co., pale green, mold roughness (SC 7)............................**385.00**

Salt dip, casket-shaped w/scroll ends, on small paw feet, strawberry diamond design, attributed to the Boston & Sandwich Glass Co., clear, 2D 2a (trace of mold roughness)....................................**121.00**

Salt dip, footed casket shape w/scrolled ends, Basket of Flowers patt., attributed to the Boston &

Sandwich Glass Co., light opalescent (BF 1f) **165.00**

Salt dip, footed casket-shape, Mount Vernon patt., attributed to the Boston & Sandwich Glass Co., aqua-light green, mold roughness (MV 1) **275.00**

Salt dip, oval w/deep sides, diamond point roundels above wide swags around the sides, fiery opalescent, attributed to the Boston & Sandwich Glass Co., OL 16a (several shallow rim flakes) **220.00**

Salt dip, oval scalloped & four-lobed bowl w/scrolls on a flaring foot, attributed to the Boston & Sandwich Glass Co., clear, OP 12 (mold roughness)......................................**495.00**

Salt dip, oval, footed, Peacock Eye patt., attributed to the Boston & Sandwich Glass Co., clear, PO 6 (unseen base chip, mold roughness) **110.00**

Salt dip, rectangular w/columnar corners & small knob feet, baskets of flowers on sides, Jersey Glass Company, clear, JY 2 (small chip, roughness at rim) **385.00**

Salt dip, rectangular w/columnar corners & tiny knob feet, basket of flowers on the sides, New England Glass Co., clear, NE 3 (small flakes on rim, mold roughness) **247.50**

Salt dip, round bowl w/leaftip design on a short hexagonal pedestal foot, golden amber, attributed to the Boston & Sandwich Glass Co., RP 25 (mold roughness) **660.00**

Salt dips, oblong boat shape on low foot, lacy scrolls in sides, attributed to Pittsburgh, clear, OL 20a (mold roughness) **77.00**

Sauce dish, Plume patt. w/acorn base, light opalescent clear, 4" d. **125.00**

Sugar bowl, cov., Gothic Arch patt., attributed to the Boston & Sandwich Glass Co., ca. 1840-60, fiery opalescent, 5¼" h. (base & cover mold roughness) **935.00**

Sugar bowl, cov., round w/gently flaring sides, domed flanged cover w/pointed button finial, Gothic Arch & Peacock Feather patt., 6⅛" h. (two scallops damaged on base & two on top rim) **385.00**

LALIQUE

Fine glass, which includes numerous extraordinary molded articles, has been made by the glasshouse established by René Lalique early in this century in

France. The firm was carried on by his son, Marc, until his death in 1977 and is now headed by Marc's daughter, Marie-Claude. All Lalique glass is marked, usually on, or near, the bottom with either an engraved or molded signature. Unless otherwise noted, we list only those pieces marked "R. Lalique" produced before the death of Rene Lalique in 1945.

R LALIQUE

FRANCE

R. LAI.IQUE

FRANCE

R. Lalique France N°3152

Stamped & Engraved Lalique Marks

Bowl, 9½" d., "Chiens," the exterior molded w/a band of dogs in a spiralling race, frosted clear, raised mark **$402.50**

Box, cov., "Cleones," wide flat bottom w/low sides fitted w/a conforming low domed cover molded w/ten opalescent scarabs among wild grasses, raised "R. Lalique" mark & engraved "France," 6⅝" d. **690.00**

"Volutes" Candlesticks

Candlesticks, "Volutes," in grey glass, each cup molded in low-relief w/rows of overlapping leafage, raised on standards w/curling serrated leaves, each acid-stamped "R. LALIQUE - FRANCE," ca. 1934, chip to edge of leaf to one, 8½" h., pr. (ILLUS.) **4,025.00**

Clock, "Moineaux," a half-round arch w/a flattened front & back, molded w/birds perched in flowering branches & framing the round dial w/Arabic numerals & molded "ATO" & stamped "MADE IN FRANCE," grey frosted, 6³⁄₁₆" h. **2,070.00**

Hood ornament, "Chrysis," frosted clear figure of a kneeling nude woman leaning back w/her arms & long hair trailing out, engraved "Lalique," 1950s, 5¼" h. **1,955.00**

Hood ornament, figural, "Libellule," cast as a dragonfly, frosted & clear grey, molded "R. LALIQUE" & "FRANCE," introduced in 1928, 6⅜" l., 2¾" h. **3,450.00**

Hood ornament, "Tete de Paon," model of a peacock's head w/upright comb, deep violet, introduced in 1928, impressed "R. LALIQUE," 7" h. **63,000.00**

Hood ornament, "Victoire," frosted clear model of a woman's head w/streaming stylized hair coming to a point, introduced in 1928, molded "R. Lalique," 10" l. **9,487.00**

Hood ornament, "Vitesse," frosted clear figure of a nude maiden stretched forward w/her hands behind her head, introduced in 1929, molded "R. Lalique," 7" h. **4,312.00**

Paperweight, figural, "Taureau Sacre," molded as a recumbent sacred cow, issued in 1938, one of 100 examples marked "Royal Dutch Mail" & "R. Lalique France," 3⅝" l. **575.00**

Pendant, rounded triangular form, molded w/a pair of large lily blossoms, opalescent w/a sepia patina, molded signature "LALIQUE" **345.00**

Perfume bottle w/flattened rectangular disc stopper, "La Belle Saison" for Houbigant, upright flattened rectangular form molded in low-relief w/a central figural panel within rayed leafy bands, frosted clear w/original brown patina, introduced in 1925, molded "R. LALIQUE - MADE IN FRANCE," 3¾" h. (chip to stopper) **1,725.00**

Ring, "Fleurs," blue glass domed form cast in low-relief w/a ring of flowers & stems running down the band, enameled in white, introduced in 1931, unsigned **1,035.00**

Vase, 5⅞" h., "Avallon," rounded cylindrical form w/slightly flaring rim, molded in medium- & high-relief w/finches perched amid scrolling branches, cherries & leafage, ca. 1927, acid-stamped "LALIQUE - FRANCE" (ILLUS. top next page) **1,265.00**

Vase, 5¾" h., "Caudebec," cylindrical, the side handles cast in low-relief w/stylized flowerheads & leafage, clear w/original light brown patina,

"Avallon" Vase

introduced in 1929, inscribed
"R. LALIQUE - FRANCE" **920.00**
Vase, 6" h., "Pierrefonds," slightly
flaring trumpet-form body flanked by
large molded full-relief spiraling
handles, amber, introduced in 1926,
inscribed "R. LALIQUE - FRANCE-
No. 990" **3,450.00**
Vase, 6⅛" h., "Chamonix," flaring
cylindrical body molded w/notched
vertical ribs, opalescent, ca. 1933,
stamped "R. LALIQUE -
FRANCE" **805.00**
Vase, 6¾" h., "Espalion," spherical
body tapering to a short, small rolled
neck, molded in low-relief
w/overlapping fern fronds, frosted
clear, introduced in 1927, inscribed
"R. Lalique - Paris" **1,610.00**
Vase, 6¾" h., "Ferrieres," flat-based
ovoid body tapering to a flattened
flaring rim, the sides molded in low-
relief w/five tiers of stylized
flowerheads & leafage, green,
introduced in 1929, inscribed "R.
Lalique - France - No. 1019" **2,012.00**
Vase, 9¼" h., "Ronces," slender ovoid
body tapering to a tiny cylindrical
neck, molded in medium-relief
w/overlapping thorny brambles,
frosted blue w/traces of original
white patina, introduced in 1921,
molded "R. Lalique"
(rim ground) **4,312.00**
Vase, 9⅜" h., "Ceylon," slightly flaring
cylindrical body molded in low- and
medium-relief w/perching pairs of
facing lovebirds around the top half,
frosted clear w/blue patina,
introduced in 1914, inscribed
"R. LALIQUE"...............................**3,737.00**
Vase, 9½" h., "Borromée," simple
ovoid body tapering to slightly flaring
mouth, molded around the upper
half w/bands of peacock heads,
opalescent w/the recessed areas
trimmed w/green patina, engraved
"R. Lalique France" **6,900.00**

LE VERRE FRANCAIS

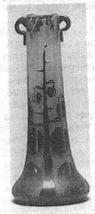

Le Verre Francais Cameo Vase

*Glassware carrying this marking was
produced at the French glass factory
founded by Charles Schneider in 1908. A
great deal of cameo glass was exported to
the United States early in this century and
much of it was marketed through
Ovingtons in New York City.*

Various Le Verre Francais Marks

Cameo planter, bulbous rectangular
form w/the rounded sides tapering
gently to the flat rectangular top,
mottled turquoise blue overlaid in
cobalt blue & acid-etched
w/blossom-filled suspended ball
forms, inscribed "Le Verre
Francais"......................................**$460.00**
Cameo vase, 5" h., ovoid body on a
cushion foot, grey cased over lemon
yellow & overlaid in orange shading
to cobalt blue, cut w/a design of
stylized foliage, inscribed "Le Verre
Francais," ca. 1925 ....**230.00**
Cameo vase, 11¾" h., slender
trumpet-form body w/a bulbous top
& closed mouth, on a cushion foot,
grey streaked w/violet, raspberry &
pale blue & overlaid in mottled
raspberry shading to burgundy & cut

w/stylized blossoms & pendent berries, signed in intaglio "Le Verre Francais," ca. 1920 ....**805.00**

Cameo vase, 13⅞" h., baluster-form body raised on a cushion foot & tapering to a flattened flaring rim, small applied purple loop handles at the neck, brown mottled w/blue base, cut from brown to mottled yellow & light brown w/stylized geese flying over marsh grasses, inscribed "Le Verre Francais," also inscribed twice on the base "France - New York - Ovington," ca. 1925 ....**805.00**

Cameo vase, 15⅜" h., squatty bulbous foot tapering to a long cylindrical neck w/applied purple handles at rim, grey ground mottled in pink & yellow, overlaid in purplish red & cut w/stylized fruiting branches, signed "Le Verre Francais - France" & stamped "FRANCE" & "OVINGTON" on base, ca. 1925 (ILLUS.) **1,150.00**

LIBBEY

In 1878, William L. Libbey obtained a lease on the New England Glass Company of Cambridge, Massachusetts, changing the name to the New England Glass Works, W.L. Libbey and Son, Proprietors. After his death in 1883, his son, Edward D. Libbey, continued to operate the company at Cambridge until 1888 when the factory was closed. Edward Libbey moved to Toledo, Ohio, and set up the company subsequently known as Libbey Glass Co. During the 1880s, the firm's master technician, Joseph Locke, developed the now much desired colored art glass lines of Agata, Amberina, Peach Blow and Pomona. Renowned for its Cut Glass of the Brilliant Period (see CUT GLASS,) the company continues in operation today as Libbey Glassware, a division of Owens-Illinois, Inc.

Champagne, Silhouette patt., clear bowl, opalescent figural squirrel stem **$162.50**

Claret, Silhouette patt., clear bowl, opalescent figural bear stem, Libby-Nash series **200.00**

Goblet, water, Silhouette patt., clear bowl, w/amber figural cat stem.....**170.00**

Maize celery vase, clear w/amber iridescent kernels & blue husks (ILLUS. top next column) **170.00**

Maize salt & pepper shakers, condiment size..................................**75.00**

Maize Celery Vase

Maize sugar shaker w/original top, creamy opaque w/yellow husks & gold trim **245.00**

Sherbet, low, Silhouette patt., clear bowl, opalescent figural rabbit stem, Libby-Nash series **75.00**

Sherbet, Silhouette patt., clear bowl, opalescent figural squirrel stem, 4" h..**110.00**

Tumblers, Currier & Ives Classics Collection, 12 oz., set of 4, mint in original box **75.00**

Vase, 10" h., turquoise zipper pattern on a clear ground, signed **425.00**

Vase, 15" h., lily-shaped, Amberina, signed **800.00**

LOETZ

Loetz Art Glass Vase

Iridescent glass, some of it somewhat resembling that of Tiffany and other contemporary glasshouses, was produced by the Bohemian firm of J. Loetz Witwe of Klostermule and is referred to as Loetz. Some cameo pieces were also made. Not all pieces are marked.

Loetz, Austria

Engraved Loetz Mark

Bowl-vase, oval boat-shaped body w/pointed tips at each end, applied at each end w/log-form feet, pale amber opalescent decorated w/bands of aubergine, silvery blue & melon trailings, design attributed to Koloman Moser, signed "Loetz - Austria," 3½" l. **$8,050.00**

Cameo bowl, 7⅛" h., oval w/slightly swelled cylindrical sides, milky white overlaid in black & cut w/an upper wide band of heart-shaped leaves & tendrils over a lower band of spaced slender bars, designed by Hans Bolek, ca. 1915, Model 661, from Series III.......................................**4,025.00**

Rose water sprinkler, bulbous pear-shaped body w/a tall slender slightly curved 'stick' neck topped w/a bulbous knob rim w/the sides pulled into two points, deep cobalt blue decorated w/turquoise blue iridescence & dark blue random trailing, ca. 1900, 11¼" h. **2,875.00**

Vase, 5⅜" h., inverted bell-form w/the lip continuing into a loop handle on each side, deep blue iridescence w/light blue oil spotting, signed "Loetz - Austria," ca. 1900....**690.00**

Vase, 6½" h., bulbous body w/bulbous ringed rim, iridescent white ground decorated w/iridescent silver spots, design attributed to Marie Kerishner, signed...................**528.00**

Vase, 8⅝" h., slightly swelled cylindrical body tapering slightly to a crimped rim, gold amber iridescent decorated w/orangish red stripes & ovals, design attributed to Koloman Moser, ca. 1900, unsigned **3,450.00**

Vase, 8¾" h., swelled cylindrical body tapering slightly at the shoulder to a wide flat mouth, pale green shaded to crimson decorated w/silvery blue iridescent trailings & overlaid w/engraved silver arabesque, rim inscribed "C.A.C. - DUTCH POOL - 1911 - SECOND PRIZE - WON BY C.A. CLAYTON," ca. 1900 ....**5,462.00**

Vase, 9" h., ovoid body w/pinched sides tapering to a flat rim, salmon pink iridescent ground decorated

w/indigo blue waves & silver spots **4,370.00**

Vase, 10" h., cylindrical body w/dimpled sides, emerald green body w/embossed rib design, metal collar w/pierced decoration of eagles on laurel swags **450.00**

Vase, 11⅛" h., paperweight-type, wide ovoid body tapering to a short flaring neck, pearlescent silvery blue & emerald green textured glass cased in clear, ca. 1900, unsigned **5,750.00**

Vase, 12½" h., of elongated goblet form w/flaring rim, amber cased to luminescent crimson-red w/lustrous golden combed iridescent surface, recessed pontil marked "Loetz - Austria" (ILLUS.)..............**2,990.00**

LUSTRES

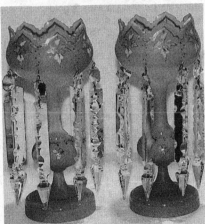

Bristol Apple Green Lustres

Lustres were Victorian glass vase-like decorative objects often hung around the rim with prisms. They were generally sold as matched pairs to be displayed on fireplace mantels. A wide range of colored glasswares were used in producing lustres and pieces were often highlighted with colored enameled decoration.

Apple green opaque, gold enameled decoration, hung w/ten 6½" l. facet-cut prisms, 10" h., pr. **$400.00**

Bristol, scalloped bulbous-form top supported by baluster-form standard on domed squared foot, apple green satin ground decorated w/gold leaves & insects, hung w/seven prisms, 4" d., 9⅝" h., pr. (ILLUS.) **450.00**

Canary cut to clear, the bowl engraved w/deer & castle scenes, hung w/faced prisms, Bohemia, pr..**545.00**

Pink Decorated Lustre

Pink exterior, white interior, decorated w/white flowers & gold leaves, two rows of prisms, inside 5½" l., outside 7¼" l., 15½" h., pr. (ILLUS. one of two).....................**910.00**

Ruby-flashed etched to clear, Deer & Castle patt., hung w/faceted prisms, 10" h., pr..............................**245.00**

MARY GREGORY

Mary Gregory Liqueur Mugs

Glass enameled in white with silhouette-type figures, primarily children, is now termed "Mary Gregory" and was attributed to the Boston and Sandwich Glass Company. However, recent research has proven conclusively that this ware was not decorated by Mary Gregory nor was it made at the Sandwich factory. Miss Gregory was employed by the Boston and Sandwich Glass Company as a decorator; however, records show her assignment was the painting of naturalistic landscape scenes on larger items such as lamps and

shades but never the charming children for which her name has become synonymous. Further, in the inspection of fragments from the factory site, no paintings of children were found.

It is now known that all wares now called "Mary Gregory" originated in Bohemia beginning in the late 19th century and were extensively exported to England and the U.S. well into this century.

For further information see The Glass Industry in Sandwich, Volume 4, by Raymond E. Barlow and Joan E. Kaiser, and the new book, Mary Gregory Glassware, 1880-1990, by R. & D. Truitt.

Atomizer, tapering cylindrical body, cranberry, white enameled decoration of a boy & girl facing each other, 5" h...........................**$360.00**

Box w/hinged lid, cobalt blue, white enameled little girl, 2" d., 1" h..........**225.00**

Cruet w/original amber stopper, footed spherical body w/a slender cylindrical neck, amber w/applied amber handle, white enameled young girl, 3" d., 8¾" h...................**245.00**

Cruet w/original amber bubble stopper, tapering cylindrical body w/a sloping shoulder to the cylindrical neck w/a tricorner rim, golden amber w/applied amber handle, Optic patt., white enameled boy...**245.00**

Decanter w/original blue bubble-shaped stopper, cushion foot supporting an ovoid body tapering to a cylindrical neck w/a flat flaring rim, sapphire blue, white enameled young girl, 3½" d., 9½" h.................**195.00**

Dresser box, cov., ovoid base w/original cover w/long teardrop-shaped finial, emerald green, white enameled young boy lying in the grass, 3⅞" d., 6½" h........................**200.00**

Ewer, spherical body w/a tall slender cylindrical neck, turquoise blue opaque, w/applied turquoise blue opaque handle, white enameled young girl, 3" d., 5" h.......................**175.00**

Lamp, table, kerosene-type, footed urn-shape, black, white enameled girl in flowing gown riding a large butterfly, electrified, 18" h. **345.00**

Liqueur mugs, amber barrel shaped body w/applied amber handle, white enameled girl on one & boy on the other, facing pr., 2½" d., 4" h. (ILLUS.) **127.50**

Pitcher, 5" h., 3" d., applied green handle, green, white enameled boy holding flower, standing among lily-of-the-valley, three-lobed rim, gold trim...**175.00**

Rose bowl, green, white enameled boy w/wings holding bird, surrounded w/lattice & gold scrolls, polished pontil, 6½" d., 6½" h. **225.00**

Sugar bowl, cov., footed spherical body, the domed cover w/a knob finial, golden amber, white enamel decoration of a young boy on the bowl & white enamel trim on the cover, 3½" d., 5" h..........................**195.00**

Tumbler, waisted cylindrical form, green, white enameled boy, 2¼" d., 3⅜" h. **40.00**

Tumbler, flaring cylindrical form, golden amber, white enameled young girl, 2⅞" d., 4" h......................**70.00**

Vase, 3⅞" h., 2" d., bulbous body tapering to a flaring cylindrical neck, cranberry, white enameled little girl **125.00**

Vase, 8" h., 3¼" d., pedestal foot supporting a bulbous body tapering to a slender cylindrical neck, cobalt blue, white enameled young girl **175.00**

Black Amethyst Mary Gregory Vase

Vase, 9¾" d., 4" d., footed, slightly flaring cylindrical body w/cupped flaring rim, black amethyst, white enameled young girl wearing hat (ILLUS.) **210.00**

Lime Green Mary Gregory Vase

Vase, 11" h., 3⅜" d., tall slender waisted cylindrical form, lime green, white enameled young boy dressed in a suit (ILLUS. bottom previous column) **85.00**

McKEE

The McKee name has been associated with glass production since 1834, first producing window glass and later bottles. In the 1850s a new factory was established in Pittsburgh, Pennsylvania, for production of flint and pressed glass. The plant was relocated in Jeannette, Pennsylvania in 1888 and operated there as an independent company almost continuously until 1951 when it sold out to Thatcher Glass Manufacturing Company. Many types of collectible glass were produced by McKee through the years including Depression, Pattern, Milk White and a variety of utility kitchenwares.

McKee

Early McKee Mark, ca. 1880

PRESCUT

McKee Prescut Mark

KITCHENWARES

Bowl, cov., 6¼" d., Chalaine Blue, marked **$100.00**

Butter dish, cov., Chalaine Blue, marked **325.00**

Pitcher, measuring, Chalaine Blue, marked, 4 cup **185.00**

PRES-CUT LINES

Candy dish, cov., Rock Crystal patt., amber, tall **63.00**

Cordial, Rock Crystal patt., clear **14.00**

Cup, custard, Rock Crystal patt., ruby **47.00**

Deviled egg plate, Rock Crystal patt., clear **55.00**

Egg cup (or sherbet), footed, Rock Crystal patt., clear, 3½ oz. **12.00**

Goblet, water, Rock Crystal patt., clear, 5¾" h..**11.00**

Mayonnaise bowl, Rock Crystal patt., ruby, 5" d..................................**60.00**

Parfait (sundae), footed, Rock Crystal patt., ruby..............................**31.50**

Pitcher, tankard, 9" h., Rock Crystal patt., clear **172.00**

Plate, dinner, 10½" d., Rock Crystal
patt., clear **45.00**
Spooner, Toltec patt., clear **29.00**
Sugar bowl, cov., Rock Crystal patt.,
clear **35.00**
Toothpick holder, Toltec patt.,
clear **33.00**
Tumbler, Rock Crystal patt., clear,
3½" h...**12.00**

MISCELLANEOUS PATTERNS & PIECES

Creamer, Gothic patt., ruby-stained.....**38.00**
Mug, Serenade (Troubadour) patt.,
custard **35.00**
Plate, 6½" d., Serenade patt., milk
white **42.00**
Spooner, Gothic patt., ruby-
stained **38.00**

MILK WHITE

Trumpet Vine Cake Stand

This is opaque white glass that resembles the color of and was used as a substitute for white porcelain. Opacity was obtained by adding oxide of tin to a batch of clear glass. It has been made in numerous forms and shapes in this country and abroad from about the first quarter of the last century. It is still being produced, and there are many reproductions of earlier pieces.

Animal covered dish, Baboon on
fleur-de-lis base, Flaccus,
6½" l..**$750.00**
Animal covered dish, Fox on ribbed
base, patent dated **170.00**
Animal covered dish, Pekinese
Dog on oblong latticework base,
3½ x 4¾"..**650.00**
Cake stand, Trumpet Vine patt.,
6½" d., 9" h. (ILLUS.) **75.00**
Compote, open, 8¼" d., 8¼" h.,

Atlas stem, scalloped rim,
Atterbury ....**75.00 to 100.00**
Compote, open, 8¼" h., 10" d.,
Open Hand patt., Atterbury................**85.00**
Covered dish, Football, modern..........**85.00**
Creamer, Paneled Wheat
patt. ....**25.00 to 35.00**
Creamer, Swan patt., 5" h. ....**25.00 to 35.00**
Jar, cov., Owl, Atterbury,
7" h. ....**125.00 to 130.00**
Match holder, hanging-type, Indian
Head, 4¾" w., 5" h. **65.00**
Model of a baseball, maker
unknown, modern ....**45.00 to 55.00**
Pitcher, 7½" h., Owl w/glass
eyes..................................**125.00 to 150.00**
Plate, 7" d., Anchor & Belaying
Pin...**35.00**
Plate, 7" d., Contrary Mule, w/gilt
paint....................................**35.00 to 40.00**
Plate, 7" d., Owl Lovers ....**45.00 to 55.00**

Three Bears Plate

Plate, 7" d., Three Bears, w/traces
of original brown, green & gilt
(ILLUS.) **37.50**
Plate, 7¼" d., Little Red Hen,
openwork lacy border ....**45.00 to 55.00**
Plate, 7¼" d., "No Easter Without
Us," rooster & hens **50.00**
Plate, 7¼" d., Spring Meets Winter,
openwork border **55.00**
Plate, 7¼" d., Yacht & Anchor **32.50**
Plate, 7½" d., Indian Head center,
Beaded Loop border............**40.00 to 50.00**
Plate, 8" d., Angel & Harp ......**25.00 to 35.00**
Plate, 9½" d., Columbus bust
center, Club & Shell border...............**65.00**
Salt dip, figural Goose **30.00**
Salt & pepper shakers w/original
tops, Medallion Sprig patt., pr. **65.00**
Sugar bowl, cov., Basket Weave
patt., dated 1874, 6" h. ......**90.00 to 100.00**
Sugar shaker w/original top,
Challinoir's Tree of Life patt. **85.00**
Syrup pitcher w/original metal top,
Scroll & Net w/Cosmos patt. **70.00**

MOSER

Moser Vase with Elephants

Ludwig Moser opened his first glass shop in 1857 in Karlsbad, Bohemia (now Karlovy Vary, in the former Czechoslovakia). Here he engraved and decorated fine glasswares especially to appeal to rich visitors to the local health spa. Later other shops were opened in various cities and throughout the 19th and early 20th century lovely colorful glasswares, many beautifully enameled, were produced by Moser's shops and reached a wide market in Europe and America. Ludwig died in 1916 and the firm continued under his sons. They were forced to merge with the Meyer's Nephews glass factory after World War I. The glassworks were sold out of the Moser family in 1933.

Basket, applied clear glass handle & foot, honey amber body decorated w/multicolored ferns inside & out, 9¼" h.................................**$865.00**

Box, cov., amethyst decorated w/raised enameling on the cover & sides, incised Moser Karlsbad mark, 3½" d., 3" h. **245.00**

Compote, open, 8¾" d., 6¼" h., "Radon," the wide bell-form bowl on a short wide pedestal & wide, thick disc foot, amethyst decorated around the stem w/a broad gold-etched band of Amazon warriors, matching gilt rim & base borders **575.00**

Cordials, cranberry ground decorated w/heavy gold highlighted w/blue dotting & white branches w/white dotted flowers, set of 4.....................**165.00**

Ewer, green body decorated overall w/multicolored ferns, 6" h.................**525.00**

Pitcher, tankard, 12¼" h., shaded apple green to clear cylindrical body decorated w/intaglio-cut poppy design on the front **765.00**

Tumbler, whiskey, facet-cut paperweight base etched w/tiny flowers, bowl acid-cut w/fighting cocks highlighted in gold trim...........**195.00**

Vase, 6¼" h., cylindrical body, overall deep intaglio-cut floral decoration, clear shaded to deep purple ground.................................**300.00**

Vase, 8½" h., clear pedestal base supporting a cranberry body decorated w/an enameled portrait, signed **250.00**

Vase, 8⅝" h., paneled body w/a cylindrical neck & raised on a domed ring foot, cobalt blue w/a center horizontal band in gold depicting Amazon warriors, etched mark "Made in Csecho Slovakia - Moser - Karlsbad," early 20th c........**575.00**

Vase, 13¾" h., slightly tapering cylindrical body w/a flat rim, deep amber acid-cut to light amber w/a continuous panel of two elephants & young under palm trees, all trimmed w/gilt, stylized floral upper & lower border, signed "Made in Szecho Slovakia - Moser - Karlsbad," ca. 1925-30 (ILLUS.) **1,840.00**

Vase, 14" h., clear ground decorated w/cut flowers & heavy gold outlining, signed **350.00**

Vase, 16" h., squatty bulbous base tapering to a tall cylindrical neck, enameled pink & blue florals & heavy gold decoration on a green ground, signed **496.00**

Vases, 6" h., 1¼" d., cranberry trumpet-form body w/a clear wafer foot, decorated w/heavy gold enameling, dainty white flowers & red & blue jewels overall, unsigned, pr. **295.00**

MT. WASHINGTON

A wide diversity of glass was made by the Mt. Washington Glass Company of New Bedford, Massachusetts, between 1869 and 1900. It was succeeded in 1900 by the Pairpoint Corporation. Miscellaneous types are listed below.

Celery tray w/original silver plate holder, acid-etched deep cranberry to clear floral design, patent dated Aug. 22, 1893, holder marked "Pairpoint," 2 pcs..............**$425.00**

Dresser box, cov., round footed silver plate box w/a hinged lid inset w/a round opal glass disc h.p. w/delicate flower clusters, satin-lined, base

w/the Pairpoint mark, 4½" d.,
1¾" h. (silver & satin worn) **230.00**

Ewer, bulbous, four-lobe melon-
ribbed base tapering to a cylindrical
neck & flaring to two-lobed rim
w/pinched spout, applied thorn
handle, blue satin ground decorated
w/large yellow daisies & delicate
foliage, 3½" widest d., 8" h.............**210.00**

Finger bowl & underplate, squatty
ovoid body w/a flat flaring ruffled
rim, satiny white ground, 2 pcs. **400.00**

Finger bowl & underplate, squatty
ovoid shaped bowl w/flat, crimped
rim, saucer w/slightly indented
center w/flaring crimped rim,
yellow satin ground, 2 pcs. **350.00**

Salt shaker w/original top, cockle
shell shape, decorated w/blue &
yellow florals on a white satin
ground..**750.00**

Salt shaker w/original top, egg-
shaped, reclining-type, h.p. floral
decoration on a white satin ground....**60.00**

Salt & pepper shakers w/original
tops, bulbous body w/embossed
creased neck, opaque white w/floral
decoration, pr. **75.00**

Salt & pepper shakers w/original
tops, egg-shaped, reclining-type,
souvenir of "Colombian 1893
Exposition," pr. **300.00**

Tazza, cornflower blue bowl
w/engraved floral decoration, silver
plate pedestal base w/three dolphin-
shaped feet, signed **450.00**

MULLER FRERES

Muller Freres Cameo Vase

*The Muller Brothers made acid-etched
cameo and other fine glass at Luneville,
France, starting in 1910 and until the
outbreak of World War II in Europe.*

Muller Freres Mark

Cameo vase, 7⅛" h., inverted bell-
form, cut w/four flecked red fish on a
frosted ground w/overall overlapping
circlets, incised "MULLER - FRES-
LUNEVILLE," ca. 1925-30 ....**$1,495.00**

Cameo vase, 7½" h., tapering ovoid
body w/a narrow flared rim, grey
shaded w/pale salmon, splashed
w/violet & yellow, overlaid w/crimson
& cut w/poppy blossoms & leaves,
signed in cameo "MULLER FRES -
LUNEVILLE," ca. 1920 ....**3,105.00**

Cameo vase, 9¾" h., spherical body
tapering to a short flaring neck, grey
shaded w/lemon yellow & overlaid in
red & cut w/rhododendron flowers &
leaves, signed in cameo,
ca. 1920 ....**3,737.00**

Cameo vase, 11" h., bulbous ovoid
body tapering to a short cylindrical
neck w/flat rim, grey mottled
w/lemon yellow & overlaid in orange
& dark red, cut w/lily blossoms &
leafage, signed in cameo "MULLER
FRES - LUNEVILLE"
(ILLUS.) **2,530.00**

Cameo vase, 12⅔" h., slender ovoid
body tapering to a flat mouth, pale
peach ground overlaid in moss
green, etched & finely wheel-carved
to depict a lake w/flowering water
lilies, a dragonfly & a bug, engraved
signature "Muller Croismare" **2,530.00**

Lamp, table, 12" d. domical
mushroom-form shade & matching
baluster-form base w/cushion foot,
each in mottled purple shaded to
yellowish amber & acid-etched
w/thorny branches w/lush berries all
enamel-decorated w/autumnal
earthtones, wrought-iron three-arm
mount, base inscribed "Muller Fres
Luneville," 19½" h. **8,625.00**

Vase, 9" h., wide spherical body w/a
short cylindrical neck, clear
internally decorated w/streaks of
butterscotch yellow, orange, brown
& flecks of black, signed on the base
"Muller Fres Luneville," ca. 1930s....**489.00**

Vase, 9½" h., bulbous ovoid body
tapering sharply to a short cylindrical
neck, clear internally layered w/gold
flecks & green & reddish orange

Cluthra-like inclusions, signed on the base "Muller Fres Luneville," ca. 1930s **546.00**

NAKARA

Tall Nakara Vase

Like Kelva, Nakara was made early in this century by the C.F. Monroe Company. For details see WAVE CREST.

Box, cov., Bishop's Hat mold, blue ground w/florals, 5" w......................**$550.00**
Pin tray, Bishop's Hat mold, yellow ground decorated w/delicate pink flowers, 4" w..................................**295.00**
Pin tray, decorated w/delicate roses, 4½" d...**295.00**
Vase, 15¾" h., tall slender baluster-form body w/a wide flaring mouth, decorated w/large pink & white flowers on a shaded pale green ground (ILLUS.) **1,910.00**

NEW MARTINSVILLE

The New Martinsville Glass Mfg. Co. opened in New Martinsville, West Virginia in 1901 and during its first period of production came out with a number of colored opaque pressed glass patterns. They also developed an art glass line they named "Muranese," which collectors refer to as "New Martinsville Peach Blow." The factory burned in 1907 but reopened later that year and began focusing on production of various clear pressed glass patterns, many of which were then decorated with gold or ruby staining or enameled decoration. After going through receivership in 1937, the factory again

changed the focus of its production to more contemporary glass lines and figural animals. The firm was purchased in 1944 by The Viking Glass Company (now Dalzell-Viking) and some of the long-popular New Martinsville patterns are now produced by this still active firm.

Basket w/applied handle, Janice patt., (No. 4500 Line), ruby red, 12" l. oval, 10" h. **$155.00**
Basket w/applied dolphin-shaped feet, Radiance patt., (No. 4200 Line), clear **45.00**
Bonbon, rolled-up handles, Janice patt., clear **15.00**
Book ends, figural, Cornucopia patt., No. 651, clear, 5¾" h., pr. **45.00**
Book ends, Ship patt., No. 499, clear, 5¾" h., pr. **85.00**
Bowl, 6" d., handled, Janice patt., clear w/silver trim **25.00**
Butter dish, cov., Radiance patt., clear w/silver overlay **120.00**
Cake stand, Princess patt. (No. 5200 Line), clear **40.00**
Creamer & sugar bowl, Moondrops patt. (No. 37 Line), ruby, pr. **20.00**
Creamer & sugar bowl, Radiance patt., ruby, pr........................**40.00**
Cup & saucer, Janice patt., light blue **18.50**
Cup & saucer, Moondrops patt., blue **18.00**
Goblet, Prelude etching, clear **14.00**
Pitcher, water, Florene patt., ruby-stained **135.00**
Plate, 8½" d., Moondrops patt., cobalt blue **18.50**
Relish, dish, divided, Janice patt., amber, 6¼" l..................................**12.50**
Sherbet, Prelude etching, clear **9.00**
Sugar bowl, individual, Moondrops patt., red....................................**17.50**
Wine, Moondrops patt., red, 4" h.........**22.50**

NORTHWOOD

Harry Northwood (1860-1919) was born in England, the son of noted glass artist John Northwood. Brought up in the glass business, Harry immigrated to the United States in 1881 and shortly thereafter became manager of the La Belle Glass Company, Bridgeport, Ohio. Here he was responsible for many innovations in colored and blown glass. After leaving La Belle in 1887 he opened The Northwood Glass Company in Martins Ferry, Ohio in 1888. The company moved to Ellwood City, Pennsylvania in 1892 and Northwood moved again to take over a glass plant in Indiana, Pennsylvania in 1896. One of his major lines made at the Indiana, Pennsylvania plant was Custard glass (which he called "ivory"). It was made in several patterns and some pieces were marked on the base with "Northwood" in script.

Harry and his family moved back to England in 1899 but returned to the U.S. in 1902 at which time he opened another glass factory in Wheeling, West Virginia. Here he was able to put his full talents to work and under his guidance the firm manufactured many notable glass lines including opalescent wares, colored and clear pressed tablewares, various novelties and, probably best known of all, Carnival glass. Around 1906 Harry introduced his famous "N" in circle trade-mark which can be found on the base of many, but not all, pieces made at his factory. The factory closed in 1925.

In this listing we are including only the clear and colored tablewares produced at Northwood factories. Specialized lines such as Custard glass, Chrysanthemum Sprig, Blue, Carnival and Opalescent wares are listed under their own headings in our Glass category.

Northwood Peach Butter Dish

Northwood Signature Mark, ca. 1898

Northwood "N" in Circle Mark, ca. 1906

Bowl, 9" d., Plums & Cherries patt., clear **$60.00**

Bowl, master berry, 10" d., Leaf Medallion (Regent) patt., clear w/gold trim **60.00**

Butter dish, cov., Leaf Medallion (Regent) patt., green w/gold trim **350.00**

Butter dish, cov., Peach patt., green w/gold trim (ILLUS.).........**125.00 to 145.00**

Candlesticks, No. 719, opaque green, 6" h., pr. **35.00**

Candy jar, cov., No. 636, paneled sides, pointed cover & finial, blue stretch glass, 1920s **50.00**

Celery vase, Chrysanthemum Swirl patt., vaseline speckled **175.00**

Compote, fruit, Grape Frieze patt., "Verre D'or" decoration on dark amethyst **275.00**

Cruet w/original stopper, Venetian (Utopia Optic) patt., green ....**225.00 to 250.00**

Model of a Bushel Basket, black amethyst, marked **90.00**

Pitcher, Aurora patt., rubina..............**175.00**

Punch cup, Memphis patt., clear........**12.00**

Salt shaker w/original top, Leaf Mold patt., vaseline w/cranberry spatter **75.00**

Salt shaker w/original top, Leaf Umbrella patt., Rose du Barry (cased mauve) **65.00**

Salt shaker w/original top, Ribbed Pillar patt., pink & white spatter **45.00**

Salt & pepper shakers w/original tops, Quilted Phlox patt., blue opaque, pr. ....**75.00 to 100.00**

Sugar shaker w/original top, Leaf Mold patt., cased blue satin **365.00**

Sugar shaker w/original top, Leaf Mold patt., Rose du Barry (cased mauve) **300.00**

Sugar shaker w/original top, Leaf Mold patt., vaseline w/cranberry spatter ....**375.00 to 425.00**

Sugar shaker w/original top, Parian Swirl patt., blue opaque **195.00**

Sugar shaker w/original top, Quilted Phlox patt., pink opaque **240.00**

Syrup pitcher w/original top, Grape & Leaf patt., green opaque.................**245.00**

Syrup pitcher w/original top, Jewel (Threaded Swirl) patt., rubina **295.00**

Syrup pitcher w/original top, Reverse Swirl patt., blue satin spatter...........**250.00**

Table set: cov. butter dish, creamer & spooner; Mikado (Flower & Bud) patt., frosted clear w/multicolored decoration on the individual flowers & gold trim, 3 pcs. **275.00**

Toothpick holder, Ribbed Pillar patt., pink & white spatter, glossy finish......**60.00**

Tumbler, Cherry Lattice patt., clear w/ruby & gold trim **16.50**

Tumbler, Diadem (Sunburst on Shield) patt., blue opalescent **125.00**

Tumbler, Leaf Medallion (Regent) patt., green w/gold trim 40.00
Tumbler, Netted Oak patt., milk white w/green band decoration 45.00
Tumbler, Plums & Cherries patt., clear w/ruby & gold trim 25.00
Water set: pitcher & four tumblers; Leaf Medallion (Regent) patt., purple, 5 pcs. 395.00
Water set: pitcher & 4 tumblers; Netted Oak patt., clear, 5 pcs. 265.00

OPALESCENT

Presently, this is one of the most popular areas of glass collecting. The opalescent effect was attained by adding bone ash chemicals to areas of an item while still hot and refiring the object at tremendous heat. Both pressed and mold-blown patterns are available to collectors and we distinguish the types in our listing below. Opalescent Glass from A to Z by the late William Heacock is the definitive reference book for collectors. Also see PATTERN GLASS.

MOLD-BLOWN OPALESCENT PATTERNS

COIN SPOT

Coin Spot Tumbler

Compote, jelly, green........................$30.00
Pitcher, 8" h., crimped rim blue..........175.00
Pitcher, water, square top mold, cranberry...150.00
Sugar shaker w/original top, Northwood mold, white 110.00
Sugar shaker w/original top, tapered mold, blue 145.00
Tumbler, cranberry (ILLUS.)................45.00

DAISY & FERN
Lamp, banquet-type, white.................489.00

Pitcher, water, cranberry 225.00
Rose bowl, cranberry 55.00
Rose bowl, white 45.00
Syrup pitcher w/original metal top, blue...250.00
Water set: pitcher & six tumblers; cranberry, 7 pcs. 475.00

HOBNAIL, HOBBS

Hobnail Celery Vase

Celery vase, ruffled rim, cranberry, 4" d., 6¼" h. (ILLUS.) 135.00
Compote, 5½ x 9", cranberry............250.00

Hobbs Hobnail Creamer

Creamer, blue, 4½" h. (ILLUS.)............55.00
Decanter w/original stopper, cranberry...85.00
Pitcher, water, cranberry 325.00
Syrup pitcher w/original top, blue 325.00
Tumbler, canary.................................95.00
Tumblers, white, set of 5 ....100.00

REVERSE SWIRL
Salt shaker w/original top, white..........45.00
Salt & pepper shakers w/original tops, canary, pr. 120.00
Syrup pitcher w/original top, blue 195.00
Toothpick holder, canary...................90.00

Tumbler, blue...............................65.00
Tumbler, white.............................58.00

RIBBED OPAL LATTICE
Celery vase, blue...........................85.00
Toothpick holder, blue....................135.00
Toothpick holder, white...................75.00

SEAWEED
Bride's bowl, tightly crimped rim,
   cranberry, 10" d. 175.00
Pitcher, water, blue.......................500.00
Sugar bowl, cov., white...................115.00
Syrup pitcher w/original top, white....130.00

SPANISH LACE
Bowl, 5½" d., canary.......................25.00
Bowl, 6½" d., ruffled rim, white..........47.50
Bowl w/upturned rim, canary..............95.00
Pitcher, water, 9½" h., ruffled rim,
   blue.......................................300.00
Rose bowl, canary..........................37.50
Salt shaker w/original top, canary.......95.00
Sugar shaker w/original top,
   cranberry.....................375.00 to 425.00
Tumbler, canary............................48.00
Vase, 6" h., canary........................75.00
Vase, blue................................225.00

STRIPE
Barber bottle, cranberry..................195.00
Bowl, 10" d., cranberry...................210.00
Sugar shaker w/original top, blue......225.00

SWIRL
Butter dish, cov., canary.................175.00
Celery vase, blue.........................105.00
Pitcher, water, 8½" h., square rim,
   applied clear handle, cranberry.......225.00
Sugar shaker w/original top,
   cranberry.................................398.00
Tumbler, cranberry.........................72.00
Tumble-up (water carafe w/tumbler
   lid), cranberry, 2 pcs. 460.00

PRESSED OPALESCENT PATTERNS

BEATTY HONEYCOMB
Sugar shaker w/original top, white....202.50
Toothpick holder, blue....................71.00
Toothpick holder, white...................54.50

CIRCLED SCROLL
Creamer, green.............................70.00
Water set: pitcher & five tumblers;
   blue, 6 pcs. 725.00

DIAMOND SPEARHEAD
Mug, green.................................50.00
Mug, canary................................55.00
Table set, green, 4 pcs. 575.00

DRAPERY
Butter dish, cov., blue...................152.50
Table set, blue w/gold trim, 4 pcs. 430.00
Tumbler, blue..............................67.00

EVERGLADES
Bowl, oblong master berry, blue........212.50
Butter dish, cov., canary.................250.00
Compote, jelly, blue.......................80.00
Compote, jelly, blue w/gold trim..........95.00
Compote, jelly, canary...................110.00
Pitcher, water, canary....................525.00
Table set, blue, 4 pcs....................550.00
Table set, canary, 4 pcs. ...500.00 to 525.00
Tumbler, canary w/gold trim...............50.00
Tumbler, white............................45.00
Water set: pitcher & five tumblers,
   white, 6 pcs. 675.00

FAN
Candy dish, green..........................30.00
Gravy boat, green..........................32.50
Sauce dish, green..........................30.00

FLORA
Bowl, master berry, blue..................77.50
Butter dish, cov., blue...................260.00
Spooner, blue..............................82.50
Sugar bowl, cov., canary.................130.00

FLUTED SCROLLS

Fluted Scrolls Butter Dish

Berry set: master bowl & six sauce
   dishes; canary, 7 pcs. 283.00
Butter dish, cov., blue...................160.00
Butter dish, cov., canary (ILLUS.)...152.50
Creamer, blue..............................65.00
Pitcher, water, canary...................240.00
Salt & pepper shakers w/original
   tops, canary, pr. 140.00
Sauce dish, blue...........................38.00
Table set, blue, 4 pcs....................502.50
Table set, canary, 4 pcs. ...450.00 to 500.00
Water set: pitcher & six tumblers;
   canary, 7 pcs. ....675.00 to 725.00

HOBNAIL (Northwood & others)
Creamer & sugar bowl, white, pr........50.00
Pitcher, water, white 95.00
Sugar bowl, cov., white 85.00
Spooner, lavender 75.00
Spooner, white...................................50.00

INTAGLIO
Bowl, berry, blue 35.00
Compote, jelly, blue 68.00
Compote, jelly, white 30.00
Creamer, blue 55.00
Spooner, blue 94.50
Table set: cov. sugar bowl, creamer,
    cov. butter dish & spooner; white,
    4 pcs. 350.00

INVERTED FAN & FEATHER
Bowl, master berry, 10" d., blue.........245.00
Candy dish, green.............................285.00
Creamer, blue 125.00
Rose bowl, canary...............................40.00
Sauce dishes, white, set of 6 ....120.00
Spooner, blue 140.00

IRIS WITH MEANDER
Bowl, 9" d., footed, blue......................35.00
Bowl, 9" d., footed, green....................41.00
Compote, jelly, canary...........50.00 to 75.00
Creamer, blue 125.00
Sauce dish, blue.................................25.00
Sugar bowl, cov., white 50.00
Toothpick holder, blue.........................79.50
Toothpick holder, green 85.00

JEWEL & FLOWER
Bowl, master berry, blue......................91.00
Berry set: master bowl & six sauce
    dishes; blue, 7 pcs. 258.00
Berry set: master bowl & six sauce
    dishes; white, 7 pcs. 135.00
Sauce dish, blue.................................35.00
Tumbler, blue......................................70.00

OVER-ALL HOBBS
Celery vase, white, 4½" d.,
    6½" h..325.00
Sugar shaker w/original top, blue........75.00
Toothpick holder, white 45.00

REGAL
Berry set: master bowl & five sauce
    dishes; white, 6 pcs. 175.00
Bowl, master berry, blue......................45.00
Table set, blue, 4 pcs.........................500.00

RIBBED SPIRAL
Bowl, 7½" d., blue................................40.00
Bowl, 7½" d., canary...........................41.50
Sauce dish, white 20.00
Toothpick holder, blue.........................97.50
Toothpick holder, canary....................60.00

SWAG WITH BRACKETS
Compote, jelly, blue.............................40.00
Compote, jelly, canary.........................35.00
Compote, jelly, green...........................35.00
Creamer, blue 105.00
Pitcher, water, amethyst....................100.00
Spooner, blue 110.00
Sugar bowl, cov., canary...................115.00
Sugar bowl, cov., green 125.00
Toothpick holder, canary, 2½" h. 165.00
Tumbler, canary...................................55.00

TOKYO
Bowl, 7" d., ruffled rim, blue.................37.50
Bowl, master berry, green....................70.00
Creamer, blue 67.50
Cruet w/original stopper, blue 145.00

WILD BOUQUET
Creamer & sugar bowl, white, pr......150.00
Cruet w/original stopper, blue 340.00
Table set, blue, 4 pcs........................825.00

WREATH & SHELL

Wreath & Shell Spooner

Salt dip, blue.....................................110.00
Sauce dish, blue.................................30.00
Spooner, blue (ILLUS.)........................84.00
Sugar bowl, open, blue 52.50
Table set, blue, 4 pcs.........................687.50
Toothpick holder, blue.......................190.00
Toothpick holder, white 150.00
Tumbler, collared base, canary 85.00

MISCELLANEOUS PRESSED
NOVELTIES

Diamond Point vase, 11" h., ruffled
    rim, blue..42.00
Diamond & Oval Thumbprint vase,
    12" h., blue..30.00
Dolphin compote, clear 209.50
**Fluted Bars & Beads toothpick
    holder,** green......................................42.00
Hilltop Vine compote, blue 52.50
Leaf & Diamond bowl, 8½" d.,
    three-footed, white 30.00
Lined Heart vase, 7" h., blue..............28.00
Lined Heart vase, 13" h., white 20.00

Lined Heart vase, green......................**33.00**
Lorna vase, blue..................................**35.00**
Many Loops bowl, ruffled rim,
    green..**25.00**
Many Loops candy dish, triangular,
    green..**45.00**
Palisades bowl, blue...........................**40.00**
Palm & Scroll bowl, three-footed,
    blue..**52.50**
Peacocks on a Fence bowl, 9" d.,
    blue..**180.00**
Pearl Flowers bowl, footed, blue.......**38.00**
Popsicle Sticks compote, 8" d.,
    4" h. **40.00**
Rose Show bowl, 9" d., blue............**120.00**
Ruffles and Rings bowl, 8½" d.,
    white **57.50**

Scheherezade Bowl

Scheherezade bowl, blue, 8" d.
    (ILLUS.) **52.50**
Twig Vase, 7" h., blue.........................**60.00**
Vintage bowl, 6½" d., 4" h., blue.........**40.00**

(End of Opalescent Section)

ORREFORS

Orrefors "Ariel" Vases

This Swedish glasshouse, founded in 1898 for production of tablewares, has made decorative wares as well since 1915. By 1925, Orrefors had achieved an international reputation for its Graal glass, an engraved art glass developed by master glassblower Knut Berqvist and artist-designers Simon Gate and Edward Hald. Ariel glass, recognized by a design of controlled air traps, and the heavy Ravenna glass, usually tinted, were both developed in the 1930s. While all Orrefors glass is collectible, pieces signed by early designers and artists are now bringing high prices.

Bowl, 8¾" l., 6" h., "Graal," thick-walled oval form w/rounded upright flattened sides, green shaded to clear, internally deco-rated w/four fish among aquatic plants, inscribed on the base "Orrefors Sweden Graal N. 380 Edward Hald" (some interior scratches) **$862.50**
Bowl & underplate, 15¼" d., clear widely flaring bowl engraved obverse & reverse w/nude male & female figures amid scrolling foliage, w/matching underplate, designed by Simon Gate, inscribed "Orrefors - Gate - 147 - 29 - R," ca. 1920, 2 pcs. **4,025.00**
Vase, 5" h., "Ariel," thick rounded body w/a wide band of sepia-colored airtrap six-petal blossoms within the crystal walls, base inscribed "Orrefors Ariel Sweden 1945 No. 335, E. Ohrstrom"...................**1,150.00**
Vase, 5¾" h., "Graal," "Fiskgraal," thick teardrop-form body in clear internally decorated w/a pattern of fish swimming through aquatic foliage in emerald green & deepest amber, designed by Edward Hald, inscribed "ORREFORS - Sweden - GRAAL No. 9940 - Edward Hald," ca. 1980 ....**575.00**
Vase, 6¾" h., "Ariel," simple ovoid body tapering to a flat mouth, thick walls enclosing a portrait of a maiden in fanciful headdress, w/leafage & sea forms, in shades of pale green & brown in clear, designed by Edvin Ohrstrom, inscribed "Orrefors Sweden - Ariel - Orv. 687 - Edvin Ohrstrom," ca. 1949 (ILLUS. right) **3,450.00**
Vase, 7" h., "Graal," clear internally decorated w/green fish swimming through seaweed, signed "Orrefors Sweden Graal #NR 2550 Edward Hald" **550.00**
Vase, 7½" d., deep rounded & slightly triangular form, the body

w/trelliswork, each cell containing
tiny captive bubbles, the rim in
opaque blue, by Sven Palmquist,
signed "Orrefors - Kraka N 342 -
Sven Palmquist"...............................**517.00**
Vase, 8¼" h., "Ariel," thick-walled
ovoid body w/small irregular mouth,
the walls enclosing a singing
gondolier w/guitar beneath a cresent
moon, the reverse w/a portrait of a
maiden, in shades of topaz & blue,
designed by Edvin Ohrstrom,
inscribed "ORREFORS - Ariel Nr
315N - Edvin Ohstrom," ca, 1950
(ILLUS. left)...............................**2,587.00**
Vase, 10" h., exposition-type, slightly
swelled cylindrical body w/wide flat
mouth, heavy walls engraved
w/minutely detailed vineyard scene
of two nude maidens picking grapes,
inscribed on reverse w/a monogram
& "19 10/25 49," base signed
"Orrefors Nils Landberg Expo
1438.1950"...............................**546.00**
Vase, 10½" h., "Graal," 'Europa & the
Bull' patt., slender ovoid body raised
on a thick applied footring, clear
decorated w/a large stylized seated
nude Europa & the bull in shades of
aubergine, designed by Vicky
Lindstrand, Inscribed "Orrefors -
1937 - Sweden - Graal - No. 103 -
W.Lindstrand" **10,062.00**

OVERSHOT

Pewter Mounted Overshot Claret

*Popular since the mid-19th century,
Overshot glass was produced by having a
gather of molten glass rolled in finely
crushed glass to produce a rough exterior
finish. The piece was then blown to the
desired size and shape. The finished piece*

*has a frosted or iced finish and is
sometimes referred to as "ice glass." Early
producers referred to this glass as
"Craquelle" and, although Overshot is
sometimes lumped together with the glass
collectors now call "crackle," that type was
produced using a totally different
technique.*

Basket, Amberina w/applied amber
thorn handle, ruffled rim,
7½ x 8½", 9½" h...........................**$650.00**
Bowl, 8" d., 3½" h., applied clear
feet & handle, pale pink **475.00**
Claret pitcher, ovoid body fitted
w/pewter foot, long handle & tall
embossed neck w/ornate spout &
hinged, domed cover, cranberry
shading to clear Rubina Crystal
w/overshot finish, 4⅜" d., 12½" h.
(ILLUS.) **295.00**
Pitcher, 8¼" h., green w/applied
amber shell handle, Boston &
Sandwich Glass Co.,
ca. 1870 ....**235.00**
Pitcher, tankard, 9½" h., w/large ice
bladder, cranberry w/applied
cranberry handle w/clear
casing **795.00**
Rose bowl, applied clear rigaree foot,
Rubina Crystal w/overshot finish,
3½" d...**110.00**

PADEN CITY

*The Paden City Glass Manufacturing
Company began operations in Paden City,
West Virginia in 1916, primarily as a
supplier of blanks to other companies. All
wares were hand-made, that is, either
hand-pressed or mold-blown. The early
products were not particularly noteworthy
but by the early 1930s the quality had
improved considerably. The firm
continued to turn out high quality
glassware in a variety of beautiful colors
until financial difficulties necessitated its
closing in 1951. Over the years the firm
produced, in a addition to tablewares,
items for hotel and restaurant use, light
shades, shaving mugs, perfume bottles and
lamps. Also see ANIMALS in the Glass
category.*

Book ends, model of a Pouter
Pigeon, clear, pr...........................**$170.00**
Bowl, cream soup, footed, Crow's
Foot (No. 412) line, amber..................**9.00**
Tumbler, Party Line (No. 191) line,
red, 3¼" h. **8.00**

Tumbler, Party Line (No. 191) line,
red, 4⅛" h. **10.00**
Tumbler, Party Line (No. 191) line,
red, 5¼" h. **12.00**
Vase, 10" h., Gazebo etching, topaz....**85.00**

PAIRPOINT

Originally organized in New Bedford, Massachusetts in 1880, as the Pairpoint Manufacturing Company, on land adjacent to the famed Mount Washington Glass Company, this company first manufactured silver and plated wares. In 1894, the two famous factories merged as the Pairpoint Corporation and enjoyed great success for more than forty years. The company was sold in 1939 to a group of local businessmen and eventually bought out by one of the group who turned the management over to Robert M. Gundersen. Subsequently, it operated as the Gundersen Glass Works until 1952 when, after Gundersen's death, the name was changed to Gundersen-Pairpoint. The factory closed in 1956. Subsequently, Robert Bryden took charge of this glassworks, at first producing glass for Pairpoint abroad and eventually, in 1970, beginning glass production in Sagamore, Massachusetts. Today the Pairpoint Crystal Glass Company is owned by Robert and June Bancroft. They continue to manufacture fine quality blown and pressed glass.

Center bowl, clear "controlled"
bubble bowl w/applied ruby pedestal
base, 12" d. **$245.00**
Compote, cov., 9", ruby w/clear
"controlled" bubble knob finial **225.00**
Compote, open, 5" h., ruby bowl
w/clear "controlled" bubble knob
pedestal base **135.00**
Compote, open, 7½" d., 4" h.,
amethyst decorated w/engraved
grape design **110.00**
Vases, 8¾" h., cornucopia shape,
ruby w/clear "controlled" bubble
knob base, pr. **450.00**
Vase, 11" h., ruby cornucopia-shaped
body w/clear "controlled" bubble
connector & applied ruby pedestal
base **185.00**

PATE DE VERRE

Pate de Verre, or "paste of glass," was molded by very few artisans. In the pate de verre technique, powdered glass is mixed with a liquid to make a paste which is then placed in a mold and baked at a high temperature. These articles have a finely-pitted or matte finish and are easily distinguished from blown glass. Duplicate pieces are possible with this technique.

WALTER
NANCY

G·ARGY ROUSSEAU

Typical Pate de Verre Marks

Bowl, 2½" h., wide rounded shallow
bowl raised on a small cylindrical
foot, turquoise blue internally
decorated w/swirls of deep purple,
molded on the exterior w/geometric
devices & concentric lines, molded
"DECORCHMENT" & inscribed
"579," ca. 1927 ....**$2,300.00**
Bowl, 8½" l., rounded bowl flanked by
wide, heavy ram horn-shaped
handles conjoined at the flaring foot,
mottled amber, molded on the sides
w/stylized flowers & leaves, signed
in the mold "G. ARGY-
ROUSSEAU," ca. 1927 ....**2,990.00**
Bowl-vase, footed rounded form
w/flat dies, tan molded w/amber-
brown, black & brick red foliate
border, impressed "G. Argy-
Rousseau," 3⅛" h. **4,312.50**
Box, cov., squatty bulbous round form
molded overall w/stylized hydrangea
blossoms, mottled shades of dusty
violet, pale white & black, signed in
the mold "G. ARGY-ROUSSEAU,"
ca. 1926, 4" d. **5,750.00**
Figure of Buddha, seated w/legs
crossed & hands in lap, pale amber,
impressed "A. Walter Nancy" on the
lower front, an Oriental symbol on
the back, 6¾" h. **1,725.00**
Pendant, round, molded w/purple &
green blossoms above a red tie on
brown stems, impressed "G.A-R,"
G. Argy-Rousseau, 2⅝" d. **1,265.00**
Vase, 3⅞" h., wide ovoid body
tapering slightly to a short wide
cylindrical neck, grey mottled
w/purple, mint green & rose, molded
in low-relief w/thistle blossoms &
leaves in deep forest green & rose,
molded "G. ARGY-ROUSSEAU" &
"FRANCE"....................................**3,450.00**
Vase, 6" h., "Plumes," swelled
cylindrical body w/a wide flat mouth,
molded w/three pairs of stylized
pheasant feathers, mottled shades
of aubergine & moss green against

a mottled grey ground, signed in the mold "G. ARGY-ROUSSEAU 13304," ca. 1922.............................**4,370.00**

Vase, 6¾" h., footed 12-paneled trumpet-form body in purple, amethyst & clear striated w/a bubbled surface, incised w/a repeating geometric border, engraved on the base "F Decorchement A679"...................**4,600.00**

Vase, 7" h., low sloping foot & tapering sides, molded in low-relief w/a band of hops in shades of mottled lemon yellow, green, red & orange, molded "A. WALTER - NANCY" & "Bergé - S.C.," ca. 1925.......................................**2,300.00**

Vase, 9" h., wide ovoid body tapering to a short flaring neck flanked by loop handles w/three graduated curls at the shoulder, grey molded in low-relief w/overlapping stylized foliage & modeled & streaked w/shades of rose, purple, brown & white, molded mark "G. ARGY - ROUSSEAU" & enameled "FRANCE," ca. 1926.....................**4,600.00**

Pate de Verre Vase

Vase, 9¾" h., baluster-shaped w/a wide flaring rim, molded w/stylized diaphanously draped dancing maidens above narrow horizontal bands, mottled shades of salmon, Tuscany red, brown & silvery grey, signed in the mold "G. ARGY-ROUSSEAU - FRANCE," ca. 1930 (ILLUS.) **40,250.00**

***Vide poche* (figural dish),** shallow oval dish molded in full-relief along one side w/a lizard perched on a rock, in shades of brilliant lemon yellow, green & black, modeled by Henri Bergé, inscribed "A. WALTER

- NANCY - BERGÉ - S.C.," 4⅜" l..**5,462.00**

***Vide poche* (figural dish),** shallow oblong dish molded in full-relief at one end w/a frog on a rock, grey w/mottled green, turquoise blue, olive green & ochre, modeled by Henri Bergé, molded "A. WALTER - NANCY - HBergé - SC - FRANCE," ca. 1925, 7¼" l., 3½" h. (rim ground) **3,737.00**

PATTERN GLASS

Though it has never been ascertained whether glass was first pressed in the United States or abroad, the development of the glass pressing machine revolutionized the glass industry in the United States and this country receives the credit for improving the method to make this process feasible. The first wares pressed were probably small flat plates of the type now referred to as "lacy," the intricacy of the design concealing flaws.

In 1827, both the New England Glass Co., Cambridge, Massachusetts and Bakewell & Co., Pittsburgh, took out patents for pressing glass furniture knobs and soon other pieces followed. This early pressed glass contained red lead which made it clear and resonant when tapped (flint.) Made primarily in clear, it is rarer in blue, amethyst, olive green and yellow.

By the 1840s, early simple patterns such as Ashburton, Argus and Excelsior appeared. Ribbed Bellflower seems to have been one of the earliest patterns to have had complete sets. By the 1860s, a wide range of patterns was available.

In 1864, William Leighton of Hobbs, Brockunier & Co., Wheeling, West Virginia, developed a formula for "soda lime" glass which did not require the expensive red lead for clarity. Although "soda lime" glass did not have the brilliance of the earlier flint glass, the formula came into widespread use because glass could be produced cheaply.

An asterisk (*) indicates a piece which has been reproduced.

ACTRESS

Bowl, cov.	$110.00
Bowl, 6" d., flat	45.00
Bowl, 6" d., footed	50.00
Bowl, 7" d., footed	60.00
Bowl, 8" d., Adelaide Neilson	65.00
Bread tray, Miss Neilson, 12½" l.	
(ILLUS. top next page)	70.00 to 75.00

Actress Bread Tray

Butter dish, cov., Fanny Davenport &
Miss Neilson ....**100.00 to 125.00**
Cake stand, Maude Granger & Annie
Pixley, 10" d., 7" h............................**112.00**
Cake stand, frosted
stem..................................**150.00 to 165.00**
Celery vase, Pinafore scene..............**180.00**
Cheese dish, cov., "Lone Fisherman"
on cover, "The Two Dromios" on
underplate ....**225.00 to 235.00**
Compote, cov., 6" d., 10" h.............**100.00**
Compote, cov., 7" d., 8½" h..............**155.00**
Compote, cov., 8" d.,
12" h. ....**175.00 to 190.00**
Compote, open, 7" d., 7" h.,
Miss Neilson **150.00**
Compote, open, 7" d., 7" h., Maggie
Mitchell & Fanny Davenport............**110.00**
Compote, open, 8" d., 5" h. **75.00**
Compote, open, 10" d., 6" h. **80.00**
Compote, open, 10" d., 9" h. **100.00**
Creamer, clear **78.00**
Creamer, frosted...............**200.00 to 250.00**
Goblet, Lotta Crabtree & Kate
Claxton...**85.00**
Marmalade jar, cov., Maude Granger
& Annie Pixley.................................**110.00**
***Pickle dish,** Kate Claxton, "Love's
Request is Pickles," 5¼ x 9¼" **37.50**
Pitcher, water, 9" h., Miss Neilson &
Maggie Mitchell ....**275.00 to 325.00**
Platter, 7 x 11½", Pinafore scene **107.00**
***Relish,** Miss Neilson, 5 x 8" **40.00**
Relish, Maude Granger,
5 x 9" ....**75.00 to 95.00**
Salt shaker w/original pewter top **56.00**
Sauce dish, Maggie Mitchell & Fanny
Davenport, 4½" d.,
2½" h. ....**15.00 to 20.00**
Spooner, Mary Anderson & Maude
Granger...**76.00**
Sugar bowl, cov., Lotta Crabtree &
Kate Claxton **97.00**

ADONIS (Pleat & Tuck or Washboard)

Bowl, master berry, canary yellow **50.00**
Celery...**26.00**
Compote, cov., 8" d. **110.00**
Creamer, blue **35.00**
Creamer, clear **25.00**
Plate, 10" d., clear **13.50**
Plate, 10" d., green..............................**35.00**
Plate, 11" d., canary yellow.................**28.00**
Relish dish **9.50**
Salt shaker w/original top **27.50**
Sauce dish...**7.00**
Sugar bowl, cov.,................................**28.00**

**ALABAMA (Beaded Bull's Eye with
Drape)**

Butter dish, cov., ...**50.00**
Cake stand, 8" d...............**100.00 to 125.00**
Castor set, 4-bottle, original silver
plate stand, green **375.00**
Celery tray, clear **38.00**
Celery tray, ruby-stained **125.00**
Compote, cov., 5" d. **125.00**
Creamer...**36.00**
Creamer, individual size, souvenir,
ruby-stained **48.00**
Cruet w/original stopper **47.50**
Pitcher, water......................................**150.00**
Relish, 5 x 8⅛"....................................**20.00**
Salt shaker w/original top **30.00**
Sauce dish..**17.50**
Spooner **48.00**
Sugar bowl, cov....................................**55.00**
Sugar bowl, cov., miniature.................**48.00**
Syrup pitcher w/original
top ....**125.00 to 150.00**
Table set: creamer, cov. sugar bowl,
spooner & cov. butter dish;
4 pcs. **200.00**
Toothpick holder **76.00**
Tray, water, 10½"................................**125.00**

AMAZON (Sawtooth Band)

Amazon Child's Creamer

Banana stand **66.00**
Bowl, 5" d..**12.00**
Bowl, 8" d., scalloped.........................**24.00**
Butter dish, cov. **77.50**

Cake stand, 8" to 9½" d. ....50.00 to 60.00
Champagne...30.00
Compote, open jelly, 4½" d.................25.00
Compote, open, 8¾" d.,
7¼" h. ....45.00 to 55.00
Compote, open, 9½" d.,
8" h. ....45.00 to 55.00
Cordial, ruby-stained 38.00
Creamer..49.00
Creamer, child's miniature
(ILLUS.) ....20.00 to 30.00
Cruet w/bar in hand stopper...............80.00
Goblet, engraved...................25.00 to 30.00
Goblet, plain...25.00
Pitcher, water...60.00
Salt shaker w/original top 20.00
Sauce dish, flat or footed, each...........10.50
Spooner..34.00
Spooner, child's miniature 26.00
Sugar bowl, cov......................................47.50
Tumbler, engraved 35.00
Tumbler, plain..22.50
Vase, double-bud 75.00
Wine..21.50

ANIMALS & BIRDS ON GOBLETS & PITCHERS

GOBLETS

Bear Climber, acid-etched.................110.00
Bird & Roses, acid-etched ....50.00 to 75.00
Birds at Fountain, pressed 55.00
Camels, acid-etched 85.00
Deer & Doe w/lily-of-the-valley,
pressed...107.50
Dog w/rabbit in mouth, acid-
etched...115.00
Elk & Doe, pressed 172.50
Falcon Strawberry, pressed 35.00
Flamingo Habitat,
acid-etched ....30.00 to 35.00
Giraffe, acid-etched 75.00
Horse, Cat & Rabbit, pressed 1,200.00
Ibex, acid-etched...................................90.50
Leopard, acid-etched..........................125.00
Lion in the Jungle, acid-
etched.............................100.00 to 125.00
Nestlings, acid-etched.........................40.00
Ostrich Looking at Moon,
pressed............................100.00 to 125.00
Owl in Horseshoe, pressed 80.00
Owl-Possum, pressed.......125.00 to 150.00
Pigs in Corn, pressed ....575.00 to 600.00
Rooster & Hen, acid-etched 172.50
Squirrel, pressed, non-Greentown 800.00
Stork & Flowers, acid-etched..............65.00
Stork Eating, acid-etched....................95.00
Three Deer..225.00
Two Herons, acid-etched 145.00

PITCHERS

Bringing Home Cows, pressed 750.00

Dog & Cat, pressed 325.00
Flamingo Habitat, acid-etched..........125.00
Fox & Crow, pressed ....250.00 to 300.00
Heron, pressed ....175.00 to 200.00
Squirrel, pressed, non-
Greentown.......................200.00 to 250.00

ASHBURTON

Ale glass, flint, 6½" h...........................82.50
Bitters bottle w/original pewter lid.......65.00
Celery vase, plain rim, flint 59.00
Celery vase, scalloped rim, canary
yellow, flint.......................700.00 to 850.00
Celery vase, scalloped rim, clear,
flint 135.00
Champagne, flint 59.00
Champagne, barrel-shaped, flint 85.00
Claret, flint, 5¼" h................................63.00
Cordial, flint, 4¼" h. ....40.00 to 45.00
Creamer, applied handle, flint...........255.00
Decanter, bar lip w/patent pewter
stopper, canary yellow, flint 1,600.00
Decanter, bar lip w/patent pewter
stopper, clear, flint 155.00
Decanter, bar lip & facet-cut neck,
clear, flint, qt. 55.00
Decanter w/original stopper, clear,
flint, qt. 97.50
Egg cup, clambroth, flint....................155.00
Egg cup, clear, flint...............20.00 to 30.00
Egg cup, clear, non-flint.......................15.50
Egg cup, disconnected ovals, clear 35.00
Egg cups, flint, set of six....................125.00
Goblet, short, flint.................................42.00
Goblet, barrel-shaped, flint 54.50
Goblet, flared, flint, clear.....................51.50
Goblet, flared, flint, clear w/gold,
6" h...100.00
Goblet, non-flint 30.00
Honey dish, 3½" d. 8.50
Mug, applied handle, 3" h....................60.00
Mug, applied handle, 4¾" h.................87.50
Pitcher, water, applied hollow handle,
flint.....................................400.00 to 450.00
Pomade jar, cov., white opaque,
flint 195.00
Sauce dish, flint......................................7.50
Sugar bowl, cov., flint 92.00
Sugar bowl, cov., fiery opalescent,
flint 1,650.00
Tumbler, bar, flint..................................66.50
Tumbler, water, flint..............................59.00
Tumbler, water, footed..........................92.50
Tumbler, whiskey, applied handle,
flint....................................100.00 to 125.00
Wine, clear, flint....................................39.00
Wine, clear, knob stem.........................85.00
Wine w/cut design, clear w/gold
trim 125.00
Wine, peacock green, flint...................650.00
Wine, non-flint 31.00

ATLANTA (Lion or Square Lion's Head)

Bowl, 5 x 8" oblong, flat 50.00

Butter dish, cov. 105.00
Cake stand 95.00
Celery vase.......................................110.00
Compote, cov., 5" sq., 6" h. 95.00
Compote, cov., 7" sq., high
  stand................................175.00 to 200.00
Compote, open, 4¼" sq., 4" h.............46.00
Compote, open, 6" sq., 7½" h.............75.00
Compote, open, 8" sq., high stand 95.00
Creamer 81.50
Egg cup 95.00

Atlanta Goblet

*Goblet (ILLUS.) 77.50
Marmalade jar, cov., w/lion's head
  finial 100.00
Relish, boat-shaped...........................27.50
Salt dip, individual size 35.00
Salt dip, master size 135.00
Sauce dish...45.00
Spooner 55.50
Sugar bowl, cov., engraved...............160.00
Sugar bowl, cov., plain 97.50
Toothpick holder 60.00
Tumbler, engraved 39.00
Tumbler, plain.....................................35.00
Wine 13.00

BABY THUMBPRINT -See Dakota Pattern

BALTIMORE PEAR
Bowl, 4 x 8"..19.00
Bread plate, 12½" l..............................48.00
*Butter dish, cov..................................53.00
Cake plate, side handles, 10"
  octagon 38.00
*Cake stand, high pedestal.................52.50
Compote, open, jelly...........................26.50
*Creamer..27.50
*Goblet...35.00
*Pitcher, water....................95.00 to 100.00
*Plate, 9" d. 28.00
Relish, 8¼" l. 22.50
*Sauce dish, flat or footed, each 13.00
Spooner 40.50
*Sugar bowl, cov. 53.00
Tray, water 28.00

BAMBOO - See Broken Column Pattern

BANDED BEADED GRAPE MEDALLION
Creamer..48.00
Dish, open, 5 x 8" oval 15.00
Egg cup 30.00
Goblet 28.50
Spooner 30.00
Tumbler, footed 40.00
Wine 85.00

**BANDED PORTLAND (Portland
w/Diamond Point Band, Virginia
(States series), Portland Maiden
Blush (when pink-stained)**
Berry set: master bowl & 8 sauce
  dishes; pink-stained w/gold trim,
  9 pcs. 295.00
Bowl, berry, 9" d.,...............................30.00
Butter dish, cov., pink-stained...........150.00
Candlesticks, pr. 87.50
Celery tray, pink-stained, 10" oval.......75.00
Celery tray, 5 x 12" 27.50
Celery vase...30.00
Cologne bottle w/original stopper 49.00
Compote, cov., 8" d., high stand........110.00
Compote, open, 8¼" d., 8" h.,
  scalloped rim ....35.00 to 40.00
Creamer, individual size,.....................29.00
Creamer & sugar bowl, individual
  size, pink-stained, pr. 70.00
Cruet w/original stopper, clear 60.00
Cruet w/original stopper, pink-
  stained 400.00
Dresser jar, cov., clear, 3½" d. 36.00
Dresser set: large tray, oval pin tray,
  cov. jar, cologne bottle w/original
  stopper & ring tree; 5 pcs.................215.00
Goblet, clear 33.00
Goblet, pink-stained............................63.00
Goblet, yellow-stained 85.00
Pitcher, water, 9½" h. 95.00
Pitcher, tankard, 11" h., pink-
  stained ....225.00 to 250.00
Pitcher, child's, clear...........................32.00
Pomade jar, cov..................................27.50
Punch cup, clear 11.00
Punch cup, pink-stained......................26.00
Relish, pink-stained, 4 x 6½" 28.00
Ring tree, gold-stained 50.00
Salt shaker w/original top, pink-
  stained ....50.00 to 55.00
Salt & pepper shakers w/original
  tops, clear, pr. 60.00
Salt & pepper shakers w/original
  tops, pink-stained, pr. ....85.00 to 100.00
Sauce dish, 4½" d. 15.00
Spooner, pink-stained..........................75.00
Sugar bowl, cov., pink-stained 112.00
Sugar bowl, individual size.................24.00
Sugar shaker w/original top, clear......50.00
Sugar shaker w/original top, pink-
  stained 135.00

Syrup jug w/original top, pink-
stained **365.00**
Toothpick holder, clear w/gold **25.00**
Toothpick holder, pink-
stained...............................**50.00 to 55.00**
Tumbler, clear..**27.00**
Tumbler, pink-stained..............................**42.50**
Vase, 6" h., flared, clear **32.00**
Vase, 6" h., flared, pink-stained...........**35.00**
Vase, 9" h., ...**42.00**
Wine, clear **29.00**
Wine, pink-stained...................................**75.00**

BARBERRY

Barberry Goblet

Bowl, 6" oval **18.00**
Butter dish, cov., shell finial **50.00**
Butter dish, cov., pattern on base
rim..**110.00**
Cake stand, 9½" d. **48.00**
Cake stand, 11" d. **125.00**
Celery vase ....**40.00 to 50.00**
Compote, cov., 6" d., high stand,
shell finial **49.00**
Compote, cov., 8" d., high stand,
shell finial **99.00**
Compote, cov., 8" d., low stand,
shell finial...............................**65.00 to 70.00**
Compote, open, 8½" d., 7" h. **42.00**
Creamer..**32.50**
Egg cup **25.00**
Goblet (ILLUS.) **25.00**
Pitcher, water, 9½" h., applied
handle **84.00**
Plate, 6" d., blue....................**40.00 to 50.00**
Plate, 6" d., clear **19.00**
Salt dip, master size **16.00**
Sauce dish, flat or footed ....**8.00 to 10.00**
Spooner, footed **32.00**
Tumbler, footed **31.50**
Wine..**30.00 to 35.00**

BASKETWEAVE

Bread plate, amber **30.00**
Bread plate, blue **29.00**
Creamer, amber......................................**35.00**
Cup, blue...**30.00**

Cup & saucer, amber............**25.00 to 30.00**
Cup & saucer, canary..........................**37.50**
*Goblet, blue **35.00**
*Goblet, canary **34.00**
*Goblet, clear **27.00**
Pitcher, milk, blue **50.00**
*Pitcher, water, amber **57.00**
*Pitcher, water, blue **70.00**
*Pitcher, water, canary **77.00**
Plate, 8¾" d., handled, amber.............**24.00**
Plate, 8¾" d., handled, blue **19.50**
Plate, 8¾" d., handled, clear **11.00**
Sauce dish..**8.50**
*Tray, water, scenic center, amber,
12"..**47.00**
*Tray, water, scenic center, blue,
12"..**55.00**
*Tray, water, scenic center, canary,
12"..**50.00**
Wine...**16.00 to 20.00**

BEADED GRAPE MEDALLION

Butter dish, cov. **50.00**
Celery vase ....**65.00 to 75.00**
Compote, cov., 8¼" d., low stand........**85.00**
Compote, open, 8¼" d., low stand......**30.00**
Egg cup **32.50**
Goblet....................................**25.00 to 30.00**
Pitcher, water, applied handle **135.00**
Salt dip, individual size **26.00**
Salt dip, master size, footed, oval.......**55.00**
Salt shaker w/original top **35.00**
Sauce dish..**9.00**
Spooner...**29.00**
Wine..**47.50**

BEADED LOOP (Oregon, U.S. Glass Co.)

Bowl, berry, 9½" l., 6¾" w., oval **25.00**
Bread platter **21.00**
Butter dish, cov. **46.50**
Cake stand, 9" to 10½" d. **46.50**
Celery vase, 7" h. **27.00**
Compote, cov., 7" d. **90.00**
Compote, open, jelly..............................**31.00**
Compote, open, 7" d..............................**26.50**
Compote, open, 7½" d., low stand.......**38.00**
Creamer...**35.00**
*Goblet ....**30.00 to 35.00**
Goblet w/gold trim..................................**32.50**
Mug, footed..**38.00**
Pitcher, pint, 7" h. **44.00**
Pitcher, milk 8½" h. **37.50**
Pitcher, water, tankard ....**45.00 to 50.00**
Relish...**16.00**
Relish, w/advertising for "Carson
Furniture, Pittsburgh" **26.00**
Salt shaker w/original top **25.00**
Sauce dish, flat or footed, each...........**13.00**
Spooner, clear **26.00**
Spooner, ruby-stained............................**65.00**
*Sugar bowl, cov. **39.00**
Toothpick holder ....**45.00 to 50.00**
Tumbler **49.00**
Vase, small ....**40.00 to 45.00**

Wine................................55.00 to 65.00

BEADED TULIP
Bowl, 6⅝ x 9½" oval 20.00
Goblet 35.50
Pitcher, milk, 1 qt. 75.00
Pitcher, water ....55.00 to 60.00
Plate, dinner, 6" d...............................19.00
Sauce, 4" d..7.50
Tray, wine, 9" d....................................26.00
Wine, amber 55.00
Wine, clear...........................25.00 to 35.00

BIGLER
Bowl, 8" d..45.00
Celery vase...77.50
Champagne...85.00
Decanter w/bar lip, qt. ....100.00 to 125.00
Goblet, 6" h...51.00
Lamp, whale oil, 10" h........................175.00
Plate, 6" d...30.00
Salt dip, master size, clear ....40.00 to 60.00
Sauce dish, 4" d. 16.50
Tumbler 67.50
Wine..55.00

BIRD & FERN -See Hummingbird Pattern

BLEEDING HEART

Bleeding Heart Spooner

Bowl, cov., 7" d., 5" h.........................110.00
Bowl, cov., flat, 8" d. 175.00
Bowl, 8" ....30.00 to 35.00
Butter dish, cov. 55.00
Cake stand, 9½" to
    11" d. ....95.00 to 100.00
Compote, cov., 8" d., high stand,
    w/Bleeding Heart finial.....150.00 to 175.00
Compote, open, 8½" d., high
    stand 37.50
Creamer...50.00
Egg cup 49.50
Goblet, knob stem ....35.00 to 40.00
Mug, 3" h...50.00
Salt dip, master size, flat, oval.............92.00
Sauce dish, flat...................................11.50
Spooner (ILLUS.) ....30.00 to 35.00
Sugar bowl, cov..................................72.00

Tumbler, bar 140.00
Tumbler, flat.......................................110.00
Tumbler, footed ....75.00 to 100.00
Wine, knob stem ....145.00 to 175.00

**BROKEN COLUMN (Irish Column,
Notched Rib or Bamboo)**
Banana stand 185.00
Basket, applied handle, 15" l.,
    12" h. ....175.00 to 200.00
Butter dish, cov. 85.00
Cake stand, 9" to 10" d.......................92.50
Carafe, water.....................................110.00
Celery vase...55.00
Compote, cov., 5" d., high stand,.........70.00
Compote, cov., 7" d., high
    stand...............................175.00 to 200.00
Compote, cov., 8" d., high stand,
    w/red notches 450.00
Compote, open, 6" d., high stand 35.00
Compote, open, 7" d., low stand..........50.00
Compote, open, 8" d., low
    stand.................................60.00 to 65.00
Compote, open, 10" d., low stand......110.00
Cracker jar, cov. 90.00
*Creamer, clear...................................38.00
Creamer, w/red notches.....................245.00
Cruet w/original stopper 85.00
*Goblet...49.00
Marmalade jar w/original cover 100.00
Pickle castor, cov., clear, original
    ornate frame ....225.00 to 250.00
Pickle castor, w/red notches,
    w/frame & tongs ....400.00 to 425.00
*Pitcher, water, clear 105.00
Pitcher, water, w/red notches 225.00
Plate, 5" d...32.00
*Plate, 8" d. 40.00
Punch cup, blue 95.00
Punch cup, clear 25.00
Relish, 3¾ x 5".....................................12.50
Relish, 6½" l..17.00
Relish, w/red notches, 9" l., 5" w. 78.00
Salt shaker w/original top 55.00
*Sauce dish, clear 10.50
Sauce dish, w/red notches 32.00
*Spooner, clear...................................31.50
Spooner, w/red notches.....................125.00
*Sugar bowl, cov., clear 72.00
Sugar bowl, cov., w/red notches........150.00
Syrup pitcher w/metal top 130.00
Tumbler, clear.....................................47.50
Tumbler, w/red notches.....100.00 to 125.00
Vase, 6½" h...30.00
*Wine..85.00

CABBAGE LEAF
Cheese dish, cov., stippled 410.00
Celery vase, clear & frosted 90.00
Creamer, amber.................................165.00
Sauce dish, frosted w/rabbit center.....37.50

CABBAGE ROSE
Bitters bottle, 6½" h. 125.00

Butter dish, cov. 95.00
Cake stand, 9½" to
   12½" d. ....45.00 to 55.00
Celery vase...62.00
Champagne...75.00
Compote, cov., 6" d., low stand...........95.00
Compote, cov., 6" d., high stand........110.00
Compote, cov., 7½" d., high stand.....105.00
Compote, cov., 8½" d., 7" h. 125.00
Compote, cov., 8½" d., high stand.......95.00
Compote, open, 7" d., low stand..........30.00
Compote, open, 7½" d., high
   stand...60.00
Compote, open, 8½" d., high
   stand..............................75.00 to 85.00
Creamer, applied handle.....................55.00
Egg cup 34.00

Cabbage Rose Goblet

*Goblet (ILLUS.) ....35.00 to 45.00
Pickle or relish, 7½" to 8½" l...............18.00
Salt dip, master size 30.00
Sauce dish..10.50
*Spooner..30.00
Sugar bowl, cov.................................62.50
Tumbler, bar 43.50
Tumbler 42.00
Wine....................................40.00 to 50.00

CANADIAN
Bowl, 6" d., handled............................28.00
Bowl, 8" d., handled............................44.50
Bowl, 9½" d..55.00
Bread plate, handled,
   10" d. ....40.00 to 50.00
Butter dish, cov. 62.50
Celery vase...70.00
Compote, cov., 7" d., low
   stand...............................125.00 to 140.00
Compote, cov., 7" d.,
   11" h. ....100.00 to 125.00
Compote, cov., 8" d., low stand...........92.00
Compote, cov., 8" d., 11" h. 150.00
Compote, open, 8" d., 5" h. ...45.00 to 50.00
Creamer..77.50
Goblet 49.50
Marmalade jar, cov............................210.00
Pitcher, milk, 8" h. ....100.00 to 125.00

Pitcher, water....................................110.00
Plate, 6" d., handled............................32.00
Plate, 7" d., handled............................45.00
Plate, 8" d., handled............................44.00
Sauce dish, flat or footed, each...........18.00
Spooner..45.00
Sugar bowl, cov. ....65.00 to 75.00
Wine....................................40.00 to 50.00

CARDINAL BIRD

Cardinal Goblet

Butter dish, cov. 90.00
Butter dish, cov., three unidentified
   birds 115.00
Creamer..36.00
*Goblet (ILLUS.) ....35.00 to 45.00
Sauce dish, flat or footed, each...........14.00
Spooner...............................30.00 to 40.00
Sugar bowl, cov..................................60.00

COLONIAL (Empire Colonial)
Celery vase, flint.................................72.50
Champagne, flint 75.00
Claret, flint, 5½" h...............................70.00
Compote, open, 9" d., 3¾" h., flint.......25.00
Egg cup, flint......................................45.00
Goblet, flint..55.00
Plate, 6¼" d., canary yellow, flint 250.00
Sugar bowl, cov., flint........................125.00
Tumbler, footed, flint...........................85.00
Wine, flint..............................50.00 to 75.00

COLUMBIAN COIN
Bowl, 8½" d., 3" h., frosted coins 75.00
Celery vase, frosted coins 110.00
Claret, gilded coins ....125.00 to 150.00
Compote, cov., 8" d., frosted coins....157.00
Creamer, gilded coins 125.00
Cruet w/original stopper, frosted
   coins 195.00
Goblet, frosted coins ....80.00 to 90.00
*Goblet, gilded coins...........................80.00
Lamp, kerosene-type, milk white,
   8" h. 400.00
Mug, frosted coins 120.00
Pitcher, milk, gilded coins 195.00
Relish, frosted coins, 5 x 8" 58.00

Sauce dish, flat or footed, frosted
coins, each.................................**43.50**
Spooner, frosted coins ....**75.00 to 85.00**
Spooner, gilded coins **77.50**
Syrup pitcher w/original top, frosted
coins ....**320.00 to 330.00**
*Toothpick holder, frosted
coins ....**150.00 to 175.00**
*Tumbler, clear coins...........................**30.00**
*Tumbler, gilded coins **55.00**
Wine, frosted coins ....**100.00 to 125.00**

COMET, EARLY
Compote, low stand ....**175.00 to 185.00**
Goblet.................................**95.00 to 100.00**
Tumbler, bar, clear **87.50**
Tumbler, whiskey, 3" h.......**150.00 to 175.00**
Tumbler, whiskey, handled................**225.00**

COTTAGE (Dinner Bell or Finecut Band)

Cottage Cruet

Bowl, master berry, 9¼" l.,
6½" w. oval **25.00**
Butter dish, cov., clear **48.00**
Cake stand, amber **75.00**
Cake stand, clear................................**35.00**
Celery vase, amber **85.00**
Celery vase, clear...............................**34.00**
Champagne **65.00**
Compote, cov., 8" d., high stand,
amber..**180.00**
Compote, open, jelly, 4½" d., 4" h.,
clear **22.00**
Compote, open, jelly 4½" d., 4" h.,
green **45.00**
Creamer, amber...................................**60.00**
Creamer, clear **23.50**
Cruet w/original stopper (ILLUS.).........**65.00**
*Goblet, amber....................................**52.50**
*Goblet, blue.......................**65.00 to 70.00**
*Goblet, clear **34.00**
Pitcher, milk, clear **35.00**
Pitcher, water, 2 qt. ....**55.00 to 65.00**
Plate, 6" d...**13.50**
Plate, 7" d...**20.00**
Plate, 10" d...**42.50**
Sauce dish, amber **25.00**

Sauce dish, clear.................................**15.00**
Tray, water, clear **47.50**
Tray, water, green **65.00**
Tumbler **19.00**
*Wine, amber **53.00**

CROWFOOT (Turkey Track, Yale)
Bowl, 10" d..**32.50**
Butter dish, cov. **45.00**
*Cake stand, 9" d................................**52.00**
Compote, cov., 7" d. **68.00**
Compote, open, 8" d **25.00**
Creamer **37.00**
*Goblet..**40.00**
Pitcher, water......................................**60.00**
Sauce dish, footed..............................**22.00**
Spooner **35.00**
Sugar bowl, cov. **35.00**
Tumbler ....**20.00 to 25.00**

CRYSTAL WEDDING (Collins)
Banana stand, 10" h............................**110.00**
Banana stand, low pedestal **108.00**
Bowl, cov., 5" sq. **58.00**
Bowl, cov., 7" sq. **75.00**
Butter dish, cov., clear **110.00**
Butter dish, cov., ruby-stained **130.00**
Cake stand, 9" sq., 8" h. **58.00**
Cake stand, 10" sq. **80.00**
Celery vase...**45.00**
Compote, cov., 4" sq., 6½" h. **37.50**
Compote, cov., 5" sq. **56.50**
Compote, cov., 7" sq., low stand **65.00**
Compote, cov., 7" sq., high
stand....................................**75.00 to 100.00**
Compote, open, 5" sq. **45.00**
Compote, open, 6" sq. **48.00**
Compote, open, 7" sq., high
stand....................................**50.00 to 75.00**
Compote, open, 8" sq., low stand........**55.00**
Creamer, clear **38.00**
Creamer, ruby-stained **125.00**
*Goblet, clear.......................**40.00 to 45.00**
Goblet w/fern engraving......................**70.00**
*Goblet, ruby-stained.............**70.00 to 75.00**
Honey dish, cov., 6" square **90.00**
Lamp, kerosene-type, 7" h. **117.50**
Lamp, kerosene-type, 9" h., frosted &
clear **145.00**
Lamp, kerosene-type, square
font, 10" h.......................................**280.00**
Lamp, kerosene-type, banquet-style,
blue base, clear font **245.00**
Pitcher, 12" h., tankard, water **85.00**
Pitcher, water, square, engraved.......**195.00**
Pitcher, water, square, plain **175.00**
Plate, 9" sq. **45.00**
Relish **21.50**
Salt dip..**45.00**
Salt shaker w/original top, clear **125.00**
Sauce dish, clear.................................**10.00**
Sauce dish, ruby-stained....................**35.00**
Spooner, clear **35.00**

Spooner, ruby-stained 95.00
Sugar bowl, cov., amber-stained.......125.00
Sugar bowl, cov., clear.........................54.00
Tumbler, clear......................................45.00
Wine..105.00

CURRANT

Currant Goblet

Butter dish, cov. 67.00
Cake stand, 9¼" d., 4¼" h.................110.00
Cake stand, 11" d. ....60.00 to 65.00
Celery vase..45.00
Compote, cov., 8" d., high stand........175.00
Compote, open, 10½" d. 50.00
Creamer...39.50
Goblet (ILLUS.).....................................24.00
Pitcher, water...90.00
Spooner...28.00
Sugar bowl, cov......................................40.00
Wine...42.50

CUT LOG

Cut Log Goblet

Bowl, 7" d..33.00
Butter dish, cov......................................64.00
Cake stand, 9¼" d., high stand............73.50
Cake stand, 10½" d., high
  stand.......................................65.00 to 75.00
Celery tray 45.00
Celery vase ....20.00 to 30.00

Compote, cov., jelly, 5½" d., high
  stand...65.00
Compote, cov., 7¼" d., high stand.......95.00
Compote, open, jelly, 5" d....................32.50
*Compote, open, 6" d., flared rim,
  high stand 35.00
Compote, open, 9¾" d., scalloped
  rim, high stand 65.00
Compote, open, 10¾" d., scalloped
  rim, high stand 72.50
Creamer...37.00
Creamer, individual size........................18.00
Creamer & open sugar bowl,
  individual size, pr. 25.50
Cruet w/original stopper, small,
  3¾" h..38.00
Cruet w/original stopper, large,
  5" h...48.00
Goblet (ILLUS.).....................................50.00
Mug, small..18.00
Olive dish, handled, 5" d. 25.00
Pitcher, water, tankard,
  clear......................................85.00 to 95.00
Pitcher, water, tankard, ruby-
  stained 240.00
Relish, boat-shaped, 9¼" l....................23.00
Salt dip, master size 65.00
Salt shaker w/original tin top 60.00
Sauce dish, flat or footed, each...........20.00
Spooner..................................40.00 to 45.00
Sugar bowl, cov......................................50.00
Sugar bowl, cov., individual size 30.00
Tumbler, juice 40.00
Tumbler, water.......................................40.00
Vase, 16" h. 58.00
Wine.......................................16.00 to 20.00

DAISY & BUTTON

Banana boat, 14" l................................45.00
Berry set: triangular master bowl & 4
  sauce dishes; canary, 5 pcs. 150.00
Berry set: master bowl & 12 sauce
  dishes; canary, 13 pcs. 225.00
Bowl, 7 x 9½", sapphire blue 30.00
Bowl, 8" d., flat......................................15.00
Bowl, 8" w., tricornered, clear 45.00
Bowl, berry or fruit, 8½" d. 35.00
Bowl, 9" sq., amber ....30.00 to 35.00
Bowl, 9" sq., Amberina.......................182.50
*Bowl, 10" oval, blue.............................65.00
Bowl, 10 x 11" oval, 7¾" h., flared,
  canary 95.00
Bowl, 11" d., amber................................38.00
Bowl, 12" l., 9" w., shell-shaped oval,
  blue 75.00
Butter chip, round, amber 12.00
Butter chip, square, amber 13.50
Butter chip, square, Amberina 75.00
Butter chip, square, blue.....................16.00
Butter chip, square, canary.................20.00
Butter chip, square, clear......................7.00
Butter chip, square, green 14.50
Butter chip, square, purple..................15.00

Butter dish, cov., scalloped base **65.00**
Butter dish, cov., square, green **60.00**
Butter dish, cov., triangular, amber **60.00**
*Butter dish, cov., model of Victorian
stove, green **215.00**
Cake stand, blue **50.00**
Cake stand, clear, 9" sq., 6" h. **45.00**
Canoe, canary, 4" **18.00**
Canoe, amber, 8" l. **35.00**
Canoe, blue, 8" l. **46.00**
Canoe, amber, 11" l. **39.00**
Canoe, blue, 11" l. **60.00**
Canoe, amber, 12" l. ....**60.00 to 65.00**
Canoe, green, 13" l. **48.00**
Canoe, canary, 14" l. **85.00**
Canoe, clear, 14" l. **21.50**
Castor set, 3-bottle, amber, clear &
blue, in clear glass frame **120.00**
Castor set, 4-bottle, blue, in glass
frame **375.00**
Castor set, 5-bottle, amber, blue &
clear bottles, in original
frame ....**100.00 to 145.00**
Castor set, 5-bottle, canary, in
original frame **495.00**
Celery tray, flat, boat-shaped,
4½ x 14" **90.00**
Celery vase, triangular, amber **65.00**
Celery vase, triangular, clear **45.00**
Cheese dish, cov., canary **165.00**
Cheese dish, cov., clear **62.00**
Creamer, child's, amber **25.00**
*Creamer, blue **40.00**
*Creamer, clear **18.00**
*Cruet w/original stopper, amber **100.00**
*Cruet w/original stopper, blue **95.00**
*Cruet w/original stopper, clear **45.00**
Cuspidor, blue **38.00**
*Dish, fan-shaped, 10" w. **35.00**
Dresser tray, amber, 8 x 11" **52.50**
*Goblet, amber **36.00**
*Goblet, blue **25.00**
*Hat shape, amber, 2½" h. **24.50**
*Hat shape, blue, 2½" h. ....**40.00 to 50.00**
*Hat shape, canary, 2½" h. **38.00**
*Hat shape, clear, 2½" h. **17.50**
*Hat shape, amber, from tumbler
mold, 4" widest diameter **40.00**
*Hat shape, clear, from tumbler mold,
4½" widest diameter **55.00**
*Hat shape, blue, from tumbler mold,
4¾" widest diameter **45.00**
Hat shape, clear, 8 x 8", 6" h. **85.00**
*Ice cream dish, cut corners, 6" sq. **8.50**
Ice cream set: 2 x 7 x 9½" ice cream
tray & two square sauce
plates; amber, 3 pcs. **85.00**
Ice tub, amber, 4¼ x 6¾" **52.50**
Inkwell w/original insert, cat seated
on cover **210.00**
Inkwell, canary **175.00**
*Match holder, cauldron w/original
bail handle, blue **25.00**

Match holder, wall-hanging scuff,
blue **75.00**
Match holder, wall-hanging scuff,
clear **65.00**
Mustard, amber ....**15.00 to 20.00**
*Pickle castor, amber insert, w/silver
plate frame & tongs **197.50**
*Pickle castor, canary insert,
w/silver plate frame & tongs **185.00**
*Pickle castor, sapphire blue insert,
w/silver plate frame & tongs **238.00**
Pitcher, water, tankard, 9" h.,
amber **125.00**
Pitcher, water, bulbous, applied
handle, clear **95.00**
Pitcher, water, bulbous, applied
handle, ruby-stained buttons **325.00**
Plate, 7" sq., blue **17.50**
Plate, 9" d., canary **40.00**
*Plate, 10" d., scalloped rim, amber **26.00**
*Plate, 10" d., scalloped rim, blue **35.00**
*Plate, 10" d., scalloped rim, canary ...**39.50**
Platter, 9 x 13" oval, open handles,
amber ....**30.00 to 35.00**
Platter, 9 x 13" oval, open handles,
canary **52.50**
Powder jar, cov., amber, 3¾" d.,
2" h. **30.00**
Powder jar, cov., blue **38.00**
Relish, "Sitz bathtub," amber **125.00**
*Rose bowl, canary **38.00**
*Salt dip, canoe-shaped, amber,
2 x 4" **19.50**
*Salt dip, canoe-shaped, canary,
2 x 4" **12.00**
*Salt dip, canoe-shaped, clear,
2 x 4" **14.50**
*Salt shaker w/original top, corset-
shaped, amber **25.00**
*Salt & pepper shakers w/original
tops, canary, pr. **57.50**
*Sauce dish, amber, 4" to 5" sq. **13.50**
Sauce dish, Amberina, 4" to 5" sq. **115.00**
*Sauce dish, canary, 4" to 5" sq. **20.00**
Sauce dish, w/amber-stained
buttons **20.00**
Sauce dish, tricornered, canary **16.00**
Sauce dish, tricornered, clear **12.50**
*Slipper, "1886 patent," amber **46.00**
*Slipper, "1886 patent," blue **47.00**
*Spooner, amber **32.50**
Spooner, Amberina, 5" h. **150.00**
Spooner, amethyst **30.00**
*Spooner, clear **37.50**
Toothpick holder, fan-shaped,
amber **35.00**
Toothpick holder, square, blue **24.00**
Toothpick holder, three-footed,
Amberina **170.00**
*Toothpick holder, three-footed,
electric blue **55.00**
Toothpick holder, urn-shaped,
canary **30.00**

Toothpick holder, urn-shaped,
clear **22.50**
Tray, clover-shaped, amber **75.00**
Tray, canary, 10 x 12" **57.00**
Tray, water, amber, 11" d....................**90.00**
Tray, water, triangular,
canary.................................**75.00 to 80.00**
Tumbler, water, amber **22.50**
Tumbler, water, blue...........................**30.00**
Tumbler, water, canary......................**30.00**
Tumbler, water, clear **19.00**
Waste bowl, canary **30.00**
Whimsey, "canoe," wall hanging-type,
ruby-stained buttons, 11" l. **110.00**
Whimsey, "cradle," amber **45.00**
***Whimsey,** "dustpan," light blue...........**42.50**
***Whimsey,** "sleigh," amber,
4½ x 7¾"...**225.00**
Whimsey, "wheel barrow," canary **125.00**
***Whimsey,** "whisk broom" dish,
blue **75.00**
***Wine**...**20.00**

DAISY & BUTTON - SINGLE PANEL
(Paneled Daisy & Button)

***Berry set:** master bowl & 5 sauce
dishes; amber panels, 6 pcs. **110.00**
Bowl, master berry, amber panels **35.00**
Butter dish, cov., amber panels **180.00**
Castor set, three-bottle, clear, in
original clear glass frame...................**85.00**
Compote, cov., 5" d., high stand..........**55.00**
Creamer, blue **35.00**
Pitcher, water, amber panels.............**215.00**
Platter, oval **125.00**
Relish, amber panels, small.................**30.00**
Relish, amber panels, 12½" l.,
5¼" w...**50.00**
Salt shaker, amber panels.................**125.00**
Spooner, amber **47.00**
Sugar bowl, cov., amber panels........**140.00**
Toothpick holder, canary....................**28.00**
Toothpick holder, clear.......................**25.00**
Tumbler, amber panels ....**65.00 to 75.00**
Tumbler, clear.....................................**28.00**

DAISY & BUTTON WITH THUMBPRINT
PANELS

Berry set: master bowl & 6 sauce
dishes; 7 pcs. **75.00**
Bowl, 7" w., heart-shaped, amber
panels **42.50**
Bowl, 8" sq., amber..............................**28.00**
Bowl, 9" sq., amber..............................**28.00**
Cake stand, canary, 10½" d.,
7¼" h...**75.00**
Celery vase, amber panels
(ILLUS. top next column) **125.00**
Celery vase, clear................................**26.00**
Creamer, applied handle, amber
panels **68.00**
Creamer, footed, clear **26.00**
***Goblet,** amber panels **55.00**

Daisy & Button w/Thumbprint Panels
Celery

***Goblet,** blue panels ....**40.00 to 45.00**
Pitcher, water, canary.......................**132.50**
Salt shaker w/original top, amber
panels **75.00**
Sauce dish, flat or footed, amber
panels, 5" sq. **20.00**
Spooner, amber panels **75.00**
Tray, water, canary **95.00**
Tumbler, amber panels.......................**38.50**
Tumbler, canary..................................**30.00**
Tumbler, clear.....................................**25.00**

DAKOTA (Baby Thumbprint)

Butter dish, cov., engraved...**70.00 to 80.00**
Butter dish, cov., plain **47.50**
Cake basket w/metal handle,
10" d. **245.00**
Cake stand, 8" d., engraved **50.00**
Cake stand, 8" d., plain........................**45.00**
Cake stand, 9" d., engraved **85.00**
Cake stand, 9½" d. **50.50**
Cake stand, 10½" d.,
engraved ....**70.00 to 75.00**
Cake stand, 10½" d.,
plain.......................................**45.00 to 55.00**
Cake stand w/high domed cover **295.00**
Celery vase, flat base,
engraved ....**35.00 to 40.00**
Celery vase, flat base, plain **36.00**
Celery vase, pedestal base,
engraved...**47.50**
Celery vase, pedestal base, plain........**42.00**
Cologne bottle w/original stopper,
7" h...**135.00**
Compote, cov., jelly, 5" d., 5" h...........**47.50**
Compote, cov., 6" d., high stand,
engraved ....**75.00 to 100.00**
Compote, cov., 6" d., high stand,
plain **58.00**
Compote, cov., 8" d., high stand,
plain **72.50**
Compote, cov., 8" d., high stand,
engraved...**190.00**
Compote, cov., 12" d., high stand,
engraved...**145.00**

Compote, open, jelly, 5" d., 5½" h.,
  engraved..**31.50**
Compote, open, jelly, 5" d., 5" h.,
  plain...**36.00**
Compote, open, 6" d. ....**25.00 to 35.00**
Compote, open, 7" d., engraved..........**40.00**
Compote, open, 7" d., plain...................**35.00**
Compote, open, 8" d., high stand........**38.50**
Creamer, table, engraved......**55.00 to 65.00**
Creamer, table, plain.............................**50.00**
Creamer, hotel **110.00**
Cruet w/original stopper,
  engraved...**145.00**
Goblet, clear, engraved.........**30.00 to 35.00**
Goblet, clear, plain ....**20.00 to 25.00**
Goblet, ruby-stained, engraved **86.50**
Goblet, ruby-stained, plain...................**65.00**
Lamp, kerosene-type **120.00**
Pitcher, milk, jug-type, engraved,
  pt. **190.00**
Pitcher, milk, tankard, engraved,
  pt. ....**150.00 to 155.00**
Pitcher, milk, tankard, clear, plain,
  pt..**95.00**
Pitcher, milk, tankard, engraved,
  qt...**115.00**
*Pitcher, water, tankard, engraved,
  ½ gal.............................**140.00 to 150.00**
Pitcher, water, tankard, ruby-stained,
  ½ gal.............................**185.00 to 200.00**
Salt shaker w/original top **50.00**
Sauce dish, flat or footed, clear,
  engraved, each **18.00**
Sauce dish, flat or footed, clear,
  plain, each **10.00**
Sauce dish, flat or footed, cobalt
  blue, each **55.00**
Shaker bottle w/original top, 5" h. **68.00**
Shaker bottle w/original top, hotel
  size, 6½" h. **65.00**
Spooner, engraved................**35.00 to 45.00**
Spooner, plain **40.00**
Sugar bowl, cov., engraved ..**70.00 to 80.00**
Sugar bowl, cov., plain........................**46.00**
Tray, water, piecrust rim, engraved,
  13" d..**125.00**
Tray, water, piecrust rim, plain,
  13" d..**95.00**
Tray, wine, 10½" d. **105.00**
Tumbler, clear, engraved ......**35.00 to 45.00**
Tumbler, clear, plain.............................**35.00**
Tumbler, ruby-stained............................**42.50**
Tumbler, ruby-stained,
  souvenir................................**25.00 to 30.00**
Waste bowl, engraved..........................**75.00**
Waste bowl, plain **58.00**
Wine, clear, engraved............**30.00 to 40.00**
Wine, clear, plain..................................**27.00**
Wine, ruby-stained................**50.00 to 60.00**
Wine, ruby-stained, souvenir...............**40.00**

DIAGONAL BAND
Celery vase ....**20.00 to 30.00**
Creamer...**30.00**

Diagonal Band Goblet

Goblet (ILLUS.) ....**20.00 to 30.00**
Marmalade jar w/original lid.................**50.00**
Pickle castor w/amber insert.............**165.00**
Pitcher, water...**40.00**
Spooner **20.00**
Tray, handled, 7¼ x 13"........................**20.00**
Wine..**22.00**

DIAMOND MEDALLION (Finecut &
Diamond or Grand)
Bread plate, 10" d................................**20.00**
Butter dish, cov....................**35.00 to 45.00**
Cake stand, 8" d...................................**35.00**
Celery vase...**25.00**
Compote, cov., 6" d., 9" h...................**65.00**
Compote, cov., 8" d., low stand...........**80.00**
Creamer, footed **22.00**
Goblet...................................**20.00 to 30.00**
Pitcher, water..**39.00**
Relish, 7½" oval.....................................**9.00**
Salt shaker w/original top **32.50**
Spooner..**22.50**
Wine......................................**20.00 to 25.00**

DIAMOND QUILTED
Bowl, 6" d., turquoise blue...................**11.00**
Bowl, 7" d., amber.................................**25.00**
Bowl, 7" d., canary................................**18.00**
Celery vase, blue ....**40.00 to 45.00**
Champagne, amethyst **37.50**
Champagne, canary **26.00**
Champagne, turquoise blue **37.50**
Claret, canary.......................................**18.00**
Compote, open, 6" d., 6" h.,
  amber ....**20.00 to 25.00**
Compote, open, 6" d., 6" h., clear.......**22.50**
Compote, open, 7" d., low stand,
  amber...**17.50**
Compote, open, 8" d., low stand,
  amethyst **45.00**
Compote, open, 9" d., low stand,
  canary...**38.00**
Cordial, amber......................................**32.50**
*Goblet, amber **47.50**
*Goblet, amethyst **41.50**
*Goblet, blue **37.50**

*Goblet, canary 32.50
Pitcher, water, amber 53.50
Relish, amber, 4½ x 7½".....................14.00
Relish, leaf-shaped, canary,
  5½ x 9"...20.00
*Salt dip, amber, master size,
  rectangular......................................32.00
*Salt dip, amethyst, master size,
  rectangular......................................22.00
Sauce dish, flat or footed, amber,
  each 11.50
Sauce dish, flat or footed, canary..........9.00
Sauce dish, flat or footed, turquoise
  blue, each 11.00
Spooner, amber..................................28.00
Spooner, canary 35.00
Sugar bowl, cov., amethyst................85.00
Sugar bowl, cov., canary....................55.00
Tray, water, clover leaf-shaped,
  amethyst, 10 x 12"..........................45.00
*Tumbler, amber.................................30.00
*Tumbler, canary 26.00
Waste bowl, blue, 4½" d.....................38.00
Wine, amethyst 42.00
Wine, canary 38.00
Wine, clear 17.00

DINNER BELL - See Cottage Pattern

DRAPERY

Drapery Spooner

Creamer, applied handle ....30.00 to 35.00
Egg cup 22.50
Goblet..28.00
Plate, 6" d..23.00
Spooner (ILLUS.) ....30.00 to 35.00
Sugar bowl, cov...................................40.00

EGG IN SAND

Bread tray, handled 36.00
Creamer..32.00
Dish, flat, swan center, 7" d. 48.00
Goblet, blue 48.00
Goblet, clear 25.00
Pitcher, milk.......................................45.00
Pitcher, water, blue............................98.00
Pitcher, water, clear...........................35.00

Platter, 12½" oblong 42.00
Spooner, amber..................................40.00
Spooner, blue 35.00
Spooner, clear 26.00
Sugar bowl, cov...................................35.00
Tray, water, flat 21.00
Tumbler 30.00

EYEWINKER

Banana boat, flat, 8½"........................90.00
Banana stand......................................115.00
Bowl, cov., 9" d. 85.00
Bowl, 6½" d...25.00
Bowl, master berry or fruit, 9" d.,
  4½" h..70.00
*Butter dish, cov. ....80.00 to 85.00
Cake stand, 8" d. 58.00
Cake stand, 9½" d. 65.00
Celery vase, 6½" h..............................55.00
*Compote, cov., 6" d., high stand 50.00
Compote, open, 4" d., 5" h.,
  scalloped rim...................................32.50
Compote, open, 5½" d., high stand 60.00
*Compote, open, 7½" d., high stand,
  flared rim ....75.00 to 80.00
Compote, open, 8½" d., high stand 75.00
Compote, open, 9½" d., high
  stand...................125.00 to 150.00
Creamer..45.00
*Goblet...25.00
Pitcher, milk.......................................70.00
*Pitcher, water 80.00
Plate, 7" sq., 1½" h., turned-up
  sides 24.00
Salt shaker w/original top 35.00
*Sauce dish, round 34.00
Sauce dish, square.............................12.00
Spooner................................35.00 to 40.00
*Sugar bowl, cov. 52.00
Syrup pitcher w/silver plate top.........135.00
*Tumbler...28.00

FESTOON

Festoon Creamer

Bowl, berry, 8" rectangle....................23.00
Bowl, berry, 5½ x 9"
  rectangle............................20.00 to 25.00

Bowl, 7" d.................................**25.00**
Butter dish, cov. **42.00**
Cake stand, high pedestal,
  9" d. ....**40.00 to 50.00**
Compote, open, 9" d., high
  stand **56.00**
Creamer (ILLUS.).....................**30.00**
Marmalade jar, cov. **32.00**
Mug, handled **58.00**
Pitcher, water ....**55.00 to 60.00**
Plate, 7" d................................**36.00**
Plate, 8" d................................**42.00**
Plate, 9" d................................**46.00**
Sauce dish...............................**10.00**
Spooner **35.00**
Sugar bowl, cov.......................**55.00**
Tray, water, 10" d. **33.00**
Tumbler **25.00**
Waste bowl...............................**53.00**
Water set, pitcher, tray & 4 tumblers,
  6 pcs. **215.00**

FINECUT & BLOCK
Bowl, round, handled, pink blocks **50.00**
Butter dish, cov., two-handled **55.00**
Celery tray, clear w/amber blocks,
  11" l......................................**85.00**
Champagne, amber...................**70.00**
Cordial **35.00**
*Creamer, clear.......................**30.00**
Creamer, clear w/amber blocks **62.50**
Creamer, clear w/pink blocks.............**75.00**
Egg cup, double.......................**29.00**
*Goblet, amber........................**52.50**
*Goblet, clear....................**35.00 to 40.00**
Goblet, clear w/blue blocks ...**60.00 to 65.00**
Goblet, clear w/pink blocks **65.00**
Goblet, clear w/yellow blocks.............**52.00**
Pitcher, water, clear w/amber
  blocks...................................**85.00**
Pitcher, water, clear w/blue blocks **125.00**
Pitcher, water, clear w/pink blocks **110.00**
Punch cup, clear w/yellow blocks........**55.00**
Salt dip....................................**12.00**
Sauce dish, amber **16.00**
Sauce dish, clear w/amber blocks.......**12.50**
Sauce dish, clear w/blue blocks **22.50**
Spooner, clear **40.00**
Spooner, clear w/amber blocks **45.00**
Sugar bowl, cov., clear w/yellow
  blocks ....**100.00 to 125.00**
Tumbler, clear w/blue blocks **40.00**
Waste bowl, amber...................**55.00**
*Wine, amber **58.00**
*Wine, blue..............................**58.00**
*Wine, clear.............................**24.00**
Wine, clear w/amber blocks **48.00**
Wine, clear w/blue blocks....................**45.00**
Wine, clear w/pink blocks....................**60.00**
Wine, clear w/yellow blocks.................**35.00**

FISHSCALE
Bowl, 6" d.................................**39.00**
Butter dish, cov. **40.00**

Cake stand, 9" d. **25.00**
Cake stand, 10" d. **35.00**
Celery vase..............................**35.00**
Compote, cov., 7½" d. **85.00**
Compote, open, jelly ....**20.00 to 25.00**
Compote, open, 6" d **20.00**
Creamer...................................**27.50**
Goblet.....................................**36.00**
Mug.............................**65.00 to 75.00**
Pickle dish...............................**18.00**
Pitcher, milk...................**40.00 to 45.00**
Pitcher, water ....**50.00 to 60.00**
Plate, 7" d................................**25.00**
Plate, 8" d................................**31.00**

Fishscale Plate

Plate, 9" sq. (ILLUS.) ....**30.00 to 35.00**
Relish, 5 x 8½".........................**20.00**
Sauce dish, flat or footed, each...........**10.00**
Spooner **25.50**
Sugar bowl, cov........................**38.00**
Tray, water, round **35.00**
Tumbler **95.00**

**FLYING ROBIN - See Hummingbird
  Pattern**

FROSTED LEAF
Celery vase ....**100.00 to 125.00**
Champagne...............................**225.00**
Egg cup ....**95.00 to 100.00**
Goblet.....................................**135.00**
Salt dip....................................**50.00**
Salt dip, master size **125.00**
Sauce dish...............................**25.00**
Sugar bowl, cov........................**175.00**
Wine..**170.00**

FROSTED LION (Rampant Lion)
Bowl, cov., 3⅞ x 6⅞" oblong,
  collared base **80.00**
Bowl, cov., 4⅝ x 7⁷⁄₁₆" oblong,
  collared base **110.00**
*Bowl, open, oval......................**61.50**
*Bread plate, rope edge, closed
  handles, 10½" d. **78.00**
*Butter dish, cov., frosted lion's head
  finial **90.00**

Butter dish, cov., rampant lion
finial ....165.00 to 170.00
*Celery vase 70.00
Cheese dish, cov., rampant lion
finial 425.00
Compote, cov., 5" d., 8½" h. 175.00
Compote, cov., 6" d., 7" h., rampant
lion finial ....200.00 to 250.00
*Compote, cov., 6¾" oval, 7" h.,
collared base, rampant lion
finial ....150.00 to 175.00
Compote, cov., 7" d., 11" h., lion
head finial 150.00
Compote, cov., 5½ x 8¾" oval,
8¼" h., rampant lion
finial ....170.00 to 180.00
Compote, open, 7" d., 6¼" h. 125.00
Compote, open, 7" oval, 7½" h..........135.00
Compote, open, 8" d.........................175.00
Creamer...80.00
*Egg cup 90.00
*Goblet ....75.00 to 80.00
Marmalade jar, cov., rampant lion
finial 135.00
Paperweight, embossed "Gillinder &
Sons, Centennial"...........100.00 to 110.00
*Pitcher, water...................475.00 to 525.00
Platter, 9 x 10½" oval, lion
handles 95.00
Salt dip, cov., master size, collared
base, rectangular 295.00
*Sauce dish, 4" to 5" d. ....20.00 to 25.00
*Spooner...62.00
*Sugar bowl, cov., frosted lion's head
finial 50.00
Sugar bowl, cov., rampant lion
finial ....100.00 to 125.00
Table set, cov. sugar bowl, creamer
& spooner, 3 pcs. 225.00

GARFIELD DRAPE
Bowl, 6" d...42.50
Bread plate, "We Mourn our Nation's
Loss," 11½" d. ....55.00 to 60.00
Butter dish, cov. 78.00
Cake stand, 9½" d. 85.00
Celery vase, pedestal base 58.00
Compote, cov., 7" d., 9½" h...............155.00
Compote, cov., 8" d., 12½" h..............185.00
Creamer................................45.00 to 50.00
Goblet 46.50
Pitcher, milk 90.00
Pitcher, water..95.00
Sauce dish, flat or footed, each..........12.00
Spooner.................................30.00 to 40.00
Sugar bowl, cov....................................80.00

GRASSHOPPER (Locust)
Bowl, cov., 7" d., footed 50.00
Bowl, open, 11" d., shallow..................35.00
Butter dish, cov., no insect, clear........45.00
Butter dish, cov., w/insect, clear 70.00
Celery vase, w/insect ....55.00 to 65.00

Compote, cov., 7" d.,
7¾" h. ....50.00 to 55.00
Compote, cov., 8¼" d. 70.00
Creamer, amber....................................65.00
Creamer, no insect................................30.00
Creamer, w/insect.................................45.00
Pitcher, water, w/insect .....100.00 to 125.00
Plate, 7½" d., footed............................18.00
Plate, 8½" d., footed............................18.00
Plate, 10½" d., footed..........................28.00
Salt dip, master size 38.00
Sauce dish, footed, no insect 14.00
Sauce dish, footed,
w/insect ....20.00 to 25.00
Spooner, no insect, clear` .....60.00 to 65.00
Spooner, w/insect, clear........75.00 to 80.00
Sugar bowl, cov., no insect 40.00
Sugar bowl, cov., w/insect...................70.00

HALLEY'S COMET
Celery vase...42.00
Goblet ....30.00 to 40.00
Pitcher, water, tankard, engraved........95.00
Pitcher, water, tankard,
plain......................................60.00 to 65.00
Spooner.................................30.00 to 40.00
Wine...16.50

HAND (Pennsylvania, Early)
Bread plate, 8 x 10½" oval 38.00
Butter dish, cov....................................125.00
Cake stand, 12¼" d., engraved 175.00
Celery vase ....35.00 to 40.00
Claret 85.00
Compote, cov., 7" d., high stand..........95.00
Compote, open, 7¾" d., 6¾" h. 40.00
Compote, open, 9" d., low stand..........36.00
Cordial 85.00
Creamer.................................30.00 to 40.00
Goblet 47.50
Marmalade jar, cov................................55.00
Mug 95.00
Pickle castor, w/silver plate frame &
tongs...110.00
Pitcher, water ....85.00 to 95.00
Relish..22.50
Sauce dish, 4½" d. 12.50
Spooner...45.00
Sugar bowl, cov.....................................65.00
Tumbler, water.......................................97.00
Wine.......................................45.00 to 55.00

HICKMAN (Le Clede)
Bowl, 6" d., green..................................25.00
Bowl, 8" d..25.00
Butter dish, cov. 35.00
Cake stand, 8½" to 9½" d. 38.00
Celery dish, boat-shaped, green 22.00
Celery tray 18.00
Compote, cov., 5" d..............35.00 to 40.00
Compote, cov., 7" d., high stand..........82.00
Compote, open, 8½" d., 12" h. 65.00
Compote, open, 9½" d., 8" h. 45.00

Condiment set, miniature: salt &
  pepper shakers & cruet w/original
  stopper on cloverleaf-shaped tray;
  clear, 4 pcs 90.00
Creamer, clear w/gold.........................25.00
Creamer, green ....20.00 to 25.00
Cruet w/triple pouring spout &
  faceted stopper 31.00
Goblet, clear 35.00
Goblet, green 75.00
Ice tub, clear 45.00
Ice tub, green......................................60.00
Pitcher, water......................................45.00
Plate, 6" d...11.00
Punch cup, clear 8.00
Punch cup, green.................................18.50
Relish, green..22.50
Rose bowl..26.00
Salt dip..22.50
Sauce dish, green 12.50
Sauce dish, ruby-stained.....................18.50
Sugar bowl, cov., clear........................65.00
Toothpick holder 38.50
Vase, 8" h., trumpet-shaped, green 18.00
Vase, 10" h., green...............................37.50
Wine, clear 30.00
Wine, green..45.00

HIDALGO (Frosted Waffle)

Hidalgo Ruby-Stained Goblet

Butter dish, cov. 50.00
Celery dish, boat-shaped, 13" l 35.00
Celery vase, amber-stained..................49.00
Celery vase, clear................................30.00
Compote, open, 7" sq., high stand 45.00
Creamer 35.00
Cruet w/original stopper,
  clear....................................70.00 to 75.00
Cruet w/original stopper, amber-
  stained 195.00
Goblet, clear 16.00
Goblet, engraved 17.50
Goblet, frosted....................30.00 to 35.00
Goblet, ruby-stained (ILLUS.) 57.00
Pitcher, water.......................................43.00
Sauce dish, handled............................12.00
Sugar shaker w/original top.................45.00

Tray, water 55.00
Tumbler, frosted 35.00

HORSESHOE (Good Luck or Prayer Rug)

Bowl, cov., 5 x 8" oval, flat, triple
  horseshoe finial................................295.00
Bowl, open, 7" d., footed.....................47.50
Bowl, open, 5 x 8" oval, footed 30.00
Bowl, open, 6 x 9" oval 27.50
*Bread tray, single horseshoe
  handles...............................40.00 to 50.00
Bread tray, double horseshoe
  handles 93.00
Butter dish, cov..................................105.00
Cake stand, 7" d. 35.00
Cake stand, 8" d., 6½" h. 76.00
Cake stand, 9" d., 6½" h. 69.00
Cake stand, 10" d. 87.00
Cake stand, 10¾" d. 127.00
Celery vase...81.00
Cheese dish, cov., w/woman
  churning butter in base 275.00
Compote, cov., 6" d., 10½" h. 250.00
Compote, cov., 7" d., high stand..........75.00
Compote, cov., 8" d., low stand.........210.00
Compote, cov., 8" d., high stand........175.00
Creamer 31.50
Doughnut stand 95.00
Goblet, knob stem................................45.00
Goblet, plain stem................................30.00
Marmalade jar, cov.............................225.00
Pitcher, milk....................125.00 to 135.00
Pitcher, water ....130.00 to 135.00
Plate, 7" d..45.00
Plate, 8" d..80.00
Plate, 10" d..86.00
Relish, 5 x 8"..5.00
Salt dip, individual size 17.50
Salt dip, master size, horseshoe
  shape..100.00
Sauce dish, flat or footed, each...........11.00
Spooner 35.00
Sugar bowl, cov. ....75.00 to 100.00
Wine...295.00

HUMMINGBIRD (Flying Robin or Bird & Fern)

Butter dish, cov., blue 110.00
Celery vase...32.50
Creamer, amber ....75.00 to 100.00
Creamer, blue.......................................85.00
Creamer, clear......................................45.00
Goblet, amber 65.00
Goblet, blue 67.50
Goblet, clear 52.50
Pitcher, water, amber 150.00
Pitcher, water, blue.............................145.00
Pitcher, water, clear.............................90.00
Spooner 30.00
Sugar bowl, cov., blue 110.00
Tray, water 50.00
Tumbler, amber 60.00
Wine...................................75.00 to 85.00

IVY IN SNOW

Ivy in Snow Wine

Bowl, 7" d. **22.00**
***Cake stand,** 8" to 10" d. **42.00**
***Celery vase,** 8" h. **35.00**
Compote, open, jelly...........................**20.00**
***Creamer,** clear...................................**25.00**
Creamer, ruby-stained ivy sprigs **85.00**
***Goblet,** clear......................................**50.00**
Goblet, green & red ivy sprigs & gold
  band at top & base..........................**175.00**
Honey dish, cov., amber-stained ivy
  sprigs **87.50**
Plate, 7" d...**17.50**
Plate, 10" d...**30.00**
***Sauce dish,** flat or footed, each **12.00**
***Spooner...28.00**
Sugar bowl, cov., clear.......................**30.00**
Sugar bowl, cov., ruby-stained..........**135.00**
Tumbler, clear......................................**26.00**
Tumbler, ruby-stained..........................**40.00**
Wine (ILLUS.).......................................**38.00**

JEWELED MOON & STAR (Moon & Star with Waffle)

***Banana boat,** w/amber & blue
  staining ....**275.00 to 325.00**
***Bowl,** 6¾" d., flat................................**13.50**
Butter dish, cov., w/amber & blue
  staining ....**130.00 to 140.00**
Cake stand, w/amber & blue staining,
  10" d..**235.00**
Carafe **38.00**
Celery vase, clear...............................**25.00**
Celery vase, frosted w/amber & blue
  staining **82.50**
***Compote,** open, 9" d., high stand.......**52.00**
***Goblet..38.00**
Pitcher, water, bulbous, applied
  handle, w/amber & blue staining......**175.00**
Salt shaker w/original top, w/amber &
  blue staining.....................................**125.00**
Spooner, w/amber & blue
  staining ....**60.00 to 65.00**
Tumbler, w/amber & blue staining.......**60.00**
***Wine..33.00**

JUMBO and JUMBO & BARNUM

Butter dish & cover w/frosted
  elephant finial, oblong .....**675.00 to 700.00**
Castor holder (no bottles) **100.00**
Creamer............................**235.00 to 250.00**
Creamer, w/Barnum head at
  handle...**295.00**
Marmalade jar w/Barnum head
  handles & cover w/frosted elephant
  finial **450.00**
Spoon rack........................**600.00 to 750.00**
Sugar bowl, w/Barnum head handles
  & cover w/frosted elephant
  finial ....**475.00 to 500.00**

KING'S CROWN (Also see Ruby Thumbprint)

King's Crown Mustard Jar

Banana stand **110.00**
Bowl, berry or fruit, 8¼" d., flared
  rim..**27.00**
Bowl, 9¼" oval, scalloped rim,
  round base..**67.50**
Butter dish, cov. **65.00**
Cake stand, 9" d. **85.00**
Cake stand, 10" d. **85.00**
Castor bottle, w/original top **16.50**
Castor set, salt & pepper shakers, oil
  bottle w/stopper & cov. mustard jar
  in original frame, 4 pcs....................**325.00**
Celery vase, engraved.........................**60.00**
Celery vase, plain...............................**61.50**
Champagne, w/amethyst
  thumbprints **25.00**
Compote, cov., 5" d., 5½" h.,
  engraved..**32.50**
Compote, cov., 7" d., 7" h. **95.00**
Compote, cov., 11" d. **145.00**
Compote, open, jelly...........................**45.00**
Compote, open, 7½" d., high stand **42.00**
Compote, open, 8½" d., high stand **85.00**
Compote, open, 9" d., low stand..........**44.00**
Cordial **50.00**
Creamer, clear **47.50**
Creamer, individual size, clear............**16.50**
Creamer, individual size, clear
  w/gold **29.50**
Creamer, individual size, w/green
  thumbprints **35.00**

Cup & saucer **55.00**
Goblet, clear **27.50**
Goblet, clear w/engraved moose, doe
& dog **95.00**
Goblet, w/green thumbprints...............**25.00**
Goblet, w/green thumbprints,
souvenir **18.00**
Lamp, kerosene-type, stem base,
10" h..**180.00**
Mustard jar, cov. ....**40.00 to 50 00**
Pitcher, 5" h., souvenir.........................**40.00**
Pitcher, tankard, 8½" h....................**110.00**
Pitcher, tankard, 13" h., engraved **122.50**
Pitcher, tankard, 13" h., plain............**195.00**
Pitcher, bulbous...............................**125.00**
Plate, 8" sq...**54.00**
Punch bowl, footed ....**225.00 to 250.00**
Punch cup **22.50**
Relish, 7" oval....................................**10.00**
Salt dip, individual size **37.50**
Sauce dish, boat-shaped.....................**22.00**
Sauce dish, round **17.00**
Spooner...**39.00**
Toothpick holder, clear......................**25.00**
Toothpick holder, clear, souvenir **50.00**
Toothpick holder, rose stain,
souvenir **30.00**
Tray, square.......................................**29.00**
Tumbler, clear....................................**22.00**
Wine, clear...**22.50**
Wine, cobalt blue ....**100.00 to 150.00**
Wine, cobalt blue, souvenir **165,00**
Wine, w/amber thumbprints **22.00**
Wine, w/amethyst thumbprints **17.50**
Wine, w/green thumbprints **15.00**

LEAF & DART (Double Leaf & Dart)
Butter dish, cov., pedestal base..........**90.00**
Celery vase, pedestal base **37.50**
Creamer, applied handle......................**45.00**
Egg cup **20.50**
Goblet..**25.00**
Pitcher, water, applied handle **95.00**
Salt dip, cov, master size....................**95.00**
Salt dip, open, master size **27.00**
Sauce dish...**9.00**
Spooner..**25.00**
Sugar bowl, cov. ....**45.00 to 55.00**
Tumbler, footed **25.00**
Wine...**34.00**

LILY-OF-THE-VALLEY
Bowl, 5½" x 8" oval.............................**32.50**
Butter dish, cov. **105.00**
Celery vase...**76.00**
Champagne **175.00**
Compote, cov., 8" d., low stand.........**126.50**
Compote, cov., 8½" d., high
stand..**137.50**
Compote, open, 7" d., low stand..........**47.50**
Compote, open, 8½" d., 5" h. **54.00**
Creamer, three-footed, molded
handle...**80.00**

Creamer, plain base, applied
handle...**61.50**
Cruet w/original
stopper ....**150.00 to 200.00**
Egg cup **43.00**
Goblet...............................**75.00 to 85.00**
Pitcher, milk, applied
handle.............................**200.00 to 225.00**

Lily of the Valley Pitcher

Pitcher, water, bulbous, applied
handle (ILLUS.)..............................**120.00**
Relish, 4½ x7"....................................**24.00**
Relish, 5½ x 8"...................................**28.00**
Salt dip, open, master size, three-
footed..**60.00**
Sauce dish..**17.50**
Spooner, plain base............................**45.00**
Spooner, three-footed.........................**55.00**
Tumbler, flat...**9.50**
Wine...**155.00**

LOCUST - See Grasshopper Pattern

MAGNET & GRAPE
Champagne, frosted leaf, flint....**176.00**
Champagne, stippled leaf, non-flint.....**45.00**
Cordial, 4" h., frosted leaf, flint..........**150.00**
Creamer, stippled leaf, non-flint **35.00**
Egg cup, clear leaf, non-flint **33.00**
Egg cup, frosted lead, flint **83.00**
Egg cup, stippled leaf, non-flint **18.00**
Goblet, clear leaf, non-flint...................**18.00**
Goblet, frosted leaf, flint......................**78.50**
Goblet, frosted leaf & American
Shield, flint **400.00**
Goblet, stippled leaf, non-flint **26.00**
Salt dip, master size, footed,
non-flint..**24.00**
Sauce dish, clear leaf, non-flint **4.50**
Sauce dish, frosted leaf, flint...............**18.50**
Sauce dish, stippled leaf, non-flint........**6.00**
Spooner, frosted leaf, flint....................**74.00**
Spooner, stippled leaf, non-flint...........**28.00**
Sugar bowl, cov., frosted leaf &
American Shield, flint **325.00**
Wine, frosted leaf, flint ....**200.00 to 225.00**

MANHATTAN

Basket, applied handle, 7 x 10",
  11½" h..145.00
Bowl, 8¼" d..25.00
Bowl, 9" d...22.00
Bowl, 10½" d..15.00
Bowl, master berry, pink-stained 40.00
Butter dish, cov......................................48.00
Cake stand..........................33.00 to 40.00
Carafe, water, pink-stained 65.00
Celery tray...26.00
Compote, open, large 47.50
Cracker jar, cov., pink-stained.............55.00
Creamer...27.50
Creamer, individual size.......................18.50
Creamer & open sugar bowl, pr.........42.00
Cruet w/original stopper.......................60.00
Dish, flat, 6 x 7" oval 22.00
Goblet...25.00
Ice bucket, pink-stained.......................50.00
Marmalade jar, cov..............................37.50
Pickle castor in silver plate frame,
  w/tongs 110.00
Pitcher, water, pink-stained 100.00
Plate, 5" d., pink-stained 25.00
Plate, 10¾" d..20.00
Punch cup...20.00
Salt shaker w/original top....................24.50
Sauce dish, flat, amber or pink-
  stained 12.50
Spooner...20.00
Toothpick holder, clear.........................30.00
Toothpick holder, purple-stained
  eyes 30.00
Tumbler...12.50
Tumbler, clear w/gold trim 25.00
Tumbler, footed 30.00
Tumbler, pink-stained 16.00
Vase, 6" h..20.00
Wine..17.50

MASCOTTE

Mascotte Goblet

Butter dish, cov., engraved................85.00
Butter pat...11.00
Cake basket w/handle 76.00
Cake stand, 10" d. 48.00

Celery vase ....30.00 to 40.00
Cheese dish, cov....................................65.00
Compote, cov., 5" d. 44.00
Compote, cov., 8" d., 12" h. ..85.00 to 90.00
Compote, open, jelly..............................32.50
Creamer...35.00
Goblet, engraved, (ILLUS.)....................39.50
Goblet, plain..30.00
Jar, cov., globe-type, embossed
  patent date, milk white.....................265.00
Pitcher, water ....145.00 to 155.00
Salt shaker w/original top 14.00
Sauce dish, flat or footed, each...........10.00
Spooner, clear, engraved 40.00
Spooner, clear, plain.............................30.00
Spooner, canary 135.00
Sugar bowl, cov., engraved.................48.00
Sugar bowl, cov., plain.........................39.00
Tray, water, engraved 65.00
Tray, water, plain...................................58.00
Tumbler, engraved 34.00
Tumbler, plain.......................................29.00
Wine, clear, engraved 35.00
Wine, clear, plain..................................25.50

MINERVA

Bread tray, 13" l....................................52.50
Butter dish, cov. 80.00
Cake stand, 8" d. ....55.00 to 75.00
Cake stand, 9" d. 95.00
Cake stand, 10½" d. 115.00
Compote, cov., 8" d., low stand.........175.00
Compote, cov., 8" d., high
  stand.............................150.00 to 175.00
Compote, open, 8" d., 8½" h. 90.00
Creamer...47.50
Goblet 96.00
Marmalade jar, cov. 150.00
Pitcher, water ....180.00 to 200.00
Plate, 8" d., Bates (J.C.) portrait
  center, scalloped rim..........................75.00
Plate, 10" d., Mars center.....................55.00
Platter, 13" oval 60.00
Relish, 5 x 8" oblong 33.50
Relish, 6 x 9" oblong 59.00
Sauce dish, footed, 4" d. 19.00
Sauce dish, flat, 5" d.............................20.00
Spooner...48.50
Sugar bowl, cov.....................................97.00

MINNESOTA

Banana bowl, flat ....55.00 to 60.00
Basket w/applied reeded handle..........75.00
Bowl, 6" sq..32.00
Bowl, 6 x 8¼" 38.00
Bowl, 8" sq..32.00
Bowl, 8½" d., clear 40.00
Bowl, 7½ x 10½".....................................38.00
Butter dish, cov. 44.00
Carafe 48.00
Celery tray, 13" l....................................41.50
Cheese dish, cov....................................58.00
Compote, open, 7"..................................40.00

Compote, open, 9" sq. 50.00
Cracker jar, cov...................87.50 to 100.00
Creamer, 3½" h. ....30.00 to 40.00
Creamer, individual size, w/gold trim ...18.00
Cruet w/original stopper 50.00
Goblet 30.00
Goblet, clear w/gold...............................35.00
Mug 22.00
Nappy, 4½" d. 12.00
Pickle dish...12.00
Pitcher, water, tankard ....50.00 to 75.00
Plate, 7⅜" d., turned-up rim 17.00
Relish, 3 x 5"...10.00
Relish, 6½" x 8¾" oblong....................21.00
Sauce dish...10.00
Spooner, clear 35.00
Spooner, clear w/gold............................52.50
Sugar bowl, cov.......................................37.00
Syrup pitcher w/original top 65.00
Toothpick holder, three-handled,
    clear.............................25.00 to 35.00
Toothpick holder, three-handled,
    green...125.00
Tumbler 18.00
Wine..23.00

NAIL
Bowl, 6" d., flat, ruby-stained 45.00
Butter dish, cov. 72.50
Cake stand 42.50
Celery tray, flat, 5 x 11".........................75.00
Celery vase, engraved...........................50.00
Celery vase, ruby-stained....................65.00
Claret 55.00
Compote, jelly, 5¼", clear...................67.50
Compote, jelly, ruby-stained...............85.00
Compote, 7" d., ruby-stained.............155.00
Compote, 8" d., clear, engraved.........85.00
Creamer, clear, engraved 35.00
Creamer, clear, plain.............................50.00
Goblet, clear, engraved 60.50
Goblet, clear, plain................................48.00
Goblet, ruby-stained 95.00
Pitcher, water, clear...............................85.00
Pitcher, water, ruby-
    stained..........................200.00 to 225.00
Salt shaker w/original top,
    w/engraving, clear..............................65.00
Salt shaker w/original top,
    w/engraving, ruby-stained.................75.00
Sauce dish, flat or footed.....................12.00
Sauce dish, flat or footed, ruby-
    stained 50.00
Spooner, clear 45.00
Spooner, clear, engraved 35.00
Sugar bowl, cov., clear.........................50.00
Sugar bowl, cov., clear w/engraved
    cover..40.00
Syrup jug w/original top........................28.00
Syrup jug w/original top,
    ruby-stained 225.00
Tumbler, clear...15.00
Tumbler, ruby-stained...........................60.00

Tumbler, ruby-stained, souvenir 42.50
Wine, clear, engraved 55.00
Wine, clear, plain....................................52.00
Wine, ruby-stained, souvenir...............59.00

NEW ENGLAND PINEAPPLE
Bar bottle, qt. 395.00
Champagne, flint ....225.00 to 275.00
Compote, open, 5" d., 8" h. 85.00
Compote, open, 9" d., flint 145.00
Compote, open, high stand, 10½"
    d., 9⅜" h. (rim chips)......................350.00
Cordial, flint, 4" h. 119.00
Creamer, applied handle, flint...........235.00
Decanter w/bar lip, flint, qt. 175.00
Decanter w/original stopper, flint,
    qt. 205.00
Egg cup, flint..56.50
Goblet, flint ....65.00 to 75.00
Goblet, lady's, flint 142.50
Honey dish, flint.....................................35.00
Pitcher, milk, 1 qt. 950.00
Pitcher, water..310.00
Plate, 6" d., flint....................................190.00
Salt dip, master size, flint.....................50.00
Sauce dish, flint......................................27.50
Spillholder, flint ....90.00 to 95.00
Sugar bowl, cov., flint 160.00
Tumbler, bar, flint.................................135.00
Tumbler, water, flint...............................75.00
Wine, flint 210.00

OAKEN BUCKET (Wooden Pail)
Butter dish, cov., amber......................70.00
Butter dish, cov., clear 65.00
Butter dish, cov., canary......................95.00
Creamer, amber......................................45.00
Creamer, amethyst................55.00 to 75.00
Creamer, blue 65.00
Creamer, clear....................25.00 to 30.00
Creamer, canary 45.00
Match holder w/original wire handle,
    2⅝" d., 2⅝" h., amber 25.00
Pitcher, water, amber 80.00
Pitcher, water, amethyst....................175.00
Pitcher, water, blue..............................100.00
Pitcher, water, clear...............................60.00
Pitcher, water, canary..........................120.00
Spooner, amber ....35.00 to 40.00
Spooner, blue 55.00
Spooner, clear 35.00
Sugar bowl, cov......................................50.00
Sugar bowl, open, amethyst................35.00
Toothpick holder, amber 30.00
Toothpick holder, clear.......................20.00

OPEN ROSE
Butter dish, cov. 65.00
Creamer..49.00
Egg cup 21.00
Goblet 30.00
Goblet, lady's...35.00
Salt dip, master size 24.00

Sauce dish...10.00
Spooner...32.00
Sugar bowl, cov...54.00
Tumbler 41.00

PALMETTE
Celery vase..53.00
Compote, open, 8" d., low stand..........24.00
Creamer, applied handle.....................58.00
Cruet..95.00
Cup plate, 3⅜" d. 45.00
Egg cup..............................30.00 to 35.00
Goblet..................................35.00 to 40.00
Lamp, kerosene-type, table model
   w/stem, clear...78.50
Pitcher, water, applied
   handle..........................100.00 to 125.00
Relish...17.50
Salt dip, master size, footed 25.00
Sauce dish...8.00
Spooner...35.00
Tumbler, water, flat...............................75.00
Wine..50.00

PANELED GRAPE
Butter dish, cov. 45.50
Compote, cov., 4" d., high stand..........30.00
Creamer..30.00
Creamer, individual size.....................25.00
Goblet...30.00
Parfait 35.00
Pitcher, water, 8¾" h. 55.00
Sauce dish...15.00
Spooner...25.00
Sugar bowl, open 28.00
Toothpick holder 38.00
Tumbler 25.00
Water set, cov. pitcher & 6 goblets,
   7 pcs. ....200.00 to 250.00
Wine..16.00

PAVONIA (Pineapple Stem)

Pavonia Engraved Goblet

Butter dish, cov., clear, engraved.......90.00
Butter dish, cov., clear, plain...............72.00
Butter dish, cov., ruby-
   stained..........................100.00 to 115.00

Cake stand, 10" d. 60.00
Celery vase, engraved.....................44.50
Celery vase, plain................................40.00
Compote, cov., 6" d., high stand..........55.00
Compote, cov., 7" d., engraved 100.00
Compote, cov., 8" d., engraved 125.00
Compote, open, 7" d.............................48.00
Creamer, engraved.............................41.00
Creamer, plain 38.00
Goblet, engraved (ILLUS.)...................42.00
Goblet, plain..29.00
Pitcher, water, tall tankard, clear,
   engraved ....95.00 to 100.00
Pitcher, water, tall tankard, clear,
   plain..60.00
Pitcher, water, tall tankard, ruby-
   stained, engraved 275.00
Salt dip, master size 16.50
Salt shaker w/original top 28.00
Sauce dish, flat or footed...................14.50
Spooner, clear 39.00
Spooner, ruby-stained.......................45.00
Sugar bowl, cov., clear......................50.00
Sugar bowl, cov., ruby-stained............85.00
Tray, water 73.00
Tumbler, clear, acid-etched...25.00 to 30.00
Tumbler, clear..25.00
Tumbler, ruby-stained.........................35.00
Tumbler, ruby-stained, engraved.......45.00
Waste bowl, clear, engraved..............47.50
Water set: tankard pitcher & 6
   tumblers; ruby-stained, 7 pcs...........375.00
Wine, clear, engraved 25.00
Wine, clear, plain................................20.00
Wine, ruby-stained 39.00

PLEAT & PANEL (Darby)

Pleat & Panel Celery

Bowl, 5 x 8"..32.00
Bowl, 6" sq., flat 28.00
Bowl, 7" d., 4½" h., footed 21.50
Bowl, 8" sq., flat 90.00
Bowl, cov., 8" rectangle, flat...............90.00
Bowl, 8" rectangle, footed....................35.00
Bread tray, closed handles, 8½
   x 13" ....40.00 to 45.00

Bread tray, pierced handles ..**25.00 to 30.00**
Butter dish, cov., footed, tab
handles ....**75.00 to 100.00**
Cake stand, 8" sq. **40.00**
Cake stand, 9" to 10" sq. **75.00**
Celery vase, footed (ILLUS.) **38.00**
Compote, cov., 7" sq., high stand........**85.00**
Compote, cov., 8" d., high stand..........**98.00**
Compote, open, 8" d., high stand **35.00**
Creamer..**25.00**
Goblet **28.00**
Lamp, kerosene-type, stem **125.00**
Marmalade jar, cov...........................**100.00**
Pitcher, milk......................................**180.00**
Pitcher, water ....**100.00 to 125.00**
Plate, 5" sq. **22.00**
Plate, 6" sq. **26.00**
Plate, 7" sq., canary **48.00**
Plate, 7" sq., clear **19.00**
Relish, cov., oblong, handled..............**65.00**
Relish, open, handled, 5 x 8½" **24.00**
Salt shaker w/original top **35.00**
Sauce dish, flat, handled....................**18.00**
Sauce dish, footed.............................**22.50**
Spooner **35.00**
Sugar bowl, cov..................................**85.00**
Tray, water, 9¼ x 14" **45.00**

**PORTLAND MAIDEN BLUSH - See
Banded Portland Pattern**

**PORTLAND WITH DIAMOND POINT
BAND - See Banded Portland
Pattern**

PRINCESS FEATHER (Rochelle)
Bowl, cov., 8" d. **85.00**
Butter dish, cov. **50.00**
Cake plate w/closed handles, 9" d.......**55.00**
Celery vase...**40.00**
Compote, cov., 8" d., low stand.........**100.00**
Creamer **60.00**
Goblet, non-flint **41.00**
Lamp, kerosene, hand-type w/finger
grip handle **120.00**
Pitcher, water, bulbous, applied
handle, flint ....**120.00 to 125.00**
Plate, 6" d., non-flint............................**29.00**
Plate, 7" d., amber, flint.....................**225.00**
Plate, 7" d., clear, non-flint **22.00**
Plate, 8" d., non-flint............................**24.00**
Plate, 9" d., non-flint............................**32.50**
Spooner, clear, non-flint **25.00**
Spooner, milk white, flint......................**48.00**
Sugar bowl, cov., clear, non-flint.........**62.50**
Sugar bowl, cov., milk white, flint **135.00**

**RAMPANT LION - See Frosted Lion
Pattern**

RED BLOCK
Bowl, berry or fruit, 8" d. **85.00**
Butter dish, cov....................**65.00 to 85.00**
Celery vase, 6½" h. **135.00**

Creamer, large......................**60.00 to 80.00**
Cruet w/original stopper **150.00**
Decanter, whiskey, w/original
stopper, 12" h..................................**175.00**
Dish, rectangular, 5 x 7½"....................**55.00**
***Goblet**..**37.50**
Mug, plain, 3" h. **26.00**
Mug, souvenir, 3" h. **42.00**
Pitcher, 8" h., bulbous.........................**225.00**
Pitcher, tankard, 8" h.........**150.00 to 175.00**
Sauce dish, 4½" **35.00**
Spooner **32.50**
Sugar bowl, cov. ....**50.00 to 70.00**
Tumbler, souvenir **32.00**
Tumbler **30.00**
***Wine** ....**25.00 to 35.00**

**REVERSE TORPEDO (Diamond &
Bull's Eye Band)**

Reverse Torpedo Bowl

Banana stand **130.00**
Basket, high stand **160.00**
Bowl, 7½" d., ruffled rim (ILLUS.) **48.00**
Bowl, 9" d., piecrust rim **75.00**
Butter dish, cov. **75.00**
Cake stand ....**75.00 to 85.00**
Celery vase...**55.00**
Compote, cov., 6" d., high stand..........**85.00**
Compote, open, jelly **40.00**
Compote, open, 5" d., flared rim,
high stand **50.00**
Compote, open, 8" d., piecrust rim,
high stand **105.00**
Compote, open, 10" d., piecrust rim,
high stand **125.00**
Creamer **67.50**
Goblet **85.00**
Goblet, w/engraved flower...**75.00 to 100.00**
Lamp, kerosene-type, 9" h. **145.00**
Pitcher, water, tankard ......**125.00 to 150.00**
Pitcher, water, tankard w/engraved
flowers **225.00**
Salt shaker w/original top **40.00**
Sauce dish...**19.00**
Spooner **52.00**
Sugar bowl, cov..................................**72.50**
Tumbler **50.00**

RIBBED PALM
Celery vase ....**95.00 to 100.00**
Champagne..**125.00**
Compote, open, 7¼" d., 4¼" h. **45.00**
Creamer..............................**125.00 to 150.00**

Ribbed Palm Egg Cup

Egg Cup (ILLUS.) 36.00
*Goblet..44.00
Pitcher, water, 9" h., applied
  handle.............................250.00 to 300.00
Salt dip, master size 38.00
Sauce dish...12.00
Spillholder..........................35.00 to 45.00
Sugar bowl, open 37.50
Tumbler 120.00
*Wine ....65.00 to 70.00

RIBBON CANDY (Bryce or Double Loop)
Butter dish, cov., flat.............35.00 to 40.00
Butter dish, cov., footed.....................50.00
Cake stand, child's, 6½" d., 3" h........125.00
Cake stand, 8" to 10½" d.....................46.50
Celery vase...45.00
Compote, cov., 7" d. 95.00
Creamer...32.00
Doughnut stand 32.00
Goblet...............................50.00 to 75.00
Pitcher, milk.......................................42.00
Plate, 8½" d..26.00
Relish, 8½" l.......................................13.00
Sauce dish, flat, 3½" d........................10.00
Sauce dish, footed, 4" d. 12.00
Spooner..24.00
Sugar bowl, cov.................................48.00
Wine..95.00

**ROCHELLE - See Princess Feather
  Pattern**

ROSE SPRIG
Bowl, 6 x 9" oblong 27.50
Bread tray, two-handled, canary 40.00
Bread tray, two-handled, clear 32.00
Cake stand, amber, 9" octagon,
  6½" h...68.00
Cake stand, blue, 9" octagon,
  6½" h...125.00
Cake stand, clear, 9" octagon,
  6½" h...70.00
Cake stand, clear, 10" octagonal.........72.00
Celery vase..44.50
Compote, open, 7" oval, amber...........58.00
Compote, open, 7" d., 5" h., canary.....47.50

Compote, open, 8" oval 50.00
Compote, open, 9" oval, high
  stand, blue 22.00
*Goblet, amber....................................50.00
*Goblet, blue 55.00
*Goblet, canary 60.00
*Goblet, clear....................35.00 to 40.00
Pitcher, milk, amber............................80.00
Pitcher, milk, blue 95.00
Pitcher, milk, clear 65.00
Pitcher, water, amber 60.00
Pitcher, water, clear............................48.00

Rose Sprig Plate

Plate, 6" sq., blue (ILLUS)...................45.00
Plate, 6" sq., canary 47.50
Plate, 6" sq., clear..............................27.50
Relish, boat-shaped, amber, 8" l.........35.00
Relish, boat-shaped, blue, 8" l............45.00
Relish, boat-shaped, canary, 8" l.........40.00
Relish, boat-shaped, clear, 8" l...........32.50
Sauce dish, flat...................................13.00
Sauce dishes, flat, sitz bath-shaped,
  canary, set of 4 ....90.00
Sauce dish, footed, amber 18.50
Sauce dish, footed, canary..................20.00
Sauce dish, footed, clear.....................17.50
Tumbler 39.00
Whimsey, sitz bath-shaped bowl,
  blue, 7 x 10"......................75.00 to 80.00
Whimsey, sitz bath-shaped bowl,
  canary, 7 x 10" 47.50
Wine..32.00

SAWTOOTH BAND - See Amazon Pattern

SHELL & TASSEL
Bowl, 7½" l., shell-shaped, three
  applied shell-shaped feet...................55.00
Bowl, 9" oval, canary 175.00
Bowl, 9" oval, clear 50.00
Bowl, 10" oval, amber..........................90.00
Bowl, 10" oval, clear 59.00
Bowl, 6½ x 11½" oval, amber 90.00
Bowl, 6½ x 11½" oval, blue................125.00
Bowl, 6½ x 11½" oval, clear.................50.00
Bowl, 8" d., cov., collared base,
  canary 120.00

Bread tray, 9 x 13"..............................55.00
Bride's basket, 8" oval bowl in silver
  plate frame......................................150.00
Bride's basket, 5 x 10" oval
  amber bowl in silver plate
  frame...............................250.00 to 275.00
Bride's basket, 8" oval blue bowl in
  silver plate frame.............................350.00
Cake stand, shell corners, 9" sq..........94.00
Cake stand, shell corners,
  10" sq. ....100.00 to 150.00
Celery vase, round, handled................90.00
Compote, cov., 4½" sq., 8" h. 45.00
Compote, cov., 5¼" sq. 60.00
Compote, open, jelly............................85.00
Compote, open, 6½" sq., 6½" h...........50.00
Compote, open, 7½" sq., 7½" h...........95.00
Compote, open, 8" sq., 7½" h..............56.00
Compote, open, 8½" sq.,
  8" h. ....50.00 to 55.00
Compote, open, 9½" d., 9" h. 90.00
Compote, open, 10" sq., 8" h...............70.00
Creamer, round....................................45.00
Creamer, square...................................60.00
Dish, 7 x 10" rectangle........................35.00
Doughnut stand, 8" sq., signed 225.00
*Goblet, round, knob stem.....55.00 to 65.00
Mug, miniature, blue...........................100.00
Oyster plate, 9½" d. ....225.00 to 250.00
Pickle jar, cov...................150.00 to 175.00
Pitcher, water, round.........150.00 to 155.00
Pitcher, water, square........................125.00
Plate, shell-shaped w/three
  shell-shaped feet, large 70.00
Platter, 8 x 11" oblong.........................52.00
Platter, 9 x 13" oval............................55.50
Relish, canary, 5 x 8".........................125.00
Salt dip, shell-shaped 18.00
Salt & pepper shakers w/original
  tops, pr..260.00
Sauce dish, flat or footed, 4" to 5" d. ...15.00
Sauce dish, footed, w/shell handle......15.00
Spooner, round ....40.00 to 45.00
Spooner, square...................................52.00
Sugar bowl, cov., round, dog finial 110.00
Tray, ice cream 125.00
Vase..................................155.00 to 165.00

SKILTON (Early Oregon)
Bread tray...32.00
Butter dish, cov., ruby-
  stained...............................90.00 to 95.00
Compote, open, 7" d.............................55.00
Compote, open, 8½" d., low
  stand, clear 24.00
Compote, open, 8½" d., low
  stand, ruby-stained 67.50
Goblet..33.00
Goblet, ruby-stained 75.00
Pitcher, milk, ruby-stained (ILLUS.
  top next column) 110.00
Pitcher, water, tankard, ruby-
  stained 115.00

Skilton Milk Pitcher

Spooner, clear 28.00
Spooner, ruby-stained 44.50
Sugar bowl, cov., ruby-stained............82.50
Tumbler, ruby-stained..........................41.50
Wine..32.50

SPRIG
Bowl, 7" oval 25.00
Bowl, 8" oval, footed 35.00
Bread platter, 11" oval.........................35.00
Butter dish, cov. 75.00
Cake stand 44.00
Celery vase..45.00
Compote, cov., 6" d., low stand 50.00
Compote, cov., 6" d., high stand..........90.00
Compote, cov., 8" d., low stand 76.00
Compote, cov., 8" d., high stand..........95.00
Compote, open, 7" d., low stand..........38.00
Compote, open, 8" d., high stand 39.00
Creamer...37.00
Goblet..33.00
Pickle castor, resilvered frame
  & tongs...85.00
Pitcher, water.......................................55.00
Relish, 6¾" oval 14.00
Relish, 7¾" oval 18.00
Relish, 8¾" oval 22.00
Sauce dish, flat or footed, each...........13.00
Spooner..25.00
Sugar bowl, cov....................................65.00
Wine......................................40.00 to 45.00

**SQUARE LION'S HEAD - See
  Atlanta Pattern**

**SQUIRREL - See "Animals & Birds
  on Goblets & Pitchers"**

TEARDROP & TASSEL
Berry set: master bowl & 5 sauce
  dishes; teal blue, 6 pcs. 200.00
Bowl, 7½" d..38.00
Bowl, 8¼" d..55.00
Butter dish, cov., clear (ILLUS. top
  next page)..65.00

Teardrop & Tassel Butter Dish

Butter dish, cov., cobalt blue.............**150.00**
Compote, cov., 5" d., 7½" h.,.............**85.00**
Compote, cov., 7" d., 11½" h..............**95.00**
Compote, open, 8½" d........................**42.00**
Creamer, clear.................................**45.00**
Creamer, cobalt blue.........................**125.00**
Creamer, Nile green ....**150.00 to 200.00**
Creamer & cov. sugar bowl,
   white opaque, pr. **175.00**
Goblet............................**145.00 to 150.00**
Pickle dish, amber.............................**90.00**
Pickle dish, clear **29.00**
Pitcher, water, clear...........................**70.00**
Pitcher, water, cobalt blue **225.00**
Pitcher, water, emerald
   green ....**250.00 to 275.00**
Relish...**35.00**
Salt shaker w/original top **125.00**
Sauce dish, clear...............................**13.00**
Sauce dish, cobalt blue **30.00**
Spooner...**50.00**
Sugar bowl, cov.................................**60.00**
Tumbler, clear...................................**37.00**
Tumbler, cobalt blue.............**65.00 to 75.00**
Water set: pitcher & 6 tumblers,
   clear, 7 pcs. **285.00**

THREE FACE
Butter dish, cov.,
   engraved ....**200.00 to 225.00**
Butter dish, cov., plain **190.00**
*Cake stand, 8" to
   10½" d. ....**160.00 to 165.00**
Celery vase ....**100.00 to 125.00**
*Champagne.....................................**165.00**
Claret, engraved **265.00**
Claret, plain.....................................**152.00**
Compote, cov., 4½" d., 6½" h. **100.00**
*Compote, cov., 6" d **125.00**
Compote, cov., 7" d **285.00**
Compote, cov., 8" d., high stand........**295.00**
Compote, cov., 10" d. **275.00**
Compote, open, 6" d., high stand **80.00**
Compote, open, 7" d., high stand **90.00**

Compote, open, 8½" d.,
   high stand.......................**100.00 to 115.00**
Compote, open, 9½" d., high
   stand, engraved **375.00**
Compote, open, 9½" d.,
   high stand, plain..............................**160.00**
*Cracker jar, cov..............................**1,250.00**
Creamer...**92.50**
*Creamer w/mask spout.....................**150.00**
Goblet, engraved **150.00**
*Goblet, plain........................**40.00 to 45.00**
*Lamp, kerosene-type, pedestal
   base, 8" h..**165.00**
Marmalade jar, cov. **225.00**
Pitcher, water....................................**550.00**
*Salt dip **44.00**
*Salt shaker w/original top **65.00**
*Sauce dish **30.00**
Spooner, engraved............**120.00 to 125.00**
*Spooner, plain **70.00**
*Sugar bowl, cov..............**125.00 to 150.00**
*Sugar shaker w/original top **155.00**
*Wine...**85.00**

THREE PANEL

Three Panel Mug

Bowl, 7" d., footed, blue......................**30.00**
Bowl, 7" d., footed, canary **31.50**
Bowl, 9" d., footed, canary **45.00**
Bowl, 9" d., footed, clear....................**22.50**
Bowl, 10" d., blue...............................**65.00**
Bowl, 10" d., canary **40.00**
Butter dish, cov., canary **50.00**
Celery vase, amber **47.50**
Celery vase, canary...........................**55.00**
Celery vase, clear..............................**35.00**
Compote, open, 7" d., low stand,
   amber...**32.00**
Compote, open, 7" d., low stand,
   canary **27.50**
Compote, open, 8½" d., low stand,
   blue..**40.00**
Compote, open, 9" d., 4¼" h.,
   amber...**40.00**
Compote, open, 9" d., canary **45.00**
Compote, open, 10" d., low stand,
   blue..**65.00**
Creamer, amber ....**30.00 to 35.00**
Creamer, blue **47.00**

Creamer, canary...................25.00 to 35.00
Creamer, clear 20.00
Cruet w/original stopper.....................155.00
*Goblet, amber......................................35.00
*Goblet, blue 42.00
*Goblet, canary.....................................40.00
*Goblet, clear 25.00
Lamp, kerosene-type, amber 145.00
Mug, blue, small (ILLUS.)....................40.00
Mug, clear, small 30.00
Pitcher, milk, 7" h.................................44.50
Sauce dish, footed, amber 17.00
Sauce dish, footed, blue......................19.50
Sauce dish, footed, canary.................15.00
Sauce dish, footed, clear....................11.50
Spooner, amber.....................................30.00
Spooner, blue 38.00
Spooner, canary 35.00
Spooner, clear......................................15.00
Sugar bowl, cov., blue..........................75.00
Sugar bowl, cov., canary......................65.00
Sugar bowl, cov., clear.........................55.00
Table set, clear, 4 pcs.......................175.00
Tumbler, amber 35.00
Tumbler, blue...40.00
Tumbler, clear.......................................12.00

Goblet, clear (ILLUS.)...........20.00 to 25.00
Pitcher, water, 7½" h.,
  amber ....60.00 to 65.00
Pitcher, water, blue..............................72.00
Relish, amber, 5⅜ x 9".........................22.50
Salt dip, master size, blue 45.00
Salt shaker w/original top,
  apple green......................................30.00
Sauce dish, footed, blue......................13.00
Spooner, amber.....................................38.00
Spooner, canary 35.00
Tray, water 25.00
Tumbler, ruby-stained..........................30.00

VIRGINIA - See Banded Portland Pattern

WAFFLE

Celery vase ....75.00 to 85.00
Champagne 140.00
Creamer, applied handle....................125.00
Egg cup 35.50
Goblet 95.00
Sugar bowl, cov...................................125.00
Tumbler, bar 95.00
Wine....................................115.00 to 125.00

WAFFLE AND THUMBPRINT

Waffle & Thumbprint Spillholder

Bowl, 6 x 8¼", flint 45.00
Celery vase, flint................100.00 to 175.00
Compote, open, 6" d., 6" h.,
  flint..................................150.00 to 175.00
Decanter w/bar lip, flint,
  pt. ....95.00 to 100.00
Decanter w/matching stopper, pt. 325.00
Decanter w/bar lip, qt. ....100.00 to 125.00
Egg cup, flint...52.50
Goblet, flint..94.00
Salt dip, master size, flint....................29.00
Spillholder, flint (ILLUS.) 100.00
Sugar bowl, cov., flint 195.00
Sweetmeat dish, cov. ....100.00 to 125.00
Tray, 8¼" l..66.00
Tumbler, bar, flint ....95.00 to 125.00
Tumbler, whiskey, handled, flint,
  3" h...275.00
Wine, flint 95.00

VALENCIA WAFFLE (Block & Star)

Valencia Waffle Goblet

Bread platter 30.00
Butter dish, cov., apple green.............55.00
Celery vase...30.00
Compote, cov., 7" sq., low stand,
  blue.....................................50.00 to 75.00
Compote, cov., 7" sq., low stand,
  clear 40.00
Compote, cov., 8" sq., low stand,
  clear 125.00
Compote, open, 6" sq., low stand,
  blue 30.00
Compote, open, 7" sq., low stand,
  amber...32.50
Compote, open, 7" sq., light blue.........55.00
Compote, open, 8" d., 8" h., amber 60.00
Compote, open, 9" d., high stand 65.00
Goblet, amber.......................................35.00
Goblet, blue 45.00

WASHINGTON CENTENNIAL

Carpenter's Hall Platter

Bowl, 8½" oval 21.00
Bread platter, Carpenter's Hall
　　center (ILLUS.) ....**100.00 to 115.00**
Bread Platter, George Washington
　　center, frosted ....**100.00 to 115.00**
Bread platter, Independence Hall
　　center 85.00
Bread platter, Independence Hall
　　center, frosted 95.00
Cake stand, 8½" to
　　11½" d. ....**55.00 to 75.00**
Celery vase...44.00
Champagne...68.00
Egg cup 39.00
Goblet 45.00
Pickle dish...34.00
Pitcher, water.....................................110.00
Relish, bear paw handles,
　　dated 1876 ....**30.00 to 35.00**
Salt dip, master size 60.00
Sauce dish, flat or footed, each...........10.00
Spooner...35.00
Sugar bowl, cov....................................72.50
Tumbler 58.00
Wine..48.00

WHEAT & BARLEY

Wheat & Barley Creamer

Bowl, open, 7" d....................................16.50
Bread plate, amber..............................30.00
Bread plate...........................30.00 to 35.00
Butter dish, cov....................................35.00
Cake stand, amber, 8" to 10" d...........44.00
Cake stand, blue, 8" d. 55.00
Cake stand, clear, 8" to 10" d. 38.00
Cake stand, 11½" d. 40.00
Compote, cov., 8½" d., high stand.......47.50
Compote, open, jelly,
　　amber ....25.00 to 35.00
Compote, open, jelly, blue 36.00
Compote, open, jelly, clear 25.00
Compote, open, 8¼" d., amber............65.00
Creamer, amber...................................45.00
Creamer, blue 55.00
Creamer, clear (ILLUS.).......................21.00
***Goblet,** amber ....35.00 to 40.00
***Goblet,** blue.......................................70.00
***Goblet,** clear......................................40.00
Mug, amber...........................30.00 to 35.00
Mug, clear 19.00
Pitcher, milk, amber ....55.00 to 60.00
Pitcher, milk, clear 45.00
Pitcher, water, amber 105.00
Pitcher, water, clear.............................53.00
Plate, 6" d...30.00
Plate, 7" d..21.00
Plate, 9" d., closed handles, amber......45.00
Plate, 9" d., closed handles, canary 35.00
Salt shaker w/original top, blue 38.00
Salt & pepper shakers w/original
　　tops, pr..38.00
Sauce dish, flat, handled, amber.........11.50
Sauce dish, flat, handled, clear 10.00
Sauce dish, footed, amber 12.00
Sauce dish, footed, clear....................11.50
Spooner, amber ....35.00 to 45.00
Spooner, clear 29.00
Sugar bowl, cov., blue.........................65.00
Sugar bowl, cov., clear ....35.00 to 40.00
Tumbler, amber 32.00
Tumbler, clear......................................20.00

WILLOW OAK

Willow Oak Pitcher

Bowl, cov., 7" d., flat **49.00**
Bowl, 7" d., amber................................**14.00**
Bowl, 7" d., blue.................................**47.50**
Bowl, 7" d., clear................................**35.00**
Bread plate, 9" d.................................**35.00**
Bread plate, 11" d................................**32.00**
Butter dish, cov., amber....................**65.00**
Butter dish, cov., clear **55.00**
Cake stand, amber, 8" to 10" d...........**61.00**
Cake stand, blue, 8" to 10" d. **65.00**
Cake stand, clear, 8" to 10" d. **35.00**
Celery vase, amber **45.00**
Celery vase, blue...............................**125.00**
Celery vase, clear...............................**48.00**
Compote, cov., 6" h...........................**75.00**
Compote, cov., 8" d. **65.00**
Compote, open, 6" d., scalloped
   top...**40.00**
Compote, open, 7" d., high stand **26.00**
Compote, open, 8" d., low stand,
   amber..**65.00**
Creamer, amber.................................**35.00**
Creamer, blue **65.00**
Creamer, canary **45.00**
Creamer, clear.....................**30.00 to 40.00**
Goblet, amber....................................**40.00**
Goblet, blue **36.00**
Goblet, clear ....**35.00 to 40.00**
Pitcher, milk, amber...........................**85.00**
Pitcher, milk, clear................**30.00 to 40.00**
Pitcher, water, amber (ILLUS.) **80.00**
Pitcher, water, blue............................**75.00**
Pitcher, water, clear...........................**48.00**
Plate, 9" d., handled, amber...............**38.00**
Plate, 9" d., handled, blue **47.50**
Plate, 9" d., handled, clear.................**35.00**
Salt shaker w/original top, amber........**40.00**
Salt shaker w/original top, blue **66.00**
Salt shaker w/original top, clear **28.00**
Sauce dish, flat or footed, each...........**10.00**
Spooner, amber..................................**35.00**
Spooner, blue **50.00**
Spooner, clear....................................**28.00**
Sugar bowl, cov..................................**41.00**
Tray, water, 10½" d.............................**32.00**
Tumbler, blue.....................................**65.00**
Tumbler, clear....................................**41.50**

**WOODEN PAIL - See Oaken Bucket
   Pattern**

X-RAY
Berry set: 8" d. master bowl & 6
   sauce dishes; emerald green,
   7 pcs. **155.00**
Berry set: 8" d. master bowl & 8
   sauce dishes; amethyst,
   9 pcs. **295.00**
Butter dish, cov., emerald green
   w/gold ....**100.00 to 150.00**
Carafe, large, emerald green
   w/gold **135.00**
Celery vase, clear w/gold **89.00**

Compote, cov., high stand, emerald
   green...**65.00**
Compote, jelly, clear **42.00**
Compote, jelly, emerald green.............**47.00**
Creamer, breakfast size, emerald
   green w/gold.....................................**60.00**
Cruet w/original stopper, emerald
   green w/gold **125.00**

X-Ray Pitcher

Pitcher, water, 9½" h., clear
   w/gold, ½ gal. (ILLUS.) **50.00**
Pitcher, water, 9½" h., emerald
   green, ½ gal......................................**65.00**
Rose bowl, emerald green w/gold **68.00**
Salt shaker w/original top, amethyst....**50.00**
Salt shaker w/original top, clear **18.50**
Sauce dish, clear, 4½" d.....................**12.00**
Sauce dish, emerald green, 4½" d. **22.50**
Spooner, emerald green w/gold **45.00**
Sugar bowl, cov., emerald green
   w/gold.................................**40.00 to 50.00**
Sugar bowl, cov., breakfast size,
   emerald green w/gold **65.00**
Syrup pitcher, clear w/gold **225.00**
Toothpick holder, emerald green **60.00**
Tray, condiment **37.50**
Tumbler, amethyst..............................**42.50**
Tumbler, emerald green **25.00**
Water set: pitcher & 4 tumblers,
   emerald green w/gold, 5 pcs...........**225.00**

(End of Pattern Glass Section)

PEACH BLOW

*Several types of glass lumped together
by collectors as Peach Blow were produced
by half a dozen glasshouses. Hobbs,
Brockunier & Co., Wheeling, West Virginia
made Peach Blow as a plated ware that
shaded from red at the top to yellow at the
bottom and is referred to as Wheeling
Peach Blow. Mt. Washington Glass Works*

produced an homogeneous Peach Blow shading from a rose color at the top to pale blue in the lower portion. The New England Glass Works' Peach Blow, called Wild Rose, shaded from rose at the top to white. Gunderson-Pairpoint Co. also reproduced some of the Mt. Washington Peach Blow in the early 1950s and some glass of a somewhat similar type was made by Steuben Glass Works, the Boston & Sandwich Factory and by Thomas Webb & Sons and Stevens & Williams of England. Sandwich Peach Blow is one-layered glass and the English is two-layered.

Another single layered shaded art glass was produced early in this century by the New Martinsville Glass Mfg. Co. Originally called "Muranese," collectors today refer to it as "New Martinsville Peach Blow."

GUNDERSON - PAIRPOINT

Barber bottle, satin finish $130.00
Bowl, footed, 5" d., 3½" h. 250.00
Champagne, 4¼" d., 5½" h. 350.00
Compote, open, 6½" d., 4¾" h. 350.00
Compote, open, 10" d., 5" h., ruffled rim, signed 350.00
Compote, open, 10" d., 7" h., pulled-up rim, signed 600.00
Nappy, triangular shape, w/applied milky white handle 175.00
Vase, cornucopia-type, 7" h., ruffled rim, satin finish................................450.00
Vase, 7½" h., jack-in-the-pulpit shape, enameled decoration 375.00
Vase, 9" h., lily-form 300.00

MT. WASHINGTON

Carafe w/original pewter top, overall h.p. floral decoration 500.00
Tumbler, satin finish, 4" h. 950.00
Vase, 7" h., glossy finish 300.00
Vase, 7" h., satin finish.......................300.00

NEW ENGLAND

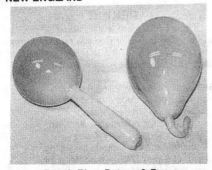

Peach Blow Darner & Pear

Bowl, 9½" d..250.00
Creamer, 2½" h..................................225.00

Darner, ball-shaped w/handle, deep rose pink shaded to white, glossy finish, 2¼" d., 6" l. (ILLUS. left) 135.00
Model of a pear, deep pink shades to white, glossy finish, 3" d., 5" l. (ILLUS. right) 135.00
Dish, leaf-shaped w/applied handle, 6½" d..350.00

New England Rose Bowl

Rose bowl, spherical, seven-crimp top, deep crushed raspberry color shading to off-white, satin finish, 2⅞" d., 2½" h. (ILLUS.) 300.00
Sugar bowl, open, marked "World's Fair 1893," 2½" h. 450.00
Toothpick holder 595.00
Tumbler, glossy finish, 4" h................395.00
Vase, square rim, two applied handles, glossy finish......................450.00

WEBB

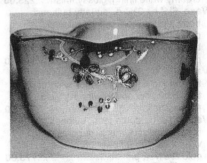

Webb Peach Blow Finger Bowl

Bowl, 4" d., 2¼" h., decorated w/gold prunus blossoms & pine needles & gold trim, white lining, satin finish......................................325.00
Finger bowl, three-lobed rim, gold prunus blossoms decoration on three sides w/small butterfly in each corner, 4½" d., 2¾" h. (ILLUS.)........260.00
Jar w/sterling silver cover, spherical squared body w/pinched-in sides, decorated w/a gilt floral sprig, hallmarked silver rim, inset cover & bail handle, 4½" h.........................172.50

Vase, 3⅜" h., 2⅝" d., pedestal footed squatty bulbous body w/short flaring rim, heavy gold florals & branches on front, gold butterfly on reverse, creamy white lining, satin finish **365.00**

Vase, 3½" h., 4" d., spherical form w/short cylindrical neck, decorated w/heavy gold prunus blossoms & leaves, gold butterfly on back side, gold band around top **345.00**

Vase, 3¾" h., 2¾" d., ovoid body w/short flared neck, gold prunus blossoms decoration, white lining, glossy finish **275.00**

Vase, 5" h., 3½" d., ovoid body tapering to a short cylindrical neck, heavy gold decoration of prunus blossoms, branches & bee in flight, creamy white lining **245.00**

Vase, 5" h., 3½" d., ovoid body tapering to a short cylindrical neck, decorated w/enameled branches of white flowers, gold leaves, two birds on branches in brown, yellow & orange, white lining, glossy finish **495.00**

Vase, 5⅛" h., 3¼" d., ovoid body tapering to a cylindrical neck w/flaring rim, overall decoration of silver flowers & heavy gold leaves, creamy white lining, glossy finish.....**295.00**

Vase, 5⅜" h., 3¼" d., spherical body tapering to a flaring, ruffled neck, decorated w/enameled white flowers & green & brown leaves, creamy white lining, glossy finish.....**225.00**

Vase, 6½" h., 3⅝" d., squatty bulbous body tapering to a cylindrical neck, decorated w/gold branches, prunus blossoms & a small butterfly, propellor mark **345.00**

Vase, 7½" h., 3⅝" d., bulbous body tapering to a tall 'stick' neck w/short flaring rim, decorated w/heavy gold florals & foliage, glossy finish...........**325.00**

Vases, 10" h., bottle-form, bulbous base w/tall 'stick' neck, decorated w/applied raised flowers & pears in gold & silver, pr. **775.00**

WHEELING

Cruet w/original stopper, 6¾" h........**1,200.00**

Pitcher, 4¼" h., bulbous ovoid body tapering to a flaring tricorner rim, applied amber handle, glossy finish **805.00**

Pitcher, 6" h., footed squatty bulbous body w/a short squared flaring neck, molded Drape patt., applied clear reeded handle, glossy finish (four potstone blemishes).......................**517.50**

Pitcher, 7¼" h., bulbous body w/quatrefoil rim, applied amber

handle, deep red shading to pale green, white lining, polished pontil (small factory imperfection bottom of handle).....................................**795.00**

Pitcher, claret, 9¾" h., tall conical body tapering to a short cylindrical neck w/a pinched spout, an applied amber reeded angled handle attached to a band of applied amber rigaree at the base of the neck (small scratch at side)...................**1,840.00**

Salt shaker w/original metal top, spherical footed shape, glossy finish, 2¾" h. **460.00**

Tumbler, glossy finish, 3¾" h............**400.00**

Vase, 3¾" h., 1⅜" d., bulbous body tapering to a short cylindrical neck **250.00**

Wheeling "Morgan" Vase

Vase, 8" h., "Morgan vase," tall ovoid body tapering to a slender ringed neck w/flaring lip, satin finish, no stand (ILLUS.)...................................**777.50**

Vase, 10⅝" h., bottle-shaped, spherical footed base tapering to a tall 'stick' neck.............................**977.50**

Vase, 11" h., stick-type.....................**895.00**

PEKING

This is Chinese glass, some of which has overlay in one to five colors, which has attracted collector interest. Peking Imperial glass is the most valuable.

Beakers, barrel-form, bright reddish orange body carved around the sides w/a pair of descending confronted foliate dragons flanked by large monster mask & ring handles, between lappets encircling the foot & pentant *ruyi* lappets at the rim, the underside inscribed w/a four character mark within a double square, Qianlong marks & period, 4⅛" h., pr. **$7,475.00**

Bowl, 6" d., rich egg yolk yellow body
skillfully carved around the exterior
w/three fan-tailed carp swimming
amid flowering & blooming lotus
stems rising from rolling waves
encircling the base, four carp
peering from beneath the waves,
Jiaqing **3,737.00**

Vase, 3⅝" h., bottle-form, overlay,
finely carved through layers of
ruby, sapphire, amber & pale green
to the opaque white ground w/a
rising sun, a bat, a pavilion & a
crane amid cloud scrolls above
wavesencircling the base,
19th c. **4,715.00**

Vase, 5½" h., slightly splaying ovoid
form, overlay, finely carved through
the yellow, ruby, emerald & sapphire
layers to the snowflake white ground
w/chrysanthemum, orchid,
cockscomb, begonia & epony stems
w/their respective leaves issuing
from layered or pierced rockwork
encircling the base, a dragonfly, &
insect, a bird & a pair of butterflies
overhead, 18th c. (hairline crack
to neck) **1,150.00**

Vase, 8¾" h., bottle-form, the swelling
rich amber sides incurving gently to
the tall cylindrical neck, the
underside incised w/a four
character Qianlong mark within a
square, 18th c. (footrim
ground) **3,105.00**

Peking Bottle-form Vase

Vase, 10¾" h., bottle-form, the deep
burgundy globular body surmounted
by a tall cylindrical neck, 18th c., tiny
chips (ILLUS.) **2,875.00**

Wine cups, brilliant egg yolk yellow,
inverted bell shape w/everted rim,
raised on a narrow footring, 19th c.,
2¼" d., pr. (one w/polished rim
chip) **1,840.00**

PELOTON

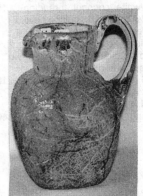

Peloton Pitcher

*Made in Bohemia, Germany and
England in the late 19th century, this
glassware is characterized by threads or
filaments of glass rolled into the glass body
of the objects in random patterns. Some of
these wares were decorated.*

Cracker jar, cov., deep pink squatty
bulbous embossed rib body
decorated w/white, blue, rose &
yellow "coconut" threading,
resilvered cover w/finial, rim & bail
handle, 7¾" h. to top
of handle **$1,170.00**

Pitcher, 6½" h., 3¾" d., squared
bulbous body tapering to cylindrical
neck w/pinched spout, clear applied
handle, clear w/pink, white, blue &
yellow "coconut" threading
(ILLUS.) **145.00**

Plate, 9¼" d., pink ground w/white
"coconut" threading.........................**125.00**

Two Peloton Vases

Vase, 3⅜" h., 2⅞" d., spherical cased
body tapering to widely flaring
ruffled neck, shaded lavender pink
w/white, blue, pink & yellow
"coconut" threading (ILLUS. left)......**175.00**

Vase, 5¾" h., 3" d., bulbous body,
pink w/white "coconut" threading **155.00**
Vase, 6⅞" h., 5½" d., bulbous ovoid
shouldered body tapering to
cylindrical neck, small handles from
neck to shoulders, clear body w/two
shades of green "coconut" threads
(ILLUS. right) **185.00**
Vase, 9½" h., double-handled, blue
ground w/white "coconut"
threading...**400.00**

PIGEON BLOOD

This name refers to the color of this glass, a deep blood-red. It was popular in the late 19th century and was featured in a number of mold-blown patterns.

Bowl, master berry, w/metal rim,
Torquay patt.....................................**$100.00**
Butter dish, cov., Torquay patt.,
clear underplate **295.00**
Creamer, Torquay patt......................**175.00**
Pitcher, water, Venecia patt.,
enameled decoration **300.00**
Salt shaker w/original top,
Bulging Loops patt. **95.00**
Salt & pepper shakers, Torquay
patt., pr...**195.00**
Sugar bowl, cov., Torquay patt. **225.00**
Sugar bowl w/metal cover, Torquay
patt...**100.00**

PILLAR-MOLDED

This heavily ribbed glassware was produced by blowing glass into full-sized ribbed molds and then finishing it by hand. The technique evolved from earlier "pattern moulding" used on glass since ancient times but in pillar-molded glass the ribs are very heavy and prominent. Most examples found in this country were produced in the Pittsburgh, Pennsylvania area from around 1850 to 1870, but similar English-made wares made before and after this period are also available. Most American items were made from clear flint glass and colored examples or pieces with colored strands in the ribs are rare and highly prized. Some collectors refer to this as "steamboat" glass believing that it was made to be used on American riverboats, but most likely it was used anywhere that a sturdy, relatively inexpensive glassware was needed, such as taverns and hotels.

Bar bottle w/pewter dispenser cap,
eight-rib, clear tapering body
w/applied collar & lip & cut-out
panels in neck, 8½" h.....................**$104.50**
Celery vase, eight-rib, clear,
elongated tulip-form bowl w/flared,
scalloped rim, applied pedestal &
round disc foot, 10¾" h. **104.50**
Syrup pitcher, cov., eight-rib, clear,
tapering cylindrical form, applied
hollow handle & collar, tin lid
w/pewter finial, 9¾" h. (wear)...........**412.50**
Syrup pitcher w/original hinged metal
lid, eight-rib, clear, footed bulbous
body tapering to a ringed neck,
heavy applied hollow strap handle,
10" h. (edge of base lightly
ground) **302.50**

POMONA

Pomona Tumblers

First produced by the New England Glass Company under a patent received by Joseph Locke in 1885, Pomona has a frosted ground on clear glass decorated with mineral stains, most frequently amber-yellow, sometimes pale blue. Some pieces bore smooth etched floral decorations highlighted with staining. Two types of Pomona were made. The first Locke patent covered a technique whereby the piece was first covered with an acid-resistant coating which was then needle-carved with thousands of minute criss-crossing lines. The piece was then dipped into acid which cut into the etched lines, giving the finished piece a notable "brilliance." A cheaper method, covered by a second Locke patent on June 15, 1886, was accomplished by rolling the glass piece in particles of acid-resistant material which were picked up by it. The glass was then etched by acid which attacked areas not protected by the resistant particles. A favorite design on Pomona was the cornflower.

Butter dish, cov., lid w/acanthus leaf
decoration, 1st patent, 8" d.,
4" h..**$540.00**

Celery vase, ruffled rim, clear applied
base, 1st patent, 6¼" h. **370.00**

Finger bowl, ruffled rim, 1st patent,
5½" d., 1¾" h. **220.00**

Pitcher, 7" h., blue cornflower
decoration, 1st patent **825.00**

Punch cup, blue cornflower
decoration, 1st patent......**150.00 to 175.00**

Tumblers, cylindrical, decorated
w/blue cornflowers, honey amber
leaves & honey amber tops, 2nd
patent, 2½" d., 3⅝" h., 4 pcs.
(ILLUS. two of four)..........................**135.00**

Vase, 5½" h., ruffled rim, clear applied
base, blue cornflower decoration,
1st patent **220.00**

ROSE BOWLS

Amber Nine-Crimp Rose Bowl

*These decorative small bowls were
widely popular in the late 19th and early
20th centuries. Produced in various types
of glass, they are most common in satin
glass or spatter glass. They are generally a
spherical shape with an incurved crimped
rim, but ovoid or egg-shaped examples
were also popular.*

*Their name derives from their reported
use, to hold dried rose petal potpourri or
small fresh-cut roses.*

Amber, Optic Ribbed patt., decorated
w/pink enamelled flowers, red
berries & green leaves, spherical
body w/nine-crimp top, 4¼" d.,
3¾" h. (ILLUS.) **$95.00**

Cased, pink hobnail exterior, white
interior, squatty bulbous body
w/eight-crimp top, 3⅞" d.,
3¼" h...**60.00**

Cased satin, rainbow mother-of-pearl
Diamond Quilted patt. exterior in

white, pink, yellow & blue, frosted
clear applied leaf tab feet w/berry
prunt, late 19th c., 5" h....................**110.00**

Cased satin, blue mother-of-pearl
Ribbon patt., white lining, spherical
body w/nine-crimp top, 3⅝" d.,
2¾" h..**245.00**

Cased satin, shaded blue decorated
w/enameled branch w/yellow buds,
lavender leaves & orange & blue
bird, egg-shaped body w/eight-crimp
top, applied frosted petal feet, white
interior, 4" d., 6¼" h. **135.00**

Cased satin, shaded pink, white
lining, decorated w/enameled blue &
white flowers w/peach scrolls &
foliage, spherical form w/eight-crimp
top, 4⅜" d., 4" h. **145.00**

Cased satin, shaded pink decorated
w/dainty blue & white flowers & lacy
gold foliage, white interior, applied
frosted petal feet, spherical body,
eight-crimp top, 4¼" d., 4¾" h..........**135.00**

Cased satin, heavenly blue
Embossed Swirl patt. exterior,
spherical body w/creamy interior,
eight-crimp top, 5⅞" d., 5¼" h..........**195.00**

Rubena Verde Rose Bowl

Rubena Verde opalescent,
cranberry opalescent to vaseline
ground decorated w/dainty white
enamelled flowers & gold scrolls &
foliage, spherical body w/eight-crimp
top, 4¼" d., 4" h. (ILLUS.) **75.00**

Verre Moire Rose Bowl

Verre Moire, Nailsea-style, opaque
white loopings against heavenly
blue frosted ground, egg-shaped,
eight-crimp top, 3¾" d., 4¼" h.
(ILLUS. bottom previous page) **165.00**

RUBY-STAINED

*This name derives from the color of the
glass - a deep red. The red staining was
thinly painted on clear pressed glass
patterns and refired at a low temperature.
Many pieces were further engraved as
souvenir items and were very popular from
the 1890s into the 1920s This technique
should not be confused with "flashed" glass
where a clear glass piece is actually dipped
in molten glass of a contrasting color. Also
see PATTERN GLASS.*

Berry set: master bowl & six sauce
dishes, Roanoke patt., 7 pcs. **$100.00**
Cheese dish, cov., Victoria patt.........**175.00**
Creamer, The Prize patt.......................**85.00**
Cruet w/original stopper, Scalloped
Six-Point patt. **250.00**
Decanter w/original stopper & serving
tray, Aurora patt., 10" d., tray,
the set **150.00**
Goblet, Block & Lattice patt. **52.00**
Mug, two-handled, Heart Band patt.,
souvenir **15.00**
Pitcher, tankard, Hexagon Block
patt...**125.00**
Pitcher, water, Horseshoe Medallion
patt...**175.00**
Pitcher, water, Pleating patt...............**120.00**
Salt & pepper shakers w/original
tops, Co-op's Royal patt., pr. **60.00**
Spooner, National's Eureka patt..........**45.00**
Straw holder, cov., The Prize patt.......**95.00**
Sugar bowl, open, Triple Triangle
patt...**50.00**
Syrup pitcher w/original top,
Truncated Cube patt. **260.00**
Table set: cov. sugar bowl, creamer,
cov. butter dish & spooner; High
Hob patt., 4 pcs...............................**185.00**
Table set, National's Eureka patt.,
4 pcs. **300.00**
Toothpick holder, Cut Block patt. **60.00**
Toothpick holder, Pleating patt. **75.00**
Toothpick holder, Rib & Bead patt. **55.00**
Toothpick holder, Summit patt. **195.00**
Toothpick holder, Truncated Cube
patt..**39.00**
Toothpick holder, Zanesville patt. **49.00**
Tray, Aurora patt. **55.00**
Water set: pitcher & six tumblers;
Hexagon Block patt., 7 pcs. **300.00**
Wine, Rustic Rose patt........................**20.00**

SANDWICH

Star & Punty Lamps

*Numerous types of glass were produced
at The Boston & Sandwich Glass Works in
Sandwich, Massachusetts, on Cape Cod,
from 1826 to 1888. Those listed here
represent a sampling. Also see PATTERN
GLASS and LACY in the "Glass" section.*

*All prices are pressed glass unless
otherwise noted.*

Candlestick, a deeply waisted
hexagonal socket above a ringed
columnar paneled shaft on a flaring
hexagonal foot, milky opalescent,
mid-19th c., 9¼" h. (minor
imperfections) **$460.00**
Candlesticks, petal-form socket
above a figural dolphin shaft on a
hexagonal foot, canary yellow,
mid-19th c., 9¼" h., pr. (chips).........**920.00**
Flat iron, toy size, cobalt blue,
ca. 1850-70, 1⅜" l., ⅞" h.................**259.00**
Lamps, whale oil, tapering cylindrical
paneled hexagonal font joined by
double wafers to the tiered flaring
hexagonal base, cobalt blue,
ca. 1850, 10" h., pr. (minor
imperfections) **1,725.00**
Lamps, whale oil, Star & Punty patt.,
paneled fonts attached w/wafers to
hexagonal baluster-form stems &
hexagonal feet, milky clambroth,
minor chips, 11" h., pr.
(ILLUS.)...**920.00**
Lamps, whale oil, pressed Four
Printie fonts on knobbed stems
w/wafer on flaring hexagonal foot,
amethyst, original pewter collars &
double burners, each w/single small
spall on side of base, one w/pinpoint
bruise, amethyst, 11¾" h., pr. **935.00**
Tumbler, Lutz-type, pink & white
candy stripe, milk white diamond
design lining, 3¾" h.........................**125.00**
Vase, 9¾" h., tulip-shaped on flaring
octagonal foot, medium amethyst,

trace of mold roughness under
base **880.00**

SATIN

Pink Satin Jam Dish

Satin glass was a popular decorative glass developed in the late 19th century. Most pieces were composed of two layers of glass with the exterior layer usually in a shaded pastel color. The name derives from the soft matte finish, caused by exposure to acid fumes, which gave the surface a "satiny" feel. Mother-of-pearl satin glass was a specialized variety wherein air trapped between the layers of glass provided subtle surface patterns such as Herringbone and Diamond Quilted. A majority of satin glass was produced in England and America but collectors should be aware that reproductions have been produced for many years.

Basket, applied thorn handle, white mother-of-pearl Diamond Quilted patt., rose interior, 7¼" d., 8½" h..**$795.00**

Bowl, 11" d., 5" h., 3⅝" d. base, heavenly blue overlay w/lavender shading on edge, decorated w/enameled white flowers w/pale green centers & gold branch, embossed border of wavy pattern 2" deep, bowl turned up at back, white underside...............................**325.00**

Ewer, bulbous stepped body below a slender flaring neck w/tri-corner rim, applied frosted clear angled handle, shaded rich pink enameled w/dainty pink & white flowers & gold foliage decoration, white interior, 4" d., 8½" h...**118.00**

Ewer, footed bulbous body tapering to a cylindrical neck w/flat flaring ruffled

tri-corner rim, applied clear rim & angular handle, Rainbow mother-of-pearl Swirl patt., white interior, 8½" h...**580.00**

Finger bowl, deep four-lobe form, deep rose red shaded to pale rose mother-of-pearl Herringbone patt., white lining, 4¼" d., 3" h....................**165.00**

Jam dish, ovoid body w/applied clear frosted shell trim around the rim, shaded pink decorated w/black incised designs of birds & berries, footed silver plate holder w/handle, 4" d., overall 6½" h. (ILLUS.) **165.00**

Perfume bottle w/original sterling silver screw-on bulbous top, lay-down teardrop-shaped body, light green decorated w/h.p. florals outlined in gold, 4¾" l......................**385.00**

Pitcher, 4¾" h., 4¼" d., bulbous spherical body w/wide cylindrical mouth, applied frosted reeded handle, heavenly blue embossed Swirl patt., white lining **175.00**

Plate, dessert, 6½" d., ruffled rim, deep peach mother-of-pearl Swirl patt., white underside.......................**175.00**

Rose bowl, bulbous body, three-crimp rim, wafer foot, rose red mother-of-pearl Ribbon patt., white lining, 2⅝" d., 3" h. **225.00**

Rose bowl, eight-crimp, shaded geranium pink mother-of-pearl Herringbone patt., 4¼" d., 3⅛" h..**310.00**

Rose bowl, squatty bulbous form, eight-crimp top, shaded lemon yellow Swirl patt., decorated w/enameled pink flowers, gold & peach foliage, white lining, 4" d., 3¼" h...................**135.00**

Rose bowl, 5" d., 4" h., footed bulbous base w/eight-crimp top, rainbow mother-of-pearl Rivulet patt., three applied frosted feet & applied frosted berry prunt on the base...................**695.00**

Tumbler, blue mother-of-pearl Raindrop patt., white lining, 3¾" h..**225.00**

Tumbler, shaded rose to white mother-of-pearl Coin Spot patt., white lining, 2⅝" d., 3¾" h................**100.00**

Vase, 2¾" h., 2⅞" d., ovoid body w/swelled rectangular-shaped top, frosted wafer foot, chartreuse mother-of-pearl Ribbon patt., white lining **195.00**

Vase, 5⅜" h., 3" d., ovoid body tapering to a fan-shaped neck w/crimped rim, chartreuse green decorated w/white lilies of the valley & gold foliage, clear frosted applied edge trim, white lining **135.00**

Vase, 13" h., footed slender ovoid body w/a crimped & ruffled rolled rim,

Tall Decorated Satin Vase

shaded pink mother-of-pearl
Raindrop patt., clear applied rim,
decorated w/white roses & leaves
around the base & colored leafy
blossom branch w/birds above
(ILLUS.) **1,650.00**
Vases, 7¼" h., 3⅜" d., ovoid melon-
lobed body tapering to a cylindrical
neck w/a flaring rim, shaded
heavenly blue decorated w/enameled
purple & blue violets & cream foliage,
applied frosted shoulder handles,
white lining, pr. **210.00**

SILVER DEPOSIT -
SILVER OVERLAY

Tall Silver Overlay Vase

*Silver Deposit and Silver Overlay have
been made commercially since the last
quarter of the 19th century. Silver is
deposited on the glass by various means,
most commonly by utilizing an electric
current. The glass was very popular during*
the first three decades of this century, and
some pieces are still being produced.
During the late 1970s, silver commanded
exceptionally high prices and this was
reflected in a surge of interest in silver
overlay glass, especially in pieces marked
"Sterling" or "925" on the heavy silver
overlay.

Card tray, clear w/silver overlay
design of a daffodil, 8" l...................**$30.00**
Relish dish, three-part, scalloped rim,
cranberry w/silver overlay of roses
& butterflies, 6" d..............................**45.00**
Vase, 12" h., slender slightly tapering
cylindrical body w/a flared base & a
short shoulder to the short wide
cylindrical neck w/a flattened rolled
rim, bright red w/opaque white
interior, overlaid in silver w/swirling
leaves & blossoms & centered by a
vacant cartouche, a silver rim,
Europe, ca. 1900 ....**1,265.00**
Vase, 14¼" h., tall slender baluster-
form body w/a flaring neck, dark
green overlaid w/tall stems of orchid
flowers centered by a heart-shaped
vacant cartouche, ca. 1900
(ILLUS.) **2,070.00**

SMITH BROTHERS

*Originally established as a decorating
department of the Mt. Washington Glass
Company in the 1870s, the firm later was
an independent business in New Bedford,
Massachusetts. Beautifully decorated opal
white glass was their hallmark but they
also did glass cutting. Some examples
carry their lion-in-the-shield mark.*

Smith Brothers Mark

Box w/hinged lid, melon-ribbed body,
white decorated w/h.p. pansies,
5½" d..**$385.00**
Cracker jar, cov., melon-ribbed body,
h.p. pansies outlined in gold on a
peach ground, silver plate cover,
marked, 6½" d., 6½" h. **400.00**
Cracker jar, cov., barrel-shaped,
creamy white ground decorated
w/h.p. daisies, silver plate rim, cover
& bail handle, signed **415.00**

Sweetmeat jar, cov., opaque white squatty melon-ribbed body & cover, decorated overall w/h.p. tiny blue flowers, silver plate rim & ball handle, signed, 5½" d., 5½" h. to top of handle **640.00**

Smith Double Pilgrim Vase

Vase, 7¼" h., 8" w., double pilgrim-style, two flattened round vases joined at the side & at the short cylindrical neck, creamy white ground decorated w/lavender wisteria blossoms traced in gold, gold beading at the top (ILLUS.) **1,220.00**

SPANGLED

Pink Spangled Bowl

Spangled glass incorporated particles of mica or metallic flakes and variegated colored glass particles embedded in the transparent glass. Usually made of two layers, it might have either an opaque or transparent casing. The Vasa Murrhina Glass Company of Sandwich, Massachusetts, first patented the process for producing Spangled glass in 1884 and this factory is known to have produced great quantities of this ware. It was, however, also produced by numerous other American and English glasshouses. This type, along with Spatter (see below) is often erroneously called "End of Day."

A related decorative glass, Aventurine, features a fine speckled pattern resembling gold dust on a solid color ground. Also see "Art Glass Baskets" under Glass.

Bowl, 8½" d., 3" h., wide shallow form w/one edge crimped & ruffled & the other pinched into two lobes & turned inward, cased shaded pink w/overall fine silver mica flecks, white underside (ILLUS.) **$165.00**
Chamberstick, baluster-form shaft w/a cylindrical socket & wide cupped rim, the flaring foot applied w/a wide clear crimped band, gold, maroon & green Aventurine cased in white, applied clear angled handle, 3½" d., 5¼" h. **75.00**
Chamberstick, baluster-form shaft w/a cylindrical socket & wide cupped rim, the flaring foot applied w/a wide clear crimped band, pink & green Aventurine cased in white, clear applied angled handle, 3½" d., 5½" h...**85.00**
Pitcher, 8" h., 5½" d., bulbous body w/six wide molded ribs & a heart-shaped pouring spout, silver mica suspended between double gather of clear & rose colored glass, applied clear handle, decorated w/hand-painted flowers & leaves, white lining, gold trim, patent dated 1883......................................**520.00**

Amber Spangled Tumbler

Tumbler, slightly tapering cylindrical form, amber Inverted Thumbprint patt. w/white spatter & silver mica flecks, 2¾" d., 3¾" h. (ILLUS.) **40.00**
Vase, 3⅞" h., 3¾" d., cranberry cup-shaped bowl w/applied clear embossed beads & clear stars w/berry centers, on clear applied

Two Ornate Spangled Vases

scroll feet, overall fine silvery mica
flecks (ILLUS. right) **150.00**
Vase, 5¾" h., 4¼" d., slender lobed
conical bowl w/upright crimped rim,
dark amber w/fine overall golden
mica flecks, on three applied looped
legs w/berry prunts at the top,
probably Thomas Webb,
England (ILLUS. left) **235.00**

SPATTER

Spatter Glass Jam Jars

*This variegated-color ware is similar to
Spangled glass but does not contain
metallic flakes. The various colors are
applied on a clear, opaque white or colored
body. Much of it was made in Europe and
England. It is sometimes called "End Of
Day."*

Cruet w/original stopper, shades of
pink & yellow spatter, white
lining **$325.00**
Jam Jar, cov., barrel-shaped w/ringed
rim & double-ringed base, squatty

rounded cover w/a clear applied leaf
finial, teal green w/controlled bands
of egg-shaped white spatter, white
lining, 3¼" d., 6" h. (ILLUS.right)........**75.00**
Jam jar, cov., barrel-shaped w/ringed
rim & double-ringed base, squatty
rounded cover w/a clear applied leaf
finial, golden yellow ground
w/maroon, white & pink spatter,
3½" d., 6½" h. (ILLUS. left) **80.00**
Jam jar, cov., barrel-shaped w/ringed
rim & double-ringed base, stepped
domed cover w/applied clear leaf
finial, maroon, yellow, green & pink
spatter w/bands of controlled white
egg-shaped spatter, white lining,
3¼" d., 6¾" h. **85.00**

Small Spatter Pitcher

Pitcher, 4½" h., 2¾" d., ovoid body
tapering to a cylindrical neck
w/pinched spout, molded Swirl patt.,
blue w/white spatter lining, applied
reeded blue handle (ILLUS.)..............**85.00**
Pitcher, 9" h., melon-ribbed body
tapering to a square rim, applied
clear handle, cranberry & white
spatter...**205.00**

Sunburst Spatter Pitcher

Pitcher, 9¼" h., 5½" d., footed

baluster-form body, molded
Sunburst patt., alternating wide
stripes of pink & white & yellow &
white spatter, cased in clear, applied
clear handle (ILLUS.) **135.00**

STEUBEN

*Most of the Steuben glass listed below
was made at the Steuben Glass Works,
now a division of Corning Glass, between
1903 and about 1933. The factory was
organized by T.G. Hawkes, noted glass
designer, Frederick Carder, and others.
Mr. Carder devised many types of glass
and revived many old techniques.*

Steuben Marks

ACID-CUT BACK

Acid Cut-Back Bowl

Bowl, 10" d., 4" h., wide rounded
sides w/a flat rim, Oriental patt.,
mirrored black Jade cut to stark
white w/a scrolling background,
fleur-de-lis mark on the base, shape
No. 5002 (ILLUS.) **$1,840.00**
Vase, 10" h., alabaster overlaid in
Jade green & cut-back w/a running
Greek key design at the rim &
dragons, flower, foliage & Chinese
characters on the body,
ca. 1920s **1,150.00**

ALABASTER

Bowl, 7" d., 4" h., squatty bulbous
body tapering to a wide short rolled
neck, creamy white lightly overlaid
w/lustrous gold Aurene & acid-
etched in a floral Chinese design,
shape No. 6283 (ILLUS. top next
column) **2,415.00**
Lamp base, the tall slender baluster-
form body w/a baluster-form neck
deeply acid-etched w/stylized florals,
raised on a scroll-cast openwork

Alabaster & Aurene Bowl

tiered round gilt-metal foot & w/gilt
metal lamp fittings, shape No. 2052,
glass 14½" h., overall 29½" h. **977.50**

AURENE

Aurene Cordial Cups

Ashtray, rounded tricorner form
w/three "spouts" at the rim, bright
gold iridescence, shape No. 7025,
autographed on the base "F. Carder
- Aurene," 4¾" w., 1¼" h.................**546.00**
Basket, ruffled crimped rim on an
unribbed base w/applied berry
prunts on the arched handle, gold
iridescent finish, signed "Aurene
455," 12½" h. **1,150.00**
Bowl, 6" h., squared form w/scalloped
rim, overall gold iridescence, etched
"Steuben" **322.00**
Cordial cups, round-bottomed
trumpet-form gold iridescent cups
fitted into elaborate pierced &
chased footed handled silver
holders, holders monogrammed &
marks, cup inserts unmarked,
2¼" h., set of 8 (ILLUS. of part) **805.00**
Lamp base, slender baluster-form
standard in smooth deep lavender
decorated w/gold Aurene trailed
threading in an overall random
design, mounted in a leafy gilt-metal
socket on a short pedestal & wide
disc base w/four scroll tab feet,

Threaded Aurene Lamp Base

electric lamp fittings at the top,
shape No. 8026, glass 10" h.,
overall 32" h. (ILLUS.)..................**2,990.00**

Punch bowl, deep rounded sides on
a small footring, brilliant gold
iridescence, shape No. 2852, signed
"Aurene 2852," 12" d., 4¾" h. **747.50**

Salt dips, gold iridescent finish,
shape No. 2660, signed, set of 6 ....**95.00**

Vase, 3½" h., bulbous ovoid body
tapering to a flaring galleried rim,
silvery gold iridescence, signed
"Aurene"...**402.50**

Vase, 5" h., waisted cylindrical form
w/a widely flaring gently ruffled rim,
bright pinkish red exterior w/gold
iridescent lines & stylized "peacock
eyes," the interior w/gold crackled
iridescence, signed "aurene
723"...**5,750.00**

Vase, 5½" h., footed lamp shade-style
trumpet-form w/ten fine ribs, overall
blue iridescent finish, signed
"Steuben"...**690.00**

Vase, 5¾" h., bulbous body w/four
deep indentations below the wide
cylindrical neck, overall silvery gold
iridescence, shape No. 158,
signed..**575.00**

Vase, 5⅞" h., the fluted floriform
vessel in Alabaster decorated
w/pulled feathering in ruby & gold
iridescence, inscribed "AURENE
548," ca. 1910.............................**5,175.00**

Vase, 6½" h., tree trunk-form,
tripartite w/three tree trunks on a
round base, overall gold
iridescence, shape No. 2744,
marked "Steuben - Aurene
2744"...**747.50**

Vase, 8" h., baluster-form body w/a
short, squatty bulbous neck tapering
to a flat mouth, olive green

iridescence shading to grass green,
decorated w/heart-shaped leafage &
undulating tendrils in rich amber
iridescence shading to silvery blue,
the interior w/amber iridescence,
signed "AURENE 255".................**4,025.00**

Vase, 8" h., flaring trumpet-form body
w/a wide angled shoulder to a short
neck w/rolled rim, silvery blue
iridescence, signed "Steuben -
Aurene 2144".................................**862.50**

Vase, bud, 8⅛" h., very slender stick
body on a round foot, overall blue
iridescence, shape No. 2556,
signed "Aurene 2556".....................**431.00**

Vase, 8½" h., 8" d., waisted cylindrical
body w/a widely flaring eight-crimp
ruffled top, overall blue iridescence,
shape No. 1952 variant,
signed "Steuben" **1,092.50**

Vase, 8⅞" h., baluster-form, gold-ruby
decorated w/gold iridescent trailings
& leafage, Alabaster lining, inscribed
"AURENE 270," ca. 1910.............**8,625.00**

Vase, 9½" h., trumpet-form, overall
blue iridescence, shape No. 2839,
marked "Aurene 2839"....................**920.00**

Vase, 10" h., 9¾" d., wide ovoid body
w/a broad shoulder tapering to a
short rolled neck, overall silvery blue
iridescence darkening toward the
edge, signed "Steuben Aurene
2683"...**1,265.00**

Vase, 12" h., wide ovoid shouldered
body w/a short neck & flattened
flaring rim, on a domed round foot,
the shoulders applied w/small S-
scroll handles, rich blue shading to
purple & gold iridescence, signed
"Steuben Aurene 6690" **1,035.00**

Vase, 14" h., footed ovoid body
tapering to a widely flaring short
neck, overall satiny gold
iridescence....................................**1,150.00**

BRISTOL YELLOW
Console bowl w/wide rolled edge,
optic design, applied clear feet,
signed...**175.00**

Goblet, black Jade reeding on lower
half of bowl, signed, 8" h..................**85.00**

Vase, 11" h., embossed Swirl Optic
design, shape No. 7001 ....**185.00**

CALCITE
Bowl, 10" d., 4" h., deep widely flaring
sides on a small round foot, white
exterior & gold iridescent interior,
shape No. 2851 ....**230.00 to 280.00**

Vase, 7" h., 7¼" d., waisted cylindrical
ribbed body w/a widely flaring six-
ruffle rim, Calcite exterior & gold
Aurene interior (ILLUS. top next
page)..**402.50**

Calcite & Aurene Vase

CERISE RUBY
Champagnes, swirl-molded bowl on a
  clear wafer stem & foot, set of 4 ......**100.00**
Compote, open, 7" h., embossed
  Swirl Optic design, clear stem,
  shape No. 6597 ....**325.00**
Goblet, clear twisted stem & foot,
  shape No. 6474, signed, 5½" h.......**125.00**

CLUTHRA

Broad Cluthra Vase

Lamp, desk, 7" d., 3⅞" h. domical
  yellow Cluthra shade w/white
  mottling interspersed w/bubbles,
  suspended in a gilt-metal harp
  above a knobbed disc base w/small
  button feet, silver "Steuben" fleur-
  de-lis mark on shade rim,14" h. **1,725.00**
Lamp base, Art Deco style, mottled
  bubbly green base w/decorative
  metal fittings & original finial,
  overall 21" h. **375.00**
Vase, 8¼" h., broad ovoid body w/a
  wide shoulder to the short rolled
  neck, cased clear & white w/overall
  bubbly inclusions, stamped
  "Steuben" on base, shape No. 2683
  (ILLUS.) **862.50**

IVRENE
Bowl, 10¾" d., 6" h., deep rounded
  sides w/a heavy rib at each side

continuing to a ruffled four-pointed
  rim, shape No. 7091 ....**295.00**
Lamp base, wide baluster-form body
  w/flaring neck, applied inwardly
  looped handles at the shoulder,
  w/original decorative fittings & finial,
  shape No. 6795, base 9½" h. **450.00**
Vase, 6" h., wide ovoid body w/a
  broad shoulder to the short rolled
  neck, shape No. 2683, signed on
  the base **805.00**

ORIENTAL POPPY

Oriental Poppy Vase

Perfume bottle & stopper, tall
  slender teardrop form on a disc foot,
  the shoulder tapering to a short
  flaring neck, pointed teardrop
  stopper, pale rose iridescent ground
  w/opalescent stripes, pale
  opalescent stem & foot,
  signed "547," 9⅞" h.......................**2,640.00**
Vase, 5" h., 6" d., broad ovoid body
  tapering to a short widely flaring &
  flattened neck, satin iridized surface
  on an opal-ribbed pastel pink
  ground, shape No. 6500
  (ILLUS.) **2,185.00**

TOPAZ
Bowl, 10" d., deep widely flaring
  rounded body on a small foot,
  shape No. 3200 ....**85.00**
Candlestick, ovoid candle socket w/a
  wide flat rim above a tall cylindrical
  twisted standard on a bulbous,
  domed foot, shape No. 6107,
  signed, 12" h. **165.00**

MISCELLANEOUS WARES
Candlesticks, crystal, a tall cylindrical
  socket w/rolled rim above a triple-
  knob standard w/a teardrop in the
  center knob, raised on a high domed
  flaring foot, signed "Steuben,"
  No.7746, 10½" h., set of 4 ....**1,495.00**
Model of a lion, crystal, the
  recumbent animal w/deeply carved

Crystal Model of a Lion

stylized details, on original walnut
rectangular stand & fitted red leather
& velvet case, designed by Lloyd
Atkins, figure 8¼" l. (ILLUS.).........**1,380.00**
Tablewares: nine champagnes, nine
goblets, nine wines, 12 dessert
dishes w/12 undertrays & four round
salt dips; crystal, the stemware
trumpet-shaped w/a teardrop stem,
No. 7737, set of 55 ....**1,840.00**
Vase, 11⅞" h., crystal, footed bulbous
body w/a wide flat rim, finely
engraved w/a stylized figure of
Circe, shells, a sailing ship & a
horse, designed by Raoul Dufy
engraved "Raoul Dufy - Steuben,"
ca. 1939 ....**9,200.00**

(End of Steuben Section)

STEVENS & WILLIAMS

Ornate Stevens & Williams Bowl

*This long-established English glass-
house has turned out a wide variety of
artistic glasswares through the years. Fine
satin glass pieces and items with applied
decoration (sometimes referred to as
"Matsu-No-Ke") are especially sought after
today. The following represents a cross-
section of its wares.*

Bowl, 12½" w. overall, 7" h., the wide
squatty bulbous body tapering to a
flaring crimped rim, shaded pink

opalescent decorated w/large
applied red strawberries & green
leaves on amber stems, applied
amber thorn handles & feet
(ILLUS.) **$2,475.00**

Stevens & Williams Striped Pitcher

Pitcher, tankard, 9½" h., 4½" d.,
slightly tapering cylindrical body
w/applied silver rim & spout, clear
body w/alternating wide stripes of
white & pale greenish yellow,
applied clear branched handle
(ILLUS.) **325.00**
Rose bowl, folded rim, pale coral
exterior decorated w/applied clear
acanthus leaf, rose interior, 4" h. **225.00**
Rose bowl, spherical satin glass,
box-pleated top, soft aqua shaded to
cream overlay, cream lining, ground
pontil, 5⅜" d., 4¼" h....................**195.00**
Vase, 8" h., four-lobed body, pink
w/applied flowers, signed................**150.00**

Large Rare Stevens & Williams Vase

Vase, 18¼" h., 7" d., bottle-form,
spherical base w/a very tall slender
'stick' neck w/flaring rim, Pompeian
Swirl mother-of-pearl satin exterior
in dark green & rose, robin's-egg
blue interior (ILLUS.)......................**895.00**

TIFFANY

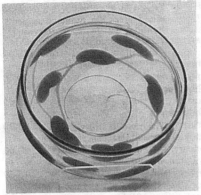

Tiffany 'Paperweight' Bowl

This glassware, covering a wide diversity of types, was produced in glasshouses operated by Louis Comfort Tiffany, America's outstanding glass designer of the Art Nouveau period, from the last quarter of the 19th century until the early 1930s. Tiffany revived early techniques and devised many new ones.

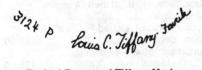

Typical Engraved Tiffany Mark

Various Tiffany Marks & Labels

Bowl, 3¼" h., round tapered sides, overall gold iridescence, signed "L.C. Tiffany Inc. Favrile" **$345.00**

Bowl, 6" d., footed, butterscotch opalescent ground w/raised diamond quiltied design, signed **575.00**

Bowl, 6¼" d., 2¼" h., 'paperweight' type, wide flat bottom w/upright sides in clear internally decorated w/heart-shaped lily pads in bright emerald green, signed "L.C. Tiffany Favrile 811 J" (ILLUS.) **1,322.50**

Bowl, 6¾" d., inverted bell-form, clear w/radiating green feathers, signed "L.C.T. Favrile - 387V," ca. 1920s **517.00**

Bowl, 8" d., ovoid form w/ribbed sides, overall gold iridescence, signed "L.C. Tiffany Favrile"............**690.00**

Bowl, 9" d., rounded sides, iridescent blue decorated w/silver-gold Egyptian chain pattern, inscribed "D766 - L.C.T. - Louis C. Tiffany," ca. 1895. ....**2,300.00**

Candlesticks, a bulbous socket w/a wide flattened rim raised on a tall slender swelled & ribbed hollow stem above a slightly domed ribbed disc foot, gold iridescent finish, signed "LCT Favrile 1825," 12" h., pr...**1,380.00**

Center bowl, low rounded sides lightly ribbed below the the slightly scalloped rim, orangish gold overall iridescence, signed "L.C. Tiffany Favrile," 9½" d., 3¾" h. **690.00**

Compote, open, 6" d., 3¼" h., wide shallow bowl raised on a short knobbed stem & wide disc foot, diamond quilted optic design w/pastel green interior & opalescent white exterior, iridized stem & foot, signed "L.C.T. Favrile" **690.00**

Goblet, wide cylindrical bowl swelled at the base & raised on a triple-knop stem above a domed foot w/disc rim, overall amber iridescence, signed "L.C. Tiffany - Favrile 3976K," ca. 1916, 9¾" h. **1,035.00**

Vase, 2⅛" h., "Cypriote," a small foot supports a wide low cushion body centered by a small rolled neck, decorated w/swirls of amber, pink & blue iridescence reserved against a deep bluish black ground, signed "L.C.T. - Louis C. Tiffany Favrile - E432," ca. 1896 ....**4,600.00**

Vase, 4¾" h., ovoid shouldered body tapering to a cylindrical neck, ten lightly molded ribs & small indented dimples around the shoulder, cobalt blue w/overall silvery blue iridescence, signed "L.C. Tiffany Favrile X89," experimental design **1,092.50**

Vase, 6½" h., 'paperweight' type, bulbous ovoid body w/a closed rim & tapering to a flared base, clear lightly tinted w/palest yellow, the upper half enclosing convolvulus blossoms & trailing leafage in shades of deep purple, puce, lavender, mustard, amber & lime green reserved against a gently shaded turquoise blue ground, signed "L.C. Tiffany Favrile 3309J," ca. 1915 (irregular hole in pontil) **48,875.00**

Vase, 7½" h., "Tel el Amarna," the waisted ovoid vessel w/bulbous neck in cased amber iridescent over white, the neck decorated w/a chain pattern in pale green & amber, inscribed "L.C. Tiffany-Favrile 8700G," ca. 1912 ....**2,760.00**

Rare Tiffany "Lava" Vase

Vase, 10" h., "Lava," squatty bulbous irregular base tapering to slender cylindrical irregular sides & a wide cupped rim, amber coated w/deep cobalt blue oxide & decorated w/a bold irregular spiral of golden iridescence, signed "L.C. Tiffany - Favrile 2336C," ca. 1908 (ILLUS.) **33,925.00**

Vase, 14¾" h., floriform, the bowl w/tall flaring & ruffled upright sides above a spherical base raised on a very tall slender slightly swelled stem above a wide low-domed foot, iridescent amber decorated w/pale violet & green pulled leaves, signed "L.C.T. - M3057," ca. 1900...........**7,475.00**

TIFFIN

Tiffin Glass Label

A wide variety of fine glasswares were produced by the Tiffin Glass Company of Tiffin, Ohio. Beginning as a part of the large U.S. Glass Company early in this century, the Tiffin factory continued making a wide range of wares until its final closing in 1984. One popular line is now called "Black Satin" and included various vases with raised floral designs. Many other acid-etched and hand-cut patterns were also produced over the years and are very collectible today. The three

"*Tiffin Glassmasters*" books by Fred Bickenheuser, are the standard references for Tiffin collectors.

Banana boat, Sandwich patt., (No. 41), milk white **$110.00**
Champagne, etched Byzantine patt., clear **20.00**
Champagne, Classic (platinum) patt., clear..**28.00**
Champagne, etched Fuschia patt., clear..**18.00**
Cocktail, etched Byzantine patt., clear..**20.00**
Cocktail, etched Persian Pheasant patt., clear, 3 oz. **15.00**
Console bowl, low, etched Byzantine patt., clear, 13" d. **35.00**
Cordials, etched June Night patt., clear, set of 4 ....**140.00**
Goblet, low, etched Cherokee Rose patt., clear **15.00**
Goblet, water, etched Flanders patt., topaz, 8¼" h.....................................**40.00**
Goblet, etched Fuchsia patt., clear **25.00**
Goblet, water, etched June Night patt., shape No. 17403, clear, 9 oz. **25.00**
Plate, torte, 14" d., etched Byzantine patt., clear **35.00**
Oyster cocktail, etched Fuchsia patt., clear **25.00**
Punch set: bowl & eight cups; Cascade patt., clear, 9 pcs. **195.00**
Rose bowl w/three ball feet, Copen blue, large, 1941-55 ....**65.00**
Sherbet, etched Cherokee Rose patt., clear **22.00**
Sherbet, etched Fuchsia patt., clear **22.50**
Wine, etched Cherokee Rose patt., clear...**35.00**

VASELINE

Vaseline Opalescent Vases

This glass takes its name from its color,

*which is akin to that of petroleum jelly
used for medicinal purposes. Originally
manufacturers usually referred to the color
as "canary." We list miscellaneous pieces
below. Also see OPALESCENT GLASS
and PATTERN GLASS.*

Butter dish, cov., blown & pressed,
cover embossed w/Inverted
Thumbprint patt. & underplate
w/pressed Daisy & Button patt.,
knob finial.....................................**$175.00**

Candlestick, pressed, flaring
scalloped base tapering to a ribbed
tapering shaft & tulip-form socket
w/ball trim, late 19th c., 3¾" d.,
5¼" h...**45.00**

Vase, 4½" h., 5¾" d., mold-blown
opalescent, spherical body w/a
widely flaring fluted rim, opalescent
scroll & flower design, polished
pontil, probably England, late 19th-
early 20th c. (ILLUS. right)...............**85.00**

Opalescent Swirl & Dot Vase

Vase, 5" h., 4" d., mold-blown
opalescent, bulbous flat-sided base
tapering to a wide cylindrical neck
w/a flattened widely flaring ruffled
rim, swirl & dot band opalescent
design, dimpled sides in base,
ground pontil, probably England,
late 19th - early 20th c.
(ILLUS.) **110.00**

Vase, 7¼" h., 4¾" d., pressed
opalescent, footed gently flaring
cylindrical ribbed body w/knobbed
rim, marked w/English registry mark
(ILLUS. left)....................................**135.00**

VENETIAN

*Venetian glass has been made for six
centuries on the island of Murano, where it
continues to be produced. The skilled glass*

*artisans developed numerous techniques,
subsequently imitated elsewhere.*

Bowl, 6" w., octagonal, golden amber
body w/twisted ball stem.................**$40.00**

Candlestick, hollow stemmed w/ball
connector, clear & cranberry
w/turquoise trim on foot, top &
bobeche **125.00**

Centerbowl, ribbed fan-shaped body
w/scalloped rim, sommerso blue &
clear internally decorated w/foil
inclusions, silky iridescent surface,
attributed to Ercole Barovier,
10" w., 5¾" h.................................**330.00**

Centerbowl, "Cordonato d'Oro,"
footed, scalloped rim, internal ribbing
w/gold twist design enhanced by
applied flared foot & blossoms on
each end, attributed to Ercole
Barovier for Barovier & Toso, 12" l,
7½" h...**247.50**

Console set: 16" d. bowl & a pair
10" h. candlesticks; Aventurine, the
wide shallow gently ruffled bowl
w/applied figural swan handles raised
on a short pedestal base, the
candlesticks w/deep flaring drip pans
centered by the socket & trimmed
w/applied gadrooning above a
tapering hollow cylindrical stem
w/applied gadrooning & flanked by
applied rings above a knob connector
on a slightly domed gadrooned wide
disc foot, all gold-flecked blush pink,
the set...**632.50**

Cups & saucers, "filigrana a retortoli,"
tall bell-form cup & widely flaring
saucers w/colored twisted vertical
ribbons alternating w/lacy white
ribbons, one set w/blue, two sets
w/pink, saucer 5" d., cup 3" h.,
set of 3..**345.00**

Model of a bird, aqua w/gold flecks &
controlled bubbles, 5" l.....................**27.00**

Model of a fish, w/paper label,
5½" h...**75.00**

Model of a swan, ruby w/dense gold
flecks in the wings & neck, 4" h. **35.00**

Model of a whale, solid frosted
sculpture w/controlled bubbles
throughout, w/partial Murano label,
10¼" l..**247.50**

Stemware service: 18 water goblets,
11 red wines, 8 white wines, 18
champagnes, 18 dessert plates & 18
finger bowls; in pale blue, the glasses
w/tall slender stems terminating in a
swirled knob enameled w/blue, green
& pink leaves, the conical bowls
enameled w/figures in 18th c.
costume, divided by flowering rose
garlands & standing rococo scrolls &
trellis, the circular bases w/gilt scrolls

Enameled Venetian Stemware

& roses, very minor imperfections,
91 pcs. (ILLUS. of part)................**4,312.00**

Venetian Champagnes

Tableware service: 12 champagnes,
12 goblets, 12 dessert bowls
w/underplates & 4 wines; each piece
w/shallow swirled bowls on a
knopped & tapering stem on a
swirled foot, clear Aventurine gold-
flecked w/applied prunts, 52 pcs.
(ILLUS. of part) **2,415.00**
Vase, 15¾" h., bulbous ovoid body
tapering to a short flaring neck,
cobalt blue w/internal bubbles, Ercole
Barovier, produced by Barovier &
Tosco, ca. 1964 ....**1,380.00**
Vase, 20¾" h., patchwork-style, wide
tapering cylindrical body composed
of large patches in random shades of
green, orange, purple, white, yellow
& blue w/internal gold foil inclusions,
in the manner of Fulvio Bianconi,
unsigned, third quarter 20th c. **5,175.00**

VICTORIAN COLORED GLASS

There are, of course, many types of

*colored glassware of the Victorian era and
we cover a great variety of these in our
various glass categories. However, there
are some pieces of pressed, mold-blown and
free-blown Victorian colored glass which
don't fit well into other specific listings, so
we have chosen to include a selection of
them here.*

Sapphire Blue Bottle

Bottle, w/original square cut sapphire
blue stopper, sapphire blue cut
square base tapering to a cylindrical
neck w/flat flaring rim, decorated
w/gold grapes & leaves,
2¾" d., 7¾" h. (ILLUS.) **$185.00**
Bowl, 9½" d., 4" h., sapphire blue
squatty bulbous form w/applied
amber rigaree around top, applied
amber drops on each side & applied
amber feet, decorated w/white
enameled sheep & baby lamb, white
fence, blue & white flowers & a
white & gold gazebo **295.00**
Creamer & open sugar bowl:
tankard-shaped creamer w/applied
clear handle & applied clear ruffled
rim, squatty bulbous, open sugar
bowl w/applied clear ruffled rim;
orange ground, 2¾" d., 4¼" h.
creamer, 5¼" d., 2½" h. sugar bowl,
pr..**165.00**
Decanter w/original pewter stopper,
footed bulbous body w/slender neck,
amber w/lacy embossed pewter
casing & handle, 4" d., 8" h..............**150.00**
Ewer, cushion foot supporting a
squatty bulbous body tapering to a
turned-down three-petal rim, applied
clear handle, cobalt blue decorated
w/gold bands w/blue & white
flowers, green leaves & garland of
pink & white flowers, 3¾" d.,
5½" h..**95.00**
Jar w/cone-shaped cover w/finial,
baluster-form w/deep shoulder &
short cylindrical neck, cobalt blue

heavily decorated overall w/gold bands & scrolls, 2¼" d., 4¾" h. **85.00**

Liqueur set: 9" h., 3½" d., baluster-form liqueur cruet w/original bubble stopper, four 1½" d., 2⅛" h. mugs & round tray; sapphire blue background w/white enameled flowers & blue leaves decoration overall, 6 pcs.....................................**265.00**

Pitcher, tankard, 8½" h., mold-blown Inverted Thumbprint patt., w/applied clear rope handle extending to encircle the rim **310.00**

Salt shaker w/original top, Challinor's Forget-Me-Not patt., pink opaque......**44.00**

Salt shaker w/original top, Clematis & Scroll patt., blue opaque on original glass stand, Challinor, Taylor & Co...**100.00**

Salt shaker w/original top, Fleur-de-Lis patt., blue opaque **32.00**

Sugar shaker w/original top, Acorn patt., blue opaque **135.00**

Sugar shaker w/original top, Challinor's Forget-Me-Not patt., opaque green..................................**150.00**

Sugar shaker w/original top, cylindrical-form, pressed Hobnail patt., amber.......................................**45.00**

Syrup pitcher w/original top, Forget-Me-Not patt., opaque blue **95.00**

Tumbler, cylindrical, clear w/irregular green threading, 2½" d., 3½" h. **55.00**

Unusual Frog Vase

Vase, 6" h., 5¾" d., cased blue Diamond Quilted patt., model of a frog w/clear legs climbing on a cased clear scalloped tree stump-shaped base, white lining (ILLUS.) **295.00**

Vase, 8⅜" h., 4⅛" d., lily-form w/flaring crimped rim, slender body sharply tapering to a clear wafer foot, alternating stripes of cranberry & amber separated w/white stripes in a swirling design **95.00**

Vase, 10" h., 4½" d., four thorny tree trunk-shaped vases joined together,

shaded pink opalescent to clear opalescent **195.00**

WAVE CREST

Baroque Shell Box

Now much sought after, Wave Crest was produced by the C.F. Monroe Co., Meriden, Connecticut, in the late 19th and early 20th centuries from opaque white glass blown into molds. It was then hand-decorated in enamels and metal trim was often added. Boudoir accessories such as jewel boxes, hair receivers, etc., were predominant.

WAVE CREST WARE

Wave Crest Mark

Box w/hinged lid, Double Shell mold, top & sides decorated w/tiny blue & yellow flowers & green leaves on an opaque white ground, 3" d. **$200.00**

Box w/hinged lid, wide spiral panels on base & edge of lid, center of lid w/a large oval reserve decorated w/a row of dancing storks, panels alternating pink & green w/dainty florals & scrolls, gilt-metal fittings, unsigned, 5½" d., 3½" h...............**1,150.00**

Box w/hinged lid, embossed scrolling top & sides, decorated w/roses on a blue background, 5½" oval **510.00**

Box w/hinged lid, Egg Crate mold, decorated w/two classical women, 6" d., 6" h. **800.00**

Box w/hinged lid, Baroque Shell mold, decorated on top w/pink daisies bordered by sky blue & all outlined in lavender, 7¼" d. (ILLUS.) **765.00**

Box w/hinged lid, Helmschmied Swirl mold, decorated w/h.p. florals, 8" d...**495.00**

Card holder, upright rectangular form w/embossed frame design, gilt-metal rim, cloth lining, decorated w/h.p. blue flowers & pink border.....**360.00**

Wave Crest Cracker Jar

Cracker jar w/metal lid, rim & twisted bail handle, smooth tapering cylindrical body decorated w/a large white & purple iris & green leaves on a cream ground bordered by scrolled panels of pale tan, unmarked (ILLUS.) **375.00**

Ferner, Egg Crate mold, decorated w/yellow wild roses, metal twisted rope rim, 7" sq.................................**650.00**

Humidor w/original brass cover w/finial & flaring base, bulbous tapering cylindrical body decorated w/enameled house & bridge scene **460.00**

Jardiniere, bulbous body tapering to a short cylindrical rim, body decorated w/h.p. mums & foliage, gold lacy trim on the rim, 9" d., 8" h...**550.00**

Salt & pepper shakers w/original tops, Helmschmied Swirl mold, opaque white ground decorated w/delicate white flowers w/yellow centers & green foliage, pr...............**485.00**

Spooner w/silver plate rim & loop handles, cylindrical paneled rib shape, decorated w/floral transfer..**285.00**

WEBB

This glass is made by Thomas Webb & Sons of Stourbridge, one of England's most prolific glasshouses. Numerous types of glass, including cameo, have been produced by this firm through the years. The company also produced various types of novelty and "art" glass during the late

Victorian period. Also see in "Glass" BURMESE, ROSE BOWLS, and SATIN & MOTHER-OF-PEARL.

Decorated Webb Satin Bowl

Bowl, footed squatty bulbous body w/deeply dimpled sides & a wide short cylindrical neck, shaded apricot satin decorated w/gold blossoms on brown branches, creamy white lining, 7½" d., 6¼" h. (ILLUS.) **$295.00**

Webb Cameo Perfume Bottle

Cameo perfume bottle w/silver rim & hinged cap, lay-down teardrop form, luminescent red overlaid in white & cut w/floral sprays on the front & back, cap w/scrolling monogram, 4" l. (ILLUS.) **977.50**

Cameo vase, 4¾" h., footed spherical body w/a small trumpet neck, bright red overlaid in white & cut w/a morning glory vine & blossoms, a butterfly at the back & linear borders, unsigned **1,035.00**

Potpourri jar w/hinged metal inner lid & ornate pierced domed outer lid, bulbous body in satin opal decorated w/a petal-form deep aqua border at the top w/gold fringe above a band of multicolored blossoms, attached brass base band w/three knob feet, 5½" h. **615.00**

Vase, 8" h., satin turquoise ground decorated w/a raised gold "snowball" on a leafy branch & three butterflies **550.00**

WESTMORELAND

The Westmoreland Specialty Company was founded in East Liverpool, Ohio in 1889 and relocated in 1890 to Grapeville, Pennsylvania where it remained until its closing in 1985.

During its early years Westmoreland specialized in glass food containers and novelties but by the turn of the century they had a large line of milk white items and clear tableware patterns. In 1925 the company name was shortened to The Westmoreland Glass Company and it was during that decade that more colored glasswares entered their line-up. When Victorian-style milk glass again became popular in the 1940s and 1950s, Westmoreland produced extensive amounts in several patterns which closely resemble late 19th century wares. These and their figural animal dishes in milk white and colors are widely collected today but buyers should not confuse them for the antique originals. Watch for Westmoreland's "WG" mark on some pieces. A majority of our listings are products from the 1940s through the 1970s. Earlier pieces will be indicated.

Early Westmoreland Label & Mark

Animal covered dish, Cat on lacy edge base, blue opaque w/glass eyes, copied from the Atterbury original ....**$150.00 to 175.00**

Animal covered dish, Cat on a lacy base, glass eyes, red & white slag, copied from antique original...............**70.00**

Animal covered candy dish, Dolphin, shell finial, milk white **37.00**

Animal covered dish, oval, cover w/full figural eagle w/wings out & three fledglings, glass eyes, Basketweave & Lattice patt. base w/beaded rim, blue opaque, 5⅞" w., 7¼" l., 6" h...........................**135.00**

Animal covered dish, Hen on nest,purple slag, copied from antique original, 7½" l., 5¾" h. **60.00**

Animal covered dish, Lion, blue opaque..**135.00**

Bowl, 10½" d., Paneled Grape patt., milk white **75.00**

Bowl, wedding, Rose & Lattice patt., milk white **48.00**

Candy box, cov., English Hobnail patt., opaque pink w/cranberry staining & gold trim, 11½" h. **85.00**

Candy dish, cov., footed, Swirl & Ball patt., milk white, 8" h..................**18.00**

Compote, 7" octagonal, Old Quilt patt...**15.00**

Compote, 12" d., Della Robbia patt., milk white, 1950s **90.00**

Creamer, English Hobnail patt., milk white **15.00**

Goblets, Della Robbia patt., colored trim, set of 6 ....**150.00**

Gravy boat & underplate, Paneled Grape patt., clear, 2 pcs. **50.00**

Model of a pig, "Porky Pig," clear, 3" d., 1¼" h. **24.00**

Pitcher, Della Robbia patt., colored trim, 32 oz. **195.00**

Planter, Paneled Grape patt., antique green, 4½" sq. **47.00**

Plate, 9" d., Della Robbia patt., colored trim **35.00**

Punch cup, Paneled Grape patt.,clear ..**8.00**

Salt & pepper shakers w/original tops, Della Robbia patt., colored trim, pr...**50.00**

Sugar bowl, cov., w/lacy edge, Paneled Grape patt., milk white.........**32.00**

Tumbler, Beaded Edge patt., clear.....**15.00**

Tumbler, iced tea, Old Quilt patt., milk white **12.00**

Tumblers, ginger ale, Della Robbia patt., colored trim, set of 5 ....**125.00**

(End of Glass Section)

GRANITEWARE

This is a name given to metal (customarily iron) kitchenwares covered with an enamel coating. Featured at the 1876 Philadelphia Centennial Exposition, it became quite popular for it was lightweight, attractive, and easy to clean. Although it was made in huge quantities and is still produced, it has caught the attention of a younger generation of collectors and prices have steadily risen over the past few years. There continues to be a consistent demand for the wide variety of these utilitarian articles turned out earlier in this century and rare forms now command high prices.

Berry bucket, cov., blue & white
   swirl...**$95.00**
Berry bucket w/tin lid, grey mottled,
   w/bail handle, large...........................**110.00**
Chamberstick, scarlet red...................**85.00**
Chamberstick, sky blue w/black trim...**65.00**
Coffeepot, cov., blue & white swirl......**95.00**
Coffeepot, cov., white w/red lid &
   handle...**45.00**
Colander, blue & white swirl...............**75.00**
Fish poacher, cover & insert, white
   w/blue trim...**65.00**
Funnel, grey mottled, 6" l....................**35.00**
Hot plate, gas, grey & white
   speckled, 8 x 8"................................**65.00**
Pitcher, milk, cobalt & white swirl......**140.00**

HEINTZ ART METAL WARES

Heintz Art Vase & Candlesticks

   Beginning in 1915 the Heintz Art Metal Shop of Buffalo, New York began producing an interesting line of jewelry and decorative items, especially vases and desk accessories, in brass, bronze, copper and silver. Their distinctive brass and bronze wares overlaid with sterling silver Art Nouveau and Art Deco designs are much sought after today. Collectors eagerly search for pieces bearing their stamped mark consisting of a diamond surrounding the initials "HAMS." Around 1935 the firm became Heintz Brothers, Manufacturers.

Boudoir lamp, the 7¾" d. domical
   bronze mushroom-form shade inlaid
   around the flaring rim w/a band of
   fine lines, wide U-form metal arm
   raised on a slender bronze base
   w/flaring foot, original patina, felt
   bottom, 10½" h............................**$1,045.00**
Compote, open, bronze, the wide

   deep bowl inlaid w/long delicate
   horizontal leafy flowers around the
   exterior, angled side handles, raised
   on a short pedestal w/a wide disc
   foot, rich brown patinated ground,
   die-stamped diamond mark &
   "1868D - STERLING ON BRONZE,"
   11½" d., 5½" h. **330.00**
Console set: 9¼" d. console bowl &
   pair 11" h. candlesticks; each piece
   w/silver floral inlay on a mottled
   green patina ground, die-stamped
   diamond mark, 3 pcs. (ILLUS.
   candlesticks, right)..........................**495.00**
Humidor, cov., slightly waisted
   cylindrical bronze body w/a low
   domed cover w/angled loop handle,
   the sides w/silver inlay of a fox
   hunting scene w/horses & riders &
   hounds, on a green & brown
   patinated ground, die-stamped
   diamond mark, 5½" d., 6" h.............**440.00**
Vase, simple cylindrical form, slender
   upright floral inlay on a dark bronze
   ground, die-stamped mark, 2½" d.,
   9" h. (ILLUS. left)............................**330.00**
Vase, tall cylindrical form swelled at
   the shoulder & tapering to a flaring
   neck, inlaid sterling silver tall
   cattails, original bronze patina,
   impressed mark & numbered
   "8798," 10¾" h. **431.00**
Vase, tall slender ovoid body tapering
   slightly to a short cylindrical neck,
   bronze inlaid w/delicate silver
   goldenrod plants, dark bronze
   ground w/original dark patina, die-
   stamped diamond mark & "3622A,"
   5½" d., 12½" h. **660.00**

HOLIDAY COLLECTIBLES

   For collectors Christmas offers the widest selection of desirable collectibles, however, other national and religious holidays also were noted with the production of various items which are now gaining in popularity. Halloween-related pieces such as candy containers, lanterns, decorations and costumes are the most sought after category after Christmas and other holidays such as Thanksgiving, Easter and the 4th of July have relatively few collectibles available for collectors. Also see CHRISTMAS TREE ORNAMENTS, EGG REPLICAS, and VALENTINES.

EASTER
Candy container, cardboard, chick
   w/spring neck, West Germany........**$35.00**

Candy container, composition,
chicken w/painted clothes, 4" h........**100.00**
Model of a bunny, china w/pin-
cushion egg, blue & white, 1¼" h.......**30.00**
Model of a bunny, sitting up on
haunches, painted features, bisque,
marked "Japan," 3" h. **35.00**
Model of a lady rabbit, molded
blouse, skirt & hat, fully painted,
bisque, Japan, 5" h. **65.00**
Model of a bunny, chalkware,
pushing buggy w/baby bunnies,
4½" h..**40.00**
Model of a chicken, hatching from
egg, relief-molded milk glass,
Victorian...**85.00**
Model of an egg, tin w/lithograph of
two children playing w/an egg, 2" l.....**60.00**

HALLOWEEN
Jack-o-lantern, papier-maché,
battery light-up type, 4½" d. **75.00**

Halloween Papier-Maché Lantern

Lantern, papier-maché, a howling
cat's head w/openings for eyes &
mouth, orange & black, some paint
chipping, early 20th c., 6½" w.,
7½" h. (ILLUS.) **60.50**
Noisemaker, "Safety Cracker,"
wooden, dated 1918, 3 x 6" **135.00**

HORSE & BUGGY
COLLECTIBLES

Bit, iron, w/models of doves on sides,
rawhide reins **$150.00**
Booklet, advertising, "Booth &
McCosker Buggies & Wagons" front
cover pictures a two-seater wagon &
back cover shows the Springfield,
Illinois factory **38.00**

Hitching post, cast iron, figural,
modeled as a standing black groom
w/one arm extended, old worn red &
black repaint, solid casting,
24½" h., plus wooden base..............**302.50**

Black Boy Hitching Post

Hitching post, cast iron, figural,
modeled as a standing black boy
wearing tattered clothes, one arm
extended holding a ring, on a thick
square base, old rusted silver paint,
small casting hole in torso, 46" h.
(ILLUS.) **3,300.00**
Hitching post, cast iron, figural,
modeled as a standing jockey w/one
arm extended, worn & rusted old
polychrome repaint, loose on a deep
rectangular base, late 19th c., 4' h...**412.50**
Hitching post, cast iron, figure of a
black jockey standing w/one hand
on his hip & the other extended, feet
apart, wearing cap, long-sleeved
shirt, vest & pants tucked into knee-
high riding boots, 4' h....................**1,380.00**
Hitching post, cast iron, a large
horse head w/ring in its mouth
raised on a reeded column w/a leaf-
cast band above the ringed foot, on
a square block base, 45" h. (crack in
base, pitted) **770.00**
Hitching post, cast iron, a small
horse head w/an open hexagonal
tube on top, resting atop a tall
slender reeded column above a
ringed base on a tall plain column,
5' 7½" h. (pitted w/rust) **1,100.00**
Hitching posts, cast iron, each cast
w/an eagle's head capital above a
slender baluster-form post cast
w/acanthus leaves above a baluster-
form base, 19th c., 43" h., pr.........**4,370.00**
Horse brasses, depicting a heart in a
circle, graduated set of four w/ring,
14" l..**49.50**
Lap robe, mohair, design of roses &
little foxes w/glass eyes **295.00**

Saddle, pony-type, J. C. Higgins..........**95.00**
Stirrup, brass, marked "E & T
Fairbanks & Co., St. Johnsbury,
VT.," 6" h...**32.00**
Wagon jack, wood & wrought iron,
19th c. **137.50**

Cast Iron Watering Trough

Watering trough, cast iron, deep
flaring oval form w/a molded ring &
flaring foot, on a thick rectangular
base marked "J. L. Mott, Iron Works
N.Y.," 19th c., 24¼ x 45½",
20⅜" h. (ILLUS.) **1,430.00**

HOUSEHOLD APPLIANCES

*Labor saving devices for the housewife
as well as appliances to improve the
quality of life of the American family began
to proliferate in the 19th century. The
introduction of electricity helped expand
the field even more and today early
appliances, especially electric models, are
increasingly collectible. Many serious
collectors search for early fans and toasters
in particular, but old coffee makers, steam
irons and vacuum cleaners also have
dedicated enthusiasts. All pieces listed are
electric unless otherwise noted. Also see
LAUNDRY ROOM ITEMS.*

Butter churn, electric-type, Sears **$65.00**
Can opener, table top model,
"Dazey," Art Deco style, red enamel
& chrome **25.00**
Casserole, cov., "Nesco," green &
cream enamel, 1933, works..............**45.00**
Coffee maker, "General Electric," Art
Deco style, red, black & chrome
w/separate heating element,
complete w/tags & instructions **45.00**
Fan, "Carleton," AC/DC electric, brass
blades & guard, 8" h. **600.00**
Fan, "The Portable Battery Fan Co.,"
battery-operated **1,800.00**
Ice cream maker, "Hamilton Beach
Iceless Freezer," w/original box,
marked, "Natl. Recovery Act,"
ca. 1934 ....**40.00**

Sewing machine, "Singer
Featherweight - Model 221,"
ca. 1952..........................**250.00 to 295.00**
Sun lamp, "Presto Electric Co.," a
wide chromed metal reflecting dish
w/a stylized zigzag wire guard,
raised on a stepped pyramidal metal
base cast w/a band of zigzags & w/a
bronzed finish, company medallion
mark, ca. 1930, 14" d., 20" h...........**172.50**
Waffle iron, "Universal," Art Deco-
style chrome w/grain design on
cover, overflow tray, Landers, Frary
& Clark **65.00**

ICART PRINTS

Winter

*The works of Louis Icart, the successful
French artist whose working years
spanned the Art Nouveau and Art Deco
movements, first became popular in the
United States shortly after World War I.
His limited edition etchings were much in
vogue during those years when the fashion
trends were established in Paris. These
prints were later relegated to the closet
shelves and basements but they have now
re-entered the art market and are avidly
sought by collectors. Listed by their
American titles, those appearing below
have been sold within the past eighteen
months. All prints are framed unless
otherwise noted.*

Cancan, 1933, 15½ x 24¾" (light
foxing, mat burned, minor edge
tears)..**$17,250.00**
Bathers (The), 1926, 17 x
20½"..**2,070.00**
Before Christmas, 1922, 9¾ x 14½"
(loose sheet, tear on upper
right side) **4,600.00**
Black Fan, 1931, 16⅛ x 20½" (age
darkened, laid down, glued to
mat)..**1,150.00**

Coursing II, 1929, 15 x 25", full
sheet **3,737.00**
Coursing III, 1930, 15⅜ x 25¼" (laid
down, glued to mat, finger
smudging) **4,025.00**
Dreaming, 1935, 18 x 25¾".............**1,955.00**
Eve, 1928, 14 x 19¾" (unframed,
glued to mat, minor foxing, slight
time darkening)..........**1,100.00 to 1,375.00**
Fair Dancer, 1939, 18¾ x 22⁵⁄₁₆" (laid
down, glued to mat, minor mat
burning)......................................**1,840.00**
Four Dears (The), 1929, 15 x 21½"
(laid down, glued to mat, time
darkening & foxing).......................**1,265.00**
Green Parakeets, 1920,
12¼ x 17⅛" **1,850.00**
Joy of Life, 1929, 15 x 23¼" (age
darkening, laid down, formerly glued
to mat)..**3,680.00**
Lilies, 1934, 18¾ x 27⅛" (laid
down, glued to mat) **4,025.00**
Little Thieves, 1926,
19½ x 25¾".....................................**927.00**
Montmarte I, 1928, 14½ x 21" (loose
sheet, small tear to top
center, discoloration top margin) ..**1,150.00**
My Model, 1932, 16½ x 21⅛" (loose
sheet, some time
darkening & soiling) **2,760.00**
Pink Slippers, 1936, 11 x 24⅛"
(laid down, glued to mat) **5,175.00**
Poem (The), 1928, 18¼ x 21⅞" (laid
down, two repairs, minor
crease, mat burn).........................**1,725.00**
Rain, The Shower, 1925, 14 x 18½"
oval (loose sheet, slight
foxing) **1,150.00**
Smoke, 1926, 14 x 19¼"..................**1,610.00**
Speed, 1927, 14⅝ x 25" (laid down,
formerly glued to mat, mat burn,
foxing, pencil marks in margin) **3,335.00**
Winter, 1928, 6¾ x 9", loose sheet
(ILLUS.) **1,035.00**
Zest, 1928, 14¼ x 19¼" (age
darkened, back paper burn, left
edge stained) **2,415.00**

ICONS

Icon is the Latin word meaning likeness or image and is applied to small pictures meant to be hung on the iconostasis, a screen dividing the sanctuary from the main body of Eastern Orthodox churches. Examples may be found all over Europe. The Greek, Russian, and other Orthodox churches developed their own styles, but the Russian contribution to this form of art is considered outstanding.

Icon of Christ Enthroned

Christ Enthroned, chased silver
oklad, Russia, ca. 1842, 10¾ x
12½" (ILLUS.) **$3,450.00**

Icon of the Crucifixion

Crucifixion, scene of Christ's
crucifixion, the corners painted w/the
Evangelists, Russia, ca. 1800,
17¼ x 21¼" (ILLUS.) **1,495.00**
The Dormition, Russia, 17th c.,
10¼ x 12¼" **1,380.00**
Kazan Mother of God, Russia,
19th c., 10¼ x 12¼" (ILLUS. top
next page) **920.00**
Kazan Mother of God, w/an
associated gilded silver oklad, by
Kozlov, Moscow, Russia, 1883,
9¼ x 11".......................................**1,035.00**
Old Testament Trinity, Russia, late
19th c., 12 x 14"...........................**1,035.00**
Resurrection and Descent into Hell,
a large central scene w/small
scenes of twelve Feast Days around
its edges, brown outer border bands
w/inscriptions & small figures of
saints in each corner, Russia,
19th c., 14½ x 17¼"......................**1,955.00**
Resurrection with Feasts, a central
scene framed by twelve Feast Day

Kazan Mother of God

scenes all within a dark gold border
band w/gilt inscriptions, Russia,
19th c., 10¼ x 12¼" **1,380.00**

St. John the Baptist, w/a gilded
silver oklad repoussé & chased
w/foliage & w/urns of flowers, by
Yegor Petrov, Moscow, Russia,
ca. 1785, 11 x 12½" l. **2,990.00**

Icon of St. Nicholas

St. Nicholas, silver oklad, by
Smirnov, Russia, ca. 1893,
10¼ x 12½" (ILLUS.) **2,300.00**

St. Nicholas Mozhaisky, the saint
standing holding a church in one
hand & a sword in the other, a
seaside landscape w/sailing ship &
church below & small figures of
Christ & Mary above, Russia,
19th c., 13½ x 15¾" **977.00**

St. Pantelemon, hagiographical-type,
a central scene of the saint framed
by 14 small scenes, Russia, early
19th c., 10½ x 15¾" **1,035.00**

St. Yerimin, three-quarter length
portrait w/a long scroll w/Cyrillic
inscription, Russia, ca. 1700,
14¾ x 20".....................................**1,725.00**

Tolga Mother of God, Mary & the
Infant Jesus against a white ground,
Russia, ca. 1700, 10 x 11¾" **3,105.00**

Vladimir Mother of God, w/a gilded
silver oklad, Moscow, Russia,
ca. 1900, 8¾ x 10½" **1,150.00**

INDIAN ARTIFACTS & JEWELRY

Jicarilla Apache Basket

Basket, Jicarilla Apache, deep oval
form w/terrace design in typical
faded aniline colors w/two coils
separated for handles, missing &
loose stitches, 15¼ x 22", 5" h.
(ILLUS.) **$88.00**

Basket, Winnebago, woven splint,
two-handled, nice patina, 5 x 8¾"......**90.00**

Book, "Fabulous Redman - The
Carlisle Indians," autographed by
the author, Jim Thorpe.......................**85.00**

Box, cov., Chippewa, quilled
birchbark, short wide cylindrical
form, the top decorated w/a red &
purple aniline thunderbird, fine
workmanship, Great Lakes region,
7" d., 2¾" h. (minor quill loss) **110.00**

Micmac Porcupine Quill Box

Box, cov., Micmac, oval, the oval bark
lid w/stitched porcupine quill
decoration in red, black, cream,
yellow & green geometric reserves
opening to a conforming interior also
decorated w/black, yellow, green,
red, cream & purple porcupine quills
in a herringbone patt., 19th c.,
3½ x 5½", 3" h. (ILLUS.) **483.00**

Concho belt, Navaho, silver squash
blossom-type, eleven sand-cast
conchos in silver w/matching buckle,

each set w/a high quality turquoise, on a black leather strap **357.50**

Cuffs, woman's, Sioux, beaded, faceted blues, red & gold on a white ground, ca. 1900, 12" l., pr. (small holes, minor bead loss)....................**203.50**

Doll, Navaho, wrapped splint body w/velvet skirt & calico shirt, painted facial features on cloth head w/black wool hair, glass beads & tin concho belt, early, 10" h. **148.50**

Knife sheath, possibly Great Lakes or Upper Plains, beaded & quilled leather, decorated w/red & green quills & a beaded edge, leather stained a dark color, sinew-sewn w/three tin cones & worn red horse-hair-dangles, probably early 20th c., 13½" l. (some quill damage) **412.50**

Moccasins, Northern Plains - Plateau, possibly Crow or Yakima, high-top beaded leather, yellow ochre-stained leather w/beaded floral designs in blues, greens, metallic, Cheyenne pink, red, etc., sinew-sewn w/brass button closures, 9½" l., pr. (small hole, some bead loss) **467.50**

"Indian With Headdress" Photograph

Photograph, "Indian with Headdress," platinum print on wove paper, signed by the photographer in ink & w/his copyright blindstamp on the image, matted, by Edward S. Curtis, ca. 1908, 11½ x 15⅞" (ILLUS.).....**4,313.00**

Photograph, "Red Cloud - Ogalala," large format photogravure, plate 103 from "The North American Indian," printed on Japan vellum, w/the letterpress title, plate number & photographer's copyright, printer's credit in margin, by Edward S. Curtis, 1905, matted & framed, 11¾ x 15½".....................................**5,463.00**

Pouch, Sioux, probably from The Standing Rock Reservation, Edith Claymore-style, beaded pictograph type, decorated w/a beaded horse in maroon & a bullhead in white, reverse w/multicolored floral design w/geometric edging, ca. 1910, 4 x 5½" (very minor bead loss, leather tassel missing) **247.50**

Rug, Navaho, serrate diamond design in dark brown, gold, red & grey on a natural ground, 32 x 47"................**715.00**

Rug, Navaho, Ganado area, Water Spider patt., composed of large diamonds in russet, natural, black & red on a carded grey background, ca. 1935, 37 x 61" (slight end wear, warp break) **385.00**

Rug, Navaho, serrate diamond designs in dark brown & tan on alternating grey & natural bands, red & dark brown border, 39 x 46" **385.00**

Navaho Storm Pattern Rug

Rug, Navaho, Storm patt., dark double-dye red, brown, natural & carded greyish brown, early 20th c., 42 x 62" (ILLUS.) **770.00**

Rug, Navaho, Klagetoh area, carded grey elongated lozenge w/red cross on a natural background, dark brown borders, ca. 1915, 42 x 77" (light stains) **605.00**

Rug, Navaho, central serrate diamond design flanked by zigzag lines & various geometric devices in faded red, brown, dark brown, grey & natural, 46 x 69" **495.00**

Rug, Navaho, Ganado area, bright red, dark brown, carded brown & natural triangular stripe design, edge lacing broken & a few warp breaks, ca. 1910, 53 x 79" (ILLUS. top next page)...**605.00**

Navaho Rug

Eye Dazzler Navaho Rug

Rug, Navaho, Eye Dazzler design w/bands of diamonds between sawtooth borders, worked in carded red, purple & orange w/dark brown & natural, red selvage cord, ca. 1900, minor end wear, small ink stains, 53 x 86" (ILLUS.) **770.00**

Santa Clara Wedding Vase

Wedding vase, Santa Clara, pottery, spherical body w/two slightly waisted cylindrical necks w/spouts, connected by a handle, black body deeply molded w/snake motif, signed on base "Teresita Naranjo," 8¼" h. (ILLUS.) **500.00**

IVORY

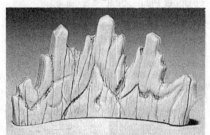

Rare Ivory Brushrest

Box, cov., ball-form, the panel-carved exterior w/a center hinge separating the two carved figural scenes, Europe, late 18th - early 19th c., 2" h. (drilled) **$632.50**

Brushrest, mountain-form, naturalistically carved along a curve w/five jagged peaks of varying heights, the smooth golden surface textured to resemble rockwork, 16th - 17th c., splits, 4⅞" w. (ILLUS.)......**2,875.00**

Figure of an infant in a sitting position, on an oval base, Europe, late 17th - early 18th c., 4¼" h. (age cracks) **460.00**

Figure of a doctor's lady, a well-carved nude woman reclining on her side, her head raised on her right hand, her left hand stretched across the body, her hair & face trimmed in black pigment, China, Ming Dynasty, 5¼" l., (dark patina & age cracks) **6,612.00**

Figure of Guanyin, the goddess seated on a rockwork base, resting her weight on her right arm leaning on pierced rockwork to the side, dressed in flowing robes, an elaborate necklace & a long veil over her high coiffure, the face w/delicate features, China, 17th c., 4⅝" h. (stained, splits)...............................**4,600.00**

Figure of an Immortal, depicted seated on a plinth, wearing long robes falling in folds around him, the rounded head w/grimacing features turned to one side & two top knots on either side of a central part, a *lingzhi* sashed to his waist on one side, China, 17th c., 5¼" h. (splits, chips) **2,875.00**

Figure of woman w/cats, female nude figure holding two kittens in her right arm while leaning over to pet a mother cat w/her tail curled around her legs, on shaped black marble base, ca. 1925, 10⅝" h. **1,380.00**

Prisoner of War-style Figure Group

Figure group, Prisoner of War-style, the group comprising of four standing women & a cradle holding a baby, behind a spinning wheel, below an intricate wheel mechanism that when cranked the figures & spinning wheel rotate, all set within a paper lined pine box w/ sliding top, probably French, late 18th c., some loses to string on spinning wheel, 4¼ x 6½", 2¾" h. (ILLUS.) **3,162.00**

Carved Ivory Triptych

Triptych, three-part, carved, depicting the Judgment of Solomon, Germany,

18th -19th c., open 8³⁄₁₆", 10" h. (ILLUS.) **2,530.00**

Knife & fork, the ivory handles carved w/female figures in naughty poses, steel knife & fork, Europe, 18th c., in a fitted case, 7" & 8" l., the set......**1,322.50**

Panel, flattened rectangular form, carved & pierced w/a pair of large soaring phoenix confronting over a rising sun supported on cloud vapors, amid scrolling clouds & beribboned auspicious symbols, all within a barbed frame, China , 18th c., 11⅞" 1. (tiny chips) **3,450.00**

Plaque, rectangular, portrait of a queen carved in high-relief, Europe, 19th c., 2¾ x 3¼" **862.50**

Plaque, round, carved portrait of George Washington, inset to a wooden frame, 19th c., 2¼" d. **690.00**

Ivory Stein

Stein, the tall slightly curved cylindrical body carved in high-relief w/a continuous battle scene w/knights, horses, etc., fitted w/silver embossed domed foot band, stepped & domed cover w/figural finial & an ornate scroll handle w/a figural caryatid, traces of gilt on the silver, silver marked w/a crowned "L" & "800," Europe, 19th c., some ivory damage, 15¾" h. (ILLUS.) **4,290.00**

JEWELRY

ANTIQUE (1800-1920)

Arts & Crafts Bar Pin

Bar pin, diamond & 14k yellow gold, designed as a scrolled foliate bar set w/rose-cut diamonds in a platinum-topped gold mount, marked "Black, Starr & Frost," Victorian **$575.00**

Bar pin, 14k gold & turquoise, centered by a row of turquoise w/bead & wire twist terminals, Victorian...**316.00**

Bar pin, moonstone & 14k gold, Arts & Crafts style, set w/three moonstones in a grape & vine mount (ILLUS.) **805.00**

Bracelet, bangle-type, diamond & 14k gold, centrally set w/a cluster of old mine-cut diamonds forming a blossom & flanked by four diamonds set in engraved starbursts, Victorian...**977.50**

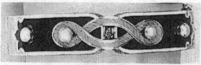

Gold & Enamel Bangle Bracelet

Bracelet, bangle-type, gold (14k), enamel & pearl, overall engraved w/red & blue guilloche center highlighted by four pearls, w/secret compartment, minor dent to one side, ca. 1840 (ILLUS.) **920.00**

Etruscan Revival Bangle Bracelet

Bracelet, bangle-type, gold (14k), Etruscan Revival style, in the archaeological style w/mythological animal head terminals accented w/wire twist & beadwork (ILLUS.) **4,600.00**

Bracelet, bangle-type, gold & enamel, the hinged bracelet centering a panel w/an enamel scene of ladies serenaded in a landscape w/mandolin player, the scene bordered w/black enamel & bright-cut gold inset w/seed pearls, late 19th c. **2,645.00**

Bracelet, coral, 18k gold, onyx, & diamonds, set w/angel skin coral

buttons, alternating w/round diamonds & square-cut onyx links highlighted by diamonds, marked "Fouquet," Edwardian **2,070.00**

Bracelet, gold, the yellow gold of braided mesh design, completed by a wire twist & beaded drop, Victorian...**460.00**

Bracelet, gold (14k) & citrine, a wide band of textured oval links, completed by a large beaded gold oval clasp set w/a large oval citrine w/eight small oval citrines around the edge, Victorian (prongs missing) **747.50**

Bracelet, gold (18k) & coral, two narrow strips of gold mesh centered by a large angel skin coral button in a gold mount, accented by wire twist details & completed by an oval clasp, Victorian **805.00**

Bracelet, gold, ruby, diamond & sapphire, the central head formed as a round textured gold crescent set w/a small ruby, diamond & sapphire, the crescent framing a spider web w/a silver spider to one edge, Victorian...............................**862.50**

Bracelet, pietra dura & braided hair, a large oval stone plaque inlaid w/a colorful perched bird & flying butterfly, framed w/an 18k gold chased scrolled framework on a wide braided hair bracelet, Victorian...**747.50**

Brooch, reverse-painted crystal, decorated w/the head of a dog, in a 14k yellow gold mount, ca. 1900 (minor solder).................................**374.00**

Brooch, garnet, ruby, emerald, diamond & 14k yellow gold, in the form of a butterfly set w/variously shaped garnets, rubies, emeralds & diamonds, the body & wings bordered in rose-cut diamonds, in a silver top gold mount, Portuguese hallmarks (solder) **2,520.00**

Arts & Crafts Brooch

Brooch, sterling silver, Arts & Crafts style, designed as two long overlapping oak leaves w/acorns & openwork scrolls to one side, centering an oblong piece of turquoise, attributed to Oakes, early 20th c. (ILLUS.).........................**805.00**

Agate Cameo Brooch

Cameo brooch, agate & gold (18k), two cameos of bearded men within wire twist gold frames & black enamel highlights, solder to clasp (ILLUS.) **1,092.00**
Cameo bracelet, carved lava, composed of six different hued 1⅛ x 1¼" cameos, each w/two full-figured classical ladies, bezel set in 14k yellow gold, ca. 1840 ....**1,850.00**
Cameo brooch, hardstone, depicting a classical bust of a woman within a half-pearl & 14k gold frame (solder)...**747.50**

Cameo Brooch

Cameo brooch, hardstone, depicting the profile of a classical figure in high-relief within a gold-filled wire twist frame, Victorian (ILLUS.) **431.00**
Choker, vermeil & clear *paté de verre* stones designed to resemble diamonds, five-strand, England, ca. 1870 ....**125.00**
Cross pendant, pietra dura, the wide pointed arms of the black cross inlaid w/a pink rose & white lily of the valley, w/a wide 14k gold pendant loop at the top, Victorian **575.00**
Cuff links, gold (18k), Art Nouveau style, designed as a curled griffin w/a leafy vine, accented w/ruby eyes, French hallmarks, pr. **632.50**
Cuff links, gold (18k) & diamond, Art Nouveau style, designed as an eagle's head centered in a scrolling foliate mount highlighted by a collet-set diamond, pr. **517.50**
Earrings, gold (14k) & enamel, a triangular loop suspending a wide oval hoop highlighted w/black enamel foliate tracery on a stippled ground, the hoop flanked by two slender urn-shaped drops, Victorian, pr...**805.00**
Earrings, gold (18k), designed as a half-sphere w/wire twist & beadwork overlay, Victorian, pr. **431.00**
Earrings, gold (18k yellow), Etruscan Revival style, designed as slender elongated classical urns w/squared loop top handles, accented around the rim w/wire twist, 19th c., pr. **2,990.00**
Lavaliere, diamond, platinum & gold, designed as an openwork pendant set w/round diamonds in a platinum top yellow gold mount, suspended from a fine platinum chain, Edwardian....................................**1,150.00**

Victorian Gold Bird Locket

Locket, emerald, ruby, diamond & 18k gold, the oval w/a pavé-set emerald, ruby, & diamond bird on a branch highlighted by small pearls, Victorian (ILLUS.) **862.50**
Locket, mourning-type, gutta percha w/tintype of a baby, geometric shape, 2½ x 3" **60.00**
Locket, mourning-type, water-color on ivory & gilt metal, the double-sided oval decorated w/a trumpeting angel before a monument inscribed "FAITH, HOPE AND CHARITY," w/three small children (ILLUS. top next page)....................................**2,070.00**
Necklace, black opal & gold (18k yellow), designed as a festoon

Ivory Mourning Locket

w/collet-set opals joined by a seed
pearl & a gold chain, Edwardian
16½" l. **3,165.00**
Necklace, cultured pearls, evenly
matched 7½ mm., 16" l. **475.00**
Necklace, garnet, set w/three rows of
faceted beads accented w/rosettes
in gilt mounts, Victorian, 17" l.
(some repairs).................................**546.00**

Victorian Gold Necklace

Necklace, gold (14k), a fancy link
bead & wire twist revival chain
w/elaborate wire twist locket,
Victorian (ILLUS.) **2,300.00**
Necklace, iron, composed of oval
scalloped frames w/applied figures
on a ground of polished steel, joined
by gold florets to floral iron links,
Berlin, Germany **1,495.00**
Necklace, turquoise & 14k gold, set
w/alternating large oval cabochons
of turquoise & small freshwater
pearls centered by a large heart-
shaped turquoise suspending a fine
chain w/a teardrop-form turquoise
drop, 14k gold mounts & chains,
ca. 1900, 23½" l. **1,380.00**
Necklace, turquoise & 14k yellow
gold, set w/turquoise beads
suspending knife-edge bars set

w/oval turquoise, on a fox link chain,
Edwardian, early 20th c. **402.50**
Pendant, enamel, tourmaline, pearls
& 14k gold, Arts & Crafts style,
designed as a festoon set w/green &
pink enamel flowers suspending a
pear-shaped pink tourmaline on a
gold link chain accented by collet-
cut pink tourmalines & freshwater
pearls, 18" l. **977.50**

Arts & Crafts Style Pendant

Pendant, sapphire, pearls & 18k gold,
Arts & Crafts style, designed as a
gold sphere w/foliate overlay
enhanced w/collet-set sapphires &
pearls, suspending tassels w/beads,
enhanced w/matching slide
(ILLUS.) **21,850.00**
Pendant, sterling silver & enamel,
Arts & Crafts style, on oval silver
frame w/inner rope twist band
framing an enameled galleon under
full sail in shades of blue, yellow &
red w/gold outlining, Boston School,
ca. 1910, 2⅛" l. **172.50**
Pendant, turquoise & diamond, an
oval turquoise drop surmounted by
two old mine-cut diamonds
suspended from an 18k gold link
chain, 17" l. **374.00**
Ring, amethyst & 18k yellow gold, a
long narrow amethyst cabochon
centering a wide gold band
w/stylized floral design, ca. 1900
(minor repair) **546.00**
Ring, bloodstone & 15k gold, an
octagonal bloodstone tablet within a
gold frame w/undulating engraved
designs down the sides, forms a
hinged compartment, Victorian **546.00**
Ring, cat's eye chrysoberyl, centered
by an oval cabochon in a 14k yellow
gold mount, ca. 1900 ....**431.00**
Ring, diamond, red spinel & platinum,
a center collet-set spinel flanked by

round diamonds within a diamond-edged platinum mount, Edwardian......................................**1,610.00**

Edwardian Topaz Ring

Ring, diamond, topaz & 14k gold, a rectangular clipped corner topaz weighing approx. 29ct., surrounded by a double tier of diamonds, in a gold & platinum mounting, Edwardian (ILLUS.) **5,750.00**

Ring, gold (14k), topaz & diamond, Arts & Crafts style, a navette-shaped top w/openwork leaf sprigs centered by a collet-set topaz & accented by seven collet-set diamonds, early 20th c....................**632.50**

Ring, pink sapphire, diamond & 14k yellow gold, a navette-shaped head centered by pink sapphires surrounded by rose-cut diamonds in a gold mount, Edwardian................**402.50**

Watch chain, gold-filled, swivel catch w/nine opals, 46" l...........................**100.00**

Watch chain & slide, gold-filled chain, fitted w/an 18K gold slide w/two pearls & one ruby, swivel catch, 46" l. **125.00**

Watch chain & slide, gold (14k) & enamel, a loop-in-loop fine chain mounted w/a large flaring shield-form slide w/a border of black enamel & a raised center bow accented w/small diamonds, Victorian, 59" l. **2,070.00**

Watch chain & slide, 18k gold, swivel catch, slide w/three pearls & one ruby, 10" l. **140.00**

SETS

Brooch & earrings: 14k gold, the brooch w/a large wide triangular plaque centered by an acanthus leaf & bead framed by rays of fine wire twist, the triangle suspending an angular bar suspending a row of fine tapering bar tassels, the matching earrings w/long narrow triangles w/similar trim & tassels, Victorian, the set (solder to back) **1,840.00**

Pendant & earrings, each in the form of a large round disc w/a pointed base drop, the disc inlaid w/a fine bouquet of blue flowers w/a foliate ground & red outline, in silver mountings, Victorian, 3 pcs...........**1,265.00**

MODERN (1920s-1960s)

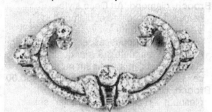

Art Deco Diamond Brooch

The bright sparkling jewelry so popular from the 1920s through the 1960s has again come into its own. The baubles of rhinestones (faceted glass with a foil backing), colored glass stones and faux pearls were affordable to a large segment of the population with prices ranging from very low—less than a dollar for a rhinestone dress clip—to well over $100 for a well-designed article utilizing sterling silver mountings with fine Austrian crystal. Some pieces were in excellent taste, resembling fine jewelry, while others were flamboyantly fake with a multitude of rhinestones interspersed with brilliantly colored glass stones.

Bar pin, crystal, onyx & diamond, Art Deco style, navette-shaped crystal w/an engraved foliate design within a calibre-cut onyx border edged w/round diamonds, marked "S. & Co."...**4,140.00**

Bracelet, Aurora Borealis rhinestones, marked "Weiss" **35.00**

Bracelet, Bakelite, bangle-type, carved rope design, brown, ⅜" w.......**35.00**

Bracelet, Bakelite, bangle-type, butterscotch, carved, ½" w................**45.00**

Bracelet, diamond & black onyx, Art Deco style, comprised of alternating diagonal rows of black onyx & old European-cut diamonds, in a platinum mount **7,150.00**

Bracelet, diamond & black onyx, Art Deco style, three openwork panels, each centered by a rectangular-cut diamond, highlighted by black onyx, joined by diamond-set rectangular links, in a platinum mount w/gold safety chain..................................**4,730.00**

Bracelet, diamond & sapphire, Art Deco style, flexible bracelet composed of square & round diamonds highlighted by sapphires (one synthetic), in a platinum mount, No. 3534, marked "Yard Inc." **8,800.00**

Bracelet, pearls, 20-strand, blue cabochon center stone surrounded by pearls & clear stones, marked "Ciner" **130.00**

Bracelet, rhinestones, individually set, four-row, marked "Weiss"............**40.00**

Brooch, diamond, Art Deco style, centered by a collet-set diamond in a semi-circle frame set w/seventy-two round diamonds, accented by half moon, baguettes & triangular-cut diamonds, in a platinum mount, ca. 1930 (ILLUS.).........................**3,450.00**

Brooch, diamond, sapphire & platinum, Art Deco style, circular, set w/round diamond & calibre-cut sapphires interrupted at either side by curved diamond-set lines centering a single diamond, in a platinum mount marked "J.E.C. & Co.," for J. E. Caldwell, No. K5609....................................**6,050.00**

Brooch, enameled flower w/rhinestones, marked "Staret," 2½ x 3⅛"..**750.00**

Brooch, flamingo under palms w/pearls in trees & bird, goldtone mount, 1¾" h..............................**45.00**

Brooch, gold (14k yellow) & citrine, designed as a leaf accented by six round faceted citrines, ca. 1940s.....**550.00**

Brooch, marquise & round amber-colored rhinestones, pavé setting, model of a butterfly, signed "Weiss," 2½"..**40.00**

Brooch, model of a leopard w/black & clear stones covering the silver metal body, marked "Kenneth J. Lane," 2½" l.......................................**90.00**

Brooch, painted Lucite, model of an umbrella **45.00**

Brooch, rhinestone, center flower of green & champagne teardrop rhinestones surrounded by large clear brilliant & marcasite stones, side pavé bow motif, 1950s, marked "Eisenberg".......................................**115.00**

Brooch, sterling silver, model of a sphinx, signed "Coro," 3" **175.00**

Clip, platinum & diamond, Art Deco style, set w/round & baguette diamonds in a pierced platinum mount marked "Cartier #03371, France," in a leather box.............**8,250.00**

Clip, Bakelite, model of an ivory-colored arrow w/set rhinestone edges **85.00**

Dress clip, gold (14k bicolor), Retro style, a long stylized leaf through a plain circle, a small ring of diamonds set in platinum at the top end of the leaf, marked "Lester & Co.".............**345.00**

Earclips, 17mm Mabe pearl within a double corded 14k white gold bezel,

retailed by J.E.C. for Caldwell & Co., pr..**935.00**

Retro Bicolor Gold Earclip

Earclips, sapphire & 14k bicolor gold, Retro style, accented w/an arrow of channel-set sapphires & diamonds, signed "Tiffany & Co." (ILLUS. one of two) **2,875.00**

Earrings, Bakelite, double hoop dangles, red, pr. **25.00**

Earrings, Bakelite, model of dice, ivory w/rhinestones, pr. **35.00**

Earrings, diamond, ruby & platinum, set w/mine-cut diamonds, each accented w/collet-set cabochon ruby, in platinum mounts, ca. 1930s, pr..**3,850.00**

Earrings, large clear stone, clip-style, ca. 1935, marked "Eisenberg," pr. **60.00**

Earrings, marquise & round rhinestones, pavé setting, signed "Eisenberg Ice," pr. **34.00**

Earrings, onyx, diamond & platinum, Art Deco style, geometric plaques surmounted by a diamond & platinum bar & onyx top, pr. **4,290.00**

Earrings, rose gold, pearl & diamond, an open wire flower design accented w/diamonds suspending two diamond & cultured pearl tassels, ca. 1940s, pr. **1,100.00**

Necklace, choker-type, sterling silver w/chalcedony & marcasite, ca. 1930, Germany **155.00**

Necklace, Bakelite, three large carved beads, ivory....................**22.00**

Necklace, Bakelite & brass filigree rounds, varicolored loops, 20" l..........**65.00**

Necklace, faux pearls, two-strands, marked "M. Haskell"..........................**65.00**

Necklace, gold (14k), Retro style, a flat narrow band of fine brickwork w/a buckle terminal accented w/small channel-set rubies & diamonds, 16" l. **1,725.00**

Necklace, rhinestones & pearls, marked "Weiss"................................**30.00**

Pendant, jade & diamond, Art Deco style, a pierced jade plaque approximately 31 x 47mm

suspended from a diamond-set
platinum filigree chain highlighted
w/black enamel **7,150.00**
Pin, Bakelite, cherries on log................**75.00**
Pin, Bakelite, geometric-shaped bow,
red & white rhinestone-set bar...........**65.00**
Pin, Bakelite, large carved flower &
leaves, custard..................................**85.00**
Pin, blue & clear rhinestones, model
of a crown, marked "Castlecliff" **115.00**
Pin, diamond & emerald, Art Deco
style, a black enamel rod
suspending carved emerald beads
w/collet-set diamonds, centered by
an emerald carved leaf within a
diamond frame (some enamel
loss) **3,080.00**
Pin, gold-filled, model of a flower,
signed "Van Dell," 3" **30.00**
Pin, gold-plated, large central pearl
surrounded by seed pearls, marked
"Miriam Haskell"...............................**200.00**
Pin, goldtone, model of a bunny head
w/bow tie, covered w/stones,
marked "Weiss," 1¾" h. **75.00**
Pin, novelty, "Kilroy," 1940s, w/3 x 4"
illustrated card **15.00**
Pin, sapphire blue rhinestones
w/black metal backing, model of
a butterfly, marked "Weiss"................**48.00**
Pin, sterling silver, model of a bow,
marked "Hobe" **26.00**
Pin, sterling silver & red enamel,
model of a boy, signed "Vogue".........**80.00**
Pin, sterling silver, modeled in the
form of a round-bodied bird in flight,
marked "Georg Jensen," No. 320,
ca. 1920 ....**385.00**

SETS
Bracelet & earrings: pearls, three-
strand bracelet; marked "Miriam
Haskell," 3 pcs. **205.00**

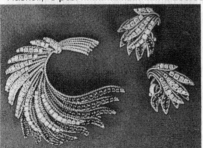

French Brooch & Earring Set

Brooch & earrings, gold (18k),
diamond & emerald, the brooch
designed as a spray set w/eighty-
nine diamonds & emeralds w/a wire
twist mount, together w/matching
earrings, set w/forty-two diamonds &
emeralds, signed by Van Cleef &
Arpels, French hallmarks,
ca. 1960s (ILLUS.) **9,200.00**
Necklace & earrings, blue stones &
pearls, marked "Lisner," 3 pcs. **25.00**

JUKE BOXES

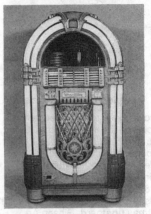

Wurlitzer Model 1015

John Gabel Entertainment, Art Deco
style, Chicago, Illinois, 24 plays, 78
rpm records, original mint condition,
electronics restored **$3,500.00**
Rock-Ola Model 1426, 1947
(restored) **5,525.00**
Rock-Ola Model 1455, 1957 ....**995.00**
Seeburg Model C, w/records
(restored, w/new chrome) **2,995.00**
Wurlitzer Model 61, table model **5,500.00**
Wurlitzer Model 750, 1941
(restored) **7,800.00**
Wurlitzer Model 1015, 1946-47
(ILLUS.) **9,200.00**
Wurlitzer Model 1080 (Colonial/Mae
West), 1947 ....**8,600.00**
Wurlitzer Model 2200-2204,
1958..**4,500.00**

KEWPIE COLLECTIBLES

*Rose O'Neill's Kewpies were so popular
in their heyday that numerous objects
depicting them were produced and are now
collectible. The following represents a
sampling.*

Advertisement, "Kewpie Pie,"
posterboard, yellow & cream
background w/blue, cream & brown
lettering, 9½ x 18½"
(ILLUS. top next page)....................**$93.50**

Kewpie Pie Advertisement

Box, cov., china, round, three action Kewpies on the lid, marked "J. C. Bavaria" 125.00

Cake plate, china, scalloped rim & molded edge handles, decorated w/colored transfer-printed Kewpies, gold & orchid accents, Germany, 1920s, 9¼" d. 230.00

Christmas postcard, Gibson Art Co., authorized by Rose O'Neill, 1920s 35.00

Creamer, jasper ware, blue ground w/white relief Kewpies, three in joyous floating position on one side, four on other, floral border around rim & under handle, butterflies in background, signed "Rose O'Neill," 5 oz., Germany 125.00

Counter display figure, cardboard, stand-up type, Kewpie Santa Claus, signed "Rose O'Neill," dated "1913," 12" h..45.00

Figure, bisque, Kewpie guitar player, signed "Rose O'Neill," 3½" h............300.00

Figure, bisque, "Little Traveler," beautiful coloring & details, incised "Germany" & original paper label.....275.00

Figure, bisque, Kewpie sitting & playing a mandolin, copyright mark........160.00

Figure, bisque, "The Thinker," signed "Rose O'Neill," 6" h. 600.00

Figure, chalkware, carnival-type, 12" h..65.00

Plate, china, depicts Kewpies playing leap frog, Royal Rudolstadt............100.00

Print, "Love is a Cozy Thing," framed, artist-signed, 21 x 25" 85.00

KITCHENWARES

Aebleskiver pan, cast iron, "Griswold No. 32," round...............................$47.50

Goodell Cherry Pitter

Apple butter stirrer, wood, long slender handle attached to broad paddle, old dark patina, 74" l. 38.50

Apple parer, cast iron, marked "Turntable 98," made by Goodell Co., Antrim, New Hampshire, 1898 patent date.......................................69.00

Apple parer, White Mountain, Goodell Co., mint in original box w/instructions, 1940s 43.00

Batter jug w/original lid, Jadite green glass, Jeanette Glass Co.......200.00

Bowl, soup, 7⅝" d., glass, Jane Ray patt., Jadite 14.00

Bread maker, tin w/clamp lid, "Universal #4," w/original directions...55.00

Breadstick pan, cast iron, "Griswold No. 23"...85.00

Bundt pan, cast iron, "Frank Hay No. 965," made by Griswold...................300.00

Butter churn, "Dazey," glass, 5 qt. 100.00

Butter churn, rocking-type, painted pine, 12½ x 34", box on legs w/attached rockers, old red paint, overall 31½" h. 275.00

Canister w/screw-on lid, glass, "Coffee," Skokie Green, McKee Glass Co., 48 oz. 128.00

Can opener, cast iron, figural bull's head & tail, 6¼" l.............................65.00

Cherry pitter, cast iron, "Goodell Co., Antrim, N.H., U.S.A.," clamp-on model, 1895 patent, 6¾" l. (ILLUS.)...47.50

Cookie cutter, tin, roller-type, six different patterns, wooden handle, 4" d., 9" l...110.00

Cookie mold, cast iron, basket w/leaves & grape hyacinth design, ca. 1830, Albany foundry, 4 x 6" oval 165.00

Cork press, "Enterprise No. 1," patent-dated 1867.............................65.00

Corn bread pan, cast iron, "Griswold
Model F"..**75.00**
Cornstick pan, cast iron, "Griswold
No. 262," miniature **97.50**
Cup & saucer, glass, Jane Ray patt.,
Jadite, Fire King................................**3.50**
Custard baking cup, glass, Jane
Ray patt., Jadite, Fire King **2.50**
Dutch oven, cov., cast iron, "Griswold
No. 8"...**79.00**
Dutch oven, cov., cast iron, "Griswold
No. 10" **105.00**
Dutch oven, cov., cast iron,
"Wagnerware No. 9" **40.00**
Food grinder, cast iron, "Griswold
No. 10" **18.00**
Fruit auger, "Sugar Devil," turned
wooden handle, patent-dated July
27, 1875, 10" d., 16" l.....................**110.00**
Griddle, cast iron, round, "Griswold
No. 8," **45.00**
Griddle w/bail handle, round, cast
iron, "Wagner No. 14," ca. 1890 ....**75.00**
Ice cream freezer, wooden bucket
w/galvanized crank container,
original green paint, "White
Mountain #2 - pat. June 2, 1923".......**45.00**
Ice shaver, "Gilchrist No. 78" **25.00**
Ice shaver, cast iron, "Griswold
No. 1"...**75.00**
Lemon reamer, carved cherry wood,
hand-held, ca. 1820, 2" d.,
5¾" h..**150.00**
Nutmeg grater, cast iron, "Bellows,"
mechanical, marked "JM Smith, pat.
June 7, 1870," complete, ca. 1870,
3 x 4 x 4"...**570.00**
Nutmeg grater w/cover, pocket-type,
tin, dark patina, ca. 1890 ....**19.00**
Pastry board, slate, 19th c.,
American, 24½" h. **192.50**
Pitcher, pottery, decorated w/scene
of two cows, yellow & green **95.00**
Pitcher, utilitarian crockery, Cherries
patt., brown glaze **65.00**
Popover pan, cast iron, "Griswold
No. 10"..**65.00**
Popover pan, cast iron, "Griswold
No. 18" **75.00**
Potato slicer, cast iron, clamp on-
type w/hand crank, painted green,
ca. 1918, Eagle Engineering Co.,
Springfield, Ohio **49.00**
Roll pan, cast iron, "Griswold No. 11"..**45.00**
Skillet, cast iron, "Griswold No. 11,"
large emblem, w/smoke ring.............**125.00**
Skillet, cast iron, "Griswold No. 12" **75.00**
Skillet, cast iron, "Griswold No. 14" ...**142.00**
Skillet, cast iron, "Griswold
No. 738" **100.00**
Skillet, cov., chrome, "Griswold
No. 8"...**50.00**
Skillet, cast iron, "Wagner No. 8".........**50.00**

Skillet, cast iron, "Wapak No. 6
Indian"...**150.00**
Skillet griddle, cast iron, "Griswold
No. 109"..**95.00**
Skimmer, brass & wrought iron,
polished brass bowl & iron handle
w/cut-out heart & brass inlay,
17¼" l. (iron pitted)..........................**148.50**
Sugar bowl, cov., glass, Jane Ray
patt., Jadite **8.00**
Sugar dredger (muffineer), raw tin,
dome top, handled, 3½" d., 5" h.........**55.00**
Tea kettle, cov., cast aluminum
w/high bail handle & wooden grip,
"Colonial" line, Wagner Ware,
Sidney, Ohio, early 20th c., 4 qts.......**30.00**
Vienna roll pan, cast iron, "Griswold
No. 26"..**95.00**
Waffle iron, cast iron, "Griswold
No. 8," w/high base **90.00**
Waffle iron, cast iron, "Griswold
No. 11," square, w/stand.................**135.00**
Waffle iron, cast iron, heart-shaped,
marked "Alfred Anderson Co." **40.00**

LAW ENFORCEMENT ITEMS

Early South Carolina Badge

*All types of objects relating to law
enforcement activities of earlier days are
now being collected, just as are fire-
fighting mementoes. The range extends
from badges and insignia to leg irons and
weapons. The following compilation
represents a cross-section.*

Badge, "City of Sunrise (Florida)
Police Officer," goldtone metal
w/black enameled lettering, center
disc w/wreath & enameled details
w/state seal, sunburst background,
2 x 2¾" **$28.00**
Badge, "Deputy Sheriff - Wyandotte
Co., KS," six-point star shape,
silvered metal w/black enameled
details, enameled state seal in
center, 2½" l......................................**27.00**

Badge, "Patrolman - Harlingen (Texas) Police," oblong, silvered metal w/black enameled details, wreath w/eagle at top, center disc w/state seal w/enameled trim, 1¾ x 2½" **37.00**

Badge, "Patrolman - South Carolina Highway Patrol," shield-shaped, gilded metal w/black enameled lettering, eagle at the top, seal in the center, early, worn, 2½" l. (ILLUS.) **244.00**

Badge, "Police Reserve - Detroit," shield-shaped silvered metal w/black enameled details, state seal in the center, 2¾ x 3¼" **21.00**

Badge, "Sergeant - Memphis Police," shield-shaped goldtone metal w/black enameled details, state seal in center, 2¼" l. **30.00**

Badge, "Special Deputy Sheriff - Pike County, Pa.," oblong, silvered metal w/black enamel details, large center disc w/state seal, eagle at top, 1¾ x 2¾" **30.00**

Ball & chain, an iron ball w/chained leg iron, old black paint (pitting) **275.00**

Book, "History of the Police Bureau, Rochester, New York - 1819-1829" ...**65.00**

Cap badge, "Metropolitan D. C. Police Reserve - Lieutenant," shield-shaped silvered metal w/gold wash & black painted details, scroll design w/eagle at top & seal in center, 2¾ x 3" **55.00**

Early Handcuffs

Handcuffs, nickel silver finish, marked "The Maltby - Mattatuck Mfg. Co.," single link 1¾" l., early, worn, lacks key (ILLUS.) **122.00**

Night stick, curly maple, turned, 16" l. **44.00**

Overcoat, Metropolitan Police, Washington, D.C., black leather, dark blue wool lining, three-quarter length, gilded metal buttons (some wear) **100.00**

Sweater, Takoma Park Maryland Police, brown virgin wool cardigan-style, two pockets, felt shield on chest w/"TPPD," includes sleeve patch, size 44, 1960s **51.00**

LIGHTING DEVICES

Also see ART DECO, CANDLESTICKS & CANDLEHOLDERS, HEINTZ ART METAL WARES, METALS, RAIL-ROADIANA, ROYCROFT ITEMS, and WORLD'S FAIR COLLECTIBLES. Also see various listings in the "Glass" and "Ceramics" categories.

LAMPS

FAIRY LAMPS

These are candle burning night lights of the Victorian era. Best known are the Clarke Fairy Lamps made in England, but they were also made by other firms. They were produced in two sizes, each with a base and a shade. The Fairy Pyramid Lamps listed below usually have a clear glass base and are approximately 2⅞" d. and 3¼" h. The Fairy Lamps are usually at least 4" d. and 5" h. when assembled and these may or may not have an additional saucer or bottom holder to match the shade in addition to the clear base.

Fairy Pyramid Lamps

Amber Glass Fairy Lamp

Amber glass w/opalescent swirl shade on clear pressed glass marked "Clarke" base, 3" d., 3⅝" h. (ILLUS.) **$95.00**

Cranberry Fairy Lamp

Cranberry mica flaked embossed swirl w/green threading shade on

clear marked "Clarke" pressed glass
base, 2⅞" d., 3¼" h. (ILLUS.) **150.00**

Frosted Apple Green Fairy Lamp

Frosted apple green embossed swirl
glass shade on clear pressed glass
marked "Clarke" base, 2⅞" d., 3½" h.
(ILLUS.) **100.00**

Pink Overshot Fairy Lamp

Pink overshot embossed hobs shade
on clear pressed glass marked
"Clarke" base, 3" d., 3¾" h.
(ILLUS.) **118.00**

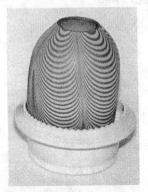

Verre Moiré Pyramid Lamp

Verre Moiré (Nailsea) glass shade,
frosted cranberry w/opaque loopings,
cream pottery base, marked "S.
Clarke's Patent Trademark Fairy
Pyramid," 3¼" d., 3¾" h. (ILLUS.)....**145.00**

Yellow Cased Glass Fairy Lamp

Yellow cased glass w/white spatter
shade on clear pressed glass marked
"Clarke" base, 2⅞" d., 3½" h.
(ILLUS.) **120.00**

Fairy Lamps

Burmese Fairy Lamp

Burmese glass epergne, flared glass
base supports three metal rings
holding clear glass candle cups
w/Burmese shades, center w/small
turned-in bowl & ruffled turned-down
vase, marked "Thos. Webb & Sons,"
10¾" h..**2,135.00**
Burmese glass shade on a matching
base marked "Thos. Webb & Sons
Queen Burmeseware Patented"
& a clear glass insert marked
"Clarke," 5½" h. (ILLUS.) **950.00**
Burmese satin glass shade on
matching square base w/folded-in
sides, supporting a clear glass
candle insert marked "Clarke,"
base 6 x 6", 6½" h. (ILLUS. top
next page) **985.00**
Citron & white Nailsea glass shade,
Nailsea glass ruffled base...............**450.00**

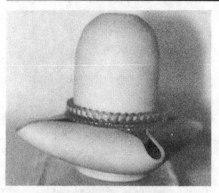

Unusual Burmese Fairy Lamp

Green satin glass shade w/crimped
top on clear marked "Clarke" base,
4" d., 5" h. **295.00**

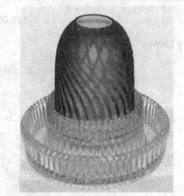

Blue Diamond Quilted Fairy Lamp

Heavenly Blue Diamond Quilt patt.
mother-of-pearl satin glass shade
on clear marked "Clarke" flower
bowl glass base, 6" d., 5½" h.
(ILLUS.) **350.00**

Figural Crown Fairy Lamp

Opalescent overshot figural crown
shaped shade on clear pressed glass
marked "Clarke" base, ca. 1887,
3" d., 4¼" h. (ILLUS.) **165.00**

Peacock blue molded Pinwheel patt.
shade on a matching swirled base,
marked "Baccarat Depose," one w/a
crystal candle cup, 5¾" d., 4⅛" h.,
pr. **230.00**

Pink satin glass shade, embossed
ribbon design, pink satin glass
base **300.00**

Pink Swirl mother-of-pearl satin
glass shade, matching ruffled
base, 5½" d., 5" h. **525.00**

Rose to pink embossed swirl satin
glass shade on clear marked
"Clarke" base, 4" d., 4¾" h. **195.00**

Large Verre Moiré Fairy Lamp

Verre Moiré (Nailsea) glass shade,
frosted cranberry w/opaque white
loopings, on matching ruffled base
w/clear marked "Clarke" candle
insert, 9" d., 6" h. (ILLUS.) **795.00**

White satin overlay glass shade,
clear cup mounted on a matching,
ruffled under base w/enameled
decoration **500.00**

HANDEL LAMPS

Forget-Me-Not Boudoir Lamp

*The Handel Company of Meriden,
Connecticut (1885-1936) began as a glass*

and lamp shade decorating company. Following World War I they became a major producer of decorative lamps which have become very collectible today.

Boudoir lamp, a 7" d. domical shade w/reverse painted blue forget-me-nots, raised on matching slightly swelled cylindrical standard w/a wide disc foot, inscribed "6454A" & "HANDEL", 14½" h. (ILLUS.) **1,840.00**

Boudoir lamp, a 6½" d. tall domical shade composed of a metal framework around four curved panels each reverse-painted w/a 'jewel' & lattice design above a base band of stylized leaves in yellow, green & red, raised on a slender reeded bronzed metal shaft w/a wide disc foot, shade signed "Handel 4359," base impressed "Handel," 15" h. ..**1,610.00**

Boudoir lamp, 7" d. domical mushroom-shaped reverse-painted shade w/chipped-ice & sanded finish, grey w/the interior decorated w/an overall design of wild rose blossoms in shades of pink, yellow, blue, green, orange & brown, on a patinated bronze tree trunk base w/open roots at the base, shade signed "HANDEL 6452," base w/woven Handel label, ca. 1917, 16" h...**1,840.00**

Handel Chandelier

Chandelier, spherical amber glass shade painted w/a tranquil forest scene w/three robins in shades of green, brown, yellow, orange & charcoal, signed "Bedigie," "HANDEL" & "6885," painted by Henry Bedigie, ca. 1923, 41" h. (ILLUS.) **4,888.00**

Pendant hanging lamp, compressed "Teroma" onion-form shade

Teroma Pendant Lamp

decorated w/two pairs of exotic birds amid foliate blossom & leaf motif, unsigned, 8" h. (ILLUS.)...............**4,312.50**

Table lamp, 16" d. domical red glass shade w/bronze sand-finish & lower border of acid-etched large pine needles, the slender bronze base cast w/heavy ribbing continuing to the flaring foot, copper-brown patina, shade signed "HANDEL 6412," base w/woven label "HANDEL Lamps," ca. 1920, 22½" h. (losses to patina) **2,875.00**

Table lamp, 16" d. domical reverse-painted shade decorated w/a wide pond-side landscape in earthtone shades of browns & greens against a dusky mauve shaded sky, inscribed "Handel 6810," mounted on a slender baluster-form copper-colored metal standard w/ribbing in the lower half & raised on a paneled disc foot, woven cloth "Handel" tag, 23" h. (base paint worn) **3,225.00**

Table lamp, 16" d. domical reverse-painted shade in grey w/a chipped & sand-textured exterior, the interior decorated w/chrysanthemums & leafage in shades of yellow, orange, red & green, the exterior w/green leafage reserved against thin yellow vines, brown patina, raised on a slender ribbed bronze standard w/a lobed cushion foot, shade signed "HANDEL - 5651," base impressed "HANDEL," 24" h...........................**4,888.00**

Table lamp, 17¾" d. domical reverse-painted shade decorated w/green, yellow, brick & grey-green daffodils & foliage among flowers & leaves, signed "7/22 HANDEL HR," mounted on a brown patinated metal base cast as an urn on a circular

stepped foot, stamped "Handel,"
24" h...**8,625.00**

Handel Peacock Table Lamp

Table lamp, 18" d. domed glass
shade decorated w/two full-length
peacocks cameo etched & enamel-
painted in metallic gold against
burgundy red background w/orange
& blue blossoms, green leaves &
amber highlights, mounted on
tripartite gilt metal shaft & simulated
onyx platform base, shade inscribed
"Handel 7126 Pal," 24" h.
(ILLUS.) **19,550.00**

Table lamp, 18" d. domical reverse-
painted shade, grey w/a chipped &
sand-textured exterior, painted on
the interior w/two perched
multicolored parrots & a butterfly
amid peony blossoms & leafage in
shades of tan, magenta & yellow,
reserved against a charcoal
background, raised on a painted
metal disc font w/three tall slender
strap legs w/curled toes resting on a
disc foot w/a lappet border, the base
painted in gold & red w/three amber
glass teardrop ornaments, shade
signed "Bedigie - Handel - 7023,"
ca. 1923, 23½" h..........................**11,500.00**

Table lamp, 18" d. domical reverse-
painted "Treasure Island" shade
painted w/shades of blue, green,
grey & browns depicting a tall-
masted sailing ship at anchor in a
moonlit lagoon surrounded by palm
trees, signed "Handel 6891," on a
metal baluster-form finely ribbed
base w/a swirled & ruffled foot & a
grey patina, marked "Handel,"
24½" h......................................**8,050.00**

Table lamp, 18" w. octagonal
tapering cylindrical leaded glass
shade composed of sixteen narrow
triangular panels, four acid-etched
w/a looping scroll design, raised on
a brass base w/a slender baluster-
form standard above a ringed ball
raised on three S-scroll legs resting
upon a flat ring w/three knob feet,
shade signed "Handel 7689,"
28" h..**1,495.00**

Table lamp, 18½" d. leaded glass
shade w/a domed top above a wide
flat border w/uneven rim, composed
of green, yellow & orangish amber
pieces arranged as bright centered
flowers within a green latticework,
mounted on a tall slender bronzed
metal base w/a bulbous top &
tapering toward the round foot, cast
w/fine ribbing, 28" h. **3,450.00**

Wrought Iron & Glass Handel Lamp

Table lamp, 20½" d. circular shade of
creamy brown slag glass & stylized,
cut-out copper flowers, suspended
on a wrought-iron circular base
w/two thick, vertical struts joined by
four balls, the base w/two spade-
shaped cut-outs, one fitted w/slag
glass, unmarked, ca. 1910, two
decorative top chains missing, one
panel of glass replaced, 30" h.
(ILLUS.) **2,310.00**

Wall sconce, an orange-tinted ball
shade reverse-painted w/an
autumnal landscape w/birds in flight,
mounted to a bronzed metal
crooked-neck electrical socket
w/foliate-decorated top rim, base
drop & oval wall plate, shade signed
"Handel 7003" **2,300.00**

MINIATURE LAMPS

*Our listings are arranged numerically
according to the numbers assigned to the
various miniature lamps pictured in Frank
R. & Ruth E. Smith's book,* Miniature

Lamps, *now referred to as Smith's Book I, and Ruth Smith's sequel,* Miniature Lamps II. *All references are to Smith's Book I unless otherwise noted.*

White Bristol Miniature Lamp

Bristol glass, white shaded to soft blue w/enameled dainty orange flowers, green leaves, square ruffled shade w/flowers, base w/flowers & brown, orange & green bird flying over flowers, opalescent shell applied feet, original burner & clear glass chimney, 4¾" d., 10" h., color plate No. V right (ILLUS.)................**850.00**

Clear glass "Time & Light, Pride of America. Grand Vals Perfect Time Indicating Lamp" & time marks from 8 to 6, unmarked burner, white embossed, Shell patt. shade, 6¾" h., No. 23..................................**153.00**

Embossed "Little Buttercup" on cobalt blue glass font w/applied handle, Nutmeg burner, clear glass chimney, 2¾" h. base, No. 36............**75.00**

Cranberry opalescent glass Spanish Lace patt. base, applied cranberry handle, Hornet burner, clear glass chimney, 3" h., No. 40 ...**425.00**

Matchholder lamp, amber glass w/embossed ribs; matchholder in Basketweave patt., Nutmeg burner, 8" h., No. 52 ....**225.00**

White Bristol glass shade, clear glass font embossed "Evening Star," applied handle, Lomsted-type burner, 3½" h., No. 57..............**150.00**

Clear glass stem lamp w/square base, Acorn burner, clear glass chimney, advertised in Butler Brothers "Our Drummer" 1912 catalog, 4" h., No. 103 ....**45.00**

Amethyst glass Fishscale patt. stem lamp, Nutmeg burner, clear glass chimney, 5" h., No. 116 ....**135.00**

Clear glass Shag or "Christmas Tree" patt. w/gold ribs, base & shade, Acorn burner, No. 125 ....**150.00**

Blue opaque glass embossed beaded panels, Acorn burner, 7" h., No. 179 ....**130.00**

George & Martha Washington Lamp

Milk glass, squatty bulbous base tapering to a ribbed shoulder, domed half-shade w/portrait decals of George & Martha Washington, clear glass chimney, 3" d., 5¾" h., No. 182 (ILLUS.) **175.00**

Cased Pink Miniature Lamp

Cased pink glass, white interior, flaring sides w/bulging panels, original brass burner w/matching chimney shade, 4" d., 7¾" h., No. 220 (ILLUS.) **622.50**

Green opaque glass w/embossed scroll leaf design, trimmed w/painted florals, Nutmeg burner, 8¾" h., No. 240 ....**275.00**

Pink opaque glass w/embossed petal design, Hornet burner, 8½" h., No. 289 ....**525.00**

Green glass orange-peel textured ground, Nutmeg burner, 9" h., No. 309 ....**400.00**

Blue shaded to white milk glass base w/globe-chimney shade w/red floral decoration, original brass

Blue & White Milk Glass Lamp

burner, 8⅜" h., No. 315
(ILLUS.) **272.50**
Blue Satin glass puffy Diamond
Quilted patt. base & umbrella-type
shade, Nutmeg burner, clear glass
chimney, by Consolidated Lamp &
Glass Co., Pittsburgh, ca. 1894,
8" h., No. 394 ....**425.00**
White opalescent w/blue "eyes"
glass, clear pedestal base, Nutmeg
burner, 7½" h., No. 510....................**250.00**
Light apple green Fleur-de-lis patt.,
foreign burner, 10" h., No. 567......**2,425.00**
Brass lantern, blue globe, unmarked
burner, 7" h., Book II, No. 9 ....**200.00**
Brass lantern, embossed on clear
glass globe "Baby," unmarked
burner, 4½" h., Book II, No. 10 ....**550.00**
Shaded pink satin glass base,
tapering cylindrical form
w/embossed leaves, scrolls & swirls,
white lining, original burner, 3¼" d.,
5¾" h., Book II, No. 517...................**118.00**

PAIRPOINT LAMPS

Pairpoint Reverse-Painted Lamp

Well known as a producer of fine Victorian art glass and silver plate wares, between 1907 and 1929 the Pairpoint Corporation of New Bedford, Massachusetts also produced a wide range of decorative lamps.

Boudoir lamp, 9" d. domical "Puffy"
reverse-painted shade, the lobed
edge molded w/rose clusters in pink
& yellow below blue butterflies &
yellow & green leafage all against a
black background, on a slender
baluster-form patinated metal
standard w/a wide disc base raised
on tiny scroll feet, ca. 1915,
15½" h...**4,600.00**
Boudoir lamp, 9¼" w. square
pyramidal "Radcliffe" shade reverse-
painted w/a colorful harbor scene
w/large sailboats, rim artist-signed
"Doran," raised on a gilt-metal
pedestal on a white marble
rectangular foot, base impressed
"Pairpoint" & numbered "E 3017,"
12½" h...**1,840.00**
Table lamp, 8¾" d. tapering drum-
shaped "Puffy" shade in the
'Stratford' patt., clusters of roses
against a latticework ground,
reverse-painted in shades of pink,
purple, yellow, green & black, on a
slender baluster-shaped copper-
patinated metal base cast w/slender
leaves, shade marked "The
Pairpoint Corp's. - Patented July 9-
13," base cast "Pairpoint C 3064,"
14" h..**2,875.00**
Table lamp, 9" d. domical "Puffy"
shade molded w/delphinium
blossoms, grey reverse-painted
w/blossoms in shades of purple,
pink, yellow & green, on a slender
baluster-form brass-patinated base
molded w/slender leaves, shade
marked "The Pairpoint Corp.," base
cast "PAIRPOINT - C 3064," w/a
maker's mark, 14" h. **4,888.00**
Table lamp, 9½" d. domical "Puffy"
shade in the 'Papillon' patt., relief-
molded clusters of roses
w/butterflies decorated in shades of
white, pink, yellow, blue, green &
black, on a simple slender baluster-
form brass base w/a dished base on
small feet, shade printed "The
Pairpoint Corp.," base impressed
"PAIRPOINT - 3047," 15" h..........**2,875.00**
Table lamp, 10½" d. clear glass
shade reverse-painted w/spider
chrysanthemums & leafage in
shades of crimson, white, yellow &
green w/pink satin overlay, patinated

metal square shaft cut w/leaves & scrolls, on a pyramid-shaped base incised w/scrolls, shade stamped "The Pairpoint Co.," base impressed "PAIRPOINT MFG. CO - 3054" & maker's mark, base repatinated, 21" h. (ILLUS.) **2,070.00**

Table lamp, 12" d. domical flat-topped "Puffy" reverse-painted shade in the 'Albemarl' patt., molded in medium-relief w/clusters of roses & two butterflies below a ribbed upper section, painted on the reverse in shades of crimson, green, yellow, orange, blue & pink, unsigned, ca. 1915, 24" h. **6,900.00**

"Puffy" Red Rose Table Lamp

Table lamp, 13" d. "Puffy" domical 'Red Rose' patt. reverse-painted shade w/vivid red roses, mounted on silvered squatty baluster-shaped metal handled base w/foliate designs, impressed "Pairpoint Mfg. Co. 3076," finish worn, minor chips to shade edge, 19" h. (ILLUS.) **9,200.00**

Table lamp, 14" d. domical flat-topped "Puffy" reverse-painted shade in the 'Devonshire' patt., grey molded in medium-relief & painted on the interior in shades of blue, yellow, mauve, pink, green & black w/a border of rose blossoms & two hummingbirds in flight, tripod scroll-legged silvered-metal base, w/finial, shade unsigned, base marked "PAIRPOINT 08084," ca. 1920, 21¼" h......................................**12,650.00**

Table lamp, 14" d. ribbed mushroom-shaped reverse-painted 'Venice' patt. shade decorated w/large roses & leaves in shades of pink, red & green reserved against an intricately painted white & ivory background, on a slender patinated metal ribbed

standard w/a lobed & squared base on small paw feet, shade signed "THE PAIRPOINT CORP.," base impressed "PAIRPOINT MF'G CO. - B 3055" w/hallmark, ca. 1915, 22" h. (losses to patina) **5,750.00**

Table lamp, 14" d. "Puffy" domical 'Papillon' patt. reverse-painted closed-top shade in frosted grey painted on the interior w/four multicolored butterflies amid stems of red roses, the leafage tinged w/blue & gold, against a white & green background, the exterior trimmed w/gilding, raised on a slender leaf-cast gilt-metal baluster-form standard w/a wide round ribbed foot, shade signed "THE PAIRPOINT CO.," base impressed "PAIRPOINT - C 3066," ca. 1915, 20" h..............................**9,200.00**

Pairpoint "Puffy" Apple Tree Lamp

Table lamp, 15" d. "Puffy" domical 'Apple Tree' patt. reverse-painted shade molded w/fruit, blossoms, bees & two butterflies in frosted grey glass painted on the interior in shades of green, orange, yellow, brown, teal, white & blue, raised on a tree trunk base, shade signed "The Pairpoint Corp.," & the base impressed "PAIRPOINT MFG. - 3091," w/hallmark, ca. 1915, 21" h. (ILLUS.) **24,150.00**

Table lamp, 21" d. slightly pointed domed shade painted on the exterior w/a wooded lakeside landscape in fall colors on a clear textured glass ground mottling to pink, on a baluster-shaped wood standard on base w/metal mounts, signed "The Pairpoint Corp.," on inner rim, ca. 1920 (ILLUS. top next page) **1,840.00**

Pairpoint Glass & Wood Table Lamp

Table lamp, 8½ x 14½" oblong
domical "Puffy" shade in the 'San
Remo' patt., grey molded in low-
relief w/a central medallion
enclosing a pansy bouquet &
meandering groups of poppies,
vines & leafage overall, painted
on the reverse in shades of
crimson, yellow, green, pink,
lavender & blue, the exterior
trimmed in gold, shade marked
"The Pairpoint Corporation - Posted
July 9, 1901," raised on a slender
ovoid gilt-metal pedestal w/a four-
lobed rectangular foot, base
impressed "PAIRPOINT MFG.
CO. - 83020," ca. 1915, 23¼" h. ...**7,475.00**
Table lamp, 16" d. tapering drum-
form open reverse-painted 'Seville'
patt. shade decorated w/a
continuous summer landscape in
shades of green, brown, yellow,
orange, charcoal & blue, raised
on a brass-patinated slender
stem flanked by U-form scroll
arms w/candle-form sockets
raised above a clear bubbly
glass ball connector on an
octagonal metal foot, shade
signed "L. H. Goreham," base
impressed "PAIRPOINT - D 3830,"
ca. 1915, 26½" h. **2,587.00**
Table lamp, "Puffy" flat-topped
conical 'Hummingbird' patt. reverse-
painted shade decorated in rose,
yellow, green & violet w/a band of
roses w/hummingbirds against a
white & yellow ground, on a slender
ribbed baluster-form gilt-metal
standard w/a stylized palmette
design & on a wide disc foot,
stamped "PAIRPOINT P C 3066,"
21½" h. **5,980.00**

TIFFANY LAMPS

Favrile & Bronze Counter-Balance Lamp

Desk lamp, spherical pivoting shade
composed of iridescent green
turtleback tiles in an overall leaf-
form design w/bronze shade mount
pierced w/stylized flowerheads at
the sides, raised between slender
curved uprights on a domed base,
greenish brown patina, impressed
"TIFFANY STUDIOS NEW YORK
7911," 10½" h. **13,800.00**
Desk lamp, Favrile glass & bronze,
counter-balance type, the domed
bronze shade w/a star-design
bronze openwork overlay set
w/milky white Favrile glass behind,
supported by a pivoting gooseneck
arm w/weighted ball support,
stamped "TIFFANY STUDIOS NEW
YORK 417," shade 7" d.,
overall 14" h. **5,520.00**
Desk lamp, "Nautilus," the leaded
glass shade in the shape of
a nautilus shell composed of
green shaded to white blocks of
glass, raised on a slender bronze
pedestal w/a wide leaf-cast disc
foot, base stamped "TIFFANY
STUDIOS - NEW YORK 25890,"
14" h...**7,187.00**
Desk lamp, counter-balance type, a
domical cased green shade
w/iridescent gold trailings supported
on a high arched two-bar arm
curving down to a large counter-
balance ball above the stepped,
domed bronze base, shade
inscribed "L.C.T.," base impressed
"TIFFANY STUDIOS - NEW YORK -
417," shade 7" d., 15½" h.
(ILLUS.) **4,600.00**
Floor lamp, "Acorn," 12" d. domical
leaded glass shade in green &
amber mounted in a swiveled socket

in a bell-form ring frame raised on a slender dark bronze shaft w/five short curved legs ending in spade feet, shade & base impressed "Tiffany Studios New York," 4' 10" h. **9,775.00**

Tiffany "Curtain Border" Floor Lamp

Floor lamp, "Curtain Border," 24" d. domical leaded glass shade composed of a geometric ground of mottled yellow glass above a curtain border of mottled amber & green rippled glass, stamped "TIFFANY STUDIOS NEW YORK 1565," the bronze base w/flattened circular foot w/reddish green patina, stamped "TIFFANY STUDIOS NEW YORK 875," 6' 7" h. (ILLUS.) **35,650.00**

Floor lamp, "Linenfold," 9" d. leaded glass 12-panel shade set w/a band of amber "linenfold" glass, shade stamped "TIFFANY STUDIOS N.Y. 1936," supported on a bronze base w/knopped standard raised on scrolled feet, stamped "TIFFANY STUDIOS NEW YORK 425," 4' 7" h. **6,325.00**

Floor lamp, "Poppy," 26½" d. domical leaded glass shade composed of a profusion of deep & variegated red poppy blossoms w/striated green foliage against a green & azure blue background, shade impressed "TIFFANY STUDIOS 1902," the base w/alligator finish in a dark gilt patina, impressed "TIFFANY STUDIOS NEW YORK 876," 6' 6" h. (ILLUS.) **288,500.00**

"Poppy" Floor Lamp

Tiffany Favrile Hanging Lamp

Hanging lamp, Favrile glass, the pierced bronze cap w/beaded border supporting a shade composed of radiating panels of green & white striated glass, impressed "TIFFANY STUDIOS - NEW YORK. D.," 1899-1928, 13" d. (ILLUS.) **3,450.00**

Lily lamp, ten-light, each long trumpet-form shade in amber iridescent glass w/intaglio finish, on a gilt-bronze base w/the slender arched stems issuing from a cluster of lily pads, shades signed, base impressed "TIFFANY STUDIOS - NEW YORK - 381," one shade w/minor crack, one w/a minor crack & chip, 21¼" h. (ILLUS. top next page) **16,675.00**

Student lamp, the swiveling upper section set w/two oval turtleback tiles w/irregular surface in gold, green & purple iridescence, surrounded by overall beading, the domed bronze base cast w/leaves &

Tiffany Favrile "Lily" Lamp

set w/a border of iridescent glass beads, impressed "TIFFANY STUDIOS - NEW YORK - D801," 1899-1929, 15⅜" h. (interior crack to one tile) **4,025.00**

Table lamp, Favrile glass & gilt-bronze, the circular base on five ball feet, cast w/a whiplash motif, supporting a cylindrical gold Favrile glass shade in an openwork gilt-bronze foliate mount, the gilt-bronze heightened w/coral enamel, stamped "TIFFANY STUDIOS NEW YORK 517," 14" h. **8,625.00**

Favrile "Acorn" Lamp

Table lamp, "Acorn," 16" d. Favrile glass shade composed of radiating graduated rectangular glass tiles w/a medial band of meandering heart-shaped leaves above three rows of brick tiles, all heavily mottled opalescent yellow, etched patina, on slender paneled standard flaring to a round base, shade impressed

"TIFFANY STUDIOS - NEW YORK - 1435," base impressed "TIFFANY STUDIOS - NEW YORK - 534," 1899-1920, 22½" h. (ILLUS.) **8,050.00**

Table lamp, "Belted Apple Blossom," 18" d. domical leaded glass shade w/a central band of pink & white striated opalescent blossoms w/yellow centers, the leaves in various shades of green against a ground of mottled pale bluish grey, on a simple bronze columnar standard w/a stepped disc foot, green patina, shade impressed "TIFFANY STUDIOS - NEW YORK 1555," base signed "TIFFANY STUDIOS - NEW YORK - 526," 22¾" h. **17,250.00**

Table lamp, "Daffodil," 15¾" d. domical leaded glass shade w/an overall pattern of daffodil blossoms in mottled shades of lemon yellow, w/emerald to lime green leafage, reserved against a striated yellow & white background, raised on a bronze base w/slender ribbed shaft above the wide cushion base cast w/ribbed leaves above the curled tab feet, greenish brown patina, shade signed "TIFFANY STUDIOS - NEW YORK," base impressed "TIFFANY STUDIOS - NEW YORK - D 805," 21" h. **13,800.00**

Table lamp, "Dragonfly," 20" d. conical leaded glass shade composed of seven dragonflies, their bodies in blue w/green 'eyes,' their wings in striated blue & plum, w/delicate openwork bronze overlay, against a mottled amber ground, set w/amber & plum cabochon 'jewels,' stamped "TIFFANY STUDIOS NEW YORK," the bronze base cast w/stylized pods & seated upon four out-turned feet, stamped "TIFFANY STUDIOS NEW YORK 395," 27" h. **29,900.00**

Table lamp, "Swirling Leaf," 18" d. low domical leaded glass shade w/a flat border band, composed of radiating bands of graduated rectangular tiles in mottled amber & green opalescent w/a medial band of swirling leaves, raised on a simple slender bronze paneled standard w/a wide dished & ribbed base w/tab feet, brown patina, shade signed "TIFFANY STUDIOS NEW YORK 1470," base signed "TIFFANY STUDIOS - NEW YORK - 531," 27" h. **10,925.00**

Table lamp, "Tulip," 16" d. domical leaded glass shade w/an overall design of tulip blossoms in striated shades of pink, rose & crimson, w/mottled green & white stems & leafage, reserved against a background shading from striated cobalt blue to green, raised on a bronze base w/an egg-form font held by three long prongs above a domed base w/a wide rectangular foot, shade marked "TIFFANY STUDIOS - NEW YORK - 1906," base impressed "TIFFANY STUDIOS - NEW YORK - 444," 22" h................................**39,100.00**

"Woodbine" Table Lamp

Table lamp, "Woodbine," 14" d. leaded glass shade comprised of predominately maroon & green w/pink & blue-purple mottled segments including ripple & drapery-fold glass arranged as woodbine blossoms & leaves, on square platform bronze two-socket base, shade marked "TIFFANY STUDIOS NEW YORK," base marked "TIFFANY STUDIOS NEW YORK 22054," 19" h. (ILLUS.) **11,500.00**

Table lamp, three-light, the bronze base w/a finely ribbed domed foot centered by a three-stem standard w/each arched stem suspending a socket w/a bell-form amber iridescent shaded w/an interior molded honeycomb design w/an opalescent finish & brownish green patina, shades signed "L.C.T.," base impressed "TIFFANY STUDIOS - NEW YORK - 399," 16" h..............**6,900.00**

Wall sconces, Favrile glass & bronze, the bronze sphere issuing two arms, each supporting an iridescent gold glass tulip shade, inscribed "L.C.T.," 9" deep, 10" w., 11" h., pr. **17,825.00**

MISCELLANEOUS LAMPS

Classical Argand Lamp

Argand lamp, brass, two-light, Classical-style, the urn-shaped font w/acanthus finial & egg-and-dart edging above a waterleaf-embellished standard issuing two candlearms over a tripartite figural griffin base, on a molded plinth, by Messenger & Son, England, ca. 1830, electrified, 21" h. **575.00**

Argand lamps, patinated bronze, one-light, Classical style, the pineapple & acanthus top over an urn-shaped font w/scrolling armature above a reeded & papyrus-ringed pillar on an anthemion & water-leafed base, all on a square plinth w/cast shaped disc feet, together w/two matching cut glass globes, probably American, ca. 1830-50, 11" w., 23½" h., pr. (ILLUS. one of two) **2,420.00**

Arts & Crafts floor lamp, wrought iron, three small angled feet support a triangular base centered by a tall slender corkscrew shaft w/a sliding arm bracket fitted w/a pointed conical mica-lined shade, original mellow dark patina, stamped "YELLIN," Samuel Yellin, early 20th c., 16" w., 5' 4" h. **4,675.00**

Banquet lamp, kerosene-type, cranberry glass & brass, the bulbous spherical font raised on twisted pedestal base, w/matching tulip-form shade w/ruffled rim & clear glass chimney, 5" d., 14½" h. (ILLUS. top next page)....................**350.00**

Betty lamp (early grease lamp) w/hanger, wrought iron, elongated spout & swivel font cover, 4" h. plus hanger & chain pick **220.00**

Betty lamp (early grease lamp) w/hanger, wrought iron, brass spade-shaped ornament w/engraved border & "J.J.," 4½" h. plus hanger ...**302.50**

Cranberry Banquet Lamp

Betty lamp (early grease lamp) w/hanger & stand, wrought iron, wide strap handle & crimped detail on stand, lamp 5" h. plus hanger, overall 12½" h. **605.00**

Betty lamp (early grease lamp), wrought iron flattened boat-shaped font w/a brass lid w/iron finial, 19th c., 5¼" h. plus hanger.....................**154.00**

Betty lamp (early grease lamp), wrought iron flattened boat-shaped font w/a hinged brass lid w/a rooster finial & inlaid brass heart crest, 7¼" h. plus twisted hanger, 19th c. (pitted iron).....................................**357.50**

Bradley & Hubbard Kerosene Lamp

Bradley & Hubbard kerosene table lamp, cast metal & opal glass, the elaborate gilt metal font cast w/scrolls, mounted on complimentary base w/tab feet, spherical opal glass shade decorated w/h.p. blue & white Delft windmill scene in

the Mt. Washington manner, clear glass chimney, 18" h. (ILLUS.) **287.00**

Bradley & Hubbard table lamp, 20" d. domical shade w/a metal framework enclosing six wide bent glass panels of ribbed frosted clear glass each acid-etched w/an urn of flowers, raised on a cast metal columnar standard on a base cast on each side w/a reclining lion, stepped rectangular foot, marked on the base, 18" h.................................**345.00**

Crusie lamp (early grease lamp), double-form, hanging-type, tin, two fitted shallow boat-shaped spouted dishes w/a flat upright handle w/stylized cut-out "thistles," 7¼" h. plus twisted hanger.........................**165.00**

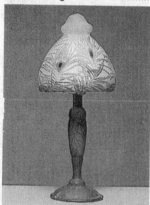

Daum Cameo Glass Table Lamp

Daum, Nancy cameo glass & metal table lamp, 17" d. domical grey shade mottled w/charcoal overlaid w/green, turquoise & navy & cut w/peacock feathers w/three-arm mount, all on baluster-shaped standard decorated w/peacock feathers, signed in cameo "DAUM - NANCY," w/cross of Lorraine, ca. 1910, 16" h. (ILLUS.) **8,050.00**

Dirk Van Erp table lamp, copper & mica, the conical shade w/four mica panels divided by flaring battens terminating in a bullet-form cap supported by four scrolling arms issuing from the riveted bulbous base w/slender neck, stamped w/the windmill mark & "DIRK VAN ERP" within a closed box, 21½" d. shade, 22" h.................................**32,200.00**

Dirk Van Erp table lamp, hammered copper & mica, the four-panel conical shade w/riveted baton dividers raised on a shaped riveted base, probably by Auguste Tiesselinck, 17" d., 25" h...............**8,050.00**

Duffner & Kimberly floor lamp,
leaded glass & polychromed metal,
the 27⅜" d. conical leaded glass
shade w/uneven border of scarlet &
cobalt blue Oriental poppy blossoms, w/large green leaves on a
fuchsia ground, the Oriental-style
base decorated w/enameled bands
of blue, red, yellow & white, 5' h. ..**6,900.00**

Duffner & Kimberly table lamp,
20" w. square pyramidal leaded
glass shade w/an irregular border,
decorated w/striated & mottled
aubergine glass panels surrounded
by intricate scrolling designs, in
mottled royal blue, violet & amber
against an amber ground, raised on
a patinated metal base w/a
columnar standard raised on a
stepped square base w/four seated
Egyptian figures, early 20th c.,
30½" h...**6,210.00**

Duffner & Kimberly Table Lamp

Duffner & Kimberly table lamp,
22" d. conical shade composed of
fiery amber, caramel, yellow & blue
colored smooth & rippled glass in
repeating drape & bellflower motif,
supported on integrated gilt-bronze
four-socket thin baluster-shaped
standard w/flaring base, base w/gold
medallion marked "The Duffner &
Kimberly Co., New York," 28" h.
(ILLUS.) **4,600.00**

Edgar Brandt torchere, wrought iron
& alabaster, the conical alabaster
shade held by four flaring cobras
alternating w/berried leafy branches
above a composite four-branch
standard each coiling at the foot,
mounted on a square heavily
hammered base raised on four
fluted feet, unsigned, ca. 1925,
5' 10½" h. **24,150.00**

Jefferson table lamp, 16" d. domical
reverse-painted shade decorated
w/a riverside landscape under a
yellow & blue sky, inscribed on
lower edge "2360 Jefferson M.G.,"
mounted on a two-socket bronze
metal slender ribbed urn-form base
w/foliate devices, 21" h. **977.50**

Jules Leleu floor lamp, painted
bronze & glass, the scrolling base
supporting a central standard
composed of three plate glass
sections w/patterned beveled edges,
supporting three scrolling arms,
each w/conical fixture, w/finial &
circular drum-shaped shade, Jules
Leleu, France, ca. 1940, shade
24" d., 6' h. **6,900.00**

Kerosene table lamp, cut-overlay
glass, the large inverted pear-
shaped font in white cut to opaque
jade green w/a row of large lancets
above a row of ovals, a brass
connector to the opaque white
pedestal base w/square foot,
original brass collar, attributed to the
Boston & Sandwich Glass Co.,
ca. 1860, 10¼" h. **990.00**

Kerosene table lamp, cut-overlay
glass, the large inverted pear-
shaped font in opaque white cut to
cranberry w/white swirled threading
w/a band of long ovals above a
horizontal band, on a columnar
brass standard w/a rope-twist
design above the square blackish
brown square marble foot, attributed
to the Boston & Sandwich Glass
Co., ca. 1860, 10⅜" h. **2,750.00**

Kerosene table lamp, cut-overlay,
the inverted pear-shaped font in
opaque white cut to deep ruby w/a
band of large lancets above a band
of thumbprints, raised on a cupped
brass connector above the flaring
reeded columnar standard w/a
round domed foot resting on a
stepped white marble foot w/brass
banded trim, attributed to the Boston
& Sandwich Glass Co., ca. 1860,
12¾" h..**990.00**

Kerosene wall hanging lamp,
tin, brass & glass, cylindrical
font w/attached reflector, brass
collar & kerosene burner, clear
glass chimney, green japanned
finish, 11" h., overall w/chimney
12½" h...**385.00**

Leaded glass desk lamp, oval shade
comprised of honeycomb-shaped
green slag glass segments in the
Duffner manner, mounted on
adjustable bronze slender baluster-

Leaded Glass Desk Lamp

form standard on wide circular base, 16" h. (ILLUS.) **747.50**

Limbert Copper Table Lamp

Limbert Arts & Crafts style table lamp, conical reticulated copper shade w/mica lining, resting on three wrought-copper arms attached to a hammered copper base w/large round riveted pulls, No. 376, unmarked, some cleaning to original finish, replaced mica, 16" d., 20" h. (ILLUS.) **3,850.00**

Peg lamps, deep robin's egg blue shaded to light blue melon-ribbed satin glass shade & body, ornate brass pedestal base, original fittings, clear glass chimney, 15" h., pr. **1,480.00**

Prairie School table lamp, a 17" w. square pyramidal shade w/slag glass panels within the oak framework, small rectangular cut-outs along the bottom edges, raised on a tall slender square oak pedestal base w/full-length 'fins' up each side, on a stepped square foot,

original dark brown oak finish, unmarked, early 20th c., 23" h. **1,870.00**

Torchere, chromed metal, flat disc base supporting a slender cylindrical standard topped by a stepped collar supporting a bowl-shaped shade, impressed "DESNY - PARIS - MADE IN FRANCE," ca. 1930, 6' h. **3,910.00**

OTHER LIGHTING DEVICES

CHANDELIERS

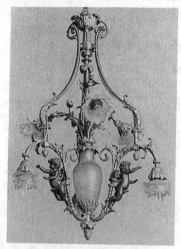

Art Nouveau Chandelier

Art Nouveau, bronze & bronze doré, six-light, the arched & leafy scroll-cast frame w/three arms from the top to the base centered by a leaf & blossom-trimmed central shaft above a tall baluster-form frosted closed shade, three vine arms terminating in frosted glass blossom shades issuing from the central shaft & two down-turned side arms w/frosted blossom shades, mounted w/figural cherubs at the base, ca. 1900, 22" w., 30" h. (ILLUS.) **2,420.00**

Arts & Crafts style, copper & chiton shell, the wide domed form w/hammered & pierced oblong reserves w/low-relief seahorses between six narrow oval Gumboot chiton shells, by Elizabeth Eaton Burton, California, ca. 1910, 25¾" d. **5,750.00**

Bronze, three-light, gasolier w/three upturned arms w/ropetwist & foliate scroll designs centering a cabochon & scroll-adorned circular base w/urn finial, suspended on a ribbed shaft w/weighted chains & fluted cap at top, mid-19th c., electrified, 20" d., 4' 8½" h. (ILLUS. top next page) ...**1,980.00**

Three-Arm Bronze Gasolier

Empire-Style Chandelier

Empire-Style, gilt & patinated bronze, four-light, a deep bowl-shaped framed w/a cylindrical base pendant, four short leaf-cast socket arms suspended from long chains to the ceiling plate, late 19th c., 17½" d., 21½" h. (ILLUS.) **770.00**

Lalique "Champs Elysees," clear & frosted glass, the wide flattened base molded w/large leaves & the upright sides formed by oversized maple leaves, w/chrome fittings, 45½" h...**4,600.00**

Muller Freres signed, molded & frosted glass & wrought iron, the central glove & three pendent shades molded in low- and medium-relief w/stylized birds in flight amid bands of leafage, within foliate cast mounts, shades molded "MULLER FRERES - LUNEVILLE," acid signature "MULLER FRES - LUNEVILLE" on

central globe, ca. 1925, center globe 10" d., 36" h.........................**2,300.00**

Ormolu Three-Light Chandelier

Ormolu, three-light, a ribbed & scroll-cast central shaft ending in a bulbous tapering font issuing three leafy scroll arms supporting molded metal fonts w/tulip-shaped frosted & engraved shades & suspending long cut prisms, the slender scroll arms at the top suspending long blossom-form cherry red cased w/white smoke bells, mid-19th c., electrified, some glass imperfections, one bell repaired, 32" h. (ILLUS.) **2,645.00**

Patinated Metal Kerosene Chandelier

Patinated cast metal, eight-light, a widely flaring two-tier design w/flattened, angular upturned arms decorated w/cast scrolls & topped by shaped finials, three arms about five arms, each arm ending in a cast cup holding a clear pressed glass font w/burner & frosted glass ball shade, ca. 1875 (ILLUS.).........................**1,650.00**

Queen Anne-Style, brass, six-light, a long ring- and baluster-turned standard w/four figure-8 form scrolls above six S-scroll arms ending in candle sockets w/wide drip pans, a turnip-form pendant below, 18th - 19th c., 19" d., 15" h.....................**2,875.00**

Schneider, glass & wrought iron, a central elongated bell-form glass shade & three smaller lily-form shades in grey internally decorated w/pink & pale amber striations, all suspended from an ornate wrought-iron frame w/three down-curved arms cast w/poppy blossoms, leaves & applied glass buds, central shade signed, ca. 1925, 33" d., 4' h. **26,450.00**

Tiffany, the wide conical leaded glass shade composed of a meandering pattern of yellow black-eyed Susan blossoms & leafage in shades of rich emerald & striated green reserved against a background shading from white to striated green, impressed "TIFFANY STUDIOS NEW YORK 614-3," 28½" d. (fittings missing) **23,000.00**

Venetian Glass Chandelier

Venetian, clear blown glass, six-light, a domed leaf-trimmed cap above a round central cylinder trimmed w/bands of rigaree & enclosed by tall upright & curved glass jonquils & serrated leaves, the dished base issuing six scrolling arms ending in floriform drip pans alternating w/down-turned leaves & hung w/a pendent floral sphere, electrified, 33" h. (ILLUS.) **2,090.00**

LANTERNS

Candle lantern, folding-type, tin w/two mica panels, original brown japanning w/gold stenciled decoration & "Minor's Pat. Jan. 24 1865," 5¼" h. **71.50**

Candle lantern, tin & glass, slender cylindrical chimney in a low footed base & wire frame w/bail handle, worn brown japanning, 9¾" h. plus bail..**357.50**

Early Glass Hall Lantern

Hall lantern, blown glass & metal, the frosted clear tulip-form shade engraved w/a leafy blossom band, suspended from a stamped metal ring decorated w/grapevine & anthemion, stamped base cap, suspended from three chains, American-made, early 19th c., electrified, 15" h. (ILLUS.).............**1,725.00**

Leaded & Stained Glass Lantern

Hall lantern, leaded & stained glass, Victorian Aesthetic Movement style, rectangular brass frame w/pierced pointed finials & ringed base drops, each side composed of a central glass panel painted w/a bird framed by round jewels & rectangular & square glass segments, the corners w/cobalt blue swirls alternating w/clear swirls, four arched supports at the top, originally gas, now electrified, ca. 1885, 10" w., 33" h. (ILLUS.) **2,310.00**

Arts & Crafts Lantern

Hanging lantern, Arts & Crafts style, copper & slag glass, the rectangular dished copper top w/ring handle above rectangular metal-framed sides enclosing mottled yellow & white slag glass, metal w/original greenish brown patina, unmarked, early 20th c., 12½" w., 18" h. (ILLUS.) **660.00**

Skater's lantern, tin & glass, tin font base & domed pierced vent cap w/wire bail handle, pear-shaped blue glass globe, 7" h. **269.50**

Tin lantern, Paul Revere-type, cylindrical body w/conical top w/ring handle, overall pierced designs, the sides w/hearts & compass flowers, the curved door w/a large diamond w/crosses & quarter circles & crosses in the corners, 12" h. plus handle **495.00**

Whale oil lantern, brass w/clear pressed glass bull's-eye globe, base & top w/decorative piercing, ring handle, 9" h. plus handle **495.00**

Whale oil lantern, tin & glass, circular collared font base w/pierced design, clear pressed paneled globe w/wire guard attached to a cylindrical pierced tin cap w/peaked top & attached ring handle, very worn dark brown japanning, 9½" h. plus handle **330.00**

Whale oil lantern, tin & glass, circular font base above a round slightly domed foot, clear blown glass globe surmounted w/a pierced tin cap w/large ring handle, probably New England Glass Co., 13" h. plus handle **302.50**

SHADES

Handel ball shade, spherical orangish amber crackled surface decorated

w/large blue stenciled parrots w/long curling tables perched on leafy branches, unsigned, 9" d. **259.00**

Early Hurricane Shade

Hurricane Shade, clear blown glass, tall baluster-form, engraved w/a band of stars over knobby chain swags w/feathered finials framing stylized blossoms above a lower band of grape clusters, early 19th c., 23½" h. (ILLUS.) **1,955.00**

Leaded glass, wide domical form w/an irregular lower edge, stylized florals on a brickwork ground in green, red, yellow smooth glass w/rippled reverse surfaces, early 20th c., 16" d..**345.00**

Lime Green Overshot Shade

Lime green glass, blown tulip-form w/deeply ruffled & crimped green rim shading to clear overshot sides, for a peg lamp, 6" d., 3⅝" h., pr. (ILLUS. of one)..**195.00**

Monot Stumpf, Pantin glass, wide swelled cylindrical tulip-shape w/deeply ruffled & crimped flaring rim, shaded pink to white opalescent swirl design, 8½" d., 6⅝" h. (ILLUS. top next page)....................**225.00**

Pairpoint, domical 'beehive' form "Danver" shade horizontally ridged & reverse-painted along the lower

Monot Stumpf Opalescent Shade

border w/a stylized fenced landscape scene w/cottages & trees, signed "H. Fisher," 15" d...........................**1,265.00**

Signed Quezal Shades

Quezal, slender trumpet-form w/lightly molded ribbing, iridescent green & gold pulled-feather design above an opal white rim band, gold iridescent interior, signed, 5½" h., set of 3 (ILLUS.) **489.00**

Steuben Gold Aurene Shades

Quezal, slender trumpet-form w/lightly scalloped rim, orangish gold iridescence w/a pebbled surface,

marked on top rim, 5¼" h., set of 5..**632.50**
Steuben, gold Aurene, ribbed squatty bell-form w/flattened flaring rim, four marked, one w/slight chip, 4¾" d., 4" h., set of 6 (ILLUS. bottom previous column) **1,210.00**
Tiffany, candlelamp-type, deeply ruffled flaring bell-form, damascene gold iridescent w/green pulled & coiled striations, top rim inscribed "L.C.T.," 7" d. (small chip at collar rim)..**805.00**

Tiffany Black-Eyed Susan Shade

Tiffany, domical leaded glass "Black-eyed Susan" patt., worked in a design of four bouquets of black-eyed Susan blossoms in mottled yellow & white glass w/amber centers & yellow & green stems, reserved against a background shading from white to striated green, frame w/brownish green patina, impressed "TIFFANY STUDIOS - NEW YORK - 1447-29," 16" d. (ILLUS.)............**10,925.00**
Tiffany, domical octagonal leaded glass "Hanging Trellis" patt., worked w/pink, red & blue flowers entwining on a lattice & incorporating drapery & fractured glass panels, unsigned, 26" w. (cracks, losses)...............**39,100.00**

(End of Lighting Devices)

LUNCH BOXES

Although there were a few character-related lunch boxes produced before World War II, it was the arrival of the television age in the 1950s that saw such boxes proliferate. Most of these vintage boxes were rectangular metal and included a matching thermos bottle with both the box exterior and thermos colorfully decorated with a picture relating to the character and their TV series. Beginning in the 1960s lunch boxes in plastic and vinyl became popular and these, as well as the earlier metal examples, are very collectible today if in top condition. References on old lunch boxes include The Illustrated Encyclopedia of Metal Lunch Boxes *by Allen Woodall and Sean Brickell (Schiffer Publishing, 1992) and* Lunch Box: The Fifties and Sixties *by Scott Bruce (Chronicle Books, 1988). Prices are for lunch boxes alone unless otherwise indicated.*

Adam 12, metal, 1972.........................**$49.00**

Archies Lunch Box

Archies (The), metal, red rim, w/thermos (ILLUS.) ....**65.00 to 75.00**
Barbie, vinyl, black, 1962 (some wear)...**60.00**
Barbie & Francie, vinyl, black, 1965 ...**75.00**
Barbie & Midge, vinyl, black, 1963......**75.00**
Batman & Robin, metal, ca. 1966.....**150.00**

Battlestar Galactica Lunch Box

Battlestar Galactica, metal, yellow rim, w/thermos, 1978, some wear (ILLUS.) **30.00**

Beatles Brunch Bag

Beatles, vinyl brunch bag, blue, w/thermos, 1966, some wear (ILLUS.) **550.00**
Bee Gees, plastic, w/thermos, 1978 ....**20.00**
Bee Gees, metal, w/thermos, 1978......**35.00**
Bonanza, metal, 1963.......................**140.00**
Boston Red Sox, vinyl, white w/Red Sox logo in red, 1960........................**85.00**
Brady Bunch (The), metal, red rim, decorated w/various scenes from the TV show, 1970 (some wear)......**150.00**
Buck Rogers, metal, red rim, close up of Buck Rogers in upper left hand corner, w/thermos, 1979 (mint condition) **39.00**
Canadian Train lunch box, metal, 1957, Ohio Art....................................**25.00**
Dagwood Bumstead, lunch bag, waxed paper, illustration of Dagwood on front, King Features Syndicate, 1952, unused **25.00**
Davy Crockett & Kit Carson, metal, red rim, 1955 (some wear)..............**240.00**
Dick Tracy, metal, 1967....................**144.00**
Doctor Dolittle, metal, 1967 (some wear)...**65.00**
Donny & Marie, vinyl brunch bag, zippered, the duo w/long hair, Aladdin, 1977................................**65.00**
Donny & Marie, vinyl brunch bag, zippered, duo w/short hair, Aladdin, 1978...**65.00**
Dukes of Hazard (The) metal, w/thermos, 1980 ....**45.00**
Empire Strikes Back, metal, scene of the swamp, w/thermos, 1980.........**40.00**
Empire Strikes Back, metal, spaceship scene, 1980 (some wear)...**18.00**
Evil Knievel, metal, 1974, Aladdin Industries, w/thermos.......................**55.00**

Family Affair Lunch Box

Family Affair, metal, black rim, w/thermos, 1969 (ILLUS.) **69.00**
Fat Albert & the Cosby Kids, metal, 1973 (some wear) **16.00**
Flipper, metal, King-Seeley, 1967 ....**88.00**
Garfield, metal, half-size, Japan, 1978...**200.00**
G.I. Joe, metal, olive green rim, 1967...**70.00**

Gunsmoke, metal, 1962 ....**225.00**
Happy Days, metal, sides w/pictures
  of the Fonz, Richie & Potsie, 1977
  (slight wear) **25.00**
Hardy Boys Mysteries, metal,
  w/thermos, 1977 ....**20.00**
Hong Kong Phoey, metal, 1975
  (wear)..**20.00**

Hopalong Cassidy Lunch Box

Hopalong Cassidy, metal, full
  lithograph, 1954, some wear
  (ILLUS.) **165.00**
Hopalong Cassidy, metal, blue
  w/small lithograph, 1950 (wear).........**90.00**
James Bond, metal, Aladdin, 1966 ...**150.00**
Jet Patrol, metal, white band, 1957
  (some wear) **300.00**
Jetsons (The), metal, dome top,
  yellow rim & handle, blue ground
  decorated w/scenes from 'The
  Jetsons,' 1963................................**600.00**
Kellogg's Frosted Flakes, metal,
  w/picture of Tony the Tiger on front,
  1969 (some wear) **165.00**
Knight Rider, metal, w/thermos...........**31.50**
Kung Fu, metal, 1974 ....**45.00**
Little Orphan Annie, metal,
  w/thermos **30.00**
Land of the Lost, metal, w/thermos,
  1975...**35.00**
Lone Ranger, metal, blue band,
  1954...**325.00**
Man From U.N.C.L.E., metal, 1967
  (some wear) **125.00**

Monkees Vinyl Lunch Box

Monkees (The), vinyl, w/thermos,
  1967, soiling & wear around edges
  (ILLUS.) **90.00**
Mork & Mindy, metal, w/thermos,
  1979..**39.00**
Partridge Family, metal, 1971 (some
  wear)..**33.00**
Pathfinder, metal, yellow rim,
  1959...**395.00**
Pee Wee's Playhouse, hard
  plastic, w/white thermos w/red
  top, 1987...**15.00**
Pigs in Space (The Muppets), metal,
  black background w/stars,
  w/thermos, 1977 ....**37.00**

Planet of the Apes Lunch Box

Planet of the Apes, metal, black rim,
  w/thermos, 1974, some wear
  (ILLUS.) **75.00**

Rare Popeye Lunch Box

Popeye, metal, black rim w/Popeye,
  Olive Oyl, Bluto & Whimpey,
  w/thermos, 1962, rare, wear
  (ILLUS.) **600.00**
Rifleman (The), metal, brown band
  w/picture of a shotgun & brown rim,
  1961 (some wear) **275.00**
Rough Rider, metal, green band,
  w/thermos, 1972, some wear
  (ILLUS. top next page)......................**55.00**
Roy Rogers & Dale Evans, metal
  w/blue band, American
  Thermos, 1954................................**245.00**

Rough Rider Lunch Box

Roy Rogers & Dale Evans, metal
w/red band, 1954 ....**250.00**
Secrets of Nimh (The), metal, 1982....**15.00**
Snoopy, dome lid.................................**35.00**
Sophisticats (The), vinyl, brown
brunch bag w/thermos, 1969 ....**95.00**

Star Trek Dome Lid Lunch Box

Star Trek, metal, dome lid, w/ther-
mos, 1967, some wear (ILLUS.) **425.00**
Star Trek, plastic, w/thermos,
1988...**15.00**
Star Wars, metal, black w/characters
on band (some wear).........................**30.00**

Star Wars Lunch Box

Star Wars, metal, stars on band,
w/thermos, 1978, some wear
(ILLUS.) **42.00**
Superman thermos, 1967-68..............**25.00**
Super Powers, metal, 1983.................**40.00**
Tarzan, metal, 1966 ....**95.00**
Trigger (Roy Rogers' horse), metal,
w/thermos.........................**50.00 to 100.00**

Tom Corbett Lunch Box

Tom Corbett Space Cadet, metal,
red, 1952, some wear (ILLUS.)........**170.00**
Wagon Train, metal, golden yellow
band & red rim, 1964 ....**225.00**
Waltons (The), metal, yellow rim
w/pictures of the family w/John Boy
on the sides, 1973 ....**65.00**
Washington Redskins, metal, brick
red w/Redskins logo in center, 1970
(some wear) **175.00**
Welcome Back, Kotter, metal, red
rim w/pictures of Mr. Kotter & the
Sweathogs on the front, picture of
blackboard w/writing on the sides,
1977...**28.00**
Wild Frontier, metal, 1977...................**22.50**
World of Barbie, vinyl, pink, 1971 ....**75.00**
World of Barbie, vinyl, blue
w/thermos, 1973 ....**80.00**
Yogi Bear & friends, metal, black
rim, 1961 ....**85.00**

MAGAZINES

First Issue of Life

*All magazines are in excellent, complete
condition unless otherwise noted*

American Boy, 1924, December, stories by Leo Edwards, Heyliger, Kelland, Mills & toy ads **$12.00**
Boy's Life, 1961, April **3.50**
Collier's, 1902, May 10, cowgirl cover, double page Charles Remington story **12.50**
Collier's, 1957, January 4, Princess Grace on cover **10.00**
Esquire, 1939, March **45.00**
Field & Stream, 1916, February **60.00**
Fortune, 1932, October **15.00**
Genii (magic), 1938, February **6.00**
Life, 1920, January 8, Norman Rockwell "Wallflower" cover **10.00**
Life, 1936, November 23, premier issue of the new version of "Life," absolutely mint (ILLUS.) **220.00**
Life, 1937, April 19, the "Queen Mary" ocean liner on the cover **30.00**
Life, 1964, December 18, Elizabeth Taylor on cover **20.00**
Life, 1969, June 20, Joe Namath on cover **9.00**
Literary Digest, 1919, January............**12.00**
National Geographic, 1939, July through December, six months bound **8.50**
National Sportsman, 1920, April **50.00**
Reader's Digest, 1922, February 11, Volume I, No. I (some wear) **65.00**
Time, 1941, September 29, Joe Louis on cover **45.00**
Time, 1948, July 19, Howard Hughes on cover **28.00**

MARBLES

Indian Swirl Marble

Glass, Akro Agate Company, original box of Royals, near mint condition **$725.00**
Glass, banded swirl, 5/8" d. **45.00**
Glass, brick (dark red oxblood), 11/16" d. **65.00**
Glass, carnelian, 23/34" d.......................**45.00**
Glass, Christmas corkscrew, green & red opaque, 5/8" d. **15.00**
Glass, clambroth w/red lines, 11/16 d. **145.00**
Glass, clear green Aventurine 9/16" d. **22.00**
Glass, divided core-type, 1 1/8" d. **150.00**
Glass, egg yolk oxblood, 11/16" d. **150.00**
Glass, hand-made, banded swirl, 11/16" d. **40.00**
Glass, German slag-type, tan, opaque blue & white, 1" d. **52.50**
Glass, green swirl, 9/16" d......................**20.00**
Glass, hand-made, opaque blue, 7/8" d. **100.00**
Glass, hand-made, double ribbon, 5/8" d. ....**20.00 to 30.00**
Glass, hand-made, mica-type, green w/mica flecks throughout, 9/16" d. **25.00**
Glass, hand-made, solid core, transparent swirl, 1" d. **35.00**
Glass, hand-made, Indian swirl, 5/8" d. **38.00**
Glass, Indian swirl, black w/red & green bands, 11/16" d. (ILLUS.) **110.00**

Joseph's Coat Marble

Joseph's coat, orange & yellow swirls, contemporary piece by Mark Matthews, 1 1/2" d. (ILLUS.) **160.00**
Glass, latticino-type, aqua w/swirled yellow bands, 13/16" d. **370.00**
Glass, latticino-type, yellow, 1 11/16" d. **120.00**
Glass, lemonade oxblood, 19/32" d. **100.00**
Glass, Lutz-type, amber, 13/16" d. **225.00**
Glass, machine-made, Persian blue opaque, 3/4" d..**10.00**
Glass, mica-type, cobalt w/mica flecks throughout, 7/8" d. **40.00**
Glass, mica-type, green w/center filament, 3/4" d. **60.00**
Glass, mica-type, green w/overall mica flecks throughout, 9/16" d. **25.00**
Glass, milky oxblood w/cane cut swirls, 1/2" d., pr. **35.00**
Glass, milky oxblood w/green swirl, 3/4" d. **150.00**
Glass, "onionskin," blue & white, 15/16" d. **125.00**
Glass, "onionskin," end-of-day-type, four-panel, 5/8" d. **55.00**
Glass, "onionskin," end-of-day-type, pink & white swirled spatter, 1 3/4" d. (ILLUS. top next page) **160.00**
Glass, "onionskin," turquoise, 5/8" d. **125.00**
Glass, Pee Wee, divided core, 1 1/2" d. **20.00**

"Onionskin" End-of-Day Marble

Glass, Popeye, fluorescent, ⅝" d. **45.00**
Glass, Popeye, purple, 19/32" d. **45.00**
Glass, red, banded opaque,
11/16" d. **125.00**
Glass, reverse double corkscrew,
green & white, ⅝" d. **50.00**
Glass, ribbon core-type, yellow &
purple, 1 1/16" d. **200.00**
Glass, slag-type, green, white double
pontil, 2" d. **300.00**
Glass, slag-type, oxblood & milky
white, ⅝" d. **30.00**
Glass, sulphide, w/bird, 1⅞" d.
(chips) **82.50**
Glass, sulphide, w/cat, seated **275.00**
Glass, sulphide, w/dog in seated
position, 1⅛" d. (wear) **82.50**
Glass, sulphide, w/perched falcon,
1 11/16" d. **190.00**

Sulphide with Numeral "2"

Glass, sulphide, w/numeral "2,"
1¼" d. (ILLUS.) **294.00**
Glass, sulphide, w/pig **75.00**
Glass, sulphide, w/sheep, 1⅞" d.
(wear) **104.50**
Glass, sulphide, w/sheep, 2" d.
(chips) **137.50**
Glass, sulphide, w/swimming fish,
1⅝" d. **275.00**

MATCH SAFES & CONTAINERS

Advertising container, wall-type,
lithographed tin, "Tubular Cream
Separators," flat rectangular plate
w/rounded arch top, decorated at
the top w/a landscape scene w/cows
above a panel showing a mother &
daughter operating the separator &

Tubular Separators Match Container

w/the wording "The Pet of the
Dairy," match container at the
bottom w/the wording "Tubular
Cream Separators," colorful scenes
& yellow, black & white lettering,
2¼" w., 7" h. (ILLUS.) **$412.50**

Patent-dated Match Container

Cast iron container, hanging-type, a
paneled urn-form container within a
scrolled cartouche-style frame
w/serrated bands at the sides,
patent-dated "Jan. 15, 1867," minor
rust, gold paint missing, 3½" w.,
6" h. (ILLUS.) **132.00**
Cast iron container, hanging-type,
hunt scene w/two men flanking
moose head at top above hanging
game & curved horn over two-
section game bag, old polychrome
repaint over black, 10¾" h. **115.50**
Pottery container, model of a black
& white pig seated by a tree stump
labeled "MATCHES," 2¾" h.
(chipped) **181.50**
Sterling silver safe, Art Nouveau
style florals **85.00**

Early Wooden Match Container

Wooden container, hanging-type, chip-carved & incised cherry, cylindrical tube pierced w/a hole for hanging, decorated on the front w/arcs, circles, shells & flowers & hearts along w/the initials "AB 1800," New England, 10¼" h. (ILLUS.) **2,415.00**

MEDICAL COLLECTIBLES

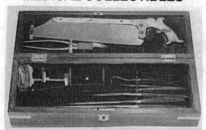

Amputating & Trepanning Set

Amputating set, metal blades w/brass inlay impressed "E.V. Chase Elsie, Mich.," in fitted wooden case, ca. 1860, case 4¼ x 15½", 3" h., the set................................**$2,530.00**

Amputating & trepanning set, metal instruments impressed "W. R. Goulding New York, ebony handles, in brass-bound fitted wood case w/purple velvet lining, small scalpel not matching, missing probe, ca. 1870, 5¼ x 15½", 3" h. (ILLUS.) **2,970.00**

Anesthesia Inhaler

Anesthesia inhaler, "Sonoform," chrome w/rubber fittings, w/instruction booklet marked "Stratford-Cookson Co...Philadelphia Revised Copyright 1930," in fitted wooden carrying case, the set (ILLUS.) **209.00**

Blood pressure instrument, "Sphygmometrique," slender metal cylinders & rubber bulbs, in fitted black carrying case, Paris, France, ca. 1900, the set **440.00**

Book, "Consumption, Nature, Prevention & Homeopathic Treatment," by Wm. Hitchman M.D., Philadelphia, PA, 1859 ....**38.00**

Early Cupping Set

Cupping set, clear cylindrical glass bottles & a cylindrical metal pump device, in a fitted wood case marked "Savigny & Co.," late 19th c., the set (ILLUS.)............................**1,980.00**

Dentist's drill, cast iron, foot pedal-driven, ca. 1870s **230.00**

Ear horn, brass & copper, a large half-round spherical horn on a long slender tapering stem w/curved end, marked "English Made," 13½" l..**93.50**

Ear horn, silver plate, beehive-shaped w/pierced front, French, ca. 1800 ....**225.00**

Electrocardiograph machine, "Sanborn Visco Cardiette," metal in wooden carrying case, case marked "Made for Dr. E.I. Schinder," ca. 1930-50, case 8¼ x 15", 11½" h. (ILLUS. top next page).....................**385.00**

Electro thermophore device, used to treat glaucoma & other eye problems, w/instructions in wooden case, ca. 1920, 3 x 4¼ x 12½"..........**577.50**

Eye surgical instrument set, three fine ivory-handled blades & hook, in original fitted wooden box, American-made, 19th c., 6½" l. (box binding separated) **214.50**

Electrocardiograph Machine

Fleam knife (blood-letting lancet),
folding-type, brass & steel, two-
blade, stamped "Borwick 3" **82.50**

Machine, "Davis & Kidder's Magneto
Electric Machine," quack medical
device, in brass-bound wooden
case, case 4½ x 10", 3" h. **330.00**

Machine, "Electrical Faradic"
apparatus, quack medical device,
made by Sears & Roebuck, in
wooden case w/instructions, ca.
1920, 7½ x 10", 9" h........................**319.00**

Machine, "Home Medical Apparatus,"
quack medical device, labeled "J.H.
Bunnell & Co., 20 Park Place, New
York," ca. 1920, w/wooden case,
5¼ x 8½", 4½" h.............................**308.00**

Machine, "No. 6 Peerless Coil,"
quack medical device, in black
carrying case w/instructions, ca
1920..**165.00**

Machine, "Polysine Generator
Electric Shock Machine," quack
medical device, w/wood case
w/four drawers & white enamel
top, ca. 1920-30 (enamel top
scratched) **385.00**

Quack Electrical Machine

Machine, "The Dow Portable
Electrical Assistant," quack medical
device, in fitted wooden case,
Braintree, Massachusetts, case
7½ x 8½", 5¼" h. (ILLUS.) **412.50**

Machine, "Voltamp Electrical Shock,"
quack medical device, made by
Montgomery Ward & Co., ca. 1910,
in oak case, 7¼ x 8", 5½" h. **209.00**

Surgeon's kit, rectangular mahogany
case fitted w/ten tools, seven
w/checkered ebony handles, three
pieces stamped "D. Kolbe, Phila."
three other marks, includes two
saws, one boring tool, pliers,
tweezers, four scalpels & a
rubber tourniquet, Civil War era,
the set **1,100.00**

Early Surgical Saw

Surgical saw, double-bladed, bone
handles, last quarter 19th c.,
10½" l. (ILLUS.) **1,320.00**

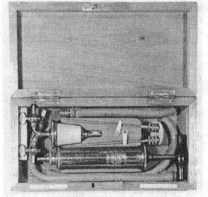

Early Syringe Set

Syringe set, metal syringe w/rubber
hose, case & instruments marked
"Down Bros.," London, England, in
fitted wooden case, last quarter
19th c. (ILLUS.)................................**247.50**

Tonsil cutters, metal w/bond handle,
in fitted black case, England, late
19th c. **440.00**

X-ray machine, portable, "General
Electric," in wooden carrying
case, ca. 1935, case 12½ x 19",
8" h...**605.00**

METALS

ALUMINUM

Bulbous Aluminum Vase

Basket w/twisted handle, embossed w/fruits & flowers, signed "Cromwell," 11" d..................**$34.50**

Bowl, 8 x 12½", scalloped, tulips design, hammered, "Rodney Kent"................................**12.00**

Console set: bowl & double candleholders; Dogwood patt., Wendell August Forge, 3 pcs..........**250.00**

Floor lamp, Modern style, the inverted bell-form elongated shade above a tall slender shaft & disc foot, spun metal w/a wood knob switch, impressed mark of Russel Wright, the designer, New York, 20th c., 5' 4½" h. (base dents).........**546.00**

Plate, floral design, hammered, "Everlast," 11¾" d. **10.00**

Punch set: 11⅜" d., 6" h. bowl, six cups & a ladle; spun deep slightly flaring bowl w/wide rolled rim w/upturned edge for the hooked wooden punch cup handles, ladle w/turned bamboo handle grip, designed by Russel Wright, impressed mark, the set (dents) **546.00**

Vanity set, in the form of an airplane opening to reveal various compartments for vanity items, stamped "D.R.G.M. MADE IN GERMANY," w/firm's mark, ca. 1930s, 10" l................................**1,150.00**

Vase, 9" h., ovoid bulbous shape w/hammered surface decorated in relief w/stylized palm leaf design, stamped "LAVEUR CHAUDRON ART," ca. 1930 (ILLUS.) **115.00**

BRASS

Card tray, Victorian-relief scene of nude lady, 3¼ x 4¾" **$85.00**

Brass & Wrought-Iron Fireplace Trivet

Fireplace trivet, the U-shaped kettle support pierced w/a phoenix & C-scrolls on wrought-iron arched legs ending in penny feet, w/baluster-turned mahogany handle, ca. 1770, 20¼" l., 10" h. (ILLUS.) **1,955.00**

Kettle, spun, iron bail handle, deep slightly flaring cylindrical sides, marked "Hayden's Patent," dark patina, 9½" d.......................................**49.50**

Kettle, spun, iron bail handle, "Hayden's patent," 12" d., 7¾" h........**60.50**

Kettle, spun-type w/iron bail handle, 13½" d., 6¾" h. **82.50**

Kettle, spun, iron bail handle, labeled "American Brass Kettle," polished, 17" d., 10" h. **93.50**

Ladle, cast-iron arm w/wooden handle & hook for hanging, 23" l., bowl 7" d., 3" deep............................**85.00**

Letter holder, Art Nouveau style w/cherubs, signed, Bradley & Hubbard **155.00**

Letter slot, cast, door-type, Victorian era..**45.00**

Model of an eagle, large spread-winged bird w/fine feather detailing, head turned to the right, tin back w/oval label "Patented Sept. 10, 1891, N.Y.," 27" l................**522.50**

Planter, Secession style, bi-level w/central plant well flanked by stylized putti, w/brickwork foliate cast border, attributed to Michael Powolny, ca. 1900, 7½" w., 15" l., 12" h..................................**2,875.00**

Stencils, for labeling barrel heads, one "Grain Alcohol," the other, "Vodka," 21" d., pr...........................**115.50**

BRONZE

Ashtray, floor model, the standard in the form of three fluted rods, continuing to a spreading circular base, stamped "TIFFANY STUDIOS NEW YORK 1658," 24" h.................**402.00**

Ewer, Art Nouveau style, wide ovoid body w/a wide shoulder tapering to a short tapering cylindrical neck, the handle cast as a large curved thistle blossom & stem, the sides cast w/large stylized thistle blossoms & leaves arching over faces in profile, inscribed "J. JOZON Salon de Beaux-Arts," impressed "BRONZE - GARANTI - AU - TITRE - C&L - DEPOSEE - 7373," brown patina, Jeanne Jozon, France, ca. 1900, 9" h...**1,610.00**

Inkwell, Zodiac patt., octagonal, Tiffany Studios, No. 1072, 6½" w. **590.00**

Jardiniere, figural, oblong base below flared-out center below tapering sides cast w/rings & scrolls below a large cluster of blossoms at the foot of a standing maiden, dark & gilt patinas, inscribed "CH. KORSCHANN - PARIS," impressed "LOUCHET," by Charles Korschann, France, ca. 1900, 12" h.................**2,875.00**

Jardiniere, the wide flat bottom w/shallow upright sides cast w/cyclamen blossoms, gilt intaglio finish, w/original metal liner, impressed "TIFFANY STUDIOS - NEW YORK - 834," 10¾" d...........**2,875.00**

Match holder, model of a beetle, tabletop-type, Bradley & Hubbard....**195.00**

Bronze Figural Tazza

Tazza, figural, shallow bowl supported by nude female w/drape tied around her waist, on a round pedestal base flanked by sphinx-like figures on a triangular base w/scroll feet, inscribed "H. WADERE," & "GUSS: C. LEYRER," & "MUNCHEN," & "Professor Dr. Theodor von Jürgensen seinen Assistenzärzten gewidmet. Tüningen 1873-1898," Heinrich Wadere, Germany, late

19th - early 20th c., 30⅜" h. (ILLUS.) **4,830.00**

Urn, Art Deco style, straight slender long handles w/turned-down tips extend from the rim of the deep rounded bowl on a small foot, the side cast w/large oval reserve of a stylized sea creature, stamped "E. BRANDT," Edgar Brandt, 10" h..**11,500.00**

Vase, figural, wide ovoid body w/a ringed neck & molded rim flanked on one side w/a nearly nude maiden w/one arm raised & on the other by a smaller figure, greenish brown & black patinas, signed "Recipon," inscribed "Susse F - Edt" w/foundry mark, designed by Georges Recipon, France, ca. 1900, 10" h..................................**1,380.00**

Bronze Tiffany Vase

Vase, 15" h., angular baluster form decorated w/vertical panels & curvilinear devices, impressed "Tiffany & Co. - 28215B" (ILLUS.) **990.00**

***Vide poche* (figural dish),** cast as an oblong shallow shell w/a figural fish in waves along one side, dark brown patina, inscribed "NEEDHAM," impressed "D. ZOPPO - FOUNDRIES N.Y.," ca. 1900, 6¾" l., 3½" h...............................**920.00**

CHROME

Bar caddy, Chase catalog No. 90141 ....**20.00**

Champagne bucket, "Bacchus" patt., Rockwell Kent, Chase catalog, 9¼" h.....................................**575.00**

Cocktail set, Art Deco style, shaker w/red Bakelite handle, four ruby chrome stemmed glasses, "Stainless Chrome," 5 pcs. **58.00**

Cocktail shaker, red lucite handle, Art Deco style **35.00**

Coffee set: elliptical double-handled

tray, coffeepot, creamer & sugar bowl; each piece w/orange Bakelite handles, early 20th c., tray 17" l., the set **161.00**

Coffee set, individual, stacking-type: coffeepot w/stacking cream pitcher & cov. sugar bowl on top; polished chromium w/white plastic handles & knob, coffeepot holds 1½ cups, manufactured by Chase, No. 90073, the set **155.00**

Creamer & sugar bowl, ivory handled, Walter Von Nesson, Chase catalog No. 17089, pr. **55.00**

Creamer & sugar bowl w/undertray, Chase catalog No. 26003 ....**140.00**

Dressing mirror, table model, a large rectangular mirror raised on a thin narrow rectangular base & flanked by stepped bars at each side, the top center mounted w/a long tapering oval stylized female head w/applied long curls & facial features, Hagenauer, ca. 1920, indistinct hallmark, 22½" h. **2,875.00**

Damon Chromed-metal Reading Lamp

Lamp, reading, globular shaped shade surrounded by two rings, on a curved circular base, adjustable, Damon, ca. 1928, 11" d., 13" h. (ILLUS.) ...**3,163.00**

Ming bell, Chase catalog No. 13007 ....**75.00**

Pitcher, beer, Chase catalog No. 90025 ....**100.00**

Pitcher, "Normandie," rounded wedge-shaped body w/strap handle, impressed "Revere - ROME - N.Y.," Designed by Peter Müller-Monk for the Revere Copper & Brass Company, ca. 1936, 12" h. (ILLUS. top next column) **2,530.00**

Salad serving set: fork & spoon; Bakelite handles, Chase, catalog No. 90076, pr. **38.00**

Tea service: cov. electric teapot, cov. sugar bowl, creamer & tray; "Comet," Chase catalog No. 90119,

"Normandie" Chrome Pitcher

teapot 7½" h. overall, 12" d. tray, the set **280.00**

Wine bottle holders, stark linear construction & standing at an angle on four square legs joined by a cylindrical handle, w/sliding & padded neck rest, designed by Jacques Adnet, unsigned, ca. 1935, 9" h., pr. **1,725.00**

COPPER

New England Copper Kettle

Ashtray, hand-hammered, square, embossed horse's head, anvil & hammer mark of maker, "Craftsman Co.," 3½" sq. **120.00**

Ashtray, hand-hammered, round w/a wide flattened rim w/oblong indentations surrounding the center round indentation, impressed mark of Gustav Stickley, Model No. 272, cleaned, 5¾" d. **172.50**

Ashtray w/matchbox holder, Arts & Crafts style, shallow rimmed bowl, matchbox holder & two cigarette rests on rim, wood-grained surface, monogrammed, w/glass liner, marked "Hand wrought by Fred

Brosi - Ye Olde Copper Shoppe San Francisco," 3¾ x 6½" **165.00**

Basket, wide canoe-shaped bowl w/a wide pierced riveted handle from side to side at the center, fine original dark patina, impressed box mark of Dirk Van Erp w/remnant of "D'Arcy Gaw," 6¾ x 10¼" **1,045.00**

Book ends, Arts & Crafts style, hand-hammered, pillow-form backs, original patina, impressed mark of Gustav Stickley, early 20th c., 5½" w., 5½" h., pr............................**660.00**

Bowl, cov., Arts & Crafts style, hand-hammered, a wide shallow rounded bowl raised on a trumpet foot, the round notched & slightly domed cover decorated w/blue, gold, green & orange enamel peacock eye boxes, the disc knob handle centered by five peacock eye medallions, blue enamel interior, designed by Rebecca Cauman, Boston, impressed mark, 7" d., 4" h..**4,025.00**

Bowl, Arts & Crafts style, hand-hammered, the wide shallow form w/closed sides, three small hanging holes around the rim & an applied silver monogram "JHW" at one side, original light brown patina, stamped "KALO - 62," The Kalo Shop, Chicago, Illinois, early 20th c., 7¼" d., 2¾" h. **165.00**

Bowl, Arts & Crafts style, hand-hammered, a thin footring below a rounded seven-lobe petal-form bowl, original brown patina, impressed mark of Karl Leinonen, Boston, 9" d., 3" h. **316.00**

Box, cov., Arts & Crafts style, hand-hammered copper & enamel, squatty rounded base w/inverted shoulder supporting a low domed cover w/a large low-relief floral medallion in shades of blue w/green trim, blue enamel interior, designed by Caroline Hay, Boston, incised "Hay Crafters," 4¾" d., 2" h...........**1,610.00**

Box, cov., Arts & Crafts style, hand-hammered, rectangular w/a curving handle & four riveted legs, second patina forming, unmarked Benedict, early 20th c., 6 x 10", 7" h...............**165.00**

Camelia basket, Arts & Crafts style, hand-hammered, the deep canoe-shaped basket centered by a wide central loop handle from side to side pierced w/a band of narrow slits, medium-light patina, Dirk Van Erp windmill mark, ca. 1915, 7⅜ x 10", 7½" h. (patina loss) **460.00**

Candy kettle, wrought-iron handle, dove-tail construction, 9½" d............**265.00**

Candy kettle, deep rounded dovetailed body, heavy iron side handles, 15½" d. **104.50**

Chambersticks, Arts & Crafts style, hand-hammered, deep dished base centered by a cylindrical shaft w/a flattened dished rim, riveted strap handle on the shaft, excellent original dark patina, Gustav Stickley stamped "Als Ik Kan" mark, Model No. 74, 9¼" h., pr........................**1,210.00**

Coal scuttle, cylindrical w/a hinged handle, America or England, 19th c., 17½" h...**345.00**

Coffee service: cov. coffeepot, creamer, cov. sugar bowl & tray; Art Deco style, each piece w/bands of raised triangles, & overall hammered finish, stamped w/mark of Wertembergische Metalwaren fabrik, coffeepot 8" h., 4 pcs. **403.00**

Dinner gong, Arts & Crafts style, hand-hammered, hand-wrought round disc hanging from a triangular wallplate showing embossed, stylized flowers, original medium brown patina, die-stamped 'anvil' mark of Mission Studios, Laguna Beach, California, early 20th c., 5¾ x 9½" **110.00**

Inkstand, Arts & Crafts style, hand-hammered silvered copper, long rectangular tray w/flaring base, fitted w/a pen tray & blotter pad & two attached square boxes w/hinged covers at the ends, affixed pen holders, stitched double border & applied monogram "R," Dirk Van Erp open box mark, early 20th c., 2¾ x 18" (wear to original patina)..**330.00**

Kettle, cov., short cylindrical form w/handle on wrought-iron feet, New England 19th c., 21½" l., 12" h. (ILLUS.) **1,265.00**

Onondaga Metal Shops Oil Lamp

Lamp, oil, hand-hammered, slightly

bulbous body w/original bronze patina & riveted wrought-iron foliate handles painted black, oil font inset supporting reddish woven wicker shade w/cloth liner, incised "OMS," Onondaga Metal Shops, East Syracuse, New York, ca. 1904, 21" h., shade 18" d. (ILLUS.) **2,070.00**

Loving cup, hand-hammered, Arts & Crafts style, flat-bottomed wide trumpet-form w/three strap handles from the rolled rim to the base, some wear to original patina, numbered on base "33," attributed to the Stickley Brothers, 6¼" d., 4¾" h..**302.50**

Pot, hand-hammered, Arts & Crafts style, wide bulbous ovoid shouldered vessel w/a wide flat rolled rim, medium brown patina, Dirk Van Erp, die-stamped "San Francisco" mark, early 20th c., 4½" d., 3½" h. (cleaned) **522.50**

Sauce pan, cov., deep cylindrical sides, dished flat cover, double cast-iron long handle, marked "L.F.D. & H. N.Y.," 7¾" d. plus handle **110.00**

Skillet, cov., dished flattened cover, cast iron handle, marked "D.H. & M. N.Y.," 12" d. plus handle.................**121.00**

Stamp box, cov., hand-hammered, Arts & Crafts style, long rectangular form w/a low-domed cover w/a center small knob, original deep bronze patina, impressed Gustav Stickley mark, early 20th c., 2¼ x 4⁵⁄₁₆", 2⅛" h. **402.50**

Tazza, Arts & Crafts style, hand-hammered copper & horn, the wide shallow bowl raised on a segmented slender pedestal comprised of a shaped brass bead between carved horn discs, on a flaring round foot, designed by Rebecca Cauman, Boston, original brown patina, impressed mark, 6¾" d., 4⅜" h...**230.00**

Teakettle, cov., dovetailed construction, wide cylindrical body w/indented foot, gooseneck spout w/flap, domed cover w/decorative finial, strap swing handle, 7¼" h. plus handle **82.50**

Teakettle, cov., wide rounded & shouldered dovetailed body w/a swan's-neck spout & low domed cover, swivel strap handle stamped "E. A. Franklin," brass finial on cover, 8" h. plus handle (some battering)..**137.50**

Teakettle, cov., dovetail construction, slightly globular base, flat shoulder, gooseneck spout, rounded swing handle, polished, 8¼" h. plus handle **220.00**

Teakettle, cov., cylindrical dovetailed sides w/a wide shoulder to the small domed cover, stationary handle w/bar grip raised on S-scrolls, swan's neck spout, 19th c., 8¾" h..**137.50**

Teakettle, cov., dovetailed construction, straight sides, gooseneck spout, fixed overhead handle, brass trim, maker's mark on bottom, overall 11" h. (dents)...........**181.50**

Tray, Arts & Crafts style, hand-hammered, oval dished form w/flat scalloped edge, two oval bone knob end handles, cleaned original finish, stamped "BERRYS CRAFT SHOP - THEIR MARK - SEATTLE - 5," Albert Berry, Seattle, Washington, 9¼ x 14¼" **247.50**

Tray, Arts & Crafts style, hand-hammered, oval w/low flared sides & a flared rim, mounted w/angled loop end handles, Dirk Van Erp mark, early 20th c., 17" l. **605.00**

Tray, Arts & Crafts style, hand-hammered, rectangular w/rounded corners & rolled rim, riveted braided end handles, restored dark patina, stamped "Als Ik Kan" mark of Gustav Stickley, Model No. 356, 12 x 17"...**715.00**

Stickley Copper Umbrella Stand

Umbrella stand, trumpet-form body w/two riveted handles & an embossed stylized floral design on each side, w/its worn original patina, die-stamped circular mark, Gustav Stickley, Model No. 382, 14" d., 24½" h. (ILLUS.) **1,650.00**

Urn, dovetailed construction, wide ovoid body tapering to a cylindrical neck flanked by large loop handles to the shoulder, decorated w/tooled brass double eagle cartouches, Russia, marked, 13¼" h...................**165.00**

Vase, Arts & Crafts style, hand-
hammered, wide squatty bulbous
base w/an angled shoulder tapering
sharply to a cylindrical neck
w/molded rim, original reddish
brown patina, by Harry Dixon,
incised "H. Dixon - San Francisco -
1920," 5" d., 5½" h. **440.00**

Vase, Arts & Crafts style, hand-
hammered, squatty bulbous body
tapering to a cylindrical neck w/a
rolled rim, aged patina, etched mark
"Harry Dixon - San Francisco," early
20th c., 4" d., 6" h. (minor
unevenness at rim) **275.00**

Vase, Arts & Crafts style, hand-
hammered & etched, bulbous ovoid
form w/a short wide cylindrical neck
w/rolled rim, etched around the neck
w/the motto "Great Oakes From
Little Acorns Grow," the sides
etched in low-relief w/large stylized
oak leaves & acorns, unsigned,
early 20th c., 7" d., 7½" h.
(patina loss) **345.00**

Dirk Van Erp Copper Vase

Vase, squatty bulbous shape w/neck
tapering to a rolled rim, rich red
patina, stamped w/windmill mark &
"DIRK VAN ERP" within broken box,
by Dirk Van Erp, ca. 1912,
8" h. (ILLUS.) **4,370.00**

Vase, Arts & Crafts style, hand-
hammered copper, a domed round
foot below the flat trumpet-form
sides flaring to a shoulder & short,
widely flaring & lightly ruffled &
flatted rim, impressed marks of
Joseph Heinrichs, New York, ca.
1910, 11¾" h.................................**172.50**

Wash boiler, double-handled, ca.
1890, 13 x 13 x 23" oval **95.00**

IRON

Cookie board, cast, rectangular
decorated w/a bird on a branch &
dotwork within an oval,
3 x 4⅞"..**165.00**

Cookie board, cast, oval, decorated
w/a swan within a circle w/an outer
framework of dots, 4¾ x 5¾" **170.50**

Cookie board, cast, rectangular
w/rounded corners, decorated w/a
pineapple & dotwork, geometric
design around outer edge,
4½ x 6"...**151.50**

Door handle, hand-wrought, featuring
a cut-out of an Indian head in a
feathered headdress.....................**1,430.00**

Door knocker, cast, model of a
basket of flowers,very good paint **130.00**

Door knocker, model of lady's hand,
holding apple, w/all hardware **65.00**

Door knocker, model of a parrot **65.00**

Cast Iron Fireback

Fireback, cast, low curved top over
molded grotesque face surrounded
by molded scrolls over narrow band
w/molded words "Ana 1763," above
elaborate C-scrolls ending in
grotesque animal heads, ca. 1763,
15½" h. (ILLUS.) **201.00**

Fireback, cast, arched scrolled top
above a tall panel w/the raised
design of a man on horseback, vine
borders down the sides, 18th c.,
24" h..**805.00**

Fruit press, "Griswold No. 110,"
wood slats......................................**250.00**

Gate hook, wrought, in the form of a
stylized serpent w/coiled body &
ending in the form of an arrow,
probably Vermont, 19th c.,
50" l...**3,105.00**

Griddle, cast, "Griswold No. 9,"
rectangular.......................................**40.00**

Hinges, wrought, scrolling ram's horn
form, 16" l., pr. **137.50**

Kitchen set, child's, waffle iron,
griddle, fry pan & pot w/bail handle,
Wagnerware, 4 pcs........................**115.00**

Lawn ornament, cast, rabbit,
11" h..**195.00**

Model of an eagle, cast, modeled
standing on a rocky base w/wings to
sides, old worn & weathered black,
white & yellow paint, 33½" h. **2,090.00**

Nail holder, cast, revolving-type w/divided cup, base marked "Star Nail Cup," 9½" d. **44.00**

Oven peel, hand-wrought, a flat squared blade w/a long slender handle ending in a ram's horn curl, 40½" l. **104.50**

Oven peel, hand-wrought, long handle w/ram's horn end, 43" l **143.00**

Oven peel, hand-wrought, squared blade w/rounded corners, long slender handle w/ram's horn end curl, 48" l. **159.50**

Patty bowl, cast, "Griswold No. 72" **60.00**

Rush light holder, wrought, tooled brass wafer at base of stem, tripod base, 9½" h. (light rust) **357.50**

Rush light holder, wrought, w/mushroom shaped counter-weight, tapering cylindrical wooden base, 10¼" h. **275.00**

Sugar nippers, scissors-type, hand-wrought, simple tooled details, 9" l. **192.50**

Sugar nippers, hand-wrought, tooled detail, 10¼" l **159.50**

Cast Iron Umbrella Rack

Umbrella rack, cast, thin baluster-and ring-turned column w/leaf detail w/loop handle at top, center ring w/six holes for umbrellas, scalloped drip pan on small feet, old worn green paint w/rust, 39½" h. (ILLUS.) **412.50**

Waffle iron, cast, "Griswold No. 0," w/coil handle **495.00**

Waffle iron, cast, child's, Stover, Jr. **115.00**

PEWTER

Basin, round w/upright sides & molded rim, marked "Townsend & Compton, London," England, late

18th c., 11" d., 2¾" h. (wear, scratches) **220.00**

Basin, Samuel Hamlin, Sr., Hartford, Connecticut & Providence, Rhode Island, polished, 5¾" d. (minor battering) **495.00**

Bowl, low hammered bulbous body raised on three strapwork legs, set w/six dark blue glazed cabochons, impressed "MADE - IN ENGLAND - TUDRIC - PEWTER - 01128 - MADE BY LIBERTY & CO.," ca. 1900, 8¼" h. **575.00**

Bowl, shallow, rampant lion touch mark of Joseph Danforth, Middletown, Connecticut, 13¼" d. (minor battering) **440.00**

Center bowl, Art Nouveau style, oval squatty sides w/flaring rim, applied w/Celtic style strapping, raised on four trefoil feet, hanging interior flower mesh screen, Liberty & Co., England, impressed marks & "0336," 9⅜ x 13¼", 5⅝" h. **517.50**

Charger, flanged rim engraved "HGI," marked on back, possibly England, late 18th - early 19th c., 13½" d. **60.00**

Charger, round, marked on base "IF" w/fleur-de-lis, Europe, 19th c., 18" d. **431.00**

Charger, round, Lawrence Langworthy, Exeter, England, before 1731, 18½" d. **690.00**

Coffeepot, cov., lighthouse-form, marked on base "R. Dunham" in rectangular cartouche, Rufus Dunham, Westbrook, Maine, 1837-61, 11" h. (imperfections) **247.50**

Coffeepot, cov., tall pear-shaped body raised on a stepped foot, domed cover, Boardman & Co., New York, Hartford, Connecticut, 12" h. **577.50**

Flagon, cov., slightly tapering cylindrical body on molded base, decorative band around middle, Sellew & Co., Cincinnati, Ohio, 8⅝" h. **577.50**

Flagon, cov., tall tapering cylindrical body w/C-scroll handle & domed cover, Thomas Danforth Boardman, Hartford, Connecticut, 1804- after 1860, 12½" h. **1,760.00**

Ladle, pointed handle, T. D. Boardman, Hartford, Connecticut, 1804- after 1860, 13¾" l. **357.50**

Measure, tankard-form, footed baluster-form body w/C-scroll handle, marked "Watts & Harton, London," England, 19th c., pint, 5¼" h. **93.50**

Measures, bellied-form, ringed foot, C-scroll handle, England, from ¼ gill

to quart, the tallest 6⅜" h., set
of 6...**825.00**

Mug, slightly tapering sides, scrolled
handle, Samuel Danforth, Hartford,
Connecticut, 1795-1813, 1 qt........**1,430.00**

Mug, tulip-shaped, crown "VR" mark,
James Yates, England, 4½" wide
from rim including handle, 4" h. **77.00**

Mug, marked "T.D." in rectangular
cartouche, Thomas Danforth III,
Connecticut & Philadelphia, 1777-
1818, 1 qt., 5½" h.........................**1,540.00**

Mug, tapering cylindrical body w/a
slightly flaring base & lower body
band, S-scroll handle, Samuel
Hamlin, Providence, Rhode Island,
1801-56, 1 qt., 6" h. **1,540.00**

Pitcher, 7¾" h., indistinct mark,
19th c. **259.00**

Pitcher, water, globular w/low base &
spreading foot, eared handle, Flagg
& Homan, Cincinnati, Ohio, 1842-
54, 9" h...**247.50**

Plate, Frederick Bassett, New York &
Hartford, Connecticut, 1761-99,
9¼" d. (wear) **742.50**

Plate, George Grenfell, London,
England, 8⅝" d. (wear, scratches).....**66.00**

Plate, engraved initials "LR," T. W.
Leeds, London, England, 12" d........**172.50**

Plate, Love touch mark, Philadelphia,
Pennsylvania, 8⅝" d. (wear &
dents) **247.50**

Plate, rampant lion touch mark of
Edward Danforth, Middletown,
Connecticut, 1786-95, 8" d. (worn
& pitted) **253.00**

Platter, oval w/wide rim, John
Townsend, London, England, 1748-
1801, marked, 20" l.
(imperfections) **770.00**

Porringer, cast crown handle,
marked "I.G.," New England,
4¾" d...**357.50**

Porringer, round bowl w/ornate
flower-pierced handle, Gershom
Jones, Rhode Island, ca. 1775,
4¼" d. (minor dent) **1,265.00**

Porringer, cast crown handle,
marked "S.G.," New England, 5½" d.
(handle w/minor edge damage) **192.50**

Porringer, scroll-cast pierced handle,
eagle touch of Samuel Hamlin, Jr.,
Providence, Rhode Island, 1801-56,
5½" d...**522.50**

Soup plate w/flanged rim, angel
touchmark, Continental, 11½" d.
(scratches) **170.50**

Tankard, flat-top, the flat-top circular
lid w/molded thumbpiece, the body
w/shaped handle w/bud terminal, on
a stepped molded foot, New York,
Henery Will, ca. 1775, 7" h.
(ILLUS. top next column) **3,450.00**

American Pewter Flat-top Tankard

Teapot, cov., footed, compressed
globular form w/ornate scrolled
handle, swan's-neck spout, domed
cover, Sellew & Co., Cincinnati,
Ohio, 6¼" h. **275.00**

Teapot, cov., bulbous footed body
w/flaring rim, painted wooden
scrolling handle, swan's-neck spout,
Boardman & Hart, New York City,
1828-53, 7½" h. (tiny split in edge
of foot)...**330.00**

Teapot, cov., pear-shaped w/high
domed cover, eagle touchmark of
Roswell Gleason, Dorchester,
Massachusetts, 7" h. (repair to
handle & edge of lid) **440.00**

Teapot, cov., pedestal base below a
tapering cylindrical body below a tall
flaring neck below a domed cover,
swan's-neck spout & double scroll
metal handle, marked "Smith & Co.,
Warranted," mid-19th c., 10" h. **203.50**

Teapot, cov., wide tapering cylindrical
body w/rounded shoulder raised on
a wide pedestal foot, short
cylindrical neck w/flared rim
supporting an inset domed cover
w/disc finial, swan's-neck spout &
S-scroll handle, John Munson,
Yalesville, Connecticut, 1846-52,
8" h. (minor battering) **247.50**

Teapot, cov., bulbous shoulder body
w/flared foot & rim, painted C-scroll
handle, swan's-neck spout, Rufus
Dunham, Westbrook, Maine,
1837-60, 8¼" h. **467.50**

Teapot, cov., the tall body w/a
pedestal foot below the slightly
flaring cylindrical mid-section below
the tapering shoulder & neck w/a
flared rim, domed cover (wood finial
missing), swan's-neck spout, ornate
scroll handle, Rufus Dunham,

Westbrook, Maine, 1837-60, 12" h.
(dents)..**275.00**
Tea & coffee service: cov. coffeepot,
cov. teapot, cov. sugar bowl &
creamer; each w/a slightly bulbous
base tapering to a cylindrical neck,
low flared foot, scroll handles, cast
flower finials, "Homan & Co.,
Cincinnati," also labeled "From Gen.
Grant's Father's Collection, Bethel,
Ohio," 4 pcs. **550.00**

SHEFFIELD PLATE
Candelabra, three-light, baluster-form
w/swing arms decorated w/leaves &
shells, 18¼" h., pr.
(dents, minor rosing) **862.50**
Candelabra, three-light, baluster-form
w/swing arms, decorated w/flower &
leaf designs, 19" h., pr.
(dents, rosing) **172.50**
Urn, hot water, paneled vasiform
w/two handles, 18½" h. (rosing).......**144.00**
Vase, trumpet-from body decorated
w/chased foliage, marked
"S (crown) E," 10⅞" h. **144.00**
Wine cooler, George III style, two-
handled, 7½" h. (minor dents,
rosing) **1,150.00**

SILVER, AMERICAN (Sterling & Coin)

DeMatteo Silver Candlestick

Basin, circular fluted bowl, the rim
applied w/a band of overlapping
spiraled wheel designs, matching
chasing around the center of the
interior, Durgin Division of Gorham
Mfg. Co., 1928, 14⅜" d. **2,013.00**
Basket, coin, oval w/engraved
scrolling foliage, monogrammed, N.
Harding, Boston, Massachusetts,
19th c., 12" l. **797.50**
Beakers, vase-shaped, on spreading
circular foot, w/flaring rim, engraved
w/the script initial "R," one engraved
under base "EGR 1847 to JHH
1905," each w/maker's mark of Hall,

Hewson & Co., Albany, New York,
ca. 1840, set of 10 ....**3,850.00**
Berry bowl, *Martelé,* circular lobed
body w/a wide rolled undulating rim
chased at intervals w/a
chrysanthemum flowerhead, the
lobed sides divided by flowering
plants, wavy-edged foot, Gorham
Mfg. Co., Providence, Rhode Island,
retailed by Spaulding & Co.,
Chicago, 1902, 11" d. **3,737.00**
Bowl, *Martelé,* shaped circular form,
the lobed spot-hammered body
w/elaborate undulating rim repoussé
& chased w/foliate scrolls,
flowerheads & buds, engraved
under base "1881 R 1906," Gorham
Mfg. Co., Providence, Rhode Island,
ca. 1906, 12¾" d. **4,950.00**
Bowl, everted rim w/paneled
neoclassical design, Wm. B. Durgin
Co., Concord, New Hampshire,
13" d., 4" h. **330.00**
Brandy warmer, in the Japanese
taste, shaped circular form, w/spot-
hammered surface & wavy molded
rim, the handle pierced w/stylized
clouds, presentation inscription
engraved under the base & dated
1883, Whiting Mfg. Co., Providence
Rhode Island, ca. 1883, 7¼" l. **990.00**
Butter dish, cover & liner, Medallion
patt., compressed spherical form,
the domed top applied w/a classical
medallion & a helmet finial, rod side
handles, monogrammed within a
strapwork cartouche, Ball, Black &
Co., New York, New York, ca. 1865,
overall 7¼" l. **1,035.00**
Butter dish, cover & liner, tureen-
form w/shallow oval base raised on
leafy scroll feet & chased w/flowers,
figural horned cow-head end
handles w/loose rings, the molded
border band w/a wrapped ribbon
design, the widely flaring domed
cover chased w/flowers & scrolls &
topped by a recumbent cow finial,
Wood & Hughes, New York, New
York, ca. 1850, engraved w/the
name "Bryan," overall 8½" l. **1,725.00**
Cake basket, round, swing handle,
acid-etched Regence decoration,
Tiffany & Co., New York, early
20th c., 10½" d. **770.00**
Candlesticks, flaring candle cup over
an openwork stem of rosebuds,
beads & ribbons on a flared foot,
maker's mark of William DeMatteo,
Sr. on base, 10" h., pr. (ILLUS.
one of two) **3,860.00**
Cann, tapering cylindrical form
w/flaring rim, on molded foot, scroll
handle, maker's mark of Peleg

Collins, Cincinnati, 1820-43,
3⅛" h...**880.00**
Card tray, square, hammered,
applied bugs & flowers, Dominck
& Haff Mfg. Co. **735.00**
Caster, baluster-form, on a molded
spreading circular foot, the high
domed cover w/panels of piercing
within engraved trelliswork,
surmounted by a baluster finial,
engraved w/a crest, maker's mark of
Eleazer Baker, Ashford,
Connecticut, ca. 1785, 5¼" h.......**3,850.00**

"Medallion" Centerpiece

Centerpiece, Medallion patt., Neo-
Classical style, the shallow bowl
w/tab handles & a classical
medallion decoration on the long
side, on hairy animal legs ending in
paw feet on a disk w/tab feet,
Gorham, ca. 1863 (ILLUS.)...........**4,675.00**
Centerpiece bowl, shaped circular
form, the spreading circular foot
chased w/a band of scrolls &
flowerheads & raised on six paw
feet headed by foliate scrolls, the
flaring sides elaborately repoussé,
chased & pierced w/foliate scrolls,
flowerheads & trelliswork on a
matted ground, the applied foliate
scroll & flowerhead rim w/openwork
floral sprays at intervals, Tiffany &
Co., New York, 1892-1902,
20" d...**11,000.00**
Coffeepot, cov., coin, baluster-form
body chased w/grapevines centering
an engraved crest, Ball, Tompkins &
Black, New York, New York,
ca. 1845, 11½" h.............................**770.00**
Coffeepot, cov., baluster-form, on a
circular foot w/chased gadrooning,
the silver scroll handle w/ivory
insulators, the spout w/similar scroll
decoration, the hinged cover
w/chased gadrooning & surmounted
by a bud finial, one side engraved
w/script initials "EMc," John David,
Philadelphia, Pennsylvania,
ca. 1770, 13¾" h.........................**11,500.00**
Coffeepot, cov., coin, vase-shaped,
the spreading circular foot applied

w/a beaded rim & raised on a
square pedestal base, the shoulder
applied w/a similar band below
engraved wrigglework bands, the
foliate scroll spout applied w/similar
bands, w/carved foliate scroll
wooden handle, the hinged cover
w/similar bands & rising to a
pedestal supporting a pineapple
finial, marked "I. DAVID," maker's
mark of John David, Philadelphia,
ca. 1790, 15½" h............................**8,250.00**
Coffee urn, cov., coin, high arched
handles, Greek key & bead detail,
bright-cut decoration, Bigelow Bros.
and Kennard, Boston,
Massachusetts, ca. 1845,
16¾" h..**2,090.00**
Compote, open, w/tied & scrolled
handles & applied leaves,
monogrammed, Gorham Mfg. Co.,
Providence, Rhode Island, ca. 1870,
7¾" d. (minor dents) **302.50**
Compotes, shaped circular form,
Chrysanthemum patt., on four scroll
feet headed by chrysanthemums,
w/compressed baluster-form stem,
the bowl w/raised center & applied
chrysanthemum rim, Tiffany & Co.,
New York, 1880-91, 9⅛" d., pr......**4,180.00**
Creamer, inverted pear-shaped body
w/a gadrooned rim & matching cast
pedestal foot, leaf-capped scroll
handle, marked on base & w/scratch
weight "5:2" & scratched initials
"FG," Richard Humphreys,
Philadelphia, Pennsylvania,
ca. 1775, 5¼" h.............................**2,587.00**
Creamer, waisted baluster-form, on
spreading circular foot w/die-rolled
leaf & bead rim, applied at the
shoulder w/a similar band, below a
geometric rim, w/reeded scroll
handle, the front engraved w/a
monogram "GJAE," maker's mark of
William Seal, Philadelphia,
ca. 1815, 6⅛" h...............................**770.00**

Art Nouveau Style Demitasse Set

Demitasse set: cov. coffeepot, open
sugar & creamer; Art Nouveau style,
all of baluster-form w/angled

shoulders, embossed w/Art Nouveau flowers & leaves, Wallace, the set (ILLUS.)............................**1,100.00**

Demitasse set: cov. coffeepot, open sugar & creamer; paneled Colonial Revival style bodies w/bright-cut decoration, monogrammed, Graf, Washburn & Dunn, New York, New York, retailed by Bigelow and Kennard, early 20th c., the set........**330.00**

Dessert spoons, coin, shell & scroll pattern, monogrammed, J.B. Jones & Co., Boston, Massachusetts, early 19th c., set of 12 ....**247.50**

Dresser set: hand mirror, comb & brush; Old Colony patt., Gorham Mfg. Co., Providence, Rhode Island, in a fitted case, the set.....................**137.50**

Ewer, the elongated inverted pear-shaped body w/a tapering neck w/a high, arched spout & C-scroll handle cast w/grape clusters, raised on a short pedestal w/domed foot, the body chased overall w/a landscape w/a chinoiserie building, a boat & birds surrounded by flowering foliage & also engraved w/contemporary arms, the base w/disc insert where previously pierced for electricity, Bailey & Co., Philadelphia, ca. 1850, 19" h. **5,750.00**

Gravy boat & undertray, footed rounded boat-shaped container w/long, wide spout & D-scroll handle, on round undertray, designed by Arthur Hartwell & David Carlson for Stone Assoc. of Gardner, Massachusetts, ca. 1918, impressed marks, monogrammed inside foot, 2 pcs.............................**825.00**

Humidor, cov., rectangular body raised on ball feet, chased w/scrolling leaves & surmounted by a horse & rider, Derby Silver Co., Derby, Connecticut, 9½" l. **660.00**

Ice cream bowl, shallow circular dish w/*bombé* sides embossed & chased w/Indian flowering foliage, raised on four shaped & matte bracket feet hung w/swags of jewelry-like beads, each leg surmounted by a three-dimensional model of a stylized peacock w/arched wings, beaded collars & standing on a winged hoop, Tiffany & Co., New York, New York, ca. 1885, 12½" d. **9,200.00**

Kettle, cover & stand, hot water, pear-shaped body w/chased leafy decoration, openwork stand w/scroll feet, Tiffany & Co., ca. 1850, lacking burner, slight dents, 13¼" h. (ILLUS. top next column) **2,310.00**

Jar, cov., spherical body w/wide domed cover, the body w/finely

Tiffany Hot Water Kettle

ribbed bands flanking a center band of chased flowers & shells, w/inscription dated "1883," Tiffany & Co., New York, 4" h. **522.50**

Meat platter, oval w/scalloped border, Chrysanthemum patt., monogram in the center, Tiffany & Co., New York, late 19th c., 22" l. (scratches, light dent)...**5,225.00**

Montieth bowl, a crown-form detachable scalloped rim on the wide shallow round bowl raised on a short pedestal above a domed foot, chased w/flowers above a band of acanthus & engraved w/a contemporary monogram "MLD," Wilson Bros., Baltimore, Maryland, late 19th c., 10" d. **1,725.00**

Mote skimmer, the oval rat-tail bowl pierced w/a pair of flowerheads, a spiraled flowerhead & symmetrical scrollwork, a long, slender tapering handle w/tiny baluster terminal, engraved near base of handle "E-W," Benjamin Brenton, Newport, Rhode Island, ca. 1730, 5¾" l. **3,220.00**

Mug, tall tapering cylindrical body w/a band of thin rings around the middle & the base, S-scroll handle, engraved w/foliate monogram, Ebenezer Moulton, Boston, Massachusetts, ca. 1790, 5¼" h. (minor imperfections) **2,640.00**

Pitcher, water, spherical body below a cylindrical neck w/small rim spout, hollow rounded handle, the body chased overall w/flowers & w/leaf columns around the base, Bigelow, Kennard & Co., ca. 1863, 8½" h. (minor dents).................................**1,870.00**

Pitcher, water, simple ovoid octagonal body w/high arched spout & angled handle, monogram on the side, ovolo border, late 19th c.,

Howard Sterling Co., Providence, Rhode Island, retailed by Bigelow and Kennard, 9¼" h. **660.00**

W. Adams Water Pitcher

Pitcher, water, coin, paneled pear-form, chased w/flowers & engraved w/scrolling cartouches, the spout supported by a mask, W. Adams, New York, mid-19th c., 9¾" h. (ILLUS.) **1,495.00**

Pitcher, vase-shaped, the rim & neck w/stylized egg-and-dart bands, w/gadrooned rim & foliate scroll reeded handle, the front repoussé & chased w/a coat-of-arms, crest & motto, maker's mark of James Thomson, New York, ca. 1834, 10¼" h..**1,650.00**

Pitcher, cover & undertray, water, the pitcher of double-skinned pear-shape raised on a flaring foot & embossed & chased overall w/flowers on a matte ground in the Kirk style, a vine-wrapped S-scroll handle, domed cover w/vine finial & short arched shellwork spout w/inner flap, on a matching undertray w/domed border band, the pitcher engraved w/arms, the stand w/a matching crest, William Wilson & Son, Philadelphia, ca. 1890, pitcher 13¼" h., 2 pcs. **4,313.00**

Plates, dinner, fluted & scalloped rims, marked on the backs "STERLING," 20th c., 10" d., set of 12 ....**1,725.00**

Porringer, child's, round bowl w/pierced scroll keyhole handle engraved "A = D" above "I = S," the front later engraved "Davis to Alice," marked near center of bowl "REVERE," Paul Revere, Jr., Boston, Massachusetts, ca. 1780, rim 4⅜" d....................**17,250.00**

Porringer, circular, the pierced keyhole handle later engraved w/block letters "I + E" & the date "1784," John Andres, Salem, Massachusetts, 1770-90, 5½" d...**1,380.00**

Porringer, circular, w/pierced keyhole handle engraved "C" over "IM," marked "W:Cowell," William Cowell, Sr., Boston, ca. 1720, 8⅛" l. **3,080.00**

Punch bowl, deep footed bowl w/the sides embossed w/a band of large hearts outlined by fine chased foliage & beading, on a matching foot, Gorham Mfg. Co., Providence, Rhode Island, 1905, marked w/special order number "236," 14¾" d..**2,875.00**

Punch cups, figural, each modeled as an orange w/twig stalk forming the handle that spreads into a spray of leaves to form a foot, silver-gilt interior, Gorham Mfg. Co., Providence, Rhode Island, 1886, 2⅛" h., set of 12............................**3,162.00**

Punch ladle, shaped oval bowl w/bifurcated & partly faceted silver handle socket & wood extension, the wood now shortened, marked in center of bowl "TEdwards" in script in a rectangle, Thomas Edwards, Boston, Massachusetts, ca. 1750, bowl 4⅜" l. **8,337.00**

Rose bowl, Regence-style, monogrammed, Tiffany & Co., New York, w/silver plated liner & frog, 12½" d., the set...............................**935.00**

Salt dips & spoons, Chrysanthemum patt., shaped rectangular form on spreading rectangular foot, w/chrysanthemum rim, the spoon w/gilt circular bowl & chrysanthemum stem, Tiffany & Co., New York, 1880-91, 4⅛" l., set of 6 ....**3,520.00**

Sauce pan, short beaker-form body w/slightly flared rim & molded base rim, the handle terminal mounted on a drop-shaped panel, the wood extension replaced circa 1825 w/a silver baluster handle w/chased borders, engraved underneath "T*Hubbard," marked on body "NHurd" in script in a rectangle w/shaped top, Nathaniel Hurd, Boston, Massachusetts, ca. 1705, rim 3½" d....................................**10,350.00**

Soup ladle, coin, Jenny Lind patt., Freeman & Bennett.........................**295.00**

Soup ladle, Orange Blossom patt., Alvin Silver Co., Providence, Rhode Island, 12" l. **522.50**

Soup ladle, coin, Fiddle Thread patt., Wm. Tenney **275.00**

Soup tureen, cov., of boat form w/beaded & key pattern rim, ring

Oval Soup Tureen & Cover

handles pendant from horned lion heads, finial formed as a stag & branch, oval pedestal foot w/four bun feet, one side engraved w/name & date 1912, Vanderslice & Co., retailed by George C. Shreve & Co., ca. 1870, length over handles 15" (ILLUS.) **4,312.00**

Sugar bowl, cov., shaped faceted oval, the rims bright-cut w/bands of foliate sprays & scrolls on a reeded band, enclosing a circular foliate cartouche engraved w/monogram "NMB" on one side & a crest on the other, the hinged flat cover w/similar foliate border, the overhead swing handle w/feather edge bands enclosing a vacant navette-shaped cartouche, maker's mark of Charles L. Boehme, Baltimore, ca. 1805, 5" l. **2,420.00**

Sugar bowl, cov., coin, ovoid w/oak leaf design, monogrammed, Curry & Preston, Philadelphia, Pennsylvania, 8½" h...**302.50**

Sugar nippers, scissor-type, the domed terminals engraved w/contemporary initials "KH," marked in each terminal "PS" in shield, Philip Syng, Jr. Philadelphia, Pennsylvania, ca. 1740, 4⅝" l. **2,645.00**

Sugar tongs, spring-form, w/shell tips & wrigglework & bead borders, engraved w/script initial "R," Paul Revere, Boston, ca. 1795-1800, 5¾" l. **4,180.00**

Tablespoon, coin, rattail handle engraved "Wiley," marked "D. Kinsey & Co.," Cincinnati, Ohio, ca. 1845, 8" l...**33.00**

Tablespoon, coin, rattail handle engraved "L.C.," marked "E. & D.

Kinsey," Cincinnati, Ohio, ca. 1845, 8¾" l..**16.50**

Tankard, cov., tapering cylindrical body w/ring-molded flaring base, stepped & domed cover w/flaming urn finial, S-scroll handle w/scrolled thumbpiece, the front engraved above the molded girdle w/"John Bray Goodwin 1799" in a bright-cut cartouche of leafy swags & pendant husks, Benjamin Burt, Boston, ca. 1799, 7⅞" h................................**10,350.00**

18th Century Silver Tankard

Tankard, cov., tapering cylindrical form on slightly flared foot w/medial relief stave, w/hinged stepped cover & S-scroll handle, marked on base, James Butler, Boston, Massachusetts, ca. 1770, restoration where spout had previously been added, 8½" h. (ILLUS.) **3,850.00**

Tankard, cov., tapering cylindrical form, on a spreading circular molded foot, applied w/a mid-band, the front engraved w/a coat-of-arms & crest within an asymmetrical foliate scroll & rocaille cartouche, the scroll handle w/molded drop, disk terminal & engraved w/initials "G" over "N*L," the hinged stepped domed cover w/scroll thumbpiece & surmounted by a flame finial, unmarked, Boston, ca. 1760, 9¼" h. **11,000.00**

Tea caddy, cov., cylindrical form, the surface w/floral repoussé decoration, the cover w/similar repoussé decoration rising to a flat-topped floral knob finial, maker's mark of Tiffany & Co., New York, 1884-91, 4⅜" h. (ILLUS. top next page)..**805.00**

Tea & coffee service: cov. teapot, cov. coffeepot, cov. sugar bowl, cream jug & waste bowl; each on molded rim foot, the body repoussé & chased w/elaborately entwined foliate grapevines on a matted

Tiffany Tea Caddy

ground between bands of reeded rocaille, the covers w/similar decoration & surmounted by a foliate bud finial, Tiffany & Co., New York, coffeepot 1891-1902, other pieces pre-1891, 5 pcs. **6,600.00**

Tea & coffee service: cov. teapot, cov. coffeepot, cov. hot water pot, cov. sugar bowl, creamer & oval tray; Classical Revival style w/die-rolled zig-zag borders, female classical head finials & engraved monograms in raised circular cartouches & applied w/cast griffin crests, matching engraving on the tray, Ball, Black & Co., New York, New York, ca. 1865-80, tray 22" l., coffeepot 8⅝" h., the set **4,025.00**

Teakettle on lampstand, Chrysanthemum patt., the squatty bulbous ribbed kettle w/a domed cover & shaped overhead swing handle, raised between floral-embossed uprights above the footed base w/lamp warmer, Tiffany & Co., New York, New York, ca. 1905, 13½" h...**5,740.00**

Teapot, cov., 18th century-style, spherical footed body chased at the shoulders w/rococo ornament, domed cover w/bud finial, C-scroll wood handle, inscribed on the bottom, Newell Harding & Co., Boston, Massachusetts, mid-19th c., 5⅜" h...**1,380.00**

Teapot, cov., vase-shaped, on three scrolling paw feet raised on ball supports & headed by acanthus, applied at the shoulder w/a foliate band, w/acanthus scroll spout terminating in an animal mask & w/acanthus scroll handle, the hinged domed cover chased w/foliate scrolls on a matted ground above a similar rim & surmounted by a bud finial, maker's mark of Gerardus

Boyce, New York, ca. 1830, 7⅞" h...**1,045.00**

Teapot, cov., baluster-form body chased w/flowers & scrolls, raised on scroll feet, monogrammed, N. Harding, Boston, Massachusetts, mid-19th c., 8½" h. (slight dents) **660.00**

Teapot stand, oval w/low flaring edge w/bead rim & raised border outlined w/lightly tooled bands of ribbon & zig-zag work, the center engraved w/contemporary monogram "EDW" in ribbon-hung shield above foliate sprays, raised on four fluted panel feet chased at the top w/beaded swags, John Avery, Preston, Connecticut, ca. 1790, 6⅞" l. **1,380.00**

Tea service: cov. teapot, cov. sugar bowl & cov. creamer; each oval vase-shaped on spreading oval foot, the body engraved below the rim w/bands of stylized foliage within scrolls on a reeded ground, enclosed by wrigglework bands, the domed covers surmounted by a pineapple finial, the teapot w/wooden scroll handle, the creamer & sugar bowl w/angular reeded handles, engraved on each side w/script initial "C," maker's mark of Ebenezer Moulton, Boston, ca. 1810, teapot 11¼" h., 3 pcs. **4,180.00**

Tea service: cov. teapot, cov. hot water pot, cov. sugar bowl, creamer & waste bowl; each w/a simple footed oval urn-form w/angled handles molded at the angle w/a ram's head, the stepped covers w/loop finials, each w/an engraved coat-of-arms, beaded borders, Shreve, Standwood & Co., Boston, Massachusetts, ca. 1860, 5 pcs. ..**3,300.00**

Teaspoon, coin, rattail handle engraved "L.C.," marked "E. & D. Kinsey," Cincinnati, Ohio, ca. 1845, 5⅝" l...**22.00**

Tea tray, oval, the applied foliate band on a reeded ground between beaded bands, the scroll handles w/laurel band on a reeded ground between similar beading & issuing from acanthus, the field engraved w/a coat-of-arms, helm & crest within foliate swags & enclosed by an elaborate foliate scroll cartouche, maker's mark of William Forbes for Ball, Black & Co., New York, 1839-50, length over handles 25½" **4,180.00**

Toast rack, the shaped oval openwork scrolling base w/bands of die-rolled foliate scrolls, flowerheads & grapes, raised on four ball feet, w/loop dividers & bifurcated scroll loop finial engraved underneath w/script monogram "MC," marked "AEW," A. E. Warner, Baltimore, & w/Baltimore assay office marks w/dominical letter D, 1818, 8¾" l. **6,600.00**

Tray, oval, monogrammed, Reed & Barton, Taunton, Massachusetts, 1945, 18" l. **440.00**

Vegetable dish, oval, raised on four winged foliate scroll matted feet, the rim applied w/a die-rolled band of entwined flowerheads on a reeded ground, the loop handles issuing from openwork scrolls & palmettes, each side engraved w/a monogram "FDE" entwined w/"AAA," maker's mark of Tiffany & Co., New York, 1867-70, length over handles 10½" **880.00**

Tray, Plymouth patt., Gorham Mfg. Co., 17" l. **850.00**

Vase, octagonal trumpet-form body w/ribbed banding, Reed & Barton, Taunton, Massachusetts, 15⅞" h. **770.00**

Vegetable dish, cov., oval, Maintenon patt., Gorham Mfg. Co., Providence, Rhode Island, 12¾" l. **990.00**

SILVER, ENGLISH & OTHERS

Bowl, "Cymric," deep rounded sides w/a closed rim, tooled in a waved design & applied w/stylized large ribbon loops above five ribbed trifid feet, Liberty & Co., Birmingham, England, 1902, 9" d. **5,462.00**

Bowl, lobed circular form, embossed w/two bands of oval beads, Georg Jensen Silversmithy, Copenhagen, Denmark, 1920, 9¼" d. **6,900.00**

Centerpiece, model of a Viking ship, w/reeded sides & rim w/frieze of conjoining shields, the bow w/mythical animal figurehead & stern w/similarly decorated tail, on a stand w/rectangular stepped feet, the crossing fluted supports w/claw & mythical animal mask ends joined by openwork scroll bar w/mythical animal heads at each end, maker's mark of David-Anderson, Oslo, Norway, 1906, 20½" l. **9,200.00**

Chalice, the domed base chased in high-relief w/strapwork on a matted ground & w/four roundels engraved w/the Evangelists, the bowl engraved w/the Savior flanked by the Mother of God & St. John, also w/an Orthodox cross, Constantin Knyazev, Moscow, Russia, ca. 1900, 12⅛" h. **1,035.00**

Compote, open, Grapevine patt., a

widely flaring smooth bowl raised on a ring of tiny grapevine above the stem w/two lobed rings flanking the spiral-twist standard, above a short funnel foot, designed by Georg Jensen, Copenhagen, Denmark, numbered "264A," ca. 1928, 10½" h. **5,750.00**

Condiment set: vase-shaped pepper, salt & mustard w/matching spoon & circular tray; Acorn patt., Georg Jensen Silversmithy, Copenhagen, Denmark, post-1945, numbered 741, over handles tray 7¼" l., the set **1,840.00**

Dinner service: 18 - 6" d. bread plates, 10 - 3½" d. butter chips or glass coasters, a 14½" l. oblong platter, a 24¼" l. shaped oval platter; plain w/rope borders, William Spratling, Mexico, ca. 1940, the set **14,950.00**

Meat platter, oval, the thin rim band molded w/stylized acorns spaced at intervals, designed by Johan Rohde in 1915, marked by Georg Jensen, Denmark, post-1945, 16" l. **4,600.00**

Edwardian Period Montieth

Montieth, scalloped edge w/ridged sides w/two ring handles hang from modeled lions' heads, Edwardian period, Charles Stuart Harris, London, 1902-03, 11" d. (ILLUS.) **3,162.50**

Pitcher, water, ovoid w/flared lip & integrated C-scroll handle, designed by Johan Rohde in 1920, Georg Jensen Silversmithy, Copenhagen, Denmark, No. 432C, post-1945, 11½" h. **4,600.00**

Pitcher, water, & undertray, spherical pitcher raised on a small cylindrical foot & tapering to a wide cylindrical neck w/small pointed spout, a wooden loop handle carved w/a stylized eagle head & trimmed around the base w/a ring of beads, on a matching round undertray w/a small band of beads along the rim,

William Spratling, Mexico, ca. 1940,
pitcher 6½" h., 2 pcs. **2,300.00**

Soup ladle, the oval bowl
w/hammered surface, the rim
chased w/overlapping leaves, ebony
handle topped by elongated silver
finial chased w/leafage & w/berry
cluster terminal, Georg Jensen,
Copenhagen, Denmark, ca. 1904-
08, marked on base of stem "826S,
GJ" in monogram & "G.I.,"
16¼" l. **4,600.00**

Soup tureen, cov., the sloping sides
divided into ten panels, plain circular
rim & block rosewood handles,
matching finial, the spreading
circular foot w/notched rim, Jean E.
Puiforcat, Paris, France, ca. 1925,
at rim 11½" d. **19,550.00**

Table gong, the gong suspended
between two curved tendrils topped
by berries & rising from a stepped
hammered circular base w/scalloped
rim, complete w/ebony-handled &
leather baton w/silver finial,
designed by Harald Neilsen, ca.
1927, Georg Jensen Silversmithy,
Copenhagen, Denmark, 1927-32,
numbered 490, 7½" h. **12,650.00**

George III Tankard

Tankard, cov., tapering cylindrical
body on slightly flared foot w/medial
relief stave, w/hinged stepped cover
& S-scroll handle engraved
monogram on handle, George III
period, probably Jacob Marsh,
London, 1766-67, 7¼" h.
(ILLUS.) **1,150.00**

Teakettle on stand, flattened ovoid
body, decorated w/birds among
bamboo plants, bombé -shaped
handle & stand, Japan, late 19th c.,
7" h. **805.00**

Teapot, cov., Blossom patt., designed
by Georg Jensen in 1905, Georg
Jensen Silversmithy, Copenhagen,
Denmark, ca. 1925, numbered 2B,
5¼" h. **3,163.00**

Toast rack, arched Celtic knot at
alternating sides w/a high pointed
knot center handle, designed by
Archibald Knox, Liberty & Co.,
England, 1908, 2⅝ x 3¼",
5⅝" h. **2,300.00**

Vase, tall tapering cylindrical body,
cast & chased w/overlapping leafy
branches half hiding vignettes of a
nymph at a waterfall, a boy drinking
below & a mother & child
w/harvester quenching his thirst,
also applied w/a butterfly,
Bourcheron, Paris, France,
ca. 1880-90, 6⅜" h. **1,150.00**

Vase, slightly waisted form embossed
& chased in low- & high-relief
w/clover plants, A. Michelsen,
Copenhagen, Denmark,
1905, 10⅜" h. **3,163.00**

Austrian Silver Vase

Vase, of flaring form on a domed
base, the rim & base joined by four

French Silver Vase

geometrically pierced supports w/similar arc-formed handle, maker's mark of Wiener Werkstätte, w/retailer's mark "SB," designed by Josef Hoffmann, Austria, 12¾" h. (ILLUS. previous page) **12,075.00**

Vase, baluster-form body chased w/peonies, maker's mark "A (wheel) R," France, ca. 1900 16¼" h. (ILLUS. bottom previous page) **2,645.00**

Urn-Shaped French Vase

Vase, urn-form w/flaring rim set w/two pierced & reeded circular handles, on a flaring cylindrical foot w/reeded bands, marked on base, Risler, Paris, ca. 1935, 22" h. (ILLUS.) **11,500.00**

SILVER PLATE (Hollowware)

Morel Silver Plate Charger

Butter dish, cov., Heritage patt., 1847 Rogers Bros. **38.00**

Candlesticks, Art Deco style, "Skyscraper," tapering square form w/stepped top & rod side handle, impressed "SKY - SCRAPER - DES. PAT. PENDING - APOLLO - E.P.N.S. - MADE BY - BERNARD

RICE'S SONS, INC. - 5720," ca. 1925, 8¼" h., pr. **920.00**

Card holder, fan-shaped, Rogers Bros., 6½" **350.00**

Charger, circular, depicting a classical beauty & her attendants in a courtyard, signed & stamped, designed by Morel, ca. 1876, 20¼" d. (ILLUS.) **440.00**

Barbour Cocktail Set

Cocktail set: cov., cocktail pitcher, ice bucket, tray & eight glasses; the cocktail pitcher of cylindrical form raised on a ribbed base & flat foot, the cover w/ribbed knob set w/amber Bakelite, the remaining pieces en suite, each impressed "Barbour - 6733," the pitcher cover impressed "PAT'D JAN. 11-1927," ca. 1930, tray 24½" l., pitcher 11⅛" h., the set (ILLUS.) **690.00**

Crumb tray set, embossed Art Nouveau lady w/flowing hair, vine & roses, Victor Silver Co., 2 pcs..........**150.00**

Humidor, cov., box-shaped, decorated w/a Setter dog w/bird in mouth, Meriden, large **675.00**

Humidor, cov., double-sided, decorated w/a Setter dog, Rogers Bros. **595.00**

Mirror plateau, the rectangular mirror plate w/cut corners & rounded ends within a molded surround, raised on a Celtic-inspired base w/stylized winged creatures at the corners conjoined by intrelac devices, Elkington & Company, England, dated 1879, impressed marks & numbered, 13 x 15¼", 3⅜" h. **2,588.00**

Mustache cup & saucer, engraved w/flowers, quadruple plate, marked "Pairpoint" **60.00**

Punch set: bowl & twelve matching cups; the circular punch bowl w/shaped rim applied w/strapwork & interspersed w/female masks, the lower body chased w/a wide sloping lobed band centering a cartouche hung from a chased rocaille band,

Silver Plate Punch Bowl

the circular foot chased w/sloping
lobes above a stepped rim, the cups
w/similar decoration, mounted
w/scroll handle, England, 19th c.,
wear, diameter of bowl 15¼"
(ILLUS. punch bowl) **1,265.00**

Pairpoint Salt Dips

Salt dips, shell-shaped bowls w/glass
  inserts on dolphin pedestals on
  round feet, w/salt spoons, marked
  Pairpoint, 2½ x 3½", 3¾" h., pr.
  (ILLUS.) **270.00**
Shield, large oval form cast w/various
  allegorical figural scenes, inscribed
  "Elkington & Co - Morel Ladenil
  Fecit 1866," England, third quarter
  19th c., 34½" l. (silver worn) **1,725.00**
Tray, Art Nouveau style, rectangular
  w/rounded tab ends, relief-molded at
  the ends w/the head of a maiden,
  her arms spread & her body
  disappearing toward the center,
  James W. Tufts, Boston, marked,
  7⅛ x 12½" **172.50**
Tureen, cov., of circular form on three
  splayed legs w/two cylindrical wood
  handles, the flat circular cover w/a
  notch for the ladle & an ebony finial,
  marked under base "P.O.D.R. - 28
  July 1880," maker's mark of Hukin &
  Heath, 1880-1883, designed by
  Christopher Dresser, ca. 1880,
  length over handles 7¾"
  (ILLUS. top next column) **3,220.00**
Vegetable dish, cov., oval w/overall

Silver Plate Tureen

repoussé floral decoration, unicorn
& shield handle, 13" l. **302.50**

SILVER PLATE (Flatware)

ALDINE (1895 Rogers Bros.)
Berry spoon, gold-washed bowl..........**30.00**
Cheese scoop, gold-washed bowl **40.00**
Pie forks, set of 6................................**45.00**

ARBUTUS (Wm. Rogers & Son)
Bouillon spoon **15.00**
Butter knife, twisted handle................**20.00**
Butter pick..**22.00**
Cocktail fork.....................................**10.00**
Cold meat fork **25.00**
Cream soup spoon **20.00**
Dinner fork **15.00**
Gravy ladle **25.00**
Luncheon fork...................................**15.00**
Salad fork **24.00**
Sauce ladle.......................................**20.00**
Sugar spoon......................................**18.00**
Tablespoon **15.00**
Youth fork...**20.00**

BERKSHIRE (1847 Rogers Bros.)
Bonbon spoon, gold-washed bowl **75.00**
Demitasse spoon................................**8.00**
Jelly trowel **48.00**
Sugar tongs.......................................**25.00**

CARNATION (W. R. Keystone)
Citrus spoon **20.00**
Cream ladle **25.00**
Pie server **45.00**
Salad fork **25.00**
Strawberry fork **25.00**

CHARTER OAK (1847 Rogers Bros.)

Charter Oak Pattern

Baby food pusher 95.00
Berry spoon 65.00
Butter knife, flat............................25.00
Citrus spoon 25.00
Cream ladle 45.00
Fruit knife 35.00
Dinner fork, hollow-handled
   (ILLUS. bottom) 40.00
Dinner knife, hollow-handled
   (resilvered blades) 15.00
Luncheon fork (ILLUS. center) 38.00
Luncheon knife, hollow-handled........27.50
Salad fork (ILLUS. top) 36.00
Salad serving fork 75.00
Salad serving set 175.00
Soup ladle 125.00
Soup spoon, round bowl 40.00

COLUMBIA (Wm. A. Rogers)
Berry spoon 30.00
Butter knife, twist handle..................19.00
Citrus spoon 22.00
Cream ladle 40.00
Fruit spoon...................................13.00
Ice spoon...................................147.50
Salad fork 45.00
Salad serving fork 150.00
Strawberry fork...............................65.00
Sugar tongs 75.00

FLORAL (1835 R. Wallace)
Cocktail fork.................................10.00
Cold meat fork 30.00
Ice cream spoon 45.00
Pie server 75.00
Salad fork 36.50
Seafood fork..................................22.00
Soup spoon, oval bowl......................15.00
Soup ladle, large 95.00
Strawberry fork...............................50.00
Stuffing spoon 70.00

GROSVENOR (Oneida Community)
Butter knife, flat.............................7.00
Carving set, large, 3 pcs. 110.00
Cream soup spoon 10.00
Dinner fork, hollow-handled 14.00
Dinner knife...................................10.00
Fruit knife 16.00
Fruit spoon....................................9.00
Ice cream spoon 20.00
Ice tea spoon.................................16.00
Luncheon fork.................................15.00
Salad fork 10.00
Sherbet spoon 16.00
Sugar tongs...................................35.00

HOLLY (E.H.H. Smith)
Bouillon spoon 45.00
Carving set, 3 pc. 350.00
Cold meat fork 90.00
Demitasse spoon..............................35.00
Ice cream fork 90.00
Luncheon fork.................................30.00

Luncheon knife 20.00
Soup ladle 300.00
Tablespoon 35.00
Tomato server...............................225.00

KING CEDRIC (Oneida Community)
Iced tea spoons, set of 12................40.00
Jelly server....................................5.00
Place setting, 4 pcs..........................56.00
Tablespoon 32.00
Teaspoon......................................12.00

LA VIGNE (1881 Rogers)
Butter spreader...............................20.00
Citrus spoon, gold-washed bowl.........25.00
Soup ladle 165.00
Sugar tongs.................................100.00
Dinner fork 9.00
Dinner knife..................................12.00
Luncheon fork................................10.00
Soup spoon...................................12.00
Strawberry fork...............................60.00
Sugar tongs...................................90.00
Tablespoon 10.00
Teaspoon.......................................7.00
Tea strainer 175.00

MARTINIQUE (Lady Beautiful)
Butter spreader, individual..................6.00
Dinner fork 8.00
Iced tea spoon 7.00
Salad fork 8.00
Soup spoon, oval bowl......................7.00
Teaspoon.......................................5.00
Vegetable serving spoon 12.00

OLD COLONY (1847 Rogers Bros.)
Cold meat fork 20.00
Dinner fork, hollow-handled 12.50
Dinner knife, hollow-handled..............20.00
Ice cream fork 30.00
Ice cream spoon 35.00
Iced beverage spoons, set of 6..........25.00
Salad serving fork 65.00
Strawberry fork...............................30.00

STERLING SILVER (Flatware)

ACORN (Georg Jensen)
Baby spoon, curved handle 115.00
Berry spoon, pierced.......................625.00
Bonbon spoon 95.00
Bouillon spoon 65.00
Butter spreader...............................75.00
Canapé server, short.......................250.00
Cheese scoop 225.00
Cheese plane 175.00
Cheese snag 55.00
Citrus spoon 85.00
Cocktail fork..................................60.00
Cold meat fork, 6⅝ " 70.00
Cream soup spoon...........................85.00
Dessert spoon................................85.00

Acorn Pattern

Dinner service: eight each dinner knives, salad forks, fruit knives, dinner forks, butter spreaders & seven teaspoons & one each serving spoon, letter opener, serving fork, iced tea spoon & a berry spoon & jam spoon w/an openwork ring & beaded terminal, in wooden table w/two drawers, 54 pcs. **4,600.00**
Dinner fork, 7¾ " 125.00
Dinner fork, 7⅜ " 85.00
Dinner knife, 9⅞ " 105.00
Dinner knife, 9" 85.00
Fish serving fork..............................85.00
Ice cream fork 95.00
Iced tea spoon 75.00
Lemon fork 75.00
Luncheon fork, 6⅝ " 40.00
Luncheon knife 52.50
Mixing spoon 250.00
Pastry fork.......................................65.00
Pie server 250.00
Pie server (engraved blade) 550.00
Salad fork, 4-tine 95.00
Seafood fork....................................55.00
Serving spoon..................................125.00
Soup spoon, oval bowl......................85.00
Tablespoon, 7½ " 95.00
Teaspoon,..57.00

AMERICAN BEAUTY
(George W. Shiebler)
Bonbon spoon 295.00
Bouillon spoon 26.00
Cheese server, large 150.00
Cocktail fork.....................................32.00
Cold meat fork 87.50
Demitasse spoon...............................15.00
Dessert spoon..................................45.00
Dinner fork 55.00
Ice cream fork 45.00
Lettuce fork......................................50.00
Luncheon fork...................................30.00
Luncheon knife 29.00
Salad fork 61.00
Sardine fork......................................50.00

Sauce ladle......................................50.00
Serving spoon...................................49.00
Serving spoon, pierced......................57.00
Sherbet spoon, 5⅜ " 40.00
Tablespoon 50.00
Teaspoon..25.50

CHRYSANTHEMUM (Tiffany & Co.)
Asparagus tongs 825.00
Berry spoon 450.00
Breakfast knife, straight blade 125.00
Cheese scoop 375.00
Citrus spoon 35.00
Claret ladle, 18" 575.00
Cocktail fork.....................................40.00
Cream soup spoon 85.00
Crumber..650.00
Demitasse spoon...............................40.00
Dessert spoon..................................85.00
Dinner service: 18 each dinner knives, fish knives, soup spoons, fruit knives, demitasse spoons, dinner forks, fish forks, dessert spoons, fruit forks & 12 teaspoons, 1 cold meat fork & 1 sauce ladle, 176 pcs. **15,870.00**
Egg spoon..75.00
Fish fork 130.00
Fruit spoon.......................................77.00
Gravy ladle 372.50
Ice cream fork, gold-washed..............85.00
Ice cream set: 11¾ " ice cream knife & six spoons; 7 pcs. 600.00
Luncheon fork....................................75.00
Mustard ladle 165.00
Olive spoon 175.00
Pastry fork..95.00
Pie server 225.00
Pie server, serrated, pierced 872.50
Salad fork 122.50
Soup ladle, fluted bowl......................1,200.00
Tablespoon 132.50
Teaspoon..63.00
Tea infuser spoon.............................495.00
Waffle server 610.00

ENGLISH KING (Tiffany & Co.)

English King Pattern

Berry spoon	175.00
Breakfast knife	58.00
Butter spreader, flat	45.00
Carving fork, roast	65.00
Carving set, large, 2 pcs.	350.00
Cheese scoop	295.00
Claret spoon, 20" l.	425.00
Cream soup spoon	60.00
Demitasse spoon, gold-washed bowl	65.00
Dessert spoon	92.50
Dinner fork	89.50
Dinner knife	70.00
Fish fork	83.50
Fish knife, hollow-handled	50.00
Luncheon knife	54.50
Olive fork	175.00
Pastry fork	77.00
Pickle fork	195.00
Pie server	662.50
Salad fork	81.50
Salad set	895.00
Seafood fork	45.00
Stuffing spoon	700.00
Tablespoon	125.00
Tea infuser spoon	295.00
Tea knife	85.00
Teaspoon	48.00

KINGS (Dominick & Haff)

Kings Pattern

Berry spoon	$110.00
Butter knife, master	52.00
Butter serving knife	70.00
Cherry fork	35.00
Citrus spoon	150.00
Cocktail fork	25.00
Cream soup spoon	26.50
Dessert spoon	45.00
Fish knife	52.50
Fruit knife	42.50
Fruit spoon	35.00
Grapefruit spoon	45.00
Gravy ladle	100.00
Luncheon fork	38.00
Salad fork	42.00
Sugar tongs	40.00

LILY OF THE VALLEY (Gorham Mfg. Co.)

Butter spreader, flat handle	16.00
Cocktail fork	18.00
Cold meat fork, 8 " l.	53.00
Dinner service for 4, 8-piece settings, 32 pcs.	640.00
Gravy ladle	38.00
Jelly spoon	21.50
Lemon fork	24.00
Pie server, hollow handle	25.00
Sugar Spoon	17.00
Tablespoon	39.00

POPPY (Gorham Mfg. Co.)

Berry fork	44.00
Berry spoon	85.00
Bouillon spoon	45.00
Butter spreader	15.00
Chipped beef	65.00
Cocktail fork	12.00
Cold meat fork	85.00
Cracker scoop	295.00
Cream ladle	18.00
Cream soup spoon	30.00
Dinner fork	30.00
Dinner knife	45.00
Gravy ladle	20.00
Luncheon fork	15.00
Mustard ladle	65.00
Salad fork	45.00
Soup spoon, oval bowl	32.00
Strawberry fork	30.00
Teaspoon	16.00

REPOUSSÉ (Samuel Kirk & Sons)

Asparagus fork	188.00
Baby fork & spoon set	39.50
Baby pusher	33.50
Baby knife, sq.. handle, all silver	40.00
Bacon fork, long-handled	58.00
Berry spoon, fruit in bowl	117.00
Berry spoon, fruit in bowl, gold-washed, large	210.00
Berry spoon, scalloped	77.50
Berry spoon, oval, large	95.00
Bonbon spoon	39.00
Bouillon spoon	22.00
Butter paddle, hollow-handle	19.50
Butter serving knife, flat handle	35.00
Cake knife, hollow handle	30.00
Casserole spoon	85.00
Cheese server	26.00
Citrus spoon	25.00
Cold meat fork, large	62.50
Corn holder	35.00
Cream ladle	65.00
Demitasse spoon	13.00
Dinner knife	30.00
Fish knife, hollow handle, silver blade	27.00
Gravy ladle, 6¼ " l.	81.00
Ice cream server	175.00
Iced tea spoon	28.50

Ice tongs..87.50
Lemon fork.......................................45.00
Lettuce fork, 7¼ " l. 68.00
Lobster shear....................................120.00
Meat fork...225.00
Nut spoon..30.00
Olive fork, 2-tine 24.00
Pickle fork, 3-tine 26.00
Salad fork..23.00
Salt spoon, individual 9.00
Salt spoon, master size.....................26.50
Serving spoon, egg-shaped bowl,
   large, 9½ " l. 119.00
Steak knife...29.00
Stuffing spoon, 12" l. 315.00
Soup spoon, oval bowl......................33.00
Sugar spoon, fluted...........................29.00
Sugar tongs.......................................31.00
Tablespoon, pierced bowl 60.00
Teaspoon..18.00
Youth fork...21.50

VERSAILLES (Gorham Mfg. Co.)
Beef fork...135.00
Berry spoon 278.00
Berry spoon, gold-washed bowl,
   large..235.00
Bouillon ladle....................................495.00
Bouillon spoon 30.50
Bread knife...31.00
Butter knives, hollow-handled,
   set of 12 ....300.00
Butter, master....................................87.00
Butter serving knife..........................110.00
Cake knife...350.00
Carving set, small (steak), 2 pcs. 157.50
Cheese scoop, large 190.00
Citrus spoon 45.00
Cocktail fork.......................................31.00
Cream ladle..85.00
Crumb knife.......................................325.00
Demitasse spoon................................25.00
Dessert spoon....................................49.00
Dinner knife..66.50
Gravy ladle.......................................126.00
Gravy ladle, gold-washed bowl 169.00
Gumbo spoon.....................................58.00
Ice cream fork....................................67.50
Ice cream knife, 10½ " l.....................162.50
Ice cream ladle.................................295.00
Ice cream slice, large.......................295.00
Ice cream slice, hollow-handled, all
   silver, 12½ " l..................................425.00
Ladle, pierced 162.50
Lettuce fork, bright-cut 185.00
Luncheon fork.....................................38.00
Luncheon knife...................................54.00
Meat fork...110.00
Mustard ladle 165.00
Olive spoon...85.00
Pastry fork...75.00
Paté spreader......................................30.00
Pie server, silver blade 274.00
Preserve spoon.................................105.00

Salad fork...62.00
Salad serving fork 225.00
Salad serving set, gold-washed
   bowls...385.00
Salad serving set, long handles........575.00
Salad serving set, shell bowls 650.00
Salad spoon......................................150.00
Sardine fork......................................135.00
Sauce ladle.......................................113.50
Seafood fork.......................................45.00
Serving fork, 8½ " 125.00
Serving spoon, shell bowl,
   medium 190.00
Serving spoon, shell bowl, large.......400.00
Serving spoon, large.........................72.50
Soup ladle, gold-washed bowl,
   14" l...650.00
Soup spoon, oval or round bowl 57.00
Sugar spoon.......................................75.00
Sugar tongs..82.50
Tablespoon...58.00
Tea knife...60.00
Teaspoon..24.00
Youth fork...60.00

WATTEAU (Wm. B. Durgin Co.)
Berry spoon 115.00
Dinner fork..30.00
Honey spoon.......................................85.00
Ice cream slice 200.00
Luncheon fork.....................................20.50
Pastry fork...45.00
Salt spoon, master 33.00
Serving fork, 9¼ " l.............................65.00
Soup spoon, oval bowl.......................21.00
Tablespoon...26.00
Tea strainer 85.00

TIN & TOLE
Bread box, tole, original worn black
   paint w/red on facade & stenciled
   label "BREAD" w/black shadowing,
   16" l...104.50
Candle box, tin, hanging-type,
   cylindrical, old black paint,
   10½" l...132.00
Candle mold, tin, six-tube,
   rectangular top & base, 10¾" h. 60.50
Candle mold, tin, ten-tube,
   rectangular top & base plates, wide
   strap handle at side of top, 11" h. 115.50
Candle mold, twelve-tube, tin,
   crimped top & bottom flange, strap
   handle, 10½" h. 440.00
Candle mold, tin, thirty-six tube,
   rectangular top & base framing the
   tubes, large eared strap handles at
   each side, 11½" h. (one handle
   resoldered)......................................137.50
Candle sconce, tin, circular, the
   mirrored reflector depicting a
   mosaic-like star in clear & amber
   glass, 12" h. (some age but not
   19th c.) 247.50

Candle sconce, tole, crimped crest above a rectangular back, very worn original dark brown japanning w/floral decoration in red, green & yellow, 13¼" h. **330.00**

Candle sconces, tin, a half-round sunburst crest above the flat rectangular backplate above the half-round pan w/candle socket, old finish, 4" h., pr. **715.00**

Octagonal Coal Hod

Coal hod, cov., tole, octagonal shape w/ornately molded feet & handles, decorated w/stylized florals in yellow, orange & green leaf designs (ILLUS.) **475.00**

Coffee boiler, cov., tin, wide tapering cylindrical body w/a rim spout & strap handle, strap swing handle across the top, low domed cover, 16" h. plus swing handle (some damage & repair) **176.00**

Coffeepot, cov., tin, wide tapering cylindrical body w/a high angled straight spout, strap handle & low domed cover, 9¼" h. **44.00**

Deed box, cov., tole, rectangular w/slightly domed cover w/small oval top ring & edge latch, original worn black ground decorated w/flowers & lyre in yellow, red & green, 6½" l. **192.50**

Document box, cov., tole, rectangular w/a domed cover & ring handle, original dark brown japanning w/swag & line decoration in red, white & yellow, 9" l. (paint on lid has some old touch up repair) **330.00**

Document box, cov., tole, slightly domed cover, worn original dark brown japanning w/stylized floral decoration in red, green, yellow & white, 9" l. **220.00**

Model of a top hat, tin, anniversary-type, cylindrical w/hatband & bow above flat brim, old blue & red paint w/red showing through blue, 11¾" d. **110.00**

Tea caddy, cov., tole, cylindrical w/a slightly rounded wide shoulder to the short cylindrical neck, original worn dark brown japanned ground decorated w/stylized flowers in red & yellow, 4" h. **148.50**

Tinder box, tin, short wide cylindrical box w/a lift-off top & small loop side handle on the base, the top centered by a cylindrical candle socket, includes damper & flint & steel, 19th c., 4½" d. **385.00**

Megaphone, tin, old worn red paint, 30" l. **93.50**

Plate warmer, tole, a bail handle above the conical open sides w/domed top raised on three cabriole legs w/domed snake feet, decorated w/clusters of fruit, leaves & a bird on a black ground, second half 19th c., width at feet 15", 21" h. **1,035.00**

Rum warmer, cov., tin, pewter finial, long turned curly maple handle, 7¼" h. **357.50**

New England Syrup Jug

Syrup jug, cov., tole, tapering cylindrical form w/shaped & domed hinged lid continuing to an inverted cup-form base, the jug w/a broad band of red, green & yellow swags & leafage all on a dark brown ground w/turned wood handle & ball finial, probably New England, 19th c., minor loses, 8" h. (ILLUS.) **172.00**

Tray, two-tier, tole, oval w/reticulated galleries, high curved overhead handle, old black repaint w/vintage & landscape scene w/classical ruins, 16½" l., overall 16½" h. **275.00**

Tray on stand, tole, oval, yellow & black centered by a figure of Ceres within a foliate border, the sides pierced for handles, the stand w/bamboo-turned legs joined by a

Regency Period Tray

stretcher, Regency period, England,
first quarter 19th c., 22 x 30",
25¼" h. (ILLUS.) **3,450.00**
Tray, tole, oval w/a raised rim pierced
w/end handles, a central narrow
oval reserve painted in polychrome
w/a landscape scene w/several
figures by the sea w/a ship & house
in the distance, the wide border
decorated w/gold grapevines on a
dark red ground, possibly American-
made, early 19th c., 24 x 32¼" **2,875.00**
Wall sconces, tin, single light, each
w/a circular concave backplate set
w/mirror tiles, 9½" d., pr. **1,610.00**

(End of Metals Section)

MILITARY COLLECTIBLES

CIVIL WAR (1861-65)

Civil War Broadside

Broadside, printed paper, titled
"Head Quarters European Brigade,"
dated "New Orleans, 27th April,
1862," notes that by the order of
Mayor J.T. Monroe, Paul Juge Fils is
taking command of all the Foreign
Troops, creasing and fading
(ILLUS.) **$770.00**
Canteen, Model 1858, bull's-eye
pattern, early worn red, white, blue
& silver paint w/stars, pewter spout,
7½" l. **412.50**
Cartridge case, leather w/shoulder
strap, U.S. brass insignia **375.00**
Clothing receipt form, signed by all
members of the company, 1865 ....**45.00**
Discharge paper, signed twice by
Union General D.T. Van Buren,
5th New York Zouaves **55.00**
Flag, silk, 4th Division Headquarters,
framed, 27 x 42" (fabric loss &
discoloration) **1,092.00**
Photographs, Civil War Corps photos
consisting of 54 - ⅞ x 1" tintypes
w/gilt liners & mounted on a white
board backing, arranged in rows
w/each person identified, a pencil
inscription reads "Camp C - 11th
Regt. Invalid Corps," most shown
wearing U.S. issue Invalid Corps
jackets & some women shown, in an
early veneered beveled rectangular
frame, 12¼" x 16¼" (some
pictures flaking & some
darkened)..**880.00**
Saddle tags, brass, one stamped
"Charleston 1862 Servant 80," the
other embossed "CS" for
'Confederate States,' 2 pcs...........**1,430.00**
Shoulder straps, Confederate Chief
Naval Engineer, decorated w/two
oak leaves, pr. **110.00**
Spur, Confederate, made in
Richmond, Virginia, complete **350.00**
Sword w/brass hilt, marked "U.S.
1863 - F.S.S.," 38" l. **220.00**

WORLD WAR I (1914-18)
Bolo knife & sheath, machine-
gunner's, mint unused condition **175.00**
Signal lantern, aluminum, brass &
celluloid, folding-type, marked "Capt.
James A. Northrup Aviation Division
Signal Corps.," patent-dated 1908,
Stonebridge **225.00**

WORLD WAR II (1939-1945)
Book, "Life's Picture History of World
War II," 1950, w/slipcase **30.00**
Bayonet, German, Army dress-type,
excellent leather..................................**95.00**
Bayonet, German, Hitler youth-type,
inscribed, maker & "RZM" marks **250.00**
Compass, "Atro-Compass MK II,"
hard black Bakelite case, Sperti,
Inc., Cincinnati, Ohio, complete
w/instruction booklet (ILLUS. top
next page)..**225.00**

World War II Navigation Compass

Dagger, German Army general's, gold-washed, w/hanger & portapee..**550.00**

Field telephone, wooden, Japanese **100.00**

Flight jacket, USN G-I, leather, size 38 ....**295.00**

Jacket, leather bomber-type w/removable beaver lining, German Luftwaffe, excellent condition............**695.00**

Map, cartograph-type, depicts 42nd Infantry Rainbow Division "Mission of the Rainbow," colorful, 1944, 19½ x 25½".......................................**90.00**

Naval range indicator, Bakelite, paddle-shaped viewer used to calculate distance & type of enemy aircraft, marked "US Navy AA," made by A.C. Gilbert Co.................**225.00**

Officer's belt, United States Navy.......**25.00**

Pennant, for German vehicle, small metal flag w/Maltese Cross, excellent condition **225.00**

Pocket watch, Longines, U.S. Army Air Force navigation master, size 18, 21-jewel movement, temp & five positions, 36 hour indicator, 24 hour dial w/sweep seconds hand, nickel-plated case w/some wear, inscription on case **785.00**

Stick grenade w/cord, German, mint condition **175.00**

MINIATURES (Paintings)

Bust profile portrait of a bearded gentleman on ivory, Europe, 19th c., framed, 4½x 5"..................**$287.50**

Bust portrait of a gentleman, water-color on ivory, blue eyes & tousled dark hair, wearing a high-collared black coat & high white stock, facing

Bust Portrait of a Gentleman

right, in a rose gold double-sided locket frame w/plaited light brown hair & the initials "J.C.B." in finely cut rose gold letters, American School, early 19th c., 2⅛ x 2¾" oval (ILLUS.).................**1,495.00**

Miniature Portrait of a Lady

Bust portrait of a lady, stated to be Jane Cook of South Carolina, water-color on ivory, her fair curly hair pulled up, facing left, wearing a white low-cut dress & red shawl, in a landscape background, bearing a later signature "Peale," attributed to Charles Fraser, ca. 1810, oval, 3¼" h. (ILLUS.) **1,093.00**

Bust portrait of a little girl, water-color on ivory, the girl holding a small toy dog, American School, 19th c., 1¾ x 2¼" **10,350.00**

Bust portrait of a young boy, water-color on ivory, large dark tresses & bangs, wearing a lace-trimmed blue costume, attributed to Joseph Steward, ca. 1795, in a later gold-colored metal oval filigree frame, 1⅜ x 1½".......................................**4,312.00**

Bust portrait of a young man on ivory, oval, shown in three-quarter view facing right, thin smiling mouth, large blue eyes, dark hair w/side-burns, wearing a high-collared jacket w/wide lapels, a cravet & white shirt, in a thin gold-filled oval frame, lock of man's brown hair under lens in back, early 19th c., 2½" h..**577.50**

Bust portrait of a young woman on ivory, oval, shown facing right but looking left, her dark hair pulled into a chignon atop her head, wearing a high lacy collar on her dark dress w/a brooch & pink ribbon at her throat, in a thin gold-filled oval frame, scrap of her dress under lens in back, ca. 1830-40, 2½" h. **715.00**

Bust portraits of a man & woman, water-color on ivory, the gentleman seated in a chair, the woman seated in a chair & holding a baby in her arms, American School, 19th c., 2⅝ x 3", pr....................................**1,150.00**

Bust profile portrait of a Peter Thacher, fabric, paper & water-color, facing left, his long dark hair cropped at his collar, wearing a blue great coat & frilled white stock, attributed to Mary B. Way, ca. 1800, in a narrow oval gold metal locket frame, 1¼ x 1½"...........................**3,450.00**

Half-length portrait of a lady, water-color on ivory, wearing a lacy white mobcap w/blue ribbons & a coral pink gown w/white kerchief, American School, late 18th c., in a narrow oval brass frame, 1¼ x 1⅝" **805.00**

Half-length portrait of a little girl, water-color on ivory, the seated girl in a frilly dress, grasping the strand of coral bead necklace she is wearing, American School, 19th c., 1⅝ x 2" **6,900.00**

Three-quarter length portrait of a youth dressed as a harlequin, signed "IBM" & "PEL," label on reverse "la petite Girard au threatre la cigale, Paris, July 1917," France, 2⁹⁄₁₆ x 4⅛"......................................**747.50**

Two maidens in diaphanous gowns & a small spaniel in a landscape, on ivory, signed "N. Zardelli," Europe, 19th c., in a molded brass frame, 3⅛ x 4⅛".......................................**517.50**

MINIATURES (Replicas)

Blanket chest, painted pine & poplar, rectangular top w/molded edge lifting above a well w/covered till &

secret drawer, dovetailed case above two small bottom drawers above the molded base on dovetailed shaped bracket feet, original brass keyhole escutcheons, cleaned down to worn old red flame graining, Pennsylvania, late 18th - early 19th c. (some edge damage, feet w/added nails).....................**$4,400.00**

Miniature Chandelier

Chandelier, wood & iron, nine-light, Baroque style, the slender turned standard w/spherical ball base & metal ring drop, supports two tiers of S-scroll iron arms w/candle cups, Europe, 19th c., 4½" h. (ILLUS.) **1,610.00**

Chippendale Chest of Drawers

Chest of drawers, Chippendale, walnut, rectangular top w/molded cornice above a pair of small drawers over three long graduated drawers w/molded edges, molded base on bracket feet, appears to retain original small round brass pulls, Pennsylvania, 1760-80, 6½ x 13½", 13½" h. (ILLUS.) **3,680.00**

Chest of Drawers, mahogany, Federal, a molded rectangular top

Federal Chest of Drawers

above a pair of stepped-back small drawers on the rectangular top above a pair of small drawers overhanging three long drawers flanked by spiral-turned columns, molded base, baluster- and ring-turned feet, New England, ca. 1825, 8½ x 16½", 18" h. (ILLUS.) **1,495.00**

Chest of Drawers, walnut, rectangular top w/low pointed backrail above four narrow graduated long drawers w/small wooden knobs, gently arched apron, old alligatored finish, square nail construction, 8 x 13½", 15" h. (added wire nails) **330.00**

Desk, George III style, mahogany, a slant-front top opening to a fitted interior above three long graduated drawers w/round brass pulls, molded base & simple bracket feet, England, late 18th - early 19th c., 14¼" w., 15" h. (repairs, feet replaced) **1,840.00**

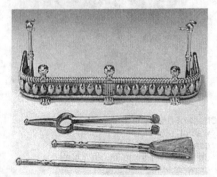

Miniature Fireplace Equipment

Fireplace equipment, brass & various metals, four D-form low brass fireplace surrounds, one gilt-bronze & polished steel, another

foliate-cast brass, w/various other tools including tongs, shovel & poker, Europe, 19th c., heights 4" to 9", the group (ILLUS. of part) **1,495.00**

Footstool, painted pine, rectangular top above wide undulating sides & cut-out ends, painted yellow & brown over earlier grey & red, New England, early 19th c., 6½" l. (top has been moved slightly in an old re-nailing)................................**460.00**

Parlor suite: settee, two armchairs & two side chairs; silver, each w/an arched back w/a tiny ribbon crest, the backs embossed w/groups of birds, on cabriole legs below decorated seatrails, France, 1838-64, ½ -inch scale, the set................**287.50**

Tea set: cov. teapot, open sugar bowl, two cups & saucers & an oval handled tray; sterling silver, tapering cylindrical forms, Chester & Birmingham, England, 1907-09, tray 5⅜" l., teapot 1½" h., the set...........**287.50**

MOLDS - CANDY, FOOD, & MISC.

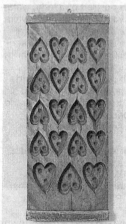

Early Maple Sugar Mold

Also see BUTTER MOLDS & STAMPS.

Cake, rabbit, cast iron, "Griswold 862"..**$275.00**

Cake, Santa Claus, nickel-plated cast iron, "Griswold" **670.00**

Chocolate, bird, tin, No. 217278, 6½" h...**88.00**

Chocolate, boy w/top hat, tin, "Anton Reiche", 7½" h. **125.00**

Chocolate, rabbit, tin, No. 26067, 8½" h..**120.00**

Chocolate, rooster, tin, No. 256,
5" h..**48.00**
Food, cow, stoneware, domed oblong
form w/a standing cow embossed in
the interior top, molded decorations
on interior sides, 5¼" l.
(small flakes)......................................**93.50**
Food, fish, cast iron, 13¼" l..................**82.50**
Food, fish, redware, slightly curved
stylized fish w/dotted scales & fin
details, clear glaze w/brown flecks &
splotches, 11⅝" l. (minor edge
chips) **440.00**
Food, fish, stoneware, domed oval
form w/a long scaley fish embossed
in an oval reserve in the inside top,
deep scalloped interior edges, tan
exterior, grey interior, 7½" l.
(minor hairline) **126.50**
Food, fish, tin, arched shape
w/detailed scales & a ruffled rim,
12¼" l. **38.50**
Food, quail, stoneware, oval domed
shape w/a small bird impressed in
the inside top, deep scalloped
interior edges, tan exterior, grey
interior, 5¾" l. (minor crazing) **82.50**
Maple sugar, hearts, carved wood,
rectangular board w/breadboard
ends, carved w/alternating rows of
inverted hearts, New England, early
19th c., 11 x 27" (ILLUS.)..............**4,313.00**
Pudding, fish, copper, curved leaping
form, 8½ x 9"....................................**120.00**

MOVIE MEMORABLIA

BOOKS
"Jane Withers" (Her Life Story),
1936...**$17.00**
"Now I Am Eight," by Shirley
Temple, Saalfield Publishing Co.,
No. 1766, 1937 ....**35.00 to 45.00**
"Rudolph Valentino Recollections,"
by Natacha Rambova (his wife), soft
cover, 1927 ....**55.00**
"Shirley Temple - Little Star,"
Saalfield Publishing Co., 1936...........**45.00**
"Shirley Temple Through the Day,"
Saalfield Publishing Co., No. 1716,
1936 ....**35.00 to 40.00**
"The True Story of Jean Harlow,"
1964, photos throughout, soft
cover **40.00**

COSTUMES
Julie Andrews, "The Sound of
Music," 20th Century Fox, 1965,
yellow wool three-piece suit,
designed by Dorothy Jeakins, the
set **7,475.00**

"Désirée" Coronation Costume

Marlon Brando, "Désirée," 20th
Century Fox, 1954, coronation
costume including cream tunic &
crimson robe completely lined
w/white fur, designed by Rene
Hubert (ILLUS.)...........................**20,700.00**
Francis X. Bushman, "Ben-Hur,"
Metro-Goldwyn-Mayer, 1925, chariot
race costume, complete...............**6,900.00**
James Cagney, "Yankee Doodle
Dandy," Paramount Pictures, 1942,
three-piece blue checkered wool
suit, inside lining stamped "Property
of Paramount Pictures," photograph
of Cagney in the suit included, the
group..**2,300.00**
Cyd Charisse, "The Kissing Bandit,"
1948, a gold w/bronze lamé dance
costume, the bustier w/open weave
fringe skirt **403.00**
Montgomery Clift, "Raintree County,"
Metro-Goldwyn-Mayer, 1958,
bronze & silver paisley vest, sewn-in
tag reads "METRO-GOLDWYN-
MAYER 1692-5095"......................**1,380.00**

Claudette Colbert Costume
Claudette Colbert, "Sign of the

Cross," Paramount Studios, 1932, elaborate floor-length grey silk crepe kimono, trimmed w/lavish gold bullion embroidery, sewn-in tag w/"Paramount Studios" (ILLUS.) **805.00**

Robert DeNiro, "Raging Bull," United Artists, 1980, boxing trunks, Everlast black satin trunks banded & trimmed in white, costumer's staining on the side bands **2,875.00**

Emerald City, "The Wizard of Oz," Metro-Goldwyn-Mayer, 1939, green & white felt undervest worn by a resident of The Emerald City, sewn-in studio tag reading "Metro-Goldwyn-Mayer Shopkeeper 1060-40-7842" **2,875.00**

Jose Ferrer, "Cyrano de Bergerac," 1950, mustard wool doublet & breeches w/gilt braid, blue ribbons, lace collar, sewn-in Brooks Costume Co. tag **575.00**

Judy Garland, "Easter Parade," MGM 1948, floor-length gown, the bodice of sleeveless gown in pale gold w/lace overlay, the body of the gown in apricot crepe, designed by Irene Sharaff, sewn-in tag reads "1418 4693 Judy Garland" **1,380.00**

Judy Garland, "The Harvey Girls," 1950, red & white striped green velvet-trimmed jacket blouse, sewn-in costumer's tag reads "Judy Garland 1348" **2,760.00**

Judy Garland Test Dress

Judy Garland, "The Wizard of Oz," MGM, 1939, test dress worn by Judy Garland, blue cotton pinafore w/a blue polka dot border attached w/white buttons, dot pattern also circles hem border, inside left hook seam, sewn-in tag reads "JUDY GARLAND 3955," w/a black & white studio photo of Garland wearing the dress, 2 pcs. (ILLUS.) **10,925.00**

Judy Garland, "The Wizard of Oz," Metro-Goldwyn-Mayer, 1939, gingham checked apron, one of several worn in the movie **14,375.00**

John Gielgud, "Julius Caesar," Metro-Goldwyn-Mayer, 1953, cream cotton crossbar weave tunic worn by Gielgud, geometric embroidery, sewn-in tag "METRO-GOLDWYN-MAYER 1599 2253" **690.00**

Charlton Heston, "Ben-Hur," Metro-Goldwyn-Mayer, 1959, beige wool bronze weave trim tunic worn by Heston, sewn-in MGM tag w/a Western Costume Company tag reading "Charlton Heston 2358-1" ...**920.00**

Charlton Heston, "Ben-Hur," Metro-Goldwyn-Mayer, 1959, chariot race costume, complete.....................**48,500.00**

Dustin Hoffman, "Papillon," 1973, three-piece cotton prisoner uniform, red & white stripes, w/a costumer's tag, photograph of Hoffman wearing the costume included, the group...**1,955.00**

Gene Kelly, "Summerstock," MGM, 1950, three-piece suit, orange wool striped jacket lined in beige silk & single breast pocket, yellow wool vest, partially lined, w/five buttons, beige trousers of wool blend w/inside cotton waistband, sewn-in tag reading "Metro-Goldwyn-Mayer Gene Kelly 1546 9037 30 314," designed by Walter Plunkett, 3 pcs. **1,150.00**

Janet Leigh "Houdini" Costume

Janet Leigh, "Houdini," Paramount Studios, 1953, mint green wool period three-piece suit, worn in the roll of Mrs. Houdini, with her name tag (ILLUS.) **460.00**

Jack Lemmon, "The Great Race," Warner Bros., 1965, cape, worn by Lemmon in his role as Professor Fate, black wool floor-length w/black satin collar, tag inside collar reads "Warner Bros. Jack Lemmon"..........**633.00**

'Lollipop Kid' (Jerry Maren), "The Wizard of Oz," Metro-Goldwyn-Mayer, 1939, Munchkin costume worn by this character, complete **23,000.00**

James Mason, "The Prisoner of Zenda," MGM, 1952, suit, the military-style jacket in blue heavy wool lined in blue satin, the front embellished w/horizontal blue & gold braid & gold-tone buttons, the trousers in blue wool w/wide stripe border on outer seams, jacket w/tag "Metro-Goldwyn-Mayer James Mason 1579 9755," trousers w/tag "Metro-Goldwyn-Mayer 1579 9755 312," 2 pcs. **978.00**

Paul Muni, "The Good Earth," MGM, 1937, two-piece tunic costume, black raw silk tunic lined in blue cotton w/braided loop closures, black raw silk trousers, collar tag reads "Muni," 2 pcs. **575.00**

Ramon Novarro, "Ben-Hur," Metro-Goldwyn-Mayer, 1925, laurel wreath worn by the Novarro character **3,737.50**

Jane Powell, "Two Weeks With Love," dress, cream-colored gauze-printed w/overall blue flower pattern w/net short sleeves, trimmed at square neck, waist & knee w/inset band of cream lace & blue ribbon, over pink silk-satin lining trimmed in lace & satin ruffles, tag marked "Jane Powell," w/movie still showing Powell wearing the dress, 2 pcs. **575.00**

Anthony Quinn, "Ride Vaquero," Metro-Goldwyn-Mayer, 1953, crimson satin shirt, sewn-in tag reads "METRO-GOLDWYN-MAYER A. Quinn 1597-2279" **230.00**

George C. Scott, "Patton," 20th Century Fox, 1970, military jacket **9,775.00**

Ann Sothern, "Three Hearts for Julie," MGM, 1943, skirt, calf-length blue & white polka dot silk, sewn-in tag reads "Metro-Goldwyn-Mayer Ann Sothern 1270-5427" **253.00**

Barbra Streisand, "What's Up Doc?," 1972, brown velvet "cavalier" type hat trimmed w/colorful feathers, photograph of Streisand wearing the hat included **2,530.00**

Elizabeth Taylor, "Raintree County," MGM, 1958, Civil War era style bathing costume, two-piece red wool blend trimmed in cream bands on short sleeves, hem & pants leg, button closure border, sewn-in tag reads "1692 5059 Elizabeth Taylor," 2 pcs. **1,380.00**

Elizabeth Taylor, "Rhapsody," Metro-Goldwyn-Mayer, 1954, pink & grey wool plaid dressing gown, quilted cuffs, tag reads "METRO-GOLDWYN-MAYER 1628" **1,035.00**

Robert Taylor "Ivanhoe" Costume

Robert Taylor, "Ivanhoe," MGM, 1952, medieval costume w/a waist-length taupe wool jacket lined in grey satin blend, the sleeves in brown suede, the front w/hook fasteners embellished w/taupe braiding, tag sewn into collar reads "M.Berman Ltd. 18 Irving St. Leicester Sq. W.C.2 Mr. Robert Taylor," the sleeveless over-tunic in burnt orange wool w/a heavily embroidered dragon on the front & back, tag sewn in collar reads "Film and Theatrical Costumes M. Berman Ltd. 18 Irving St. Leicester Sq.W.C. 2 Robert Taylor," 2 pcs. (ILLUS.) **805.00**

Lana Turner, "Green Dolphin Street," MGM, 1947, gown, two-piece floor-length in heavy pale gold satin, the bodice designed w/like material tassel yoke, trimmed w/three bands of satin, the skirt w/muslin slip w/a wide draped sash, tags inside bodice read "LANA TURNER CHANGE 15," & "1394 LANA TURNER," the skirt tag reads "LANA TURNER CHANGE 15," & w/a clip tag w/"MGM 34943 16," 2 pcs. **690.00**

Van Trapp children's outfits, "The Sound of Music," 20th Century Fox, 1965, the 'curtain' play clothes for the children, the complete set.....**18,400.00**

Johnny Weissmuller, "Tarzan," MGM, 1930s-40s, loincloth worn in the role of Tarzan, four panels of brown wool & chamois w/four string ties, 17 x 60"..**4,025.00**

Orson Welles, "Citizen Kane," 1941,

Orson Welles Frock Coat

gentleman's frock coat worn by Welles (ILLUS.)...........................**10,350.00**

Orson Welles, "MacBeth," 1948, three-piece costume w/a long white & brown wool plaid cape & matching "balloon" leg pants & a dark rose wool floor-length tabard **2,300.00**

Ornate Mae West Hat

Mae West, "I'm No Angel," 1933, lavender & white hat, net & straw weave ornately trimmed w/large feathers & maribou plumes, embellished w/strips of sequins & paillettes, 24" h. (ILLUS.) **483.00**

Esther Williams, "Million Dollar Mermaid," MGM, 1952, bathing costume, one-piece rayon blend embellished w/large clear paillettes, rear zipper seam, sewn-in tag reading "1567 9566 Esther Williams" **2,760.00**

LOBBY CARDS

"After the Thin Man," starring William Powell & Myrna Loy, MGM, 1936, 11 x 14", set of 8 ......**1,265.00**

"All About Eve," starring Bette Davis, Anne Baxter, George Sanders & Celeste Holm, scene of the four main characters in formal attire, 20th Century Fox, 1950, 11 x 14"..**1,150.00**

"Beau Geste," starring Gary Cooper, Ray Milland & Robert Preston, Paramount, 1939, 11 x 14", set of 8...**2,300.00**

"Cleopatra," starring Claudette Colbert, Warren William & Henry Wilcoxon, central bust portrait of Colbert wearing an ornate headdress, single card, Paramount, 1934, 11 x 14"................................**633.00**

"The Devil is a Woman," starring Marlene Dietrich, pictured in an embrace w/a handsome man, single jumbo card, Paramount, 1935, 14 x 17"...**1,495.00**

"Dinner At 8" Lobby Card

"Dinner At 8," starring Jean Harlow, Wallace Beery, Marie Dressler & John Barrymore, a colored photo showing Harlow confronting Beery, MGM, 1933, 11 x 14" (ILLUS.) **2,070.00**

"Dracula" Lobby Card

"Dracula," starring Bela Lugosi, horizontal format w/three tall vignette scenes, Dracula in the center scene, Universal, 1931, 11 x 14" (ILLUS.) **6,325.00**

"Gone with the Wind," starring Vivian Leigh & Clark Gable, scene

of Mammy lacing Scarlett, MGM,
1939, 11 x 14".............................**1,380.00**

Famous "Public Enemy" Lobby Card

"**Public Enemy**," starring James
Cagney & Mae Clark, color photo of
the classic movie scene where
Cagney shoves a grapefruit into
Mae Clark's face, Warner, 1931,
11 x 14" (ILLUS.) **5,462.00**
"**Sunset Boulevard**," starring Gloria
Swanson, William Holden & Erich
von Stroheim, scene depicting
Swanson clinging to Holden as von
Stroheim looks on, single card,
Paramount, 1950, 11 x 14" **920.00**

"Superman" Lobby Cards

"**Superman**," starring Kirk Alyn, set
of four cards from Chapter 4 of the
serial, "The Man of Steel vs the
Spider Lady," each w/a different
scene in sepia & white, Columbia,

1948, each 11 x 14" (ILLUS. two
of four) **287.00**
"**They Died with Their Boots On**,"
starring Errol Flynn & Olivia
DeHavilland, battlefield scene w/one
man standing & firing a pistol while
others fight off Indians & many lay
dead, Warner Bros., 1941,
11 x 14"...**1,265.00**
"**The Thin Man**," starring William
Powell & Myrna Loy, bust portrait of
Powell & Loy cheek-to-cheek,
MGM, 1934, 11 x 14" **1,265.00**

"Wizard of Oz" Title Card

"**The Wizard of Oz**," starring Judy
Garland, title card w/color head
portraits of the stars across the top
& the title in oversized letters below,
MGM, 1939, 11 x 14"
(ILLUS.) **5,175.00**

POSTERS

"Atom Man vs. Superman" Poster

"**A Bill of Divorcement**," starring
John Barrymore, Katharine Hepburn
& Billie Burke, dramatic depiction of
the three main characters, six-sheet,
RKO, 1932, linen-backed,
81 x 81"...**9,200.00**
"**A Day at the Races**," starring the
Marx Brothers with Allan Jones &

Maureen O'Sullivan, caricature of the Marx Brothers w/a horse leaning across their shoulders beneath the title & list of cast members, one-sheet, MGM, 1937, linen-backed, style C, 27 x 41"............................**3,450.00**

"The Adventures of Robin Hood," starring Errol Flynn, Olivia DeHavilland, Basil Rathbone & Claude Rains, scene of Robin Hood aiming w/his bow, a lovely maiden in the background above a shield-shaped device w/the movie title, one-sheet, Warner Bros., 1938, linen-backed, 27 x 41" **8,050.00**

"A Letter To 3 Wives," starring Jeanne Crain, Linda Darnell & Ann Southern, half-sheet, 1949, 22 x 28"...**50.00**

"Atom Man vs. Superman," starring Kirk Alyn, colorful cartoon-style design w/a large figure of Superman, a black & white photo vignette marked "Chapter 6" in the lower left, one-sheet, Columbia, 1950, linen-backed, 27 x 41" (ILLUS.) **1,840.00**

"The Big Sleep" Poster

"The Big Sleep," starring Humphrey Bogart & Lauren Bacall," centered by a photo of Bogart & Bacall embracing, framed w/a wide red square, one-sheet, Warner Bros., 1946, 27 x 41" (ILLUS.) **862.00**

"Call Her Savage," starring Clara Bow, color lithograph w/a bust portrait of the red-headed star, one-sheet, 20th Century Fox, 1932, linen-backed, 27 x 41" (ILLUS. top next column) **1,265.00**

"Casablanca," starring Humphrey Bogart, Ingrid Bergman & Paul Henreid, bust portrait of Bogart holding a gun against a background of portraits of various cast members above the title, three-sheet, Warner

"Call Her Savage" Poster

Bros., 1942, linen-backed, 41 x 81".......................................**16,100.00**

"City Lights," starring Charlie Chaplin, colorful drawing showing Chaplin standing in the corner of a boxing ring, one-sheet, United Artists, 1931, linen-backed, 27 x 41"...**8,625.00**

"The Country Flapper," starring Dorothy Gish, color scene of a young couple & another young lady in a wooded landscape, one-sheet, 1922, linen-backed, 27 x 41" **575.00**

"Creature from the Black Lagoon," starring Richard Carlson & Julia Adams, scene depicting the creature menacing the heroine above three vignettes, the title & cast listing superimposed over the scene, three-sheet, Universal, 1954, linen-backed, 41 x 81" **8,625.00**

"Dinner At Eight" Poster

"Dinner At Eight," starring Jean Harlow, Wallace Beery, Marie Dressler & John Barrymore, cast members names beside a vignette

w/their heads above a full-length
seductive portrait of Harlow at the
bottom beside the title, in dark blue
& black on a yellow background,
one-sheet, MGM, 1933, 27 x 41"
(ILLUS.) **11,500.00**

"Dr. No" James Bond Poster

"Dr. No," starring Sean Connery, first
James Bond film, color half-length
portrait of Bond & four seductive
ladies, quad, United Artists, British,
1962, linen-backed, 30 x 40"
(ILLUS.) **2,300.00**
"The Eagle," starring Rudolph
Valentino, portrait of Valentino as a
Russian Cossack, one-sheet, United
Artists, 1925, linen-backed,
27 x 41"......................................**8,625.00**

Rare "Gone With The Wind" Poster

"Gone With The Wind," starring
Clark Gable & Vivien Leigh,
described as the "ultimate" 'Gone
With The Wind' poster, color full-
length photographs of the four major
cast members at the bottom below a
color half-length portrait of Gable &
Leigh flanked by color painted
vignette scenes, the title & credits
across the top, MGM, 1939,
linen-backed, 43 x 65"
(ILLUS.) **71,250.00**

"His New Profession," starring
Charlie Chaplin, scene of Chaplin
w/his trade-mark hat & cane
standing beside a portly gentleman
in a wheelchair, three-sheet, Mutual,
1914, linen-backed, 41 x 81" **10,350.00**

"Hold Your Man" Poster

"Hold Your Man," starring Jean
Harlow & Clark Gable, painted half-
length portraits of Harlow & Gable at
the bottom below their names & the
title, all on a black background, one-
sheet, MGM, 1933, linen-backed,
27 x 41" (ILLUS.) **6,325.00**
"Holiday," starring Cary Grant &
Katharine Hepburn with Doris Nolan,
the two women depicted in a double
picture frame effect w/Grant looking
down at them from above, one-
sheet, Columbia, 1938, linen-
backed, framed, 27 x 41" **1,495.00**
"Invasion of the Saucer-men,"
starring Steve Terrell & Gloria
Castillo, scene of large-headed bug-
eyed monsters carrying off a lovely
young woman, one-sheet, American
International, 1957, 27 x 41".........**2,300.00**

"It Happened One Night" Poster

"It Happened One Night," starring
Clark Gable & Claudette Colbert,
large color bust photos of the stars

at one side, small vignette of them
on the other, display size, Columbia,
1934, 22 x 28" (ILLUS.) **6,327.00**

"Jerry and the Lion," cartoon
starring Tom & Jerry, scene
depicting large seated lion w/Jerry
sitting in front of him, Tom peeking
around the corner, one-sheet, MGM,
1949, linen-backed, 27 x 41" **805.00**

"Jezebel," starring Bette Davis
w/Henry Fonda & George Brent,
portrait of Davis gazing over one
shoulder w/a sultry expression, one-
sheet, Warner Bros., 1938, linen-
backed, 27 x 41" **16,100.00**

"Just Neighbors," starring Harold
Lloyd, scene of an angry Lloyd
holding a dog & talking to a man
across a broken fence holding a
chicken, one-sheet, Pathé, 1919,
linen-backed, 28 x 40" **920.00**

"Kiki," starring Mary Pickford, color
lithograph w/a half-length portrait of
Pickford in a jazzy costume, one-
sheet, United Artists, 1931, linen-
backed, 27 x 41" **1,380.00**

Rare Large "King Kong" Poster

"King Kong," starring Fay Wray &
Robert Armstrong, lithographed
colorful scene of Kong destroying
airplanes atop the Empire State
Building, three-sheet, Style A, RKO,
1933, linen-backed, 41 x 81"
(ILLUS.) **112,500.00**

"The Mark of Zorro," starring
Douglas Fairbanks, depicting the
masked Fairbanks as Zorro leaning
on an oval frame w/a bust portrait of
Fairbanks, one arm across the
likeness holding a sword, one-sheet,
United Artists, 1920, linen-backed,
27 x 41"......................................**8,625.00**

"The Mummy's Curse" Poster

"The Mummy's Curse," starring Lon
Chaney, color lithograph w/half-
length portrait of the Mummy & other
cast members, one-sheet,
Universal, 1944, 27 x 41"
(ILLUS.) **2,587.00**

"Mysterious Mr. Moto," starring
Peter Lorre, portraits of various cast
members around the title & cast list,
one-sheet, 20th Century Fox, 1938,
linen-backed, 27 x 41" **575.00**

"Perfect Understanding," starring
Gloria Swanson, Art Deco style
w/three-quarter profile of Swanson
to one side beneath her name &
movie title, one-sheet, United
Artists, 1933, linen-backed,
27 x 41"..**575.00**

"The Phantom of the Opera,"
starring Lon Chaney, scene
depicting a masked gentleman
looking down on the throng of
opera-goers on a grand stairway,
one-sheet, Universal, 1925, linen-
backed, 27 x 41" **24,150.00**

"The Phantom of the Opera,"
starring Lon Chaney, central scene
of the phantom wearing his red-lined
cape swimming underwater in the
underground of the Paris Opera
House, one-sheet, Universal, 1925,
linen-backed, 27 x 41" **41,400.00**

"Queen Christina," starring Greta
Garbo & John Gilbert, bust portrait
of Garbo center, one-sheet, MGM,
1934, linen-backed, 27 x 41" **5,750.00**

"Sabrina," starring Humphrey Bogart,
Audrey Hepburn & William Holden,
three main characters pictured, one-
sheet, Paramount, 1954, linen-
backed, 27 x 41"...........................**1,150.00**

"The Singing Cowboy," starring
Gene Autry, sketch of Autry playing
the guitar w/Western vignettes

above & to one side, three-sheet, Republic, 1936, linen-backed, 41 x 81"...**1,150.00**

"Son of Frankenstein," starring Basil Rathbone, Boris Karloff & Bela Lugosi, scene of the monster standing w/one arm raised, the title & cast superimposed on the image, lower scene of the monster, Dr. Frankenstein & Igor, one-sheet, Universal, 1939, linen-backed, 27 x 41"......................................**20,125.00**

"The Son of the Sheik," starring Rudolph Valentino with Vilma Banky, color scene of Valentino carrying Banky in his arms against a stylized desert background, one-sheet, United Artists, 1926, linen-backed, 27 x 41".........................**16,100.00**

"Square Deal Sanderson," starring William S. Hart, bust portrait of Hart wearing broad-brimmed cowboy hat & kerchief above his name & movie title, one-sheet, Artcraft Pictures, 1919, linen-backed, 27 x 41".........**3,450.00**

Shirley Temple "Stowaway" Poster

"Stowaway," starring Shirley Temple, a half-length portrait of Shirley at the bottom w/the heads of the other characters in a plume of smoke above, Style B, one-sheet, 20th Century Fox, 1936, linen-backed, 27 x 41" (ILLUS.) **1,150.00**

"Tarzan the Fearless," starring Buster Crabbe with Jacqueline Wells & Edward Woods, scene w/Tarzan & a lovely blonde Jane reclining in a jungle setting, one-sheet, Principal, 1933, 27 x 41" **4,600.00**

"To Kill A Mockingbird," starring Gregory Peck, scraps of paper shown mounted on a wooden board background, one-sheet, Universal, 1963, linen-backed, 27 x 41" **1,380.00**

"Through the Back Door," starring Mary Pickford, scene of Pickford as

the kitchen maid tiptoeing through a garden, three-sheet, United Artists, 1921, linen-backed, 41 x 81" **2,070.00**

"The Wasp Woman," starring Susan Cabot, Fred Eisley & Barboura Morris, scene of a man in the clutches of a huge wasp w/the head of a beautiful woman, Film Group, 1960, linen-backed, 40 x 60" **805.00**

"The Wizard of Oz" Poster

"The Wizard of Oz," starring Judy Garland, colorful design w/head color portraits of the stars in the upper left, a black & white & color vignette at the right, all on a black background, display size, MGM, 1939, 22 x 28" (ILLUS.) **21,850.00**

MISCELLANEOUS

Monroe & DiMaggio Autographs & Photo

Academy Award (Oscar) for 1945 'Best Actress' presented to Joan Crawford for her performance in "Mildred Pierce," gold-plated britannia metal **68,500.00**

Army jacket, short flight jacket worn by Clark Gable during his tenure as a pilot in World War II, dark green wool blend lined in brown satin w/two front flap button pockets & waist buckle, tag inside collar reads

"E. Abinton & Sons - Rushden & Kimbolton," hand-written tag by Mr. Gable in black ink "Capt.Clark Gable" **2,070.00**

Autographs & photograph of Marilyn Monroe & Joe DiMaggio, the original wire photo of the couple at their wedding, matted w/a note paper signed by both, framed together, 2 pcs. (ILLUS.) **3,680.00**

Booklet, promotional, "Birth of a Nation" 1916 ....**75.00**

Box, sterling silver, nearly square w/smooth slightly domed top engraved in script "For Louella with my love Clifton," opens to a cedar-lined compartmented interior, gift to Louella Parsons by Clifton Webb, 3¼ x 4" **1,035.00**

Cigar cutter, steel & mother-of-pearl pocket-style, owned by Groucho Marx, 6" l. **2,530.00**

Coloring book, "Gone With the Wind," 1940, unused, excellent condition **150.00**

Compact, pink enameled cover, complete w/rouge & lipstick in compartments, owned by Jean Harlow, w/letter of authenticity & photo of Harlow, 3 pcs. **575.00**

Condiment dish, Charlie Chaplin, bisque, a figure of Charlie surrounded by two egg-shaped condiment cups, the cups in white w/gold trim & Chaplin dressed as the Little Tramp in black & white, probably British-made, 4½" h. **207.00**

Clark Gable's Dressing Robe

Dressing robe, personal property of Clark Gable, calf-length cream raw silk robe w/black piping bordering the sleeves, pockets & front collar, the left breast pocket mono-grammed "C.G.," made by A. Sulka & Co. of New York, ca. 1940s (ILLUS.) **5,750.00**

Figure, Charlie Chaplin, "Little Tramp" figure, chalkware, painted highlights, coin inset in base reads, "Sold by Mark Hampton Co., Inc., Copyright 191, ...," 7" h. **125.00**

Flacon, sterling silver, flattened oblong form w/an engraved stripe design, removable screw cap, inscribed on the front "Louella," owned by Louella Parsons, 2 x 3¾" **345.00**

Game, board-type, Charlie Chaplin, "Tramp," beautiful graphics, 1930s, Chad Valley, mint condition **90.00**

Golf clubs & bag, personal property of Clark Gable, a set of fourteen clubs including 10 irons (Ralph Guldahl, Wilson & Tommy Armour) & four wooden drivers (Patty Berg, Ralph Guldahl), also four fancy club covers & a MacGregor black leather golf case w/zipper compartments & shoulder strap, the set **9,200.00**

Hat, blue knit in tight-fitting 'flapper' style, overall black buttons applied, ending w/a bow at the front, owned by Bette Davis, w/a photo of Davis, 2 pcs. **230.00**

Hat, gold-colored silk velvet shirred, worn by Carole Lombard, w/letter of authenticity & photo of Lombard, the group **403.00**

Hat, grey felt fedora w/black band, marked "Royal Stetson," w/Warner Bros. Pictures tag on inside w/ "J. Cagney" printed in black ink, w/photo of Cagney wearing the hat, 2 pcs. **1,150.00**

"The Wizard of Oz" Insert Card

Insert Card, "The Wizard of Oz," starring Judy Garland, long design w/color head portraits of the stars down the right side & small photo vignette scenes at the left side, the title down the center, MGM, 1939, 14 x 36" (ILLUS.) **11,500.00**

Magazine, "Modern Screen," 1939, Myrna Loy on cover & "Wizard of Oz" ad **33.00**

Magazine, "Modern Screen," 1940, Jeanette MacDonald on cover **30.00**

Magazine, "Modern Screen," 1952, October, Elizabeth Taylor on cover, stories on Lucy & Desi, Mario Lanza **8.50**

Magazine, "Modern Screen," 1953, Marilyn Monroe on cover **50.00**

Magazine, "Motion Picture," 1953, January, Marilyn Monroe on cover **75.00**

Magazine, "Movie & Radio Guide," 1940, May 24, colored photo of Gene Autry on cover **20.00**

Magazine, "Movie Fan," 1952, December, Marilyn Monroe on cover **75.00**

Magazine, "Movieland," 1952, July, Marilyn Monroe full color photo........**100.00**

Magazine, "Photoplay," 1940, December, Judy Garland on cover, Charlie Chaplin story **15.00**

Magazine, "Photoplay," 1952, April, Marilyn Monroe on cover **65.00**

Magazine, "Photoplay," 1957, Jayne Mansfield on cover..............................**22.00**

Magazine, "Pic," 1940, January 9, Negro movies & Shirley Temple articles **20.00**

Magazine, "Pic," 1944, Linda Darnell on cover, Deanna Durbin feature story **25.00**

Magazine, "Screenland," 1952, August, Marilyn Monroe on cover **85.00**

Magazine, "Screen Romance," 1936, April, Clark Gable & Myrna Loy on cover **15.00**

Magazine, "Screen Stories," 1954, November, Marilyn Monroe on cover....................................**35.00 to 45.00**

Magazine, "Song Fan," 1954, Marilyn Monroe on cover **32.00**

Membership card, Nelson Eddy, "Nelson Eddy Fan Club," 1940 ....**20.00**

Movie contract, original Clark Gable agreement for playing Rhett Butler in "Gone With the Wind," between Gable & Loew's Inc. & Selznick International Pictures, 1939 ....**4,830.00**

Movie contract, typed on paper, original signed agreement between Margaret Mitchell and Selznick International Pictures, Inc. for the exclusive & complete & entire rights to "Gone With The Wind," also an agreement signed by Mitchell by which Loew's Inc. was assigned an interest in her contract w/Selznick Pictures, 1939, the group............**23,000.00**

Movie contract, original Laurence

Olivier agreement for the movie "Rebecca," between Olivier & Selznick International Pictures, contains original black ink signatures of Daniel O'Shea & Laurence Olivier, 1939.................**1,035.00**

"Casablanca" Cafe Chair

Movie prop, chair used in Rick's Cafe in "Casablanca," Warner Bros., 1942, brown cane w/a square back above a red-painted wood seat on four slender & gently flaring legs, the back w/a cane weave design below a figure-8 braid across the top, a photograph of Humphrey Bogart & Ingrid Bergman with a similar chair included, 2 pcs. (ILLUS.) **4,830.00**

Movie prop, sword used in "Samson and Delilah," Paramount, 1949, used by George Saunders in the role of Lord King Sirhan of Gaze and The Five Cities, cold-painted & gilt metal hilt formed as Mycenaean snake goddess, the polished blade w/a central channel on each side, w/gilt-metal & chamois sheath, 31" l., 2 pcs. **2,530.00**

Movie prop, Winkie spear from "The Wizard of Oz," MGM, 1939, cast-metal painted silver head attached to a long reddish wood pole, 102" h..**8,050.00**

Movie slide, glass, from the movie "Manhattan," starring Richard Dix......**25.00**

Nightgown, black sheer material trimmed in red, worn by Marilyn Monroe, w/letter of authenticity, 2 pcs. **2,185.00**

Photograph of Judy Garland, black & white portrait of Judy Garland wearing a full-length velvet coat & leaning on a step ladder, by photographer Richard Avedon, 1951, matted & framed, 7 x 9" **5,750.00**

Photograph of Vivian Leigh, titled "Aurora," Surreal silverprint portrait of Leigh in classical garb floating in

Surreal Photo of Vivian Leigh

the clouds, by Agnus McBean,
mounted, signed in lower left in
pencil "Angus McBean London,"
12 x 16¾" (ILLUS.) **2,588.00**
Photograph of the Marx Brothers,
black & white group shot of Harpo,
Gummo, Zeppo & Groucho wearing
farmer outfits, when they owned a
farm, ca. 1916, framed, 8 x 10".......**403.00**

Signed Photo of Marilyn Monroe

Photograph of Marilyn Monroe,
black & white shot featuring Monroe
standing on a globe wearing a
negligee, signed in green ink "To
Gregory 'My Ardent Fan' Love &
Luck Marilyn Monroe," 8 x 10"
(ILLUS.) **1,725.00**
Pin, gold accessory pin initialed "GG,"
originally from a purse, in a swirling
script design, owned by Greta
Garbo, w/letter of authenticity &
photo of Garbo, 3 pcs. **460.00**
Pipe, silver w/a cut-out design
engraved on the bottom & engraved
"Gary Cooper".................................**690.00**
Preview folder, "Bright Eyes," Shirley
Temple, theater premium, 1934.........**40.00**

Puzzle, jigsaw-type, "Man's Favorite
Sport," starring Rock Hudson **15.00**
Ring, gold & diamond, 14k gold w/a
round diamond in the center,
initialed "EF" on the inside band,
owned by Errol Flynn, w/letter of
authenticity, 2 pcs. **2,300.00**
Scrapbook, filled w/newspaper
clippings & photos of Shirley
Temple, Saalfield Publishing Co.,
No. 1722, ca. 1936 ....**125.00**
Shoe horn, sterling silver engraved
w/ornate Art Deco design at the top
w/initials "CG" in the center, owned
by Clark Gable, w/letter of
authenticity, 5½" l., 2 pcs. **230.00**

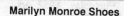

Marilyn Monroe Shoes

Shoes, worn by Marilyn Monroe,
Italian-made size 38½ black satin
pumps w/four inch heels, inside of
each marked "CREAZONI DAL
CO.," w/a letter of authenticity from
The Lee Strasberg Theatre Institute,
1950s, pr. (ILLUS.) **3,220.00**
Souvenir book, "The Eagle," 1926,
starring Rudolph Valentino, sixteen
pages of film photos.........................**115.00**
Souvenir book, "The Longest Day,"
giant cast including John Wayne,
1962..**50.00**
Souvenir book, "Solomon & Sheba,"
starring Gina Lollobrigida & Yul
Brynner, 1950s **25.00**
Telephone directory, cream leather
book-form, personal property of

Prince David Tumbler

Judy Garland & used in the 1950s, contains the names & addresses of many Hollywood notables, 6½ x 9" **5,750.00**

Tumbler, clear glass w/red decoration, Prince David from "Gulliver's Travels," animated feature from Paramount, 1939 (ILLUS. bottom previous page) **57.00**

Dorothy "Wizard of Oz" Tumbler

Tumbler, clear glass w/blue decoration, shows "Dorothy" from 'The Wizard of Oz,' released at the period of the movie, 1939 (ILLUS.) **110.00**

Window card, "Angels with Dirty Faces," starring James Cagney, Pat O'Brien, Humphrey Bogart & the Dead End Kids, sketch of the main characters against a background crowd scene, Warner Bros., 1938, 14 x 22" **3,163.00**

Window card, "Applause," starring Helen Morgan, drawing of the head of a bobbed-hair flapper w/silhouetted clapping hands in the background, black, orange & green lettering & green hands, reads "She gave youth and beauty for Applause - with Helen Morgan," Paramount, 1920s, 15" w., 18" h. (minor soiling, edge tear) **60.50**

Window card, "Doctor Terror's House of Horrors," starring Christopher Lee & Peter Cushing, 1965, 14 x 36"........**30.00**

Window card, "Flying Down to Rio," starring Dolores Del Rio w/Fred Astaire & Ginger Rogers, theatre name & dates across the top above a busy colorful design, top right corner missing, top left corner w/small cut, framed, 19 x 25½" (ILLUS. top next column) **825.00**

Window card, "Footlight Parade," starring James Cagney, Joan Blondell, Ruby Keeler & Dick

"Flying Down to Rio" Window Card

Powell, stylized dance scene w/two women in abbreviated costumes & two men in formal attire w/top hats & canes, Warner Bros., 1933, 14 x 22" **10,350.00**

Window card, "The Gold Rush," starring Charlie Chaplin, a colored lithograph of a dejected Chaplin sitting atop a pile of snow next to a sign reading "My Claim," theatre information & dates across the top, United Artists, 1925, 14 x 22" **6,325.00**

"It's A Wonderful Life" Window Card

Window card, "It's A Wonderful Life," starring James Stewart & Donna Reed, featuring a large portrait of the young couple, RKO, 1946, 14 x 22" (ILLUS.) **920.00**

Window card, "The Mask of Fu Manchu," starring Boris Karloff & Myrna Loy, bust portrait of Karloff above a sketch of a seductive woman w/a long cigarette holder above the title & cast names, MGM, 1932, 14 x 22" **4,025.00**

Window card, "The Private Life of

Charles Laughton Window Card

Henry VIII," starring Charles
Laughton, theatre name & dates
across the top, a head portrait of
Laughton near the top & a larger
photo of him & one of his wives
across the bottom, London Films,
1933, upper left corner missing,
14 x 22" (ILLUS.) **302.50**

(End of Movie Memorabilia Section)

MUCHA (Alphonse) ARTWORK

Biscuits Lefevre-Utile Poster

*A leader in the Art Nouveau movement,
Alphonse Maria Mucha was born in
Moravia (which was part of
Czechoslovakia) in 1860. Displaying
considerable artistic talent as a child, he
began formal studies locally, later
continuing his work in Munich and then
Paris, where it became necessary for him to*

*undertake commercial artwork. In 1894,
the renowed actress Sarah Bernhardt
commissioned Mucha to create a poster for
her play "Gismonda" and this opportunity
proved to be the turning point in his career.
While continuing his association with
Bernhardt, he began creating numerous
advertising posters, packaging designs,
book and magazine illustrations and
"panneaux decoratifs" (decorative pictures).*

Poster, "Biscuits Lefevre-Utile,"
lithographed in colors featuring a
seated portrait of a young blonde Art
Nouveau maiden holding a plate of
biscuits, signed in the plate, 1896,
framed, 17 x 23½" (ILLUS.) **$7,475.00**

Flirt Biscuits Poster

Poster, "Flirt - Biscuits Lefevre-Utile,"
lithographed in colors by F.
Champenois, Paris, a tall narrow
scene of a young couple flirting in a
flower-filled conservatory, ca. 1899,
slight foxing, 10 x 23" (ILLUS.) **2,875.00**
Poster, "Job," lithographed in colors
by F. Champenois, Paris, a bust
portrait of an Art Nouveau maiden
w/long curling hair smoking a
cigarette, rare pencil signature &
signed in the print, framed, ca. 1896,
18¼ x 26¼" (several small tears at
borders, restorations, minor
corner creasing, minor stains) **6,612.00**
Poster, "Lorenzaccio," lithograph in
color depicting a standing figure of
Sarah Bernhardt in the role of
Lorenzaccio, signed in the plate,
1896, framed, 30 x 80¼" **12,650.00**
Poster, "Theatre de la Renaissance -
Amants...," lithographed in colors by
Camis, Paris, a long rectangular
scene of elegant couples at a party,
laid down, 1895, framed, 44 x 57½"
(restorations, creases, tears, time
darkening, minor water stains) **9,487.00**

Print, "Evocation," lithographed in sepia by F. Champenois, Paris, portraying the figure of an elegantly draped Art Nouveau lady holding a basket of flowers, 1897, framed, 9⅛ x 42⅛" (trimmed margins, taped to mat) 2,300.00

Print, "Ivy," a bust profile of an Art Nouveau maiden w/ivy vines in her hair, within a round reserve framed by stylized leaves, signed in the plate, framed, 1901, 17" sq. 2,070.00

Print, "Tetes Byzantines (Brunette)," lithographed in color by F. Champenois, Paris, bust profile portrait of an Art Nouveau maiden w/long hair wearing an ornate coronet, trimmed to fit original round molded frame, France, 1897, 10⅝" d. (slightly time-darkened, minor foxing) 2,070.00

Print, "Zodiaque La Plume," lithographed in colors by F. Champenois, Paris, a large bust profile of an Art Nouveau crowned maiden before a large disc w/the signs of the zodiac, titled at the top & w/columns detailing the zodical signs across the bottom, loose sheet, laid down on canvas, 1896, framed, 18½ x 24¾" (margins trimmed, time-darkened, small tear at top center) 5,750.00

"Heather" & "Sea Holly" Prints

Prints, "Heather" & "Sea Holly," lithographed in colors by F. Champenois, Paris, each depicting a different young woman in French regional costume holding a flower, 1902, framed, margins trimmed slightly, each 11⅞ x 27", pr. (ILLUS.) 5,462.00

MUSICAL INSTRUMENTS

Fleta Acoustic Guitar

Accordian, "Hohner Diatonic," boxed $250.00

Acoustic/electric guitar, 1930s Vivi Tone model, sunburst finish, spruce top & recessed spruce back w/f holes, mahogany neck, twenty fret bound ebony fingerboard w/dot inlays, cream headstock featuring Vivi Tone logo, wooden bridge, metal tailpiece & tortoiseshell pickguard, w/internal pickup accessed by drawer in side of instrument, label w/"Vivi Tone Guitar No. 577 manufactured by Vivi Tone Company Kalamazoo, Michigan," w/hardshell case 3,450.00

Acoustic guitar, 1944 Ignacio Fleta archtop model, single cutaway mahogany body w/sycamore bindings, carved spruce top w/f holes & circular sound hole, 19 fret bound ebony fingerboard w/diamond inlays, wooden bridge & metal tailpiece, "sunburst" finish, label w/"Ignacio Fleta Barcelona 1944 no. 8," & name stamped in the wood inside, w/a hardshell contoured case (ILLUS.) 28,750.00

Acoustic guitar, 1951 Martin F-1 archtop model, "sunburst" finish, mahogany body, carved spruce top w/f holes, mahogany neck, twenty fret ebony fingerboard w/dot inlays, wooden bridge & metal tailpiece, serial No. 76735, once owned by Andy Summers, w/black hardshell case 1,380.00

Acoustic guitar, 1956 Gibson J-200 model, natural finish maple body, spruce top, maple neck, twenty fret bound rosewood fingerboard w/crested block inlays, Kluson tuners, moustache-shaped pin

bridge & floral pickguard, serial No.
A 22050, w/brown hardshell
case **5,750.00**

Early Martin Acoustic Guitar

Acoustic guitar, Martin 2-27,
rosewood body, spruce top
w/marquetry purfling, rosette w/
abalone ring, mahogany neck, 18
fret bound ebony fingerboard, tuner
w/ivory buttons, ebony pyramid
bridge, "C.F. Martin New York"
stamped in the wood, ca. 1860s,
w/hardshell coffin case, once owned
by Steve Howe (ILLUS.) **3,220.00**

Dulcimer, w/a grain-painted wooden
case, 19th c.,42½" l. **489.00**

Electric guitar, 1953 Gibson Les
Paul model, metallic gold finish,
single cutaway solid mahogany
body, maple top, mahogany neck,
twenty-two fret bound rosewood
fingerboard w/crown inlays, Kluson
tuners, two P90 pickups, four
controls, selector, trapeze bridge-
tailpiece & cream pickguard, serial
No. 3 1034, w/brown hardshell case,
w/photograph of vendor w/guitar in
the 1950s **5,520.00**

Electric guitar, 1954 Gibson ES-350
archtop model, white finish, single
cutaway body, arched top w/f holes,
twenty fret bound rosewood
fingerboard w/double parallelogram
inlays, Kluson tuners, two P90
pickups, four controls, selector,
Tune-O-Matic bridge, metal tailpiece
& black pickguard, w/factory order
No. X 7452 15, serial No. A17026,
w/brown hardshell case **5,520.00**

Electric guitar, 1955 Gretsch 6193
country club archtop model, natural
finish, single maple cutaway body,
maple top, maple neck, twenty-one
fret bound rosewood fingerboard
w/block inlays, Bowen tuners, two

DeArmond pickups, four controls,
selector, metal bridge, metal
tailpiece & tortoiseshell pickgaurd,
serial No. 14000, w/hardshell
case **3,220.00**

Harmonica, "The Bugle Call," made
in Germany, in box............................**28.00**

Harmonica, "Hohner - Choromonica,"
w/original box....................................**30.00**

Piano, baby grand, Steinway "Model
L," mahogany case w/old dark
brown heavily alligatored finish,
Serial #240459, made in 1926,
70" l..**7,150.00**

Steinway Grand Piano

Piano, grand, "Steinway & Sons,"
ebonized base on square tapering
legs w/spade feet on casters, early
20th c., together w/a round Victorian
style stool, 2 pcs. (ILLUS.) **7,150.00**

Early Aschenberg Upright Piano

Piano, upright, "Emil Aschenberg,"
satinwood case w/extensive
marquetry decorations, the central
panel above the keyboard inlaid in
various woods, mother-of-pearl,
brass & copper w/a scene of a
maiden playing an instrument on a

terrace w/a garden beyond, the flanking panels inlaid w/swags, the fallboard & the side panels inlaid w/musical trophies amid floral scrollwork, two gilt-metal candleholders, the seven octave keyboard, AAA to a^4, w/ivory naturals & ebony occidentals, two pedals controlling forte & piano stops, inscribed on interior of fallboard & w/the serial number W5710, ca. 1860, 64½" w., 4' 6" h. (ILLUS.)............................**7,475.00**

Piano, upright, "Erard," parcel-gilt satinwood case, the rectangular case fitted w/gilt-bronze leaftips, flowerheads & a pair of candlearms, carved w/foliage, columns & a lyre & incised decoration, the whole w/panels fitted to simulate grillwork, by Erard, cabinetry by L.W. Collman, France, 19th c., 61" l., 45" h............................**6,325.00**

Piano forte, "Alpheus Babcock," Classical (American Empire) style, inlaid mahogany, rectangular top w/rounded front corners, the front half opening (warped), fold-down front section over keyboard, the front w/rosewood inlaid panels & stamped brass band inlays & a brass plaque inscribed "made by A. Babcock for G.D. MacKay, Boston," three narrow drawers w/bail pulls across the base above the ring-turned & ribbed tapering legs on brass casters, by Alpheus Babcock, Boston, ca. 1820, w/an ebonized & gilt-wood round upholstered piano stool on four slender ring-turned legs joined by cross-stretchers & a center screw for raising the seat, piano 27 x 66", 35" h., 2 pcs. **4,140.00**

Piano forte, "Dubois and Stodart," inlaid mahogany & satinwood, the rectangular case w/hinged front opening to the keyboard, a plaque w/maker's name behind, on brass-mounted ring-turned & reeded tapering legs ending brass casters, Dubois and Stodart, New York, New York, ca. 1820, 27½ x 69½", 34" h..............................**1,150.00**

Piano forte, "Gibson & Davis," Classical style, inlaid & brass-inlaid mahogany, rectangular brass-inlaid case w/rounded corners, inlaid panels & crossbanded stringing, the front top opening at one end to an ebony & ivory keyboard w/inlaid panels, two backed by mirrors w/foliate tracery centering a string instrument & flanking a central tablet w/h.p. gilt floral garlands & an oval

w/inscription "Patent Grand - Gibson & Davis, New York," on double urn waterleaf-carved pedestals on downswept waterleaf-carved & reeded legs w/paw brass casters, joined by a brass-ended & turned & swelled reeded & waterleaf-carved medial rail centering a waterleaf-carved lyre w/mirrored back & brass string rods, base attributed to Duncan Phyfe, New York, ca. 1801-20, 30¼ x 71¼", 37¼" h. ...**16,100.00**

Loud Brothers Piano Forte

Piano forte, "Loud Brothers," Classical (American Empire) style, rosewood veneer & stenciled rectangular case w/outset round front corners, on baluster- and ring-turned acanthus leaf-carved legs on casters, golden anthemion scrolls & striping & stamped brass outline, gilded tablet above keyboard inscribed "Loud Brothers - Philadelphia," ca. 1825-37, minor surface imperfections, 70" l. (ILLUS.) **2,070.00**

Daniel Thomas Piano Forte

Piano forte, "Daniel Thomas," Classical (American Empire) style, carved mahogany & rosewood, rectangular inlaid lid w/rounded corners opening above a conforming rosewood case w/mahogany panels, delineated w/light wood string inlay over an arched skirt flanked by a single short drawer w/carved floral pulls, the lid opening to reveal an ivory & ebony keyboard decorated w/stencil & hand-painted designs & signature tablet inscribed "Daniel Thomas warrented: 87 New York," on waterleaf-carved & inlaid lyre w/brass rod strings & acorn-shaped pedal, 1815-25, 27⅛ x 68", 36¼" h. (ILLUS.) **3,680.00**

Saxophone (alto), "Buescer," (reconditioned) **550.00**

Saxophone (C-melody), "Buescher," silver plate..**200.00**

Steel guitar, 1938 Gibson EH 150 electric Hawaiian lap model, "sunburst" finish, maple body, twenty-nine fret rosewood fingerboard w/dot inlays, Charlie Christian pickup, two controls, metal tailpiece w/cover, serial No. DGE 4811, once owned by Steve Howe, w/hardshell case.........**863.00**

Tenor Guitar, 1940 Gibson model, "sunburst" finish, mahogany body, carved spruce top w/f holes, mahogany neck, nineteen fret bound rosewood fingerboard w/dot inlays, Charlie Christian pickup, two controls, wooden bridge, metal tailpiece & tortoiseshell pickguard, serial No. FGE 2335, w/case **1,150.00**

Trumpet, brass, "Bundy," w/original case **95.00**

MUSICAL INSTRUMENTS, MECHANICAL

Band organ, "Artizan," console cabinet, 61 key, w/15 rolls **$28,000.00**

Band organ, "Limonaire Freres," Paris, France, console cabinet, 49 keys **27,500.00**

Band organ, "Wurlitzer Model 103," ca. 1923 (restored) **13,500.00**

Barrel organ, hand-cranked, "James Davis" of Chelsea, London, rosewood Gothic-style cabinet w/exposed non-functional pipe in the upper portion of the cabinet, six barrels in the base, 1795-1815 .....**7,900.00**

Barrel organ, "Molinari & Sons," wooden cabinet, 26 keys **8,000.00**

Coin-operated piano, upright, "Capitol Piano and Organ Co.," oak case w/art glass, w/pipes, w/rolls...**8,000.00**

Coin-operated piano, upright, "Coinola C-2," oak case w/two rectangular art glass panels, piano keyboard w/rank of wooden flute pipes mounted in an inverted position under the keybed, mandolin, two octaves solo flute pipes, snare drum, bass drum & cymbol, plays solo O music rolls **26,000.00**

Coin-operated piano, upright, "Peerless Style D," art glass case, w/three "A" rolls (restored) **10,000.00**

Coin-operated piano, upright, "Seeburg Style A," w/xylophone & mandolin attachment, hardwood rectangular cabinet w/square columns down the sides, art glass panel, 5' 3" h. **9,000.00**

Coin-operated piano, upright, "Seeburg Style C," w/xylophone & mandolin attachment, Art Deco oak cabinet w/five art glass panels forming a scene of a swan on a lake, ca. 1925, 5' 6½" h..............**15,000.00**

Coin-operated piano, upright, "Seeburg Style E," w/xylophone attachment, quartered oak rectangular cabinet w/square columns down the sides, an art glass scene w/wooded landscape, 4' 9" h. **7,700.00**

Coin-operated piano, upright, "Seeburg Style G," oak cabinet w/four arched stained-glass panels, uses style "G" 65-note, ten-selection music rolls, 6' 7½" h. **65,000.00**

Coin-operated piano, upright, "Seeburg Style L," keyboardless, oak case w/leaded glass panels (restored) **10,500.00**

Coin-operated piano, upright, "Wurlitzer Style C," Grecian-style case, complete w/two sets of pipes (violin & flute), snare & bass drum, triangle, mandolin & wonder light, rebuilt stack (restored) **21,500.00**

Coin-operated piano, upright, "Wurlitzer Style I," cabinet w/art glass panel....................................**7,500.00**

Hammer dulcimer, wood, lyre-shaped, "The Bosstone Grand," w/music & original box, 13 x 20" **295.00**

Orchestrelle, "Mortier," 639 pipes & six percussion instruments, upright case decorated w/three animated figures, 14' w..........................**118,000.00**

Orchestrelle, "Wilcox & White," Meriden, Connecticut, oak cabinet **3,000.00**

Orchestrion, "Seeburg Style G," w/piano, flute pipes, snare drum, bass drum, timpani & cymbals, in golden oak case, the front w/four art glass panels, the outer panels w/projecting flaming torches, central arched panels w/upper roundels containing cottages & windmills in

landscapes, serial No. 162413,
w/three rolls, 6' 7½" h.................**65,000.00**
Orchestrion, "Seeburg Style K,"
w/piano, mandolin & flute, upright
oak cabinet w/art glass windows,
5' 2" h...**16,000.00**
Orchestrion, "Universal," piano,
mandolin & a 10-note section of
bells or xylophone bars, ca.
1920s **11,000.00**
Orchestrion, "Wurlitzer Style C,"
piano w/mandolin attachment, 38
violin pipes, 38 flute pipes, & bass
drum & snare drum, automatic roll
changer, Grecian-style case,
ca. 1921, 7' 4" h. **23,000.00**
Photoplayer, "American Photo Player
Company - Style 20," piano
w/several other instruments within a
large upright cabinet, photoplayer
operator could switch rolls to provide
the appropriate accompaniment &
background music (restored) **20,000.00**
Player organ, "Aeolian Solo
Orchestrelle Style V," mahogany
case, w/200 rolls (restored) **6,900.00**
Player organ, "Reproduco," pipe
organ & piano, upright cabinet
w/square columns down the sides,
plays "OS or "NOS" rolls
interchangeably **16,000.00**
Reproducing piano, grand, "Apollo
Ampico," decorated art case
w/twelve legs, 6' 2" l....................**20,000.00**
Reproducing piano, grand,
"Chickering Ampico A," w/rolls, 6' 5"
(restored) **16,000.00**
Reproducing piano, baby grand,
"Marshall & Wendell Ampico Model
B," small art case (restored) **8,500.00**
Reproducing piano, grand,
"Steinway Duo-Art XR," Italian
Renaissance walnut art case
w/matching bench, ca. 1928,
2 pcs. (restored)........................**25,000.00**
Street organ, 40 key-type, "Carl Frei,"
Waldkirch, Germany, ca 1900
(professionally restored) **18,000.00**

MUSIC BOXES

Automaton-type, singing bird box,
ormolu, rectangular case w/rounded
corners, scroll-pierced top & sides,
the lid centered by a large oval
panel decorated w/flowers, the sides
w/small oval panels w/flowers, on
pierced scroll feet, Europe, late
19th c., w/key, damages, 5¼ x 7⅛",
4⅞" h. (ILLUS. top next
column) **$6,325.00**

Automaton Music Box

Criterion Disc Music Box

Criterion disc music box, table
model, rectangular mahogany case
w/chamfered corners, the case
w/beaded top edging & a stepped
base w/beaded edging, the sides of
case w/floral reserves, original label
inside side, w/discs (ILLUS.).........**1,850.00**

Swiss Music Box on Stand

Langdorff & Fils (Swiss) cylinder
music box on stand, inlaid burl
walnut, rectangular case w/burl
walnut panels within inlaid banding,
a diamond reserve inlaid on the

front, gilt metal end handles, resting upon a rectangular stand w/molded edges over a serpentine apron w/burl panels raised on simple cabriole legs on casters & w/a heavy baluster-form central leg, single comb, separate handle winder, w/seven interchangeable 18¾" l. cylinders playing six tunes each, late 19th c., 28 x 44½", 39" h. (ILLUS.) **5,775.00**

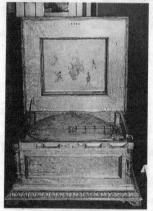

Regina Disc Music Box

Regina disc music box, table model, rectangular oak case w/a band of small rectangular blocks along the top of the base over rectangular raised panel reserves flanked by ring-turned corner pilasters, the stepped flaring base w/an acanthus leaf-carved band & small scroll feet, refinished case, plays 16" d. discs, w/a disc (ILLUS.) **4,000.00**

Swiss cylinder music box, table model, rectangular rosewood case inlaid on the top w/trophies & flowers & on the front w/a guitar & florals, six-tune, single comb, late 19th c., cylinder 18⅛" l., case 27" l..**862.50**

Swiss Cylinder Music Box

Swiss cylinder music box, table model, rectangular rosewood case

w/inlaid hunting trophies on the lid & front & line-inlaid panels, six-bells & two drums, late 19th c. (ILLUS.) **4,400.00**

NAPKIN RINGS

Napkin rings were popular dining table adjuncts in the late 19th and early 20th century. The most valuable today are the figural silver plate examples produced in abundance between 1880 and 1900. All rings listed here are silver plate unless otherwise noted.

Boy fairy w/ butterfly wings, Wilcox, No. 2206 ....**$220.00**
Cat w/amber glass eyes, Babcock Silver Co. **270.00**
Chick & wishbone, Derby Silver Co. **120.00**
Chick & wishbone, inscribed "Best Wishes" (some wear) **75.00**
Cow standing by engraved ring, round base **140.00**
Egyptian busts flanking ring & extending into hoofed legs, bud vase tops ring, 6" h. **125.00**
Barrel-shaped, engraved "Father".......**13.00**
Lion, resting on base, ring on back....**155.00**
Owl perched on leafy branch **135.00**
Turtle, ring supported on the back, three-tiered rectangular base, Derby **235.00**
Wishbone on filigree-edged triangle w/four ball & claw feet, engraved florals & "Best Wishes," Meridan **75.00**

NAUTICAL ITEMS

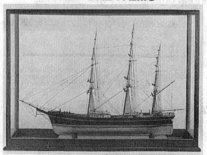

Model of the "Flying Cloud"

The romantic lure of the sea, and of ships in general, has opened up a new area of collector interest. Nautical gear, especially items made of brass or with brass trim, is sought out for its decorative appeal. Virtually all items that can be associated with older ships, along with items used or made by sailors, are now considered collectible for technological advances have rendered them obsolete. Listed below are but a few of the numerous nautical items sold in recent months.

Binnacle cover, brass, John Bliss Co., New York, 19th c., 20¾" d., 12½" h.................................**$247.50**

Booklet, "SS United States," contains facts & pictures of ship's interior, 1952.....................................**30.00**

Chest, seaman's, pine w/hand-forged fittings, name inside, 19th c., small **135.00**

Map, Coast Guard Geodetic coastal navigation, Stratford Shoal to New York, 1902, large **35.00**

Marine chronometer, eight-day, unusual two-tier fusee & chain movement in the style of Westwood w/later spring detent escapement & bi-metallic compensation balance, free sprung blued steel helical hairspring, latched silvered matte dial, Roman numeral subsidiary seconds & sector for up & down scale, weighted brass case w/winding shutter inscribed "windup to the left hand once a week," gimballed in mahogany case, signed by Arnold, London, England, No. 436, ca. 1825 (movement w/alterations) **4,888.00**

Model of a whale boat, painted wood, complete w/sails & equipment, 20th c., boxed, 18¼" l.....................................**201.00**

Octant, cased ebony & brass, marked "Hemsly Tower Hill London," case labeled "...R.L. Shaw...Beekman N.Y.," 19th c., 11¾" l.....................**440.00**

Octant, signed "Heath Erith Kent," case cover inlaid w/an ivory ship's anchor, case labeled "W.F. Chisholm, Gloucester, Mass.," 19th c. **690.00**

Sextant, brass, cased, signed "Owen Owens Liverpool," England, 19th c., 9" l.....................................**522.50**

Sextant, signed "Spencer, Browning & Rust, London," case labeled "David Baker...New Bedford," 19th c. (repaired split in case).......**1,035.00**

Ship diorama, carved & painted pine, carved in relief w/a three-masted sailing vessel at full-sail on the open seas, flying an American flag & another flag inscribed "Nawadana," a smaller vessel sailing towards it, in a shadow box frame, America,

19th c., 5" deep, 35" l., 21¾" h.....................................**4,600.00**

Ship half-model, carved & painted wood, model of the British clipper ship "Cutty Sark," shown fully rigged under sail, in a shadowbox frame, England, 19th c., frame 3³⁄₁₆ x 20⅝", 11⅝" h. (some paint flaking) **460.00**

Ship half-model, carved & painted wood, the three-masted British ship "Mary Ann" depicted under full sail, mounted in a shadowbox frame, 19th c., 40" w., 22⅛" h. **1,540.00**

Ship half-model, carved & painted wood, model of the schooner "The Mayflower" of Gloucester, Massachusettes, shown under full sail against a painted seascape, in a shadowbox frame, 20th c., 5¼ x 34¼", 24½" h........................**862.50**

Ship model, carved & painted wood, the three-masted sailing ship "Flying Cloud" of Boston, labeled "by E.F. Tanner," fully-rigged, in a glass-sided case, 20th c., 14½ x 91", 29⅝" h.(ILLUS.) **3,190.00**

Shipwright's caulking mallet & steel caulking wedge, 2 pcs. **82.50**

Telescope, single-draw, brass, cased, retailed by Pinkham R. Smith Co., Boston, Massachusetts, 19th c., 26" h.................................**357.50**

NUTTING (Wallace) COLLECTIBLES

In 1898, Wallace Nutting published his first hand-tinted pictures and these were popular for more that 20 years. An "assembly line" subsequently colored and placed a signature and (sometimes) a title on the mat of these copyrighted photographs. Interior scenes featuring Early American furniture are considered the most collectible of these photographs.

Nutting's photographically illustrated travel books and early editions of his antiques reference books are also highly collectible.

BOOKS

"Connecticut Beautiful," second edition, brown cover, signed **$50.00**

"England Beautiful," second edition **50.00**

"Maine Beautiful," second edition w/dust jacket **45.00**

"Massachusetts Beautiful," second edition...................................**28.00**

"New Hampshire Beautiful," first
edition **50.00**
"New York Beautiful," second
edition w/dust jacket **55.00**
"Pennsylvania Beautiful," second
edition **35.00**
"Vermont Beautiful," second edtion
w/dust jacket (some tears in dust
jacket) **40.00**
"Virginia Beautiful," second
edition **40.00**
"Wallace Nutting's Biography,"
1936, first edition, w/dust jacket.......**110.00**

PRINTS
Apple Row, 10 x 12", exterior
scene **115.00**
Birch Paradise (A), 13 x 16", exterior
scene **135.00**
Callers at the Squire's, 14 x 17",
exterior scene **200.00**
Coming Out of Rose (The), 18 x 22",
exterior scene **275.00**
Dykeside Blossoms, 11 x 14",
foreign exterior scene, blue canal &
country lane merge as they run
towards a Dutch village, five very
tiny people in roadway **165.00**
Eventful Journey (An), 14 x 17",
exterior scene **600.00**
Fair Autumn, 13 x 16", exterior
scene **145.00**
Golden Twilights, 11 x 17", exterior
scene **145.00**
Honeymoon Blossoms, 11 x 14",
exterior scene **75.00**
Informal Call (An), 11 x 14", interior
scene **275.00**
Into the Birchwood, 17 x 20",
exterior scene **125.00**
Little River (A), 20 x 30", exterior
scene **275.00**
Maple Sugar Cupboard (The),
13 x 16", interior scene **190.00**
Morning Duties, 14 x 17", interior
scene **325.00**
Oak Curves, 10 x 12", exterior
scene **135.00**
Plymouth Curves, 13 x 22", exterior
scene **150.00**
Scotland Beautiful, 10 x 13", foreign
exterior scene **175.00**
Spring Colors, 10 x 16", exterior
scene **135.00**
Stitch in Time (A), 18 x 22", interior
scene **325.00**
Street Border (A), 12 x 16", exterior
scene **225.00**
Vermont Road (A), 13 x 22", exterior
scene **150.00**
Vermont Spring (A), 10 x 12",
exterior scene **125.00**
Woodland Cathedral (A), 11 x 14",
exterior scene **125.00**

MISCELLANEOUS ITEMS
Miniature, Natural Bridge (The),
4 x 5", exterior scene **60.00**
Miniature, 4 x 5", exterior scene,
large stone bridge crosses blue river
near blossom tree **60.00**
Silhouette, 4 x 4", girl snips potted
plants while standing by table............**40.00**
Silhouette, 4 x 4", girl w/feather quill
in hand writes letter at slant front
desk **40.00**
Silhouette, 4 x 4", girl near bonsai
tree looks at a hanging birdcage........**40.00**

OCCUPIED JAPAN

*American troops occupied the country of
Japan from September 2, 1945, until April
28, 1952, following World War II. All
wares made for export during this period
were required to be marked "Made in
Occupied Japan," Now these items, mostly
small ceramic and metal trifles of varying
quality, are sought out to be a growing
number of collectors.*

Ashtray, metal, model of a baseball
catcher's mitt, 3" w. **$85.00**
Bowl, china, latticed rim, pink floral
decoration, 6¾" d. **20.00**
Cigarette lighter & tray, metal,
2 pcs. **25.00**
Cup & saucer, child's, china, Blue
Willow patt., cup 2¼" d., saucer
3½" d. **18.00**
Figure of a boy w/his dog, china,
2¾" h. **12.00**
Figure of a girl w/flowers, china,
2¾" h. **12.00**
Figure of a Colonial man, china,
4" h. **8.00**
Figure of a man smoking a pipe,
china, 4¼" h. **15.00**
Jam jar, cover & spoon, china, figural
black Mammy, 3 pcs. **175.00**
Model of a bird, china, 2" h. **10.00**
Models of a cartoon-style pig girl &
duck girl, china, 4" h., pr. **45.00**
Opera glasses, metal & plastic...........**45.00**
Plate, china, scenic decoration of
trees & a brook, 8" d. **22.00**

OFFICE EQUIPMENT

*By the late 19th century business offices
around the country were becoming
increasingly mechanized as inventions*

such as the typewriter, adding machine, mimeograph and dictaphone became more widely available. Miracles of efficiency when introduced, in today's computerized offices these machines would be cumbersome and archaic. Although difficult to display and store, many of these relics are becoming increasingly collectible today.

Adding machine, "Remington Rand," hand-operated, serial No. 73-651433 ....**$100.00**
Adding machine, "Wolverine," No. 39, w/original box **80.00**

Early Edison Dictating Machine

Dictating machine, "Ediphone," rectangular metal case w/cylindrical recording mechanism & flexible metal tube w/speaker cup, ca. 1900, 7½ x 13", 10½" h. (ILLUS.) **467.50**
Handstamp, "Bates," numbering stamp, 1906 ....**25.00**
Stapler, "Acme," heavy duty, ca. 1890s **68.00**
Stenotype, "Master Model Four"........**166.00**

PAPER COLLECTIBLES

Also see BLACK AMERICANA, CHARACTER COLLECTIBLES, FIRE FIGHTING COLLECTIBLES, FRATER- NAL ORDER ITEMS, MAGAZINES, MUCHA ARTWORK, PAPER DOLLS, POLITICAL ITEMS, POP CULTURE COLLECTIBLES, RADIOS, RADIO & TELEVISION MEMORABILIA, ROY- CROFT ITEMS, SIGNS & SIGN- BOARDS, SPACE AGE COLLECTIBLES, STEAMSHIP COLLECTIBLES, TOBAC- CIANA, WESTERN CHARACTER COL- LECTIBLES, and WORLD'S FAIR COL- LECTIBLES.

Bond certificate, "Logan Rapid Transit," Utah, 1913, unissued.......**$105.00**
Book, "Empire State Building," 1931, pictorial record of construction, illustrated by Vernon Howe Bailey, published by Edwin Rudge, limited edition, 12½ x 17½" **325.00**
Broadside, hand-printed, titled "A Dialogue Between a Reverend Clergyman and Daniel Wilson, a young Man, aged Tweny-five Years, who was tried at Providence, in the Colony of Rhode-Island, in March Term, for a Rape, found guilty, condemned and executed on the Twenty-ninth of April, 1774. Published as a solemn Caution and Warning to Youth. Boston: Printed and Sold by E. Russell, 1774," 11⅝ x 18⅛" **8,625.00**
Calligraphic drawing, pen & ink on paper, Spencerian-style bird, pen & flourishes in red & black ink, signed "By K.L. McLean," in modern grained frame, 12" w., 9½" h...........**242.00**

Early Calligraphic Specimen

Calligraphic specimen & advertisement, water-color & pen & ink on paper, a large center circle w/smaller circles in each corner, the center circle titled "The Writing Masters Invitation & Instruction...," signed, inscribed & dated "Betsy Drake., Epping, Nov. 4 1791," 12¾ x 15¾" (ILLUS.) **1,610.00**
Criminal complaint, from a Montana mining camp, charging a man w/sexual assault & describing the incident, 1890 ....**227.00**
Cutwork pictorial, a cutwork inscription across the top reading "The American Republican - Victory in New York Nov the 5th - 1844," above a spread-winged eagle

Dated Cutwork Pictorial

clutching crossed red, white & blue painted American flags over a coiled hissing snake set in an oak leaf-cut ground w/four corner rosettes, all above the inscribed cut name "Elias Striker," 13¾ x 17½" (ILLUS.) **3,680.00**

Land grant, printed & handwritten on parchment, signed by John Floyd, Governor of the Commonwealth of Virginia, 1830, framed, 14 x 18" (fold lines) **110.00**

Land grant, Presidential-type, from Oklahoma to "Skunk Running - A Cheyenne & Arapahoe Indian," 1910..**92.00**

Legal document, signed by noted New Mexican Albert J. Fountain who was Billy the Kid's defense lawyer during his trial **550.00**

Letter, Civil War era, soldier's description of chasing Confederate General John Morgan's raiders through Ohio & Tennessee, 1863....**175.00**

Letter, Military Surgeon stationed at Fort Cameron, Utah Territory, he writes "Surrounded by mountains, Mormons, mines and sagebrush - my family is small for a resident of Utah as I have but one wife and two little girls," 1881................................**100.00**

Letter, soldier's, from Fort Stanton, New Mexico, w/Indian-related content, 1885 ....**270.00**

Military Sharpshooter's certificate, signed by Major-General Adna Chaffee, noted Indian fighter, a bull's-eye was scored **125.00**

New Mexico Territory check, signed by James J. Dolan, one of the leaders of the Lincoln County War **675.00**

Newspaper, "The Pennsylvania Packet & Daily Advertiser," 1785, includes advertising for fire engines by Mason & Gibbs & illustrations of pumpers, 4pp.....................................**55.00**

Playbill, "The Entertainer," starring

Laurence Olivier, New York, New York, 1958 ....**30.00**

Slave document, estate appraisal of William Kennedy of Tattnal County, Georgia, sixty-six entries w/twelve named slaves valued between $200 to $700, 1848, 1pp., 8 x 12"....**105.00**

Souvenir program, "13th Annual Convention of International Brotherhood of Magicians," Cincinnati, Ohio, 1938, w/original paper wrap, 32pp., 6 x 9"..................**12.00**

Stagecoach way bill, mentions a Chinese passenger, from Oregon, 1891...**135.00**

Stock certificate, "Hughes River Oil Co.," West Virginia, 1864................**125.00**

Stock certificate, "Red Hill Hydraulic Mining & Water Co.," California, 1877...**125.00**

Stock certificate, "Selby Hill Mining Co.," California, 1878, uncancelled....................................**125.00**

Stock certificate, "Winnemucca Chief Silver Mining Co.," Nevada, 1872...**180.00**

Will of Ebenezer Devotion, written in his own hand, listing seven family portraits by Winthrop Chandler, dated November 2, 1827, framed, 8 x 8¼"...**690.00**

Will, Last of Will & Testament of Narcissa Bell of Hall County, Georgia, twelve bequests w/five slaves by name, sex & owners (three allowed a bed & usual furniture), brown paper w/large brown ink writing, 1861, 3pp., 8 x 12½"..**75.00**

PAPER DOLLS

Ballet Dancers, uncut book, Merrill, No. 3447, 1947 ....**$50.00**

Judy Garland, uncut book, by Tom Tierney, modern, 32pp......................**24.00**

Hedy Lamarr, uncut book, Saalfield, No. 2600, 1951 ....**185.00**

"Precious Paper Dolls," uncut, Musser, signed by author, 1985 ....**30.00**

"Sweet Abigail," Raphael Tuck, w/original folder & additional clothes, dated 1894......................................**95.00**

PAPERWEIGHTS

Advertising, cast iron, "Thomas Drills," model of a rooster on an oval

base lettered w/company name, old
gold painted finish, 3¼" h..............**$137.50**

Baccarat "Closepack Millefiori"
weight, tightly arranged & colorful
complex canes including Gridel
silhouette, whorls, arrows,
honeycomb & stars, dated "B1848,"
3" d. (small cullet inclusion) **1,980.00**

Baccarat "Pansy" weight, a white
star-centered purple & yellow
blossom w/a green leafy stem, star-
cut base, 2½" d. **431.00**

Baccarat "Scattered Millefiori"
weight, nine colorful silhouette
canes including lovebirds, a rooster,
dog, swan & hunter w/other complex
millefiori canes, over an upset
muslin ground dated "B1848," 3" d.
(few tiny bubbles, tiny piece of cullet
in glass) **1,870.00**

Baccarat "Snake on Rock" Weight

Baccarat "Snake on Rock Ground"
weight, clear set w/a coiled green
snake w/mottled red spots & black
eyes edged in white, set on a beige,
silver & green crackled rock ground,
19th c., repolished, small cracks to
rock ground, 3⅛" d. (ILLUS.) **6,900.00**

Bacchus "Concentric Millefiori"
mushroom weight, clear set w/three
rows of pastry mold & cogwheel
canes in pastel shades of red, blue
& white about a shaded red
composite pastry mold cane center
within a basket of elongated white
pastry mold canes lined in green
w/red & white cogwheel cane
centers encompassed by a white
corkscrew cable surrounded by a
cobalt blue & white spiral thread,
19th c., 3⅞" d. (minor chips,
repolished) **6,325.00**

Clichy "Chequer" weight, 19 brightly
colored canes including two pink &
green Clichy roses w/stars, whorls &
pastry mold canes, on a white

muslin ground, 3¼" d. (some tiny
bubbles, tiny piece of cullet) **2,750.00**

Clichy "Closepack Millefiori"
weight, colorful selection of complex
canes including a white & green, an
all-white & a pink & green Clichy
rose w/florets, whorls, stars, arrows
& pastry mold canes w/a white &
light blue signature "C" cane, all
within a cobalt blue & white stave
basket ground, 2⅝" d. (few
surface scratches) **357.50**

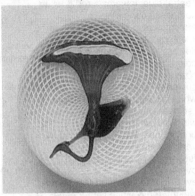

Clichy "Morning Glory" Weight

Clichy "Morning Glory" weight,
clear set w/a blue flower formed w/a
ribbed shaded trumpet-form
blossom lined in white, growing from
a curved green stem w/a large
green leaf, set on a white latticinio
ground, 19th c., bad bruise to side,
scratches, repolished, 2⅞" d.
(ILLUS.) **14,950.00**

Clichy "Pansy" weight, clear set w/a
flower formed w/two shaded upper
purple petals & three lower ecru
petals w/purple & white stripes &
purple markings about a green
stamen, growing from a curved
green stem w/a cluster of five green
leaves at the base & a purple bud
growing from a shorter green stem,
set on a white latticinio ground,
19th c., 2⅞" d. (repolished,
bruises, chips).............................**3,105.00**

Kaziun (Charles) "Pedestal Rose"
weight, fourteen pink petals on four
green leaves, "K" signature cane,
2¼" d., 3" h. **660.00**

New England "Cross" weight, clear
set w/two rows of overlapping
shaded lavender petals forming a
Latin cross intersected by composite
cogwheel canes in shades of cobalt
blue & white about a red cogwheel
cane center above a green stem, set
on a white latticinio ground, 19th c.,

3⁵⁄₁₆" d. (repolished, minor chips & scratches) **4,025.00**

New England "Crown" weight, light green & white center cane w/white latticinio twists alternating w/yellow & blue & red & white twisted ribbons, 2⅜" d. (small center bubble & scattered tiny bubbles, flat dome)..**660.00**

New England "Faceted Double-Overlay Upright Bouquet" weight, clear set w/an arrangement of a central blue flower w/a red & white composite cane stamen encompassed by a similarly formed & colored flower, a red & a white flower divided by two similarly colored millefiori canes & one in shades of yellow & green joined by six green leaves, set on an opaque white ground, overlaid w/a layer of red over white, cut w/a decorative window, leaf designs & various size printies near the base, divided by vertical ribs, 19th c., 2¹¹⁄₁₆" d. (severe chips & losses to overlay) **5,750.00**

New England "Spaced Concentric" weight, red & white center cane surrounded by four rings of canes in white, orange & blue containing a total of 29 tiny running rabbit canes, over a clear ground, 2¾" d. (some light surface scratches) **385.00**

Pantin "Rose" weight, dark pink shading to white folded petals surrounding a yellow stamen center on five light green leaves & stem w/one pink bud, on an opaque white ground, 3" d. (few minute bubbles, bit of ash on ground) **3,575.00**

St. Louis "Double Clematis" Weight

St. Louis "Double Clematis" weight, clear set w/a flower composed of two rows of overlapping ribbed white pointed petals about an orange & red stamen, growing from a curved

green stem w/four leaves about the flowers, set on a red & white jasper ground, 19th c., 3" d. (ILLUS.) **2,070.00**

St. Louis "Faceted Nosegay" weight, three blossoms on a green leafy stem above an amber ground, the clear side w/five wide facets, the top w/a circle of punties around a central punty, smooth base, 3⅛" d...**517.50**

St. Louis "Miniature Garlanded Sulphide Portrait" weight, clear set w/a small sulphide profile portrait of Queen Victoria facing dexter, the truncation signed "Victoria" in blue script, encompassed by a garland of alternating blue & amber composite cogwheel canes lined w/florets, set on an amber-flash ground, 19th c., 1⅝" d. (minor chip & scratches) **862.00**

St. Louis "Molded Gilded Lizard" weight, the naturalistically formed green & white jasper gilded lizard coiled above a green & white jasper ground weight base, 19th c., 3⁷⁄₁₆" d. (wear to gilding, small crack to center of lizard) **12,650.00**

St. Louis "Pear" weight, green-centered pink & yellow pears w/green leaves arranged on a white latticinio ground, 2⅛" d., 2⅛" d...**1,092.50**

Sandwich "Blue Rose" weight, red-centered white rose surrounded by cobalt blue petals & green leaves & stem, 3⅛" d., 2" h. (small chip at base edge) **489.00**

Sandwich "Poinsettia" weight, flower w/ten light blue petals surrounding a blue & white center cane w/two green leaves & straight stem, on a clear ground, 3" d. (one bubble, minute speck of cullet) **522.50**

Stankard (Paul) "St. Anthony's Fire Bouquet" weight, three flowers w/buds, green leaves & stems over an opaque light blue ground, signed w/"S" cane & scratch-dated "1978," 2⅞" d...**935.00**

PAPIER-MACHÉ

Various objects including decorative adjuncts were made of papier-maché, which is a substance made of pulped paper mixed with glue and other materials, or layers of paper glued and pressed and then molded.

Candy container, figure of a standing policeman, painted black eyes, molded & painted mustache & molded & painted tall police hat, one-piece body w/molded & painted uniform, early 20th c., 12" h. **$125.00**

Uncle Sam & Rabbit Candy Container

Candy container, figural Uncle Sam riding a large rabbit, the nodding-head Uncle Sam wearing a blue & white star design cloth jacket & red & white striped pants, astride a large shaded brown rabbit, early 20th c. (ILLUS.) **8,250.00**

Candy containers, figurals of Snow White & the Seven Dwarfs, 1930s, 8 pcs. **495.00**

Regency Tray on Stand

Tray on stand, rectangular w/rounded corners, decorated w/scrolling stencil border bands, set in a later stand w/slender bamboo-turned legs & stretchers, Regency period, England, first quarter 19th c., restored, 22½ x 30½", 18¼" h. (ILLUS.) **4,888.00**

Tray on stand, oval, gilt diaper

border, on a later Regency style mahogany base, late 19th c., 23 x 30½", 19½" h., 2 pcs. **834.00**

Papier-maché Wig Stand

Wig stand, figural, in the form of a bust of an elegantly dressed gentleman wearing white tie, late 19th - early 20th c., probably French, 17½" h. (ILLUS.) **3,105.00**

PARRISH (Maxfield) ARTWORK

During the 1920s and 1930s, Maxfield Parrish (1870-1966) was considered the most popular artist-illustrator in the United States. His illustrations graced the covers of the most noted magazines of the day - Scribner's, Century, Life, Harper's, Ladies' Home Journal and others. High quality art prints, copies of his original paintings usually in a range of sizes, graced the walls of homes and offices across the country. Today all Maxfield Parrish artwork, including magazine covers, advertisements and calendar art, is considered collectible but it is the fine art prints that command the most attention.

Advertisement, magazine, 'Review of Reviews,' 1922, "JELL-O," 6½ x 9½" **$30.00**

Blotter, for Edison-Mazda lamps w/artwork by Maxfield Parrish............**35.00**

Book, "The Arabian Nights," nine color illustrations by Maxfield Parrish, 1942, Scribners **110.00**

Book, "The Golden Treasury of Songs & Lyrics," illustrated by Maxfield Parrish, 1911, first edition..**185.00**

Book, "Knave of Hearts," by Louise Saunders, illustrated by Maxfield Parrish, spiral bound **750.00**

Book, "Poems of Childhood," by Eugene Field, eight color

illustrations by Maxfield Parrish,
1955, published by Scribners **175.00**
Book, "Wonder-Book and
Tanglewood Tales (A)," by Nathaniel
Hawthorne, illustrated by Maxfield
Parrish, 1928 ....**150.00**
Calendar, 1925, for Edison-Mazda,
entitled "Dreamlight," small,
complete **950.00**
Calendar, 1927, for Edison-Mazda,
entitled "Reveries," large, framed,
complete **575.00**
Calendar, 1928, for Edison-Mazda,
entitled "Contentment," large,
framed, complete.............**700.00 to 800.00**
Calendar, 1938, for Albany Creamery
Association, Albany, Oregon,
entitled "Only God Can Make A
Tree" **175.00**
Calendar print, 1923, for Edison-
Mazda, entitled "Lampseller of
Baghdad," large...............**750.00 to 800.00**
Calendar print, 1928, for Edison-
Mazda, entitled "Contentment,"
large ....**675.00 to 700.00**
Calendar print, 1922, for Edison-
Mazda, entitled "Egypt," small,
cropped...**500.00**
Calendar print, 1926, for Business
Man's Calendar, entitled "Cadmus
Sowing The Dragon's Teeth" **200.00**
Calendar print, 1929, for Edison-
Mazda, entitled "Golden Hours,"
small, framed **300.00**
Greeting card, "The Twilight Hour,"
w/original envelope, for Brown &
Bigelow Publishing Company **25.00**
Magazine, Ladies' Home Journal,
1916, Maxfield Parrish color
advertisement for Djer-Kiss
Cosmetics (cover as is) **48.00**
Magazine cover, Saturday Evening
Post, 1904, November 5 ....**12.50**
Playing cards, for Edison-Mazda,
"Waterfall," 1931, full deck **275.00**
Print, "Air Castles," for Ladies' Home
Journal, 1904, 12 x 16",
framed ....**250.00 to 275.00**
Print, "The Chimera (Bellerophon),"
P.F. Collier & Son, from "A Wonder-
Book and Tanglewood Tales," 1909,
9¼ x 11½" ....**125.00 to 150.00**
Print, "Daybreak," House of Art -
Reinthal Newman, 1923, large,
18 x 30"..**325.00**
Print, "Evening," House of Art -
Reinthal Newman, 1922, large,
12 x 15" ....**250.00 to 275.00**
Print, "Garden of Allah," House of Art
- Reinthal Newman, 1918, medium,
original frame, 9 x 18"......**150.00 to 165.00**
Print, "Hilltop," House of Art - Reinthal
Newman, 1927, medium,
framed, 12 x 20" ....**300.00 to 350.00**

Print, "Morning," House of Art -
Reinthal Newman, 1926, large,
framed, 12 x 15" ....**175.00 to 200.00**
Print, "The Page," House of Art -
Reinthal Newman, 1928, framed,
10 x 12" ....**125.00 to 175.00**
Print, "Pierrot's Serenade," P.F.
Collier & Son, from "The Golden
Treasury of Songs and Lyrics,"
1908, 9½ x 11¼" ....**125.00 to 150.00**
Print, "The Prince," House of Art -
Reinthal Newman, 1928, framed,
10 x 12"..**150.00**
Print, "With Trumpet and Drum," from
"Poems of Childhood," Charles
Scribner's Sons, 1905, 5 x 7"............**50.00**
Print, "Wynken, Blynken & Nod," from
'Poems of Childhood,' Charles
Scribner's Sons, 1905, framed,
10¼ x 14½" ....**350.00 to 400.00**

PERFUME, SCENT, & COLOGNE BOTTLES

Cobalt Blue Cologne Bottle

*Decorative accessories from milady's
boudoir have always been highly collectible
and in recent years there has been an
especially strong surge of interest in
perfume bottles, Our listings also include
related containers such as pocket bottles
and vials, tabletop containers & atomizers.
Most readily available are examples from
the 19th through the mid-20th century, but
earlier examples do surface occasionally.
The myriad varieties have now been
documented in several recent reference
books which should further popularize this
collecting specialty.*

BOTTLES & FLASKS
Blue cut crystal glass w/frosted
stopper (ground rod), depicting a

curious goose watching a posturing nude w/scarf, Czechoslovakia **$235.00**

Canary yellow glass, square shape, mold-blown in Buttons & Panels patt., original cruciform stopper, attributed to New England Glass Co., 6" h. to top of stopper **375.00**

Citron glass, pedestal base, decorated w/three large applied snake-like fish, aquatic plants & coral, original stopper, 9" h. **275.00**

Clear glass, "Mitsouko," by Guerlain, Baccarat bottle, 4" h..........................**95.00**

Clear glass w/frosted top, "Aimee," by Richard Hudnut, label w/mother & child, ca. 1902, 5" h. **85.00**

Cobalt blue blown glass, paneled ovoid body tapering to cylindrical neck w/two neck rings & ball stopper, all on a pontilled base, ca. 1850, 6½" h. (ILLUS.) **230.00**

Monumental Cobalt Blue Bottle

Cobalt blue glass, pyramid-shaped body w/brick-like surface, short cylindrical neck w/tooled lip & smooth base, ca. 1870, 8" h. (ILLUS.) **550.00**

Ruby Cut Cologne Bottle

Lalique glass, "Deux Fleurs," 4" h.......**95.00**

Lalique glass, "Faroucha," by Ricci, heart-shaped....................................**137.00**

Lalique glass, "Dans La Nuit," by Worth, blue.................................**145.00**

Opalescent turquoise blue, tapering twelve-sided body w/rolled lip & smooth base, American, ca. 1870-80, 5½" h..**357.50**

Ruby cut glass, paneled ovoid body w/gold trim, matching ruby cut stopper, 3½" d., 6¾" h. (ILLUS. bottom previous column) **138.00**

Sterling silver, two-handled ovoid body, applied w/stylized flowers & leaves suspended from a clip w/chain, Tiffany & Company, New York, New York, late 19th c., 4 " l. ...**747.00**

PEZ DISPENSERS

PEZ, an abbreviation for the German word pfefferminz, *meaning peppermint, was 'discovered' by Eduard Haas as he experimented with peppermint oil in 1927. Haas developed a small brick-shaped candy and marketed it towards adults as an alternative to smoking. Although PEZ became quite fashionable, production ceased with the onset of World War II. The first PEZ dispensers were not produced until its re-introduction in 1949. The first PEZ dispensers were not like the cartoon head dispensers produced today, but resembled cigarette lighters and are known today as 'headless regulars.' Unfortunately, PEZ did not regain its popularity following World War II and quickly failed.*

In 1952, Haas introduced a new and improved PEZ to America. He altered the shape of the dispenser, changed the formula of the candy and marketed his new product towards children. PEZ's popularity soared. Over the years, more than 200 PEZ dispensers have been produced. A sampling is listed below.

CHRISTMAS

Angel...**$15.00**

Angel w/halo **25.00**

Rudolph the Red Nosed Reindeer **25.00**

Santa, one-piece head, no feet...........**90.00**

Santa, small head, no feet...**80.00 to 125.00**

Santa, white face..................................**50.00**

Santa, black face, white hat, white stick..**500.00**

Santa, black face, red hat, red stick...**300.00**

Snowman, without feet...........**5.00 to 10.00**

CIRCUS

Clown with Collar

Big top elephant
w/flat hat ....**50.00 to 100.00**
Big top elephant w/hair.....................**120.00**
Big top elephant w/pointed hat...........**30.00**
Clown w/chin..**35.00**
Clown w/collar (ILLUS.) **45.00**
Gorilla **30.00**
Li'l Lion **35.00**
Mama Giraffe ....**50.00 to 75.00**
Mimic Monkey **30.00**

Monkey Sailor

Monkey Sailor (ILLUS.) **30.00**

CRAZY FRUIT
Orange.................................**75.00 to 125.00**
Pear (ILLUS. top next column) **690.00**
Pineapple (ILLUS.
next column) ....**750.00 to 900.00**

DISNEY
Baloo...**15.00**
Baloo, dark pink w/copyright...............**250.00**
Bambi..**25.00**
Bouncer Beagle, 1992 ....**6.00**
Goofy, removable teeth ....**10.00 to 20.00**

Pear PEZ Dispenser

Pineapple PEZ Dispenser

Goofy, removable teeth & nose **50.00**
Goofy, white face.................**50.00 to 100.00**
Gyro Gearloose, 1992...........................**6.00**
Jiminy Cricket.....................................**60.00**
King Louie, brown face **15.00**
King Louie, green head
w/copyright.....................................**250.00**
Li'l Bad Wolf..**15.00**
Mary Poppins....................**500.00 to 600.00**
Mickey Mouse, white or pink painted
face...................................**100.00 to 150.00**
Mickey Mouse, removable nose..........**15.00**
Mowgli **15.00**
Peter Pan **125.00**
Pluto, tan or flesh colored
head ....**10.00 to 15.00**
Scrooge McDuck, Donald Duck head
w/feathers, hat & glasses...................**15.00**
Snow White.........................**50.00 to 100.00**
Thumper w/copyright.........................**600.00**
Tinkerbell...**125.00**
Winnie the Pooh **20.00**
Zorro w/logo.......................................**125.00**

EASTER

Bunny, original ....200.00 to 300.00
Bunny w/flat ears....................5.00 to 10.00
Bunny, pink, 1994............................125.00
Bunny, purple, 1994 ....250.00
Duckie ....35.00 to 40.00
Lamb, yellow......................................20.00
Rooster..30.00

FULL BODY

Full Body Yellow Space Trooper

Santa Claus......................................100.00
Space Trooper, yellow
   (ILLUS.) ....175.00 to 200.00

HALLOWEEN

Blob octopus ....25.00 to 40.00
Fishface............................125.00 to 150.00
Mr. Ugly ....10.00 to 20.00
One-Eyed Monster ....30.00 to 50.00
One-Eyed Monster, pink face 125.00
Witch, regular....................................500.00

HUMANS

Pilot PEZ Dispenser

Cowboy..400.00
Football player...................................75.00

Pilot (ILLUS.) 75.00
Spaceman 125.00
Stewardess..75.00

BI-CENTENNIAL

Bicentennial PEZ dispensers

Betsy Ross (ILLUS. center left)...........75.00
Captain 75.00
Daniel Boone....................................150.00
Indian Brave......................................150.00
Indian Chief (ILLUS. right) ....25.00 to 50.00
Indian Squaw 55.00
Pilgrim (ILLUS. center right) 80.00
Uncle Sam (ILLUS. left) 75.00
Wounded Soldier................................75.00

LICENSED CHARACTERS

MOVIE MONSTERS

Movie Monsters

Creature from the Black Lagoon
   (ILLUS. center) 175.00
Frankenstein (ILLUS. left) 155.00
Wolfman (ILLUS. right) 175.00

PEANUTS (1990)
Charlie Brown w/eyes
   closed ....30.00 to 50.00
Charlie Brown w/frown..........................6.00
Charlie Brown w/tongue.....................10.00
Lucy w/white eyes ....10.00 to 15.00

Lucy w/white facial markings 30.00
Woodstock w/feathers..........................10.00

SMURFS
Papa Smurf, 1989.................................6.00
Smurf, white hat, 1986..........................6.00
Smurf, red hat, 1986 ....10.00
Smurfette, 1989..................................8.00

SUPERHEROES
Batman...................................1.00 to 10.00
Batman, black cape 400.00
Batman, black cowl, mask & stick........15.00
Batman, blue cape..............................110.00
Batman, soft.......................................75.00
Captain America, blue mask...............30.00
Green Hornet ....175.00 to 340.00
Hulk, dark green.................................15.00
Thor..100.00
Wonder Woman, red hair 125.00
Wonder Woman, soft 75.00

WARNER BROTHERS
Bugs Bunny ....1.00 to 10.00
Cool Cat, hot pink 330.00
Cool Cat, orange..................................25.00
Foghorn Leghorn..................................25.00
Henry Hawk..25.00
Merlin Mouse..6.00
Petunia Pig...15.00
Speedy Gonzales..................................6.00
Sylvester the Cat...................1.00 to 10.00
Will E. Coyote......................................25.00

MISCELLANEOUS

Little Orphan Annie PEZ Dispenser

Asterix 600.00
Bozo the Clown ....75.00 to 125.00
Bullwinkle, yellow stick.....................175.00
Bullwinkle, brown stick......................200.00
Casper the Friendly Ghost...............100.00
Muselix 1,800.00
Obelix...600.00
Little Orphan Annie (ILLUS.)..............50.00
Peter PEZ (ILLUS. top next
    column)...75.00
Peter PEZ, 1993...................................2.00

Peter PEZ

MERRY MUSICAL MAKERS
(Whistle Heads)
Camel...25.00
Frog...25.00
Indian..6.00
Koala...15.00
Monkey 15.00
Pig 25.00

PEZ PALS

Various PEZ Pals

Bride (ILLUS. second from right) 500.00
Doctor (ILLUS. left)............................55.00
Engineer 40.00
Fireman..30.00
Groom (ILLUS. center) 150.00
Knight (ILLUS. right) ....75.00 to 125.00
Nurse (ILLUS. second from left) 55.00

PREMIUMS
Donkey Kong Jr...............................125.00
Golden Glow (ILLUS. top next
    page)..125.00
Stand by Me w/package 150.00

MISCELLANEOUS
Baseball glove ....200.00 to 250.00
Baseball glove w/bat & base
    (ILLUS. next page) ....300.00 to 400.00

Golden Glow PEZ Dispenser

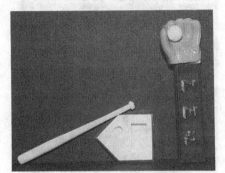

Baseball bat with Glove

Candy shooter gun, blue & white
grip **400.00**
Candy shooter gun, black & brown
gun ....**70.00 to 125.00**
Candy shooter gun, orange w/white
grip **60.00**
Candy shooter gun, red w/white
grip **60.00**

Psychedelic Eye PEZ Dispenser

Psychedelic Eye (ILLUS.) **500.00**
Psychedelic Flower **500.00**

Regular PEZ Dispenser

Regular, many color variations
(ILLUS.) **125.00**
Regular w/advertising **350.00**
Space Gun, 1950s.............**125.00 to 300.00**

1980s Space Gun

Space gun, 1980s (ILLUS.) **75.00**

(End of PEZ Section)

PHONOGRAPHS

Columbia Type B Cylinder
Graphophone, "Eagle," w/original
aluminum horn, Serial No.
150,716..**$360.00**
Edison Amberola Model 30, table
model, oak case..............................**422.50**
Edison Home Cylinder model
w/red morning glory horn **500.00**
Edison Opera, table model, walnut
case w/metal bail end handles,
wooden horn, ca. 1912 (ILLUS.
top next page) **3,500.00**

Edison Opera Table Model

Polly portable phonograph, fold-out
paper horn **375.00**

PHOTOGRAPHIC ITEMS

Expo Watch Camera

Camera, Ansco No. 1 Readyset
Royal, 1926 (minor wear outside) **$65.00**

Camera, Kodak No. 1A Gift, chrome
case w/a geometric design
enameled in chocolate brown & red,
w/manufacturer's label & original
wooden box w/conforming
enameled metal design on the lid,
designed by Walter Dorwin Teague,
ca. 1930, 9" w., 4½" h. **1,093.00**

Camera, Eastman Kodak Brownie
No. 3A, folding-type, ca. 1909-13 ......**37.50**

Camera, Konica C-35, automatic,
w/Vivitar flash, w/original box &
instructions...**45.00**

Camera, Rolleiflex, 4 x 4, 3.5 lens,
w/original box & papers, 1931 ....**350.00**

Camera, novelty type, Expo watch
camera, outside case of camera
engraved w/"EXPO," box marked
w/"EXPO - Watch Camera -
Guaranteed to take Perfect Pictures"
(ILLUS.) **467.50**

Carte de visite, General Thomas **25.00**

Carte de visite, outdoor view of a
courthouse w/dozens of Union
soldiers on roof, in belltower & lined
along the street, also what appears
to be a line of Confederate
prisoners, by Th. Gubelman,
Pulaski, Tennessee **165.00**

Carte de visite, John Sutter, pictures
Sutter on river bank w/shovel
w/hand-written ink legend, "The
Exact Spot Where the Gold Was
Found," cream mount, original mat &
frame, photo, 4 x 7¼",
mount 7 x 9"................................**1,200.00**

Daguerreotype of a Locomotive

Daguerreotype, locomotive, sixth
plate, America, mid-19th c., crack
to case (ILLUS.) **1,265.00**

Daguerreotype, sixth-plate image of
Tom Thumb & his parents, flesh
tones lightly tinted & jewelry touched
w/gold, sealed in an embossed
leather case, the lining of the case
w/stenciled name "Mary Byington,"
only known image of Tom Thumb
w/both his parents & only known
photo of his mother, ca. 1848 .....**12,650.00**

George Washington Daguerreotype Case

Daguerreotype case, brown
thermoplastic, square, each side

embossed w/a round medallion framing a bust profile of George Washington w/the inscription "First in Peace…," a small star at each corner within a delicate chain border band, no photo, mid-19th c., 3⅜ x 3¾" (ILLUS.) **330.00**

Wash. Monument Daguerreotype Case

Daguerreotype case, black thermoplastic, front molded w/a scene of the Washington Monument in Richmond, Virginia w/eagles in bottom corners, spandrels & angels w/trumpets in top corners, back molded w/same border design but inside oval w/scroll design, glass plate photo of bearded gentleman standing beside chair, 5 x 6¼" (ILLUS.) **632.50**

Columbus Daguerreotype Case

Daguerreotype case, black thermoplastic, w/intricate scene of the landing of Columbus, tintype of Niagara Falls, wear & chips, 7¼ x 9¼" (ILLUS.) **2,475.00**
Locket, gutta percha, contains a 1" tintype of a young man **65.00**
Tintype, cased, soldier or cadet seated wearing white cross belts & epaulettes, a Shako helmet on the table beside him, in a thermoplastic

case w/a leaf design, 2¾ x 3¼" (edge chips) **247.50**

PIE BIRDS

A pie bird is a small, hollow device with a stem that allows steam to escape from a double-crust pie. Usually in the form of a bird with an open beak, they can be found in china, pottery or metal. Various figural examples are listed below.

China, bird, pink, green & yellow **$60.00**
China, Blackbird, blue & black **30.00**
China, black chef holding rabbit by ears **63.00**
China, chicken, yellow **60.00**
China, duck, yellow **60.00**
China, elephant w/shamrock.............**100.00**
China, elephant, white ....**50.00 to 100.00**
China, frog, sitting up, brown w/open mouth & beady eyes, England...........**51.00**
China, hen carrying basket of eggs **57.00**
China, pelican on stump, England **53.00**
Stoneware, blue & white.....................**55.00**

PINCUSHION DOLLS

Graceful China Half Figure

These china half figures were never intended for use as dolls, but rather to serve as ornamental tops to their functional pincushion bases which were discreetly covered with silk and lace skirts. They were produced in a wide variety of forms and quality, all of which are now deemed collectible, and were especially popular during the first quarter of this century.

Our listings are arranged numerically, when possible, according to the code numbers assigned in The Collector's Encyclopedia of Half-Dolls *by Freida Marion and Norma Werner.*

China half figure of a lady w/grey hair dressed in an ornate style w/curls & single loop rising at top, wearing a low-cut bodice w/elbow-length sleeves, holding a closed fan in one hand, incised "21633" (MW517-361) **$110.00**

China half figure of a lady, ornate grey coiffure w/rows of curls on top & curls cascading to her shoulders, arms away from her body, both hands raised to her breast, impressed "14753," 3" d., 4¾" h., MW 730-225 (ILLUS.) **135.00**

China Harlequin Lady

China half figure of a Harlequin lady wearing an orange hat & white bodice w/blue trimmed ruffle, holding a yellow mask, 3½" h., 2" d. (ILLUS.) **125.00**

China Half Figure with Green Purse

China half figure of a lady wearing an orange hat w/green bow tie, orange off-the-shoulder bodice w/white ruffle, holding a green purse, 2¼" d. 3⅝" h. (ILLUS.) **150.00**

China half figure lady wearing a wide-brimmed white hat w/green band & an orange bodice w/green

China Half Figure with Wide Hat

shawl-like collar, 2⅜" d., 3⅞" h. (ILLUS.) **150.00**

Dutch Half Figure Lady

China half figure of a Dutch lady wearing white Dutch hat w/pink band & green flowers, a green bodice w/a pink wide collar holding a brown basket full of yellow fruit, 2½" d., 4" h. (ILLUS.) **150.00**

Two China Half Figures

China half figure lady, powdered-white wig, heavy make-up around the eyes, arms away from her body

holding pink flower, 2½" d., 5" h.
(ILLUS. left).....................................**265.00**
**China half figure of a Spanish
dancer,** one hand at her waist, the
other raised above her head,
wearing a comb in her hair, a red
flower at the base of her neck, a
black dress w/a green & pink shawl,
2" d., 5" h. (ILLUS. right).................**165.00**

Three Half Figure Whiskbrooms

China half figure of a "flapper"
whiskbroom, her head tilted back
wearing a white hat w/green trim
w/heavily made-up eyes, white
loose collar over a pink & green
dress, 2" d. overall, 8¼" h.
(ILLUS. center) **88.00**
China half figure whiskbroom, chin-
length blonde hair, wearing a pink
bodice w/wide white collar holding a
pink flower, 2" d. overall, 8" h.
(ILLUS. left).......................................**75.00**
China half figure whiskbroom, light
brown chin-length hair wearing a
pink dress, her hands resting on her
hip, 2¼" d. overall, 8" h.
(ILLUS. right) **75.00**

PIN-UP ART

*For most of the past century advertisers
have used sensuous depictions of young
ladies to help sell their products. Modern
"pin-up" art really came of age about the
1920s and soon artists such as Alberto
Vargas, George Petty, Rolf Armstrong and
others were churning out provocative
portraits of young beauties to grace
calendars, magazines covers and other
advertising art. In more recent years male
"beefcake" has also been used to sell
products, but it is the earlier female
portraiture which is most sought-after by
collectors today.*

Calendar, 1940, Alberto Vargas
illustration, 12 pp., 10 x 14"
(mint)..**$80.00**
Calendar, desk-type, 1946, Vargas,
complete **50.00**

Warren Beauty & Barber Supply Calendar

Calendar, 1947, advertising, "Warren
Beauty & Barber Supply," w/portrait
of "Judy," signed "J. Erbit," January
page missing & minor soiling,
10 x 17" (ILLUS.) **32.50**

1948 MacPherson Calendar

Calendar, 1948, MacPherson
artwork, various pictures of pin-up
girls, very minor soiling, 9½ x 12½"
(ILLUS.) **38.50**
Calendar, 1951, Al Moore artwork,
for "Esquire," w/envelope..................**15.00**
Calendar, 1962, "Playboy Playmate
Calendar," w/Tina Louise, w/jacket....**52.50**
Calendar, 1966, wall-type, "Playboy,"
w/jacket...**69.00**
Calendar, 1968, "Playboy" **25.00**
Calendar top, 1930s, by Rolf
Armstrong, 12 x 18" **150.00**

Magazine, "Playboy," 1954,
September **125.00**
Photo book, flip-type, 1940s strip
tease photos **25.00**
Puzzle, jigsaw-type, pictures Marilyn
Monroe...**25.00**
Sheet music from Zeigfeld Follies,
illustrated by Alberto Vargas in his
early years, 1931 ....**65.00**

POLITICAL, CAMPAIGN & PRESIDENTIAL ITEMS

Also see BOOKS, PRESIDENTIAL & HISTORICAL FIGURES

CAMPAIGN

Book, "Nixon Yearbook," 1968,
contains Nixon's life story &
hundreds of full color photos,
100 pp. **$15.00**
Badge, 1856 campaign, John C.
Fremont, first Republican
presidential candidate, 3 x 7½"........**150.00**
Ballot, 1884 campaign, New
Hampshire presidential, Cleveland &
Hendricks...**22.00**
Doll, 1964 campaign, Barry
Goldwater, in original box **58.00**
Guest ticket, June 14, 1916, Wilson,
(Woodrow), Marshall, (Thomas R.),
for the closing session of the
Democratic National Convention,
St. Louis...**45.00**
Hat, straw, Panama-style, 1960
campaign, Nixon-Lodge on hat band
ribbon **50.00**
Letter, 1968 campaign, typed by
Gerald Ford on House of
Representatives stationery, content
concerning Republican National
Convention, signed "Jerry"...............**100.00**
Stereoview card, 1908 campaign,
Bryan (William Jennings) & Kern
(John), portrait of Bryan & his wife,
by Keystone View Company..............**45.00**
Token, 1856 campaign, portrait of
John C. Fremont w/Free Soil
slogans, Eagle half dollar size **30.00**
Watch fob, 1904 campaign, Alton
Parker & John Davis **37.50**
Watch fob w/strap, 1920 campaign,
James Cox...**125.00**

NON-CAMPAIGN

Air mail sheet, a block of 50 10¢
United States Air Mail stamps,
autographed by Franklin D.
Roosevelt & Harold Le Claire Ickes,
Secretary of the Interior, w/photo

United States Air Mail Stamps

inserts of FDR & Ickes, gilt frame,
ca. 1940, Ickes signature faded &
tear over "Franklin" & "D.," some
paint loss, 19 x 23¼" d.
(ILLUS.) **467.50**
Book, "PT 109," by John F. Kennedy,
first edition, paperback w/photos,
1962...**20.00**
Clock, figural Franklin D. Roosevelt,
full-figure, nautical theme, ca.
1940s **225.00**
Dance card, book & attached pencil,
Theodore Roosevelt inaugural ball ..**135.00**
Game, "Who Can Beat Nixon," 1970....**55.00**
Lithograph, mourning, portrait of
Abraham Lincoln above draped
shield, 15 x 20" **45.00**
Newspaper, *Chicago Tribune,*
"Dewey Defeats Truman,"
November 3, 1948, complete...........**600.00**
Pass, U.S. Senator gallery guest for
1929 session......................................**40.00**
Photograph, albumen print of
Ulysses S. Grant in uniform, signed
by the photographer Frederick
Gutekunst, mounted & w/studio
label, taken ca. 1860s, printed ca.
1880, framed, 15½ x 17½"...........**3,163.00**

Abraham Lincoln Photograph

Photograph, mammoth platinum print of Abraham Lincoln, enlarged & printed by George B. Ayres from the negative by Alexander Hesler, the printer Ayre's copyright blindstamp twice in the image, mounted, inscribed, signed & dated by Ayres in ink on the reverse "Copyright, 1897. Enlarged from the original negative, owned by Geo. B. Ayres, Artist, Philadelphia," a portrait of the beardless Lincoln taken in 1860, printed in 1897, in old oak frame, 20½ x 26" (ILLUS. bottom previous page) **18,400.00**

Picture card, Theodore Roosevelt & family, 1906 ....**15.00**

Plate, blue on white spongeware pottery, flanged & scalloped border, the center molded in relief w/a bust of James Garfield w/an ivy border, back marked "Burford Bros. E.L.O.," East Liverpool, Ohio, 10½" d. (small flakes, short internal hairline) **385.00**

Teddy Roosevelt Plate

Plate, Staffordshire china, commemorative, center portrait of Theodore Roosevelt w/"Theodore Roosevelt - 26th President of the U.S." written in script below, surrounded by smaller portraits of the White House, the Capitol, Theodore Roosevelt Jr., Roosevelt's farewell, Roosevelt's home & Roosevelt as a Rough Rider, very minor crazing, 10" d. (ILLUS.)..........**110.00**

Plate, china, transfer-printed oval picture of William McKinley surrounded by eagles & flags **50.00**

Print, "Washington Family," hand-colored lithograph, by Kellogg & Comstock, mid-19th c., in old gilt shadowbox frame, 13½ x 17½" (stains on print) **71.50**

Ribbon, pale green silk, printed in black w/an oval portrait of George Washington & titled "Centennial Anniversary - of the birthday of - WASHINGTON - 1832 - Tiller and Winship," 2 1/16 x 8¼" (some creasing) **66.00**

Snuff box, cov., papier-maché, the cover w/a copy of the Trumbull portrait of Washington in full dress uniform, titled "Washington," 3⅜" d..**3,850.00**

Watch fob w/strap, 1917, inauguration commemorative, Governor James Cox......................**280.00**

Wrist watch, Spiro Agnew.................**75.00**

POP CULTURE COLLECTIBLES

The collecting of pop culture memorabilia is not a new phenomenon; fans have been collecting music-related items since the emergence of rock and roll in the 1950s. But it was not until the 'coming of age' of the post-war generation that the collecting of popular culture memorabilia became a recognized movement

The most sought after items are from the 1960s, when music, art and society were at their most experimental. This time period is dominated by artists such as The Beatles, The Rolling Stones and Bob Dylan, to name a few. From the 1950s, Elvis Presley is the most popular.

Below we offer a cross section of popular culture collectibles ranging from the 1950s to the present day. Also see RECORDS and RECORD JACKETS, LUNCH BOXES and CHARACTER COLLECTIBLES

Alice Cooper lyrics, handwritten for the song "Trash," three verses in black ink w/corrections in blue ball point pen, two additional verses in blue ball point pen, written on yellow legal size paper, composed in studio, ca. 1989 ....**$299.00**

B-52's (The) stage pants, red cotton blend, worn by band member Fred Schneider, size 32, signed in silver felt pen, "Cindy Wilson - Hey Shake A Leg, Fred S III - Hey! Oh Save The Forest Yes! Love Kate".............**575.00**

Beach Boys (The) acoustic guitar, spruce top, twenty fret rosewood fingerboard w/dot inlays, pin bridge & black pickguard, signatures include Carl Wilson & Mike Love, Hohner MW 400N (ILLUS. top next page)......................................**978.00**

Beach Boys Acoustic Guitar

Beach Boys (The) photograph,
black & white Capital Records
promotional, signed "Al Jardine -
Carl Wilson - Love Mike Love" in
bright red marker, "Bruce Johnston"
in blue Sharpie & "Brian Wilson" in
black marker, 8 x 10" **184.00**

Bill Graham Series concert poster,
featuring The Doors, Chuck Berry,
Big Brother & the Holding Co. &
Winterland, marked "Six Days of
Sound - Dec. 26-New Year's Eve
1967," design by Bonnie MacLean
(slight rounding at corners) **121.00**

Blue Meanie Animation Cel

Beatles animation cels, from *Yellow
Submarine,* gouache on celluloid,
group of eight, including two large
images of the Blue Meanie, one of
the Blue Meanie's henchmen &
Glove, one a large image of George
& John, one of the Blue Meanie
w/one of his henchmen, the
remaining three of various
characters, seven w/certificates of
authenticity, King Features Studio,
1968, the set (ILLUS. of one)........**2,587.00**

Beatles bank, date register, 1964 ....**25.00**

Beatles banks, plastic, Yellow
Submarine set w/colorful bust
figures of each Beatle, 1960s,
7½" h., set of 4 (repainted chip on
John's jacket, stickers missing
from bottoms)................................**1,400.00**

Beatles Banner

Beatles banner, printed nylon,
depicts all four Beatles in black
w/large heading "The Beatles" in
blue print, Memphis, 1966
(ILLUS.) **1,150.00**

Beatles billfold, red w/four
signatures in white on one side &
their picture on the other, mint
condition **90.00**

Beatles cake decorating kit, figurals
of each one playing their
instrument, set of 4, mint in box.......**195.00**

Beatles Christmas tree ornaments,
delicate blown-glass figures of the
Beatles, three in red, one in blue,
w/three plastic guitars, ca. 1960s,
7" h. (minor rubs) **925.00**

Beatles Nodder Dolls

Beatles dolls, nodding-type, each
figure dressed in light blue suit
standing on gold base w/signatures
printed on them, Ringo Starr on
drum, Paul McCartney w/bass
guitar, John Lennon w/guitar,

George Harrison w/guitar, Japan,
ca. 1964, 8" h., the set (ILLUS.).......**368.00**
Beatles game, paddle ball **100.00**
Beatles magazine cover story,
"Saturday Evening Post," August 27.
1966, cover pictures the Beatles in
matador costume, six page spread
includes full page photos w/British
Empire medals **35.00**
Beatles magazine cover & story,
"Sixteen," 1966, August **15.00**
Beatles magazine cover & story,
"Teen World," 1965, July **15.00**
Beatles mug, ceramic, close-up bust
photos of the group wearing blue
jackets, England, ca. 1964, 3" d.,
4" h..**85.00**
Beatles notebook, three-ring binder,
red vinyl cover, by Standard Plastic
Products...**132.50**

Rare 'Sgt. Pepper's' Cover Photo

Beatles photograph, from the
legendary "Sgt. Pepper's Lonely
Hearts Club Band" cover shot,
shows the Beatles in different poses
& includes the image of 'Bowery
Boy' Leo Gorcey, who was later
removed, small crease in lower right
corner, 20" sq. (ILLUS.) **402.50**
Beatles pins, guitar-shaped, 1964,
set of 4, mint on card **65.00**
Beatles puzzle, Yellow Submarine,
mint **55.00**
Beatles phonograph record
w/picture sleeve, "Got To Get You
Into My Life," 45 rpm **10.00**
Beatles rings, flasher-type, 1960s,
set of 4 ....**23.50**
Beatles scrapbook, NEMS, 1964,
covers in mint condition, some
writing inside **50.00**
Beatles sheet music, "Day Tripper,"
1964 ....**20.00**
Beatles signatures, a piece of paper
signed in ink & pencil by each
member of the Beatles & addition-

The Beatles Signatures

ally inscribed "XXX Beatles," in
McCartney's hand, 4 x 4½"
(ILLUS.) **1,265.00**
Beatles sweatshirt, white, NEMS,
1963 ....**150.00**
Beatles tour program, features the
Beatles pictured in playing cards,
tour also included Mary Wells, 1964
British tour (folded w/some surface
abrasions) **230.00**
Beatles window card, "Hard Days
Night," rare version of band
performing...**150.00**
Billy Joel beige stage jacket, linen
w/satin lining & matching brown-on-
beige buttons, worn by Joel on
"Nylon Curtain" tour, inscribed on
left lapel in black felt pen "Nylon
Curtain Tour 1982," on right lapel, in
same ink, "Billy Joel," ca. 1982,
mounted in a shadowbox w/plaque,
40¼ x 45¼"....................................**1,495.00**
Black Crowes (The) electric guitar,
Fender Stratocaster, white finish,
double cutaway body, maple neck,
twenty-one fret rosewood
fingerboard w/dot inlays, three pickups, three controls, selector, tremolo
bridge - tailblock & white pickboard,
signed on body by Rich Robinson,
Chris Robinson, Jeff Cease, Steve
Gorman & Johnny Colt **1,495.00**
Boy George doll, by LJN, 1984, mint
in box **100.00**
Bruce Springsteen vest, black wool,
signed "To Brian - Bruce
Springsteen - The River Tour" in
silver felt tip pen, worn by
Springsteen during the 1981 "The
River" tour in England, mounted in
shadowbox w/plaque, 27½ x 39"
(ILLUS. top next page)..................**1,840.00**
Buddy Holly postcard, handwritten
in pencil & addressed to his parents,
discusses his shows & a phone call

Bruce Springsteen Vest

from his parents, signed "Love
Buddy," matted & framed w/a photo
of Holly & The Crickets, postmarked
"May 10, 1956," overall
10½ x 18".....................................**1,735.00**

Concert Poster Featuring Janis Joplin

Concert poster, "Hells Angels Party,"
featuring Big Brother, Gold, Main
Squeeze & Janis Joplin, May 21
1970, design by Don Moses (toned,
various bends, corners w/holes,
reinforced w/masking tape on
reverse)..**345.00**
David Bowie stage suit, forest green
cotton - linen double-breasted suit
jacket w/goldtone emblem buttons &
matching pleated style trousers,
jacket pocket w/ "KANSAI
JOURNEY" emblem patch, jacket
lining signed in black felt pen, "David
Bowie '91," w/letter of authenticity
from Isolar Productions, 3 pcs. **1,725.00**
Doors (The) drumhead, h.p. over
pencil outline in black paint on the
upper left hand side "THE" in small

The Doors Drumhead

type above "doors" in large type,
marked on the rim "Professional
Drum Shop, Inc.," this drumskin was
specially made for the Doors'
appearance on WNET-TV in New
York City in 1971, jagged crack
appears above & through lettering,
21" d. (ILLUS.) **13,800.00**
Ella Fitzgerald autograph, signed
"Best Wishes - Ella Fitzgerald" in
blue ball point ink on small piece of
bluish paper, affixed to black & white
photograph (various tears &
soiling) **244.00**
Elvis Presley AM radio, figural,
depicts the 'old' Elvis in suit, holding
a microphone, stands atop a plastic
base which serves as an AM radio,
marked "ELVIS PRESLEY" on front,
made in Hong Kong, ca. 1977,
base 1¼ x 3 x 5", figure 8" h. **37.00**
Elvis Presley army hat, khaki Army
dress hat worn by Presley in
Germany, manufactured in 1956 &
issued to him in 1958, size 7¼,
stamped "CO254." w/a photo of
Elvis wearing the hat, 2pcs. **8,050.00**
Elvis Presley button, flasher-type,
"Love Me Tender" changes to a
performing pose, 1956, 2½" d...........**24.00**
Elvis Presley calendar, 1963,
premium from "RCA," unused............**75.00**
Elvis Presley charm bracelet, charm
reads "Loving You," 1956, mint on
card **80.00**
Elvis Presley color photograph,
white plastic frame embossed
w/guitars, musical note & "Love Me
Tender" in raised gold, issued by
Elvis Presley Enterprises, 1956 ....**250.00**
Elvis Presley credit card, Elvis'
original American Express card,
dated 6/73 through 5/74..............**41,400.00**
Elvis Presley dog tag anklet, on
original card, dated 1956.....**25.00 to 50.00**
Elvis Presley handkerchief, black

silk, worn by Presley in the 1962-63 movie "It Happened at the World's Fair," together w/a photo of Presley w/the handkerchief in his breast pocket & a letter of authenticity, the group.......................................**575.00**

Elvis Presley movie poster in original stand-up sidewalk movie marquee, "Easy Come, Easy Go".......**80.00**

Elvis Presley newspaper, "Memphis Press," dated "August 17, 1977" (the day of his death), mint condition **30.00**

Elvis Presley perfume bottle, "Teddy Bear," 1957, mint in original box...**158.00**

Elvis Presley photograph, black & white still from movie "Jailhouse Rock," boldly signed in blue ball point pen, matted, 8 x 10" **920.00**

Elvis RCA Promo Photo

Elvis Presley photograph, RCA Victor color promotional photo collage, boldly signed in blue ball point pen, ca. mid-1960s, matted, few small creases, 10½ x 12½" (ILLUS.) **1,322.00**

Elvis Presley program menu, Sahara Tahoe, 1970s, large (mint) **45.00**

Elvis Presley sheet music, "Love Me Tender" **35.00**

Fleetwood Mac, presentation "gold" disc, for song "Tusk," R.I.A.A. certified, strip plate format, plaque inscribed "Presented to FLEETWOOD MAC," disc signed, "Best wishes & love Stevie Nicks," framed, 16¾ x 20¾".........................**518.00**

Grateful Dead concert poster, "Skull in Sand," poster for the 1981 European Fall tour w/venues listed at bottom, design by Stanley Mouse 22½ x 27"...**80.50**

Grateful Dead poster, featuring the "Skeleton & Roses" design from the cover of the 1971 LP "Grateful Dead," signed "Jerry Garcia" in gold ink, 21¾ x 33" **184.00**

James Brown Leather Vest

James Brown stage vest, black leather w/gold round buttons, lined in white felt, on the front left side of the vest in cut white leather are the initials "JB," on the front right side in white leather letters "MR D" (ILLUS.) **1,840.00**

Jerry Garcia Electric Guitar

Jerry Garcia electric guitar, 1959 Fender Stratocaster, sunburst finish, double cutaway body, maple neck, rosewood fingerboards w/dot inlays, three pickups, three controls, selector, non-tremolo metal bridge - tailpiece & white pickguard, serial No. 44987, letter of authenticity from Jerry Garcia & a photo of him w/guitar, a sales tag & original receipt (ILLUS.).........................**17,825.00**

Jimi Hendrix meal receipt, signed & inscribed on back in pencil, "Love to you Jimi Hendrix," 3½" x 5¾"..........**920.00**

Jimi Hendrix stage pants, purple crushed velvet, vents on both lower leg seams sewn closed w/five matching fabric-covered buttons, inside waistband two small pockets of purple & tangerine fabric, w/signed letters of authenticity from

road manager Eugene McFadden &
band member Noel Redding.........**7,475.00**

Jim Morrison drawing, pencil on
paper, head of a man, wide-eyed
w/beard, inspired by Jim's
fascination w/writer Jack Kerouac,
handwritten caption "Good Lord!,"
9¼ x 12"......................................**1,380.00**

John Lennon beret, black, worn by
Lennon at the 1975 Grammy
Awards, mounted in shadowbox
w/plaque & a black & white
photograph of Lennon wearing the
hat, standing w/Yoko Ono, Simon &
Garfunkel & David Bowie,
22 x 40½".....................................**3,150.00**

John Lennon drawing, black felt
pen, in same ink a doodle & "John
Lennon" & "1978," 8 x 10½".........**2,990.00**

John Lennon musical arrangement,
handwritten arrangement for the
song "Imagine," probably in the
hand of arranger Torrie Zito, pencil
written w/annotations in red pencil,
written on the first page in black felt
tip pen "John Lennon - Imagine -
Torrie Zito," & in pencil "7/4/71,"
1971...**3,680.00**

John Lennon ring, flasher-type,
1960s **15.00**

John Lennon shirt, green "Army"
style, cotton, garment w/a "U.S.
ARMY" strip over the left breast
pocket, on right breast pocket a red,
yellow & black patch, on upper left
shoulder a black & white patch
featuring an American Indian head,
on both shoulders there are yellow &
black inverted Sergeant stripes,
worn by Lennon ca. 1972, inscribed
in blue ink on inside back panel,
"'May 1 to 1' - John Lennon 23 Aug
1972," includes two color
photographs **20,700.00**

John Lennon trenchcoat, green

Johnny Cash Acoustic Guitar

"Army" style, cotton, wide waist belt
& double row of buttons, Lennon
wore the coat throughout the 1970s,
sewn-in tag on inside collar "38R
8405 965 2135," mounted in a
shadowbox w/plaque & a black &
white photograph of John Lennon
wearing the coat, 42½ x 62" **5,520.00**

Johnny Cash acoustic guitar,
mahogany body, spruce top, twenty
fret rosewood fingerboard w/dot
inlays, pin bridge & black pickguard,
signed on the body "Johnny Cash,"
Yamaha fg300A (ILLUS. bottom
previous column) **863.00**

"Kiss" Dolls

Kiss dolls, includes Ace, Peter Criss,
Gene Simmons & Paul Stanley,
wearing original outfits, also
includes *Kiss* albums "Alive!,"
"Double Platinum," "Dynasty,"
"Destroyer," "Love Gun," "Peter
Criss" (solo w/poster), dolls near
mint, albums all discolored w/some
wear, the group (ILLUS. of dolls) **450.00**

Led Zeppelin concert poster, "Bill
Graham Presents - Led Zeppelin -
July 23-24 1977 - Oakland
Stadium," design by Randy Tuten &
William Bostedt (small corner
bends) **172.50**

**Lynyrd Skynyrd portrait
photograph,** the inner sleeve of
their LP "Nothin' Fancy," signed
"Allen Collins - Leon Wilkinson" in
red ball point pen, "Artimus 'Lynyrd
Skynyrd' - Ronnie Van Zant" in blue
bal! point pen, "Billy Powell - God
Bless You" in black marker, each
signed on their respective photos,
ca. 1975..**345.00**

Madonna baseball glove, Wilson
brown leather, well-worn, used by
Madonna in "A League of their
Own," signed in black felt pen,
"Madonna - Penny Marshall - Tom
Hanks - Geena Davis" **1,380.00**

Madonna 'hoop' skirt, a pink satin

Madonna Pink Ruffled Skirt

moire knee-length ruffled skirt,
elaborately decorated w/coins, dice,
shiny pinwheels, toy money, grapes
& brightly colored letters, stamped
on the inside waistband "Western
Costume Co. Hollywood, California,"
on the inside lining signed
"MADONNA," from the 1987 "Who's
That Girl" tour (ILLUS.) **6,900.00**

Madonna Stage Shorts

Madonna stage shorts, low waisted,
high-cut purple shorts made of
ribbed stretch knit, the legs lined in
black satin, completely decorated
w/purple sequins, from the 1992
"Girlie Tour" (ILLUS.) **1,725.00**
Michael Jackson fedora style hat,
white, worn in "Smooth Criminal,"
inside band stamped in gold letters
"MICHAEL JACKSON," signed on
underside of brim "All My Love
Michael Jackson 1988"...................**805.00**
Miles Davis photograph, black &
white promotional, signed in lime
green marker, some corner creases,
8 x 10" (ILLUS. top next column) **230.00**
Monkees bracelet on card **25.00**
Monkees button, guitar-shaped
w/"Monkees" in red, ca. 1960s...........**10.00**
Monkees puzzle, jigsaw-type, "Hey-
Hey," w/official autographed pictures
on box, mint in original box **35.00**

Signed Miles Davis Promo Photo

Monkees ring, flasher-type.................**30.00**
Montery Pop Festival pre-concert
program, features numerous essays
by such rock notables as Jan
Wenner, Derek Taylor, Al Kooper,
Bob Shelton & Leonard Bernstein,
nice photographs of performers, 80
pgs. (minor surface scratches) **218.50**
Pat Boone charm bracelet,
w/records, shoes, framed photo &
TV **30.00**
Paul McCartney baseball, official
American League model, signed in
blue ink on the sweet spot, "Paul
McCartney," in the same ink a
doodle of a smiling face **690.00**
Paul McCartney guitar, acoustic
model, signed by McCartney in blue
Sharpie, Washburn Model D-10N,
serial #92070333D.......................**2,300.00**
Paul McCartney handwritten original
lyrics for "When I'm 64," from the
1967 'Sgt. Pepper' album, shows
lyrics in variant sequence
w/revisions **40,250.00**
**Pete Townshend smashed acoustic
guitar,** top-of-the-range Gibson J-
200 model, in a natural finish,
played & then smashed on national

Pink Floyd Cymbal

television on "The David Letterman Show," inscribed & signed on base of guitar, "Pete Townshend On David Letterman Show June 17, 1993," framed, 23 x 34" **5,520.00**

Pink Floyd cymbal, China type, signatures in black felt pen include "David Gilmore" & "Nick Mason" in 'bubble letters,' Paiste 2000, 16" d. (ILLUS. bottom previous page) **1,093.00**

"Rock Groups" Photograph

Photograph, "Rock Groups (San Francisco), Big Brother & the Holding Company & The Grateful Dead," Janis Joplin, Big Brother & the Holding Company standing on one side w/The Grateful Dead on the other, platinum-palladium print, mounted on aluminum, signed, titled, dated, numbered "28/50" & w/printing notations by the photographer in pencil & his copyright stamp on the reverse, matted, framed, no. 28 in an edition of 50, ca. 1967, printed 1979, by Irving Penn, 19 x 19¾" (ILLUS.) **3,335.00**

Rascals (The) in-house presentation "gold" disc, "Freedom Suite," R.I.A.A. certified, plaque inscribed "Presented to Atlantic Records," framed, 17½ x 21½"........................**748.00**

Rolling Stones (The) calendar page,

'Pretty Vacant' Promo Poster

dated "Wednesday, September 8, 1965 - Thursday 9," w/original ink signatures of Mick Jagger, Bill Wyman, Charlie Watts, Brian Jones & Keith Richards, 3 x 4½" **920.00**

Sex Pistols (The) promotional poster for the single "Pretty Vacant" on Virgin Records, lightly toned, tack holes in corners, slight wear, 28⅜ x 39⅞" (ILLUS. bottom previous column) **264.50**

Stevie Ray Vaughan photograph, Epic Records promotional, boldly signed in gold marker, matted, 11 x 14"...**374.00**

Stevie Nicks Stage Coat

Stevie Nicks stage coat, red puff shoulder-style floor length coat ornately embellished w/red sequins, beads & rhinestones, bead fringe border & red lace, worn on several tours (ILLUS.) **1,265.00**

The Supremes Concert Poster

Supremes (The) concert poster, "Trude Heller and G. Keys present - The Supremes - Lincoln Center -

Philharmonic Hall - Friday October 15,1965," design by Eula, 25 x 38" (ILLUS.) **489.00**

Talking Heads bass guitar, Veillette Citron model, green finish, double cutaway body, twenty-two fret rosewood fingerboard w/dot inlays, two pickups, four controls, selector, metal bridge & tailpiece w/hardshell case, signed on body in silver ink by David Byrne **1,955.00**

Signed U2 Promo Photo

U2 promotional photograph, black & white, signed "Bono" in black Sharpie & "Edge - Adam - Larry" in blue Sharpie, framed, minor smudging, 10½ x 12½" (ILLUS.) **287.50**

(End of Pop Culture Collectibles Section)

POSTCARDS

Advertising, "Standard Oil," pictures an oil truck, 1910 ....**$55.00**
Bangkok & Japan, 1928, set of 15 in wooden album **55.00**
Baron Wrangel, real photo **75.00**
BPOE Elks Reunion, Portland, Oregon, 1912......................................**25.00**
Buffalo Bill, wearing buckskins w/rifle **15.00**
Father Christmas, embossed, blue, 1908, Raphael Tuck artwork..............**16.00**
Father Christmas, embossed, green, Germany **18.00**
General Bogaevsky & Don Ataman, real photo..**45.00**
General Lukomsky, real photo **45.00**
General May Maevsky, real photo **75.00**
Halloween, Clapsaddle little girl in red witch costume w/Jack o' lanterns **22.00**
Helen Keller & braille alphabet............**7.50**
Lake Washington, Seattle, 1920s.........**5.00**
Oklahoma, Seminole, pictures Main Street **40.00**
Sally Rand Nude Ranch, 1939 ....**25.00**

Santa Claus, blue suit, driving old red roadster, 1916.....................................**13.00**
Santa Claus, wearing black suit, No. 3025, Rotograph Co., fine condition....................................**100.00**
Sunbonnet Baby, unused, seven days, complete set............................**70.00**

POSTERS

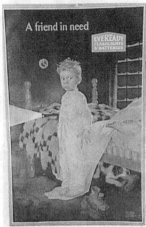

Eveready Batteries Poster

Batteries, Eveready flashlights & batteries, a small boy standing in his bedroom w/flashlight, "A friend in need" printed across top, pink, red, cream, green, blue, yellow & white lettering, signed by Frances Tipton Hunter, cloth-backed, 19½ x 30" (ILLUS.) **$550.00**

Palace Hotel Poster

Hotel, "Palace Hotel - St. Moritz - In Switzerland," depicting the 'smart set' relaxing beside an ice rink w/a skater in the background, by Emile Cardinaux, ca. 1920, 35½ x 50⅜" (ILLUS.) **2,760.00**

Ocean liner, "Normandie - Cie. Gle. Transatlantique - French Line - Le Havre - Southampton - New York," a large image of a stylized ocean liner approaching, signed & dated in the plate, A.M. Cassandre, 1935, France, 24¼ x 39½" **2,990.00**

Russian Propaganda Poster

Propaganda, "Workers of All Countries, Unite," printed in Russian, lithograph & offset lithograph printed in black & two shades of red, ca. 1939, D. Moor & Senkin, creasing, a few tears around edges, 23⅞ x 36¾" (ILLUS.).........**3,738.00**

"Exactitude" Poster

Railroad, "Exactitude," large stylized image of an oncoming train, signed & dated in the stone, Pierre Fix-Masseau, 1932, France, 24½ x 39¼" (ILLUS.) **5,520.00**

Travel, "Bordeaux - Son Port - Ses Monuments - Ses Vins," stylized

portrait of a nude female standing amid symbols of the French city, signed in the plate, Jean Dupas, 1937, France, framed, 27⅝ x 43"......................................**3,450.00**

Liberty Bonds Poster

World War I, "Hun or Home? Buy More Liberty Bonds," cream & black, Edward & Deutsch Litho Co. Chicago, very minor soiling, 19½ x 30" (ILLUS.) **49.50**

World War I Poster

World War I, "I Want You For The Navy...," standing woman wearing a naval jacket & hat, signed "Howard Chandler Christy - 1917," cloth-backed, edge tears & creases, touch-up on top center edge, 26½ x 41" (ILLUS.) **110.00**

World War I, "Remember Belgium - Buy Bonds - Fourth Liberty Loan," silhouetted figure of a fat German soldier dragging a young screaming girl against a fiery background, by Ellsworth Young, 1918, 20 x 30"........**55.00**

World War II, "For a Secure Future - Buy War Bonds," brilliant colors of

War Bonds Poster

blue, red, white, green, orange,
brown, signed by Amos Seweil, ca.
1945, creased corners, 20 x 27½"
(ILLUS.) **93.50**

POWDER HORNS & FLASKS

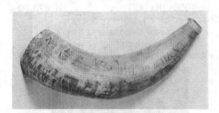

Hand-carved Powder Horn

Copper flask, embossed fanned shell
design framed by long slender leafy
scrolls, brass spout stamped "Dixon
& Sons - Sheffield," England,
19th c., 8⅛" l. **$82.50**

Copper & brass flask, embossed
shell design, 7½" l. (dents)................**60.50**

Horn, engraved w/a scene of the
Siege of Boston, inscribed "Gediton
Dennison his horn made at Roxbury
November the 9th AD 1775 - Liberty
or Death," 7½" l. (cut mark)..............**920.00**

Horn, engraved w/hex signs, Masonic
symbols, sun & an eagle, 8½" l.........**460.00**

Horn, hand-carved, depicts Boston
Harbor w/ships, the city commons &
municiple buildings, engraved "A
View of the City of Boston - John
Boyle made at Roxbury 1775,"
18th c., part of carved lip missing,
8½" l. (ILLUS.) **825.00**

Horn, engraved "James McIntyre
1816 - Derry Twp. Westmoreland
Co. Penna.," peg construction
w/screw tip spout & turned cherry
end plug, good patina, 10½" l.
(small age cracks at spout) **907.50**

Horn, incised "Palitar Crooker"
w/geometric & vine decoration plug
incised "RB," America, late 18th c.,
10¾" l. **431.00**

New York State Powder Horn

Horn, hand-carved, depicts a crude
map of New York State, Albany,
Saratoga and the state seal, carved
"Henry Dodge 4th Regt. 1761,"
18th c., 11" l. (ILLUS.).....................**935.00**

18th Century Powder Horn

Horn, hand-carved, depicts a map of
New York State w/Fort George, Fort
Edward & Fort Henry, etc., marked
"Isaac Horton - 1st Regt. - Orange
City Militia - 1778 - New York,"
18th c. (ILLUS.)............................**1,320.00**

Horn, boldly relief-carved near the top
w/"Phillip Challis - 1749," domed
pine plug w/dark finish & a staple,
spout w/raised rings for strap & old
cracks w/sinew repair, good color,
11¼" l. (minor ring chip)..................**330.00**

Horn, engraved "Sam' Beach Eus^n of
Capt Burroughs's Com^p Col^o
Warners Reigh Sam^{el} Jones facit
Sep^t ye 17th AD 1778 the plan of
Fort Starks....," 12" l. (small
hole) **4,125.00**

Horn, decorated w/a three-masted
ship & schooner, late 18th c.,
13½" l..**517.50**

Horn, inscribed w/scenes of a duck
hunter & a deer hunter, possibly
Long Island, 14" l. **345.00**

Horn, long curved form w/flat pine

plug w/incised carving & chip-carved edges, carved spout w/eight flats, wooden peg construction, 19th c., 14" l. **165.00**

PURSES & BAGS

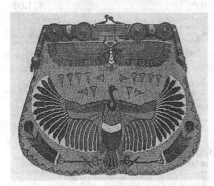

Egyptian Revival Beaded Handbag

Alligator shoulder bag, head & body, Cuba **$95.00**
Beaded, Egyptian Revival style, decorated w/colorful Egyptian Benu bird, brass frame w/faience scarab inserts, mounted in display frame, minor bead loss (ILLUS.) **2,875.00**
Armor mesh, chatelaine-style, ball drops, German silver, women w/flowing hair & roses, frame & plaque, 4½ x 10¼" **185.00**
Beaded, cut steel, decoration of house & trees, 5 x 9" **175.00**
Canvaswork, double-sided, flattened rectangular form worked w/red, coral, green, yellow & brown wool flame stitch w/a series of spade-like devices on a black-brown ground, the interior lined w/olive green worsted, signed "Ebnr Ward" on

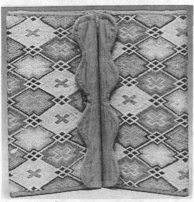

Canvaswork Purse

interior, probably Salem, Massachuttes, ca. 1786, 4½ x 8¾" **4,600.00**
Canvaswork, stitched in a bargello design in shades of red, green, violet, yellow & black; now in two-sided frame, stitched monogram "WG 1769," ca. 1769, 8½ x 9½" (ILLUS. bottom previous column) **1,955.00**

Crocodile Handbag

Crocodile, envelope-style, grey, grey lambskin lining w/goldtone closure, stiff handle, Hermes, Paris, ca. 1950s (ILLUS.) **2,875.00**
Enameled mesh, tapestry design w/red & yellow diagonals, scene of building w/American flag, chain handle, Whiting & Davis, 5½ x 6" **125.00**

Gold Mesh Purse

Gold mesh, rectangular w/diamond & emerald set clasp & chain handle (ILLUS.) **2,250.00**
Gold mesh, 14k tri-color gold, engraved yellow gold frame centered by a pierced sapphire & diamond-set platinum top enhanced

by a cabochon sapphire thumbpiece
& slide suspending a seed pearl
tassel, marked Beline &
Glasser **4,312.50**
Gold mesh, 18k yellow gold,
designed as a coin purse, accented
by a rose-cut frame.........................**460.00**
Gold mesh, 18k yellow gold, mesh
pattern w/gold chain handle..........**4,945.00**
Leather, Arts & Crafts style, flattened
rectangular style, black w/the front
flap stamped along each end w/a
blossom & band of leaves painted
dark red & green, a large single
blossom in red at the center edge
above the metal latch, early 20th c.,
unmarked, 6 x 8"...............................**77.00**
Suede, black cylindrical vanity purse
w/top which lifts to reveal compact,
opening beneath compact reveals
partition for comb, lipstick, matches,
etc., bottom swivels & raises vanity
to eye level, La Vadelte, France **295.00**

RADIO & TELEVISION
MEMORABILIA

Baby Snooks Doll

*Not long after the dawning of the radio
age in the 1920s, new programs were being
aired for the entertainment of the national
listening audience. Many of these
programs issued premiums and
advertising promotional pieces which are
highly collectible today.*

*With the arrival of the TV age in the
late 1940s, the tradition of promotional
items continued and in addition to
advertising materials, many toys and
novelty items have been produced which
tie-in to popular shows.*

Below we list alphabetically a wide

*range of items relating to classic radio and
television. Some of the characters
originated in the comics or on the radio
and then found new and wider exposure
through television. We include them here
because they are best known to today's
collectors because of television exposure.*

*Also see CHARACTER COLLECTI-
BLES, LUNCH BOXES, POP CULTURE
COLLECTIBLES, MOVIE MEMORA-
BILIA and WESTERN CHARACTER
COLLECTIBLES.*

Addams Family (TV) card game,
Milton Bradley, 1965.........**$40.00 to 50.00**
Adams Family (TV) gum cards, set of
62 different...**95.00**
Agent 99 (Get Smart, TV) spy purse,
plastic, comes w/a two-way mirror,
ID card holders, film & secret rose
button, Miner Industries, 1960s, in
original box (box cellophane torn)....**115.00**
Amos & Andy sheet music, "The
Perfect Song," 1929..........................**35.00**
Amos & Andy yard long print,
includes advertising from a
drugstore, orange & black,
outstanding graphics, premium from
CBS Radio **100.00**
Baby Snooks (Fanny Brice) doll,
composition head w/painted blue
eyes, open-closed mouth w/bottom
teeth, molded & painted brown hair
w/loop for bow, wooden torso & feet,
metal flexy arms & legs, composition
hands, back of head marked "Ideal
Doll," paper wrist tab reads "Flexy -
An Ideal Doll - Fanny Brice's Baby
Snooks - Ideal Novelty & Toy Co. -
Long Island City, N.Y. - The Doll of a
Thousand Poses," in original outfit,
unplayed-with condition, some
cracks in finish, 12½" h. (ILLUS.).....**160.00**
Batman (TV) automobile, Batmobile,
model kit, unbuilt, in box **50.00**
Batman (TV) belt, leather w/metal
buckle reading "Batman," mounted
on original card w/illustrations of
Batman & Robin & the Batman logo,
1960s, card 5 x 12"...........................**60.00**
Batman (TV) coloring book, Whitman,
1967, 80+ pp., 8 x 11" (unused) **29.00**
Batman (TV) lamp, model of the Bat
Cave, 1966 ....**95.00**
Batman (TV) magazine, "Life," March
11,1966, Adam West as Batman on
the cover **20.00**
Batman (TV) mug, china, 1966,
Washington Pottery **45.00**
Batman (TV) store display, die-cut
cardboard full-figure stand-up of
Batman, 1966, 5' 10" h. (some tape
on the back) **80.00**
Beany (Beany & Cecil cartoons) doll,

talking-type, stuffed cloth body w/soft vinyl head, hands & shoes, molded vinyl head, hands & shoes, molded vinyl hat w/small plastic propeller, pull-string on one leg which activates internal voice box, speaks several phrases, Mattel Inc., ca. 1960, 18" h............................**60.00**

Ben Casey (TV) "Photo Scrapbook," 1962 w/color photo on cover.............**35.00**

Bewitched (TV) sheet music, show theme, 1964.....................................**38.00**

Bewitched (TV) writing tablet, color photo of the cast on the cover, 1964, 8 x 10", mint....................................**15.00**

Bozo the Clown tablecloth, paper, several illustrations of Bozo in circus performances, 1950, unused in original packaging, 52 x 102".............**29.00**

Bugs Bunny cartoon cel, gouache on celluloid, depicts Bugs wearing a long robe & walking towards his hole & carrying a chamberstick in a wintery landscape, dated in lower right "April 1946," applied to a gouache Warner Bros. background, possibly a publicity cel, 9 x 12" **2,875.00**

Bugs Bunny planter, ceramic, Bugs standing next to wheelbarrow, in shade of brown & grey, marked "Warner Bros. Cartoons Inc.".............**45.00**

Captain Midnight (radio) decoder, 1948, "Miro-Magic Code-O-Graph," Ovaltime premium.............................**65.00**

Captain Midnight (radio) decoder manual, 1942.....................................**65.00**

Captain Midnight (radio) decoder manual, 1948 (clipped corners) **40.00**

Captain Midnight (radio) handkerchief, w/Secret Squadron emblem **225.00**

Captain Midnight (radio) membership token, brass, 1940 ....**17.50**

Captain Midnight (radio) decoder, 1945, "Magni-Magic Code-O-Graph," Ovaltine premium **90.00**

Captain Midnight (radio) decoder, 1946, "Mirro-Flash Code-O-Graph," Ovaltine premium..............................**65.00**

Captain Midnight (radio) decoder, 1947, "Whistling Code-O-Graph," Ovaltine premium ....**70.00 to 80.00**

Captain Midnight (radio) mug, Ovaltine premium, red plastic (ILLUS. top next column) **55.00**

Captain Midnight (radio) patch, "SQ 15th Anniversary," cloth, 1957 ....**50.00**

Captain Midnight (radio) stamp album w/stamps, "Air Heroes," Skelly Oil premium, w/16 stamps, 1940, 5 x 6½"......................................**55.00**

Charlie McCarthy book, "A Day with Charlie McCarthy & Edgar Bergen," Whitman, 1938...................................**40.00**

Captain Midnight Mug

Charlie McCarthy book, "Speaking for Myself," by Charlie McCarthy, 1939, mint **50.00**

Charlie McCarthy game, "Radio Party," 21 pcs. complete w/spinner & envelope, Chase & Sanborn Coffee premium, 1938, in original mailer **70.00**

Charlie McCarthy soap figure, mint in box..............................**125.00 to 145.00**

Charlie McCarthy teaspoon, embossed "Inspector," 1938.............**35.00**

Charlie McCarthy "Benzine Buggy"

Charlie McCarthy toy, windup tin, "Benzine Buggy," Charlie at the wheel, lithographed in black & white, w/box, 8" h. (ILLUS.) ....**400.00 to 500.00**

Charlie McCarthy ventriloquist dummy, marked "Edgar Bergen, Charlie McCarthy, An Effanbee Product," composition shoulder head, painted brown eyes, painted upper lashes, single stroke brows, accented nostrils, open mouth w/movable jaw, cloth body w/composition hands & feet, dressed in original white shirt, vest, tuxedo & top hat, w/original

monocle, 17" h. (light crazing
on face & hair) **400.00**
Charlie McCarthy & Edgar Bergen
tumbler, decals illustrating both
characters, 1930s **75.00**
Charlie McCarthy & Mortimer Snerd
picture, advertising "Bergen's Better
Bubble Gum".....................................**75.00**
Crusader Rabbit (cartoons) coloring
book, cartoon graphics, Saalfield,
1967...**50.00**
Daniel Boone (TV) coloring book,
color photo of Fess Parker on the
front & back, Saalfield, 1964,
80+ pp., 8 x 11", mint......................**59.00**
Dark Shadows game, board-type,
illustrates Barnabas Collins on box
cover, 1969 ....**45.00**
The Deputy (TV) puzzle, jigsaw-type,
picture includes Henry Fonda, from
England, mint in box **85.00**
Dr. Kildare (TV) pencil-by-number
set, six pre-numbered pictures & six
colored pencils, Standard Toykraft,
1962, box 9 x 13" **39.00**

Grinch Animation Cel

Dr. Seuss animation cel, from *How
The Grinch Stole Christmas,*
gouache on celluloid, publicity cel of
the Grinch in his Santa costume w/
Max (wearing his antler) perched on
one knee & Cindy Lou Who on the
other, inscribed within mat at bottom
right "Merry Christmas to Bill Patterson from Chuck Jones & Dr. Seuss,"
1966, 7¾ x 11" (ILLUS.) **2,587.00**
Dragnet whistle, "Jack Webb,"
plastic..**10.00**
Family Affair (TV) dolls, "Buffy & Mrs.
Beasley," blonde character doll
w/her own smaller doll, Mattel, 1967,
never removed from box, small tear
in cellophane (ILLUS. top next
column) **210.00**

"Buffy & Mrs. Beasley" Dolls

Flintstones Animation Cel

Flintstones animation cel, gouache
on celluloid applied to a gouache
production background, shows Fred
& Barney driving along w/their golf
clubs in the back, ca. 1965, 7 x 9"
(ILLUS.) **920.00**
Flintstones coloring book, 1978,
17 x 22"...**25.00**
Flintstones (TV) cookie jar, cover
w/Dino finial, pictures Fred &
"Flintstones" impressed on upper
part of jar, American Bisque
Company, base marked
"USA" ....**1,200.00 to 1,400.00**
Flintstones night-light, in original
package **22.00**
Flintstones projector, "Give A
Show," battery-operated, w/box &
112 color slides **65.00**
Fred Flintstone toy, dart game &
target gun, Trans-O-Gram Co., Inc. **48.00**
Get Smart (TV) bumper sticker, reads
"Get Smart - Wear Your Seat Belt!,"
w/a photo of Don Adams talking into
his shoe, released by Motor
Vehicles, 1960s, 4 x 12" **25.00**
Green Hornet (TV) playing cards,
mint in box **45.00**
Gumby jack-in-the-box, 1966, mint
in box **150.00**

Hawaiian Eye (TV) puzzle, jigsaw-
type, England, mint in box **85.00**

Honey West Doll

Honey West (TV) doll, vinyl figure
representing star Anne Francis,
brown hair, wearing black judo
leotards & gold belt w/holster,
Gilbert, w/box, doll w/small neck
split, box slightly worn & damaged,
missing pistol, black boots &
instructions, 11" h. (ILLUS.) **115.00**
Howdy Doody bank, ceramic, a
figure of Howdy astride a small,
smiling pig, 7" h...............................**525.00**
Howdy Doody camera, "Sun Ray,"
mint in original package.......**75.00 to 85.00**
Howdy Doody coloring book, Poll
Parrot Shoes premium.....................**40.00**
Howdy Doody "Cookie-Go-Round"
container, tin, pictures Howdy &
friends riding carousel, 1950s,
large ....**175.00 to 200.00**
Howdy Doody cookie jar, cov.,
ceramic, head of Howdy w/winking
eye, Vandor....................**450.00 to 500.00**
Howdy Doody figure, wood &
composition, composition head
w/blue eyes painted looking to the
side, single stroke brows, painted
freckles, closed smiling mouth,
molded & painted red hair, wood
segmented body, arms & legs, label
on chest "Howdy Doody, © Bob
Smith," 13" h....................**200.00 to 275.00**
Howdy Doody figure, wood-jointed
push-up type, Howdy shown in front
of an N.B.C. mike, w/rare
original box......................**175.00 to 200.00**
Howdy Doody game, bean bag,
original box **175.00**
Howdy Doody game, bowling
w/Howdy, Clarabel, Dilly Dally &
Flub-a-dub, mint in box....**125.00 to 150.00**
Howdy Doody game, "Electrical
Carnival Game," by Wiry Dan
Electric Games, w/original box **95.00**
Howdy Doody handkerchief,

colorful, pictures Howdy,
8 x 8¼" ....**50.00 to 75.00**
Howdy Doody light fixture, glass,
pictures Howdy sitting on a chimney
w/Santa standing next to him,
w/original box ....**175.00 to 225.00**
Howdy Doody marionette,
composition hands, head & feet,
dressed in original cowboy
outfit, 16" h. ....**175.00 to 200.00**
Howdy Doody puppet, hand-type,
Howdy face w/moving
eyes.....................................**45.00 to 65.00**
Howdy Doody puppet set, "Howdy
Doody Puppet Show," includes six
characters including Mr. Bluster,
Howdy, Clarabell Clown, Flub-a-dub
& Dilly Dally, complete &
unpunched, Kagran, 1950s,
w/original box, the set (box water-
stained on bottom, front cover
bottom damaged).............................**95.00**
Howdy Doody rocking chair, child's,
w/original bell on base **250.00**
Howdy Doody tumblers, Musical
Notes Series, verses include "We all
agree," "Parade each day," "You'll
like it swell," "Helps make you
strong," "Favorite treat" & "Hits the
spot," different illustrations on each
glass, Welch's premium, 1953, set
of 6...**84.00**
Incredible Hulk (TV) game, board-
type, unused **45.00**
Jack Armstrong (radio) "Explorer
Telescope," radio premium **35.00**

Jack Armstrong "Hike-O-Meter"

Jack Armstrong pedometer, "Hike-
O-Meter," 2¾" d. (ILLUS.) ...**25.00 to 30.00**
Jack Armstrong (radio) "Secret
Bomb Sight," black & green wood
w/yellow sticker-decal of meters &
dials, w/one red wood bomb, 1942,
2½ x 3½", 1" h. (minor surface
wear)..**195.00**
Jackie Gleason (TV) doll, molded
face, wearing uniform & cap, 1950s,
30" h...**750.00**

Jetsons (TV) paint book, Whitman,
1962..**100.00**
Jetsons (TV) toy, "Jetsons Magic
Slate," die-cut cardboard w/magic
erasable slate & pencil, features a
scene of the family in a spaceship,
Watkins - Strathmore, 1963, 8 x 14",
mint..**59.00**
Lassie (TV) kit, "Lassie Forest
Rangers Membership Kit," contains
photos of Lassie & Corey Stuart &
letter from Corey, in original mailer....**45.00**
Magilla Gorilla (TV) game, board-
type, Ideal, 1964, complete in
10 x 20" box (slight lid dent on
box, nearly repaired corner split) **98.00**
Man From U.N.C.L.E (TV) card
game, 1965, complete in original
box..**50.00**
Man From U.N.C.L.E (TV) gum card
wrapper, colorful fuschia paper
w/black & white photo of Napoleon
Solo holding U.N.C.L.E. gun..............**49.00**
Mighty Mouse charm bracelet,
brass charms of comic characters
including Gandy Goose, Terry Bear,
Mighty Mouse & others, 1950s,
w/original card (card damage) **45.00**
Mr. Magoo (TV) game, board-type,
Lowe, 1961, complete in box, box
10 x 20"...**79.00**
Mr. Novak (TV) game, board-type,
1963...**40.00**
Mod Squad (TV) model kit, "Mod
Squad Station Wagon," plastic, by
Aurora Plastics, copyright 1969,
mint in original box..........................**400.00**
My Favorite Martian (TV) coloring
book, softbound, Whitman, 1964,
128 pp., 8 x 11" (minor coloring) **22.00**
My Little Margie (TV) coloring book,
1954 ....**35.00**
Ozzie & Harriet coloring book,
1955..**42.00**
Princess SummerFall -
WinterSpring (Howdy Doody)
marionette, w/original box................**175.00**
Ricky Jr. (I Love Lucy) doll, 1950s,
mint in box **275.00**
Robin Hood (TV) cloth patch on card,
1956..**15.00**
Rootie Kazootie (TV) Club button,
lithographed tin, picture of Mr.
Deetle Dootle, 1950s, 1" d. **45.00**
Scooby Doo (TV) doll, stuffed cloth in
light orangish brown w/dark brown
accents, w/original illustrated tag,
J.S. Sutton and Sons, 1970, 14" h.
(unused, ¼" tear on one side of
head)..**59.00**
Sea Hunt (TV) game, board-type,
"Lloyd Bridges in Underwater
Adventures," 1961 ....**85.00**
Sergeant Preston (TV) comic book,

miniature, "How He Became a
Mountie"..**23.00**
Sergeant Preston comic book,
miniature, "How Yukon King Saved
Him From The Wolves"......................**23.00**
Sergeant Preston distance finder,
1955..**65.00**
Tarzan puzzle, jigsaw-type,
cardboard w/photograph of Buster
Crabbe as Tarzan, 1930s, w/original
box..**85.00**

RADIOS & ACCESSORIES

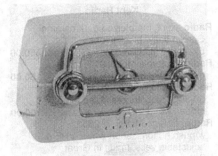

Crosley Radio

Book, "Drakes Encyclopedia of Radio
Electronics," Manly & Gorder,
1943, eleventh edition
w/dust jacket **$20.00**
Book, "Elements of Radio," Charles I.
Hellman, 1943, second printing
w/dust jacket **18.00**
Book, "Radio Operating - Questions
& Answers," Arthur Nilson & J.L.
Hornung, 1936, sixth edition **18.00**
Book, "Radio Telegraphy &
Telephony," Rudolph Duncan &
Charles E. Dres, second edition **20.00**
Book, "Understanding Radio,"
Wattson, Welch & Eby, 1940, first
edition **20.00**
Radio, Addison Model 2, maroon &
white Catalin case............................**450.00**
Radio, American Bosch Model 515,
table model, wood..............................**50.00**
Radio, Crosley, light green plastic
w/gold colored front w/knobs, some
paint wear, 7½ x 12" (ILLUS.) **88.00**
Radio, Crosley Model M-151, battery-
operated w/earphones **65.00**
Radio, FADA Model 263, wooden
cabinet w/one rounded end,
veneered w/various tropical woods,
tambour door, paper label,
6⅝ x 14½", 8" h. (abrasion) **165.00**
Radio, General Electric Model
P-1850A, nine transistor **18.00**

Radio, General Electric Model
P-808G, transistor, ca. 1960 ....**18.00**

Kent Radio

Radio, Kent, marbleized dark caramel
Catalin body, black knobs,
5¼ x 7½" (ILLUS) **550.00**
Radio, Motorola Model 9T1, table
model, Bakelite case........................**150.00**
Radio, Philco Superhetrodyne Model
60-505, tombstone-shaped table
model, wood **100.00**
Radio, Phillips Model BA2553,
w/push buttons, short wave, VHF &
adjustable volts, made in Great
Britain..**95.00**
Radio, RCA Model 8R75, brown
marbelized Bakelite case, 1949.........**47.50**
Radio, Sampson Model SC4000,
pocket-type w/case **85.00**

Sentinel Radio

Radio, Sentinel, Catalin body, green
& gold metal front, back of case
opens, minor soiling & scratches,
8 x 10" (ILLUS.) **176.00**
Radio, Stewart-Warner Model 3044A,
Art Deco style bird's-eye maple case
w/turquoise wraparound grill, dial &
knobs, original paper
label, ca. 1935, 7½ x 12" (wear) **259.00**
Radio, Tom Thumb, portable-type,
rectangular army green case
w/rounded corners & brown vinyl
front & sides, front opens to turn dial

w/orange lettering & numbering,
back opens, 4½ x 5", 9" h. (minor
overall soiling) **55.00**
Radio, Zenith Model H725-6723,
working condition **50.00**
Radio, Zenith Trans-Oceanic
w/wave magnet.................................**60.00**

RAILROADIANA

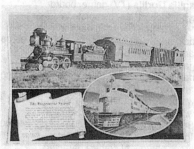

Union Pacific Folder

Advertising folder, "Union Pacific
Railroad," paper, opens to show a
black & white photo of a 19th
century train above a modern train,
titled "The Progressive Spirit," the
reverse w/a listing of Pennzoil
distributors, compliments of
Pennzoil, ca. 1940s, 12 x 17"
(ILLUS.) **$33.00**
Book, "Santa Fe Steel Rails through
California," 1963, 184 pp. **20.00**
Booklet, "Erie Railroad," 1915 ....**20.00**
Booklet, "Southern Pacific Co., -
California Route," 1948......................**12.00**
Booklet, "Union Pacific Railroad,"
1931, Zion, Bryce & Grand Canyon,
first booklet w/color photos, also
maps & articles, linen-finish pages,
48 pp..**85.00**
Bouillon cup, "Pennsylvania
Railroad," china, Broadway
patt. ....**25.00 to 35.00**
Boullion cup, "Union Pacific
Railroad," china, Winged
Streamliner patt. **24.00**
Bowl, "Baltimore & Ohio Railroad,"
china, Capitol - Black & Gold patt.,
10" d..**90.00**
Bowl, "SP" (Southern Pacific), china,
Prairie-Mountain Wildflowers patt.,
6" d..**75.00**
Butter pat, "Chicago, Burlington &
Quincy Railroad," china, Violets &
Daisies patt. **30.00**
Calendar, 1929, "Pennsylvania
Railroad," paper, a large upper color
photograph of a speeding train
above a narrow route map above

Pennsylvania Railroad 1929 Calendar

the long, narrow calendar sheets
w/each page displaying three
months, calendar reattached to
background, tears to edges, water
stains, 29" w., 30" h. (ILLUS.) **231.00**

Undated Missouri Pacific Calendar

Calendar, undated, "Missouri Pacific
Lines," metal over cardboard, a
color scene of a speeding train
above "Missouri Pacific Lines"
above a metal bracket holding
original large month & day cards,
early 20th c., (minor soiling &
scratches,) 13 x 19" (ILLUS.) **385.00**
Lantern, "Cleveland, Cincinnati,
Chicago & St. Louis Railroad,"
amber etched globe, tall **250.00**
Menu, "Union Pacific Railroad," Bryce
Canyon illustration, 1954 ....**11.00**
Pass, annual, "Western Pacific
Railroad," 1930, framed **19.00**
Plate, "New York Central Railroad,"
china, DeWitt Clinton patt.,
9" d. ....**50.00 to 75.00**
Plates, "Chesapeake & Ohio," china,

a central oval colored portrait of
George Washington, the wide outer
rim gold-encrusted & etched, by
Buffalo Pottery, 10¾" d., set of 3
(one w/portrait wear) **1,237.50**
Platter, "Atchinson, Topeka & Santa
Fe Railroad," china, Adobe patt.,
7 x 9" ....**75.00 to 100.00**
Playing cards, "Denver & Rio
Grande," sealed deck **59.00**

Early Railroad Crossings Postcard

Postcard, "Cross Crossings
Cautiously" across the top above a
scene of a speeding train about to
collide w/a racing open sedan,
printed in the lower right "In Five
Years 9,101 Killed - 24,208 Injured,"
ca. 1923, minor soiling, 3½ x 5½"
(ILLUS.) **44.00**
Schedule, "Chicago - Northwestern
Railroad," 1924 season, Grand
Teton Mountains to Yellowstone........**35.00**
Schedule, "Great Northern Railroad,"
1949...................................**14.00**
Soup plate, "Union Pacific Railroad,"
china, Desert Flower
patt. ....**75.00 to 100.00**
Soup spoon, "Union Pacific," silver
plate w/engraved winged
streamliner logo, International
Silver ....**15.00 to 25.00**
Ticket, "South Carolina Railroad,"
1873, money design, rag paper,
signed **30.00**

Pennsylvania Railroad Tie Tac

Tie tac, "Pennsylvania Railroad,"
enameled metal, long rectangular
form w/a red & white train & the
keystone emblem w/"PRR" in red &
yellow, marked "Hook-Fast-Prov.RI,"
2" l. (ILLUS.) **55.00**
Timetable, "Minneapolis & St. Louis
Railroad," 1886, w/full map **65.00**

Timetable, "New York & Boston
Railroad," 1906 ....**24.00**

RECORDS & RECORD JACKETS

*Since the late 1870s when Thomas
Edison invented the first phonograph
machine, literally millions of records have
been produced. Early wax cylinders were
soon followed by 78 rpm disc records,
which became the industry standard.
Later 33⅓ rpm and then 45 rpm records
evolved and today these have nearly been
superceded by CDs (compact discs). Since
there are so many old records still around,
collectors need to understand that even
very early cylinder and disc records may
have only a minimal collector value -
especially if they are in poor playing
condition.*

*Below we list a sampling of records of
various styles and vintages. Listings are
alphabetical by the first name of the artist
or group.*

CYLINDERS

BROWN WAX
Cal Stewart, "Uncle Josh Comments
On The Signs In New York City,"
Columbia NY & P No. 14023
(small needle drops) **$13.00**
Columbia Orchestra, "Zenda Waltz,"
Columbia NY & P No. 15077,
original record slip (1% mold) **12.00**
Edison Grand Concert Band,
"Pizzicato Polka," No. 61
(1% mold) **28.00**
Gilmore's Band, "America (My
Country Tis of Thee)," Columbia
NY & P No. 1514 ....**28.00**
Gilmore's Band, "Miserere from 'Il
Trovatore,'" Columbia CPC
No. 1508 (few light mold spots,
2" hairline).....................................**17.00**
Gilmore's Band, "1900 March,"
Columbia CPC No. 1677, possible
master cylinder, original record slip
taped to side of box **63.00**
Imperial Minstrels w/Steve Porter,
"The Old Log Cabin In The Dell,"
Columbia CPC No. 13002 ....**41.00**
J.W. Myers, "Minnie Ha Ha,"
Columbia CPC..............................**13.00**
Len Spencer, "If They'd Only Fought
With Razors In De War," Columbia
CPC No. 7452, master cylinder,
original record slip taped to box
(very light mold) **119.00**

EDISON BLUE AMBEROLS
Ada Jones & Billy Murray, "I Wish
That You Belonged To Me," Edison
No. 26069, original box w/lid.............**11.00**
Albert Farrington, "Rule Britannia,"
Edison No. 2486, no box **18.00**
Billy Jones, Steve Porter & Co.,
"Christmas Morning At Clancy's,"
Edison No. 5071, original box w/lid....**30.00**
Billy Murray, "Casey Jones," Edison
No. 1550, original box w/lid...............**25.00**
Collins & Harlan, "Snookey
Ookums," Edison No. 1796, no box....**14.00**
Duke Rogers, "Save A Little Dram
For Me," Edison No. 4565, no box.....**16.00**
Edward Meeker, "Rap, Rap, Rap,
Rap On Your Minstrel Bones,"
Edison No. 1576, original box w/lid....**11.00**
Edward S. Wright, "A Little Christmas
Basket & Howdy, Honey, Howdy,"
Edison No. 2152, no box **24.00**
E.V. Stoneman, "Tell Mother I Will
Meet Her," Edison No. 5382,
no box...**34.00**
Harry Humphrey, "The Night Before
Christmas," Edison No. 2464,
no box **51.00**
Harry Lauder, "Good-Bye Till We
Meet Again," Edison No. 1818,
no box **9.00**
Harry Lauder, "McGregor's Toast,"
Edison No. 5258, original box w/lid....**47.00**
Joe Belmont, "Oh! You Circus Day
Medley," Edison No. 1534, original
box w/lid.......................................**8.00**
Kimball, Miller & Croxton, "Trio from
'Faust,'" Edison No. 1502, no box......**13.00**
Liberati's Band, "Suffragettes
March," Edison No. 2413, original
box w/lid.......................................**25.00**
Tennessee Happy Boys, "I Miss My
Swiss," Edison No. 5039, original
box w/lid.......................................**18.00**
Tuxedo Dance Orchestra, "I'm
Forever Blowing Bubbles," Edison
No. 3841, no box **13.00**
United States Marine Band, "Ride of
The Thuringia Hussars," Edison
No. 1729, no box **7.00**
Vincent Bach (cornet solo),
"Nightingale Song," Edison
No. 2611, original box w/lid...............**35.00**
Vincent Lopez's Orchestra, "Parade
of The Wooden Soldiers," Edison
No. 4614, original box w/lid...............**22.00**
Waikiki Hawaiian Orchestra, "Love
Dreams of Lula Lu," Edison
No. 5087, no box **8.00**

TWO MINUTE CYLINDERS
Arthur Collins, "H-A-S-H, Dat Am
The Word I Love," Albany
Indestructible No. 800, w/original
Columbia box.................................**9.00**

Arthur Collins, "I've Got A White Man Workin' For Me," Edison No. 7779, w/original box **58.00**

Billy Murray, "Lazy Bill," Columbia No. 32376, original box **22.00**

Bob Roberts, "In The Lives Of Famous Men," Edison No. 8634, flat edge, w/original box **26.00**

Bob Roberts, "Tain't No Disgrace To Run When You're Skeered," Columbia No. 32398, original box w/lid..................**30.00**

Cal Stewart, "Uncle Josh And The Lightning Rod Agent," Columbia No. 14029, moulded brown wax, original box (small scratches & skips)..................**14.00**

Clarke & Hazel (cornet duet), "The Friendly Rivals," Edison No. 9125, w/original box **29.00**

Columbia Fife, Drum & Bugle Corps, "The Girl I Left Behind Me," Columbia No. 12800, moulded brown wax, origianl box (25% light mold) **8.00**

Edison Concert Band, "Titania (Air de Ballet)," Edison No. 9209, w/original box..................**8.00**

Edison Military Band, "School Days," Edison No. 9625, w/original box **12.00**

Edison Symphony Orchestra, "Wiener Blut Waltz," Edison No. 633, original box **20.00**

Harlan & Stanley, "Two Rubes And The Tramp Fiddler," Edison No. 8988, w/original box **20.00**

Harry Spencer, "Stump Speech On Love," Columbia No. 10501, moulded brown wax, original box (1% mold) **22.00**

Invincible Quartette, "Laughin Medley," Edison No. 8504, w/original box..................**8.00**

James White, "Casey At The Telephone," Edison No. 8069, w/original box..................**17.00**

Jones & Murray, "Smile, Smile, Smile," Albany Indestructible No. 681, w/original Columbia box **14.00**

William Howard Taft, "Unlawful Trusts," Edison No. 10,000, w/original box..................**200.00**

William Jennings Bryan, "Imperialism," Edison No. 9920, w/original box..................**127.00**

William Jennings Bryan, "The Trust Question," Edison No. 9917, w/original box..................**187.00**

THREE MINUTE CYLINDERS
Albert Campbell, "'Neath The Old Acorn Tree, Sweet Estelle," Columbia 20th Century No. 85158, w/original box, 6" l, (3" hairline)........**166.00**

Billy Murray, "Sweethearts In Every Town," Columbia 20th Century No. 85028, w/original box, 6" l. (small pits) **221.00**

Henry Burr, "Face To Face," Columbia 20th Century No. 85138, w/original box, 6" l. (medium mold, pits) **130.00**

Prince's Military Band, "Yankee Land," Columbia 20th Century No. 85008, w/original box, 6" l. (few small pits)..................**166.00**

FOUR MINUTE CYLINDERS
American Symphony Orchestra, "Popular Songs of 1908," Edison No. 74, w/original box **18.00**

Anthony & Chapman, "For Your Bright Eyes," Albany Indestructible No. 3091, original Oxford box **7.00**

Bob Roberts, "I Want To Sing In Opera," U.S. Everlasting No. 1213, no box **16.00**

Cal Stewart, "Uncle Josh and Aunt Nancy's Courtship," U.S. Everlasting No. 1346, Lakeside, no box **19.00**

Cal Stewart, "Uncle Jose Keeps House," Edison No. 75, w/original box **5.00**

Edgar Davenport, "Lasca," Edison No. 296, w/original box & lid **4.00**

Edison Comic Opera Company, "Favorite Airs from 'Mikado,'" Edison No. 465, w/original box **17.00**

Ester Ferrabini, "Cavalleria Rusticana, Voi lo sapete," Edison Wax Operatic No. B-180, w/original box **61.00**

Frank Coombs, "Do They Think Of Me At Home," U.S. Everlasting No. 1135, Lakeside, no box **6.00**

Golden & Hughes, "My Uncle's Farm," U.S. Everlasting No. 1137, Lakeside w/original box & lid **10.00**

Henry Burr, "Star of Bethlehem," U.S. Everlasting No. 1021, no box.....**10.00**

Jose Ramirez, "La Madrilena Danze," U.S. Everlasting No. 21808, no box...**48.00**

Karl Jorn, "Lohengrin, Abschied," Edison Wax Operatic No. 40025, original box w/lid..................**56.00**

Leo Slezak, "La Boheme, Wie eiskalt is das handchen," Edison Wax Operatic No. B-158, original box w/lid..................**110.00**

Lucrezia Bori, "Boheme, Mi chiamano Mimi," Edison Wax Operatic No. 40039, w/original box & lid..................**85.00**

Peerless Quartette, "My Old Kentucky Home," U.S. Everlasting No. 1077, Lakeside, no box **7.00**

Sousa's Band, "Elfentanz, Concert

Valse," Edison No. 656, w/original
box & lid **9.00**
Spencer & Jones, "Ludwig's
Aircastle," Albany Indestructible
No. 3048, no box **4.00**
U.S. Symphony Orchestra,
"Cavalleria Rusticana," U.S.
Everlasting No. 1028, no box..............**6.00**

78 RPM DISC RECORDS

BLUES 78 RPMs
Big Bill, "I Want You By My Side -
Sweetheart Land," Vocalion (blue
label) No. 04041 ....**9.00**
Big Bill, "Keep Your Hands Off Her -
Sun Gonna Shine In My Door Some
Day," Bluebird No. B-6188.................**20.00**
Black Ivory King, "Working For The
PWA - The Flying Crow," Decca
(sunburst label) No. 7307 ....**52.00**
Blind Boy Fuller, "Big Leg Woman
Gets My Pay - I Want Some of Your
Pie," Columbia No. 37683 (small
lamination crack) **9.00**
Blind Boy Fuller, "Snake Woman
Blues - New Louise Louise Blues,"
Melotone No. 7-11-58 ....**40.00**
Bumble Bee Slim, "New Mean
Mistreater Blues - Rough Road
Blues," Vocalion (gold label)
No. 02829 ....**29.00**
Bumble Bee Slim, "When The Sun
Goes Down - I Done Lost My Baby,"
Vocalion No. 03054 ....**6.00**
Charlie Jackson, "Salt Lake City
Blues - Salty Dog Blues,"
Paramount No. 12236........................**18.00**
Clara Smith, "Low Land Moan -
Woman To Woman," Columbia
No. 14580-D **26.00**
Coley Jones, "The Elder's He's My
Man - Drunkard's Special,"
Columbia No. 14489-D **24.00**
Hokum Boys, "Nancy Jane - I'm
Gonna Tell My Mama On You,"
Vocalion No. 03265 ....**36.00**
Kokomo Arnold, "Your Ways And
Actions - Midnight Blues," Decca
No. 7510 ....**30.00**
Lil Johnson, "That Bonus Done
Gone Thru - Take It Easy Greasy,"
Melotone No. 6-05-52 ....**19.00**
Little Brother, "Never Go Wrong
Blues - Tampa Red: Someday I'm
Bound To Win," Bluebird (buff label)
No. B-6825 (light writing on label)......**55.00**
Mary Dixon, "Black Dog Blues - Fire
and Thunder Blues," Columbia
No. 14459-D (light scratches) **33.00**
Minnie Wallace & Her Night Hawks,
"Field Mouse Stomp - The
Cockeyed World," Vocalion
No. 03106 (ILLUS. top next
column) **350.00**

"Field Mouse Stomp" Record Label

Pinetop & Lindberg, "East Chicago
Blues - Farish Street Jive," Bluebird
No. B-10177...**7.00**
Red Nelson, "Empty Bed Blues -
What A Time I'm Havin'," Decca
(sunburst label) No. 7185 (grainy) **23.00**
Sara Martin w/Clarence Williams on
piano, "Numbers On The Brain -
Shipwrecked Blues," Okeh
No. 8412 ....**75.00**
State Street Boys, "Don't Tear My
Clothes - She Caught The Train,"
Vocalion No. 03002 ....**38.00**
Tampa Red & the Chicago Five, "My
Za Zu Girl - If It Wasn't For You,"
Bluebird (buff label) No. B-6787 ....**9.00**
Teddy "Big Boy" Edwards, "W.P.A.
Blues - Louisiana," Decca (sunburst
label) No. 7184 ....**22.00**
Wee Bea Booze, "These Young Men
Blues - So Good," Decca No. 8658
(bubbles)..**4.00**

CHILDREN'S 78 RPM RECORDS
Frankie Laine, "Robin Hood -
Champion, The Wonder Horse,"
Columbia No. J-275, original sleeve,
10" d..**7.00**
Frank Luther, "Raggedy Ann's Songs
- Part 1 & 2," Victor Scroll No. 218,
7" d. (small needle drop)....................**8.00**
Frank Luther, "Raggedy Ann's
Songs, Part 5 & 6," Victor Scroll
No. 220, 7" d.......................................**5.00**
Frank Luther, "Winnie the Pooh,
Christopher Robin Songs," RCA
No. 221-223, 7" d., set of 3 ....**24.00**
Gene Autry, "Rudolph, The Red-
Nosed Reindeer - If It Doesn't Snow
On Christmas," Columbia No.
38610, nice Christmas sleeve,
10" d..**8.00**
Jimmy Blaine, "Hi-Diddle-Dee-Dee,
An Actor's Life For Me - The Little
Tin Soldier and The Little Toy

Drum," Peter Pan No. 527, original
sleeve, 10" d. **4.00**

Jolly Good Scouts' Quartette, "Sing
Another Song - Bow Wow!," Official
Boy Scout Record #2, label
w/Scouts doing semaphore, 10" d. **20.00**

Mel Blanc, "I Taut I Taw A Puddy Tat
- Yosemite Sam," Capitol No. CAS-
3104, nice original picture sleeve,
10" d..**8.00**

Pennsylvania Railroad, "Call on the
Flag Leaving Crestline -
Pennsylvania's Broadway Limited:
At Union Station," Senco No. 297,
10" d...**17.00**

Red Raven Orchestra, "Rudolph,
The Red-Nosed Reindeer - Frosty
The Snowman," Red Raven No.
M-17/18, red wax, 8" d. (label &
record scratches) **20.00**

Red Raven Orchestra, "Sidewalks of
New York - Bicycle Built For Two,"
Red Raven No. M-7/8, yellow &
black swirled wax, 8" d......................**18.00**

CLASSICAL & OPERATIC 78 RPMS

Brunswick Records

Edith Mason, "Oh For The Wings of a
Dove - Serenade (Tosti)," No.
10243, 10" d. (graininess,
light scuffs)...**62.00**

Nina Koshetz, "Eastern Romance -
Humoresque," No. 10138, 10" d. **121.00**

Renate Muller, "An der Donau, Wenn
der Wein Bluht - Wenn der Lanner
Spielt einen Walzer," No. 53050,
10" d. (light scuffs) **3.00**

Toronto Mendelssohn Choir,
"Adoremus Te - Exultate Deo," No.
3248, 10" d. (light graininess,
very light scuffs) **11.00**

Walter Fischer (organ), "Organ
Concerto No. 4, Op. 4 (Handel),"
No. 25023-25, two records, 12" d.
(light graininess) **6.00**

Columbia Records

Amelia Karola, "Manon, Guizzar
vid'io - Ancor son jo," Magic Notes
label No. A1644, 10" d. **24.00**

Arcangelo Rossi, "Il Barbiere di
Seiglia, Aria Bartolo - Gina
Ciaparelli: Semiramida, Bel raggio
lusinghier," Magic Notes label
No. A535, 10" d. (grainy) **22.00**

Bernice de Pasquali, "Linda di
Chamounix - O luce di quest'anima,"
Banner label No. 30880, 12" d...........**11.00**

Charles Hackett, "Dear Old Pal of
Mine," Banner label No. 79196,"
10" d. (grainy) **6.00**

Ettore Brancaleoni, "La Forza del
Destino - Maledizione," Milano,

Black & Silver label No. 10208,
10" d. (edge flake not to grooves,
lamination crack, needle drop)...........**16.00**

Gerolamo Galbiero, "La Boheme -
Mimi e tanto malata," Milano, Black
& Silver label No. 10220, 10" d. **31.00**

Jeanne Gordon, "Samson and
Delilah, Mon coeur s'ouvre a ta
voix," Banner label No. 49752,
12" d..**9.00**

Marcel Journet, "Le Chalet," Black &
Silver label No. 3136, 10" d. **16.00**

Toscha Siedel (violin), "Orientale
(Cui)," Banner label No. 78138,
10" d..**8.00**

Walter Wheatley, "Maritana, Yes! Let
me like a soldier fall - There is a
flower that bloometh," Banner label
No. A1422, 10" d. (light graniness) **19.00**

Gramophone Company Records

Agustarello Affre, "Parais a ta
Fenetre (Grieg)," Paris,
Gramophone & Typewriter Co.
Black label No. GC-2-32686 (Fr),
10" d..**16.00**

Alf. Grunfeld (piano),
"Fruhlingsstimmen (Straus),"
Vienna, Gramophone & Typewriter
Co. Black label No. 045503, 12" d. **22.00**

Enrico Caruso, "Carmen, Romance
de la fleur," pre-dog Pink label
No.052087, 12" d. (hairline crack) **24.00**

Enrico Caruso, "Mefistofele - Giunto
sul passo estremo," Milan, stamper
II, Gramophone & Typewriter Co.
Red label No. GC-52347," 10" d.
(very small crack)..............................**103.00**

Enrico Caruso, "Pagliacci, Vesti la
giubba," Milan, Gramophone &
Typewriter Co. Red label No. GC-
52440," 10" d. **40.00**

Fernando De Lucia, "Rigoletto, La
donna e mobile," Milan,
Gramophome & Typewriter Co.
Red label No. GC-52411, 10" d. **132.00**

Gualtiero Pagnoni, "Rigoletto, Deh!
non parlar al misero," Milan,
Gramophone & Typewriter Co.
Black label No. GC-52395, 10" d. **19.00**

Jan Kubelik (violin), "Last Movement
from 'Carmen,'" London,
Gramophone & Typewriter Co.
Black label No. GC-7968, 10" d. **58.00**

Nellie Melba, "Rigoletto, Caro nome,"
London, Gramophone & Typewriter
Co. Mauve label No. 03025, Melba
label, 12" d. (hairline crack, needle
drop repeats) **28.00**

Pathe Records

Ellen Gulbranson, "Thannhauser,
Elisabeth halsing - Traume,"
No. 90290, 11¾" d. **184.00**

Emma Calve, "Carmen, L'amour est enfant de Boheme - Air des cartes," No. 0273, 11¾" d. **26.00**

Henri Albani, "Aida, O celeste Aida - Rigoletto, Comme la plume au vent," No. 10, 11¾" d. **13.00**

Henri Albers, "La Chanson des Sonneux (Delabre) - Marie Boyer: Les Vieilles de Chez Nous (Levade)," No. 241, 10¾" d. **14.00**

Hippolyte Belhomme, "The Barber of Seville, Air de la calomnie - Le Domino Noir, Deo gratias," No. 26006, 10¾" d. **17.00**

Olga Carrara, "La Boheme, Mi chiamano Mimi - Grand Opera Sextet of Milan: Lucia, Chi mi frena," No. 40184, 11¾" d. **10.00**

Robert Lassalle, "La Favorite, Me voici donc pres d'elle - Lapeyrette, Lassalle, Albers & Poumayrac: De son sort…," No. 1561, 11¾" d. **10.00**

Rudolph Ganz (piano), "Sweddish Wedding March No. 1 (Soderman) - La Fileuse (Raff)," No. 27015, 10¾" d...**47.00**

Yvonne Gall, "William Tell, Sombre foret - Aida, Ritorna vincitor," No. 60081, 11¾" d. **10.00**

Victor Records

Adelina Patti, "Home Sweet Home," Deluxe Red Seal No. 95029, original 'Patti' label, 12" d. **35.00**

Andres Segovia (guitar), "Tremolo Study (Tarrega) - Fandanguillo (Turina)," Scroll Red Seal No. 6767, 12" d. (very light graniness) **20.00**

Bernachi, Colazza & Caronna, "Trovatore, Di beloso amor sprezzato (Act 1, No.4)," Black label Import No. 61156, 10" d.......................**8.00**

Edmond Clement, "Bergere Legere & L'adieu Matin," Patents Red Seal No. 64223, 10" d. (lightly grainy, writing on label)....................................**6.00**

Ellen Beach Yaw, "Lakme, On va la jeune Hindoue," Grand Prize Red Seal No. 74090, 12" d. (small bubble, light scuffs)..........................**20.00**

Emma Eames, "Love In May & I Once Had A Sweet Little Doll, Dears," Grand Prize Red Seal No. 88131, 12" d. (bubble)................**28.00**

Emma Juch, "Serenata (Tosti)," Grand Prize Red Seal No. 74015, 12" d...**67.00**

Emmy Destinn, "Magic Flute - Pamina's Air," Bat Wing Red Seal No. 88510, 12" d. **11.00**

Enrico Caruso, "Giocondo, Cielo e mar," Grand Prize Red Seal No. 85055, 12" d. **23.00**

Enrico Caruso, "La Favorita - Spirito gentil," Grand Prize Red Seal No. 88004, 12" d. (small scratches) ...**11.00**

Enrico Caruso, "La Mia Canzone (Paoli-Tosti)," Monarch Red Seal No. 5011, 10" d. **52.00**

Enrico Caruso, "Largo (Handel)," Bat Wing Red Seal No. 88617, 12" d. **11.00**

Enrico Caruso, "Requiem Mass - Ingemisco," Bat Wing Red Seal No. 88514, 12" d. **18.00**

Enrico Caruso, "Rigoletto - La donna e mobile," Patents Red Seal No. 87017, 10" d. (faded label) **9.00**

Enrico Caruso, "Tosca - E lucevan le stelle," Patents Red Seal No. 87044, 10" d. (writing on label) **10.00**

Ernestine Schumann-Heink, "Love's Lottery - Sweet Thoughts of Home," Grand Prize Red Seal No. 85092, 12" d. (small bubbles) **18.00**

Ernestine Schumann-Heink, "The Rosary (Nevin)," Grand Prize Red Seal No. 88108," 12" d. (label crack) ...**7.00**

Evan Williams, "Elixir of Love - A furtive tear," Patents Red Seal No. 74150, 12" d. (small needle drop) **14.00**

Ezio Pinza, "Vespri Siciliani - O tu Palermo - Don Carlos - Dormiro sol nel manto," Scroll Red Seal No. 6709, 12" d. (grainy) **9.00**

Farrar & Homer, "Madama Butterfly - Duet of the Flowers," Grand Prize Red Seal No. 89008, 12" d. (hairline crack, grainy) **26.00**

Fernando de Lucia, "Manon, Il sogno," Monarch Red Seal No. 91020, 10" d. **27.00**

Frances Alda, "Carmen - Micaela's Air," Bat Wing Red Seal No. 74353, 12" d...**12.00**

George Hamlin, "Lolita - Spanish Serenade," Patents Red Seal No. 74248, 12" d. **6.00**

Giacomelli, Mileri & Martinez-Patti, "Il Trovatore, Ha quest infame (Act 4, No. 20)," Black label Import No. 71031 (cracks) **6.00**

Giuseppina Huguet, "Huguenots - O vag suol della Turenna - Giacomelli & Martinez-Patti: Dillo ancor," Patents Black label Import No. 35123, 12" d. (hairline crack) **11.00**

Giuseppina Huguet, "Mignon - Polonese," Grand Prize Black label Import No. 58338, 12" d. **26.00**

Gluck & Zimbalist, "Elegie," Patents Red Seal No. 87101, 10" d. (small scratch, writing on label) **7.00**

Jan Kubelik (violin), "Serenade (Drdla)," Monarch Red Seal No. 91024, 10" d. **28.00**

Jascha Heifetz (violin), "Gypsy Airs No. 1 & 2 (Sarasate)," Bat Wing Red Seal No. 6153, 12" d. **10.00**

Johanna Gadski, "Stabat Mater - Inflamatus," Grand Prize Red Seal No. 88059, 12" d. **17.00**

Josef Hollman (violon cello solo), "Serenade (Blockx)," Grand Prize Red Seal No. 74045, 12" d. **12.00**

La Scala Chorus, "Ernani - beviam - de Angelis & Cigada: Da quel di che t'ho veduta," Patents Black label Import No. 35168, 12" d. **14.00**

Lawrence Tiffett, "Pagliacci - Prologue, Part 1 & 2," Scroll Red Seal No. 6587," 12" d..........................**4.00**

Leo Slezak, "Der Lenz (Hildach)," Patents Red Seal No. 64111, 10" d. (writing on label) **5.00**

Lina Mileri, "Il Trovatore, Condotta ell'era in ceppi (Act 2, No.7)," Black label Import No. 71030, 12" d. (one inch crack) **11.00**

Linda Brambilla, "Pescatore di Brahma, gran Dio," Patents Red Seal No. 58301, black label, 12" d. (bubble).....................................**7.00**

Madame Michailowa, "Serenade (Gounod), "Monarch Red Seal No. 91037 ....**22.00**

Marcel Journet, "Favorita - Splendon piu belle in ciel le stelle," Patents Red Seal No. 74273, 12" d. (small needle drop)..**4.00**

Maud Powell (violin), "St. Patrick's Day," Deluxe Red Seal No. 85039, 12" d. (small bubble) **30.00**

M. Battistini, "Tannhauser, Aria Delia Stella," Monarch Red Seal No. 5119, 10" d..**66.00**

Mischa Elman (violin solo), "Gavotte (Bohm)," Patents Red Seal No. 61184, 10" d. **10.00**

Mischa Elman (violin), "Humoresque (Dvorak)," Bat Wing Red Seal No. 74163, 12" d. **3.00**

Mme. A. Michailowa, "Lucia di Lammermoor, Mad Scene," Black label Imports No. 61129, 10" d. **6.00**

Nellie Melba, "Old Folks At Home," Monarch Red Seal No. 94005, cream-colored Melba label, 10" d. **39.00**

Nielson & Constantino, "Traviata - Parigi o cara," Bat Wing Red Seal No. 74075, 12" d. **10.00**

Pol Plancon, "Damnation de Faust - Voici des roses," Grand Prize Red Seal No. 85117, 12" d. (small bubbles, scratches)..........................**18.00**

Van Hoose, de Gogorza & Journet, "Faust - Le duel," Patents Red Seal No. 74004, 12" d. **11.00**

COUNTRY & COUNTRY WESTERN
78 RPMs

Allen Brothers, "Ain't That Skippin' and Flyin' - Cheat' Em," Columbia No. 15270-D **56.00**

Arthur Tanner, "Gather The Flowers - Tanner & Pucket: Bring Back My Blue-Eyed Boy," Columbia No. 15577-D **41.00**

Bill Boyd & His Cowboy Ramblers, "Ain't She Coming Out Tonight? - You Shall Be Free, Monah," Bluebird (buff label) No. B-6694 ....**9.00**

Bud Billings (Trio), "Red River Valley - Little Cabin In The Cascade Mountains," Victor Scroll label No. V-40267....................................**20.00**

Carter Family, "Lulu Wall - Sweet Fern," Victor Scroll label No. V-40126....................................**41.00**

Carter Family, "Railroading On The Great Divide - Little Moses," Acme No. 992 ....**17.00**

Carter Family, "River of Jordan - Keep On The Sunny Side," Victor label No. 21434..................................**11.00**

Carter Family, "Ship Ahoy - Hill, Lone and Grey," Acme No. 999 (scratches,scuffs)........................**8.00**

Dock Walsh, "I'm Free At Last - The East Bound Train," Columbia No. 15047-D **4.00**

Frank Hutchinson, "Lightning Express - All Night Long," Okeh No. 45144 ....**19.00**

Frankie Marvin, "Dust Pan Blues - Miss Moonshine," Columbia No. 15518-D **3.00**

Gene Autry, "Ride Tenderfoot Ride - The Old Trail," Conqueror No. 9058 ..**11.00**

Holland Pucket, "Little Bessie - The Old College Home," Supertone No. 9324 ....**4.00**

Jimmie Rodgers, "Blue Yodel - Away Out On The Mountain," Bluebird (buff label) No. B-5085..............**10.00**

Jimmie Rodgers, "Blue Yodel - Away Out On The Mountain," Montegomery Ward No. M-3272 (small bubble side 1) **28.00**

Jimmie Rodgers, "For The Sake of Days Gone By - A Drunkard's Child," Montgomery Ward No. M-4221 ....**121.00**

Jimmie Rodgers, "Mother, The Queen of My Heart - Miss The Mississippi and You," Montgomery Ward No. M-4206 ....**66.00**

Jimmie Rodgers, "Roll Along Kentucky Moon - Why Should I Be Lonely?," Bluebird (buff label) No. B-5082 (crack) **4.00**

Jimmie Rodgers, "Sweet Mama

Hurry Home or I'll Be Gone - Blue Yodel No. 11," Montgomery Ward No. M-4726 ....**173.00**

Jimmie Rodgers w/The Carter Family, "The Carter Family Visits Jimmie Rodgers - The Wonderful City," Montgomery Ward No. M-7137 ....**72.00**

Leake County Revelers, "In The Good Old Summertime - My Bonnie Lies Over The Ocean," Columbia No. 15227-D **7.00**

Oscar Harper & Doc, "Terrell Texas Blues - Dallas Bound," Okeh No. 45420 ....**77.00**

Pete Wiggins, "A Gay Caballero - Barnacle Bill The Sailor," Okeh No. 45295 ....**7.00**

Riley Puckett, "It's Simple To Flirt - Wish I Was Single Again," Columbia No. 15036-D **4.00**

Sanders Terry (harmonica), "Train Whistle Blues - New Love Blues," Columbia No. 417-M.........................**23.00**

Sunshine Four, "Beautiful Land - In My Heart," Columbia No. 15119-D **3.00**

Vel Veteran, "Common Bill - Merrymakers: Button Buster," Broadway No. 8223 ....**41.00**

Vernon Dalhart, "Who Said I Was A Bum? - Wanderin'," Columbia No. 1585-D **4.00**

EARLY BERLINER 78 RPMs
A.P. Stengler (clarionet), "Clog Dance," Oct. 11, 1898, No. 302 ....**62.00**

Banjo duet, "Twin Star March," Washington, D.C., Dec. 24, 1897, No. 496-W..**51.00**

Charles P. Lowe (xylophone), "The Mocking Bird," New York, Oct. 12, 1897, No. 3259 ....**46.00**

Ferruccio Giannini, "Trovatore- Miserere," No. 930-Y **138.00**

George Graham, "Talk On Money," Sept. 24, 1896, No. 645-Y **77.00**

Graham & Terell, "Minstrel Show," June 1898, No. 6010 ....**37.00**

John Terrell, "The Chimes of Trinity," Aug. 1898, No. 1699-Z **26.00**

Jos. Cullen (banjo), "Marriage Bells," Oct 1898, No. 473-X **56.00**

J. Yorke Atlee, "Laughing Song," Oct. 1, 1898, No. 404-XX.................**95.00**

Mr. Knoll & Miss McNeil (cornet duet), "My Coal Black Lady," New York, No. 3647 ....**32.00**

Sousa's Band, "Selection from 'Robin Hood,'" Zono hole, No. 131-Z..**36.00**

Trumpet Quartette, "Lutzow's Charge from 'The Fortune Teller,'" Zono hole, No. 844 ....**26.00**

EARLY COLUMBIA 78 RPMs
Bert Williams, "Nobody from 'Abyssinia,'" No. 3423, Conditions label, 10" d. (light warp, needle drop, grainy).....................................**11.00**

Bert Williams, "Play That Barber Shop Chord - Something You Don't Expect," No. A929, Magic Notes label, 10" d. (scratches) **6.00**

Billy Murray, "Teasing," No. 3043, Conditions label, 7" d. (needle drop repeats)...**4.00**

Billy Williams, "Giving A Donkey A Strawberry - Mr. John Mackenzie, O," No. A1787, Magic Notes label, 10" d...**4.00**

Bob Roberts, "The Poo Bah of Blackville Town," No. 1147, Conditions label, 10" d. **23.00**

Cal Stewart, "I'm Old, But I'm Awfully Tough," No. 22, Ring label, 10" d.........**3.00**

Collins & Harlan, "Under The Bamboo Tree," No. 970, Conditions label, 7" d. (needle drop repeats).........**9.00**

Columbia Band, "Tell Me Pretty Maiden," No. 82, Conditions label, 7" d..**7.00**

Columbia Band, "The Watch On The Rhine," No. 354, Columbia Fleur-de-lis label, 10" d....................................**3.00**

Columbia Orchestra, "March 'Soko' (A Moorish Intermezzo)," No. 1755, Conditions label, 10" d. **3.00**

George Alexander, "Holy, Holy, Holy Lord God Almighty - Anthony & Harrison: Looking This Way," No. A5035, Magic Notes label, 12" d. (grainy). **3.00**

Golden & Hughes, "Unlucky Mose - I'se Gwine Back to Arkansaw," No. A5578, Magic Notes label, 12" d. (grainy) **6.00**

Hager's Orchestra, "Susie, from 'The Girl from Up There,'" No. 279, Gold & Black Climax label, 7" d. (grommet, label applied on top of embossed label information)..............**10.00**

Harry Macdonough, "I've A Longing In My Heart For You, Louise," No. 226, Victor Talking Machine (VTM) stamp, Ring label, 7" d...........**14.00**

Harry Macdonough, "The New Born King," Gold & Black Climax label, 7" d. (grommet)..................................**13.00**

Henry Burr, "For All Eternity," No. 412, No Ring label, 7" d. **13.00**

Jules Levy (cornet), "Alice, Where Art Thou?," No. 918, Ring label, 10" d. (one inch crack) **30.00**

Jules Levy (cornet), "Robin Adair," No. 919, Conditions label, 10" d. (small bubbles) **67.00**

J.W. Myers, "Come Take A Trip In My

Airship," No. 3034, Conditions label,
7" d...**9.00**

J.W.Myers, "I'll Be With You When
The Hawthorn Blooms Again," No.
726, Ring label, 10" d. (internal
hairline, light warp)..............................**3.00**

J.W. Myers, "In The Shade of The
Palm from 'Florodora,'" No. 402,
Ring label, 7" d................................**33.00**

Len Spencer, "Making the Fiddle Talk
- Collins & Harlan: Alabam,"
No. A650, Magic Notes label,
10" d...**11.00**

**Len Spencer & Prince's Military
Band,** Roosevelt's Inaugural
Parade," No. 3198, Conditions label,
10" d...**7.00**

Margaret Keyes, "Angel's Serenade -
Ever of Thee," No. A5244, Magic
Notes label, 12" d. (grainy) **6.00**

Minstrels, "Old Folks At Home,"
No. 804, Ring label, 7" d.
(grommet) **16.00**

Miss Vivienne, "Madame Butterfly -
One Fine Day - Miss Vivienne & Mr.
Stiles: Love Duet," Magic Notes
label, 12" d. (scratches) **9.00**

Mr. & Mrs. Cal Stewart, "Christmas
Time At Pumpkin Center - Mixed
Quartette: Home Sweet Home,"
No. A387, Magic Notes label,
10" d...**23.00**

Orquestra Mexicana de Curti,
"Marcha de Cadiz," No. 5386,
Columbia Fleur-de-lis label, 10" d.
(blisters) **3.00**

R.H. Burnside, "A New York
Hippodrome Rehearsal - Porter,
Jones & Harlan: The Band Festival
at Plum Center," No. A2057, Magic
Notes label, 10" d................................**7.00**

Stanley & Harlan, "A Scene In A
Country Store," No. 1558, Grand
Prize label, 10" d.................................**5.00**

Steve Porter, "Mrs. Reilly's Troubles
With The Dumb-Waiter," No. 3472,
Grand Prize label, 10" d. (internal
lamination crack)................................**6.00**

Vess Ossman (banjo), "Anona,"
No. 1619, Conditions label, 7" d.
(hairline crack) **3.00**

Will C. Pepper (banjo), "Dinky's
Patrol," No. 25732, Conditions label,
10" d...**4.00**

EARLY VERTICAL 78 RPM RECORDINGS

Pathe 78 RPMs

Alan Turner, "The Irish Emigrant -
The Distant Shore," No. 5175,
Etched label, center start, 11½" d........**9.00**

Carrie Herwin, "Guide Me To The
Light - Lead, Kindly Light," No. 5432,
Etched label, center start, 11½" d........**6.00**

Collins & Harlan, "On The Ozark
Trail - Premier American Male
Quartet: Chong," No. 22113,
10½" d...**6.00**

David Irwin, "America, Here's My Boy
- Lewis Piotti: The Man Behind The
Hammer And The Plow," No. 20187,
10½" d...**7.00**

Eubie Blake Trio, "American Jubilee
- Hungarian Rag," No. 20326,"
10½" d. (small scratch on side 2).......**26.00**

George Jessel, "Dolls - Marcelle,"
No. 22418, 10" d. (edge chipping not
to grooves) **6.00**

Golden & Marlowe, "Two New Coons
in Town - By, By, Ma' Honey," No.
29136, 11½" d. (light scratches
on side 2) **11.00**

Imperial Symphony Orchestra,
"Passing of Salome - The Monk and
The Woman," No. 5228, Etched
label, center start, 11½" d. **10.00**

Imperial Symphony Orchestra,
"Tres Doggy - Secrets," No. 30044,
11½" d...**3.00**

Isabelle Patricola, "I Ain't Gonna Be
Nobody's Fool - When Francis
Dances With Me," No. 20639, 10" d.
(small bubble) **7.00**

Jack Norworth, "Ten Little
Bridesmaids - I Stopped And I
Looked And I Listened," No. 29208,
11½" d...**19.00**

Jules Levy Jr.'s Brass Quartet,
"Ben Bolt - In The Gloaming,"
No. 20548, 10" d. (small label tears)....**3.00**

**Lavina Turner & Jas. P. Johnson's
Harmony Seven,** "He Took It Away
From Me - If I Were Your Daddy,"
No. 20627, 10" d. **28.00**

**Lt. Jim Europe's 369th U.S. Infantry
Band,** "Russian Rag - St. Louis
Blues," No. 22087, 10½" d.................**28.00**

Noble Sissle's Southland Singers,
"Hallelujah To The Lamb - Steal
Away To Jesus," No. 20483, 10" d.
(very small label tear) **61.00**

Pathe Dance Orchestra, "You're
Here And I'm Here - Leg of Mutton,"
No. B5029, Etched label, center
start, 11½" d..**8.00**

Pathe Orchestra, "Joaquina,
Argentine Tango - El Choclo,
Argentine Tango," No. 5499, Etched
label, center start, 11½" d. **13.00**

Peerless Quartette, "Are You From
Dixie? - Collins & Harlan: Honey
Bunch," No. 30381, 11½" d...............**10.00**

Rube Goldberg, "Father Was Right -
Billy Williams : Blame It On Poor
Old Father," No. 20279, only
recording by Goldberg, 10½" d.
(ILLUS. top next page)....................**110.00**

Unique Rube Goldberg Record Label

Russell Hunting, "Casey's Fight With Oney Goeghen - The Bureau," No. 35083, 11½" d. **4.00**

Sergeant Leggett (cornet), "Nearer My God To Thee - Somewhere A Voice Is Calling," No. 30014, 11½" d. **3.00**

Thomas Malin (banjo), "Comical Coons - Billy Whitlock (bells): Scotch Hot," No. 22136, 10½" d. **9.00**

Thomas Malin (banjo), "The Darkies' Dream - John Pidoux: A Plantation Episode," No. 22055, 10½" d. **9.00**

Sergeant Leggett (cornet), "The Rosary - Good-Bye," No. 10012, 10½" d. **6.00**

Tuxedo Syncopaters, "Linger Longer Letty - In And Out," No. 22308, 10" d. **4.00**

Van Eps Banjo Orchestra, "Queen of the Movies - All Aboard For Dixieland," No. 29045, 11½" d. **7.00**

Willie Weston, "Over There - Irving Kauffman: Never Forget To Write Home," No. 20225, 10½" d. (light label needle run) **6.00**

EARLY VICTOR 78 RPMs
American Band of Providence, "Messiah - Hallelujah Chorus," No. 1670, later dog label, 7" d. **11.00**

American Quartet, "Dancing On The Old Barn Floor," No. A-911, Improved pre-dog label, 7" d..............**8.00**

Arthur Collins, "Every Race Has A Flag But The Coon," No. 538, later dog label, 7" d. **25.00**

Arthur Collins, "Helen Gonne," No. 1632, Monarch label, 10" d **6.00**

Billy Murray, "Robinson Crusoe's Isle," No. 4547, Grand Prize label, 10" d. **6.00**

Bob Roberts, "You're Always Behind Like An Old Cow's Tail," No. 2917,

later dog label, 7" d. (heavy scratch) **10.00**

Cal Stewart, "Uncle Josh and The Lightning Rod Agent," No. 667 , later dog label, 7" d. (sticker on label, internal cracks) **9.00**

Cal Stewart, "Uncle Josh's Trip to Coney Island," No. 664, Grand Prize label, 8" d. **27.00**

Charles P. Lowe & Miss Jottie, "Vaudeville Specialty," No. 963, early dog Victor label, 7"d. **15.00**

Collins & Harlan, "The Dude and The Farmer," No. 2116, later dog label, 7" d...**9.00**

Dan W. Quinn, "Bill Bailey, Won't You Please Come Home," No. 1411, early dog Victor label, 7" d. **17.00**

Dan Quinn, "R-E-M-O-R-S-E from 'The Sultan of Sulu,'" No. 2194, Monarch label, 10" d. **17.00**

Edith Elena, "Laughing Song," No. 4283, Grand Prize label, 10" d. **11.00**

Evening with the Minstrels, No. 6, "The Cakewalk in Coontown," No. 31132, Deluxe label, 12" d. **13.00**

Georgia Minstrels, "Minstrel 1st Part, No. 3," No. A-508, Victor pre-dog label, 7" d...**16.00**

Harry Lauder, "Mary of Argyle - Auld Scotch Sangs," No. 45256, Blue Bat Wing label, 12" d. (small label tear) **3.00**

Harry Macdonough, "Sweet Annie Moore," No. 3314, Eldridge Johnson pre-dog label, 10" d...........................**16.00**

Harry Macdonough, "While The Band Is Playing Dixie," No. A-654, Victor Pre-dog label, 7" d. **10.00**

Haydn Quartet, "A Night Trip to Buffalo," No. 43, Grand Prize label, 10" d...**9.00**

Haydn Quartet, "A Sleighride Party," No. 3088, Eldridge Johnson pre-dog label, 10" d. **33.00**

Haydn Quartet, "Carry Me Back to Old Virginny," No. 656, Grand Prize label, 8" d. **14.00**

Haydn Quartet, "Old Uncle Ned," No. 1259, early dog Victor Monarch label, 7" d. **17.00**

Haydn Quartet, "'Round the Campfire," No. 4046, Monarch label, 10" d...**7.00**

John J. Kimmel (accordian), "Medley of Irish Jigs," Grand Prize label, 8" d. **15.00**

Joseph Natus, "I Wonder If It's Springtime," No. 1113, Victor Monarch pre-dog label, 7" d..............**19.00**

Jules Levy (cornet), "The Blue Bells of Scotland," No. 1059, Victor pre-dog label, 10" d. (light needle run) ...**193.00**

J.W. Myers, "Bashful Betsy Brown,"

No. 1234, early dog Victor Monarch label, 7" d. **10.00**

J.W. Myers, "Minnie Ha-Ha," No. 1147, later dog label, incorrect label, 7" d. **9.00**

Nazzareno Franchi, "Serenata, Mephisto from 'Faust,'" No. A-1003, Improved pre-dog label, 7" d. **7.00**

Reinald Werrenrath, "Pagliacci, Prologue - Carmen, Chanson du toreador," No. 55068, Blue Bat Wing label, 12" d. (small label needle run)....**8.00**

Richard Jose, "Belle Brandon," No. 2554, Monarch label, 10" d. **7.00**

Richard Jose, "She Fought By His Side," No. 31345, Deluxe label, 12" d...**17.00**

S.H. Dudley, "Parody on 'The Soldiers In The Park,'" No. A-198, Improved pre-dog label, 7" d.............**56.00**

S.H. Dudley, "Yuba Dam," No. A-36, Victor Monarch pre-dog label, 7" d. ...**24.00**

Silas Leachman, "Turkey In De Straw," No. A-804, Victor pre-dog label, 7" d. **17.00**

Sousa's Band, "Chopin's Waltz," No. A-317, Victor pre-dog label, 7" d........**22.00**

Sousa's Band, "Hands Across The Sea," No. 300, early dog label, 10" d...**10.00**

Sousa's Band, "Jolly Fellows' Waltz," No. 1174, Victor Monarch pre-dog label, 7" d. **12.00**

Sousa's Band, "King Broadway March," No. 1222, early dog Victor Monarch label, 7" d. **21.00**

Spencer & Girard, "Story for Little Folks - A Trip to The Circus," No. 3461, Eldridge Johnson pre-dog label, 10" d. (needle drop)..................**16.00**

Vess Ossman (banjo), "Finale to William Tell Overature," No. 1293, early dog Victor label, 7" d. **18.00**

Victor Orchestra, "Polly Prim March," No. 4827, Grand Prize label, 8" d. **8.00**

Walter B. Rogers (cornet), "Old Black Joe," No. 2736, Monarch label, 10" d. **11.00**

EARLY MISCELLANEOUS AMERICAN LABELLED 78 RPMs

American Record Company
Arthur Collins, "What's The Matter With The Mail," No. 031077, blue wax, 10¾" d. **26.00**

Billy Heins, "I'Aven't Told 'Im," No. 030556, blue wax, 10¾" d. **26.00**

Billy Murray, "Cheyenne," No. 031317, blue wax, 10¾" d. **26.00**

Collins & Harlan, "My Yankee Irish Girl," No. 031200, blue wax, 10¾" d.(writing on label, needle runs, skips) **4.00**

Collins & Harlan, "Whoa Bill," No. 031082, blue wax, 10¾" d **3.00**

Early Columbia Client Labels
Armanini & Parvis, "Madame Butterfly: Addio, Fiorito Asil," Silvertone No. 11386, 10" d. **7.00**

Bob Roberts, "My Hindoo Man (Coon Song)," Manhattan No. 3296, 10" d. **7.00**

David Bispham, "Faust - Dio possente," Manhattan No. 30037, 12" d. (heavy graininess, faded label) **5.00**

Mme. Jose Grayvill, "The Bird Carol," Manhattan No. 30102, 12" d. (light graniness) **9.00**

Male Quartette, "Down By The Old Mill Stream," Silvertone No. 19410, 10" d...**3.00**

Rosa Linde Wright, "Les Huguenots - Liete signor," Manhattan No. 30031, 12" d. (grainy, label tears **13.00**

William Halley, "Sit Down, You're Rocking The Boat," Silvertone No. 39152, 10" d. **8.00**

Leeds & Catlin Pressings
Collins & Harlan, "It Looks Like A Big Night - Bambazoo," Nassau No. D134, 10" d. **21.00**

Frank C. Stanley, "Afterwards," Oxford No. 16109, 7" d. **9.00**

George J. Gaskin, "Miss Maloney," Concert No. 7636, 10" d. **12.00**

Henry Burr, "Scots Wha Hae," Imperial No. 44572, 10" d. **8.00**

Tenor Solo, "A Good Cigar Is A Smoke," Oxford No. 16141, 7" d........**32.00**

Leeds Embossed Gold Foil Label
Len Spencer Minstrels, "Mother's Watch By The Sea," announced, No. 4066, 10" d. (label scuffs)............**10.00**

Spencer Minstrels, "My Heart Is Yours And Yours Alone," No. 4077, announced, small label, 10" d. **24.00**

Wilson, "The Tragic Tale," No. 4169, announced, 10" d.................................**18.00**

FLEXIBLE 78 RPM RECORDS
Arthur Collins, "Pretty Desdamone," Marconi No. 0306, 10" d. (needle drop repeats) **11.00**

Ben Pollack's Orchestra, "Cryin' For The Carolines," Hit-of-the-Week No. 1027 ....**24.00**

Columbia Band, "Strauss Autograph Waltz," Marconi No. 048, 10" d. (original sleeve somewhat tattered at top)...**11.00**

Dick Robertson's Orchestra, "By The River Sainte Marie," Hit-of-the-Week No. 1149 ....**7.00**

Don Voorhee's Orchestra, "Go Home And Tell Your Mother," Hit-of-the-Week No. 1091 ....**4.00**

Harlem Hot Chocolates, "Sing You Sinners," Hit-of-the-Week No. 1045...**10.00**

Hit-of-the-Week Orchestra, "Across The Breakfast Table," Hit-of-the-Week No. 1071 ....**12.00**

Hotel Pennsylvania Music, "University of Maine Stein Song," Hit-of-the-Week No. 1036 ....**16.00**

Male Vocal Quartette, "Down On The Farm," Marconi No. 0388, 10" d.........**12.00**

Reser's Radio Band, "Sweet Jennie Lee!," Hit-of-the-Week No. 1122........**22.00**

Vincent Lopez Orchesta, "Little White Lies," Hit-of-the-Week No. 1088 ....**3.00**

Vincent Lopez Orchestra, "Springtime In The Rockies," Hit-of-the-Week No. 1050 ....**5.00**

JAZZ & DANCE BAND 78 RPMs

Bunny Berigan, "All Dark People Are Light On Their Feet - Tommy Dorsey: Wanted," Victor Scroll label No. 25557....................................**9.00**

Benny Goodman, "I Gotta Right To Sing The Blues - Ain't Cha' Glad?," Columbia Blue Wax No. 2835-D........**23.00**

Benny Goodman, "Love Me Or Leave Me - Why Couldn't It Be Poor Little Me," Columbia Blue Wax No. 2871-D (scratches)......................**25.00**

Benny Goodman, "Madhouse - The Devil And The Deep Blue Sea," Victor Scroll label No. 25268 ....**8.00**

Benny Goodman, "Tappin' The Barrel - Your Mother's Son-in-Law," Columbia Blue Wax No. 2856-D........**47.00**

Benny Goodman, "The Dixieland Band - Down Home Rag," Columbia Blue Wax No. 3033-D (scratches) **30.00**

Cab Calloway, "Evenin' - Harlem Hospitality," Victor Scroll label No. 24414 ....**19.00**

Cab Calloway, "Farewell Blues - Mood Indigo," Banner No. 32152.........**8.00**

Cab Calloway, "Jitter Bug - Harlem Hospitality," Bluebird No. B-5676 (very light scuffs & small bubbles) **12.00**

Casa Loma Orchestra, "Alexander's Ragtime Band - Put On Your Old Gray Bonnet," Okeh No. 41476 ....**41.00**

Charlie Johnson, "Hot Bones And Rice - Harlem Drag," Victor Scroll label No. V-38059 (ILLUS. top next column) **194.00**

Charlie Johnson, "The Boy In The Boat - Walk That Thing," Bluebird No. B-10248 (heavy graniness) **14.00**

Chicago Footwarmers, "Sweep 'Em Clean - My Girl," Okeh No. 8792 .....**114.00**

"Harlem Drag" Record Label

Chicago Rhythm Kings, "Sarah Jane - The Martins And The Coys," Bluebird (buff label) No. B-6400 ....**12.00**

Chick Bullock & His Levee Loungers, "My Melancholy Baby - Somebody Loves Me," Melotone No. M-13434 (grainy) **12.00**

Clarence Williams & His Jazz Kings, "Red River Blues - Need You," Columbia No. 14326-D (small half-moon lamination crack)..............**84.00**

Clarence Wiliams & His Jazz Kings, "The Keyboard Express - Walk That Broad," Columbia No. 14348-D (crack, faded label) **44.00**

Duke Ellington, "East Saint Louis Toodle-Oo - Black Beauty," Bluebird (buff label) No. B-6430 (light scratches) **7.00**

Duke Ellington, "Moonglow - Solitude," Brunswick No. 6987.............**8.00**

Duke Ellington, "The Dicty Glide - High Life," Bluebird (buff label) No. B-6269..**4.00**

Duke Ellington, "Tishomingo Blues - Yellow Dog Blues," Brunswick No. 3987 ....**19.00**

Dick McDonough, "Way Down Yonder In New Orleans - Dear Old Southland," Melotone No. 6-09-08.....**23.00**

Dixieland Jug Blowers, "If You Can't Make It Easy, Get A Job and Go To Work - When I Stopped Runnin' I Was At Home," Victor Scroll label No. 20770 ....**136.00**

Earl Hines, "Chicago Rhythm - Everybody Loves My Baby," Victor Scroll label No. V-38042 ....**68.00**

Fats Waller, "Ain't Misbehavin' - Moppin' And Boppin'," VDP (La Voce del Padrone, Gramophone Co.) No. SH 1, 12" d. (light label scuff) **9.00**

Fats Waller, "Muscle Shoals Blues -

Birmingham Blues," Okeh
No. 4757 ....**40.00**
Fats Waller & His Rhythm, "Truckin'
- The Girl I Left Behind," Victor
Scroll label No. 25116.........................**16.00**
**Glen Gray & His Casa Loma
Orchestra,** "White Jazz - Blue
Jazz," Brunswick No. 6611
(scratches) **22.00**
Glenn Miller, "I Got Rhythm - Sleepy
Time Gal," Vocalion (blue label)
No. 5051 (scratch on side 1)...............**9.00**
Glenn Miller, "Peg O' My Heart - I'm
Sitting On Top Of The World,"
Decca (sunburst label) No. 1342 ....**14.00**
Glenn Miller, "Why'd Ya Make Me
Fall In Love - Don't Wake Up My
Heart!," Brunswick (silver label)
No. 8152 (small needle drop) **17.00**
Guy Lombardo, "Too Many Tears -
Love, You Funny Thing," Brunswick
No. 6261 (grainy) **11.00**
Guy Lombardo, "Without That Gal -
How The Time Can Fly!," Columbia
No. 2475-D (needle run) **6.00**
Harlem Hamfats, "Lake Providence
Blues - Oh! Red," Decca (sunburst
label) No. 7185 (label scuffs, warp) ...**15.00**
**Irving Aaronson & His
Commanders,** "An Evening In June
- Way Back Home," Columbia Blue
Wax No. 3037-D **42.00**
**Jelly-Roll Morton & His
Incomparables,** "Mr. Jelly Lord -
Duke Ellington: Wanna Go Back
Again Blues," Champion No. 15105 ..**44.00**
**Jelly-Roll Morton & His Red Hot
Peppers,** "Blue Blood Blues
Mushmouth Shuffle," Bluebird
No. B-8201...**8.00**
**Jelly-Roll Morton & His Red Hot
Peppers,** "Smoke-House Blues -
Steamboat Stomp," Bluebird
No. B-8372...**11.00**
Jim Clarke, "Fat Fanny Stomp - Dan
Stewart: New Orleans Blues,"
Vocalion No. 1536 ....**501.00**
Joe Haymes, "Lime House Blues -
Shine On Harvest Moon," Bluebird
(buff label) No. B-5133........................**3.00**
Joe Venuti, "Something - Nothing,"
Decca No. 2312 ....**22.00**
King Oliver, "West End Blues - Duke
Ellington: The Mooche," Victor
Scroll label No. V-38034 (light
scratches) **30.00**
King Oliver, "What You Want Me To
Do - Too Late," Victor Scroll label
No. V-38090.....................................**110.00**
Louis Armstrong, "I Wonder Who -
That's My Home," Bluebird (buff
label) No. B-6644 ....**7.00**
Louis Armstrong, "Love, You Funny

Thing! - New Tiger Rag," Columbia
Blue Wax No. 2631-D **44.00**
Louis Armstrong, "Rockin' Chair - I
Ain't Got Nobody," Okeh No. 8756 ....**20.00**
McKinney's Cotton Pickers, "Shim-
Me-Sha-Wabble - Milenberg Joys,"
Victor Scroll label No. 21611 ....**26.00**
Memphis Jug Band, "Bob Lee Junior
Blues - I Packed My Suitcase,
Started To The Train," Victor Scroll
label No. 21412................................**270.00**
New Orleans Rhythm Kings, "Maple
Leaf Rag - Sweet Lovin' Man,"
Gennett No. 5104 ....**39.00**
New Orleans Rhythm Kings, "Tin
Roof Blues - San Antonio Shout,"
Decca (sunburst label) No. 161 ....**7.00**
Original Dixieland Five, "Clarinet
Marmalade - Bluin' The Blues,"
Victor Scroll label No. 25525 ....**8.00**
Original Memphis Five, "Bad News
Blues - Shufflin' Mose," Perfect
No. 14150 (lightly grainy) **14.00**
Ozzie Nelson, "I'll Never Say 'Never'
Again - I'm Just An Ordinary
Human," Brunswick No. 7426 ....**10.00**
Ozzie Nelson, "Mountain Music -
Satan Takes A Holiday," Bluebird
(buff label) No. B-6965.......................**4.00**
Paul Whiteman, "Broadway -
Manhattan Mary," Victor Scroll label
No. 20874 (grainy) **6.00**
Paul Whiteman, "Driftwood - Out-O'-
Town Gal," Columbia No. 1505-D,
picture label **17.00**
Paul Whiteman, "Felix The Cat -
Mother Goose Parade," Columbia
No. 1478-D..**32.00**
Ray Noble, "Love Locked Out - On
The Other Side Of Lover's Lane,"
Victor Scroll label No. 24485 (light
scratches) **9.00**
Red Nichols & His Five Pennies,
"The New Yorkers - I May Be
Wrong," Brunswick No. 4500 ....**20.00**
Reginald Foresythe, "Angry Jungle -
Serenade For A Wealthy Widow,"
Columbia Blue Wax No. 2916-D........**21.00**
Teddy Wilson w/Billie Holiday,
vocal, "If You Were Mine - Eeny
Meeny Miney Mo," Brunswick
No. 7554 ....**8.00**
Teddy Wilson w/Billie Holiday,
vocal, "I'm Painting The Town Red -
Sweet Lorraine," Brunswick
No. 7520 ....**24.00**
Ted Lewis, "I Ain't Got Nobody - A
Good Man Is Hard To Find,"
Columbia No. 1428-D (small scuffs) ..**17.00**
Ted Lewis, "Unfortunate Blues -
Steppin' Out," Columbia No. 48-D
(scratches) **6.00**
Tommy Dorsey, "I'm Getting

Sentimental Over You - I've Got A Note," Victor Scroll label No. 25236.....**9.00**

Tommy Dorsey, "Now You've Got Me Doing It - Weary Blues," Victor Scroll label No. 25159..........................**4.00**

MOVIE RELATED 78 RPM RECORDINGS

Alice Faye, "Yes to You - My Future Star?," movie promo record for '365 Nights In Hollywood,' Fox Movietone No. F-119, 10" d. (internal cracks) **23.00**

Bing Crosby, "Friendly Mountains - The Kiss In Your Eyes," movie promo for 'The Emperor Waltz,' Paramount No. RR 16173 - RR 16174, 12" d. (light label scuffs).........**13.00**

Bing Crosby, "Song of Freedom," movie promo for 'Holiday Inn,' Paramount No. P32952, 10" d. **11.00**

Bing Crosby & Bob Hope, "Put It There" & Dorothy Lamour "Personality," movie promo for 'Road To Utopia,' Paramount No. RR 13332 - RR 13334," 10" d. **50.00**

Ezio Pinza & Chorus, "Boris Godunov, Coronation Scene, Part 1 & 2," from 'Tonight We Sing,' film rehearsal record, 20th Century Fox No. 13/13, 1953, acetate, 12" d. **36.00**

Gene Kelly, "I'll Go Home With Bonnie Jean, Part 1 & 2," from 'Brigadoon,' film rehearsal record, MGM No. 29160-29161, 1954, 12" d. (light scratches) **34.00**

Gene Kelly, "MacConnachy Square - Almost Like Being In Love," from 'Brigadoon,' film rehearsal record, MGM No. 29158-29159, 1954, 12" d. **31.00**

Helen Morgan, "It's Home - Song of a Dreamer," promo record for 'Marie Galante,' Fox Movietone No. F-120, 10" d. (scratches, edge chips on grooves on side 2) **24.00**

Movie Rehearsal Record Label

Isaac Stern, "Zigeunerweisen, Violin Concerto (Wieniawski)," from 'Tonight We Sing,' film rehearsal recording, 20th Century Fox No. 26-27, 1953, acetate, 12" d. (ILLUS. label, bottom previous column) **50.00**

Jan Pierce, "Mattinata" & Ezio Pinza, "Boris Godunov, Death Scene," from 'Tonight We Sing,' film rehearsal recording, 20th Century Fox No. 11/14, 1953, acetate, 12" d. **46.00**

PICTURE RECORDS

Art Kassel, "If I Could Be With You - Jeannine," Vogue No. R-771 ....**89.00**

Art Kassel, "Let's Get Married - Touch Me Not," Vogue No. R-780 ...**113.00**

Art Kassel, "The Whiffenpoof Song - If That Phone Ever Rings," Vogue No. R-770 ....**75.00**

Art Mooney, "In The Moonmist - I Don't Know Why," Vogue No. R-732 ....**113.00**

Ben-Baruch, "Zochrenon Lachaim - Zechor," foreign picture record, Saturne No. S-214, dramatic black & white picture of the sacrifice of Isaac, 12" d. **530.00**

Don Large Chorus, "The Bells of St, Mary's - Star Dust," Vogue No. R-710 (light scratches) **68.00**

Enric Madriguera, "So It Goes - The Minute Samba," Vogue No. R-760.....**66.00**

Enrico Caruso, "A Granada - Noche Feliz," RCA Victor No. 17-5001 ......**579.00**

Frankie Masters, "Everybody Knew It But Me - Sweet I've Gotten On You," Vogue No. R-724 ....**178.00**

Hour of Charm All Girl Orchestra, "Rhapsody In Blue - Alice Blue Gown - Blue Skies," Vogue No. V-100, two-record set w/original album **120.00**

Joan Edwards, "This Is Always - Love Means The Same Old Thing," Vogue No. R-767 ....**76.00**

Kiddie Picture Record, "A-Hunting We Will Go - London Bridge Is Falling Down," Record Guild No. G4012, 7" d. **17.00**

Kiddie Picture Record, "Happy Birthday - Happy Birthday Party," Picture-Play PR 2, 10" d. **166.00**

Kiddie Picture Record, "Muffin Man - The Farmer In The Dell," Record Guild No. 3001 P, 7" d. **14.00**

Kiddie Picture Record, "Red River Valley - Working On The Railroad," Record Guild No. M5020, 7" d. **20.00**

Le Quintette Guy Rios, "Vents - Reste Encore," foreign picture record, Saturne No. J-306, 10" d. **168.00**

Marion Mann, "Long, Strong and Consecutive - You're Gonna Hate

Yourself In The Mornin'," Vogue
No. R-758 ....**101.00**

M. Fauchet, "Lauda Jerusalem - Ave
Maria de Lourdes," foreign picture
record, Le Disque Religieux No.
50.137/138, black, white & red
flexible disc w/photo of Lourdes,
10" d...**530.00**

Nat Shilkret & Company, "Selections
from 'Music in the Air'," RCA Victor
No. 39001, 12" d. **200.00**

POPULAR RECORDING ARTISTS ON 78 RPMs

Al Jolson, "Hallelujiah, I'm A Bum -
April Showers," Harmony No. 1005 ...**58.00**

Al Jolson, "Sonny Boy - There's A
Rainbow 'Round My Shoulder,"
Brunswick No. 4033...........................**6.00**

Al Jolson, "You Made Me Love You -
Pullman Porters' Parade," Columbia
No. A1374 (grainy)...........................**22.00**

Beatrice Lillie, "Like He Loves Me -
Nicodemus," original cast recording,
Victor Scroll label No. 20361 (needle
drop, light graininess) **23.00**

Billie Holiday, "They Can't Take That
Away From Me - Let's Call The
Whole Thing Off," Vocalion (blue
label) No. 3520 ....**20.00**

Bing Crosby, "Ridin' Around In The
Rain - May I?," Melotone No.
M 13167 (very small bubbles)............**13.00**

Bing Crosby, "The Last Round-Up -
Home On The Range," Brunswick
No. 6936 ....**3.00**

Bing Crosby w/the Mills Brothers,
"My Honey's Lovin' Arms - Mills
Brothers: Smoke Rings," Brunswick
No. 6525 ....**12.00**

Boswell Sisters, "You Oughta Be In
Pictures - I Hate Myself," Brunswick
No. 6798 (needle drop)......................**15.00**

Cliff Edwards (Ukelele Ike), "What Is
'Good Morning?' - No Fooling,"
Perfect No. 11615 (grainy).................**11.00**

Dolores Del Rio, "Ramona - Ya Va
Cayendo," Victor Scroll label
No. 4053 (light graininess) **14.00**

Ethel Waters, "Am I Blue -
Birmingham Bertha," Columbia
No. 1837-D (scratches)......................**9.00**

Ethel Waters, "Please Don't Talk
About Me When I'm Gone - When
Your Lover Has Gone," Columbia
No. 2409-D (needle drop, crack) **39.00**

Ethel Merman, "You're The Top - I
Get A Kick Out Of You," Brunswick
No. 7342 (light scratches, edge flake
not to grooves) **36.00**

Fanny Brice, "I'd Rather Be Blue - If
You Want The Rainbow," Victor
Scroll label No. 21815 (light
graininess) **18.00**

Happiness Boys, "She Knows Her
Onions - It Won't Be Long Now,"
Victor Scroll label No. 20208
(grainy)...**9.00**

Jan Peerce, "A Beautiful Lady In Blue
- My Romance," Brunswick No. 7635 ..**8.00**

Josephine Baker, "J'ai Deux Amours
- La Petite Tonkinoise," Columbia
DF No. 229, England (label tear) **20.00**

Kate Smith, "When The Moon Comes
Over The Mountain - Makin' Faces
At The Man in The Moon,"
VelvetTone No. 2423-V **13.00**

Marian Anderson, "Deep River - My
Way's Cloudy," Victor No. 19227.......**19.00**

Maurice Chevalier, "My Love Parade
- Nobody's Using It Now," Victor
Scroll label No. 22285 (graininess) **9.00**

Mildred Bailey, "Georgia On My Mind
- Ro Chair," Bluebird (buff label)
No.6945 ....**26.00**

Mills Brothers & Ella Fitzgerald,
"Dedicated To You - Big Boy Blue,"
Decca Sunburst label No. 1148
(light graininess) **9.00**

Noel Coward, "I Like America - Why
Does Love Get In The Way,"
Columbia DB No. 3078, England
(small scratches) **13.00**

Rudolph Valentino, "El Relicarlo -
Kashmiri Song," CRS No. 17
(light scratches)...............................**62.00**

Rudy Vallee, "Outside - Jack Miller:
Weary River," Diva No. 2857-G **4.00**

**Rudy Vallee & His Connecticut
Yankees,** "Bye and Bye Sweetheart
- My Time Is Your Time," Victor
Scroll label No. 21924 (grainy) **17.00**

**Rudy Vallee & His Connecticut
Yankees,** "Life Is Just A Bowl of
Cherries - This Is The Missus,"
Victor Scroll label No. 22783 (light
scratches) **7.00**

Sophie Tucker, "He Hadn't Up Till
Yesterday - Aren't Women
Wonderful?," Columbia No. 5064,
England...**29.00**

Sophie Tucker, "I'm Doing What I'm
Doing For Love - I'm Feathering A
Nest," Victor Scroll label No. 21993
(grainy)...**18.00**

Whiteman's Rhythm Boys, "So The
Bluebirds and The Blackbirds Got
Together - Louise," Columbia Blue
Wax label No. 1819-d (lamination
crack) **16.00**

Will Rogers, "Timely Topics - A New
Slant On War," Victor 45347 ....**28.00**

POST-WORLD WAR II 78 RPMs

Bill Haley, "Rock Around The Clock
Tonight - Thirteen Women,"
Brunswick No. 05317 ....**33.00**

Bill Haley & His Comets, "Birth of
The Boogie - Mambo Rock," Decca
No. 29418 ....**5.00**

Bill Haley & His Comets, "I'll Be True
- Ten Little Indians," Essex No. 340
(small bubbles) **40.00**

Chuck Berry, "School Days - Deep
Feeling," Chess No. 1653 ....**31.00**

Drifters, "Warm Your Heart - Honey
Love," Atlantic No. 1029 ....**34.00**

Eddie Fisher, "Don't Stay Away Too
Long - Song of The Dreamer," RCA
No. 20-6196 (small edge flake not to
grooves) **3.00**

Elvis Presley, "Hound Dog - Don't Be
Cruel," RCA No. 20-6604 ....**40.00**

Elvis Presley, "I Want You, I Need
You, I Love You - My Baby
Left Me," RCA No. 20-6604 ....**88.00**

Elvis Presley, "Love Me Tender -
Hound Dog," RCA No. 1143,
Argentine (heavy scratches) **34.00**

Elvis Presley, "Make Me Know It -
Fever," RCA No. 2135 (Uruguay) **36.00**

Elvis Presley, "Mystery Train - I
Forgot To Remember To Forget,"
RCA No. 20-6357 ....**72.00**

Elvis Presley, "Raised On Rock - For
Ol' Times Sake," 45 rpm, RCA
promotional issue w/light yellow
label & "DJA0-0088," released 9/73,
w/brown sleeve (light wear on
sleeve w/2" edge split) **22.00**

Elvis Presley w/Scotty & Bill,
"That's All Right - Blue Moon of
Kentucky," Sun No. 209 ....**633.00**

Four Tunes, "Sometime, Someplace,
Somewhere - Where Is My Love,"
Manor No. 1077 (grainy) **12.00**

Frankie Lymon & The Teenagers,
"Teenage Love - Paper Castles,"
Gee No. GG 1032 ....**16.00**

Frankie Lymon & The Teenagers,
"Why Do Fools Fall In Love - Please
Be Mine," Gee No. GG-1002 ....**30.00**

**Jimmy Bowen w/the Rhythm
Orchids,** "Ever Lovin' Fingers - I'm
Stickin' With You," Roulette
No. R-4001 ....**26.00**

**Johnny Cash & The Tennessee
Two,** "I Walk The Line - Get
Rhythm," Sun No. 241 ....**28.00**

Nat King Cole, "A Blossom Fell - If I
May," Capitol No. 3095 ....**7.00**

Pat Boone, "Sugar Moon - Cherie, I
Love You," Dot No. 15750 ....**3.00**

Patti Page, "A Poor Man's Roses -
The Wall," Mercury No. 71059...........**3.00**

Penguins, "Earth Angel - Hey
Senorita," Dootone No. 348 ....**28.00**

Ray Price, "Crazy Arms - You Done
Me Wrong," Columbia No. 21510 ......**23.00**

Rex Allen, "As Long As The River
Flows - The Waltz of the Roses,"

Decca No. 27952, disc jockey
(tape on label) **4.00**

Ricky Nelson, "Be-Bop Baby - Have I
Told You Lately," Imperial No. 5463,
black label side 2 ....**10.00**

Sammy Davis Jr., "Back Track! - It's
Bigger Than You And Me," Decca
No. 29649 ....**9.00**

Sammy Davis Jr., "The Birth of The
Blues - Love," Decca No. 29393.........**4.00**

Spiders, "Bells In My Heart - For A
Thrill," Imperial No. 5354 (light
scratches) **16.00**

Tune Weavers, "Happy, Happy
Birthday Baby - Ol Man River,"
Checker No. 872 ....**52.00**

V-DISCS
World War II Armed Forces Records

**Arturo Toscanini & the NBC
Symphony Orchestra,** "Garibaldi's
War Hymn - Stars and Stripes
Forever," No. 31 ....**39.00**

Benny Goodman, "Dinah -
Henderson Stomp & Goodman,
Krupa & Stacey: Limehouse Blues,"
No. 159 ....**9.00**

Benny Goodman Sextet, "Good
Enough To Keep - Gene Krupa Trio:
Liza & Hodge Podge," No. 33 ....**20.00**

Benny Goodman Sextet," Good
Enough To Keep - Gene Krupa Trio:
Liza & Hodge Podge," No. 253 ....**6.00**

Benny Goodman Trio, "Poor
Butterfly & The World is Waiting For
The Sunrise - Lee Castle: I Get The
Blues When It Rains," No. 54 (large
lamination crack) **6.00**

**Capt. Glenn Miller & the AAFTC
Orchestra,** "Embraceable You &
G.I. Jive - Duke Ellington:
Sophisticated Lady & Azure,"
No. 183 ....**12.00**

**Capt. Glenn Miller & the AAFTC
Orchestra,** "The Squadron Song &
Tail End Charlie - Don't Be That
Way & Blue Champagne," No. 144......**8.00**

Charlie Spivak, "I'll Remember April -
Woody Herman: Lazy River &
There'll Be Some Changes Made,"
No. 268 ....**13.00**

Duke Ellington, "I Never Felt This
Way Before & Live and Love
Tonight - Paul Baron: The Story of
Two Cigarettes & Cabaret," No. 453....**9.00**

Harry James, "Eli Eli & Trumpet
Rhapsody - Les Brown: Bizet Has
His Day," No. 213 ....**10.00**

Jimmy Dorsey w/Kitty Kallen, "That
Wonderful, Worrisome Feeling -
Woody Herman: By The River of
The Roses," No. 157.........................**6.00**

Jo Stafford & Her V-Disc Play Boys,
"Bakery Blues - Frank Sinatra:

You'll Never Walk Alone & The Charm of You," No. 537 ....**9.00**

Spike Jones & His City Slickers, "Blue Danube & Toot Toot Tootsie Goo'Bye - Les Paul Trio: How High The Moon & Begin The Beguine," No. 540 ....**27.00**

Tommy Dorsey, "I've Got Rhythm & Count Basie: G.I. Stomp - Count Basie: Dance of the Gremlins," No. 34 ....**17.00**

Tommy Dorsey, "Melody In A & Chicago - Benny Goodman & His V-Disc All-Star Band: After You've Gone," No. 322 ....**9.00**

Tommy Dorsey, "Minor Goes A'Muggin & Losers Weepers - Not So Quiet Please," No. 220 ....**17.00**

Woody Herman, "Red Top - Guy Lombardo: Poor Little Rhode Island & Come With Me My Honey," No. 382 ....**8.00**

RECORD JACKETS

Beatles Picture Sleeve

Record jackets have minimal value unless they are rare, unusual or autographed. Below are listed a select number of jackets, both with and without records.

Beatles "The Beatles Story," two record set **35.00**

Beatles, picture sleeve for the single "I Want to Hold Your Hand/I Saw Her Standing There," signed by Paul McCartney, George Harrison, John Lennon & Ringo Starr, all in blue ball point pen, slight aging & small staple hole (ILLUS.) **3,450.00**

Beatles, "Sgt. Peppers Lonely Hearts Club Band" **35.00**

Cream, cover of 1970 LP "Live Cream," signed "Jack Bruce" in blue Sharpie, "Eric Clapton '94" in silver Sharpie & "Ginger Baker" in gold Sharpie (edge wear) **345.00**

Creedence Clearwater Revival, picture sleeve of their 1970 single "Lookin Out My Back Door," signed "John Fogerty" & "Doug Clifford" in gold ink, "Tom Fogerty" (deceased) in black ink & "Stu Cook" in blue Sharpie on the group portrait (some creasing at edge, upper left corner missing) **264.50**

Crosby, Stills & Nash, cover of their 1969 self-titled debut album, signed "David Crosby" in silver marker, "Steven Stills" in gold marker & "Graham Nash" in red marker **195.50**

Eagles (The), cover of their 1976 multi-platinum LP "Hotel California," signed "Don Henley" & "Joe Walsh" in blue marker, "Don Felder '92" in gold marker, "Glen Fry" in silver marker & "Randy Meisner" in black marker **632.50**

Elvis Presley EP, cardboard gate-fold black & white record cover, opens to reveal small black & white photo & text, while reverse features a third photo, contains set of two 45 rpm records on RCA label, each w/two songs per side including "Blue Suede Shoes" & "Tutti Frutti," record No. EPB-1254, released April 1956, cover 7 x 7" (back cover w/some writing & small name sticker on record label) **127.00**

Everly Brothers (The), cover of 1962 compilation "The Golden Hits of the Everly Brothers," signed "Phil Everly" & Don Everly" in blue marker **218.50**

Janis Joplin, jacket of 1967 "Cheap Thrills," signed in red ball point pen w/heart flourish near her portrait on the back cover (minor soiling & wear) **1,035.00**

John Cougar Mellencamp, "Uh-huh," autographed, includes 33⅓ rpm record, Riva Records Inc., 1983, signed in 1988 ....**45.00**

Lou Reed, "Lou Reed," autographed, includes 33⅓ rpm record, Sire Records Co., 1989 ....**30.00**

Nat King Cole, cover of "Wild is Love," nicely signed in blue ball point pen near his artistically rendered portrait on the back cover (near mint) **287.50**

Partridge Family, "The Partridge Family Up to Date" record, colorful cardboard cover contains 33⅓ rpm record on the Bell label, release 1971, cover 12¼ x 12¼" (some wear) **17.00**

Partridge Family, "The Partridge

Family Shopping Bag" album, gate-fold cover w/black & white photo inside plus information on the 1972 fan club, comes w/thin white plastic shopping bag w/same color design on each side that appears on album cover, contains 33⅓ rpm record on Bell label, cover 12¼ x 12¼", bag 11 x 15" (minor color rubs & inked name on cover, some color loss on bag) **50.00**

Paul McCartney, cover of 1988 LP "Live in Russia," signed neatly in blue Sharpie on the cover **207.00**

Peter Tosh, promotional copy of 1978 LP "Bush Doctor," which features appearances by Mick Jagger & Keith Richards, signed "Peter Tosh - Rasta" **402.50**

Roy Orbison, jacket of 1969 LP "The Original Sound," neatly signed in blue ball point pen on front cover (minor edge wear)...........................**121.00**

Tiny Tim, "With Love and Kisses From Tiny Tim - Concerts in Fairyland," sealed album, nice illustrated front w/black & white illustrations & text on reverse, record on Bouquet label, ca. late 1960s-early 1970s, cover 12¼ x 12¼" (original shrink wrap missing, some wear) **25.00**

Van Morrison, "Astral Weeks," autographed w/dedication, includes 33⅓ rpm record, Warner Bros. - 7 Arts Records, Inc. (some storage wear) **45.00**

(End of Records Section)

ROYALTY COMMEMORATIVES

QUEEN VICTORIA (1837-1901)

1897 Diamond Jubilee Mug

Mug, pottery, 1897 Diamond Jubilee commemorative, cylindrical w/angled handle, printed in black & white w/an oval bust portrait of Queen Victoria framed by flags & banners, marked on the bottom "Wood & Hulme, Burselm," 4" d., 4" h. (ILLUS.) **$145.00**

Pitcher, stoneware, 1897 Diamond Jubilee commemorative, marked "Doulton - Lambeth" ....**350.00 to 400.00**

EDWARD VII (1901-10)

Magazine, "Collier's," 1902, August 23, cover pictures Royal family & double page color of the coronation of the new king.................................**15.00**

Mug, porcelain, lithophane bottom, 1902 coronation commemorative **125.00**

Pitcher, jug-type, ceramic, commemorating the 1863 wedding of Prince Edward & Princess Alexandra.......................................**225.00**

GEORGE V (1910-36)

Newspaper, "London Illustrated News," 1935 Silver Jubilee special issue, red & gold cover, color & black & white illustrations, fine condition **45.00**

Plate, china, 1911 coronation commemorative Royal Worcester **120.00**

Plate, china, 1935 Silver Jubilee commemorative, Shelley China.........**55.00**

Postcards, 1911 coronation commemorative, large size, published by Valentine, set of 6.......**100.00**

EDWARD VIII (1935, Abdicated)

Bowl, china, 1937 coronation commemorative, Paragon China ....**275.00 to 325.00**

Mug, china, 1911 investiture commemorative **125.00**

Teapot, cov., china, 1937 coronation commemorative **139.00**

ELIZABETH II (1952-)

Biscuit tin, cov., commemorating 1957 "State Visit to the United States & Canada," colorful depiction of Elizabeth on horseback, Huntley & Palmer **40.00**

Box, cov., tin, 1953 coronation commemorative, Sharp & Son...........**20.00**

Cigarette jar, cov. & 4½" d. ashtray, jasper ware, 1953 coronation commemorative, royal blue, Wedgwood, set **180.00**

Cup & saucer, china, 1953 coronation commemorative, Paragon China...................................**52.00**

Cup & saucer, china,
commemorating 1957 royal visit to
Canada & United States **65.00**

Cup & saucer, porcelain,
commemorating the 1959 royal visit
to Canada, portraits of Queen
Elizabeth II & Prince Philip................**30.00**

Goblet, crystal, 1977 Silver Jubilee
commemorative, Brierley, 8½" h. **135.00**

Matchbook, 1953 coronation
commemorative **12.00**

Mug, china, 1953 coronation
commemorative, 3½" h. **24.00**

Pitcher, jug-type, china, 1953
coronation commemorative,
Royal Doulton **250.00**

ROYCROFT ITEMS

Roycroft Tall Chest of Drawers

Elbert Hubbard, eccentric entrepreneur of the late 19th century, founded Roycroft Shops and established a craft community in East Aurora, New York in 1895. Individuals were trained in the trades of bookbinding, leather tooling and printing. Craft-style furniture in the manner of Gustav Stickley and known as "Aurora Colonial" furniture was produced. A copper workshop, begun in 1908, turned out numerous items. All of these, along with those pieces of Buffalo Pottery china which were produced exclusively for use at the Roycroft Inn and carry the Roycroft symbol, constitute a special category associated with the Arts and Crafts movement.

Bench, "Ali Baba," ash, half-round top
w/bark exterior, on two legs joined
by long center stretcher, exposed
keyed tenons, orb mark, Model

No. 046, 14½ x 42",
19" h. ....**$5,500.00 to 6,500.00**

Book, "Little Journeys to the Homes
of Great Business Men," by Elbert
Hubbard, 1909, Volume 25, three-
quarter vellum hand-tooled binding
w/gilded spine, the text w/hand-
illuminated pages & polychrome
frontispiece designed & signed by
Dard Hunter, w/original box,
221 pp. **165.00**

Book, "'The Motto Book' - Being A
Catalog of Epigrams by Fra
Elbertus," brown kraft paper cover
w/red poppies & green leaves, uncut
pages, 64 pp., 5 x 7¼" **110.00**

Bookcase, oak, the rectangular top
above a case w/two single pane
glass doors, the interior fitted w/two
shelves, orb mark, 13 x 50",
4' 8" h. **4,370.00**

Book ends, hand-hammered copper,
embossed stylized floral designs,
rick dark original patina, orb mark,
4¼ x 4¾", pr. **192.50**

Book ends, brass-washed hand-
hammered copper, the square
upright plates w/a riveted strap w/a
ring loop, impressed orb & cross
mark, 4" w., 5" h., pr. (minor surface
wear) **275.00**

Book ends, hand-hammered copper,
rectangular upright plates fitted
w/narrow metal ribbed slats topped
by circular pulls attached w/rivets,
feathered border band, original
patina, orb & cross mark, 4" w.,
5¼" h., pr. **302.50**

Bookstand, "Little Journeys"-type,
oak, rectangular top overhanging
slant sides w/two lower shelves
w/through-tenons & keys, original
dark finish, metal tag, 26¼" l.,
26¼" h. **770.00**

Bracelet, hand-hammered sterling
silver, flattened bangle-style
stamped in the center w/a stylized
diamond-form flower flanked by
hammered bands, impressed marks,
2³⁄₁₆" d. **374.00**

Buffet, Mission-style (Arts & Crafts
movement) style, a high plate rack
above the rectangular top above a
single long drawer w/copper plate &
ring pulls above a pair of
geometrically leaded glass doors
opening to a shelf, copper plates &
knobs on the doors & large
"butterfly" form copper hinges, flat
apron, short legs w/chamfered ends,
thick quarter-sawn boards w/a
lightened finish, branded orb mark,
20 x 42", 45½" h..........................**6,875.00**

Candlesticks, hand-hammered copper, a cylindrical candle socket w/flaring rim above widely flaring dished drip pan over the square shaft composed of four slats w/attached ball rivets & curving out at the base to form angled, short legs, wear to original brass-washed finish, orb & cross mark, 3½" w., 12" h., pr. **1,320.00**

Center bowl, hand-hammered copper, squatty wide rounded form w/wide rolled rim, original dark brown patina, on tiny knob feet, early orb mark, 10" d., 4" h. **880.00**

Chandelier, copper & mica, conical w/circular rim of hammered copper panels riveted together, the rim set w/four sections of mica of five panels each, stamped mark, w/ceiling cap & chains, 34" d., 18" deep.....................................**24,150.00**

Chest of drawers, tall, Mission-style (Arts & Crafts movement), oak, a flat crestboard between short square stiles on the rectangular top overhanging a case of six long graduated drawers w/iron plates & bail pulls, original medium to dark finish, carved mark, ca. 1905, rear post crack, 25¾ x 29⅝", 5' 3" h. (ILLUS.) **10,925.00**

China cabinet, Mission-style (Arts & Crafts movement), oak, rectangular top above a pair of tall geometrically-leaded glass doors opening to three shelves, flat apron, large exterior copper hinges, short legs continue from stiles, vibrant quartersawn flaking w/a lightened finish, branded orb mark, 21 x 45½", 4' 9" h...**9,350.00**

Desk, oak, rectangular top overhanging a plain skirt w/one drawer above a shaped stretcher w/double keyed tenons each side, orb mark, 33 x 49¾", 30" h. **2,990.00**

Dining chairs, Mission-style (Arts & Crafts movement), oak, the back w/a wide rail above a narrow lower slat between square stiles, replaced cloth seats, lightened finish, branded orb mark, 37" h., set of 6..............**2,200.00**

Dining table, Mission-style (Arts & Crafts movement), oak, the round divided top above a deep molded apron raised on five heavy square legs w/flattened flaring square reeded feet, lightened finish, w/four leaves, branded orb mark, 48" d., 29" h...**4,125.00**

Lamp, table model, wrought iron, the double-domed shade decorated w/bands of tight scrolls between

Roycroft Table Lamp

curved straps & lined w/taffeta, raised on a slender flaring base composed of panels of pierced scrolls alternating w/straps, possibly by Dard Hunter, white paper label, 11" d., 20" h. (ILLUS.) **1,320.00**

Letter rack, hand-hammered copper, the round-topped riveted flat side panels decorated in repoussé w/a large poppy blossom, original medium brown patina, orb & cross mark, 7¼" w., 6½" h. (center divider missing) **330.00**

Library table. oak, rectangular top above an apron w/a pair of drawers w/shaped copper plates & bail pulls, square legs joined by a medial shelf, shaped squared feet, original medium finish, incised orb mark, Model No. 76, ca. 1906, 33¼ x 52⅛", 30" h.........................**1,955.00**

Nut set, hand-hammered copper, a wide shallow bowl w/a center cylindrical shaft holding a matching nutcracker & four picks, unmarked, 8" d., 4½" h., the set.........................**330.00**

Tray, hand-hammered copper, Arts & Crafts style, round w/a wide flanged rim & riveted loop side handles, brass-washed finish, Model No. 806, impressed mark, ca. 1917, 15⅞" d. (finish loss).....................................**259.00**

Trunk, flat-top, stained mahogany & wrought iron, rectangular w/the lift-lid fitted w/a wrought-iron clasp & w/wrought-iron corners on the base, carved Roycroft monogram in the lid, ca. 1910, 12½ x 23", 9¾" h. **747.00**

Vase, hand-hammered copper, wide squatty bulbous base w/a flat bottom, the shoulder tapering to a short flaring neck, Model No. 239, original patina, 6" d. (ILLUS. top next page) **385.00**

Wide Roycroft Vase

Vase, hand-hammered copper, cylindrical w/an incurved closed rim, applied near the top w/a double band of silver overlay w/geometric drops, original medium brown patina, orb & cross mark, 3" d., 6" h...**1,100.00**

Vase, hand-hammered copper, slender ovoid body w/a scalloped flaring rim, original dark patina, early orb mark, 3¾" d., 8¾" h. **770.00**

Cylindrical Roycroft Vase

Vase, hand-hammered copper, tall cylindrical form w/an incised band of diamond devices around the rim w/long pendant bands down the sides, 10" h. (ILLUS.)....................**2,200.00**

Vase, hand-hammered copper, 'American Beauty'-type, footed, w/compressed body & cylindrical neck w/everted rim, orb mark, 18¾" h...**2,760.00**

Vase, hand-hammered copper, 'American Beauty'-type, bulbous squatty footed base w/a flattened shoulder tapering to a tall cylindrical neck w/flaring rim, impressed orb mark, 19½" h...............................**1,725.00**

RUGS - HOOKED & OTHER

HOOKED

Rug with Animals & Flowers

Animals & flowers, a center design of scattered animals w/a horse & birds among stars, flowers & other designs w/a large central four-petal design & fans at each corner, within a wide border band, dated 1893, rebacked, 30 x 46" (ILLUS.)........**$1,092.50**

Cat & Flowers Hooked Rug

Cat & flowers, a recumbent black & white cat in the center flanked by colorful flowers & leafy branches, wide border band, early 20th c., some fiber loss, rebacked, 21½ x 40½" (ILLUS.) **1,495.00**

Cats, two cats facing one another centered on a black and brown ground, enclosed by a white crossed inner border, early 20th century, 31¼ x 53½"...................................**1,955.00**

Dog & Cat Hooked Rug

Dog & cat, a large walking dog beside a small seated cat, hearts at each corner, early 20th c., some fiber loss, rebacked, 20¾ x 37" (ILLUS.) **2,530.00**

Eagle perched on rockwork in center, the large bird framed by an oblong C-scroll border & diamond cross-hatched corners, worked in cream, red, green, black & taupe cottons & wools, 19th c., 35⅜ x 51" **863.00**

Floral Design Hooked Rug

Floral design, the long rectangular center panel w/four large stylized blossoms & several buds on slender stems w/scattered leaves, wide edge band of serrate design w/two rows of contrasting triangles, 19th c., rebacked, 31½ x 67½" (ILLUS.) **1,035.00**

Florals, clusters of stylized flowers within a diamond lattice design all within a chain link border band, Grenfell-type, early 20th c., 25½ x 37" (some fiber loss, edge bound) ...**920.00**

Flowers in pot, rectangular, striped pot holding large stylized blossoms, in shades of grey, taupe, red, black, yellow & lighter green wools, grey ground w/red inner border & taupe outer border, early 20th century, 28½ x 44"..**920.00**

Dated Hooked Rug with Horse

Horse, rectangular w/a horse stepping off a small block marked "1880" in the center, wide double sawtooth border band, worked in multicolored wool & cotton, dated 1880, 36½ x 53" (ILLUS.) **4,600.00**

Lions, underneath trees made of colorful yarn within wide border of diamonds & corner blocks, 21½ x 38½".....................................**345.00**

Lions, worked in yellow, brown, green, red, black & beige wool

depicting a central recumbent lion & another standing to one side in an exotic landscape of palm trees & flowering plants within a three-quarter striped border of red, green, yellow & black, 20th c., 28 x 61"..**1,495.00**

Mary & her lamb, a Sunbonnet-type girl w/a white lamb running ahead of her, good colors, wide black border band, 16½ x 23½"...........................**159.50**

Rooster, standing on a 'shingled' ground in a crowing stance, worked in browns, yellows & green w/red & white on a light blue ground w/black border, 20 x 24½" **522.00**

Yawls racing, the two sailing boats on a stylized wavy sea below abstract patterned skies, diagonally banded border, early 20th c., 37 x 67" (fiber loss, rebacked) **6,325.00**

OTHER

Early "Penny" Rug

Penny rug, hexagonal, black, grey, maroon & olive green wool on a natural burlap ground, embroidered details, 29 x 33" (sewn repairs)........**154.00**

Penny rug, wool & flannel, lozenge-shaped, appliqued w/a series of wool & felt circles in tones of brown, navy blue, red & blue patches, each appliqued w/a star, New England, late 19th c., some fabric loss & wear, 14 x 32¾", (ILLUS.)...............**920.00**

Reed-stitch all-wool rug, rectangular, a large flower-filled bowl at the center w/scattered blossoms around the sides, all within a large leaf border band, shades of reddish brown, dark brown, black & white, probably New England, 19th c., 34 x 57½" (ILLUS. top next page).................**6,900.00**

Early Reed-Stitch Wool Rug

Woven rag runner, bluish grey
w/white & blue warp, Pennsylvania,
3 x 15' **88.00**

SALESMAN'S SAMPLES

Rare Old Town Canoe Model

The traveling salesman or "drummer" has all but disappeared from the American scene. In the latter part of the 19th century and up to the late 1930s, they traveled the country calling on potential costumers to show them small replicas of their products. Today these small versions of kitchenwares, farm equipment, and even bathtubs, are of interest to collectors and are available in a wide price range.

Canoe, wooden, original green paint,
red lettering & decals, reads
"Genuine Old Town Canoe Co.
Canoes," excellent condition,
9½ x 50", 4" h. (ILLUS.) **$9,350.00**
Cider press, walnut & poplar w/metal
fittings & spring, mortised & pinned
construction, w/dovetailed poplar
storage box labeled "Samson Cider
& Vine Press, Pat. by E. Stoner &
Co. Oct. 5th, 1869," 13¾" l. (some
damage)..**467.50**
Cooking pan, aluminum, "Royal
Super Ware," inside w/information
about waterless cooking, 1½" d.,
3" l...**135.00**
Door lock, wood & brass, Corbin
Lock Co., upright wood panel w/the
doorknob, lock & key, scratches,
6½" w., 12½" h. (ILLUS. top next
column) **22.00**
Egg carrier w/one dozen eggs, "Star
Egg Carrier," American, Canadian &
English patent dates, 1½ x 3½ x
4½"...**160.00**

Corbin Lock Co. Door Lock

Nesbitt's Fanning Mill

Fanning mill, wood & cast iron, the
wooden box machine w/mahogany
varnish finish & black & gold
lettering reading "M.T. Nesbitt's
Improved Fanning Mill, Patented
June 11th 1872," cast-iron & other
metal fittings, square nail
construction, some damage & old
repair & replaced pieces, 17¾" l.
(ILLUS.) **467.50**

Evinrude Outboard Motor Model

Outboard motor, "Evinrude," metal,
blue & black w/yellow lettering,

electric starting, marked "Japan," ca. 1950s, minor wear, 1½ x 2¾", 5½" h. (ILLUS.) **110.00**

Sugar cane slicing machine, walnut, a long rectangular box w/a lever mechanism at one end, raised on a trestle base w/a foot pedal at one end, metal fittings, wire nail construction, old finish, 11½" l. **357.50**

Early Spiller Buckboard Wagon

Wagon, buckboard-type, wooden, the rectangular platform w/seat raised on metal springs & large wheels, painted deep reddish brown & inscribed in gold "A.H. Spiller. Builder," 19th c., imperfections, 29" l. (ILLUS.) **1,955.00**

Wagon jack, mahogany w/metal fittings, an upright plank w/stepped top edge, a spring mechanism on the side w/a long wooden turned handle, on a rectangular base, old dark finish, 9" h. **137.50**

Washing machine, cherry, pine & hickory w/metal fittings, a round slat-sided tub w/two metal bands, rests on a rectangular platform on baluster-turned legs, a tall turned upright lever at each end of the platform, the tub fitted w/a screw mechanism, old varnish finish, 12" l. **330.00**

SCALES

Fairbanks Balance Scale

Balance scale, cast iron & brass, a ratcheted arm w/scale extending from balance platform raised on upright supports & a heavy molded base, decorated w/green flowers on each side of the bottom, marked "Fairbanks," minor wear & fading, 16 oz. scale, 10¼" l., 4" h. (ILLUS.) **$66.00**

Sidewalk scale, painted metal, tall upright rectangular case in red w/white trim & two long rectangular mirrored panels, marked "Peerless Weighing & Vending Corp. - New York," 16" w., 5' 4" h. (overall scratches) **60.50**

Sidewalk scale, red & cream metal w/a mirror, tells fortune & weight , Watling, ca. 1920s, excellent working order, 17" l., 4' 4" h. **975.00**

Steelyard scale, iron, red decoration, 18" l. **175.00**

SCIENTIFIC INSTRUMENTS

Lettey Stick Barometer

Altazimuth, pocket-type, cased, dial signed "L. Casella, London," w/printed instructions, England, late 19th c., 5¾" l. **$172.50**

Barometer, stick-type, mahogany, the molded pitched pediment centering a brass finial above a hinged glazed door opening to the weather indicator inscribed "Cetli & Co., 25 Red Lion, A. HO...London," the temperature indicator inscribed "blood heat, sumr heat, tempe rate" & "freezing," the weather indicator inscribed "very dry, set fair, change, rain, m. rain" & "stormy," the elongated center drop above a turned pendant, mercury glass broken, England, last quarter 18th c., 5" w., 38½" h. **805.00**

Barometer, stick-type, mahogany case, the broken-swan's-neck pediment above a molded frieze over a line-inlaid baluster-form neck fitted w/moisture gauge, thermometer & quicksilvered convex glass over a line-inlaid pendant inverted baluster base fitted w/barometric gauge & level, marked by J. & N. Lettey, Dunster, 19th c., 10" d., 38½" l. (ILLUS.) **1,495.00**

Barometer, stick-type, mahogany case w/a broken-scroll pediment centering a brass urn finial above the rectangular plate over the top of the tube, the long slender case ending in a bulbous shield-form base, J. Watkins, Charing Cross, London, England, 19th c., 41" h....**1,495.00**

Fine French Barometer

Barometer, wheel-type, Louis XVI-Style, giltwood, the tall crest molded & pierced w/ribbons continuing down to long relief-molded oak leaf pendants flanking the arched case centered by a round dial above a leaf-carved panel w/a small center oval reserve w/figures, the molded platform w/central scrolling leaves above leaf swags framing a rectangular panel in the base drop, dial marked "Charpentier - Paris," France, 19th c., damage, repairs, 36½" h. (ILLUS.) **1,265.00**

Barometer, wheel-type, inlaid mahogany, the banjo-shaped case w/an inlaid edge & four inlaid sunburst medallions, polished steel engraved thermometer & similar barometer below, marked "Thos. Ripley & Son, Hermitage, London," England, ca. 1830...........................**357.50**

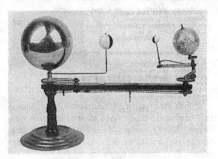

Trippensee Orrery

Orrery, metal & wood, marked "Trippensee Planetarium, Detriot, Michigan," early 20th c., 14 x 25½" (ILLUS.) **1,495.00**

Pedometer, cased, made by A.M. LaFontaine, Paris, France, w/printed instructions, late 19th c., 2½" d........**230.00**

Slide rule, brass & mahogany, cylindrical w/printed paper-covered drum, Keuffel & Esser, mahogany case measures 6½ x 6½ x 23¾" (some stains) **550.00**

Early Surveyor's Compass

Surveyor's compass, wood, glass & metal, marked "Made by Thomas Greenough, Boston N. England," mid-18th c., minor imperfections, 13" l. (ILLUS.) **1,210.00**

Surveyor's compass, brass, dial engraved "Benj Pike & Son New York," 19th c., 15" l. **115.00**

Telescope, brass, retailed by Andrew J. Lloyd Company, Boston, w/wooden tripod stand, w/case, early 20th c., case 40½" l..............**1,955.00**

Telescope, brass, engraved "Bardou & Son, Paris," on a tall wooden tripod stand, barrel 38" l., overall 5' h. **990.00**

Transit level, brass, the silvered face engraved "Henry Ware Maker, Cincinnati, Ohio," on a wooden tripod stand, w/original wooden case

w/Henry Ware paper label, overall
5' 6" h. **907.50**

SCOUTING ITEMS

Scout rules and regulations, handbooks and accouterments have changed with the times. Early items associated with the Scouting movements are now being collected. A sampling follows.

BOY SCOUTS

Belt buckle, copper-finished metal, C.A.C. Award, framed high-relief image of Boy Scouts founder, Baden Powell, w/rope border, early 1900s **$65.00**

Book, "Boy Scout Explorers At Headless Hollow," by Don Palmer, Cupples and Leon Company, 1957 .....**8.00**

Compass, made in Sweden for Silvia, Inc., Laporte, Indiana **22.50**

Handbook, 1940 ....**20.00**

Handbook, 1943, cover illustrated by Norman Rockwell..............................**30.00**

Handbook, 1954, cover illustrated by Norman Rockwell..............................**10.00**

Identification card w/envelope, 1933 ....**12.00**

Pocket knife, Remington Model No. RH 51..**65.00**

Early Boy Scout Knife

Pocket knife, stamped metal, on side w/a relief scene of a standing Scout holding an American flag, the reverse w/a long camping scene, early 20th c., larger blade missing, rust, soiled (ILLUS. two views) **33.00**

Scarf holder, 1937 Jubilee, bronze, Waltham Watch Company **125.00**

GIRL SCOUTS

Compass, official, nickel, 1943, mint in box **25.00**

Uniform dress & jacket, complete ca. 1920s **175.00**

SEWING ADJUNCTS

Early Needlework Pincushion

Pincushion, needlework, worked in queen stitch w/bands of zigzag lines around a two-story house, in shades of yellow, blue, green & earthtones, signed "J.S.," 18th c., 7" sq. (ILLUS.) **$4,600.00**

Pincushion, white metal, figural, cast in the form of a small standing terrier dog, worn original greyish paint w/red trim, cloth cushion in the back, stamped "Germany," 3½" l. **16.50**

Sewing box, inlaid wood, rectangular, the front & lid inlaid w/geometric designs & floral marquetry w/cross-banded trim, the lid interior lined w/a mirror above a compartment fitted w/a tray w/ivory-handled lids & spools of thread w/a hidden pincushion, 12¾" l. (some damage)..**236.50**

Sewing box, walnut, rectangular w/an inset pincushion top of worn blue velvet, single drawer w/porcelain knob in front, applied molding on base, old varnish finish, square nail construction, 7⅛" l. **104.50**

Sewing case, mother-of-pearl, shell-shaped w/a ribbed center & delicate engraved scrolls around the edge, the interior fitted w/a mirror & lined in velvet, holds gold scissors, spools, perfume flacon & other implements, early, some implements missing, interior mirror cracked, 5½" w. (ILLUS. top next page)........**805.00**

Tape measure, celluloid, model of a pig **39.00**

Mother-of-Pearl Sewing Case

Advertising Tape Measure

Tape measure, metal, one side w/a color picture of Queen Louise dressed in red & white, the reverse printed w/advertising reading "J.E. Gubb - Queen Quality - Shoes - Sole Agent - Batavia, N.Y.," side opens, early 20th c., 1½" d. (ILLUS. two views) **38.50**

Pease Thread Caddy

Thread caddy, turned-wood, squatty bulbous base on wide disc foot, w/two compartments, old worn varnish finish, signed & numbered "C.G. Pease Mfg., Concord, Lake Co. Ohio 593" (ILLUS.) **275.00**

SHAKER ITEMS

Shaker Child's Armchair

The Shakers, a religious sect founded by Ann Lee, first settled in this country at Watervliet, New York, near Albany, in 1774 and by 1880 there were nine settlements in America. Workmanship in Shaker crafts is an extension of their religious beliefs and features plain and simple designs reflecting a chaste elegance that is now much in demand though relatively few early items are available. Also see FURNITURE.

Armchair, child's, three gently arched slats between round stiles w/pointed finials above flat curved arms w/mushroom handgrips above baluster-turned supports, old red & black worn taped seat, double stretchers on three sides, No. 1 size, Mt. Lebanon, New York, 1880-1930, imperfections, 27½" h. (ILLUS.) **$1,840.00**

Early Shaker Baskets

Basket, woven brown ash splint, deep oval sides w/rectangular bottom, ash handle & rim, probably Mt. Lebanon, New York, ca. 1840, 12" l., overall 13½" h. (ILLUS. right) **2,300.00**
Basket, apple-type, woven ash splint, deep rounded sides w/a squared bottom w/ash rim & handle, probably

New Lebanon, New York, ca. 1850-70, 13½" l., overall 15" h. (ILLUS. left) **1,725.00**

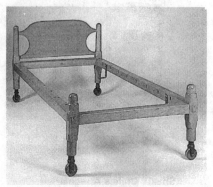

Shaker Low-Poster Bed

Bed, low-poster, turned maple & pine, the shaped pine headboard flanked by tapered headposts, the legs raised on cast-iron & turned wood casters, New Lebanon, New York, 19th c., 37¼ x 78½", 29½" h. (ILLUS.) **977.00**

Blanket chest, cherry & tiger stripe maple, a rectangular top hinged above a deep well above a case w/two long bottom drawers w/wooden knobs, short turned feet on casters, signed "Built by W.D. Shimnway 1835 when he was 18 years old," 18 x 42", 39½" h..........**1,265.00**

Box, cov., miniature, oval bentwood w/two finger lappets, 19th c., 3¾" l..**690.00**

Decorated Shaker Box

Box, cov., painted maple & pine oval bentwood, the fitted lid w/a single lappet, the base w/four finger lappets, the top painted w/a geometric grid in black on a brown ground, the base painted brown, probably Maine, mid-19th c., 7½ x 10", 4¼" h. (ILLUS.) **1,150.00**

Box, cov., 'gift'-type, round bentwood w/fitted pine lid & bottom, the sides fastened w/small copper tacks &

painted bluish green, attributed to Elder Joseph Johnson, Canterbury or Enfield, New Hampshire, ca. 1850, 14" d., 6½" h..................**2,875.00**

Box, cov., painted pine & hardwood oval bentwood, single lappet construction on cover & three lappets w/copper tacks on base, old blue paint w/very good color, 11¾" l. (very minor damage to bottom edge)................................**2,200.00**

Box, cov., oval bentwood w/finger lappet construction, salmon brown paint, 13½" l. **2,990.00**

Chest of drawers, walnut, rectangular top w/molded edge over a case w/five graduated long drawers, each w/turned wood knob pulls, shaped skirt, bracket feet, varnish finish, probably Union Village, Ohio, mid-19th c., 23 x 43½", 4' 7" h. (minor imperfections) **9,350.00**

Rug, knitted wool 'sampler' type, knitted in bands of red, yellow, blue, pink, orange, black, grey, purple, green & beige wool square & rectangular patches within striped bands, sewn to mattress ticking, now mounted on a wood frame, attributed to Sister Elvia C. Hullett, Hancock, Massachusetts, ca. 1890, 35½ x 44½".......................**3,737.00**

Sewing box, butternut, rectangular w/a hinged lid & spring locking mechanism opening to a well, exposed dovetail construction on a molded base, the lid interior inscribed "Made July 1843 New Lebanon," 9¾ x 19", 7" h. **920.00**

Early Shaker Sewing Desk

Sewing desk, pine, the tall enclosed back flanked by downswept rounded sides to the rectangular top over a pull-out shelf above a case w/three

graduated long drawers w/wooden
knobs, bootjack sides, old refinish,
Canterbury, New Hampshire, early
19th c., imperfections, 17 x 22",
30½" h (ILLUS.) **1,725.00**

Sewing table, mahogany, rectangular
top widely overhanging a deep case
w/two short over two long drawers,
paneled ends, on swelled circular
legs, inscribed on the underside "Bilt
by Brother Frank Libby, Alfred,
Maine, 1894," 24 x 35", 28" h......**10,925.00**

Side chair, maple, turned oblong
finials on turned stiles flanking three
curved slats, woven rush seat, box
stretchers, old finish, marked
w/Roman numeral "II," found in
Harvard, Massachusetts, 19th c.,
39½" h...**374.00**

Sill cupboard, painted pine,
rectangular top on the tall upper
section w/a long narrow double
raised-panel door opening to an
interior fitted w/three shelves, the
projecting lower section w/a single
raised-panel long door opening to
an interior fitted w/two shelves,
small wooden knobs & wooden
thumb latches, New Lebanon, New
York, early 19th. c., original red
paint, 17 x 21", 6' 3¼" h. **65,750.00**

SHEET MUSIC

*Also see ADVERTISING ITEMS,
CHARACTER COLLECTIBLES and POP
CULTURE COLLECTIBLES.*

"Anchors Aweigh," Franklin Delano
Roosevelt on cover, 1935 ....**$21.00**
"Animal Crackers in My Soup,"
Shirley Temple on cover **16.00**
"Girl Shy," 1924, Harold Lloyd on
cover **28.00**
"Good Night My Love," Shirley
Temple on cover **25.00**
"Hers to Hold," 1943, Deanna
Durbin on cover **8.00**
"Mad About Music," 1938, Deanna
Durbin on cover **8.00**
"Meet Me in St. Louis," 1944, Judy
Garland on cover **22.00**
"Mounted Police Two Step," 1909,
illustrated cover................................**23.00**
"My Sunshine Rose," cover by Rolf
Armstrong **17.00**
"Songs of Safety," 1937, cover
illustrated by Rose O'Neill.................**25.00**
"Thanks For The Memory," Shirley

Ross photo & drawings of Bob
Hope, Alice Faye, W.C. Fields, etc.
on cover **20.00**
"Tipperary Guards March," 1915,
cover by E.T. Paull............................**35.00**
"When the Lusitania Went Down,"
1915, by McCarron & Vincent,
photos of full ship & two parlors
on cover **10.00**

SIGNS & SIGNBOARDS

Ruppert's Beer Sign

*Also see ADVERTISING ITEMS,
BREWERIANA and COCA-COLA COL-
LECTIBLES.*

Beer, "Moose Beer," wood,
rectangular flat board painted w/gold
& red lettering reading "Better Than
Ever" - Moose Beer - "The Pride of
the Monongahela Valley," 15" l.
6⅞" h. (top left corner filled, overall
paint chipping, soiling & fading) **$93.50**
Beer, "Pabst Blue Ribbon,"
lithographed cardboard, a color
scene of a smiling, portly elderly
gentleman pouring a glass of beer,
printed across the bottom "Pabst -
Blue Ribbon - The Beer of Quality,"
printed in blue, green, red & yellow,
copyright 1933, framed, 23 x 29"
(chip to cardboard at one side,
scratch in one letter) **231.00**
Beer, "Ruppert's Beer," reverse-
painted glass, oval, black ground
w/white & silver lettering reading
"Jacob Ruppert's New York Beer," in
a wide oval frame, minor scratches
on frame, 12½ x 18" (ILLUS.) **143.00**
Boarding house, painted poplar,
rectangular w/a black ground
painted w/gold block lettering
reading "Boarding - by the Week,
Day or Meal," 22¾ x 36" **687.50**
Bottling company, "Star Bottling
Works," painted metal, narrow

Star Bottling Works Sign

rectangular form decorated w/a tall bottle w/the label reading "Star - Bottling - Works - Sudbury Ont.," in blue, orange, yellow & cream, very minor scratches, 11 x 35½" (ILLUS.) **104.50**

Kellogg's Corn Flakes Sign

Breakfast cereal, "Kellogg's Toasted Corn Flakes," cardboard, rectangular, printed in red & green, reads "36 One-half Pound Packages - Kellogg's - Toasted Corn Flakes - None Genuine Without This Signature - W.K. Kellogg - Kellogg Toasted Corn Flake Co. - Battle Creek, Mich.," overprinted in large open letters "Waxtite," soiled, bent corners, 11 x 17" (ILLUS.) **33.00**

Butcher, "Hodson - Superior - Pork - Butcher," carved giltwood, model of a large fat hog, carved half-round, stenciled inscription, 19th c, some loss to gilding, age cracks, tail loose, 57" l., 38½" h. (ILLUS. top next column) **3,737.00**

Butcher Trade Sign

Chocolates, "Samoset Chocolates," cast iron, round plaque-style, a three-dimensional Indian paddling a canoe emerging from the center of a ring border embossed w/"Samoset Chocolates - Trade Mark," 18" d. **302.50**

Old Gold Cigarette Sign

Cigarettes, "Old Gold," cardboard in metal frame, rectangular, printed in color w/a seated "flapper" reaching for a pack of cigarettes as a round-headed cartoon man in a raccoon coat looks on, lady wearing orange & red, the man a black coat, black & orange lettering, printed across the top "Riled by Raccoon Rah-Rah? - light an Old Gold," printed at the bottom "for young ideas!," ca.1920s, water stains, 31" w., 42½" h. (ILLUS.) **412.50**

Cigars, "Napoleon Cigars," embossed painted metal, round, colorful bust portrait of Napoleon in the center framed by a wreath below "Napoleon" w/"Cigars" below, the scroll-decorated outer border band printed in red on white w/"Powell & Goldstein - Oneida, N.Y.," in red, yellow, green, blue, gold & brown, touch-ups, 20" d. (ILLUS. top next page)...**1,320.00**

Napoleon Cigars Sign

Luden's Cough Drops Sign

Hy-Quality Coffee Sign

DeLaval Cream Separators Sign

Coffee, "Hy-Quality Coffee," die-cut cardboard, a colorful design w/a rectangular box at the top printed in black & gold on white w/"Our Suggestion Roth's - Hy-Quality - Coffee - Delicious to the Last Sip," box suspends strings w/cut-out of a young lady holding a cup of coffee & seated on a swing, wearing a red floral-sprigged pale blue dress w/a pink sash, early 20th c., creases, 24" w., 42½" h. (ILLUS.) **605.00**

Cough drops, "Luden's," painted tin, rectangular w/scroll ends, dark green ground w/a yellow box of the product, printed in red & cream "Luden's - Menthol Candy - 5¢ - Cough Drops - Give Quick Relief," minor edge wear, 6¾ x 9" (ILLUS. top next column) **1,045.00**

Cream separators, "DeLaval," printed metal, ornate color design w/"De Laval - Cream Separators" across the top above four color

vignettes of cattle & a separator framing an oval reserve w/the head of a maiden & cow, further advertisements across the bottom, in an ornate gilt plaster frame, "green" version, minor scratches, denting, rust spotting, 24" w., 35" h. (ILLUS.) **770.00**

McCormick Dairy Equipment Sign

Dairy equipment, "McCormick," embossed painted metal, rectangular, printed in the upper left w/the small "International Harvester" logo beside "McCormick Dairy Equipment - Used On This Farm,"

"Dibble Hardware - Meshoppen, Pa." at the bottom, red & black lettering on a yellow & black ground, minor scratches, 14¼ x 23" (ILLUS.) **77.00**

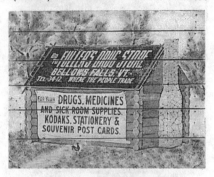

Drugstore Trade Sign

Drugstore, "Fuller's Drug Store," painted wood, rectangular composed of six planks decorated w/a log cabin & trees, the cabin inscribed "Go To Fuller's Drug Store - Bellows Falls, VT. - Tel. 3412 Where The People Trade." - "For Your Drugs, Medicines - and Sick room Supplies. - Kodaks, Stationery & - Souvenir Post Cards," ca. 1920, wear & scratches, 47½ x 60" (ILLUS.) **1,150.00**

Rare Aunt Jemima Flour Sign

Flour, "Aunt Jemima Pancake Flour," die-cut cardboard, a large figure of Aunt Jemima in color seated on a wooden swing w/boxes of the product beside her, a plate of pancakes on her lap & advertising printed on her apron including "Ise In Town, Honey," early 20th c. (ILLUS.) **5,940.00**

Hair cutting, "Ladies Hair Cutting," neon, a neon arched frame around a profile of a lady's head w/the wording "Ladies Hair Cutting" in blue, pink & white neon, mounted on plywood, 36" w., 39" h. (neon repair) **192.50**

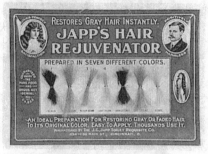

Japp's Hair Rejuvenator Sign

Hair dye, "Japp's Hair Rejuvenator," tin over cardboard, rectangular, colorful design w/a small oval bust portrait of a lady & man at the top corners flanking advertising "Restores Gray Hair Instantly. - Japp's Hair - Rejuvenator," a rectangle at the center w/real samples of colored hair & marked "Prepared In Seven Different Colors - Black Dark Brown Light Brown Dark Chestnut Light Chestnut Blonde," further printing across the bottom, very minor scratches, 9¼ x 13¼" (ILLUS.) **330.00**

Stanley Hardware Sign

Hardware, "Stanley Hardware," cardboard, rectangular, printed w/gold block lettering on a red & blue ground, very minor soiling, 5 x 12" (ILLUS.) **55.00**

Ice cream, "Hershey's Ice Cream," posterboard, printed in color, a large scrolled banner across the top reading "Peaches 'N Ice Cream - Peach Sundae Supreme" above a large sundae glass, a circle in the lower left printed "Hershey's Ice Cream," in green, grey, orange, red & cream w/red lettering, 13 x 20" (ILLUS. top next page) **66.00**

Ice cream, "Keystone Ice Cream," porcelain, bracket-hung type,

Hershey's Ice Cream Sign

rectangular, deep red ground w/white lettering framing a keystone logo, white border, hung from a scrolled wrought-iron bracket, double-sided, 28" l., 20" h. (edge wear, minor chipping & soiling) **154.00**

Ice cream, "Primrose Ice Cream," color die-cut cardboard, a pretty girl wearing a cream dress w/pink flowers & darker pink tie belt sitting on a wooden plank swing & eating a dish of ice cream, swing suspended from upper rectangle w/wording "I Love It - 'Primrose' Ice Cream - Made by Kenosha Ice Cream Co., red & black lettering, mounted in a gold frame, 21¼ x 40¾" (creases, edge wear) **880.00**

Theroux's Ice Cream Sign

Ice cream, "Theroux's Ice Cream," painted metal, rectangular, blue center reserve showing a package & dish of neapolitan ice cream, cream lettering on a red background above & below reading "Theroux's - Ice Cream - Taunton, Mass.," minor scratches & soiling, dent at bottom & sides, 19¼ x 27¾" (ILLUS.) **198.00**

Eskimo Pie Sign

Ice cream bar, "Eskimo Pie," painted metal, rectangular, two-sided, yellow & silver w/blue & red lettering, center oval w/"Eskimo Pie - 'M-m-m-melts in your mouth!'" & a picture of the bar, ca. 1948, scratches, minor rust, 24 x 36" (ILLUS.) **264.00**

Rare Carter's Ink Sign

Ink, "Carter's Ink," self-framed tin, rectangular wood-grained frame w/narrow gilt scroll border surrounds an oval color scene of an elderly man wearing a brown suit & a red tie & sitting writing in a large book, a red ink bottle on the desk & blue Carter's ink bottle on shelf in background, 18½ x 25" (ILLUS.) **1,210.00**

Insurance company, "Delaware Underwriters," painted wood, red & gold lettering on a brown ground, reads "Automobile Fire Tornado - Delaware - Underwriters - Philadelphia, Pa.," wide flat wood frame, very minor soiling, overall paint crazing, 14¾ x 21½" (ILLUS. top next page)......................**192.50**

Livestock feed, "Roe Feeds," embossed painted metal, rectangular w/rounded corners, a dark background printed in color w/a

Early Insurance Company Sign

Havoline Motor Oil Sign

Motor oil, "Havoline," porcelain flange-type, rectangular w/a round disc projecting at the top center, white lettering on dark blue reading "Havoline - the power oil - Indian Refining Company, Incorporated," rust to flange, edge chipping & scratches, 19 x 24" (ILLUS.) **660.00**

Roe Feeds Sign

cartoon-like scene of a "seed-bag" man & various farm animals, in green, red, brown, black & white, very minor scratches & edge chipping, 23 x 28" (ILLUS.) **253.00**

Socony Air-Craft Oils Sign

Motor oil, "Socony Air-Craft Oils," porcelain, rectangular, white lettering on a dark ground w/a flying monoplane at the center, professionally restored, scratches, very minor chips to one mounting hole," 30" w., 20" h. (ILLUS.) **1,540.00**

Rare Mincemeat Sign

Mincemeat, "None Such Condensed Mince Meat," tin, printed in color w/a large bust portrait of an American Indian chief above the wording "None Such - Condensed Mince Meat. - Merreel & Soule, Syracuse, N.Y.," in an old wooden shadowbox frame (ILLUS.) **8,250.00**

Benjamin Moore Paint Sign

Paint, "Benjamin Moore Paint," die-cut cardboard, a half-length cut-out portrait of a house painter at the top holding a can of paint & saying "I use Moore Paint," a colorful framed rectangular street scene below w/a panel in the lower left reading "Picture your home in Moore's Paint," 22½ x 33" (ILLUS. bottom previous page) **88.00**

Dutch Masters Paint Sign

Paint, "Dutch Master Paints," porcelain, round, the bust portrait of a Dutch master in the center, wording in the border band, red, white & black background, black lettering, minor scratches, 26" d (ILLUS.) **203.50**

Indian Root Pills Sign

Patent medicine, "Dr. Morse's Indian Root Pills," stand-up cardboard, three-fold, triple-arch top, contin-uous landscape w/American Indian seated figure & tepees, in red, green, yellow, blue, brown & pink w/blue & red lettering, 42" w., 27" h. (ILLUS.) **269.50**
Patent medicine, "Dr. Pierce's Family Medicines," lithographed paper, rectangular, a colorful detailed scene of a Victorian interior w/am older couple & a younger couple w/their daughter around a table

Dr. Pierce's Medicines Sign

w/the product, boxes of the products along the bottom, in a walnut shadowbox frame, ca. 1870s (ILLUS.) **17,600.00**
Phonograph, "RCA Victor," colored lithograph print of the famous logo scene of Nipper listening to 'His Master's Voice,' green, brown, blue, gold & white, in narrow wooden frame, 7½ x 10" (two minor creases) **55.00**

Baldwin Piano Sign

Pianos, "The Baldwin Piano," reverse-painted glass, rectangular, gold lettering on a brick red ground, in a wooden frame, minor soiling & flaking, 16 x 27½" (ILLUS.) **121.00**
Post office, painted wood, oval w/weathered black ground & large white lettering in three lines reading "Plainville Post Office" on one side, Ohio, 31" l., 18¼" h. **247.50**
Rope, "Columbian Manila Rope," cardboard stand-up type, 3-D effect w/a large round disc at the top framing a large sailing ship on a rectangular water-design base printed w/a picture of the product & "Columbian - Pure Manila Rope," red & black lettering, w/original mailing box, bottom corners slightly bent, 40½" w., 42" h. (ILLUS. top next page) **165.00**
Scales, "Fairbanks Scales," porcelain, white lettering on narrow rectangular

Columbian Manila Rope Sign

Fairbanks Scales Sign

blue ground, minor edge chipping, 44" l., 9" h. (ILLUS.) **82.50**
Shoes, "Hamilton, Brown Shoe Co.," lithographed paper, half-length color portrait of a pretty young woman w/long dark hair draped over one shoulder, wearing a low-cut red dress & holding a bunch of fruit to her bosom, green background, printed "Compliments of Hamilton Brown Shoe Co. - St. Louis, U.S.A.," ornate molded gilt plaster & black banded frame, 25½ x 30" (frame edge chips) **176.00**

Jettlicks Neon Shoe Sign

Shoes, "Enna Jettlicks," neon, the brand in yellow neon letters above a printed band reading "America's Smartest Walking Shoes," 8 x 27½" (ILLUS.) **231.00**
Soft drink, "Canada Dry," painted die-cut & embossed tin, company shield logo in green, white & yellow w/red letters, 15" w., 14½" h. (ILLUS. top next column) **88.00**
Soft drink, "Grapette Soda," porcelain, oval, red & white lettering on a navy blue ground w/red & white

Canada Dry Die-Cut Sign

Grapette Soda Sign

border, reads "Grapette Soda - Imitation Grape Flavor," metal insert missing on mounting hole, 10 x 17" (ILLUS.) **154.00**
Soft drink, "Moxie," self-framed tin, rectangular, a scene of the racing Moxiemobile w/horse figure & rider, going past a large roadside billboard reading "Drink Moxie - Distinctively

Moxie "Hall of Fame" Sign

Different," in blue, red, gold, green, yellow & cream, 27" l., 19" h. (nail holes overall, paint loss at edges, scratches) **385.00**

Soft drink, "Moxie," self-framed embossed metal, tall rectangular form w/a scene of a classical temple housing a giant bottle of Moxie, reads "Eclipses Everything - Moxie - Hall of Fame - Drink Moxie - Distinctively - Different," colorful, minor paint chips to edges & at bottom lettering, 18" w., 53" h. (ILLUS. bottom previous page) **550.00**

Early Moxie Sign

Soft drink, "Moxie," pressed cardboard, glass & metal frame, rectangular, large gold letters on a black ground, under glass, in a gilt metal frame w/hanging chain, pre-1900 (ILLUS.) **1,012.00**

Moxie Sign with Victorian Lady

Soft drink, "Moxie," embossed tin, rectangular, colorful scene of a Victorian lady pouring a glass of Moxie from a large bottle, blue & red lettering on a white ground, reads "'Of Course' You'll Have Some - Moxie - It's so Healthful, So

Strengthening.," slight corner damage & overall dirt & light wear (ILLUS.) **2,950.00**

Soft drink, "Royal Crown Cola," painted tin, rectangular, yellow & white embossed lettering reading "Drink Royal Crown Cola - Best by Taste-Test," oval reserve w/a bottle to the right, all on a red background, 12 x 30" (very minor scratches) **66.00**

R-Pep Sign

Soft drink, "R-Pep," painted embossed tin, rectangular, red, yellow & orange w/cream & green lettering, reads "Drink R-Pep - 5¢" & shows bottle, minor scratches, paint chips & denting, 17½ x 36" (ILLUS.) **110.00**

Oval 7 Up Sign

Soft drink, "7 Up," painted tin, oval, orange center w/silver edge, reads "'Fresh up' with 7 Up," scratches, edge rust, 30 x 40" (ILLUS.) **181.50**

Soup, "Campbell's Condensed Vegetable Soup," porcelain, designed as a large labeled soup can in red & white, 14" w., 22½" h. (ILLUS. top next page)..................**2,420.00**

Spark plugs, "Superior Spark Plug Co.," painted tin, rectangular, center design of a half-length man behind a large spark plug, wording reads "Meet A Superior" at top, "Superior Spark Plug Co." at bottom, red ground w/white & black lettering, 7" w., 18" h. (minor edge rust) **209.00**

Campbell's Soup Can Sign

The French Line Sign

Rare Peoria Starch Sign

Dixon's Stove Polish Sign

Stove Polish," marked in the lower right corner "Joseph Dixon Crucible Co. Jersey City, NJ Established 1827," framed, creases, tear at 'Dixon's,' ca. 1890s, 15½ x 31¼" (ILLUS.) **522.50**

Starch, "Peoria Starch Co., framed lithographed paper, large sepia & white center w/a portrait of two pretty Victorian children, brown ground w/white lettering, reads at top "Superb Gloss - Improved Corn - Starch," at the bottom w/"Manu-factured by - Peoria Starch Co. - Peoria, Ills.," in a narrow wood-grained & gold frame, very minor creases & edge tears, 22½ x 28½" (ILLUS.) **1,980.00**

Steamship line, "The French Line," self-framed metal, a wide flat serpentine wood-grained frame around a colorful rectangular scene of the ocean liner "Great Ocean Flyer," some fading & scratches, 28 x 38" (ILLUS. top next column) ...**467.50**

Stove polish, "Dixon's Stove Polish," lithographed paper, a colorful scene of a pretty Victorian maiden peeking around a large tree, printed in green, blue, red & yellow w/cream lettering, reads "Dixon's Carburet of Iron

D.B. Clark Tavern Sign

Tavern "D.B. Clark," painted wood, double-sided, rectangular, one side painted w/a scene of a man hooking a white horse up to a carriage, the reverse shows an American eagle surmounting a panoply of flags, name inscribed across the bottom, 19th c., imperfections, wear, 43½" l., 35½" h. (ILLUS.) **3,190.00**

Tavern, "Golden Fleece," carved & painted pine, a swell-bodied ram sheep w/carved fur & curled horns suspended from a bow knot, the whole within oval wrought-iron frame, gilded, probably England, 19th c., 21" w., 28" h. **3,738.00**

Red Rose Tea Sign

Tea, "Red Rose Tea," embossed painted tin, rectangular, features a large colored box of the product, printed on the sides "Red Rose Tea 'is good tea'," green, cream & red on a black ground, very minor scratches & denting, 19 x 29" (ILLUS.) **110.00**

Telephone, "Bell System," round porcelain, blue on white, blue bell emblem in the center, outer ring printed w/"Public Telephone," 7" d..**137.50**

Tires, "Firestone Cycle Tires," painted metal, flange-mounted, rectangular w/navy blue ground w/red & white lettering reading "Firestone Cycle Tires - For Sale Here," early 20th c., 22" l., 11½" h. (overall minor scratches, chipping).........................**330.00**

Good Year Tires Sign

Tires, "Good Year Tires," self-framed tin, flat rectangular wood-grained frame around a scene of a large foot w/winged sandal, reads "Agency - Good Year - Akron, Ohio. - Tires," blue & red lettering on a grey & pale

blue ground, minor scratches & minor edge chipping, 10 x 16½" (ILLUS.) **1,540.00**

Diamond Tire Service Sign

Tire service, "Diamond Tire Service," flange-type, die-cut painted metal, a half-round tire above a rectangular shield printed w/"Diamond Tire Service," cream, red, gold, blue & grey, rust spotting, paint chipping, 17½ x 27" (ILLUS.) **522.50**

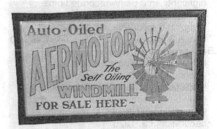

Aermotor Windmill Sign

Windmill, "Aermotor Windmill," framed cardboard, the head of a large windmill to the right of the wording "Auto-Oiled - Aermotor - The Self Oiling - Windmill - For Sale Here," yellow ground w/red & black lettering, grey & red windmill, very minor soiling, 11½ x 19½" (ILLUS.) **495.00**

(End of Signs & Signboards Section)

SILHOUETTES

These cut-out paper portraits in profile were named after Etienne de Silhouette, Louis XV's unpopular minister of finance and an amateur profile cutter. As originally applied, the term was synonymous with cheapness, or anything reduced to its simplest state. These substitutes for the more expensive oil paintings or miniatures were popular from about 1770 until 1850 when daguerreotype images replaced the vogue. Silhouettes may be either hollow-cut, with the head cut away leaving the white paper frame for mounting against a dark background, or the profile itself may be cut from black paper and pasted to a light background.

Bust portrait of a gentleman, hollow-cut, portly man wearing a wing collar, black ink & gilded detail, back marked "Mr. Minney, Butler to his Majesty George IV," black lacquer frame w/gilded detail, 4⅞" w., 5½" h.................................**$357.50**

Bust portrait of a young woman, red & gilt detail, back dated 1826, black lacquer frame w/gilded detail, 4¼" w., 5" h. (wear & minor surface damage)..**412.50**

Bust profile portrait of an elderly gentleman, hollow-cut, shown wearing a high stock & tie, mounted over black fabric, pen & ink highlights, in a paint-decorated pine frame in black w/free-hand gold leaf sprigs at the corners, ca. 1830, image 3" w. **1,495.00**

Bust profile portrait of a young boy, hollow-cut, wearing a black jacket w/white Eton collar, mounted over black fabric, water-color trim, in early black-painted pine frame w/stencilled gilt leaves & free-hand decoration, ca. 1825, 2⅞ x 3½"....................................**2,013.00**

Silhouette of Robert Wright

Bust profile portrait of a young man, hollow-cut, shown facing right & wearing a high-collared jacket, inscribed at bottom w/his name "Robert Wright," dated 1830, in a

rectangular carved stone frame, 3 x 4½" (ILLUS.) **805.00**

Bust profile portrait of a young man, hollow-cut, facing left, wearing a high collar, w/pencil & ink detail, printed label "Worcester Farr, Aged 22, 1829, framed, 4½" w., 5½" h......**330.00**

Bust profile portrait of a young officer, hollow-cut, in uniform w/epaulets, w/charcoal gouache, blank ink & gilt detail, black lacquer frame w/gilded detail, 4½" w., 5⅜" h...**220.00**

Bust Portrait of a Young Woman

Bust profile portrait of a young woman, hollow-cut, facing right, her hair pulled back into a chignon, wearing a dress w/a high ruffled collar, in a gilt sunburst églomisé border & giltwood frame, American school, 19th c., 3⅛ x 4½" (ILLUS.) **460.00**

Bust profile portrait of a young woman, hollow-cut, facing right, her hair pulled up into a chignon, wearing a high-collared dress, pen & ink detailing, worn oval églomisé glass & an embossed oval frame, early 19th c., 5⅛ x 5⅞".....................**203.50**

Bust profile portrait of a young woman facing right, hollow-cut, her hair in an upsweep held w/a comb, wearing a narrow white collar, pencil detail, églomisé glass & gilded frame, 5½" w., 7" h.......................**1,017.50**

Full-length portrait of a gentleman, free-cut, standing facing right & wearing a black frock coat & carrying a top hat, mounted on white paper w/pencil & wash, in a fine heart & star-inlaid maple frame, written on the back is "'Pinxt by P. Lord 14 Central St. Lowell Mass. July 17 1843,' an itinerant profilist Lord was born in Newburyport 1814-

Fine Full-Length Silhouette

1888," by Philip Lord, 5¾ x 10"
(ILLUS.) **12,650.00**
Full-length portrait of a gentleman
w/top hat & walking stick, cut black
paper against a sepia ink
background on paper, signed "Aug.
Edouart fecit New Orleans, Augt.
1843," matted & framed, 11" w.,
14¼" h...**467.50**
Full-length portrait of a girl gathering
flowers, hollow-cut, depicted in
profile wearing a full skirt &
pantalets, holding a basket of
flowers in her right hand & a flower
in her left hand, strip of cut-out
flowers in the foreground &
"Elizabeth" & then an ink-wash
ground, old gilt frame, 10" w.,
12½" h. (minor stains) **770.00**
Full-length portrait of a military
officer, standing facing right &
wearing a low cap, long coat &
carrying a long sword under one
arm, inscribed "Lt. W.B. Knipe 5th
drag. Gs. Birmingham 12th June,
1838," England, rebacked in ogee
maple frame, 10¼ x 13¾" **302.50**

SNUFF BOTTLES & BOXES

*The habit of taking snuff (powdered
tobacco meant for inhaling) began in 17th
century France and reached its peak
during the 18th century, spreading to
England, elsewhere on the Continent, and
even to China, probably introduced there
by Spanish or Portuguese traders. In
Europe, tightly hinged porcelain or metal
boxes were considered desirable containers
to house the aromatic snuff. Orientals
favored bottles of porcelain or glass, or
carved of agate, ivory or jade. By mid-19th
century the popularity of snuff declined.*

BOTTLES

Chinese Ivory Snuff Bottle

Amber, flattened rectangular form
w/rounded corners, carved on each
side w/a phoenix amid flowering tree
peony, China, 1750-80 ....**$1,265.00**
Bamboo node, flattened rounded
form, carved in the form of a lobed
pod w/a cluster of fleshy leaves
issuing from each side of the small
mouth, the material of finely spotted
warm brown, China, 1800-80...........**805.00**
Banded agate, swelled cylindrical
form w/a short neck, translucent
grey w/a band of white around the
middle & brown striping at the base,
China, 1800-80 ....**12,650.00**
Brass, egg-shaped w/short cylindrical
neck, a disc-form depression on one
side flanked by two incised
archaistic dragons & a flaming pearl,
disc-form handles on the sides,
China, by Cheng Rongzhang, dated
to Shunzhi Sixth year (1649) **10,350.00**
Cobalt blue Aventurine glass,
flattened shouldered ovoid form,
deep cobalt blue flecked w/gold,
China, 18th c.............................**2,760.00**
Inside-painted glass, flattened
rectangular form w/rounded
shoulders, painted on one side in
tones of *grisaille* w/the half-length
portrait of a Chinese official, the
reverse w/an inscription, by Ma
Shaoxuan, China, dated to midsummer of the dingwei year,
1907 ....**8,050.00**
Ivory, finger citron-form,
naturalistically carved as a finger
citron, w/a leafy branch extending
down one side, an insect on the
other, China, 18th c. **1,092.00**
Ivory, flattened ovoid form, finely
carved on one side w/Liu Hai, his

string of cash & his toad, the reverse
w/an official & a candle pricket,
China, 19th c. (ILLUS.) **1,725.00**

Lacquer, flattened rounded form in
dark green, carved on one side w/a
pheasant in magnolia branches, the
reverse w/a phoenix amid peony
branches, China, 19th c. **1,265.00**

Limestone, flattened ovoid form, dark
grey material w/fine horizontal
banding in brown & light grey,
China, 19th c. **5,520.00**

Malachite, flattened ovoid form, dark
green w/black striations, China,
19th c **460.00**

Rare Overlay Glass Snuff Bottle

Overlay glass, carved through the
blue layer to white w/a bird soaring
over lotus on one side, the reverse
w/a flowering peony & *lingzhi*
emerging from rockery, China,
1750-1850 (ILLUS.) **13,800.00**

Overlay glass, carved through the
blue layer to clear w/a carp & lotus
on each side, the rim & foot in blue,
China, 1780-1850 (tiny rim
chip) **1,725.00**

Overlay glass, carved through the
emerald green to the bubble-
suffused frosty clear ground, on one
side w/a frog among lotus plants,
the reverse w/a carp emerging from
the waves & water plants,
China **2,875.00**

Overlay glass, carved through the
red overlay to a milk white ground
w/a continuous scrolling vine
bearing double-gourds, China,
1750-1850.....................................**1,380.00**

Porcelain, blue-glazed, flattened
ovoid form, finely molded around the
sides w/a continuous design of a
five-clawed dragon chasing a
flaming pearl amid formalized
clouds, the eyes of the dragon
painted in white w/black pupils,
attributed to Jingdezhen, China,
1820-70...**4,025.00**

Porcelain, *Famille Rose,* flattened
rounded form, painted on each side
w/the Eighteen Lohans & their
attributes in a garden setting, in
various attitudes, the shoulders
adorned w/mock mask & ring
handles, Daoguang, China, 1821-50
(slight chip to foot rim) **920.00**

Root amber, gourd-form, tall slender
ribbed ovoid shape, carved through
the translucent & ochre matrix as a
gourd w/pendant leafy tendrils & a
butterfly on one side, China, 1800-
80...**862.00**

Yellow faceted glass, round
flattened form w/octagonal facets at
the edges, China, 1750-1800 ....**9,200.00**

BOXES

German Wooden Snuff Box

Brass w/engraved mother-of-pearl
sides & tortoiseshell top, slender
rectangular shaped w/cut corners,
the top centered by a small oblong
silver medallion engraved "C.C. to
J.B.," 2⅝" l. **357.50**

Burl wood, rectangular, the top
carved in bold relief w/a humorous
interior bedroom scene, an
inscription across the bottom,
Germany, early 19th c., 2¾ x 4"
(ILLUS.) **431.00**

Gold, presentation-type, shaped oval
form, engine-turned, the hinged
cover set w/scattered diamonds
centering an oval enamel plaque
painted w/a bust portrait miniature of
a young lady bordered by diamonds,
a diamond-set coronet above,
maker's mark "L.T.," Paris, France,
ca. 1860, 3¾" l. **11,500.00**

Gold, rectangular, top-opening,
chased w/foliage on a matted
ground, Switzerland, ca. 1810,
3½" l..**1,610.00**

Gold & enamel, narrow rectangular
form, the cover enameled w/figures
by a river, the surround & the base

engine-turned, Switzerland, ca.
1805, 3¼" l. **5,750.00**
Ivory, figural, carved as a pug dog's
head shown licking its lips, the eyes
set w/tiger's eye agate, w/a gilt-
metal mount, ca. 1765, 1⅞" l. **1,380.00**
Papier-maché, black round box, the
lid inset w/a miniature on ivory of a
young man in the 18th c. attire,
3½" d. (lens missing) **137.50**
Papier-maché, round, the cover w/a
bust portrait of a uniformed army
officer titled "Alexander Macomb,"
early 19th c., 3⅝" d. **660.00**
Purpurine & micro-mosaic,
rectangular, the cover w/a micro-
mosaic depicting the Colosseum
within a silver-gilt mounting, in
original fitted green leather case w/a
presentation inscription, Luigi
Mascelli, Rome, Italy, ca. 1820,
3½" l. **6,325.00**
Silver, shallow oval form, the slip-on
cover engraved w/a two-handled
vase of flowers within a border of
overlapping leaftips, the base
engraved w/contemporary initials
"IS" centered by a flowerhead, later
scratched w/initial "P," apparently
unmarked, American-made, 18th c.,
3" l. **1,955.00**
Silver, rectangular w/hinged lid,
engraved design, gilt interior,
Vienna, Austria, 1847, 3½" l. **316.00**
Wood, thin rectangular box carved on
the top w/three male figures within a
scroll border, France, early 19th c.,
2½ x 3½" **287.50**

SODA FOUNTAIN COLLECTIBLES

*The neighborhood ice cream parlor and
drugstore soda fountain are pretty much a
thing of the past as fast-food chains have
sprung up across the country. Memories of
the slower-paced lifestyle represented by
the rapidly disappearing local soda
fountain have spurred the interest of many
collectors today. Anything relating to the
soda fountains of old and the delicious
concoctions they dispensed are much
sought-after.*

APPLIANCES
Malted milk mixer, "Hamilton Beach,"
marble base, brass mixer shaft, rare
early model **$225.00**

ICE CREAM SCOOPS & SERVERS
"Benedict Indestructo No. 14" **32.00**

"Crisscraft No. 31" **28.00**
"Fisher Motor Co., Ltd., Orilla,
Ontario, Canada," 'Cold Dog'
cylinder-type, German silver,
wooden handle, 1920s, 9½" l. **750.00**
"Gilchrist No. 30," size 24, nickel-
plated brass, metal squeeze-type
handle, patented in 1914,
10½" l. ....**50.00 to 75.00**
"Gilchrist No. 31," size 6, round,
nickel-plated brass, wooden handle,
patented in 1915, 11" l. **95.00**
"Hamilton Beach Model 60-B,"
round **65.00**
"Hamilton Beach Model 65," size
20, stainless steel w/black Bakelite
handle **22.00**
"Royal No. 5," cone-shaped, key
release **30.00**

CONTAINERS & DISPENSERS

Grapine - Orangenectar Cooler

Cooler, "Grapine - Orangenectar,"
metal & glass, two barrel-shaped
clear glass jars w/domed metal
covers sit atop a wide cylindrical
metal base molded w/ornate scroll
bands & w/clusters of grapes &
oranges flanking the wording
"California Grapine - Orangenectar -
5¢," very minor paint wear, 14" d.,
26" h. (ILLUS.) **1,430.00**
Ice cream cone dispenser, counter-
type, "Turnball Cones & Cups,"
cylindrical tin, orange w/round cover,
side handles, from "Dairy Queen
Fountain Ohio," depicts dispenser &
cones, 16" d., 26½" h......................**130.00**
Syrup dispenser, "Brazilla,"
stoneware, barrel-shaped, white
w/blue rings & red lettering reading
"Drink - Brazilla - 5¢," very minor
soiling, 8" d., 11½" h. (ILLUS.
top next page) **990.00**

Brazilla Syrup Dispenser

SPACE AGE COLLECTIBLES

Although fiction novels about space exploration have been around since the 19th century, and such space fantasies as "Flash Gordon" and "Buck Rogers" were popular in the 1930s, the modern Space Age started after World War II. There have been dozens of space science fiction movies and television shows produced since the early 1950s when Russia and the United States were locked in the "Space Race." Our listings are divided into 'Space Exploration Memorabilia,' relating to actual historical events and 'Space Fantasy Items,' which were produced to tie-in to all the movies, TV shows and works of fiction released since the early 1950s. These 'fantasy' listings are arranged alphabetically by the name of the character, show or movie.

Also see CHARACTER COLLECTIBLES, TOYS and LUNCH BOXES.

SPACE EXPLORATION MEMORABILIA

Coloring book, "Apollo Man on the Moon," by Saalfield, unused, 1969..**$40.00**

Document, "Man on the Moon," blue satin, commemorative of the 1969 moon landing **25.00**

Jigsaw puzzle, Space Shuttle Columbia, Jaymar, mint in unopened box **20.00**

Model kit, "Challenger," sealed box.....**75.00**

Pencil clip, "International Association of Machinists & Aerospace Workers," depicts tools, patriotic colors, early **15.00**

Phonograph record, 45 RPM, Hugh Downs narrates the landing of the "First Man on the Moon," 1969 ....**16.00**

Pinback button, "Man's First Landing On The Moon," w/ribbon attached, Apollo 11, pictures three astronauts **19.00**

Print, 1969 moon landing commemorative, silver on blue, 5½ x 8½"....................................**15.00**

Record & book set, "To the Moon," Time-Life records presentation, "The Story in Sound, Picture & Text, July 20, 1969, mint in box **75.00**

SPACE FANTASY ITEMS

"Forbidden Planet" Insert Card

Chewbacca (Star Wars) bank, figural, ceramic, Sigma **65.00**

"Forbidden Planet" movie insert card, large scene of Robby, the

"Invasion of The Saucer-Men" Poster

Robot carrying a scantily clad woman, MGM, 1956, above average condition, 14 x 36" (ILLUS.) **2,070.00**

"Invasion of The Saucer-Men" movie poster, three-sheet, colorful design of a big-headed creature holding a scantily-clad woman, AIP, 1957, linen-backed, 41 x 81" (ILLUS. bottom previous page) **1,610.00**

"Not of This Earth" Poster

"Not of This Earth" movie poster, three-sheet, large scene of a huge screaming woman's head beside an alien grasping the Earth, Allied Artists, 1957, linen-backed, above average condition, 41 x 81" (ILLUS.) **805.00**

Rocky Jones, Space Ranger (TV), coloring book, 11 x 15", unused.........**48.00**

Space Cadet (TV) coin, plastic flasher-type, red & white, front features rocket ship launching, back w/"Space Cadet Rocket Ship," 1950s, 1¼" d.....................................**25.00**

Space Cadet (TV) membership card, "Rocket-Lite Squadron," 1950s, 3 x 5"...**20.00**

Space 1999 (TV) game, board-type, 1976, boxed **65.00**

Space Patrol (TV) Diplomatic Pouch, complete ....**225.00 to 250.00**

Space Patrol (TV) ring, "Hydrogen Ray Gun" **200.00**

Space Patrol (TV) spaceship, long flat two-dimensional plastic shaped spaceship in color, from the Lunar Fleet set, 1950s, 2¾" l. (minor scratches) **25.00**

"Space Race" card game, color lithographed, each card w/different scenes, w/instructions, 1952, boxed **45.00**

Star Trek (movie) coloring book, 1978, mint condition.........................**20.00**

Star Trek Communicator Prop

Star Trek (TV) communicator prop, the original prop finished in hard grey plastic w/gold hinged mesh cover, dual knobs, three simulated indicator lights, 3-D wave screen & Velcro holding tape, ca 1967, 2½ x 4" (ILLUS.) ....**3,000.00 to 4,000.00**

Star Trek (movie) model kit, "The Bridge," 1975, unassembled, complete **40.00**

Star Trek (TV) model kit, "USS Enterprise," plastic, AMT, 1968, mint in box **120.00**

Star Wars calendar, 1978, in illustrated cardboard mailer **55.00**

Stars Wars collector's case, "Return of the Jedi" figural C-3PO, No. SW-1825, 1983, by Kenner, in original box & shrink wrap (shows some wear from storage).............................**39.00**

Stars Wars comb & keeper, "Rebo Band," plastic comb fits into base,

C-3PO Cookie Jar

small plastic star attached by string to one end, Rebo Band shown on base, marked w/Stars Wars logo, mint in package..................................**14.00**

Star Wars comb & keeper, "Speeder," plastic comb fits into base, small plastic star attached by string to one end, comb decorated w/R2-D2 & C-3PO, base shaped like a landspeeder, marked w/Star Wars logo, mint in package.........................**14.00**

Star Wars cookie jar, cov., figural C-3PO, gold finish, Roman Ceramics (ILLUS. bottom previous page) ....**350.00 to 450.00**

"Darth Vader" Mask & Helmet

Star Wars face mask & helmet, "Darth Vader," molded black plastic, two-piece construction, marked "Don Post Studios 20th Century Fox" (ILLUS.) **91.00**

Stars Wars doll, "Princess Leia Organa," wearing white outfit w/silver belt, white knee socks & white shoes, Kenner, near mint, 11½" h. (hair rubberbands broken)...**60.00**

Star Wars figure, Han Solo, small, complete **200.00**

Star Wars figure, Jawa, small, complete **85.00**

Star Wars figure, Luke Skywalker, small, complete **65.00**

Star Wars magnet, colored plastic magnets of Darth Vader, Chewbacca, R2-D2 & Yoda, w/Jedi logo, 1", mint in package, set of four....**5.00**

Star Wars mug, ceramic, figural Darth Vader, large **60.00**

Star Wars plate, 10th Anniversary Commemorative, colorful applied stencil shows characters from the movie, gold lettering around the edge, limited edition to 14 days, numbered, 1987 ....**66.00**

Star Wars pop-up comb, comes w/flip-up mirror which locks closed

when inserted, decorated w/C-3PO & R2-D2 w/Star Wars logo, mint in package **14.00**

Star Wars pop-up comb, comes w/flip-up mirror which locks closed when inserted, decorated w/Darth Vader & Jedi logo, mint in package **14.00**

Star Wars toy, 'Return of the Jedi' B-Wing fighter, molded plastic, by Kenner, 1984, 22" l **32.00**

Star Wars night-light, plastic, figural head of C-3PO, marked w/Jedi logo, mint in package..................................**15.00**

Star Wars night-light, plastic, figural head of Darth Vader, marked w/Jedi logo, mint in package.........................**20.00**

Star Wars night-light, plastic, flat w/color image of C-3PO, Jedi logo, mint in package...................................**10.00**

Star Wars night-light, plastic, flat w/color image of Yoda, Jedi logo, mint in package...................................**10.00**

Star Wars "At-At" Transport

Star Wars toy, 'Empire Strikes Back' "At-At" armored transport, molded plastic, No. SW-1550, by Kenner, 1981 (shows some play wear) (ILLUS.) **40.00**

Star Wars toy, "Land Speeder" vehicle, molded plastic, No. SW-1520, 1977, by Kenner, in original box (box & toy show some storage wear) **60.00**

Star Wars toy set, "Duel at Death Star Race Set," complete, original box **75.00**

"The Day The Earth Stood Still" movie lobby cards, each w/a different color scene from the movie, 20th Century-Fox, 1951, 11 x 14", set of 8 (ILLUS. top next page).....**2,070.00**

"The Man From Planet X" movie poster, three-sheet, the spaceman confronting an earthwoman, large spaceship in the background, United

Movie Lobby Card Set

"The Man From Planet X" Poster

Artists, 1951, linen-backed, 41 x 81"
(ILLUS.) **7,130.00**
Tom Corbett, Space Cadet (TV)
photo, in original mailer......................**40.00**
Tom Corbett, Space Cadet (TV) rifle,
"Atomic Ray," Louis Marx & Co.,
original box **300.00**
Tom Corbett, Space Cadet (TV) wrist
watch, original cardboard rocketship

"2001" Movie Poster

display card, Ingraham,
1951 ....**150.00 to 200.00**
"2001: A Space Odyssey" movie
poster, three-sheet, large painting of
a space station, MGM, 1968,
average condition w/some tears &
wear, 41 x 81" (ILLUS.)....................**287.50**

(End of Space Age Collectibles Section)

SPORTS MEMORABILIA

1949 NY Yankees Signed Baseball

Baseball, 1949 New York Yankees
team ball, an official American
League baseball signed by twenty-
seven members of the World
Champion 1949 New York Yankees,

Joe DiMaggio signed the sweet spot, others include, Yogi Berra, Rizzuto, Henrich, Dickey, Reynolds, Lopat, Bauer & Woodling (ILLUS.) **$1,265.00**

1970 NY Mets Signed Baseball

Baseball, 1970 New York Mets team baseball, an official National League baseball signed by twenty-nine members of the 1970 New York Mets, this team was almost identical to the 1969 World Championship team, Gil Hodges on the sweet spot, others include Nolan Ryan, Tom Seaver, Yogi Berra, Bud Harrelson, Jerry Koosman, Tommy Agee & Jerry Gote (ILLUS.)..........................**299.00**

Baseball bat, hand-made bat signed by over ninety former Negro League players, including Buck Leonard, Hank Aaron, Josh Gibson Jr., Leon Day, Double Duty Radcliffe, Cool Papa Bell, Monte Irvin, Minnie Minoso & Ray Noble, made by Lyman Bostock Sr.........................**1,840.00**

Baseball bat, Lou Brock game-used Louisville Slugger 125, Model M-110, signature Lou Brack bat (3 inch crack 13" from the knob)..................**127.00**

Book, "Zupke of Illinois," by Red Grange, first edition, one of a thousand copies, copy number 793 inscribed by Grange w/"Sincerely to my friend Christy Walsh from Red Grange"...**391.00**

Booklet, "America's Cup," 1899, illustrated **90.00**

Book, "Training for Boxers," by Nat Fleischer, contains photos of famous boxers, 1937 ....**32.00**

Christmas card, 1990-91 season card from the Chicago Bulls, pictures drawing of the team caroling w/"Silver Bulls" on the front

Chicago Bulls Christmas Card

& "Silver Bulls, Silver Bulls, It's basketball time in the City," signed by Michael Jordan (ILLUS.) **483.00**

Sid Luckman Signed Football

Football, signed by Hall of Fame Quarterback Sid Luckman (ILLUS.) **460.00**

Football Official Program, 6th annual All-Star game, college All-Americans vs. New York Giants, 1939..**150.00**

Football program, for a game between the University of Southern California & Washington State University at the Los Angeles Coliseum on October 9, 1926, featuring a tackle named Marion Morrison (John Wayne), his picture on page six **173.00**

Glass, "Kentucky Derby," 1949..**150.00**

Glass, "Kentucky Derby," 1954..**150.00**

Glass, "Kentucky Derby," 1956..**125.00**

Glass, "Kentucky Derby," 1957..**100.00**

Glass, "Kentucky Derby," 1958, gold bar...**117.50**

Glass, "Kentucky Derby," 1960..**52.50**

Glass, "Kentucky Derby," 1961..**72.00**

Glass, "Kentucky Derby," 1963..**45.00**

Glass, "Kentucky Derby," 1964 (ILLUS. top next page).....................**39.00**

1964 Kentucky Derby Glass

Glass, "Kentucky Derby,"
1966...**39.00**
Glass, "Kentucky Derby,"
1967...**36.50**
Glass, "Kentucky Derby,"
1968...**31.00**
Glass, "Kentucky Derby,"
1970...**45.00**
Glass, "Kentucky Derby,"
1972...**22.00**
Glass, "Kentucky Derby,"
1973...**22.00**
Glass, "Kentucky Derby,"
1976...**12.00**
Glass, "Kentucky Derby,"
1978...**9.00**
Glass, "Kentucky Derby,"
1982...**6.00**
Glass, "Kentucky Derby,"
1984...**6.00**

Lombardi Glass

Glass, Vince Lombardi, Green Bay
Packers, from Pizza Hut
(ILLUS.) **25.00**

Golf club, putter, wood shaft w/brass
head, Otey Crisma...........................**150.00**
Golf clubs, "MacGregor," wood
shafts, two woods, six matching
irons, putter, bag, balls, tees &
glove, ca. 1930s, the set.................**450.00**
Golf clubs, stainless steel w/wood
shafts, Shaler, three irons &
putter, the group **95.00**
Golf score cards, depicts pro, tips,
etc., 1939, set of 6 ....**10.00**
Guide, "Spaulding's Ice Hockey
Guide," 1937 ....**35.00**

Pele's Soccer Jersey

Jersey, 1970s, Pele Cosmos game
used New York Cosmos jersey,
bears the number "10" & a
"Cosmos" patch on the front
w/"PELE" & number "10" on the
back (ILLUS.) **3,220.00**
Jersey, 1989, Darryl Strawberry
home Mets jersey, all tags & labels
authentic **518.00**
Plate, aluminum, depicts a golfer in
action, Wendell August Forge,
8" d...**65.00**
Poster, "Sammy Harris," black boxer,
ca. 1920s **45.00**
Program, boxing, 1927, program for
the famous "long count"
championship fight between
heavyweight champion Gene
Tunney & ex-champion/challenger
Jack Dempsey at Soldier's Field,
Chicago, on September 22, 1927,
slight soiling on cover
(ILLUS. top next page)....................**690.00**
Program, football, 1969, Packers &
Falcons Hall of Fame game..............**10.00**
Program, football, 1982, Cardinals &
49ers..**10.00**
Program, football, 1982, Cardinals &
Giants **10.00**
Program, football, Super Bowl IV **125.00**
Program, football, Super Bowl V **250.00**

Tunney vs. Dempsey Boxing Program

Program, hockey, 1925, first issue for the 'new' Madison Square Gardens in New York City, featuring the first public event, a hockey game between Tex Rickart's New York Americans & the Montreal Canadians, an elaborate "Historical Book" program w/photos of the teams & other notable persons congratulating the new Garden, dated December 15, 1925 ....**575.00**

Program, hockey, 1940-41, Boston Bruins vs. Toronto Maple Leafs, autographed by seventeen Boston players including six hall of famers, (program w/center fold)..................**460.00**

World Cup Soccer Program

Program, soccer, 1930, first World Cup Program, pictures leading teams & players, offered w/a souvenir medal from the games, 2 pcs. (ILLUS.).............................**805.00**

Photograph, 1955 Cleveland Indians, signed by thirty-four players & coaches, including Bob Feller, Ralph

Kiner, Herb Score, Larry Doby, Don Mossi, Al Lopez, Bob Lemon, Ferris Fain & Sal Maglie, 14½ x 19"..........**518.00**

Print, boxing, original color print of the match between Heeman & Sayer for the first international boxing championship of the world (print w/several scrapes & marks in the image) **173.00**

Poster, boxing, original site poster for the heavyweignt bout between Muhammad Ali & Alfredo Evangelista on May 16, 1977, pictures on the underside of Roberto Duran & Javier Nuniz, 14½ x 22¾"....................................**633.00**

Shirt collar, vintage men's detachable collar w/hand-written inscription "Compliments of John L. Sullivan - To Whoever gets the collar - March 3, 1907 - To Stop Arguments - size - 21 inches," the other side w/"The Noblest Roman of Them All - Now will you be good -That's all" (worn & aged)..**633.00**

Tennis ball, signed by Arthur Ashe in black marker **138.00**

Ticket stub, 1960, Oakland Raiders, from their first regular season game ever against the Houston Oilers in their American Football League debut at Kazar Stadium in San Francisco **345.00**

STATUARY

Bronzes, and other statuary, are increasingly popular with today's collectors. Particularly appealing are works by "Les Animaliers," the 19th century French school of sculptors who turned to animals for their subject matter. These, together with figures in the Art Deco and Art Nouveau taste, are available in a wide price range.

BRONZE

Beach, Chester, figure of a standing female nude, inscribed "KUNST-FOUNDRY. N.Y. - BEACH@" & foundry mark, w/marble base 9¾" h...**$460.00**

Bitter, Ary, figure group, two young children seated on a mound w/two recumbent fauns, rich greenish patina, inscribed "Ary. Bitter" & stamped "SUSSE FRES CIRE PERDUE," on a green marble base, 23" l., 11" h..................................**345.00**

Art Deco Cockatoo

Blanc, Pierre, model of an Art Deco cockatoo, bronze & black patina, inscribed "PIERRE BLANC - 5," Switzerland, ca. 1920-30s, 16¾" h. (ILLUS.) **2,760.00**

Patinated Bust of Longfellow

Brock, Thomas, bust of Longfellow, bronze, patinated, signed & dated London 1884, further inscribed "Elkington & Co. Founders," 32" h. (ILLUS.) **1,955.00**

Bugatti, Rembrandt, panthers, a pair of panthers striding on a narrow rectangular base, one behind the other, greenish brown patina, inscribed "R. Bugatti," w/foundry seal "CIRE PERDUE A.A. HEBRARD," & numbered, one of an edition of three, ca. 1904, 44¾" l., 9½" h. **123,500.00**

Chiparus, Demetre, figure of a dancer "Jupettes," a young woman toe dancing & wearing a close-fitting scally costume covering her from head to toe & flaring out into three wide, tiered skirts at her hips, carved ivory face & hands, on an oblong arched, blocked & step brown onyx base, stamped "Made in France," signed on base "Chiparus," France, early 20th c., 23¼" h......**11,500.00**

Chiparus, Demetre, "Testris," figure of an exotic female dancing posed on tip-toe w/other leg raised, her torso leaning back w/one arm straight up & the other straight down, her head turned to the side, wearing a close-fitting cap, a long pleated skirt w/a tight bodice, ivory head, neck, arms & feet, silver-gilt & polychrome finish, raised on a high & wide stepped brown marble rectangular base, inscribed "Chiparus - Made in France," ca. 1920s, 26⅝" h **46,000.00**

Bust of "Grand Dame Patricienne"

Colombo, Grang, bust of "Grand Dame Patricienne," Neopolitan lady in Renaissance costume, multicolored bronze plaque on onyx base engraved "Grand Dame Patricienne Florentine au XIV Eme Siecle," France, ca. 1905, 15½" h. (ILLUS.) **2,530.00**

Colombo, R., bust of Napoleon, depicted w/a stern expression, wearing a hat & high-collared coat, signed "R. Colombo 1885," w/garanti au titres foundry mark, 23" h...**2,310.00**

Cormier, Joseph Descomps, model of a couple kissing, nude except for a drape, parcel-gilt, inscribed "Cormier" & "Ier epreuve 1929," w/artist's monogram, 31" h **3,450.00**

Fiot, Maximilien, group of panthers, one reclining languorously, the other standing, black patina, inscribed "M. Fiot - Susse Frs. Edts. Paris - circe perdue," ca. 1925, 25" l................**5,750.00**

Gérome, Jean-Léon, "La Joueuse de Cerceau," a young lady wearing a classical robe walks & holds a large ring around her head & neck, gilt finish, on a green onyx socle, signed "J.L. GEROME," impressed "SIOT - DECAUVILLE - FONDEUR -PARIS G532," ca.1895, 12½" h...............**2,530.00**

Diana & the Hounds by Gilbert

Gilbert, Alfred, figural group of Diana & the Hounds, silvered-bronze, on a shaped black marble base, inscribed "A. Gilbert," impressed "MADE IN FRANCE," ca. 1925, one tail & bow loose, 13½" h. (ILLUS.).................**3,163.00**

Gratchev, equestrian group, depicting a Cossack standing & kissing his sweetheart goodbye, the couple embracing beside his saddled horse, signed & w/the Woerffel foundry mark, St. Petersburg, Russia, late 19th c., 13½" h. **2,185.00**

Cossack & Gypsy Woman on Horseback

Gratchev, Alexei, Cossack & Gypsy woman on horseback, dark patina, St. Petersburg foundry, Russia,

imperfections on base, 12" w., 13¾" h. (ILLUS.) **3,450.00**

Grath, Anton, Europa & the Bull, a nude woman seated cross-legged atop a large bull, gold & brown patina, inscribed "EUROPA - ANT. GRATH," on a stepped black marble base, early 20th c., 24" h. **9,200.00**

Gregoire, Jean Louis, figure of Mozart as a young boy, tuning his violin, brown patina, inscribed "L.Gregoire," titled, France, late 19th c., 30½" h. **4,888.00**

Gregory, Catherine, model of a giraffe, the recumbent animal w/its head raised & looking straight ahead, signed below the front leg "Catherine Gregory," on a black lacquered wood base, ca. 1925-30, 15¼" h.....................**2,300.00**

Guiraud-Riviere, Maurice, allegorical figure of "The Comet," a nude woman extended in a flying pose w/one arm extended straight ahead, the other on her breast, her very long hair fanned & streaming back over her body, raised on a column of flat, rounded clouds above a black stepped rectangular base, the figure parcil-gilt, the clouds cold-painted in silver & blue, inscribed "GUIRARD-RIVIERE" and "ETLING PARIS," France, early 20th c., 21¾" h......**11,500.00**

Hatvany, Christa Winsloe, model of a doe, inscribed "CHRISTA WINSLOE HATVANY - Susse Frs. Edts Paris circe perdue," w/foundry seal, brown patina, 20th c., 15" h..**1,840.00**

Kalish, Max, figure of a nude female sprawled facedown on a rockwork mound, rich greenish brown patina, inscribed "M. KALISH 24" & "ANDRO FONDEUR PARIS," on rectangular marble base, 15¼" l., 7" h..**1,035.00**

Lanceray, Eugene, equestrian group, depicting a mounted herdsman w/a child herding three horses, on an oval base, signed & w/Shtange foundry mark, late 19th c., 22" l. ...**5,750.00**

Le Faguays, Pierre, figure of a muscular male athlete throwing a javelin, mounted on a rockery base, greenish brown patina, inscribed "P. LE FAGUARY - 23," France, ca. 1925, 22" l., 13¼" h.................**2,300.00**

LeMoyne, F., figure of a dancer, poised en revelé w/arms outstretched to the sides & standing on tiptoes, her head & arms well carved in ivory, gilded, on a mottled white socle, impressed "F.

LEMOYNE" & "UNIS - FRANCE"
w/foundry marks, ca.1900,
14" h.............................**1,840.00**

Lepage, Celine, figure of a Moroccan
woman, tall slender ovoid form of a
standing woman w/her cloak pulled
tightly around her, on a rectangular
base, rich greenish brown patina,
inscribed "Celine Lepage," stamped
"3" & impressed w/the LaStele
foundry mark & w/a separate tag
inscribed "A. ETIENNE D'AMOUR
en souvenir du Xe anniversaire de D
. . . ceux de l'an V," France, early
20th c., 20¼" h..........................**5,750.00**

Muller, H., bust of a maiden in a
garland of flowers, inscribed "H
MULLER," 5" h................................**230.00**

Nachtmann, F., figure of a kneeling
nude Amazon wearing an ancient
Greek helmet & holding a bow,
medium brown patina, inscribed "F.
NACHTMANN. MUNCHEN,"
stamped "LAUCHHAMMER
BILOGUSS 15," w/foundry insignia,
20th c., Germany, 12" h...............**1,093.00**

Omerth, G., model of a cat playing
w/a ball, on a slate base, dark
patina, signed, 3¹³⁄₁₆" l., 4¼" h..........**172.50**

Pompom, Francois, model of a
stylized bird, perched w/a
streamlined body, the head raised
high & the breast continuing into a
curved wide strap forming webbed
feet, incised "POMPOM," on a
rectangular mottled black marble
base, 7⅜" h.................................**1,380.00**

Pozene, L., figure group depicting a
group of peasants including two
women & a child resting by their
wagon, a cow & their horse nearby,
signed "Sculp. L. Pozene," Russia,
late 19th c., 31½" l. **6,613.00**

Pradier, Jean Jacques, "Sappho,"
figure of a woman wearing a flowing
off-the-shoulder gown seated &
leaning forward clasping one leg,
light brown patina, inscribed "J.
PRADIER" & stamped "SUSSE
fres. - A. VS," 11½" h. **3,795.00**

Preiss Johann Philipp Ferdinand,
'Autumn Dancer,' figure of a young
woman dancing, posed on one tip-
toe w/other leg raised & arms up &
away from the body, her head
turned to the side, ivory head, neck,
arms & legs w/gilt-bronze cap & long
draped robe, on a square green
onyx pedestal & octagonal base,
inscribed "F. Preiss," Germany,
early 20th c., 14½" h. **7,360.00**

Privat, Auguste Gilbert, figure of a
nude kneeling woman, her arms
raised above her head holding a

large cluster of fruit w/two birds
perched atop it, natural patina
trimmed w/black, inscribed
"GILBERT PRIVAT - Suisse Fes.
Edt. Paris - lere Epreuve,"
ca. 1925, 31¼" h. **6,613.00**

Bronze Figure of Lalique

Riviére, Théodore Louis August,
figure of Rene Lalique standing
w/his hands in the pockets of his
jacket, dark brown patina, inscribed
"á mon ami Lalique - THEODORE
RIVIERE," 14" h. (ILLUS.).............**8,050.00**

Roch, Georg, model of a seal, the
sleek animal balancing a striped ball
on his nose, dark brown patina,
green marble base, signed "GEORG
ROCH.," ca. 1925, 14½" h. **1,035.00**

Strnad, Oskar, figure group, "Adam
und Eva," standing nude figures, he
with his arm behind her & she
holding an apple in one hand,
mounted on a bronze decorated
shaped grey marble base applied
w/a serpent, impressed "WIENER
WERKSTATTE - MADE IN
AUSTRIA" w/rose hallmarks,
ca. 1920, 23½" h. **10,350.00**

Sykes, Charles, "The Spirit of
Ecstasy," a young woman wearing a
diaphanous gown leans forward
w/her arms & robes flying behind
her, on a waisted green marble
socle, silvered finish, inscribed
"Charles Sykes," England, early
20th c., 27½" h...........................**3,450.00**

Sylvestre, Paul, 'Leda & the Swan,'
the nude Leda seated w/her legs
straight out & leaning against a large
swan which leans back against her,
dark patina, inscribed "Sylvestre -
Susse F Edts. Paris - 1854 - Fonte
sur platre," France, 29¾" l. **2,875.00**

Verschneider, Jean, figure of a
female athlete, the woman
depicted in a running stance w/one

arm thrust out in front, the other behind her & one leg bent & held high the other stretched out behind her, nude but for a drape flying straight out to the back, gilt bronze w/a dark patina, on a rectangular green marble base, inscribed "Jean Verschneider, France," ca. 1925, 30" l. (losses to gilding) **7,188.00**

Vienna bronze, model of an elephant, on stand **135.00**

Watrin, Etienne, Elizabethan maiden, the young woman standing wearing a large cap, wide lacy collar & close-fitting gown, ivory head & hands, gilt-bronze finish, late 19th - early 20th c., 13" h. **4,025.00**

Zach, Bruno, figure of a girl on a prancing horse, her torso, arms & legs of ivory, inscribed "Zach Austria," early 20th c., drilled as a lamp base, 16" l., 26½" h. **3,450.00**

MARBLE

White Marble Figure of Ariadne

Bust of a woman, shown w/an elegant coif & beaded necklace, late 19th c., 26" h. **1,495.00**

Figure of Ariadne, nude & seated on a draped panther, white marble, late 19th c., small chips, repair, 15½" l., 18" h. (ILLUS.) **1,092.00**

Figure of a woman, standing, wearing a classical dress adorned w/flowers, white marble, Europe, 19th c., chips, 24½" h. (ILLUS. top next column) **1,380.00**

Figure of a Gypsy woman holding a mandolin, Italian white marble, on a Carrara marble pedestal, late 19th c., overall height 76" (ILLUS. middle next column) **14,950.00**

Figure of Woman in Classical Dress

Figure of a Gypsy Woman

Grey Marble Horse's Head

Lombardi, G.B., figure of a woman in classical dress, seated w/an outstretched arm, signed "G.B. Lombardi fece Roma," late 19th c., 45" h. (some losses) **2,530.00**

Model of the head of a horse, Art Deco, grey marble, mounted on a stepped black & purple marble base, unsigned, ca. 1925, 23½" h. (ILLUS. bottom previous page) ...**16,100.00**

Petrille, Prof., bust of Cleopatra, shown wearing an elaborate necklace, diadem & arm bracelet, her hand holding a snake, signed "Prof. Petrille Firenze," Italy, 26" h..**3,737.00**

OTHER

Terra Cotta Reclining Woman

Ivory, figure of a young girl holding a rabbit, the nude child kneeling & cradling a rabbit in her arms, · mounted on a green onyx base, inscribed "F. Preiss," Germany, ca. 1925, 3½" h. **1,150.00**

Terra cotta, bust of a young woman, inscribed "Carrier Belleuse," raised on an ebonized wooden socle, 19th c., 23¼" h.............................**2,070.00**

Terra cotta, figure of a nude woman reclining on a bed of grass, cast in full relief in tan-brown glazes, inscribed "RAOUL LARCHE," foundry stamp "SISSE FRES. - PARIS," ca. 1900, 28" l. (ILLUS.) **3,737.00**

STEAMSHIP MEMORABILIA

The dawning of the age of world-wide airline travel brought about the decline of the luxury steamship liner for long-distance travel. Few large liners are still operating, but mementoes and souvenirs from their glamorous heyday are much sought-after today.

Advertising sign, Cunard Line, depicting the steamship Aquitania at

Cunard Line Advertising Sign

sea, multi-color on board, ca. 1900-1920, 26 x 42" (ILLUS.) **$577.50**

Advertising sign, "Hudson River Day Line Between New York & Albany," depicting New York steamboat, West Point lighthouse & crow nest mountain, multicolor on board, ca. 1880-1900, 35 x 49" (some stain & imperfections) **330.00**

Advertising sign, "Scandinavian-American Line - New York, Norway - Sweden," depicting old steamliner (Frederik III), multicolor on tin, ca. 1890-1910, 30 x 41" (weathered, rust & pitting)....................................**467.50**

Broadside, depicts four-masted steamship, "Red Star Line" carved in frame, colorful lithograph, ca. 1870s 3' x 4'...**1,700.00**

Coin, bronze, "Lusitania," shows torpedoed ship sinking, skeleton selling tickets, 1915, 2½" d., Germany **150.00**

Cruise book, "Canadian Pacific," cover art by A. Cloutier, 72 pp., 1930-34, 8 x 11".................................**30.00**

Cruise book, "Cunard Mediter-reanean Cruise Line," color & black & white photo illustrations of ships & points of interest, 78 pp., 1913-14, 5 x 8".................................**17.00**

Normandie Deck Chair

Deck chair, teak, "Normandie," designed to collapse for storage, the back & footrest w/vertical slats w/the

ocean liner's plaque, ca. 1934,
22½ x 56", 36" h. (ILLUS. bottom
previous column) **748.00**

Menu/postcard, "T.S.S. Caledonia,"
Anchor Line, 1910..............................**22.00**

Painting, R.M.S. Titanic, decks of
ship inlaid w/mother-of-pearl, made
at the time of the sinking of the
Titanic, framed, 7½ x 9½" **175.00**

Pamphlet, "Alaska Steamship," 1935 ....**8.50**

Passenger list & menu, "S.S.
Advance," 1916.................................**20.00**

Poster, "United States Lines," 1921,
depicts sailing of U.S. George
Washington, showing staterooms,
etc., 12 x 19".....................................**95.00**

STEIFF TOYS & DOLLS

Steiff Bear on Wheels

*From a felt pincushion in the shape of
an elephant, a world-famous toy company
emerged. Margarete Steiff (1847-1909), a
polio victim as a child and confined to a
wheelchair, planned a career as a
seamstress and opened a shop in the family
home. However, her plans were
dramatically changed when she made the
first stuffed elephant in 1880. By 1886 she
was producing stuffed felt monkeys,
donkeys, horses and other animal forms.
In 1893 an agent sold her toys at the
Leipzig Fair. This venture was so
successful that a catalog was printed and a
salesman hired. Margarete's nephews and
nieces became involved in the business,
assisting in its management and the
design of new items. Through the years,
the Steiff Company has produced a varied
line including felt or plush animals, Teddy
Bears, gnomes, elves, felt dolls with
celluloid heads, Kewpie dolls and even
radiator caps with animals or dolls
attached as decoration. Descendants of the
original family members continue to be
active in the management of the company
still adhering to Margarete's motto "For
our children, the best is just good enough."*

Baboon, puppet, hand-type, white
mohair w/blue, green & orange h.p.
highlights, original tag & ear
button..**$50.00**

Bear on wheels, brown mohair,
brown glass eyes, black floss nose
& mouth, applied ears, body
w/hump, unjointed legs standing on
a wire metal frame w/wooden
wheels, pull-ring for growler on
back, original leather collar, early
20th c., wear (ILLUS.) **900.00**

Camel on wheels, felt & mohair,
black steel eyes, button in ear, ca.
1913, 9¾" l., 9½" h. (slight moth
damage to muzzle, slight fiber
loss) **747.50**

Cat, seated, beige mohair w/dark
stripes, swivel head w/green glass
eyes, pink floss nose & mouth,
unjointed body, red floss claws,
button in left ear, "U.S. Zone
Germany" on tag, 8" h.....................**105.00**

Dog, Boxer, U.S. Zone tag, 8" h.,
(mint condition) **150.00**

Dog: "Mopsy," tan mohair plush
w/dark markings, black & white
eyes, black floss nose, orange felt
tongue, jointed neck, in sitting
position, paper tab at neck, hole in
left ear from button, 8" h. **85.00**

Dog: "Peky," terrier, 8" h. **75.00**

Dog, Poodle, black, fully jointed,
14" h..**250.00**

Steiff "Inga" Doll

Doll: "Inga," pressed felt head, set
blue eyes, single stroke brows,
accented nostrils, open-closed
mouth w/white space between lips,
original blonde mohair wig, cloth
body jointed at shoulders & hips,
dressed in tagged original dress,
underclothing, socks & shoes,
w/original Steiff tag a & yellow tag
w/button on red wrist band, tiny hole

below mouth, on left temple, right
side of neck & lower back, slight
aging, 12" h. (ILLUS.) **275.00**
Doll, Dwarf, "Lucki," rubber face, felt
body **75.00**
Donkey, tan w/black mane, button
eyes, 11½" **225.00**
Elephant: "Jumbo," w/chest tag &
button in ear, 1950s, 8½" h.............**265.00**
Giraffe, w/original button in ear & tag,
14" h. (mint condition) **165.00**
Giraffe, w/original buttons, 1950s,
30" h...**425.00**
Goat, long white mohair plush body
w/black shaved mohair face
w/curling felt horns, green glass
eyes, pink floss nose & mouth, black
shaved mohair legs & tail,
unmarked, 6" h.................................**65.00**
Leopard, reclining, old mohair,
buttons, 13" l. **195.00**
Lion cub, standing, gold mohair
w/brown spots, red embroidered
nose, fully jointed, 1950-60s, 4" h.
(no identification) ....**60.00 to 80.00**
Rabbit: "Niki," mohair, 13" h..............**175.00**
Skunk, velvet & mohair, 1950s, (no
identification, otherwise mint) **145.00**
Zebra, black & white felt, 1950s, 5" ...**100.00**

TEDDY BEARS

Steiff Teddy Bear

Teddy bear, yellow mohair, fully-
jointed, black steel eyes, straw-
stuffed, button in ear, wearing an
olive green velvet cape & crocheted
bonnet, ca. 1905, tiny size
(extensive fur loss)..........................**316.00**
Teddy bear: "Zotty," long brown
mohair plush w/swivel head, brown
glass eyes, shaved mohair muzzle
w/brown floss nose, open-closed
mouth, five-piece body jointed at
shoulders & hips, gold mohair on

chest, gold felt pads, button in ear,
9" h. (chest tag missing) **155.00**
Teddy bear, white mohair, 1914,
10" h. (excellent condition except
foot pad)..**625.00**
Teddy bear, white mohair, w/growler,
16" h..**210.00**
Teddy bear, golden mohair, original
button in ear & tag, 1919,
18" h..**2,250.00**
Teddy bear, tan mohair, jointed body,
brown glass eyes, brown floss nose
& mouth, vertical stitching on nose,
applied ears, elongated arms w/felt
pads, four brown floss claws, legs
w/large feet, nice hump on back,
excelsior stuffing, marked "Steiff" in
left ear, some wear spots on head,
arms & torso, small repairs to each
paw, small moth holes, 20" h.
(ILLUS.) **2,300.00**

Yellow Mohair Teddy Bear

Teddy bear, yellow mohair, jointed
body, black button eyes,
embroidered nose & mouth, felt
pads, excelsior stuffing, ear button,
ca. 1904-10, some fiber loss, moth
damage on pads, 29" (ILLUS.) **5,462.50**

STEINS

Character, bust of a fat man w/pipe
wearing hat forming the cover,
pottery, inscribed at the bottom "Die
Kehl Kost Vell," 6" h. **$185.00**
Character, "Sad Radish," china,
marked "Musterschutz" **450.00**
Character, model of a skull, pottery,
inlaid pewter lid, Germany
(ILLUS. top next page)....................**210.00**

Skull Stein

China Monk Scene Stein

Glass Stein Encased in Pewter

Three Glass Steins

China, squatty cylindrical body w/slightly tapering rim w/domed pewter lid, scene of a monk w/stein & large keg in the background, all in rust brown, marked "C.P. & CO." & "Manning Bowman & Co. Meriden, Conn." on base, 3⅞" d., 4¾" h. (ILLUS.) **95.00**

Delft-type pottery, cylindrical, decorated in polychrome w/a figure of a winged angel grappling w/a bearded figure, flanked by large palm trees, low domed pewter cover w/large ball thumb rest & a domed pewter band around the base, Germany, late 18th c., 9¾" h. **1,265.00**

Glass, amber encased in pewter, egg-shaped body tapering to slightly flaring cylindrical neck, encased in pewter frame w/four ram heads embossed around the center, low domed hinged pewter lid, 7" d., 15¾" h. (ILLUS. top next column) **495.00**

Glass, blue shaded to clear threaded glass, slightly bulbous cylindrical body w/clear applied handle, hinged figured pewter lid & thumbpiece, scroll-cut pewter base, .3 liter, 2⅞" d., 7½" h. (ILLUS. right) **175.00**

Glass, cranberry, slightly tapering cylindrical body w/clear glass applied handle, cranberry inset lid, pewter mount & pewter ball thumbpiece, 3¾" d., 6½" h. (ILLUS. left) **225.00**

Glass, iridized honey amber, cylindrical body w/four raised bands on slightly flaring foot, figured pewter hinged lid & pewter thumbpiece, white enamelled scroll decoration, ½ liter, 3⅞" d., 9¼" h. (ILLUS. center) **245.00**

Glass, overlay, tall cylindrical form w/the blue ground cut w/oval medallions below a paneled decoration of shields & weapons, hinged pewter-framed lid w/a porcelain medallion of a fox, Germany, late 19th c., 8¾" h. **2,300.00**

Glass, overlay, tall cylindrical form w/an amethyst ground w/cut leafy

scrollwork surrounding paneled
decoration of shield & weapons,
hinged pewter-framed lid
w/porcelain medallion of a fox,
Germany, late 19th c., 8¾" h. **2,300.00**

Mettlach Steins No. 1467 & No. 2823

Mettlach No. 1467, four panels of
relief-molded scenes of people
picking fruit, hunting, farming &
weaving, tan & grey, pottery inset
matching lid, marked, ½ liter,
4½" d., 5¾" h. (ILLUS. left) **295.00**

Mettlach No. 1923, relief-molded
scrolls & medallions, inlaid lid,
.3 liter **100.00**

Mettlach No. 1932, etched, Cavaliers
drinking scene around body, signed
"Warth," inlaid lid, ½ liter **450.00**

Mettlach No. 1997, etched & PUG,
bust portrait of George Ehret,
brewer, inlaid lid, ½ liter **250.00**

Mettlach No. 2002, etched, Munich
stein, upper half w/Munich Child &
cityscape, lower half w/long German
inscription, inlaid lid, ½ liter **450.00**

Mettlach No. 2077, relief-molded
coat-of-arms w/owl, inlaid pewter lid,
½ liter **150.00**

Mettlach No. 2090, etched, Club
stein, man at table in his club
smoking a pipe, signed "Schlitt,"
inlaid lid, ½ liter **500.00**

Mettlach No. 2363, relief-molded
decoration, "In the Whale at
Ascalon," inlaid lid of turtle,
ca. 1898, ½ liter **125.00**

Mettlach No. 2391, incised
decoration of The Wedding March of
the Swan King from Lohengrin,
inlaid pewter lid, ½ liter **770.00**

Mettlach No. 2823, tapestry, scene of
a woman sharp-shooter on a grey
ground, original pewter figural lid,
castle mark, ½ liter, 3¾" d., 5" h.
(ILLUS. right) **375.00**

Stein No. 2951

Mettlach No. 2951, cameo, sage
green ground decorated w/the
Prussian Eagle, original pewter top,
1 liter, 4" d., 10¼" h. (ILLUS.) **795.00**

Norwegian Birch Stein

Wood, birch, cylindrical w/low domed
cover, heavy S-scroll handle, all on
four stylized lion feet, carved bas-
relief scenes from the life of King
David, Norway, ca. 18th c., 6¼" h.
(ILLUS.) **4,887.50**

STRING HOLDERS

*Before the widespread use of paper
bags, grocers and merchants wrapped their
goods in paper, securing it with string. A
string holder, usually of cast iron was,
therefore, a necessity in the store.
Homemakers also found many uses for
string and the ceramic or chalkware wall-*

type holder became a common kitchen item.

Cast iron, beehive-form w/pierced lattice sides, marked "Patented April 11, 1861," 4¾" h. **$82.50**
Chalkware, bird & birdhouse, marked "String Swallow"................................**12.00**
Chalkware, head of a chef..................**30.00**
Chalkware, model of apple w/worm.....**30.00**
China, model of a cat head.................**35.00**

TEA CADDIES

Tiffany Tea Caddy

Harewood, oblong hexagonal form w/each side centered by an inlaid patera, ivory inlaid keyhole escutcheon on front & small ivory button finial, England, George III style, late 18th c., 6" w. **$690.00**
Mahogany & rosewood, rectangular, the stepped hinged top opening to a later glass mixing bowl flanked by lidded compartments, the tapering case raised on later bun feet, Regency period, England, first quarter 19th c., 7 x 13", 9" h. **1,150.00**
Rosewood, parquet & Tunbridgeware, rectangular w/parquetry lid, the top & front w/stylized floral borders, Victorian, mid-19th c., 4¾" l. **1,100.00**
Silver & copper, ovoid body w/cylindrical neck, decorated w/wisteria seed pods & insects, marked "TIFFANY & CO. 5246 M 94," by Tiffany & Co., New York, 5" h. (ILLUS.) **4,370.00**
Tortoiseshell, rectangular top enclosing a lidded container w/ivory banding, on ball feet, Regency period, England, early 19th c., 4¾" l..............................**1,950.00**
Tortoiseshell, the rectangular lid enclosing two lidded containers, scalloped front, on a conforming plinth & compressed ball feet, Regency period, England, 19th c., 9" l..............................**4,180.00**
Tortoiseshell, rectangular w/cut corners, the domed cover w/silver plate ball finial opening to two lidded caddies, the whole w/panels of tortoiseshell divided by thin silver plate bands, raised on small silver plate ball feet, Regency period, England, early 19th c., 7" l. **1,150.00**
Tortoiseshell w/ivory inlay, rectangular body w/break-front outline & a hinged lid opening to two lidded compartments, the conforming body on a shaped plinth, England, first quarter 19th c., 4½ x 8", 5" h.....................................**920.00**

TEDDY BEAR COLLECTIBLES

Knickerbocker Teddy Bear

Theodore (Teddy) Roosevelt had become a national hero during the Spanish-American War by leading his "Rough Riders" to victory at San Juan Hill in 1898. He became the 26th President of the United States in 1901 when President McKinley was assassinated. The gregarious Roosevelt was fond of the outdoors and hunting. Legend has it that while on a hunting trip, soon after becoming President, he refused to shoot a bear cub because it was so small and helpless. The story was picked up by a political cartoonist who depicted President Roosevelt, attired in hunting garb, turning away and refusing to shoot a small bear cub. Shortly thereafter, toy plush bears began appearing in department stores labeled "Teddy's Bears" and they became an immediate success. Books on the adventures of "The Roosevelt Bears" were written and illustrated by Paul Piper under the pseudonym of Seymour Eaton and this version of the Teddy bear became a popular decoration on children's dishes. Also see STEIFF.

Plate, porcelain, Roosevelt Bears at the White House scene, 5" d. **$130.00**

Teaspoon, souvenir, silver plate, from "Harlem Opera House," w/embossed image of early jointed Teddy bear..**95.00**

Teddy bear, brown mohair, swivel head w/brown glass eyes, brown floss nose & mouth, applied ears, five-piece body w/felt paws, hump on back, non-working squeaker in torso, "Made in U.S. Zone Germany" tag, 11" h...**475.00**

Teddy bear, pale golden mohair head & body, swivel head, brown glass eyes, vertically stitched black floss nose & mouth, applied ears, jointed arms & legs, pads on feet, working growler, Herman Teddy Original tag on neck, "Herman - Teddy - Original - Made in West Germany," on original tag on seam of right arm, 13" h...**95.00**

Teddy bear, yellow mohair, fully-jointed, black steel eyes, embroidered nose & mouth, excelsior stuffing, felt pads, early 1920s, 13" h. (one eye replaced, some fiber loss & moth damage) **402.50**

Teddy bear, blonde mohair, fully-jointed, glass eyes, embroidered nose & mouth, felt pads, probably England, 1930s, 17½" h. (one eye damaged, some fiber loss) **230.00**

Teddy bear, light brown mohair, fully-jointed, glass eyes, short arms & modified hump, straw stuffing, possibly American-made, ca. 1920s, 18" h. (some fiber loss, replacement jersey nose) **489.00**

Teddy bear, shaggy brown mohair w/blue tips, swivel head, brown glass eyes, gold shaved muzzle w/vertically stitched brown floss nose, open-closed mouth w/beige felt inside, jointed arms & legs w/beige felt pads, working tummy squeaker, Herman Zotty, w/green & gold paper neck tag, 19" h. **110.00**

Teddy bear, yellow mohair, fully-jointed, glass eyes, embroidered

nose & mouth, long oval body, short curved arms, straight legs, excelsior stuffing, pink & white knit sweater, 19" h. (fiber loss & repairs) **316.00**

Teddy bear, gold mohair head & body, black button eyes, horizontally stitched black floss nose & mouth, applied ears, swivel head, jointed arms & legs, velour pads on hands & feet, excelsior-stuffed, striped knit scarf around neck, 20" h. (wear) **160.00**

Teddy bear, gold mohair swivel head & body, brown glass eyes, horizontally stitched black floss nose & mouth, applied ears, jointed arms & legs w/mohair paws, large plaid bow around neck, 20" h. **150.00**

Teddy bear, brown mohair head & body, brown glass eyes, inset round flannel muzzle w/black felt triangular nose, embroidered mouth, applied ears, jointed arms & legs, flannel pads on hands & feet, excelsior & kapok stuffing, marked "Knickerbocker Toy Co. Inc., New York, Animals of Distinction, Made in USA" on satin factory tag in stomach seam (ILLUS.) **275.00**

TEXTILES

BEDSPREADS

Daisy Pattern Bedspread

Cotton, all-white w/a candlewick pattern of a series of eight-point stars outlined w/latticework borders, tatted fringe, probably New England, mid-19th c., 83" sq. **$920.00**

Cotton batiste, all-white w/white embroidery, 70 x 106"........................**60.00**

Cotton, ecru w/wide strips of hand-crocheted popcorn stitch panels & gathered drops, full-size **125.00**

Crewel-embroidered linen,
composed of three widths of white
linen stitched together, embroidered
at the center w/a brilliant bouquet of
roses, tulips, pansies & irises, the
field interspersed w/sprays of single
flowers & clusters, the borders w/a
meandering vine of lilies, grape
clusters & open roses, all in bright
tones of rose, pink, green & blue
wool crewel threads, worked
predominantly in Roman & stem
stitches, attributed to Esther
Meacham Strong, Massachusetts,
late 18th c., 88 x 92" **9,200.00**
Crib spread w/matching pillowcase,
twelve squares made from sugar
sacks, dated "1903", 2 pcs.................**90.00**
Hand-crocheted, child's, "Now I Lay
Me" alternating w/squares of girl
w/candle, children skipping, bed,
Teddy bear & toys, cream colored,
52 x 96" **195.00**
Hand-crocheted, Daisy patt., 95 x
95" (ILLUS.) **93.50**
Organdy spread w/matching pillow
shams, partially embroidered,
pastel, 1930s-40s, Royal Society kit
No. 565, the set **45.00**

COVERLETS

Fruit & Peacock Jacquard Coverlet

Jacquard, one-piece, bands of
compotes of fruit surrounded by
peacocks & flowers, woven in red,
white & blue, early 19th c.,
72 x 78" (ILLUS.) **632.50**
Jacquard, one-piece, patriotic design,
edges inscribed "UNDER THIS WE
PROSPER," corner block inscribed
"United We Stand, Divided We Fall,
Alice Williams," woven in red
w/Washington on horseback, mid-
19th c., 78 x 92" (ILLUS. top next
column) **1,092.00**

Patriotic Jacquard Coverlet

Single Weave Jacquard Coverlet

Jacquard, single weave, one-piece,
central medallion & floral border
w/edge label inscribed "Made by
Wm. Ney, Myerstown, Lebanon Co.
Pa," woven in red & white, 78 x 84"
(ILLUS.) **330.00**
Jacquard, single weave, one-piece,
flower blossom medallions
w/feathery leaves, leafy sprig border
band, corners signed "Made by J.
Hausman in Lobachsville, 1846,"
red, olive green, deep yellow &
natural white, 78 x 101" **495.00**
Jacquard, single weave, one-piece,
bands of stars within five-petal
flower wreaths, vintage grape
border, corners signed "Made by
Samuel Dornbach, Sugarloaf,
Luzerne for....Penn. 1845," red,
navy blue, medium green & natural
white, fringed, 82 x 89" (stains,

some color bleeding, slight fringe
loss) **440.00**

Jacquard, single weave, one-piece,
rows of large floral medallions each
framed by small stars, within double
bird on tree border, corners labeled
"Made by Samuel Dornbach,
Sugarloaf, Luzerne for....Penn.
1845," red, navy blue, medium
green & natural white, fringed,
85 x 88" (minor stains & moth
damage, slight fringe loss) **302.50**

Jacquard, single weave, two-piece,
four-rose medallions, bird & rose
border w/corner labels "C Boden,
Montgomery County, Ohio 1848,"
navy blue, tomato red & natural
white, 74 x 94" (worn, small holes &
stains, fringe on one end) **192.50**

Jacquard, single weave, two-piece,
four-rose medallions & stars w/eagle
border & "Eagle," corners signed
"Martin B. Breneman, Washington
Township, York County, Pa. 1838,
Katherine Filler," navy blue, tomato
red, yellow & natural white, 76 x 92"
(minor wear, fringe on two sides, no
fringe on slightly frayed bottom
edge).................................**412.50**

Jacquard, single weave, two-piece,
rows of four-rose medallions,
vintage grape borders, corner blocks
signed "Andrew Hoover Han-r 1843,
E. Uhrich," deep reddish pink, olive
green, navy blue & natural white,
82 x 92" (minor stains) **385.00**

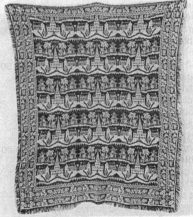

Double Weave Jacquard Coverlet

Jacquard, double woven, one-piece,
Boston town design & vintage
borders, navy blue & natural white,
minor wear & moth damage, minor
stains, 62 x 74" (ILLUS.) **385.00**

Jacquard, double woven, two-piece,
delicate vining floral medallions,
stylized blossoms & fanned leaves
vining around the border, navy blue,
tomato red & natural white,
attributed to Ohio, 74 x 78" (minor
stains & wear) **330.00**

Jacquard, double woven, two-piece,
overall central design of various
medallions, "Hempfield Railroad"
borders, identified in corners, navy
blue & tomato red, 75 x 88" (minor
wear & a little fringe loss)..............**3,520.00**

Overshot, geometric optic design of
quatrefoils around squares, wavy
band border, tomato red, navy blue
& natural, 72 x 86" **330.00**

Overshot, two-piece, snowflakes &
pine trees patt., navy blue, tomato
red & natural white, fringe at one
end, 76 x 84" **770.00**

Overshot, two-piece, optical pattern
bands framing squares composed of
tiny blocks, red, blue & natural
white, 79 x 94" **176.00**

Overshot, three-piece, bold optic
pattern w/Op Art effect, wine red,
charcoal, black & natural white,
81" sq. (minor wear).......................**495.00**

Overshot, star design in navy blue,
olive green, tomato red & natural
white, 90 x 95" (minor fringe
damage)...**357.50**

LACE

Battenburg

Tablecloth, grape cluster patt.,
66" d...**200.00**

Table runner, 5 to 7" w. Battenburg
border all around, very lacy,
18 x 54" **168.00**

Table runner, three plain squares
down the center, all surrounded by
Battenburg lace, 17 x 54" **195.00**

Tea cozy, floral design, 12 x 16" **85.00**

Other Laces

Bobbin lace tablecloth, 44" d. **115.00**

Filet lace table runner, 5½" square
panel flanked by cherubs, torches &
arrows, 16½ x 42" **135.00**

Filet lace table runner, a large
design of ladies w/flower baskets at
each end, 6 x 23" filet lace oval
center, overall 16 x 50" **185.00**

Tuscany lace tablecloth, very lacy,
beige, 56 x 84" **275.00**

LINENS & NEEDLEWORK

Bed sheet, linen, finely embroidered
panel w/exceptional hemstitching,
69 x 98"..**95.00**

Centerpiece, Arts & Crafts style,
round, w/embroidered ivory, green &
blue geometric designs outlined in
black around the edge, against a

beige ground, fringed border, early
20th c., 40" d....................................**440.00**

Embroidered Petticoat Border

Petticoat border, Deerfield School,
linen, worked in shades of blue blue
silk, embroidered "Lydia Safford,
1793," 96" l. (ILLUS. detail)..........**2,645.00**

Pillow, Arts & Crafts style,
embroidered w/a stylized floral
design in red, green, black & pink on
a neutral ground, green backing,
fringed end, early 20th c.,
14 x 18" **137.50**

Pillow, Arts & Crafts style,
embroidered w/red roses & green
leaves on a dark brown linen
ground, early 20th c., 17 x 23"
(some wear).....................................**220.00**

Pillow face, Arts & Crafts style, linen
embroidered w/stylized geometric
flowers & leaves against geometric
banding, in blue, black, yellow &
green on a beige ground, unmarked,
early 20th c., 17 x 24" **110.00**

Pillow face, Arts & Crafts style, linen,
embroidered w/a floral medallion in
blue, green, yellow & buff on a tan
ground, signed "M. Heminway &
Sons Silk Craft Design No. 380 - 7,"
18 x 21½" (some soiling) **33.00**

Pillow face, Arts & Crafts style, linen,
embroidered w/a wide band of
conventionalized geometric floral
designs in gold & green on a brown
ground, unmarked, early 20th c.,
23 x 24" **385.00**

Lancaster County Show Towel

Show towel, embroidered linen,
decorated w/flowering pot, deer, a
peacock & inscribed on the top "The
property of Anna Reist, Harison
Township, Lancaster County, March
7 1846," worked w/red, blue, green,
brown, pink & yellow wool threads,
Pennslyvania, 1846, some minor
staining, 17¾ x 60" (ILLUS. bottom
previous column) **3,737.00**

Table centerpiece, Arts & Crafts
style, oval, embroidered linen,
decorated around the border
w/angular stylized flowers & a ball &
link design embroidered in light blue,
green & gold on a natural ground,
early 20th c., 20 x 32" (minor
staining) **330.00**

Table centerpiece, Arts & Crafts
style, round, linen, finely
embroidered w/large white lilies &
lily pads in a silvery white on a white
ground, w/gallon fringe, early
20th c., 33" d. plus fringe **385.00**

Table centerpiece, Arts & Crafts
style, round, embroidered linen,
decorated w/torches & laurel
wreaths tied w/ribbons embroidered
in green & gold on a natural ground,
fringe border, early 20th c., 36" d.....**522.50**

Tablecloth, Arts & Crafts style, linen,
bands of large chevrons & small
diamonds embroidered in pastels
within black line borders, on heavy
linen trimmed w/lace at each end,
early 20th c., 21 x 51" **275.00**

Tablecloth, Arts & Crafts style,
embroidered w/gold & teal blue
geometric designs on a burgundy
ground, probably English, 52" sq. **165.00**

Tablecloth, linen, cross-stitch
embroidered roses, ribbons,
53 x 68" (excellent condition).............**47.50**

Tablecloth & napkins, Arts & Crafts
style, white linen, embroidered in
yellow w/stylized tulip blossoms
within line borders, all within wide
yellow border bands, early 20th c.,
tablecloth 38" sq., tablecloth & six
napkins, the set.................................**99.00**

Table runner, Arts & Crafts style, felt,
a deep purple runner embroidered
at each end w/a large square design
of stylized, swirled orange & yellow
roses & green floral sprays within
orange & yellow border lines, early
20th c., 11½ x 49" (some moth
damage & soiling) **99.00**

Table runner, Arts & Crafts style,
embroidered natural linen w/small
clusters of white daisies & gold leafy
stems & long leaf-like devices along
the border, 15½ x 52" (loose
fringe)...**192.50**

Table scarf, Arts & Crafts style, rectangular, white, gold & green embroidered stylized blossoms on a neutral linen ground w/fringe border, early 20th c., 32 x 74" **220.00**

Stickley Table Scarf

Table scarf, grey natural fabric embroidered at either end w/the 'China Tree' patt., depicting stylized trees in pale blue & ivory thread, by Gustav Stickley, 15 x 68" (ILLUS.) **2,070.00**

QUILTS

Appliqued Album Quilt

Appliqued Album quilt, composed of green, red, yellow, orange & blue calico patches arranged in a series of squares decorated w/wreaths of oak leaves, flowers, tulips & baskets of flowers, within green calico sawtooth borders, some squares w/verses & signatures & dates "1854" & "1856", Cecil County, Maryland, dated 1854-56, minor stains, 83" sq. (ILLUS.) **2,587.00**

Appliqued Album quilt, worked primarily in turkey red & green calico on white cotton & bearing 25 appliqued squares w/various designs including President's wreath, lovebirds, dove on wreath, lyre in wreath & basket of flowers, centering a yellow & blue ship w/American flags, on diamond quilted ground enclosed by red double-stepped border w/scrolling feather & diamond quilting, probably mid-Atlantic States, second quarter 19th c., 109" sq. **4,620.00**

Pennslyvania Album Quilt

Appliqued Album quilt, worked in thirty-six blocks of variously alternating printed cotton calicoes including compass stars & glazed cotton chintz including bunches of flowers, a bird of paradise & several 'Moorish' & 'Hindoo' squares, some w/ signatures; enclosed in a printed cotton calico border appliqued as an Irish chain, the border w/conforming quilting, the central field w/diagonal quilting, Pennslyvania, ca. 1830-50, 97½ x 98½" (ILLUS.) **3,450.00**

Appliqued bold floral design w/nine round medallions in dark greyish blue, red & goldenrod w/vining border on three sides, quilted flower designs & simple four-leaf, two-leaf & one-leaf appliques in dark royal blue, 77 x 85" (stains & minor wear)...**1,045.00**

Appliqued 'broderie perse' Star of Bethlehem patt., composed of orange, blue, red, brown & green printed fabrics w/compotes of fruit in glaze chintz around the sides, the border band of printed red, blue, green, yellow & white glazed floral chintz on a white ground decorated w/floral & diamond quilting, Baltimore, Maryland, ca. 1850, 110 x 112" (some minor imperfections) **4,600.00**

Appliqued design w/four stylized urns of flowers w/puffed berries & embroidery, composed of brown, goldenrod & green patches & quilted w/feather wreaths & meandering border, 75 x 78" (wear, stains & small holes near one corner) **550.00**

Cotton & Velvet Flower Basket Quilt

Appliqued Flower Basket patt., composed of brightly colored red, yellow, blue, green & orange printed & solid calico cotton & velvet patches arranged in a Flower Basket patt., the central reticulated yellow basket standing on a stepped pedestal w/brown velvet base filled w/a profusion of summer blossoms & a brown velvet book surrounded by a luxuriant oval floral wreath, the borders w/floral arcs & smaller baskets of flowers; all mounted on a white cotton field w/shell & fruit vine quilting within red swag borders, probably Pennslyvania, mid-19th c., some minor discoloration & stain & fabric loss, 104 x 112" (ILLUS.) **6,613.00**

Calico Flower Basket Quilt

Appliqued Flower Basket patt., composed of red, yellow, green & pink printed & solid calico patches arranged in a series of woven baskets filled w/brightly colored rose blossoms in ruched patches all mounted on a white cotton field w/meandering vine & floral quilting, Miss Mary Chappell, Jenkinsville, South Carolina, 1848, some stain & fabric loss, 100 x 104" (ILLUS. bottom previous column) **3,450.00**

Royal Hawaiian Flag Quilt

Appliqued Royal Hawaiian Flag patt., composed of brightly colored red, yellow, navy blue & white patches, at center the Royal Hawaiian insignia w/the inscription "KUUHAE ALOHA," the borders w/stylized Union Jacks, the field heightened w/diamond & diagonal line stitching, late 19th - early 20th c., some minor staining, 72" sq. (ILLUS.) **3,450.00**

Oak Leaf Pattern Quilt

Appliqued Oak Leaf patt., composed of blue, brown & red calico patches of circles of oak leaves within a trailing oak leaf & trapunto berries on a vine border, one patch signed "Sarah Northup Lewisboro March 1847," losses to red fabric & minor staining, 84 x 100" (ILLUS.) **517.00**

Appliqued Princess Feather patt., composed of green, pink & red printed & solid calico patches, the feathers in the form of seaweed w/starfish centers, the whole mounted on a white cotton ground w/finely scaled diamond & diagonal line quilting, Cape Cod, Massachusetts, ca. 1860, 96 x 100" (minor fading)................**1,380.00**

Appliqued Princess Feather & Snowflake patt., composed of brightly colored red & slate blue patches, all mounted on a white cotton ground w/heart & flower quilting, signed along border "I. Franklin W.," probably Pennsylvania, dated 1865, 100" sq. (minor discoloration & wear) **2,070.00**

Appliqued Rose of Sharon patt., composed of red, yellow, grey & brown printed & solid calico patches arranged on a white cotton field w/oak leaf & diagonal line quilting, third quarter 19th c., 80 x 84" **1,725.00**

Appliqued Rose Wreath patt., composed of blocks in red & green printed calico separated by white cotton sashing all on a white cotton background, with white cotton border, the whole enclosed by green printed cotton sawtooth binding, the worked squares w/diamond quilted, the sashing and border w/princess feather quilting, Mid-Atlantic States, 19th c., 70 x 90½" **1,265.00**

Appliqued Sampler Quilt

Appliqued Sampler quilt, comprised of thirty-six appliqued squares of green, red, yellow & blue cotton printed calicoes, including two flower baskets w/butterflies, a bird w/album

book, crossed flags & Baltimore's Battle Monument flanked above by the letters "IO - OF" & below by an Oddfellows Triple Chain & Heart-in-Hand motif, w/several squares inscribed w/names, each square separated by green calico sashing & enclosed on three sides by a green & red calico tassel-and-swag border, the whole bound w/green calico; the border worked in diamond & swag quilting, the central field variously quilted, inscribed "Baltimore," dated 1845, 90¾ x 102½" (ILLUS.) **2,300.00**

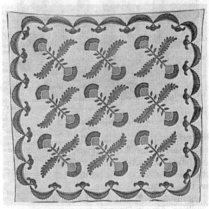

Thistle Variant Pattern Quilt

Appliqued Thistle variant patt., comprised of nine stylized floral medallions & swag border in red, orange & green w/red binding, overall wear, light stains & a little fading, 81 x 86" (ILLUS.)................**935.00**

Appliqued Urns of Flowers patt., four urns w/large branching bouquets w/puff berries & embroidery in brown, goldenrod & green on a white feather-quilted ground w/meandering vine border, 75 x 78" (wear, stains, small corner holes) **632.50**

Crib-size, pieced Nine Patch patt., composed of colorful light & dark blocks in black, red & goldenrod, 35 x 47" **148.50**

Pieced Barn Raising patt., composed of narrow strips in multicolored prints & calico w/salmon pink & red center, 75" sq...**577.50**

Pieced Bars patt., composed in red & teal woven cotton & blue crepe w/red & teal repeating Diamond-in-Square inner border surrounded by red outer border w/contrasting teal corner blocks, enclosed by a blue crepe binding, the inner field &

border w/diamond quilting, the outer border & corner blocks quilted in an alternating flower basket & triple tulip pattern, Amish, Lancaster County, Pennsylvania, early 20th c., 67¼ x 68" **1,039.00**

Amish Bar Quilt

Pieced Bar patt., composed of alternating blue & brown wool bars within red banded border further bordered in wide blue panels w/brown square corners, the field heightened w/baskets & diamond quilting, Amish, Pennsylvania, last quarter 19th c., 80" sq. (ILLUS.) ...**4,312.00**

Pieced Basket patt., composed of twenty blocks in purple & black plain & satin woven cottons w/purple inner border surrounded by black outer border w/slate blue binding, the central field w/princess feather & channel quilting, the outer border w/rope twist quilting, Amish, Indiana or Ohio, ca. 1910, 70 x 81" **1,495.00**

Pieced Diamond-in-the-Square patt., composed of pastel tones of pink, green, lavender & coral patches on a white cotton field w/diamond & pretzel quilting, probably Pennsylvania, ca. 1930, 76 x 80" **690.00**

Pieced Diamond-in-the-Square patt., worked in shades of blue, lilac, burgundy, teal & purple wool & cotton, the blue star, heart & Princess Feather wreath-stitched diamond framed by grapevine-quilted robin's egg blue sashing w/purple corner blocks & blue tulip-stitched spandrels surrounded by a lilac & burgundy grapevine-stitched inner border framed by teal princess feather stitched sash & purple corner blocks, w/a burgundy binding, initialled "MMI," Amish,

Lancaster County, Pennsylvania, ca. 1920, 78 x 80" **5,280.00**

Pieced Double Four-in-Nine Patch patt., composed of brown, navy blue, pale blue, lavender, maroon & green cotton patches, the field heightened w/flowerhead, cable & diagonal line stitching, Amish, probably Indiana, early 20th c., 68 x 88" **3,450.00**

Pieced Double Nine Patch patt., composed of lavender, green, pink, blue, black, red, purple & taupe patches arranged as four rows of four blocks each, the field dark blue & purple decorated w/double stitched basket quilting along w/flowerheads & diamonds, red wool binding, Amish, signed "K.S." (Katie K. Stoltzfus), Lancaster County, Pennsylvania, 1920-35, 84" sq. **12,650.00**

Pieced Flying Goose patt., composed on one side in pale blue, pink & grey plain woven cottons on a black satin woven cotton ground, enclosed by a pale blue inner border surrounded by a black outer border w/pale blue binding, the reverse worked in a single border plain pattern, w/navy outer border w/pale blue binding, the whole quilted in an alternating princess feather & channel pattern, w/teacup & princess quilted borders, Amish, probably Ohio, early 20th c., 44 x 61" **690.00**

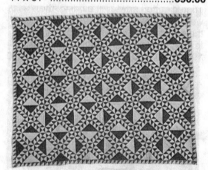

Lady of the Lake Quilt

Pieced Lady of the Lake patt., composed of red calico & white patches arranged in the Lady of the Lake patt., w/sawtooth border, the field heightened w/diamond, circle & floral quilting, late 19th c., some minor staining, 72 x 88" (ILLUS.) **747.00**

Pieced Lone Star patt., composed of large star surrounded by twelve smaller stars in red, green, blue & pink calico & solid yellow, intricately quilted design w/flowers & scrolled foliage, stains, 89" sq. **1,155.00**

Pieced Nine Patch patt., composed of calico & chintz patches in pink, green, beige & brown floral & geometrically-printed designs, bands of blocks alternating w/wide stripes, the field highlighted w/herringbone in square quilting, probably New England, mid-19th c., 100" sq. (some fabric loss) **546.00**

Pieced Ohio Star variant patt., composed of alternating colored chintz & white blocks, signed & dated "Anna M. Staeffer September 1, 1852" in ink on the back, 81 x 85" (scattered discoloration) **1,265.00**

Pieced Pineapple patt., composed of small patches in two shades of brown calico & solid medium blue, late 19th c., 77 x 95" **660.00**

Pieced Rose Wreath patt., friendship quilt, composed of solid red, yellow & green calico cotton patches, the center of each wreath w/a signature, all on a white ground heightened w/outline quiliting, late19th c., 84 x 84" (minor staining) **2,588.00**

Pieced Snail's Trail patt., composed in pale blue & black plain & satin woven cottons, surrounded on a black inner border & pale blue outer border w/black binding, the central field quilted in alternating channel & rosette pattern, w/ocean waves quilted border, Ohio, ca. 1910, 83 x 84½" **1,150.00**

Pieced Star of Bethleham variant patt., composed of numerous small graduated diamond-shaped multi-colored patches arranged in eight wide arms w/serrated tips & w/an eight-point star in a block in each corner, 19th c., 87 x 89" (minor fiber loss & discoloration)..............**1,035.00**

Pieced Triple Irish Chain patt., composed of black, rose, cornflower, green & salmon satin cottons w/black binding, rose outer border, cornflower inner border & cornflower, green & salmon worked inner field, diagonal, princess feather & diamond quilting, Amish, Mifflin County, Pennsylvania, late 19th - early 20th c., 86½ x 92" **2,530.00**

Pieced Tumbling Blocks patt., child's quilt, composed of solid blue & black cotton patches, Amish, modern, 45 x 52" **192.50**

Pieced & appliqued Star of Bethleham patt., composed of red, blue, yellow & green printed cotton fabrics, the field appliqued w/tulips, stars & leaves on a white ground elaborately heightened w/floral, diamond, hearts & diagonal line quilting, late 19th c., 114 x 116" (some stains) **1,840.00**

Pieced & embroidered Wreath & Leaf patt., composed of 101 squares of alternating wreath & leaf design in white on red & figural embroidery featuring either a woman or a bird, w/a central larger square embroidered w/a couple & a child in a scrolling foliage surround w/the embroidered name below, "Euphemia Kichlein, 1832," Bucks County, Pennslyvania, 80 x 85¾" **32,200.00**

SAMPLERS

Nancy Forrest's Sampler

Alphabets above a pious inscription, above a pictoral scene centering a weeping willow flanked on one side by a Federal house & the inscription, "Hannah M. Elkins Born in - Windham Oct 15th 1814," over wrought verse, the whole surrounded by a border of meandering flowers & urns, worked in silk threads in black, green, yellow, cream, white & beige on linen, unframed, 16½ x 25" **2,185.00**

Alphabets above "Roxana M'Gee's sampler - Franklin, Tenn. August, 1839," over wrought verse "May I govern my passions with absolute sway, - And grow wiser and better as life wears away," above central urn w/fruit flanked on either side by wreaths dated "1793" & "1799," the whole flanked by three sides of garland flowers, worked in silk thread in cream, light & dark green,

yellow, black & red on linen,
unframed, 16¼" sq.......................**2,070.00**

Alphabets & numerals above
"Nancy Forrest's sampler wrought in
the fourteenth year of her age,
1811," the whole surrounded by
meandering leafy vine w/urns of
flowers in the upper corners, worked
in silk thread on linen w/a solidly-
worked background, minor thread
loss, 16¼ x 21" (ILLUS.) **34,500.00**

1821 Framed Sampler

Alphabet & numerals w/inscription
"When this you see Remember me -
Abigail Knowlton, age 12 - Wrought
in the year of our Lord 1821 -
Searsport, Maine," includes a
farmhouse & farmer in field,
framed (ILLUS.) **2,750.00**

Alphabets, numerals & pious verse,
a large central oval reserve filled
w/rows of alphabets & numerals
above a short pious verse & the
inscription "Sedate Foote's
Sampler," a wide border of vining
flowers w/two long-tailed birds at the
bottom, early 19th c., framed,
16 x 19" **977.50**

Landscape scene of a tree flanked
by flowers above wrought verse,
above a building flanked by trees,
flowers & birds, above "Margaret
Rimmington - 1842," flanked by
baskets of flowers, surrounded by a
floral border, framed 12½ x 16½"
(ILLUS. top next column) **1,150.00**

Pious verse, basket of fruit & flowers
& grapevines, an arch of
meandering flowering vines &
grapes up the sides & across the top
above a pious verse & inscription
"Mary A. Fairbairn age 12 years
New York 1836," a large basket of
flowers & grapes at the bottom,

Landscape Sampler

worked in polychrome silk threads
on linen, framed, 17¼ x 17¾"
(some discoloration) **2,300.00**

Pious verse & building in
landscape, a running floral vine
border around a square panel w/a
pious verse flanked by urns of
flowers above a large three-towered
building flanked by larger pots of
flowers, the building atop a steep hill
lined w/fir trees & small figures &
sheep, worked in polychrome silk on
linen, signed "Catherine Cassady's
work Washington City Feb. 16,
1814," unframed, 16 x 18" (minor
staining in lower left edge) **37,950.00**

Unframed Early Sampler

Pious verse flanked by flowers
above a building atop a hill covered
w/trees & animals surrounding
"Margaret A. Cassady's work
Washington Oct. 3, 1826," flanked
by urns of flowers, worked in vivid

polychrome silk threads on linen ground, unframed 16¾ x 17½" (ILLUS.) **54,050.00**

(End of Textiles Section)

THEOREMS

Sarah Stodard Theorem

During the 19th century, a popular pastime for some ladies was theorem painting, or stencil painting. Paint was allowed to penetrate through hollow-cut patterns placed on paper or cotton velvet. Still-life compositions, such as bowls of fruit or vases of flowers were the favorite themes, but landscapes and religious scenes found favor among amateur artists who were limited in their ability and unable to do freehand painting. Today these colorful pictures, with their charming arrangements, are highly regarded by collectors.

Apples, cherries & blue grapes on a marble slab, water-color, pen & ink on paper, inscribed, signed & dated "Summer fruit - painted by Sarah

Basket of Flowers Theorem

I.G. Stodard for her dear Mother March 1847," 13½ x 17" (ILLUS.) **$3,450.00**

Basket of flowers, water-color on velvet, still life w/basket of flowers, American school, 19th c., 15 x 16" (ILLUS. bottom previous column) **1,035.00**

Basket of fruit, water-color & pen & ink on paper, an openweave straw basket filled w/yellow & dark blue grapes, peaches & pears, framed, early 19th c., faint inscription on back of frame, 7⅝ x 9⅝".............**2,070.00**

Basket of Fruit Theorem

Basket of fruit, water-color on linen, a yellow basket w/peaches, plums, berries & a green pear, stencilled, initialed "D.B." & dated "1836" on back, American school, 9¾ x 7⅞" (ILLUS.) **11,500.00**

Bowl of fruit, pen & ink & water-color on paper, the long blue & white bowl w/a rolled & scalloped edge overflowing w/a wide variety of colorful fruit including peaches, pears, blue grapes & a pineapple, in a boldly painted & stencilled black & yellow frame w/corner blocks, ca.1830, 9 x 11" **19,550.00**

Tray of Fruit Theorem

Tray of fruit, water-color on velvet, a toleware tray w/watermelon, basket of strawberries & a yellow bird, attributed to David Ellinger, 20th c., 18⅞ x 22" (ILLUS.) **4,887.00**

TOBACCIANA

Although the smoking of cigarettes, cigars and pipes is controversial today, the artifacts of smoking related items - pipes, cigar and tobacco humidors, cigar and cigarette lighters and, of course, the huge range of advertising materials - are much sought after. Unusual examples, especially fine Victorian pieces, can bring high prices. Below we list a cross section of Tobacciana pieces recently offered. Also see ADVERTISING ITEMS and CANS & CONTAINERS.

ADVERTISING ITEMS

'Bull' Durham Bull Figure

Ashtray, brass, "Chicago Auto Club" **$45.00**
Ashtray, chrome, "Phillip Morris," held by figural Johnny the Bellboy, original paint, 35" h. **125.00**
Cigarette lighter, "Clark Candy Bar," Zippo...**55.00**
Cigarette lighter, "Mobil Oil Company," slim design, Zippo, mint in box **30.00**
Cigarette pack, "Kent," complimentary pack from TWA Airlines **20.00**
Counter display, figure, 'Bull' Durham, bull standing on oval base marked "For Three Generations - The Standard Smoking Tobacco - of the World," signed "I. Bonheur," 7½ x 22", 17¾" h. (ILLUS.) **1,760.00**

CIGAR & CIGARETTE CASES, HOLDERS & LIGHTERS
Cigar box, silver, designed to resemble a commercial cigar box

w/the cover engraved w/the Imperial Russian eagle & simulated paper tax bands, the corners engraved w/strapwork, the front engraved w/geometric borders, Moscow, Russia, ca. 1900, 6½" l. **6,900.00**
Cigar case, silver & niello, rectangular w/rounded corners, chased to simulate basketweave & w/a wide center lengthwise band inscribed in Cyrillic "Cigars," nielloed to simulate a paper tax band, Moscow, Russia, 1877, 4¼" l........**1,380.00**
Cigar holder, funnel-shaped, "Wm. F. Brookmeyer Cigar & Tobacco Co., St. Louis, MO.," giveaway item **200.00**
Cigar holder - ashtray, decorated w/golfing scene, signed "Brown" **225.00**

Bust of Lady Cigar Lighter

Cigar lighter, electric, burnished bronze metal, bust of a lady, mouth w/coils that get hot to light cigar, ca. 1930s, burn marks at mouth, soiled (ILLUS.) **192.50**
Cigar lighter, silver & enamel, egg-shaped, the body enameled overall in dark blue, raised in a decorated narrow silver band supporting three slender square legs w/paw feet, the top fitted w/a ribbed star-form silver mount centering the columnar wick support, marked w/the initials of Workmaster Anders Nevalainen, & the 88 standard, Fabergé, St. Petersburg, ca. 1900, 5" h. **20,125.00**
Cigarette case, gold (18k), rectangular w/rounded edges, decorated w/alternating red gold & yellow gold stripes, also w/match compartment & tinder compartment, cabochon sapphire thumbpiece, bearing a signature for Cartier, France, ca. 1900, 3¾" l................**3,450.00**
Cigarette case, gold & enamel, rectangular, the cover enameled in

red w/an ancient Egyptian char-
ioteer on a black ground, the
borders enameled in green, the
base enameled w/a scarab,
Lacloche Freres, Paris, France,
signed on the thumbpiece,
w/London import marks
for 1925, 3¼" l.................................**1,955.00**

Silver & Enamel Cigarette Case

Cigarette case, silver & enamel,
depicts two putti among clouds, E.H.
Stockwell, London, 1879, 3⅜" l.
(ILLUS.) **1,840.00**
Cigarette case, silver & enamel,
flattened rectangular form, the
cover enameled w/a large
rectangular reserve of a partly
draped young woman in brown,
her black hair pulled up to the
sides of her head,Europe, ca.
1910, 3½" l....................................**1,610.00**
Cigarette case, silver & enamel,
rectangular, the cover enameled w/a
scene of Leda & the swan, curved to
fit the pocket, Europe, ca. 1910,
3⅝" l..**1,495.00**
Cigarette case, silver & translucent
enamel, rectangular, enameled
translucent oyster of a sunray
ground, the cover set w/a gold
coin of the reign of Tzarina
Elizabeth, "1756," bordered
by red stones, three corners
of the case applied w/gold rococo
scrolls, red hardstone thumbpiece, marked "Faberge" in
Cyrillic w/Cyrillic initials of Workmaster August Holming & 88
standard, St. Petersburg, ca.
1910, 3½" l. **23,000.00**
Cigarette case & lighter com-
bination, metal, press golf ball to
ignite **125.00**
Cigarette holder, amber, the
tip enameled w/white bands &
set w/diamonds, the central
band chased w/berried leaftips,
marks unclear, ca. 1900, in
original fittedholly wood case,
3" l...**5,750.00**

Cigarette holder, Meerschaum,
carved horses, amber stem & fitted
case, marked "Austria," 5" l.............**115.00**
Cigarette humidor, bronze,
rectangular, carved figural,
geometric & fruit decoration, E.F.
Caldwell & Co., New York,
4¼ x 6⅛", 2¼" h.............................**345.00**
Cigarette lighter, chrome, figural
airplane **55.00**
Cigarette lighter, copper, wall-type,
figural sea captain w/pipe in mouth
that lights a cigar, Germany **140.00**
Cigarette lighter, 14k gold plated,
Florentine finish, unused...................**22.00**
Cigarette lighter, "Penciliter," gold-
filled, Ronson, 1948.........................**35.00**
Cigarette lighter, table model,
Barcroft, Zippo, no logo, mint in box ..**75.00**
Cigarette lighter, table model, figural,
dark grey metal, full-figure standing
knight in a suit of armor, on a square
base, base marked "Patent #84335.
Demley New York," 3" w., 9¾" h........**60.50**
Cigarette lighter, table model, red
cast metal, model of fire pumper on
wheels, 4 x 4½"...................................**85.00**

CIGAR & TOBACCO CUTTERS

Wrought-Iron Horse Tobacco Cutter

Counter-type, cast iron, Brown's
mule, R.J. Reynold Tobacco Co. **85.00**
Counter-type, cast iron, marked "The
Champion Knife Improved,"
Enterprise Mfg Co., excellent
condition **65.00**
Counter-type, cast iron, "Master
Mason," painted red w/yellow
highlights, 18" l., 20" h. (minor paint
chipping) **88.00**
Counter-type, pine & wrought-iron,
fashioned from a flat wrought-iron
sheet, the silhouette of a white
painted horse w/black socks
mounted on a rectangular pine
handled chopper affixed to a
baluster-turned wrought-iron finial,
mounted on a rectangular oak block,
America, first half 19th c., 18½" l.,
12" h. (ILLUS.) **1,150.00**

PIPES

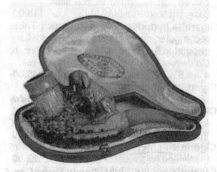

Meershaum Pipe with Dog in Case

Figural, Meerschaum, carved as the
head of a bearded man wearing a
turban, w/a fitted case, Turkey,
early 20th c., 22¼" l. **460.00**

Figural, Meerschaum, dog, w/case,
relatively used, minor soiling to
case, 4" l. (ILLUS.) **88.00**

SIGNS & SIGNBOARDS

Dutch Masters Cigar Sign

Cigars, "Castle Hall - Twin Cigars,"
cardboard, rectangular, color
lithographed vignette w/a stork flying
& carrying two babies in a scale
across a lake to a large castle,
"Castle Hall" across the top & "The
New Arrivals - Twin Cigars" in the
vignette, printed in orange, blue,
white & black w/black & orange
lettering (shrink-wrapped, minor
soiling) **82.50**

Cigars, "Dutch Masters Cigars,"
painted tin, oval, six Dutchmen in
black at red table, dented rim &
minor scratches, 11" w., 9" h.
(ILLUS.) **77.00**

Cigars, "El Moriso Cigar," cardboard,
yellow w/gold border black & red
lettering, "Cellophane Wrapped" in

white, 10¼ x 13½" (white powder
marking, minor edgewear) **44.00**

Imperial Club Cigar Sign

Cigars, "Imperial Club Cigar,"
embossed tin, depicts cream
w/silver open box of Imperial Cigars
next to "Smoke the - Imperial Club -
5cts - Cigar - The Best for the
Money," marked "Sentenne &
Green, New York, NY, U.S.A. Wolf
& Co. Selling Agents" at bottom,
slight bend, minor scratches &
fading, 10 x 13½" (ILLUS.) **66.00**

Roosevelt Cigar Sign

Cigars, "Roosevelt - Highest Grade -
5¢ Cigar - D.B. Long & Son.
Makers," embossed tin, oval portrait
of Theodore Roosevelt in uniform
flanked by vignettes of Roosevelt's
career as Assistant Secretary of the
U.S. Navy & "in the field"
(ILLUS.) **14,300.00**

Cigars, "Y-B Webster Admiration
Cigars," reverse-painting on glass,
printed gold block lettering on a dark
red ground reading "'The Quality
Trio' - Y-B - Webster - Admiration -
Quality Cigars," narrow metal frame,
28½ x 33" (denting to frame) **242.00**

Cigarettes, "Egyptienne Straights Cigarettes," cardboard, depicts woman w/bonnet & a pack of cigarettes, original wood frame, 20 x 31" (slight stains)......................**125.00**

Cigarettes, "Murad Cigarettes," lithograph, shows the "Vanderbilt Cup Race," three cars racing down track, pack of Murad Turkish Cigarettes in bottom corner, marked "Copyright 1909 By S. Anargyros," 10½ x 14½" (minor wear)................**605.00**

Piedmont Cigarettes Sign

Cigarettes, "Piedmont - For Cigarettes Virginia Tobacco is the Best," porcelain, blue w/white lettering, cigarette box in white w/blue lettering & yellow highlights, chipping to edges & overall, scratches, 30 x 49" (ILLUS.)............**176.00**

Cigarettes, trolley car-type, "Chesterfield," cardboard, portrays women athletes smoking, ca. 1940...**100.00**

Tobacco, "Beech-Nut Chewing Tobacco," porcelain, rectangular, a striped package of the product at the left w/"Beech-Nut Chewing Tobacco" to the right, printed in red & white on a dark blue ground, 22" l., 10½" h. (chipping at hanging holes & along edges) **214.50**

Tobacco, "'Bull' Durham," lithographed canvas, rectangular, a circle at the left w/a portrait of a large bull & reading "Gold Old 'Bull' - It's Pure," a large silhouette of a male golfer wearing knickers & swinging a club, advertising copy to the right reading "'On every green' they all roll "Bull" - It's easy for YOU to roll your own - Genuine - "Bull" Durham - Tobacco," printed in orange, yellow, white, green & black, newly framed, 61" l., 25½" h. (touch-up around edges & lettering at bottom corner) **440.00**

Tobacco, "Mail Pouch Tobacco," die-cut cardboard, a large owl perched on a tree stump in front of a full moon, a box of the product in the front left, printed on the moon "You're wise to chew Mail Pouch Tobacco," colorful printing w/a black, red & cream box & red & black lettering, 7½ x 12¼" (minor soiling) **231.00**

Tobacco, "Nevada Klingenberg," paper, centered w/circular portrait of 19th century woman, surrounded by tobacco leaves, coins & two cherubs, banner reading "Nevada" above, below "Gebr. Klingenberg," 7½ x 9½" (some tears)......................**25.00**

TOBACCO JARS

Scotsman Head Tobacco Jar

Ceramic, figural bust of man drinking from a stein as cover, base a bunch of figural cigars tied w/a ribbon, Czechoslovakia, 9¼" h. **225.00**

Ceramic, figural bust of a man smoking pipe, Royal Austria **68.00**

Ceramic, figural head of a winking Scotsman wearing a blue cap w/plaid band, 3½" d., 5½" h. (ILLUS.) **125.00**

Majolica, Art Nouveau floral decoration w/applied pipe on lid **155.00**

MISCELLANEOUS

Ashtray, ceramic, "Snuf-a-rette," cobalt blue glaze w/"Stand burning cigarettes in 1 of the cells, count ten, it's out," patent dated 1937 ....**28.00**

Ashtray, metal, figural standing kangaroo, top hat, jacket, bow tie, open mouth & nostrils, 5" h...............**50.00**

Ashtray, model of a Volkswagen "Bug"...**25.00**

Cigar band, "Baltimore Belle," Warner
& Brown Co., Baltimore **35.00**
Cigar band, campaign-type, "William
H. Taft" (crease)...............................**26.00**
Cigar band, marked "The Home of
Baseball - Cooperstown, NY,"
w/picture of baseball player
(small tape mark) **30.00**
Cigar band, "Publicos," Jose Lovera
Co., depicts woman sitting at harp,
silver-embossed................................**25.00**
Tobacco label, "'Bull' Durham,"
depicts a bull standing behind a
fence inscribed, "Rich & Rare
Flavor"...**95.00**
Tobacco label, "Lucky Duck Cigars,"
original artwork for can label, key
line drawings & documentation,
Hepburn, Ohio, 8 pcs. **176.00**

(End of Tobacciana)

TOKENS & MEDALS

Bronze, official coronation commem-
orative medal of Alexander III,
Russia...**$65.00**
Gilt-plated brass, negro liveryman
holding horse **20.00**
Gilt-plated metal, San Francisco
World's Fair - 1939 ....**5.00**
Metal, Indian Trading Post,
Blanding, Utah **25.00**
Metal, International Harvester, for
the Centennial of the reaper,
1831-1931...**35.00**
Silver, official commemorative medal
of Nicholas II, Russia **85.00**

TOOLS

Calipers, marked "Athol, Mass -
1855," 5" **$15.00**
Hoof knife, w/iron handle.......................**9.00**
Marking gauge, "Stanley
No. 64½" **24.00**
Measuring chain, surveyor-type,
iron, w/handles & tags, 30 ft. **55.00**
Plane, "Bedrock No. 605½"..................**75.00**
Plane, "Stanley No. 4½".......................**65.00**
Plane, "Stanley No. 10".........................**65.00**
Plane, "Stanley No. 30".........................**35.00**
Plane, "Stanley No. 35".........................**52.50**
Plane, "Stanley No. 45," w/21 bits,
in original box....................................**85.00**
Plane, "Stanley No. 62" **100.00**
Plane, "Stanley No. 72" **160.00**
Plane, "Stanley No. 194" **45.00**
Plane, "Winchester No. 3205," 10" l...**145.00**

Rule, "Chapin-Stephens No. 36,"
inclinometer **150.00**
Rule, folding-type, "Stanley No. 40,"
ivory **125.00**
Rule, folding-type, "Stanley No. 62,"
brass & basswood, four-fold **25.00**
Traveler, crude scorings, wooden
handle, 6½" d. **30.00**
T-square, sliding-type, "Stanley
No. 25," 8" **10.00**
Wood file, cooper's convex-type **45.00**
Wood file, cooper's straight-type,
w/wooden knob handles **45.00**

TOOTHPICK HOLDERS

Basket Pattern Toothpick Holder

*Reference numbers listed after the
holders refer to the late William Heacock's
books,* Encyclopedia of Victorian Colored
Pattern Glass, Book 1 *or* 1000 Toothpick
Holders.

Blue speckled w/white glass,
Reverse Swirl patt.........................**$135.00**
Clear glass, pressed Rising Sun patt.
(1000, No. 612) ....**25.00 to 35.00**
Clear glass w/amber stain, Scroll
with Cane Band patt. (Book 1, No.
282)...**75.00**
Custard glass, pressed Bees on a
Basket patt., 1000, No. 312
(ILLUS.) **54.00**
Pink opaque glass, pressed One-O-
One patt. (Book 1, No 187)...............**69.50**
**Pink shaded to white opaque
glass,** Acorn patt. (Book 1,
No. 3) **75.00**
Ruby-stained glass, pressed Ribbed
Thumbprint patt. (Book 1,
No. 254) **35.00**
Ruby-stained glass, Trophy patt.,
(1000, No. 235) **18.00**

TOYS

Also see ADVERTISING ITEMS,
CHARACTER COLLECTIBLES, COCA-
COLA ITEMS, DISNEY COLLECTI-
BLES, MARBLES, RADIO & TELE-
VISION MEMORABILIA, STEIFF TOYS,
WESTERN CHARACTER COLLECTI-
BLES, & DOLLS and TEDDY BEAR
COLLECTIBLES.

African Safari animal,
Hippopotamus, wooden, glass eyes,
Schoenhut & Co. (Philadelphia, Penn-
sylvania), regular size **$575.00**

Two Cast Iron Airplanes

Airplane, "Friendship," painted cast
iron, Fokker tri-motor seaplane,
painted yellow w/"Friendship"
embossed on the single wing in
blue, features three exterior motors
whose propellers can be made to
turn by pushing the toy on its hidden
wheels, Hubley Mfg. Co. (Lancaster,
Pennsylvania), 10½" l. (ILLUS.
bottom)..**4,830.00**

Airplane, cast iron, silver monoplane
w/red accents, wheels, black radial
engine & single propeller, embossed
"LUCKY BOY" on top of wing, Dent
Hardware Co. (Fullerton, Pennsylvania), ca. 1930, w/original Dent
sample room tag, 10½ x 12".........**2,070.00**

Airplane, monoplane, cast iron, grey,
embossed on top of the wing
"LINDY," single propeller, rubber
tires, propeller turns as the wheels
move forward, tagged "Spirit of St.
Louis," Hubley, ca. 1929,
11½ x 13¼" (decal worn,
replacement tires) **1,955.00**

Airplane, pressed steel, airmail
passenger model in mustard yellow
w/a silver nickled propeller, red
wheels w/rubber tires & a
noisemaker activated when moving,
Keystone Mfg. Co. (Boston, Massachusetts), ca. 1929, 9½ x 24 x 24"...**920.00**

Airplane, "Tat," painted cast iron, a
tri-engine passenger airplane

finished in green & beige, the plane
features three exterior nickeled
motors & streamlined "fenders"
on two wheels, Kilgore Mfg. Co.
(Chesterville, Ohio)
(ILLUS. top) **6,325.00**

Airplane construction set, tinplate,
parts for a twin cockpit biplane,
painted cream & red, still affixed in
the original box w/directions sheet,
Meccano (Dinky Toys - Liverpool,
England), ca. 1938,
box 2 x 9 x 13" **230.00**

Airplane construction set, wood, US
Army Stinson 0-49 Observation
model, unbuilt, original box **45.00**

Automobile, cast metal, long
streamlined two-door sedan w/silver
paint & white rubber tires, Tootsietoy
(Dowst Mfg. Co., Chicago, Illinois),
ca. 1930s, 5" l., 1½" h. (soiling,
scratches) **49.50**

Automobile, Chevrolet coupe, cast
iron, two-door closed model painted
black w/gold belt piping, nickeled
driver, white tires w/spoke wheels &
rear spare, Arcade Mfg. Co.
(Freeport, Illinois), ca. 1926,
6¾" l...**253.00**

Automobile, Chevrolet roadster, cast
iron, painted black, nickeled driver &
white rubber tires, Arcade, ca. 1926,
6¾" l. (very rough hood casting) ...**1,150.00**

Automobile, Chevrolet roadster, cast
iron, painted black, chromed driver,
white-painted tires & rear spare,
Arcade, 6¾" l. **437.00**

Automobile, Ford Model T Phaeton,
cast iron, painted black w/top up,
nickeled driver, white painted tires,
Arcade, 6¼" l. (some paint
wear)...**219.00**

Automobile, Ford Model T sedan,
cast iron, four-door style painted
black w/gold belt piping & white tires
on spoke wheels, w/nickeled driver,
Arcade, ca. 1920s, 6½" l. **138.00**

Tin Bandai GT

Automobile, Grand touring-style, tin
friction, red w/black plastic hood,
w/box, minor scratches to car,
Bandai (Japan), 8¼" l., 2½" h.
(ILLUS.) **27.50**

Automobile, limousine w/driver, cast iron, the sedan painted red w/yellow wheels & open chauffeur's compartment, closed rear quarters, molded side lamps & headlamps, Kenton Hardware Co. (Kenton, Ohio), ca. 1915, 7¾" l. (paint chipped, some rust) **575.00**

German Tin Limousine

Automobile, limousine, lithographed tinplate, finished in dark green lined w/yellow & black, w/bevelled glass windshield, opening rear doors, white rubber tires, hand brake & start/stop lever, two pairs of lamps, adjustable front wheels, clockwork motor driving rear wheels, h.p. tinplate driver, George Carette, (Nuremberg, Germany), ca. 1910, 15¾" l. (ILLUS.) **8,050.00**

Automobile, Packard convertible, remote-control tinplate, light green & beige, turning front wheels, rubber tires & a detachable remote control unit, Schuco Toy Co. (Nuremberg, Germany), ca. 1956, w/box, 11" l..**863.00**

Automobile, Plymouth, cast metal, white tires, Arcade, 1933, 4¾" l. **225.00**

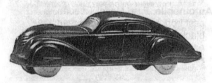

Green Sun Rubber Sloped-back Car

Automobile, slope-backed, green rubber, Sun Rubber Mfg. Co. (Barberton, Ohio), very minor paint chips & one nick to back bumper (ILLUS.) **38.50**

Automobile, touring car, cast iron, open car w/overhead roof, painted in blue w/grey seats, gold piping & yellow spoke wheels, two sets of lamps, w/a driver at tiller & lady passenger in a red dress in the rear seat, Jones & Bixler Co. (Freemansburg, Pennsylvania), ca. 1912, 9" l..**1,495.00**

Automobile, touring car, steamdriven tinplate, a beige car w/front head lamps & center steering wheel w/a steam mechanism attached to the rear, Bing, Gerbruder (Nuremberg, Germany), early 20th c., 11" l..**3,680.00**

Automobile & trailer, LaSalle sedan & matching Art Deco-style trailer, pressed steel, green paint w/white rubber tires, Wyandotte Toys All Metal Products Comp. - (Wyandotte, Michigan), 2 pcs., 26" l. overall **650.00**

Automobile & trailer, cast iron, a Lincoln Zephyr in red w/a separate grill & whitewall rubber tires, pulls a trailer, Hubley, ca. 1937, overall 13½" l., 2 pcs. **437.00**

Automobiles, race cars, die-cast metal, each w/chromed drivers, painted light blue, yellow & red, Hubley, set of 3 in original box, each 7" l., the set **207.00**

Balance toy, painted tinplate, a white horse w/an American flag attached to his back raised high & counterbalanced by a tinplate weight & raised on slender rods above a flat base w/four open-spoked metal wheels, American-made, ca. 1870, 7" h..............................**1,955.00**

Battery-operated, airplane, "United Air Boeing 737" **45.00**

Battery-operated, automobile, "Jaguar," stunt car w/tumble-over lever..**157.50**

Battery-operated, automobile, taxicab, yellow, side door opens showing passenger, blinking light, fare meter runs, mint in box **120.00**

Battery-operated, automobile, "Mercedes Benz," blinking lights, mint in box **75.00**

Battery-operated, automobile, Volkswagen "Love Beetle" race car, blinking lights, many advertising logos, mint in box.............................**125.00**

Battery-operated, "Balloon Blowing Monkey," Japan **125.00**

Battery-operated, "Barney Drumming Bear," plush & tin, remote control, turns head, plays the drum & the eyes light up.......................................**93.00**

Battery-operated, "Bingo Clown" **110.00**

Battery-operated, "Blushing Willy," eyes roll, pours from bottle & drinks, Y Company (Japan), 1960s, 10" h.....**87.00**

Battery-operated, "Bubble Blowing Monkey," plush & tin, w/light-up eyes, Alps Shojo Ltd. (Tokyo, Japan), mint in box **136.00**

Battery-operated, "Captain Blushwell," pours drink, blushes &

rolls eyes, Japan, mint in box,
11" h.,..**127.00**
Battery-operated, "Charlie Weaver,"
bartender, six actions, 1962, T-N
Co. (Japan), 12" h..........................**50.00**
Battery-operated, "Chippy
Chipmunk," mint in box **60.00**
Battery-operated, "Dolly Dressmaker,"
girl seated at sewing machine **130.00**
Battery-operated, "Fire Chief's Car"
w/siren & flashing dome light, Barlos
(Japan) mint in box, 7¼" l. **110.00**
Battery-operated, "A Gambling Man,"
roulette, Cragston (Japan), mint in
box **250.00**
Battery-operated, "Hungry Baby
Bear," mint in box............................**272.50**
Battery-operated, "Maxwell Coffee-
Loving Bear" **210.00**
Battery-operated, "McGregor,"
dressed in cloth Scotsman outfit &
smokes a cigar, Japan, 11" h..........**162.50**
Battery-operated, "Mr. Magoo Car,"
tin, plastic & cloth, auto wobbles
forward as Mr. Magoo bounces up &
down in seat, Hubley Mfg. Co.........**280.00**
Battery-operated, "Old Sleepy Head
Rip," w/original box **350.00**
Battery-operated, "Papa Bear,"
w/lighted pipe, smoke comes from
mouth **95.00**
Battery-operated, "Rosko Bartender,"
shakes cocktail, drinks, smoke
comes from ears, mint in box.............**75.00**
Battery-operated, "Roulette Player,"
five actions, includes small ball &
detachable table, Cragston, ca.
1950, 9½" h.....................................**197.50**
Battery-operated, "Royal Cub,"
w/original box..................................**100.00**
Battery-operated, "Sandy the Sniffy
Pup," six actions, in original box **190.00**
Battery-operated, "Santa on Globe,"
w/original box..................................**450.00**
Battery-operated, Santa Claus,
sitting on a house, four actions,
No. M-750, H.T.C. Co., 1960s,
8" h..**165.00**
Battery-operated, school bus, both
doors open, flashing headlights,
"Alps," mint in box **120.00**
Battery-operated, sewing machine,
child's, "Sew Mistress," in original
carrying case, mint & in working
condition **60.00**
Battery-operated, space capsule
w/three astronauts, one astronaut
w/air pressure floating mechanism &
two astronauts in the space capsule,
Japan, mint in box, 9" l.....................**198.00**
Battery-operated, "Space Patrol
Tank," tin, 1960s, mint in box.............**92.50**
Battery-operated, "Two Gun Sheriff,"
Cragston **170.00**

Battery-operated, "Walking Rhino,"
RC...**40.00**

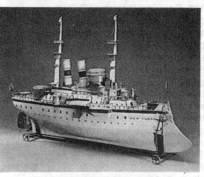

"New York" Marklin Battleship

Battleship, "New York," tinplate,
painted ocean grey & red w/two
smokestacks, dual masts, four
lifeboats, battle cannons
strategically placed around the
vessel, rests on tinplate four wheel
stand, rudder stamped w/Marklin
logo, Marklin (Germany), 36" l.
(ILLUS.) **32,200.00**
BB gun, "Benjamin," nickel over
brass, pump action, Benjamin
(Air Rifle), ca. 1900 ....**195.00**
BB gun, "Columbian Helprin," cast
iron & brass lever action, ornate
animal scenes, ca. 1900, excellent
condition **650.00**
BB gun, Daisy Model 21, double-
barreled, Daisy Manufacturing
Co. **408.00**

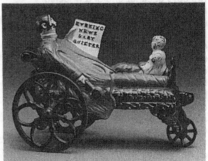

"Baby Quieter" Bell Ringer Toy

Bell ringer toy, "Baby Quieter,"
painted cast iron, a father reads his
evening newspaper on a lounging
couch while moving his left leg up &
down to amuse his baby sitting on it,
thereby ringing a bell, on three-
wheel cast base, J. & E. Stevens
(Cromwell, Connecticut), 8" l.
(ILLUS.) **2,070.00**
Bell ringer toy, "Billy's Bell Ringer,"
cast iron, a four-wheeled base w/two

goats, one black & one white, which butt heads to ring the bell, Gong Bell Mfg. Co. (East Hampton, Connecticut), late 19th c., 7½" l. **863.00**

Bell ringer toy, cast iron, a dressed & capped monkey riding a high-wheel early three-wheel velocipede which rings bell as the monkey appears to pedal, J. & E. Stevens, late 19th c., 8¼" l. **3,680.00**

Bell ringer toy, cast iron, model of a turtle w/a low domed shell painted green w/a large tan bell on its back, on small wheels, a pull string from the head, late 19th - early 20th c., 6¼" l. **575.00**

Bell ringer toy, cast iron, two black horses jump from a yellow-painted platform causing a clown, on a road between them, to somersault wildly, ringing his bells, Hubley Mfg. Co., late 19th - early 20th c., 6" l. **805.00**

Bell ringer toy, cast iron, a wheeled platform w/the standing figure of a blue & yellow-painted clown w/a white poodle on a leash w/a bell in its mouth, Gong Bell Mfg. Co. (East Hampton, Connecticut), late 19th c., 8" l. **1,150.00**

Bell ringer toy, cast iron, a white pig on three wheels & a clown on its back, running along ringing a bell attached to the pig's snout, Gong Bell Mfg. Co., 6" l. **1,035.00**

Bell ringer toy, "Ding Dong Bell, Pussy's Not in the Well," cast iron, two boys at either end of a wheeled platform, one of whom has just rescued a cat from the well between them ringing a bell, Gong Bell Mfg. Co., 9¼" l. **1,495.00**

Bell ringer toy, "Hunter and Rabbit," cast iron, when the four-wheeled base is pulled a rabbit pops out of a hole in the turf ringing a bell & confronting a hunter whose rifle is aimed directly at him, N.N. Hill Brass Co. (New Jersey), late 19th c., 6" l. **4,600.00**

Bell ringer toy, "Saw the Watermelon," cast iron, a four-wheeled base w/heart-shaped spokes surmounted by two young black boys who maneuver a large saw back & forth over three watermelons, Gong Bell Mfg. Co., 8½" l. (worn paint) **2,415.00**

Bell ringer toy, "Trick Pony," painted cast iron, white horse wearing a red blanket swings on a pedestal & rings a bell, on four-wheeled platform, Gong Bell Mfg. Co., 8" l. (ILLUS. top next column) **575.00**

"Trick Pony" Bell Ringer Toy

Bell ringer toy, "Uncle Sam," cast iron, a formally dressed Uncle Sam strikes a bell as he is pulled along on four cast wheels, Gong Bell Mfg., Co., 6½" l. **460.00**

Bell ringer toy, "Wild Mule Jack," cast iron, a man clinging to the back of a running wild mule whose tail pops up & down ringing a large bell, Gong Bell Mfg., Co., late 19th c., 8½" l. **1,495.00**

Blocks, building-type, "Crandall's Building Blocks," in wooden dovetailed box w/color lithograph of children playing w/blocks, ½ x 7 x 11" **300.00**

Chicago Limited Blocks

Blocks, novelty-type, lithographed paper-on-wood, Chicago Limited train set, consisting of an engine, tender, two passenger cars & one baggage car all w/vestibules & handsomely lithographed, ca. 1895, some paper loss on tender, 46" l. overall (ILLUS.) **2,185.00**

Blocks, nesting-type, covered w/red paper & colorful chromolithographic paper squares w/children, animals, birds & scenes from children's stories, marked "Lungers, Hausen," graduated from 2½ to 8¾", set of 8 (next to smallest block missing) **302.50**

Blocks, nested-type, lithographed paper-on-wood, brightly colored blocks picturing circus arts & performers on the sides & letters of the alphabet on the top, Milton Bradley & Co. (E. Longmeadow &

Nested-type Blocks

Springfield, Massachusetts),
ca. 1910, 5¾ x 6 x 6", set of 6
(ILLUS.) **460.00**
Blocks, picture-type, "Little Workers
Picture Cubes," lithographed paper
on wood, the cubes fitting together
in a series to picture Victorian boys
& girls following various
occupations, together
w/lithographed sheets showing the
finished pictures, McLoughlin
Brothers, (New York, New York),
ca. 1890, w/box, 3 x 8 x 10½",
set of 12 ....**552.00**
Bobsled, "Flexible Flyer," wood &
steel, 3' l...**60.00**
Britains (soldiers), cast metal, "Boer
War Royal Horse Artillery," No. 126,
small scale, shown at gallop in
active service dress, w/original box,
pre-war, the set (box in poor
condition) **259.00**
Britains (soldiers), cast metal,
"Middlesex Regiment - Parade
Series," No. 439, set of nine
w/original box, pre-war, the set (two
helmet spikes missing) **747.50**
Britains (soldiers), cast metal,
"Types of the World's Armies," No.
27, tied in original box, late 1940s,
set of 12 (one helmet spike
missing) **316.00**
Buckboard wagon, wood & tin, worn
old cream-colored paint w/red
striping, 12" l. plus rods (wheels
damaged).......................................**170.50**
Bus, double-decker, cast iron, painted
turquoise blue w/an orange stripe,
contains seven seats in the open top
area, rear stairwell, Kilgore, ca.
1930, 6" l. (paint worn, some rust) ...**633.00**

Arcade Double-Decker Yellow Bus

Bus, double-decker, cast iron
w/rubber tires, painted in browns &
black, marked on the side "Yellow
Coach," Arcade Mfg. Co., ca. 1920s,
replaced tires, one seat missing on
top, 11½" l., 5" h. (ILLUS. bottom
previous column) **2,475.00**

Arcade Double-Decker Bus

Bus w/passengers & driver, double-
decker, cast iron, painted green
w/driver & two passengers seated in
the upper deck, nickel headlights &
bumper, original rubber wheels,
marked "318R" inside bus, Arcade
Mfg. Co., minor paint chipping, one
passenger missing, 7¾" l., 3¼" h.
(ILLUS.) **665.50**

Buddy-L Steel Bus

Bus, pressed steel, painted bluish
green, w/decal, gold, black & red
lining on sides, solid cast wheels,
adjustable front axle, chromed
bumper & headlights, opening
doors, Buddy-L (Moline Pressed
Steel Co., E. Moline, Illinois),
surface paint loss & rust, 28¾" l.
(ILLUS.) **2,185.00**

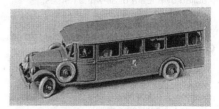

Buddy-L Passenger Bus

Bus, pressed steel, passenger-type,
large green painted multi-seated bus
w/opening door, sidemounts, large
headlamps, turning front wheels & a
front bumper, Buddy-L, ca. 1929,

paint distressed toward the rear,
29" l. (ILLUS.) **680.00**
Cap pistol, dagger Derringer, Hubley,
mint in box **100.00**
Cap pistol, "Lawmaker," Kenton
Hardware Co.....................................**115.00**
Cap pistol, "Navy Colt 45," Hubley **175.00**
Cap pistol, "Pluck," cast iron, 4" h. **115.00**
Cap pistol & holster set, "Ric-O-
Shay Jr.", in original box **250.00**
Carpet sweeper, Bissell's "Little
Helper," Mother Goose on top **75.00**

Brake Style Carriage

Carriage, four seat Brake style, cast
iron, consisting of two white horses
& two light brown horses pulling a
black painted four-seated Brake on
four large yellow cast wheels; eight
cast figures, w/a driver in a long
robe, black & orange side lamps,
Pratt & Letchworth (Buffalo, New
York), ca. 1892, some paint wear,
28" l. (ILLUS.) **9,775.00**

Hubley Horse-Drawn Carriage

Carriage, Landau w/driver, cast iron,
the black enclosed landau trimmed
w/gold on yellow-spoked wheels
pulled by a team of all-white horses,
separate coachman atop the
carriage, Hubley, ca. 1900, 17" l.
(ILLUS.) **4,370.00**
Carriage, Landau-type, cast iron, a
single lady sits in a four-wheeled
open carriage painted black & red
w/yellow foot rug, pulled by a single
trotting horse, Wilkins Toy Co.
(Keene, New Hampshire),
late 19th c., 17" l. **1,610.00**
Carriage, two seat Station style, cast
iron & steelplate, painted black
w/yellow wheels, w/top-hatted
driver, the wagon pulled by a tan &
yellow horse wearing an off-white

Two Seat Station Style Carriage

blanket, Pratt & Letchworth, 14" l.
(ILLUS.) **1,265.00**
Cart, horse-drawn, cast iron, a boy
driver sporting a tri-color cap, sits in
a yellow open cart w/a sleeping dog
at the rear, he drives a white horse
by waving a stick in his right hand,
J. & E. Stevens, late 19th c., 9" l......**633.00**
Chariot, cast iron, red & gold ornately
cast chariot w/a standing driver &
pulled by three galloping horses,
Hubley, ca. 1920, 11" l. **345.00**
Chariot toy, cast iron, a figure of
Uncle Sam stands in an eagle-
shaped silver chariot on two red
wheels, pulled by two galloping
black horses, Jones & Bixler Co.,
ca. 1900, 11½" l. **1,380.00**
Chemistry set, No. 1 "For Boys,"
contents & instructions, 1943, A.C.
Gilbert (New Haven, Connecticut),
some box wear **65.00**

Rare Cinderella Coach

Cinderella coach, lithographed reed
paper-on-wood, w/a colorfully
elaborate coach picturing Cinderella
inside & two outside drivers, pulled
by a pair of horses, ca. 1900, blocks
missing, 26" l. (ILLUS.) **2,760.00**
Circus animal, Buffalo, wooden,
carved mane, painted eyes,
Schoenhut, regular size **356.00**
Circus animal, Elephant, wooden,
painted eyes, Schoenhut, regular
size, 8¼" l. **175.00**
Circus wagon, lithographed reed
paper-on-wood, two dapple grey
horses pull a large circus wagon
inside of which is a trainer w/whip &
a white polar bear who moves up &

Rare Paper-on-wood Circus Wagon

down as the wagon is pulled
forward, ca. 1897, 26" l.
(ILLUS.) **7,475.00**
Circus band wagon, cast iron, six
musicians play atop a red, yellow &
gold band wagon w/driver, pulled by
twin white & gold horses w/individual
riders, marked "Overland," Kenton
Hardware Co., ca. 1940, overall
16" l. **403.00**
Circus cage wagon, cast iron,
"Overland Circus" bear wagon,
w/driver, two horses & two out
riders, Kenton Hardware Co.,
13½" l. (minor paint wear)................**330.00**
Circus calliope wagon, cast iron,
twin white horses w/individual riders
pull a red & yellow calliope wagon
manned by two men, one a driver,
the other the calliope player, marked
"Overland Circus," Kenton Hardware
Co., ca. 1940, 14½" l. **978.00**
Circus performer, Bareback Rider,
lady, wooden w/bisque head,
Schoenhut, 8½" h. **406.00**
Circus performer, Lion Tamer,
wooden, Schoenhut, regular size **325.00**
Circus set, cast metal, "Mammoth
Circus," eight painted circus
personnel & thirteen circus animals
w/ring & stand, all affixed in the
original box, Britains (William) Ltd.
(London, England), ca. 1955,
figures 4" h., the set......................**1,265.00**
Circus set: complete boxed set
w/painted wood-jointed figures
including the Ring Master, girl
acrobat, clown, elephant, donkey,
tiger & horse as well as the tent, ring
poles, bar, trapeze, ring set, string of
18 colorful pendants, three barrel
stands, three chairs & one ladder;
"Humpty Dumpty Circus,"
Schoenhut, ca. 1915, the set........**2,185.00**
Circus wagon, paper-on-wood,
"Mammoth Show Circus Wagon," a
printed wooden four-wheeled wagon
w/sliding top containing figures of
three large circus animals & two
trainers, all colorfully lithographed,

w/bases, W.S. Reed Toy Co.
(Leominster, Massachusetts),
ca. 1890, wagon 6 x 6¾ x 14",
the set **1,955.00**
Clicker, birds feeding babies,
lithographed tin **30.00**
Clockwork mechanism, Alfa Romeo
race car #2, tinplate, classic racer
finished in blue w/turning front
wheels, rubber Michelin tires, a
water & gas can, knock-off hubs,
front springs, wire grille, fitted seats
& a brake, C.I.J. (France), ca. 1929,
21" l...**2,070.00**

Ives Clockwork Toy

Clockwork mechanism, "Curzner
Trotter," tinplate, painted red
carriage w/canted back, beige
horse, figure w/red tin hat wearing
red striped trousers & grey jacket,
cast spoked wheels, Ives Corp.
(Bridgeport, Connecticut), patented
March 7, 1871, very slight paint
loss, 11½" l. (ILLUS.) **3,450.00**
Clockwork mechanism, ocean liner,
painted tinplate, the hull painted red
& blue, white lining & upper decks,
three funnels in orange & black,
w/tin masts, four lifeboats, four
ventilators, gold-stamped portholes,
twin three-black screws, adjustable
rudder, Bing (Gebruder), 1920s,
16" l. (slight retouching, flags
replaced) **2,300.00**

Clockwork U-Boat

Clockwork mechanism, U-boat,
tinplate, the submarine w/a

periscope & lifeboat, the rudder marked w/the Marklin logo, 30" l. (ILLUS.) **8,625.00**

Clown "roller" push toy, a wooden jointed donkey pulls a round roller w/large wheels decorated w/colorful clowns, kittens, etc., a wooden clown figure stands atop the roller & holds the reins of the donkey, Schoenhut, 15" l., 13" h. (some wear, reins replaced, wire support added to barrel end) **675.00**

Connestoga wagon w/two horses & driver, cast iron, one black & one white horse, cloth canopy, metal wheels, Kenton Hardware, unused in original box, 15" l.........................**440.00**

Cork gun, metal, Captain Commando, 1940s, mint in box **95.00**

Erector set, A.C. Gilbert Model No. 3, dated 1913, original cardboard box w/manual **45.00**

Erector Set, A.C. Gilbert Model No. 7½ **65.00**

Farm set, painted wood, miniature farmhouse, barn, shed, various farm animals, fencing, as well as cut & painted heavy paper plants & trees, Fiske Farm (Lexington, Massachusetts), 19th c., all contained in a wooden crate, farm house 3¾" h., approximately 25 pcs. **1,495.00**

Fire chief's wagon, cast iron & steelplate, horse-drawn, a figure wearing a red shirt drives a galloping black horse pulling a four-wheel maroon steelplate wagon, Wilkins, ca. 1885, overall 12" l. (worn paint on driver) **1,150.00**

Fire hook & ladder wagon, horse-drawn, cast iron, a bronzed wagon on yellow wheels w/five ladders, pulled by one white & two black galloping horses, Hubley, early 20th c., 31" l. **3,680.00**

Fire hook & ladder wagon, horse-drawn, cast iron, a black & red ladder wagon No. 45 w/two drivers, ladders & pails, pulled by a team of galloping horses, one white, one black on an eccentric wheel, Ives, ca. 1885, 28" l. (some crazing on the white horse) **1,840.00**

Fire hose reel wagon, horse-drawn, cast iron, the red fire wagon w/hose reel mounted by two firemen & pulled by a white & a tan detachable horse, the reel in tan w/red piping, Wilkins Toy Co., 16" l....................**2,530.00**

Fire horse reel wagon, horse-drawn, cast iron, ornate brown, gold & red hose reel carriage w/two firemen, pulled by a white & two black

galloping horses on eccentric wheels, Dent, ca. 1900, 25" l. **2,760.00**

Fire ladder truck, cast iron, red truck w/two drivers cast into the vehicle, turning front wheel section, gold eagle embossed at sides, w/two wooden ladders, Hubley, ca. 1920, 15½" l. **460.00**

Kingsbury Fire Ladder Truck

Fire ladder truck, steelplate, truck w/double ladder which can be raised forty inches & can be rotated, steering front wheels, black simulated leather driver's seat, white rubber tires w/"Kingsbury" molded into them, Kingsbury Mfg. Co., (Keene, New Hampshire), 35" l. (ILLUS.) **2,760.00**

Fire pumper wagon, horse-drawn, cast iron, the red water pumper wagon w/handles at either end for manual power to work the two pumps at the center of the four-wheeled wagon, w/rubber hose, marked "Friendship 1774," 4¼ x 9 x 16" **1,093.00**

Fire pumper wagon, horse-drawn, cast iron, the red fire wagon w/two firemen pulled by one white & one tan horse, the pumper finished in bronze, Wilkins Toy Co., 18" l.......**3,450.00**

Fire pumper wagon, cast iron & tinplate, the red, black & gold pumper w/gauges & four red cast wheels pulled by two black & one white galloping horses, Wilkins, early 20th c., 19" l. **1,265.00**

G.I. Joe "Action Pilot," complete w/air manual, mint in box, 1964...............**322.00**

G.I. Joe, "Black Commander Adventure Team," w/gun & holster, mint, 1974 ....**138.00**

G.I. Joe, "Green Beret," complete w/rifle, mint, 1966...........................**288.00**

G.I. Joe, "Japanese Imperial Soldier," complete w/pack & case, mint, 1967 (ILLUS. top next page)...................**322.00**

G.I. Joe, "Mike Powers, Atomic Man," atomic flashing eye model, complete w/jacket, shorts & hand helicopter, sealed on card, 1975 ....**127.00**

G.I. Joe, "Police Officer," complete w/whistle & violation tickets, mint, 1967 ....**345.00**

G.I. Joe, "Race Car" figure, complete w/racing goggles, mint, 1967 ....**219.00**

Japanese Imperial Soldier

G.I. Joe, "Royal Guard," complete
w/helmet, sword & royal outfit,
mint, 1967 ....**460.00**
G.I. Joe, "Shore Patrol," complete
w/accessories, mint, 1964 ....**219.00**
G.I. Joe set, "Army Combat
Construction & Engineer Set," figure
& accessories, mint, 1967................**460.00**
G.I. Joe set, "Australian Jungle Set,"
figure & complete accessories,
mint, 1967 ....**230.00**
G.I. Joe set, "Deep Freeze Set,"
figure & complete accessories,
mint, 1967 ....**196.00**
G.I. Joe set, "Heavy Weapons Set,"
figure & complete accessories,
mint, 1967 ....**253.00**
G.I. Joe set, "Jungle Fighter Set,"
figure & complete accessories,
very fine, 1967 ....**437.00**
G.I. Joe set, "Official Combat Jeep
Set," includes a battery-operated
jeep w/detachable cargo trailer &
various accessories, mint in box,
1965..**184.00**

Russian Infantryman

G.I. Joe set, "Russian Infantry Set,"
figure & complete accessories,
mint, 1967 (ILLUS.)..........................**345.00**

Iron, electric-type, red-painted tin
w/black wood handle, "Sunny Suzy,"
Wolverine Co. (Pittsburgh
Pennsylvania), 1940s,
5½" l. ....**15.00 to 20.00**
Jack-in-the-box, wooden box
w/colorful chromolithographed paper
sides showing children & animals,
the clown in papier-maché w/original
polychrome trim & cloth ruff, 11" h.
(some wear & edge damage) **55.00**

The Magic Car & Garage

Keywind, "The Magic Car & Garage,"
by Louis Marx & Co. (New York,
New York), mint in box (ILLUS.) **180.00**
Lincoln Logs, w/original box, 1923 .....**78.00**

Soldier in Armor Marionette

Marionette, soldier in armor, dressed
in full set of armor w/shield & sword,
19th c., 44" h. (ILLUS.) **935.00**
Marionette set, "Alice in
Wonderland," wood, papier-maché
& cloth, including Alice, Duchess &
baby, March Hare, Cook, White
Rabbit, Mad Hatter, Fish & Frog,
Pelham Puppets, Ltd., (Marlboro,

Wiltshire, England), ca. 1951, w/original boxes & two w/instructions by Jan Bussell of the Hogarth Puppets, the set **977.50**

Matchbox van, No. 47 Trojan Brook Bond Tea, die-cast, mint condition **30.00**

Milk wagon, tinplate, a front pivot-hitch wagon w/six milk containers, a pair of horses accompanies the lot, 15" l. **1,380.00**

Model kit, "Mummy," 1963, Aurora, (Brooklyn, New York), sealed in box **365.00**

Red Motorcycle with Driver

Motorcycle, cast iron, w/driver, red w/white rubber tires, tires cracked & minor paint chips, 3¾" l., 2½" h. (ILLUS.) **165.00**

Motorcycle w/sidecar, cast iron, painted red & blue w/rubber tires, ca. 1930s, 4" w., 2½" h. (tires cracked, minor rust & paint loss) **198.00**

Motorcycle w/sidecar, cast iron, w/a driver & passenger, red & blue paint w/rubber tires, cycle numbered "7-1723," sidecar numbered "1724B," 4" l., 2½" h. (minor rust & paint loss, tires cracked) **198.00**

Ocean liner, live-steam tinplate, h.p. red, white & tan w/stenciled portholes, dual cabins, open bridge, twin stairs, two lifeboats, two masts & a single smokestack, attributed to Carette, 32" l. **6,900.00**

Pedal airplane, Murray Ohio Mfg. (Murray, Ohio), original condition & paint..**2,595.00**

Sky King Tricycle & Steelcraft Pedal Plane

Pedal airplane, pressed steel, body painted light olive green lined w/red

& yellow, wings & tail painted red & yellow, lettered on sides in yellow "Spirit of St. Louis," w/red propeller, pierced steel disk wheels w/black rubber rims, Steelcraft, ca. 1927, rebuilt & restored, 45" l., wingspan 30" (ILLUS. right) **2,990.00**

Pedal car, "Chrysler," Airflow, Steelcraft, 1937............................**3,883.00**

Phonograph, RCA Victrola Model 6-JM-25, Ding Dong School...............**125.00**

Piano & stool, upright-model, painted white, glass window above the keyboard, w/a white four-legged round-topped stool, Schoenhut, 11 x 16", 24" h., 2 pcs. (some dark stains on top, slightly yellowed paint)...**80.00**

Pinball game, "Poosh-M-Up Big 5," 13 x 23"...**40.00**

Pop-Up Kritter, "Tailspin Tabby," black cat w/yellow face & feet on red guitar-shaped base, Model 400, Fisher-Price, Inc. (East Aurora, New York), 1931-39 (mint condition) **150.00**

Pull toy, bee on wheels, "Buzzy Bee," Model 325, Fisher-Price, Inc., 1950-55 ....**35.00 to 45.00**

Pull toy, cow on wheels, wood & papier-maché animal w/worn suede covering in tan & white & glass eyes, on a rectangular wooden base w/red & black wood-graining & tiny cast-iron wheels, a voice box activated when head is turned, tin reservoir in hind quarters for 'milk,' late 19th c., 11¾" l. (horns mis-matched, wear, some damage) **577.50**

Pull toy, dog, "Fido Zilo," lithographed puppy plays xylophone w/four nickel keys on a pivoting platform, Model 707, Fisher-Price, Inc., 1955-57 ....**65.00 to 75.00**

Pull toy, dog, "Snoopy Sniffer," lithographed wood, Model 181, Fisher-Price, Inc., 1961 ....**55.00**

Pull-toy, elephant on wheels, tinplate, the grey elephant, wearing an orange & gold-painted rug, stands on a four-wheeled green platform, George Brown & Co. (Forestville, Connecticut), late 19th c., 6¼" l. **368.00**

Pull toy, farm wagon & two horses, low-sided tin buckboard-style wagon w/original red & black paint, pulled by two lithographed wood horses in dapple grey w/black & red, wagon marked w/decal "Art Craft Fixture Co.," overall 20½" l..........................**412.50**

Pull toy, hen on wheels, "Katy Kackler the Red Hen," wings & feet move up & down, plastic comb & "cluck, cluck, squawk" sound mechanism, Model 140, Fisher-Price, Inc., 1954-56 ....**85.00**

Pull toy, horse, "Dandy Dobbin," Fisher-Price No. 765, 1941 ....**75.00**

Pull toy, horse on wooden platform w/small steel wheels, brown mohair animal w/steel eyes, leatherette & cloth tack, Germany, early 20th c., 13½" h. (some damage & fiber loss) **345.00**

Pull toy, horse & cart, the wood & composition horse w/white flannel coat & leatherized cloth harness on a thin rectangular base w/tiny wheels, pulls a low-sided wooden cart w/two large wheels, cart w/original red & yellow paint, 9½" h. (wear, damage, mane & tail incomplete, one wheel on horse replaced) **220.00**

Horse & Jockey Pull Toy

Pull toy, horse w/jockey, h.p. tinplate, a red semiformed jockey straddles a black horse w/grey mane on a green four-wheeled platform, Fallows (James) & Sons (Philadelphia, Pennsylvania), ca. 1875, some rust, 7" l. (ILLUS.) **920.00**

Pull toy, lion, "Leon the Drummer," lion w/ movable arms swings wooden mallets & beats on a metal-topped drum, Model 480, Fisher-Price, Inc., 1952-53 ....**112.50**

Santa Claus Pull Toy

Pull toy, Santa Claus & two reindeer, painted cast iron, a thin Santa sits in a dark blue elaborate curved runner

sleigh pulled by two galloping white reindeer, Hubley Mfg. Co., 16½" l. (ILLUS.) **1,265.00**

Pull toy, train, "Fisher-Price Choo Choo," comprised of an engine, three cars & a caboose, w/wobbling action & unbreakable steel connectors & axles, Model 215, Fisher-Price, Inc., 1955-57, 17" l. **45.00**

Pull toy, train, "Huffy Puffy," engine w/moving eyes, pistons & realistic sound, w/coal car, cattle car w/sliding doors & caboose w/plastic brakeman who swings his lantern, Model 999, Fisher-Price, Inc., 1958-70, 4 pcs. **52.50**

Riding toy, bus, large, Keystone Mfg. Co., Boston, Massachusetts (professional restoration) **2,650.00**

Riding toy, donkey, stands on four-wheeled red cart, w/original bridle & cloth saddle, Dean's Rag Book Co., (Great Britain) **375.00**

1950s Road Grader

Road grader, heavy pressed metal, painted w/functional steering & blade, six rubber tires, marked "Models Toys - Charles Wm. Doepke Mfg. Co. Inc. Rossmoyne, O.," ca. 1950s, overall paint chipping & wear, 25¾" l., 8" h. (ILLUS.) **44.00**

Battery-operated Robot

Robot, battery-operated, tin & plastic, silver body w/clear plastic revolving head, shapes inside head spin, moving color bands in mouth, ca. 1950s (ILLUS.)..............................**1,300.00**

Robot, "Capt. Robot," windup, Line Mar (Japan), in original box **35.00**

Robot, Commando, battery-operated, tin, 1961, Ideal (Brooklyn, New York) **185.00**

Robot, "Marvelous Mike," battery-operated, silver figure at the controls of a large yellow bulldozer, mint in box..**295.00**

Robot, "Mighty Robot," battery-operated tin & plastic, robot's head lights up & 16 gears spin in it, arms swing, bump-&-go action **132.50**

Robot, "Sparky Robot," 1950s, Yoshiya, (Japan)............................**240.00**

Robot, "Super Space Commander," w/space scenes on big screen..........**95.00**

Painted Rocking Horse

Rocking horse, painted & decorated wood, the full-bodied figure of a horse w/leather saddle & bridle mounted on a green painted rocker, 19th c., 34" l., 21" h. (ILLUS.) **1,610.00**

Rocking toy, painted wood, a sleigh-form seat raised on a low platform w/four large curved triangular "rockers," the front w/two small cut-out silhouetted horses fitted w/horse-hair manes & tails, original red & black paint w/yellow striping, 36" l. (minor repairs) **660.00**

Roller chimes, complete w/clappers on the top roller that strike revolving, brightly finished steel xylophone bars, mounted on multicolored sound pipes, threaded handle, Model No. 123, Fisher-Price, Inc., ca. 1953, handle 16½" l. **115.00**

Sad iron & trivet, cast iron, w/removable handle, marked "Pat. May 21, 1895," 2 pcs. **115.50**

Sand pail & shovel, decorated w/clowns, Ohio Art Company (Bryan, Ohio), 6" h., 2 pcs...............**200.00**

Sewing machine, "Little Mother," red metal, Artcraft Metal Products, 4 x 7⅜ x 8"....................................**75.00**

Sled, child's size, painted wood, the narrow wooden platform w/rounded end decorated w/stenciled bands of flowers near each end & h.p. flowers at the center all on the original red ground, sheet metal-tipped runners, underside marked in pencil "Enola M. Brownell, Feb. 5, 1909," 33½" l...**385.00**

Sled, child's size, painted wood, the narrow wood platform w/rounded end decorated w/worn red paint w/a stenciled design, sheet metal-tipped high runners, underside labeled "Paris Mfg. Co…," 38" l. (well done repair) **247.50**

Steam plant, a sheet steel boiler w/escape valves, steam discharge valve, glass water gauge & tinplate smokestack, the boiler mounted horizontally on a high tinplate burner which features three circular ventilation ports & the Marklin crest; a steam pipe leads from the escape valve to a dual piston apparatus w/dual nickel-plated machine cast steel flywheels mounted next to the boiler, 'The Dynamo', an electric motor that converts steam energy to electricity also mounted w/the other pieces on the tinplate base w/flared sides, a saw & original paper directions included, Marklin, Germany, early 20th c., 21½" sq. **5,175.00**

Stove, kitchen, cast iron, in original box, 1950s, Greycraft **35.00**

Stove, kitchen range, cast iron, "Star Range," a piercedwork warming shelf above a rectangular top fitted w/six removable burners & a griddle above an oven & rotisserie, on animal paw feet, together w/a group of toy cooking utensils including a griddle, two skillets, a wooden potato masher & a waffle iron, late 19th - early 20th c., 19½ x 20", 18¾" h., the group **368.00**

Tool chest, miniature, rectangular, machine-dovetailed case w/molded base, chromolithographed label inside lid reads "Elite tool Chests for Boys," includes two cast-iron tools, a monkey wrench & a hammer, 11¼" l., the set.................................**71.50**

Tractor, live-steam type, brass, steel & cast iron, finished in green & black, w/red & yellow detailing & lining, maroon-painted spoked 14" d. flywheel, finely detailed including ball governor, single slide valve cylinder, eccentric driven, water pump, chimney, brass banding on boiler, opening firebox doors, screw adjustable steering, Whitney

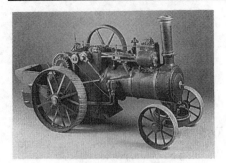

Steam Tractor Engine

(London) pressure gauge, water gauge glass, brake, Stephenson's lever & quadrant reverse, safety valves, regulator, England, early 20th c., overall 56¼" l. (ILLUS.) **978.00**

Train accessory, mountain fortress w/overpass, tinplate, a center passageway for the railway tracks & an overhead bridge connect both sides of the mountain, the taller side features a small village set up w/a road that leads down to the sides of the first mountain & across the bridge to the second lower mountain, 20" l., 20½" h...............**4,370.00**

Train car, caboose No. 7546, red tinplate, Ives, 12" l...........................**184.00**

Train car, coal car No. 7648, tinplate, dark green, marked "Pennsylvania Coal and Coke Co.," Ives, 12" l. (some paint flaking) **58.00**

Train car, logging car, tinplate, a flat cargo car w/a set of wooden logs, Marklin logo on underside, Marklin, 12" l...**138.00**

Train car, petroleum tanker car, tinplate, dark grey, marked w/the Bing "Bavaria" diamond trade-mark, Bing, 12" l......................................**161.00**

Lithographed Train Engine

Train engine, lithographed, friction-powered, Japan, minor soiling & scratches, 16" l., 5" h. (ILLUS.)..........**38.50**

Train set, "American Flyer," lithographed tin, a tank locomotive, two passenger cars each w/six windows & marked "Empire Express," coal car marked "Limited," ca. 1925, minor scratches (ILLUS. top next column) **275.00**

American Flyer Train Set

Train set, tinplate, a live-steam engine w/boiler, tender & single passenger car, w/original box & circular tracks, Germany, ca. 1890s, overall 23" l., the set **2,070.00**

Train station, lithographed tin w/cast iron window & door frames, roof sign reads "Grand Central Station," Bing, Germany, ca. 1916, 20¾" l., 8⅝" h. (some wear & dents, interior partition missing)..............................**747.50**

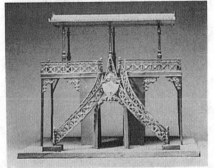

Tinplate Train Station

Train station, tinplate two stories w/covered upper level, center archway below dual staircases leading to upper level, Goerling, Germany, base 14¾ x 19⅝", 16" h. (ILLUS.) **2,185.00**

Train station, pressed fiberboard & wood, the long red roof w/raised "Railroad Station" sign above sides resembling grey blocks w/white cement mortar, white wood door & window frames, wooden door & two windows w/metal cages, one window marked "Telegraph Office," the other "Ticket Office," simulated wooden floor inside, celluloid plate on base marked "Manufactured by The A.Schoenhut Co., Philadelphia, Pa.," early 20th c., 13 x 17", 10" h...**475.00**

Tricycle, "Sky King," pressed metal, streamlined cycle finished in red & black w/wide black edging & accent stripes, black handlebars w/inset

light, sprung flat seat, red spoked
wheels w/black rubber rims, ca.
1935, restored & rebuilt, 38" l.
(ILLUS. left with pedal airplane)....**1,725.00**
Truck, Bell Telephone Ford truck,
cast iron, Hubley **225.00**
Truck, dump, cast iron, original red &
green paint & white rubber tires,
Hubley Mfg. Co., 3¾" l. **237.50**
Truck, dump truck, pressed steel, red
cab & yellow load compartment,
Tonka Toys, ca. 1950s, 13½" l.,
6¼" h. (minor scratches) **55.00**

Hathaway Bakery Truck

Truck, "Hathaway Bakery," w/original
driver, cast iron, painted w/"Hathaway Bread Cafe" on sides, rear door
opens, original rubber tires, Arcade
Mfg. Co., paint chipping & soiling,
9½" l., 3½" h. (ILLUS.) **1,622.00**

Lincoln Ice Delivery Truck

Truck, ice delivery, green pressed
metal, "Lincoln Ice Delivery" printed
on the sides, rubber tires, marked
"Lincoln Toys - Made in Canada,"
paint chips & scratches, 14½" l.,
4¾" h. (ILLUS.) **60.50**
Truck, "Jewel Tea," pressed steel,
1954, Tonka Toys **695.00**
Truck, oil & gas tanker, cast iron,
painted green w/raised letters on
sides of tank "Oil - Gas," gold
accents, yellow spoke silvered cast-
iron wheels, Kenton Hardware
Company, 1927, 9¾" l. (paint fair
to good, driver missing) **920.00**
Truck, oil tanker, "Phillips 66
Gasoline," red cast iron, premium
from Okie Oil Co., Arcade Mfg. Co.,
13" l. (ILLUS. top next column) **2,200.00**
Truck, semi-trailer, "G.M.C.," Smith-
Miller Toy Co. (Los Angeles, Cal.) ...**395.00**

Phillips 66 Gasoline Truck

Typewriter, "Tom Thumb," maroon
w/original case **40.00**
Washing machine, painted wood, a
tub-type w/deep sides & a rounded
bottom, raised on angled legs,
galvanized tin bottom, fitted w/a
wooden wringer, the exterior painted
blue w/white stenciling of a girl
hanging wash on a clothesline
below "Wee Washer," 18½" h. **210.00**
Wheelbarrow, child's size, painted
wood, the nailed wooden sides
w/worn original red paint w/white
striping & stenciled w/a black
running horse, four-spoke wheels,
34½" l. **412.50**
Windup celluloid, minstrel monkey,
Occupied Japan..................................**125.00**
Windup celluloid traveling camel,
Occupied Japan, in original box.........**75.00**
Windup celluloid & felt "Tumbling
Pete Monkey," Japan, in original
box **65.00**
Windup celluloid & tin turtle,
Occupied Japan..............................**200.00**

Marx Plastic Windup Race Car

Windup plastic race car, "Silver
Streak," rubber tires, w/original box,
Louis Marx & Co. Inc., box w/
minor wear, 6" l. (ILLUS.).................**71.50**
Windup plastic & metal, "Mr
Machine," w/original key,
assembled, Ideal Toy Co., ca.
1960s, 17½" h...............................**110.00**
Windup tin "Andy Walker", a man
wearing a bowler, blue suit & striped
pants walks holding a cane, Louis
Marx, ca. 1930s, 11" h. **115.00**
Windup tin "Animal Barber Shop,"
a bear barber shaves a costumer
reclining in a chair, polychrome
lithographed decoration, Japan,
w/original tape-repaired box, ca.
1950s **192.50**

Windup tin "Bucking Bronco," the white horse on a wheeled, rectangular base appears to try to throw his cowboy rider, Ernest Lehmann Co. (Brandenburg, Germany), ca. 1912, 7½" l. **650.00**

Windup tin bus, "Bus Deluxe," lithographed in color w/a driver & double row of seats, numbered "105," Ferdinand Strauss Corp. (New York, New York), ca. 1920s, w/original box, 13½" l. **1,380.00**

Windup tin carnival shooting gallery, tin, rotating disk, moving ducks, clown & other circus lithographs, original gun & darts, Ohio Art Co. (Bryan, Ohio), mint in original box..................................**175.00**

Windup tin "Cowboy Rider," cowboy w/lariat, Marx, ca. 1941, mint in original box **272.50**

Windup tin ferris wheel, J. Chein & Co. (New York City), 16½" h. **395.00**

Windup tin "G.I. Joe & His Jouncing Jeep," Unique Art Mfg. Co., Inc. (New York, New York), ca. 1940, w/box, 8" l. **256.00**

Windup tin "G.I. Joe & the K-9 Pups," Unique Art Mfg. Co., Inc. 9" h. **244.00**

Windup tin "Honeymoon Express," Louis Marx & Co., 1929, 9½" l. **247.00**

Windup tin "Honeymoon Express," Louis Marx & Co., 1947 ....**333.00**

Windup tin "Jackee the Hornpipe Dancer," jointed sailor dances on the plain yellow planked deck of a simple red, white & blue ship, start/stop lever on deck, ca. 1920, fair condition, signs of play & wear to surface, 9" h. **288.00**

Windup tin "Kiddy Cyclist," steers in figure 8 patterns & rings bell, Unique Art Mfg. Co., Inc., 1930s, 8¾" h. **290.00**

Windup tin "Knock-out Prize Fighters" w/box, Ferdinand Strauss, 1921 patent, 7" h. (overall surface rust & soiling, box w/soiling & tears) **302.50**

Windup tin Lincoln Tunnel, featuring six vehicles shuttling between tunnel entrances, one marked "New York" depicting skyscrapers w/a zeppelin overhead, the "New Jersey" side w/trees & a country town, w/original lithographed box, Unique Art Mfg. Co., Inc., ca. 1935, 24" l. **415.00**

Windup tin Louis Armstrong playing trumpet, cloth costume, plastic head, hands & horn, marked "T.N.," Japan, 9½" h. **425.00**

Windup tin "Mechanical Tractor," metal wheels w/rubber treads, Louis Marx, ca. 1940s, minor wear, earth grader accessory missing, working, w/original damaged box, 8½" l. **60.50**

Windup tin monkey, "Bombo the Monk," w/tree, Unique Art Mfg. Co., Inc., monkey 5½" l., tree 9½" h., ca. 1930, 2 pcs. **145.00**

Windup Ocean Liner

Windup tin ocean liner, "Kronprinz Wilhelm," h.p. burnt orange & black w/portholes painted on either side of the ship, four smoke stacks, ten lifeboats, dual decks, a pair of masts, companionway ladders & tinplate four-wheel stand, the rudder stamped w/the Marklin logo, includes three menus from S.S. Brenan, 37" l. (ILLUS.)................**23,000.00**

Windup Leviathan Ocean Liner

Windup tin ocean liner, "Leviathan," specially built h.p. red, white & black hulled two-deck, three-finished ocean liner w/six lifeboats, eleven ventilators, twin masts w/ladders, two skylights, two cast anchors & four flags, 27" l. (ILLUS.)...............**2,530.00**

Windup tin "Play Golf," lithographed figure putting ball toward nine holes on rectangular lithographed green, spring motor, ca. 1925, base 12" l., in original cardboard box **460.00**

Windup tin "Quack Quack," duck pulling basket of ducklings (3), Lehmann, 7½" l. **395.00**

Windup tin "Range Rider," Louis Marx & Co., 1940s **287.50**

Windup tin roller coaster, "Jet Roller," Wolverine Co. (Pittsburgh, Pennsylvania), 21" l. **250.00**

Windup tin roller coaster, "Loop-A-
Loop," includes small cars,
Wolverine Co., ca. 1930, 19" l.,
mint in box **375.00**

J.E.P. Windup Seaplane

Windup tin seaplane w/pilot,
lithographed, the pilot in an open
cockpit of this single wing, single
engine seaplane, decorated in red,
blue & white, riding on large
pontoons, JEP (Jouets en Paris -
Paris, France), ca. 1935
(ILLUS.) **2,185.00**
Windup tin "Whoopie Car," graffiti-
covered flivver featuring a spinning
head driver & two flappers seated
on "trunk," w/erratic movement &
oversized rear wheels, Marx,
w/original box, 7" l. **475.00**
Windup tin submarine, "The Sea
Wolf Atomic Submarine," yellow,
Sutcliffe Model (England), mint in
box, 10½" l. **207.00**

Windup U.S. Mail Truck

Windup tin truck, "U.S. Mail"
delivery, early electric powered-type,
lithographed, the black & yellow
truck features a driver, opening rear
door & "U.S. Mail" & "Parcel Post"
on the sides, red spoked wheels,
Gilbert, ca. 1916, 8¼" l. (ILLUS.) **552.00**
Zeppelin, "Los Angeles," polished
aluminum, finished in silver &
chrome w/three wheels, two

"Los Angeles" Zeppelin

simulated motors & a rear gondola,
Dent Hardware Co., ca. 1929,
12½" l. (ILLUS.) **288.00**

(End of Toys Section)

TRADE CATALOGS

Abercrombie & Fitch, 1923,
136 pp. **$48.00**
Abercrombie & Fitch, Christmas,
1938, 32 pp. **25.00**
Aldens, 1964, Christmas **35.00**
Art Metal Tools & Supplies, 1933 .....**25.00**
Avery Steel Threshers, 1928, 32 pp...**19.00**
Boston Varnish Co., ca. 1938,
Kyanize paints, varnishes, etc.,
216 tipped-in swatches, 42 pp.,
10 x 13" **43.00**
Bramhill (Deane), 1899, cooking,
heating & ventilating apparatus,
French ranges, ovens, etc., 140 pp.,
9¾ x 13¾" **177.00**
California Perfume Co., 1914, color
illustrations, 68 pp. **65.00**
Charles Williams Stores, 1926,
Spring & Summer, some color
pages of fashions...............................**20.00**
J.B. Clow & Sons, 1916, modern
plumbing for schools, profusely
illustrated, along w/photos & names
of schools as clients nationwide, 88
slick pp., 9½ x 12"............................**45.00**
Columbia Bicycles, 1894, Pope
Manufacturing Company, 46 pp.........**75.00**
"Der Jugend Spiel und Arbeit"
(toys), German catalog, dated 1910,
featuring examples of live-steam
plants, trains & accessories, optical
toys, boats & automobiles, Leipzig,
Germany, 7 x 9¼" (some
yellowing) **115.00**
Fitz Water Wheel Co., 1935, 8 pp. **18.00**
Gowing Dietrich, Syracuse, 1918,
creamery machinery & supplies,
322 pp., 6 x 9"...................................**35.00**
Hoegee (William), Sporting Goods,
1938, guns, fishing tackle, outing
clothing in Volume I, telescope &
gun parts in Volume II, 230 pp., set ...**85.00**
Larkin Premiums, 1910, furniture **35.00**
LL Bean, Spring, 1927, 52 pp. **69.00**

LL Bean, Spring, 1951 ....**20.00**
Montgomery Ward, 1966,
   Christmas...**42.00**
Narragansett Machine Co., 1928,
   gymnastic apparatus, 240 pp.............**75.00**
Poppy Plumbing Fixtures, 1937,
   16 pp...**20.00**
Port Huron Engine & Thresher Co.,
   1895, 24 pp. **39.00**
Russell's Army, Navy & Sporting
   Goods, 1921, rifles, shotguns,
   pistols, ammunition, air rifles **60.00**
Savage (M.W.), 1933-34, Fall &
   Winter, 153 pages..............................**20.00**
Schoenhut, 1912, toys, pictures
   Humpty Dumpty Circus, dolls, Rolly
   Dollys, etc. **95.00**
Sears, Roebuck and Co., 1907,
   stoves, 56 pp. **87.00**
Sears, Roebuck and Co., 1915,
   August sale **35.00**
Sears, Roebuck and Co., 1924-25,
   Fall & Winter, sporting goods.............**50.00**
Sears, Roebuck and Co., 1936,
   Summer Savings, 80 pp. **22.00**
Sears, Roebuck and Co., 1956,
   Christmas catalog, 450 pp. **38.00**
Sears, Roebuck and Co., 1961,
   Christmas..**23.00**
Shakespeare Fishing Tackle, 1949,
   32 pp..**22.00**
Schrieber Co., Chariton, Iowa, 1910,
   carriages, 20 slick pp., 8 x 9½" **65.00**
Simplex, 1916, theater movie
   projectors, 70 slick pp., 6 x 9" **35.00**
Spiegel, 1937, Spring & Summer **28.00**
Standard Cast Iron Pipe & Foundry
   Company, 1916, Bristol,
   Pennsylvania **28.00**
Starrett Tool, 1938, No. 26..................**65.00**
Western Metal Supply Co., ca. 1938,
   embossed hard cover, San
   Diego, California, 903 pp., 9 x 12" ...**125.00**
Williams Co. (J.H.), 1937, tools, titled
   "Tools of Industry," Buffalo, New
   York **20.00**

TRAMP ART

   *Tramp art flourished in the United
States from about 1875 into the 1930s.
These chip-carved woodenwares, mostly in
the form of boxes or other useful items,
were made mainly from old cigar boxes
although fruit and vegetable crates were
also used. The wood is predominately
edge-carved and subsequently layered to
create a unique effect. Completed items
were given an overall stained finish which
was sometimes further enhanced with
painted highlights. Though there seems to
be no written record of the artists, many of
whom were itinerants, there is a growing
interest in collecting this ware.*

Picture frame, large rectangular form
   w/wide borders, the top & bottom
   edges w/long thin tiered & scalloped
   bands, the sides w/chip-carved &
   painted designs of hearts & a long
   leaf sprig, decorated w/old varnish
   trimmed w/silver, gold & bronze
   paint, 28 x 35½" **$715.00**

Tramp Art Cupboard Panel

Cupboard panel, carved pine, the
   rectangular form divided in two
   framed recessed panels, the top
   decorated w/a stylized grapevine
   w/leaves & pendant bunches of
   grapes, the lower rectangular panel
   decorated w/a stylized tree all
   rendered in characteristic chip-
   carved & concentrically layered
   style, Ohio, ca. 1930, 25" w., 6' h.
   (ILLUS.) **3,738.00**
Model of the Eiffel Tower, in four
   parts, comprising a gilded & glazed
   polygonal capital w/rounded-arch
   windows above painted arch
   windows over an arcaded balcony
   above a second arcaded
   observatory all over the eleven-story
   flaring tower embellished w/stairs &
   fences above an arcaded landing
   over an arched trapezoidal base,
   each corner fitted w/spiral stairs,
   Paul George Keilberg, Fond du Lac,
   Wisconsin, ca. 1915,
   7' 11½" h. **5,750.00**
Picture frame, composed of seven
   chip-carved layers, 8¾ x 10"..............**75.00**

TRAYS, SERVING & CHANGE

Both serving & change trays once used in taverns, cafes and the like and usually bearing advertising for a beverage maker are now being widely collected. All trays listed are heavy tin serving trays, unless otherwise noted.

Anheuser-Busch, "Budweiser Beer," St. Louis, Missouri, Mississippi River levee scene of 1870s, w/copyright of 1914, issued 1934 ....**$225.00 to 250.00**

Bohemian Beer, Detroit, depicts girl w/glass, etched "beer" in gold, 1911 ....**125.00**

Fehr's Ambrosia Beer, Roman garden scene, 1917 ....**250.00**

Hires Root Beer, rectangular, beautiful girl by Haskell Coffin **145.00**

Thomas Moore Whiskey Tray

Moore (Thomas) Whiskey, round colored center scene of a nude woman reclining near a bottle, wording around the border reads "Take A Little Moore - Old Possum Hollow," some light rust (ILLUS.) **660.00**

Nu-Grape Soda Tray

Nu-Grape Soda, rectangular, pretty blonde lady wearing orange & green holding a bottle, purple border w/yellow lettering at top & bottom reading "A Flavor You Can't Forget," 1920s, minor scratches & some paint loss, 10½ x 13" (ILLUS.) **49.50**

Rubsam & Horrmann Beers Tray

Rubsam & Horrmann Bottled Beers - New York City - Stapelton, S.I., colored scene of a semi-nude lady seated on a rock in a landscape (ILLUS.) **715.00**

Ruhstaller's Beer Tray

Ruhstaller's "Gilt Edge Lager," Sacramento, California, square, man pouring beer for ladies in touring car, pre-prohibition, 13" w. (ILLUS.) **522.50**

"Success" Manure Spreader Tray

"Success" Manure Spreader, Kemp & Burpee, Syracuse, New York, rectangular w/flanged rim, colorful scene of a team of horses pulling a wagon, round lion head logo in the corner, wording around border, minor scratches & soiling, change (ILLUS.) **176.00**

Virginia Dare Wines, pictures a bottle & figures of Paul & Virginia running...**295.00**

Wieland's Pale Lager Tray

Wieland's "Extra Pale Lager," San Francisco, California, round, portrait of Indian maiden 1900-10, (ILLUS.) **330.00**

TRUNKS

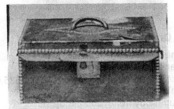

Small Flat-Top Trunk

These box-like portable containers are used for transporting or storing personal possessions. There are many styles to choose from since they have been made from the 16th century onward. Thousands arrived in this country with the immigrants and more were turned out to accommodate the westward movement of the population. The popular dome-top trunk was designed to prevent water from accumulating on the top. Hinges, locks and construction, along with condition and age, greatly determine the values of older trunks.

Cylindrical, hide-covered wood w/leather trim & brass stud trim, brass stud initials "A.W." in an oval

on the lid, wrought-iron lock & hasp & end handles, 19th c., 24" l. (wear, damage).....................................**$203.50**

Dome-top, painted wood, decorated w/swags on a green ground, 19th c., 24½" l., 10" h.......**1,092.50**

Dome-top, painted wood, black decoration on a reddish brown ground, 19th c., 24½" l., 12½" h. (imperfections) **575.00**

Dome-top, vinegar-grained wood, green striping on a light ochre ground, 19th c., 30" l., 13½" h..........**316.00**

Dome-top, rawhide w/leather trim w/brass studs, w/"C.S.," wrought-iron lock w/hasp, lined w/1859 New York newspaper, 24" l. (wear & slight damage) **77.00**

Flat-top, leather military cap style, rectangular w/a leather handle on top, the sides & top brass-studded, the interior lined w/blue-dotted wallpaper, labeled by James Boyd, Boston, Massachusetts, first half 19th c., 10¼ x 16", 7" h. (ILLUS.) **172.00**

Flat-top, pine, decorative wrought-iron banding & old worn & weathered finish, inside of lid w/old floral decoration on a blue ground & decorative strap hinges, 41" l..........**357.50**

Fine Leather & Brass Trunk

Flat-top, brass & leather-mounted camphorwood, rectangular, the hinged lid decorated w/an oval in brass tacks, opening to an aromatic camphorwood-lined interior, the front decorated w/a swag in brass tacks, the sides fitted w/carrying handles, 19th c., 21 x 41¾", 19¾" h. (ILLUS.) **2,645.00**

VALENTINES

Children's, 1940s, unused set of 25...**$22.00**

Fold-out-type, honeycomb tissue & standing Cupid, ca. 1926 ....**45.00**

Early Auto Valentine

Fold-out-type, cut-out model of an
early blue car carrying children
dressed in blue, white, green & red,
w/honeycomb tissue, Germany,
early 20th c., soiling, very minor
edge wear, 11¼" w., 7½" h.
(ILLUS.) **55.00**

Early Shellwork Valentine

Shellwork, in hinged double
octagonal case, one half featuring a
design of a large basket of flowers,
the other half w/triangular panels
framing a round center reserve
w/"Home Sweet Home" spelled
out in shells, 19th c., minor
imperfections, 10" d. (ILLUS.).......**3,575.00**

VENDING & GAMBLING
DEVICES

Arcade, "Babe Ruth Baseball," a
baseball player moves into position
to catch the falling ballbearing,
Stephens Novelty Co. **$1,900.00**
Arcade, "Electricity is Life," Mills
Novelty Co., 1904 ......**2,000.00 to 2,500.00**
Candy vendor, tall square upright
heavy metal cabinet in green &
yellow, original red & gold decals on
the sides reading "5¢ Candies,"
glass front window for selections,
minor wear, works, 9" w., 44" h.
(ILLUS. top next column) **165.00**
Gambling, Buckley's "Diamond
Fronts" countertop slot
machine, 50-cent play, late
1940s......................**1,350.00 to 1,500.00**

Tall Candy Vendor

Groetchen "Columbia Standard"

Gambling, Groetchen "Columbia
Standard" countertop slot machine,
5-cent play, ca. 1937 (ILLUS.) **625.00**
Gambling, Jennings' "Operator Bell"
(Dutch Boy front), countertop slot
machine, 25-cent play, 1926.........**1,900.00**
Gambling, Jennings' "Sportsman Golf
Ball Vendor Bell" countertop slot
machine, ca. 1932 (restored)........**4,995.00**
Gambling, Jennings' "Standard
Chief" countertop slot machine,
5-cent play, 1946-56 ....**1,950.00**
Gambling, Mills' "Blue Front"
countertop slot machine,
5-cent play................**1,500.00 to 2,000.00**
Gambling, Mills' "Bonus Bell" (Horse
Head front) countertop slot machine,
10-cent play, 1937 & 1943
(unrestored) **1,750.00**
Gambling, Mills' "Brown Front"
countertop slot machine, 10-cent
play, ca. 1938-44, 25" h. **1,320.00**
Gambling, Mills' "Check Boy"
countertop slot machine, 5-cent
play, ca. 1907-16 ....**4,500.00**

Gambling, Mills' "Cherry" ("Bursting Cherry") countertop slot machine, 5-cent play, 1937 ....**1,200.00**

Gambling, Mills' "Cherry" ("Bursting Cherry") countertop slot machine, 50-cent play, 1937 (restored)........**1,300.00**

Gambling, Mills' "Dewey" upright slot machine, 5-cent play, ca. 1900 (restored) **11,500.00**

Gambling, Mills' "Diamond" countertop slot machine, 5-cent play, 1937 ....**1,395.00**

Gambling, Mills' "Futurity" countertop slot machine, 5-cent play **3,500.00**

Gambling, Mills' "Golden Falls" countertop slot machine, 5-cent play **1,495.00**

Gambling, Mills' "Jackpot" (Poinsettia front) countertop slot machine, 1-cent play, ca. 1929-31 ....**1,800.00**

Gambling, Mills' "Jackpot" (Poinsettia front) countertop slot machine, 5-cent play, ca. 1929-31 ....**1,800.00 to 2,000.00**

Gambling, Mills' "Silent Gooseneck" (Lion front) countertop slot machine, 5-cent play, ca. 1930s.................**1,795.00**

Gambling, Pace's "The Kitty" countertop slot machine, 10-cent play, 1937 ....**3,995.00**

Gambling, Watling's "Lincoln De Lux" countertop slot machine, 5-cent play, 1926-29 ....**1,795.00**

Gambling, Watling's "Rol-A-Top Bell" countertop slot machine w/cornucopias of coins, etc., 5-cent play, 1935-46 ....**4,695.00**

Gambling, Watling's "Rol-A-Top Front Vendor," countertop slot machine w/two column mint vender, 5-cent play, ca. 1935 ....**4,000.00 to 4,500.00**

Watling "Treasury" Slot Machine

Gambling, Watling's "Treasury" countertop slot machine, 1-cent play, ca. 1936-41 (ILLUS.)............**4,495.00**

Gambling, Watling's "Treasury" countertop slot machine, 10-cent play, 1936-41 ....**2,500.00 to 3,000.00**

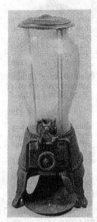

Rare Early Gum Vendor

Gum vendor, "Climax 10," footed cast-iron base, baluster-form clear glass globe, patent dated 1902 & 1904, ca. 1910, some wear (ILLUS.) **1,375.00**

Gum vendor, "Clown," case w/clown inside, Pulver Mfg. Co.,1930s..........**500.00**

Gum vendor, "Columbus Model V," clear glass cylindrical dome w/cylindrical metal base & cover, Columbus Vending Co., 1930..........**325.00**

Gum vendor, "Cop & Robber (or Hobo)," 1-cent operation, ca. 1930, Pulver Mfg. Co. **1,650.00**

Gum vendor, "Ford," formed metal body w/chrome finish, Ford Gum and Machine Co., Inc., ca. 1950 ....**65.00**

Gum vendor, "Kayem Products Co.," wall-mount metal cabinet for Beech Nut Gum, painted label, red, yellow, blue & cream, 5¢ action, late 1940s - early 1950s, 3½ x 8", 13½" h. (minor paint chips & scratches, left side wing slightly bent)...**302.50**

Gum vendor, "Kenney Magic Clock," Art Deco case w/yellow clock face w/black & white numbers, yellow label at bottom tells how to get gum & fortune, 7" d., 12" w., 14" h. **440.00**

Gum vendor, "Little Duke," 1-cent operation w/gumball dispenser, O.D. Jennings Co., 1932, original condition **2,395.00**

Gum vender, "Northwestern Model 33 Gum," porcelain over cast iron w/glass container, red & yellow, 1-cent operation, 1933, 14" h..........**400.00**

Gum vendor, "Topper," painted square cast-metal base, squared clear glass globe w/metal lid &

Topper Gum Vendor

original label reading "Topper - 1¢,"
Victor Vending Corp., Chicago,
Illinois, some label damage, paint
chipping on base, 6¼" w., 16" h.
(ILLUS.) **154.00**

Peanut vendor, "Northwestern Model
33 Peanut," porcelain, Northwestern
Corp., 1-cent operation,
1933 ....**175.00 to 200.00**

Pinball machine, "Bally Hoo," 1-cent
play, Bally, 1931 ....**550.00**

Postage stamp vendor, tall upright
metal case w/wood-grained front, on
stepped base, front w/printed signs
reading "4-1¢ Stamps For A Nickel -
Insert Nickel Pull Plunger," "3-3¢
Stamps For A Dime - Insert Dime
Pull Plunger," "Buy U.S. Postage
Stamps in Sanitary Folders - Pull,"
marking at base for the Postage
Stamp Machine Co. of New York,
7" w., 15½" h., w/key (very minor
wear) **82.50**

Trade stimulator, "Ciga-Rola Bell,"
combination-type, cigarette vendor
or a gambler could put his money in
& win from 1 to 10 packs, O.D.
Jennings & Co. **2,000.00**

Trade stimulator, "Saratoga
Sweepstakes," horse race game,
H.C. Evans and Co., Chicago,
Illinois, 1933-35...........................**1,500.00**

VIENNA ART TIN PLATES

*These decorative tin plates were
generally printed in the center with
colorful bust portraits of lovely and exotic
young ladies and were most often used as
advertising promotional items in the early
20th century. The names used here are*

*those given in Jane and Howard
Hazelcorn's book* Hazlecorn's Price Guide
to Tin Vienna Art Plates *(H.J.H.
Publications, 1987).*

Beautiful young mother holding
child w/another child standing near,
entitled "Madonna Della Sedia,"
manufactured by H.D. Beach Co.,
1904, 10⅛" d................................**$135.00**

"Ethel," bust portrait of a young
woman w/long brown hair draped
over both shoulders & wearing a
rose above her ear, ornate border
w/a five-lobe design filled
w/spiderwebbing, swags & basket
design between each lobe,
advertising on the back for
"Anheuser Busch's Malt Nutrine,"
ca. 1910, 10⅛" d. **125.00**

Jamestown Exposition Tin Plate

Jamestown Exposition souvenir,
center scene of an Indian attack,
"Jamestown" at top, portraits of John
Smith & Pocahontas at sides & open
book w/dates "1607 - 1907" at
bottom, manufactured by H.D.
Beach Co., 1905 patent date,
10⅛" d. (ILLUS.) ....**100.00 to 125.00**

"Marguerite," bust profile portrait of a
young woman wearing a cap on her
long , dark hair, in a low-cut gown,
gilt scroll border, "Western Coca-
Cola Bottling Co.," advertising on
the back, H.D. Beach Co., ca. 1906,
10⅛" d..**850.00**

"The Nude," lovely lady seated half-
nude w/a drape around her legs,
H.D. Beach Co., ca. 1908,
10⅛" d..**475.00**

WARTIME MEMORABILIA

Since the early 19th century, every war

that America has fought has been commemorated with a variety of war-related memorabilia. Often in the form of propaganda items produced during the conflict or as memorial pieces made after the war ended, these materials are today quite collectible and increasingly important for the historic insights they provide. Most commonly available are items dating from World War I and II. Since 1995 marked the fiftieth anniversary of the end of World War II, there should be added interest in this collecting field. Also see MILITARY COLLECTIBLES and POSTERS.

CIVIL WAR (1861-65)
Banner, cloth, decorated w/a calligraphic drawing of an American eagle w/a wreath, framed **$85.00**
Boots, youth's or drummer boy's high-top style, unused, pr. **300.00**
Document, clothing receipt from 156th Illinois Volunteer Infantry **35.00**

SPANISH-AMERICAN WAR (1898)
Bandanna, cloth, depicts Admiral Dewey..................................**85.00**
Lamp, tin, bullet-shaped, flag medal & Admiral Dewey medal w/wreath on front, glass chimney..........................**235.00**

WORLD WAR I (1914-18)
Trench art, fluted brass cannon shell vase w/"World War" & "Chateau Thiery" embossed on a textured background, 13½" h......................**150.00**
Trench art, fluted brass cannon shell vase from 4.71 gun, 16½" h. ....**25.00 to 50.00**

WORLD WAR II (1939-45)

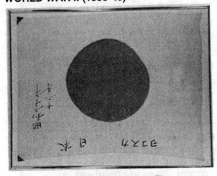

World War II Japanese Flag

Badge, German, tunic-type, silver braid...................................**55.00**
Dog tags, American, from German prisoner of war camp, Stalag-marked...............................**45.00**
Flag, captured Japanese flag,

Japanese inscriptions, framed, minor water stains, 30 x 39" (ILLUS.) **93.50**
Flare gun, German double-barrel type **150.00**
Gravy boat w/handle, metal, German Luftwaffe markings...........................**65.00**
Police helmet, German, dark blue w/Nazi emblems **360.00**

WATCHES

Jules Jorgensen Pocket Watch

Hunting case, lady's, Lady Humbert, serial no. 5254, stem wind lever set movement, porcelain enamel dial w/Roman numerals & subsidiary seconds dial, engraved 18k yellow gold case (crystal cracked) **$275.00**
Hunting case, man's, American Waltham Watch Co., Waltham, Massachusetts, lever set, coin silver case, size 18....................................**145.00**
Hunting case, man's, American Waltham Watch Co., serial no. 7316350, porcelain enameled dial w/Roman numeral hour & Arabic numeral rings, subsidiary seconds dial, 14k yellow gold case, late 19th c., together w/a 14k gold curb link chain, 2 pcs. **495.00**
Hunting case, man's, American Waltham Watch Co., serial no. 1004043, P.S. Bartlett keywind movement, porcelain enameled dial w/painted bouquet, Roman numerals, subsidiary seconds dial, engraved gold case, late 19th c.......**220.00**
Hunting case, man's, Elgin National Watch Co., Elgin, Illinois, serial no. 326596, "H.L. Culver" stemwind movement, porcelain enamel dial w/Roman numerals & subsidiary seconds dial, late 19th c. **412.50**
Hunting case, man's, Jules Jorgensen, Copenhagen, Denmark, 18k yellow gold case, glass dust cover, porcelain enameled dial

w/Roman numerals & subsidiary
seconds dial, serial no. 12959,
monogrammed case, ca. 1875
(ILLUS.) **1,870.00**

Hunting case, man's, H.L. Matile,
Switzerland, gold case, highly
jeweled nickel lever movement,
some jewels carried in screwed gold
chatons, w/later automaton figures
of a cavalier & lady striking bells
above the center white enamel dial
w/Arabic numerals, engraved later
case **4,025.00**

Hunting case, man's, Tiffany & Co.,
five-minute repeating-type, ultra-thin
18k gold case, highly jeweled
nickel lever movement, bi-metallic
compensation balance, gold cuvette,
white enameled dial w/Arabic
numerals & subsidiary seconds dial,
polished case, No. 78641, case,
dial, cuvette & movement signed,
ca. 1900 ....**4,313.00**

Open face, man's, E. Howard & Co.,
Boston, gold-filled case, 23 jewel
movement, Roman numerals &
subsidiary seconds dial, serial
No. 1078880 ....**345.00**

Open face, man's, Longines, 18k
gold case, gilt lever movement, bi-
metallic compensation balance,
highly jeweled, slide repeat, white
enameled dial w/Roman numerals &
subsidiary seconds dial, gold
cuvette, engine-turned case, case,
cuvette, dial & movement signed,
ca. 1900 ....**3,738.00**

Open face, man's, Patek Philipp &
Co., Geneva, Switzerland, 18k gold
case, nickel lever movement, bi-
metallic compensation balance, gold
cuvette, white enameled dial
w/Arabic numerals & subsidiary
seconds dial, blued-steel moon-style
hands, polished case, case, dial,
cuvette & movement signed, dial
signed "Patek Philipp & Cie. -
Geneve, Suisse," w/original
mahogany base, certificate &
additional mainspring, No. 199361,
ca. 1920 ....**2,530.00**

Open face, man's, J.P. Stevens
Watch Co., Atlanta, Georgia, 14k
gold case, 16 size, three-quarter
plate damascened nickel movement,
club tooth lever escapement,
Stevens patent micrometer
regulator, bi-metallic compensation
balance, jeweled white enamel dial
w/Arabic numerals, gold cuvette,
polished case engraved w/a
monogram, case, dial & movement
signed, No. 44, ca. 1885.............**4,600.00**

Open face, man's, Vacheron &
Constantin, Geneva, Switzerland,
18k gold case, nickel lever
movement, bi-metallic compensation
balance, eight adjustments, 29
jewels, gold cuvette, white
enameled dial w/Arabic numerals &
subsidiary seconds dial, polished
monogrammed case, case, dial,
cuvette & movement signed, ca.
1900...**7,188.00**

WEATHERVANES

Sheet Metal Pig Weathervane

Angel Gabriel, sheet metal,
horizontal figure blowing a horn,
vestiges of paint, early 20th c.,
48" h,..**$3,335.00**

Arrow banner, molded & painted
copper, the shaft w/sheet copper
curlicues & a ridged tail terminating
in a molded arrowhead w/traces of
gilding & old yellow paint, late
19th c., 49" l., 11" h......................**2,070.00**

Horse, running hackney-type, molded
& gilded copper, swell-bodied
animal w/cropped tail raised, the
surface w/much original gilding,
verdigris & traces of old yellow paint,
mounted on a rod in a cast-iron
base, J.W. Fiske & Co., New York,
ca. 1893, 36" l., vane 22¾" h. (old
repairs)..**7,763.00**

Horse & jockey, molded copper &
zinc, full-bodied racing horse
w/jockey, mounted on a rod in a
black metal base, late 19th c., 32" l.,
19½" h. (some restorations to
gilding) **6,900.00**

Pig, sheet metal, silhouetted standing
animal, 19th c., 42" l. (ILLUS.) **2,070.00**

Polar bear, painted & gilded molded
copper, the swell-bodied walking
animal w/open jaw & cut teeth,
applied sheet metal ears & eyes,
traces of white paint & gilding, now
mounted on a sheet metal rod &
black metal base, third quarter
19th c., missing an ear, some rust,
19" l. (ILLUS. top next column) **3,450.00**

Polar Bear Weathervane

Ram, molded copper & zinc, swell-
bodied animal w/applied sheet
copper curled horns & cast zinc
head, the surface w/ pock-marked
fur, mounted on a rod, weathered
overall verdigris, attributed to
Cushing & White, Waltham,
Massachusetts, third quarter 19th c.,
23½" l., 28¼" h............................**12,650.00**

Rooster, carved pine, grey-painted
silhouetted bird w/a wide arched tail
& flat comb, mounted on a rod
above a pine orb, probably
Pennsylvania, 19th c., now on a
turned circular base, 18½" h. **1,093.00**

Rooster, copper, full-bodied, gilt
verdigris surface, 19th c., 23" h.
(bullet hole) **1,840.00**

Swan, wood, long stylized bird w/hole
eyes, open beak & articulated four-
finger tail, Pennsylvania, ca. 1889,
70" w., 15" h., (neck repaired).......**8,280.00**

WESTERN CHARACTER COLLECTIBLES

*Since the closing of the Western frontier
in the late 19th century the myth of the
American cowboy has loomed large in
popular fiction. With the growth of the
motion picture industry early in this
century, cowboy heroes became a mainstay
of the entertainment industry. By the
1920s major Western heroes were a big
draw at the box office and this popularity
continued with the dawning if the TV age
in the 1950s. We list here a variety of
collectibles relating to all American
Western personalities popular this century.
Also see LUNCH BOXES.*

Allan "Rocky" Lane photograph,
black & white, 8 x 10"........................**$1.50**

Andy Clyde photograph, black &
white, 8 x 10" **1.50**

Andy Devine arcade card, black &
white, 1950s, No. 116, 3¼ x
5½"..**1.50**

Annie Oakley costume, cowgirl outfit
consisting of blouse, vest, skirt,
neckerchief band, mid-1950s, the
set **105.00**

Audie Murphy arcade card, black &
white, 1950s, No. 106, 3¼ x 5½"
(mint condition) **1.50**

Audie Murphy photograph, black &
white film studio still from "The Guns
of Fort Petticoat," scene w/U.S.
cavalryman w/Kathryn Grant holding
rifle, Columbia Pictures,
1956, 8 x 10" (fine condition) **2.50**

Bat Masterson playsuit: hat, vest,
shirt, tie, pants, belt & cane; mint in
original box, the set ....**50.00 to 75.00**

Ben Cartwright (Bonanza, TV)
record, cardboard, Chevrolet
premium, pictures Ben, in original
envelope, ca. 1960s, 7" d...............**45.00**

Bob Steele photograph, pistol in one
hand, black & white, 8 x 10".................**1.50**

Bonanza game, table top-type,
Rummy, mint in box **95.00**

Bonanza (TV) toy, Bonanza Rub-On
Transfers Set, partially used, in
original box w/cast characters on the
cover, Hasbro, ca. 1960s **112.00**

Buffalo Bill Cody figure, metal,
wearing Wild West Show costume &
holding rifle, Blenheim Military
Models, England, 1977, 2¼" h..........**20.00**

Buffalo Bill Cody postcard, black &
white photo image of Cody standing,
leaning on rifle, pistol at waist,
wearing full suit of fringed
buckskins, signed **125.00**

Buffalo Bill Jr. (TV) puzzle, "Cocoa
Malt" premium **65.00**

Buster Crabbe movie handbill, "The
Drifter," PRC movie, black ink on
color paper stock, 9½ x 13" **2.50**

Buster Crabbe photograph, black &
white, 8 x 10" **1.50**

Cisco Kid (TV) gun, paper clicker-
type, Tip Top Bread premium,
"Cisco Kid" printed on handle,
1950s, 8" l. **45.00**

Cisco Kid lobby card, "Robin Hood
of Monterey," Monogram, 8 x 10" **1.50**

Cisco Kid movie handbill, "Beauty
and the Bandit," Monogram
Pictures, starring Gilbert Roland,
black ink on color paper stock,
9½ x 13"..**3.50**

Cisco Kid (TV) ring, brass w/gold
finish, club item **175.00**

Clayton Moore lobby card,
"Message of Death," chapter 10,

serial movie "Ghost of Zorro,"
8 x 10" **1.50**

Clint Walker arcade card,
"Cheyenne," black & white, 1950s,
No. 110, 3¼ x 5½" **1.50**

Dale Evans cowgirl outfit & hat,
w/picture of Dale & horse, in original
box **185.00**

Dale Evans necklace, on original
card **25.00**

Dale Evans wrist watch, Ingraham,
1951 .... **357.00**

Dale Evans & Buttermilk figures,
plastic, Hartland, 1950s, 2 pcs **180.00**

Dale Robertson arcade card, "Wells
Fargo," black & white, 1950s, No.
115, 3¼ x 5½" **1.50**

Daniel Boone pocket knife, two
blades, color drawing of Daniel
Boone on handle, 1970 .... **5.00**

Dave O'Brien lobby card, "The
Whispering Skull," PRC Pictures,
8 x 10" **1.50**

Don "Red" Barry photograph, black
& white, 8 x 10" **1.50**

Gabby Hayes ring, cannon-type,
complete **175.00**

Gary Cooper arcade card, black &
white, 1950s, No. 127, 3¼ x 5½" **1.50**

Gene Autry arcade card, black &
white photograph of Gene wearing
sheriff's badge, 1950, 3¼ x 5½" **2.50**

Gene Autry arcade card, multi-
photo, two photographs of Gene &
photographs of Tom Tyler & Leo
Mahoney, blue, 3¼ x 5½" **2.00**

Gene Autry book, "Champion the
Wonder Horse," a Daily Mirror Book,
1959, printed in England, hard cover
w/color front & back cover, 125 pp.,
8 x 11" **3.50**

Gene Autry book, "Gene Autry & the
Thief River Outlaws," 1944 .... **17.00**

Gene Autry book, "Gene Autry
Makes a New Friend," hardback,
Tell-A-Tale Books, 1952, full-color,
28 pp., 6 x 7" **15.00**

Gene Autry boots, rubber, w/box **295.00**

Gene Autry cap pistol, leather
holster & belt, made by Leslie
Henry **150.00**

Gene Autry cap pistol, repeating
Jr. Model, three-shooter, cast iron,
w/jeweled leather
holster .... **150.00 to 200.00**

Gene Autry comic book, No. 93,
Dell Publishing Co. **175.00**

Gene Autry jigsaw puzzle, frame
inlay, color w/sleeve, 1948, large
size **22.00**

Gene Autry movie handbill, "Mule
Train," Columbia Pictures, Gene
riding Champion, black ink on color
paper stock, 9½ x 13" **3.50**

Gene Autry movie poster, "Loaded
Pistols," Columbia Pictures, Gene in
three scenes w/Champion, black ink
on color paper stock, 9½ x 13" **3.50**

Gene Autry photograph, holding
pistol, black & white, 8 x 10" **1.50**

Gene Autry postcard, advertisement
for Gene's Western shirts, glossy
photograph of Gene, 1950s **3.50**

Gene Autry ring, horseshoe nail-
type, mint on original card **175.00**

Gene Autry sheet music, "Phantom
Empire," 1935 .... **45.00**

**Gene Autry & Champion arcade
cards,** blue, different scenes, set of
12 .... **7.50**

Gene Autry & Champion pennant,
cloth, "Back In The Saddle Again,"
purple **45.00**

**Gene Autry & Champion
photographs,** different color Kodak
photographs, 3¼ x 5", set of 3 .... **5.00**

Gene Barry arcade card, "Bat
Masterson," black & white, 1950s,
No. 102, 3¼ x 5½" **1.50**

Gene Barry & Adele Mara arcade
card, "Bat Masterson," black &
white, 1950s, No. 99, 3¼ x 5½" **1.50**

George Houston lobby card, "The
Lone Rider in Ghost Town," shows
Houston on horseback, PRC,
8 x 10" **1.50**

Gunsmoke (TV) puzzle, jigsaw-type,
1950s, boxed **16.00**

Guy Madison arcade card, black &
white, 1950s, No. 104, 3¼ x 5½" **1.50**

Guy Madison photograph, black &
white film studio still from "Reprisal,"
love scene w/Felicia Farr, Columbia
Pictures, 1956, 8 x 10" (fine
condition) **2.50**

Harry Carey lobby card, "Rustler's
Paradise," AJAX Pictures, 8 x 10" **1.50**

Have Gun Will Travel (TV) play set,
Paladin ring & calling card, mint in
package **22.00**

High Chaparral (TV) album of songs
& black & white photographs of all
the series stars, color front & back
cover w/photographs of the stars,
1970, West Coast Publishing Inc.,
8½ x 11", 52 pp. (complete, very
good condition) **7.50**

Hopalong Cassidy badge, "Eat Bond
Bread," advertising premium, black
& silver w/picture of Hoppy **10.00**

Hopalong Cassidy bath mat,
chenille, w/Hoppy & Topper image,
red & brown lettering, 24 x 28" **165.00**

Hopalong Cassidy bedspread,
chenille, w/image of Hoppy & Topper
jumping fence, "Hopalong Cassidy"
printed across bottom, 90 x 106" **250.00**

Hopalong Cassidy bedspread, cotton poplin, w/image of Hoppy & Topper jumping fence, "Hopalong Cassidy" printed on bottom, 90 x 106"...**275.00**

Hopalong Cassidy Billfold

Hopalong Cassidy billfold, vinyl, picture of Hoppy & Topper on front (ILLUS.) **65.00**
Hopalong Cassidy birthday postcard, 1950 ....**7.50**
Hopalong Cassidy book, "Hopalong Cassidy & Two Young Cowboys," Whitman, 1951....................................**12.00**
Hopalong Cassidy book, "Hopalong Cassidy & The Singing Bandit," book & two record set, Capitol Records, Inc.....................................**115.00**

Hopalong Cassidy Camera

Hopalong Cassidy camera, Galter Products Co., 1940, original box (ILLUS.) **212.50**
Hopalong Cassidy candy bar wrapper...**100.00**
Hopalong Cassidy cereal bowl, white china w/multicolored picture of Hoppy & Topper, backstamped

Hopalong Cereal Bowl & Mug

"Hopalong Cassidy by W.S. George," 5" d. (ILLUS. left) **85.00**
Hopalong Cassidy coloring kit w/figural paints, crayons, stencils, etc., in original box..........................**250.00**
Hopalong Cassidy cookie jar, cov., "Bar 20 Cookie Corral," pottery, decal & embossed designs, 8" d., 6½" h...**295.00**
Hopalong Cassidy drapes, chenille, near mint, pr.....................................**250.00**
Hopalong Cassidy game, "Chinese Checkers," w/original box **254.50**
Hopalong Cassidy game, "Dominoes," Milton Bradley, ca. 1950 ....**187.50**
Hopalong Cassidy game, target-type, tin w/great graphics, Marx.......**145.00**
Hopalong Cassidy ice cream carton, "Weber's Ice Cream - My Favorite Kind," cardboard, pictures Hopalong, ½ gal. (mint) **120.00**
Hopalong Cassidy lamp, wall-type, gun in holster, Alacite glass, Aladdin ....**300.00 to 350.00**
Hopalong Cassidy milk bottle, clear glass w/black & red graphics, Dairy-Lee Milk, ½ pt. **85.00**
Hopalong Cassidy milk bottle, black & red graphics, Dairy-Lee Milk, qt......**72.50**
Hopalong Cassidy milk carton, three photographs, ½ pint **3.50**
Hopalong Cassidy milk carton, two photos show Hoppy drawing guns, 1 qt..**3.50**
Hopalong Cassidy movie handbill, "Doomed Caravan," starring William Boyd, shown in two scenes, black ink on color paper stock, 9½ x 13".......**3.50**
Hopalong Cassidy mug, opaque white glass w/color decal picture (ILLUS. right w/cereal bowl)..............**35.00**
Hopalong Cassidy night light, Hoppy riding Topper, yellow & black, 3" d..**7.50**
Hopalong Cassidy notebook binder, ring-type, loose leaf, picture of Hoppy & Topper on front & back w/Hoppy Western Guide inside, hard cover.......................................**120.00**

Hopalong Cassidy pencil case, ca. 1950, 5 x 11"................................**145.00**

Hopalong Cassidy penknife, miniature, black, one side w/picture of Hoppy on Topper, other side w/his name, 1950s, 2" l....................**65.00**

Hopalong Cassidy bust photograph, black & white, 8 x 10"........................**1.50**

Hopalong Cassidy photograph, holding two pistols, black & white, 8 x 10"....................................**1.50**

Hopalong Cassidy plate, china, signed "To My Friend, Hoppy," marked W.S. George Mfg., 10" d.......**75.00**

Hopalong Cassidy Plate

Hopalong Cassidy plate, milk white glass w/black decal of Hoppy & Topper, Anchor Hocking, 7" d. (ILLUS.) **77.50**

Hopalong Cassidy postcard, Savings Club birthday, tan & brown w/photograph, 1950s **6.00**

Hopalong Cassidy puzzle, jigsaw, color frame tray-type, inlay picture puzzle w/sleeve, ca. 1950.................**29.00**

Hopalong Cassidy rug, chenille, horsehead & fence, 2 x 4' **175.00**

Hopalong Cassidy scrapbook, tan vinyl covers, center embossed colorful picture of Hopalong on horse, two embossed side pictures & Western symbols, cord tie binding, unused (brittle blank pages) **132.00**

Hopalong Cassidy token, "Lucky Coin" **25.00**

Hopalong Cassidy tumbler, milk white glass, "Dinner" **37.00**

Hopalong Cassidy water-color set, mint in box **200.00**

Hopalong Cassidy wrist watch, picture of Hoppy on face, black strap, die-bossed "Good Luck from Hoppy," U.S. Time, 1950-67, w/box **246.50**

Hugh O'Brian arcade card, "Wyatt Earp," black & white, 1950s, No 101, 3¼ x 5½"................................**1.50**

Jack Kelly arcade card, "Maverick," black & white, 1950s, No. 130, 3¼ x 5½"................................**1.50**

Johnny Mack Brown movie handbill, "Oklahoma Justice," shown w/pistol in one hand, black ink on color paper stock, 9½ x 13"......**3.50**

John Wayne note card w/envelope, black & white photograph of John laughing, 1963, 4 x 7" **5.00**

John Wayne photograph, wearing U.S. Cavalry uniform, black & white, 8 x 10"................................**1.50**

John Wayne photograph, sitting w/rifle across lap, rolling a cigarette, black & white, 8 x 10"........................**1.50**

Keith Larson, Buddy Ebsen & Don Burnett arcade card, "Northwest Passage," black & white, 1950s, No. 120, 3¼ x 5½" **1.50**

Kit Carson (TV) bandanna, Coca-Cola premium **60.00**

Lash LaRue photograph, whip around arm, pistol in one hand, black & white, 8 x 10"........................**1.50**

Lash LaRue photograph, shown on horseback, black & white, 8 x 10"........**1.50**

Lee Powell lobby card, "Texas Man Hunt," Bill Boyd & Art Davis also shown, PRC, 8 x 10"........................**1.50**

Lex Barker arcade card, black & white, 1950s, No. 125, 3¼ x 5½".........**1.50**

Lone Ranger badge, brass, horseshoe-shaped, "Lone Ranger Club," 1930s **30.00**

Lone Ranger book, "The Lone Ranger and the Outlaw Stronghold," by Fran Striker, 1939, Grosset & Dunlap, hard cover, 214 pp. (very good)................................**7.50**

Lone Ranger book, "The Lone Ranger and Tonto," by Fran Striker, 1940, Grosset & Dunlap, hard cover book w/fly leaf photograph, 215 pp. (very good)........................**7.50**

Lone Ranger Bookbag

Lone Ranger bookbag, leatherette, multicolored picture on tan, 10 x 12" (ILLUS. bottom previous page)........**160.00**

Lone Ranger comic book, miniature, entitled "Lone Ranger & The Story of Silver"...**25.00**

"The Lone Ranger Game"

Lone Ranger game, board-type, "The Lone Ranger Game," w/five metal horses & riders, directions, etc., Parker Bros., 1938, board opens to 18½" sq. (ILLUS.) **65.00**

Lone Ranger Gum Store Box

Lone Ranger gum store box, "Lone Ranger Bubble Gum," the cover & all side panels, including the bottom, printed w/color images of the Lone Ranger, Tonto & Silver, the cover w/the Lone Ranger on a rearing Silver, ca. 1940, depression tear in lower right of cover (ILLUS.) **3,450.00**

Lone Ranger pencil box, rectangular simulated leather cardboard, embossed image of the Lone Ranger on Silver on the lid w/"HiHo Silver," silver trim, opens to top tray & sliding tray, American Pencil Co., 1949, 5 x 9"..**79.00**

Lone Ranger pencil, Silver Bullet-type, on original card ....**25.00 to 35.00**

Lone Ranger photograph, w/radio schedule on reverse, radio premium, 1936...**125.00**

Lone Ranger photograph, both guns drawn, black & white, 8 x 10"..............**1.50**

Lone Ranger pocket knife, red w/picture, slogans & three-dimensional silver bullet....................**55.00**

Lone Ranger pocket watch, New Haven Clock Co., 1939 ...**300.00 to 350.00**

Lone Ranger Premium Cards

Lone Ranger premium cards, each depicts a full-color action scene, cards were obtained by sending in wrappers from Lone Ranger gum, 1940, rare, some wear & tape marks, each 8 x 10", set of 5 (ILLUS. of one) **2,875.00**

Lone Ranger ring, "Atom Bomb," w/instructions **85.00**

Lone Ranger ring, saddle-type, w/original filmstrip **155.00**

Lone Ranger ring, "Six-shooter," Cheerios premium, 1940s.................**79.00**

Lone Ranger sleeping bag, 1978......**45.00**

Lone Ranger teaspoon, silver plate, ca. 1938 ....**30.00**

Lone Ranger toothbrush holder, dated 1938......................................**100.00**

Lone Ranger Wind-up Toy

Lone Ranger toy, wind-up tin, "Range Rider," rocker base, No. C-8, 10½" h., Marx, 1938 (ILLUS.) **565.00**

Lone Ranger wrist watch, New Haven, 1939 ....**295.00**

Lone Ranger & Silver photograph, black & white, 8 x 10"............................**1.50**

Lone Ranger & Tonto photograph, helping a wounded man, black & white, 8 x 10"..**1.50**

Lorne Green & Pernell Roberts arcade card, "Bonanza," black & white, 1960s, No. 100, 3¼ x 5½" **1.50**

Mark Stevens arcade card, black & white, 1950s, No. 123, 3¼ x 5½ **1.50**

Maverick (TV) paint-by-number set, contains three pre-numbered sketches & 24 vials of paints & brush, black & white photo of James Garner on the cover, Hasbro, 1958, box 14 x 18", unused **98.00**

Maverick photograph, James Garner & TV show cast, black & white, 8 x 10"..**1.50**

Maverick (TV) token, metal, James Garner & Jack Kelly on front, Kaiser Aluminum...**5.00**

Michael Landon arcade card, "Bonanza," black & white, 1960s, No. 133, 3½ x 5½" **1.50**

Nick Adams arcade card, "The Rebel," black & white, 1950s, No. 111, 3¼ x 5½" **1.50**

Peter Graves arcade card, "Fury," black & white, 1950s, No. 134, 3¼ x 5¼"..**1.50**

Randolph Scott arcade card, black & white, 1950s, No. 121, 3¼ x 5½"..**1.50**

Red Ryder paint book, 1947, unused **45.00**

Red Ryder suspenders, child size......**70.00**

Rex Allen arcade card, "Man From the West," black & white, 1950s, No. 105, 3¼ x 5½" **1.50**

Richard Coogan arcade card, "The Californians," black & white, 1950s, No. 138, 3¼ x 5½ **1.50**

Rifleman (TV) game, board-type, 1958, mint in original box ....**25.00 to 50.00**

Robert Horton arcade card, "Wagon Train," black & white, 1950s, No. 132, 3¼ x 5½" **1.50**

Rory Calhoun photograph, black & white film studio still from "The Gun Hawk," bust photograph, wearing Western clothes, Allied Artists, 1963, 8 x 10" (fine)............................**2.50**

Rough Riders (The) photograph, Buck jones, Tim McCoy & Raymond Hatton, black & white, 8 x 10"..............**1.50**

Roy Rogers arcade card, multi-photo, full figure of Roy Rogers drawing gun & photographs of Monte Hale, James Warner & Jack Padjeon, signed, blue, 3¼ x 5½" **2.00**

Roy Rogers arcade cards, two show Roy riding Trigger, blue, signed, three different scenes, set of 3 (mint)..**5.00**

Roy Rogers blanket, woven, brown & white, pictures Roy & Trigger **250.00**

Roy Rogers book, "Roy Rogers & The Outlaws of Sundown Valley," 1950...**20.00**

Roy Rogers camera, box-type, Herbert George Company, ca. 1950, w/box ....**100.00 to 200.00**

Roy Rogers coloring book, No. 1186 ....**20.00**

Roy Rogers costume, official cowboy outfit, color illustrations on box, Yankiboy **165.00**

Roy Rogers cowboy shirt, child's, Western-style plaid shirt w/contrast yoke & piping, yoke embroidered w/a design of Roy lassoing cactus as Trigger rears, Roy Rogers Frontier Shirts, early 1950s...............**98.00**

Roy Rogers figure, bobbing head-type, composition, cowboy outfit painted in aqua, red & white, mounted on green base w/facsimile signature decal on front, 1960s, 6½" h.......................................**250.00**

Roy Rogers movie handbill, "Don't Fence Me In," Republic Pictures, Roy playing guitar, black ink on color paper stock, 9½ x 13" **3.50**

Roy Rogers movie press book, 1940s, contains extremely large film photographs, publicity, etc., in color, 20-30 pp................................**50.00**

Roy Rogers phonograph record album, "Pecos Bill," 1949 ....**75.00**

Roy Rogers photo cards, bubble gum premium, black & white scenes of Roy & Trigger from 1955 Republic Pictures movie "In Old Amarillo," Times Confectionary Co., England, 1½ x 2½", complete set of 24 ....**15.00**

Roy Rogers photograph, standing in front of "Mutual" microphone, black & white, 8 x 10"..............................**1.50**

Roy Rogers pocketknife & key chain, diamond-shaped, w/picture of Roy in horseshoe............................**10.00**

Roy Rogers toy, stagecoach w/tool chest for taking off the wheels, gun & whip & other accessories in original colorful display box, the stagecoach, 14" l., the set................**425.00**

Roy Rogers Viewmaster reel, No. 945, 1950 ....**15.00**

Roy Rogers & Dale Evans, paper doll book, Whitman No. 998, 1950, Trigger on back cover, uncut **115.00**

Roy Rogers & Dale Evans wrist watch, Bradley, 1970, mint in box **32.00**

Roy Rogers, Dale Evans & Gabby
Hayes photograph, black & white,
8 x 10"......................................**1.50**

Roy Rogers, Dale Evans, Trigger &
Bullet sticker book, rodeo fun book,
uncut....................................**75.00**

Roy Rogers & others calendar, full
figure black & white illustrations of
Roy Rogers, Hopalong Cassidy,
Gene Autry, Tom Mix, John Wayne
& others, also notes Western stars'
birthdates, 11 x 17".....................**5.00**

Roy Rogers & Trigger figures,
plastic, Hartland, complete **210.00**

Roy Rogers & Trigger lamp, figural,
plaster base, color painted figure of
Roy on a rearing Trigger, cardboard
shade, base 8½" h., shade
5½" h..................................**215.00**

Roy Rogers & Trigger pull-toy,
lithographed wood & metal **300.00**

Roy Rogers, Trigger & Trigger Jr.
play set, tin, includes figures, truck
cab & horse trailer, Marx, the set.....**175.00**

Sunset Carson movie handbill,
"Deadline," starring Sunset Carson,
shown holding pistol in each hand,
black ink on color paper stock,
9½ x 13"................................**3.50**

Tex Ritter photograph, black &
white, 8 x 10"..........................**1.50**

Tom Mix belt buckle, Ralston
championship...........................**65.00**

Tom Mix belt buckle w/decoder &
secret compartment, Ralston
premium, 1946.........................**95.00**

Tom Mix book, "Tom Mix Died for
Your Sins," by Darryl Ponican, 1975,
Delacorte Press, novel based on life
of Tom Mix w/black & white
photographs, hard cover, 300 pp........**6.50**

Tom Mix cigar box, small, color
lithograph shield-shaped label, ca.
1930s, 2 x 3"..........................**40.00**

Tom Mix comic book, "Straight
Shooters," No. 10, Ralston
premium................................**50.00**

Tom Mix decoder badge, "Six Gun
Decoder," 1941 ....**75.00**

Tom Mix "I.D." bracelet w/initial
"W," Straight Shooter's **35.00**

Tom Mix manual, "Life of Tom Mix
and the Ralston Straight Shooters
Manual," 1933 w/original
mailer...........................**65.00 to 75.00**

Tom Mix photograph in silver plate
frame, Ralston premium, 1938 ....**85.00**

Tom Mix photograph, on Tony,
waving hat, black & white, 8 x 10" **1.50**

Tom Mix postcard, black & white
photograph of Tom Mix w/guns
drawn, scene from movie "The
Unknown," 1920s.......................**2.50**

Tom Mix spinner, "Good Luck,"
1933, 1¼ x 1½".........................**50.00**

Tom Mix telescope, bullet-type,
w/bird call, original box
w/instructions.........................**75.00**

Tom Mix toy, "Rocket Parachute," in
original mailer, 1936 ....**165.00**

Tom Mix toy, television viewer,
w/instructions & original mailer **85.00**

Tom Tyron arcade card, "Texas
John Slaughter," black & white,
1950s, No. 108, 3½ x 5½"...............**1.50**

Tonto costume, "Suedine," by Pla-
Marker, mint in original box.............**150.00**

Tonto model kit, Aurora, unopened ..**100.00**

Tonto soap figure, Kirk Guild
Company, in original box **65.00**

Ward Bond arcade card, "Wagon
Train," black & white, 1950s,
No. 107, 3¼ x 5½"......................**1.50**

Ward Bond & Robert Horton arcade
card, "Wagon Train," black & white,
1950s, No. 98, 3¼ x 5½".................**1.50**

Wyatt Earp (TV) coloring book,
softbound, nice color cover painting
of Hugh O'Brian as Earp, Saalfield,
1957, 44+ pp., 8 x 11" (some minor
coloring)..............................**24.00**

Wyatt Earp (TV) game, board-type,
"The Life and Legend of Wyatt
Earp," complete w/playing board,
cardboard figures, discs & spinners,
Trans-O-Gram, 1958, box 13 x 16"....**79.00**

**(End of Western Character
Collectibles Section)**

WIENER WERKSTATTE

Wiener Werkstatte Bust

*The Wiener Werkstatte (Vienna
Workshops) were co-founded in 1903 in
Vienna, Austria by Josef Hoffmann and
Koloman Moser. An offshoot of the Vienna
Secession movement, closely related to the*

Art Nouveau and Arts and Crafts movements elsewhere, this studio was established to design and produce unique and high-quality pieces covering all aspects of the fine arts. Hoffmann and Moser were the first artistic directors and oversaw the work of up to 100 workers, including thirty-seven masters who signed their work. Bookbinding, leatherwork, gold, silver and lacquer pieces as well as enamels and furniture all originated from these shops over a period of nearly thirty years. The finest pieces from the Wiener Werkstatte are now bringing tremendous prices.

Box, cov., tooled leather, the top w/four stylized mythological heads within brickwork borders, the apron w/various coats-of-arms, brown dye, the interior in tan pigskin, stamped "WIENER - WERK - STATTE - HF," possibly designed by Ferdinand Heider, ca. 1910, 9 x 10¾", 2¾" h..**$2,300.00**

Bust of a woman, glazed terra cotta, modeled as a lady wearing a close-fitting cap & framed by a blue scarf, designed by Knorlein, painted on the base "Austria" & incised on the side "Knorlein," 6¾" w., 12½" h. (ILLUS.) **1,925.00**

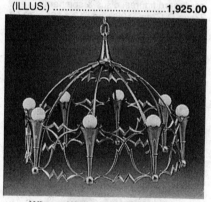

Wiener Werkstatte Chandelier

Chandelier, 8-light, brass, the domed foliate cap & pendent central section w/eight curved arms each ending in a stylized trumpet flowerhead socket, conjoined by a stylized foliate open framework, designed by Dagobert Peche, ca. 1920, 26" d., 4' h. (ILLUS.).................................**6,900.00**

Compote, open, silver plate, the deep flat-bottomed bowl w/gently flaring ringed sides, decorated around the rim w/triangles enclosing grape clusters, raised on a wide domed pedestal foot, designed by Dagobert

Peche, impressed mark "WIENER - WERK - STATTE" w/designer's hallmark, ca. 1925, 5⅞" h. **1,380.00**

Ladle, silver & lapis lazuli, the deep bowl formed w/two spouts & a long slender sloping notched handle, the terminal inset w/a lapis lazuli stone, designed by Koloman Moser, marked, ca. 1925, 6" l...................**1,035.00**

Vase, pottery, wide pyramidal sides topped by a small sphere w/tab handles, the base pierced overall w/scattered geometric openings outlined in orange against a grey ground, impressed "WW - Made in Austria - 446," 6¾" w., 7½" h. **770.00**

Vase, silver, slender trumpet-form body on a domed foot, the rim & edge of base joined by four geometrically-pierced straps w/a similar high arched handle, designed by Josef Hoffmann, marked on base, retailer's mark "SB," 12¾" h. **12,075.00**

WOODENWARES

Early Wooden Canteen

The patina and mellow coloring, along with the lightness and smoothness that come only with age and wear, attract collectors to old woodenwares. The earliest forms were the simplest and the shapes of items whittled out in the late 19th century varied little in form from those turned out in the American colonies two centuries earlier. A burl is a growth, or wart, on some trees in which the grain of the wood is twisted and turned in a manner which strengthens the fibers and causes a beautiful pattern to be formed. Treenware is simply a term for utilitarian items made from "treen," another word for wood. While maple was the primary wood used for these items, they are also abundant in pine, ash, oak, walnut, and other woods. "Lignum Vitae" is a species of wood from the West Indies that can always be identified by the contrasting colors of dark heartwood and light sapwood and by its heavy weight, which causes it to sink in water. Also see KITCHENWARES.

Apple butter stirrer, hand hewn & carved, long handle, shaped paddle at right angle w/pierced holes, ca. 1800, 5½' l. **$95.00**

Blueberry picker, one-piece, pine, U-shaped handle, ca. 1860, 3¾ x 5½ x 10½" **395.00**

Bowl, carved burl, oblong boat-shaped w/high cut-out end handles, 19th c., 10" l., 5¼" h. **517.00**

Bowl, curly maple, gently curved sides, refinished w/traces of old red, 17" d., 5¼" h. (wear & age crack in rim) **357.50**

Bowl, burl w/good figure, gently rounded sides w/incised lines, soft grey scrubbed finish, 17" d., 5¾" h. (small edge break w/old nailed repairs) **660.00**

Bowl, curly maple, deep rounded sides w/thin edge band, 18¾ x 19¾", 6¾" h. (refinished) **440.00**

Bowl, dense burl w/good figure, oval, curved sides w/high raised cut-out handles, old dark patina, 14 x 18", overall 9" h. (old repairs in both side rims) **1,650.00**

Bowl, ash burl, oval w/slanted sides, carved end handles, good interior ware, 16" l. (revarnished) **412.50**

Bowl, burl, gently rounded sides w/wide band at rim, on a slightly raised foot, first half 19th c., 19½" d. **1,495.00**

Butter churn, dasher-type, stave construction, pine barrel w/brass hoops, ca. 1840, 19½" h. **140.00**

Butter firkin, cov., round bentwood, pine & poplar, single finger-lappet construction on base & cover, the top decorated in polychrome w/a flowerhead, the sides painted w/the inscription "CATHARINE V.P.," all on a dark green ground, probably New Jersey, ca. 1775, 5" d., 2⅝" h. **4,600.00**

Butter paddle, ash burl, wide shallow rounded bowl w/integral upright side handle w/curved tip, good figure, soft finish, 8½" l. **302.50**

Butter paddle, curly maple, shallow oblong bowl w/long slender slightly tapering handle w/hook end, nut brown refinishing, 8¾" l. **165.00**

Butter scoop, bird's-eye maple, old worn refinishing, 8½" l. **44.00**

Canteen, circular form w/flat sides fitted in three locations w/tacked leather loops as well as a drinking hole, the entire piece painted blue w/a large white star surrounded by a small rosette border on one side, American-made, possibly 18th c., 6½" d., 2⅛" h. (ILLUS.) **1,265.00**

Chalice, hand-turned, a flaring bell-form bowl on a short ring-turned stem & round domed disc foot, old varnish finish, attributed to Pease of Ohio, 3" h. **104.00**

Cookie board, hardwood, narrow rectangular board carved w/two rows of six blocks each, each block w/a different animal, bird or flower, 3⅜ x 12⅝" (some edge damage)..............................**192.50**

Cookie board, hardwood, rectangular, carved w/three large stylized coiled snakes bordered in tin, 7⅛ x 10¼" (few worm holes) **121.00**

Cookie board, carved mahogany, nearly square, a round medallion in the center carved w/a standing figure of George Washington flanked by figures of Justice & Columbia & two large cornucopia below a large spread-winged American eagle w/shield breast & a long slender banner reading "E. Pluribus Unum" & five stars, probably by Conger, early 19th c., 11¾ x 12" (minor edge chip).........**3,630.00**

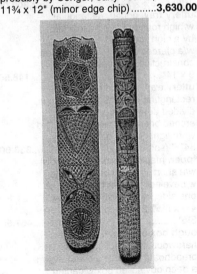

Carved Corset Busks

Corset busk, chip-carved maple, wide flattened slightly tapering board rounded at the bottom & w/a flattened scalloped top, chip-carved w/designs of pinwheels, hearts, flowerheads & geometric patterns, signed "Eunice Davis," & dated "1787," North Weymouth, Massachusetts, 2¾" w., 12¾" l. (ILLUS. left)............................**575.00**

Corset busk, chip-carved maple, long wide & flat board slightly tapering to a slightly rounded end, the opposite end incurved, carved on the obverse w/hearts, pinwheels & stellate devices, the reverse inscribed "July Ye 17 1764 a busk made at Ye Grand Bank," 3 x 12½" **2,588.00**

Corset busk, chip-carved maple, shaped triangular form w/chip-carved hearts, pinwheels, fans & a flowering tulip, the reverse signed & dated "Hannah Goodell 1727," New England, 13" l...............................**460.00**

Corset busk, chip-carved maple, long slender flattened board w/a rounded base & double-lobed top, overall chip-carving of hearts, stars, flowers, trees & a hot air balloon w/flags, inset w/a brass plaque initialed "MAF," the reverse w/sprigs of leaves, New England, early 19th c., 14" l. (ILLUS. right)............**460.00**

Corset busk, chip-carved maple, long flat thin board rounded at one end & incurved at the other, decorated w/incised flowering vines, pinwheels & a heart, inset w/a glass panel, probably New England, early 18th c., 2½ x 14½"..............**2,300.00**

Cutlery tray, poplar, rectangular w/high rounded end boards joined by a high scalloped central divider w/a pierced hand-hold, dovetailed construction, old brown finish, 9 x 14".................................**148.50**

Cutlery tray, painted poplar, rectangular w/slightly canted sides, divided down the center w/an arched board w/cut-out handle, old worn light greyish paint, 15½ x 34½" (some edge damage) **330.00**

Dipper, maple, long deep oval bowl w/a short straight oblong handle w/beveled edges at the center of one side, old varnish finish, bowl 4½ x 5½", 2½" deep, handle 3½" l.....................................**467.50**

Dough box on frame, pine & hardwood, long rectangular breadboard top widely overhanging a deep dovetailed box w/canted sides, on a deep frame raised on heavy baluster-turned legs w/bun feet, 26 x 48", 27" h. (minor edge damage, age cracks) **715.00**

Painted Hickory Drying Rack

Drying rack, painted hickory, two-bar style, slender square bars between slender square uprights on arched trestle feet, overall grain-painted in shades of ochre, New England, 19th c. (ILLUS.)...............................**546.00**

Firkin (tab-handled bucket), cylindrical, old blue, green, red & yellow paint over original blue, 19th c., 9¾" h. **1,725.00**

Flax hatchel, mounted on an oak board, punch-dated in tin "1816," decorated w/hex signs, 4¼ x 10½", 7" h..**150.00**

Funnel, speckled ash burl, one-piece, 18th c., 3 x 5", ¾" d. opening, ...**495.00**

Grain shovel, poplar, one-piece, long slightly curved rectangular blade, rounded handle w/flattened rectangular end, old worn natural patina, branded "E.J.S.," 40½" l. (some edge damage).......................**71.50**

Jar, cov., wide inverted bell-form body raised on a short stem above a domed foot, the wide mouth supporting a stepped & domed cover w/button finial, attributed to Pease of Ohio, old varnish finish, 7" h...**275.00**

Jar, cov., tall cylindrical body w/a wide ring below the flat mouth, boldly stepped & domed cover w/button finial, attributed to Pease of Ohio, worn old varnish finish, 7¼" h. (age cracks in base) **93.50**

Jar, cov., painted & decorated poplar, cylindrical body turned from one piece of wood, carved ring at base & top, top rim w/added reinforcement, original red & yellow sponge graining, 11" d., 11½" h. (minor age cracks in base & lid)..............**3,850.00**

Jars, cov., miniature, urn-shaped

body w/tooled ring at midsection, on low standard & flat circular foot, ring-turned cover w/pointed finial, attributed to Pease of Ohio, 19th c., graduated sizes from 2¼" to 3" h., set of 4 (one w/glued foot) **726.00**

Mortar & pestle, slightly tapering cylindrical burl body on low base, plain wood pestle w/simple turning, refinished, 4½" h., 2 pcs. (age cracks) **99.00**

Rolling pin, springerlee-type, short cylinder carved w/twelve shallow designs including starflowers, leaf sprigs & a cross, turned wood handles, 13" l. **203.50**

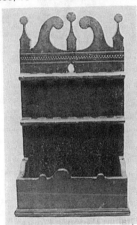

Carved & Painted Spoon Rack

Spoon rack, painted pine, the tall flat back w/a broken-scroll carved crest ending in carved rosettes & flanked by three painted finials w/carved rosette terminals all above a narrow band of chip carving over two slotted bars for spoons, an open rectangular box at the base, painted green, possibly Connecticut, ca. 1800, imperfections, 21½" h. (ILLUS.) **4,950.00**

Spoon rack, Chippendale style, the high arched & stepped crest above two slotted bars for spoons flanked by incurved sides, a rectangular open box at the base, painted black, New England, late 18th - early 19th c., 23¾" h. (ILLUS. top next column) **2,875.00**

Sugar bucket, cov., stave construction w/wooden bands, swivel handle, brown stain, 9" h. **135.00**

Sugar bucket, cov., stave construction, slightly tapering cylindrical sides w/two bands, flat fitted cover, old worn light green repaint, 12" h. plus swivel bentwood strap handle **247.50**

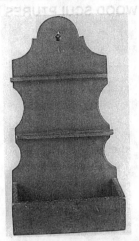

Early New England Spoon Rack

Sugar bucket, cov., stave construction w/black painted metal bands, wire bail handle w/wooden handgrip, old green paint, tattered paper label inside lid, 14" h. **220.00**

Early Watch Hutch

Watch hutch, carved & inlaid cherry, Federal style, a swan's-neck cresting above a scrollboard pierced w/a heart, a glazed & inlaid cupboard door below, all on a molded base, together w/a watch paper inscribed to "Deborah Cutler, New England" & dated "April 15, 1806," inscribed on both sides in ink in contemporary script surrounded by a laurel wreath "By Eliza Ann Cutler April 15, 1806," hutch 3¼ x 6", 10" h. 2 pcs. (ILLUS. of hutch)..**1,725.00**

WOOD SCULPTURES

Carved Figure of a Hunter

American folk sculpture is an important part of the American art scene today. Skilled wood carvers turned out ship's figureheads, cigar store figures, plaques and carousel animals of stylized beauty and great appeal. The wooden shipbuilding industry, which had originally nourished this folk art, declined after the Civil War and the talented carvers then turned to producing figures for tobacconist's shops, carousel animals and show figures for circuses. These figures and other early ornamental carvings that have survived the elements and years are eagerly sought.

Bust of a bearded gentleman,
painted pine, carved in the round, the man w/delicately rendered features, hair & costume, the details picked out in blue, black & green, probably New England, third quarter 19th c., 6¾" h. **$6,325.00**

Cigar store figure of an Indian chief, carved & painted pine, the standing figure wearing a feathered head-dress & orange & blue costume w/a fur cloak, grasping a bunch of cigars & a block of tobacco in one hand & a dagger in the other, mounted on a green-painted pine pedestal base, third quarter 19th c., overall 6' 5" h. (cracks & chips & restorations to paint) **14,950.00**

Cigar store figure of an Indian
princess, carved & painted pine, standing wearing a feathered headdress & brown dress w/red sash, holding a bunch of cigars inscribed "HABANA" in her right hand, mounted on a rectangular brown-painted composition base

inscribed "DRAKE'S" in yellow, the front & back w/bail carrying handles, attributed to Samuel Robb, New York City, third quarter 19th c., overall 6' 5" h. (cracks & restoration to paint) **32,300.00**

Figure of a hunter & his dog, maple & pine, carved in the full round, the hunter w/relief-carved facial features wearing a hat & tie w/engraved decoration, holding a rifle in his right hand, the separate figure of his small dog by his feet, on a footed octagonal base, 20th c., overall 20½" h. (ILLUS.) **1,955.00**

Italian Madonna Figure

Figure of a Madonna, Renaissance style, parcel-gilt & polychrome, the standing figure wearing a cape & long robes, on a square base, Italy, 17th c., repainted areas, worming, 44" h. (ILLUS.) **7,700.00**

Carved Model of a Dove

Model of a dove, carved & painted pine, the standing bird carved in the round, on wire feet, fitted w/glass eyes, painted white, probably New England, late 19th c., 7¼" h. (ILLUS.) **1,265.00**

Model of an eagle, long spread-winged bird w/the head curved up, below a long arched banner reading "Don't Give Up The Ship," banner on a long pole, painted decoration, partial label on back "...Captain Clark," attributed to John H. Bellamy, Kittery Point, Maine, together w/two tools purportedly belonging to Bellamy, one marked "B.H.J.," model 25¼" l., the group..**16,100.00**

Early Ship's Figurehead

Ship's figurehead, a bust portrait of a lady, her dark hair pulled to the back, wearing a wide-collared bluish green dress continuing to a leaf-carved socle, paint losses, New England, ca. 1840, 16" h. (ILLUS.) **19,550.00**

Ship's figurehead, a bust portrait of a dark-haired lady w/blue eyes & finely carved features, the coiffure continuing to a scrolled socle w/anthemia leaves, details picked out in blue, green & gold, mounted on an oblong pine base, New England, mid-19th c., 16" deep, 18" h..**23,000.00**

Ship's sternboard, carved & painted, long shaped & arched board w/a central shield carved w/a scrolled banner marked "SPERO" above a profiled griffin's head, flanked by long thistle clusters & scrolling leaves, Europe, 19th c., 57" l. (imperfections) **862.50**

Wall plaque, painted pine, rectangular, carved in the half-round w/a gadrooned compote filled w/polychrome-painted pears, oranges, a melon, a pineapple & two red flowers, possibly New York State, ca. 1840, 8 x 8¾"................**3,737.00**

Whirligig, carved & painted wood, figure of an American Indian in full red & green feather headdress & articulated face w/white bead eyes & paddle baffles above bent legs

seated in a brown dugout canoe, mounted on square base, 19th c., 6" w., 15¾" l., 16¼" h...................**2,990.00**

'Keystone Cop' Whirligig

Whirligig, carved & painted pine & sheet metal, figure of a 'Keystone Cop,' carved in the full round w/relief-carved face w/black sheet metal cap, white painted sheet metal hands w/articulated arms, brass tack buttons, mounted on a black stand, probably New England, ca. 1900, one foot repaired, 17½" h. (ILLUS.) **2,875.00**

Whirligig, carved & painted pine & metal, depicting a man on a 'bone shaker' bicycle, the stylized figure of a man wearing a yellow cap & jacket & grey pants seated atop a yellow & grey painted metal bicycle, his legs bend & pedal when the wind moves the wheels set w/finned spokes, fitted w/a mounting brace, early 20th c., 39" l., 40" h......................**5,175.00**

Lighthouse Whirligig

Whirligig, painted wood, model of a lighthouse, molded in the full round, the octagonal lighthouse painted white w/red roof, blue louvred windows & two red tiered galleries, a red fan & blue tail w/a white bird attached to the top w/articulated wings, late 19th - early 20th c., 5' 9" h. (ILLUS.)................................**805.00**

WORLD'S FAIR COLLECTIBLES

There has been great interest in collecting items produced for the great fairs and expositions held through the years. During the 1970s, there was particular interest in items produced for the 1876 Centennial Exhibition and now interest is focusing on those items associated with the 1893 Columbian Exposition. Listed below is a random sampling of prices asked for items produced for the various fairs.

1876 PHILADELPHIA CENTENNIAL

Centennial Hand Vase

Banner, cloth, showing buildings, people & seals, blue & white..........**$150.00**

Book, "Frank Leslie's Illustrated Historical Register of the Centennial Exposition - 1876," 320 pp., 11 x 16" (spine poor)........................**150.00**

Book, "History of the Centennial Exhibition," by James D. McCabe, hard cover, contains over 300 illustrations, including full page and a few fold-out double-page size, published by Jones Brothers & Co., 6 x 9" (some cover scuffing, contents extra fine) **75.00**

Book, "The National Ode July 4, 1876 Bayard Taylor," hard cover, printed one side only in script form, gold

lettering on blue cover, 12 pp., 10 x 12"................................**25.00**

Book, "The Centennial Diary 1876," contains general information, eclipses for 1876, interest laws, postal rates, populations, etc., plus dated blank pages for memorandums, 22 pp., 3 x 6" (cover split, contents fine) **20.00**

Book, "Treasures of Art, Industry and Manufacture at the International Exhibition, 1876," 14 x 19½" **170.50**

Cloth, printed beige cotton, red border w/stars, brown design of eagle w/spread wings at top, shield on breast, "E Pluribus Unum" on banner, large building pictured across cloth w/"Memorial Hall Art Gallery 1776 Centennial 1876" below, 19 x 25" (a couple of very small holes in field area, not affecting design................................**85.00**

Cloth, beige cotton w/thirty-seven multicolored flags & country names shown underneath each, eagle w/spread wings in center, shown at top & bottom margins, "Flags of the Nations which participate in the - Centennial Exhibition of the United States in 1876," 15 x 24½" (very minor staining) **85.00**

Cloth, printed w/a large central vignette of the main fair building w/a round vignette in each corner showing a different fair scene, a spread-winged American eagle at the top center, printed at the bottom center "Centennial International Exhibition, Phila...," black & white w/a blue border band, unframed, 25 x 26¾" (minor stains) **71.50**

Cup, china, white w/multicolored view of "Centennial Memorial Building" & "1776-1876," 3½" d., 3½" h...............**95.00**

Medal, bronze, awarded by United States Centennial Commission, Philadelphia MDCCCLXXVI, 3" d. ...**250.00**

Medallion, walnut, relief-molded bust of "Gen'l Joseph R. Hawley, President U.S. International Exposition," on reverse in raised lettering, "The 100th Anniversary of American Independence" & "Great International Exhibition Fairmount Park Philadelphia 4th of July 1876," 2½" d...**75.00**

Mug, pressed glass, embossed w/the Liberty Bell on the front & back side & the Centennial dates "1776-1876" between the two bells, milk white, 2" h...**300.00**

Photograph, view card of Machinery Hall at the Exhibition **45.00**

Photographs, view card of Machinery Hall, Ohio State Building, New Hampshire State Building, New Jersey State Building, Art Gallery, Japanese Dwelling, Interior of Machinery Hall, Illinois State Building, Michigan State Building, Massachusetts State Building, Pennslyvania Building, Horticultural Hall & German Government Hall, 4½ x 6½", set of 13 ....**75.00**

Program, paper, single page w/design of Liberty Bell & "1776-1876" & "Centennial Exposition Philadelphia - Machinery Hall" at top, pre-printed message relative to the exhibits, imprinted w/addressee's name, the sender's name & "August 8th 1876," 5 x 6¼" **22.50**

Sheet music, "Centennial Music," cover w/black & white lithograph of the main building..................................**45.00**

Stereo view cards, No. 496, Corliss Engine, No. 999, Mrs. Maxwell's Rocky Mountain Museum, No. 1821, Mrs. Maxwell's Rocky Mountain Museum (different view), Centennial Photographic Co., each 4 x 7", set of 3 ....**35.00**

Stud pin, brass, embossed building w/"Art Gallery 1876" beneath, 1" d. (minor discoloration of finish) **22.50**

Ticket, front overprinted in red "Fifty Cents," back depicts female figure w/sword, eagle, cornucopia, printed by Philadelphia Bank Note, 1¼ x 3¾" **12.50**

Vase, frosted pressed glass, model of a hand holding a sheaf of wheat, Gillinder & Sons, 7" h. (ILLUS.) **85.00**

1893 COLUMBIAN EXPOSITION

Booklet, "World's Columbian Exposition Official Guide," illustrated, 1893 ....**40.00**

Bookmark, woven silk, "Stars & Stripes," in original Phoenix Silk Manufacturing folder **110.00**

Cabinet photograph, shows the Ferris Wheel **52.00**

Coin, U.S. Government Treasury Building depicted, large **15.00**

Napkin ring, silver plate, embossed "World's Fair, Chicago" **25.00**

Pass for "Chicago Day," dated October 9, 1893, "Ft. Dearborn Chicago, 1833" depicted on reverse, 4" l., 2⅛" h...**8.00**

Pass to dedication ceremonies, September 17, 1892 ....**45.00**

Salt & pepper shakers w/original lids, glass, egg-shaped, Mount

Washington Glass Co., New Bedford, Massachusetts, pr. **245.00**

Tapestry, Egyptian applique, scene of Egyptian Pavilion, 18 x 55" **195.00**

Teaspoon, sterling silver, advertising "Casler's Dry Goods" **30.00**

1901 PAN-AMERICAN EXPOSITION

Coin, copper, aluminum encased cent, marked "Good Luck Souvenir, Pan-American Exposition," 1½" d. **15.00**

Coin, copper, elongated cent, Electric Tower design **12.50**

Envelope, multicolored design of "U.S. Government Building," showing ship, canon, etc., 3½ x 6½" (light blemish streak)..........**15.00**

Envelope, multicolored circular design of two ladies as the continents, North & South America, return address of "The Buffalo Review" (The People's Paper) cancelled "Aug. 18, 1899 Buffalo, N.Y.," combined w/pre-fair slogan oval cancel "Pan-American 1901 Exposition," 2¢ red stamp **12.50**

Letter opener, metal, made from a large nail, partially flattened to form blade which shows design of globe, marked "Pan-American Souvenir 1901"..**20.00**

Matchsafe, nickel-plated, embossed design of Manufacturers & Liberal Arts Building on front, reverse w/design of female w/arms outstretched in front of a waterfall, hinged top w/striker, cigar cutter on bottom (very slight plating wear)........**50.00**

Medal, official, brass, front w/design of Indian w/arm raised, astride an eagle, relief map of North & South America on reverse, marked "Pan-American Exposition, Buffalo, N.Y., U.S.A., May 1 - Nov. 1 MDCDI," designed by Brewster, struck in Mint Exhibit on expo grounds, 1⅜" d. **25.00**

Napkin ring, aluminum, impressed design of a buffalo, marked, "Pan-American Exposition, Buffalo, USA 1901," engraved floral design w/beaded border **20.00**

Paperweight, glass, round, encased seashells, large shell in center lettered in script, "Souvenir Pan-American Exposition, Buffalo 1901"...**20.00**

Paperweight, glass, rectangular, photo of Government Building, marked "Empire Art Co."...................**37.50**

Paperweight, glass, rectangular, photo of Temple of Music Building & portrait of President McKinley............**25.00**

Pinback button, celluloid, multi-colored design of two ladies in shape of North & South American continents, marked "Official Button" on edge, Whitehead & Hoag paper label still intact, 1¼" d. **17.50**

Playing cards, single deck in original two-part slip case, "Pan-American Exposition, Buffalo 1901" in semi-circle above frosted design of the Electric Tower, backs of cards w/typical design of two ladies as North & South America, w/different exposition building or scene on face of each card, the deck **70.00**

Postcard, official souvenir w/multicolored scene of Mines, Horticulture and Graphic Arts buildings, etc., handwritten message "Saw McKinley's funeral procession this afternoon...," 1901 flag cancellation tied to 1¢ Pan-Am commemorative stamp **20.00**

Ribbon, woven silk, Electric Tower scene in tones of grey, 3½ x 5", in original mat 6 x 9" **60.00**

Stickpin w/metal buffalo figure suspended at top **28.00**

Tumbler, clear glass, "Pan-American Exposition Buffalo 1901" in semi-circle above frosted design of the Electric Tower **35.00**

Whimsey, pressed glass, model of a frying pan, the round pan molded w/two eggs designed to appear as North & South America, the long flat handle w/hanging hole designed to hold a thermometer, milk white w/paint trim, 6⅞" l. (thermometer missing) **45.00**

1904 ST. LOUIS WORLD'S FAIR

St. Louis World's Fair Tumbler

Dish, china, depicts Machinery Building, Victoria Carlsbad mark........**95.00**
Napkin ring, brass & pewter................**35.00**
Paperweight, glass, colored scene of Festival Hall **65.00**
Plate, clear pressed glass, depicts Festival Hall & Cascade Gardens,

openwork rim, good gold, 7¼" d. ....**45.00 to 55.00**

Souvenir spoon, sterling silver, "Louisiana Purchase Exposition" on handle, "St. Louis Festival Hall & Cascades" in bowl **45.00**

Stein, pottery w/pewter lid, depicts Cascade Gardens, made in Germany **175.00**

Tumbler, clear pressed glass, tapering cylindrical form molded w/various fair scenes within scroll borders, 5" h. (ILLUS.) **22.00**

1915 PANAMA-PACIFIC INTERNATIONAL EXPOSITION

Admission button on ribbon, closing day...**65.00**

Medal, "Mississippi Women Dollar" exhibit w/Jefferson Davis **25.00**

Paperweight, square, "California Invites the World Panama Pacific Exposition" **65.00**

Photograph book, "Views of the Panama-Pacific International Exposition," San Francisco **20.00**

Print, "After the lights went out," Palace of Arts & Duck Baby statue, framed...**50.00**

Scarf, woven silk, gold, "Panama-Pacific International Exposition".........**45.00**

Teaspoon, sterling silver, "Panama-Pacific International Exposition" on handle, bowl plain **55.00**

1933-34 CHICAGO "CENTURY OF PROGRESS"

Novelty Toothpick Holder

Ashtray, enameled red & black **35.00**
Ashtray, model of rubber tire w/amber glass insert, FirestoneTire ....**40.00 to 50.00**
Bank, metal, model of an "Under-wood" typewriter, 2½ x 11¼" **150.00**
Book, 1934 Century of Progress Expo official guide book, color photos **10.00**

Bracelet, bangle-type, metal, stamped fair scenes...........................**20.00**

Clothes brush, round w/celluloid top, depicts fair scenes **23.00**

Employee photo identification & pass...**45.00**

Handerchiefs, silk w/fair logo, Japanese-made, package of 3 ....**24.00**

Playing cards, depicting "Avenue of Flags" on back, in original box, the deck **20.00**

Salt & pepper set w/tray, silver plate, 3 pcs.....................................**20.00 to 25.00**

Scrapbook, includes 30 pp. of clippings from "The Chicago Daily News," 30 newspaper stamps & 16 postcards **45.00**

Thermometer, metal, key-shaped w/fair scenes depicted **24.00**

Toothpick holder, porcelain, figure of a Dutch boy standing beside a large basket for toothpicks, decorated in light & dark blue, fair souvenir sticker on the bottom, 4¼" w., 5" h. (ILLUS.)..**11.00**

Wagon, toy size, coaster-type, "Radio Flyer," pressed steel, red w/white rubber tires, all decals intact **185.00**

1939-40 NEW YORK WORLD'S FAIR

New York World's Fair Teapot

Banner, cloth, outdoor-type, Richfield gas station, depicts Trylon & Perisphere, plus 1939 New York Bingo, Trylon & Perisphere on box (some wear to both) **85.00**

Book, "Railroads on Parade," 1939 .....**10.00**

Book ends, alabaster, figural Trylon & Perisphere, from the Italian exhibit, pr. **95.00**

Button, chrome-plated & enameled, orange & blue, on original card..........**40.00**

Compact, goldtone metal w/imitation mother-of-pearl, American Airlines, Schildkraut, 2¼" d. **50.00**

Compact, Lucretia Vanderbilt, blue enamel w/butterfly, paper liner, 1½ x 2¼"...**50.00**

Pencil, mechanical, 1940, 10½" l.........**40.00**

Pin, wooden, figural flat Mr. Peanut w/Trylon & Perisphere, w/original card...**55.00**

Plate, china, depicts Hall of Communications, blue & white, first edition, Abraham & Straus, 10½" d. **55.00**

Playing cards, two decks, sealed in original box w/stamps **75.00**

Saxophone, toy, tin, souvenir, 1940....**30.00**

Swizzle stick, glass, marked "Dinty Moore" w/logo **20.00**

Teapot, cov., china, footed spherical body w/short angled spout, D-form handle, molded in relief w/a large scene of the Trylon & Perisphere w/color trim, marked "Porcelier Vitreous - Hand Decorated China - Made in U.S.A.," minor wear, 8" h. (ILLUS.) **148.50**

Ticket book, souvenir stubs, Trylon & Perisphere logo, in color **50.00**

Toothpick holder, chrome, depicts Trylon & Perisphere **75.00**

Tray, lithographed, tin, "Medaglia D'Oro Coffee," 10 x 16" ....**50.00 to 65.00**

1939-40 GOLDEN GATE INTERNATIONAL EXPOSITION

Bookmark, copper **15.00**

Coaster, Bakelite **10.00**

Compact, lady's, goldtone w/enameling, decorated w/a fairscene..............**33.00**

Ice pick **25.00**

Medallion, metal, depicts Treasure Island **17.00**

Letter opener, silver plate, ornate handle, 1939 ....**26.50**

Teaspoon, sterling silver, shows the Tower of Sun & Court of Pacifica.......**40.00**

1964-65 NEW YORK WORLD'S FAIR

Flash cards, 1964, set of 28 in original box **25.00**

Map, three-dimensional, elaborate pictorial & visitor's guide to New York City **20.00**

Snowdome, shows "Vatican Pavilion" **25.00**

Swim air mattress, child's, inflatable plastic, mint in box **25.00**

Tumblers, glass, each w/different scene, set of 8 ....**48.00**

(End of World's Fair Collectibles Section)

WRITING ACCESSORIES

Early writing accessories are popular collectibles and offer a wide variety to select from. A collection may be formed around any one segment - pens, letter openers, lap desks or inkwells - or the collection may revolve around choice specimens of all types. Material, design and age usually determine the value. Pen collectors like the large fountain pens developed in the 1920s but also look for pens and mechanical pencils that are solid gold or gold-plated.

INKWELLS & STANDS

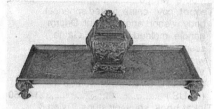

Brass Inkstand

Blown Glass stand, free-blown clear fountain-form, double-lobed bowl w/small upper dished holder for sander trimmed w/strawberry prunts, each lobed font w/short-necked opening & decorated w/a prunt & a band of applied vertical rigaree, short pedestal & round disc foot, probably Pittsburgh, Pennslyvania, ca. 1830, 4⅛" h. **$715.00**

Blown glass well, tapering cylinder, disc mouth, pontil scar, olive green, possibly Keene Marlboro Street Glassworks, Keene, New Hampshire, 1800-30, 3⁹⁄₁₆" d., 2¾" h...**302.50**

Blown-three mold glass well, geometric, cylindrical body w/disc mouth, pontil scar, medium olive green, attributed to the Mt. Vernon Glass Co., ca. 1825-30, 1¾" h.........**777.00**

Blown-three mold glass well, cylindrical w/rounded shoulders & flat collar, geometric diamond point design, plain base w/pontil, dark amber, 2⅜" d., 1⅞" h., GII-2............**137.50**

Blown-three mold glass well, short cylindrical form, geometric design,dark olive green, GII-16, 2⅜" d..**137.50**

Brass stand, long rectangular tray w/elaborate cast leaf & butterfly scene, centered by a footed bulbous inkwell cast w/dragons, the tray raised on elephant head feet, glass well insert missing, 13" l., 5½" h. (ILLUS.) **82.50**

Bronze stand, figural, an oval tray w/two inkwells centering an eagle perched on a rocky ledge, signed "A. MARIONNET," 16" l. **460.00**

Bronze stand, Wild Carrot patt., a

flat disc leaf-cast base centered by a bulbous ovoid plant-form well w/a small domed cover opening to a clear glass insert, base impressed "TG & D Co. 29 230" & double striked "Tiffany Studios, New York,"early 20th c., 5¼" d., 3¾" h...**6,900.00**

Bronze well, figural, a nude male in deep waves leans against a large spiral shell while pulling another one through the waves, one shell w/a cap opening to the inkwell, rich reddish brown patina, inscribed "H. Muller," 15" l., 8½" h.....................**920.00**

Tiffany Crab Inkwell

Bronze well, figural, cast as a full-bodied crab w/a hinged body holding in his claws a shell-form inkwell w/beaded trim & hinged lid, original dark patina, impressed "Tiffany Studios - New York - 893," possibly missing one bail handle, 8" l., 3½" h. (ILLUS.) **4,312.50**

Bronze & glass well, Grapevine patt., the large squat vessel overlaid w/leaves & tendrils against a green glass ground, impressed "TIFFANY STUDIOS - NEW YORK - 847," 1899-1928, 6¾" h. **805.00**

Cut Glass Inkwell

Coral pink cut glass well, square w/dimpled sides, matching hinged lid, brass mountings, 2¾" d., 4½" h. (ILLUS.) **245.00**

Coral pink cut glass well, tapering

cylindrical shape w/matching hinged lid, brass mountings, 2¾" d., 4¾" h..**225.00**

Gallé Cameo Inkwell

Gallé cameo glass well, wide squatty round form in clear cased to bright yellow & overlaid in reddish amber, etched overall w/berries & leafy branches w/a glossy 'fire-polished' surface, signed in cameo, w/original gilt-metal double cover, 5¾" d., 2" h. (ILLUS.)....................**1,725.00**

Gilt-bronze stand, Art Nouveau style, depicting two nude women in the surf, the inkwell lid in the form of a crab, brown composition base, attributed to Vve-Leonie Ledru, France, ca. 1900, 12" w., 6⅞" h.......**522.50**

Gilt-bronze well, cast as three nude men pulling a rope-tied octagonal chest from the sea, the chest enclosing an inkwell & w/hinged cover set w/red & green cabochon 'jewels,' w/glass liner, stamped "TIFFANY STUDIOS NEW YORK 1038," 11" l....................................**4,600.00**

Rare Tiffany Inkstand

Gilt-bronze & 'turtleback' tile stand, rectangular bronze box inset w/ten Favrile glass purple iridescent tiles & four on a central drawer, the hinged lid opening to two wells w/gold Favrile glass inserts inscribed "L.C.T." & pen or brush holder hooks, on four pad feet, base inscribed twice "Tiffany Studios - New York - 10388," 4 x 8¾", 4½" h. (ILLUS.)..........................**12,650.00**

Louis XV-Style stand, lacquer, gilt-

bronze & Meissen porcelain, the shaped lacquer platform base decorated w/bamboo, dogwood & exotic birds, centered by an oval porcelain well & fitted along the back edge w/a figure group of two Chinese men w/umbrella flanked by kneeling figures of Chinese children, the base bordered w/gilt-bronze scroll-cast & footed border & a gilt-bronze border band around the central well, Europe, late 19th c., 15½" l., 12" h...............................**3,450.00**

Mahogany & silver stand, rectangular silver tray top fitted w/a square diamond point-cut inkwell & sander w/silver lids flanking a round silver taperstick holder, on a narrow mahogany case w/a narrow drawer w/small silver knob, all raised on tiny silver claw feet, Regency period, England, early 19th c., 9½ x 13"......................................**4,025.00**

Malachite & ormolu stand, the rectangular malachite base w/twig-like ormolu mounts holding a glass inkwell & sander, each w/ormolu covers, 19th c., 11¼" l. **2,875.00**

Mold-blown glass well, Pitkin-type, 36 broken ribs swirled to the right, tapering cylindrical form, pontil scar, tooled disc lip, medium yellowish olive green, early 19th c., 1¾" h. **660.00**

Mold-blown glass well, w/18 vertical ribs, aqua, tooled opening, bubbly glass, ca. 1850, 1⅞" h. **264.00**

Blown Well with Bubbles

Periwinkle blue blown glass well, squatty bulbous body w/spherical hinged lid, controlled bubble decoration, brass mountings, 3¾" d., 4" h. (ILLUS.).......................**245.00**

Periwinkle blue cut glass well, squatty angled panel-cut sides, matching hinged lid, brass mountings, 3½" d., 3⅞" h................**235.00**

Pewter stand, an oblong slightly dished tray cast in low-relief w/lotus lilies & a dragonfly, holding two tapering cylindrical wells w/domed covers, the sides cast w/large tulip blossoms, Kayserzinn, Germany, impressed mark & "4256," ca. 1900, tray 8¾ x 13½" (cleaned) **506.00**

Pigeon Blood Glass Well

Pigeon blood blown glass well, squatty bulbous body w/spherical hinged lid, controlled bubble decoration, brass mountings, 3⅞" d., 3¾" h. (ILLUS.) **265.00**

Sevres Porcelain Inkstand

Sevres porcelain & bronze stand, a rectangular porcelain platform w/molded leaf band & scroll borders centered by bronze bands cast w/rosettes & scroll bars, the stepped top fitted w/two round bronze & porcelain wells w/domed covers centering a rectangular compartment w/leaf-molded domed cover w/loop handles, bronze loop end handles on the base & cast winged eagle corner legs, dark green enamel ground w/gilt leaf borders, France, mid-19th c., painted mark, 10" l. (ILLUS.) **1,840.00**

Silver inkwells, in the form of realistically modeled seated camels, w/glass liners, Theodore H. Starr, New York, ca. 1905, 8" l., pr. **4,025.00**

Silver well, traveling-type, straight-sided oval section, the cover inscribed "Baradell A Paris," in original fitted leather case, Louis XV period, Baradell, Paris, 1753, 1¼" l. **2,875.00**

Staffordshire pottery well, figural, a

reclining whippet in orangish tan on an oblong well base in underglaze-blue trimmed w/a gold band, 19th c., 6½" l. **247.50**

Sterling silver stand, shaped oval form w/applied scrolling rim, fitted w/a central wafer box w/detachable taperstick & flanked by two silver-mounted squatty bulbous diamond-cut glass inkwells, on four scroll feet, maker "HW," London, England, 1870-71, 9¼" l. (snuffer missing) **632.50**

Sterling silver stand, replica of the one used at the signing of the Declaration of Independence, given to John Wanamaker, Jr. from Rodman Wanamakers, Philadelphia, December 31, 1926, 10¼" l. **862.50**

Teal blue pressed glass well, ribbed design, matching hinged led, brass mountings, 3½" d., 3¾" h. **225.00**

Treenware, waisted cylindrical form w/incised rings at center, worn original brown sponging w/stenciled gold vintage decoration, 4½" d. **126.50**

LETTER OPENERS

Copper, hand-hammered Arts & Crafts design, the flattened, round-tipped handle w/a large applied monogram "R," original light brown patina, Dirk Van Erp 'open box' mark, San Francisco, California, early 20th c., 10" l. **220.00**

Ivory w/silver mounts, Art Nouveau designs, Russia, late 19th c., 11½" l. **747.50**

Nephrite & silver, the long flat dark green nephrite blade w/a rounded end, the silver handle in the form of an Imperial crown, each side w/a red stone cabochon, Nicholls and Plincke, St. Petersburg, Russia, ca. 1890, 8¼" l. **2,070.00**

Silver, figural cherub at the top, Georg Jensen, Denmark....................**95.00**

PENS & PENCILS

Conklin "Endura" mechanical pencil, blue, small **45.00**

Conklin fountain pen, marbleized Bakelite, original silver nib, leather holder & box....................................**15.00**

Faberge fountain pen, silver, decorated w/neo-rococo scrolls & flowerheads, marked w/Cyrillic initials of workmaster Julius Rappoport & Faberge in Cyrillic, St. Petersburg, ca. 1900, 8" l. **1,840.00**

Parker, "Duofold Lucky Curve" lady's fountain pen, orange body.......**60.00**

Parker, "Duo-Fold Sr." fountain pen, black chased hard rubber, ca. 1920, 6½" l. **250.00**

Parker "51" fountain pen, black barrel, sterling silver cap **60.00**

Sheaffer "Lady Sheaffer No. 500" fountain pen, grey pearl, ca. 1940 .....**30.00**

Sheaffer "Lifetime No. 875 White Dot" fountain pen, golden brown, gold-filled trim, military clip, ca. 1941 ....**65.00**

Sheaffer "Lifetime White Dot" fountain pen, brown & gold stripes, ca. 1930 ....**30.00**

Wahl-Eversharp "Skyline" fountain pen, gold & blue, 14k gold tip, ca. 1940 ....**85.00**

Waterman "No. 452 ½ V," sterling silver cap & barrel, lever filler, ribbon ring, ca. 1923 ....**149.00**

POUNCE SANDERS

Holly or boxwood, turned slightly tapering base rising to a ringed waist & flaring sharply to the top, 2½" h. (minor age crack) **104.50**

Maple, barrel-shaped, tooled bands top & base, ca. 1820, 2 x 2¾" **45.00**

Maple, cylindrical, pierced star in top, ca. 1810, 3 x 3⅛" **85.00**

WAX LETTER SEALS

Amber stone, engraved "Better Late Than Never," 1850s **90.00**

Bloodstone, silver-gilt & enamel, the fluted bloodstone handle w/collar enameled translucent salmon over a *guilloché* ground, unmarked, probably Fabergé, ca. 1910, 4" h...**3,105.00**

Clear stone, engraved "Absence Pains But Cannot Alter," 1850s **100.00**

Rock crystal & 18k gold, faceted crystal handle & chased gold collar **385.00**

YARD LONG PRINTS

These out of proportion colorful prints were fashionable wall decorations in the waning years of the 19th century and early in the 20th century. Horizontal types are 36" wide and between 8" and 10" high. Vertical examples are about 25" to 30" tall. A wide variety of subjects, ranging from florals and fruits to chicks and puppies, is available to collectors. Prices for these yard-long prints have shown a dramatic increase within the past years. All included in this list are framed unless otherwise noted.

"Alluring," beauty product premium, panel depicts lovely lady standing, turned & looking to her left, signed

"Bradshaw Crandell," 1928 or 1929, Pompeian Co., Cleveland, Ohio, unframed, 7" w., 16" h....................**$170.00**

"A Yard of Cats," by Guy Bedford, Chicago, Illinois, framed **235.00**

"A Walk-Over Girl," depicts a young girl seated, signed "R. Ford Harper," ca. 1912, Walk-Over Shoes store stamp on back, 10" w., 27" h. **275.00**

"The Bride," beauty product premium, panel depicts half-length figure of beautiful bride holding bouquet, flowers in her hair, signed "Rolf Armstrong," ca. 1927, Pompeian Co., Cleveland, Ohio, unframed, 7" w., 26" h.....................**275.00**

"The Clay, Robinson & Co., Army of Employees," beauty product premium, panel shows three-quarter figure of young lady, wearing coat & hat, her right hand holding the collar of a dog, signed "H. Dirch," 1916, Pompeian Co., Cleveland, Ohio, unframed, 12" w., 28" h....................**275.00**

"Foot Rest Hosiery," beauty product premium, lovely lady standing, 10" w., 27" h...............................**137.00**

"Girl with Laughing Eyes," beauty product premium, full-length figure of young woman smiling, signed "F. Carlyle," 1910, Pompeian Co., Cleveland, Ohio, unframed, 6" w., 25" h..**302.00**

"Honeymooning in the Alps," beauty product premium, panel depicts elegantly dressed couple w/mountains in background, signed "Gene Pressler," ca. 1923, Pompeian Co., Cleveland, Ohio, unframed, 7" w., 27" h.....................**137.00**

"Honeymooning in Venice," beauty product premium, seated couple, his arm around her shoulder, signed "Gene Pressler," 1922, Pompeian Co., Cleveland, Ohio, unframed, 7" w., 26" h...................................**176.00**

"Liberty Girl," beauty product premium, figure of seated girl holding a banner, by Forbes w/verse by Daniel M. Henderson, 1922, Pompeian Co., Cleveland, Ohio, unframed, 7" w., 26" h.....................**330.00**

"Pabst American Girl," figure of lovely young lady wearing long gown, signed "C. Allan Gilbert," 1914, 7" w., 36" h............................**203.00**

"Selz Good Shoes," depicts lovely lady standing w/left hand on her neck, wearing long draped gown, signed "Haskell Coffin," ca. 1920, 9" w., 37" h...............................**187.00**

"Selz Good Shoes," depicts lovely lady standing w/stole over her arm, ca. 1921, 10" w., 32" h....................**187.00**

INDEX